THE NOVEL
An Alternative History

BOOKS BY STEVEN MOORE

*A Reader's Guide to William Gaddis's
"The Recognitions"* (1982)

William Gaddis (1989)

*Ronald Firbank: An Annotated Bibliography
of Secondary Materials* (1996)

BOOKS EDITED WITH AN INTRODUCTION
BY STEVEN MOORE

In Recognition of William Gaddis (with John Kuehl, 1984)

The Vampire in Verse: An Anthology (1985)

Edward Dahlberg, *Samuel Beckett's Wake
and Other Uncollected Prose* (1989)

Ronald Firbank, *Complete Short Stories* (1990)

Ronald Firbank, *Complete Plays* (1994)

The Complete Fiction of W. M. Spackman (1997)

*Beerspit Night and Cursing: The Correspondence of
Charles Bukowski and Sheri Martinelli* (2001)

Chandler Brossard, *Over the Rainbow? Hardly* (2005)

THE NOVEL
An Alternative History

Beginnings to 1600

STEVEN MOORE

continuum

The Continuum International Publishing Group Inc
80 Maiden Lane, New York, NY 10038

The Continuum International Publishing Group Ltd
The Tower Building, 11 York Road, London SE1 7NX

www.continuumbooks.com

Library of Congress Cataloging-in-Publication Data
A catalog record for this book is available from the Library of Congress.

ISBN: 978-1-4411-7704-9 (hardcover)

Typeset by Pindar NZ, Auckland, New Zealand
Printed in the United States of America

Contents

INTRODUCTION

The Novel Novel

Although I unwittingly planted the seeds for this book in a short promotional piece I wrote in 1993, and tilled the ground with a few notes later in the '90s, it wasn't until 2002 that I began thinking seriously of writing it, for two things happened that year: the first was my discovery of Francesco Colonna's *Hypnerotomachia Poliphili* — an extravagant novel dating from the end of the 15th century — and the second was a three-pronged attack on the kind of fiction I love. Colonna's vast dream-novel is a kind of Renaissance forerunner of *Finnegans Wake*, which reminded me, yet again, that avant-garde, experimental novels are not a 20th-century development, as is commonly believed, but instead have a long, rich history, one never properly told. Someone should write a comprehensive history of the novel, I thought, so that curious readers like me wouldn't have to learn belatedly and haphazardly of such glories as the *Hypnerotomachia Poliphili*.[1]

But as I was drooling over my copy of Colonna's work — a heavy, oversized volume handsomely produced by Thames & Hudson in 1999 — the literary tradition he exemplifies was coming under attack. First there was B. R. Myers's *A Reader's Manifesto*, an exposé of perceived pretentiousness in some contemporary writers. (It first appeared as an article in the July/August 2001 issue of the *Atlantic Monthly*, but I didn't learn of it until it came out in book form in 2002.) Then came Dale Peck's essay "The Moody Blues" in the 1 July 2002 issue of the *New Republic*; the occasion was a review of Rick Moody's memoir *The Black Veil*, but Peck used the opportunity to discredit

a bankrupt tradition. A tradition that began with the diarrheic flow of words that is *Ulysses*, continued on through the incomprehensible ramblings of late Faulkner and the sterile inventions of Nabokov (two writers who more or less sold out their own early brilliance), and then burst into full, foul life in the ridiculous dithering of John Barth and John Hawkes and William Gaddis, the reductive cardboard constructions of Donald Barthelme, the word-by-word wasting of a talent as formidable as Thomas Pynchon's, and finally broke

---

1 Two years later Colonna's novel would find unexpected fame as the basis for a best-selling novel, *The Rule of Four*, by Ian Caldwell and Dustin Thomason. The *Hypnerotomachia* was reissued as a trade book and this bizarre, proto-modernist novel enjoyed solid sales for a while. You can't make this stuff up.

apart like a cracked sidewalk beneath the weight of the stupid — just plain stupid — tomes of Don DeLillo. (185)

But the unkindest cut of all was delivered by Jonathan Franzen (because I thought he was *one of us*) in the 30 September 2002 issue of the *New Yorker*; this time the occasion was William Gaddis's posthumous publications, but it expanded to include substantially the same hit list that Peck had compiled, though more in sorrow than in anger. What all the writers attacked by these three have in common is a yen for innovation, a showy prose style, and a perceived disregard for the common reader.

These three had their own attackers and defenders — and of course similar arguments have been made in the past, and will be made in the future — but it struck me that a fundamental misassumption about the purpose of fiction was at the heart of the problem. Make that *purposes*: fiction can be many things, but MPF (an abbreviation I'll use from now on for "Myers, Peck, Franzen, and readers like them") seemed to hold a very narrow view of fiction's function, and a historically uninformed one at that.[2] Anyone who thinks linguistic extravagance in novels began with *Ulysses* in 1922 hasn't done his homework. Mr. Peck, may I introduce Messrs. Petronius, Apuleius, Achilles Tatius, Subandhu, the anonymous Irish author of *The Battle of Magh Rath*, Alharizi, Fujiwara Teika, Gurgani, Nizami, Kakuichi, Colonna, Rabelais, Wu Chengen, Grange, Lyly, Sidney, Nashe, Suranna, the Scoffing Scholar of Lanling, Cervantes, López de Úbeda, Quevedo, Tung Yueh, Swift, Gracián, Cao Xueqin, Sterne, Li Ruzhen, Melville, Lautréamont, Carroll, Meredith, Huysmans, Wilde, Rolfe, Firbank, Bely, et al.? "The model for those who thought that high literature should be allusively obscure and complex," Robert Irwin suggests, is not Joyce but the 11th-century Arabic fictionist al-Hariri;[3] a Sanskrit scholar would nominate the 7th-century novelist Bana for that distinction. Of López de Úbeda's linguistically extravagant *Justina* (1605), critics have approvingly noted that "the work was written for the amusement of a cultured audience, a small minority of readers capable of deciphering the novel's obscure allusions, leaving the less ingenious reader, of course, totally bewildered."[4] Experts in other fields could offer other models, all predating Joyce by centuries. I dallied for a year or so (no — make that *dithered*, like Barth and the others) thinking about writing this book, but did nothing until early 2004, when Irish novelist Roddy Doyle raised a stink by attacking *Ulysses*. (Not *Ulysses* again! Never thought I'd have to defend Joyce, of all people. Now I know how a Christian feels when an atheist attacks his god.)

---

2 I want to emphasize "and readers like them": by the time this book is published, Myers and Peck (if not Franzen) may be long forgotten, but their complaints are typical of many readers and reviewers, and hence make convenient talking points.

3 *The Arabian Nights: A Companion*, 80.

4 Damiani, 59, paraphrasing French critic Marcel Bataillon.

That was the final straw. Knowing full well I was on a fool's errand, I decided to attempt a complete history of the novel, with special attention to the innovative, unconventional ones; if I couldn't convince MPF of the superiority of such novels over the kind they prefer — *de gustibus non est disputandum* — I could at least try to refute these insulting, ill-informed assumptions about the writers who create such novels, and the readers who cherish them.

THE OTHER GREAT TRADITION

First, a little history lesson. The standard history of the novel — the one that MPF seem to believe in, and the one I was taught as an English major in the early 1970s — goes something like this: The novel was born in 18th-century England, the offspring of a questionable marriage between fiction and nonfiction (Defoe's *Robinson Crusoe* and Swift's *Gulliver's Travels* pretended to be true travel accounts), gained respectability with Samuel Richardson's epistolary novels named after prudish virgins (*Pamela, Clarissa*), sowed some wild oats (Fielding, Smollett, Sterne) and went through a goth phase (Walpole, Radcliffe, Mary Shelley) before settling down into domestic life (Austen) and becoming the preferred entertainment of the middle class. Scott invented the historical novel with *Waverley*, while over in France Balzac launched the realistic novel: straightforward, lightly romanticized stories of recognizable people out of everyday life, usually narrated in chronological sequence and in language no different from that of the better newspapers and journals. The novel matured during this time, dramatizing the great moral issues of the day (Dickens, Eliot, and Hardy in England; Hugo, Flaubert, and Zola in France; Tolstoy, Dostoevsky, and Turgenev in Russia; Hawthorne, James, and Dreiser in the United States) and providing trenchant social commentary. Things got a little out of hand during the 1920s and 1930s (Joyce's *Ulysses*, Woolf's *Jacob's Room*, Faulkner's *Sound and the Fury*), but soon settled back on track, though not before spawning a lunatic fringe that still remains. (Most of them are confined to small presses and hence easily ignored, though every once in a while one of them will fake his or her way onto a reputable New York publisher's list.) And today our best novelists follow in this great tradition:[5] that is, realistic narratives driven by a strong plot and peopled by well-rounded characters struggling with serious ethical issues, conveyed in language anybody can understand.

Wrong. The novel has been around since at least the 4th century BCE (Xenophon's *Cyropaedia*) and flourished in the Mediterranean area until the coming of the Christian Dark Ages. The earliest novels were Greek romances

---

5 *The Great Tradition* is a 1948 book by F. R. Leavis lauding Austen, Eliot, James, and Conrad.

and Latin satires, where the plot was a mere convenience that allowed the author to engage in rhetorical display, literary criticism, sociopolitical commentary, digressions, and so on. It was an elastic form that made room for interpolated poems, stories within stories, pornography, and parodies, where the realistic and fantastic blend together. (In other words, "magic realism" was not invented in the 1960s by the Latin American "Boom" writers, but instead has *always* been a property of the novel.) These novels peaked with Apuleius's *Golden Ass* and Heliodorus's *Ethiopian Story*, and even the early Christians produced a novel before the fall of Rome ended this phase of the novel's history. (That Christian novel was called *Recognitions*, remembered today only because it may be the first instance of the Faust theme in Western literature, and because it gave its name to one of the greatest American novels of the 20th century.[6])

The European novel went underground during the Middle Ages but continued to mutate in interesting ways. The Irish began converting their heroic stories into book-length fictions, and in England and France legends of King Arthur inspired prose romances, forerunners of the modern novel. By then Icelanders had invented the realist novel, seven centuries before Balzac — they're called sagas, but they're essentially realistic novels, despite the occasional appearance of a troll — which was then reinvented by Thomas Deloney in Elizabethan England. In 13th-century Spain, Moses de León wrote a vast, mystical novel called the *Zohar*, misunderstood by most as a commentary on the kabbala but actually a road novel like Kerouac's, with a band of religious nuts dissecting the Torah and running into crazy characters in the same spirit as Sal and Dean digging a Dexter Gordon saxophone solo while on the road. In the east, novels in Sanskrit started appearing in the 6th century, and in the Middle East Arabs began producing vast adventure novels and stringing short novels into story-cycles like *The Arabian Nights*. In 11th-century Japan, Murasaki Shikibu composed a huge novel (*The Tale of Genji*) more sophisticated than anything produced in the West until the Renaissance. In 14th-century China, gentlemen-scholars began producing ambitious, 2000-page novels, arguably the greatest body of fiction before the modern era. "The Chinese have thousands of them," Goethe told Eckermann, "and had them when our forefathers were still living in the woods."[7]

During the Renaissance, the novel experienced its own rebirth, reviving the tradition established 15 centuries earlier by the Greeks and Romans to create extravaganzas like Colonna's *Hypnerotomachia Poliphili*, Rabelais's

---

6 *The Recognitions* (1955) by William Gaddis. Get used to seeing that name; I've written several books and essays on him, and Gaddis is held up by opposing camps as an example of everything that's good and bad about innovative fiction.
7 *Conversations with Eckermann*, 31 January 1827. Mein Herr exaggerates somewhat.

Gargantua and Pantagruel, and of course Cervantes's *Don Quixote,* which introduced metafiction into the mix. England soon caught up with the Continent with the appearance of novels by George Gascoigne, John Lyly, Robert Greene, and others we'll meet later in this book. In other words, by the time Daniel Defoe was born in 1660, the novel was 2,000 years old and included thousands of examples of the genre.

A traditional critic would stop me right here to object that I haven't defined the novel yet, nor differentiated it from other kinds of fiction, like the romance, the confession, and the anatomy, as Northrop Frye did in his classic *Anatomy of Criticism* (303–14). That's because, in biological terms, Frye is working at the genus and species levels, whereas I'm speaking of the novel as a family classification. Besides, I find those distinctions too tidy, too often ignored by novelists who refuse to color within the lines. They are more pedantic than useful, a doomed attempt to nail down what Mikhail Bakhtin correctly called "this most fluid of genres."[8] Even though Hawthorne labeled some of his book-length fictions "romances" rather than "novels" — and in his preface to *The House of the Seven Gables* distinguished between the two — a critic can hardly be said to commit a literary crime by calling them all novels. As Frye himself admits, most novels are mixed bags anyway, combining elements from many genres, and resist definition. In my ecumenical view — schooled by the wild variety of forms the novel has taken in the last century — any book-length fictional narrative can be called a novel. I like E. M. Forster's minimalist definition of a novel as "any fictitious work over 50,000 words," and like better the vaguer, more inclusive one Forster based his on, French critic Abel Chevally's Gallic shrug "a fiction in prose of a certain extent."[9] Novelist Jane Smiley also kept it simple: "A novel is a (1) *lengthy,* (2) *written,* (3) *prose,* (4) *narrative* with a (5) *protagonist,*" though *narrative* needs to be more sharply defined to distinguish fictional ones from nonfictional.[10] I'll expand on these qualifications at the end of the introduction, but for now let's just call the novel *a prose composition longer than a short story, either fictitious in content or in its treatment of historical events, "worked out with an eye toward a strategy of effects."* The quoted phrase is from novelist Italo Calvino's *Uses of Literature* (109) and encompasses form, technique, style, tone, rhythm, intention, and other aspects of the novel. (Content doesn't matter: a novel can be about anything.) And lest that sound too dry, I second Jane Austen's proud defense of the novel as, at its best, a "work in which the greatest powers of the mind are displayed, in which the most thorough knowledge of human nature, the happiest delineation of its varieties, the liveliest effusions

8 *The Dialogic Imagination,* 11.
9 *Aspects of the Novel,* 17. However, Forster's 50,000-word minimum would exclude shorter novels like *Candide* and *A Red Badge of Courage.*
10 *Thirteen Ways of Looking at the Novel,* 14.

of wit and humour are conveyed to the world in the best chosen language" (*Northanger Abbey*, chap. 6).

Throughout its long history, the novel has evolved by way of stylistic and formal innovation, taking advantage of the genre's elasticity to try new approaches, new techniques. Literary historian Arthur Heiserman provides a pertinent etymology for the word *novel*:

> Latin *novellus*, a diminutive of *novus* ("new" or "extraordinary"), yielded the late Latin substantive *novella*, an "addition to a legal code." This in turn yielded the French *nouvelle* and Italian *novella* — a diminutive story whose material is fresh, untraditional, and whose resolution is extraordinarily surprising.[11]

Fresh, untraditional. "An experiment is attempted in this novel, which has not (so far as I know) been hitherto tried in fiction" — that's not the boast of one of our brash postmodernists but Wilkie Collins in his 1860 preface to *The Woman in White*. As far back as 1592, conservative critics were railing against the "monstrous newfangledness" of certain novels,[12] but innovation has kept the novel fresh and surprising. The novel has always been a work-shop, not a museum. What links a novelist like Collins with one today like Mark Danielewski "is chiefly the desire to escape a sclerosis," Alain Robbe-Grillet once wrote, "the need for *something else*." The French novelist goes on to ask:

> Around what have artists always grouped themselves, if not the rejection of the outworn forms still being imposed on them? Forms live and die, in all the realms of art, and in all periods they have had to be continually renewed: the composition of the novel of the nineteenth-century type, which was life itself a hundred years ago, is no longer anything but an empty formula, serving only as the basis for tiresome parodies. (*For a New Novel*, 134–35)

The newfangled realistic novel popularized by Balzac in the 1830s peaked later in the 19th century and quickly lost its novelty in the hands of lesser talents. Yet it became rooted in the mind of the reading public as *the* form of the novel henceforth, marginalizing more inventive fictions. At that point, fiction-writing branched into two streams — bourgeois fiction for the masses and belletristic fiction for the elite — and, in one of life's little ironies, the stream that deviated from the long tradition of innovation in fiction became the "main" stream, while the other, older tradition became a misunderstood tributary. Instead of enjoying a brief fad and then losing favor, like the

---

11 *The Novel before the Novel*, 221.
12 Gabriel Harvey, *Four Letters and Certain Sonnets*, cited in the introduction to Greene's *Planetomachia*, xvi.

18th-century epistolary novel, the realistic novel became thought of as the norm in fiction, instead of what it actually is: only one of many mutations in the evolution of the novel, and one less concerned with exploring new techniques and forms than with pleasing audiences and enriching authors and publishers. Entertainment rather than art.

ART AND/OR ENTERTAINMENT

Because the novel can be both a work of art and a form of entertainment, misunderstandings and recriminations will arise when readers fail to distinguish between the two, or don't even realize there is a difference. Graham Greene divided his published fictions into "novels" and "entertainments"; anyone picking up *The Power and the Glory* for a light read will probably be disappointed, as will the serious critic who approaches *Our Man in Havana* as a profound work of art. I remember in 1987 eagerly diving into Tom Wolfe's *Bonfire of the Vanities* under the assumption he would be applying the innovative, experimental techniques of his new journalism to fiction for some sort of kandy-kolored combo of Gaddis and Hunter S. Thompson, but after 20 pages I realized Wolfe had opted for entertainment rather than art, and adjusted my expectations accordingly.[13] Some novels can be rigorously artistic yet enjoy popular success — A. S. Byatt's postmodern *Possession* springs to mind — but most writers choose between art or entertainment: very few can serve both the muse and mammon. Nor is this a contemporary development; writing of the Akkadian *Epic of Creation*, Stephanie Dalley says that, unlike the more popular *Gilgamesh*, it was "designed to impress rather than to entertain" (231). MPF's complaints boil down to resentment toward those who want to be artists rather than entertainers.

When not applied strictly to painters, "artist" does have a pretentious sound to it — "It's *artiste* to you!" an impudent voice on an old Holy Modal Rounders song proclaims[14] — and any discussion of art vs. entertainment in the present cultural climate invites accusations of elitism and snobbery. But

13 Wolfe was angered when John Updike, reviewing his 1998 novel *A Man in Full*, described it as "entertainment, not literature," but Updike was simply making a taxonomic distinction. James Wood makes that distinction even clearer in his harsh but just assessment of "Tom Wolfe's Shallowness and the Trouble with Information" (in *The Irresponsible Self*, 210–22). But I loved *The Electric Kool-Aid Acid Test*.

14 On their 1968 acid-folk album *The Moray Eels Eat the Holy Modal Rounders*. Listening to noncommercial music like this at a young age — and poring over the trippy lyrics of Bob Dylan, Keith Reid, Syd Barrett, Jim Morrison, Robin Williamson, Tom Rapp, Nico, and Pete Sinfield — prepared me for the noncommercial fiction I would start reading a few years later. In fact it was my admiration of the avant-garde rock group Soft Machine that led me to pick up Burroughs's novel of the same name, my first encounter with experimental fiction.

the distinction between the two should be a matter of taxonomy, not necessarily of quality. Great entertainment is better than bad art; but one shouldn't condemn artistic works for not being more entertaining, nor entertainment for not being more artistic. We hold these truths to be self-evident. But I find MPF condemning writers who follow the dictates of art rather than those of entertainment — that is, who follow their muse rather than the marketplace — and I'm not sure they understand the difference.

Franzen at least senses the difference, but gets it wrong. He feels there are "two wildly different models of how fiction relates to its audience," the Status model and the Contract model — that is, art vs. entertainment. In the former, the author has either "disdained cheap compromise and stayed true to an artistic vision" or has placed "his selfish artistic imperatives or his personal vanity ahead of the audience's legitimate desire to be entertained," depending on how you feel about such novels. Similarly, the Contract novel can be either "a recipe for pandering, aesthetic compromise" or "a pleasurable experience" that fulfills "the deepest purpose of reading and writing fiction . . . to sustain a sense of connectedness, to resist existential loneliness."

I have several problems with these distinctions. First, Status and Contract are odd word choices, having their origin in Marxist theory. (*Status* means having a legitimate, inherited place in society, which lasted up until the bourgeois era; *Contract* sacrifices this security for mobility: the son of a blacksmith doesn't inherit his father's smithy but instead contracts his labor to one factory or another.) The historical transition in society from Status to Contract (a theme in Gaddis's *J R*[15]) is usually considered a bad thing, a fall from grace, which makes Franzen's advocacy of the Contract model surprising. Second, entertainers may have a contract with their audiences, but artists only with their muses. If I go to Las Vegas to see Tom Jones perform, he'd *better* sing "What's New, Pussycat?" or else I'll demand my money back, but if I go to a club to hear Robert Fripp, he can play whatever his muse prompts him to play, and I'll follow. The only contract artists have with their audiences is to perform at the top of their abilities in the expectation we will raise ourselves

---

15 Franzen quotes from my 1989 monograph *William Gaddis* a few times; on pp. 70–71 I discuss status vs. contract in *J R*. All quotations from Franzen are from p. 100 of his essay. (A slightly revised version appears in his collection of essays *How to Be Alone*, and in an interview posted on the online edition of the *New Yorker* Franzen distanced himself from Peck, calling his dismissal of DeLillo "stupid" and stating "Peck undervalues the excitement and potential of some of that modern and postmodern formal experimentation.") Three years after Franzen's article appeared, fiction writer Ben Marcus published a smart rebuttal entitled "Why Experimental Fiction Threatens to Destroy Publishing, Jonathan Franzen, and Life as We Know It: A Correction" (*Harper's*, October 2005, 39–52). Keeping it rolling, Cynthia Ozick responded to both with an essay entitled "Literary Entrails" (*Harper's*, April 2007, 67–75), in which she complains that the main problem with literature today is the absence of good critics who can, among other things, trace "the descent of literature not only from one nation to another but from one writer to another" (74).

to their level, not pout because they haven't lowered themselves to ours.[16] Third, he implies pleasure is to be found only in Contract novels, that Status novels are work — an onerous task either imposed by a professor for a literature class or undertaken as an act of self-flagellation for the good of one's soul. He apparently finds it hard to believe that some of us actually *enjoy* demanding novels, find them intellectually stimulating, even exhilarating. For me, reading *J R* for the first time was like taking a thrilling roller-coaster ride; reading Marguerite Young's 1,200-page *Miss MacIntosh, My Darling* was like slipping into a luxurious opium dream; and as the old ballad says, "There's lots of fun at *Finnegans Wake*." Reading Joyce, Barth, Pynchon, et al. is a treat, not a task; nor is it something one does (unless you're a poseur) just to claim bragging rights afterward: at your next social gathering, try announcing you've just finished Hermann Broch's *Death of Virgil* and see how far that gets you. These novels are admittedly not for everyone, but they are for some of us. And finally, we don't read such novels "to sustain a sense of connectedness, to resist existential loneliness." We read them for the same reason we might go to the opera or the ballet: to be dazzled by a performance.

Think of the novel as an opera, with the author singing all the parts and playing all the instruments, or as a ballet, with the author dancing all the roles. Think of Sloppy in Dickens's *Our Mutual Friend*, praised by his mother for his dramatic readings from the newspaper: "He do the Police in different voices" (1.16). Dickens is praising himself; his novel is a one-man show where *he* does all the voices.[17] Cervantes posted the same advertisement for himself centuries earlier; speaking through a canon, he admits most novels of chivalry are nonsense, but "he found one good thing in them, which was *the opportunity for display* that they offered a good mind, providing a broad and spacious field where one's pen could write unhindered . . ." (1.47, trans. Grossman, my italics).

Literature is a rhetorical performance, a show put on by someone who possesses greater abilities with language than most people. Any literate person can write, just as anyone can sing and dance; what distinguishes artists from the rest of us is they can do these things *better* — and art is a demonstration of *how* much better they can. The reason some of us consider *Ulysses* the greatest novel ever written is not because it has a gripping story, lovable characters, or unique insights into the human situation, but because it is the most elaborate

---

16 In Gaddis's *J R*, the composer Edward Bast improvises a lecture on Mozart and berates popularizing efforts "—to humanize him because even if we can't um, if we can't rise to his level no at least we can, we can drag him down to ours . . ." (42). Later in the novel, Jack Gibbs (a mouthpiece for the author) expresses exasperation at lazy readers: "—Ask them to bring one God damned bit of effort want everything done for them they get up and go to the movies" (290).

17 "He Do the Police in Different Voices" was Eliot's original title for *The Waste Land*, a career-making ventriloquist act by an enthusiastic patron of the music hall.

rhetorical performance ever mounted, making wider and more masterful use of all the forms and techniques of prose than any other novel. An anonymous Amazon.com reviewer of *The Museum of Unconditional Surrender* by Croatian novelist Dubravka Ugrešić complains that "the author seemed more intent upon demonstrating her knowledge of literary technique than in getting the message, whatever it was, across to the readers." Well, yeah. As the old Hollywood producer said, if you want to send a message, call Western Union. The literary artist has a different agenda: "Much of his writing consists of *tour de force* demonstrations of the art of rhetoric rather than expressions of deeply felt conviction," says Robert Irwin of the great medieval Arabic author al-Jahiz,[18] though he may as well be speaking of Joyce. Samuel Johnson had lousy taste in novels — he derided those of Swift, Fielding, and Sterne — but he was on to something when he told Boswell, "Why, sir, if you were to read Richardson for the story, your impatience would be so much fretted that you would hang yourself. But you must read him for the sentiment, and consider the story as only giving occasion to the sentiment." The thought of (re)reading Richardson makes me want to hang myself, but substitute "rhetorical performance" for "sentiment" and you have the right approach to literary fiction. As the Russian Formalist critic Viktor Shklovsky insists in italics, "*Art is a means of experiencing the process of creativity. The artifact itself is quite unimportant.*"[19] Or as Joyce put it, "The important thing is not what we write, but how we write it."[20] Even Peck knows this, though he fails to apply it; speaking of drag queens and their tacky dresses in another of his hatchet jobs, he observes: "what elevates some drags to the status of divas while others remain mere queens is the quality of performance. In other words, the dress isn't as important as what you do once you've got it on" (60).

If this sounds too trendy, too reminiscent of the inconsequential "performance art" of recent decades, it's worth noting that literature has always been performative in nature. You can see it at line 871 of the Anglo-Saxon epic *Beowulf*, the morning after our hero's first encounter with the monster Grendel. The anonymous author self-consciously introduces a *scop* (poet) into the proceedings, whereupon this wordsmith

> found new words,   bound them up truly,
> began to recite   Beowulf's praise,
> a well-made lay   of his glorious deed,
> skillfully varied   his matter and style. (trans. Chickering)

---

18 *Night and Horses and the Desert*, 84.
19 *Theory of Prose*, 6. (I was the copy-editor for this translation, one of the toughest assignments I ever had.)
20 Power, *Conversations with James Joyce*, 95.

Suddenly the reader realizes the previous 870 lines have not been a historical account of Beowulf's actions but a fanciful re-creation — a literary *performance*; the poet, having "unlocked his word-hoard" (l. 259), has armored himself with words to perform a glorious linguistic deed to rival if not outdo Beowulf's wrestling match of the night before. For the *story* of Beowulf's deeds, you can read the CliffsNotes; the poem is a *performance* of the story, a showy display of the poet's wrestling match with words in which he emerges triumphant. (Beowulf only tears off an arm.) Look at me, at *my* prowess, the word-warrior proclaims, not at Beowulf, and it's the poet's achievement that still commands our attention after 1,300 years, not the deeds of a Swedish he-man.

Poetry of course has a bardic tradition of performative recitation, but I would argue literary prose possesses the same property and allows us to distinguish between art and entertainment. The difference between mainstream fiction and literature is what their writers do with words; the former places its emphasis on the story rather than the language used to tell that story; in literature, the language *is* the story; that is, the story is primarily a vehicle for a linguistic display of the writer's rhetorical abilities. Exercises in style. Nabokov critic Alfred Appel, Jr., gives an amusing but instructive example of the difference between the languages of art and entertainment; he was stationed with the U.S. army in France in the Fifties when *Lolita* was first published by Olympia Press, known for its pornography. He took the book with its distinctive green cover back to base, where it was pounced upon:

> "Hey, lemme read your dirty book, man!" insisted "Stockade Clyde" Carr, who had just earned his sobriquet, and to whose request I acceded at once. "Read it aloud, Stockade," someone called, and skipping the Foreword, Stockcade Clyde began to make his remedial way through the opening paragraph. "'Lo . . . lita, light . . . of my life, fire of my . . . loins. My sin, my soul . . . Lo-lee-ta: The . . . tip of the . . . tongue . . . taking . . . a trip . . .' — *Damn!*" yelled Stockade, throwing the book against the wall. "*It's God-damn Litachure!!*" (*The Annotated* Lolita, xxxiv)

MPF share Stockade Clyde's aesthetics. Peck longs for "the traditional satisfactions of fictional narrative — believable characters, satisfactory storylines, epiphanies and the like" (129). Myers, whom Peck quotes with approval (173–74), wants "the reader [to be] addressed as the writer's equal, in a natural cadence and vocabulary" (44); he wants "no pseudo-Joycean tomfoolery with punctuation — just crisp, believable dialogue" (54). Whatever "point" the writer wants to make should be made quickly and efficiently (60), and there should be no "name-dropping . . . historical and literary figures, titles of books, etc." (64). A writer should "speed his readers along" (77) with "a vigorous, fast-moving plot . . . written in careful, unaffectedly poetic prose"

(88). (That is, metaphors and imagery are acceptable if used sparingly and modestly.) The ideal is "strong stories told in an unaffected fashion" (116). I would argue just the opposite: the story is unimportant, and the style can be as affected as the writer wants, for too often "unaffected" means plain, modest, simple — admirable qualities in a repair manual, but not in a work of literature.

Let's take the story of Romeo and Juliet, best known from the play by a writer whose style Dryden considered "affected." It's a good one, but when you go to a performance of *Romeo and Juliet*, you're not going for the story; you already know the story. Nor do you go to receive a message about tolerance; you're already as tolerant as you'll ever be. And you don't go to empathize with the characters, unless you're a teenager seeing it for the first time. You don't go for the story but for the *performance* of the story. If it's Shakespeare's play, you'll divide your attention between the extraordinary language and the theatrical presentation (the actors' abilities, the costumes, the lighting, the director's interpretation, and so on). If it's Gounod's opera, you'll focus on the singers' abilities, wondering if Romeo will hit that optional high C at the end of the third act. If it's a ballet, based on either Berlioz's or Tchaikovsky's music, you'll focus on the dancers' abilities, wondering if Juliet's extensions can possibly match those of leggy Sylvie Guillem, former *étoile* of the Paris Opéra Ballet and the sexiest Juliet ever. Same with any of the movie versions, from that old 1936 one featuring middle-aged actors portraying teenagers to Baz Luhrmann's 1996 rock-video version. And with any adaptation — from *West Side Story* to the Dire Straits song "Romeo and Juliet" to Sonia Leong's manga version (2007) — the appeal will come not from the story but the imaginative presentation of the story.

The literary development of the Romeo and Juliet story allows us to mark the point where it was transformed from popular fiction to literature. Shakespeare scholar David Bevington gives this compact summary:

> The story of Romeo and Juliet goes back ultimately to the fifth-century A.D. Greek romance of *Ephesiaca*,[21] in which we find the motif of the sleeping potion as a means of escaping an unwelcome marriage. Masuccio of Salerno, in his *Il Novellino*, in 1476, combined the narrative of the heroine's deathlike trance and seeming burial alive with that of the hero's tragic failure to receive news from the friar that she is still alive. Luigi da Porto, in his *novella* (c. 1530), set the scene at Verona, provided the names of Romeo and Giulietta for the hero and heroine, added the account of their feuding families, the Montecchi and Cappelletti, introduced the killing of Tybalt (Theobaldo), and provided other important details. Luigi's version was followed by Matteo Bandello's famous *Novelle* of 1554, which was translated into French by Pierre Boaistuau (1559). The French version became the

---

21 Aka *An Ephesian Tale* by Xenophon of Ephesus (usually assigned to the 2nd century), a simplistic novel I'll mention in chapter 1.

source for Arthur Brooke's long narrative poem in English, *The Tragical History of Romeus and Juliet* (1562).[22]

And that's where Shakespeare got the story; he made some further modifications to the plot, but the reason we read his version today and not his predecessors' is the language. The earlier Italian versions are simple tales told in a straightforward manner; Brooke was the first to attempt to turn it into art, but another Shakespeare scholar, Stephen Greenblatt, describes his version as "long, leaden," and there the story may have sunk from literary history. What makes Shakespeare's *Romeo and Juliet* great is not so much the story or the characters, which he filched from elsewhere (as he did for most of his plays), but his matchless rhetorical powers. As Greenblatt says,

> *Romeo and Juliet* is saturated with language games: paradoxes, oxymorons, double entendres, rhyming tricks, verbal echoings, multiple puns. The obvious question is, why? One possible answer, proposed as early as the eighteenth century, is that Shakespeare could not resist: verbal wit was an addiction, an obsession, the object of an irrational passion. He could indulge this passion because a display of wit would appeal to those segments of the audience most attuned to rhetorical acrobatics.[23]

"An irrational passion": commercial writers merely *use* language, while artistic writers *love* language. In his afterword to *Lolita*, Nabokov writes: "an American critic suggested that *Lolita* was the record of my love affair with the romantic novel. The substitution 'English language' for 'romantic novel' would make this elegant formula more correct" (318). At one point in Alexander Theroux's novel *Darconville's Cat*, the magniloquent Dr. Crucifer interrupts himself to say, "How I adore the language that can tell you this" (544). And of course this love for language easily turns erotic in the hands of artistic writers: in the same afterword, Nabokov speaks of the "aesthetic bliss" that results from a satisfying work of fiction (316), and in her unconventional erotic novel *Aureole*, Carole Maso establishes the equivalence of "lovemaking, language making" (15), where reading and writing are aphrodisiacal acts, and where sexual energy becomes a goal to strive for in writing: as the writer/narrator says to her lover, "And I'd like to do with any sentence what I am about to do to you . . ." (10).

Back (after a cold shower) to *Romeo and Juliet*: Greenblatt gives other reasons for the lavish language of the play, but "rhetorical acrobatics" are what Myers and Peck seem to hate most about contemporary fiction. Myers

---

22 *The Necessary Shakespeare* (NY: Longman, 2002), 444. (I want to limit this book's bibliography to fictions and literary criticism, so bibliographic details for other books and essays in most cases will be given in the footnotes.)

23 *The Norton Shakespeare* (NY: Norton: 1997), 866. All Shakespearean citations will be to this edition.

criticizes Paul Auster for "trying so hard to draw attention to his fancy-pants language" (63), just as Peck dismisses Moody's "transparent attempts at linguistic virtuosity." But isn't virtuosity what we value most in a singer, a musician, a dancer? Would you want to watch an actor merely phoning in a performance, or a dancer merely going through the motions? Would you accuse ice skaters of "showing off"? That's what they're paid to do, and that's why you're watching. Yet writers who have developed extraordinary linguistic skills are expected by MPF to suppress those skills, or use them sparingly, like a gifted architect confining himself to building only doghouses.[24] Don't you want singers/musicians/actors/dancers/ice skaters/architects/chefs/designers/ et al. to exert themselves to the utmost of their abilities? And if so, shouldn't writers be allowed to display their virtuosity? to use every rhetorical trick in the book? to plan and execute grand structures? to set themselves difficult challenges and then allow us to watch as they triumph over those challenges? to load every rift of their subject with ore (as Keats put it)? For many critics, the answer to all these questions is No. Reviewing Byatt's *Little Black Book of Stories* in 2004, Carolyn See (a novelist herself) recognized the lavish artistry on display but complains "a little fine writing can go a long way . . . you want to say [to authors like Byatt], OK, I get it! We don't make enough use of the language! Our minds are largely dead! Thank you for sharing! You've made your point!" Cast not your pearls before swine, as the man said.

Back (again) to our star-crossed lovers: the story of Romeo and Juliet is familiar, one might object; with a new novel, there's the attraction of an unfamiliar plot. Not necessarily; "life, my fine friend, is made up strictly of four or five situations," the narrator of a quirky Brazilian novel informs us, "which circumstances vary and multiply in people's eyes,"[25] and the same can be said for fiction. In fact, most plots are just variations on one masterplot: "The novel records the passage from a state of innocence to a state of experience," critic Maurice Z. Shroder wrote many years ago, "from that of ignorance which is bliss to a mature recognition of the actual way of the world."[26] This is why so many novels in world literature feature protagonists in their teens or twenties, the time when one moves "from innocence to experience, ignorance to knowledge, naïveté to maturity."[27] In his *Seven Basic Plots* Christopher Booker suggests all stories are variations of (1) overcoming a monster, (2) rags to riches, (3) the quest, (4) a voyage and return, (5) comedy, (6) tragedy, or (7) rebirth; but don't all of these have in common some sort of confrontation with "the actual way of the world," as Shroder says, and at least a partial recognition

---

24 See Kurt Vonnegut's story "Harrison Bergeron" (1961), set in a future where dancers and musicians are deliberately handicapped so that they appear no better than anyone else.
25 Machado de Assis, *Quincas Borba*, 259.
26 "The Novel as a Genre" (1963), rpt. in Stevick, 16.
27 Heath, "Romance as Genre in *The Thousand and One Nights*" (1987), in Marzolph's *Arabian Nights Reader*, 197.

of how it really works? This is why critic Lionel Trilling claimed "all prose fiction is a variation on the theme of *Don Quixote*," that paradigm-shifting Spanish inquisition into illusion vs. reality (203). I would argue further that this should be the lifelong goal of every intelligent person: to see through the polite lies promulgated by political, corporate, media, and religious entities, the often irrational customs, beliefs, and prejudices of one's social group — everything that makes up "the curtain," as Milan Kundera calls it in his recent study of the novel — to arrive at a clear understanding of the true nature of things. This is why the novel is invaluable, for more than any other art form it encourages and assists us on that goal. Traditionally, the sacred scriptures of various cultures have claimed that prerogative, but they are merely fictions of a different sort — giving a false view of the world and promoting repression — inferior to the "secular scriptures" of imaginative literature.

But I don't want to overstate the novel's potential as a vehicle for enlightenment, or wholly endorse the Marxist view of writers as agitators for social change; novelists are not necessarily wiser than anyone else, and if fiction were truly enlightening, then literature professors would be veritable buddhas of wisdom and equanimity. (N.B.: they're not. In fact there's a whole subgenre of novels that quite rightly mocks them.) Sure, fiction can wise you up, although it can also trick you into thinking the world is other than it is, as in *Don Quixote*. Rather, the novel is essentially a delivery system for aesthetic bliss. The variations on the ignorance-to-knowledge masterplot differ so little in substance from novel to novel that *"something else"* is needed to make a choosy reader want to pick up yet another coming-of-age novel, for example, and that something is artistry, an aesthetically pleasing display of language and/or form. Both make Joyce's *A Portrait of the Artist as a Young Man* more satisfying than, say, John Grisham's *A Painted House*; the latter's predictable language, unrealistic dialogue (for a seven-year-old narrator), and by-the-numbers form offer little to the art crowd, though its melodramatic plot and social commentary appeal to those with mainstream tastes. As if to save such readers time and effort (and make them go away), Nabokov began one of his novels thus:

> Once upon a time there lived in Berlin, Germany, a man called Albinus. He was rich, respectable, happy; one day he abandoned his wife for the sake of a youthful mistress; he loved; was not loved; and his life ended in disaster.
>
> That is the whole of the story and we might have left it at that had there not been profit and pleasure in the telling; and although there is plenty of space on a gravestone to contain, bound in moss, the abridged version of a man's life, detail is always welcome.

The opening paragraph of *Laughter in the Dark* fulfills all of Myers's requirements; anyone reading for the plot and the moral point can stop right there.

(He would earn Myers's ire for giving away the plot, however.[28]) In the second, we see Nabokov switching from the commercial mode to the literary: one long, grammatically involved sentence rather than two short, choppy ones; the use of alliteration ("profit and pleasure") and fanciful imagery ("bound in moss"), and attitude: this will not be a straightforward story, but a clever writer putting on a show for us. The tale may be an old and predictable one, but the telling will be new and unpredictable. Predictability is fine in entertainment fiction — we know Hercule Poirot will eventually solve the mystery, Jeeves will extricate Bertie Wooster from the soup — but art thrives on novelty. British dance critic Nicholas Dromgoole admires dancer Sylvie Guillem even more than I do and reviewing her in the London *Sunday Telegraph* (July 1996) had this to say about one of her performances:

> Sylvie Guillem had chosen a show-off piece by Victor Gsovsky to music by Auber, run-of-the-mill choreography to put it mildly, but when shot through with her gleaming intelligence, it was transformed. It became a vehicle through which she captivated us, conveyed the fun of moving with incredible virtuoso skills, wrenching the music out of context and making it a part of something else: dance, nothing but lovely dance. . . . Gsovsky's steps really amount to little more than choreographic junk, a frayed piece of very old rope, but Guillem seems to be saying, "Yes, of course it is old rope, but just watch what I can do with it, and now, and this will surprise you, I am going to try this . . ." and her audience sits elated with surprise and delight.

With this in mind, let's now turn to an example Myers gives of pretentious prose, a passage that outraged him so much that he entitled an earlier version of his book after it (*Gorgons in the Pool*). It's from Cormac McCarthy's 1992 novel *All the Pretty Horses*; two young men named Rawlins and John Grady sit out a rainstorm in Mexico drinking bad booze:

> By dark the storm had slacked and the rain had almost ceased. They pulled the wet saddles off the horses and hobbled them and walked off in separate directions through the chaparral to stand spraddlelegged clutching their knees and vomiting. The browsing horses jerked their heads up. It was no sound they'd ever heard before. In the gray twilight those retchings seemed to echo like the calls of some rude provisional species loosed upon that waste. Something imperfect and malformed lodged in the heart of being. A thing smirking deep in the eyes of grace itself like a gorgon in an autumn pool.

28 Some publishers of literary classics are now affixing a spoiler alert at the head of the introduction, like this one from Penguin's 2004 edition of Gogol's *Dead Souls*: "*New readers are advised that this introduction makes the details of the plot explicit.*" I think customers who requested such alerts (there must have been complaints) are mistaking literary novels for Hollywood movies. If you're one of them, you'd better put my book down right now because I spoil the plots of the 200-plus novels I discuss.

Now, here's Myers reaction to this extraordinary (literally: beyond ordinary) paragraph:

> It is a rare passage in a rare book that can make you look up, wherever you may be, and wonder if you are being subjected to a diabolically thorough *Candid Camera* prank. I can *just* go along with the idea that horses might mistake human retchings for the call of wild animals. But "wild animals" isn't epic enough; McCarthy must blow smoke about "some rude provisional species," as if your average quadruped had table manners and a pension plan. Then he switches from the horses' perspective to the narrator's, though just what "something imperfect and malformed" refers to is unclear. The last half-sentence only deepens the confusion. Is the "thing smirking in the eyes of grace" the same thing that is "lodged in the heart of being"? And what is a gorgon doing in a pool? Or is it peering into it? And why an *autumn* pool? I doubt even McCarthy can explain any of this; he just likes the way it sounds. (48–49)

This reminds me of those smug TV announcers in the early days of rock who would recite the lyrics of pop tunes as poetry to the old farts in their audience and all have a good laugh over them. First, McCarthy could obviously explain all this; artists may be able to fling paint at a canvas and decide later whether they like the results, but writers don't do that, and Myers's contempt for McCarthy (and other such writers, *and* their lapdog reviewers) is obvious and is itself contemptible. Second, even though I'm no fan of McCarthy's writing — this happens to be the only novel of his I've read; I started a few others but couldn't get interested — it's obvious what he's doing here. *All the Pretty Horses* has its comic moments, and when it comes to describing a hangover, every writer feels at liberty to have some fun with it. They will reach for the most ludicrous simile they can find; Kingsley Amis described waking up with a hangover as "being spewed up like a broken crab upon the tarry shingle of the morning" — that sort of thing. McCarthy is no P. G. Wodehouse, so he's not going to get too goofy, but having reached a point in his novel where he can describe a hangover, he's obviously going to have some fun with this old staple. Like la Guillem, McCarthy is saying, "Yes, of course it is old rope, but just watch what I can do with it, and now, and this will surprise you, I am going to try this. . . ." The paragraph starts with some sequential alliteration (storm/slacked/ceased), and narratively winks at the reader with the clownish adverb "spraddlelegged," hinting at the fun to come. The boys' vomiting is enough to attract the attention of the horses, but the point of view doesn't change there. (I don't know why Myers thinks it does; and witness his feeble attempt to get a laugh out of it.) McCarthy, not the horses, comically compares the sound of their retching to the calls of some prehistoric species to underscore how wretched the boys feel. He could have stopped there — he's made his point and can speed the reader along to what's next — but no; "this will surprise you, I am going to try this." Pushing the simile even further, he conjures "something imperfect and malformed lodged in the heart of being." He could have stopped there too, but no; he's going to see if he can push it even further, like an aerialist attempting a triple somersault after accomplishing a single and a double. So now the money shot: "A thing smirking deep in the eyes of grace itself like a gorgon in an autumn pool." The eyes are compared to a pool (a traditional trope), and the smirking "thing" within finally identified as a gorgon, a monster from Greek mythology "imperfect and malformed." Note the alliteration between "grace" and "gorgon," and the assonance in "gorgon" and "autumn," both trochees. (Some adjective was necessary to modify "pool"; "autumn" is the right complement to "grace," evoking the stillness befitting the quiet chaparral. Plus "autumn pool" does indeed sound good.[29]) Yes, Mr. Myers, the "thing smirking in the eyes of grace" is the same thing that is "lodged in the heart of being." It's an extended metaphor — "retchings" become the "calls of some rude provisional species" that lodge themselves in and thus profane the "heart of being," just as a "rude provisional species" like a gorgon would profane with its presence an autumn pool. The "imperfect" gorgon is the perfect literary equivalent to a stomach-emptying, chaparral-echoing retch.

There are no doubt other, better ways to read this paragraph — I haven't looked to see what McCarthy specialists have made of it — but the point is I'm acting on the assumption McCarthy knows what's he's doing, rather than assuming he's a fake just because the passage doesn't make *immediate* sense. Though carefully constructed, the passage lacks the clarity of an instruction manual or of the prose of conventional writers, but literary writers take that chance. The best don't play it safe but push themselves, reaching for and even exceeding the best of their abilities. Sometimes they may go too far, like the dancer who occasionally slips while attempting a difficult combination, or a singer who has to slide up to a high note, but the proper reaction to such efforts is not to sneer but to applaud their daring, their willingness to give it their all. After holding up several of Annie Proulx's metaphors to ridicule, Myers quotes with scorn *Time* magazine reviewer John Skow, who actually demonstrates the correct attitude toward such writing: "Annie Proulx twirls words like a black-hat badman twirling Colts, fires them off for the sheer hell of it, blam, blam, no thought of missing, empty beer cans jump in the dust, misses one, laughs, reloads, blams some more. Something like that" (19). When it goes right, when the writer hits her targets, "her audience sits elated with surprise and delight," not looking around to see if they're on *Candid Camera.*

Now I've never read any Proulx, but I prefer such trick shots. The Canadian

29 It also sounded good to the author of the 14th-century Chinese novel *The Water Margin,* who says of a woman warrior: "The eyes are calm like autumn pools. . . ." (chap. 63). It's a common image in classic Chinese literature.

storyteller Alice Munro once furnished a blurb for a novel that read: *"The Man of My Dreams* is so free of tricks, the honesty is so startling, you feel there's a writer here who isn't trying to beguile you but to lay out some plain, raw truth about emotions and sex." But if I want the "plain, raw truth" on a topic, I'll read *nonfiction*; when I read fiction, I *want* to be tricked, I *want* to be beguiled. "Be wily, be twisty, be elaborate," the narrator is advised in Vikram Chandra's fabulous *Red Earth and Pouring Rain.* "Forsake grim shortness and hustle. Let us luxuriate in your curlicues" (24). Give me fat novels stuffed with learning and rare words, lashed with purple prose and black humor; novels patterned after myths, the Tarot, the Stations of the Cross, a chessboard, a dictionary, an almanac, the genetic code, a game of golf, a night at the movies; novels with unusual layouts, paginated backward, or with sentences running off the edges, or printed in different colors, a novel on yellow paper, a wordless novel in woodcuts, a novel in first chapters, a novel in the form of an anthology, Internet postings, or an auction catalog; huge novels that occupy a single day, slim novels that cover a lifetime; novels with footnotes, appendices, bibliographies, star charts, fold-out maps, or with a reading comprehension test or Q&A supplement at the end; novels peppered with songs, poems, lists, excommunications; novels whose chapters can be read in different sequences, or that have 150 possible endings; novels that are all dialogue, all footnotes, all contributors' notes, or one long paragraph; novels that begin and end midsentence, novels in fragments, novels with stories within stories; towers of babble, slang, shoptalk, technical terms, sweet nothings; give me many-layered novels that erect a great wall of words for protection against the demons of delusion and irrationality at loose in the world:

> When the Balinese prepare a corpse for burial, they read stories to one another, ordinary stories from collections of their most familiar tales. They read them without stopping, twenty-four hours a day, for two or three days at a time, not because they need distraction but because of the danger of demons. Demons possess souls during the vulnerable period immediately after a death, but stories keep them out. Like Chinese boxes or English hedges, the stories contain tales within tales, so that as you enter one you run into another, passing from plot to plot every time you turn a corner, until at last you reach the core of the narrative space, which corresponds to the place occupied by the corpse within the inner courtyard of the household. Demons cannot penetrate this space because they cannot turn corners. They beat their heads helplessly against the narrative maze that the readers have built, and so reading provides a kind of defense fortification surrounding the Balinese ritual. It creates a wall of words, which operates like the jamming of radio broadcasts. It does not amuse, instruct, improve, or help while away the time: by the imbrication of narrative and the cacophony of sound, it protects souls.[30]

30 Robert Darnton, *The Great Cat Massacre and Other Episodes in French Cultural History* (NY: Basic Books, 1984), 216. (I am grateful to Karen Elizabeth Gordon for sharing this

I'm reluctant to cite any French literary theorists, for I hold them largely responsible for turning literary criticism into the laughingstock it's become to most people outside the profession; 40 years ago they sashayed over like flirty foreign-exchange students and began seducing English and American critics into making fools of themselves.[31] However, Roland Barthes made a valuable distinction between "readerly" and "writerly" texts. A readerly (*lisible*) text is a conventional narrative with a beginning, middle, and end, one that can be passively consumed without much effort. A writerly (*scriptible*) text, however, is *un*conventional, more original, is open to a wider variety of interpretations, and requires some work on the reader's part, the purpose being "to make the reader no longer a consumer, but a producer of the text."[32] People like Myers are either unaware of this distinction or try to pound the square peg of a writerly text into the round hole of a readerly one, a fundamental mistake people usually don't make in other fields. A newspaper doesn't send its rock critic to review a symphonic concert, or its beret-wearing art-film critic to review the latest popcorny blockbuster down at the multiplex. Like movies, perhaps novels should have a rating printed on them — **R** for readerly, **W** for writerly — so that they attract the appropriate audience. Of course, many novels are mongrels — "pure" readerly and writerly novels are found at the extremes: Harlequin romances vs. *Finnegans Wake* — but most fall predominantly into one camp or the other. Most novels belong of course to the readerly camp: thousands are published each year in a variety of genres, they dominate the best-seller list and library waiting lists, and they are what most people think of when they use the term "novel." The writerly version is a rarer breed: 200 years ago the German critic Friedrich Schlegel idealized it as "a purely intellectual *jeux d'esprit*, sheer poetry and fancy, as much an abstraction from reality as the arabesque, which Kant had extolled as the highest form of art, because it does not copy any object in nature but is pure form."[33] Barthes himself described a writerly text as a "paradise of words," where "every kind of linguistic pleasure exists." He loses his head over Severo Sarduy's dazzling novel *Cobra*, which

---

passage with me.) All of the novels described in the preceding paragraph are real, by the way.

31 Terry Eagleton's *After Theory*, Daphne Pattai and Will H. Corral's *Theory's Empire*, and Brian Boyd's bluntly titled essay "Getting It All Wrong" survey the damage done. See also Frederick Crews' *Postmodern Pooh* (NY: North Point, 2002); his parodies of hip, academic critics and their theory-addled works are funny, accurate, and terribly depressing.

32 Barthes, *S/Z*, 4. Aptly enough, it requires some work on the reader's part to extract this meaning from Barthes's obfuscatory prose.

33 Thus Harry Steinhauer in his introduction to *Twelve German Novellas*, summarizing views put forth in Schlegel's essay on Boccaccio (1801). The arabesque — not the kind Sylvie Guillem executes so perfectly but the literary kind — will be discussed in my next volume.

is in fact a paradisiac text, utopian (without site), a heterology by plenitude: all the signifiers are here and each scores a bull's-eye; the author (the reader) seems to say to them: *I love you all* (words, phrases, sentences, adjectives, discontinuities: pell-mell: signs and mirages of objects which they represent); a kind of Franciscanism invites all words to perch, to flock, to fly off again: a marbled, iridescent text; we are gorged with language, like children who are never refused anything or scolded for anything or, even worse, "permitted" anything. (*The Pleasure of the Text*, 8)

But Myers mocks such aspirations, holding up the following quotation from Mark Leyner for ridicule, though it indicates exactly why I and many others treasure his work: "It's because I want every little surface to shimmer and gyrate that I haven't patience for those lax transitional devices of plot, setting, character, and so on, that characterize a lot of traditional fiction" (133). The most disturbing implication of criticism like MPF's is that there should be no such thing as writerly fiction, period, and that anyone attempting such stuff is either wasting his time (Roddy Doyle's verdict on *Finnegans Wake* after reading three pages), or indulging in pretentious showmanship, or just being difficult. Readerly texts are by definition reader-friendly, while writerly texts can often be difficult, and for many readers and reviewers, there is no greater sin in literature than difficulty.

IN PRAISE OF DIFFICULTY

"Art is not difficult because it wishes to be difficult," Donald Barthelme once wrote, "but because it wants to be art" (*Not-Knowing*, 15). Difficulty is the principal charge leveled against Joyce, Pynchon, Gaddis, and other ambitious novelists; perceived difficulty is what keeps many people from reading Proust or (as Franzen admits) from finishing *Moby-Dick*. Difficulty is nearly always considered a fault: it's the result of a writer trying too hard to be intellectual, too eager to show off a large vocabulary or specialized knowledge, or mistaking obscurity for profundity, or wanting to lord it over the reader, to rub his or her superiority in the hapless reader's face. Franzen says "literary difficulty can operate as a smoke screen for an author who has nothing interesting, wise, or entertaining to say." Myers and Peck would substitute "does" for "can."

Only in literature, however, is difficulty considered a fault rather than a virtue. Only readers resist what Yeats called "the fascination of what's difficult." In diving competitions and gymnastics, ratings depend on the degree of difficulty. Magicians who pull off difficult feats get more applause than the guy who merely pulls a rabbit out of a hat, as do jugglers who keep a dozen objects in the air rather than two or three oranges. Experienced climbers and skiers prefer the challenge of a difficult mountain over an easy one; for a good golfer, a "difficult" course is an exciting one. If you enjoy working jigsaw puzzles, do you want a simple one with 30 pieces, or a "difficult" one with 300? A crossword puzzle from *TV Guide* or the *New York Times*? Add your own examples. But when it comes to literature, many readers want to be spoon-fed; they want the bunny slope rather than the challenging one, miniature golf rather than the real thing. No wonder movies usually portray bookish types as pansies.

Some readers regard difficult writers as though they were difficult people, as Franzen put it elsewhere, their books as appealing as a difficult pregnancy. Critic Jack Green addressed "The 'Difficult' Cliché" in a section of his book *Fire the Bastards!* that defends Gaddis against his critics. (Franzen dubs him "Mr. Difficult" in his *New Yorker* piece, a charge that dogged Gaddis all his career.) Green points out that a novel is difficult only if you read it like a textbook, in which each paragraph has to be mastered before moving on to the next. Another critic, Sven Birkerts, admits this is exactly what kept him from appreciating Gaddis for so long: "It seems that I am wired in such a way that I cannot proceed with a book — a novel, say — so long as I feel that there are things I should be getting but am not. I cannot move to C until I've absolutely nailed A and B."[34] Great advice if following a cookbook. But we don't watch movies or listen to music that way. Can you imagine watching a movie with someone who kept stopping and rewinding it every time he wasn't 100 percent sure he had completely understood what had just happened and noted every detail on the screen? The first time you listened to one of Bob Dylan's lyrically abstract songs, did you hit the pause button after every verse to make sure you "absolutely nailed" it before letting the song continue? ("With your mercury mouth in the missionary times . . ." Huh? What's a "mercury" mouth? What or when are the missionary times? Is that a newspaper, the *Missionary Times*? Am I on *Candid Camera*?) Those who attended the riotous premiere of Stravinsky's *Rite of Spring* fell into two groups: those who didn't immediately understand the difficult music and started booing, and those who didn't immediately understand the difficult music but were intrigued enough to go on listening.

It isn't a matter of submitting uncritically to a difficult work; it's about trusting that the artist knows what he/she is doing, even if you don't apprehend it right away. Just keep reading: even the most difficult novel will eventually make some sense, and if you realize you missed things, you can always go back for a second try if still curious. As the late David Foster Wallace once wrote, "some art is worth the extra work of getting past all the impediments to

34 *Conjunctions* 41 (2003): 387–88.

its appreciation."[35] I suspect the difficulty with difficulty is largely a matter of personality: some people like a challenge, some don't; some people are open to new, initially puzzling experiences, others are scared off by them. In 1966, the poet John Ashbery returned to New York City from Paris to take in Andy Warhol's multimedia show the Exploding Plastic Inevitable; bewildered by the lights, the dancers, and Velvet Underground's loud, anarchistic music, he cried, "I don't understand this at all" and burst into tears.[36] Others were enthralled.

"Difficulty" is the wrong word; a better one is "complexity." Writers like Joyce and Gaddis planned their novels on an ambitious scale — cathedrals, not trailer homes — and probably knew that with every new level of complexity they added, they would lose a few more readers. But they did so because "the work required it," as it says on the last page of Gaddis's *Recognitions*, not to impress the gullible or to be difficult. Literary critics have been chastised in recent years for applying ill-understood scientific concepts to literature — see Sokal and Bricmont's scolding *Fashionable Nonsense* (1998) — but I can't resist quoting planetologist David Grinspoon on what's called "complexity theory": "All the significant developments in our cosmic story can be seen as leaps to new levels of complexity."[37] Likewise, all the significant developments in the novel can be seen as leaps to new levels of complexity. Those who bemoan complexity/difficulty in modern literature remind me of fretful fathers who don't want to see their little girls grow up; a 17-year-old is more complex, more "difficult" to understand than a seven-year-old in pigtails, but this is a necessary, positive development, not a loss. Dad may despair, but she can't wait to discuss Camus with college boys while showing off her new bustier.

When the Beatles released *Sgt. Pepper's Lonely Hearts Club Band* in June 1967, some criticized its complexity. Writing to the official Beatles fan magazine, Joanne Tremlett of Welling, Kent, complained, "I can't tell you how disappointed I was when I played it through. Of all the songs, only 'When I'm 64' and 'Sgt. Pepper's Lonely Hearts Club Band' itself come up to standard. Everything else is over our heads and The Beatles ought to stop being so clever and give us tunes we can enjoy."[38] Like that British bird, MPF tell authors "Please Please Me," but would the Fab Four have become the cultural icons they are today if they had stuck to exhilarating but simple songs like that? It was their willingness to experiment, to explore new directions that made them more popular than Jesus, not their allegiance to fans like

---

35 *Consider the Lobster*, 263. Originally I had written, "As my favorite living writer says," but sorrowfully revised it after Dave hanged himself in September 2008. What a devastating loss to modern literature.

36 Steven Watson, *Factory Made: Warhol and the Sixties* (NY: Pantheon, 2003), 277.

37 *Lonely Planets: The Natural Philosophy of Alien Life* (NY: Ecco, 2003), 270. Grinspoon's breezy but informed approach to his topic kick-started my book.

38 Quoted in John Harris's "The Day the World Turned Day-Glo," *Mojo*, March 2007, 87.

Joanne Tremlett of Welling, Kent. If most older fans applauded the Beatles' progression from "I Want to Hold Your Hand" to "I Am the Walrus," why is Joyce vilified for progressing from *Dubliners* to *Finnegans Wake*? Tell me why literary authors aren't allowed to be as ambitious as pop musicians.

Do you want to know a secret? Literature is not for everyone. People grant that about the other arts — serial music isn't for everyone, nor is Balinese shadow dancing — but when it comes to fiction, there's a democratic assumption that anyone with a basic education should be able to read and enjoy any novel. Perhaps this stems from high school, where everyone is assigned classic novels to read, whereas classes in art or music have to be elected, and opera and dance not offered at all. Hence some feel it's reprehensible to write a novel beyond a high-school reading level. (And of course the idea that some novels require a little extra work to understand is anathema, despite the fact that readers surely remember from school how much more a novel reveals with a little study.) Franzen, criticized himself for writing novels over the heads of "the average person who just enjoys a good read" (the complaint of a Mrs. M—, quoted in his "Mr. Difficult"), states that "Fiction is the most fundamental human art. Fiction is storytelling, and our reality arguably consists of the stories we tell about ourselves. Fiction is also conservative and conventional, because the structure of its market is relatively democratic . . ." (108), and hence writers should eschew difficulty or any impulse to elevate this populist, market-driven entertainment into an art form. Peck feels the same way; with the arrogance of one who assumes his own personal reaction is a universal one (and displaying again his ignorance of pre-20th-century fiction), he complains:

> My generation has inherited a tradition that has grown increasingly esoteric and exclusionary, falsely intellectual and alienating to the mass of readers, and just as falsely comforting to those in the club. In place of centuries of straightforward class discrimination, the twentieth century invented an elitist rhetoric intelligible to only the most diligent and educated of readers — a club that doesn't exclude anyone per se, but makes you work very, very hard to join. In the process they lost not just the eye but the respect of a more general reading public, a respect that every generation since modernism has striven for unsuccessfully, trying to entice the common reader back into the fold with delicately carved morsels of rotting flesh they try to pass off as prime rib. (222)

Why this bleeding-heart concern for "the mass of readers," "the common reader"? They have more than enough to satisfy them, as the best-seller lists indicate; most of the publishing industry caters to their tastes. Why this intolerance for the minority of readers with a different textual orientation who prefer an alternative kind of fiction, one that they genuinely enjoy (a concept MPF can't fathom, for some reason), and which is neither "falsely intellectual" nor "falsely comforting"? Such fiction is challenging and unconventional, granted, but the fact that it's not for everyone doesn't make it elitist, snobbish, pretentious, arrogant, or wrong-headed. It's simply not for everyone.

QUIZ: ARE YOU READER ENOUGH FOR DIFFICULT FICTION?

In the early 1990s I was an editor at Dalkey Archive Press, which specialized in what one bookseller disparaged as "egghead" fiction. The most difficult and demanding novel we published was probably Julián Ríos's *Larva: Midsummer Night's Babel*, sort of Spain's answer to *Finnegans Wake*. It received fine reviews across the country, including a spirited one from Michael Dirda in the *Washington Post*, but since the *New York Times Book Review* adamantly ignored it (despite Carlos Fuentes's pleading) and a promised review in the *Voice Literary Supplement* fell through, I decided to try to reach their hip demographic with an ad in the *VLS* captioned "Are You Reader Enough for *Larva*?" The mock-macho appeal was intended to attract those who like a literary challenge, as well as those who are open to new artistic experiences. Since I'm convinced those who malign innovative fiction do so more for personal, temperamental reasons than for the aesthetic ones they publicly espouse, here's a test you can take to see if you're the right kind of reader for writerly texts:

1. You are an average Joe or Jane and have moved to a big city offering lots of culture. One night you're strolling past an art-house theater and the manager is out front giving away tickets to fill the house (the money's in the concessions). Having nothing better to do, you take a seat and soon learn the movie is in a foreign language and has no subtitles. Do you:
   (a) automatically get up and leave, knowing you won't completely understand it?
   (b) stay and get what you can out of it: appreciate the cinematography, the background music, the way an actress holds her purse, the possibility of a sex scene, etc.?
2. A neighbor gives you a free ticket to the ballet in gratitude for babysitting her cat last week. You go and discover it's not a simple story ballet like *Gisele* or *Swan Lake* but an evening of abstract dance. Do you:
   (a) give your ticket away because you don't "understand" modern dance?
   (b) stay and enjoy the show: the unusual choreography, the beautiful bodies poured into bodystockings, the weird music, etc.?
3. Speaking of weird music: you go to a club hoping for some good ol' rock 'n' roll, but instead of a long-haired band there's a bald DJ spinning some techno-ambient concoction unlike anything you've ever heard before. Do you:

    (a) pull an Ashbery by crying, "I don't understand this at all" and burst into tears?

    (b) let the music wash over you, let yourself find the pulse, maybe even ask that purple-haired girl in the striped tights to dance?

4. You've had enough of the big city and decide to return home. Waiting for a bus, you pick up a discarded copy of *Larva* and, because you have a long bus-ride ahead of you, begin reading. You quickly discover it is not a conventional novel. Do you:

    (a) discard it and stare out the window all the way back home?

    (b)

It's not necessary to go on, or to provide an answer key. An openness to innovative fiction is an openness to any new experience, a willingness to try new things, knowing full well you may not completely understand them at first but always willing to give interesting things a shot. We all know people who prefer to stick to the tried and true, who automatically reject anything that doesn't conform to their pre-established tastes (or, more often, the pre-established tastes of their social group; such people are not exactly Ayn Randian pillars of individuality). These are the people who mock anything new *because* it is new, anything different *because* it is different. Of course it can be equally brainless to champion novelty merely for its own sake, to don and discard fads like a fashion slave. Just because something's new and different doesn't necessarily mean it's good. But a willingness to give the new a chance distinguishes fans of writerly texts from those of readerly texts, and individualists from the masses: "The human spirit requires surprise, variety, and risk in order to enlarge itself," writes novelist Tom Robbins in one of his essays. "Imagination feeds on novelty. As imagination emaciates, options diminish; the fewer our options, the more bleak our prospects and the greater our susceptibility to controls" (*Wild Ducks Flying Backward*, 72–73). Hell, even animals thrive on novelty, as Temple Grandin tells us:

> Animals find novelty both fear-provoking and attractive. Normal development of the brain requires novelty and varied sensory input. Novelty-seeking behavior is hard-wired in the brain and guides the animal to explore their environment in order to access their safety and discover new food sources.[39]

Indifference I could understand; there's no law that anyone interested in culture *has* to champion the avant-garde. Hostility from the uncultured I can also understand; they always feel threatened by the new and different. But hostility from the cultured is the most puzzling for several reasons, most of

---

39 *Humane Livestock Handling: Innovative Plans for Healthier Animals and Better Quality Meat* (North Adams, MA: Storey, 2008), 19.

them ugly. Recall Myers's prescription for ideal fiction ("strong stories told in an unaffected fashion"; "no pseudo-Joycean tomfoolery with punctuation — just crisp, believable dialogue"), then read Dubravka Ugrešić's description of one society that enforced that literary ideal with a vengeance:

> Stalinist writers had to take great care to follow the rules of the game: the rules of socialist realism. And those rules were not just ideological but also commercial. Literature had to be comprehensible to the broad reading masses; there was no place for avant-gardism and the antics of experimentalism. . . . One had to squelch through a muddy *kolhoz*, and then at the request of some publisher write a novel which would be convincing to the vast Soviet masses. One had to know how to use narrative techniques, to control one's own creative impulses and literary taste, to clench one's teeth and write within the framework of the given norm. Only a true professional could agree to something like that. Writers who were unable to adapt to the demands of the ideological market ended tragically: in camps. Nowadays, writers who cannot adapt to commercial demands end up in their own personal ghetto of anonymity and poverty. (44)

That last part's not always true — many experimental writers in the U.S. at least seem to be tenured professors — but this is why the hostility shown by MPF smacks of totalitarianism; or, if that's too strong, of deep conservatism. (It's probably only coincidental that all three essays by MPF appeared during the second Bush presidency; then again, Tom Wolfe's earlier and similar screed appeared during the first Bush presidency, so maybe not.[40]) Those who protest at museums or movie theaters, try to remove books from school libraries (and, if they can, burn them), and/or phone television stations to complain of anything that departs from their provincial Puritan values rarely read innovative fiction, but they don't need to: it's being trashed by book journalists who are probably liberal in most matters but conservative when it comes to literature. To label MPF's attitude toward unconventional fiction "fascist" would be going too far, but it's no coincidence that the kind of fiction they condemn is the same kind always banned by totalitarian governments. As a character in one of Arno Schmidt's novels sneers, "Art for the people ? ! : leave that slogan to the Nazis and Communists" (*Nobodaddy's Children*, 115).

Then there's what we might call the Salieri syndrome, where an artist regards another artist's superior abilities as a personal insult. As "ballet's bad girl" Sylvie Guillem snaps in her French accent, "Jealous people get mean. Your success reflects their failure." In the 1984 movie *Amadeus*, Mozart represents the flashy, "difficult" artist — his music contains "too many notes"

---

40 See Wolfe's "Stalking the Billion-Footed Beast: A Literary Manifesto for the New Social Novel" (*Harper's*, November 1989), and *then* see Mikhail Epstein's "Tom Wolfe and Social(ist) Realism" (*Common Knowledge*, 1:2 [1992]; on the Web), where the same parallel to Stalinist fiction is explored.

and makes "too many demands on the royal ear," which is essentially the complaint made against Gaddis et al. — and earns the jealous resentment of rival composer Antonio Salieri. Novelist John Gardner, the Dale Peck of his day, lambasted Gaddis, Barth, Gass, and other superior writers in *On Moral Fiction* (1978) but later admitted jealousy played a big part: "I wrote [most of] that book in 1964," he said in 1983. "I had not yet been published. I was furious — just enraged at those guys with big reputations. . . . Most of it I got wrong. . . . I'm ashamed of my mistakes, and it's full of them."[41] "*I apologize if I got it all wrong*" Peck says on the dedication page of his *Hatchet Jobs,* and in a few years his toes will probably curl in embarrassment at such statements as this:

> Moody starts his books like a boxer talking trash before the bout, as if trying to make his opponent forget that the only thing that really matters is how hard and how well you throw your fists after the bell rings. But in reality the clash between Moody and the reader is less pugilistic competition than pissing contest, particularly if that reader happens to be a man; and if that reader happens to be a writer then the experience becomes even more inflammatory. For me, the beginning of a Rick Moody book is a bit like having a stranger walk up and smack me in the face, and then stand there waiting to see if I am man enough to separate him from his balls. (176)

Oh dear. What does one do with a psychotic reaction like that to a work of art? Shake the head and move on to something more common but equally repulsive. William Gaddis died on 16 December 1998; five days later, book critic Carlin Romano published in the *Philadelphia Inquirer* a mean-spirited obituary — punk didn't have the balls to call Gaddis out while he was still alive (as Peck might say) — that exposes the ugly arrogance of readers who can't admit they're not as smart as they think they are. Assuming Gaddis was out "to torture readers for their own good" with his "derivative pseudo-European modernism," Romano calls his novels shapeless and unorganized and clotted with "untethered arcana." (Can't recognize the organization of a novel? Assume there isn't one. Baffled by "arcana" — i.e., stuff you don't already know? Call the author pretentious. Find a book hard-going? Assume the author is deliberately torturing you.) Setting aside the utter tastelessness of attacking a writer while the corpse is still warm, the viciousness of Romano's attack betrays something else at work. He's a bright, well-read guy who thus assumes that he should be able to comprehend any novel he takes up; when he can't — as his snide summaries of Gaddis's novels certainly suggest — he is psychologically unable to admit he may have intellectual shortcomings, that some writing is over his head, so instead he blames the author for willful obscurity and meanness. I've seen it before. I once taught Nabokov's story

41 Quoted in Silesky's *John Gardner,* 278.

"The Vane Sisters" to some undergraduates, and when I showed on the chalkboard how the initial letters of the words in the final paragraph of the story form an acrostic spelling out a message, a female student exploded with rage, as though a dirty trick had been pulled on her. (I reacted with amazed delight when I first learned of Nabokov's gambit; imagine how difficult it must have been to compose that paragraph, even working in the word "acrostics" into his acrostic!)

For some people, resentment rather than modesty is the ego's way of protecting itself; play them some unconventional music and they dismiss it as noise, show them some nonrepresentational art and they claim their kid could do as well. You know the type. There's a better way to respond to what you don't understand: When I was 30, having already published a few short articles on *Finnegans Wake* and with my first book under contract to an academic press, I was feeling pretty cocky about my critical abilities. Then an acquaintance studying modern literature at Denver University — Margaret Whitt, who later wrote a book on Flannery O'Connor — asked me to read an assigned story that she couldn't make heads or tails of: Donald Barthelme's "Indian Uprising." I had never read it but promised an explication next time I saw her. I read the story, and was humbled. I couldn't make heads or tails of it either. I *liked* it, even though I didn't understand it, and immediately recognized Barthelme as an original stylist. I didn't look around to see if I was on *Candid Camera*, I didn't feel betrayed that Barthelme hadn't fulfilled an implied author–reader contract, didn't feel like I'd been smacked in the face by a stranger, nor did I attack him as a lousy writer because the meaning of his story wasn't immediately apparent to a bright guy like me. I was humbled.

Of course, a lot of mediocre stuff that calls itself art gets produced, in literature as well as other fields, and one needs to develop an aesthetic sensibility to distinguish the good from the bad, innovative novels from mere novelties. I remember once reading a novel that avoided any form of the verb "to be," but I stopped after 30 pages because it was still a lousy novel, despite this challenging formal constraint.[42] But that same sensibility needs to be able to recognize when something is good but incompatible with one's personal tastes, and such recognitions should result in toleration rather than condemnation. I have zero interest in polka music, for example, but I can tell a good polka band from a bad one, and the former will have my respect even as I race for the exit to avoid those obstreperous accordions. To condemn polka music (and its fans) as inferior simply because I personally don't care for the music would be arrogant beyond belief. Yet it's arrogance and intolerance I hear when MPF launch their attacks, not a defense of standards (as they seem to think). I'm sure those hecklers at the premiere of *The Rite of Spring*

---

42 It wasn't Christine Brooke-Rose's *Between* (1968), which works under the same constraint, but some other novel, with a half-hearted blurb by novelist Walter Abish.

arrogantly assumed they were upholding standards, just like those folkies who booed Dylan when he went electric at Newport in 1965. (They must have forgotten his advice in their old favorite, "The Times They Are A-Changin'": "Don't criticize / What you can't understand.") To admit that certain novels are excellent but not to one's taste requires an honesty and humility seldom seen in critics, and an ability to distinguish between objectivity and subjectivity, seldom seen in anybody.

THE STRANGE SURPRIZING ADVENTURES OF THE NOVEL

Objectivity may be possible when evaluating a mathematical equation or a chemistry experiment — either it works or it doesn't — but subjectivity by necessity obscures any literary judgment. Personal tastes, background, and expectations will always trump critical claims for the merit or deficiency of any writer, no matter how strong the argument. But I remain convinced that negative reactions to unconventional modern fiction can be blamed partly on ignorance of the novel's long, colorful, and decidedly unconventional history. No one familiar with Lyly's *Euphues* is likely to accuse a contemporary writer of being showy and pretentious; Lyly makes them all look as modest as nuns. Gaddis's alleged difficulty is a walk in the park compared with Subandhu's *Vasavadatta*. Those who balk at the length of some of today's literary mega-novels (*Gravity's Rainbow*, *Infinite Jest*, *2666*) might be chastened to learn that the best novels in China, Arabia, and France during the late medieval period are *thousands* of pages long.

One legitimate excuse for this ignorance is the paucity of books on the subject. There are dozens of histories of painting, opera, sculpture, ballet, and the other arts, but almost no general histories of the novel, only specialized studies (Saintsbury's *History of the French Novel*, Watt's *Rise of the Novel* [in England, that is], Hsia's *Classic Chinese Novel*, etc.).[43] This is a gap my book obviously hopes to fill. I'd like to think a greater tolerance for writers who depart from the norm will be possible once it becomes apparent the novel never really had a norm, until recently. Nor should it: the novel is "the most anarchical of all forms of literature," Orwell once noted, and the late British

---

43 The only comprehensive histories in English I know of are Dunlop's pioneering study, *The History of Fiction* (1814), a three-volume survey from the ancient Greeks down to his own time; Warren's *History of the Novel Previous to the Seventeenth Century* (1895), also beginning with the Greeks; and Doody's *True Story of the Novel* (1996), which traces the influence of ancient Greek and Roman novels on later ones. Doody in particular covers a lot of territory, but passes over just as much that is irrelevant to her thesis. Even more ground is covered in *The Novel* (2006), a two-volume collection of essays edited by Franco Moretti (reduced from the five-volume Italian original), but its collective nature (about a hundred contributors) preempts a coherent narrative and consistent point of view. Besides, it's priced for the library market and intended for researchers, not general readers.

critic (and early champion of *The Recognitions*) Tony Tanner agreed: "The novel, in its origin, might almost be said to be a transgressive mode, inasmuch as it seemed to break, or mix, or adulterate the existing genre-expectations of the time."[44] And to this day the novel remains defiantly lawless; as the experimental novelist Julio Cortázar once joked, "in reality, the novel has no rules, except to keep the law of gravity from going into effect and allowing the book to fall from the reader's hands."[45] Establishing a continuum between anarchical, transgressive, innovative novelists past and present offers a much-needed sense of perspective for contemporary readers, if only to prevent them from making stupid remarks like this one from Gardner: "When the artist has moved as far from the tradition of the novel as either of these novels has moved [Bely's *Petersburg* and Beckett's *Malone Dies*], he has nothing to guide him but his feelings as he writes" (*On Moral Fiction*, 170). The tradition is wider and weirder than that, and if artists didn't move away from the tradition from time to time, literature would never have progressed beyond tales told around campfires. In the last essay she wrote, Susan Sontag warned of the danger of assuming (as Gardner and MPF do) that "the tradition of the novel" is only a few centuries old:

> The long prose fiction called the novel, for want of a better name, has yet to shake off the mandate of its own normality as promulgated in the 19th century: to tell a story peopled by characters whose opinions and destinies are those of ordinary, so-called real life. Narratives that deviate from this artificial norm and tell other kinds of stories, or appear not to tell much of a story at all, draw on traditions that are more venerable than those of the 19th century, but still, to this day, seem innovative or ultra-literary or bizarre.[46]

What follows is a history of the various forms and permutations the novel has taken over the centuries, a survey of the infinite variety of this versatile, venerable genre. It's both an alternative history of the novel and a history of the alternative novel. It's not an exercise in multicultural revisionism, but simply an attempt to tell the complete story of the novel, not the abridged version most people know. This volume takes the novel from its beginnings up to the end of the 16th century, just before the publication of *Don Quixote*, which some call the first novel. Volume 2 will begin with Cervantes's antic masterpiece and then track those novelists who continued to refresh the genre up to the present.

You will have noticed I have not yet expanded on my preliminary definition of the novel offered earlier, and that I have been using various modifiers

---

44 "Inside the Whale," 239; *Adultery in the Novel*, 3.
45 From Ernesto González Barmejo's *Conversaciones con Cortázar* (1978), as quoted by Peavler in his *Julio Cortázar*, 94.
46 "A Report on the Journey," *New York Times Book Review*, 20 February 2005, 16 (reprinted as the introduction to Halldór Laxness's *Under the Glacier*, also 2005).

(innovative, noncommercial, unconventional, avant-garde, experimental, alternative) almost interchangeably. This is because none of those modifiers is quite right, and because every definition of the novel I've come across disqualifies several books on my groaning shelves labeled "novels" by their authors or publishers. It doesn't help that even the most basic features of the novel are hard to pin down. One could say a story is short and deals with one incident while a novel is long(er) and deals with a series of incidents, and go on to state the novel is written in prose, not poetry, and consists either of fictitious events or historic events treated fictitiously. But exceptions immediately occur, beginning with length. Pynchon considers his *Crying of Lot 49* a story, while his publishers and most readers consider it a novel.[47] Ronald Firbank's *Santal* was published as a novel, yet it occupies some 20 pages in *The Complete Firbank*; none of the three "novels" gathered in Samuel Beckett's *Nohow On* is much longer. Poet Jack Spicer's *Fake Novel about the Life of Arthur Rimbaud* — in three books of 10 chapters each — runs 17 pages. Yuri Tarnawsky has written what he calls "mininovels," short fictions 10 to 40 pages long that have the *effect* of full-length novels. The 10 novels collected in Stephen Leacock's *Nonsense Novels* average 15 pages each; the odd couple comprising Canadian writer bpNichol's *Two Novels* (1969) are even shorter. Gertrude Stein wrote a piece entitled "A Little Novel" that is slightly over a page long, and wrote stories that she called "novelettes." *The Grand Passion* by Edward Gorey is subtitled "A Novel"; it consists of 15 captioned drawings that occupy two and a half pages of *Amphigorey Also*. Most of these authors are of course toying with the term "novel," but who is authorized to set a minimal length?

And prose vs. poetry? There are hundreds of novels written in verse, novels that alternate between prose and poetry, and book-length prose poems. Fielding called his *Joseph Andrews* a "comic epic-poem in prose." Mark Z. Danielewski's *Only Revolutions* looks and reads like a 360-page poem, yet is categorized as a novel.

And fiction vs. nonfiction? There are fictitious works masquerading as nonfiction — Geoffrey of Monmouth's *History of the Kings of Britain* and the *Book of Mormon* are obvious examples — and the "nonfiction novel" popularized by Capote and Mailer in the 1960s can be traced back for centuries. (Literary historian Elaine Showalter says Mary Rowlandson's 1682 Indian captivity narrative "really is a novel.") Frederick Exley called his heartbreaking *A Fan's Notes* "a fictional memoir"; Jack Kerouac called his beat books "true story novels," but his collected fiction a "legend." Gore Vidal's *Two Sisters*

---

47 See his introduction to *Slow Learner* (Boston: Little, Brown, 1984), 22. And page counts are not helpful when making distinctions; *The Crying of Lot 49* is about 50,000 words, and though his original publisher was able to spread that out over 183 pages, it would occupy only 83 pages if set in the same layout as Wallace's *Infinite Jest*. Wallace himself wrote "stories" the length of novellas.

is subtitled "A Memoir in the Form of a Novel." There are works that have undergone the equivalent of a sex-change operation — Kenneth Gangemi's *Volcanoes from Puebla* was published as nonfiction in 1979, but billed as fiction when reprinted a decade later — and books that swing both ways: when Peck sold his book *What We Lost* to his publisher, he told them, "I didn't care if they published it as a novel or as a memoir."[48] The opening chapters of Fay Weldon's *Mantrapped* (2004) alternate between fiction and memoir, an example of what she calls "the new reality novel"; after her female protagonist swaps souls with a man, the fiction and memoir start bleeding into one another, providing an interesting exercise in both gender- and genre-bending.[49] What is *What Is the What* by Dave Eggers (2006), fiction (as marketed) or nonfiction (which it mostly is)? Wayne Koestenbaum's *Hotel Theory* (2007) is printed in two columns, one nonfiction and one fiction; how do you classify *that* book, Sir Critic? Alexandra Lapierre's *Artemisia* was first published in England as a biography, then as a historical novel in America in 2001.

That same year David Markson published a brilliant novel provocatively entitled *This Is Not a Novel*; well, is it or isn't it? Is Carlyle's *Sartor Resartus* fiction or philosophy? Are Laurence Sterne's *Sentimental Journey* and E. E. Cummings's *EIMI* novels or travelogues? Is *Winesburg, Ohio* a novel or a collection of stories? Is *Go Down, Moses* a short-story collection, as its original publisher called it, or a novel, as Faulkner insisted?[50] Is Andy Warhol's *a* (1968), a book of tape-recorder transcriptions, really "a novel," as its subtitle claims? Tolstoy didn't consider *War and Peace* a novel and begged his editor not to call it one. George Singleton confidently called his 2005 novel *Novel: A Novel*, but an uncertain A. J. Perry entitled his quirky 2000 book of fiction *Twelve Stories of Russia: A Novel, I Guess*. Choplogic critics have complicated matters further by subdividing the novel into special categories: the romance, the anatomy, the confession, the historical novel, the naturalist novel, the novel of manners, the French *récit*, the antinovel, the meganovel, and so forth.[51] And then there are hypertext and graphic novels, manga and cellphone novels (big in Japan), the "new-media novel" (see Steve Tomasula's mystic *TOC*, a DVD from FC2), instant-messaging novels (click

---

48 Interview with Robert Birnbaum (2003). Occasionally there's a scandal in the publishing world when a nonfiction memoir is exposed as being largely fictitious; sometimes said works were submitted as novels but published as memoirs to attract greater attention (i.e., sales).

49 The cover of the original British edition uses only the title and features family photos, looking very much like a memoir; the American edition that followed a few months later has "a novel" printed on the cover and indeed looks like one.

50 And speaking of Faulkner: Is *If I Forget Thee, Jerusalem* a novel, or two novellas sliced and diced together? Is *Requiem for a Nun* a play or a novel?

51 The "antinovel" is associated with postwar French novelists — Sartre used it to describe a novel by Nathalie Sarraute — but the term was actually coined by the experimental novelist Charles Sorel in 1633. (Yes, there were experimental novelists in the 17th century.)

Lauren Myracle's *ttyl, ttfn,* and/or *l8r, g8r*), digi-novels, and other species of fictions that have emerged in recent years. Coming up with a definition that encompasses all these works is beyond me; I'd rather let authors show me what a novel can be than to impose a definition on them. Henry James famously described certain novels as "large loose baggy monsters," and if the movies have taught us anything it's that monsters come in all shapes and sizes, many unimaginable until they burst onto the screen. I want to rethink what we mean by a "novel," and to look at the various ways writers have kept the novel novel over the centuries. In his review of Pynchon's *Against the Day*, Luc Sante stated "the size and sprawl of Pynchon's canvas proceed from an impatience with the limits of the novel form";[52] but there have never been limits to the novel form, as I will show. The sky's always been the limit for the best novelists, who couldn't care less how critics label their fictions.

Finally, most older novels have been the victims of antiquated nomenclature. Until a few centuries ago, "literature" meant only poetry or drama; most cultures didn't even have a word (much less a critical rhetoric) for long prose fictions, whose authors were operating in a kind of Wild West outside the laws of sanctioned literature. Consequently, there are older book-length prose "romances," "sagas," "tales," "pastorals," "legends," "acts," "picaresques," and "folk epics" that are novels in everything but name. When critics argue that these earlier forms aren't really novels, they mean *conventional, modern* novels, a provincial view that ignores the wild diversity of fiction in our own time as well as in the past. Just because older, foreign novels don't exactly resemble those on the *New York Times* best-seller list, it doesn't mean they're not novels; the earliest European travelers to the Far East sometimes dismissed the complex music there as barbaric noise simply because it didn't sound like the music back home. Defending Firbank's capricious novels against the charge of "artificiality," British critic Philip Toynbee argued (in a 1961 *Observer* review) "there is no such thing as a 'natural' novel; there are simply various methods, tones and styles which appear to us in varying degrees of familiarity." The aesthetics of a 7th-century Sanskrit novel may be unfamiliar to us in the West, but it still qualifies as a novel.

I want to emphasize that I'm not foisting a private, eccentric notion of the novel on older works, but rather am working backward from recent developments in the genre. If we can call Nabokov's *Pale Fire* a novel — which the Victorians would not have — we can bestow that description on other unusual fictions of the past that mix fiction and poetry. Similarly, if we call Gilbert Sorrentino's episodic, stylistic tour de force *Blue Pastoral* a novel — and

---

52 "Inside the Time Machine," 8. Sante of course means the "traditional" or "conventional" novel; I'm starting to think the noun "novel" is incomplete without a qualifying adjective, like "conventional," "experimental," "graphic," "romantic," "Western," "detective," "cyberpunk," or even (as David Breskin describes his *Supermodel* [2006]) "self-contextualizing turbo-novel."

it says so, right on the cover — then we can call Judah Alharizi's episodic, stylistic tour de force *Sefer Tahkemoni* one too. More important, this reverse-engineering allows us to see that *Pale Fire* and *Blue Pastoral* don't so much make radical departures from the genre (as MPF would complain) as recover features that were dropped centuries ago in favor of more mainstream narratives. Nor am I showing much originality, much less eccentricity, for these identifications. I'm certainly not the first to call the longer Icelandic sagas novels, and earlier critics called the anonymous Irish *Pursuit of Diarmaid and Gráinne* and Zabara's 12th-century *Book of Delight* novels long before I'd ever heard of them. Nearly a century ago, my idol George Saintsbury described the medieval *Lancelot-Grail* as a novel with no sense of anachronism. It was the great kabbala scholar Gershom Scholem who first called the *Zohar* a mystical novel, not me. Now and again I'll be stretching the term a bit to include some borderline cases, but not much further than other historians of the novel.

My specialty is 20th-century fiction, so I spend most of this book tramping through many fields where (some academics might say) I don't belong, though I should point out in my defense that I read pretty widely in world literature before I settled on contemporary fiction. When studying for my master's degree in the early 1970s I became enamored with medieval literature: I learned to read Middle English with some ease — I dedicated my first book to my Middle English professor, a flamboyant man named Sam Freeman, who died under mysterious circumstances the summer I studied Chaucer with him — then learned Anglo-Saxon from a former nun — she liked my translation of "The Battle of Maldon" but went medieval on my commentary — and ate up things like the Welsh *Mabinogion* and Jackson's *Celtic Miscellany*. After graduating, I made a list of all the major literary works I had not read yet — I had been a history major my first two years of college, hence got off to a late start — and spent the next few years working my way through *Gilgamesh*, Greek and Latin classics, the Bible,[53] the complete Burton translation of *The Arabian Nights* (but only the first half of *The Tale of Genji*), Dante, Rabelais, Cervantes, Li Yu's *Prayer Mat of Flesh* (1657), Sade, the great Russian novelists, George Borrow's Gypsy novels, etc., all while supporting a serious Joyce habit and trying my hand at a few novels myself.[54] Returning to college a decade later to earn a doctorate allowed me to fill in other gaps.

53 I wouldn't mention this except that I continue to be surprised at how few people, even among Christians, have read the whole thing. In fact, reading the Bible led to my first scholarly publication, a short note suggesting one aspect of the Buckley and the Russian general episode in *Finnegans Wake* was based on an incident in 1 Samuel: see "David in Crimea," *A Wake Newsletter* 13 (December 1976): 115–16.

54 One finished but unpublished, a second abandoned after a few hundred pages, though there's nothing like writing a novel yourself to sharpen your appreciation for those who do it well.

Thus the challenge for me is not unfamiliarity with earlier literature but with foreign languages. I know only a little Spanish and a soupçon of French, so I've had to rely on translations for all but a handful of the novels discussed in this book — a major drawback for someone like me in it for the language. Even the best translation is merely a ventriloquist's act, a cover version leaving the reader wondering what the original sounded like. As that old rake Goethe memorably put it, translators are like "enthusiastic matchmakers singing the praises of some half-naked young beauty: they awaken in us an irresistible urge to see the real thing with our own eyes." (I'm relying on a translator for that line, and yes I'm aware of the irony.) The first thing lost in translation is figurative language and nuances of style; Flaubert would spend all day searching for *le mot juste,* but how many translators devote that much time to one word? But don't get me wrong; I'm grateful to them, for without the profusion of translations that have appeared over the last 50 years I couldn't have written this book. Unless the translation is exceptionally faithful, then, formal and thematic matters will be the focus; given the formal variations of the modern novel, it will be possible to recognize kindred spirits from the past, prose works often excluded even from inclusive histories of the novel.

The emphasis throughout is on innovation and experimentation, renovations to the house of fiction, reports from the research and development wing of the writing community. In this volume, I'll be casting my net fairly wide into the ocean of story and dragging in anything that remotely resembles a novel in order to demonstrate the genre's age and infinite variety. (In the next, I'll be more selective, tightening the net to fish mostly for innovative, unconventional novels.) For obvious reasons, covering 3,500 years of fiction in 700 pages allows for only an overview of the topic, a general introduction rather than an exhaustive treatment. Consider this book a literary traveler's diary, or postcards from exotic fictional locales that readers can explore later on their own.

Finally, while I don't want to disparage the traditional novel — I still prefer Dickens's *Great Expectations* over Kathy Acker's *Great Expectations,* though I'll take Lauren Fairbanks's *Sister Carrie* over Dreiser's any day — there's a whole other world of novels out there most people never even hear of, much less read. Let's go see.

CHAPTER 1

The Ancient Novel

Sorting through the various ancient writings that have come down to us on cuneiform tablets, papyri, scrolls, and ostraca (potsherds or limestone flakes), it is not difficult to find prototypes for literary fiction and what would eventually be called the novel. What's difficult is sorting prose from poetry, and fiction from mythology and theology. The Egyptians had no term for narrative or story or poem, only a general term equivalent to belles-lettres. The Akkadians who gave us *Gilgamesh* had no word for epic or myth. The ancient Hebrews had no words for history or literature, nor distinguished between the two. These are modern labels and distinctions that don't really apply to ancient literature.

For example, I own eight anthologies of ancient Egyptian literature — edited by Erman, Lewis, Pritchard, Simpson, Lichtheim, Foster, Parkinson, and Quirke — all containing what their editors call tales.[1] Five of them present the tales as prose, two as poetry (though the latter two don't mount very convincing arguments for their choice), and one (Quirke) line-by-line transcriptions from the originals without regard to genre. Like ancient Hebrew, ancient Egyptian was written out continuously, without punctuation or vowels, breaking lines only when required by the width of the column or ostracon on which the scribe was writing. John L. Foster, the anthologist most wedded to poetry, admits the writings lack meter or end-rhymes and resist scansion. R. B. Parkinson, the other anthologist using verse, bases his approach on metrical principles proposed by an Egyptologist named Gerhard Fecht, but admits these principles are problematic and still being debated. Similarly, Stephanie Dalley in her splendid collection *Myths from Mesopotamia* notes that meter as we understand it is absent in Akkadian literature, and that "Length of line on a tablet is not directly connected to the concept of a metrical line, as various arrangements in different versions show" (xvii). And yet most anthologies of Akkadian literature and editions of *Gilgamesh* are in verse form, a choice made by other translators of early literature as well. In his introduction to *Stories from Ancient Canaan*, Michael

---

1 See bibliography for details. Lichtheim has the smoothest translations, Simpson the widest one-volume selection, and Parkinson the most commentary. Quirke is for specialists only.

David Coogan explains that the 14th-century BCE originals were inscribed in columns on clay tablets, "each column containing about fifty lines of text written continuously without spacing according to meter or sense" (11), yet he sets these vibrant stories of gods and kings in verse largely because of their use of parallelism. When the 11th-century Russian epic *The Lay of Igor's Campaign* was discovered and translated at the end of the 18th century, it was described as a "poetic masterpiece," but as Serge A. Zenkovsky warns, "The word 'poetic' should not be understood here in its narrower sense, since the *Lay* is neither rhymed nor organized in verses, nor does it follow any metrical pattern. The rhythm and the length of the sentences to some extent replace verse organization" (*Medieval Russia's Epics*, 167). Similarly, the Mayan *Popol Vuh* is routinely described as a great epic poem, even though its translators admit the writing "is not based on rhyme or metrical rhythms,"[2] which are the most basic properties of poetry.

I wonder if the decision to use verse rather than prose to translate older works isn't due to the lingering prejudice that poetry is nobler and finer than prose, perhaps related to the same decision made by the first translators of these works to adopt an archaic, "poetic" diction echoing Milton and the King James Bible. In the 19th century, when Egyptian and Akkadian literature was rediscovered and deciphered, the novel was still considered an upstart, lowbrow form by many, and prose a medium more suitable to newspapers than to literature. But the qualities all these editors ascribe to ancient narratives are also those of artful *prose*: parallelism, cadence, syntactic balancing of independent and dependent clauses, recurring imagery, wordplay, literary and historical allusions, and so forth. For that reason, it's easy to turn such prose into "poetry," as with Abraham Lincoln's famous 1858 speech (riffing on Mark 3:25):

> "A house divided against itself cannot stand":
> I believe that this Government cannot endure
>   permanently half-slave and half-free.
> I do not expect the Union to be dissolved.
> I do not expect the house to fall —
> but I do expect it will cease to be divided.
>   It will become all one thing,
>   or all the other.

In *The Defense of Poesy* (1595), Sir Philip Sidney defined a poet as a maker of imaginative fictions, whether written in prose or verse; "poetry" meant a writerly style, not a genre. Early literary narratives seem to hover somewhere

---

2 Christenson, *Popul Vuh*, 42; cf. Tedlock's *Popol Vuh*, 202–5. Both chose prose for their translations.

between poetry and prose, based more on the storyteller's dramatic needs (ease of memorization and effectiveness of presentation) than on an alliance to a particular genre. All early literature was meant to be recited, not read, and the line breaks created by later editors indicate only the breathing places a performer might use, not a reflection of poetic form. Miriam Lichtheim, the grande dame of ancient Egyptian literary studies, felt that, aside from some obvious lyric poems and prayers, most Egyptian writers used "symmetrically structured speech" or an "orational style" halfway between prose and poetry, and occasionally mixing the two (1:11). Literary Akkadian is similar: as in the prose of Joyce and Nabokov, "Punning and wordplay are revelled in, and sometimes they are crucial to the plot; at other times they are highly esoteric and would only have been appreciated by expert scribes. Alliteration, rhetorical questions, chiasma, inclusio,[3] similes; verb pairs with contrasting tenses; a build-up of tension through repetition with slight variation . . ." (Dalley xvii) — this describes *Lolita* as neatly as it does *Gilgamesh*. It makes more sense to consider these ancient works "pre-genre," just as some contemporary writers display a "post-genre sensibility."[4] Addressing the difficulty of assigning modern genres to ancient literature, the editors of *The Literature of Ancient Sumer* write, "Nowadays, we think of literature as comprising poems, novels, and plays. Something resembling all three can be found within Sumerian literature, *often within the same composition*."[5] Consequently, until a better case can be made for them as poetry, I'm going to consider the narratives that follow as prose, specifically as the world's first examples of *writerly* prose.[6]

ANCIENT EGYPTIAN FICTION

The earliest examples of literary fiction, and perhaps of the novel itself, are four anonymous tales that have come down to us from Egypt's Middle Kingdom. Composed during the middle of the 12th Dynasty (that is, between 1990 and 1800 BCE), each between 10 and 20 pages long in translation, they establish the forms and techniques that fiction writers follow to this day. Of the four, the most highly regarded is "The Tale of Sinuhe," a sophisticated

---

3 *Chiasma:* the inversion of the order of words in parallel clauses; *inclusio:* use of the same word or phrase at the beginning and end of a sentence or passage as a bracketing device.

4 The latter phrase is taken from the back cover of Thalia Field's *Point and Line* (NY: New Directions, 2000), consisting of works that "represent a confluence of genres (fiction, theater, and poetry)."

5 Black, Cunningham, et al., xxiii (my italics).

6 I won't be making the same argument when I reach Greek literature (or later epic poems); even though prose translations of Homer's epics certainly look and read like novels, and even though some (like T. E. Lawrence) have called the *Odyssey* in particular the world's first novel, there's no question (as there is with Egyptian and Akkadian works) they're poetry.

fiction that has led one of its translators to call its author "the Shakespeare of ancient Egypt" (Foster 124). It's only a dozen pages long, but its scope far exceeds the single-incident confines of the short story. Tell me if this doesn't sound like the plot of a full-length novel:

An attendant of the historical King Amenemhet I named Sinuhe has accompanied the king's son, Sesostris, to Libya on a military expedition. Word reaches them that Amenemhet has died (which occurred around 1960), so Sesostris returns to the capital to assume the throne. Then Sinuhe overhears messengers giving more details to the other royal sons; we're not informed what he overhears, though the original audience would have known that Amenemhet didn't die peacefully but was assassinated. The news throws Sinuhe into an unexplained panic, whereupon he flees the camp.[7] Skulking like a fugitive, he makes his way across Egypt and heads northward into Upper Retjenu (modern Lebanon), where he is unexpectedly welcomed by the Egyptian expatriate community there. The local ruler knows Sinuhe by reputation and takes him under his wing, marries him to his eldest daughter, gives him land and even a tribe to lead. Sinuhe prospers there over the next 20 years or so, sees his sons grow into manhood, and fights a decisive duel with a rival leader and confiscates his lands. But his homesickness is obvious and reaches the ear of King Sesostris back in Egypt, whom Sinuhe has praised enthusiastically. Still fond of his former attendant despite his unexplained flight, the king invites Sinuhe back to Egypt, where he is warmly received, given a fine dwelling and a pyramid of his own, and lives happily ever after "until the day of landing came," when he dies.

At least one Egyptologist feels "it deserves to be called a novel";[8] let's call it a mininovel. What's remarkable about "The Tale of Sinuhe" is the variety of genres it includes: it begins like a formal tomb inscription (the Autobiography genre that is the earliest form of Egyptian writing), at which point Sinuhe begins speaking from beyond the grave, as it were, telling his story in compact, imagistic language. Sesostris's return to the capital is conveyed by "the falcon flew with his attendants" (Parkinson 27) because the new king now embodies the falcon-god Horus. The tale contains "narratives of conquest and combat, eulogies of the king, a royal decree, meditative prayers, and ceremonial lyrics, culminating in the description of the tomb in which Sinuhe's Autobiography is supposedly inscribed" (Parkinson 22). It establishes the ideal for writerly fiction: "Its author employs every sentence construction and literary device known in his period together with a rich vocabulary to give variety and color to his narrative," notes Bernard Lewis (31). It's like a pocket anthology of

---

7 In his modern version of the story, "The Return of Sinuhe" (1941), the late Egyptian writer Naguib Mahfouz supplied a romantic rivalry between Sinuhe and Sesostris.

8 Georges Posener, "Literature," in J. R. Harris's *Legacy of Egypt* (Oxford: Oxford UP, 1971), 232.

Egyptian literary forms. As one of the tale's earliest translators says, the author "was less concerned with the contents than with the form of his work" (Erman 14), that is, he was an artist rather than an entertainer. Sinuhe's panic attack, which is never really explained and which he blames on some god, feels very modern in its ambiguity, as are the circumstances of his return to the Egyptian court: the royal princesses he had abandoned two decades earlier are still young, as if the whole experience was a bad dream, like something out of Kafka or Borges. The scope, depth, and rhetorical variety of "The Tale of Sinuhe" are impressive and display in compact form all the characteristics of the literary novel.

Rhetorical skill is also the chief attraction of "The Tale of the Eloquent Peasant," the longest of the four tales under discussion. Here, a landowner named Nemtinakht swindles a peasant named Khunanup, who complains to Rensi, the high steward. The latter is so surprised and impressed by the peasant's elaborate, metaphoric complaint that he tells the king of it, who orders Rensi to keep the peasant coming back and to write down what he says for the king's entertainment. (They both know Khunanup has been wronged but suspend judgment for entertainment purposes.) The tale consists of nine petitions by the eloquent peasant on the nature of justice, each employing extended metaphors and rhetorical fireworks. Khunanup is finally vindicated, as much for his eloquence as the justice of his case, and is awarded Nemtinakht's property. The Egyptians enjoyed didactic tales and instructional literature, but valued rhetorical skill above all.

Aside from the unexplained ability of a peasant to speak like a seasoned rhetorician, his tale and that of Sinuhe are realistic stories in recognizable settings. The other two Middle Kingdom tales are antirealistic, even surrealistic. In "The Tale of the Shipwrecked Sailor," an attendant tries to cheer up a high official who has just returned from a failed expedition with a marvelous adventure involving shipwreck on a mysterious island inhabited by a giant talking snake that shows how adversity can sometimes turn into success. This is the earliest example of a frame-tale, which embeds further tales within a unifying structure, like *The Arabian Nights*, and in fact this tale reads like one of Sindbad's adventures. Not only does the attendant tell a tale, but within that the human-headed snake tells a tale (with clues hinting at an esoteric allegory), both dramatizing what Parkinson calls the role of art: "the telling and retelling of misfortune enable people to overcome or endure it. In the Tale as a whole, literature acts as a redress for suffering: the man saves himself by his quick and skilful speech. The Tale is thus about the value of telling tales" (90), which anticipates by almost four millennia the strategies of modern metafictionists like John Barth.

Even closer to the spirit of *The Arabian Nights* is *The Tale of King Cheops' Court*, reminiscent of the more outlandish tales told by Shahrazad. The frame of this cycle of five tales is set in the 4th Dynasty (c. 2600–c. 2450 BCE), seven centuries before it was composed in the 12th. Unfortunately, most of the first tale is missing, and the fifth breaks off abruptly — a shame because this work is easily the most playful of the four surviving Middle Kingdom tales. The king is bored, so his sons try to entertain him with increasingly outrageous tales, each trying to outdo the other. The damaged manuscript begins just where the nameless first son's tale concludes. The second son, Khaefre, then tells a tale of adultery that occurred in Cheops's father's time, in which a magician makes a crocodile out of wax and animates it to attack the adulterer. Then the third son, Baufre, stands up to deliver another story of Cheops's father, Snefru. The main portion has many points of interest and is worth quoting at length:[9]

> One day King Snefru wandered through all the rooms of the palace in search of relaxation and found none. Then he said: "Go, bring me the chief lector-priest, the scribe of books, Djadja-em-ankh!" He was brought to him straightway. His majesty said to him: "I have gone through all the rooms of the palace in search of relaxation and found none." Djadja-em-ankh said to him: "May your majesty proceed to the lake of the palace. Fill a boat with all the beautiful girls of your palace. Your majesty's heart will be refreshed by seeing them row, a rowing up and down. As you observe the fine nesting places of your lake, as you observe its beautiful fields and shores, your heart will be refreshed by it."
>
> Said his majesty: "Indeed, I shall go boating! Let there be brought to me twenty oars of ebony plated with gold, their handles of sandalwood plated with electrum. Let there be brought to me twenty women with the shapeliest bodies, breasts, and braids, who have not yet given birth. Also let there be brought to me twenty nets and give these nets to these women in place of their clothes!" All was done as his majesty commanded.
>
> They rowed up and down, and his majesty's heart was happy seeing them row. Then the one who was at the stroke oar fingered her braids, and a pendant of new turquoise fell into the water. Then she stopped rowing, and her side of women stopped rowing. Said his majesty: "Why don't you row?" Said they: "Our leader has stopped rowing." Said his majesty to her: "Why have you stopped rowing?" Said she: "Because the pendant of new turquoise fell into the water." Then his majesty said to her: "Row! I shall replace it for you!" She said: "I prefer my thing to one like it." Said his majesty: "Go, bring me the chief lector-priest Djadja-em-ankh!" He was brought to him straightway.
>
> Said his majesty: "Djadja-em-ankh, my brother, I did as you had said. My majesty's heart was refreshed seeing them row. Then a pendant of new turquoise of one of the leaders fell into the water. . . . [He retells the incident word for word.]
>
> Then the chief lector-priest Djadja-em-ankh said his say of magic. He placed one side of the lake's water upon the other; and he found the pendant lying on a shard. He brought it

---

9 In Lichtheim's translation, 1:216–17. For ease of reading I've eliminated her various brackets showing emendations and parenthetical manuscript reference numbers. (Coincidentally, Lichtheim died in March 2004 just as I began work on this section.)

and gave it to its owner. Now the water that had been twelve cubits deep across had become twenty four cubits when it was turned back. Then he said his say of magic and returned the waters of the lake to their place. His majesty spent the day feasting with the entire palace. Then he rewarded the chief lector-priest Djadja-em-ankh with all good things.

Several interesting things going on here, not the least of which, as Parkinson points out, is what "sounds like the invention of fishnet tights" (104), which to my mind ranks up there with the greatest achievements of Egyptian civilization. He's referring to the king's plan to dress the twenty beauties only in net outfits, like strippers.[10] In fact, you could almost call the episode Egyptian porn: the boating excursion parodies a ritual involving the Egyptian sex-goddess Hathor, and when the tale concludes with "His majesty spent the day feasting with the entire palace," Parkinson informs us this means he had an orgy on board with the palace babes (121–22, nn17 and 21). Also interesting is the equation of writers with magicians, literary creation with a conjuring act: Djadja-em-ankh is both "the scribe of books" *and* an enchanter with miraculous powers. But the most striking detail is Djadja-em-ankh's magical displacement of one side of the lake atop the other, which reminded me of the "Cleveland Wrecking Yard" chapter of Richard Brautigan's quirky masterpiece *Trout Fishing in America* (1967), where lengths of a Colorado trout stream are stacked up for sale in a junkyard. When I first read Brautigan, I thought this was an astounding act of imagination, not realizing he'd been anticipated by some writer four millennia ago.[11] In other words, what came to be called magic realism in the 20th century has been around since the 20th century BCE.

After these tall tales, the next son insists he'll tell a "true" story about a magician still living, "a man of a hundred and ten years who eats five hundred loaves of bread, half an ox for meat, and drinks one hundred jugs of beer to this very day." This wizard is brought before the king and demonstrates his ability to join severed heads before prophesizing the wondrous birth of the three kings who would found the next dynasty, the subject of the fifth and final tale of this cycle. The sun-god Re has chosen a mortal woman named Ruddedet to bear his incarnations, and he sends Isis and a few other goddesses down to assist with the birth. (They disguise themselves as dancing girls, a *huge* improvement over the Three Wise Men of Christian mythology.) The tale breaks off just as a servant who plans to inform King Cheops of the

---

10 Parkinson gives further fashion details: "*Nets* of beads were sometimes worn over dresses as jewelry, but Sneferu enthusiastically dispenses with the dresses, making the women near-nude" (122).

11 One Egyptologist compares the author not to Brautigan but to an earlier comic American novelist: see E. S. Meltzer's "The Art of the Storyteller in Papyrus Westcar: An Egyptian Mark Twain?" in *Essays in Egyptology in Honor of Hans Goedicke*, ed. Betsy M. Bryan and David Lorton (San Antonio: 1994), 169–75.

miraculous birth is eaten by a crocodile, recalling the avenging agent of the second story in the cycle.

By the end of the 19th century, then, all the elements of the novel were in place: sustained narrative, dialogue, characterization, formal strategies, rhetorical devices, even parody, pornography, metafiction, and magic realism.[12] Unfortunately, Egyptian fiction dried up after that for about six centuries, no doubt due to political unrest and foreign invasions, though perhaps intervening work has never been recovered.

When fiction-writing resumed during the Ramesside period (c. 1292–1070 BCE, the setting for Norman Mailer's huge novel *Ancient Evenings*), Egyptian writers invented a few more genres, like the war story, the ghost story, and the fairy tale, but mostly pushed magic realism to bizarre lengths. In "The Tale of Two Brothers," for example, an upright young man named Bata lives with his older brother Anubis, a landowner. (These are also the names of Egyptian gods, but they're introduced as average citizens.) One day, Anubis's wife makes a pass at Bata but is rebuffed. As in the later Hebrew story of Joseph and Potiphar's wife, the scorned woman tells her husband that Bata tried to assault her. Anubis then hides himself behind the stable door to kill his brother when he returns from the fields, but a talking cow warns Bata of Anubis's plan. He runs off but is pursued by his brother, so he prays to the sun-god for protection, who obliges by creating a wall of water between the two brothers, infested with crocodiles.[13] Then things *really* get weird.[14] To demonstrate his innocence, Bata cuts off his phallus and throws it into the water (where a catfish swallows it), which convinces his brother that his wife lied to him. Then Bata goes off to live alone in the Valley of the Cedar, where he cuts out his heart and puts it on top of a cedar tree for safekeeping. The gods pity him and so create a beautiful woman for him (even though the catfish still has his *ankh*); one day the sea surges up to try to drown her but misses, and so instructs the cedar tree to grab her — and it just gets stranger after that. (Like a god in Ovid, Bata later metamorphoses into a bull, then a Persea tree, a splinter from which enters the mouth of the pharaoh's wife, who then gives birth to . . . Bata! who eventually becomes king of Egypt.) It's a remarkable testament to the colorful imagination of one Egyptian fantasist.

Even weirder is "The Contendings of Horus and Seth," which reads like a

12 And these are merely from the tales that have survived; Quirke transcribes fragments of a dozen more tales from the end of the 12th Dynasty, too short to make much sense of but testifying to the popularity of fiction at this early age.

13 Recall the displacement of the lake in *The Tale of King Cheops' Court*, then compare it and this example of the magical use of water to the Hebrew myth of Moses parting the Red Sea.

14 Of course this may be more myth than story, and ancient myths follow a narrative logic that is different from that of fiction. For an explanation and examples, see Elizabeth and Paul Barber's *When They Severed Earth from Sky: How the Human Mind Shapes Myth* (Princeton: Princeton UP, 2004).

Monty Python takeoff on Egyptian mythology, adding farce to literature's repertoire. Even Simpson, who includes it in his anthology, says, "The behavior of some of the great gods is at points so shocking that it is hard to imagine that no humor was intended" (91). He's referring to the goddess Hathor exposing her genitals to her father the "Universal Lord," who just laughs at her, and also to a sticky homosexual encounter between Horus and Seth — add gay lit to Egyptian literature's other genre inventions.

In addition to magic realism, the Egyptians also invented literary realism, as demonstrated by two other stories from the Ramesside era discovered by a fellahin in a clay vessel around 1890, both of which mimic nonfiction forms. "The Report of Wenamun" is a highly realistic account of a humiliating business trip spread out over several months.[15] Wenamun travels north from Thebes to Lebanon and eventually to Cyprus, with one thing after another going wrong, largely because Egypt no longer commands the respect it once had. The business negotiations are rather tedious, but the dialogue is remarkably lifelike; as Lichtheim notes, "The Late-Egyptian vernacular is handled with great subtlety. The verbal duels between Wenamun and the prince of Byblos, with their changes of mood and shades of meaning that include irony, represent Egyptian thought and style at their most advanced" (2:224). It contains sentences that would be at home in a contemporary novel — "I found him seated in his upper chamber with his back against a window, and the waves of the great sea of Syria broke behind his head" (2:226) — and it's not surprising to read that ancient businessmen "took care" of important clients the same way they do today: "He sent his secretary out to me, bringing me two jugs of wine and a sheep. And he sent me Tentne, an Egyptian songstress who was with him, saying, 'Sing for him! Do not let his heart be anxious'" (2:229). Unfortunately the tale breaks off just as Wenamun meets a princess of Cyprus who invites him to spend the night. It probably wasn't long enough to be called a novel, but the realism of the tale is the earliest instance of what traditional critics consider the defining characteristic of the novel.

Shorter but just as realistic is the papyrus translator Ricardo Caminos has entitled "A Tale of Woe." It's a story in the form of a letter from a priest named Wermai to his friend Usima're'nakhte, a scribe attached to the royal court. Opening with an elaborate salutation and unctuous wishes for a prosperous life, Wermai then relates a series of unfortunate events: after losing his job (unfairly, he implies, without going into detail), he also lost his wife and his property, was abandoned by his friends, beaten up by thugs, and kicked out of town. Like Sinuhe he wandered throughout Egypt, winding up in some hellhole in the desert rife with corruption and crime, an unwelcome outcast

---

15 I'll be quoting Lichtheim's version (2:224–29). It can also be found in Erman (174–85), Pritchard (16–24), and Simpson (117–24). Goedicke's book-length translation-cum-commentary is for scholars only.

on the brink of starvation. Writing from there in despair, Wermai hopes Usima're'nakhte will pass his letter along to a person of influence (perhaps the pharaoh). It's a bleak tale, for Wermai's hardships are shared by a population at large suffering from famine, war, and overtaxation, and cleverly structured: by praising his friend's prosperous state at the beginning, Wermai gives his own miserable situation greater bite and poignancy. "A Tale of Woe" is only three pages long, but as Caminos argues, it has an important place in literary history: "Dating back, therefore, to some time or other between 1300 and 1000 B.C., the story of Wermai's misadventures is by far the earliest extant tale or piece of fictional narrative which employs the literary device known as 'the epistolary technique': the use of an imaginary letter or series of letters as a vehicle to convey a narrative work of fiction" (78). But after the Ramesside period, unfortunately, Egyptian fiction went through another dry spell for about five centuries.

Some Egyptologists throw around the term "king's novel," introduced by Alfred Hermann in his 1938 monograph *Die ägyptische Königsnovelle*, but this is misleading, referring not to any novels per se (or per anyone's definition) but merely to literary documents in which the pharaoh is the protagonist.[16]

The earliest book-length fictions were frame-tale narratives in the tradition of *The Tale of King Cheops' Court*. Only tantalizing fragments remain of *The Story of Petese, Son of Petetum, and Seventy Other Good and Bad Stories*, which is frustrating because it sounds fantastic. As reconstructed by Kim Ryholt, it features a priest-magician of Heliopolis named Petese and his wife Sakhminofret: Petese has learned from a ghost he has only 40 days to live, and initially plans to spend those days, sensibly enough, enjoying sex with his wife. But then he decides to extort money from his fellow priests in exchange for explaining what the occult texts in their temple mean. All but one agree, so Petese fashions a cat and a falcon out of wax to intimidate the holdout like a pair of Mafia enforcers. He buckles, Petese gets paid, and then makes his own special funeral arrangements. He creates two baboons out of wax and orders them to go out and collect 70 stories, half that praise women, and half that condemn them. After Petese dies, the baboon anthologists meet daily with the widow Sakhminofret to recite these tales, alternating each day between a positive and negative tale. One of Petese's motives may have been to keep his wife on the straight and narrow via these didactic tales, but since 70 days was the ideal period for embalming a corpse, the tales were probably intended as a way of preserving his memory: pyramids were for kings and nobles, but for writers, as an ancient Egyptian poem has it, "Books of wisdom were their pyramids."[17]

---

16 See, if really interested, Antonio Loprieno's essay "The 'King's Novel'" in his useful critical anthology *Ancient Egyptian Literature*, 277–95.
17 "The Immortality of Writers," in Foster, 226.

The extant fragments are too sketchy to appreciate, especially in Ryholt's overliteral translation; typical is this comic one in which a man named Merire falls for the daughter of Prince Wadjhar; Merire tries to hide the fact he's already married by rendering his wife unconscious and ditching her in a coffin. When she awakes, she is mistaken for a goddess by some bystanders, and is cut off just as she begins to give her husband hell:

> Wadjhar came out in front of Merire [—
> saw the daughter of the King's Son Wadjhar. He desired her very much [—
> He went to the place in which his wife was [—
> If the King's Son Wadjhar learned about me that [—
> wife into a coffin. He shut its lid. He gave it to the Overseer of the Necropolis [—
> her father. The Overseer of the Necropolis carried it. He went up there [—
> The woman awoke with a start. She found herself in the coffin [—
> [.........] her, and they were in great distress thinking that she was a goddess [—
> [.........], while she had very evil thoughts and she said: The wrath of [—[18]

A more coherent example of the kind of tales the baboons tell can be found in Herodotus's *Histories* (c. 430 BCE), which contains a plot summary of one of the tales from *The Story of Petese* (fragment C1):

> When Sesostris died, he was succeeded by his son Pheros [i.e., Pharaoh], a prince who undertook no military adventures. He went blind, and the reason for it is explained in the following story: one year the Nile rose to an excessive height, as much as twenty-seven feet, and when all the fields were under water it began to blow hard, so that the river got very rough. The king in insensate rage seized a spear and hurled it into the swirling waters, and immediately thereafter he was attacked by a disease of the eyes, and became blind. He was blind for ten years, and in the eleventh he received an oracle from the city of Buto to the effect that the time of his punishment being now ended, he would recover his sight, if he washed his eyes with the urine of a woman who had never lain with any man except her husband. He tried his wife first, but without success; then he tried other women, a great many, one after another, until at last his sight was restored. Then he collected within the walls of a town, now called Red Clod, all the women except the one whose urine had proved efficacious, set the place on fire, and burnt them to death, town and all; afterwards he married the woman who had been the means of curing him.[19]

18 Page 122 in *The Petese Stories II*. If you still have the demotic text edition of *The Story of Petese* (Copenhagen: Museum Tusculanum, 1999), dump it, for shortly after he published that Ryholt discovered a further group of manuscript fragments, incorporated into this expanded edition.
19 2.111, p. 137 in Sélincourt's translation. Since Herodotus presents many fictions like this as fact, some historians have suggested his book should be classified as fiction rather than nonfiction: see note 82 below. I was tempted to make a case for the *Histories* as a fanciful historical novel, but resisted.

This is one of the earliest examples of the folkloric motif of the difficulty of finding a faithful woman, and we'll see other examples as we progress, as well as other frame-tale narratives recited by animals. The inclusion of this story in Herodotus implies *The Story of Petese* is older than the 5th century BCE, and while that's possible, this could be merely an old folktale that the author added to his work; Ryholt guesses *Petese* was compiled sometime in the 4th or 3rd century, though allowing that many of its individual tales might be much older. But the framing narrative, the careful structure of the work, the recurring characters, the metafictional account of its own making, and its length — it was probably in the range of 150 to 200 pages — qualify *The Tale of Petese* as the first full-length Egyptian novel.

There is another longish frame-tale narrative from the same period entitled *The Myth of the Sun's Eye*, which (as Lichtheim explains)

> tells how Tefnut, the daughter and "eye" of the sun-god Re, who after quarreling with her father had left Egypt and settled in Nubia, was persuaded to return to Egypt. The sun-god had sent Thoth, the counsellor and mediator among the gods, to appease the angry goddess and bring her back. Tefnut at first resisted the blandishments of Thoth, and there ensued lengthy debates in the course of which Thoth told her several animal fables, each designed to teach a moral lesson. Eventually, the goddess relented and, on the journey back to Egypt, Thoth continued to entertain her with fables. (3:156–57)

Lichtheim follows this with one such fable, "The Lion in Search of a Man" (157–59), but I'm not aware of a complete English translation of the entire work. The fact that Thoth was often depicted with the head of a baboon suggests the two narrators in *The Story of Petese* are his avatars; and as the god of learning, invention, and magic, Thoth is a suitable patron for the creative writer.

By the Ptolemaic Period (c. 332–30 BCE), Egyptian fiction had degenerated into mere entertainment, mostly occult stories trading on Egypt's reputation as the land of sorcerers and magic. They are a bit longer than the earlier tales, and one of them, "The Romance of Setna Khaemuas and the Mummies," has the dubious distinction of inspiring the 1932 movie *The Mummy*, via Gilbert Murray's 1911 verse translation, *Nefrekepta*. "Setna" even has a typical B-movie scene where our hero becomes enamored with a mysterious femme fatale, who exchanges spicy double entendres with him before disappearing to slip into something more comfortable; she returns wearing "a dress of sheer royal linen. Setna beheld all her limbs within it. His desire surged even in excess of what he had been in previously" (Simpson 465; sounds like the translator fell under the same erotic spell and forgot how to use words, which can happen). This is one of two surviving tales apparently from a cycle of occult stories about Ramses II's fourth son, a high priest fascinated by magic texts and ancient sacred monuments. But the contrast between the Shakespearean "Tale of Sinuhe" and this schlocky stuff is the same writerly/readerly contrast we'll see throughout the history of the novel. The last interesting piece of Egyptian fiction is "The Fable of the Swallow and the Sea," an example of both epistolary narrative and the animal fable. But as the Egyptian language died out and was replaced by Coptic, the old writings were forgotten, and with them all these early prototypes of the novel.

In his surprisingly well-informed capsule history of the novel, the Marquis de Sade rightly credits Egypt with the invention of the novel, and insists all stories of gods are creative fictions, novels in spirit if not in form:

> Let there be no doubt about it: it was in the countries which first recognized gods that the novel originated; and, to be more specific, in Egypt, the cradle of all divine worship. No sooner did man begin to *suspect* the existence of immortal beings than he endowed them with both actions and words. Thereafter we find metamorphoses, fables, parables, and novels: in a word, we find works of fiction as soon as fiction seized hold of the minds of men.[20]

I don't know how seriously the ancient Egyptians took their tales of gods and mummies, but the inability of other ancient peoples to recognize their own sacred tales as fictions would prove to be the true original sin.

ANCIENT MESOPOTAMIAN FICTION

The literature of the Mesopotamian region (modern Iraq) follows a trajectory similar to that of ancient Egyptian literature: it originated in the 3rd millennium BCE in the form of hymns to the gods and songs of praise for heroic kings, expanded into longer narratives during the 2nd millennium, then deteriorated and vanished during the 1st, not to be recovered for 2,000 years. (The day English scholar George Smith broke the linguistic code of the Babylonian flood story in the 1870s, he became so excited he began running around the room and stripping off his clothes, shocking his colleagues.[21]) The longer narratives, however, continued to concern themselves with gods and kings and never really lost their earlier function as hymns and incantations; nor did they shake off their origins as oral performance pieces intended for royalty. So even though there are several surviving examples of fictitious narratives, it's a little harder to make a case for them as fictions in the modern

20 "Reflections on the Novel" (preface to *The Crimes of Love*), in *The 120 Days of Sodom and Other Writings*, 98.
21 In a recent book on *Gilgamesh*, David Damrosch says Smith may have only loosened his collar, but I like to think he went further than that. Smith was a working-class man, after all, not an uptight blueblood.

sense, with a few possible exceptions. And since, unlike the anthologies of ancient Egyptian literature, virtually all editors of Mesopotamian literature follow the line breaks of the cuneiform tablets, it's harder to make a case for them as prose tales, even though they may read more effectively that way. On the one hand, poetry is easier to memorize and deliver in performance; on the other hand, as Stephanie Dalley points out, we should consider the surviving texts "as bare skeletons which were fleshed out in practice by skilled narrators, rather as early musical notation gave only the guidelines needed to remind the musician of appropriate melody and rhythms, leaving embellishments and flourishes to his own skills and popular taste" (xvi) — like jazz musicians today. That is, what may look like poetry may have become prose narrative in performance, and given the strong narrative line of longer Mesopotamian works, I'm going to consider them novellas in verse.

The earliest writings from this region come from Sumer, in what is now southern Iraq. Like the first mythographers everywhere, certain imaginative Sumerians personified the sometimes puzzling phenomena of nature as "gods" — larger-than-life versions of people like themselves, prey to the same emotions of anger, pride, lust, jealousy, and so on — then started making up stories about them. After the invention of cuneiform writing, the more popular of these oral hymns and tales were preserved in permanent form. In Thorkild Jacobsen's excellent anthology *The Harps That Once . . . : Sumerian Poetry in Translation*,[22] he presents a number of hymns and love songs that are obviously poetry, but also translates some longer narratives that he calls myths or epics, which have many characteristics of prose fiction. One of the longest and most impressive of these is "Enmerkar and the Lord of Aratta," which opens with a splendidly vigorous evocation of the city of Kullab:

> In that fierce bull of a city, imbued with dignity and great awesomeness, Kullab, bellowing holy hymns, place where at dawn decisions by the gods are made, in Uruk the great mountain carried in Inanna's heart, destined in the days of yore to be at workday's end An's dining hall: in Uruk, in Kullab, in Urugal, proudly the great princes of the gods convened, and plenteous precipitation, producing carp-floods and rainshowers, producing mottled barley, they joined together for Uruk and for Kullab in their decisions.[23]

This gong-like opening occupies 26 lines of verse in Jacobsen's anthology but

22 Though he doesn't identify it, his lovely title comes from Thomas Moore's poem of the same name, which begins "The harp that once through Tara's halls / The soul of music shed, / Now hangs as mute on Tara's walls / As if that soul were fled." Some anthologists of ancient Mesopotamian literature exhibit a touching nostalgia for ancient Babylon.

23 Jacobsen 280 (as with Lichtheim earlier, I've eliminated brackets and parentheses for ease of reading); Uruk was a nearby town that later absorbed Kullab; Inanna (aka Ishtar) is the Sumerian goddess of love and patroness of Kullab; An is the sky-god, and Urugal the name of his temple in Uruk.

loses nothing, I think, as prose. It almost sounds like Saul Bellow's Chicago. In fact, one reason why this literature is not better known is the difficulty of reading the direct transcriptions specialists insist on, resulting in passages like this a page later in "Enmerkar":

> [The people] bathed not for the feasts
> [under copper ewers]
> [the . . . .] who sat [not]
> on [. . . . .]
> spent the day in [. . . . .]
> [. . . . .]
> [. . . . .][24]

Useful for the scholar, but not for the average reader. In other Sumerian tales we behold the origins of familiar stories: "Inanna's Descent" is an early version of the Demeter/Persephone myth and perhaps contains world literature's first striptease scene.[25] "The Eridu Genesis," written sometime around 1600 BCE, anticipates all the plot-lines of the Hebrew Genesis written centuries later; "The Birth of Man" gives a different version, one that admirably assigns useful roles in society to the handicapped and acknowledges "the equality of the sexes' contributions to healthy propagation" (Jacobsen 153) — a concept rejected by the later Hebrews, who preferred a mateless male god who could create life by himself, thereby setting in motion millennia of misogyny. In translating these works, Jacobsen "used a high prose and short lines, resulting in a kind of free verse," even though the "Sumerian poets did not, as far as one can see, use rhyme. Meter and rhythm, which must be assumed to be a prominent feature since the poetry was sung, are not sufficiently recognizable from the texts to invite attempts at imitation" (xiv–xv). These demurrals suggest to me that written Sumerian literature, like its contemporary Egyptian literature, is closer to what Lichtheim called "symmetrically structured speech" or an "orational style," but until someone more familiar with the intricacies of Sumerian literature makes this case, I won't insist.

The longest and most impressive narrative in Sumerian literature is a cycle of four tales that a recent translator calls the Matter of Aratta (after medieval designations like the Matter of Britain), which includes the aforementioned

---

24 The American poet Armand Schwerner (1927–1999) wrote a book-length poem called *The Tablets* (Orono: National Poetry Foundation, 1999) in which he imitated this scholarly presentation, sometimes to comic effect, while paying tribute to the earthy vitality of Mesopotamian literature.

25 As she descends lower in the underworld, Inanna goes through seven doors, at each of which she has to remove an article of clothing, until she is nude. Scholars have suggested Salome's Dance of the Seven Veils derives from this myth.

"Enmerkar and the Lord of Aratta."[26] It dramatizes the rivalry between Enmerkar, priest-king of Sumer, and his counterpart in distant Aratta (identified by some with Iran); the cycle demonstrates the superiority of Sumer as Enmerkar outwits his rival and emerges as the worthier ruler, and more deserving of the sexual favors of the patroness of both cities, the goddess Inanna. "He may meet with Inana in his dreams at night," Enmerkar smirks, "but I shall converse with Inana between her gleaming legs" ("Enmerkar and Ensuhgirana," 31–32). We are shocked and awed by the startling imagery throughout the cycle, with metaphors so unexpected they sound like sun-baked surrealism at times.

> Sleep then overwhelmed the king.
> Sleep is the realm of darkness;
> It is a towering flood; like the hand that demolishes a brick wall
> Its hand is overpowering, its foot is overpowering;
> It covers all that it finds before it like syrup;
> It overflows all that it finds before it like runny honey;
> It knows no lieutenant, no captain,
> Yet it strengthens the warrior.
>
> ("Lugalbanda in the Wilderness," 327–34)

These lines come from an episode featuring a saintly figure named Lugalbanda, one of the least of Enmerkar's men, who apparently dies only to be resurrected three days later — by analogy with the moon's three days of darkness at the turn of the lunar cycle — and who gains godlike powers thanks to a giant talking "thunder-bird" (not a dove). Another subplot concerns a magic contest between a sorcerer and a sorceress. The entire cycle is about 50 pages long, the length of a novella, but it belongs more to the genres of myth and nationalistic epic than fiction, and so, like the pack-asses transporting grain from Sumer to Aratta, we move on.

By the beginning of the 2nd millennium BCE, the Sumerian language had been replaced by Akkadian (from Akkad, now central Iraq), lingering only as a scholarly language, like Latin during the Middle Ages. Akkadian literature continues the principal themes and topics of its predecessor — stories of gods and heroic kings — and contains four long narratives that can be included in the development of literary fiction. The earliest is "Atrahasis" (or "The Story of the Flood"),[27] written around 1700 BCE by the first author for whom

---

26 See Herman Vanstiphout's bilingual edition *Epics of Sumerian Kings*, henceforth cited by tale and line number. A communal work developed over several generations, the Matter of Aratta assumed its final form in the 20th century BCE.

27 Like many ancient literary compositions, Akkadian works were known by their opening line (their *incipit*); these titles are those of modern anthologists. (Italo Calvino's 1979 novel *If on a winter's night a traveler* follows this ancient practice; can you think of any

we actually have a name: Ipiq-Aya. (I should say "compiled" rather than "written"; like most ancient authors, Ipiq-Aya took various older tales and edited them into a coherent narrative.) Set in prehistory, "Atrahasis" relates how the gods created human beings to serve them, and the flood they later sent to reduce overpopulation. It's a lively piece, with a revolt of the younger working-gods against their elders and lots of arguments between the deities as they try to quell the noisy humans who are robbing them of sleep. To reduce their numbers, the gods first send illness, then starvation, before Enki secretly unleashes the flood, but not before warning his favorite human Atrahasis to build a large boat to save himself. After Atrahasis revives humankind, the gods decide on some measures for population control, folkloric explanations why not all women can give birth. Like most mythographers, Ipiq-Aya tried to explain puzzling natural phenomena; floods were fairly common in southern Mesopotamia, but as Dalley points out, "the idea of a universal flood may well have arisen to explain observations in different places of marine fossils in rocks high above sea level. At a time when there was no conception of how geological change took place, nor of how vast was the time-scale of evolution, . . . an enormous flood which man by chance survived would be the only way to account for the presence of such marine fossils, and may have been thought up by more than one inquiring mind" (7).

Atrahasis appears under the name Utnapishtim in the greatest work of Akkadian literature, *Gilgamesh*. I would love to claim this as the world's first novel, for it's nearly long enough and dramatizes the central concern of the novel: "The Gilgamesh Epic is a story about growing up,"[28] about moving from a state of innocence to one of experience and accepting the way things really are. Especially in the definitive version compiled in the mid-2nd millennium by the scribe and incantation-priest Sin-leqi-unninni, we have the first extended example of the bildungsroman.[29]

It certainly has a novel's worth of action: young King Gilgamesh of Uruk (modern-day Warka) is a royal hell-raiser, mistreating his subjects so badly that they complain to the gods, who oblige by creating a wild man named Enkidu as a worthy rival and distraction. Growing up in the wild, Enkidu disrupts the local hunting, so a hunter convinces Gilgamesh to send a woman to domesticate

others?) Throughout this section I rely primarily on the translations in Dalley's *Myths from Mesopotamia*, supplemented by Foster's *From Distant Days*.

28 The concluding sentence of Thorkild Jacobsen's fine essay "'And Death the Journey's End': The Gilgamesh Epic" (1976), rpt. in Foster's Norton Critical Edition of *Gilgamesh*, 207.

29 *Gilgamesh* developed from various oral folktales and Sumerian "short stories" (as Dalley calls them) about this semilegendary king; many of these were compiled early in the 2nd millennium into what is now called the Old Babylonian Version of *Gilgamesh*, which was reworked by Sin-leqi-unninni a few centuries later into the Standard Babylonian Version. After that, Akkadian writers continued to write further stories about Gilgamesh.

him. He sends a religious sex worker named Shamhat,[30] who easily seduces him: "Shamhat loosened her undergarments, opened her legs and he took in her attractions" we're told with admirable frankness. "For six days and seven nights Enkidu was aroused and poured himself into Shamhat" (Dalley 55). After this rite of passage, he loses his rapport with animals, signaling his transition from innocence to maturity, from nature to civilization.

Shamhat closes shop and sends Enkidu back to Uruk, where he and Gilgamesh become fast friends after a wrestling match. (This is a very macho work, despite the presence of several interesting female characters.) Together they go off to slay a monster named Humbaba, a feat that so impresses the goddess Ishtar that she proposes marriage to Gilgamesh. He spurns her because of her promiscuous past, so she rushes off to complain to daddy, the sky-god Anu, and convinces him to unleash a wild bull on the heroes.[31] But they kill the bull, and Enkidu heaps further insults on Ishtar. The gods decide one of the heroes must die for this act and settle on Enkidu, who curses Shamhat for civilizing him in the first place. Enkidu's death hits Gilgamesh hard, and wishing to avoid his own death, he goes in quest of the secret of immortality. This takes him to Utnapishtim (aka Atrahasis), survivor of the great flood and now living on the edge of the world. In an awkward insert in a different style, Utnapishtim relates the story of the flood — abridged from "Atrahasis" — then tests Gilgamesh's worthiness for immortality. He fails, but Utnapishtim's wife convinces her husband to give him a consolation prize: a plant at the bottom of the sea that causes rejuvenation. Gilgamesh finds the plant, but in a moment of neglect loses it to a snake that swallows it (and then sheds its skin — a folkloric explanation for that phenomenon). Realizing all his efforts have been in vain, Gilgamesh resigns himself to the inevitability of death and realizes the only true immortality is for work that endures: for him, it is the walls of Uruk he has erected; for the author, it is the definitive version of *Gilgamesh* he has carefully crafted.[32]

Though *Gilgamesh* is filled with gods and supernatural events, the all-too-human concern for death lifts the story out of mythology and sets it in the realm of the novel. It's about male friendship, about putting off and reluctantly accepting maturity and civic responsibilities, about coming to terms with one's mortality and limitations, all topics more common to the novel than to the epic, the genre it is usually placed in. It's not surprising that some

---

30 That is, a cult prostitute who served in the temple devoted to the sex-goddess Ishtar, a respected position that doesn't carry any of the modern, pejorative implications of "prostitute." Think of her as a sexual nun. In her translation of the Akkadian version of "The Descent of Ishtar to the Underworld," Dalley cattily refers to such women as "party girls" (160, 162 n22), which is probably nearer the truth.

31 In his translation of *Gilgamesh* Foster notes that Ishtar uses "jarring colloquialisms" and consequently he makes her sound like a spoiled teenager (48).

32 See Vanstiphout's "The Craftsmanship of *Sîn-leqi-unninnī*."

modern novelists have drawn from it (Gardner's *Sunlight Dialogues*, Lerman's *Call Me Ishtar*, Roth's *Great American Novel*, Silverberg's *Gilgamesh the King*, London's *Gilgamesh*). The language is closer to poetry than prose, as I'll admit Andrew George demonstrates in his splendid edition of *Gilgamesh*, but the narrative drive, variety of incident, and sociological concerns earn it a place in the development of the novel. Call it a novel in verse, and one of the best.

The *Enuma Elish*, or "Epic of Creation," returns us to the origin of the world. It is an impressive if somewhat chilling work, less concerned with the actual creation of gods and humans than with praising the Babylonian hero-god Marduk and demonstrating the need for authoritarianism. Like "Atrahasis" it tells of a war in heaven between the gods, but they behave in more subdued fashion, like executives of a multinational corporation fighting off a hostile takeover. The old guard is represented by the matriarch Tiamat, mother of the gods and a personification of the sea, but also associated with primordial chaos; she is challenged and defeated by Marduk, a brash representative of the new order, whose praises are sung at length by the learned if sycophantic author. Written in the latter part of the 2nd millennium, it is (like the Sumerian Matter of Aratta) a nationalistic piece that places Babylon at the center of the world and Marduk at the center of the universe, a glaring example of the ethnocentrism nearly every society displays. (Every primitive tribe considered itself *the* people, just as cheerleaders today proclaim their school is # 1 no matter how many games they've lost.) The work celebrates the defeat of female chaos by male order, and Marduk's sole creation of mankind without female help anticipates the dour Priestly author of the Hebrew Genesis, who apparently heard and approved of the work.[33]

The last major work of Akkadian literature was written in the early 8th century BCE by Kabti-ilani-Marduk. "Erra and Ishum" is interesting for several reasons, not the least of which is that it's told almost exclusively in dialogue, a set of declamatory speeches that are true rhetorical performances. Throughout the history of the novel there are occasional examples of narratives told entirely in dialogue; Kabti-ilani-Marduk sets the pattern in this story warning against the dangers of violence. Erra, the god of war, is introduced (like Gilgamesh) as a hothead itching for a fight, but too lazy to pick one; he asks his cooler-headed advisor Ishum to stir him up, but after Ishum points out the drawbacks to violence, Erra allows himself to be worked up instead by "the Seven," a gang of gods who also like to fight. Mayhem ensues, with

---

33 Marduk splits the defeated sea-goddess Tiamat in half, making the sky of the upper half and the sea of the lower (Dalley 255). Cf. Gen. 1:6–8: "God said, 'Let there be an expanse in the midst of the water, that it may separate water from water.' God made the expanse, and it separated the water which was below the expanse from the water which was above the expanse. And it was so. God called the expanse Sky." (Unless otherwise noted, all quotations from the sacred writings of the Jews are from the New JPS translation of the Tanakh.)

Erra destroying most of the known world. Ishun gives a long speech trying to curb Erra's violence, succeeding finally with an appeal to his vanity by claiming that Erra (like a vain gangleader) has finally won the respect he deserves. The author experiments with point of view — shifting between third-person omniscience to first- and second-person narration — and pushes the Akkadian language to outlandish extremes. Foster defends Kabti-ilani-Marduk's innovations: "The diction of this text seems strange, or at least idiosyncratic, to some modern readers. They are inclined to regard this as indicative of an author untutored in the finer points of Akkadian poetics. One might equally consider it a determined effort to refurbish a rich inventory of inherited expressions to lend them greater force, to do such violence, so to speak, to traditional usage as to command attention" (*From Distant Days*, 132–33) — the kind of showing off that would get Kabti slapped down by some of today's literary gatekeepers. But the author saves his most audacious move for the end; after he finishes Erra's story, he adds this advertisement for himself:

> The one who put together the composition about him was Kabti-ilani-Marduk son of Dabibi. Some god revealed it to him in the middle of the night, and when he recited it upon waking, he did not miss anything out, nor add a single word to it. Erra heard and approved it, and it was pleasing also to Ishum who marches in front of him. All the other gods gave praise with him. And the warrior Erra spoke, saying, "Wealth shall be piled up in the shrine of the god who praises this song! But whoever discards it shall never smell the *qutrinnu*-offering! . . . Let this song endure forever, let it last for eternity!" (Dalley 311–12)

It's a bold author who not only claims to have written something in his sleep but also to have it blurbed by the gods, but he was right: mighty Babylon has fallen, but his daring work is still being read 2,700 years later.

ANCIENT HEBREW FICTION

They left behind no spectacular monuments or golden treasures like the Egyptians, made no discoveries in astronomy, agriculture, or mathematics like the Babylonians, but the ancient Hebrews left behind a magnificent body of literature, exceeding that of most of their more civilized neighbors. Their writing followed the same path of development: Hebrew storytellers composed some poems and tales, heard others from Egyptian and Akkadian travelers (Israel was located on the trade routes between Egypt and Assyria), adapted them by changing names and adding local color, passed them along to others of their profession who added their own touches, until eventually priests decided they should write these poems and tales down and preserve them. As with *Gilgamesh*, these priest-editors often had a variety of related but contradictory stories to choose from, so they kept the ones that served their purposes (political/theocratic/nationalistic) and discarded the rest, edited them together (not always very skillfully), and then — and here's the unbelievable part — proclaimed the result not literature but history. And even more unbelievably, there are hundreds of millions of people today who continue to regard these writings as history, even divine revelation, despite the overwhelming evidence against their historicity. No one believes anymore in Horus or Isis or Marduk or Anu or Erra, but in the 21st century of the Common Era there are educated citizens with responsible jobs who still believe in Yahweh and his angels, Baal and Satan, Joshua stopping the sun in its tracks with the help of his sky-god, and other fanciful creations. Incredible, isn't it? Only this inability or unwillingness to distinguish fact from fantasy has prevented ancient Hebrew authors from being accorded their rightful place in the development of literary fiction, for the decision of those editor-priests to convert oral tales and hymns into written prose narratives is the Big Bang in the history of the novel. This "shift from the medium of the spoken to the written word" is key, Robert S. Kawashima notes: "In exploiting this new medium, the biblical writers developed a literary sense of prose style and of formal technique surprisingly akin to that of the modern novelist" (14). The traditional categorization of these ancient Jewish narratives as history rather than literature is not only taxonomically wrong, but has encouraged denigrating remarks like this one from André Gide in 1914: "Why Jewish literature hardly goes back more than twenty years or at most fifty."[34] This is a shame, because within the collection of Hebrew writings called the Tanakh there are at least two novels and a few novellas by some of the finest writers of the ancient world.

The Tanakh is a massive anthology of works — everything from sacred myths to dietary regulations to erotic poetry — written between the 8th and 3rd centuries BCE, at which time it was edited into its final form. The title is an acronym taken from its three main divisions: Torah ("Instruction," aka "The Five Books of Moses": myths and legends about tribal origins), Nevi'im ("Prophets": a highly biased and historically inaccurate account of the conflicts between two minor kingdoms in present-day Israel from roughly the 11th through 6th centuries: Israel in the north and Judah in the south), and Kethuvim ("Writings": a miscellany of works on religious themes). Textually, it's a mess, a patchwork of writings by dozens of authors at the mercy of various editors and "redactors" who later revised and reshaped the writings to suit their doctrinal needs, and then further tinkered with by generations of anonymous scribes who felt at liberty to alter the texts.[35] For example, the

---

34 A journal entry quoted in Stern and Mirsky's *Rabbinic Fantasies*, 364.

35 They're even criticized within the Tanakh: at one point Jeremiah fulminates, "How can you say, 'We are wise, since we have Yahweh's Law'? Look how it's been falsified by the lying pen of the scribes!" (Jer. 8:8, *New Jerusalem Bible*). Similarly, the author of Deuteronomy twice warns scribes not to add or delete anything (4:2, 12:32), hip to their lowdown revising

first work in the Torah, Genesis or "In the Beginning" (from its opening line, the same practice as in Akkadian literature), combines texts written over a 200-year period by three principal authors, four if you count the incompetent editor that later stitched them together, who filled in a few cracks but left all sorts of glaring inconsistencies and contradictions in the final text. Same with the other books of the Torah, except for Leviticus, written by a single author with minimal editorial interference. The so-called Deuteronomistic History that runs from Deuteronomy through the books of Kings isn't quite as chaotic, though later editors honked it up by inserting the book of Ruth in the middle. The remaining writings have various problems, like the speeches by Elihu that were inserted by an inferior author into the sublime book of Job (chaps. 32–37), or the Greek material added to the Hebrew book of Esther, in addition to the usual problems of editorial tampering and scribal transmission.

For the last 200 years, scholars and archaeologists have been reverse-engineering the Tanakh, untangling the various narrative sequences and assigning them to distinct authors, now known by their initials: the J author (via the German form of Yahweh, J's local god), from Judah in the south, wrote one version of the tribal myth, from the creation through the death of King David; the E author (so called because he prefers the plural Elohim for his gods), from Israel in the north, wrote a shorter, spottier account, beginning at Genesis 20 and petering out after Exodus. (The E author may have written a longer account that mostly wound up on the cutting-room floor because later editors preferred other versions.) Then there's the P author, a no-nonsense guy obsessed with priesthood; he apparently obtained a text that combined J and E together and decided he could do better. That's his version of the creation at the very beginning of Genesis, and his hand can be detected through Numbers. (Leviticus, the most Talibanic book in the Tanakh, is all his, except for the Holiness Code in chapters 17–26, which he adapted from an earlier text.) The J and E texts were written in the 8th or 7th centuries BCE; the P document, which takes up the lion's share of the Torah, was written a little later. Finally, D was assigned to the authors of Deuteronomy and the rest of the Deuteronomistic History, written in the late 7th century BCE, then revised during the 6th (perhaps by the same author, perhaps by another). The entire sequence was then edited into its present form by the Redactor (R) in the 4th century, who may have been the prophet Ezra.[36] The miscellaneous

---

ways. For an eye-opening account of their role, see Toorn's *Scribal Culture and the Making of the Hebrew Bible*; as he puts it, "The Hebrew Bible as we know it is the result of a series of scribal interventions" (6).

36 See Friedman's *Who Wrote the Bible?* for a fascinating account of all this. His edition of the Torah, *The Bible with Sources Revealed*, uses different colors and typefaces for the various documents so that you can see at a glance who wrote what. While some details are still in dispute, this "documentary hypothesis" is known and accepted by most biblical scholars today; the only people who don't are head-in-the-sand fundamentalists and of course the

writings comprising the final section of the Tanakh were composed between the 8th and 3rd centuries, and a few centuries later the immense three-part work was canonized as it now stands (in Hebrew bibles that is, not Christian), with other similar writings downgraded to apocrypha.

Embedded within the Tanakh are two accomplished novels — a magic-realist one (J) and a family saga (D) — that *should* be considered the first examples of the genre. They're long enough, and written in prose (intermixed with some poetry); only their alleged status as nonfiction and/or divine revelation prevents them from taking their deserved place at the beginning of the novel tradition. But *of course* they're fiction; otherwise they must be classified as religious propaganda, pious frauds perpetrated by self-serving priests who rewrote history as perniciously as Soviet historians rewrote theirs in the last century and with a similar totalitarian agenda.[37] I'm going with fiction.

A few attempts have been made to extract the J document from its surroundings and to present it as the independent work it once was. The best known is *The Book of J*, translated by David Rosenberg with extensive commentary by Harold Bloom, who made news by suggesting the author was a woman. (Actually, Friedman had suggested this a few years earlier in *Who Wrote the Bible?* [86].) Their version of J is a little over a hundred pages long, from Gen. 2:4b through the death of Moses at the end of Deuteronomy. But the most convincing is Richard Elliott Friedman's version, which occupies pages 67–291 of *The Hidden Book in the Bible*, starting from the same point in Genesis but extending to the death of David and ascension of Solomon in the second chapter of 1 Kings. Following ancient literary practice, he entitles it *In the Day* after its opening line ("In the day that YHWH made earth and skies . . .") and proudly calls it the first extended prose masterpiece in world literature. And he's right.

It begins with a god and ends with a king, both demanding unquestioning obedience from a people portrayed as dishonest, petty, arrogant, inhospitable, suspicious, and cruel, a people who can't be trusted to do what's right and consequently need the iron hand of a dictator to force them to do so.[38] Deception and disobedience are the principal themes; the deception begins

---

vast majority of Jews and Christians, who don't know jack about the origins of their own sacred writings.

37 Don't believe me; read Finkelstein and Silberman's illuminating *Bible Unearthed*, which uses the latest findings in archaeology and extrabiblical sources to demolish any claims to historicity in the Tanakh. (The totalitarian slant is mine, as I'll explain later.) It is gracefully written and free of my sneering, irreligious tone.

38 The Abraham and Isaac story (written by E) is a parable promoting unquestioning obedience to authority; only an absolute dictator could order a citizen to kill his own son and expect to be obeyed, and Abraham's willingness to do so marks him as a model apparatchik in YHWH's totalitarian state. (A "test of faith"? — every dictatorship uses euphemistic doublespeak.) More admirable is the Abraham of Bob Dylan's "Highway 61 Revisited": "God said to Abraham, 'Kill me a son'/ Abe says, 'Man, you must be puttin' me on.'"

with YHWH himself, who warns the human he has just made not to eat from "the tree of knowledge of good and bad" or else "you'll *die!*" — a threat the human disobeys at the suggestion of the woman who was created for him, and a sly snake that knew YHWH was lying about the tree. In contrast, *In the Day* ends with King Solomon warning Shimei not to leave Jerusalem or "you'll *die!*"; when Shimei disobeys three years later and goes to Gath, Solomon coldly reminds him of his earlier threat and has an *obedient* servant kill him. And on that chilling note, *In the Day* ends.

That deliberate verbal echo of "you'll *die!*" and the formal elegance of contrasting acts of deception/disobedience in the beginning with honesty/obedience at the conclusion are only a few of the numerous rhetorical clues that *In the Day* was composed not by a historian or theologian but by a writerly artist. Even stripped of the sumptuous robes of the King James translation and presented in Friedman's nakedly literal one, the text's verbal dexterity is evident. In fact it reads as though the author set out to compile a straightforward tale of the Israelites (from a Judean perspective) from whatever old sources were at hand — legends of mythic heroes, folktales, myths "borrowed" from neighboring Egyptians and Akkadians,[39] songs, poetry collections like *The Scroll of the Wars of YHWH* and *The Book of Yashar* — and discovered the art of the novel in the process. It's an enormous leap from a one-dimensional character like Noah to the complex David, from a creation myth inferior to those of other Near Eastern countries to a scene like this:

> And the people were not willing to listen to him. And the man took hold of his concubine and brought her to them outside. And they knew her and abused her all night until morning and let her go at sunrise. And the woman came toward morning and fell at the entrance of the house where her lord was, until it was light. And her lord got up in the morning and opened the doors of the house and went out to go on his way, and here was the woman, his concubine, fallen at the entrance of the house, and her hands on the threshold.
>
> And he said to her, "Get up, and let's go."
>
> And there was no answer.[40]

There's nothing like that in ancient Egyptian or Akkadian literature; only the author(s) of the *Iliad*, living about the same time, could have written something like that.[41] This scene — which deliberately echoes the more famous

---

39 The extent of these borrowings can be seen in a useful anthology edited by Matthews and Benjamin entitled *Old Testament Parallels*, which shows how profoundly *unoriginal* the stories and theology of the Torah are. (Then again, originality is a fairly recent concept; it didn't count for much until about 200 years ago.) See also Callahan's *Secret Origins of the Bible*, a thorough, erudite study of extrabiblical sources and parallels.

40 *In the Day*, 186–87 (Judges 19:25–28). You don't want to know what he does with the corpse.

41 Like the Torah, the Homeric epics are now thought to be the work not of one author but of many writers and editors working over a long period.

one of Lot in Sodom, though, as with Solomon and Shimei, with an uglier twist — occurs halfway through *In the Day*; from that point on, it reads more and more like a modern novel exploring the quagmire of moral issues an increasingly complex cast of characters find themselves in. This isn't history: as the authors of *The Bible Unearthed* point out in relentless detail, there's no evidence that *anything* portrayed in the Tanakh prior to the monarchy of Saul actually happened, and that everything else from then until the Assyrian conquest of Israel in 722 BCE "must be considered more of a historical novel than an accurate historical chronicle" (175). It's fiction because it shows instead of tells — the first lesson a novelist learns.

What it shows is a people for whom lying and deception seem to be a way of life. YHWH lies to his human; Eve lies that she was deceived; Cain deceives his brother, then lies to YHWH; Abraham lies when claiming his wife Sarah is actually his sister (as his son Isaac will later do);[42] Sarah laughs at YHWH then lies and says she didn't; Lot's daughters deceive their father by getting him blind drunk and raping him (the same father who offered to throw his daughters to the crowd to be raped — bizarre people); Jacob takes advantage of Esau to obtain his birthright, then disguises himself as his brother to con their father into blessing him; Jacob is himself conned by his uncle Laban into working twice as long for him, and in turn tricks his uncle out of a flock; Jacob's sons deceive Shechem and Hamor and then murder their entire tribe; Joseph's brothers lie to their father about selling him to the Ishmaelites; Tamar disguises herself as a religious sex worker to deceive her father-in-law into impregnating her (who *are* these people?!);[43] Potiphar's wife lies after Joseph spurns her advances; Joseph repeatedly deceives and tricks his brothers after they come to Egypt for help, and after revealing himself encourages them to lie to the pharaoh who nurtured Joseph — and we haven't even left Genesis yet![44] Yes, I know: the Torah is supposed to celebrate YHWH's eternal covenant with the Israelites — basically an ethnocentric excuse to kill their neighbors and steal their land — but what is told is offset by what is shown.

42 J develops characterization by analogy: if Moses is a great man who led his people across the dried-up Red Sea, then Joshua can be assumed to be a great man because he leads his people across the dried-up Jordan river. J counts on the reader to hear these verbal echoes and make the connection.

43 The answer is these aren't people but mythic figures; Lot's daughters and Tamar gave birth to the eponymous founders of various tribes. (If I didn't know better, I'd say J wanted to portray these tribes as literal sons of bitches.) It's worth noting all these tales of sexual transgression appear only in J, not E or P.

44 In the 6th-century midrash *Genesis Rabbah* (8.5), YHWH informs the angels of his plans to create a man, but the Angel of Truth objects: "Let him not be created for he will be all lies." YHWH "flung him to the earth" and went ahead anyway, apparently less disgusted with liars than I am. (See Holtz's *Back to the Sources*, 191–92.) In Buddhism, *three* of their "ten commandments" (*daśākuśala*) forbid using deceitful language, as opposed to only one in the Jewish list (Deut. 5:17), and even that is limited to giving false testimony during legal proceedings.

YHWH is so disgusted early on at what he hath wrought that he decides, like Enki before him, to destroy humankind with a flood. Again like the Akkadian god, he relents and allows one human to survive and repopulate the land, but his continued disappointment with his creation thereafter is obvious; like a stern father disappointed in his disobedient offspring, he becomes more and more distant — literally. The author cunningly shows this by portraying a god in the beginning as a palpable presence: he strolls in his garden, sews clothes for his humans, and appears before Abraham and others; but as his people continue to lie and deceive each other, he withdraws into a burning bush and other manifestations, warns people to keep their distance from him, and finally becomes only a bodiless voice — like Echo in the Greek myth, or like the Great Oz.

Why would J portray the national god in this way? Because *In the Day* is what the French call a *roman à thèse*, its thesis being that people are not capable of moral behavior on their own and have to be coerced into it by a strong theocracy. They need to *submit* to authority, which would likewise later become the basis of Islam (which means "submission," not "peace" as sometimes alleged — unless referring to the lobotomized peace of mind that comes from just following orders and allowing others to do your thinking for you), and which is of course the basis of every totalitarian government. Halfway through the novel we start hearing the refrain "In those days there was no king in Israel. Each man would do what was right in his eyes," the author's voice dripping with sarcasm because that meant each man would do what was ethically wrong. Since the people won't follow a god — that is, an internal moral compass pointing them in the right direction — they'll be cursed with a king and a priesthood, an external authority that will force them to toe the line. (We have to remember that both J and E were written first and foremost as nationalistic charters for a reunited monarchy.) In a remarkable antimonarchist speech that Thomas Jefferson might have penned, YHWH pretty much *curses* his people with kingship for abandoning him (*In the Day*, 207; 1 Sam. 8:7–18), just as he cursed Adam and Eve for disobeying him in the beginning. J seems to suggest the Israelites deserve nothing better, and ultimately seems to have been more interested in establishing the divine right of kings than in revealing the divine love for a chosen people. Harold Bloom calls J an ironic humorist, like Kafka, but she strikes me more as a satiric misanthropist, like Swift.[45]

But Bloom is right in calling J "a narrator on the grandest scale who combines, for the first time in Hebrew or indeed in any language, every genre available to her in Near Eastern literature" (318). Even discounting Bloom's

---

45 Bloom's identification of the author as a woman doesn't sound very convincing to me, but since this early period is dominated by male authors, I'll go along with it for variety's sake.

usual hyperbole — "The Tale of Sinuhe" and *Gilgamesh* also incorporate a number of genres — *In the Day* displays examples of myth, folklore, fable, fairy tale, travelogue, children's stories, theology, poetry, history, romance, legal codes, sermons, and etiological fictions, along with some illicit sex scenes and assorted bizarreries.[46] This very heterogeneity has led some commentators to suspect many authors are at work here, but *In the Day* could actually be an early example of Menippean form, which mixes prose, poetry, and whatever nonfiction genres the author fancies. (Laurence Sterne's *Tristram Shandy* is the classic example, while Gilbert Sorrentino's *Mulligan Stew* is a more recent one.) The language itself is heterogeneous, ranging from understatement to what Bloom calls "the wordplay of false etymologies and puns" (286), which are not merely verbal rim-shots but generate much of the narrative. Imaginative language creates this tale of creation; in the beginning was the word. The author is also a master of dramatic irony and is capable of great subtlety: compare the graphic scene of sexual awakening in *Gilgamesh* with Adam and Eve's, which is almost abstract: the phallic snake whispering sweet nothings, Eve's hesitancy, the sudden awareness of the body, the opening of eyes, the "knowing" of sex — the scene is a delicate ballet of symbols and epiphanies, in stark contrast to Enkidu and Shamhat's X-rated performance.[47] As history, *In the Day* is unreliable, as theology it's reprehensible — it justifies misogyny, xenophobia, genocide, body-shame, and totalitarianism — but as literature, it's fascinating.

The last quarter of *In the Day* concerns King David, and is so good that it was transferred almost intact into the middle of the other novel contained within the Tanakh, the Deuteronomistic History. I wish it had a better title: I'd suggest either *A Tale of Two Kingdoms* (after Dickens) or *A Blessing and a Curse* (after Deut. 11:26), though *Yahweh or the Highway* best sums up its terse religious message.[48] Following Near Eastern literary practice, let's call it *These Are the Words*, after its opening line: "These are the words that Moses addressed to all Israel. . . ."[49] Of course these *aren't* the words of Moses but of someone writing late in the reign of King Josiah of Judah (ruled 639–609)

---

46 I'm thinking of that weird night scene where YHWH decides to kill Moses but is scared off by his wife Zipporah, who circumcises her son, smears the blood on Moses' genitals, then declares him to be her "bridegroom of blood" (*In the Day*, 129; Ex. 4:24–26).

47 Though the actual sex *follows* this scene, it's implied that eating of the tree of good and bad is a sexual act. In Michelangelo's painting *The Fall of Man and the Expulsion from the Garden of Eden* (c. 1510), it looks like Eve's temptation occurs as she's in the middle of performing oral sex on her mate, eating of Adam's Tree of Life, so to speak.

48 Everett Fox entitled his translation of Samuel 1 and 2 *Give Us a King!*, which is appropriate.

49 In fact one ancient Jewish designation for Deuteronomy was *Sefer Devarim*, or "Book of Words," short for "The Book of 'These are the words . . .'" (*Jewish Study Bible*, n. to Deut. 17:18).

some six to eight centuries after the alleged time of Moses.[50] The author began with the brutally fundamentalist law code that now occupies chapters 12–26 of Deuteronomy (probably written a little earlier in the 7th century), wrote the chapters before and after the code, adapted material from J, E, and P, worked in some old poems, and extended the story from the time of Solomon down to Josiah (i.e., from Deuteronomy through 2 Kings 23:25); then, some 20 years later, he or someone else wrote the final chapters of Second Kings on the collapse of Judah in 587 and the exile to Babylon, and went back to revise some earlier portions to "prophesize" this final tragedy.[51] Friedman feels it's possible that one person wrote/adapted/edited the entire thing, and further suggests that person may have been Baruch ben Neriah, a scribe associated with the prophet Jeremiah (and perhaps the author of the book of Jeremiah as well; he's mentioned in Jer. 32:12, 36:4). For simplicity's sake, let's adopt Friedman's thesis that this is what happened and that Baruch is our author.[52] In a nutshell, *These Are the Words* is the story of a tiny nation that blew its chance at greatness by breaking its contract with its benefactor.

The 350-page work gets off to a clumsy start. Moses gives a long synopsis of Our Story So Far — recapitulating material from Exodus and Numbers with the usual contradictions and inconsistencies — before launching into the 20-page legal corpus. And it doesn't get better. One problem is Deuteronomy is made up of too many documents revised by too many editors to serve too many functions. It's the last part of the Torah, concluding the legend of Moses, but the first book of the Deuteronomistic History, an idealized, Judahite legend of the nation from its resettlement by Moses's successor Joshua down to its dispersal after 587. As history, it's as unreliable as *In the Day* and even contradicts parts of the Torah, which the author presumably had available; plus the Levite priesthood has its fingerprints all over it as they justify their role in Israelite society and insist, over and over again, on keeping those offerings coming.[53] ("Follow the money" Deep Throat advised of suspicious

---

50 *If* Moses even existed — see Finkelstein and Silberman, who argue convincingly that he probably didn't and that the Exodus never happened.

51 Like Friedman's *Bible with Sources Revealed*, Campbell and O'Brien's *Unfolding the Deuteronomistic History* provides an annotated text using different fonts and typefaces to suggest the various levels of source documents, revisions, and editorial additions.

52 *Who Wrote the Bible?* 101–49. In the first edition of his book, Friedman suggested Jeremiah was the author, but 10 years of additional research led him to propose Baruch instead in the second edition. In his recent monograph on the scribe, J. Edward Wright says only that Baruch was "an integral member of . . . the deuteronomistic circle of Yahwists who were ultimately responsible for . . . the 'Deuteronomistic History'" (33–34).

53 Commenting on the "coevolution of religion with social structure" in most early societies, Nicholas Wade explains that "the elites coopted the ritual practices as another mechanism of social control and as a means of justifying their privileged position. Making the religion more exclusionary gave the elites greater power to control the believers. To justify the ruler's position, new truths, also unverifiable and unfalsifiable, were added as subtexts to the religion's sacred postulates, such as 'The chief has great *mana*,' 'Pharaoh is the living

situations like this.) As fiction, it's deadly: Deuteronomy is basically a two-hour monologue by an old man who frequently forgets whom he's addressing — mistaking the present generation of his audience for the previous generation he led through the desert — often repeats himself, and occasionally misremembers his own past. He even garbles the Ten Commandments that were thundered into his brain 40 years earlier (cf. Deut. 5:6–17 with Ex. 20:1–14). If this were intended as a characterization of forgetful, garrulous old age, then it would be spot-on, even comic: one can imagine members of the audience looking impatiently at their sand-clocks, wondering how much longer the old coot was going to continue haranguing them, asking one another, "What was that he just said about crushed testicles and cut-off members?" (Deut. 23:2), eyeballing their teenage daughters when Moses says any girl who commits fornication while still living under her father's roof must be stoned to death by the community (22:2), and looking at one another in puzzlement when Moses insists, "You shall make tassels on the four corners of the garment with which you cover yourself" (22:12) and making that circular motion with the finger at the side of the head.[54]

But the author is serious, and serious damage was done to the text by later editors who inserted material awkwardly, sometimes disrupting the point of view as a result. The law code (chaps. 12–26), which Baruch was probably forbidden to change in any way, contains too much undigested material from alien sources, like the Babylonian Code of Hammurabi and the Vassal Treaty of Esarhaddon (the key to 28:27–35, 49–57). Only the concluding scene of Moses's burial, written by J, touches us: in the beginning she depicted YHWH forming a human from the earth, and here completes the circle by showing YHWH burying one in the earth. The rest of Deuteronomy we leave to the rabbis.

If *These Are the Words* is the world's first historical novel, then we can cut Baruch some slack. He faced the same formal problem every historical novelist must deal with: providing enough background as quickly as possible to establish the historical setting. Straight exposition, as here, is the clumsiest way; I'm reminded of the opening of Shakespeare's *Comedy of Errors*, where everyone onstage has to stand around while Egeon provides the long backstory. Great novelists handle this more efficiently; in *Notre-Dame de Paris* Victor Hugo sets us down amid the tolling bells of Paris on the morning of 6 January 1482 and away we go (he'll fill us in later); in *A Tale of Two Cities* Dickens masterfully sets the stage with three pages of sarcasm and whimsy before proceeding with his tale. Baruch begins the book of Joshua the same

---

Horus,' or 'Henry is by the Grace of God King'" (*Before the Dawn: Recovering the Lost History of Our Ancestors* [NY: Penguin, 2006], 167).

54 Moses is repeating fashion tips he gave to a previous generation (Num. 15:37–40); the younger generation he's addressing here wouldn't necessarily know what he's talking about.

clumsy way as Deuteronomy, with a clump of exposition, but keeps it brief this time; the cleaner narrative line running through Joshua and Judges allows him to learn his craft before he embarks on the more subtle David story in the book of Samuel and the tricky dual narrative of the book of Kings.[55]

Joshua is a rather flat tale of imperialistic military conquest, and Joshua himself a flat character. The book is neither good fiction, nor good theology, nor good history, as scholars and archaeologists have noted.[56] Judges is more colorful, largely because it features a wider cast of interesting characters: we have the legends of Deborah the prophetess, Barak the army commander, Jael the murderess, Jephthah and his doomed daughter, and of course the story of Samson and Delilah, a grim fairy tale. There are parables, angels performing tricks, more etiological fables, snappy dialogue, riddles, rapes and abductions. Baruch was still relying on J and older material like the lost *Book of Jashar*, but we can see him moving away from older, poetic traditions and exploring the possibilities of literary prose. The two modes are contrasted in competing versions of the same incident (deliverance from the Canaanites), a carefully composed prose account in Judges 4 followed by Deborah's improvised poetic version in chapter 5. The third-person prose account is detailed, nuanced, character-driven, and builds to a terrific climax; Deborah's first-person hymn is bombastic, religiose, archaic, and frequently obscure. Novelistic prose wins the day; epic poetry, like the Canaanite commander Sisera, is left for dead.[57]

The opening of the book of Samuel shows how far Baruch has progressed in narrative skill. Before this, whenever a barren woman prayed for a child, she was answered by her god or one of his angels. But when Hannah silently prays, Eli the priest sees her moving her lips and assumes she's drunk — an

---

55 Both Samuel and the book of Kings were originally single narratives; only later were they divided into 1 and 2 Samuel and 1 and 2 Kings because of the space limitations of a scroll.

56 In her notes to Joshua in the splendid *Jewish Study Bible*, Carol Meyers has several variants of this understatement: "This discrepancy between text and archaeology . . . points to the Joshua narratives as serving ideological purposes rather than preserving historical sequences of events" (n. to Jos. 12:9–24). Ahem, yes. Like Friedman, Finkelstein and Silberman, and other reverent scholars, she doesn't take this to the logical conclusion and admit that since the Tanakh is filled with mistakes and outright lies and is obviously the work of ideologues, their YHWH is also obviously a poetic invention "serving ideological purposes." Seems to me a lot of people in biblical studies are in denial, or intellectual cowards. Prof. Hector Avalos agrees: see his disgusted call for *The End of Biblical Studies* (Amherst, NY: Prometheus, 2007) because his colleagues can't free themselves from "a bibliolatrous orientation that is manifested in a persistent effort to privilege the biblical text" (77) that would be grounds for ridicule and dismissal in any other academic discipline. For a sad example of the intellectual knots a biblical scholar can tie himself in, see *How to Read the Bible* (NY: Free Press, 2007), an erudite study by James L. Kugel, an Orthodox Jew. His cognitive dissonance is quite rightly exposed by Richard Friedman in a merciless review in the *Biblical Archaeological Review*, January/February 2008, 62–67.

57 See chap. 2 of Kawashima's *Biblical Narrative* for a brilliant analysis of this dramatization of "the transition from oral poetry to literary prose *within* the biblical corpus itself" (15).

understandable, even comic error indicating we've left the divine realm for the human. YHWH's still around, of course, but he's offstage; center stage is taken by people rather than archetypes and angels, people with recognizable, even modern traits: Saul suffers from clinical depression, the young David practices music therapy, Samuel exemplifies the priggish religious type, and the politics of establishing and maintaining a monarchy introduces politicians and advisors we recognize all too well from the media. And these characters are rounder than the mostly flat characters we've seen until now. Technically, the writing gets better: chapters 8–12 are artfully arranged, and one begins to see more novelistic detail, hear more realistic dialogue, and admire the author(s)' use of foreshadowing, symbolism, allusion, and iterative imagery. And note how subtly David is introduced in chapter 16: no semimiraculous birth from a previously barren woman, just a shepherd boy who remains nameless for a while. From this point on, the text reads almost like a modern novel, with the modern novel's emphasis on the mystery of personality: David's complex relationship with Saul; psycho Saul's violent mood-swings and the cat-and-mouse game he later plays with David; and David's intriguing relationships with Saul's son Jonathan and his daughter Michal, who is given to him in marriage. (Michal is the only woman in the entire Tanakh said to actually love a man; isn't that strange?) The narrator stumbles with the David and Goliath story, an old fairy tale that contradicts surrounding material (2 Sam. 21:19 says Goliath was killed by Elhanan, not David), but recovers nicely with the help of J. (Remember, Friedman argues that about half of Samuel was taken from *In the Day.*)

The beginning of 2 Samuel seems to contradict the end of 1 Samuel, but the narrator drops enough hints to suggest the young Amalekite is a lying opportunist, a risky narrative move because it depends on the reader's perspicacity. (These are the chances a writerly author takes; a readerly one spells things out.) 2 Samuel reaches its peak in chapters 11–20, one of the most brilliant narratives in all of ancient literature, so masterfully done that it should be taught in creative writing classes. Sometimes called the Succession Narrative, this comprises the related stories of David and Bathsheba and the revolt of David's favorite son Absalom, a nuanced study of familial relationships, of Catullus's *odi et amo* (love/hate) paradox, and a demonstration that, as a character in Gaddis's *Carpenter's Gothic* says, "that Clausnitz was wrong, it's not that war is politics carried on by other means it's the family carried on by other means."[58]

The narrative is too famous to require extended comment — for that I'd recommend Robert Alter's annotated translation *The David Story* and Baruch Halpern's brutally critical *David's Secret Demons* — but I want to point out a few stylistic masterstrokes. Note, for example, how the narrator handles

---

58 Page 241; another character corrects the name to von Clausewitz.

David's interview with Uriah, husband of the woman he has just impregnated: "When Uriah came to him, David asked him how Joab and the troops were faring and how the war was going. Then David said to Uriah, 'Go down to your house and bathe your feet'" (2 Sam. 11:7–8). Uriah's reply to David's questions is unrecorded; why? Because David doesn't really hear it; he's too preoccupied with getting Uriah to have sex with Bathsheba to cover up the pregnancy, and so *we* don't hear it either. The very *absence* of Uriah's reply conveys meaning, which is a clever narrative move. And note how, when Absalom returns from exile and is welcomed by his father David, we're told that Absalom "came to the king and flung himself face down to the ground before the king. And the king kissed Absalom" (2 Sam. 14:33b). Not *David*, not *his father*, but "the king," repeated three times. A lesser writer would avoid the repetition, but the gifted narrator wants to hammer home the point that Absalom's revolt against *a king*, YHWH's anointed, is worse than his disobedience as a son (which is deserving of stoning to death according to Deuteronomy) and that this is merely a formal, temporary reconciliation. In this 20-page sequence there are dozens of these brilliant narrative and stylistic choices that come through even in translation. Then some editor had to spoil it by tacking on four pages of leftover material (2 Sam. 21–24), breaking the spell — as if we really needed to hear about genocidal YHWH sending an angel to destroy 70,000 innocent Jews on a technicality.

The final section of *These Are the Words*, the two books of Kings, begins with the death of David and the ascension of ruthless Solomon. (Like any dictator, first thing he does is kill a bunch of people.) There J's contribution ends, and what a difference: the style reverts to the simpler, repetitious one of Deuteronomy and Joshua. Baruch's account of Solomon's construction of the Temple and palace in Jerusalem is an overheated architectural fantasia (like Colonna's *Hypnerotomachia Poliphili*) unsupported by archaeological evidence,[59] so this is still fiction, but it's no longer great literature. After Solomon's death, the land splits into two kingdoms — Israel in the north, Judah in the south — and the rest of Kings shuttles between the two as Baruch judges the kings that ruled during the next few centuries. (As a Judean, he's unfairly harsh on the northern kings, subverting the historical record to fit his theological agenda.) They are judged solely on their adherence to the proper worship of YHWH and intolerance of polytheism, and as a result much of this is formulaic and perfunctory. The narrative is enlivened somewhat by legends of two wonder-working prophets, hairy Elijah and bald Elisha, heroes of flashy anecdotes to wow the rubes.[60]

---

59 See Finkelstein and Silberman's *David and Solomon*, their sequel to *The Bible Unearthed*.

60 Those of Elisha in particular were plagiarized by the Christian authors of the New Covenant for their wonder-working prophet, Yeshua ben Yosef.

These Are the Words reaches its climax with the ascension of pious King Josiah, who finds a neglected copy of an early version of Deuteronomy, reads it aloud and panics, and then turns Judah into the fundamentalist theocracy recommended therein. Josiah embodies the ideal king described in Deuteronomy 17:14–20, linking the first and last sections of *These Are the Words* in an aesthetically pleasing narrative arc. There the original version concluded (2 Kgs 23:25), a happy ending for supporters of institutionalized superstition, xenophobia, racial purity, and totalitarianism. Then the unthinkable happened: Josiah was killed in battle before he could reunite the two kingdoms, his successors slid back into multicultural polytheism and interracial marriage, and then the Babylonian forces destroyed Jerusalem and sent its people into exile. An older, humiliated Baruch (or a member of his circle) wrote the two remaining chapters, ending *These Are the Words* on a grim note of defeat. All in all, an interesting prototype of the multigenerational historical novel, even if it didn't end the way the author(s) originally intended.

In addition to these two novels, a few novellas might be extracted from the Tanakh, but perhaps it's better to leave them where they are. Chronicles, a 90-page work composed in the 4th century BCE, is a revision of Samuel–Kings, but reads more like the P version of the Torah; that is, a theological document that uses narrative form but few novelistic or artistic techniques. Then there's the book of Job, a sophisticated rhetorical performance of the highest order, perhaps the finest thing in the entire Tanakh; at 60 pages, it approaches the length of a novella, but since it's written mostly in verse, it belongs to the history of narrative poetry rather than to that of the novel. Recently Lawrence M. Wills published an anthology entitled *Ancient Jewish Novels*, but with one exception,[61] the selections — such as the books of Ruth and Esther from the Kethuvim section of the Tanakh, noncanonical writings like Tobit and the Testament of Job — are too short to be considered novellas, much less novels.[62] He's right, however, to emphasize the importance of storytelling in the Hebrew scriptures, parts of which were intended to entertain as well as edify. Adele Berlin, one of the editors of the *Jewish Study Bible* I've been citing, goes so far as to suggest "Esther is best read as a comedy" (1623).

The Tanakh reached something close to its final form in the 2nd century BCE when the Greek Septuagint translation was completed, but that didn't stop literary-inclined Jews from writing further religious fictions. For the next few centuries, they revised, expanded, and improvised on biblical themes,

---

61 *The Marriage and Conversion of Aseneth* (121–62), which I'll discuss later under its more common title, *Joseph and Aseneth*.

62 I made allowances earlier for ancient Egyptian and Akkadian tales, but we're at the point where we need to start insisting on a certain length — otherwise I might also have dealt with the Ugaritic "Tale of Aqhat" (14th cent. BCE) and the Aramaic "Words of Ahikar" (7th–6th cent. BCE). These interesting narratives can be found in Coogan (32–47) and Charlesworth (2:494–507), respectively.

churning out things like "The Life of Adam and Eve," "The Treatise of Shem," "The Apocryphon of Ezekiel," "The Apocalypse of Abraham," "The Ladder of Jacob," "The Testaments of the Twelve Patriarchs," "The Book of Baruch" (our tentative author of *These Are the Words*), and "The Martyrdom and Ascension of Isaiah."[63] Ranging from the sublime to the ridiculous, most of these works are short, but there is one extended narrative that can be called a novel, perhaps even the origin of the modern occult novel. Anne Rice admits to having studied it, and today it sells thousands of copies a year in a variety of editions.

The Book of Enoch purports to be the first-person account of the visions and celestial travels of Enoch, the seventh descendant of Adam and Eve, grandfather of Noah, and one of only two people in the Tanakh said to have been transported to heaven without dying first. Actually the book was written — or compiled, because it seems to be another composite work — in Judea sometime in the 2nd century BCE. The anonymous work is notorious for several reasons — for its tales of the fallen angels, for its geographies of heaven and hell, for its messianic prophecies — but it interests me because it sows the seeds of several genres that would bloom with later novelists. After an introductory warning of the apocalypse to come, the author turns his attention to the first four verses of the sixth chapter of Genesis, a mysterious reference to the "sons of God" mating with mortal women that puzzles scholars to this day. From his vantage point in heaven, Enoch gives us the inside story:

> And it came to pass, when the children of men had multiplied, in those days there were born to them beautiful and comely daughters. And watchers, children of heaven, saw them and desired them, and lusted after them; and they said to one another: "Come, let us choose for ourselves wives from the daughters of earth, and let us beget us children." (6:1–2)[64]

The author shows the angels hesitating a bit, then after giving all the names of the angels — whom he calls "watchers," though "voyeurs" might be more apt — he has them swoop down on their victims:

> These leaders and all the rest of the two hundred watchers took for themselves wives from all whom they chose; and they began to cohabit with them and to defile themselves with them, and they taught them sorcery and spells and showed them the cutting of roots and herbs. And they became pregnant by them and bore great giants of three thousand cubits; and there were not born upon earth off-spring which grew to their strength. These

---

63 The best anthologies where these and many more can be found are Vermes's *Complete Dead Sea Scrolls*, Barnstone's *Other Bible* and *The Gnostic Bible*, and Charlesworth's two-volume mother lode of apocrypha, *The Old Testament Pseudepigrapha*.

64 From Matthew Black's translation; here and in the quotations that follow, verse numbers and brackets have been edited out.

devoured the entire fruits of men's labour, and men were unable to sustain them. Then the giants treated them violently and began to slay mankind. They began to do violence to and attack all the birds and the beasts of the earth and reptiles that crawl upon the earth, and the fish of the sea; and they began to devour their flesh, and they were drinking the blood. (7:1–5)

Rape! Pillaging! Witchcraft! Cannibalism! Bestiality?! Vampirism! No wonder *The Book of Enoch* is popular with Anne Rice fans. The author goes on to enumerate the various arts and crafts the angels taught the people: how to make weapons, how to use makeup, knowledge of jewelry, alchemy, incantations, astrology, divination, astronomy, and other "eternal mysteries preserved in heaven" (9:6). But as in Genesis, knowledge (via sexuality) is equated with sin, which must be punished. Having "defiled" themselves by fornicating with women — and apparently for teaching Hebrew farmgirls how to look like Babylonian babes — the angels are bound hand and foot and cast into a hole in the desert to await the day of judgment, when they will be consigned to eternal fire.

The notion of superior beings who have mingled with humans would give rise in the 20th century to sci-fi stories of aliens among us, and to this day *The Book of Enoch* is a key text for those who believe that the old tales of angels actually describe visits from extraterrestrials. But another sci-fi genre the author of *Enoch* contributes to is the "fantastic journey." Enoch is given a tour of the heavens by the angels in order to satisfy his Faustian desire to learn the secrets of the universe, and in some of the most impressive passages of the book he struggles as hard as Dante to describe the indescribable celestial realms.[65] *Enoch* predates Lucian's *True Story*, often called the first sci-fi novel because of its description of a trip to the moon, and anticipates other fantastic journeys, both mundane and celestial, from *Faust* and *Gulliver's Travels* through H. G. Wells and H. P. Lovecraft and beyond. Then the author retells the entire history of the Jewish people as an animal fable (chaps. 85–90), an, er, interesting contribution to the genre popularized by Aesop centuries earlier and expanded upon by the Indian *Panchatantra* (c. 300 CE), La Fontaine, Kipling, Orwell in *Animal Farm*, and best-sellers like *Watership Down*. What noble animal does the author of *Enoch* compare the Jewish people to? The lion? the eagle? the horse? No — the cow. And later, sheep.

Which brings us to the last literary genre the author employs: the apocalypse. At the end of *Enoch*, the prophet assembles his sons and delivers a

---

65 *Enoch* is a dumb comic book compared to *The Divine Comedy*, yet one sees the same motivation there, especially the fantasy revenge scenarios against one's enemies. Poor Dante, that lovesick fool. It's a shame most people, me included, read the *Comedy* without first (or ever) reading *La Vita nuova*, where it's plain that the whole epic is a paean to unrequited love. Paradise is Beatrice's smile, and the Celestial Rose that part of her he never got to enter.

fire-and-brimstone sermon, echoing standard Jewish themes — walk in righteousness, avoid idols of wood or gold, yadda yadda yadda — and anticipating the Christian book of Revelations as he envisions the final days when "fathers shall attack their children, and brother with one another shall fall in mutual destruction, until their blood flows like a river. . . . From dawn until sunset they shall slay one another together. And the horse shall walk up to its breast in the blood of sinners, and the chariot shall be submerged to its axles" (100:1, 3). Like all apocalyptic writers, the author despises people in general and fantasizes about the destruction of everyone different from him and his chosen group. Although the genre originated in a religious context — the book of Daniel was written around the same time as *Enoch*, and dozens of apocalypses were written over the next few centuries — the genre was eventually revived by secular American novelists of a sardonic disposition — Melville, Hawthorne, Twain, Nathanael West, Vonnegut, Elkin, Gaddis, to name a few — to render judgment on a corrupt society, though of course it remains popular with self-righteous religious novelists as well.

Though rejected by the editorial committee that assembled the final version of the Tanakh, *The Book of Enoch* was wildly popular in its day: numerous copies of the original Aramaic manuscript were made and passed around (several portions were in the library of the Qumran community in Israel, part of the larger body of writings known as the Dead Sea Scrolls); it gained wider currency when translated into Greek, and it was eventually translated into Ethiopic (the language of the texts discovered in 1773 used for the first English translation in 1821). Some of the authors of the New Covenant knew the work — it is cited in the epistle of Jude (1:14) — and some have argued that even Yeshua ben Yosef did too. Most of the Church Fathers not only knew *Enoch* but approved of it, giving it the same authority and respect as the older Jewish scriptures. Tertullian — known for his breathtakingly irrational defense of the resurrection: "It is certain because it is impossible" — was quite taken by *Enoch* and used it to preach against the unholy art of makeup and adornment. In another essay of his, "On the Veiling of Virgins," Tertullian urged women to cover their hair when praying in order to avoid attracting the lust of angels, which he picked up from the apostle Paul, who apparently knew *Enoch*, for in his first letter to the Corinthians he urged women to wear a veil in church "because of the angels."

But a backlash against Enoch's strange, lusty narrative soon set in. One of the first to attack *The Book of Enoch* was the 3rd-century historian Sextus Julius Africanus, who decided the "sons of God" mentioned in both Genesis and *Enoch* were not angels but the upper-class descendants of Seth who "fell" by marrying the lower-class descendants of Cain. The Syrian authority Ephraem seconded this motion, and then others weighed in: Hilary of Tours dismissed Enoch's version, and the Syrian theologian Theodoret said people who believed Enoch's tale were "stupid and silly." Then some real heavyweights passed judgment: Jerome said Enoch's version was a form of Manichaeanism, which he considered a heresy, and Chrysostom mocked "such insane blasphemy, saying that an [angel's] incorporeal and spiritual nature could have united itself to human bodies!" Filastrius added Enoch's tale to his list of heresies, and Augustine agreed with Julius Africanus's snobbish explanation and declared the whole idea of angels having sex with mortals impossible. Even Jews, whose Tanakh is filled with stories of angels taking bodily form — Jacob even *wrestles* with an angel in Genesis — abandoned *Enoch*; a 2nd-century rabbi named Simeon bar Yohai actually pronounced a curse on anyone who believed Enoch's story. After that, *The Book of Enoch* was consigned to the rubbish heap of unorthodox apocrypha and disappeared. But upon its rediscovery and publication in 1821, it regained something of its old popularity. Lord Byron knew of Richard Laurence's English translation and was inspired to write a poem inspired by it, "Heaven and Hell — A Mystery," as did Thomas Moore, who wrote *The Loves of the Angels* (1822), a verse-novel about three of the original fallen angels, each of whom recites how, "Won down by fascinating eyes, / For woman's smile he lost the skies."[66]

And on that lovely note, let's leave the grim, god-ridden legends of the Jews for the sunny, sensual world of the Greeks.

ANCIENT GREEK FICTION

Among the glories of Greek civilization is world literature's first "real" novel: not a tale, not a prose poem, not a religious work, but a bona fide 250-page secular prose novel. And we not only know who the author is, but also know a lot about him. It's a shame, then, that the world's first novel has a reputation for being "uncommonly dull."[67]

The Education of Cyrus (*Cyropaedia*) is one of the last works written by Xenophon of Athens (431–354 BCE), a historian best known for the *Anabasis*, based on his military service with other Greek mercenaries under the Persian king Cyrus the Younger. No man of the people, Xenophon left Athens in disgust in 401 when democracy was re-established there, and moved to Sparta, whose authoritarian, militaristic ways were better suited to his political ideology. When Athens and Sparta became allies against Thebes 35 years later, he returned to Athens and began writing a novel showing the benefits of benevolent despotism.

---

66 See Shadduck's *England's Amorous Angels, 1813–1823*, which includes the complete text of Moore's work (342–432).

67 John Tatum, "The Education of Cyrus," in Morgan and Stoneman's *Greek Fiction*, 16.

Like a writer today choosing Napoleon as a model ruler, Xenophon looked back two centuries to the reign of Cyrus the Elder, who expanded the Persian empire in the middle of the 6th century until it reached from Egypt to India. Xenophon tells Cyrus's story from boyhood to death, with an emphasis on his military conquests. It's an unhistorical, idealized portrait, and the reason the novel is considered dull is because of the absence of any dramatic conflict. Young Cyrus is a perfect little Boy Scout, beloved by everyone, and grows into a model young man. He has no faults, does everything well, and is wise beyond his years. Everything goes his way. When Persia is threatened by an alliance led by Assyria, he gains permission from his uncle to go to war, but every battle is a walkover, his tactics are always superior to the enemy's, and he never makes a wrong move. Of course he's religious. Not only does he seem to be free of any faults, he's not even tempted: at one point his army captures a noblewoman described as the most beautiful in the land; invited to feast his eyes on her (and take her for his own, if he desires), he refuses, lest she distract him from erecting his empire. After ascending to the throne and achieving his far-flung empire, he rules in Oriental splendor and dies happily in bed, surrounded by his loving children and friends. Xenophon tips his hand on the first page by saying Cyrus exemplifies the perfect ruler, and the novel is one example after another of his perfect rule. (The historical Cyrus decreed in 539 that the exiled Jews could return to Israel, for which he is praised in the Tanakh, but Xenophon didn't consider that worth mentioning.)

Xenophon marches his didactic bildungsroman along in tight formation, and only occasionally seems to remind himself he's not writing another military history and to inject some comic relief or romance, like a stern general briefly relaxing with his men for a little R&R. One romantic subplot is brief but important: the beautiful noblewoman mentioned above is named Panthea, the wife of an Assyrian commander named Abradatas. So strong is his love for his captive wife that Abradatas deserts the Assyrians to join Cyrus's army; and so strong is her love for her husband that after he dies in battle, she refuses Cyrus's offer of assistance and commits suicide at her dead husband's side, earning Cyrus's profound admiration. For Greek writers thereafter, Abradatas and Panthea became the model for a noble couple utterly devoted to each other.

The only surprise in this success story comes at the very end: after Cyrus's death, his two sons begin bickering, and the empire soon collapses. Only then does the novel get interesting, because that collapse forces the reader to reconsider Cyrus's career. Only then does it become clear that Cyrus was concerned all along not with establishing a lasting empire or doing away with injustice (which the Assyrian king was guilty of), but solely with winning enough influential friends and allies to strengthen his personal position. His lauded benevolence was just a cover for buying friends, as was his piety:

Cyrus sacrifices to whatever gods are local to buy their support as well, and his frequent oath "By Zeus" is as meaningless as a CEO's expletive. At one point, Cyrus's father uses "educate" as a synonym for "deceive" with his son (1.6.39), and thus *The Education of Cyrus* tells us not only how he learned to rule, but how the prince deceived his subjects into serving him. (No wonder Machiavelli admired this book.) Only afterward does it become clear why Cyrus shows no interest in women throughout the novel (aside from many hints that he is gay):[68] all of his erotic desire is focused on political conquest, not romantic conquest. It's unlikely that Xenophon deliberately undercut his narrative with this sort of dramatic irony (as some modern authors do), for his other writings support the ideals Cyrus represents. He apparently felt there was no such thing as *institutional* political stability, that stability was always dependent upon a strong leader and obedient followers, and that Cyrus's sons simply failed to follow their father's example in this regard. And if the novel remains dull by modern standards, we have to remind ourselves Xenophon didn't set out to write a "novel" — there was no such thing yet in his culture — but was feeling his way to a new form somewhere between factual history and fanciful epic. Our hat is always off to innovators.

Also feeling his way to a new, hybrid form was Xenophon's exact contemporary and fellow Athenian, Plato. They had much in common, for both studied under Socrates and were contemptuous of the democracy that condemned him to death. Deciding to write philosophy (after failing at poetry, legend has it), Plato bypassed the standard expository approach and instead borrowed elements from the mimes of Sophron of Syracuse and from the great Greek dramatists of the 5th century, especially Aristophanes, to create the dialogue form.[69] Of the two dozen dialogues he wrote, two are book-length, the *Republic* and the *Laws*; can we consider them novels? Nietzsche thought so. In his first book, *The Birth of Tragedy*, he spoke contemptuously of the decline of poetry to fiction:

> The Platonic dialogue was, as it were, the barge on which the shipwrecked ancient poetry saved herself with all her children: crowded into a narrow space and timidly submitting to the single pilot, Socrates, they now sailed into a new world, which never tired of looking at the fantastic spectacle of this procession. Indeed, Plato has given to all posterity the model of a new art form, the model of the *novel* — which may be described as an infinitely enhanced Aesopian fable. . . . (section 14, trans. Kaufmann)

68 There's another romantic subplot running through the novel concerning Cyrus and a gay wag named Artabazus. Cyrus eventually marries and sires two sons, but the marriage is dismissed in one line and the unnamed wife is conspicuous in her absence from his deathbed. Plus there's Cyrus's habit of wearing makeup and using lifts in his shoes.

69 There are philosophical dialogues in ancient Egyptian and Mesopotamian literature, but these are brief dialogues between a man and his god, or his soul. The Book of Job resembles Platonic dialogue, though Plato wouldn't have known the work.

Leaving aside Nietzsche's objections to the new form, I think a tentative case can be made for including one of Plato's book-length dialogues in the history of the novel. Which one will be apparent from their openings; here's how the *Laws* begins:

ATHENIAN: To whom is the merit of instituting your laws ascribed, gentlemen? To a god, or to some man?

CLINIAS: Why, to a god, sir, indubitably to a god — in our case to Zeus, in the case of Lacedaemon, to which our friend here belongs, I believe, according to their own story, to Apollo. That is so, is it not?

MEGILLUS: Certainly.

ATHENIAN: You mean that Minos, just as Homer relates, used to repair to a conference with his father every ninth year, and that his legislation for your Cretan cities was based on his father's oracles?

CLINIAS: So our local story has it. It adds the further detail that Rhadamanthus, the brother of Minos — his name will, of course, be familiar to you — was conspicuous for his justice. Well, as we Cretans insist, it was his ancient administration of our judicial business which earned him this deserved reputation.

ATHENIAN: An honorable distinction indeed, and most appropriate to a son of Zeus. But as you and our friend Megillus have both been brought up under such venerable legal institutions, I trust you will not find it disagreeable to spend the time, as we walk this morning, in conversation on questions of politics and jurisprudence. The distance from Cnossus to the cave and chapel of Zeus is, I understand, quite considerable, and there are presumably shady resting places, such as the sultry season demands, on the way, among the lofty trees, where it will be a comfort, at our age of life, to make frequent halts and entertain one another with discourse. Thus we may reach the end of our long journey without fatigue.

And it continues like that for 300 pages, basically three talking heads exchanging views with almost no further reference to their setting or any attempt at characterization beyond their stated views. Now compare the opening of the *Republic*:

I went down yesterday to the Piraeus with Glaucon, the son of Ariston, to pay my devotions to the goddess, and also because I wished to see how they would conduct the festival, since this was its inauguration.

I thought the procession of the citizens very fine, but it was no better than the show made by the marching of the Thracian contingent.

After we had said our prayers and seen the spectacle we were starting for town when Polemarchus, the son of Cephalus, caught sight of us from a distance as we were hastening homeward and ordered his boy run and bid us to wait for him, and the boy caught hold of my himation from behind and said, "Polemarchus wants you to wait."

And I turned around and asked where his master was.

"There he is," he said, "behind you, coming this way. Wait for him."

"So we will," said Glaucon. And shortly after Polemarchus came up and Adimantus, the brother of Glaucon, and Niceratus, the son of Nicias, and a few others apparently from the procession.

Whereupon Polemarchus said, "Socrates, you appear to have turned your faces townward and to be going to leave us."

"Not a bad guess," said I.

"But you see how many we are?" he said.

"Surely."

"You must either then prove yourself the better men or stay here."

"Why, is there not left," said I, "the alternative of our persuading you that you ought to let us go?"

"But *could* you persuade us," said he, "if we refused to listen?"

"Nohow," said Glaucon.[70]

That's how a novel might open: a first-person narrator recalling a memorable occasion, setting the scene, introducing characters, alternating between relaxed narration and direct/indirect dialogue, and establishing via playful banter the book's theme: proposing alternatives to the common wisdom and trying to persuade his listeners of the validity of his alternatives. Book 1 continues in this vein: Socrates and Glaucon accompany the others to Polemarchus's house, where they find several other students of philosophy. Socrates has a chat with Polemarchus's father Cephalus, when the theme of justice is introduced. The father then leaves and the son "inherits" the discussion, which proceeds politely until the brilliant but caustic Thrasymachus hurls himself into the conversation like "a wild beast" and tears apart Socrates' argument. At other points, Polemarchus and Clitophon jump in, and once Thrasymachus calms down, Socrates announces that further inquiry into the nature of justice will be like undertaking a great adventure — "For it is no ordinary matter that we are discussing, but the right conduct of life" (352d) — and makes himself sound like a knight rescuing a maiden in distress: "For I fear lest it be actually impious to stand idly by when justice is reviled and be fainthearted and not defend her so long as one has breath and can utter his voice" (368c).

Book 1 certainly sounds like the beginning of an intellectual adventure story, a novel of ideas, but in book 2, the *Republic* changes into a talking-heads dialogue like the *Laws*, with the intelligent but respectful Glaucon and

70 From the Hamilton/Cairn edition of *The Collected Dialogues*, with the *Laws* translated by A. E. Taylor and the *Republic* by Paul Shorey. I've inserted quotation marks into the latter, as in some editions.

Adimantus (Plato's real-life brothers) as the only interlocutors.[71] Thrasymachus speaks up briefly in book 5, but only to indicate he's still listening. So even though Socrates announces that he'll continue "just as if we were telling stories or fables" (376d), Plato makes little use of the novel's possibilities and techniques thereafter, especially since a page later he begins talking about censoring poets who resort to fictitious inventions. Once Plato/Socrates starts issuing ayatollahoid pronouncements on what writers can and cannot say, indifferent to how well they say it, it's clear his interest in art is limited to its propaganda value. So we'll leave him to the philosophers and not try to make a novelist of him against his will; he excluded innovative artists from his ideal republic, so we'll exclude him from our republic of fiction.[72]

But as the fledgling novel continues to grow by feeding on other genres, it is worth keeping the *Republic* and some of the shorter dialogues like the *Symposium* in mind. Nearly 2,000 years later, the Spaniard Fernando de Rojas would write a novel in dialogue called *Celestina* that would found a subgenre called the conversational novel. At the beginning of the 19th century, Shikitei Sanba wrote two imitating the chatter of Japanese bathhouses and barber-shops, and later that century Thomas Love Peacock wrote several in which characters do little more than sit around and discuss lofty topics, as in Plato. In the 20th century, novelists like Ronald Firbank and Ivy Compton-Burnett also wrote novels almost entirely in dialogue, as did early Aldous Huxley and late Henry Green, culminating in 1975 with William Gaddis's *J R*, a 726-page novel in dialogue that mentions Plato a few times and whose theme is "the right conduct of life," thus completing an arc between Platonic dialogue and the modern novel. The *Republic* can also be seen as a model or prototype for the utopian and dystopian novel, philosophical novels in general, and perhaps even legal novels with extensive courtroom scenes: it's easy to picture Socrates as a country lawyer.

Sometime in the 3rd or 2nd century BCE another biographical novel like *The Education of Cyrus* was written (or, more likely, compiled from several sources), one as lively and low-browed as Xenophon's is dull and high-browed. The *Alexander Romance* is a comic-book version of the life of Alexander the Great; embroidered from the basic facts of Alexander's life is a colorful tapestry of legends and fancies, calling to mind those laughable Italian Hercules movies from the Fifties. (It was falsely ascribed to Alexander's court historian Callisthenes, so the author is sometimes called Pseudo-Callisthenes.) The

---

71 For this reason scholars believe Plato wrote book 1 early in his career and then added books 2 through 10 toward the end of his life, when he wrote the *Laws*.

72 The great critic George Saintsbury stopped short of calling these works novels but observed "there are the makings of a great novelist in the *Dialogues*" (*History of the French Novel*, 1 n2). Similarly, in *The Dialogic Imagination* Bakhtin acknowledges the influence on the developing novel of "the Socratic dialogues, which may be called — to rephrase Friedrich Schlegel — 'the novels of their time'" (22).

ludicrous tone is set at the beginning in the account of Alexander's birth: instead of being the legitimate son of Philip of Macedon, he is the illegitimate by-blow of an Egyptian sorcerer named Nectanebo, who gulls Philip's wife Olympias into thinking she's mating with the Egyptian god Ammon. (The morning after this bedtrick, the postorgasmic queen eagerly asks the magician, "But will the god come to me again? For it was very sweet with him.") The novel remains at that farcical level throughout as Alexander grows up and kills the sorcerer, competes at the Olympics, and then goes off on his ambitious conquests, encountering all sorts of strange beasts and magic stones, exploring the sea in a diving bell and the sky in a basket borne by eagles, and meeting with Amazons, sirens, centaurs, and Indian gymnosophists; he eventually discovers the fountain of youth but fails to drink from it, and fathers a daughter who turns into a mermaid. It's noteworthy mainly for its use of letters: Alexander writes home to Mother to tell of his adventures, and in fact the earliest version of the *Alexander Romance* may have been an epistolary novel — the first (pace the Egyptian "Tale of Woe") in literary history.[73]

It would be another two centuries before other Greek writers would find a workable form that lay between the extreme examples of the historical novels about Cyrus and Alexander and the Platonic dialogue, but when they did, their influence was palpable. The next extant Greek novel, Chariton's *Chaereas and Callirhoe*, uses dialogue extensively and alludes to Xenophon's *Cyropaedia*; the author of *An Ephesian Tale* so admired the latter that he called himself the Xenophon of Ephesus. Then, taking several cues from the New Comedy popularized by Menander and other dramatists in the 4th and 3rd centuries, and perhaps even material from the ancient Sumerians, later Greek novelists stumbled upon the most popular and longest-lasting genre of prose fiction, the romantic novel. From the 1st century BCE through the 4th century of our era, the Greeks developed and refined the novel as we now know it. Unfortunately, only about a dozen complete novels survive from that period, along with fragments from a dozen others. Most of these are contained in a splendid anthology edited by B. P. Reardon entitled *Collected Ancient Greek Novels* (1989), a huge, Trojan horse of a book filled with fascinating authors and characters that belongs in the library of every lover of literature.[74]

It is surprising how compulsively readable is the earliest of these, *Chaereas and Callirhoe* (set in the 4th century BCE but written sometime between

---

73 See Stoneman's introduction to his translation for the complicated textual history of the novel; no original version survives, and there are major differences between the extant manuscripts as the novel was adapted by later writers. Patricia Rosenmeyer analyzes the use of letters in the *Alexander Romance* in chap. 7 of her *Ancient Epistolary Fictions*.

74 Unless otherwise noted, all translations of Greek novels are from this anthology. These and all subsequent novels in this chapter are cited following the conventions of classical scholarship: by book and/or chapter rather than by page number, to facilitate reference to other translations and the originals.

25 BCE and 50 CE). You could slap a shiny cover on it featuring a hot couple with designer tunics slashed to their navels and sell thousands at Wal-Mart. Within the first 20 pages, handsome but hotheaded Chaereas and supernaturally beautiful Callirhoe fall in love at first sight, overcome the *Romeo and Juliet*-like rivalry between their families to get married, and have their love tested by Callirhoe's resentful ex-suitors; in a jealous rage Chaereas kicks his bride in the chest and sends her into a coma; thinking he's killed her, he volunteers to be tried for murder and buries her in a tomb by the sea, where she later wakes, as freaked out as Juliet to find herself in a burial vault, only to have some pirate/tomb-raiders break in and kidnap her, eventually selling her into slavery in Turkey. And that's just the first chapter! Chariton, who introduces himself as a law clerk from Aphrodisias (in southwestern Turkey), has a soap-opera screenwriter's knack for melodramatic plot twists, and what may strike us today as hackneyed must have been a thrilling innovation for the first readers of Chariton's novel.

Chaereas sets off in search of his abducted wife, who meanwhile is fending off the amorous but honorable attentions of her new owner, a powerful widower named Dionysius. Both endure a number of humiliations, frequently contemplate suicide, and have unexpected adventures before eventually reuniting and living happily ever after. But the soon-to-be stereotypical plot isn't nearly as interesting as what Chariton does with it. He follows Callirhoe's story up to the dramatic point when she agrees to marry Dionysius in order to fool him into thinking her unnoticed pregnancy is his doing, but then leaves the reader hanging in order to resume Chaereas's story, and keeps narrative suspense alive thereafter by toggling between the two. Chariton also introduces the buddy system into the novel: all the main characters are paired with a friend or confidante who advises or manipulates them: Callirhoe has a crafty maid named Plangon who tells her how to hide her pregancy; Chaereas has a noble companion named Polycharmus who keeps his hotheaded friend from acting stupid (a full-time job); Dionysius has a steward named Phocas who watches out for him; and King Artaxerxes of Persia, who plays a major role in the second half of the novel, has a clever eunuch named Artaxates working both for and against him. Chariton sensed the usefulness of having dramatic foils to his main characters, an innovation that would spawn numerous famous pairs in literature, from Don Quixote and Sancho Panza to Bertie Wooster and Jeeves.

Chariton also makes extensive use of literary allusion — mostly to the Homeric epics, but also to various Greek historians and dramatists — partly to create characterization by analogy (as in ancient Hebrew fiction) but also to establish the intertextuality of literature: novels are based as much on earlier books as on real life or imagination, if not more so. When Chariton writes of the reunited couple "But when they had had enough of weeping and describing their adventures, they fell into each other's arms and 'Gladly turned to the pact of their bed as of old'" (8.1), he quotes a line from the *Odyssey* describing the reunion of Odysseus and Penelope (23:296), suggesting Chaereas's adventures have been as various as the wily Greek's, and that Callirhoe has withstood her many suitors and remained faithful as successfully as Penelope. That Chariton doesn't identify the line says something about his intended audience: he was writing for readers who knew their classics, not for the masses. (Books were luxury items back then; only the rich could afford them.) *Chaereas and Callirhoe* is the earliest example of my favorite genre, the learned novel; it is filled with literary allusions and historical references, and Chariton is not shy about showing off how much he knows about the law in several courtroom scenes.

The novel's final sentence suggests that it was originally called simply *Callirhoe*, like later novels named after their heroines (Richardson's *Pamela*, Austen's *Emma*, Galloway's *Clara*), which would be appropriate since she dominates most scenes. Hers is the face that launched a thousand novels, the beautiful heroine who attracts as much danger as devotion from her admirers. Her beauty is described several times as "superhuman" and is literally stunning: men often fall to the ground upon beholding her, people mistake her for Aphrodite and worship her as a goddess, and even women can't take their eyes from her. But her overwhelming beauty is more of a curse than a blessing: every man who sees her develops an irresistible urge to copulate with her and begins scheming how to attain that end. Callirhoe's various ruses to preserve her chastity set the pattern for besieged beauties in novels to come, especially in the Gothic novel, all the way up to *Infinite Jest*'s Joelle van Dyne, the acronymed P.G.O.A.T. ("prettiest girl of all time") whose beauty is so lethal she wears a veil. But Callirhoe is no femme fatale: far from using her beauty to her advantage (except for attracting Chaereas initially), she several times curses her beauty as the cause of all her troubles. Sexual allure is a primordial force in the novel, making men sick with lust, and Chariton's descriptions of the erotic despair his characters feel are superb.[75] He makes sure the reader is as smitten with her as the characters are by inserting a nude scene early in the novel, lingering on sensual details as Callirhoe takes a bath: "Her skin gleamed white, sparkling just like some shining substance; her flesh was so soft that you [yes, reader: *you!*] were afraid even the touch of a finger would cause a bad wound" (2.2). Callirhoe submits to this bath reluctantly, and when the serving women praise her, she is "distressed by their praise; it was ominous." Rightly so: remember what happened to Bathsheba after her bathing scene.

Chariton makes some clumsy moves at times — he begins chapters 5 and 8 with unnecessary plot recapitulations, as though not trusting his readers'

---

75 It's important to note Greek novelists don't demonize sexuality, as later Christian writers would. Eros may be an annoying pest, but he's not the Devil.

memories, and gives away the ending while doing so — but he also displays an artistry lacking in his less talented imitators. Throughout, he follows the basic Creative Writing 101 advice of showing rather than telling, rarely using description but effectively dramatizing his events. Although C & C are reunited at the end as promised, Chariton introduces some moral ambiguity by suggesting Dionysius is actually a more suitable match for Callirhoe than the emotionally immature Chaereas. (Chariton lets a crowd debate this point to make sure readers consider it as well.) Callirhoe craftily convinces Dionysius to refrain from remarriage, perhaps keeping him on hold as a replacement husband for the next time Cheareas gets violent. (She leaves her son by Chaereas with Dionysius for upbringing.) And while this isn't a psychological novel, Chariton shows insight into human behavior with the occasional aside. His characters' frequent appeals to the gods and fate are undercut by his observation "people always believe what they want to be the case" (3.9) — the psychology of religion in a nutshell — and a little later: "Human beings are constituted to believe what they want to happen" (6.5). This may be Chariton the jaded lawyer talking rather than the novelist, but he and other novelists play with reader expectations, working with and against "what they want to happen" in a novel. Chariton may have written more novels — the remaining fragments of two others may be his — but *Chaereas and Callirhoe* is enough to ensure his place in the history of the novel.

Speaking of less talented imitators: The next surviving novel, *An Ephesian Tale of Anthia and Habrocomes* (*Ephesiaka*), written sometime in the 2nd century by the guy who called himself the Xenophon of Ephesus, is a cheap knockoff of *Chaereas and Callirhoe* and need not detain us long. It's basically the same story: two beauties fall in love at first sight, get married but then get separated, are abducted by pirates, made slaves, survive shipwrecks and assaults upon their virtue, etc. etc. until reuniting at the end and living happily ever after. It approaches plagiary at times: Anthia goes into the same deathlike coma as Callirhoe, and is "rescued" by pirates in the same way. (Her coma is induced not by a violent husband but by a physician-administered sleeping potion, a plot device borrowed by Shakespeare 1,500 years later.) Callirhoe is a classy young lady who doesn't take advantage of her beauty; 14-year-old Anthia, by contrast, after spotting 16-year-old Habrocomes in a temple, "paid no attention to modesty: what she said was for Habrocomes to hear, and she revealed what she could of her body for Habrocomes to see" (1.3). What's the Greek word for slut?[76] And unlike C & C's wedding night, which is passed over in decorous silence, we're told our randy teens "relaxed in each other's

---

76 Just kidding. I venerate women willing to share their beauty and sexual allure with the world; they've enriched my life beyond measure. In fiction, such women are bold rebels against patriarchal religious strictures forbidding them to "flaunt their charms" (Quran 24:31; cf. 33:33, as well as Gen. 3:7; Isa. 3:16–24; 1 Tim. 2:9, 1 Pet. 3:3) and thus are heroes in my book.

arms and enjoyed the first fruits of Aphrodite; and there was ardent rivalry all night long, each trying to prove they loved the other more" (1.9).

Unlike Chariton, Xenophon tells his story rather than shows, and tells it so baldly that some scholars suspect *An Ephesian Tale* is merely a summary of a lost novel. The only admirable thing about it is the nonjudgmental treatment of homosexuality: the love affairs of several gay characters are portrayed no differently than those between the straight ones and are considered just as legitimate. Aside from that and perhaps a useful dating tip for women (if pressured for unwanted sex, fake an epileptic seizure), *An Ephesian Tale* only goes to show that the Greeks had their hack writers just as we do.[77]

Having established the conventions of the romantic novel, the Greeks developed two more variants: the epistolary novel and the fantasy-adventure story. *The Letters of Themistocles* and *Chion of Heraclea* are anonymous novellas written in the early 2nd century CE consisting solely of letters. The technical challenges of the epistolary novel are great: the first letter has to quickly introduce characters and their circumstances without unrealistically spelling out things two correspondents would take for granted; there is also the challenge of a limited point of view, and — when only one side of the correspondence is given, as here — of conveying the essence of the other correspondents' replies without clunkily repeating them in detail, challenges met by these two anonymous writers.

The Letters of Themistocles, the longer and more complex of the two, consists of 21 letters purportedly written by the 5th-century BCE Athenian soldier-statesman Themistocles during a period of banishment when he was under suspicion of treason.[78] In these letters written on the run, Themistocles reveals two sides of his personality: the ambitious politician who wants to be in power, and the patriot who still believes in Athens' democratic principles, yielding an astute analysis of the type of politician we still see today who praises democracy in public but undermines it behind closed doors. The anonymous author of *Themistocles* distinguishes between the two structurally: the first 12 letters, written while Themistocles travels from Argos to Persia (where he seeks political asylum), feature the conniving politician, outraged at his ostracism, while letters 13 through 21, written at the same time as the first set, feature the statesman reflecting on democratic principles and concluding he will remain true to his city-state. The achronological structure was a daring move on the author's part, and one not followed by any epistolary novelist since that I know of.

Themistocles bristles with resentment toward the Athenian people in the

---

77 My low opinion of this novel is shared by most classical scholars, but for a defense of it, see David Konstan's "Xenophon of Ephesus: Eros and Narrative in the Novel," in Morgan and Stoneman, 49–63.

78 Translated in Rosenmeyer's *Ancient Greek Literary Letters*, 56–82.

first set of letters, makes arrangements for the wife and family he left behind, accuses his business partner of fraud (then apologizes in the next letter when he learns he misjudged him), commiserates with old friends, and expresses anxiety over his plan to seek asylum in Persia (Greece's old enemy). The final nine letters have less to do with his actual journey to Persia than with the larger political issues his exile raise, revealing more backstory to the Athenian crisis. There are some contradictions between the two sets of letters, under-standable as Themistocles tailors his responses to different correspondents. He gives a long account of his tense reception at the Persian court, where he cons the king into thinking he's come to help the Persians defeat the Greeks. His bluff is called when the king asks him to lead an army against Athens, which causes a resurgence of Themistocles's patriotism; "Many other things will come about, but this? Never!" The political novella concludes with a brief letter by Themistocles enigmatically instructing an Athenian contact to send him some wine jars, incense holders, and iron breastplates — for what purpose we're not told.

As an imaginative re-creation five centuries later of what might have gone through Themistocles's mind during his first months of exile, the novella is convincing both in historical detail and in the various psychological states — anger, revenge, resignation — that such a character would experience. And it contains indications that the pitfalls of a democracy by the people haven't changed much in 2,000 years, as when Themistocles disagrees with a correspondent that the Athenians "vote randomly and select leaders from the worst pool of candidates" (letter 9). No, that never happens, especially here in America.

Chion of Heraclea, though shorter, covers a greater span of time and, as a result, has greater room for character development. It is set in the 4th century BCE, when a tyrant named Clearches took over the city of Heraclea (modern Ayvalik, Turkey) and was assassinated 12 years later by a group led by a man named Chion. In the first of 17 letters — like most of them, addressed to his father Matris — we learn that a young man named Chion has been sent by his father from Heraclea to Athens to study philosophy under Plato. Writing en route from Byzantium, Chion notes an inspirational meeting with Xenophon, and once in Athens describes his lessons with Plato. Five years elapse, and though Chion was initially unwilling to be sent abroad to study, he's now an enthusiastic convert to Plato's conviction that philosophy should be applied to civic life, and that freedom is worth fighting for. When he learns from his father that his hometown has been taken over by Clearches, he decides to return home and kill the tyrant. In his final letter, Chion writes to his mentor Plato to confirm that he has learned his lessons well; filled with bad omens and visions, the letter (and history) suggests Chion dies shortly after assas-sinating the tyrant.

Over the course of five years Chion matures from a weak, unwilling student to a brave defender of his country. One modern reader considers him "an arrogant and self-serving prig,"[79] but even this evaluation is possible because the epistolary form, as Patricia Rosenmeyer notes, "allows the novel more introspection and deeper character delineation than most ancient non-epistolary narratives achieve; instead of struggling only against external interference (e.g. pirates, robbers), the protagonist struggles also with his own opinions and decisions."[80] She also catalogs *Chion's* aesthetic sophistication:

> The novel is full of literary devices that unify the parts: repeated imagery (unfavorable winds in *Letters* 2, 3, 4, 12, 13), foreshadowing (violence in *Letters* 4, 13 anticipates a violent end), parallelism (recommendations in *Letters* 2, 7, 8; great men in *Letters* 4, 5), and a sustained focus (Chion's father as main addressee, Plato in *Letters* 6, 10). On the level of diction, many letters are written in a circular pattern, with word or phrase repetition at beginning and end (e.g. *Letters* 1, 2, 4, 8); elsewhere, one particular word (e.g. profit, *kerdos*) reappears in different letters. The letters are composed or edited to create a consistent and carefully structured story. . . . (245)

In its close imitation of actual letters and its psychological insights into the development of a sheltered rich kid into a political activist, *Chion of Heraclea* is one of the most realistic of ancient Greek novels.

One of the most *unrealistic* but intriguing of the lost Greek novels is *The Wonders beyond Thule* by Antonius Diogenes. A long work of 24 chapters apparently written in the 1st or 2nd century, it is known only from a six-page summary in the *Bibliotheca* by Photius, a 9th-century patriarch of Constantinople. Whereas Enoch took an incredible journey through the heavens, Antonius Diogenes sent his travelers on a terrestrial journey from the Black Sea to Thule (Iceland) and beyond, telling of a city whose inhabitants can see by night but are blind by day, of horses that change color, of an Amazon-like tribe known as the Artabri, of a vampiric people who awake at night but are corpses by day, all the while insisting on the veracity of his account. Given the scope of the material and the novel's size — at 24 chapters it would have been three or four times longer than the Greek novels I've discussed so far (that is, around 500 pages) — editors Stephens and Winkler speculate that *The Wonders beyond Thule* resembled a fantastic encyclopedia.[81] If so, that would make it the earliest example of what would later be called the encyclopedic novel, those huge, erudite works (*Gargantua and Pantagruel, The Plum in the Golden Vase, Moby-Dick, Ulysses, The*

---

79 Pervo, "Romancing an Oft-Neglected Stone," 33.
80 *Ancient Epistolary Fictions*, 250. Her translation of *Chion* occupies pp. 82–96 of her *Ancient Greek Literary Letters*.
81 *Ancient Greek Novels: The Fragments*, 103–4.

Recognitions, Gravity's Rainbow, Palinuro of Mexico, Darconville's Cat, Now Voyagers) that weave vast amounts of specialized knowledge into the fabric of their novels.

The Greek satirist Lucian (c. 120–85) apparently read it and/or novels like it — remember, only a handful of Greek novels survive; who knows how many more were written — and decided to have some fun with the genre. His *True Story* describes a trip he and his companions took that is literally out of this world. Setting out from the Pillars of Hercules, their ship is swept up from the sea by a whirlwind and after seven days and nights lands on the moon, an inhabited land ruled over by Endymion, who is preparing for war against the Sun-dwellers led by Phaethon. Lucian describes the wonders of the moon in a manner reminiscent of L. Frank Baum's friendly fantasies, though I won't soon forget the gigantic moon spiders that spin a web between the moon and Venus. Interestingly enough, there are no women on the moon; men pair up and reproduce via the calf of the leg (an etymological joke in Greek). After describing this and many other customs, Lucian and his crew tour the rest of the solar system, pass by Aristophanes' Cloudcuckooland, and eventually make it back to Earth's ocean, where they are swallowed by a whale 200 miles long. They find an inhabited island in the belly of the whale and again take part in a battle with others living elsewhere in the whale's stomach before eventually escaping. They next reach the Island of the Blessed, the Greek heaven where they meet Homer and the characters in his epics, Aesop, all the major philosophers, and pretty much everybody who is anybody in Greek history. Then they voyage to Hades, to the Island of Dreams and to Calypso's isle (where Lucian delivers a letter from Odysseus to the nymph promising, in essence, to call her someday), and finally to a land of male Ox-heads (like the Minotaur) and female Donkey-legs ("decked out like courtesans"); there the novella ends, with Lucian promising to continue the story in further books — the last lie in this delightful book of lies ironically called *A True Story*.

Lucian has been called the Swift and the Voltaire of his age, but *A True Story* lacks the satiric bite of *Gulliver's Travels* or *Micromegas*, Voltaire's tale of a giant from the star Sirius who visits Earth. It's basically a *jeu d'esprit*, an imaginative attempt by Lucian to concoct even bigger whoppers than Homer and Herodotus and their ilk, and to tease readers who pay too much respect to these revered masters.[82] For Lucian, as for the canon in *Don Quixote*,[83]

---

82 In an appendix to the Loeb edition of Longus's *Daphnis and Chloe*, Stephen Gaselee suggests that the "first appearance in Greek of relations that can be called prose fiction is in Herodotus" (406), and that the various historians Parthenius summarizes in his *Love Romances* (1st cent. BCE) have a tendency, like Herodotus, to confuse fiction with history.

83 As I noted earlier, the "one good thing" the canon likes about novels "was the opportunity for display that they offered a good mind, providing a broad and spacious field where one's pen could write unhindered" (1.47).

the novel is a playground, a literary space for writers to let their imaginations run wild and show off, amusing their readers with inside jokes. (The more you know about Greek lit the better you'll appreciate *A True Story*.) Lucian's trip to the moon would eventually lead to science fiction, but his playfulness anticipates the ludic approach of some postmodernists, who want to show that the novel doesn't always have to be a serious inquisition into the human condition.

Until recently, Lucian was assumed to be the author of another novella entitled *The Ass*, but the consensus now is that it is merely an adaptation by someone else of a lost earlier work by Lucius of Patrae, and hence its author is called Pseudo-Lucian. Like *An Ephesian Tale*, it's the work of a hack; it trots out the story of a man named Lucius who is transformed into an ass, but for a brilliant *performance* of the story, we'll have to wait for the Roman writer Apuleius's *Golden Ass* (discussed in the next section): one more instructive example of the difference between commercial fiction and literature. *The Ass* is fun to read, bawdy and occasionally gruesome, but it's more like a well-told bar story than a well-wrought novel.

Even more bawdy and gruesome are two intriguing novels also written in the 2nd century that survive only in fragments or summary. *A Phoenician Story* (*Phoinikika*) by Lollianus was apparently a seedy pulp fiction involving orgiastic dancing, human sacrifice, cannibalism, nudity, and all sorts of lowlife behavior. *A Babylonian Story* (*Babyloniaka*, c. 165–80), written by a Syrian named Iamblichus, sounds like dumb fun:

> The hero and heroine roam throughout the Near East pursued by two eunuchs whose noses and ears have been cut off. They encounter bees with poisoned honey, a Lesbian princess of Egypt, a cannibalistic brigand, look-alike brothers named Tigris and Euphrates who happen to be exact doubles for the hero, and a rather dignified farmer's daughter whom the heroine forces to sleep with an executioner who is really a priest of Aphrodite who helps his son Euphrates break jail by dressing in the farmer's daughter's clothes. Considering the emotional tension that is constantly breaking out between the hero and heroine, culminating in her leaving him to marry another man before their final reconciliation, it is a wonder that anyone could ever refer to this work as an "ideal romance."[84]

Not ideal, perhaps, but certainly stimulating: a 4th-century medical writer named Theodorus Priscinanus recommended *A Babylonian Story* to men as a cure for impotence.

Several extremely well-wrought novels survive from the golden age of the Greek novel, the so-called Second Sophistic period between roughly 150

---

84 Stephens and Winkler, *Ancient Greek Novels*, 179. See Reardon 785–97 for Photius's summary and the surviving fragments.

and 300.[85] All three are romantic novels like Chariton's, and demonstrate a great willingness to experiment and expand the boundaries of the genre. In *Leucippe and Clitophon* (c. 150–200), for example, Achilles Tatius takes the conventions of the romantic novel and pushes them to extremes, distorts and subverts them, and covers them in sequins and glitter. His style is more ornate than that of any previous novelist, and his subject matter both more realistic and more fantastic. From its first paragraph, there's a striking contrast to the mundane openings of *Callirhoe* and *An Ephesian Tale* as Achilles starts things off with a rhetorical bang:

> Sidon is a city beside the sea. The sea is the Assyrian; the city is the metropolis of Phoenicia; its people are the forefathers of Thebes. Nestled in its bosom, discretely refusing the ocean's advances, is a broad double harbor: where the bay curves round on the right, a second entrance has been channeled, a further inlet for the tidewater, a harbor within the harbor. There the great freighters calmly wait out the storms of winter and in the summer ply the harbor's forebay.

Assuming translator John J. Winkler has accurately reproduced Achilles' diction,[86] note the balanced inversion of city/sea and sea/city (Achilles loves this sort of mirror imaging), the archaic use of "Assyrian" (which is like a writer today calling England "Albion"), and especially the sexual imagery: "Nestled in its bosom, discretely refusing the ocean's advances" like the stereotypical romantic heroine, the rounded curves, the inlet and channel, the phallic freighter like the stereotypical romantic hero eager to "ply the harbor's forebay," "the storms of winter" anticipating the dramatic events of the novel to be happily resolved by its summery conclusion, when Clitophon can ply his Leucippe with foreplay. (And *Clito*phon?! I'm reminded of Biggus Dickus in Monty Python's *Life of Brian*.[87]) In the next paragraph, the unnamed

85 None of these Greek novels has a firm publication date, and scholars differ in their proposed dating. I'm following the chronological tables in Reardon (5) and Doody's *True Story of the Novel* (xv–xvi). Also, none of these Greek novelists actually lived in Greece proper; they lived in Greek-speaking colonies in Turkey, Syria, and Egypt.

86 This is an example of why I hate to rely on translations. Tim Whitmarsh begins his: "Sidon is a city on the sea. The sea is the Assyrian, the city is the Phoenicians' mother-city, and its people fathered the Thebans," which introduces an additional parallel mother/father, but both translations avoid the interesting fact that Achilles begins with a series of verbless sentences, meaning it should read something like: "Sidon a city by the sea, the sea the Assyrian, the city mother of the Phoenicians, its people father of the Thebans" (adapted from Anderson's *Ancient Fiction*, 28). Both translators "help out" the reader by inserting verbs rather than reproducing Achilles' terse, *Dragnet*-style opening. (Sixteen hundred years later, Charles Dickens would begin *Bleak House* in the same verbless manner: "London. Michaelmas Term lately over and the Lord Chancellor sitting in Lincoln's Inn Hall. Implacable November weather. . . .")

87 To be fair, AT may have simply taken the name from a minor character in Plato's *Republic*, but the similarity between the Greek *Kleitophon* and *kleitoris* couldn't have escaped this bawdy author.

narrator notices a painting of Europa's abduction by Zeus in the form of a bull and spends the next *seven* paragraphs describing it. This is a seismic shift in narratology: instead of using art to describe real life, here we have art describing art; the narrator is no longer looking through a window and describing what he sees but instead describing the window itself, as though it were stained glass. And he does so using the same balanced inversion of diction as in his opening sentence: "I saw a votive painting whose scene was set on land and sea alike: the picture was of Europa; the sea was Phoenicia's; the land was Sidon." This rhetorical elaboration is new to the Greek novel, as is Achilles' use of *ekphrasis*, a descriptive set-piece (like the lengthy description of the shield of Achilles in the *Iliad*) prized in Greek poetry but rarely seen in novels until this one. Achilles thus announces he's not merely going to tell us a story but dazzle us with a tour de force of rhetoric.

Concluding his long description of the painting, the narrator remarks aloud how powerful Eros is; he's overheard by a man who offers to tell him of "all the indignities Love has made *me* suffer," at which point Clitophon takes over as narrator. (This opening frame, which is not closed at the end, reminds commentators of dialogues like *Phaedrus* and the *Republic*, another reason to consider Plato a proto-novelist.) Only at this point does Achilles revert to the conventional form of the romantic novel — Clitophon's narrative begins exactly like those of Chariton and Xenophon — but it's not long before he subverts it. Clitophon is engaged to another woman but falls in love at first sight with his visiting cousin Leucippe, who reminds him of a painting "of Selene on a bull" — Achilles will continue to refer to paintings throughout the novel — and who elicits from him descriptions worthy of Wilde on Salome: "Her mouth was a rose caught at the moment when it begins to part its petal lips" (1.4). Clitophon courts her with peacocky displays of rhetoric — Achilles self-consciously makes a case for the writer as peacock (1.16) — and talks her into letting him initiate her into "the rites of Aphrodite" *before* marriage, unheard of in novels until now.[88] Clitophon sneaks into Leucippe's bedroom late one night, but before his freighter can enter her harbor the virgin's mother wakes the house screaming about a dream "in which she saw a bandit with a naked sword seize her daughter, drag her away, throw her down on her back, and slice her in two all the way up from her stomach, making his first insertion at her modest spot" (2.23). This seems like a shocking and gratuitous use of violent sexual imagery at first — and it is — but it

---

88 In addition to eroticizing nature in his descriptions, Achilles deifies human urges and actions by blaming or praising the gods for nearly everything that happens, though these appear to be rhetorical flourishes rather than expressions of a religious sensibility. Indeed, Clitophon begins one prayer, "O gods and spirits, *if* you do exist and hear our prayers . . ." (3.10, my italics). I'm not going to mock the Greek gods as I did the Jewish one because no one believes in them anymore and, more important, no one today legislates morality or conducts politics based on imagined mandates from Zeus.

foreshadows almost exactly what will literally happen later in the novel after Clitophon and Leucippe escape to elope in Egypt. This disturbing nightmare is followed by an example of French farce, a narrative mood-swing typical of this wild novel, in which Clitophon dashes out the bedroom door just as the mother enters, knocking both her and his own servant down. Quick-thinking Leucippe then mounts an ethical high horse and is shocked — *shocked!* — at her mother's accusation that she was fooling around, and claims the escaping man must have been "a god or a spirit or a burglar" (2.25). At times like these, it's hard to decide if Achilles is parodying the romantic novel or simply trying to make it more realistic.

Assuming that Leucippe's collaborating maid will tell all after being tortured (standard procedure for menials then), the romantic couple hop a ship for Egypt, and again Achilles reverts to the conventions: they remain chaste onboard, then there's the obligatory shipwreck, and although they miraculously make it to the shore, they are then captured by bandits, separated, and Leucippe apparently beheaded. (In addition to anticipating French farce, Achilles also introduces Grand Guignol.) Six months later, a desolate Clitophon is on the verge of marrying a wealthy widow of Ephesus named Melite — a reversal of the situation in *Callirhoe* — when a disheveled Leucippe appears out of nowhere, her hair cut short like a boy's, and tells a harrowing tale of enslavement. At this point Achilles again subverts the conventions of romantic fiction: Clitophon has been holding out against the widow's elegant pleas for sex — almost every speech in this novel is an elaborate aria — but he now gives in with typical male sophistry, which Achilles cleverly captures with paratactic clauses as Clitophon fumbles toward justification ("And . . . and . . . and . . ."):

> When she released me and embraced me, weeping, I had a normal human reaction. And I was genuinely afraid that the god Love might exact a terrible vengeance; and in any case I had now recovered Leukippe, and would very soon be separated from Melite, and the act could no longer be considered precisely a marital one but was rather a remedy for an ailing soul. So when she embraced me, I did not hold back; when our limbs drew close, I did not refuse the touch. . . . The casual in sex is far more sweet than the carefully prepared: its pleasure springs up like an untended plant. (5.27)

— the old "Devil made me do it" ploy combined with an act of charity rising to an epigrammatic defense of casual sex. (He doesn't try this argument on Leucippe, however, but keeps the incident to himself.) After Dr. Clitophon "had successfully treated Melite's complaint," he finds himself back in French farce, escaping wearing a dress. He now looks like a girl, Leucippe still looks like a boy, and they are surrounded by openly gay friends who try to convince Clitophon of the superiority of gay sex over straight; all this casual sex, cross-dressing, and glorifying of homosexuality makes *Leucippe* sound like something written in the late 20th century rather than the late 2nd.[89] After this violation of the rules about chastity, Achilles gets back on track with a courtroom scene as in *Callirhoe*, with lawyers setting off more rhetorical fireworks, until finally the young would-be lovers are legally wed, climactic for them, no doubt, but anticlimactic for the reader after all their sensational adventures.

There's some clumsiness in the novel, some violations of the first-person point of view, but Achilles' achievement is amazing: he uses every rhetorical trick in the book and tests how far one can push the conventions of the novel as they then existed. "Charm, elegance, and utter diversity are the goals," says translator Winkler: "the story and characters, though consistently developed, are just an occasion" (Reardon 173–74). Achilles Tatius made the most of the occasion and paved the way for even more elaborate experiments with the novel.

While Achilles occasionally halts his narration to describe an emblematic painting, Longus takes this to an extreme: his entire novel *Daphnis and Chloe* (c. 200) is a description of a painting. In a brief prologue in cadenced prose, the narrator explains he was once hunting on the island of Lesbos when he came upon a grove sacred to the Nymphs; among the votive offerings was a narrative painting depicting "women giving birth, others dressing the babies, babies exposed, animals suckling them, shepherds adopting them, young people pledging love, a pirate's raid, an enemy attack — and more, much more, all of it romantic. I gazed in admiration and was seized by a yearning to depict the picture in words." Like Nabokov in *Laughter in the Dark*, Longus tells you the plot up front because he will be concerned not with the plot but with technical innovation. To the usual elements of the romantic novel Longus introduced something unusual: the aesthetics of pastoral poetry, adapted from the *Idylls* of Theocritus (3rd cent. BCE).

This was a bold experiment; novels depend on narrative momentum and artificial contrivances, whereas pastoral poetry idles in neutral, idolizes the natural. (There's a potential Joycean pun in there somewhere: idyls au naturel?) Longus pulls this off with a delicate balancing act: he creates an artificial, bucolic setting, but reminds us occasionally it contains bothersome flies, smelly dung, and in one key scene a rotting carcass — "imaginary gardens with real toads in them," in Marianne Moore's famous definition of poetry. There is temporal movement, but it is calibrated to the natural progression of the seasons. (*Daphnis* consists of four long chapters, but they

---

89 In this frank novel, Leucippe even notes at one point she's having her period, "one of the rare occasions when this is mentioned in any work of fiction before the twentieth century" (Doody 55). Can you imagine a Jane Austen heroine declining an invitation to dance because she's having her period? Can you imagine how much saner our society would be if she had?

extend from spring of one year to autumn of the next. It would have been too easy to assign one chapter to each season; like any good artist, Longus set himself a challenge to overcome.) The principal characters are rustics, but their progress (*not* fall) from innocence to experience is accomplished only with the help of city-dwellers. Nature is improved by art.

Daphnis and Chloe were both exposed to die as infants, but were rescued by shepherds and reared as their own; Daphnis is 15 when the novel proper gets underway, Chloe 13, and unlike couples in previous romantic novels they gradually grow to love one another rather than falling in love at first sight. This leads to kissing and fondling, and they sense it should lead to something more but they are ignorant of the mechanics of copulation, despite the fact they herd flocks that are described mounting each other (3.13). They roll around naked together, but Daphnis can't quite figure out how to connect, and deservedly weeps "at the thought that he was more stupid than the rams at making love" (3.14). As in *Leucippe*, an older woman from the city named Lycaenion ("Little She-wolf"!) teaches Daphnis how to find "the road he had been searching for until now" (3.18), but when she tells him that Chloe will experience pain and shed blood when he hits the road with her, Daphnis recoils at the thought of harming his young girlfriend, thereafter "preserving" Chloe's virginity until the two are properly wed at the end of the novel.

As this suggests, Longus has as much fun with the conventions of the romantic novel as Achilles Tatius did. Some pirates abduct Daphnis, along with some cows, but as soon as they're onboard Chloe blows her pipes and the cows jump off the ship and capsize it, allowing Daphnis to swim easily to shore. The whole thing lasts about a half hour, and the revolting cows add a ludicrous tone to the incident. Longus is more interested in "the piracy of love" (1.32) than any literal piracy. Another shepherd named Dorcas makes the traditional attempt on Chloe's virginity, but his brilliant plan is to hide under a wolf's hide; as soon as he gets close to her, her dogs pick up the scent and maul him. Assuming Dorcas is just playing a pastoral game, Daphnis and Chloe actually rescue the would-be rapist from the dogs and dress his wounds. While the conventional elements of the romance are thus gently mocked in *Daphnis and Chloe*, the supernatural element is given much more respect. Eros rules over the novel — both over the characters and Longus himself, who considers his novel an offering to Eros — sometimes in his male aspect as Pan, sometimes as the nurturing Nymphs, but throughout a palpable presence, as active as the gods in Homer. Ultimately, Eros is a personification of the biological drive to reproduce — we don't need some god to tell us "Go forth and multiply": it's in our genes — but Longus gives divine beings much more interesting roles to play than they have in other novels of the period.

Technically, *Daphnis and Chloe* may be the most accomplished of the ancient Greek novels, and it is certainly one of the most famous due to numerous translations in several languages, as well as Ravel's lovely ballet version and Chagall's lithographs. Elizabeth Barrett Browning's *Aurora Leigh* considered it an "obscene text," but Bryan Reardon is closer to the mark when he calls it "a fairy story written by a Nabokov."[90]

It was at this time that the older *Alexander Romance* achieved its present form. Reading it on the heels of *Daphnis* is like following Ravel's ballet with a high-school marching band's rendition of the theme from *Rocky*. It's another example of trashy commercial fiction, "but eighty versions in twenty-four languages testify to a popularity and diffusion exceeded only by the Bible," as one of its translators notes (Reardon 650). Among its sources was a life of Alexander written shortly after his death, and the same translator admits: "It comes as a shock to realize how quickly historians fictionalized Alexander" (651), a process worth keeping in mind when we get to ancient Christian fiction. *The Story of Apollonius King of Tyre*, written by an anonymous author in Greek around the same time (3rd century) but surviving only in a Latin translation, is another crude novel in the vein of *An Ephesian Tale* and is noteworthy only for its frank treatment of incest and for its wide-reaching literary influence. (It was one of the sources for Shakespeare's *Pericles*.) Once again, artistic shortcomings didn't prevent readers from gobbling it up: "an indication of the work's exceptional popularity can be found in the existence of over a hundred manuscripts of the Latin version of the story" (Reardon 737). In contrast, only one manuscript survives of the artistically superior *Chaereas and Callirhoe*.

Two more eccentric and therefore more interesting works from this same period are worth looking at. Sometime in the early 3rd century the Greek author Athenaeus compiled a huge work called *The Learned Banqueters* (*Deipnosophistae*), which has the same tenuous claim to being classified as a novel as Plato's dialogues. It begins like the *Phaedo* with Athenaeus telling his friend Timocrates of the conversation at a banquet held in Rome by a nobleman named Larensius over the course of three days. Two dozen of the most learned men of the time were invited to bring their books and share their knowledge on a variety of topics, and Athenaeus relates what they said. The book is huge, around 1,250 pages long in the first English translation, and encyclopedic in range: with copious illustrative quotations from writers, the banqueters discuss food, wine, banquets of the past, dancing, bathing, games, drunkenness, water, furniture, fruit, plants, vegetables, music and musical instruments, fish, foreign customs, ships, famous men, fishmongers, dishware and eating utensils, jewelry, flatterers, slavery, unusual words, birds, temperance, fashion, riddles, literature, drinking cups, pleasure, luxury, profligacy, women, love, sex, philosophy, finances, desserts, jesters, perfumes, scholarship, parody, torches: everything but politics. Book 13 on women is pretty

---

90 See his insightful essay in Tatum's *Search for the Ancient Novel*, 135–47.

lively,[91] but otherwise most of the material is of antiquarian interest only.

While Athenaeus wasn't consciously writing fiction in the way Chariton and Achilles Tatius were, *The Learned Banqueters* could be called a novel because it resembles the later conversational novels of Peacock and Huxley, has a central character named Ulpian who presides over the banquet but dies at the end, includes some dramatic conflicts between the characters (especially between Ulpian and the Cynic philosopher Theodorus), and has a unifying theme: remembrance of things past as Hellenic culture was on the point of extinction. The book is a grand attempt to gather and preserve fading ideas and customs, dead words and forgotten practices, and to acknowledge the pleasures of knowledge. James Davidson writes "the *Deipnosophistae* can be viewed as a kind of anti-*Phaedo*, a celebration of the sensual world to counter Socrates's contempt for it,"[92] the same contempt Athenaeus may have noted in the Christian cult that was spreading like a virus at that time. It can also be viewed as the earliest extant example of the encyclopedic novel, since we can't be certain of *The Wonders beyond Thule*. The anonymous medieval editor who provides a summary of the first two books of *The Learned Banqueters* — lost, along with portions of books 3, 11, and the conclusion of book 15 — notes that the banquet setting is symbolic of "the delicious feast of words [*logodiepnon*] which this admirable master of the feast, Athenaeus, has prepared for us" (Yonge trans., 1–2). Readerly novels such as the *Alexander Romance* and *Apollonius* are like junk food; writerly novels are like elaborate feasts of words, and Athenaeus's influential book — Rabelais cites it seven times, Voltaire admired it, and gastronomes have studied it over the centuries — deserves at least honorary mention in the history of the novel.[93]

And then there's *Joseph and Aseneth*, the strangest, most mysterious of early Greek novellas. It's an odd hybrid of Jewish midrash, Greek romance, and Christian hagiography that has been dated everywhere from the early 1st century BCE to the early 4th century CE.[94] It was generated from a single verse in Genesis: "Pharaoh then gave Joseph the name Zaphenath-paneah [God speaks; he lives]; and he gave him for a wife Asenath daughter of Poti-pherea, priest of On" (41:45). Wondering how Joseph could have sidestepped his tribe's rules against miscegenation and married an Egyptian woman — the daughter of an idolatrous priest, no less — the anonymous Jewish author

---

91 Prostitutes are a hot topic, and Madeleine Henry has argued that Athenaeus was the first pornographer, and first to use that word (*pornographos*), both for describing prostitutes and for comparing them to food to be consumed. See her "Athenaeus the Ur-Pornographer" (503–10) in a useful collection of essays entitled *Athenaeus and His World* (2000).

92 "Pleasure and Pedantry in Athenaeus" (293), in the same collection.

93 Two Latin works from roughly the same period, Aulus Gellius's *Attic Nights* (2nd cent.) and Ambrosius Macrobius's *Saturnalia* (4th cent.), are similar smörgåsbords of learning and lore but lack the fictional elements of *The Learned Banqueters*.

94 The best book I've seen on the novella, Ross S. Kraemer's playfully entitled *When Aseneth Met Joseph*, argues for a very late date.

first imagined an 18-year-old virgin living a theatrically chaste life in Egypt. Aseneth is a heroine out of 19th-century decadent literature, like Sara de Maupers in Villiers de l'Isle-Adam's *Axel*, or like the Salome described in Huysmans's *Against Nature*. "More beautiful than any young woman on earth," she lives at the top of a tower in a penthouse suite containing 10 rooms, extravagantly decorated, and is waited upon by seven virgins all born on the same night as she, and all "as beautiful as the stars of heaven."[95] None of them, including Aseneth, has ever spoken to or even been seen by a man; in fact, Aseneth despises men and has no interest in marrying. (Another writer would further imagine what those eight isolated teenage girls would get up to in that luxurious penthouse, but not our chaste auteur.)

Enter Joseph. Now the pharaoh's prime minister, he stops by her father's house one day, and when Aseneth glimpses him and his phallic golden staff from her tower window, she is floored by his beauty and quickly abandons her anti-male views. Joseph is as proud of his virginity as she is of hers, and though he allows her to be introduced to him, he will not allow his fellow virgin to bestow a brotherly kiss, revealing himself as a religious prude in language reminiscent of John the Baptist's in Wilde's *Salomé*:

> But as Aseneth tried to kiss him, Joseph held out his right hand and placed it upon her chest, between her breasts, which were already standing up like ripe apples.[96] "It is not proper," he said, "for a man who worships God, and who blesses the living God with his lips, and eats the bread of life that has been blessed, and drinks from the cup of resurrection that has been blessed, and is anointed with the oil of incorruptibility that has been blessed, to then kiss a foreign woman who blesses dead, silent idols with her lips, eats bread of strangulation from their tables, drinks the cup of wickedness from their libation, and is anointed with the oil of destruction. (8)

"Cut to the heart" by this priggish rejection, confusing religion with eroticism (not the first or last girl to do so), Aseneth realizes conversion is the only way to win Joseph, so she throws all her idols and finery out the tower window, strips off her gown and dresses in black (close attention is paid to the girl's extensive wardrobe throughout), steals some ashes and scatters them on her floor, lets down her hair, and then wallows in misery and tear-stained ashes for a week, refusing to eat. At the end of that week, when the average person would be hallucinating from hunger, she is visited by a shining angel. He first tells her to clean herself up — once again we're privy to our beautiful heroine changing clothes — and in a sexually charged episode, the angel leads her

---

95 Section 2 in Wills's translation in his *Ancient Jewish Novels* (124–62), hereafter cited by section. The novel was originally written in Greek, which is why I'm treating it here rather than earlier with other Hebrew fictions.

96 A classical Greek simile that can also be found in Aristophanes and Theocritus, but one is reminded of the apple(s) with which Eve tempted Adam.

through a strange conversion process.[97] A mystical scene follows involving a honeycomb and some bees, apparently an invocation of the sun-god Helios, and then the angel leaves just as Aseneth gets word that Joseph has returned for another visit. Like the spoiled rich girl she still is at heart, she decides to change *again*, this time into a wedding gown "which was like lightning in appearance" (18). Wow! When Aseneth goes to wash her face, she sees the physical effects of her conversion via more over-the-top imagery:

> When Aseneth leaned over to wash her face, she saw her face in the water. It was like the sun, and her eyes like the rising morning star, her cheeks like the fields of the Most High, with a blush as red as blood, her lips were like a rose of life, rising out of its greenery, and her teeth like soldiers standing in battle array. The hair of her head was like a vine in the Garden of Eden, bearing abundant fruit, her neck like a towering cypress, her breasts like the mountains of the Most High God. (18)

Hot damn! I had no idea that's what conversion to Judaism does to a girl's figure! Joseph is naturally amazed at her appearance, and after the angel informs him he's primed the pump, Joseph takes her into his arms and "kissed Aseneth and gave her the spirit of life, then kissed her again and gave her the spirit of wisdom, and kissed her a third time and gave her the spirit of truth" (19). They marry shortly thereafter, which is where the Greek romance usually ends; but this one then jumps ahead eight years to when the pharaoh's son, who wanted to marry Aseneth before she met Joseph, catches a glimpse of her and contrives to kidnap her. Aseneth then undergoes the kind of standard adventure that would normally occur in the middle of a romance; she escapes by way of a miracle and is reunited with her husband. This second half lacks the decadent atmosphere and imagery of the first half of the novella. Hard to tell whether the author was trying something new, or whether this is a composite work (probably the latter). But in its anticipation of 19th-century symbolist literature and its use of striking imagery — the bread of strangulation! a dress like lightning! breasts like the mountains of God! — *Joseph and Aseneth* is a curious and fascinating work.

The last and most remarkable ancient Greek novel is the *Aithiopika* of Heliodorus. Sometimes translated as *Theagenes and Charikleia* but best known as *An Ethiopian Story* (or *History* or *Romance*), it is longer than most Greek novels and aesthetically more sophisticated, treating the conventional romantic conventions with techniques that wouldn't be seen again until the Renaissance. Heliodorus combines the best qualities of all his predecessors: he's as erudite and allusive as Chariton (but not Athenaeus, who seems to have

---

97 At one point, "Aseneth extended her right hand and placed it upon his knees and said to him, 'This bed is pure and undefiled, and no man or woman has ever sat upon it. I beg you, Lord, sit a while on this bed'" (15). Authors too can confuse religion with eroticism.

read and retained *everything* written in Greek up to his time), as rhetorically gifted as Achilles Tatius, as experimental as Longus, and as conversant with mysticism and fashion as the author of *Joseph and Aseneth*. Writing in Syria during the 3rd or 4th century, he had all these earlier works as an inspiration, but also as a challenge: What could he add to a form as well-established as the romantic novel? How could he interest readers in yet another tale of a beautiful hero and heroine undergoing the usual adventures before the inevitable marriage? His solution was to complicate the narrative and make the reader work at deciphering it, to convert novel-reading from a passive experience to an active one, and to introduce sociocultural considerations that had been largely absent from the novel until then.

An Ethiopian Story has the most stunning opening scene of any Greek novel:

> The smile of daybreak was just beginning to brighten the sky, the sunlight to catch the hilltops, when a group of men in brigand gear peered over the mountain that overlooks the place where the Nile flows into the sea at the mouth that men call the Heracleotic. They stood there for a moment, scanning the expanse of sea beneath them: first they gazed out over the ocean, but as there was nothing sailing there that held out hope of spoil and plunder, their eyes were drawn to the beach nearby. This is what they saw: a merchant ship was riding there, moored by her stern, empty of crew but laden with freight. This much could be surmised even from a distance, for the weight of her cargo forced the water up to the third line of boards on the ship's side. But the beach! — a mass of newly slain bodies, some of them quite dead, others half-alive and still twitching, testimony that the fighting had only just ended. To judge by the signs this had been no proper battle. Amongst the carnage were the miserable remnants of festivities that had come to this unhappy end. . . . [gory but beautifully described details omitted]
>
> They stood on the mountainside like the audience in a theater, unable to comprehend the scene.

Every previous Greek novel starts by politely introducing the characters and setting, and proceeds in linear fashion. Heliodorus begins in the middle of a baffling scene, leaving the reader as puzzled as the brigands about what happened. Nor is any authorial explanation forthcoming; the brigands are next "confronted by a sight even more inexplicable than what they had seen before. On a rock sat a girl, a creature of such indescribable beauty that one might have taken her for a goddess," especially since she is dressed like Artemis and posed like Isis over her wounded male companion.[98] Before the brigands or the reader learns who she is, a second band of brigands arrives,

---

98 Heliodorus doesn't name names, but as translator Morgan notes, these identifications "would be implicit for an ancient reader in the iconography of the descriptions of the heroine" (Reardon 355, n3).

chases off the first, and takes the girl and her companion prisoner; she doesn't understand their language, and it is not until she meets a fellow captured Greek that she and the reader begin to learn what in the world is happening. As in a play (note the final line of the extract above), only when she speaks do we learn that her companion is named Theagenes, and only when he replies do we learn that she is Charikleia, the most admirable of Greek fiction's pantheon of heroines.

It's a daring way to begin a novel, probably as baffling to its first readers as the opening of *The Sound and the Fury* is to the modern reader. Like Faulkner, Heliodorus then allows several narrators to tell their tales, out of temporal sequence, each providing pieces of the narrative puzzle of that opening scene. The fellow Greek, named Knemon, explains how he came to leave Greece and wind up in Egypt (a variant of the Hippolytus–Phaedra story); later he meets an old man named Kalasiris, who unfolds "an Odyssey of woe" (2.21 — the novel is filled with Homeric allusions) with further stories, leading Knemon and the reader through a narrative maze covering the previous 17 years that eventually circles back to the opening scene, with the last piece of the puzzle falling into place *at the exact midpoint of the novel.* My jaw dropped.

It's a dazzling piece of narrative architecture, structurally more complicated than any novel before it (and most that would follow). After my jaw returned to its normal position I realized Heliodorus was imitating the *Odyssey*, which likewise opens in medias res, devotes the first half to flashbacks, then resumes in the present at the midpoint of the book. But no previous *novel* attempted such an involved structure, and Heliodorus was understandably proud of his achievement. At one point in Kalasiris's narrative, he suggests postponing the tale to go to sleep, but Knemon protests: "if the story being told is the love of Theagenes and Charikleia, who could be so insensitive, so steely-hearted, that he would not be spellbound by the tale, even if it lasted a whole year. So please continue," speaking for the reader as well as for himself (4.4). I'm reminded of that moment near the end of the Doors's "Soft Parade" when, amidst the feverish funk and cacophony of voices, Jim Morrison yells out, "We're doing great!" The second half of the novel is narrated in more linear fashion, but even there Heliodorus introduces temporary puzzles to keep the reader alert.[99] Heliodorus wants us to become better readers in order to appreciate more demanding novels like his; he relents at some points and tells us too much (e.g., at 7.12), as though not trusting the reader to keep up, but on the other hand he kills off one of his chief narrators/interpreters three-fourths of the way through, leaving Theagenes and Charikleia to cope on their own as well as the reader, who by this point should be able to do without the training wheels.

99 Translator Morgan has an insightful essay on this tactic in Morgan and Stoneman, 97–113.

While the form of *An Ethiopian Story* is innovative and demanding, the content is fairly standard: like Chloe, Charikleia had been abandoned at birth and raised by foster parents — first a man named Charikles, then Kalasiris — and like Aseneth, she grew up to be a proud virgin uninterested in marriage until the day she spotted handsome Theagenes. Like every romantic couple before them, they face parental disapproval, undergo adventures and threats to their chastity, and several times face death before getting married at the end. But Heliodorus adds an interesting twist that allows him to question the common wisdom of the time: Charikleia is white (and thus assumed to be Greek), but was born to black (Ethiopian) parents.[100] We're told that while she was conceived her mother was staring at a painting of Perseus and Andromeda, and as a result her daughter came out as white as the future constellation.[101] Fearing she would be accused of adultery, she abandoned her child with many misgivings. Also filled with misgivings 17 years later is Charikleia's father, who as king of Ethiopia must sacrifice his child to fulfill his country's religious rituals. Racial differences, cultural differences (Greek vs. Ethiopian vs. Persian), the barbarity of some religious practices, and the need to temper (if not overthrow) patriarchy with matriarchy all come into play, with Heliodorus displaying a very modern, liberal attitude. He favors integration of the races, cosmopolitanism over nationalism, and the reform of religion. This is one of the the first novels to question the way things are and to suggest more sensible alternatives, one of the first to feature the novelist as social critic.

Realizing the novel could be a vehicle for social change as well as intelligent entertainment inspired Heliodorus to make great claims for the genre. Near the middle of the novel, a merchant named Nausikles provides a feast for Kalasiris and Knemon; when "the revelries were at their height," Nausikles tells Kalasiris: "As you can hear, the ladies have begun to dance to entertain themselves as they drink, but we, if you are agreeable, could want no finer accompaniment to our revels than the story of your travels, far sweeter than any dancing or flute music." As Kalasiris's traveling companion chimes in, Heliodorus asserts the superiority of fiction over other forms of entertainment, evoking the god of eloquence, Hermes Logios:

> "Blessings be upon you, Nausikles!" interrupted Knemon. "At your behest all sorts of musical instruments are in attendance at our festivities, yet now you do not give them a second thought and leave them to people with less taste, preferring to hear of things that

100 In the introduction to his translation of the novel, Moses Hadas emphasizes the racial element: "In effect the book is a glorification of a dark-skinned race and an obscure sect [the gymnosophists]. It is easy to believe that the author was a colored man" (ix — Hadas was writing in 1957).

101 The ancients believed visual impressions at the time of conception would influence the offspring; cf. Jacob breeding his lambs in Genesis 30:37–40.

are truly mystical and imbued with a pleasure that is indeed divine. You are, in my view, showing a very fine understanding of the ways of the gods when you ensconce Hermes beside Dionysos and spice the wine you pour us with the sweet flow of words. I was much impressed by the great expense you had been to in your sacrifice, but I am sure that there is no better way to propitiate Hermes than by bringing as your contribution to the festivities that which is his own special concern — words." (5.16)

Blessings be upon you, Heliodorus, for bringing the novel into full intellectual maturity and for showing what this newfangled genre could be in the hands of a master.

ANCIENT ROMAN FICTION

Ancient Greek fiction would lead to medieval romances — especially those satirized at the beginning of *Don Quixote* — and Elizabethan love stories, the moral novels of Samuel Richardson and Frances Burney (and even the "immoral" ones of Sade), Gothic thrillers, Sir Walter Scott's historical sagas, eventually degenerating in our day into paperback romances, formulaic sci-fi and fantasy novels, and the soap operas of daytime television, *telenovelas* as they're aptly called in Spanish. Ancient Roman fiction, on the other hand, would lead to Rabelais and *Don Quixote* itself, to Sorel, Swift, Sterne, and Fielding (*Joseph Andrews* begins as a parody of the romance novel before changing horses), to Voltaire, Huysmans, and Wilde, and eventually to *Ulysses*, to Céline and the Beats, culminating in the ambitious meganovels of Gaddis, Barth, Pynchon, Coover, Theroux, Vollmann, and Wallace. One complete novel and the ruins of an earlier one are all the Romans left behind, but their importance for the kind of fiction celebrated in this book cannot be overestimated.

When classicists bewail all the lost works from ancient Greece and Rome, they cite the hundreds of vanished plays by Aeschylus, Sophocles, and Euripides, the poems of Sappho, Ovid's *Medea*, or the missing books from Tacitus's *Annals*. For me, the greatest loss is the complete *Satyricon*. The 150 or so pages that survive represent only a fraction of the whole, and are so tantalizing that the mind boggles at what the entire work must have been like. The *Satyricon liber* (Book of Satyrlike Adventures) was written in the seventh decade of the 1st century by Titus Petronius, the "Arbiter of Elegance" at the court of Nero until a conspiracy pressured him to commit suicide in 66 in one of the great death scenes of the ancient world (recorded in the above-mentioned *Annals* of Tacitus and reprinted in the introductions of virtually every edition of the *Satyricon*). The surviving portions of his novel are said to be from the 14th and 15th books (chapters), which means the complete novel must have been gigantic, as long as *Ulysses* if not longer. Like Joyce's novel, the *Satyricon* is based loosely on Homer's *Odyssey* and is narrated in a variety of styles, incorporates a number of genres (from both prose and poetry), and alludes to a wide variety of other literary works. Again like *Ulysses*, it has been condemned as disgusting and pornographic because of its candor, yet it is one of the most honest and life-affirming novels ever written.

Petronius drew inspiration from everywhere. The Greek novel was still in development, though he might have known of the earliest of them — the fragmentary *Ninus Romance* dates from the 1st century BCE, and Chariton's *Callirhoe* was probably completed by Petronius's time — but his models came mostly from Homeric epics, raucous New Comedy plays, tales of the supernatural, mimes, Menippean satire, and bawdy anecdotes known as Milesian tales.[102] Stylistically, it's a literary orgy. Closest at hand, however, was the *Apocolocyntosis* of Lucius Annaeus Seneca — roughly, "The Apotheosis of a Pumpkinhead" — a brief skit included in some editions of the *Satyricon*. Mixing prose and poetry, Seneca wrote this satire shortly after the death and deification of Emperor Claudius in 54; Petronius surely knew it and adapted its freewheeling approach to parody. And as Petronius's title indicates, the satyr plays of ancient Greece were an important inspiration; these followed performances of tragedies and served as comic relief: instead of wrestling with moral dilemmas like tragic heroes, satyrs were hedonists who devoted their lives to wine, women, and song, as anti-Establishment as hippies. Stirring all these ingredients into his mulligan stew, Petronius topped it off with a big dollop of hard-core realism, which is what makes him sound like the most modern of the ancients.

First, the realism (always an artistic choice, not a given of the novel); compare any passage from any novel I've quoted so far with these observations from one of the guests at a wild party:

> "Shit, it's getting worse every day. This town's got it all ass backwards. Why do we have this mayor who's not worth a fig? He'd sell us down the river for small change. He sits there at home, happy as a clam; pockets more money in a day than most of us have in the bank. (I happen to know where he got a grand in cash.) If we had any balls, we'd wipe that smile off his face. Nowadays, everyone's a lion at home, a fox on the street."[103]

That could come straight out of a Charles Bukowski novel. And note the homely details in this passage near the end:

---

102 The lost *Milesiaka* of Aristides of Miletus (fl. c. 100 BCE) was a collection of racy tales, anecdotes, and what we'd now call urban legends, very popular in its day.
103 From the Branham/Kinney translation, section 44. The older translations by Heseltine, Arrowsmith, and Sullivan are just as earthy.

> Oenothea put an old table in the middle of the altar, which she filled with live coals, and proceeded to use some melted pitch to mend a cup cracked from age. Then she stuck back in the smoke-stained wall a wooden nail that had fallen out when she took the cup down. Next she put on a square apron, placed a huge kettle on the fire and used a wooden fork to lift a bag down from a meat-hook; inside were some beans and the remnants of an old pig's jowl all carved up. (135)

No writer before this would have dreamed of mentioning that nail (which serves no further purpose); what an extraordinary thing to include! "If the history of the novel can be told as the development of free indirect style," James Wood suggests, "it can no less be told as the rise of detail."[104] If so, that history begins with Petronius's nail, not 1,800 years later with Flaubert, as Wood writes. Realistic language, realistic details, and realistic sex (you'll have to read the *Satyricon* yourself for those bits): these are things we take for granted in novels today, but in Petronius's time they were radical innovations, and remained so in the West for nearly 1,500 years.

Realism happens to be the topic under discussion in the opening scene of the novel as we have it. Encolpius — like Joyce's Stephen Dedalus, a well-educated young man down on his luck — is arguing with a professor of rhetoric about the ridiculous way the subject is taught, specifically the unrealistic topics students are given for purposes of oration:

> "Why are young minds so completely stultified in college? Because they neither hear nor see anything they can use: instead they study pirates wielding chains on a beach, tyrants ordering sons to decapitate their own fathers, oracles that require the sacrifice of at least three virgins to fend off a plague — sticky gobs of speech, every word and deed slathered with poppy and sesame seeds." (1)

These unrealistic topics were the stuff of drama, but not here. Encolpius, the novel's rattled, heartbroken narrator, is more concerned with finding his next meal and retaining the fickle love of Giton, a 16-year-old male prostitute who has also caught the eye of Ascyltos, their thuggish traveling companion. (Nearly every character in this novel is bisexual, which was considered the normal state of man in Petronius's culture.) Just as Ulysses had offended Poseidon by blinding his son Polyphemus and suffers the god's wrath thereafter, Encolpius suffers the wrath of Priapus, whom he had somehow offended in the missing beginning of the novel and whom he continues to offend by accident in the surviving portion. The god of fertility curses him with impotence, and much of the novel consists of his embarrassing sexual encounters while trying to restore his manhood.

---

104 *How Fiction Works*, 73. "Free indirect style" is third-person narration told from a single character's point of view, "close to stream of consciousness" (9).

This divine curse is treated about as seriously as superspy Austin Powers's loss of his mojo in that silly movie; it's merely a vehicle for Petronius's vibrant account of the manners and mores of the Mediterranean world in his day. It's a different world from that of the Greek novel: everyone's on the make and no one is concerned with chastity. It's the first novel in which the size of a male character's genitals is noted, a detail you hardly ever get in George Eliot's novels. Girls lose their virginity as early as age seven, and quickly learn the way of the world: when a gold-digging mother drops off her young, pretty daughter for "moral instruction" at the hands of a lecherous poet named Eumolpus masquerading as a rich man, the girl not only goes along with his decision "to initiate the girl in the rites of anal Venus" (or "ritual buttock-thumping," as Arrowsmith puts it), but she's already "skillful enough to match him, thrust for thrust" (140). Religion is a muddle of magic and superstition, and morality just another con: "There is nothing falser than the silly prejudices of mankind, nothing sillier than affected virtue," Encolpius sneers after improvising a poem addressed in anticipation to his censors after arguing with his limp dick (132).

As in a Pynchon novel, characters are always breaking into song or reciting verse, giving the novel the feel of a burlesque revue. (As in Heliodorus, there are theater metaphors throughout.) There are only two things Petronius takes seriously: good taste and death. It's not immorality but bad taste that earns the lash of satire, and immorality withers before the reality of death. Both themes are at work in the novel's most famous (and most complete) section, the wild party thrown by Trimalchio, a former slave turned nouveau-riche vulgarian. Encolpius is appalled at the bad taste his host displays in all matters (literary, culinary, decorative), but his mood changes when Trimalchio begins bragging about the lavish tomb he's having built for himself and then reads aloud the epitaph he's already composed.

> As he finished his epitaph, Trimalchio started to weep uncontrollably. And Fortunata [his wife] wept. And Habinnas [his close friend] wept. And then all the slaves wept, as if invited to a funeral, filling the room with sobs. Even I had started to cry, when Trimalchio said, "Well then, since we know we're going to die, why don't we try living? And since I want to see you happy, let's take a bath together!" (72)

Death is unreal for most people, for most of their lives, but there comes a day when the brute reality of your eventual extinction hits you, and no philosophy or theology can prevent that animal panic at the realization. Trimalchio and his guests may be drunk and tired by this point, but I like to think that's what happens here. And I don't think the author is mocking him, because Trimalchio responds to the knowledge of his death as Petronius did the day he committed suicide: "he opened his veins and then, as the fancy took him, he bound them up or re-opened them, and all the while talked with his friends, but not on serious topics or anything calculated to win admiration for his courage. He listened to their contributions — not discussions about the immortality of the soul or the opinions of philosophers, but simply gay songs and light verses" (Tacitus's *Annals* [16.19], trans. Sullivan, 11–12).

In the novel's second-most famous episode, the tale of the widow of Ephesus, the *carpe diem* theme is sounded again. Eumolpus tells of a woman "so famous for her virtue" that when her husband died, she followed his corpse into a vault and mourned there day and night, apparently intending to starve herself to death in wifely devotion. A sentry watching over some crucified thieves notices the beautiful widow one night in the tomb and tries to talk her out of her suicidal plan. "Could ashes or dead souls care less for mourning?" he asks (echoing Anna's question to Dido in Virgil's *Aeneid*). "Don't you want to live again? Don't you want to shake off this womanish weakness and enjoy the good things of life while you can? Let this corpse lying here be a warning to you — to live!" (111). The widow gives in and consumes the food and wine the handsome young soldier has brought. "But you know what appetite remains when stomachs are full," winks Eumolpus. "So the same beguiling arguments that the soldier had used to make the widow want to live, he used again to lay siege to her virtue." She again capitulates, and while the couple has sex in the tomb[105] the family of one of the crucified takes down the corpse. Knowing he'll be punished for this dereliction of duty, the soldier takes out his sword and is about to kill himself when the widow convinces *him* it's better to live. She suggests using the corpse of her husband to take the place of the crucified. "The soldier adopted the sensible woman's plan, and the next day everyone wondered how a dead man had climbed up on that cross!" (112).[106] Everyone laughs at what Eumolpus intended to be a satire on the fickleness of women, but again life is chosen over death, more specifically, the enjoyment of life (food and sex) over grief and artificial notions of virtue and fidelity. The robust affirmation of life and its pleasures in the *Satyricon* at a time when a growing cult was using another crucified man to condemn life and its pleasures is one of the most appealing features of the novel. If Peter and Mary Magdalene had gotten it on in the tomb of their crucified friend instead of making up a story about some angels, we'd be living in a different world.

Eumolpus's story is an example of the bawdy Milesian tale, just one of many genres Petronius incorporates into his work; that allusion to Virgil is likewise just one of hundreds of intertextual references, as any well-annotated

---

105 The powerful symbolism of this act is complicated but not compromised by the fact Roman prostitutes often conducted their business in cemeteries (Courtney, *A Companion to Petronius*, 172).

106 This is the most charming episode in Fellini's *Satyricon* (1969), which otherwise distorts Petronius's novel. The film is amazing to look at, but way too gloomy.

edition of *Satyricon* attests; and throughout Petronius uses a variety of styles, from low slang to literary elegance. Trimalchio's feast thus becomes an ana-logue for Petronius's feast of words: a variety of literary courses (picaresque, farce, poetry in a number of styles and meters, literary criticism, pornography, parody, a werewolf story, mythology, etc.) served up by a colorful cast of char-acters. Trimalchio broods on death but ends his feast with an affirmation of life, and the *Satyricon* likewise deals with loss but ends with a restoration of Encopius's manhood — this occurs a few pages before the manuscript breaks off; presumably an Odyssean return and homecoming concluded the novel. But the real achievement is the bravura demonstration by Petronius that the novel had the potential to be the grandest genre of literature, capable of bringing any form of discourse under its vast circus tent.

Because of its incomplete state, the *Satyricon* allows only tentative judg-ments of its aesthetic merits, as obvious as they may be. (Perhaps what remains of the novel are the only good parts.) Thanks to the survival of a single manuscript, we have a complete Roman novel in the superb *Metamorphoses* of Apuleius (c. 124–after 170), but any judgment of this tricky novel remains just as tentative because of the puzzles the canny author left behind.[107] Better known as *The Golden Ass* — Augustine said that's how the author referred to it, even though the manuscript is entitled *Metamorphoses* — it was written about a century later than the *Satyricon* (that is, c. 160) by a well-educated, well-off citizen of Madauros, in modern Algeria. (*Golden* in this instance means "admirable, excellent," and refers more to the book than to the asinine protagonist.) Apuleius read either *The Ass* of Pseudo-Lucian or the lost original on which that was based and decided he could do better — and he did. His version of the adventures of a young man who is magically transformed into an ass and back again is infinitely better, in the same way that Shakespeare's *Romeo and Juliet* is better than its predecessors and for much the same reason: its superior use of language. *The Ass* is narrated in simple, straightforward prose; but *The Golden Ass*, according to its first English translator, is written "in so dark and high a style, in so strange and absurd words and in such new invented phrases, as he seemed rather to set it forth to show his magnificent prose than to participate his doings to others."[108] Arguing readability is more important than fidelity to the original, few English translators have been brave or talented enough to replicate this style.[109] But the notes to any annotated

---

107 In older sources, Apuleius is given the first name of his narrator, Lucius, but no *praenomen* is attested, as classical scholars would say.

108 William Adlington (1566), quoted by Robert Graves in the introduction to his own transla-tion, vii.

109 Joel Relihan comes closest, and for that reason I'll be citing his translation (by book and section). Jack Lindsay is the only previous translator to emulate Apuleius's style, though another translator, P. G. Walsh, says it "contains many errors and some infelicities" (xlix). Walsh's own translation is rather stiff and unidiomatic in places; I gave up during the first

edition cite numerous examples of wordplay, puns, neologisms (many of the words Apuleius uses appear nowhere else in Latin literature), and a steady stream of parodic literary allusions. What puzzles the contemporary reader is not the language but the unexpected conversion scene in the last chapter of the novel, which forces the reader to rethink everything that has gone on before it.

Apuleius planned it that way: like Heliodorus after him, he wanted to teach readers to read more carefully, so he deliberately tells two stories simultaneously, one for the pit and one for the gallery. Opening in mid-conversation, the novel begins:

> And I — well, let me string some tales together for *you*, stories of all sorts, in what they call *that Milesian manner*. Let me whisper them ever so elegantly in your ears — provided they're well-disposed, of course — let me give those ears a proper, soothing relaxation — provided you're not too proud to stick your nose in this papyrus roll — it comes from Egypt, and is inscribed with the precision of a reed-pen from the Nile. . . . [¶] What we begin is a Greek fiction, after a fashion. You, with the papyrus in your hands — pay close attention, and joy shall be yours.[110]

For the yokels up in the gallery, Apuleius will merely tell some titillating Milesian stories — and they're good ones, believe me — but for those in the pit paying closer attention, he will unfold a Platonic fable involving Egyptian mysteries and the progress of the soul, which should give greater pleasure than horselaughs at donkey sex. As he proceeds, Apuleius drops hints that don't mean much during a first reading — like the Egyptian references above, the fact that the horse of his narrator Lucius is white, and that he is related to the Greek essayist Plutarch. As in *The Ass*, *The Golden Ass* concerns a young man so consumed with curiosity about magic and the occult that he seduces a witch's maid in order to witness the witch's transformation into an owl. He convinces the maid to transform him as well, but she botches the potion and turns him into a donkey instead. He endures a number of painful and humiliating experiences in that form until he comes across the antidote: roses. In *The Ass*, Lucius gobbles up some roses, turns back into a man, and there the story ends. But at the end of *The Golden Ass*, the donkey falls asleep and has a dream about the Egyptian mother-goddess Isis, who has taken pity on him and will direct him to some roses and restore him to human form if he becomes a member of her cult, to which he enthusiastically agrees. He regains his form — exposed naked in a religious procession, a final

---

chapter and switched to E. J. Kenney's, which is better, but he doesn't attempt to match what Lindsay identifies as Apuleius's "experimental attitude to language, his remarkably florid and vivid style" (6).

110 An entire book with 25 contributors is devoted to this opening paragraph: see Kahane and Laird's *Companion to the Prologue to Apuleius' Metamorphoses*.

humiliation — and is last seen in Rome joyfully performing his functions with a shaved head, a dutiful disciple of the goddess.

Thus the novel seems to be an allegory about spiritual growth, a pilgrim's progress away from gross appetites (there's lots of food and sex in the novel) toward a free, purified state where one can contemplate the divine (which requires fasting and chastity). The reference to Plutarch now makes sense: he not only wrote an essay "On Curiosity" (Lucius's downfall) but one "On Isis and Osiris" (his salvation); his white horse is the Snowy Servant of his dream of Isis. All of the donkey's trials and tribulations in this fallen world — and Apuleius paints a grimly realistic picture of his times — can now be seen as metaphors for man's unregenerate condition. This is the way many readers have taken it, including Robert Graves, for whom Isis was a shining example of his beloved White Goddess. (He quotes Lucius's splendid vision of Isis in his famous book of that name.) While Apuleius clearly intended his novel to be read on two levels, there are problems with this religious reading.

First, Apuleius undercuts the dignity of the Isis cult by harping on its financial angles. A priest informs Lucius he has to *pay* to join the cult, verified by Isis in another dream as she specifies "what costs I would need to incur to procure the proper invocations" (11.22). Then he learns he also needs to be initiated into the cult of Osiris, Isis's consort, which requires an additional outlay of funds. And then he finds out that although he belongs to the Greco-Egyptian cult of Isis, as a Roman citizen he needs to be initiated into the mysteries of the *Roman* Isis — for an *additional* fee! Anyone familiar with the modus operandi of cults and televangelists will recognize the scam; far from attaining a higher level of being, Lucius has simply turned from one kind of dumb ass into another; Doody correctly compares him to "a sort of antique equivalent of a modern Western follower of Hare Krishna" (123). Apuleius's punch-line to his joke comes when he notes the Temple of Isis in Rome is located in the Campus Martius, which would have raised a smirk from his original readers; "like other Isiac temples," Kenney informs us, "it was notorious as a lovers' rendezvous" (259), and about as chaste as the Temple of Priapus depicted in the *Satyricon*.[111]

OK, but why? Why would Apuleius hint at a loftier meaning behind his medley of bawdy stories only to undercut it at the end? Danielle Van Mal-

---

111 "During the reign of Tiberius (14–37 C.E.), for example, an unsigned note was delivered to a Roman noblewoman called Paulina. She was invited to the temple of Isis, the Egyptian goddess of fertility, where the jackal-headed god Anubis promised to grant her the privilege of bedding down with him. When she dutifully appeared at the temple, the figure wearing the mask of Anubis turned out to be a thoroughly mortal man — a Roman knight who was either the seducer of a gullible woman or the lover of a conniving woman" (Kirsch, 43). You'll recall a similar trick was played on the mother of Alexander the Great in the *Alexander Romance* (1.4–7). *The Bedtrick* by Wendy Doniger wittily catalogues hundreds of examples of this dodge in myth and fiction.

Maeder has suggested that chapter 11 is perhaps not the end, and that a concluding chapter, now lost, followed.[112] Perhaps he wanted to teach us that a majestically written conversion scene at the end of a novel isn't necessarily to be taken seriously, that a religious conversion isn't a loftier act after all but just another crazy thing humans do. Perhaps a clue can be found in the novel's most famous inset tale, the myth of Cupid and Psyche. It seems to be an allegory of Lucius's situation: like him, Psyche (Soul) is consumed with curiosity, in her case about the appearance of her lover Cupid (Love), who comes to her only in the dark of night. When she takes a lamp to examine him as he sleeps, she accidentally spills a drop of hot oil from the lamp onto his shoulder and wakes him; he abandons Psyche, who undergoes torments as galling as those Lucius the ass endures. Eventually, Cupid and Psyche are reconciled and married, and the union of Love and Soul produces a child with an allegorical name. Would you guess Wisdom? Righteousness? Faith, Hope, or Charity? No, the darling girl is named Pleasure. In Latin, it's Voluptas: pleasure, joy, delight, enjoyment, with a sensual overtone — it's the root of *voluptuousness*. This is what Apuleius promised the attentive reader at the beginning. Not mere entertainment, not a moral lesson about the perils of delving into the occult — every other horror movie teaches us that — and certainly not a Sunday school lesson about staying away from good food and better sex: the delightful and graphic sex scene between Lucius and the witch's maid (2.16–17) couldn't have been written by anyone planning on giving up sex in his lifetime. No, Apuleius seduces us into a state of what Nabokov called "aesthetic bliss." This comes from watching an agile writer who performs with "much skill and quick leaping from one thing to another, like circus performers on their two trick horses" (1.1), not confining his work to a single or even double meaning, but raising multiple possibilities to occupy readers for as long as they want to play the game. *The Golden Ass* is a textbook example of Umberto Eco's definition of a novel as "a machine for generating interpretations."[113]

The Cupid and Psyche story is set in the middle of the novel (4.28–6.24), occupying some 40 pages of this 250-page novel. Although it ends happily, it is important to remember that it is enclosed by the story of Charite and Tlepolemus (4.23–8.14), two noble characters straight out of a Greek novel. This young couple were planning their wedding when Charite, like many a Hellenic heroine, was abducted by robbers. (An old woman guarding her tells her the story of Cupid and Psyche to cheer her up.) Tlepolemus heroically rescues his fiancée, but instead of the happy ending of the typical Greek

---

112 See her "'*Lector, intende: laetaberis*': The Enigma of the Last Book of Apuleius' *Metamorphoses*" (1997), cited in Hofmann's *Latin Fiction*, 100. Most classical works and novels have an even number of chapters, plus she notes chapter 11 lacks the scribe's concluding subscription, usually a sign that pages are missing.

113 "Postscript" to *The Name of the Rose*, 505.

novel, the two meet a grisly end soon after their marriage because of a jealous suitor. The form of the novel suggests one thing, the content another. Is that another clue that Lucius's religious conversion isn't the happy ending it appears to be?

Then again, Apuleius himself was a devotee of Isis. He was also once accused of witchcraft. Who knows what he intended his novel to mean? A postmodernist *avant la lettre*, Apuleius created a text that resists confident interpretation; as John J. Winkler notes in his brilliant book on *The Golden Ass*, "the reader's flailing about in dismay is exactly what Apuleius had in mind. It is one of the most exciting and original gambits in the history of narrative" (*Auctor & Actor*, 207). What we do know is that Apuleius, like Petronius before him, greatly expanded the novel's repertoire, adding a gruff sense of reality as well as a playful sense of a text's status as fiction to the burgeoning genre. (Apuleius is said to have written another novel entitled *Hermagoras*, which tragically hasn't survived.) These two Roman writers and the Greek novelists already at work were well on their way to establishing the novel as the sophisticated art-form it later became when a great disaster devastated the ancient world, bringing novel-writing to a halt. Like dumb-ass Lucius, the Roman emperor Constantine had a religious vision.

ANCIENT CHRISTIAN FICTION

Augustine thought *The Golden Ass* might have been a true story (*City of God* 18.18), so it should come as no surprise that he also thought an even more outlandish tale of a Jewish man metamorphosed into a god was also true. In Augustine's defense, this sort of deification was standard operating procedure in the ancient world. The historical Gilgamesh became two-thirds divine when transformed into a literary hero; to boost Cyrus's stature, Xenophon claimed the king was descended from the mythic hero Perseus; Ovid ended his *Metamorphoses* with the deification of Julius Caesar, while Seneca mocked the deification of Emperor Claudius; and a little after Apuleius's time, an Athenian writer named Flavius Philostratus (c. 170–c. 245) wrote a kind of biographical novel about a 1st-century wonder-worker whose birth was attended by miraculous portents, who is credited with many wise sayings and miraculous cures, who shuns sex, expels demons, who is tried in court for his activities, and after his death ascends to the divine realm and appears in a young man's dream to confirm the immortality of his soul. I don't know whether Augustine ever read *The Life of Apollonius of Tyana*, but the point is that stories like these were common in his time. This tendency to mythologize someone is not so different from what admirers of George Washington were up to with that lie about chopping down a cherry tree and refusing to lie about it, or what any public relations firm today does for a client. It's only natural to exaggerate the good qualities of someone you admire, especially when recommending that person to others: as a blind date, a candidate for office, or as a savior.

Yeshua ben Yosef (c. 5 BCE–30 CE) was reportedly born to a Jewish peasant woman named Miryam and an uncertain father, later agreed to be Yosef, a carpenter. He grew up to become a prophet with a radical new vision of "the kingdom of God" that offered a countercultural challenge to the status quo (both Judaism and Roman rule), spread his views via cryptic sayings and parables, rubbed the wrong people the wrong way, and for that got himself crucified (a common form of punishment in those days, as seen in many Greek and Roman novels). Like any charismatic preacher, he attracted many followers, especially uneducated women, and after his death they tried to preserve his teachings and share them with others. Memories and anecdotes were assembled in brief documents — scholars have reconstructed the Sayings Document Q (from German *Quelle*: source), miracles stories, pronouncement stories — enhanced with parallels and miracles taken from the Tanakh and neighboring mythologies. During the 30s and 40s his followers split into factions depending upon their interpretations of Yeshua's sayings: those of a mystical bent adapted them to the Gnostic quest for inner light (see the Gospel of Thomas and — if you're *really* interested — the 800 pages of writings assembled in Barnstone and Meyer's *Gnostic Bible*); others assimilated the teachings into standard Jewish theology (later expressed in Matthew's gospel); others broke with Judaism and founded a Christ cult. After the catastrophic destruction of the Second Temple in 70, more than 40 years after Yeshua's death, some members of the new sect calling themselves Christians decided to compose accounts of his life, not so much to preserve his deeds and sayings as to have a document that could be used to win others to their cause. Propaganda, that is, not biography. Or perhaps the best term would be fiction; as the 3rd-century Greek scholar Porphyry was one of the first to note, "The evangelists were fiction-writers — not observers or eyewitnesses of the life of Jesus."[114] Like the different accounts of Genesis written by J, E, and P, these accounts contradicted each other in details and theological orientation, but unlike them, they were not edited together as a single document by a redactor but allowed to co-exist side by side.[115] Eventually, some of these "gospels" (good news) were discarded as too weird (the gospels of Thomas, of Mary, of Judas, of the Hebrews, etc.), and the four most mainstream ones were settled on as the canon. These and other writings were gathered together

---

114 *Against the Christians*, quoted (in Hoffman's translation) in Ehrman's *Misquoting Jesus*, 199.

115 Actually a 2nd-century Christian named Tatian did harmonize all four into a *Diatessaron*, but it never caught on beyond the Syrian Church.

and became known (in English) as *The New Covenant*, a codicil to (if not a replacement of) the old covenant between Yahweh and the Jews enshrined in the Tanakh.[116]

As in the Tanakh, a few novellas and one full-length novel can be extracted from *The New Covenant*. Named after their alleged authors, the gospels of Mark (written c. 71–73), Matthew (c. 80), and John (c. 100) are novella-length accounts of Yeshua ben Yosef's life and death. The most literary is the gospel according to Luke (c. 90, or maybe as late as 125), which with its sequel, the Acts of the Apostles, constitutes a 150-page historical novel that has some points in common with the Greek and Roman novels being written at the same time.[117] The concluding Revelation of John can be considered a novella-length apocalypse that anticipates fantasy and occult fiction; Northrop Frye snarkily assesses its intellectual level by noting its "fairytale atmosphere of gallant angels fighting dragons, a wicked witch, and a wonderful gingerbread city glittering with gold and jewels" (*The Secular Scripture*, 30) — though Thomas Jefferson was probably closer to the mark when he dismissed it as "the ravings of a maniac." I want to focus on the novel, which scholars call *Luke–Acts* but which might more appropriately be called *The Acts of Jesus and His Apostles*.[118]

There's a telling moment near the end of Acts when the convert Paul is enthusiastically describing his new religion to the Roman governor Festus, citing Moses and the prophets, when an exasperated "Festus said in a great voice: Paul, you are mad. Too many books are driving you mad" (26:24). Books — specifically Jewish prophetic books like Isaiah but also the epic books of

---

116 Of the dozens of books detailing this complex process, I'll list a few I found enlightening; if you're under the impression the gospels are "true" in the sense you normally use that word, any of the following will set you straight: *The Nazarene Gospel Restored* by Robert Graves and Joshua Podro (1954); *Ancient Christian Gospels* by Helmut Koester (1990); *The Unauthorized Version: Truth and Fiction in the Bible* by Robin Lane Fox (1991); *Gospel Fictions* (1988) and *Who Wrote the Gospels?* (1997) by Randel Helms; *Who Wrote the New Testament?* by Burton L. Mack (1995); *Saint Saul* by Donald Harmon Akenson (2000); *From Jesus to Christianity* by L. Michael White (2004); *The Mythic Past* (1999) and *The Messiah Myth* (2005) by Thomas L. Thompson; the texts of Robert Funk and the Jesus Seminar, especially *The Five Gospels* (1994) and *The Acts of Jesus* (1998), and any of Bart Ehrman's recent books. These scholars differ on details, but all agree (and demonstrate beyond a shadow of a doubt) the gospels are primarily literary compositions based only loosely on actual events. If you read only one book on the topic, make it Mack's.

117 The page count comes from the North Point Press edition of Richmond Lattimore's translation of *The New Testament* (1996), which is typeset like a novel. All subsequent quotations are from this literal and nondenominational translation; it's not perfect — Lattimore avoids the historical present tense used by Mark and allows some anachronisms — but it has deservedly won widespread praise.

118 I'm not the first to call *Luke-Acts* a novel; for example, White says of it: "there are many features of the story and the style . . . that seem to fit better with the ancient genre of the 'novel' or 'romance'" (*From Jesus to Christianity*, 250), and Pervo devotes most of his book *Profit with Delight* to detailing the novelistic qualities of Acts.

Homer and Virgil[119] — provided the outline for Luke's hero and allowed the evangelist to turn the Jewish peasant Yeshua ben Yosef into literature's first Christ figure. Once his earliest followers convinced themselves Yeshua was the messiah foretold by Scripture, the literate ones began combing the Tanakh for descriptions of this figure, so by the time "Mark," "Matthew," and "Luke" began writing, the backstory was already assembled.[120] The messiah will belong to the dynasty of David (Isa. 7:13ff)? Luke provides Yeshua with a genealogy that goes back not only to David (as Matthew does) but all the way back to Adam (3:23–38). He will be born in David's city of Bethlehem (Mic. 5:2)? Yeshua was actually a native of Nazareth in Galilee, "so Luke borrows the census of Quirinius as the fictional occasion to get Mary and Joseph to Bethlehem in time for the birth of Jesus. In this," the authors of *The Acts of Jesus* go on to say, "as in other instances in the gospels, the story of Jesus is accommodated to prophetic texts" (521).

A Brief Digression on Nomenclature

Up to this point, as in the earlier section on ancient Jewish fiction, I have been deliberately trying to defamiliarize and desanctify these overly familiar sacred texts by avoiding titles like the Old and New Testament and using instead authentic but archaic-looking names like the Tanakh, Yahweh, and Yeshua ben Yosef. By now, this rhetorical ploy may be getting tiresome so I'll drop it, but the purpose was to take these religious writings out of their familiar, modern context and return them to their Near Eastern origins so they would sound as exotic as the Egyptian "Contendings of Horus and Seth" or the Akkadian *Enuma Elish*. Which they are. Reading the Torah in a translation like Everett Fox's — which uses spellings like YHWH, Avraham, Yitzhak, and Moshe, and retains the syntax of the original — or Willis Barnstone's of the New Testament, which uses Yeshua ben Yosef, Miryam, Yohanan for John the Baptist, etc. — reminds us of their place with other archaic mythologies.

---

119 See MacDonald's *Does the New Testament Imitate Homer?* and Bonz's *Past as Legacy* for Virgil.

120 Though the gospels are traditionally ascribed to these figures, these are of course pseudonyms for anonymous authors. It was common practice back then for a writer to name a recognized figure as the "author" of his work as an act of homage; we really should speak of them as Pseudo-Mark, Pseudo-Luke, etc. And then there are all the anonymous editors and scribes that added their two shekels as they copied manuscripts, problems with translations — Yeshua spoke Aramaic, yet his words are reported in Greek: the first casualty of translation is subtle, metaphoric language like his — meaning it's anyone's guess who actually wrote what. A key verse you may cite for an important argument may not be the words of the savior but the contribution of some religious drone that lived in a hut in 2nd-century Galatia. For example, Joseph B. Tyson argues persuasively that our version of Luke is a revision made in the 120s of an earlier version of that gospel, updated to combat the teachings of Marcion of Pontus (see chap. 4 of his *Marcion and Luke-Acts: A Defining Struggle* [Columbia: U South Carolina P, 2006). For an excellent general discussion of this problem, see Ehrman's *Misquoting Jesus*.

Like the *Satyricon* and *The Golden Ass*, *Luke–Acts* is laced with literary allusions, though deployed for the opposite purpose. Petronius and Apuleius wanted to mock their protagonists by contrasting their ludicrous odysseys to the noble ones of Homer's and Virgil's heroes, but Luke wanted to ennoble his peasant protagonist by aligning him with the messiah foretold in the Tanakh. He's not very subtle about it: in chapter 4 Jesus enters a synagogue and is handed a copy of Isaiah to read from that *just happens* to be opened to the part foretelling the messiah's ministry. A few chapters later (9:22) Luke has him quoting his own prophetic end from Scripture, as though his life were no longer his own and he's just following a script. (It's like an actor in a modern play turning to the audience and saying he feels like he's in a play.) By the time the gospels were written, the transformation of Yeshua ben Yosef into Jesus the Christ was so extensive, and Jesus so weighed down with literary/religious antecedents, that the historical figure was all but lost. Treating *Luke–Acts* as a novel, then, is an act of charity; the other choice is to denounce it as religious propaganda at best, at worst another pious fraud.

Both Luke and Acts begin with a brief address to someone named Theophilus ("god-lover"), reminiscent of the brief prologues in *The Golden Ass* or *Daphnis and Chloe*. Luke notes that numerous accounts have already been written of the life of Jesus, but that they are misleading: he's going to tell the "truth concerning those stories of which you have been informed." Then Luke embarks on a mythic fiction about the miraculous births of John the Baptist and Jesus, using the same technique of characterization-by-analogy used by the Old Testament writers. Luke was a well-read man and had a wide array of models to choose from; for the birth of John the Baptist, the Septuagint translation of the Old Testament offered several versions of the barren-wife-whose-husband-is-visited-by-an-angel story; for Jesus, Luke had numerous stories of virgin birth from local and even world mythology to select from.[121] Like Chariton, Luke then begins a dual narrative, switching back and forth between John and Jesus, before abandoning this interesting technique for a more linear, episodic account. This procedure is rather boring — Jesus goes to Capernaum and does this, Jesus goes to Nain and does that — but the story that unfolds is anything but.

---

121 Fifty pages of examples are given in the "Birth Legends" chapter of Frederick Cornwallis Conybeare's *Magic, Myth and Morals: A Study of Christian Origins* (1909); see also the "Virgin Birth" chapter in Joseph Campbell's classic *Hero with a Thousand Faces*. For more recent accounts, see Robert J. Miller's *Born Divine: The Births of Jesus and Other Sons of God* (Santa Rosa, CA: Polebridge, 2003) and Charles H. Talbert's "Miraculous Conceptions and Births in Mediterranean Antiquity" in Levine et al.'s *Historical Jesus in Context* (2006), 79–86. The whole nativity fairy tale is gently debunked in Geza Vermes' *Nativity: History & Legend* (NY: Doubleday, 2007). I'm going a little heavy on the scholarly citations in this section because I want to emphasize that my objections to the veracity of the gospels are not a cranky personal bias but are shared by an army of scholars who know more about early Christianity than you or I ever will.

If you look past all the scripted parallels — Jesus' 40 days of resisting temptation in the desert (chap. 4) was invented to provide a contrast to the 40 years the Israelites wandered in the desert giving in to temptation, but is too contrived to work — there emerges a type rather rare in ancient literature but very recognizable in modern fiction: the nonconformist at odds with society, and sometimes so critical of the status quo and its community standards that he is perceived as a threat to society and killed. Two thousand years later people are still arguing over whether the Jews or the Romans were responsible for the death of Jesus, but it almost doesn't matter: it's the old story of the many against the one, of the blinkered, conventional community against the visionary, unconventional individualist who suggests that there's something rotten in the state and offers a daring alternative. "Do you think that I came to give peace on earth?" Jesus asks his disciples defiantly. "No, I tell you, dissention rather" (12:51). This mysterious stranger defies the purity codes, works on the sabbath, claims the poor are better than the rich, spurns family for friends, hangs out with rebels, denounces hypocrisy, capitalism, and remarriage, and encourages his followers to give up the responsible life of a good citizen for the freedom of a vagabond. Is there a more radical document than the Beatitudes? He speaks in riddles, using parables and paradoxes as puzzling as Kafka's, and challenges his followers to interpret them, almost like a modernist author. (The miracles are also to be understood as parables, not for the disciples but for the reader.) Naturally, The Powers That Be (especially the Sadducees) will have none of this; "the scribes and Pharisees began to hate him terribly," and after failing to push him off a cliff early in his ministry (4:29) they finally convince the Roman authorities to crucify him. Jesus' concept of a "kingdom of God" is deliberately, intriguingly vague, but it is clearly more a state of mind than the theocratic state contemporary fundamentalists would like to impose on the rest of us. Listen:

> When he was asked by the Pharisees when the Kingdom of God was to come, he answered them and said: The Kingdom of God is not coming in an observable way, nor will they say: Look, it is here; or: There. For see, the Kingdom of God is inside you. And he said to his disciples: Days will come when you will long to see one of the days of the son of man, and you will not see it. And they will say to you: Look, it is there; or: See, this way. Do not follow them. For as the lightning flashes and lights up, from one side to the other, what is under the sky, such will be the son of man. (17.20–24)

His literal-minded followers later cranked this up to Apocalypse Now, but what emerges from Jesus' parables and extended similes is more a new way of being, of seeing, a way of positioning yourself outside of conventional society — with the tax collectors and prostitutes (Matt. 21:31) rather than with "respectable" folks — a kind of alertness to possibility; above all, a call for the end of social hierarchies in favor of universal equality. Thomas L. Thompson describes this kingdom as "a utopian and idealistic metaphor for a world of justice,"[122] not unlike the yearnings of most social reformers and activists. But the authorities were as threatened by Jesus' proposed "countercultural lifestyle" (Mack 49) as their uptight counterparts would be in the 1960s, and come down on it just as hard. He is crucified, an especially humiliating form of execution reserved for rebels against the system. It's a powerful, edifying story — one needs to discard the supernatural happy ending tacked on after the crucifixion — and it's easy to see why it has mesmerized readers ever since, and why the figure of Jesus has inspired writers:

ESUS begat Cu Chulainn, begat King Arthur, begat Perceval, begat Galahad, begat Njal Thorgeirsson, begat Hamlet, begat Faust, begat Don Quixote, begat Heathcliff, begat Ishmael and Billy Budd, begat Uncle Tom, begat Sydney Carton, begat Prince Myshkin and two of the Karamazov brothers, begat Ivan Ilych, begat Twain's mysterious strangers, begat "Lord" Jim, begat Alissa Bucolin, begat Stephen Dedalus, begat Josef K., begat John the Savage, begat Joe Christmas, begat Pietro Spina, begat Miss Lonelyhearts and Tod Hackett, begat Jim Casy, begat Merseult, begat Greene's whiskey priest, begat Lowry's Consul, begat Tessie Hutchinson, begat Winston Smith, begat Holden Caulfield and Seymour Glass, begat Santiago, begat the corporal in Faulkner's *Fable*, begat Wyatt Gwyon and Stanley, begat Simon, begat every third character in Flannery O'Connor's Christ-haunted South, begat Sal Paradise and the naked angels of the Beats, begat Oskar Matzerath, begat Mordecai Himmelfarb, begat Randle Patrick McMurphy, begat Giles the goat-boy, begat Billy Pilgrim, begat Steve Chance, begat Tyrone Slothrop, begat Elizabeth Booth, begat Bug, begat Owen Meany, begat Mario Incandenza, begat Eugene Eyestones, *et hoc genus omne.*

The sequel to Luke, the Acts of the Apostles, tells a different story, but not the one Luke intended to tell. ("Never trust the artist," D. H. Lawrence advises. "Trust the tale" [2].) The first half of *Luke–Acts* told how a visionary and his followers were persecuted by the status quo; the second half tells how those followers started on the road to becoming the next status quo, the one that would eventually triumph as the Church Militant and persecute future visionaries such as Jesus. Like the New Testament as a whole, *Luke–Acts* is less about the teachings of Jesus than how those teachings were interpreted and institutionalized.

---

122 *The Messiah Myth*, 198. See Tod Lindberg's *Political Teachings of Jesus* (NY: HarperCollins, 2007) for the argument that Jesus was teaching his followers how to live in *this* world, not how to qualify for admission into the next.

Dostoevsky's Grand Inquisitor argues that Jesus gave his followers too much freedom, a gift perhaps for some but a burden for most, who would prefer to be told what to do. As the enigmatic teachings of Yeshua ben Yosef were molded by coarser hands into Christian doctrine, the apostles began insisting on a party line, and woe to anyone who challenged it. Chapter 5 of Acts relates the menacing example of a new convert named Ananias, who "sold some property but, with the connivance of his wife, withheld some of the proceeds and brought only a part and laid it at the feet of the apostles." Like the leader of a revolutionary cell demanding total obedience, Peter accuses Ananias of disloyalty not only to them but to God. "When Ananias heard these words he fell down and died; and great fear came upon all those who heard." (Right, he *fell down* and died.) Then the wife Sapphira is likewise arraigned and likewise "falls" dead. (Both corpses are quickly buried by Peter's muscle, some nameless "young men.") "And great fear came upon the whole congregation and on all who heard about these things" (5:1–11). Not a great start for a new religion supposedly based on love and forgiveness. Soon they are squabbling over petty doctrinal matters and purity codes like a bunch of Pharisees, deciding that any gentiles who want to join their cult must "abstain from the pollution of idols, and from lechery, and from what has been strangled, and from blood" (15:20), as though they were back in the grim old days of Leviticus. The rest of Acts deals with the missionary activities of Paul (né Saul of Tarsus), the real founder of Christianity.

While the implications of Acts are scary, the actual narrative is rather lively as it tracks the apostles throughout the Mediterranean. There are several sea voyages, dire prophecies, and a riot. In Caesaria, Paul visits the evangelist Philip and his four prophetic daughters, all virgins (21:9). "It must have been quite an evening," snickers Robin Lane Fox in *The Unauthorized Version* (210). Paul gets arrested many times, accumulating quite a rap sheet. There's even an exciting storm at sea right out of a Greek novel, which reminds me of a funny story: During his oral exams at Oxford, Oscar Wilde was told to translate this scene from the Greek — a tough text chosen by his hostile examiners because of the technical nautical terms. Wilde's flawless translation was reluctantly interrupted by "That will do, Mr. Wilde," to which he cheekily responded, "Oh, please, do let me go on — I am longing to know how the story finishes."[123] Acts ends rather abruptly with Paul alive and proselytizing away, just as the Deuteronomistic History originally ended with Josiah's reforms in full swing. Luke surely knew Paul was martyred shortly after, but probably didn't want to end his book on a downer. As history, Acts is often unreliable, as scholars have shown.[124] Luke's accounts of Paul's activities

---

123 A. N. Wilson, *Paul: The Mind of the Apostle*, 21–22.
124 See especially Lüdemann's *Acts of the Apostles* for a merciless, verse-by-verse accounting. He concludes: "By interweaving history and legend, Luke confused facts, fiction, and

sometimes contradict Paul's own accounts in his letters. But Luke's use of fictional techniques to enliven his doctrinal message was a brilliant decision. Like the *Satyricon*, it's a story of life on the road, of life on the run even, and its dramatic interest is heightened by the use of trial scenes, daring escapes, and incidents like the above-mentioned shipwreck. Luke wasn't intentionally writing a novel, of course, but *Luke–Acts* became the model for a later generation of writers who decided to express their Christian faith not in the form of a theological tract but in that of the newfangled novel that was sweeping the Greco-Roman world in the 2nd and 3rd centuries.

Collectively known as the Apocryphal Acts of the Apostles, the Acts of Andrew, of John, of Paul, of Peter, and of Thomas are novella-length narratives of poor quality, episodic accounts filled with ludicrous miracles and sermons, and are regarded by most scholars today as novels meant as edifying entertainment rather than theological treatises.[125] Imagine some Jehovah's Witnesses today deciding to spread their message in the form of religious novellas, and then imagine how godawful they'd be. They're worth looking at only to demonstrate why the early Christians soon gave up on novel-writing, not to mention the dangers of wedding fiction with theology — a shotgun marriage that rarely works.[126] The literary novel is generally about growing up, about learning how to live in this world; religious fictions — romanticized conversion stories, martyrologies, hagiographies, apocalypses — are not about growing up but about regressing to a childish state and yearning for the next world, watched over by a heavenly father and "virgin" mother, with sexless angels as imaginary friends. ("In truth I tell you, unless you change and become like little children you will never enter the kingdom of Heaven" — Matt. 18:3 [*New Jerusalem Bible*].) Characters in the Apocryphal Acts, as in so many religious fictions that followed, display a gnostic-like (or merely cowardly) desire to withdraw from the world, to avoid the problems mature adults face and retreat instead to an infantile Never-Neverland

---

faith. He blended historical and suprahistorical fact, thereby falsifying history for the sake of piety, politics, and power. This was clearly an offense against the rules of critical historiography even in his day" (363) — but is perfectly consistent with the more relaxed rules of fiction.

125 See, e.g., chap. 6 of Hägg's *The Novel in Antiquity*, Pervo's "Early Christian Fiction" in Morgan and Stoneman (239–54), and the lengthy introductions to the individual Acts in Wilhelm Schneemelcher's rather daunting edition of *New Testament Apocrypha*, the source of the quotations that follow. The relationship between ancient novels and early Christian writings has been a hot topic in classical scholarship since the 1990s and continues to generate numerous publications.

126 As one of many examples, remember how Julia's late confessional scene throws a wet blanket over Waugh's otherwise enjoyable *Brideshead Revisited*? And who reads his *Helena* anymore?

Where springs not fail,
To fields where flies no sharp and sided hail
And a few lilies blow.

And I have asked to be
Where no storms come,
Where the green swell is in the havens dumb,
And out of the swing of the sea.[127]

But that doesn't mean religious novels can't sometimes be fun to read.

The Acts of Paul is especially enjoyable, in the way a charmingly inept grade-school play can be enjoyable. Originally a bit longer than Luke's Acts (about 60 percent of it survives), it likewise takes Paul as its hero, glorifying his ministry from just after his legendary conversion on the road to Damascus — see Mack (103) for what probably really happened — until his beheading in Rome. Written between 185 and 195 by an anonymous presbyter in Asia Minor (who lost his job because of this work, Tertullian tattles), it is largely about Paul's appeal to the ladies. Like an inverted Don Juan, Paul goes about seducing women into accepting Christianity and practicing chastity, much to the anger of their husbands and boyfriends. The most popular section of *The Acts of Paul* is chapter 3, concerning a virgin named Thecla, engaged to a man named Thamyris but dazzled by Paul's preaching. Paul is riffing on the Beatitudes and catches her ear with: "Blessed are the bodies of the virgins, for they shall be well-pleasing to God and shall not lose the reward of their purity" (3.6). Thecla listens "night and day to the word of the virgin life as it was spoken by Paul," and the author goes out of his way to note that "she had not yet seen Paul in person but only heard his word" (3.7). He wants to emphasize the lack of any physical appeal of Paul himself, and even inserts this novelistic but unflattering description of the apostle: "a man small of stature,[128] with a bald head and crooked legs, in a good state of body, with eyebrows meeting and nose somewhat hooked, full of friendliness; for now he appeared like a man, and now he had the face of an angel" (3.2). This is a deliberate departure from the stereotypical handsome hero of the Greek novel; Paul sounds more like George Costanza from *Seinfeld*.

Yet Thecla's reaction to Paul can only be called erotic, more like a groupie's reaction to a rock star: "when she saw many women and virgins going in to Paul she desired to be counted worthy herself to stand in Paul's presence" (3.7), and after Paul is thrown in prison for disturbing the peace, Thecla

127 Gerard Manley Hopkins, "Heaven-Haven: A Nun Takes the Veil." Beautiful, isn't it?
128 The Hellenic name Paul means "small" or "little" (Akenson 59), hence the description is more likely to be etymological than historical. This Paul is a literary character, not the Paul of history. The author seems to have known Luke's Acts, but he draws more on current legends and his own imagination for the bulk of his narrative.

bribes her way into his cell, where she "kissed his fetters" as he proclaims the mighty acts of his god. Her angry fiancé tracks her down at the prison "and found her, so to speak, bound with him in affection" (3.18–19). If this were Apuleuis writing, that "so to speak" would mean Paul and Thecla were caught in flagrente delicto. And after Paul is taken to court, Thecla remains behind in his cell and "rolled herself upon the place where Paul taught as he sat in prison" (3.20).

This misdirected (hence perverse) sexuality and the fetishism of virginity that Paul keeps banging away at inverts the paradigm of the Greek novel, which was entering its glory years at this time.[129] Instead of preserving her chastity for her future husband, Thecla saves it for her future with her god; instead of tests of fidelity, we're given tests of faith; instead of smooth-talking her into engaging in sex, Paul smooth-talks her into *disengaging* from sex. (Some feminist critics, like Doody [74–77], applaud this: Thecla takes control of her body and abandons traditional married life for an unconventional alternative. But it's a *man* who cons her into this alternative lifestyle — nothing liberating about that, just a different kind of seduction of a naïve girl.) Instead of celebrating eros as a force of nature, we see it demonized as a snare of Satan and an abomination to the Christian god. And instead of the daring adventures of the Greek novels we get preposterous miracles: Paul baptizes a talking lion, who thereafter avoids the advances of a slutty lioness (no, really! see Schneemelcher 265); Thecla is ordered to be burned at the stake, naked, for her rebellious behavior, but her god sends a downpour to douse the flames; she is later thrown to the beasts — again, naked: something our author likes to dwell on — but a lioness (a good girl, not like that other one) protects her against them; Thecla throws herself into a pool of water filled with man-eating . . . seals, but they are killed by lightning;[130] when Paul is beheaded in the final chapter, milk spurts from his gushing neck. And so on.[131] These ludicrous elements didn't prevent many early Christian authorities from taking *The Acts of Paul* as gospel, so to speak, and citing it as solemnly as they did the canonical writings. Thecla was later canonized as a saint and enjoyed cult status for centuries.

Like *The Acts of Paul*, those of Andrew (c. 150), of Peter (c. 180–90), and of John (c. 200) are incomplete and consist likewise of miracles and sermons,

---

129 In his recent dissertation, Barrier insists *The Acts of Paul* is a Christian novel with many points in common with the Greek novel then in circulation.

130 While in the pool Thecla baptizes herself, which is what got the author into hot water. Can't have people baptizing themselves without the benefit of clergy, and sure as hell can't have *women* baptizing anyone.

131 Some have tried to read allegorical meaning into these incidents, suggesting the lion represents death and sexuality, but others argue more persuasively that the author was simply providing Aesop-like entertainment value. To paraphrase Freud, sometimes a talking baptized lion is just a talking baptized lion. C. S. Lewis got a lot of mileage out of just such a critter.

mostly against the pleasures of sex, enclosed in an episodic novella form. *The Acts of Thomas* (c. 225) is the only complete example, and is the most sophisticated of the Acts in its use of rhetoric and symbolism. Starting with the legend that the apostle Thomas traveled to India to convert the heathen, and supplemented with material from Tatian's *Oratio ad Graecos* (an apology for Christianity) and Bardaisan's *Book of the Laws of the Countries* (on India), our anonymous Syrian author composed another novella that, unfortunately, amounts to little more than miracles and sermons against sex.[132] However, the prose is extremely rich: there are long sentences stacking apostrophes to Jesus up to heaven; elaborate extensions of biblical metaphors showing masterful use of balance, antithesis, paronomasia, and parallelism; and iterative imagery that lashes his narrative together and anchors it to that of the New Testament. Thomas generates most of this rhetoric, but nearly every character delivers theological arias as fiery as a Southern preacher's:

> "But to you crowds who stand by and expect those that are cast down to be raised up I say: Believe the apostle of Jesus Christ! Believe the teacher of truth! Believe him who shows you the truth! Believe in Jesus! Believe in Christ, who was born that the born might live through his life, who became a child and was raised up that the perfect manhood might become manifest through him. He taught his own teacher, for he is the teacher of truth and the wisest of the wise, who also offered the gift in the temple to show that all offering is sanctified through him. This man is his apostle, the revealer of truth. This is he who performs the will of him who sent him. But there shall come false apostles and prophets of lawlessness, whose end shall be according to their deeds, who preach indeed and ordain that men should flee from impieties but are themselves at all times found in sins; *clothed* indeed *with sheep's clothing, but inwardly ravening wolves.*" (8.79)

This happens to be spoken by a wild ass (long story), but it's typical of the high rhetoric found throughout — and which can get old in a hurry. As in pornography, where a thin plot exists only as an excuse to get from one sex scene to another, the vigorous sermons are linked merely by typical missionary

---

132 At one point, all these Acts of the Apostles were ascribed to one Leucius Charinus, and though their stylistic diversity makes this unlikely, the single-minded obsession with sex certainly unifies them all. This whole notion that the presence of a thin membrane or the avoidance of orgasms defines a decent, ethical person is one of those antiquated absurdities that makes one shake the head in wonder at the silly human race. For a scholarly account of how this perversion of nature came about, read Kathy Gaca's *The Making of Fornication: Eros, Ethics, and Political Reform in Greek Philosophy and Early Christianity* (Berkeley: U California P, 2003), and for further follies see Hanne Blank's sensible *Virgin: The Untouched History* (NY: Bloomsbury, 2007). If you're going to be irrational about it, better to adopt the old Japanese view: "it was firmly believed that any girl who remained virgin for long had been possessed by an evil spirit, and this was hardly a reputation that a self-respecting family, or the girl herself, would welcome" (Morris, *The World of the Shining Prince*, 213).

activity — there is no local color drawn from the Indian setting — in which Thomas, like that heartbreaker Paul, talks women into leaving their husbands and bestows upon them a "seal" that in effect restores their virginity for their new roles as brides of Christ. His conquests are all pushovers: Thomas delivers his spiel and the women (and asses) swallow it whole with none of the hesitation or philosophical struggle found in truly great religious novels like *The Brothers Karamazov*. Eventually even the Indian husbands come around, all except the king, who orders Thomas to be executed. Like Jesus, Thomas then returns from the dead to comfort his followers, who can't wait to die and join him and his twin brother Jesus in heaven. (Did I mention they're twins? This is the author's clumsy, overliteral way of identifying the apostle with his master.) With little characterization, conflict, or attention to setting, *The Acts of Thomas* sinks under its theological weight, despite the author's rhetorical prowess.[133]

The Acts of Peter is the crudest of these early Christian novellas, the most inhuman in its emphasis on chastity,[134] and memorable only for a ludicrous WrestleMania-like battle between Peter and Simon Magus, dueling sorcerers who perform miracles to show the citizens of Rome whose sponsor is greater, the god of the Christians or the devil. This popular taste for the supernatural led other Christian writers to try their hand at works of fantasy and the occult during this same period. The best known is the apocalyptic nightmare tacked onto the end of the New Testament, a stunning work by a sour religious nut who possessed an enviable gift for epic fantasy (but also, like all apocalyptists, a misanthropic streak). It's not quite a novella — just 35 pages in Lattimore's edition, like one of H. P. Lovecraft's longer tales of cosmic chaos and written in a similar visionary style — so we'll skip it. The least known might be the *Testament of Solomon*, not much longer but too fascinating to pass over. Written in the 2nd or 3rd century by an anonymous Christian well-versed in the black arts, it is a first-person account by King Solomon of how he built the Temple in Jerusalem with the help of demons.

It begins like the world's first vampire story: every evening at sunset, a

---

133 The novella is famous for including "The Hymn of the Pearl" — a key text for Gnostics — but this poem was written earlier by someone else and merely inserted by the author at an appropriate (but unmotivated) point in his story.

134 Though capable of curing his own paralyzed daughter, Peter chooses to leave her in that condition so that she won't be a temptation to men. And when a peasant asks Peter to pray for his only daughter, she falls dead at the apostle's word. "O reward worthy and ever pleasing to God, to escape the shamelessness of the flesh and to break the pride of the blood!" the narrator exults, convinced it is better for her to die now than to become sexually active later. It could be argued that all these pleas for chastity are merely metaphoric pleas for fidelity to God; the prophets of the Old Testament often portray Yahweh as a jealous husband and the Israelites as loose women. (See Ezek. 16 and the first three chapters of Hosea for particularly disgusting examples of Yahweh as a wife-beater.) But the authors of these Acts sound as literal and sex-negative as the "Just Say No" abstinence-only prudes of our day.

demon named Ornias approaches the building supervisor's boy and sucks blood out of his thumb.[135] When Solomon learns of this, he asks for help from his god, who sends the archangel Michael to deliver a magic seal ring to Solomon, who then uses it to summon Ornias and other demons to appear before him to confess the nature of their activities and how they can be thwarted. One after another, a fantastic parade of demons, spirits, monsters, and "heavenly bodies" are interviewed and then sent to work on the Temple. (I would think a demonic, non-kosher work crew would taint the sanctity of the Temple, but apparently this didn't bother the author.[136]) As the demons explain the grief they cause, it becomes clear that the author is attempting to account for all the trials and tribulations that plague mankind: a demoness named Obyzouth goes around at night strangling newborn infants (as in sudden infant death syndrome); Kunopegos, "who had the form of a horse in front and a fish in back," causes shipwrecks; a demon with the supervillain name of Lix Tetrax boasts, "I create divisions among men, I make whirlwinds, I start fires, I set fields on fire, and I make households non-functional." Some are narrow specialists: Sphendonael produces "tumors of the parotid gland and tetanic recurvation." (The author apparently knew the works of Hippocrates and Galen.) Rhyx Anatreth sends "gas and burning up in to the bowels," while Rhyx Autoth instigates "jealousies and squabbles between those who love each other."[137]

Unacquainted with the principles of science or medicine, puzzled by unexpected disasters and inexplicable behavior, people of that time blamed demons for everything that went wrong; living in a world where an infant died or a ship sank *for no reason* was as intolerable for them as it is for most people today. "If there is something comforting — religious, if you want — about paranoia," writes Thomas Pynchon in *Gravity's Rainbow*, "there is still also anti-paranoia, where nothing is connected to anything, a condition not many of us can bear for long" (434). The author of the *Testament of Solomon* suggests that most people create a demon-haunted world to make sense of natural phenomena and natural disasters they can't otherwise understand, rather than suspend judgment until empirical evidence can supply accurate, non-demony answers.[138] He himself may have known better; the wide range

135 Sucking a phallic thumb is a more blatant way than biting a neck to signal the sexual symbolism at the heart of most vampire tales.

136 As a Christian, perhaps he meant this as a deliberate slur against the Jews. Rabbis later explained that Solomon built the Temple with the help of a *shamir*, "a creature about the size of a grain of barley." See the various traditions gathered in Bialik and Ravnitzky's massive *Book of Legends*, 124–26.

137 From D. C. Duling's translation of the *Testament of Solomon* in Charlesworth's *Old Testament Pseudepigrapha*, 1:960–87.

138 *The Demon-Haunted World* is a book by Carl Sagan, published the year he died (1996), that exposes the many unscientific, irrational beliefs held by today's citizens, such as astrology, witchcraft, faith-healing, channeling, UFO abductions, and of course religion. The

of ancient lore on display here about astrology, magic, medicine, angelology, demonology, astronomy, and superstitions, along with references to Classical literature and the Bible, points to an extremely well-read person, someone who knew Greek medical texts well enough to know that detached tendons were not the fault of the demon Rhyx Ichthuon. Moreover, he drops all supernatural excuses in the novella's touching conclusion: after the completion of the demon-built temple, Solomon travels to the kingdom of the Jebusites and falls head over heels for a young Shummanite woman. He wants to add her to his harem but is told he can't have her unless he converts to the Jebusite religion (which involves sacrificing five locusts to Raphan and Moloch). He holds out for a while, but eventually caves: "So because I loved the girl — she was in full bloom and I was out of my senses — I accepted as nothing the custom of sacrificing the blood of the locusts." He gets the girl but loses his god. Even though mention was made earlier of various demons who inspire lust in men, no demonic excuses are given here for Solomon's apostasy, only the very real beauty of an irresistible girl. "She was in full bloom and I was out of my senses" — over the gulf of nearly 2,000 years, that cry rings true.

The last and longest Christian fiction of this period is a novel (not a novella) called *Recognitions*, in which Peter and Simon return for a grudge match. It was originally ascribed to the 1st-century Clement of Rome and for that reason is still referred to as the Clementine *Recognitions*, but it was actually written in Syria sometime in the 4th century.[139] Tomas Hägg provides a convenient plot summary:

> The young Roman, Clement, is a seeker after truth. He goes to Palestine in order to hear about Jesus. In Caesarea he meets Peter and accompanies him on a preaching tour in Phoenicia. He is present at a theological debate between Peter and Simon the Magician (who also appears in Acts, 8). Clement tells the story of his life to Peter: when he was a child, his mother left home together with her two elder sons, who were twins, and they have been missing ever since; later on his father went away to search for them, and he too has not returned; this happened twenty years ago. Now, through Peter's agency, something wonderful takes place: on the island of Aradus — where Chariton too set his recognition scene ([*Chaereas and Callirhoe* 8.1]) — Clement is reunited to his mother, and in Laodicea in Syria he meets up again his two older brothers; they had been separated from their mother by a shipwreck, sold as slaves by pirates, but then adopted by a rich woman

---

adjective "demony" is from the demon-haunted world of *Buffy the Vampire Slayer*, where such nonsense belongs.

139 Like *The Golden Ass*, it was based on an earlier document about the travels of Peter that inspired two versions: the *Homilies* and the *Recognitions*. The former survives in its original Greek form, but the latter only in the somewhat abridged Latin translation by Rufinus, an opponent of Jerome. It was very popular in its day — more than 100 manuscripts have been preserved, and it was translated into Syriac, Arabic, and Ethiopic — perhaps because it's more novel-like than the similar *Homilies*.

and given a good education. At last they are all reunited with their father, and the complex threads are disentangled. (163)

It is these recognition scenes between family members that give the novel its title and align it with the Greek novels of the period, along with the incidents of separation, shipwreck, pirates, and slavery. What the above summary doesn't reveal, however, is that most of the novel is given over to long disputations and lectures on Christian doctrine and competing heresies, which robs it of much entertainment value. I don't think the author was trying to elevate the novel into a more serious art form; more likely he merely borrowed the outward form of the popular Greek novel as a vehicle to deliver his theological message in a more palatable form. The fictional elements seem to have been almost an afterthought — for example, we're not given the story of Clement's family desertion until three-fourths of the way through the novel, and the "recognitions" take place rather quickly, telegraphed in such a way that the slowest Christian reader can see them coming — but the author sows seeds that would flower in better novels centuries later.

Recognitions begins with Clement tormented by the nature of mortality, desperate to know whether there is life after death and concerned for the future of his soul. Having a scholarly bent of mind, he frequents the philosophers of Rome, but they're only interested in dialectics and can't give him a satisfactory answer. He studies Greek myths, but dismisses them as "fables." So he decides to travel to mysterious Egypt and "win over a magician by money and entreat him, by what they call the necromantic art, to bring me a soul from the infernal regions" to learn whether his soul is immortal (1.5). "Yes, it's really the beginning of the whole Faust legend," says a character in William Gaddis's own Faustian novel *The Recognitions* (373), which is not only named after the original but cites it occasionally. Like Clement, both Marlowe's Faustus and Goethe's Faust are dissatisfied with the philosophers of their day and are willing to call up a demon from hell to satisfy their thirst for hidden knowledge. (Coincidentally, Clement's father is named Faustinianus, and his older twin brothers Faustinus and Faustus, but variants of this name were common in Roman times.) As it happens, Clement is dissuaded from going to Egypt and goes to Judea instead to investigate reports of a new message from the heavens delivered by Jesus and propagated by Peter. He's instantly converted, and after joining Peter's followers Clement fades into the background for most of the novel thereafter, much like Ishmael in *Moby-Dick*. Like Ahab, Peter is a powerful presence and becomes a father figure for Clement. The search for a father (real or spiritual) is one of the central themes of classic novels (*Tom Jones, Ulysses*) and finds one of its earliest expressions here.

"Mostly talk, talk, talk" is how the same character in Gaddis describes *Recognitions* (373), which is perhaps 80 percent dialogue. But unlike Gaddis's lively dialogue, it's deadly here; unless you're fascinated by ante-Nicene theology, the endless disputations and sermons render much of the novel static. As any director knows, dialogue-heavy scenes require some movement, some bits of "business," to retain the audience's attention, which our author fails to provide. During Peter's three-day disputation with Simon, one almost yearns for the ludicrous miracles the two threw against each other in the *Acts of Peter*; the two other three-day discussions in *Recognitions* are more polite but (for that reason) more tedious. These long discourses allow the author to show off his extensive knowledge, not only of theology but of Greek mythology and philosophy, of demonology, astrology, anthropological lore, and other unusual topics. It's a very learned novel, as much so as those by Achilles Tatius and Heliodorus, but the material is dumped on the page in clumps rather than integrated into the narrative as in those superior authors' works. And so concerned is the author with his theological message that he ignores a number of promising elements of his story: nothing is made of the fact Clement's brothers are twins — even the lugubrious author of the *Acts of Thomas* exploits the twinship of Thomas and Jesus — and very little is seen of the most intriguing female character in this male-dominated novel, Simon's flashy consort Luna. In the *Homilies* version she is named Helena and identified with the beauty that caused the Trojan War (and who later became the dream-girl of the Faust legend). Simon claims he "brought her down from the higher heavens, and that she is Wisdom, the mother of all things" (2.12), but no sooner is she introduced than she's dropped from the narrative. Three-fourths of the way through we learn that Peter has a wife who accompanies him on his journeys, but this unlucky woman is likewise ignored. It should come as no surprise that the author expresses a low opinion of the imagination (2.61–65) and shares Plato's antagonism toward poets (10.38); it is precisely this lack of imagination that prevents him from rounding out his flat characters and finding a way to dramatize his ideas rather than deliver them as soporific sermons. Though the Clementine *Recognitions* is more ambitious and more successful than the Apocryphal Acts, they all suffer from this same fault. As though this were an insurmountable barrier for the Christian writer, the ancient Christian novel was pretty much abandoned at this point.

While not very successful at it, Christian writers added the theological novel to the impressive number of variants the genre had accumulated by the 4th century: we've seen historical novels, biographical and magic-realist ones, epistolary novels, romances, parodies and satires, metafictional fables, pornography, learned novels, family sagas, novels in dialogue, gay novels, science fiction and fantasy — nearly every genre active today. Fourteen centuries ago the novel was poised to join if not exceed poetry and drama as the highest form of literature when, suddenly, novel-writing and novel-reading came to a halt.

In October 312, on the eve of a battle against a rival emperor of Rome, Constantine had a dream. A handsome man and a superb soldier, he was poorly educated and superstitious, dependent on divine signs for guidance. In the most likely of several versions of the incident (that of Lactantius), Constantine dreamt that Jesus instructed him to mark the shields of his soldiers with a particular sign (the letter P superimposed over an X), promising "*In hoc signo vinces*": By this sign you shall conquer. Constantine was victorious for the same reason he had won battles before — because of his military prowess — but the superstitious bastard (he'd been born out of wedlock) was grateful for the inspirational dream and put an end to the persecution of Christians. (Ironically, Christians then began viciously persecuting each other for alleged heresies.) Though not baptized until hours before his death in 337, Constantine found it politically expedient to favor Christianity, for its theology "provided the rationale for absolute monarchy — a single all-powerful deity reigned in heaven, and a single all-powerful monarch reigned on earth" (Kirsch 172, who provides a very readable account of all this).

Constantine's relative and eventual successor, Julian — much better educated but just as superstitious — withdrew the imperial favor from Christianity and restored it to the gods of Homer and Plato, and to polytheism in general. (He had been initiated into several mystery cults, and even began rebuilding the temple in Jerusalem for the benefit of his Jewish subjects.) Unlike Constantine, Julian looked like a hippie and was a writer — his surviving works fill three Loeb volumes — though no fan of the novel.[140] This admirable, tolerant man fought the good fight until June 363, when he was killed in battle against the Persians. Within a generation, Christianity was not only reinstated but was made the official religion of the Roman Empire, which by then extended from England to Egypt, and from Spain to Syria. And a generation after that, Rome fell to the barbarians; one by one, the lights went out over Europe and the aptly named Dark Ages descended. The extraordinary advances in mathematics and astronomy ground to a halt; painting, engineering, and medicine were abandoned; and in 390 a mob of Christian zealots stormed the famous library of Alexandria and torched it, inadvertently burning manuscripts of the Bible and other Christian writings along with some 700,000 volumes and scrolls preserving the glory that was Greece and the grandeur that was Rome. There and elsewhere novels were destroyed; Christians couldn't write them very well, nor did they want anyone reading them. (On a parchment from the early 7th century, a Coptic sermon is written on top of a partly erased copy of Chariton's *Callirhoe*.) Thus the rocky but remarkable growth of the novel, from "The Tale of Sinuhe" to *An Ethiopian Story*, came to a temporary end.

---

140 "In a letter of advice to a priest of the old religion, Julian advises him to shun made-up stuff (*plasmata*) of seeming history such as love stories and all that kind of nonsense" (Doody 21).

CHAPTER 2

The Medieval Novel

At first there was no place for the sophisticated, worldly novel in the naive, provincial culture of Christian Europe, but it didn't disappear entirely: it just played dumb for a while. Hagiography adopted the general features of the simplest novels, the ones with the most linear form and clearest moral. As critic Roderick Beaton points out, "It has often been observed that precisely during the centuries in which the secular narrative of love and adventure was in abeyance, the saints' lives provided a narrative literature in which adventures continued to abound and the love of ordinary men and women for one another was replaced by the saint's love for God."[1] Some Christian writers continued to spin tales of Jesus and the apostles, but others began writing edifying if fanciful stories about the model citizens of their brave new world: monks, hermits, god-dedicated virgins, martyrs, and all the other fanatics eventually canonized as saints. Some are bare-bones accounts based on whatever details were at hand, but many of them are so tricked out with miracles and wonders that they resemble the "news reports" one sees in supermarket tabloids: "Mermaid Found in Sardine Can," "Mummy Found in Phone Booth," "Vampires Attack U.S. Marines," or (more to the present point) "Stigmata Priest Can Tell Future."[2] Magic realism for the masses.

Many hagiographies are novella-length and consist of more fiction than fact — "extravagant and indecent fictions," Gibbon called them — despite their authors' stated intentions of merely preserving the biography of a saintly person, and for this reason they have a marginal place in the history of the novel. But the distinction we make between fact and fiction apparently didn't exist for the authors of hagiographies. For example, in one of the earliest and most famous of them, Athanasius's *Life of Antony* (356), the Alexandrian patriarch begins by claiming "I am concerned about the truth," but within a few pages he is recounting lurid tales of the devil assaulting young Antony's virtue by appearing in his dreams in the form of a beautiful woman. Like many in his time, Athanasius believed wet dreams, epileptic seizures, mental

---

1 *The Medieval Greek Romance*, 30. Reminds me of the joke about the failing rock band that becomes a successful Christian-rock group simply by replacing "Baby" with "Jesus" in their lyrics.

2 All from the 7 May 2002 issue of the *Weekly World News*, which I bought for the mermaid story.

disorders, and puzzling diseases were the result of demonic possession, and so was apparently convinced he was indeed telling the truth when describing Antony's victorious battles against these "demons" and other miraculous events. Many of these are generated from Paul's numerous descriptions of demons in the New Testament; the power of suggestion will cause people to see (and write about) the strangest things. Antony's encounter with a centaur and his heavenly visions are likewise treated as real (instead of the results of excessive fasting, sleep deprivation, malnutrition, and/or the author's imagination). In addition to validating the use of these fantastic elements, Athanasius also established the template for hagiography: the typical protagonist is a goody-goody child, wise beyond his years though not always educated — Athanasius several times notes that Antony was a simple, uneducated man who read nothing but the Bible — who, upon attaining maturity, abandons his heritage and/or an unwanted marriage, devotes himself to the religious life — which alternates between performing miracles, beating off demonic attacks, and delivering sermons — and eventually dies either peacefully or in a bloody martyrdom, his body afterward remaining incorrupt and providing magical relics for future believers. Athanasius's *Life of Antony* isn't art — we'll have to wait for Flaubert's *Temptation of Saint Antony* for an artistic treatment of this hermit's life — but he set the pattern for the hundreds of hagiographies that would follow over the next thousand years.

Some later examples have an even higher fiction quotient, but when the narrative element is abandoned, it's difficult to allow hagiographies even a peripheral place in the history of the novel. (Not that their authors would want to be associated with the profane things anyway.) Take Adomnán's *Life of Saint Columba* (c. 700), for example. Adomnán had read the *Life of Antony* and so supplied his Irish abbot with the requisite pious childhood and miraculous death, but departs from Athanasius's model by organizing the rest of his material thematically rather than chronologically. Book 1 collects anecdotes concerning Columba's prophetic abilities, book 2 those concerning his miracles, and book 3 his angelic visitations. Even though Adomnán begins with a mission statement similar to that of Athanasius — "No one should think that I would write anything false about this man, nor even anything doubtful or uncertain" — his novella consists almost entirely of fictitious anecdotes like this:

> Once, when the praiseworthy man was living in the island of *Hinba*, he saw one night in a mental trance an angel of the Lord sent to him. He had in his hand a glass book of the ordination of kings, which St Columba received from him, and which at the angel's bidding he began to read. In the book the command was given him that he should ordain Áedán as king, which St Columba refused to do because he held Áedán's brother Éoganán

in higher regard. Whereupon the angel reached out and struck the saint with a whip, the scar from which remained with him for the rest of his life. (3.5)

Columba apparently had a scar, a follower made up a story about it (unless Columba himself did), another more imaginative person added some colorful details (a glass book, an angel with a whip), and a century later Adomnán records it all as fact, also working in a subtle allusion to Samuel choosing David as Saul's successor to make the case that Irish kings should likewise be anointed by holy men, rather than via pagan ritual.[3] Aside from the facts that there was indeed a man named Columba (aka Columcille, c. 521–97) who eventually left Ireland to found a monastery on the Scottish island of Iona, almost nothing in Adomnán's account is "true" even though I'm sure he was convinced he was writing a true account, not a mélange of hearsay, wish-fulfillment, propaganda, and legend.[4] So while the *Life of Saint Columba* is a 130-page prose narrative filled with fictitious events, the author's credulous attitude toward his material disqualifies it from being considered a novel.

The one bona fide novel to be written by any of these Christian propagandists is Ramón Lull's *Blanquerna* (c. 1285). Lull, sometimes known by his Anglicized name Raymond Lully (1235?–1315?), was born in Majorca off the coast of Spain, the only son of a good family. He led a dissolute life until a married woman he was chasing repulsed his efforts by revealing her chest eaten away by breast cancer; in revulsion, he turned away from real women and embraced the unreal Virgin Mary and the cult of Catholicism, devoting the rest of his life to missionary work, alchemy, and writing. (He was especially keen on converting Muslims; fed up with his pesky proselytizing, an Algerian mob stoned him to death.) *Blanquerna* is a kind of pilgrim's progress recounting the life of a Christian extremist: like Lully, Blanquerna is the only son of a wealthy family, but spurns the good life to become a wandering religious nut; he later becomes (against his wishes) the abbot of a monastery, the bishop of a diocese in Spain, and eventually pope, which he finally gives up to become a hermit. As fiction, *Blanquerna* is tedious, a real martyrdom to read: there's little dramatic conflict, no character development, and its theology — the novel is essentially one long sermon — is dumbed down into numerous Sunday school lessons. However, *Blanquerna* can claim several firsts: it is the first novel written in a Romance language (Catalan), the first to mention knights and courtly love (Lull also wrote a book on chivalry), and the first to use theological concepts as formal devices. The novel is divided into five books "in signification of the five Wounds which Our Lord God Jesus received upon the Tree of the True Cross" (prologue); they also treat the five

---

3 So argues translator Richard Sharpe (355).
4 It contains the first account of the Loch Ness monster (2.27); the latest account can probably be found in the *Weekly World News*.

acceptable forms of Christian life: noncarnal marriage (Blanquerna's parents abstain from sex after his birth), simple religious life (monks, nuns), the prel-acy, the papacy, and hermitism. Book 3 is structured on the eight Beatitudes, and book 4 on the 15 clauses of the *Gloria* from the Latin Mass. Other nar-ratives are structured on the Seven Deadly Sins and Ten Commandments. The novel also includes some modernist, self-reflexive references: throughout the novel, the narrator recommends certain books that happen to have been written by Lull himself — the first instance of product placement? — and in book 5 Blanquerna turns author and includes two tractates in the novel, *The Book of the Lover and the Beloved* (a Sufi-influenced marvel of displaced eroticism, with 365 sections corresponding to the year) and a précis of Lull's own immense *Art of Contemplation*. But none of this alleviates the tedium of the 500-page novel; it's a sobering study of religious extremism, a scary look at what a Christian utopia might look like, but I suspect even a Christian fundamentalist — moving her lips as her finger slowly traces the words on the page — would find it too religiose.

Leafing through other medieval hagiographies and collections like Jacobus de Varagine's *Golden Legend* (13th century) and John Foxe's blood-drenched *Book of Martyrs* (16th century), one occasionally catches glimpses of a genuine literary imagination at work, trapped in the wrong genre, though the ultimate impression is one of wasted talent on wasted lives. I suppose someone could trawl through the 383 volumes of Migne's *Patrologiae Cursus Completus* and extract some book-length hagiographies that qualify as novels — there had to be a few protonovelists who adopted hagiography as the only game in town, as painters of religious subjects learned to do — but that someone isn't me. Reading too much of this stuff can rot the brain. Much more attractive are the imaginative fictions that Columba's pagan Irish countrymen began writing down at this time.

MEDIEVAL IRISH FICTION

In 1996 Thomas Cahill published a popular book explaining *How the Irish Saved Civilization*; I don't know if I'd go that far (and I'm Scots-Irish), but one could argue the Irish saved the novel. Patrick's introduction of Christianity to Ireland in the 5th century was a mixed blessing, but it brought at least two clear benefits: the end of human sacrifice and the advancement of the new religion's official language, Latin. Irish scribes abandoned the unwieldy ogham system of writing for the more versatile Latin alphabet, and soon began supplementing the copying of theological documents with preserving Ireland's rich heritage of oral literature. Older poems, prose narratives, his-tories, genealogies, legal tracts, and glossaries were committed to parchment in the 7th and 8th centuries, and new material was composed in the 9th and 10th centuries. Though much of this material is lost, a good deal is preserved in several anthologies that were compiled later in the Middle Ages like *The Book of the Dun Cow*, *The Book of Leinster* (both 12th century), and *The Yellow Book of Lecan* (14th century). The anonymous prose tales, set in the early centuries of the Common Era, are a mélange of legend and mythology with perhaps some vestiges of actual history, and while most are short, there are a few — the best, in fact — that are the length of novellas and novels.

Unfortunately, Irish fiction didn't pick up where Greco-Roman fiction left off. Instead, the earliest Irish tales take us back to *Gilgamesh* and Genesis, with one-dimensional, larger-than-life characters and stories largely concerned with aggrandizing tribal history and accounting for the origins of place-names. As in ancient Hebrew fiction, the supernatural plays a large part: humans interact with gods and other divine beings — here, fairies (the Síde) instead of angels — and many individuals are capable of shape-shifting. What distinguishes old Irish fiction is the unabashed love of verbal decoration: as one anthologist says, "descriptive passages flower into luxuriant growths out of all proportion to their narrative importance (perhaps owing to the storyteller's showing off)."[5] It's the same "showing off" on glorious display in illuminated Irish manuscripts like the stunning *Book of Kells*, where the decorative elements overwhelm the text. For example, in the novella-length *Destruction of Da Derga's Hostel* (*Togail bruidne Da Derga*, 8th cent.?), the narrator opens his story with a two-page description of a young woman named Étaín[6] at the well:

> She had a bright silver comb with gold ornamentation on it, and she was washing from a silver vessel with four gold birds on it and bright, tiny gems of crimson carbuncle on its rims. There was a crimson cloak of beautiful, curly fleece round her, fastened with a silver broach coiled with lovely gold; . . . [115 words later:] As white as the snow of a single night her wrists; as tender and even and red as foxglove her clear, lovely cheeks. As black as a beetle's back her brows; a shower of matched pearls her teeth. Hyacinth blue her eyes; Parthian red her lips. Straight, smooth, soft and white her shoulders; pure white and tapering her fingers; long her arms. . . . [118 words later:] A gentle, womanly dignity in her voice; a steady, stately step, the walk of a queen. She was the fairest and most perfect and most beautiful of all the women in the world; men thought she was of the Side, and they said of her: "Lovely anyone until Etain. Beautiful anyone until Etain."[7]

---

5 Gantz, *Early Irish Myths and Sagas* (61), a good collection of shorter medieval Irish fiction.

6 Henceforth I'm eliminating the accents from all Irish names except for book titles because they're useless without an extensive key to Irish pronunciation. Names are spelled according to the translations I cite, which can differ from other translations.

7 Gantz 62–63; *The Destruction of Da Derga's Hostel* occupies pp. 61–106.

A Hebrew novelist wouldn't have described her at all — even the Queen of Sheba gets no face-time — and a Greek novelist would have confined himself to the final sentence or two. And she's not even a major character; the novella concerns a king named Conare who puts up at a large hostel run by Da Derga of the Lagin. While there, he is spied upon by a marauder named Ingcel Caech, who reports back to his fellow plunderers. There follows a 23-page sequence (i.e., 50 percent of the tale) in which Ingcel describes one roomful of people after another and a man named Fer Rogain explains in elaborate detail who they are and what they are capable of in battle.[8] When they finally attack the hostel, the battle is treated almost as an afterthought; it's over within two pages. Some commentators describe the Ingcel/Fer Rogain sequence as "tedious," and it does remind me of those 15-minute drum solos rock bands in the 1970s used to indulge in. But we sat through those, and this sort of showmanship in Irish fiction can be enjoyable if you're in no rush to reach the story's end.

There are similar descriptive sequences in the second-longest and most famous of medieval Irish narratives, *The Cattle Raid of Cooley* (*Táin Bó Cúalnge*, 9th/12th cent.). Again, the emphasis is on the telling rather than the tale itself, which is easily told: a proud queen of Connacht named Medb discovers she's not quite as rich as her husband, King Aillil: he owns a huge bull and she doesn't. She learns of an even better bull over in Ulster owned by Daire mac Fiachna, and sends her herald to ask Daire for a year's loan of the bull to achieve parity with her husband, offering sex along with the usual gifts. Daire agrees, but when he learns that Medb's drunken messengers boasted they would have taken the bull by force had he disagreed, he changes his mind and keeps the bull. Infuriated, Medb convinces her husband and the rest of the men of Ireland to go on a cattle raid and steal the bull and his heifers. For a season, the men of Ulster are detained by a mysterious illness, so the invading forces are held off by one 17-year-old brute, the great Ulster hero Cu Chulainn (pronounced koo-CHULL-in), a sort of Irish Achilles. Eventually the Ulstermen recover and attack the Connacht forces and defeat them. As a symbolic coda, the bull of Ulster that Medb had craved likewise attacks and defeats the bull of Connacht belonging to her husband.

It would be easy to read the *Táin* (rhymes with *coin*) as a polemic against women, if men didn't start wars for reasons as flimsy as hers. But she's clearly the villain of the piece: she ignores the warnings of both her druid and of the prophetess Feidelm (and in Irish fiction those people are never wrong); after the Gailioin tribe joins her, she fears they will show up her other allies and orders their slaughter, but her advisor and lover Fergus more reasonably

---

8 This is a standard set-piece for storytellers — there's one in book 3 of the *Iliad*, another in chapter 63 of the Icelandic *Saga of the People of Laxardal* (discussed later in this chapter) — but our Irish author pushes it to extraordinary lengths.

suggests simply dispersing them among the other tribes; she consistently underrates Cu Chulainn's abilities (and loses many of her best warriors as a result), and when he challenges her army to a series of single combats, she uses her daughter Findabair as sexual bait to attract combatants; she has pimped her daughter to numerous Ulstermen as well, and when Findabair realizes she's caused the deaths of 800 men, she literally dies of shame. Not so her mother, who brazens it out until the bloody end. Fergus contemptuously dismisses the whole mess as an example of what happens when men allow themselves to be led by a woman: "This host has been plundered and despoiled today. As when a mare goes before her band of foals into unknown territory, with none to lead or counsel them, so this host has perished today."[9] Medb shrugs off the countless deaths she has caused and returns home.[10]

Fergus is an Ulsterman and the foster-father of Cu Chulainn, but was exiled from his home and not only works for the enemy but reluctantly has to fight his foster-son at one point, exemplifying the greater theme of the *Táin*: the pain of divided loyalties. The most poignant moments in the novel are those when a character must choose between conflicting allegiances: Cu Chulainn's final single combat is against a childhood friend named Fer Diad. The first two days of their epic, three-day battle end with: "each of them went towards the other and put an arm around the other's neck and kissed him thrice" (223). But loyalty to his king trumps loyalty to his friend and Cu Chulainn kills Fer Diad in a particularly gruesome way, then delivers a noble eulogy in verse. Medb, in contrast, is loyal to no one but herself — not to her cuckolded husband, not to her allies — and for that reason (rather than for being a woman) she earns the author's contempt. Even the Morrigan, the sexy goddess of war who makes several nightmarish appearances, chooses a side and suffers for it.

The style of the *Táin* (especially in the later version) is the one Joyce identified as the technique for the Cyclops episode of *Ulysses* — gigantism. The novel starts modestly, even charmingly, with some bantering pillow-

---

9 Page 270 in Cecile O'Rahilly's translation of the *Book of Leinster* version (today known as Recension II); this was composed by a monk in the 12th century who wanted to preserve a complete, consistent version of the incomplete, inconsistent versions scattered in *The Book of the Dun Cow* and *The Yellow Book of Lecan* (Recension I). Thomas Kinsella published a splendid translation of those earlier materials, but it's a patchwork of different texts, broken up into chapters, with passages moved around or sometimes eliminated for the sake of coherence. Ciaran Carson's recent translation also follows Recension I and is similarly eclectic (though the result is excellent). The later Recension II translated by O'Rahilly is a *composed* — as opposed to an assembled — work, more stylistically daring, and more consistent with the novel form.

10 Ann Dooley defends Medb against the text's overt misogyny in chapter 6 of *Playing the Hero*; contra Fergus, she points out, "Herds led by mares are the rule not the exception, they cannot seriously be made to represent a world upside down no matter how much men try" (182).

talk between Medb and her husband, but soon come the detailed lists, the excessive use of the superlative — Medb's messengers are served the choicest food, their host is the most generous in Ulster, etc. — the baroque descriptions. Characters break into poetry to express heightened emotions; some of these passages of *retoiric* (rhetoric) are so convoluted and obscure they defy translation. The few humorous scenes are likewise hyperbolic: in a flashback concerning Cu's childhood, the warriors of Emain are terrified of the seven-year-old champion and can think of only one way to disarm him: they send 150 naked women to confront him (not one, not a handful, but an armada of nudes), and when the boy turns his head in embarrassment, they grab him and dip him in three different vats "to quench the ardour of his wrath" (171). All of Cu Chulainn's actions are described in Paul Bunyanesque terms that make him sound more like a comic-book superhero than an epic figure. For example, when enraged he goes into a "warp-spasm" similar to Dr. Bruce Banner's transformation into the Incredible Hulk:

Then his first distortion came upon Cu Chulainn so that he became horrible, many-shaped, strange and unrecognisable. His haunches shook about him like a tree in a current or a bulrush against a stream, every limb and every joint, every end and every member of him from head to foot. He performed a wild feat of contortion with his body inside his skin. His feet and his shins and his knees came to the back; his heels and his calves and his hams came to the front. The sinews of his calves came on the front of his shins and each huge, round knot of them was as big as a warrior's fist. The sinews of his head were stretched to the nape of his neck and every huge, immeasurable, vast, incalculable round ball of them was as big as the head of a month-old child. Then his face became a red hollow. He sucked one of his eyes into his head so that a wild crane could hardly have reached it to pluck it out from the back of his skull on to the middle of his cheek. The other eye sprang out on to his cheek. His mouth was twisted back fearsomely. He drew the cheek back from the jawbone until his inner gullet was seen. His lungs and his liver fluttered in his mouth and his throat. He struck a lion's blow with the upper palate on its fellow so that every stream of fiery flakes which came into his mouth from his throat was as large as the skin of a three-year-old sheep. The loud beating of his heart against his ribs was heard like the baying of a bloodhound or like a lion attacking bears. The torches of the war-goddess, the virulent rain-clouds, the sparks of blazing fire were seen in the clouds and in the air above his head with the seething of fierce rage that rose above him. His hair curled about his head like branches of red hawthorn used to re-fence the gap in a hedge. Though a noble apple-tree weighed down with fruit had been shaken about his hair, scarcely one apple would have reached the ground through it but an apple would have stayed impaled on each single hair because of the fierce bristling of his hair above him. The hero's light rose from his forehead so that it was as long and as thick as a hero's whetstone. As high, as thick, as strong, as powerful and as long as the mast of a great ship was the straight stream of dark blood which rose up from the very top of his head and became a dark magical mist like the smoke of a palace when a king comes to be attended to in the evening of a wintry day. (201–2)[11]

(Wild applause.) He is so strong that he *picks up* a chariot and whales on the enemy with it until it's down to a broken wheel. Fergus is so furious that he deflects his wrath from his fellow Ulstermen and lops off the tops of three hills instead. The battle scenes are *Clash of the Titans* extravaganzas that cry out for a heavy-metal soundtrack to match the author's verbal special effects. The whole thing is at once garish and magnificent, which seems also to be the scribe's conflicted assessment. At the end of the manuscript, he writes (in Irish), "A blessing on every one who shall faithfully memorise the *Táin* as it is written here and shall not add any other form to it," then adds (in Latin), "But I who have written this story, or rather this fable, give no credence to the various incidents related in it. For some things in it are the deceptions of demons, others poetic figments; some are probable, others improbable; while still others are intended for the delectation of foolish men." The Irish short-story writer Frank O'Connor called the *Táin* "a simply appalling text, which I cannot fully read much less interpret" in *The Backward Look* (though he goes on to devote an insightful chapter to it), but I prefer the judgment of the *Táin*'s most recent translator (himself a fine novelist): "In its abrupt shifts from laconic brutality to moments of high poetry and deep pathos, from fantastic and vividly imagined description to darkly obscure utterance, from tragedy to black humour, it has no parallel in Irish literature, with the possible exception of another multilayered, polyphonic tale, James Joyce's *Ulysses*" (xx–xxi).

The *Táin* and *The Destruction of Da Derga's Hostel* both belong to what is now called the Ulster Cycle of medieval Irish literature, much of which deals with Cu Chulainn. The Fenian Cycle deals with the legendary exploits of Finn mac Cumaill; if Cu is the Irish Achilles, Finn is their King Arthur, a noble, generous, fearless leader of a band of warriors called the Fiana, less pompous counterparts to the Knights of the Round Table. (Finn may or may not be historical — one Irish chronicler said he died in the year 283 — but such warrior bands actually existed in medieval Ireland.) The longest work of the Fenian cycle is the *Acallam na Senórach*, traditionally known as *The Colloquy of the Ancients* but most recently translated as *Tales of the Elders of Ireland*.[12] Composed around 1175 by an anonymous scribe, it's an

---

11 This provides a convenient example of the stylistic differences between Recension II (translated here) and Recension I: in Carson's translation, this passage is only eight lines long (37–38). In his introduction, he writes that Recension II "has a florid and prolix style less congenial to modern taste than the laconic force of Recension I" (xiv). Not to all tastes, my boyo.

12 Translated by Ann Dooley and Harry Roe in 1999, surprisingly the first complete English translation of this major Irish work (hereafter cited by page number). But wait till I tell you. No sooner did this appear than — like Manhattan buses — a second translation showed

ethereal, convoluted narrative that moves effortlessly between paganism and Christianity, between the human and the supernatural. Years after the death of the great Finn, two of his followers named Oisin (one of Finn's sons) and Cailte are wandering despondently through the east of Erin with a few bedraggled survivors of the Fiana, mourning

> with drooping head
> Companions long accurst and dead,
> And hounds for centuries dust and air.[13]

After visiting Finn's old nurse, Oisin and Cailte separate, the son to the north to visit his mother — one of the otherworldy Tuatha De Danaan — and old Cailte to the south, where he soon runs into Patrick, who is in the process of converting the Irish to Christianity. Born in Roman Britain and taken to Ireland as a slave, Patrick doesn't know the country very well, and after baptizing Cailte begins asking him the meaning of various place-names, which invariably are named after some exploit of the Fiana. As the two travel through Ireland, Cailte relates the stories behind every place they visit, yielding a hundred or so anecdotes; eventually they link up with Oisin, who tells similar tales, resulting in a rich anthology of old Irish literature. Critic Gerald Murphy compared "the *Acallam* to a reservoir into which a brilliant late-twelfth-century innovator had diverted several streams of tradition which previously had normally flowed in separate channels; for in the *Acallam* folk motifs, mythological motifs, warrior motifs, *senchus* (history) and *dinnshenchus*, lyric poetry, ballad poetry, and learned poetry, are found harmoniously united in a single whole" (25).

But the *Acallam* is more than a mulligan stew of etiological anecdotes: there's a contemporary work called the *Dinnshenchus Érenn* (The Place-lore of Ireland) that is little more than that, and for that reason is of interest today only to antiquarians. Linking all these anecdotes are several overarching narrative lines: the rivalry between Finn and Goll mac Morna, another Fiana leader; the education of a musician named Cas Corach; the romantic story of Cael and Crede; the story of Aed, a king's son miraculously restored to life by Patrick; and other tales and themes that weave in and out of the shorter narratives. The author employs a technique known in Arthurian criticism as *entrelacement*, which consists "of the regular suspension of one story line to pick up one or more others; when those are in turn suspended, the text may take up another narrative or return to the original one to elaborate it further,

---

up: Maurice Harmon's *Colloquy of the Old Men*. The Dooley/Roe is more scholarly, the Harmon more readable.

13 From Yeats's "The Wanderings of Oisin" (1889), a dialogue between Oisin and Patrick similar to (but apparently not directly based on) those in the *Acallam*.

again dropping it one or several times before tying it up with others."[14] Some tales are paired with others on the same theme, and most of them are followed by a summary in verse. (These poems were apparently the inspiration for the prose tales, but the author chose to retain them, despite their redundancy in most cases.) The effect is very musical, with themes and variations and repeats, which is appropriate given the exalted place music enjoys in the *Acallam*: its bards and musicians are not mere entertainers but one grade away from divine beings. Even Patrick blesses them even as he admits they distract him from his religious duties.

Patrick is enchanted by the Fenian tales, and it's this ecumenical spirit that makes the *Acallam* a refreshing change from most colonialist narratives. In much Christian literature there's a tendency to demonize pagans and their gods, but Patrick (that is, our 12th-century Catholic author) not only respects them but treats the transition from druidism to Christianity as merely a gentlemanly changing of the guard, not a triumph over the heathens. In a metafictional gesture, Patrick instructs his scribe to write down the various tales Cailte and Oisin share with him — compare his book-burning brothers in Christ around the Mediterranean — and is even encouraged in this decision by his guardian angels, Aibelan and Solusbrethach, who instruct Patrick (presumably in an Irish brogue): "Have these stories written down on poets' tablets in refined language, so that the hearing of them will provide entertainment for the lords and commons of later times" (12). Patrick's miracles are treated no differently than the miraculous feats of the Fenians, and in fact Cailte and Patrick assist each other with miracles in stark contrast to the bitter contests of dueling magicians one reads about in the Bible, the *Acts of Peter*, and other ideologically strident works.

The range of characters is also ecumenical in its breadth: humans like Patrick and his followers intermingle with the giant Fenians — the author literalizes their heroic stature by making them twice the size of humans — just as the Fenians intermingle with mermaids, miniature people (like Finn's harpist Cnu Deroil and his doll-size wife), a 50-foot woman named Be Binn, female werewolves, and especially with the Tuatha De Danaan ("Ana's people," after the goddess of pre-Christian Ireland), immortal beings who live beneath fairy mounds but who often interact with mortals, like the angels of Hebrew mythology. While the author of the *Tales of the Elders* was clearly a Christian, he discriminates against nobody and, in fact, clearly admires the old Ireland of heroic legend, romanticizing it in much the same way Yeats and other brooding revelers in the Celtic Twilight would at the end of the 19th century.

Nevertheless, Christianity emerges as the dominant power at the end of the novel, when Patrick performs the first Christian wedding in Ireland. The

---

14 Lacy, *The Lancelot-Grail Reader*, xi.

bride and groom are bedecked with symbolism: Aed, the young man Patrick had brought to life (i.e., he died to paganism and was reborn in Christ), has become king of Connaught and is married to the king of Leinster's daughter, the intriguingly named Aife Ilchrothach ("of Many Shapes"). Aed is later approached by a beautiful woman of the Tuatha De Danaan with another intriguing name, Aillenn Fhialchorca ("of the Purple Veil"). In swinging old Ireland, there wouldn't be a problem, especially since Aed and Aife have grown apart. But now that he is an Irish Catholic, Aed can neither divorce Aife nor take Aillenn as a mistress (much less engage in a *ménage à trois*): the Christian way is for all three to live in misery. "Aillenn went off to her *síd* [her fairy mound residence] after that, and remained there until the story alludes to her again" (181) is the author's odd way of putting it, as though she were an actress waiting in the wings, smoking a cigarette, until her next entrance. (There are several such passages, reminding us that this isn't a story but a *performance* of a story, similar to what a bard may have performed for the royal court.) As it happens, Aed's first wife dies eventually, and patient Aillenn takes the stage again; after Patrick extracts a promise from her to forsake "her false and druidical belief and [do] homage to the Gospel of the King of Heaven and of Earth" (217), the Adze-Head (as Patrick is affectionately known) weds Aed to Aillenn, who gives up her immor(t)ality to bind herself to a mor(t)al man. This priggish submission to ecclesiastical authority would eventually grip Ireland in the "spiritual paralysis" Joyce and other Irish writers will rail against eight centuries later. As though sensing this, our conflicted author can't help but follow the wedding ceremony with a few more wondrous tales of pre-Christian Ireland before the manuscript breaks off.

The conflict between paganism and Christainity is also at the heart of the strangest and most fascinating of medieval Irish novellas, a work from the Historical Cycle called *The Frenzy of Suibhne (Buile Suibhne)*. Like the *Acallam*, it was composed in the 12th century but is based on earlier material and is likewise a mixture of prose and poetry. But rather than tacking poems at the end of his prose vignettes, often redundantly, as the *Acallam* author did, the more sophisticated author of the *Buile Suibhne* integrates poetry into his narrative as an organic product of his protagonist's development.

The Frenzy of Suibhne is actually the third of a trilogy of novellas inspired by the battle of Magh Rath (Moira) in 637; as stories accrued over the centuries, three writers in the 12th century compiled them into linked narratives that, together, constitute one of the most dazzling novels in medieval literature.[15] The first, *The Banquet of Dun na n-Gedh (Fleadh Duin na n-Gedh)*

---

15 The first two parts were published in 1842 in a bilingual edition by John O'Donovan as *The Banquet of Dun na n-Gedh and The Battle of Magh Rath: An Ancient Historical Tale* (which I'll be citing by page number). *Buile Suibhne* follows *The Battle of Magh Rath* in at least one manuscript, but the only book that prints the three together is an anthology I

is a fanciful account of the causes of the battle. Mixing historical figures like King Domhnall of Ireland (ruled c. 628–42) and his rebellious foster-son Congal Claen with gigantic apparitions, prophetic dreams, magic stones, and mysterious strangers who turn out to be long-lost sons, the author tells how King Domhnall constructed a new palace at Dun na n-Gedh on the banks of the Boyne river and then threw a lavish banquet, ostensibly to celebrate its completion but in reality to collect hostages from all the tribes of Ireland in response to a dream that warned they would soon rise up against him. Eager to have every kind of food, the king sends his people out to procure goose eggs, rare that time of year, which they confiscate from Bishop Erc of Sliane. The bishop spends his day "immersed in the Boinn, up to his two arm-pits, from morning till evening, having his Psalter before him on the strand, constantly engaged in prayer" (19); after a hard day's worship he likes to dine on an egg and a half, and so curses anyone who eats of his stolen eggs. (A saint had cursed Domhnall's royal residence at Tara, which is why he had to relocate, and another saint curses Suibhne with madness; holy men in these tales are akin to irritable sorcerers.) At the banquet, Congal's goose egg is magically transformed into a hen's egg, which he takes as the latest in a long series of insults from his foster-father, and so sweeps off in a rage and goes to Scotland to raise an army. Sounds silly, I know, but it's a beautifully told tale and whets our appetite for the battle to follow

The next novella, *The Battle of Magh Rath* (*Cath Muighe Rath*), is the longest of the three and a rhetorical tour de force. While the *Banquet* begins "Once upon a time," appropriately enough, the *Battle* begins with a complex "proem" combining literary theory with theology and philosophy, in which the author promises not merely a historical account but a bravura rhetorical performance of this "excellent, mighty-worded battle." And while the *Banquet* is narrated in relatively straightforward prose (for the Irish), the mighty-worded *Battle* contains sentences like this one:

Ah me! it were easy for one acquainted or unacquainted with Erin to travel and frequent her at this period, in consequence of the goodness of her laws, the tranquility of her hosts, the serenity of her seasons, the splendour of her chieftains, the justice of her Brehons, the regularity of her troops, the talents of her Olaves, the genius of her poets, the various musical powers of her minstrels, the botanical skill of her physicians, the art of her braziers, the useful workmanship of her smiths, and the handicraft of her carpenters; in consequence of the mild bashfulness of her maidens, the strength and prowess of her lords, the generosity and hospitality of her good Brughaidhs [*victuallers*]; for her Brughaidhs were generous and had abundance of food and kine; her habitations were hospitable, spacious, and open for company and entertainment to remove the hunger and gloom of guests; so that authors

---

once edited, *Medieval Epics and Sagas*, where they appear under the collective title *The Battle of Magh Rath* on pp. 431–572.

record that one woman might travel Erin alone without fear of being violated or molested, though there should be no witnesses to guard her (if she were not afraid of the imputations of slander) from the well-known Osgleann, in Umhall, in the west of the province of Connaught, to the celebrated remarkable rock of Carraic Eoghainn, in the east [*of Erin*], and from the fair-surfaced, woody, grassy-green island of Inis Fail, exactly in the south of Banba [*Ireland*] of the fair margin, to the furious, headlong, foaming, boisterous cascade of Buadh, which is the same as the clear-watered, snowy-foamed, ever-roaring, particoloured, bellowing, in-salmon-abounding, beautiful old torrent, whose celebrated, well-known name is the lofty-great, clear-landed, contentious, precipitate, loud-roaring, headstrong, rapid, salmon-ful, sea-monster-ful, varying, in-large-fish-abounding, rapid-flooded, furious-streamed, whirling, in-seal-abounding, royal, and prosperous cataract of EAS RUAIDH, and thence northwards by Teinne Bec an Broghadh, or by the great plain of Madh Ininnrighe, to the loud-roaring, water-shooting cliffs of Tory. (103–7, O'Donovan's brackets)

I think that's bloody brilliant; note how it moves from civil order to wild nature and imitates the noisy cataract with a riot of compound adjectives and epithets. It presages Rabelais's gargantuan catalogs, Lyly's euphonious prose, even Shakespeare's munificent "art of surfeit,"[16] but some (like translator O'Donovan) find such passages tautological and turgid. Whatever. Our flamboyant author continues in this vein as he describes the six-day battle in Homeric detail, inserting numerous poems in a variety of lengths and meters and displaying his remarkable erudition: not only does he allude to earlier Irish works but he quotes from Pliny's *Natural History* and evokes figures from Greek mythology. In this Irish *Iliad*, Congal Claen plays the part of Achilles — angry and petulant, valiant but doomed — and while no gods take part, supernatural phenomena accompany the epic battle. *The Cattle Raid of Cooley* is usually hailed as Ireland's national epic, but I think *The Battle of Magh Rath* has a greater claim to that honor.

A brief account is given in the *Battle* of the madness that overcame one of its participants, a minor king named Suibhne (Anglicized Sweeney), but in the sublime *Frenzy of Suibhne* we are given the full story. It begins just before the conflict when Suibhne is alarmed to learn that a cleric named Ronan is marking the boundaries for a future church in his territory. Suibhne's wife grabs at his cloak in an attempt to restrain him as he rushes out of his house, but he slips out of the cloak to confront the cleric in the nude. The naked pagan seizes the (clothed) Christian's Psalter and throws it into the lake and grabs Ronan intending violence when a messenger pops up to summon him to the upcoming battle at Magh Rath. Suibhne abandons Ronan, who is so insulted that he curses him: "Be it my will, together with the will of the mighty Lord, that even as he came stark-naked to expel me, may it be thus

---

16 As Stephen Dedalus calls it in *Ulysses* (9:626) by way of Walt Whitman, which of course doubles as Joyce's description of his own style.

that he will ever be, naked, wandering and flying throughout the world."[17] On the battlefield, Suibhne is struck with madness and flies off like a bird, flitting from treetop to treetop, and wanders throughout Ireland for the next seven years as an outcast. (The author is vague on whether Suibhne is actually transformed into a bird or just thinks he's one; according to O'Donovan, the Irish used to believe "that lunatics are as light as feathers, and can climb steeps and precipices like the Somnabulists" [*sic*, 234].) He eventually regains his reason and tries to return to his people, but Ronan, fearing further persecution, sends some headless apparitions to frighten Suibhne off. He finally finds refuge at the monastery of a more enlightened cleric named Moling, who records Suibhne's fantastic story and baptizes him, and then gives him a Christian burial after he dies as the final result of unforgiving Ronan's original curse.

Although the author was apparently a Christian, he was less concerned (if at all) with telling an edifying sermon about the conversion of a pagan — remember the lesson we learned from Apuleius's *Golden Ass*, another tale of transformation — than with exploring the relationship between madness, exile, and art. After Suibhne is struck mad and exiled, he begins to create art — some of the most beautiful poems in medieval literature — and the author seems to suggest the artist is someone who needs to separate himself from others to create art, and that the masses will likely interpret his devotion to art as a form of madness. Note how at the moment Suibhne goes "mad" his imagination begins to soar:

Now, when Suibhne heard these great [battle] cries together with their sounds and reverberations in the clouds of Heaven and in the vault of the firmament, he looked up, whereupon turbulence, and darkness, and fury, and giddiness, and frenzy, and flight, unsteadiness, restlessness, and unquiet filled him, likewise disgust with every place in which he used to be *and desire for every place which he had not reached.* His fingers were palsied, his feet trembled, his heart beat quick, his senses were overcome, his sight was distorted, his weapons fell naked from his hands, so that through Ronan's curse he went, like any bird of the air, in madness and imbecility. (11, my italics)

If I didn't know better, I'd swear Shakespeare had this passage in mind when he made his famous equation of the madman and the poet:

17 From the old O'Keeffe translation, section 5 (hereafter cited by section). Flann O'Brien adapted this translation for his abridged version in *At Swim-Two-Birds* (1939), anglicizing many names and exaggerating the medieval Irish love of alliteration ("he was beleaguered by an anger and a darkness, and fury and fits and frenzy and fright-fraught fear" [62]). Seamus Heaney's *Sweeney Astray* (1983) is a masterful translation of the *Buile Suibhne* as far as it goes, but the poet admits he eliminated many stanzas of poetry, "occasionally abbreviated the linking narrative and in places have used free verse to render the more heightened prose passages" (vii). Reluctantly, then, I'll be quoting O'Keeffe's dated but more faithful translation.

The lunatic, the lover, and the poet
Are of imagination all compact.
One sees more devils than vast hell can hold:
That is the madman. The lover, all as frantic,
Sees Helen's beauty in a brow of Egypt.
The poet's eye, in a fine frenzy rolling,
Doth glance from heaven to earth, from earth to heaven,
And as imagination bodies forth
The forms of things unknown, the poet's pen
Turns them to shapes, and gives to airy nothing
A local habitation and a name.

(*A Midsummer Night's Dream*, 5.1.7–17)

As Suibhne wanders in exile, his "poet's eye, in a fine frenzy rolling," allows him to see his countryside in a new way and to witness the travails of other outcasts, resulting in poems on nature and the human condition that would never have occurred to him in his previous state. "Much Madness is divinest Sense — / To a discerning eye," Emily Dickinson assures us, and while a conventional mind would interpret Suibhne's situation as that of a sinner undergoing purgation to achieve Christian holiness, a discerning eye sees a portrait of the artist. As Heaney writes in the introduction to his translation, "it is possible to read the work as an aspect of the quarrel between free creative imagination and the constraints of religious, political, and domestic obligation" (vi), a quarrel as contentious today as it was in 12th-century Ireland. Ask Salman Rushdie, or any woman artist yearning for a room of her own.

At one point Suibhne travels to England, where he encounters another "madman" named Ealladhan, who explains he was pronounced mad merely because of his aesthetic eye for fashion:

> "Once upon a time [note the conversion of experience to artistic narration with that literary opening] two kings were contending for the sovereignty of this country, . . . There was then convened a great assembly to give battle to each other concerning the country. I put *geasa* [spells] on each one of my lord's people that none of them should come to the battle except they were clothed in silk, so that they might be conspicuous beyond all for pomp and pride. The hosts gave three shouts of malediction on me, which sent me wandering and fleeing as you see." (48)

The poet and the couturier spend a year together until Ealladhan is drowned in a waterfall, leaving Suibhne alone again. His laments on such themes as loss, loneliness, and exile and his gorgeous poems praising nature (you'll want Heaney's translation for those) are obviously not the mumblings of a madman but affecting poems composed with rigorous artistry,[18] yet he is kept at arm's length by those he encounters. (Miss Dickinson continues: "'Tis the Majority / In this, as All, prevail — / Assent — and you are sane — / Demur — you're straightway dangerous — / And handled with a Chain —") Even though Suibhne eventually capitulates by returning to Ireland and becoming a Christian, even the cleric who baptizes and buries him realizes Suibhne's religious conversion is nothing compared to his artistic achievement, and like Patrick in the *Acallam* makes sure Suibhne's story is preserved for the ages.

The last medieval Irish fiction of any length is another Fenian novella written during this same period, *The Pursuit of Diarmaid and Gráinne* (*Tóruigheacht Dhiarmada agus Ghráinne*), which is not only one of the finest specimens of medieval Irish literature but closest to what we now consider a novel. This was recognized as far back as 1897; in an enthusiastic lecture given in March of that year, scholar Padriac Pearse proudly proclaimed: "The *Tóruigheacht Dhiarmada agus Ghráinne* is neither more or less than a novel — a novel with a regular and most artfully contrived, yet perfectly natural, plot. It is, as a matter of fact, one of the greatest and one of the most interesting historical novels ever written."[19] The basic story comes from an older tale in the Ulster Cycle entitled "The Exile of the Sons of Uisliu," concerning the fabled Irish heroine Deirdre. Witnessing her birth, a druid predicts many men will die on account of her great beauty; she is raised by King Conchubar to be his concubine, but when she comes of age she falls in love with a handsome young man named Noisiu and convinces him to elope with her. He and his companions are eventually killed and she returned to the old king, but she refuses to have anything to do with him and kills herself at the first opportunity.[20]

In *Diarmaid and Gráinne*, Finn mac Cumaill is now a lonely widower looking for a new wife, and likes what he hears about Grainne, the daughter of Cormac, high king of all Ireland. She agrees to marry Finn sight unseen, trusting her father's judgment, but she is shocked when she meets Finn and realizes he is even older than her father. But one of Finn's companions catches her eye, the dashing Diarmaid o Duibhne, so Grainne prepares and

---

18 Of one of the longest, Myles Dillon says of the original: "This poem of sixty-five quatrains is in a bold meter, lines of seven syllables ending in a trisyllabic word alternating with lines of five syllables ending in a monosyllable, and the meter is well handled" (98).

19 "Gaelic Prose Literature," to be found in his collected works as one of *Three Lectures on Gaelic Topics*. Only 18 when he delivered this lecture, Pearse showed special enthusiasm for the battle scenes in the *Táin*, which he compared to Homer's and which perhaps led eventually to his becoming commander-in-chief of the Irish forces in the failed Easter Rebellion in 1916. He was shot by a British firing squad.

20 The original story can be found in Gantz's anthology (257–67) and among the preliminary tales in Kinsella's translation of the *Táin* (8–20) but is best known from modern play versions by Yeats and Synge and from James Stephens's lovely novel *Deirdre* (1923). It also parallels the Tristan and Iseut story.

passes around a potent drink that puts all but Oisin and Diarmaid to sleep. She offers her love to each in turn, but both refuse to accept someone promised to Finn. She then puts a *geis* on Diarmaid — a weird combination of taboo, spell, and debt of honor — and since no Irishman dares violate a *geis*, Diarmaid reluctantly leaves with the scheming lass. After waking from the drink and realizing what has happened, a jealous and insulted Finn gathers the Fiana and goes in pursuit of the outlaws.

We're back in legendary, pre-Christian Ireland, and, as in the *Táin*, divided loyalties provide much of the drama. Diarmaid is torn between his loyalty to Finn and his obligation to Grainne and is so conflicted that he resignedly waits in his first hiding place for Finn to find and kill him; Diarmaid's companions are likewise torn between their loyalty to their friend and to their chieftan and try to persuade Finn to desist even as they help him surround Diarmaid. When he realizes Finn is being unjust, self-preservation and defiance kick in as Diarmaid boldly kisses Grainne three times in front of Finn and the Fiana before making a spectacular escape. Aside from those kisses, Diarmaid has nothing to do with the troublemaker; they sleep apart in their various hideouts and he pointedly refuses to carry her when she's tired. Fortunately for her, they soon meet a young man named Muadhan, who is eager to serve as Diarmaid's retainer, and he shoulders the sweet burden.

It's fascinating to watch the anonymous author blend older, adventure-story exploits in this portion of the novella with more modern concerns with characterization. Diarmaid's various battles are both fabulous and a little ludicrous — he tricks Finn's allies into killing themselves by rolling on a barrel and balancing on a spear tip, influences a chess game by tossing berries from a treetop on the chess pieces, fights a one-eyed giant guarding a magical tree, and tells a tall tale of a hundred-headed snake[21] — but his relations with Grainne are quite realistic. The author establishes her duplicitous nature early on; she has to ask who Diarmaid is when she sees him at Finn's gathering, but after asking Oisin first to elope with her, she tells Diarmaid that she had fallen in love with him once while watching him at a hurling match. (Diarmaid doesn't fall for this improvised story.) They are both rather annoyed with each other at first and snipe at each other but she nearly faints with joy when Diarmaid escapes a close call; she nags and taunts him, but then asks to borrow his knife to trim her nails with domestic familiarity. And she instigates one of the most famous seduction scenes in Irish fiction with a daring use of semen imagery:

---

21 These last two incidents recall two of the 12 labors of Hercules — killing both the dragon that guards the tree of the Hesperides and the Lernaean Hydra — which the author must have known from one source or another.

Grainne was getting tired, and when she realised that she had no man to carry her except Diarmaid, since Muadhan parted from her, she gained courage and a lively spirit and she began to walk boldly by Diarmaid's side until an errant little splash of water sprang up beside her leg, so she said:

"Diarmaid," said she, "though your valour and your bravery be great in conflicts and in battle-places I think myself that that little drop of errant water is more daring than you are."

"That is true, Grainne," said Diarmaid, "though I have been for a long time keeping myself from you through fear of Fionn I will not suffer myself to be reproached by you any longer; and it is hard to trust women," he said. And it was then for the first time that Diarmaid o Duibhne of the bright-tooth made a wife of Grainne, daughter of the king of Ireland.[22]

But like Deirdre and Queen Medb, Grainne brings destruction to countless men, including Diarmaid. After Finn loses hundreds of warriors in the pursuit, he reluctantly makes a truce with Diarmaid, who then settles down with Grainne and fathers five children over the next 16 years. They seem set to live happily ever after when Grainne once again stirs things up by inviting Diarmaid's two worst enemies — her father Cormac and Finn, still resentful — for a visit in an attempt at reconciliation. Henpecked Diarmaid reluctantly agrees, and one day runs in to Finn alone on a hill, where the bitter old man informs him that Diarmaid's life is magically bound with that of a wild boar on the rampage nearby; nevertheless, Diarmaid suicidally kills the boar just after it mortally wounds him. Finn taunts him mercilessly in a way grimly satisfying to any older man who has lost a lover to a young stud: "'I like to see you like that, Diarmaid,' said he, 'and I regret that all the women of Ireland are not looking at you now, for your beauty is turned to ugliness and your good form to deformity'" (91). And then the author makes a brilliant move: Finn possesses the magical ability to cure Diarmaid if he chooses, so Diarmaid pleads for his life by reminding Finn of his long service to him. The author chose to wait until a few pages before the end of the novella to fill in the backstory of their relationship — Diarmaid tells the heroic tale of how he saved Finn from attacks by "the King of the World and the three kings of Inis Tile" — which makes Finn's final act all the more heartless. Finn need only bring some water cupped in his hands from a nearby well to save Diarmaid, and after first pretending he's unaware of any well, he makes two slow trips and allows the water to run through his hands; during his third

22 Page 47 in Nessa Ní Shéaghdha's translation. For such a famous tale, there aren't many translations (as opposed to adaptations) to choose from. Aside from this fusty but reliable 1967 translation from the antiquarian Irish Texts Society, the only other modern one I could find is in Cross and Slover's 1936 *Ancient Irish Tales* (370–421), which omits this crucial scene. As my notes indicate, medieval Irish fiction is sore in need of fresh translations. (Yes, I'm looking at you, Penguin and Oxford University Press.)

trip, Diarmaid expires. The dramatic conjunction of Diarmaid's dying speech and Finn's brutal act was a stroke of genius on the author's part and heightens the tragedy of Diarmaid's death. When Grainne learns the news she suffers a miscarriage, and though hundreds have already died because of her initial decision to leave Finn at the altar, she gathers her children around her and urges further destruction in a grim poem ending

> Kill women and children
> to spite Fionn of the Fiana
> do not do treachery or deceit,
> make strife and arise. (105)

There the definitive Ní Shéaghdha translation ends; the Cross and Slover translation follows a different manuscript that has Finn comfort and seduce the bereaved widow à la Shakespeare's Richard III and Lady Anne, ending with a rather humiliating marriage. Either way, it's a morally complex story, leaving open the question of whether Grainne is a villain responsible for countless deaths out of a selfish reluctance to marry the man her father chose for her (per the custom of the day), or a heroine who fights for her right of self-determination with the only weapons at her disposal: beauty and brains. We despise old Finn, pity poor Diarmaid, but remain awed by Grainne, daughter of the king of Ireland.

Many Irish writers of this period refer to the Otherworld, "a realm beyond the senses, usually a delightful place, not knowable to ordinary mortals without an invitation from a denizen."[23] This is the fairy realm, the land of the eternally young Tuatha De Danaan. Thinking of the scribes who composed the works I've discussed in this section, and of how boring their daily lives must have been aside from the occasional Viking raid, I've come to realize that their literature is the true Otherworld, these artists the denizens who invite us in to peer through the windows of Da Dergal's hostel, to fight with Cu Chulainn, to listen wide-eyed to the tales of the elders and to the poems of mad Sweeney, to live on the run with Grainne in the caves and bee-loud glades of old Ireland. The Otherworld is the collected works of the literary imagination, and lucky we mortals who are invited to enter and dwell there.

MEDIEVAL ICELANDIC FICTION

While some Vikings were terrorizing Ireland and destroying books, Vikings of the better sort settled in Iceland and eventually began writing books. Icelandic literature developed much as Irish literature did: oral tales circulated for the

---

23 MacKillop's *Dictionary of Celtic Mythology*, 359 — an extremely useful reference book.

first 130 years, from around 870 when the first settlers arrived until around 1000, when they converted to Christianity. As in Ireland, Christianity brought literacy, and some Icelandic writers began committing to vellum their myths, histories, and legal codes. Beginning in the 13th century, certain innovators began giving literary form to the old stories about life in pre-Christian Iceland in the form of "sagas" (from the verb *sagja*, "say, tell"), narratives based on family histories but arranged like tales. In doing so, Icelandic writers basically invented the social realist novel, some 600 years before Balzac introduced the genre in continental Europe. A hundred or so sagas and tales survive from the 13th and 14th centuries. Most of them are short stories ranging from a few pages to 40 in length, but there are also about a dozen novellas (i.e., in the 40–70-page range) and a half-dozen book-length works, which are rightly considered the crowning achievements of the genre. It is this last group I'd like to look at in order to give them their long overdue place in the history of the novel.

But before turning to those realistic novels, I want first to sing the praises of a gloriously unrealistic Icelandic novella, *The Saga of the Volsungs* (*Völsunga saga*), which may or may not be the first of the sagas to be written but is certainly based on the oldest materials.[24] Like much medieval Irish fiction, it is mostly in prose but contains some poetry — the original sources for the tale — and doesn't distinguish between the natural realm and the supernatural, or between history and legend. It's a primal, rough-hewn work, but it contains powerfully symbolic episodes that would be adopted centuries later by Richard Wagner for his four-part opera *The Ring of the Nibelung*, which draws more from it than from the *Nibelungenlied*, and by J. R. R. Tolkein for *The Lord of the Rings*, which is steeped in Norse mythology. Although *The Saga of the Volsungs* takes place entirely in continental Europe, it deals with the Icelanders' oldest myths while introducing the multigenerational family saga that would dominate their medieval fiction.

The central story will be familiar to those who know Wagner's *Ring*: Sigmund and Signy (Wagner's Siegmund and Sieglinde) are siblings, the offspring of King Volsung, the progenitor for whom the saga is named. Sigmund eventually fathers Sigurd (Siegfried), who slays the gold-hoarding dragon Fafnir and rescues the valkyrie Brynhild, a sleeping beauty enclosed in a wall of flames. He promises to marry her, but before he can do so he is drugged and tricked into marrying Gudrun (Gutrune); Brynhild reluctantly marries Gudrun's brother Gunnar (Gunther) and later urges him to kill Sigurd in revenge; remorseful, she commits suicide by joining Sigurd on his flaming funeral pyre.

---

24 Translator Jesse Byock guesses it was written sometime between 1200 and 1270; the bulk of Icelandic sagas were composed in the century between 1225 and 1325, though none of them can be dated precisely.

But this is only half the story. Like the Hebrew Tanakh, *The Saga of the Volsungs* begins in myth but eventually resembles recorded history, namely, the tumultuous 4th and 5th centuries in central Europe. (Attila the Hun [d. 453] is a character in the last part of the saga.) It begins with an episode that recalls Cain's murder of Abel: a son of the Norse god Odin named Sigi goes out hunting one day with a slave named Bredi, who bags more game than Sigi. "He said he wondered that a thrall should outdo him in hunting. For this reason he attacked and killed Bredi and then disposed of the corpse by burying it in a snowdrift."[25] Like Cain, Sigi tries to conceal the murder but is soon found out and banished; but instead of being punished by his heavenly father, Sigi is spirited out of the country, given troops and warships, and eventually becomes king of Hunland. He marries and produces a son named Rerir, but his in-laws become envious of the king and kill him. As soon as Rerir is able, he revenges his father's death by wiping out his maternal uncles, even though the act violates familial bonds. Within two pages, then, all the major themes of the saga are set in play: jealousy, inequality, violence, and conflicting loyalties. Variations on these themes generate the plot of the novella, the act of that first murder setting in motion a curse that will last several generations.

Volsung is born in the same miraculous manner as many biblical and mythical figures. Rerir's barren wife prays to the gods for a son, and Odin responds not with an angel but a "wish-maiden," who assumes the shape of a crow and drops a fertility-inducing apple into the king's lap, who then shares it with his queen. A six-*year* pregnancy follows before the exhausted woman gives birth to Volsung, by which time Rerir has died. Not surprisingly, the queen dies after giving birth, but the orphan nevertheless becomes king of Hunland eventually. Volsung then marries Hljod, the wish-maiden who had provided the apple responsible for his birth; she grants wishes easily and they quickly produce 10 sons and one daughter, including the above-mentioned Sigmund and Signy. All this happens in the *first three pages*; as the author progresses, he'll learn to slow down and spend more time showing than telling, provide more motivation, and flesh out the skeletal poetry on which he based his story.

When Volsung gives his daughter Signy in marriage to a king named Siggeir (*sig-* is an Old Norse prefix meaning "victory" and appears in many names), it is the first of many unwanted marriages in the novella; like Deirdre and Grainne, nearly every bride in *The Saga of the Volsungs* marries under duress and expresses her resentment by betraying her husband and/or killing their children. Alliances are thus unwisely made and broken, mirroring the unstable political conditions in Europe in the early Middle Ages, where the

---

25 Chap. 1 in Byock's fine translation, hereafter cited by chapter. Unlike medieval Irish literature, the Icelandic sagas have been translated often into English and are readily available in a variety of editions.

personal was the political. After Siggeir is slighted by Sigmund, his army attacks and kills Sigmund's father Volsung, which is all Signy needs to plot her husband's death with her brother's help. There follows a strange scene in which she changes shapes with a sorceress and sleeps with her brother, which results in the birth of their son Sinfjotli, who grows up to join his outlaw father in seeking vengeance against Siggeir. Ghastly mass-murders ensue, orchestrated largely by Signy, who walks into the conflagration that has already burned her unwanted husband. Sigmund reclaims his father's kingdom, Sinfjotli covers himself in glory, and all seems well.

By this point the author is in better control of his material, dramatizing his scenes effectively (rather than merely converting his poetic sources into prose) and using dialogue for more than stilted utterances. In chapter 9, for example, two male characters trade insults for half a page — erudite Icelandic zingers that amount to calling each other a fag — and in chapter 10 the author imitates a drunk's talk. He complicates his plot with further misalliances and battles, further betrayals and outrages, and with mysterious appearances by Odin in various disguises and by a gallery of shield-maidens, Norns, and "spaewomen." (In this novella, the supernatural is largely a feminine realm, a rainbow of male projections from obliging wish-maidens to deadly female werewolves.) Heroic events become complicated by moral issues: when Sigurd slays the dragon Fafnir and inherits the gold, the dying dragon warns him that gold can be a curse, an anticapitalist screed that caught Wagner's attention but wouldn't have occurred to the average adventure-story writer. Sigurd was able to kill Fafnir only with a sword forged by another (Fafnir's brother Regin), diluting his heroic independence. And when he "rescues" Brynhild, she rescues him from ignorance by teaching him wisdom, which she delivers in a long, runic poem. Brynhild weaves tapestries depicting Sigurd's adventures, a double for the author of *The Saga of the Volsungs* as he weaves this enthralling tapestry of woe.

In a novella filled with strong, no-nonsense women, Brynhild especially stands out. She is single because she would rather fight on the battlefield than run a household, preferring a coat of mail to a housecoat. (But she has a femme fatale's fashion sense: when Sigurd first sees her, "She was in a coat of mail so tight that it seemed to have grown into her flesh" [21].) She had been cursed by Odin for striking down a king in battle whom the god had intended for victory, and after being awakened by Sigurd (who strips her of that fetishistic outfit) she is reluctant to marry him because of a foreboding that she will cause his ruin: "It is wiser counsel not to put your trust in a woman, because women always break their promises" (25) she says in self-condemnation, accurately predicting her later actions. Sigurd wins her hand by passing through a second wall of prophylactic flames, but he is disguised as Gunnar (just as Signy had disguised herself as the sorceress to sleep with

Sigmund), whom she marries after his sister Gudrun, who has eyes for Sigurd, gives the dragon-slayer a drink that erases his memory of his earlier vow to the valkyrie. Brynhild's rage when she discovers the subterfuge is operatic, and like Signy she throws herself onto Sigurd's blazing funeral pyre after arranging for his death. Wise, proud, and fiercely independent, as beautiful and grave as "a swan on a wave" (29), Brynhild is an unforgettable creation.

Wagner ends his *Ring* with the deaths of Siegfried and Brünnhilde, but the sagaman continues with the fate of the family those two reluctantly married into. Sigurd's wife Gudrun marries then betrays Atli (Attila the Hun), but not before Brynhild's husband Gunnar is captured by Atli and thrown into a snakepit. *The Saga of the Volsungs* stops rather than concludes with the deaths of Gudrun's sons as the next turn of the endless cycle of revenge and retribution that apparently continues on after the story's end. It's left to the reader to decide whether all that conflict was the result of the Volsung ancestor Sigi's original criminal act, or just a supernaturally heightened reflection of life among the warring royal families of 5th-century Europe. (Rumor has it that Attila the Hun died at the hands of a vengeful wife very much like Gudrun.)

The Volsung saga is an example of Icelandic *fornaldarsögur*, legendary tales; *Egil's Saga* (*Egils saga Skallagrímssoner*) is the earliest of the great family sagas, or *Íslendingasögur*. Written around 1230, perhaps by the historian and literary critic Snorri Sturluson (1179–1241), *Egil's Saga*, like *The Saga of the Volsungs*, positions a central character in the middle of a multigenerational story, emphasizing both his uniqueness and his similarities to his ancestors and descendants. Unlike Sigurd, however, Egil Skallagrimsson is no hero; in fact, he may be the novel's first antihero. He's an ugly brute of a man, a drunk and a murderer from age six onward, greedy and violent — but also a poet with a rare gift for words. He sets the mold for such outlaw/poet figures in later literature as François Villon and Arthur Rimbaud. Several of his poems are featured in the novel, and though they (like the Irish poems embedded in the *Táin*) are so complex and metaphorical that they almost defy translation, they impress his auditors immensely and in one instance save his life. How can this hideous ruffian also be a sensitive poet? The author doesn't say.

Like many saga-writers, Snorri doesn't judge or analyze his characters, or even suggest how his readers should take them. With unadorned, minimalist prose, he simply tells you who a character's people were, what he did, who he married, how other characters interacted with him, and eventually how he died. Occasionally he will describe a woman or a ship as "beautiful," but that's all you get out of these tight-lipped authors. No descriptive passages, no philosophizing, no milking of dramatic scenes, no special effects. As Michael Dirda notes, "They sound so laconic and unemotional you might imagine they were set down by a thirteenth-century Hemingway" (*Classics for Pleasure*, 44). Snorri was somewhat constrained by the historical facts — nearly all the characters in the family sagas were real, and there are maps showing where they lived — and was largely content to let the facts speak for themselves. But the sagas are not raw transcriptions of oral histories; artistic choices were made regarding which facts to include and to highlight, which is what distinguishes these tales from the straightforward chronicles Snorri and other Icelanders were writing at the time.[26]

For example, there are the family details he chose to relate. Egil isn't born until chapter 31, about a quarter into the saga named after him, but the early history of his family is telling. Egil's grandfather, a hulking Viking raider named Ulf, is rumored to be a shape-shifter, a werewolf as his byname Kveldulf (Night Wolf) suggests. His aunt is named Hallbjorn Half-troll, which doesn't bode well.[27] Kveldulf marries the daughter of a "berserk," one who (like Cu Chulainn in the *Táin*) undergoes a violent transformation during battle. Both Kveldulf and Egil's father Skallagrim are at odds with Norway's King Harald Fair-hair (ruled 860–930), whose dictatorial ways compelled many of his subjects to settle Iceland in the first place, and both are murderers. (Though in 10th-century Norway, who wasn't? Almost everyone in these sagas seems to kill someone at some point.) The product of this bad blood, Egil follows in their footsteps, his poetry and sorcery skills derived from his supernatural grandfather and his great-uncle (a court poet), and his antimonarchist tendencies and stinginess from his father. (Before Skallagrim dies, he sneaks out and buries his personal treasure chest; Egil does the exact same thing before he dies.) An intelligent, cultured man, Snorri probably had his doubts about the veracity of these rumors of werewolves and trolls in Egil's family, but as an author he recognized a good backstory when he saw one.[28] There are also several pairs of good/evil brothers, which sounds too storybookish to be historically true; Egil's brutish actions are thereby contrasted to those of his handsome, cheerful brother Thorolf, like their father and his brother before them. Snorri (and/or his sources) seems to have been as interested in biological determinism and Cain/Abel dramatic possibilities as in correctly recording Icelandic genealogy.

The story itself of Egil's thuggish career is eventful and garishly colorful

---

26 Snorri also wrote the *Heimskringla*, a chronicle of Norwegian history, and the *Prose Edda*, a study of Norse mythology and Eddic poetry. He later got involved in political intrigues and was assassinated in September 1241.

27 Characters in the sagas are saddled with some unusual nicknames, not always flattering: Grim Hairy-cheeks, Solvi [the] Chopper, Olvir Hump, Thord the Cat, Thorhalla Chatterbox, Hallgerd Long-legs, Ketil Flat-nose, and Ivar Horse-cock. In this spirit, William T. Vollmann assumed the persona of William the Blind for his postmodern saga *The Ice-Shirt* (1990).

28 He also saw the relevance of the tensions between Norway and Iceland to his own time, when the two countries were once again at each other's throats; see Andersson's *Growth of the Medieval Icelandic Sagas*, 109–10.

in a crime-novel sort of way, with turf wars and divided loyalties pulling him and other characters in different directions, with treacheries paid back with extreme violence, but with Viking raids on neighboring lands occurring mostly offstage; characters go off on raids the way characters in modern novels go off to the office, the terror and mayhem the Vikings inflicted of as little interest to the author as the daily routine of a data-entry clerk. The contentious activities of these brutal, superstitious people are elevated only by Egil's poetry, which is considered among the best in medieval Icelandic literature. Late in the novel Egil overcomes his depression at the loss of his sons by giving poetic form to his feelings, "carry[ing] from my word-shrine / the timber that I build / my poem from, / leafed with language."[29] After he composes another poem, he brags in the concluding stanza: "I have piled a mound / of praise that long / will stand without crumbling / in poetry's field" (chap. 80), but Snorri doesn't suggest Egil's artistic accomplishments redeem an otherwise thuggish life; shortly after composing this poem, he tries to create a riot at the annual Althing (general assembly) just for the hell of it, and then deprives his family of his chests of silver by burying them right before he dies. He's a jerk to the end, blind and pushed around by servant-women, but he was right: a thousand years later we are still reading his poetry.

Like the Greeks, Icelanders also had novels that aspired no higher than escapist entertainment. The short novel *Arrow-Odd* (*Örvar-Odds saga*), written around the middle of the 13th century, begins like a knockoff of *Egil's Saga*. A thuggish Norwegian named Odd goes around looting villages and challenging people to fight, occasionally tossing off poems (like Egil) to commemorate his achievements. (He's especially skillful with arrows and possesses several magic ones, hence his nickname.) But as one of his opponents aptly observes, "there can't ever have been a meeting of such stupid people; we're fighting over nothing but our own pride and ambition."[30] Either mocking the traditional saga or (more likely) realizing he's no Snorri Sturluson, the anonymous author then turns his novel into a fanciful adventure story. A prophetess had told Odd that he would live for 300 years, and he spends the centuries fighting giants in Russia, abducting/marrying a fairy in Ireland, marauding in France, bathing in the river Jordan, impregnating a young giantess, living in the forests as "Barkman," winning contests, becoming king of Greece, conquering Russia — an outlandish series of events in the tradition of Lucian's *True Story*, the voyages of Sindbad, or the tales of brave Ulysses. An Oddysey, if you will. Odd's dalliance with the giantess even anticipates the relations between Gulliver and Glumdalclitch in part 2 of Swift's novel.

---

29 Chap. 79 in Bernard Scudder's translation of *Egil's Saga*, in *The Sagas of Icelanders*, 8–184.
30 Chap. 9 in the Pálsson/Edwards translation (1970); the novel is also included in their *Seven Viking Romances* (Penguin, 1985), 25–137.

But unlike Swift with his Struldbruggs, our Icelandic author doesn't explore the implications of Odd's extended lifespan; the prophetess had also told Odd how he would die, and waiting to see how her prediction will be fulfilled provides the only narrative tension in this entertaining but otherwise ludicrous, misogynistic novel.[31]

Women play very minor roles in *Egil's Saga* and *Arrow-Odd*; not so in *The Saga of the People of Laxardal* (*Laxdœla saga*), which not only features many prominent women characters, but pays such close attention to them that — inevitably, nowadays — some scholars have suggested it must have been written by a woman.[32] Composed somewhere between 1250 and 1270, it takes place during the same time period as *Egil's Saga* — Egil even makes a brief appearance early in the novel — and is largely set in the Laxardal region in western Iceland. It has a cast of hundreds, hard to keep track of during a first reading, but the women dominate the action: first there is Unn the Deep-minded, the matriarch who first settles in the Lax River valley and distributes lands to her supporters, those who followed her there via Norway, Scotland, and the Faroe Islands. (Her father Ketil Flat-nose left Norway for the same reason many did — because of King Harald's iron fist — but never made it to Iceland: "I do not intend to spend my old age in that fishing camp," he sneers, heading for Scotland instead.[33]) A tall, forceful woman, Unn prospers over the years, and gives all of Laxardal as a dowry to her granddaughter Thorgerd. (Years later, after her husband's death, Thorgerd takes her substantial fortune and moves to Norway, remarries, and lives happily ever after; these women take care of themselves.) Thorgerd's daughter Jorunn is the first of many unhappily married women in the saga; her husband goes off to an assembly one summer and buys himself a concubine (trying out the merchandise that very night) and brings her home, which doesn't set well with Jorunn. Matters become worse when they discover the concubine is actually an abducted Irish princess named Melkorka (i.e., Mael-Curcaich, daughter of King Muirchertach). The husband is delighted at the revelation, and lavishes affection on the son she soon bears him, a boy later known as Olaf the Peacock (a snappy dresser by 10th-century Icelandic standards). To provide means for Olaf to travel to Ireland and find his grandfather, Melkorka

---

31 I mean misogynistic even by medieval Icelandic standards. It's too easy to criticize older authors for being misogynistic by today's stringent standards — and/or elitist, racist, patriarchal, homophobic, etc. — but I reserve this term only for those who denigrate women more harshly than usual for their times.

32 I'm all for attributing anonymous works to women when there's solid evidence for doing so, but ultimately it undermines and underestimates the abilities of all writers to insist that men can't create convincing female characters, or women male characters, or blacks white characters, or Jews Christian characters, or homosexuals heterosexual characters, or humans animal characters.

33 Chap. 2 in Keneva Kunz's translation of the Laxardal saga, which occupies pp. 276–421 of *The Sagas of Icelanders*, hereafter cited by chapter.

later marries a rich but dull farmer. Olaf eventually returns, marries another Thorgerd (Egil's daughter), and fathers a son named Kjartan, and foster-fathers his half-brother's son Bolli. The two boys become fast friends, but are destined to kill each other over a woman.

And what a woman. Enter Gudrun Osvifsdottir, "the most beautiful woman ever to have grown up in Iceland, and no less clever than she was good-looking. . . . She was the shrewdest of women, highly articulate, and generous as well" (32). It's Gudrun's show from here on: at about age 14 she asks a seer to interpret four troubling dreams she's had recently; after she relates them, the seer says they symbolize the four husbands she's destined to have, and the rest of the novel records her relationships with these four men. Prophetic dreams are common in the sagas, and are the writerly authors' way of saying: I'm telling you in advance *what* is going to happen so that you can pay attention instead to *how* I tell it.

As predicted, Gudrun's first marriage is made against her will at age 15 to one Thorvald, "a wealthy man but hardly a hero" (34). The unhappy teen burns through his money but takes a shine to a family friend named Thord, and so divorces Thorvald after two years of marriage. Thord happens to be a married man, but 17-year-old Gudrun convinces him to divorce his wife and marry her instead.[34] (His spurned wife gets her revenge a year later by breaking into Thord's house one night and stabbing him in the arm with a sword.) Gudrun and Thord are happy together, but he rubs a family of sorcerers the wrong way and with their "powerful incantations" they cause him to drown. The young widow then meets the love of her life, Kjartan Olafsson; he falls for her too, but is so anxious to find fame abroad that he insists on postponing marriage, much to Gudrun's displeasure. Kjartan's friend Bolli accompanies him to Norway but Bolli returns early, and when he tells Gudrun how chummy Kjartan has become with a Norwegian princess, she gives in to both anger and family pressure and marries Bolli instead. Kjartan returns, says nothing about the Gudrun-Bolli affair and marries a nice local girl, and upsets Gudrun so much that she persuades her husband (whom she no longer likes that much) to kill his best friend. Afterward, Kjartan's brothers, egged on by their mother Thorgerd (as I said, the women call most of the shots in this novel), kill Bolli, after which Gudrun marries husband number four, a man named Thorkel, whom she then pressures to avenge Bolli's death, maintaining the endless cycle of blood revenges. Thorkel, as predicted in another

34 He divorces his wife "on the grounds that she had taken to wearing breeches with a cod-piece like a masculine woman"; earlier, Thord suggested that Gudrun make Thorvald "a shirt with the neck so low-cut that it will give you grounds for divorcing him," to which the translator appends this note: "Wearing clothing considered suitable for the opposite sex was sufficient grounds for divorce, and either men or women could advance such a claim" (chap. 34, n.). The ancient Jews likewise considered cross-dressing an abomination (Deut. 22:5).

dream, drowns while transporting timber back to Iceland from Norway to build a Christian church.[35]

After Thorkel's death, "Gudrun became very religious. She was the first Icelandic woman to learn the Psalter, and spent long periods in the church praying at night" (76). In her old age she also becomes Iceland's first nun and anchoress, but she's not dead to passion. The novel ends superbly when her son asks her which man she loved the most. She gives capsule reviews of her four *husbands*, but the boy knows she's being evasive, so she answers: "Though I treated him worst, I loved him best" (78). In a novel where everything is spelled out in sometimes tedious detail, the author's daring decision to simply use a pronoun and trust his readers will know who "him" refers to is sublime. The Gudrun-Kjartan-Bolli love triangle looks back to the Brynhild-Sigurd-Gunnar one in the Volsung saga, and sideways to the various triangles in chivalric romances that had made their way to Iceland by the 13th century (Iseut-Tristan-Mark, Guinevere-Lancelot-Arthur), but the complexity of relationships in *The Saga of the People of Laxardal* is much richer, complicated further by various familial and territorial relationships, which is why it is rightly considered one of the greatest of the Icelandic sagas.

Gudrun's advisor Snorri Thorgrimsson is a secondary character in the Laxardal saga but takes center stage in *The Saga of the People of Eyri* (*Eyrbyggja saga*, c. 1270), set nearby. We're back in the violent, contentious world of men in this short novel, which is basically an account of the endless brawls and revenge-killings in the Eyri region just before and after the adoption of Christianity in 1000. Snorri is a godi — once a priest but at this time a local chieftain who had legal and administrative responsibilities — and thus gets dragged into these various disputes, while causing a few himself. He's a complex, contradictory character, more modern than medieval; eager to impose order on his thuggish countrymen, he leads the efforts to adopt Christianity — like Machiavelli, more attracted to its potential for social control than its spiritual benefits. In fact, the most overtly Christian character in the saga evokes a rain of blood, dies, and then returns from the dead to haunt her coffin-bearers. Stark naked.

The Saga of the People of Eyri is an Icelandic forerunner of the Gothic novel. The Laxardal saga had its share of supernatural elements: seers can predict the future; a disagreeable character named Hrapp returns after death as a malignant ghost; Gudrun's second husband, as I said, is done in by sorcerers; there's a magic sword that can be used only under special conditions; a giant female "fetch" (spirit guide); even a hooded cloak that utters prophecies while

---

35 The reason Kjartan stayed so long in Norway is because he was detained by the king until he converted to Christianity; that delay cost him Gudrun and eventually his life. Thorkel drowns in the attempt to build a church. The author was undoubtedly a Christian, but most events connected with Christianity in this saga are disastrous. All the saga writers display a guarded admiration for Iceland's "pagan" past.

drying on a wall. But the author of the Eyri saga (who knew the Laxardal saga: he cites it in the final chapter) goes even further: some characters speak creepily in verse, a shepherd has a Dantean vision of the otherworld, and the novel is bedeviled by numerous ghosts, witches, berserks, shape-shifters, demons, and weird creatures, even a possessed bull. It's almost as though a kind of spiritual warfare is being fought as Christianity drives out the old Norse gods, though the author treats these events as normal. Here, the typically laconic style of the sagas heightens the horror; as Vésteinn Ólason notes, "On one level the stories of ghosts and monsters become even more effective or shocking when not distinguished from the reality of the everyday world than they would be in the consciously wrought setting of, say, a Gothic novel."[36] When combined with the taming of the wild west of Iceland, the result is a kind of Gothic Western. (If that hybrid genre is hard to imagine, check out Richard Brautigan's *Hawkline Monster* [1974].) Sir Walter Scott considered the Eyri saga the most interesting of the Icelandic sagas.

But by common consent the most impressive Icelandic novel is *Njal's Saga* (*Brennu-Njáls saga*), one of the greatest works of the Middle Ages in any genre. It's the longest saga (around 300 pages in most editions), features the largest cast (the "Index of Characters" in the Cook translation I'll be citing runs to eight double-columned pages), covers the widest geographic range (all of Iceland, as well as Norway, Denmark, the Orkneys, Scotland, and Ireland), boasts the most intricate plot and most adept characterization, and overall is the most aesthetically sophisticated of the sagas. It was written by an unknown genius around 1280, about 20 years after civil strife caused Iceland to lose its independence and come under the control of Norway, and the author comments obliquely on those events as he narrates a tale of similar civil strife three centuries earlier.

Though the novel is named after him, Njal Thorgeirsson is only one of four male characters who dominate *Njal's Saga*, and who in turn are dominated by their women. The novel begins in the same flat, police-report style of the other sagas, but the author drops two significant details in the first chapter: we're introduced to a man named Mord who was "strong in pressing lawsuits. He was so learned in the law that no verdicts were considered valid unless he had been involved."[37] The law is a major concern in *Njal's Saga*; Njal is also admired for being learned in the law and acts as a legal advisor to all his friends, insisting "with law our land shall rise, but it will perish with lawlessness" (70), which indeed was what happened and one of the main reasons Norway took control of the island in 1262. (It wouldn't regain its independence until 1944.) Lawsuits, legal maneuverings, and courtroom scenes

36 Introduction to his edition of *Gisli Sursson's Saga* and *The Saga of the People of Eyri*, xxxiv. Judy Quinn's translation of the latter occupies pp. 71–199.
37 Chap. 1 in Robert Cook's translation (2001), hereafter cited by chapter.

fill the novel, alternating with bloody scenes when characters take the law into their own hands to avenge a murder or an insult to their honor. (Those Icelanders were very touchy people; the slightest thing set them off.) There are some courtroom scenes in ancient Greek novels, especially in *Chaereas and Callirhoe* (written, you'll recall, by a law clerk), but *Njal's Saga* is the first of Western literature's great legal fictions, setting a precedent for Dickens's *Bleak House*, Kafka's *Trial*, and Gaddis's *A Frolic of His Own*, as well as for legal thrillers of the John Mortimer/Grisham sort.

We then meet the first major male character, Hrut Herjolfsson from the Laxardal saga, whose story occupies the first 18 chapters of the novel, and his niece Hallgerd: "She was tall and beautiful, with hair as fine as silk and so abundant that it came down to her waist"; asked by his brother what he thinks of her, Hrut is silent, but when pressed says, "The girl is quite beautiful, and many will pay for that, but what I don't know is how the eyes of a thief have come into our family" (1). Hrut's right: Hallgerd (nicknamed Long-legs when she grows up) brings grief to many men and later will order a slave to commit a theft for her (chap. 48); her long hair, no casual detail, will play a part in the death of her third husband. Hrut's cutting remark is typical of the author, who throughout displays what one critic has called a "macabre sarcasm" that, combined with the reportorial style of the saga and its sudden eruptions of supernatural weirdness, makes him sound like William S. Burroughs at times. During some of the many fights, described in gruesome Homeric detail, opponents even exchange witty barbs à la *Buffy the Vampire Slayer*.

Legs Hallgerd burns through two husbands in a hurry; each one slaps her for making a bitchy remark, and as a result each is killed by her brutal foster-father Thjostolf (who is eventually killed by Hrut, to the reader's grim satisfaction). The femme fatale then marries the heroic Gunnar Hamundarson, the second major male character (his story occupies chapters 19 through 81) and a close friend of Njal. Hallgerd soon quarrels with Njal's wife Bergthora, and the two instigate a spiraling blood feud that results in the deaths of several of their kinsmen and servants. ("Hallgerd does not let our servants die of old age," cracks one of Njal's sons [38], another example of the author's black humor.) Gunnar likewise slaps Hallgerd at one point, which she never forgets: during a home invasion later, Gunnar breaks the string on his bow and asks Hallgerd for a few strands of her long hair as a replacement, but she refuses and lets her husband be slaughtered. (Unlike *Arrow-Odd*, *Njal's Saga* isn't misogynistic; Hallgerd is a total bitch; even the other female characters despise her.) Wise, compassionate Njal tries to keep the peace amid the growing number of feuds around him in chapters 82 through 130 — too complicated to summarize here but intricately linked by the masterful author — always urging arbitration by law over lawless violence. But soon he too becomes enmeshed in the turmoil, largely because of the actions of his sons, and his attempts at the annual Althing to find legal solutions to these troubles fail. Finally, his enemies surround him at his homestead and burn it to the ground, killing Njal and all of his family except for his son-in-law Kari Solmundarson, the fourth major male character. Kari's adventures — which entail tracking down and killing most of the arsonists, but reconciling with their leader and even marrying the widow of a man he killed at an earlier stage of the feud — occupy the final 28 chapters of the novel.

The author of *Njal's Saga* cast a cold eye on human nature and found it wanting. Neither law nor religion can check, much less improve people driven by greed, jealousy, pettiness, pride, or plain stupidity — which describes most of the characters in this novel. For example, Hrut becomes engaged to a woman named Unn — "beautiful, well mannered and gifted" (1) — but puts her on hold when he learns he has inherited some property in Norway. Even though he's already wealthy and Unn has a large dowry, greed makes him ask her to wait three years. In Norway, he has an affair with the notorious Queen Gunnhild;[38] not only is Hrut unfaithful to his fiancée back in Iceland, he lies to his royal lover who consequently curses him with a comically appropriate spell that takes effect after Hrut returns to Iceland and marries Unn. As the unblushing bride complains to her father, "When he comes close to me his penis is so large that he can't have any satisfaction from me, and yet we've tried every possible way to enjoy each other, but nothing works. By the time we part, however, he shows that he's just like other men" (7). The frustrated woman divorces him (a simple procedure in pre-Christian Iceland), runs through her inheritance after her father's death, marries a "devious and unpopular" chieftain named Valgerd the Grey, and gives birth to Mord Valgardsson, the Iago-like villain of *Njal's Saga*. Virtually all of the tragedies in the novel could have been averted had Hrut simply married Unn and settled down instead of chasing after an inheritance abroad.

Unn's cousin Gunnar is one of the few decent men in the novel, despite a period as a Viking raider (regarded back then the way a hitch in today's army is now, with any atrocities that may have been committed patriotically swept under the rug), and consequently he attracts the envy and jealousy of his inferiors. The young widow Hallgerd sets her sights on him, and dresses to kill: "she had on a red gown, much ornamented; over that she had a scarlet cloak trimmed with lace down to the hem. Her hair came down to her breasts and was both thick and fair" (33). Entranced, Gunnar proposes to her the day he meets her, a mistake in judgment that will lead to years of miserable

---

38 She also appears in *Egil's Saga* and *The Saga of the People of Laxardal*, always portrayed as a sexy older woman with an eye for strapping young men. The situation is similar to the one in the Laxardal saga when Kjartan puts Gudrun on hold and gets involved with that Norwegian princess, which likewise ends badly. Moral: A gentleman never keeps a lady waiting.

marriage and eventually cost him his life.[39] And Hrut and Gunnar are the *good* characters; the rest of the novel is populated by the same kind of "stupid people" as in *Arrow-Odd*, constantly "fighting over nothing but our own pride and ambition." The best, most moral character in the novel, Njal himself, is burned to death by his fellow citizens as a reward for being the voice of law and reason.

The introduction of Christianity into Iceland in 1000 occupies several chapters about two-thirds of the way through *Njal's Saga* (100–105); Njal and most of the others welcome the new religion because the old one was obviously not working, but it has little impact on human nature. The immoral characters now worship Jesus instead of Thor and cut back on exposing unwanted babies to die, but otherwise continue with their scheming, violent ways. Amundi the Blind is cured of his affliction when he evokes the new god's name, but first thing he does is bury an ax in the head of another character. "Praise be to God, my Lord," he proclaims. "Now it can be seen what He wants" (106). Most of the scoundrels who torch Njal's homestead are Christian converts. Although the author was undoubtedly a Christian, he — like the other saga-writers — seems to have had mixed feelings and was especially reluctant to give up the supernatural machinery of the old religion. Several characters (including Njal) have "second sight" — the ability to see the future — and the novel is rife with dreams, portents, and prophecies; ominous ravens accompany men bent on revenge; there are apparitions, a witch-ride, visions of hell, and a rain of blood as in *The Saga of the People of Eyri*; for a Grand Guignol climax, a dozen valkyries set up a loom near a battlefield — "Men's heads were used for weights, men's intestines for the weft and warp" — and chant a four-page dirge before dispersing, "six to the south and six to the north" (157). Hanging over the entire novel is an air of Nordic doom, rendering appeals to law and religion futile in the face of intransigent human nature.

Although the novel ends on a note of reconciliation in the early 11th century, the 13th-century author knew that greed, ambition, and pride would continue to tear his country apart and eventually rob Iceland of its independence. Many of his characters evoke Fate as an excuse for their actions, but the author knew that character is fate, and *Njal's Saga* is a mordantly brilliant condemnation of the choices most people make, and of the political ramifications of personal shortcomings.

The last novel-length Icelandic work, *Grettir's Saga* (*Grettis saga*), was written a century after *Njal's Saga*, and thus is even farther removed from

---

39 Why he doesn't divorce Hallgerd after she reveals her true nature is a mystery. As noted above, it was absurdly easy; at Gunnar's wedding party, his uncle Thrain spots a beautiful 14-year-old girl, tells his wife he's divorcing her, and arranges to marry the Icelanderette all in the space of an hour. Must have been Hallgerd's long blonde hair and longer legs that kept Gunnar in thrall.

the time it describes, the same transitional period just before and after the adoption of Christianity. But the anonymous author uses this distance to his advantage: not only does he draw upon the same historical chronicles as the earlier saga-writers did, but he also draws upon the sagas themselves, resulting in a kind of meta-saga that is more self-consciously literary than the earlier ones, and constructed more like a modern novel.

Grettir's Saga begins like all the others with a brief account of the protagonist's ancestors, for Icelanders very much believed that personality traits were passed along like genes. Special attention is given to Grettir's great-grandfather Onund Tree-Foot, who got his nickname after his lower leg was chopped off and replaced by a wooden stump. A Viking raider, Onund is valiant but brutal, a poet but also an outcast, and after his land in Norway is confiscated by King Harald, he leaves for Iceland, preferring freedom in the wilds to servitude in society. While Onund is successful in his goal — "He was the most valiant and deft of all the one-legged men who have been in Iceland," says the tongue-in-cheek author[40] — his great-grandson will have difficulty reconciling the desire for freedom with civic responsibility.

Grettir Asmundarson is born in chapter 11, and the account of his childhood — only Egil's Saga devotes as much space to a protagonist's early years — sets the pattern for his adult life. "As a child he was self-willed, taciturn and harsh, sardonic and mischievous," the author tells us (more than previous saga-writers would have said). "His father was not very fond of him, but his mother loved him dearly" (14). This distinction is prophetic: throughout the novel Grettir will have problems with the patriarchal sphere (law, social obligations, Christianity) but feels at home in the matriarchal one. His first heroic deed will be defending a group of unprotected women from an attack of berserks, and throughout he finds women more accommodating and forgiving than men, even though a woman will eventually cause his death. In that same introductory chapter 14, which is heavy with foreshadowing (the child is father to the man), Grettir mistreats animals, plays tricks on his father and talks back to him (usually with impudent proverbs), and composes libelous poems. Like Egil, Grettir grows up to possess great strength, and like that antihero he kills another man while still young. It's an act of self-defense, but it nevertheless gets him banished and begins his alienation from society.

Grettir wanders back and forth between Iceland and Norway for the rest of his life, getting into one fight after another, sometimes to show off his strength, but often because of an imagined insult to his honor; the author sets one such incident in a church to underscore the incompatibility of "pagan" honor with Christian humility. But his brawls differ from those of

---

40 Chap. 11 in the Fox/Pálsson translation. Earlier, the author notes: "Onund was so brave that few men with two legs could stand up to him" (10), another joke at Onund's expense and typical of the author's sometimes sarcastic attitude toward his material.

Egil and other Icelandic thugs. The author arranges Grettir's conflicts with an eye for their symbolic value: the berserks Grettir battles take their name from the Icelandic word for "bear-shirt," because they fight like enraged animals ("putting on the bear-shirt" is a kenning — a pictorial metaphor — for a change in temperament); soon after that, Grettir fights an actual bear, and after that initiates a duel with a man named Bjorn, who points out that his name means "bear." The first two represent the wild world of nature in which Grettir's natural aggression is acceptable, but Bjorn is a bear in name only and thus needs to be treated differently — a distinction Grettir is unable to make. Bjorn's kinsmen, representing society, appeal to authority and get Grettir sent back to Iceland. Grettir also fights several demons — an undead mound-dweller as well as two monsters very reminiscent of Grendel and his dam from *Beowulf*, which the author may have known — and when he mortally wounds another demon named Glam, it is suggested that Grettir is actually fighting what a therapist today would call his inner demons. Glam curses Grettir so that henceforth he will be afraid of the dark, always a victim to his darker impulses. Consequently, Grettir spends most of his life as an outlaw, winding up on an isolated island cut off from society. But even there he transgresses the law — the island belongs to nearby farmers, whose livestock he steals along with their land — and the property owners eventually get their revenge by siccing a sorceress on him, a member of the same pre-Christian world he belongs to.

Because he's an arrogant bully who survives by robbing people during his outlaw years, Grettir earns our contempt, but like Robin Hood he commits enough good deeds to soften our opinion of him. And even though, unlike the Irish Suibhne, he brings his exile upon himself, the author enlists our sympathy for him. Late in the novel, Grettir hears about a nearby assembly and leaves his island in disguise to watch their games, longing for society but forced to watch from afar. (In chapter 15, when Grettir was 14, he was invited to join in a game but proved to be a spoilsport and got in a fight.) When some men spot him and try to talk him into competing in a wrestling match, he first makes them promise him safe-conduct home afterward, for as an outlaw he can be killed with impunity by anyone who recognizes him. A "very eloquent man" named Hafr then announces the terms of their agreement in deliberately high-flown language that, unknown to him but obvious to the reader, cruelly mocks Grettir's exiled state:

"He shall have peace at every place, specified or unspecified, as long as he has need of it for a safe journey home, while this truce is in force. . . .

"He shall be branded a truce-breaker who violates this pledge or destroys this peace — to be banished and driven away from God and good men, from heaven and all holy men; he shall be deemed unfit to live among men, and, like a wolf, shall be an outlaw everywhere — wherever Christians go to church or heathens hold sacrifices, wherever fire burns, the earth grows, a speaking child calls his mother and a mother bears a son, wherever people kindle fires, where a ship sails, shields glitter, the sun shines, snow drifts, a Lapp goes on skis, a fir tree grows, where a falcon flies on a long summer's day with a fair breeze blowing under both wings, where the heavens turn, where lands are lived in, where the wind washes water down to the sea, where men sow seed — in all those places the trucebreaker shall be barred from churches and Christians, from heathens, from houses and holes, from every place except Hell alone." (72)[41]

This beautiful catalog of all the things the trucebreaker Grettir has missed out on in life begins to melt our hearts until we remember Grettir has just tricked Hafr and the others; he identifies himself to them, but they are bound by the truce to let him escape. The law protects civilized society, and by making a mockery of the law, Grettir has once again demonstrated he doesn't belong in society.

Then the author makes a mockery of the saga form by ending *Grettir's Saga* somewhere between bedroom farce and Christian hagiography, like *Othello* morphing into *The Merry Wives of Windsor*. Thorbjorn Ongul, who arranged for the sorceress to weaken Grettir so that he and his henchmen could kill him, goes to Norway and then down to Constantinople to join the Varangian Guard, an elite corps of Scandinavians at the service of the Byzantine emperor. (Several of the other sagas mention Icelanders joining the Guard.) Grettir's brother Thorstein tracks Thorbjorn down there, kills him, and is thrown in prison. So far, so good: Grettir has been avenged in standard saga style. Thorstein begins singing in his cell, conveniently situated on a busy street, and is overheard by a rich Byzantine noblewoman named Spes (Latin for "hope, expectation"), who is unhappily married to Sigurd — no dragon-slayer, just a nouveau-riche boor. "Are you outstanding in other things as you are in singing?" she asks Thorstein flirtatiously (through the prison wall, apparently), and after he tells her his story, she uses her influence to spring him from prison and then hides him at her place. Her husband soon notices her mood has improved and that she's spending a lot of money suddenly, and we get a chapter's worth of farcical attempts by the suspicious husband to find the man she's hiding (in a coffer, beneath a heap of cloths, under a trapdoor). Brazen Spes offers to go to the bishop and proclaim her innocence, and on the day of the interview she is helped across a ditch by a beggar who accidentally touches her thigh in the process. She then swears before the bishop that no man but her husband has ever touched her, except for that beggar earlier; the bishop grants her a divorce and all of her husband's fortune in punishment for his false accusation, whereupon we learn that the beggar

---

41 The author apparently borrowed this truce from an earlier document; his originality lies in the superb dramatic irony that results from his use of it in this scene.

was Thorstein in disguise.[42] Technically she was telling the truth, then, and like Grettir earlier she has subverted the law to her advantage, which earns this condemnation from the author: "Thus it turned out, as is often the case, that the weaker must suffer defeat. There was nothing [Sigurd] could do about it, although the truth was on his side" (89). *Njal's Saga* had dramatized the growing trivialization of Icelandic law as certain criminals got off the hook because they were prosecuted in the East Quarter Court instead of the North Quarter Court and other such technicalities, and the author of *Grettir's Saga* is just as contemptuous of those whose subversion of the law eventually led to Iceland's loss of independence.

But the author lets his adulterous, law-scoffing couple off easy. Thorstein and Spes get married, move to Norway, have a wonderful life, then get religion and make a pilgrimage to Rome where they confess "how they had contrived their marriage by trickery," get absolution, and live out the rest of their lives in smug penance in two custom-built stone huts. In a brief epilogue, the author notes: "Sturla the Lawman has said that in his opinion there was never an outlaw as distinguished as Grettir the Strong" (93). Hard to say whether the author shares that opinion, for he provides enough evidence to both praise and condemn Grettir. Similarly, he could be praising the earlier sagas by writing an engaging new one in tribute — and for a modern reader *Grettir's Saga* may be the most appealing of them all — or he could be mocking them by exposing the holes in their code of honor and their cult of physical prowess. The puzzling ending certainly supports the case for mockery, as do various incongruous bits in the novel. When Grettir's sympathetic brother Atli has a spear driven into him, Atli quips: "Broad swords are becoming fashionable nowadays" and drops dead (45) — which trivializes the horrible murder. The great warrior Grettir is afraid of the dark, we recall, and when a maidservant spots him sleeping in the nude, she disses him: "He is certainly big enough in the chest, but it seems to me very odd how small he is farther down. That part of him isn't up to the rest of him" (75). Atli's final quip may instead demonstrate heroic cool, and when Grettir wakes, he yanks the maid up on the bench and shows her he's not so small down there after all, but the novel is filled with enough ambiguities that it's difficult to say what the author finally thinks of his protagonist — a very modern narrative stance. It's somehow appropriate that the last major saga both celebrates and problematizes the genre.

One section of Heather O'Donoghue's *Old Norse–Icelandic Literature* is entitled "Are Family Sagas Medieval Novels?" After analyzing the story of Hrut's Amazing Expanding Penis in *Njal's Saga* (my characterization, not hers), she answers No. The sagas switch too often from naturalism to

---

42 Variants of this trick can be found throughout medieval literature, including the Hebrew *Tales of Sendebar* and the two versions of *Tristan* discussed later in this chapter.

supernaturalism and operate according to societal norms too different from ours; more important, they lack any authorial commentary or guidance on how to evaluate the characters and events, and lack "the unspoken thoughts and feelings of the characters" that true novelists provide (35), presumably like this (which I plucked at random from Thackeray's *Vanity Fair*):

> Emmy's mind somehow misgave her about her friend. Rebecca's wit, spirits and accom-
> plishments troubled her with a rueful disquiet. They were only a week married, and here
> was George already suffering *ennui*, and eager for others' society! She trembled for the
> future. How shall I be a companion for him, she thought — so clever and so brilliant, and
> I such a humble foolish creature? (chap. 25)

While it's true many classic and mainstream novels provide such guidance, more daring writers from Flaubert on have dispensed with it, removing their authorial presence from their novels and leaving their readers in much the same position as the listeners to sagas, forced to evaluate characters and events without authorial prompting. The sagas may not resemble mainstream novels but they do resemble modernist ones, that is, the novels that dispensed with the cozy moralizing and sociological padding of Victorian novels. With all due respect to O'Donoghue's knowledge of Old Norse and Icelandic literature, she has too old-fashioned a conception of the novel; Crane's *Maggie* and Gaddis's *J R* are as void of authorial guidance as any saga. As Stephen Dedalus tells Lynch in Joyce's *Portrait of the Artist as a Young Man*, "The artist, like the God of the creation, remains within or behind or beyond or above his handiwork, invisible, refined out of existence, indifferent, paring his fingernails" (chap. 5). I prefer the summary judgment of another expert in this field, Magnus Magnusson (himself a translator of *Njal's Saga*):

> These Sagas of Icelanders . . . can best be described as historical novels — the first novels
> to be written in Europe. They were not, strictly speaking, histories; they were imaginative
> works of art created around an historical framework and using many different sources: writ-
> ten records and genealogies, traditional oral stories, earlier sagas, fragments of remembered
> verses uttered on special occasions. Their purpose was to entertain their audience, like the
> great novels of the nineteenth century. (*Iceland Saga*, 21)

MEDIEVAL BYZANTINE FICTION

At the other end of Europe, where Thorbjorn and other Icelanders had gone to join the Varangian Guard, the ancient Greek novel was enjoying an unexpected revival. The Eastern Empire (Byzantium) reached its peak in the 10th century, and during this time of military and economic prosperity scholars like Photius and Suidas began investigating the remains of Hellenic culture, including its novels. Things started deteriorating after that, ending in the sack of Constantinople by the Fourth Crusade in April 1204, but in the century before that calamitous event several Byzantine writers produced novels modeled on those of Achilles Tatius and Heliodorus.

Before they appeared, the only Byzantine novel of note was the wildly popular *Barlaam and Josaphat*, a 300-page Christian fantasy "composed" (I'll explain anon) in the 1020s by Euthymius the Georgian (c. 955–1028), abbot of a monastery in Greece. You'll recall the *Acts of Thomas* told of the apostle's attempt to convert India to Christianity; *Barlaam and Josaphat* begins a few centuries later with an Indian king named Abenner, who alternates between persecuting the Christians in his land and doting on his baby son, Josaphat. He decides to shelter his son from "the annoys of life, neither death, nor old age, nor disease, nor poverty, nor anything else grievous that might break his happiness."[43] The boy is raised in an isolated palace that he never leaves, surrounded by young tutors and companions (replaced at the first sign of age or illness), completely sheltered from the world.

Abenner's plan works until his son reaches his twenties, when he begins to wonder about the outside world and comes to regard his palace more as a prison. His father reluctantly lets him leave the palace grounds, and Josaphat soon witnesses examples of poverty, old age, sickness, and death. Meanwhile, an older Christian anchorite named Barlaam, "learning by divine revelation the state of the king's son" (6), leaves the desert to visit the prince to convert him. From this point on, the novel becomes an endless infomercial for Christian fundamentalism: in a series of long-winded lectures, Barlaam retells the Bible and sets out the party line that was locked down at the Council of Nicaea in the 4th century, all of which Josaphat accepts as unquestioningly as the Indian women in the *Acts of Thomas*. (Thomas went after the women, which is perhaps why Christianity didn't take hold in India; our author goes after the men in power, with almost no mention of women at all.) Josaphat's conversion enrages his father, of course, and after trying to win his son back from the cult he's joined by tempting him with a bevy of beautiful women, he reluctantly gives him half of his kingdom, hoping the realities of governing will cure him of his religious extremism. But Josaphat proves to be a model ruler, and after converting his father near the end of his life, he inherits the other half of the kingdom of India. But he misses Barlaam and the idea of desert life, so he turns over the kingdom to another, wanders in the desert for two years in search of his master, then spends the rest of his life out there

43 Chap. 3 in the old Woodward and Mattingly translation in the Loeb Library (1914), hereafter cited by chapter. (In their text, Josaphat is spelled "Ioasaph," but I'm using the more familiar form.) The Loeb edition follows the traditional attribution of the work to a monk named John Damascene (c. 676–749), but that's just another example of the pseudepigraphy common in religious writings.

with him. After the deaths of Barlaam and Josaphat, their corpses are brought back to the capital and placed in elaborate tombs, where their bodies remain incorrupt and bestow miracle cures on visitors.

Like the ancient Greek *Alexander Romance*, also set in India, the popularity of *Barlaam and Josaphat* is in inverse proportion to its artistry. It's all fairly predictable, the characters flatter than a prayer mat, and written in complete ignorance of what India was actually like at that time. (The author confuses it with both Ethiopia and Arabia, and all of his examples of heathen gods are taken from Greek and Roman mythology.) All of the Christians are flawless heroes, all the Indians deluded sensualists. But none of this hindered its popularity: not only was it the literary sensation of 11th-century Constantinople, but in its Latin translation it swept through Europe and was adapted into nearly every European language, including Middle English. The Catholic Church, typically failing to distinguish between fact and fiction, canonized Barlaam and Josaphat, and they remain to this day on their calendar of saints (feast day 27 November). When Jesuit missionaries infested Japan in the 16th-century, a Japanese translation of *Barlaam and Josaphat* intended as a teaching tool was one of the first books published on the imported printing press (1591).[44] But the Japanese Buddhists must have smiled when they read it, because it turns out the tale of Josaphat was based on the life of Gautama Siddhartha, meaning the Church had canonized the founder of Buddhism. Oops.

Even though Euthymius put his own stamp on *Barlaam and Josaphat*, it had a long pedigree. He translated it from a Georgian work called the *Balavariani*, derived from an Arabic work called *Kiteb Bilawhar wa-Yudasaf*, which was based on "one of the popular lives of Buddha, possibly the *Lalita Vistâra*, possibly the *Jātakas*, but more probably a version derived from the *Buddhacarita*, a work attributed to the 2nd-century AD Sanskrit poet Asvaghosa."[45] Moreover, Euthymius inserted (without attribution) the entire *Apology* of Aristides (a 2nd-century Christian work by an Athenian philosopher) as well as a number of popular apologues (moral fables).[46] But Euthymius united all this disparate material by way of a colorful, imagistic prose style and a consistent, if sanctimonious and repulsive, theology: with a Buddhist sense of the impermanence of things, he calls for a rejection of the best things in life (food, sex, companionship, art, health) in the hope of finding permanence in an afterlife — the sad delusion of someone rejecting the real for the unreal. (*Of course* life is transitory: all the more reason to enjoy it to the fullest, maybe even find ways to *reduce* poverty, sickness, etc., rather than turn away from it.) The author reveals an unhealthy fascination with

44 See Keiko Ikegami's *Barlaam and Josaphat* for the Japanese version.
45 Hirsh, *Barlaam and Iosaphat*, xvi; see also David Lang's introduction to the Loeb edition.
46 One of them, the story of some deceptive-looking caskets, found its way into Shakespeare's *Merchant of Venice*.

renunciation, with the hardship of a hermit's life, the poor diet, and shows an anorexic's sick pride in the toll these deprivations take on the body:

> Ioasaph therefore begged the elder to shew himself in his wonted apparel. Then did Barlaam strip off the mantle that he wore, and lo, a terrible sight met Ioasaph's eyes: for all the fashion of his flesh was wasted away, and his skin blackened by the scorching sun, and drawn tight over his bones like an hide stretched over thin canes. (18)

Even though Josaphat in essence becomes a Buddhist monk, even a kind of bodhisattva, an ugly intolerance for other religions runs through the work,[47] as well as ugly misogyny: the only women in the novel are the courtesans Abenner sends to seduce his son, nameless sex toys who literally take their orders from demons. (The author defines women as "Devils that deceive men" [30].) Although there are instances of careful use of imagery — a demon instructs Josaphat's temptress "that she should spread under his feet the nets of deceit to drag his blessed soul into the pit of lust" (30) in contrast to the fishermen evangelists who "enclosed the whole world in their nets for Christ" (34) — ultimately the novel resembles many best-sellers of our own time: formulaic trash.

While the Byzantine masses gobbled up *Barlaam and Josaphat*, a better-read, more sophisticated minority discovered the ancient Greek novel and was inspired to create their own versions. Three complete novels survive from the middle of the 12th century — *Rhodanthe and Dosikles* by Theodorus Prodromos, *Drosilla and Charikles* by Niketas Eugenianos, *Hysmine and Hysminias* by Eustathius Makrembolites — and fragments of a fourth, *Aristandros and Kallithea* by Konstantinos Manasses. As you might guess from their titles, all of them are romantic adventure novels along the lines of *Chaereas and Callirhoe* and *Leucippe and Clitophon* (the latter was especially influential). Only the Makrembolites is in prose; the others are verse narratives but are considered novels by all scholars of the period.[48] And all are written not in the Byzantine Greek of the 12th century but in imitation of the literary Greek of the 3rd century; this is not art imitating life but art imitating art, contributions to "the artifice of eternity" that W. B. Yeats yearns for in "Sailing to Byzantium."

Some have dismissed these novels as poor imitations of the originals. They certainly made no effort to develop new story-lines, and in fact the plot seems

---

47 On this point especially, see G. MacQueen's fine essay "Changing Master Narratives in Midstream: *Barlaam and Josaphat* and the Growth of Religious Intolerance in the Buddhalegend's Westward Journey," *Journal of Buddhist Ethics* 5 (1998): 144–66.

48 My principal sources for the rest of this section are Beaton's *Medieval Greek Romance*, MacAlister's *Dreams and Suicides*, both published in 1996 (in Beaton's case, a revision of his 1989 book), Nilsson's aptly named *Erotic Pathos, Rhetorical Pleasure* (2001), and, to a lesser extent, Roilos's bizarrely named *Amphoteroglossia* (2005).

to have held little interest for these writers. Eugenianos, for example, gives away the whole story in the opening lines, indicating his will be no different from his models:

> Here are the contents of Drosilla and Charikles' story:
> flight, wandering, storms at sea, abductions, violence,
> robbers, prisons, pirates, hunger,
> dreadful dark houses
> full of gloom under a bright sun,
> iron fetters wrought with the hammer,
> a pitiable, unlucky separation from one another,
> and in the end bridal chambers and nuptials.[49]

Like Nabokov at the beginning of *Laughter in the Dark*, like all writerly authors, Eugenianos is less interested in the *what* than the *how*, less interested in the plot than in ringing variations on the themes of the ancient Greek novels and showing off his linguistic abilities. In *Rhodanthe and Dosikles*, Prodromos imitates Heliodorus by likewise starting his novel in medias res and juggling two intricate flashback narratives, but he rejects the ancients' reliability on dreams; instead of regarding dreams as the vehicles by which a god communicates with a character, his hero Dosikles considers them merely hallucinations based on personal preoccupations — the view put forth by Aristotle in his *Parva naturalia* and much closer to our present understanding of dream-mechanisms.[50]

In *Drosilla and Charikles*, Eugenianos is more self-consciously literary than his predecessors, ostentatiously so, inserting several poems within his verse narrative as performance pieces, and pushing extended metaphors further than usual. (His entire novel burns with fire imagery.) He has one character allude to several earlier Greek novels, and even uses some biblical quotations in a pagan context that must have raised some eyebrows in the repressive Christian culture of his 12th century, which (as MacAlister tells us) saw "condemnations for heresy increase dramatically" (158). The virginal title characters speak more frankly about sexual matters than earlier characters; in book 8, Charikles poetically begs Drosilla for sex, but she tells him (rather clinically), "you shall not obtain coition from Drosilla. . . . I will not give up my virginity, as a prostitute does, / without thought for my family, my parents"

---

49 From Burton's 2004 translation, the first (and as of this writing, the only) of the 12th-century novels to be published in English. (Reportedly Elizabeth Jeffreys has translated them all.) Burton uses verse, though Nilsson, reviewing her *Drosilla* in *Ancient Narrative*, suggests prose would be "the right form to represent the [Byzantine] novel in a modern language." Betts translates the later Byzantine romances into prose without comment.

50 See MacAlister's *Dreams and Suicides*; as her title indicates, she focuses on the many uses of dreams in the novels.

(8:140–46). That sounds noble, but the author slyly follows this declaration with news that the virginal girlfriend of another character has just died, not only robbing him of the chance to "obtain coition" from her, but implying it is sometimes better to seize the day, especially given the wildly uncertain world these characters live in. Luckier than his friend, Charikles's patience is rewarded and he weds Drosilla at the novel's end: "And the girl who was still a virgin in the evening / was a woman when she rose at dawn from her bed" (9:299–300).

No one pushed the sexual envelope further than Eustathius Makrembolites. The only novel of this group narrated in the first person, *Hysmine and Hysminias* has a typical plot: after a rocky start, H & H fall in love with each other, but when Hysmine's father arranges for her to marry someone else, the homonymic couple run off to elope. Storm, pirates, slavery, separation, reconciliation, marriage. But *H & H* is not a typical Greek novel: "the story is strikingly uneventful," Nilsson notes; "the emphasis lies on the emotional or mental level rather than on external action" (50). And Hysmine is not a typical heroine; when Hysminias visits her father's house for the first time, this is how the girl introduces herself to the handsome stranger:

> She stood beside me and, with her hand, placed the drinking cup into my hand and, with her eyes, she held my eyes. I reached out my hand for the cup and she pressed my finger, and when she pressed it she sighed, and exhaled a light breath as if from her heart. . . . And the maiden Hysmine crouched down on her heels and, taking hold of my feet, began to wash them with the water. . . . She kept on holding them — restraining, embracing, squeezing, silently fondling — and she stole a secret kiss. And finally, she ran her finger-nails across them and tickled me.[51]

Good golly, Miss Molly, how did that get by the censors!? Like some guys (the dumb ones), Hysminias is put off at first by Hysmine's bold advances, but that night he dreams that Eros gives her to him in marriage; he wakes, thinks about her actions earlier that day — who could ever forget those fingernails! — then drops off to sleep and has a wet dream about her, this time with the capitalized Eros transformed into the lower-case sexual drive:

> I touch her hand, but she attempts to draw it back and hide it in her dress; but, in this too, I conquer. I draw her hand to my lips, I kiss it and I nibble it, but she pulls it back again and shrinks away from me. I embrace her around her neck, I press my lips to her lips and fill them with kisses, and I let my desire pour over her. She makes a play of closing her mouth but nips me on my lip in an erotic way and steals a secret kiss. I kissed her eyes and let my soul flood with utter passion — for the eye is the source of *eros*. I occupy myself with the girl's breasts as well . . . (MacAlister 137)

51 MacAlister's translation, in *Dreams and Suicides*, 136.

My glasses are fogging up so I'll stop here, but you get the picture. This represents an extraordinary advance in sexual realism for the novel; none of the earlier Greek romances had scenes like these, and even the franker Roman novels lack this sort of delicacy and refinement in sexual matters. Elsewhere, Makrembolites is not so delicate; Hysminias spends time aboard a pirate ship and witnesses the sexual orgies that take place there, shocked that "the women were lying flagrantly with the barbarians: the ship was a hostel full of obscenity, and a feast of blood" (trans. Roilos, 243). Unfortunately, after this time the open treatment of sex — as natural as sleeping, eating, or any other activity — would be forbidden, subject to censorship (both institutional and self-), banished by a culture crazed by neurotic notions of shame and prudery, and would survive largely in the underground world of pornography, and aboveground mostly in highly sublimated and symbolic form. (Compare Hysmine's hand-job with the spermy "Squeeze of the Hand" chapter in *Moby-Dick*.) It wouldn't be until the 20th century that Western writers could write again with this kind of freedom about the joy of sex. And like Podromos, Makrembolites understands how dreams really work: the first dream acknowledges the older conception of them as external, divine visitations, but it's trumped by the second, more realistic one, which recognizes dreaming as an internal, psychic process.

These novels are paradoxically more realistic and more artificial than any that came before them. Describing a long-vanished world known only through fanciful novels and writing in an antiquated, allusive language that few could comprehend, these novelists resemble the Byzantine artisans who created artificial trees and mechanical songbirds. From their 12th-century perspective they could see through the superstitions behind some Greek notions of fate and dreams, but recognized they could be salvaged as metaphors for aesthetic purposes. Written for a very small audience, they were probably too artificial to last — too much icing and not enough cake — and after about 1160 we have no further examples of the genre. And after the sack of Constantinople in 1204, we have few examples of any literary activity except by religious writers (who, like cockroaches, seem capable of surviving any catastrophe).

However, in 1261 the Byzantines regained control of Constantinople and held on to it until the Ottoman conquest of 1453. As a result of this relative stability, the ancient Greek novel made yet another comeback, this time in everyday Greek (still in verse form, not prose) but just as artificial as their 12th-century predecessors, if not more so. Five novellas survive from the early 1300s; two are negligible historical ones based on Homeric characters (the *Tale of Achilles* and *Tale of Troy*), and three are romances: *Kallimachos and Chrysorrhoe* by Andronikos Palaiologos, and two anonymous ones, *Belthandros and Chrysantza* and *Libistros and Rhodamne*. Although their plots are rather different from those of their predecessors, they resemble each other so closely that Beaton can sum them all up in a short paragraph:

> The stories of the five romances are built upon a common and limited stock of narrative incidents. In each of them a royal prince, ignorant or scornful of Eros, sets out from his home. In a fabulous castle he first sees the princess with whom he is fated to fall in love. About half-way through the series of their adventures their love is consummated, but a setback follows. In two of the five romances the setback proves fatal and a happy ending is thwarted. In the other three, hero and heroine are separated for a time, one or both is believed dead but the pair are reunited after hair-raising adventures, with the aid of a woman helper who comes to a sticky end. (109)

The shortest and least impressive is *Belthandros and Chrysantza*. Tiring of his royal father's verbal abuse, Prince Belthandros leaves home (which may be Constantinople) in search of adventures and eventually comes to Tarsus in southeast Turkey. The fairly realistic novella then shifts into fairytale mode as the young man stumbles upon the Castle of Eros, filled with paintings and statues depicting love's difficulties. One statue in particular has an inscription predicting he will fall in love with a woman named Chrysantza, and another saying she will fall in love with him — the first of many indications in these later Byzantine novels that love is a kind of doom one is powerless to avoid, the same role Fate played in ancient Greek novels. A cupid summons the wonderstruck lad to appear before the god Eros himself, who commands Belthandros to choose the most beautiful of 40 women he has assembled and to award her a wand. Taking seriously his position as judge of this Miss Tarsus contest, Belthandros is brutally honest as each contestant appears before him: "He looked at her and replied, 'If you were without that flabby and superfluous flesh you would obtain the wand and hold it alone.' She received the decision and joined the others, her body drenched with much perspiration."[52] Belthandros narrows the group to three finalists; each of the two he dismisses (there are no runners-up) curses him to suffer the pangs of love, adding witchcraft to the doom of love. The winner turns out to be Chrysantza, daughter

---

52 From Betts's translation in *Three Medieval Greek Romances*, 16. (The novella occupies pp. 5–30; reflecting actual pronunciation, Betts entitles it *Velthandros and Chrysandza*, but I'll stick with the standard spelling.) Betts provides an interesting historical note: "The beauty contest which Velthandros conducts with considerable aplomb is in itself an echo of a former Byzantine practice. It reflects in considerable detail the manner in which the wife of the crown prince was chosen in eighth and ninth century Byzantium. At that time a number of candidates were assembled and were judged according to the same principles of beauty as Velthandros uses. When a girl was dismissed she was told the grounds for her rejection and the final choice was made from a field of three; Velthandros's procedure is much the same. The main difference between the historical reality and our romance was that the crown prince's mate was chosen by his mother, not by himself" (xxv). And the main difference between this case and the beauty contest in the biblical book of Esther is that the Persian king spent the night with each of the candidates first before making his choice.

of the king of Antioch; he hands her his heart as he hands her the wand and launches into an ecstatic description of her for the benefit of Eros, at which point the god and the girl disappear.

Determined to find her, Belthandros travels to Antioch and joins the king's retinue. He and Chrysantza don't recognize each other at first — an annoying carryover from the ancient Greek novel, where no one recognizes anyone until it's dramatically convenient — but when they do, they decide to keep their mutual love secret, for some reason. After two years and two months of chastity, both are ready to burst, and after Belthandros steals into her garden one night, where she is conveniently professing her love of him to the stars, they exchange some double entendres about his "wand" and enjoy a night of sex al fresco. In the morning, the girl manages to sneak back inside but Belthandros is captured by guards; he gets off by pleading (at Chrysantza's suggestion) that he was there to dally with her maid — whom he is then forced to marry, much to the couple's chagrin. They keep up this charade for a while — Belthandros doesn't have sex with the loyal maid but continues having it often with Chrysantza — but eventually they decide to escape Antioch. But while crossing a turbulent river, everyone in the escape party is drowned except for Belthandros and Chrysantza, who lose only their clothes. (The author harps on the beauty queen's nudity at every opportunity thereafter.) Eventually the naked couple is rescued by a ship sent by his father in search of his son, and they return home and are legally married at last.

The lazy author relies way too much on coincidence and plot contrivances to move his story along, and the characters are as flat as figures in Byzantine paintings. What *is* interesting about the novella — aside from its refreshing candor about sex — is its use of iterative imagery: the first thing the author tells us is that Belthandros "was an exceptional hunter and a bowman always on target" (5), but he becomes the target when he reaches the Castle of Eros and reads the description on the gate: "The man never touched by the shafts of the cupids will straightway be subjected to ten million woes by them when he sees Love's castle from the inside" (10), and once inside notices that one of the statues has, "fixed in its heart, an arrow which had been shot through the air by Love" (12). Belthandros notes the god Eros holds a golden arrow when he meets him, and he later wins the king of Antioch's favor by a display of his bowmanship. The novella is likewise unified by bird imagery, ranging from the mechanical birds (a Byzantine specialty) at the castle, to the turtledoves that come to the aid of the separated lovers after the river disaster, to the king's statement on the final page upon being reunited with his son: "Know, all you lords and nobles, that I have found my hawk, which I had lost" (30). The author's descriptions of the castle and its contents are elaborate and baroque, and his lavish praise of Chrysantza's beauty is wonderfully over-the-top: "That woman fell from the bosom of the moon and she broke off its brightest part and took it with her. . . . If a man casts a glance at her eyes they immediately tear at the roots of his heart. In the depths of their lake tiny cupids swim, shoot their arrows and sport" (17–18). If the author had spent as much time on plot and characterization as he did on verbal decoration and titillation, *Belthandros and Chrysantza* would be a longer and better novel.[53]

Longer and better and even more titillating is *Kallimachos and Chrysorrhoe*, written sometime between 1310 and 1350 by a member of the Byzantine royal family named Andronikos Palaiologus. Like some hell-raising royals today, he apparently had decadent tastes, for his novel is rather shocking; it reads like one of Perrault's fairy tales as rewritten by the Marquis de Sade, or like something that might have appeared in the Yellow Nineties alongside Wilde's *Salomé* and Beardsley's *Under the Hill*. Call it literature's first sadomasochistic erotic thriller. An aging king in a mythical country can't decide which of his three sons should succeed him, so he sends them off to prove themselves. The brothers come to a forbidding mountain, and while the two older ones want to turn back, the youngest convinces them to scale it. (In fairy tales, it's always the youngest, bucking conventional primogeniture.) At the top of the mountain they find a beautiful meadow, but also an even more forbidding castle protected by serpents, dragons, and wild beasts. That does it for the elder brothers, who return home, but brave Kallimachus insists on exploring it. Finding an unprotected hill next to the castle, he uses his lance to vault over the walls into the courtyard, where he beholds "strange objects of charm, beauty, delight, all supernatural."[54] A long, glittering description follows, describing the flowers, a pool surrounded by mirrors, and a golden dome set with jewels. Further wonders greet him inside the castle: a table filled with a sumptuous feast, a couch with gold coverings, and farther inside, a room of solid gold, its ceiling depicting the constellations in pearls and precious stones, and in the middle of the room . . . a beautiful nude woman hanging by her hair.

Palaiologus has so masterfully aestheticized the scene that the reader, like Kallimachus, almost takes her for another work of art: "He told himself that she too was one of the paintings. Such is the power of beauty [and a superior writing style] to uproot the soul, to bewitch the tongue and voice, and to overwhelm the heart. . . . Saying nothing, he stood gazing at her with conflicting feelings" (46), much like the reader, admiring the stunning image while at the same time deploring its cruelty.[55] Since Kallimachus remains dumbstruck,

---

53 Only one manuscript of the novella survives; where several manuscripts of a Byzantine novel are available, they show considerable differences. "This suggests that the original text of a romance, as it came from the author's pen, was regarded as something which could be changed at will and did not merit careful preservation" (Betts xxix). So perhaps the original was longer and better, and what we have is an inferior redaction.

54 Betts, 42; hereafter cited parenthetically. (The novella occupies pp. 37–87.)

55 Perhaps I should modify that to "the heterosexual male reader"; a female reader might jump right to the cruelty, indignant at any talk of aesthetics.

the girl addresses him despondently: "My body, as you see, has been delivered to tortures," she says (Palaiologus hasn't named her yet, deliberately keeping her a little longer among the other nameless "strange objects of charm"), and tells him she's being kept by a dragon, who is approaching as she speaks.[56] At her suggestion, Kallimachus hides, and then watches as the dragon whips the hanging beauty with a thin osier stick. Afterward, he eats and goes to sleep, and the girl convinces a terrified Kallimachus to slay him, which he does with the dragon's own sword. "Then he freed the hanging lady. He released her persecuted body from its torture, and rescued her voluptuous beauty in all its splendid perfection from the miseries of her prison" (48). Still naked, she expresses her fear that Kallimachus too will begin torturing her, but he protests: "What are you saying? I alone shall clean your wounds. Today I shall serve your lovely body" (49). Only then does he fetch her clothes, at which point she tells her story.

These Byzantine novellas were read aloud at court gatherings — *Belthandros* begins: "Come! Attend a moment all you young people" — and it's fun to imagine the audience's reaction as Palaiologus (or a professional *rhetor*) read this scene, especially among the ladies. Must have been like a night at the Playboy Mansion. Chrysorrhoe, now dressed, explains that she is the daughter of an emperor whose land had been besieged by the dragon. Falling in love with Chrysorrhoe, the dragon had cut off the kingdom's water supply to force her parents to agree to a marriage; they were willing but she wasn't, so the dragon began devouring the kingdom's animals, then its populace, and finally her parents before dragging the girl off to his castle. "But after so many tortures and woes," she boasts, "I conquered the dragon's pitiless heart and have kept myself[,] up to now, a spotless virgin (50–51; I love that flirty "up to now"). The dragon expressed his love by beating her, but she directs her wrath not at him but at Fortune, a malignant force that simply used the dragon as part of its grand design to make her life miserable — the kind of psychological evasion one hears from battered wives. Kallimachos wins her over, and after vowing eternal love to each other, they strip and bathe in a pool together, where the author goes on at great length about Chrysorrhoe's "most noble body, her crystal skin," and on the edge of the mirror-encircled pool the couple has sex for the first of many times. (It really *is* like a night at the Playboy Mansion.)

The second half of the novel sees a reversal of roles. A king who spots Chrysorrhoe on the castle's wall falls in love with her and employs a witch to incapacitate Kallimachus and steal his girl. Again, Chrysorrhoe refuses to have sex with her abductor, and he allows her to stew in misery in the hope that she'll come around. Given imperial power, the persecuted girl now

---

56 Beaton calls him an "ogre," but Betts insists the word is "dragon." Like Wagner's Fafnir, perhaps he alternates between a dragon and a human.

becomes the persecutor: she orders everyone in the kingdom to wear black and shave their heads in mourning to match her mood. (A ploughman calls her a "dragoness," appropriately enough.) Kallimachus eventually makes his way to the kingdom and becomes a royal gardener so that he can spy on his lady; the king has conveniently gone off to fight a war, and once the couple is reunited, bossy Mistress Chrysorrhoe orders a pavilion to be built where she and Kallimachus can continue their steamy affair, with her now in the dominant position. The king finds out, however, and returns vowing mayhem, but when he hears their story, he steps aside like a gentleman. Kallimachos and Chrysorrhoe decide to return not to either of their own kingdoms but to the dragon's castle, the scene of her degradation, to live happily ever after.

"The fruit of the bitter orange gave her an indescribable joy. From the tree she took a blend of happiness and pain" (71): this is a remarkable exploration of the psychological dynamics of sadomasochism and of the aestheticization of sexual allure. Just as Dante was whitewashing sex appeal into heavenly radiance, Palaiologus was painting it black; the Italian was content with Beatrice's smile, but the Byzantine stripped his heroine and had her tortured by a dragon; both represent the extremes of male fantasy — the beloved as virgin vs. whore — and while Palaiologus's artistry can't hold a candle to Dante's, *Kallimachos and Chrysorrhoe* offers a kinky alternative to the standard love story and anticipates by six centuries the seamy genre exemplified by *Venus in Furs*, *The Story of O*, and their ilk.

Libistros and Rhodamne is the longest and most complex of these 14th-century Byzantine novellas, and also the most artificial. Like Prodromos's *Rhodanthe and Dosikles* (and like Heliodorus before them) it begins in the middle of the story. A self-exiled Armenian named Klitovon is wandering through a meadow (we won't find out exactly why until much later) when he spots a sorrowful young man whom he suspects has undergone the same experience he has: "I too had left my country, hounded by passion, afflicted by love, and burnt by desire. In my grief I had gone and was roaming the world to find relief and ease from my many woes."[57] With some reluctance, the sad stranger, named Livistros (to use Betts's spelling), begins to tell his tale, which takes up the first half of the novella. As yet unacquainted with passion — which is treated here almost like a disease — he was happily hunting when, that night, he had a dream, the first of many in this novel: he dreams of entering a castle of Eros like that in *Belthandros and Chrysantza*, seeing many marvels and meeting many allegorical figures, and eventually is told he will develop love for "a virtuous lady of supreme beauty; passion for Rodamni, the daughter of King Chrysos" (115). Moreover, he is told he will succeed Chrysos and rule over his kingdom before losing Rodamni to kidnappers, and will spend two years searching for her. Livistros wakes, and there's a

---

57 Betts, 96; hereafter cited parenthetically. (The novella occupies pp. 95–185.)

modern-sounding description of the fluctuation of consciousness as he tries to shake off the dream: "I was here, there, and in the world beyond. I wanted to consider this but reflect on that, to think about something else but not to let another thing escape me. Believe me, my mind was breaking into a hundred pieces" (107). Although the author ignores the advances in dream psychology made by his 12th-century predecessors and reverts to the ancient notion of dreams as supernatural prophecies, there are other similar depictions of a hyperactive mind that represent a small breakthrough in psychological realism, about the only realistic element in this fanciful work.

Livistros tells his dream to a kinsman, who happens to know where this dream-girl Rodamni lives. There follows a long, rather tedious courtship after Livistros arrives at Silver Castle: shooting arrows with messages into her room, winning her love, making her angry, earning her forgiveness, exchanging love letters, but without the two actually meeting. Both are following the courtly rules of love in which the actual presence of the beloved is superfluous. At one point he asks rhetorically, "And when shall I stretch my hands over her entire body and make her dance with desire as I feel her every limb?" (128), but that one electric line is buried under pages of courtly rhetoric. Eventually they do meet, but before they can wed Livistros has to joust with a rival suitor: Verderichos, the king of Egypt. After both brandish their lances in phallic display, Livistros unseats the Egyptian king, marries Rodamni, and rules happily for two years. (Unlike other Byzantine novels, there are no sex scenes; we never get to see Rodamni "dance with desire" in her husband's hands.) A sore loser, the Egyptian bides his time until a witch helps him to kidnap Rodamni and rush her off to Egypt. Livistros goes in search of her, and that's when Klitovon meets him and asks to hear this long story.

Klitovon now takes over as narrator; he first tells *his* own backstory — he had fallen in love with his cousin Myrtani, which didn't sit well with her husband — and then narrates how he and Livistros ran into the old witch, who tells them where to find Rodamni. Refusing to allow the Egyptian king to touch her, and like Chrysorrhoe beaten as a result (though not in such graphic terms), she eventually talks the king into allowing her to operate an inn for a few years, apparently so that she can acclimatize herself to her fate and to gain solace from travelers' tales. When Livistros and Rodamni are finally reunited, they are so overwhelmed they can barely stay conscious: first he faints and recovers, then she faints and recovers, then it's his turn again, and so on, leading Klitovon to observe: "To my astonishment, I witnessed something fearful: Love and Death were fighting one another. He fainted and she recovered, then she fell unconscious and he revived. They were making frequent switches between consciousness and unconsciousness from him to her, from her to him" (174). The relationship between *eros* and *thanatos* is a profound one that will continue to occupy writers, but here as elsewhere in the novella the author's overly literal treatment is rather ludicrous.

The reunited couple make their way back to Silver Castle, improvising songs and reciting the letters they had written each other during their courtship, where Livistros rewards Klitovon with the hand of Rodamni's twin sister, Melanthia. (Neither is consulted first about this arrangement.) They live happily until her death, at which time he returns home to learn that his first love, Cousin Myrtani, is now a widow and available. At that point he addresses her directly, and we realize the entire novella has been a flashback, like Livistros's long one during the first half of the novella, rather than a narrative in the historical present, as the reader may have assumed. Klitovon concludes coyly by hoping some writer will someday tell his story, which of course is what we've just read — not Klitovon's actual narrative but the new creation of a writer who "refashion[ed] it according to his wish and fancy" (185) — adding yet another narrative level. The complex structure of stories-within-stories and atemporal plotting is an impressive achievement.

As in the 12th century, political instability and other factors in the 14th century led to a decline in literary production; instead of artificial novellas like these, translations of romances from Europe became popular with Byzantine audiences for a while, but it all came to an end in 1453 when Constantinople fell to the Turks and became part of the Ottoman Empire.

MEDIEVAL JEWISH FICTION

When we left off with ancient Hebrew fiction in chapter 1, creative Jewish writers were composing short stories based on biblical characters, expanding upon the rather laconic original narratives, and inventing new adventures for their heroes and villains.[58] This kind of writing may have led eventually to full-length novels had not historical circumstances intervened. After the destruction of the Jerusalem temple in the year 70, the Jews were forced to leave Israel and settle elsewhere, a continuation of the Diaspora that began with the Babylonian exile six centuries earlier, and that would continue until the Zionist resettlement of Israel in the 20th century. Given the fundamentalist, theocratic nature of Jewish culture, imaginative, secular literature never really developed in the scattered communities of the Diaspora until the late Middle Ages, when some Jewish writers began imitating foreign literature; in fact, there was not much of a secular side to the culture at all, except for whatever legal obligations Jews owed to their host nations during those two millennia. All other aspects of life were ruled by religion, as interpreted by the rabbis, and consequently most Jewish writing until the 13th century was

---

58 "Laconic" was the term Erich Auerbach used in his famous book *Mimesis* (1953) to distinguish the bare Hebrew narratives from the more detailed Homeric epics.

limited to religious themes, aside from some popular poetry that was deemed too inconsequential to preserve. But the urge to tell stories is universal, and within the vast theological writings of the Jews during the Middle Ages there are some imaginative narratives that bear some resemblance to the fiction being composed elsewhere in Europe and Asia.

Even before the contents of the Jewish Bible were agreed upon, commentaries and interpretations of the sacred writings had flourished. Rabbis insisted with arrogant self-aggrandizement that the "Oral Torah" they had been concocting and passing along from one generation of rabbis to the next was just as important as the written Torah taken down by Moses at YHWH's dictation. These oral teachings, mostly concerned with legal matters, were organized and written down in the 2nd century and became known as the Mishnah. Further interpretations and clarifications of the Mishnah ensued, which led to the compilation of the two gigantic collections of Talmud: the Jerusalem (or Palestinian) Talmud was compiled during the first half of the 5th century, and the bigger, better-known Babylonian Talmud a century or two later. Predictably, rabbis continued to write commentaries, and when the first Talmud was eventually published in book form, the printed page reflected this centuries-long accrual of commentary: in the upper middle in larger type there is a passage from the old Mishnah, and surrounding it in smaller type are various commentaries on it, along with later commentaries on the earlier ones.[59] As the rabbis attempted to explain problematic verses and puzzling contradictions in the Torah, they often resorted to fiction, telling a little fable or parable (*mashal* in Hebrew) to illustrate their argument, or expanding upon narratives already in the Bible. Like their Christian counterparts writing hagiography, the rabbis made no distinction between truth and fiction; a fable was "true" if it supported their beliefs and inspired others. These fictions were "inspired" by the Torah, already anticipated by it, in fact, and thus (they would argue) they were extensions of that perfect work by a perfect Author, not creative departures by individuals with a strong imagination. David Stern reminds us that "before the twelfth century the Hebrew language had no word for the imagination" (*Rabbinic Fantasies*, 4).

For example, Genesis 1:27 states: "And God created man in His image, in the image of God He created him;[60] male and female He created them." But at Genesis 2:7, "the Lord" (not "God") creates only a man; not until 2:22 does he create a woman. We now know these are two separate accounts — written

---

59 In recent years Benjamin Zucker published a trilogy of oversized novels — *Blue* (2000), *Green* (2002), and *White* (2007, all from Overlook Press) — that used the same page layout: the main narrative is in the middle of each recto page, and commentaries arranged around it in smaller type, with the added innovation of illustrations on the facing verso pages and additional notes at the end of each volume.

60 Note the syntactic mirror-imaging, grammatically replicating the act of creation — brilliant.

by P and J, respectively, a century apart and with different purposes — but the rabbis, ignorant of the composition history of the Torah and hobbled by the misassumption it was the unified, coherent work of a single Author, sought to harmonize the two accounts, and thus was born the notion that Adam had a previous wife named Lilith who ran away before Eve was created. This fundamental error about the nature of the text they were studying (and of course their assumption that it was an inerrant historical document, not just a collection of myths and legends) pretty much reduces all rabbinical writings to quaint curiosities. As a character in an Elizabethan novel points out, "to grant one false proposition is to open a door to innumerable absurdities," which describes the history of theology in a nutshell.[61] Consequently, the Talmud is like an ancient map depicting the world as flat, with sea-dragons in the oceans and anthropomorphic gods blowing winds: interesting as an artifact but utterly useless as a map for today's traveler. Unbeknownst to rabbis, the ingenious authors of the Talmud were not justifying the ways of YHWH to men but inventing fictions to justify the Tanakh to themselves.

This tendency to fictionalize is even more pronounced in midrash, the generic name for the interpretative commentaries and even more imaginative expansions of biblical narratives that began appearing at the same time the Talmud was assembled. Cynthia Ozick has called them "fictive commentaries";[62] as commentary, they have only antiquarian interest today (as in the Adam and Eve example above), but their fictive nature is intriguing and gives them a place in narrative literature. Midrashim were written throughout the Middle Ages — and, it could be argued, continue to be written to this day. Any work about biblical characters could be called a midrash in that it expands upon the stories in the Bible by offering more details and background, deeper character analysis, and more authorial interpretation than given in the original.[63] Joseph Heller's outrageous novel about King David, *God Knows* (1984), could be called a midrash, though chances are it will never be studied in any yeshiva. One critic has called Oscar Wilde's *Salomé* a "perverse midrash."[64] An older, more apt example would be the *Book of Enoch* discussed in chapter 1, a novella generated from a few mysterious verses in Genesis and out of curiosity about what Enoch saw when he was taken up to Heaven.

At first, commentators made modest use of fiction for illustrative purposes.

61 Robert Greene, *Gwydonius* (1584), 126.
62 In "Bialik's Hint" (*Commentary*, 1983), rpt. in her *Metaphor & Memory*, 223.
63 I alluded to Milton's *Paradise Lost* in the previous paragraph; think of it as a Puritan midrash on Genesis. The "Sermon" chapter in *Moby-Dick* could be considered a midrash on the Book of Jonah.
64 See Katherine Brown Downey's *Perverse Midrash: Oscar Wilde, André Gide, and Censorship of Biblical Drama* (NY: Continuum, 2004). In *American Talmud: The Cultural Work of Jewish American Fiction* (Albany: State U New York P, 2007), Ezra Cappell suggests writers like Malamud and Roth have been codifying a new Talmud.

In a midrashic text known as *Lamentations Rabbah* (5th or 6th century), the anonymous author attempts to explain a verse from Lamentations (3:21: "But this do I call to mind, / Therefore I have hope") by citing an earlier rabbi's comparison of the Torah to a marriage contract (*ketubah* in Hebrew) and then using that simile to generate a fable:

> R[abbi]. Abba b[en]. Kahana said: This may be likened to a king who married a lady and wrote her a large *ketubah*: "so many state-apartments I am preparing for you, so many jewels I am preparing for you, and so much silver and gold I give you."
>
> The king left her and went to a distant land for many years. Her neighbors used to vex her saying, "Your husband has deserted you. Come and be married to another man." She wept and sighed, but whenever she went into her room and read her *ketubah* she would be consoled. After many years the king returned and said to her, "I am astonished that you waited for me all these years." She replied, "My lord king, if it had not been for the generous *ketubah* you wrote me then surely my neighbors would have won me over."[65]

As far as fiction goes, this doesn't amount to much (even the eroticization of the relationship between YHWH and his people was a cliché by then), but in the various collections of midrashim there are longer, more developed narratives. Unfortunately, none of these are long enough to be considered novels, but these short stories at least demonstrate that the powerful gift for narrative displayed in the Jewish Bible hadn't died out.

But there are several extended fictional narratives worth mentioning; they don't much resemble the novels we've discussed so far, but some have a golem-like resemblance to certain fictional hybrids. An early example of the fantastic journey can be seen in the *Sefer Hekalot (The Book of Palaces)*, a 5th- or 6th-century work now known as 3 Enoch because of its similarity to the earlier *Book of Enoch*. It purports to be the first-person account of a mystical trip made to heaven by Rabbi Ishmael, a Palestinian scholar who died around the year 130; once there, he meets Enoch, now called Metatron, who gives him the grand tour. The style is gaudy, baroque, excessive; here is Enoch describing the extreme makeover YHWH gave him when he first arrived:

> In addition to all these qualities, the Holy One, blessed be he, laid his hand on me and blessed me with 1,365,000 blessings. I was enlarged and increased in size till I matched the world in length and breadth. He made to grow on me 72 wings, 36 on one side and 36 on the other, and each single wing covered the entire world. He fixed in me 365,000 eyes and each eye was like the Great Light. There was no sort of splendor, brilliance, brightness, or beauty in the luminaries of the world he failed to fix in me.[66]

65 Quoted in the "Midrash" chapter of Holtz's *Back to the Sources* (183–84), my principal source for this section so far.

66 Chap. 9 in P. S. Alexander's translation, in Charlesworth's *Old Testament Pseudepigrapha*, 1:255–315.

There are rabbinical sources for some of these details — the author isn't just making it up as he goes along — but the luxuriance of detail is striking. There are extensive lists of the names and attributes of angels, who resented Enoch's presence at first; he tells the rabbi the snooty angels "smelled my odor 365,000 myriads of parasangs off; they said, 'What is this smell of one born of a woman? Why does a white drop ascend on high and serve among those who cleave the flames?'" (6). The 70 names of YHWH are revealed, along with detailed lessons in celestial geography. There's not much narrative development to it — Enoch shows the rabbi this, then shows him that — and it simply stops rather than concludes. We're not told how the rabbi made it back to Palestine, though of course he never really left: perhaps the sudden ending marks the instant he snaps out of his vision.[67] If nothing else, the *Sefer Hekalot* registers the change in style from the laconic to the flamboyant that distinguishes later Jewish writings.

More down to earth is *The Chapters of Rabbi Eliezer* (*Pirke de Rabbi Eliezer*, c. 800), which begins like a historical novel: Eliezer ben Hyrcanus was a famous conservative teacher at the turn of the 1st century CE. We're told Eliezer's father came upon him weeping one day because, at age 28, Eliezer was upset he didn't know the Torah. After fasting for two weeks, he hallucinates seeing the prophet Elijah, who advises him to go to Jerusalem to study under Johanan ben Zakai, which he does with such devotion that he's soon ready to begin exegesizing. This backstory occupies only the first two short chapters of the book; the remaining 50 is a lengthy midrash on Genesis, dropping any further pretense to narrative for a 400-page excursion into what its English translator calls "Rabbinic mysticism."

We lurch from the mystical to the outrageous in *The Alphabet of Ben Sira*, an erudite parody of midrash written by an anonymous Jewish wag (perhaps even a rabbi) sometime around the 9th century, possibly in north Africa or another Muslim area. This tall tale of a hitherto unknown prophet from the time of Nebuchadnezzar (d. 562 BCE) not only satirizes stories of the Old Testament prophets but the wonder tales of rabbis and sages that were popular at the time (no different from the miraculous stories of Christian apostles and saints). Mark Jay Mirsky quotes an example from the Moed Katan section of the Talmud (where R.=Rabbi):

When the soul of R. Abbahu went into repose, the columns at Caesarea ran with tears. At [the death of] R. Jose the roof gutters at Sepphoris ran with blood. At the [death of] R. Jacob

---

67 In *Brain Fiction: Self-Deception and the Riddle of Confabulation* (Cambridge: MIT, 2005), William Hirstein examines the strange phenomenon of "confabulation," when neurological patients construct false stories they genuinely believe in. Hirstein doesn't discuss religion, but confabulation would certainly account for the heavenly journeys of Enoch, Paul, Muhammad, et al. In fact "brain fiction" would be an appropriate name for religious belief in general.

stars were visible in daytime. At that of R. Assai [all cedars] were uprooted. . . . at that of
Rabbah and R. Joseph the rocks of the Euphrates kissed each other.[68]

Equally miraculous stories were told of the precocious childhoods of these
rabbis, the principal target of the author's satire. Beginning by cheekily
criticizing a line from Job for its redundancy, the author then relates the
not-so-immaculate conception of Ben Sira. The prophet Jeremiah goes to
a bathhouse one day and catches several "wicked men from the tribe of
Ephraim" all masturbating; they threaten to sodomize the prophet if he
doesn't join them, so he jacks off into the water. Later that day, his daughter
visits the bathhouse and lo! her father's semen enters her vagina and, seven
months later, she gives birth to a boy.

He's no ordinary boychick. From the moment he's born, Ben Sira lectures
his mother in a rabbinical manner, twisting lines from Torah into comically
inappropriate contexts, and turning up his nose at his mother's milk: "I have
no desire for your breasts," he kvetches. "Go and sift flour in a vessel, knead
it into fine bread, and get fatty meat and aged wine — and you can eat with
me!" (172). At the ripe age of 12 months, he is taken to the local synagogue
to be taught Torah; the rabbi is naturally reluctant, but egged on by the baby,
he attempts to teach him the Hebrew alphabet, to which the toddler responds
with alphabetic proverbs:

> א The teacher said to him, "Say alef."
> Said Ben Sira, "Abstain from worrying in your heart, for worry has killed many."
> The teacher was immediately thrown into a panic. "I don't have a worry in the world,"
> he said, "except for the fact that my wife is ugly."
>
> ב "Say bet," he said to Ben Sira.
> "By a beautiful woman's countenance many have been destroyed, and numerous are
> her slain ones."
> The teacher said to Ben Sira, "Are you telling me this because I revealed my secret and
> told you that my wife is ugly? Do you find it wrong that I told you my secret?" (172–73)

They continue through the 22 letters of the alphabet, Ben Sira expressing (*not*
parodying) the misogyny found throughout rabbinical writings as the guilty
rabbi unfolds his plan to leave his ugly wife for an attractive young widow "who
flaunts herself in front of me." It's a hilarious set-piece, and an early example
of an abecedarium (or abecedary). Several of the Psalms are organized
alphabetically (25, 34, 37, 111–12 [perhaps the author's principal model],
the elaborate 119, and 145), as are the first four chapters of Lamentations.

---

68 Quoted in his afterword to *Rabbinic Fantasies*, 357. Norman Bronznick's translation of
   The Alphabet of Ben Sira occupies pp. 167–202 of this anthology, hereafter cited by page
   number.

Primers have long used the alphabetic structure, but several 20th-century authors have composed ingenious fictions based on the alphabet and it is these that this section of *The Alphabet of Ben Sira* most resembles.[69]

The boy prophet develops quickly: by age seven he has mastered the Tanakh, the Mishnah, and the Talmud, but also "the different languages spoken by palm trees, the ministering angels, and the demons" (177). The kid's fame spreads widely and he is summoned to the court of Nebuchadnezzar to demonstrate his wisdom, which he does in a series of 22 answers to questions the Babylonian king asks (paralleling the 22 alphabetic proverbs he had delivered earlier). They read like travesties of rabbinical thinking, but most of them can be traced back to revered teachings in the Talmud. Ben Sira's first answer, for example, faces the bristly theological question of how King Solomon depilated the Queen of Sheba's pubic hair, for which the editors of the aptly named *Rabbinic Fantasies* provide this annotation:

> This passage is clarified in the light of a well-known rabbinic tradition, according to which the Jewish women, up to the time of Isaiah (when they became sinful), had virtually no pubic hair (B. Sanhedrin 21a). Interestingly enough, one who has coitus with a woman with pubic hair is viewed as risking castration by having his genital organ become entangled in the hair (B. Sanhedrin 21a and B. Gittin 6b). The Talmud interprets the phrase *pathein yeareh* (Isaiah 3:17) to mean that as a result of the women's sinfulness, God "will afforest with hair their pubic regions" (B. Shabbat 62b). For this reason, as well as for the sake of beauty, women in talmudic times were in the habit of shaving their pubic hair (B. Nazir 59a). (199 n23).

Betcha didn't know that. Answer #5 is the first written version of the story of Lilith, Adam's original mate. Ben Sira tells us she objected to assuming the missionary position during sex; the world's first feminist, she rightly asserts: "We are equal to each other inasmuch as were both created from the earth" (per Gen. 1:27). Adam is adamant, so she lights out for the Red Sea and takes demons for lovers (who presumably allow her to be on top), and YHWH creates the more submissive Eve for him. This sublime story is followed by a ridiculous one in which Ben Sira cures the king's daughter of farting a thousand times an hour. After Ben Sira answers a series of animal questions ("Why are the cat and dog enemies?" "Why does the raven copulate by mouth?"), the novella ends with Nebuchadnezzar's solemn praise for the ultimate source of

---

69 I'm thinking of several of Edward Gorey's works (*The Fatal Lozenge, The Gashlycrumb Tinies, The Chinese Obelisks, The Utter Zoo, The Eclectic Abecedarium*), Richard Horn's *Encyclopedia*, Goffrido Parise's *Abecedary*, Gilbert Sorrentino's *Splendide-Hôtel*, Walter Abish's *Alphabetical Africa*, Milorad Pavić's *Dictionary of the Khazars*, a few of Karen Elizabeth Gordon's delightful books (*The Red Shoes, The Disheveled Dictionary*), Han Shaogong's *Dictionary of Maqaio*, Ciaran Carson's *Fishing for Amber*, Xiaolu Guo's *Concise Chinese-English Dictionary for Lovers*, and Alistair McCartney's *End of the World Book*.

all these ribald tales: "Blessed is He who gave of His wisdom to those who fear him, and revealed to them hidden and profound matters" (197).

Naturally, many rabbis condemned *The Alphabet of Ben Sira*, but others regarded it as a guilty pleasure; some portions of it actually found their way into respectable rabbinic commentaries and the *Zohar*. But it is as a literary tour de force that it commands our attention, anticipating as it does Rabelais's ribald erudition by six centuries and contemporary Jewish black humor by 10. "In fact," writes David Stern in his introduction to *Rabbinic Fantasies*, "the sophistication of both its parodies and its narrative technique suggests that this work is actually as close to an example of 'high' literary art as can be found in medieval Jewish literature" (21–22).

An example of low literary art is the anonymous *Tales of Sendebar* (*Mishle Sendebar*), assembled sometime in the 12th century, probably in one of the Jewish communities in Provence (southern France). I use "assembled" because the novella has a complicated textual history: at the core is the biblical book of Esther (specifically the part about King Ahasuerus and his seven counselors), which apparently made its way to India and eventually provided the frame for a collection of fables put together circa 800 called *The Book of Sindibad*, which was then translated into Pahlavi (an Iranian language), then into Arabic by Musa (or Musos), and finally into Hebrew.[70] The novella is peppered with phrases from Esther and other books from the Tanakh, many no doubt added by the 12th-century adapter, but others were apparently embedded in the earlier versions and indicate that some Indians and Arabs were familiar with "the Torah of the Jews," as one character calls it (229).

Reading like one of the longer tales in *The Arabian Nights* — partly because it now is: the Arabic version of the novella was eventually added to the sprawling collection[71] — it relates how King Bibar of India entrusted his son to be tutored by a sage named Sendebar, one of seven counselors attending the king. Sendebar finishes the course of instruction just before the prince's 20th birthday, at which time he is expected to demonstrate his newfound wisdom to his father; but Sendebar casts his horoscope and learns "that should the youth open his mouth before seven days had passed, he would be instantly killed" (75). Consequently, the prince remains mute when presented at court, which distresses his father, who assumes Sendebar has been unable to teach him anything. The king's favorite concubine offers to take the prince aside and learn the reason for his silence; when she gets him alone, he remains mute, so she plays the sex card:

70 See the extensive introduction and appendices in Morris Epstein's critical edition of *Tales of Sendebar* for the various theories of transmission; further citations will be by page number to this edition (dated 5727/1967 — amazing to think there are still *educated* Jews who believe the world is only about 5,800 years old.)

71 It is entitled "The Wiles of Women: The King and His Seven Viziers" in the Lyons translation (nights 578–606).

Then she continued to talk to him and then she embraced him and kissed him. And she bared her flesh before him, saying:

"Have you seen any woman as beautiful as I? Speak to me and lie with me and we will slay your father for he is an old man, a hundred years old, and you will reign, and I will be your maidservant!" (83)

But the prince covers his eyes and refuses to play along, so the spurned woman, fearing she'll be killed if the prince reveals what just happened, "rent her clothes and disheveled her hair" and tells the king his son tried to rape her. The outraged but gullible king orders his execution, but the seven counselors don't buy the concubine's story and try to dissuade him with a series of stories illustrating "the wiles of women"; the concubine counters with a series of stories about the untrustworthiness of sons *and* counselors. They go back and forth over the next seven days, after which time the prince is free to speak up and tell what really happened. The counselors want to torture and kill the concubine, but the young prince demonstrates his acquisition of wisdom: "Let her not be condemned to die, for every man fights for his life" (295); just as Shahrazad spins tales to fight for her life in *The Arabian Nights* and is eventually rewarded, the concubine's weeklong storytelling marathon makes up for her original transgression. Quoting a variant of the Golden Rule, the prince pardons her, and eventually he succeeds to his father's throne. "And he was wiser than all the sages of India, under the guidance of Sendebar" (299).

The tales the counselors tell mostly concern clever nymphomaniacs who betray their husbands and thus could be considered misogynistic if such tales didn't belong more to folklore than sociology (nymphomaniacs are mostly a male fantasy, alas), and since these women are simply using what limited means they had in patriarchal societies to accomplish their ends. At any rate, their sexual shenanigans are no worse than the more violent tales of male betrayal the concubine tells, and are much more entertaining. *Tales of Sendebar* is a pleasant frame-tale narrative, nothing more, but its principal contribution to literature is its introduction of Oriental storytelling techniques to an Occidental audience; it wouldn't be long before the appearance of superior versions of this genre such as the *Decameron* and *The Canterbury Tales. Tales of Sendebar* is a low-art version of those high-art masterpieces, but it remained popular throughout the Middle Ages, not only with Jewish audiences but, in translation as *The Seven Sages of Rome*, with all European audiences.

In 1140, after twenty years' labor, Judah ha-Levi (1075–1141), a Spanish-Jewish poet, physician, and businessman, completed a theological work that its most recent translator admits is "in part a historical novel."[72] *The Kuzari: In*

---

72 Page 28 of Korobkin's introduction; he spells the author's name Yehudah HaLevi, but I use the Library of Congress's transliteration. The book was originally written in Arabic and translated into Hebrew in 1167 by Judah ibn Tibbon, the version mostly widely read.

Defense of the Despised Faith tells the story of an 8th-century king of Khazaria (today overlapping eastern Ukraine and southern Russia) who has developed doubts about his Khazar religion — shamanism, animal sacrifice, sacred trees — and so summons and interviews first an Aristotelian philosopher, then a Christian scholar, then a Muslim — none of whose arguments satisfy him — and finally a rabbi. The bulk of the novel consists of their Q&A sessions, a detailed exposition of Judaism. The king is upset at the end to learn the rabbi plans to leave Khazaria for Jerusalem; but after the Zionist explains "the land of Canaan is especially reserved for the God of Israel, and one's deeds cannot be entirely complete in any place but there" (5:23.2), the converted king wishes him bon voyage. More catechism than literature, *The Kuzari* is nevertheless another example of medieval Jewish writers' willingness to adapt fictional techniques for their religious propaganda.

Judah ha-Levi lived in Toledo and Cordoba, and indeed the most creative Jewish community at this time was located not in Provence but in Spain, where three more noteworthy works of fiction appeared in the 12th and 13th centuries — one of them a dazzling masterpiece. The earliest and shortest of them, Joseph ben Meïr ibn Zabara's *Book of Delight* (*Sefer Shaashuim*), has been described as "a primitive novel" by one commentator,[73] but it's more complex than that. Written in the second half of the 12th century, it's an innovative hybrid of the frame-narrative like *Tales of Sendebar*, the visionary journey like *Enoch* and *The Book of Palaces*, and an Arabic literary form called *maqama*, an episodic narrative in elaborate, rhymed prose. (The oldest suras of the Quran are written in this style.) The novel begins in the third person by introducing Joseph ben Zabara, a physician living in Barcelona and a well-regarded member of the community. Then Joseph takes over as narrator and relates how, while asleep near dawn, "I saw an appearance before me in my dream, in the likeness of a man exceeding tall," bringing him food and wine.[74] He eats the food but refuses the wine, which they argue about — the first of many conflicts between this odd couple. The mysterious stranger calls himself Enan Hanatas — which bothers Joseph for a reason he can't put his finger on; an alert reader would know why — and offers to take the physician to his own land where Joseph will be better appreciated, "for here they appreciate neither thy worth nor thy skillful wisdom" (2). Joseph is reluctant to go away with him, "lest there befall me what befell a certain leopard with a fox."

"'What pray,' said he to me, 'was this happening you speak of?'" and with that formula — common to *Tales of Sendebar* and *The Arabian Nights*

---

73 Raymond P. Scheindlin, in *Rabbinic Fantasies* (255).
74 Chap. 1 in Moses Hadas's translation, hereafter cited by chapter. Unfortunately, Hadas chose not to attempt to imitate the rhyming prose style of the original; to translate the content but not the style of a work is a disservice.

— we're told the first of 15 fables scattered throughout the novel, most from Arabic sources, along with the Widow of Ephesus story from Petronius and a version of the apocryphal book of Tobit.[75] Joseph relates five fables having to do with trust, but in the end abandons his mistrust and goes off with the tall stranger, for reasons left unspoken but probably having less to do with finding fame abroad than finding peace within. Although the cunning author never mentions it again after the first page, Joseph is still dreaming, and thus he embarks on what could be considered a psychological voyage of self-discovery and renewal.

As soon as they leave Barcelona, Enan makes a puzzling remark that suggests this is a heuristic text, not just a travel narrative. Each is riding on an ass, so Enan says, "Do thou carry me or I will carry thee." Joseph takes the remark literally and responds, "But thou art riding upon thine ass and I upon mine: how then may I carry thee or thou me?" Enan is speaking metaphorically, as he illustrates in another tale: a king's messenger is on his way to a wise man to interpret a troubling dream of the king's and comes alongside a country bumpkin riding on an ass and asks him the same question Enan had; the bumpkin responds in the same literal-minded way Joseph does. But when the bumpkin later relates the odd question to his 15-year-old daughter, she grasps the metaphorical significance:

> "In truth, father, the man is wise and understanding. 'Tis thou hast failed to attend to him properly. Thou didst not understand the sense of his words, for that his speech was spoken in wisdom and his saying in knowledge and understanding. . . . As for 'carry thou me or I thee,' his meaning was that everyone that goeth upon the way with his neighbor and relateth sayings and stories, and cites puzzles and proverbs, doth thereby carry his neighbor and lead him on, and relieve him of his weariness of the journey and remove him from troubling thoughts." (3)[76]

Out of the mouth of babes: just as Joseph will be relieved of his "troubling thoughts" and acquire wisdom only when he learns to decode metaphors and symbolism, the reader of *The Book of Delight* needs to see past the "sayings and stories . . . puzzles and proverbs" that make up the bulk of the novel. The girl is telling us how to read literary fiction.

Joseph continues to be challenged by things he doesn't understand, and is chastised accordingly by Enan. But about two-thirds of the way through, Joseph demonstrates he has been learning from the various fables and proverbs he's listened to during his journey, and when they reach Enan's city, he

---

75 Most of the sources are identified in Merriam Sherwood's plodding but informative introduction to Hadas's translation.

76 The same riddle-metaphor appears in Budhasvamin's *Emperor of the Sorcerers* (21:11), a Sanskrit narrative from the 8th or 9th century that I'll discuss in chap. 4.

begins to turn the tables on his teacher. He successfully answers 32 questions about medicine (Zabara's specialty, after all), but Enan is unable to answer a single one of the 21 questions Joseph asks on various matters. After this reversal, Enan reveals himself to be a reformed demon, which is why his name had bothered Joseph: Enan Hanatas reversed is Enan the Satan. Joseph not only passes his metaphysical test but even finds Enan a new wife. He doesn't like Enan's city, a bizarro world where everything is reversed, and plans to return to Barcelona and compose the book we've just read. And there the novel ends.

Less midrash than mishmash, *The Book of Delight* is a heterogeneous mixture of lectures on diet and medicine (with copious citations from ancient authorities), animal fables, numbered quizzes, and a chapter of 99 "parables and saws." It even offers a quick religious excuse if you're caught ogling another woman: "Not for love nor desire do I gaze, but to behold in her form the craftsmanship of the Creator." "Turn her inside out; then wilt thou understand her ugliness," his companion sneers (2). There are some similarly harsh remarks about women throughout, but most of them are of the Borsch Belt "Take my wife — please" variety, not expressions of misogyny. Then again, Enan was scared straight by a particularly vicious woman; he realized that a mere spawn of Satan was no match for a truly evil woman. Like *Tales of Sandebar*, Zabara's novel is another example of the fruitful cross-pollination of Eastern and Western narrative techniques in the air at the time, and while some claim "Zabara's stories were for moral instruction, rather than for amusement" (Sherwood's introduction, 14), the novel is accurately entitled *The Book of Delight*, not *The Book of Wisdom*.

The latter is one way to translate *Sefer Tahkemoni*, one of the most astonishing literary achievements of the Middle Ages. It was written around 1220 by an erudite Jew living in Spain named Judah Alharizi (1165–1225). A practiced translator — he translated Maimonides' lengthy *Guide of the Perplexed* from Arabic into Hebrew — he decided after translating al-Hariri's *Maqamat* that he could do better. The *maqama* genre — introduced by al-Hamadhani (969–1008) and refined by al-Hariri (1054–1122), both of whom will be discussed in chapter 4 — are episodic works in rhymed prose featuring a rogue rhetorician who uses his skills for both instruction and mischief. It anticipates the picaresque novel that would develop in Spain a few centuries later, though the rhyming style didn't survive. In English, we tolerate it in musical poets like Poe and Swinburne, but nowadays it chimes only in the ringing rhymes of Dr. Seuss. *The Book of Tahkemoni* is three times the size of those Arabic works and burns with nationalistic fervor. In his introduction, Alharizi declares he wants to rescue the Hebrew language from neglect — by then it was only a scholarly language, like Latin; most Jews spoke the local patois of whatever country they lived in and couldn't understand their own

Bible — and to show that it is even better than Arabic. Or as he puts it in his magniloquent language:

> So roused by the Divine Mind, I put fear behind, struck fires that soared to heaven to sight the blind, that all earth might know our Holy Tongue beyond compare. Prisoners of hope, I cried, Israel has a son and heir who can, with loving care, with words and song and parables rare, front Hebrew, the abandoned bride, and loud declare, You are fair, my love, you are fair! I clear the way that our Holy Tongue might lead her chariots down victory's thoroughfare to her rivals' despair; fright her foes like a ravening bear and all our wastes repair, stripping Esau and Ishmael bare. See her conquer, take heroes in her snare; yea, we have sons of the giant there.[77]

Like Zabara's novel (which Alharizi undoubtedly knew), *The Book of Tahkemoni* is a miscellany that revels in variety:

> Now I have included in this work matter of all manner: anthems for Love's banner, riddles and saws, lore and laws, reflection, censure, the wayfarer's adventure, tales of times past or death's blast, the grace of every season, the way of reason or treachery and treason, godly wrath and the penitent's path, the beloved's face and hot embrace, wooing and bedding and holy wedding — and divorce as well.
>
> Yes, I tell of teetotalers and drinkers, of warriors and thinkers, spin tales of journeys, of kings and poets' tourneys, prayers and supplication, praise and protestation, the rebuke of the wise and good fortune's demise, the role of Love's gazelles and the cool of desert wells, stint's harsh breeze and beggars' pleas, wind and water, sword and slaughter, harts' hunt and heart's want, travellers' treks and slippery decks and vessels' wrecks, slandering, pandering, and Youth's meandering, Nazirites' vows and drunken carouse, paramours, ills and cures, blockheads and boors, guile's school and the gulled fool, gibe and jeer and snub and sneer, song enchanted, wine discanted, witty invention, brazen contention — all this, that this book might be Song's manse and garden, wherein every seeker might sate his quest, every petitioner gain his behest: herein shall the weary rest. Then enter, all, my dazzling manor, each in his camp, each man beneath his banner. (Introduction, 15–16)

Readers brave enough to accept Alharizi's invitation to enter his mansion of song are led through fifty "gates" or chapters with nearly the same setup: an intellectually curious, wanderlusty character named Heman the Ezrahite tells of a time he encountered a group of men debating one topic or another, when a mysterious stranger trounces them with his superior rhetorical skills and then reveals himself as Heman's old friend Hever the Kenite, "heart's

---

77 From David Simha Segal's stellar translation, in which he goes to great lengths to recreate Alharizi's musical, allusive style. (There are eight allusions to the Tanakh in that short paragraph.) Segal's award-winning edition contains more than 300 pages of commentary on the 400-page work; hereafter cited by chapter.

delight, larkspur and riddling raconteur, who graced my ears with tales of what his eye had seen through his long years" (7). Each chapter is an occasion for rhetorical display; the actual topic can be trifling (the difference between an ant and a flea [4]) or serious (a philosophical discussion of mind vs. body vs. spirit [13]), and like a seasoned debater, Hever can argue either side of a question (the pros and cons of drinking [27]). Much of the time, Hever is considered a wise man, but on some occasions he's little more than a conman, using rhetorical tricks to fleece hicks: in gate 30 he is literally a snake-oil salesman.

Heman rarely recognizes his friend until he reveals himself at the end of the gate; this is perhaps because Hever is essentially a symbolic figure, an embodiment of rhetoric rather than a recognizable character, and because rhetoric can take many forms. Heman's growing realization of the varied uses of rhetoric provides what little character development there is in the novel: though Heman usually expresses admiration for Hever's verbal abilities, he begins to have his suspicions about his silver-tongued friend. At the end of gate 30, after hearing Hever's snake-oil spiel, he is "so nonplussed by his wit and his chicanery" that he's speechless, and at the end of gate 41 (a man vs. woman debate) he chastises his friend as "the font of Cunning and Pretension. At once I knew his claims to be absurd, knew I had heard the very weasel's word." In the penultimate 49, Heman takes the stage for the first time to show off his own rhetorical skills, at which point his mentor steps aside: "You are joyous blest; only now have you come to your inheritance and rest." Since this is the narrative end of *The Book of Tahkemoni* — the concluding gate 50 is basically an appendix, a gathering of miscellaneous poems Alharizi had left over, outtakes — it's possible to see the book as a bildungsroman charting Heman's education in the art of rhetoric. From uncritical praise of Hever's verbal acrobatics to a realization that rhetoric is not always a vehicle for wisdom, is sometimes a mere show, and other times dangerously misleading, Heman (and the reader) emerges a wiser man, not so much because he's heard wise sayings but because he's learned how sayings can *appear* wise with the right verbal spin.

And boy can Alharizi spin words: in one gate he constructs a letter that can be read backward and forward with opposing meanings (8), and in another he not only offers a trilingual poem but gives a two-page speech in which every single word uses the letter *o*, then follows it with two more pages in which not a single word uses *o* (11); he creates double-homonym poems, organized in acrostic form for good measure (33) and sets up numerous contests between word-slinging poets. Many passages are complex echo chambers of verbal roots — Segal includes several charts detailing them — resulting in a Joycean riot of puns, abounding in assonance and alliteration, and throughout there are countless quotations from the Tanakh, usually yanked out of their original contexts to perform in Alharizi's verbal circus.[78] And he never stops rhyming! Like a fireworks display that goes on too long, *The Book of Tahkemoni* can become tiresome if read straight through, but it certainly fulfils the author's boast that Hebrew can hold its own as a literary language with Arabic. It has historical value for its discussions of Spanish-Jewish poetry (3) and medieval Jewish communities in Spain and the Near East (46), but its greatest value is as a linguistic tour de force, with every syllable chosen with care, a temple of text in honor of the Hebrew language. Only one other Jewish work of the Middle Ages possibly overshadows it — or rather, outshines it.

Sefer ha-Zohar (The Book of Radiance/Enlightenment) is a vast mystical novel written principally (if not entirely) by a Spanish Jew named Moses ben Shemtov de León (c. 1240–1305).[79] A kabbalist who was distressed over the growing rationalistic tendencies of his coreligionists and their neglect of tradition, he decided to write a book that would celebrate the more esoteric traditions of Jewish thought and demonstrate how rich the Torah is in occult meanings. Rather than write in his own voice and language, de León decided to pretend he was translating an ancient book written in Aramaic a thousand years earlier by the famous teacher Rabbi Shim'on (Simeon bar Yohai) and his followers, a book that had been handed down from master to disciple over the centuries until it came into his hands. (This "rediscovered manuscript" ploy has been used often in theology and literature, it goes without saying.) He wrote a first draft in the 1270s called *Midrash ha-Ne'elam* before hitting his stride in the *Zohar*, which occupied him throughout the 1280s. Beginning in 1290, he began peddling portions of this ancient book to interested customers — never allowing anyone to see the "original" — and in his other writings began to cite it, a prepublicity campaign for the complete work, which unfortunately didn't appear in his lifetime. Just before his death, de León was challenged by a young kabbalist from Israel to produce the original; the author agreed but died before he could do so. Asked about it afterward, his exasperated widow let the cat out of the bag:

> Thus and more may God do to me if my husband ever possessed such a book! He wrote it entirely from his own head. When I saw him writing with nothing in front of him, I said to him, "Why do you say that you are copying from a book when there is no book? You are writing from your head. Wouldn't it be better to say so? You would have more honor!" He answered me, "If I told them my secret, that I am writing from my own mind, they would pay no attention to my words, and they would pay nothing for them. They would say: 'He is inventing them out of his imagination.' But now that they hear that I am copying from

---

78 Alharizi's use of the Tanakh is not irreverent, however; it resembles Wodehouse's witty misappropriations of Shakespeare, whom he revered.

79 In calling the *Zohar* a "mystical novel" I am following the lead of such giants of zoharic studies as Gershom Scholem, Arthur Green, and Daniel C. Matt.

The Book of Zohar composed by Rabbi Shim'on son of Yohai through the Holy Spirit, they buy these words at a high price, as you see with your very eyes!"[80]

Spoken like a true author. While some suspected the book from the beginning, many kabbalists not only believed the *Zohar* was an ancient work, but elevated it by the time the complete work was published (1560) to the standing of the Torah and the Talmud. (And there are people *today* who still believe it was written by Rabbi Shim'on.)

But de León was no forger or conman; he was a literary artist dazzled by the endless possibilities of Torah interpretation and daring enough to concoct a new language to express his vision. Like all serious theosophists and kabbalists, he was also a religious nut, but a well-read one; if Señora de León is correct that her husband was writing from memory, he not only had the entire Tanakh memorized, but much of the Talmud, assorted midrashim, and medieval philosophy as well. De León ingested all these mind-altering texts and spent 10 years speaking in tongues, as it were, inventing his own artificial Aramaic and making up new words as he went along, playing with syllables and letters, dazzled by lights and colors, until the texts finally wore off. The result is a mindblowing performance, almost a medieval *Finnegans Wake*.[81]

The plot is fairly simple, the only thing about the *Zohar* that is. A group of rabbis (called the Companions), led by the charismatic Rabbi Shim'on, wander through the hills of 2nd-century Galilee enthusiastically explicating the Pentateuch and retelling biblical tales. The disciples exchange kabbalist readings of biblical verses and episodes, competing in a friendly way to outdo each other and impress their master. (With breathtaking chutzpah, they even believe their new interpretations of Torah impress YHWH and members of the heavenly yeshiva.) On the road, they encounter various individuals — donkey drivers, strange old men, precocious children — who invariably turn out to be mystic masters willing to share their insights with the wanderers. Near the end, three of the eight disciples are so blown away by their insights that they literally die from mystical ecstasy, and the novel concludes with the death of the master, Rabbi Shim'on, as they finish their explication of the Pentateuch, deliberately paralleling the death of Moses at the end of Deuteronomy.

80 From Isaac ben Samuel's diary *Sefer Divrei ha-Yamin*, quoted in Matt's introduction to *Zohar: Book of Enlightenment*, 4. (This is a brief selection from the *Zohar*; in late 2003 Matt began publishing a complete, annotated translation, still in progress.)

81 I doubt Joyce read the *Zohar* itself — the first English translation didn't appear until 1931–34, by which time he was nearly blind — but he was familiar with kabbalist thought: the schoolroom chapter of *Finnegans Wake* (260–308) refers to kabbalist concepts like the *Ein Sof* ("Ainsoph" [261.23]) and happens to resemble the page layout of the Talmud, with the principle text in the middle, commentary in the margins by the twins Shem and Shaun, and mischievous footnotes by the daughter, Issy.

Like a novel in dialogue by Compton-Burnett or Gaddis, the *Zohar* begins in the middle of one of the Companions' interpretation fests. This introductory section is a kind of overture, a flashy display of de León's style and lightning-fast word-association manner of explication. It begins:

> Rabbi Hizkiyah opened, "*Like a rose among thorns, so is my beloved among the maidens.* Who is *a rose?* Assembly of Israel. For there is a rose, and then there is a rose! Just as a rose among thorns is colored red and white, so Assembly of Israel includes judgment and compassion. Just as a rose has thirteen petals, so Assembly of Israel has thirteen qualities of compassion surrounding Her on every side. Similarly, from the moment God is mentioned, it generates thirteen words to surround Assembly of Israel and protect Her; then it is mentioned again. Why again? To produce five sturdy leaves surrounding the rose. These five are called Salvation; they are five gates. Concerning this mystery it is written: *I raise the cup of salvation.* This is the cup of blessing, which should rest on five fingers — and no more — like the rose, sitting on five sturdy leaves, paradigm of five fingers. This rose is the cup of blessing."[82]

Not the most inviting opening paragraph for a novel, and to be blunt, it's crazy talk. The Song of Songs reads "like a lily," not a rose, and the *last* thing the talented author of that erotic prose-poem had in mind when comparing a girl to a flower was the "Assembly of Israel." (The Jews twisted the lovely Song into an allegory of the relationship between YHWH and his people, while the Catholics read it as the love of God for his church. Both are dead wrong, of course; it's erotic poetry, period, and some of the loveliest ever written. Placing a fig-leaf over it by calling it a religious allegory is an insult to its author.) What's interesting about Rabbi Hizkiyah's riff on the rose is the imaginative metaphoric thinking, linking texts via common phrases and images to create something new. De León's characters are not so much explicating the Pentateuch as constructing a verbal collage from it and other rabbinical writings, raising up a tower of babble where words lose their nominative meaning (rose = flower) and become private codes (rose = "the cup of blessing"). As the rabbi says, pace Gertrude Stein, "There is a rose [the real thing], and then there is a rose!" — the verbal icon he has created at the end of the paragraph. Reading the *Zohar* is challenging because the novel's characters use words not to communicate but to dazzle and inspire, deconstructing the language of the Pentateuch to uncover what they're convinced is the secret meaning hidden in its deceptively plain words. In fact, it resembles some of the obscurantist academic criticism written in recent years;

---

82 From Matt's complete translation (1:1a), shorn of its footnotes, parenthetical citations, and Aramaic/Hebrew originals, all of which make for difficult reading (though absolutely necessary for the serious student). Italicized phrases are quotations from the Tanakh (in this instance, Song of Songs 2:2 and Psalm 116:13). Cited hereafter per the original three-volume edition, traditional in zoharic studies.

in 1975 (right about when such criticism hit the fan) Harold Bloom published a short book called *Kabbalah and Criticism* that opened with a particularly imaginative passage from the *Zohar* and went on to draw a parallel between kabbalistic and academic explication, and at times de León's Companions do indeed sound like eager grad students at Yale "misreading" texts in an attempt to impress their professor.

Following Rabbi Hizkiyah, "Rabbi Shim'on opened" — though it sounds like they're playing poker, each speaker *opens up* a biblical verse to reveal its true (kabbalistic) meaning. Next up is his son Rabbi El'azar, who is interrupted and tutored by his father, the first dramatic interaction in the novel; then follows Rav Hamnuna Sava — not one of the Companions but a 3rd-century Babylonian teacher who anachronistically appears in the *Zohar* from time to time — who tells the tale of how each letter of the Hebrew alphabet approached YHWH before the Creation and asked to be the first letter in the first word of Genesis (*Be-reshit*): for the kabbalists as well as for the evangelist John, in the beginning was the word. Like a group of children clamoring for attention — "Me first!" "No, *me* first!" — each letter presents her case for the honor, but YHWH rejects each one. Finally, little *bet* approaches her master and gets the nod. (Letters are feminine in Hebrew; the procession of letters to and from YHWH is like moppets visiting a department-store Santa.) For de León and other kabbalists, even the individual letters of Scripture had meaning; they had anthropomorphic qualities and numerical values that further "opened" biblical verses to those acquainted with the secret code. Some of the remaining rabbis introduce themselves with similar displays of logomania — scrambling the letters of words to create new ones as though playing Scrabble, literalizing metaphors, counting words — often prefacing their readings with "Come and see," as in "Watch this!" These are verbal performances, not dry theological readings; the Companions are like members of a jazz group taking turns on solos, each trying to outdo the other.

The second half of the overture is dominated by Rabbi Shim'on; as he explicates Psalm 19, everyday diction and meaning dissipate in his testament to the creative force of words:

> *"There is no speech, there are no words* — any other, mundane words, not heard in the presence of the holy King, nor does He wish to hear them. But as for these words, *their line extends throughout the earth* — these words extend a cord, measuring above and below. From some of them skies are made; from others, earth, through that praise. Do not suppose that those words stay in one place; they roam the world: *Their words extend to the end of the world.* Once transformed into skies, who dwells in them? The verse goes on to say: *In them He set a tent for the sun* — that sacred sun abides in them, is crowned by them. Dwelling in those skies, crowned in them, *he is like a groom coming forth from his chamber,* running joyously through those skies. Emerging from them, He enters and runs through a certain

other tower at another site. *His going forth is at one end of the heaven* — indeed He emerges from the upper world, *the end of heaven* above. *And his circuit* — who is *his circuit? The end of heaven* below, who is *the circuit of the year*, encircling all endings, linking heaven with this sky. *Nothing is hidden from his heat* — from the heat of this *circuit* and the *circuit* of the sun, encircling all sides. *Nothing is hidden* — not one of the supernal rungs is concealed from Him, for they all come encircling Him; not one of them hides from Him, *from his heat*, when He arouses himself, desiring them totally. All this praise and exaltation stems from Torah, as is written: *The Torah of YHVH is pure.* Six times YHVH is written here, and there are six verses from *Heaven declares* to *The Torah of YHVH is pure.* Concerning this mystery it is written: *In the beginning [Be-reshit]* — look, six letters! *God created the heavens and the earth* — look, six more words, corresponding to the six times YHVH appears! Six verses for six letters here; six names for six words here." (1.8b–9a)

The overture concluded, the narrative proper begins with "Parashat Be-reshit" as de León himself pulls out all the stops and launches the opening line of Genesis into cosmic space (the last extended quotation, I promise; and you might want to listen to Pink Floyd's "A Saucerful of Secrets" as you read this):

At the head of potency of the King, He engraved engravings in luster on high. A spark of impenetrable darkness flashed within the concealed of the concealed, from the head of Infinity — a cluster of vapor forming in formlessness, thrust in a ring, not white, not black, not red, not green, no color at all. As a cord surveyed, it yielded radiant colors. Deep within the spark gushed a flow, splaying colors below, concealed within the concealed of the mystery of *Ein Sof.* It split and did not split its aura, was not known at all, until under the impact of splitting, a single, concealed, supernal point shone. Beyond that point, nothing is known, so it is called *Beginning,* first command of all.

Radiance! Concealed of concealed struck its aura, which touched and did not touch this point. Then this *beginning* expanded, building itself a palace worthy of glorious praise. There it sowed seed to give birth, availing worlds. The secret is: *Her stock is seed of holiness.*

Radiance! Sowing seed for its glory, like the seed of fine purple silk wrapping itself within, weaving itself a palace, constituting its praise, availing all.

With this *beginning,* the unknown concealed one created the palace. This palace is called *God.* The secret is: *With beginning, _____ created God.*

Radiance! From here all commands were created through the mysterious expansion of this point of concealed radiance. If *created* is written here, no wonder it is written: *God created the human being in His image.*

Radiance! Mystery! *In the beginning,* first of all. *I will be,* a sacred name engraved in its sides; *God,* engraved in the crown. *Who* — a hidden, treasured palace, beginning of the mystery of *beginning.* Head, emerging from *beginning.* When afterward point and palace were arrayed as one, then *beginning* comprised supernal *beginning* in wisdom. Afterward the color of the palace transformed and it was called house, while the supernal point was called *head*, merging in one another in the mystery of *beginning*, when all was as one in one entirety, before the house was inhabited. Once it was sown, arraying habitation, it was called *God* — hidden, concealed. (1:15a–b)

Though this be madness — de León's counterpart today would be the leader of a flying saucer cult, intoning messages from the planet Clarion — there's method to it. Matt's extensive annotations show how the author drew upon centuries of rabbinical speculation for this alternative creation myth, but his choice of biblical verses and sefirotic imagery (don't ask) is unique, and very dramatic: the above reads like an ancient account of the Big Bang.

This fanfare continues for 20 pages until Rabbi El'azar jumps in and the novel resumes its conversational form, which it maintains thereafter. It contains numerous arresting images — *"The earth was chaos and void* — dregs of an inkwell in seepage"* (1:30a) — but most surprising is the extensive sexual imagery. You might have noticed that in the earlier passage YHWH is compared to an eager "groom coming forth from his chamber," encircled by vulval rings "when He arouses himself, desiring them totally," and that the act of creation is described in such terms as "thrust in a ring . . . the spark gushed a flow . . . There it sowed seed." Later in the novel, two messengers from heaven tell Rabbi Shim'on lascivious tales of midnight orgies in heaven: "Every night all of them gather as one. For the hour of coupling is in the middle of the night — both in this world and in that world. The coupling of that world is the cleaving of the soul: light with light. The coupling of this world is body with body. And all is as is proper, species after species, coupling after coupling, body after body." And the name of this swinging spot? "The Halls of the Trusting Daughters."[83] Love it. Near the end of the *Zohar*, Rabbi Shim'on compares the Torah to a clothed woman and praises the true student as one who can mentally undress her: "Fools of the world look only at that garment, the story of Torah; they know nothing more. They do not look at what is under that garment. Those who know more do not look at the garment but rather at the body under that garment" (3:152a). Someone needs to slap that peeping rabbi. A female figure called the Shekhinah, often called the Bride, heats up the *Zohar* and is lusted after by YHWH as well as by the Companions, for whom studying (undressing) Torah, usually done at night, is almost a sexual experience. *Zohar* scholar Arthur Green wonders about this:

We have referred several times in this essay to the strong erotic element in Kabbalah and especially in the Zohar. The frank and uncensored use of bold sexual language for talking

---

83 From the translation of an excerpt from the *Zohar* in *Rabbinic Fantasies* entitled "Love in the Afterlife" (243–50). The Muslim heaven is likewise a sexual paradise, the opposite of the sexless Catholic heaven Dante describes in *Paradiso*.

about the inner life of God is a major part of the Zohar's legacy and found throughout the later mystical tradition. Such phrases as "to arouse the feminine waters" or "to serve with a living limb" became so much a part of the conventional language of later Kabbalah that one almost forgets how shocking it is that the divine life is being described in terms of female lubrication or maintaining an erection. How did it happen that such unbridled eroticism was allowed to enter the domain of the sacred? How especially could this have happened in a circle that was at the same time so very cautious and extreme in its views of sexual transgression or temptation?[84]

He answers that for 13th-century Jews, the Shekhinah played the same role as the Virgin Mary did for Catholics, a theologically acceptable figure for displaced erotic sentiments. And of course we have to remember the *Zohar* opens with a discussion of the Song of Songs, the fount of sublimated eroticism in Judaism and Christianity. The confusion of the erotic with the sacred is nothing new, but the *Zohar* almost qualifies for an X-rating for its daring.

The theology of the *Zohar* is ludicrous and not worth discussing; de León's true achievement is his creation of an alternative literary world, like Lovecraft's Cthulhu Mythos or Tolkein's Middle Earth. Formally, the *Zohar* exists on a line (or a cord, as it would say) stretching between Plato's *Symposium* and Peacock's conversation novels, with a detour through *Don Quixote*, another road novel. Aryah Wineman argues that it belongs with what Northrop Frye calls encyclopedic works (the Bible, *The Divine Comedy*, *Gargantua and Pantagruel*, *Faust*, *Moby-Dick*, *Ulysses*), and there's some justice to that.[85] Stylistically it may have been inspired by the Song of Songs and other rhetorical showpieces in the Tanakh (especially the thundering prophets Isaiah, Jeremiah, and mystifying Ezekiel) but it has affinities with Blake's prophetic books, the automatic writing of the Surrealists,[86] and especially *Finnegans Wake*: Joyce's parody of kabbalistic writing isn't that far from de León's own style:

> Ainsoph, this upright one, with that noughty besighed him zeroine. To see in his horror-scup he is mehrkurios than saltz of sulphur. Terror of the noonstruck by day, cryptogram of each nightly bridable. But, to speak broken heaventalk, is he? (261).

Reading all 2,500 pages of de León's "broken heaventalk" can be exhausting, the sexual references to the sexy Shekhinah — his "noughty . . . zeroine . . . each nightly bridable" — not enough to offset the hundreds of pages of wacky theosophy. The interested reader may want to turn to an anthology

---

84 *A Guide to the Zohar*, 93. On sexuality in the *Zohar*, see the "Nocturnal Delights" chapter of Hellner-Eshed's *A River Flows from Eden*. She has drunk the Kool-Aid and regards the *Zohar* as a profoundly spiritual work, but her scholarly study is enlightening nonetheless.
85 *Mystic Tales from the Zohar*, 13; see Frye's *Anatomy*, 315–26.
86 See Matt's introduction to his abridged *Zohar* (27–29) for this intriguing suggestion.

of *Zohar* excerpts, like Matt's earlier *Zohar: The Book of Enlightenment* or Wineman's *Mystic Tales from the Zohar*, both adding enough commentary to appreciate de León's astonishing erudition and verbal ingenuity. The *Zohar* has yet to be included in any history of the novel that I'm aware of; perhaps by the time Matt finishes his translation and celebrities have abandoned it for the next spiritual fad, this mystical monster of a novel can be recognized for what it really is: not an esoteric text revealing the secrets of the universe to the initiated, but an imaginative literary creation demonstrating the power of metaphor to create its own universe — "a world elsewhere," as Shakespeare's Coriolanus says.

One final work of medieval Jewish fiction deserves to be noted: it was eventually published in an English translation as *King Artus: A Hebrew Arthurian Romance of 1279*. A Jewish version of King Arthur sounds like the premise of a Mel Brooks movie, but the anonymous author's translation of courtly romance into Old Testament terms is interesting: for example, he uses biblical allusions to draw a parallel between the Uther Pendragon/Igerne affair and that between David and Bathsheba. *King Artus* is incomplete and too short to be considered even a novella, but it offers further testimony to the receptivity of some Jewish writers to foreign genres, and provides a convenient segue to:

MEDIEVAL ARTHURIAN FICTION

Blame it all on Geoffrey of Monmouth. Anxious to glorify his native land, this 12th-century British historian concocted a fantasia entitled *Historia regum Britanniae* (*The History of the Kings of England*, c. 1136), in which he elevated a 5th-century chieftain he called Arthur into a national hero. Mixing together scraps of chronicles, Welsh legends, and personal fancies, Geoffrey tells of the prophet-magician Merlin, the birth and boyhood of Arthur, his ascension to the throne as a teenager, his marriage to Guinevere and foundation of an order of knighthood, his betrayal by his nephew Mordred, and of his uncertain fate after crushing Mordred's rebellion: "Arthur himself, our renowned King, was mortally wounded and was carried off to the Isle of Avalon, so that his wounds might be attended to" — leaving open the possible return of the messianic ruler.[87] None of this is historically true, of course, except for the shadowy existence of a British war-chief in the late 5th century who defeated the Saxons, but no matter: the story of King Arthur and his knights opened the medieval imagination and inspired a flood of texts from

---

87 Conclusion of part 7 in Thorpe's translation. I've listed this in my bibliography under non-fiction but I could have just as easily treated it as a novel, so fanciful is much of Geoffrey's "history."

the 12th century onward, continuing to this day in fantasy fiction as well as adaptations for the stage and screen. Most of the medieval works are in verse, especially the first and finest Arthurian creations: the verse romances of Chrétien de Troyes composed between 1170 and 1190. Those inspired writers even more than Geoffrey's work did, resulting in a kind of Arthurmania that flourished for about 50 years and, to a lesser extent, for the rest of the Middle Ages. In addition to all the narrative poems, however, there are a half-dozen prose romances — fantasy/adventure novels in all but name — including a few gigantic works unlike anything seen before in the history of the European novel.[88]

The Matter of Britain (as it came to be called) provided imaginative writers at the courts of Europe with a new cast of characters and a new set of themes. The ancient Greeks and medieval Byzantines had taken the teen romance far enough; those Hell's Angels in Iceland were too uncouth for continental tastes; and of course Jewish mystics were beyond the pale. The Arthurian mythos, developed out of Celtic legends, provided a repertory company that could be used over and over: the noble but flawed leader (Arthur), his brave but unimaginative right-hand man (Gawain), the admirable but adulterous wife (Guinevere), the cunning advisor (Merlin), the romantic hero (Lancelot), the witchy woman (Morgan), the naïve youth (Perceval), the sarcastic sidekick (Kay), the rebellious son (Mordred), and the rest, as stereotyped as characters in television soap operas but flexible enough to adapt to endless variations on the standard novelistic themes of love, power, and betrayal. It also gave the writers a way to Christianize (and thus make "respectable") the fascinating body of Celtic legends that French travelers brought back after the Norman conquest of England in the 11th century.

The earliest book-length prose work on Arthurian themes is a bit of a mongrel in its present form, a novel by default. Inspired and intrigued by Chrétien's unfinished *Story of the Grail*, a Burgundian writer named Robert de Boron apparently wrote circa 1200 a three-part narrative called *The Book of the Grail*; I say "apparently," for all that remains is part 1 of a narrative poem ("Joseph of Arimathea") and the first 500 lines of part 2 ("Merlin"). There also survives a 170-page prose version containing all three parts ("Perceval" is the third), and until recently scholars assumed Robert wrote a verse narrative in three parts that an admirer adapted into prose a few years later. Robert's verse romance (or what remains of it) has been criticized rather severely for its garbled phrases and inconsistencies — the eminent Arthurian critic Roger Sherman Loomis was convinced Robert "must have been drunk or subject to

---

88 It could be argued that many of the narrative poems are novels like the Byzantine ones discussed earlier — Denis de Rougemont, for example, refers to Chrétien's romances as "genuine *novels*" (126) — but that would be to privilege their subject matter over their form; while the Byzantine writers consciously imitated ancient Greek prose novels, Arthurian poets followed the metrical *chansons de geste*. So no.

fits of dementia" when he wrote certain parts, and calls him "a man whose head was not screwed on too tight"[89] — but it has nonetheless been treated as the original, with the prose version relegated to a mere redaction. But in a 1970 essay, Richard O'Gorman demonstrated that the prose version is much more coherent and better written than the poetic one, and more recently Linda Gowans has made the bold suggestion that Robert originally wrote in *prose*, and that the poetic version came later from the quill of a hack versifier. She also suggests that Robert wrote only the first third of the three-part work, and that someone else finished it.[90] This makes sense, for there's a marked tonal difference between the religiose first third and the more worldly rest. At any rate, since the complete prose version has survived and the poetic one hasn't, let's call it a collaborative novel by "Robert de Boron" (meaning Robert and an anonymous partner) and refer to it by the title translator Nigel Bryant has bestowed upon it, *Merlin and the Grail*, taken from its concluding sentence ("Here ends the romance of Merlin and the Grail").[91] And since it is the source for most succeeding Arthurian novels, it deserves a somewhat detailed plot summary.

Since Chrétien says very little about the grail — he apparently came up with the idea himself, suggested by Welsh myths of the cornucopia, a magical horn of plenty — Robert decided to provide a complete history for it and, in the process, to Christianize the entire Arthurian legend. Drawing upon two works of Christian apocrypha — *The Gospel of Nicodemus* and *The Vengeance of the Savior* — Robert opens his narrative on the night before Christ's crucifixion; at the house of Simon the Leper, Jesus endures his last supper, using a "vessel" to serve the bread and wine of communion. After Jesus is betrayed by the Jews — and Robert places the blame squarely on them, absolving the Romans entirely — this vessel is given to a secret admirer of the Christ's, a Roman soldier named Joseph; he receives the vessel from Pilate along with permission to take down Christ's crucified body, which bleeds into the vessel. To make a long story short: the resurrected Jesus appears to Joseph and entrusts him with the now-capitalized Holy Grail, so Joseph forms a cult with his sister Enigeus, her husband Bron, and other converts. All goes well with the community for a while until "misfortune and misery had befallen them because they had embarked upon a sinful course which cost them very dearly:" — if you guess murder, kidnapping, robbery, fraud, lying, betrayal,

---

89 *The Grail*, 233, 234. Elsewhere Loomis called Robert "a stupid rimester."

90 O'Gorman's essay appeared in *Romance Philology* and Gowans's "What Did Robert de Boron Really Write?" in Wheeler's *Arthurian Studies in Honour of P. J. C. Field*, 15–28. Neither mentions the part in "Perceval" when the author seems to assert the superiority of prose over poetry: "But Chrétien de Troyes says nothing of this — nor do the other trouvères who have turned these stories into jolly rhymes" (p. 147 in Bryant's translation).

91 Page 172 (hereafter cited parenthetically); within the text, Merlin calls it *The Book of the Grail* (71) and is said to have dictated the entire book to a scribe named Blaise.

assault and battery, torture, or any of the other truly terrible things people do to each other, then you still don't get the religious mind — "it was the sin of unbridled lust" (34). Joseph then consults the vessel, which acts as a conduit for divine communication, whereupon Jesus commands Joseph to build a table for the grail, one that looks back to the one used at the last supper and forward to King Arthur's most famous piece of furniture.[92] Bron is told to catch a fish for a reenactment of the last supper (and thus becomes known as the Fisher King), and by replicating the original seating arrangement Joseph is able to smoke out the lusty sinners in his cult, for they feel nothing in the presence of the holy vessel. Those who remain derive spiritual refreshment from it, and for that reason they call it the Grail (a pun, translator Bryant notes, on the Old French verb *agreer* — to delight — though Loomis dismissed that as "an absurd etymology" [231]).

Time passes, time enough for Bron and Enigeus to rear a dozen sons, one of whom, Joseph prophesizes, will be the father of the final keeper of the Grail. The catch is, it will be the son who doesn't want to marry; 11 of the boys are eager to get hitched, but one, Alain li Gros, declares with what today sounds like an excess of gay pride that he would rather be flayed alive than marry. This apparently establishes his purity, so he is put in charge of his brothers, and all depart for "the West" (that is, Britain). Bron goes with them and will guard the Grail until Alain's son appears to claim it. End of part 1.

Part 2 opens dramatically in the pit of Hell, where Satan and his demons are still grumbling about the Harrowing of Hell: that weekend between Christ's crucifixion and his resurrection when he descended to Hell and released Adam and Eve, Jewish prophets, and other worthies (mentioned briefly on p. 19 of part 1, and the highlight of *The Gospel of Nicodemus*). The demons decide to get their revenge by tricking a mortal woman to conceive "a man who would work to deceive others," so they hatch an elaborate plan to convince a married woman with three nubile daughters to ruin her husband, which she does; then they double-cross her and hang her, which causes her husband to die of grief. Then the demon who has been chosen to be the father (not all have this capacity, the author notes) sets his sights on the unguarded daughters: he gets a young man to seduce the middle one and then spreads the word to ruin her reputation. "At this time it was the custom that if a woman was taken in adultery, she should either give herself to all

---

92 Part 1 is top-heavy with typology and symbolism: the three tables represent the trinity, Bron's 12 children represent all the other dozens in the Bible (tribes of Israel, disciples, etc.), and . . . well, here's Jesus himself: "As I said at that table, several tables will be established in my service, to make the sacrament in my name, which will be a reminder of the cross; and the vessel of the sacrament will be a reminder of the stone tomb in which you laid me, and the paten which will be placed on top will be a reminder of the lid with which you covered me, and the cloth called the corporal will be a reminder of the winding-sheet in which you wrapped me" (22).

men or be put to death" (47), and the judges decide to honor her father by burying her alive one night. The youngest sister is next to be seduced, but she takes the "give herself to all men" option and becomes a wild party girl.[93] The eldest sister solicits the help of a confessor named Blaise, who convinces her to avoid making her sisters' mistakes. Like a Sadean villain, the demon is attracted by her chaste resolve and comes to her one night as an incubus and impregnates her. (The author goes out of his way to note twice that she slept "fully clothed.") The girl realizes something happened, and — again to cut to the chase — she gives birth to an exceedingly hairy boy she names Merlin. As the son of a demon he has supernatural knowledge of the past, but as the son of a devout Christian he also has knowledge of the future and a propensity to do good rather than evil. (Naturally, the demons aren't happy about this unforeseen turn.) Like Ben Sira, he is a precocious child, speaking like an adult at 18 months and defending his mother in court at 30 months. He takes up with Blaise and tells him he wants to write a book and so dictates the story of Joseph and the Grail, and thereafter will dictate further install- ments shortly after they happen, making Merlin the putative author of the novel we're reading. He and Blaise then leave for Britain, for Merlin knows that's where his destiny awaits.

After narrating the story of Merlin's "miraculous" birth, we get the equally miraculous birth of Arthur. First we hear of his grandfather Vortigern and his battles, then of his sons Uther and Pendragon (after the latter's death, the former assumes both names) and their battles, and then how Utherpendragon falls in love with the duke of Cornwall's wife, Igerne. By this time Merlin has joined the court as the king's advisor — he magically transported the gigantic stones of Stonehenge from Ireland to Britain as a tomb for Pendragon — and helps Utherpendragon assuage his lust for Igerne by magically transforming him into the duke's shape (the same magic act that allowed Signy to have sex with her brother Sigmund in *The Saga of the Volsungs*), in which form he impregnates her.[94] As it happens, the real duke conveniently dies that night, so Utherpendragon makes an honest woman of Igerne and marries her. From her previous marriage come some of the other future stars of Camelot: one of her daughters is Morgan le Fay, who goes off to Avalon to study magic, and another gives birth to evil Mordred and noble Gawain. Igerne then gives birth

---

93 This is where the poetic version breaks off, which may be significant: Gowans speculates, "This is not at all the type of material that the versifier had been working on, and by now he may have felt that enough was enough" (24).

94 Offstage, the woman-hating Alain somehow engenders a son named Perceval. All these miraculous births are meant to recall Christ's and make Merlin, Arthur, and Perceval special, but you have to wonder if such tales were a quick-thinking medieval woman's explanation for why her child looked nothing like her husband. "Oh but I thought it was *you*, dear husband, who entered my chamber that night!" or "It must have been a what-chamacallit, *an incubus!*"

to Arthur, who is named and claimed by Merlin per an earlier agreement with Utherpendragon. Part 2 ends with Arthur's ascent to the throne after pulling the sword from the stone and establishing the knighthood of the Round Table.

The Grail, neglected throughout most of part 2, returns as the object of a quest in part 3, the story of Perceval. After his father Alain dies, Perceval decides to join the court of King Arthur, a decision that breaks his name-less mother's heart and causes to die of grief. There follows a cracking, allegorical tale of mighty jousts, imperiled damsels, and some splendid supernatural scenes, all of which may be old hat now — especially to anyone who has sat through a dinner-theater production of *Camelot* or guffawed at *Monty Python and the Holy Grail* — but which must have been thrilling to 13th-century audiences. The first time Perceval arrives at the castle of the Fisher King (his grandfather Bron, remember) and witnesses the procession of the Grail, he feels it would be bad manners to ask about it, which is exactly what he needs to do to cure the king of his illness and inherit the Grail. Seven years of further wanderings follow in which he nearly loses his religion, but when he finds the castle again, he says the magic words and wins the prize. The novel ends with an account of King Arthur's European conquests and his return to England to put down his nephew's rebellion; and just as Merlin and Arthur entered the world in a supernatural way, they leave it under the same mysterious circumstances: wounded Arthur goes off to Avalon to be nursed by his half-sister Morgan, and Merlin visits Perceval in Wales a final time and tells him that since he's not allowed to die until the end of the world, he will build an *esplumoir* outside his house and disappear into it.[95]

Robert de Boron mounts a powerful argument for engaging in noble deeds not for vain fame, as the pagans did, but for a higher cause and self-improvement. There's something rather ramshackle and forced about his mixture of Christianity and Celtic myth, ancient British history and 12th-century French chivalry; the characters are still types rather than people; and chronologically it's a mess — Bron, born in the 1st century, is still alive in Arthur's time four centuries later — and yet *Merlin and the Grail* works both as an engaging piece of fiction and as an ambitious attempt at multivalent symbolism, capable of inspiring not only further Arthurian novelists — they all borrow from Robert — but a wide variety of readings, even conspiracy theories and Jungian interpretations. It begins like one of the clumsy Acts of the Apostles but ends beautifully with a superb sense of the sublime. However Robert and his collaborator managed it, they created an intriguing work that laid the foundation stone for Arthurian fiction.

95 Bryant: "This untranslatable — and probably invented — word has wonderful resonances. Its root is 'the shedding of feathers,' implying moulting, transformation, renewal" (172). In John Cowper Powys's immense novel *A Glastonbury Romance* (1932), a scholar goes mad trying to figure out the "esplumoir Merlin." I'm reminded of the phoenix's nest and Celtic fairy mounds.

It was followed a few years later by a somewhat longer, more exciting novel known as *Perlesvaus*, which Nigel Bryant has translated as *The High Book of the Grail*.[96] Drawing on both Chrétien and Robert (as well as Celtic mythology), the anonymous author outdoes both in the stridency of the Christian theme and the violence of the adventures. For this author — probably a cleric of northern France or Belgium — knights were superhero versions of saints, confronting heathens with a lance rather than a sermon. Written around the time of the Fourth Crusade (1202–04), *Perlesvaus* dramatizes the triumph of the New Law (Catholicism) over the Old Law (Judaism and paganism) with Arthurian knights personifying the Church Militant. Fortunately, this doctrinaire theme is offset by considerable formal artistry and an exuberant imagination.

Opening with a capsule version of the origin of the Grail as concocted by Robert de Boron, the author begins his story on Ascension Day with a domestic dispute between King Arthur and his wife Guinevere, in which she accuses him of shirking his divine mission by abstaining from acts of chivalry. Arthur is in a state of ennui, so his queen convinces him to regain their god's favor by seeking new adventures. (Guinevere dies in the course of the novel, which causes Arthur to relapse into ennui; she's obviously his conscience, his Jungian anima.) And then the author does something daring to justify the otherworldly dreamscape in which the rest of the novel takes place: Arthur decides to set out the next morning with a squire named Cahus, who dreams that night that Arthur leaves without him; he pursues his lord to a chapel, where he steals a candlestick, and then encounters a giant who stabs him in the side. Cahus wakes screaming, and when Arthur and others come to find out what's wrong, the squire produces the candlestick he stole in his dream and displays his knife wound — collapsing on the fifth page of the novel the distinction between dream and reality, and allowing the rest of the novel to float free of verisimilitude, even though the author periodically insists he's telling the unvarnished truth. Then again, he states he got the story from the 1st-century Jewish historian Flavius Josephus, who "recorded it at the behest of an angel" (1). Loomis accuses the author of being deranged and paranoid for making such statements (*The Grail* 97), but it's more likely the old ploy of ascribing one's own work to a revered authority to give it credibility, as de Léon did with his *Zohar*. Actually ascribing it to *an angel* is appropriate from this audacious author.

Perlesvaus is only partly concerned with the quests for the Grail by Arthur's three greatest knights, even that of the title character.[97] When the novel opens,

---

96 Published in 1978 and hereafter cited by "branch" (chapter). Loomis dismisses the old 1898 translation by Sebastian Evans entitled *The High History of the Holy Grail* as "inaccurate" (279).

97 Translator Bryant uses the standard form Perceval instead of the original's "Perlesvaus," which means "He Who Has Lost the Vales" (*per-les-vaus*) of Camelot, his father's domain.

Perceval has already visited the Fisher King and failed to ask the meaning of what he sees, which would have restored the ailing king and his kingdom; he is now wandering the countryside making amends by doing good deeds. The king's mysterious illness contaminates the countryside, the Waste Land made famous centuries later in Eliot's long poem (based partly on Jessie L. Weston's analysis of *Perlesvaus* and other Arthurian works in *From Ritual to Romance* [1920].) Gawain is the next knight to visit the Grail Castle, but he too fails to ask the question, instead slipping into a religious reverie at the sight of the holy relics (a lance that occasionally bleeds from the tip as well as the Grail itself). Then Lancelot approaches the castle but is not allowed to view the relics because he is unrepentantly in love with Arthur's wife. The true Christian, the author implies, is sinless and seeks an intelligent understanding of the symbolism of his religion. The author's heuristic text makes the same requirements of his audience, who shouldn't approach it with sinful thoughts about blatant phallic symbols and displaced eroticism, or lose themselves in the wonder of it all, but interrogate and understand the author's extensive symbolism. Periodically a wise hermit will explain to Gawain or Perceval the meaning of the baffling sights they've seen, but it's up to the reader to make sense of the rest.

The novel recounts the various adventures of Arthur and these knights, most of which are undertaken as affairs of honor. Any knight asked by a maiden to right a wrong done to her — and this novel is thick with wronged maidens — is duty-bound to help her, at the expense of whatever personal quest he may be on. Invariably, such assistance leads to further complications, for a dastardly knight killed for his wrongdoings usually has a wife or son now obligated to avenge his death, which leads to further encounters. Consequently, adventures don't simply follow one another but are linked, as in Icelandic sagas; the novel's events are not just sequential but consequential. The author masterfully juggles all these linked events while maintaining the overarching quests for the Grail that each knight is engaged on, suspending one narrative strand to pick up another, then returning to an earlier one in a dazzling feat of narrative engineering.

The adventures themselves are often ritualized and ceremonial, rich in symbolism, all taking place in a land of enchantment.[98] Medieval conventions of allegory enabled the author to make *Perlesvaus* dreamy and strange; much of the time, it's like reading *Alice in Wonderland*. Indulging in his audience's love of the *merveilleux* imported from Celtic legendry, the author will, for example, fill a cart with "the heads of 150 knights, some sealed in gold, some in silver and others in lead," drawn by three strange maidens who sound like

---

98 Eric Rohmer's 1978 film *Perceval le Gallois* (adapted from Chrétien) brilliantly captures this effect with its stylized acting and fairground sets, but the film is pretty and charming, whereas *Perlesvaus* is often weird and brutal.

they're on their way to a lesbian nightclub: one has a shaved head, another is dressed like a man, and the third "wore a short skirt, and carried a whip in her hand" (2). (They show up periodically throughout the novel, and near the end we get the story of those 150 heads.) Every castle is a marvel: in one, time slows down; others are guarded by lions or griffins, inhabited by madmen, or spin on their foundation. There are giants, dwarfs, dragons, telepathic lions, magic chessboards, places called Waste City, the Perilous Cemetery (surrounded by the ghosts of "knights, all black, with burning, flaming lances" [8]), another city that is perpetually burning, a copper tower inhabited by prophesying demons, and a variety of exotic tortures that suggest our author was a medieval Edgar Allan Poe at heart.[99] There is some comic relief by way of a cowardly knight, and one scene where Gawain and Lancelot wear women's clothes. There's even some sexual innuendo, surprising from such a devoutly religious writer: at one point, Gawain does a favor for the two "Maidens of the Tent," who eagerly offer "their service" to him that night in gratitude. The good knight spurns their sexual advances, and the next day one of the frustrated maidens watches with envy as Gawain attacks a knight "and thrust his lance two spans into his body." "'By my life,' said the elder maiden, 'the false Sir Gawain is doing better than he did last night!'" (5).

Some critics have attempted to explain everything in *Perlesvaus* in terms of Christian allegory, and while the author was partly engaged on just such a mission, his soaring imagination propels the novel far beyond paint-by-numbers allegory. His artistic choices are much closer to those of a novelist than an allegorist; for one thing, he delights in detail and description far beyond the needs for allegory — where Robert merely states Bron had 12 sons, the *Perlesvaus* author gives them names and attributes — and exults in brutal, technical accounts of the endless battles between knights. More novelistic is his habit of withholding information: often characters are not identified until it's dramatically right; sometimes friends will unwittingly battle one another because they've concealed their identities, and numerous deceptions are practiced by those withholding information, thereby generating a good deal of novelistic suspense. In his eagerness to tell a dramatic story rather than merely a Christian allegory he frequently forgets the doctrines of the New Law (especially forgiveness toward one's enemies) and indulges in bloody acts of punishment and eye-for-an-eye revenge scenarios that make for thrilling reading but characterize the very Old Law he is ostensibly trying to overturn. Perceval in particular spends most of the last part of the novel behaving more like an Islamic fundamentalist than a Christian hero, beheading people right left and slaughtering anyone unwilling to convert to his religion.

Though its theology may be confused and contradictory — what theology

99 "*Perlesvaus* is the product of a baroque, violent, even grotesque imagination" writes Richard Barber (in Dover's *Companion to the* Lancelot-Grail Cycle, 10–11).

isn't? — *Perlesvaus* is a dazzling work of fiction and compulsively readable. As Loomis says, "it is by no means free of flaws and aberrations" (97), but its strengths outweigh its flaws. It's the first extensive use of the art of enlacement — juggling multiple story-lines — that characterizes all Arthurian fiction and shows a sophisticated grasp of narrative architecture, which would prove useful to succeeding authors as the Arthurian romances grew longer and more complicated. *Perlesvaus* occupies a contested place in the Matter of Britain — nearly every specialist of that subject uses a term like "unconventional" or "singular" to describe it, not always favorably — but it can claim an uncontested place in the history of innovative fiction.

Despite their extensive borrowings from pagan mythology, both *Merlin and the Grail* and *Perlesvaus* are overtly Christian works, in which chivalry is regarded as a kind of violent missionary work, "muscular Christianity" if you will, with the holy fool Perceval held up as the model of the saintly knight. The Arthurian novel then took a brief detour from the sacred to the secular before returning to holy ground, and who better to star in such productions than the all-too-human Lancelot? Barely mentioned in *Merlin and the Grail*, tolerated in *Perlesvaus* because of his valor but denied access to the Grail because of his adultery, Lancelot is the protagonist of the next two Arthurian novels that survive, both of them huge: *Lancelot of the Lake* (c. 1215) is as long as *Moby-Dick*, but it is dwarfed by the gigantic *Lancelot-Grail* (c. 1215–35), which is as long as Proust's *In Search of Lost Time*.

Lancelot was introduced to the literary world in Chrétien de Troyes's *The Knight in the Cart*, in which he rescues Queen Guinevere from abduction. Chrétien doesn't tell us much about his background other than to say he had been raised by a fairy who gave him a magic ring to be used in times of danger. In another verse romance written shortly after, the Swiss poet Ulrich von Zatzikhoven filled in the backstory (probably taken from a lost work) to explain that Lancelot had been abducted as a child and raised by a water fairy, who kept him ignorant of his name and ancestry. In the anonymous prose *Lancelot of the Lake* (*Lancelot do Lac*) we're given a more novelistic treatment of the story. Lancelot is the son of King Ban of Benwick in Gaul (modern France), who dies en route to King Arthur to seek assistance; as his queen mourns his sudden death, a fairy named Niniane — aka the Lady of the Lake — scoops up the infant and disappears with him by jumping feet-first into a lake. (She doesn't take him to an aquatic world but to what we'd now call a parallel dimension, similar to the Otherworld of Irish mythology; the lake is a portal to this other dimension.) The Lady of the Lake rears the boy until he is 18, at which time she sends him off to the court of King Arthur to be knighted.

When Lancelot sets eyes on Queen Guinevere, it's love at first sight for both parties, and from that point on, everything he does is for her sake — not for Christ's sake as in the earlier Arthurian narratives, a significant shift. While Lancelot is being introduced at court, a wounded knight calls for someone to avenge him, but none of Arthur's knights is foolish enough to accept this stranger's odd conditions, for he "will have to swear, on holy relics, that he will do his best to avenge me on all those who say they love the man who gave me these wounds more than they do me."[100] As Arthur points out, that could take years and involve killing dozens of people, and the knight hasn't even divulged the source of the conflict. But so anxious is Lancelot to begin knightly adventures and (more important) to impress the queen that he accepts the challenge. The bulk of the novel consists of Lancelot's adventures, after each of which he makes sure word gets back to Guinevere of his achievements. His exploits are so splendid that halfway through the novel he wins the affection of a powerful king named Galehot, who is waging war against Arthur. Galehot's attraction to Lancelot seems homosexual — he sneaks into Lancelot's bed on several occasions, shares his clothes with him, and at least once kisses him on the mouth, though admittedly male friendship was expressed differently back then — and is so desirous of having Lancelot as his friend that he surrenders to Arthur, even though his army has the upper hand. When Galehot learns of Lancelot's overriding affection for Guinevere, he gallantly arranges a tryst for the two, at which time they exchange their first kiss. This is an expertly paced scene, with the author indulging in narrative foreplay until the reader is panting for them to kiss, and it's this passage that Dante later memorialized in the *Inferno*: Paolo and Francesca call the author of *Lancelot of the Lake* a pimp for inspiring them to kiss and go to Hell (5:127–37).

The sexual dynamics in this novel are surprisingly varied and make it the most modern-sounding of the Arthurian narratives. Near the end of the novel Lancelot joins the Knights of the Round Table and is publicly acknowledged as Guinevere's lover without condemnation, a very French arrangement. Arthur seems OK with that, for as it happens he has a son from a previous relationship, and during the novel's final battle he gets himself captured by falling for a seductress who happens to be the lady of the castle he's besieging. And at the end of the novel he is duped into having an affair with a "false Guinevere" who claims to be his true wife. Galehot is similarly OK with the arrangement, because he gets to "share" Lancelot with the queen for a portion of the year. It should also be noted that Guinevere is much older than the teenage Lancelot, as is the Lady of Malohaut, who also takes a Mrs. Robinson interest in the young knight. Relationships between older men and younger women are common enough — in novels as in life — but this older woman/younger

100 Page 62 in Corin Corley's translation (1989), hereafter cited by page number since it's not divided into chapters. This is an abridged translation — there is no unabridged translation in English; its 418 pages represent about two-thirds of the complete work — and is based on Elspeth Kennedy's definitive two-volume edition, *Lancelot do Lac: The Non-Cyclic Old French Prose Romance* (Oxford UP, 1980).

man variant is new to the novel. (In ancient Greek novels, older women were sex-starved schemers, never treated as Guinevere is here as a suitable object of affection.) There's lots of sexual symbolism — inevitable with all those phallic lances and swords[101] — and even some kidding about homosexual attraction after Gawain blurts out he'd change into a woman if that meant securing Lancelot's love; the queen is amused and says she can't top that:

> "By the Lord," she said, "Sir Gawain has made every offer that a lady can make, and no lady can offer more."
> And they all began to laugh. (303)

And the author makes some very modern-sounding, even Proustian observations about love: "It is always the way that the thing one desires is denied one the most, and there are some people who are reluctant to let others enjoy the thing they most love" (308); "one cannot love someone without fearing them" (321). The novel ends on a somber, if not homosexual note: a damsel tells Galehot that "she saw Lancelot killed the in Forest of Adventures," and the news kills Galehot (418).

Turns out the lady was lying (we're not told why), but by that time Lancelot was such a beloved character that even if he had died, he — like Sherlock Holmes — would have been brought back to life by popular demand. And thus he became the central character in the most ambitious literary project of the Middle Ages, the vast *Lancelot-Grail* cycle.[102] Written and assembled sometime between the years 1215 and 1235, it consists of five branches (or books): *The History of the Holy Grail* (*L'Estoire del sant Graal*, about 300 pages long), *The Story of Merlin* (*L'Estoire de Merlin*, 465 pages), *Lancelot* (*Le livre de Lancelot del Lac*, 1,300 pages), *The Quest of the Holy Grail* (*La Queste del sant Graal*, 200 pages), and *The Death of King Arthur* (*La Mort le roi Artu*, 190 pages).[103] We don't know exactly how it was composed or by whom, but the scholarly consensus is that it came about on this wise: with encyclopedic ambition and the Old Testament as a model, a northern French author or

---

101 E.g.: "The knight was holding his lance by the middle, and when he heard the queen speak, he looked up, and his hand relaxed and the lance fell, so that its head passed through the samite of the queen's cloak" (218). In our post-Freudian era it's easy to see sexual symbols in older works where none were intended, but sentences like this suggest the author knew exactly what he was saying. When Lancelot becomes Guinevere's lover he also acquires Arthur's sword — wink wink, nudge nudge.

102 This five-part novel has gone under a variety of names in the past — the Pseudo-Map Cycle (under the mistaken assumption it was composed by a cleric named Walter Map), the Prose *Lancelot*, and most often the Vulgate Cycle — but nowadays scholars prefer the *Lancelot-Grail*, the title of the first complete English translation (1993–96).

103 The page counts are from H. Oskar Sommer's seven-volume edition of the Old French original, *The Vulgate Version of the Arthurian Romances* (1908–16), for the recent English translation uses a large, double-column layout and a tiny point size, making its page counts misleading.

(more likely) team of authors decided around the year 1215 to synthesize all the tales and "histories" of Arthur and his knights that had accumulated by then into an all-encompassing master narrative, one that would nip in the bud the secular drift of *Lancelot of the Lake* and reassert the sacred nature of chivalry.

They began in the middle with *Lancelot*, keeping it virtually intact but converting the hero's love for Guinevere from a virtue to a vice, and then more than doubled its length with further adventures aligning Lancelot with the quest for the Holy Grail (which was mentioned only in passing in the original [413]), resulting in a work about the size of *War and Peace*. They then added the shorter *Quest of the Holy Grail* and *The Death of Arthur* to form a trilogy, and then finally circled back to the beginning to recount *The History of the Holy Grail* and *The Story of Merlin*: in essence a 700-page amplification of the first hundred pages of Robert de Boron's *Merlin and the Grail*. The scope and achievement of the completed work is awe-inspiring; Saintsbury considered it "to be the greatest, most epoch-making, and almost the originating conception of the novel-romance itself."[104] It is the Chartres Cathedral of Arthurian literature (whose construction overlapped that of the *Lancelot-Grail*) and the primary source for all works of chivalry that followed.[105]

And like Chartres Cathedral, the *Lancelot-Grail* is a religious work. The Old French savoir faire of Chrétien and the author of *Lancelot of the Lake* was toned down by the new authors, some of whom were as pious as Robert de Boron and the *Perlesvaus* author. Their doctrinaire agenda is clear from the beginning: in a first-person prologue, an unnamed hermit tells how one Good Friday around the year 750 he was visited by the tripartite Christian god (he harps on the importance of the Trinity as a doctrine) who hands him "a small book no longer or wider than the palm of a man's hand," which (like an e-book reader) miraculously contains the entire *Lancelot-Grail*.[106] After being swept up to the third heaven and shown the sights — the incident is modeled on Paul's boast that he did likewise (2 Cor. 12) but reads like *The Book of Enoch* — the hermit begins to transcribe the contents of the minibook. The *Perlesvaus* author claimed an angel gave him his story, but our author goes him one better and claims the Trinity wrote it; at any rate, it's made clear

---

104 *A History of the French Novel*, 29. His superb discussion of the novel (pp. 27–54) is worth seeking out.

105 With the massive *Lancelot* proper supported on both sides by shorter works, the *Lancelot-Grail* even resembles a cathedral; Arthurian critic "Jean Frappier likened the configuration to the west façade of the great Gothic cathedrals, with their large central portal flanked on either side by two smaller portals" (Carol Dover, in her *Companion*, 88 n7).

106 The quotation is from p. 6 of *The Lancelot-Grail Reader*; since the complete five-volume edition is prohibitively expensive and somewhat inaccessible, I'll be quoting from this paperback abridgment of the same translation for the first three branches. This 400-page book represents only one-sixth of the complete work, but it contains all the key episodes and summaries of the excluded parts.

from this fanciful prologue that the *Lancelot-Grail* will not be merely a long adventure story but an epic religious parable.

Following the prologue, we're given an expanded version of Robert de Boron's "Joseph of Arimathea," differing in some details but following the main story-line. As in some of the clunkier apocrypha, the heavy-handed use of typology and an overreliance on miracles is tiresome and often tasteless: after Jesus makes Joseph's pious son Josephus the first bishop, he teaches him how to administer communion the hard way — by literalizing the metaphors until Josephus is ready to gag (and inadvertently exposing the barbaric origins of the Eucharist in human sacrifice):

> "Take this and eat it; this is My flesh, . . ." These words were said by Josephus over the bread he found prepared on the paten covering the chalice; and the bread immediately became flesh, and the wine, blood. Then Josephus saw clearly that he was holding between his two hands a body just like that of a child, and it seemed to him that the blood he saw in the chalice had fallen from the child's body. Seeing this frightened him so much that he did not know what to do. So he remained silent and began to sigh and weep in great anguish because of his great fear.
>
> Then Our Lord said to him, "You must break apart what you are holding so that there are three pieces."
>
> Josephus replied, "Oh, Lord, have mercy on your servant, for my heart could not bear to break apart such a beautiful figure."
>
> And Our Lord said to him, "If you do not obey My commandment, you will have no part in My heritage."
>
> Then Joseph took the body and, putting the head to one side, broke it off from the trunk as easily as if the flesh of the child were cooked like meat when it has been forgotten on the fire; next, fearfully, he broke the rest into two parts. . . .
>
> When he stood up again, all he saw before him on the paten was a piece in the semblance of bread. He took it, raised it on high, and after giving thanks to his Creator, opened his mouth to put it inside. He looked and saw that it was still an entire body. When he started to pull it back, he could not, for he felt it was being put inside his mouth before he could close it. (26–27)

Had enough of this sublime theology? No?

> Then the angel who was carrying the paten came before Joseph, who knelt and received with joined hands his Savior in visible form, as did each of the others, for it seemed to each one that when the piece in the semblance of bread was put in his mouth, he saw a completely formed child enter his mouth. (27)

Such crude nonsense as this and too many lectures from a heavenly voice spoil the beginning of the *Lancelot-Grail*; it's like entering a cathedral but having first to pass through a gift shop hawking tacky religious gewgaws. The authors make one sensible improvement to Robert's version: the man told to catch a fish for the miraculous meal is not Bron but his chaste son Alan the Fat (Robert's Alain li Gros), who thereby begins the line of "Rich Fishermen" that eventually produces the Fisher King of Arthur's time. Having already compiled the Lancelot cycle allowed the authors to plant many foreshadowings in this early section, strengthening the artistic unity of the entire cycle, but mostly they just pad out Robert's version with more missionary activity and miraculous conversion tales.

Branch 2, *The Story of Merlin*, is infinitely more interesting and creative. The first fifth closely follows Robert's "Merlin" up to the point where Arthur pulls the sword out of the stone and becomes king of England. But several decades elapse between that event and the appearance of Lancelot; since the *Lancelot-Quest-Death* trilogy had already been written, the authors were challenged to fill in the gap and explain how Arthur became the noble warrior-king of Geoffrey's history, how he met and married Guinevere, how he assembled the Knights of the Round Table, and also how the seeds of his later failures were sown during this period. The authors had been working on this vast fiction for 15 or so years by this point and needed only this final section to complete their labors, so they gave it their all.

They provided rousing accounts of Arthur's many military campaigns to establish his warrior credentials, and emphasized his bravery by way of supernatural battles in France against a giant at Mont-Saint-Michel and a huge devil-cat at the Lake of Lausanne. His political skills are obvious as he wins over rebellious barons, makes alliances with other kings, and adopts a band of young heroes led by Gawain. But Arthur's eventual downfall, and those of Merlin and Lancelot as well, is due to lust, which comes in many sordid varieties in *The Story of Merlin*. Both Arthur and Merlin, remember, were born illegitimately via rape; no sooner does young Arthur ascend the throne than he letches after his married half-sister, and sneaking into her room one night and pretending to be her absent husband, he engenders a son: Mordred, the bastard (literally) who will betray him in branch 5. We're also told that on the same night when King Leodagan impregnated his wife with Arthur's future queen, he also raped his seneschal's wife, who later gave birth to a daughter identical to his own Guinevere (the "false Guinevere" of later episodes). And when Arthur meets Guinevere, it's her physical beauty that enflames him, not her mind or personality. After giving us a detailed, half-page description of Gwen's "very fine body," the authors add almost as an afterthought that she was considered "the wisest woman in Great Britain," but Arthur focuses only on the fact "her body was very well put together, for her waist was slender and her hips low . . . her breasts were firm and hard like little apples" (78). All this lust and rape and near-incest undermine the noble achievements of Arthur and his court and eventually cause its ruin.

Lust proves to be Merlin's undoing as well, but it results in one of the finest episodes in the entire *Lancelot-Grail*. Wandering in Brittany one day, Merlin spies a young woman named Viviane by a lake.[107] "And when Merlin saw her, he looked at her for a long time before he said a word. And he said to himself that he would be most unwise to fall asleep in sin and lose his mind and his knowledge just to know the delights of a young lady, to shame her and to lose God." He hesitates, but then "went forward and greeted her nevertheless" (79).[108] Viviane is polite but standoffish, so Merlin tries to win her over by teaching her magic. Intrigued, she agrees to be his friend — but "without any wrongdoing or baseness" — if he'll teach her everything he knows. Eager to show off for her (as men have always done, and always will), Merlin draws a wide magic circle by the lake, which attracts a band of aristocratic merrymakers (also his creation) from the forest, singing and dancing; once they enter the circle, Merlin raises up "a castle fair and strong, and beneath it an orchard with all the good smells in the world" (80). Viviane is suitably impressed, but complains *she* hasn't learned anything yet, so Merlin vows to teach her "more wonders than any woman has ever known," suggesting she write it all down in a book (just as Merlin has been dictating the whole novel to Blaise in installments). Then we get this remarkable scene:

> While the maiden and Merlin were talking together, the ladies and maidens gathered together and went off dancing toward the wood, along with the knights and squires. And when they got to the edge, they rushed in so fast that they did not know what might become of them. Indeed, the castle and everything had all faded into nothing, but the orchard stayed some time afterwards because of the maiden, who sweetly entreated Merlin. (80–81)

Having conjured up these merrymakers, Merlin forgets to end the spell, inadvertently releasing his magical creatures into the wilds of the real world, much as the characters in Flann O'Brien's *At Swim-Two-Birds* and other 20th-century metafictions (Alfau's *Locos*, Sorrentino's *Mulligan Stew*, MacNamara's *Book of Intrusions*) take on a life of their own when their creator neglects them.

Viviane pledges her eternal love and proves to be a good student, mastering Merlin's magical art as quickly as she did his heart, writing it all down in her own spellbook. Merlin leaves her temporarily to assist Arthur in his military

---

107 The lake is important, as later events will reveal. In legendry and myth, lakes and water are the dangerous domains of mermaids and Nereids, Rhinemaidens and other bathing beauties.

108 If she looked anything like the Viviane in Edward Burne-Jones's gorgeous painting *The Beguiling of Merlin* (1874), I can't blame him; in my twenties, I had a reproduction of this on my wall. Merlin looks old enough to be her father, and his face superbly reflects the despair of an older man in unrequited love with a younger woman.

campaign in Brittany, and also befriends Morgan the Fay and offers to teach her some spells as well — his standard pick-up line, apparently. By the time he returns to Viviane, he knows she will betray him but is powerless to resist her fatal attraction. As she strings him along, he teaches her more magic tricks, until finally she asks him "to teach me how I might keep a man imprisoned without a tower or walls or irons, but through wizardry, so that he could never get away but through me" (88). Thoroughly 'whipped, embracing his doom, he tells her what she wants to know, which she of course turns against him, imprisoning him in an imaginary tower in the Forest of Broceliande. She rewards him by promising, "Dear friend, I will come here often, and you will hold me in your arms and I you, and you will do forever whatever you please" (89). And, *mirabile dictu*, she keeps her word.

It's an enchanting episode for several reasons: first, there is the literalizing (if not origin) of several standard romantic tropes like being "spellbound," "enthralled," or "bewitched" by someone, under the spell of "that ol' black magic" crooners used to sing about. Then there's the *All about Eve* reversal whereby the adoring student betrays her beguiled mentor. But most intriguing is the emergence of Merlin as a symbol of the writer.[109] Merlin loses the world and his god because of his love for a woman, but the authors go easy on him, because they must have realized he is one of them. In earlier Welsh mythology, Merlin is a warrior-chief who went mad after the battle of Arferdydd and fled to the woods, where he became a poet-seer (exactly like Suibhne). Merlin is dictating (to Blaise) the very story we're reading — a surrogate for the *Lancelot-Grail* authors — and his conjuration of castles and knights and maidens out of thin air is analogous to the art of literary creation. Near the end of *The Story of Merlin*, Gawain seeks out Merlin in the Forest of Broceliande, at which time the lovesick enchanter is no more than a voice: words on a page. Nearing the end of their mammoth task, the anonymous authors of the *Lancelot-Grail* thereby acknowledge that they too will soon disappear, leaving only their voices, but permanently enshrined in a fantastic creation of their own making — and like Merlin, all for a woman: the Virgin Mary.[110]

A different, less charming account of the Merlin-Viviane affair is given at the beginning of *Lancelot*, the enormous centerpiece of the *Lancelot-Grail*. (Despite the authors' attempt to harmonize all the Arthurian legends, there are numerous discrepancies throughout.[111]) Here she's called Ninianne, and

---

109 Tennyson certainly regarded him that way. He signed a few of his early poems "Merlin," and in his late poem "Merlin and the Gleam" (1889) identifies himself with the "gray Magician."

110 See Joseph Goering's *The Virgin and the Grail: Origins of a Legend* (New Haven: Yale UP, 2005) for the importance of this Catholic goddess to the grail myth.

111 But E. Jane Burns asks us to bear in mind the nature of our text: "When we consider that the Arthurian prose romance was typically recorded in many manuscript versions, that the

instead of imprisoning him in a beautiful tower in Brittany and visiting him occasionally, she "sealed him in a pit in the perilous forest of Darnantes" in Wales, where he is never heard from again.[112] Years later, Ninianne becomes the Lady of the Lake, the water fairy who abducts the baby Lancelot and raises him as her own child. The first third of *Lancelot* is virtually identical to *Lancelot of the Lake*, which took us up to Lancelot's induction into the Knights of the Round Table; in the second third, he goes on further adventures, endures further separations from Guinevere, suffers at the hands of Morgan (Arthur's evil half-sister, who loves Lancelot but punishes him for loving Guinevere instead), all interlaced with related adventures by Arthur's other knights (Gawain, Yvain, Bors, Sagremor, Lionel, Hector). Lancelot becomes "the world's best knight" (274) but not Heaven's best knight because of his ongoing affair with Guinevere. Everything he does is for her sake, and while that's one reason the book was so popular in the Middle Ages, especially with the ladies,[113] the authors periodically remind readers that he's not the prophesized Good Knight that is needed; as a resident of the Grail castle tells Bors, "if your cousin Lancelot had kept himself [chaste], as you intended to keep yourself, at the beginning of his knighthood, he would have brought to an end everything from which you now suffer, for he is so illustrious in knighthood that he's unequaled in all the world. But on the other hand he is so debased that all the virtues that should be in him have declined and died through the frailty of his loins" (272). The final third of *Lancelot* introduces the knight who will succeed where Lancelot failed: as a result of yet another bedtrick — and yet another rerun of the Immaculate Conception, complete with symbolic dove — Lancelot impregnates the virgin daughter of the Grail-keeper (he thinks he's in bed with Guinevere), who gives birth to Galahad. (When Lancelot discovers the deception he is ready to kill her, but she pleads, "Oh, noble knight, don't kill me! Have pity on me as God did on Mary Magdalene" [242] — interesting that she would compare herself to Christ's groupie.) We're given an account of Galahad's boyhood, along with that of young Perceval, while elsewhere Lancelot and Arthur cross the sea to Gaul to defeat the king who had dispossessed Lancelot's father of his kingdom, neatly connecting the end of the vast book with its beginning while setting the stage for the next generation's quest for the Holy Grail.

The authors offset the potential monotony of 1,300 pages of knightly

---

story committed to writing was subsequently reproduced on multiple occasions by a reciter reading aloud before an audience, and that the written version of any tale was subject to frequent rewriting and recasting by different authors across several centuries, it becomes clear that the medieval 'text' shares little of the narrative autonomy and 'coherence' that we ascribe to printed works by named authors" (*Arthurian Fictions*, 2).

112 Quoted from the unabridged edition (2:12); the episode is not included in the *Reader*.

113 Chaucer's Nun's Priest insists his tale is as true "As is the book of Launcelot de Lake, / That wommen holde in ful gret reverence" (7:3212–13).

adventures with a number of dramatic dualisms and oppositions: *Lancelot* opens with two warring kings (Lancelot's father and Claudas of the Waste Land); Lancelot has two names (his baptismal name is Galahad), two mothers (his birth mother and the Lady of the Lake), and divided loyalties (Arthur and Guinevere); there is pagan sorcery vs. Christian miracles; Britain vs. Gaul; chastity vs. normalcy; male friendship vs. female, and perhaps heterosexual vs. homosexual (confirmed bachelor Galahaut remains ardently attached to Lancelot and dies of a broken heart when he hears the false rumor of his death); and ultimately, courtly ideals vs. religious ideals. "Too bad Our Lord pays no heed to our courtly ways," Guinevere tells Lancelot, "and a person whom the world sees as good is wicked to God" (161). Lancelot's exemplary behavior shines so brightly throughout the long novel that only a mean-spirited prude would consider him wicked, but the tension is there nonetheless.

As in *The Story of Merlin*, *Lancelot* exhibits a metafictional self-awareness about the act of creation. A wise man speaks of the power of language when he shows Galehaut "a little book which treats the meaning and mystery of all the great spells that can be cast with words" (159) — and what are novels if not spellbooks that make us believe in things that never were? — and from time to time the knights recount their adventures to Arthur's scribes to be "put into writing, so that they would be remembered after their death" (218). But the greatest tribute to the power of art occurs after Lancelot is imprisoned by Morgan; he borrows some paint and brushes from an artist and covers the walls of his prison cell with pictures illustrating scenes from his life, especially those with Guinevere; "this would be a great comfort in his sufferings," we're told, and art even affords some pornographic relief for the prisoner: "When he saw the image of his lady, he bowed in front of it, saluted it, came over and kissed it on the mouth, and took more pleasure in that image than in any woman except his lady" (262–63). Art as magic, as memorial, as consolation: Lancelot's paintings are the secular equivalent of stained-glass windows depicting scenes from the Bible, and as they did with Merlin, the authors celebrate their own artistry in these various acts of composition.

As if aware they may have made the profane courtly ideal a little *too* appealing, the authors bring back religion with a vengeance in the fourth branch, *The Quest of the Holy Grail*. Depending on your tastes, this is either the most sublime or the most ridiculous part of the *Lancelot-Grail*. This branch is evidently the work of a single author: if not a Cistercian monk, someone committed to their ideology.[114] Picking up where *Lancelot* left off, he describes the arrival one Pentecost of young Galahad at the court of King Arthur. (The

---

114 The Cistercian cult followed the teachings of Bernard of Clairvaux (1091–1153), a bitter opponent of Abélard's rationalistic philosophy and the instigator of the disastrous Second Crusade, thus responsible for countless unnecessary deaths.

text states that 454 years have passed since the first Pentecost, setting the story around the year 484.) In a slight return to the original event, thunder strikes, the interior of Arthur's palace lights up, and the Holy Grail hovers in like a UFO, circling the hall and furnishing a banquet for the dumbstruck onlookers before disappearing. Gawain leads the assembled knights in declaring a new quest for the Holy Grail, which Arthur takes hard: considerably older now, he knows this is the beginning of the end of Camelot, and that most of his knights will never return from this quest. Also saddened are the ladies of the court, especially "those who counted husbands and lovers among the companions of the Round Table."[115] They all volunteer to accompany their knights, but "an old and venerable man wearing the religious habit" steps up and issues the first of this branch's many misogynistic statements: "none may take maid or lady with him on this Quest without falling into mortal sin" (46–47). No girls allowed.

There follows a variety of adventures and dreams that puzzle the participants until they find a Cistercian monk or hermit to explicate their meaning. Every event or dream is an allegory based on Catholic typology and symbolism (with a few Celtic myths awkwardly shoehorned in), and every religious recluse is a prescient theologian. As one Arthurian critic puts it, "the whole romance is infested by hermits,"[116] and the numerous sermons and lectures quickly grow tiresome. Once a monk has explained the meaning of a dream, the knight often stays with him a few days to receive further instruction. A typical chapter opens thus: "Now the story relates that the holy man persuaded Lancelot to stay with him three days, and took advantage of his presence to exhort him ceaselessly with homily and discourse, saying: . . ." (134). What these monks ceaselessly exhort is the importance of virginity — not merely abstention from sex (chastity) but the complete extinction of any interest in it — and the knights' sexual histories will henceforth determine who will find the Holy Grail. All those with wives and/or lovers are automatically disqualified, naturally — no need for them to even leave Arthur's castle — along with ladies' man Gawain and especially Lancelot, now in his early forties. He is denounced harshly on several occasions for his love for Guinevere, whom he ungallantly repudiates. (However, Lancelot is last seen heading back to Camelot; mark the sequel.) That narrows the competition down to the three noblest knights, whose adventures take up most of the Quest: Bors, Perceval, and Galahad. Although Bors has led a good and holy life, we are told he "had never sinned in the flesh, save the once when he had begotten Elyan the White" (179; cf. Lancelot-Grail 269). But once is enough, so he's

---

115 Page 46 of Matarasso's translation; from this point on I'll be using her translation and Cable's Death of King Arthur for the remaining two branches of the Lancelot-Grail because they're unabridged and widely available.
116 Barber, The Holy Grail, 154.

out. Pious Perceval manages to keep it in his pants through most of the quest but then drinks a little too much and is attracted to a beautiful woman aboard an anchored ship (who turns out to be a fiend in disguise — pretty much the author's opinion of all women); even though he repents before taking the plunge, the fact he was even *tempted* suspends him from the game. Among Arthur's 150 knights, only Galahad remains "a virgin both in fact and in intent" (247).[117] Galahad has all the personality of a robot, programmed by the author to demonstrate the Cistercian ideal, but is rewarded at the end with a glimpse of the divine enshrined in the Holy Grail, whereupon he dies in religious ecstasy, like the Torah-crazed students at the end of the equally symbolic *Zohar*. The grail has been interpreted in recent years (especially by Jungians) as a symbol of wholeness, psychic integration, and at-one-ment with the universe, but Galahad's disengagement with humanity and early death suggest the concept is closer to suicidal solipsism than to the Catholic nirvana the author intended.[118]

The *Quest* is interesting for several technical reasons: by making his monks the sole explicators of the symbolic episodes and dream sequences, the author gives them narrative control of the text, taking it out of the hands of the secular narrators of *Merlin* and *Lancelot* and bestowing on them a kind of first-person omniscience. Their blocks of explication stop the narrative flow but solve the problem of providing background information out of temporal sequence; bits and pieces of the previous history of the Holy Grail are fed to the reader at different times, not only reminding the reader of what happened 2,000 pages earlier in the cycle but bringing it up to date as well. (Bors, Perceval, and Galahad take a magic ship back to Sarras, the Saracen city to which Joseph of Arimathea took his followers after leaving Israel.) As in any allegory, the author forces us to read on at least two levels, and his extensive use of biblical citations reminds us that the Bible must also be read on at least two levels to qualify as a living guide and not dead history. "Text and meta-text are brought into continuity," notes Tzvetan Todorov in an interesting commentary on the novel.[119] And the author juggles those two levels while handling as masterfully as any of his fellow *Lancelot-Grail* authors the typically interlaced story-lines of Arthurian narrative.

But his ideology is repulsive and inhuman. For other writers, knighthood

---

117 Actually that phrase is used to describe Perceval's nameless sister, who plays a small but important role near the end of the *Quest*, and then dies. In fact, aside from Elyan and a brief reference to Guinevere, none of the female characters in the *Quest* is personalized with a name.

118 For the Jungian angle, see *The Grail Legend* by Emma Jung and Marie-Louise von Franz.

119 *The Poetics of Prose*, 120–42. He concludes, "the Grail is nothing but the possibility of narrative," which would have surprised the author of the *Quest*, but no matter: "So that if the author could not quite understand what he was writing, the tale itself knew all along" (139, 142).

is an inspiring example of an honorable, principled life, with compassion for the needy at the foremost; a knight vowed "always to come to the aid of widows, maidens, and impoverished and disinherited noblemen, if ever he was summoned to do so or there was need" (*Lancelot-Grail* 258). For the author of the *Quest*, knighthood is a symbol of the soul's quest for ecstatic union with its god, an inward-directed concern for one's soul rather than an outward-directed concern for others. At several points in the story a monk will chastise a knight for rushing off to help someone instead of attending to the more immediate needs of his own soul. "For this service in which you are entered does not pertain in any way to the things of earth, but of heaven," a monk tells Lancelot, "whence you can see that he who would embrace it and attain his goal must firstly purge and cleanse himself of the corruption of this world, so that the enemy may have no part in him" (134–35). That is, he should withdraw from the world and live like . . . a monk! The author elevates priests to symbolic knighthood by describing their vestments as "armor," and describes angels as "knights of heaven."[120] But the simple fact the real world does include widows and the impoverished but does *not* include devils or heaven reduces all this to a pathetic fantasy where monks are held in higher regard than knights — a pathetic *misogynistic* fantasy when one realizes his reference to "the enemy" more often than not means a beautiful woman.

The Death of King Arthur returns us to the real world of mature men and women for the somber conclusion of the *Lancelot-Grail*. The greatest possible quest now over, the *Death* is a brief envoi, a sad farewell to the world of Arthur. It has the fewest supernatural elements, the most insight into psychological motives, and the cleanest narrative line, making it the closest of the five branches to what most readers would consider a novel. The style differs from the preceding four, making more use of dialogue, dramatic speeches, and soliloquies, but with more subdued use of diction and virtually no narrative suspense. In fact, just as Joyce wrote *Ulysses* in a variety of styles, it's possible to see the *Lancelot-Grail* displaying the chief prose forms of its day:

The History of the Holy Grail — apocryphal act
The Story of Merlin — legendary chronicle
Lancelot — courtly romance
The Quest of the Holy Grail — allegory
The Death of King Arthur — apocalypse

Since the quest for the Holy Grail has depleted the ranks of Arthur's knights, and since Galahad has disenchanted and shut down the remaining marvels of Arthur's "land of adventures," the king knows the end is near, so he vainly tries to keep up appearances by calling for a new tournament. But what follows is

120 Cf. Kierkegaard's "knight of faith" in *Fear and Trembling.*

a tragedy of errors, a series of mistakes and misunderstandings that results in the death of King Arthur and the dissolution of his kingdom.

The allegedly reformed Lancelot has returned to court, but "it took him less than a month to become just as deeply and ardently in love as he had ever been, and he fell back into sin with the queen just as before" (24–25). He decides to travel incognito to the tournament (otherwise no one would dare fight him), and then lodges at the castle of a rich citizen of Escalot whose young daughter promptly falls in love with the aging but famous knight. (He's now pushing 50.) He reluctantly agrees to the pesky girl's request to wear her sleeve as a love-token in battle, and when word reaches Guinevere that Lancelot was so adorned, she flies into a jealous rage "because she really imagined that Lancelot had deserted her, and loved the girl whose sleeve he had worn at the tournament" (48), an error of judgment that has a domino effect. The queen tries to enlist Bors's help to revenge herself on Lancelot, but he refuses to believe the lie and leaves in disgust along with Hector, the first of many to abandon Arthur's court. The queen then ironically becomes the victim of an equally baseless lie when she hands an apple, which had been poisoned by a scoundrel named Avarlan and intended for Gawain, to a knight named Gaheris, who dies. Everyone assumes the deadly apple was GuinEVEre's idea (recalling the unpleasantness in the Garden of Eden), including Arthur, who rashly condemns her to be burned like a witch. The only knights who would have defended her are the ones she drove away (Lancelot, Bors, and Hector), compounding the irony. Gawain clears up the queen's jealousy by telling her the true story of the girl of Escalot, who has killed herself from unrequited love,[121] but then himself goes insane with rage when he is misled into thinking Lancelot deliberately killed his best friend Gaheriet while rescuing Guinevere from her fiery execution. Because of this error, Gawain urges an increasingly befuddled and Lear-like Arthur to wage war against Lancelot, first in England and then later in Gaul, where Gawain will meet his death.

Mistrust, pride, jealousy, lying, treachery, and jumping to conclusions: these are the mundane causes of the fall of Camelot, not Lancelot's original adultery or the machinations of Fortune (which is often evoked in this final branch). Hypocrisy, too: Arthur seemed fine with Lancelot as his wife's gallant as long as everyone politely looked the other way; it is only when Lancelot's enemy Agravain (Gawain's brother) threatens to go public with the liaison that Arthur becomes outraged. I don't want to defend adultery, but the authors make it pretty clear that Guinevere was merely a trophy wife for Arthur; the true love of her life was and always will be brave Sir Lancelot, and his sterling

---

121 This incident became the basis for Tennyson's famous poem "The Lady of Shalott," and of J. W. Waterhouse's beautiful painting of the same title, a reproduction of which I've owned all my adult life because of the unsurpassed loveliness of the redheaded subject.

devotion to her — from the time he first met her but especially here in the final branch — is enough to make any female reader's knees go weak. So even though their adultery is the "official" reason for the end of the Arthurian era, the author's heart really isn't in this explanation, hence all the references to the pagan Wheel of Fortune and to the faults of other characters in the novel.[122] In a splendid speech in defense of Lancelot, Bors (speaking for the author?) urges the queen to stand by her man and not become one of those women who dishonors him, evoking the biblical hussies who betrayed David, Solomon, and Samson, as well as the example of Helen of Troy (perhaps another source for that apple of discord). The haste with which Arthur, on the other hand, condemns the queen to death overrides his protests of love for her and reminds the reader of the "false Guinevere" episode in *Lancelot*, where he likewise condemned her on the flimsiest of evidence. In contrast, Lancelot and Guinevere may experience lovers' squabbles — he renounces her while under the influence of a cult leader, she believes he's run off with a younger woman — but they remain deeply devoted to each other over a 30-year period. They challenge the conventions, the polite fiction of state-sponsored marriage, and that — not the "sin" of adultery — gets them in trouble. As we learned from *Luke–Acts*, the status quo always protects itself, no matter how false and hypocritical it may be.

When Arthur goes off to Gaul to fight Lancelot, his Oedipally complex "nephew" Mordred (another polite fiction — actually his bastard son) takes over the country and spreads the lie that Arthur has been killed so that he can marry Guinevere. (If anyone's "sin" of adultery is to be blamed, it is Arthur's with Mordred's mother, as Malory will insist.) As in Robert de Boron's version, Arthur returns to Britain and, at the end of an epic battle on Salisbury Plain, "the father killed the son, and the son gave his father a mortal wound" (220). At this point, the author makes several intriguing narrative choices to end this huge Arthuriad, some predictable, some not. The mortally wounded Arthur makes his way to the seashore, and after instructing the last remaining knight of the Round Table to throw his sword Excalibur into a nearby lake — out of which an arm catches the sword and brandishes it, one of the few supernatural occurrences in the *Death* — he is met by a magic ship containing Morgan the Fay and other women; but instead of taking him off to Avalon and leaving open the possibility of his messianic return (as in *Merlin and the Grail*), they bury him at the nearby Black Chapel, apparently negating that possibility. Out of fear of Mordred, Guinevere has retreated to a nunnery — just as Perceval's aunt retreated to a hermitage in fear of a warring king in the *Quest* (102), suggesting the religious life is a cowardly retreat from the world, not a noble

---

122 In fact, the medieval concept of romance took adultery for granted: see *The Art of Courtly Love*, the 12th-century manual by Andreas Capellanus and an invaluable companion volume to Arthurian fiction.

spiritual choice — where she soon dies, separated from both her husband and her lover. Lancelot, on the other hand, has a triumphant end: after defeating the rest of Arthur's enemies, he learns of the deaths of Guinevere and his cousins, which plunges him in despair. Riding at random "where adventure carried and took him" as in the good old days (231), he arrives at a hermitage and decides to devote his remaining years to the religious life — not from fear like the ladies but from the conviction there's nothing and no one left for him in the world.[123] After four years of holy living, he dies, and a fellow hermit has a vision of a host of angels carrying him to heaven — the adulterer whose sin allegedly caused the destruction of Arthur's world! But that's not all. Lancelot asks to be buried not next to Guinevere or back in Gaul, as one might expect, but in the same tomb as Galehot, his greatest male admirer! Hmm. Whether this is meant to parallel the spiritual ascendancy of his son Galahad at the end of the *Quest* or to surpass it — a repentant sinner is more welcome in the Christian heaven than one who has led a blameless life according to Luke 15:7, which has always struck me as monstrously unfair — *The Death of King Arthur* is a curious but satisfying conclusion to this massive memorial in remembrance of things past.

During Bors's speech about dishonorable women, he reminds Guinevere "it is less than five years since the death of Tristan, the nephew of King Mark, who loved fair Yseut so faithfully that he never did anything to harm her in all his life" (78). Tristan is the other great romantic hero of medieval literature, and although he began as an independent character out of Celtic legendry, he soon was drafted into the ranks of the Arthurian fellowship. Around the same time Chrétien was writing his verse narratives, Tristan became the subject of narrative poems that, unfortunately, have come down to us only in fragments: one by the French poet Béroul that seems to be closest to the Celtic origins of the character, a more courtly one written in Old French by the English poet Thomas, and the longest an adaptation of Thomas's work by the German poet Gottfried von Strassburg, the finest treatment of the story but left unfinished. The earliest complete version, and the earliest one in prose, is a translation/ adaptation of Thomas's version into Norwegian by a Friar Róbert in 1226 entitled *The Saga of Tristram and Isond (Tristrams saga ok Ísöndar)*.[124]

---

123 James Burge notes: "It was not uncommon for high-ranking people in the Middle Ages to take holy orders as a kind of retirement strategy" — *Heloise and Abelard: A New Biography* (NY: HarperCollins, 2003), 79.

124 I'll be quoting from Paul Schach's 1973 translation by chapter number, but will be dropping the diacritical marks from names. The hero's name (based on the French word for sad, *triste*) varies from Tristan to Tristram in different sources — cf. Kerouac's *Tristessa* or Stereolab's "You Used to Call Me Sadness" — as does that of Yseut/Isond/Isolde.

Róbert abridged some of Thomas's material and pared down its introspective and moralizing tendencies, resulting in a serviceable account of Tristan's career before he was Arthurianized. The hero's father was a nobleman of Brittany named Kanelangres who sailed to England to pay his respects to its ruler, King Markis of Cornwall. Kanelangres takes part in a tournament and impresses everyone, especially the ladies, which allows the author to announce his theme:

> . . . all the maidens and ladies in that great crowd cast affectionate eyes on him. All of them desired his love, even though they had never seen him before and did not even know from what country or family he came or what his name was. Yet they inclined their hearts and minds toward him, for that is the way of women. They prefer the fulfillment of their desires rather than moderation, and often desire what they cannot obtain while they reject and neglect that which is theirs to have and to hold. Thus it was with Dido, who was so ardently in love that she burned herself to death when her dearest, who had come from a distant land, deserted her.
>
> Thus misfortune has befallen many who willingly abandoned themselves to such great sorrow. (4)

Bonjour tristesse. Love at first sight, a virtue elsewhere in literature, is a vice here in this cautionary tale about the dangers of sexuality. The king's sister Blensinbil is especially attracted to Kanelangres, and the author devotes an entire chapter to her physical torment as lust grips her like a fever (6). Blensinbil's explanation for this is revealing:

> "Surely," she said [to herself], "this man is endowed with sorcery and evil powers, since I am tormented so grievously by the mere glimpse and sight of him. Oh, God, be Thou the shield and protection of my dreadful love, for terrible troubles will come from this knight. And if all who look at him experience the same feelings as I do, then he surely possesses evil arts and venomous torments with which to destroy people — for I tremble all over my body and burn inwardly from the sight of him." (7)

This is the first of several symbolic displacements of the causes of lust. Nowadays, a minority of educated people know that sexual arousal is due to visual stimuli to the ventral striatum section of the brain and involuntary chemical and neurological reactions — hormones and pheromones, dopamine and norepinephrine, the reduction of serotonin, etc.[125] — but in the Middle Ages (as in many pockets of America today) Christians believed lust

---

In chapter 4 I'll discuss an 11th-century Persian novel that anticipates the Tristan story in so many particulars that some critics feel it, rather than Celtic legendry, is the true origin.

125 See Helen Fisher's *Why We Love: The Nature and Chemistry of Romantic Love* (NY: Holt, 2004).

was a demonic urge, the genitals Satan's own power plant.[126] When Guinevere first suspects Lancelot of cheating on her, she likewise assumes "some lady or girl has caught him with a magic potion or spell" (*Death* 49), and throughout medieval literature we see these psychological projections of lust outward — to a spell, potion, or demonic being — in a blatant attempt to avoid personal responsibility for one's sexual attraction to others. The famous love potion that occurs later in the Tristan story was no symbol for the medieval author or his audience, but a recognition of its symbolic value is what has made the story so attractive to later writers and composers, first in Swinburne's verse-narrative *Tristram of Lyonesse* and reaching its apotheoses in Wagner's great opera and in Joyce's *Finnegans Wake*.[127]

Blensinbil puts Kanelangres under her spell the more mundane way — with her banter and ventral striatum-stimulating beauty — so he hangs around King Markis's court longer than he had planned. He is badly wounded in a battle, and when Blensinbil comforts him, they get carried away and she conceives Tristram "in the anguish of her love" (12), but father and mother die soon afterward. Sad Tristram is raised by a foster-father, becomes as skilled and accomplished as his father (especially on the harp), but then is abducted by Norwegian merchants and winds up back in Cornwall and joins Markis's retinue, without either of them knowing they're related until the foster-father likewise shows up and tells the story. Tristram later kills a fierce Irishman named Morold, who had been collecting tribute from Markis for years, leaving a segment of his sword in the Irishman's skull but not before becoming poisoned by it. Turns out Morold is the brother of Queen Isodd of Ireland, the only one capable of curing anyone poisoned by that sword, so Tristram sails to Ireland and sneaks into the royal palace to get the cure. His harp-playing charms the Irish court, especially the queen's daughter Isond, who begins taking harp lessons from him. Eventually it is decided to send Isond to Cornwall under Tristram's guard to marry Markis and thus end the hostilities between the two nations. But during the voyage over the Irish Sea a love potion intended for the honeymoon is mistakenly drunk by Tristram and Isond, who immediately fall in love with each other and have sex out on

---

126 The authors of the Church-approved witch-hunting manual *Malleus Maleficarum* (1488) assure us "that the power of the devil lies in the privy parts of men" (Summers trans., 26a). The funniest expression of this belief can be found in Boccaccio's *Decameron* (day 3, story 10), in which a monk convinces a naïve girl that his erect penis is a sign of demonic possession, which can be cured only by plunging his "devil" into her "Hell." The girl quickly develops a passion for "putting the devil in Hell" and thinks it's a splendid way to "serve God." See p. 264 below.

127 Though *Finnegans Wake* isn't strictly a new version of the Tristan story like Swinburne's and Wagner's, Joyce drew upon it heavily: Tristan appears on the very first page ("Sir Tristram, violer d'amores") and one of the first episodes Joyce wrote was a dialogue between Tristan and Iseut, which eventually resulted in the loveliest chapter of the novel (2.4: pp. 383–99).

the open sea, beginning "for both of them a life filled with grief and enduring distress, with carnal desire and constant longing" (46).[128]

In some versions of the Tristan story, the potion lasts only a few years (an acknowledgment of the real-life waning of lust for the same partner?), but in this version the potion unites them for life. Isond persuades her virginal maid Bringvet to sub for her on the wedding night — Markis first has her, then a few hours later has Isond, and can't tell the difference in the dark: they never do in these bedtricks — and thereafter Tristram and Isonde enjoy a Lancelot and Guinevere–type clandestine relationship, with Markis occasionally getting suspicious but, like Arthur, generally ignoring it. At one point the couple is banished from the court, and significantly they move into "a secluded place by a certain river in that cliff that heathen men had had hewn out and adorned in ancient times with great skill and beautiful art" (64). The heathen hideaway predates Christianity, just as their relationship is outside conventional Christian norms. In one of many echoes from the Irish *Pursuit of Diarmaid and Gráinne*, the king finds them sleeping in their cave with a sword on the ground between them, and convinced they weren't having sexual relations, he forgives them and welcomes them back to court. (Actually, the author implies the couple had just had sex outside and retired in the cave to sleep it off.) But when the king finally discovers the two are more than just good friends, Tristram takes leave of his beloved (who gives him a ring, symbolically wedding him) and returns to Brittany.

After wandering for a while, Tristram becomes friends with a duke who has an unmarried sister named Isond, and in an effort to take his mind off the other Isond, he rashly agrees to marry her. But on the wedding night he comes to his senses and makes excuses not to have sex with her in order to stay true to his beloved. Like Lancelot in prison painting pictures of his paramour, Tristram finds a fortress of solitude and has craftsmen create lifelike statues of Isond, her maid, and others from his life, and spends much time talking to and fondling the statue of his lover. Once again Tristram is wounded by a poison sword, from which only the Irish Isond (who inherited her mother's abilities) can cure him; he sends for her, but her return is delayed by rough weather; his spurned, still-virginal Breton wife lies to Tristram and tells him the only ship she sees in the distance has a black sail, which causes him to die from grief because the signal was supposed to be a white sail. When the Irish Isond finally arrives and finds Tristram dead, she utters a wildly inappropriate prayer (apparently inserted by the pious author to offset the profane subject matter) and then dies brokenhearted on top of him. The Breton Isond spitefully buries them on opposite sides of a church. "But it came to pass that an oak tree grew up from each of their graves, so high that their branches

---

128 "Constant *craving*" would have preserved the alliteration, and for some would evoke that gorgeous, Tristanic song by k.d. lang.

intertwined above the gablehead of the church. And from this it could be seen how great had been the love between them" (101) — the heathen oak (venerated by the Druids) transcending the Christian church.

Tristram isn't transported by angels to heaven like Lancelot, but the adulterer is likewise treated with surprising respect and admiration by his Christian author, who makes only perfunctory protests about the immorality of sex outside of marriage. (In those days of arranged marriages, many found their true loves in others anyway.) The language retains some of the alliteration and rhymes from the Old French original, and many scenes have the prettiness of a ballet, but otherwise Róbert lets the story tell itself. Aside from adapting it somewhat to the tastes of his patron, King Hakon Hakonarson of Norway, he apparently didn't feel at liberty to make it his own. Because it's a translation/adaptation of an incomplete original, it's difficult to evaluate *The Saga of Tristram and Isond*, but by preserving the key elements of the story it provides a basis for comparison to the more ambitious versions that followed.

And not until Wagner would there be a more ambitious version than what's known as the Prose *Tristan*, a 1,500-page novel written in Old French shortly after the completion of the *Lancelot-Grail*, and with a similar encyclopedic impulse to incorporate all romances into Arthur's fictional domain. (Arthur is mentioned a few times in passing in the *Saga*, but only as a conquering king.) It is apparently the work of two men, if the text can be believed: according to its English translator, a knight named Sir Luce of Gat Castle (near Salisbury) began the work between 1230 and 1235 but then died, and in the 1240s it was completed by the Frenchman Helie de Boron, who claimed to be related to Robert de Boron; Luce was primarily concerned with Tristan's original career, but Helie more concerned with transforming him into one of Arthur's knights of the Round Table. Later copyists and redactors added their two francs, and the result is a sprawling work somewhat inconsistent with itself, but it was this one that became the best-known version of the Tristan legend in the Middle Ages, easily eclipsing in popularity (if not artistry) the verse narratives of the 12th century on which it was based.

Luce certainly had no qualms about making the tale his own, nor of complicating its theme. The Tristan and Iseut relationship is only one of several cases of passionate love in the novel, all of them disastrous, but in the case of the title character thrilling enough to complicate the question of adulterous love. In this account, Tristan is not a bastard but the legitimate son of King Mark's sister Elyabel and Meliadus, the king of Leonois.[129] The queen

---

129 Translator Curtis provides this intriguing note: "Probably *Lyonesse*, a prosperous kingdom widely thought to have been submerged between Cornwall and the Scilly Isles. It was described in early English chronicles as flourishing until its sudden disappearance beneath the sea" (327) — a Celtic Atlantis. At 326 pages, Curtis's abridged translation *The Romance*

is pregnant when King Meliadus goes hunting one day; he encounters "a young lady from that region, very beautiful, and so much in love with him that she could feel no love for any other man." She tricks him into following her back to her castle: "As soon as he was inside, his heart and his will changed so completely that he could remember no one in the world except the lady he saw in front of him. And you should know he was so bewitched that he did not recall his wife nor his land nor anything on earth apart from the one who was holding him captive" (4–5). This is Luce's way of introducing his theme of extramarital love as bewitchment, a dangerous loss of any sense of responsibility to others. Queen Elyabel goes in search of him and runs into Merlin, who tells her she'll never see her husband again, which causes her so much grief that she goes into labor and delivers a child, whom she names Tristan "because of my sadness and the sadness of your birth" (7), and then dies. As he did with Arthur, Merlin assigns a man named Gorvenal to raise Tristan and predicts he will become famous as Galahad and Lancelot, bringing the original Celtic story into alignment with the French Arthurian mythos. The king is rescued from the bewitching Cornishwoman and returns to find his wife dead and himself the father of a beautiful boy.

King Meliadus eventually marries a woman straight out of Central Casting for the role of evil stepmother. After she tries repeatedly to kill Tristan, he escapes with Gorvenal to Gaul, where he is taught how to conduct himself as a knight and how to play the harp. (His musicianship is part of his rock-star appeal to women.) When Tristan is 12, his host's daughter falls in love with him, and his indifference almost gets him killed by the scorned teen, who soon commits suicide, ratcheting up the theme of sexual attraction as a deadly force. He returns to Cornwall at age 16 and defeats the Irish enforcer demanding tribute, as in Friar Róbert's *Saga*, is poisoned by the sword, and makes his way to Ireland, to be cured not by the Irish king's wife but (in an aesthetically more efficient choice) by his stunning daughter, "Iseut the Blonde, the most beautiful young girl alive and also one of the most intelligent. . . . She was not yet fourteen years old" (42). That spells trouble. A visiting knight named Palamedes falls in love with the Blonde, so Tristan — who until now has shown no interest in her — decides he wants her too, which earns him the condemnation of the author: "Thus pride and arrogance took hold of Tristan for love of my lady Iseut" (46). Incognito like Lancelot, Tristan humiliates Palamedes and sends him packing (though this lovefool will be back for an important episode); then the queen discovers Tristan's the one who killed her brother and nearly kills him herself, but the sympathetic king merely banishes him from Ireland. My lady Iseut couldn't care less at this point.

Back at King Mark's court in Cornwall, Tristan gets ensnared in a messy

---

of Tristan represents only a fifth of the original, but it's the only one in English; hereafter cited by page number.

affair that prefigures his betrayal of his uncle. Tristan catches the eye of a neighboring noblewoman, whom Mark also lusts for; she makes an assignation with the younger man, which of course makes Mark jealous, for he considers himself much worthier of her favors by any rational account. Her dwarf[130] tells him, "Love doesn't choose in accordance with what is right but with what it wants; the only reason it follows is the pursuit of its inclination" (59), stressing the selfishness and irrationality of lust, a major theme of *Tristan*. Selfishly and irrationally, Mark insists on ambushing his nephew and almost loses his life in the conflict; Tristan makes it to the noblewoman's castle and experiences "great pleasure and delight" in her bed, but is interrupted by the arrival of her husband; he flees, the husband goes after him, and Tristan is wounded a second time that night, this time almost fatally. The cuckolded husband is badly wounded and is sure to punish his unfaithful wife when he returns: everyone looks bad in this farcical incident, another indication of the author's critical opinion of Tristan and extramarital flings, and another indication of Luce's artistry: this conflict adds dramatic resonance to the later romantic triangle between Mark and Tristan and Iseut.

When Mark eventually decides to remarry, he sends Tristan to Ireland to acquire Iseut: partly because he hopes he'll get killed there — Tristan is still banned — and partly because he's heard Tristan praise Iseut's beauty and wants to steal her from his hated nephew and thus reassert his superiority. Tristan promises to do so before grasping Mark's motives, and rather naively hopes that by delivering the girl to him he can win back his uncle's favor. (You can see the author setting his trap of irony here.) After a digressive Arthurian interlude indicating the author's close familiarity with the *Lancelot-Grail*, Tristan returns to Ireland, now in the good graces of the Irish king because of a favor he performed during that interlude. Iseut, a few years older now and even more beautiful, impresses Tristan, who briefly considers taking her for himself, but he decides that would be disloyal and so fulfills his assignment. This is clearly the moral thing to do, as well as politically the right thing to do: everyone rejoices that Ireland and Cornwall will no longer be in conflict, and Tristan shows character in his willingness to put the wishes of the community before his own personal "inclination," as the dwarf put it. (The author does not record Iseut's opinion of all this, her silence telling us her place in this patriarchal society; fond of playing chess, she's just a silent ivory chess-piece being moved by others across a board.) But then the queen provides the love potion for the return voyage, and the author milks the famous mistaken-potion scene for all it's worth, writing rapturously of their newfound feelings

---

130 I've neglected to mention that there are more dwarfs per page in Arthurian literature than in any other literature. Most of them are scoundrels, a victim of the courtly prejudice that beautiful people are noble and ugly, malformed ones evil. Morgan the Fay, for example, is a fright.

for each other and the joy with which they dispense with Iseut's virginity, contrasting their private joy with the public joy that had preceded this scene for maximum foreboding.

Mark is furious to learn Tristan survived the trip, but is knocked out when he sees Iseut and falls in love with her because of her beauty — not her personality or intelligence, of which she's shown very little so far. On the wedding night, Iseut and Brangain perform their bedtrick to dupe Mark, and Tristan and Iseut begin their clandestine love affair. The author tells us, tellingly, that everyone is struck by how right Tristan and Iseut look together, and how surprised they are he "had handed Iseut over to his uncle; they were more suited to one another both as regards their beauty and their age" (94). Just as Lancelot is a more suitable mate for Guinevere than her legal husband Arthur, there is a clash here between what's legal and what's natural; throughout the novel, the author skillfully plays upon his audience (his readers as well as the Cornish citizens) to alternately condemn and condone the adulterous couple; we're outraged that they are breaking the law but thrilled to see them escape Mark's many attempts to catch them in the act. Soon Palamedes returns to remind us of the danger of obsessive love; after stalking the queen, he kidnaps Iseut and locks her in a tower. Guarding her, he lapses into erotic trances from which he cannot be roused, as will Tristan later — more creepy reminders that this is no healthy love. Palamedes's case prefigures Tristan's end: Iseut is "the lady of ladies; it was to his misfortune that he ever set eyes on her beauty, for since he was unable to have even a part of what he wanted, there was no way in which he could escape from dying of it in the end" (104). Tristan attempts to rescue her, but it is only when Iseut tricks Palamedes into obeying her command to leave — in effect, slapping a restraining order on him — that he lets her go, though he persists in his doomed love throughout the rest of the novel.

One of Mark's many attempts to expose Iseut's adultery indicates almost comically the courtly attitude toward sex outside of marriage. A knight brings to court a magic drinking horn (created by Morgan le Fay) from which no unfaithful woman can drink without spilling its contents, symbolizing the excessive, extramarital semen she's been indulging in. Libidinous Iseut puts her lips to the phallic horn and "a large part of the wine spilt all over her, so that she was quite soaked by it" (139). The rest of the ladies are also tested, and guess what? "All the ladies present, of which there were at least a hundred or more, tried to drink from the horn, but only four managed it without spilling the wine all over themselves" (140). In most Jewish or Arabic tales, as in the Egyptian *Story of Petese*, that revelation would lead to mass beheadings, which is what Mark proposes, but the husbands of the wet wives shrug it off: "My lord, my lord," they urge with worldly sophistication, "you can put to death whom you wish, but whatever you do to the Queen who is yours, we shall keep our wives. God forbid that we should have them killed for such a poor reason as this one seems!" (140). Mark loves Iseut and doesn't *really* want to kill her — he's more concerned with his reputation — so he agrees with the barons that the test results are inconclusive (though I imagine there were some heated arguments that night between all but four couples).

So the Tristan story is not about adultery or even loyalty but about neurotic obsession, and the author piles on further examples of unhinged sexual attraction. A young Cornish girl falls in love with Tristan, is spurned, and so turns her love to hate and helps Mark's loyal retainer Audret capture (again) the lovers in the act. Later, the brother of Iseut of the White Hands accompanies Tristan back to Cornwall and falls fatally in love with Iseut; she likewise spurns him, which eventually kills him, though not before he causes a serious rift between the lovers, which drives Tristan mad — not just distraught, but literally mad: "he so lost his reason and his memory that he did not know what he was doing. Like a madman he began to tear the clothes he wore, so that he went around the Forest of Morroiz more or less naked, crying and howling, leaping and running as though he were a mad beast. . . . he existed on raw meat, for he spent his time catching animals here and there, and then ate them quite raw, flesh and hide" (286). The ancient Greek novels often showed lovers becoming sick from passion, but Tristan's madness strips erotic longing of any pretty romantic notions to expose it as a longing for death.[131] Our author doesn't handle this insight as artistically as Béroul did before him, or as theatrically as Wagner would six centuries later, but it's what separates Tristan from Lancelot, with whom he is often compared in this novel. Lancelot keeps his adulterous longings within civilized bounds, and goes to Heaven in the end; Tristan recovers from his madness, is caught in bed with Iseut, and is poisoned again (by Mark) and suffers a long, painful death. Mark and Iseut visit him on his deathbed — he's still in Cornwall; the author skipped the whole return-to-Brittany, white sail/black sail thing — and Tristan challenges his beloved, proposing a suicide pact: "Dear lady, now that I'm dying, what *will* you do? Won't you die with me? Then our souls will leave our bodies together" (323). As death-obsessed as Tristan, Iseut bends over him to give a final hug: "Then he clasped her to his breast with all the strength he had in him, so that her heart stopped beating; and he himself died at that precise moment." No angels transport Tristan to heaven: "They both died of love; there was no other comfort for them" (324).

131 See the first 50 pages of de Rougemont's *Love in the Western World* for a classic (if somewhat overbearing and Catholic) analysis of this *Liebestod* theme in the Tristan narratives. Lancelot likewise goes mad for love temporarily (*Lancelot-Grail Reader* 296–301), but it's milder than Tristan's case. Translator Curtis has written an interesting essay on the topic: "Tristan *Forsené*: The Episode of the Hero's Madness in the *Prose Tristan*," in Adams's *Changing Face of Arthurian Romance*, 10–22.

What should have been a tragic, cautionary tale became one of the greatest love stories in Western literature, though with little help from our authors. The writing is often clumsy and repetitious, especially in the later portions written by Helie, who dilutes the intensity of the dramatic story with countless Arthurian digressions and subplots — Tristan even joins the quest for the Holy Grail, for which our author lifted entire portions of the *Lancelot-Grail* version. The authors do contribute to the notion that art and grief (if not madness) are related: during their most suicidal moments, Tristan, Iseut, and the brother of Iseut of the White Hands compose lengthy poems, inspired by the same despair that is destroying them. And this is the only Arthurian novel I know of to make use of letters within the text, rhetorical set-pieces that allowed one of the authors to show off his style. But the long novel was immensely popular during the Middle Ages despite its artistic shortcomings, and rather than discouraging obsessive, lawless passion, the story (as popularized by Malory) inspired later writers to explore at greater psychological depth the bizarre relationship between eros and death.

As though the encyclopedic *Lancelot-Grail* and Prose *Tristan* had exhausted all the possibilities of Arthurian fiction, no major prose works followed in their wake, only numerous adaptations and translations. The anonymous Anglo-Norman author of *The History of Fulk Fitz Warine*, a novella composed in bad French around 1320 (apparently adapted from an earlier verse version), incorporated Arthurian elements into this historical romance about a rebellious English baron of the late 12th/early 13th centuries. He relied on Geoffrey of Monmouth for an account of early Britain, stages a Merlin-like prophecy, describes some jousts, and alludes to characters like Kay the seneschal. This artless novella represents a transition from fanciful Arthurian romance to more realistic fiction, but otherwise holds only antiquarian interest for its similarities to the Robin Hood cycle.

But in the 14th century there appeared one more Arthurian meganovel that outdid even the gigantic *Lancelot-Grail*. After he finished *Moby-Dick*, Melville wrote to Hawthorne: "Leviathan is not the biggest fish; — I have heard of Krakens."[132] *Perceforest* is a kraken of a novel, some seven *thousand* pages long. It was written in the 1330s and '40s by an unknown cleric at the court of William I in Hainaut (on the Belgian-French border); it was popular enough to go through two editions in France (1528, 1532) and to be translated into Italian and Spanish, but it has never been edited in its entirety. A multivolume French edition has been underway since 1979, but I'll be dead

---

132 Letter dated 17 November 1851 (included in the Norton Critical Edition of *Moby-Dick*, 546), referring to a fabulous Norwegian sea monster "said to be capable of dragging down the largest ships and when submerging to suck down a vessel by the whirlpool it created" — *Brewer's Dictionary of Phrase and Fable*, ed. Adrian Room (NY: HarperCollins, 1999), 665.

before an English translation ever appears — *hélas!* — so what follows has been gathered from secondary sources.[133]

Robert de Boron boldly began the Arthurian mythos in 1st-century Israel, but the *Perceforest* author goes back even farther for an even more surprising genesis: he asserts that at one point in his brief but illustrious career, Alexander the Great was swept by a storm at sea to Britain, which he found inhabited by the descendants of refugees from the Trojan War. (He didn't make that second part up; Geoffrey of Monmouth and other early historians believed that Aeneas's great-grandson Brutus led a band of Trojans to Albion and renamed it Britain after himself.) Finding the kingdom in a state of anarchy, Alexander appoints two Greeks to rule over them: his brother Betis assumes the name Perceforest to become king of England, and Gadifer takes Scotland. I'll let Jane H. M. Taylor describe the rest:

> The dynasties that [Alexander] founds and the son whom he fathers while in Britain are to be the direct ancestors of King Arthur. This grandiose historical sweep has been lost to view, the author contends, because of successive invasions of the country; it has been his good fortune to rediscover the facts, and his only role has been to embellish the stark historical record.
>
> The audacity of the original conception is matched by the execution. One of the most remarkable features of the romance is the sense of discipline that the writer achieves in controlling his vast canvas. Two distinct matrices are developed. The first is sociopolitical: the history of this pre-Arthurian Britain is presented as a search for political stability and religious purity. Under Perceforest and his heirs, the country undergoes a series of cyclical vicissitudes: ideal chivalric kingdom, invasion and devastation by the Romans under Julius Caesar, regrowth and pacification, new devastation by the Danes. Always in the background, the unscrupulous forces of evil, often using sorcery, threaten the peace and stability that the writer posits as the ultimate political good and preach a dangerous polytheism. Against these forces stand chivalry, courtliness, and an ideal, austere religion preaching a single God. The romance culminates with the coming of the Grail to Britain and the propagation of the new Christian faith. The second matrix is structural. Not only does the romance explain the Arthurian kingdom, it also prefigures it. Thus, for instance,

133 Dunlop's *History of Fiction* (1:238–50); Jane H. M. Taylor's entry in *The New Arthurian Encyclopedia* (355–56) as well as two of her essays, "Faith and Austerity: The Ecclesiology of the *Roman de Perceforest*" (in Adams's *Changing Face of Arthurian Romance*, 47–65) and "La Reine Fée in the *Roman de Perceforest*: Rewriting, Rethinking" (in Wheeler's *Arthurian Studies*, 81–91); Delcourt's "The Laboratory of Fiction: Magic and Image in the *Roman de Perceforest*"; and Huot's monograph *Postcolonial Fictions in the* Roman de Perceforest. The American critic F. M. Warren long ago dismissed *Perceforest* as the work of someone too eager "to give to the reading public something that was new, and in carrying out this desire he jumbled together fact and fancy, erudition and superstition, in the most ridiculous way. . . . *Perceforest* is merely a literary crazy-quilt, and only bewilders its readers . . ." (119–20), which sounds too much like the knee-jerk reaction to experimental novels to take seriously.

Perceforest introduces the Order of the Franc Palais, which mirrors the Round Table; Perceforest's son Betides, who betrays Britain to the Romans, is a reflection and prefiguration of Mordred; and Gallafur, the perfect knight, prefigures Galahad.

Within the broad sweep of these two guiding threads, the work is a tissue of romance themes and motifs. Quests and tournaments, adventures chivalric and supernatural, proliferate and interlace across some 200 years of supposed history. But these too the writer is able to vary and animate: he has an endlessly inventive fantasy and a lively sense of the ridiculous, and his huge cast of characters includes a number who are vividly imagined and original, from the accident-prone Estonné to the delicate and subtle young girl Lyriope, from the Rabelaisian child Passelion to the Puck-like Zéphir. It is a measure of the writer's remarkable success that the reader's sympathies engage with the heroes and heroines, and that we arrive at the end of the sixth book breathless perhaps, but neither lost nor bored. (*New Arthurian Encyclopedia* 355–56)

Doesn't that sound phenomenal?! This vast prequel to the *Lancelot-Grail* is fascinating for several reasons. The earliest form of the Sleeping Beauty fairy tale appears somewhere in it (though the waking of Brynhild by Sigmund in *The Saga of the Volsungs* may be the true origin). One of "accident-prone Estonné"'s gaffes involves being turned into a bear, taking part in several ursine adventures, and then being turned back again and thinking it was all just a weird dream. The "subtle young girl Lyriope" is actually a sorceress, and King Gadifer's quiet wife Lydoire (who was a pupil of Aristotle back in Greece) begins studying the magic arts and eventually becomes the Fairy Queen, with magical powers and prophetic abilities to rival Merlin's and Morgan the Fay's. (As in the Icelandic sagas, sorcery/enchantment is largely a feminine domain.) "Puck-like Zéphir" takes the reader on a wild tour of Hell and even introduces us to Lucifer. An Oz-like king named Aroès keeps his subjects enthralled by stunning light shows and film images from a hilltop projection booth. At jousting tournaments, women perform stripteases to encourage their favorites: "Caught up in the excitement of combat, women offer one piece of jewelry after another; when the game is over, they sit there bare-headed with their arms stripped of their sleeves."[134] There are "ladies of the forest" who dwell in invisible castles that prove to be utopias of sexual fantasy and bliss for the lucky knights invited therein. (Alexander mates with the owner of one such establishment, a woman named Sebille, on whom he fathers a son.) In addition to dangerous lions and serpents, there is a bizarre animal called the *beste glatissant* or "baying beast." (It appears as the Questing Beast in earlier Arthurian romances.) "This creature is described as a hybrid mixture of different animals," Huot explains, "having the body of a leopard, the feet of a stag, the hindquarters of a lion, and the head of [a] serpent, together with" — and here's our author's innovation — "a fantastic

---

134 Huizinga, citing *Perceforest* in *The Autumn of the Middle Ages*, 88.

neck whose iridescent colours, shimmering in the sunlight, entrance all who behold it, humans and animals alike" (55). The hallucination-inducing neck is like a virtual reality program catering to personal fantasies:

> And so it might seem to them that in this blaze of colours they saw maidens, ladies or damsels, or knights, depending on what was in the hearts of the beholders. And then they were so entranced by this delightful vision that they lost their senses. [...] And when this beast saw these birds or other animals, men, or women, and that they were completely absorbed in gazing upon it, by its nature it would pounce on them and kill them, and it had no other way of catching its prey. (*Perceforest* book 2, trans. Huot, 56)

Many knights loses themselves in the erotic visions they see in the beast's neck, and Perceforest himself is so addicted to what he sees that he chases after it like a drug before a hermit stages an intervention.

Pre-Christian Britain is filled with such dangerous illusions, which function both as symbols of the imperialistic gaze of colonizers entranced by the exoticism of a conquered land, unable or unwilling to see it for what it actually is, as well as a metafictional allegory about the creation of art. Like King Aroès, like Sebille, like the baying beast, the artist is a creator of illusions, of fanciful creations that are entrancing but unreal. If misread or misinterpreted, a work of art can be dangerous, as was the case when Goethe's *Sorrows of Young Werther* led to a series of suicides, or Hitler adopted Wagner's operas as his theme music. But if read correctly, a work of art can be instructive. *Perceforest* contains numerous beautiful but baffling lays whose meanings are unraveled in dramatized displays of critical analysis, heuristic lessons in close reading that the author intends his audience to apply to the entire work. Unlike most earlier Arthurian romancers, the *Perceforest* author used his fanciful history to comment on current events; in protest against the excesses of the Catholic church in the 14th century, he urged fewer priests and sacraments and more meditation and contemplation, and in simple settings rather than lavish cathedrals. As Taylor writes above, the author had a sociopolitical agenda in mind, and to ignore that is to fall under the spell of the beast.

Washington Irving pronounced *Perceforest* a "delectable romance" and records an anecdote from it in his *History of New York* (book 5, ch. 7). I'm as sad as Tristan that I'll never be able to read this stupendous work.[135]

---

135 There are two other interesting-sounding Arthurian novels that have never been translated into English, a prequel and a sequel to the Tristan legend: *Palamedes* (or *Guiron le Courtois*) predates the Prose *Tristan* and deals with his father's generation, while *Ysaÿe le Triste* (late 14th cent.) asserts Tristan and Iseut produced a child shortly before they died, Ysaÿe the Sad, who deals with the anarchy that followed in Britain after the death of King Arthur. For comic relief he has a sidekick dwarf named Tronc, said to be the lovechild of Julius Caesar and Morgan the Fay! It sounds like a big, inventive work that deserves translation.

I want to look at one more Arthurian novel, as short as *Perceforest* is long, before concluding this survey of prose treatments of the Matter of Britain with a few remarks on Malory's *Morte Darthur*.

The Knight of the Parrot (*Le Chevalier du papegau*) is a delightful, hundred-page novel written in France sometime in the 14th century. It is the only Arthurian narrative that focuses solely on Arthur, and specifically on his early career, though it's filled with so many folkloric episodes that it's a departure from (rather than an addition to) the Arthurian mythos. It opens on the day of young Arthur's coronation; a damsel approaches the festive court to request a knight to aid her lady, and too new to the job to delegate adventures to other knights, as he will do later, Arthur turns over the reins of his kingdom to a regent and goes off with the damsel. He is distracted by another damsel who requests his assistance in a battle, which results in Arthur winning a prized parrot and its keeper, yet another dwarf. This is no ordinary pet, but a garrulous, well-informed parrot who henceforth acts as Arthur's advisor, advocate, and minstrel, singing songs while Arthur is traveling. (In one scene, when Arthur is being undressed by some giddy 15-year-old girls, the bird even plays the pimp.) He's also something of a party animal, "for he did not want to do, hear, or see anything but sing, dance and have a good time."[136] Arthur is so delighted with it that henceforth he calls himself the Knight of the Parrot — perhaps a takeoff on Chrétien's Knight with the Lion.

He finally returns to the first damsel in distress, enticingly known as the Lady of the Blonde Hair, residing in the Amorous City. After the Knight of the Parrot defeats her monstrous enemy — a bizarre half-giant, half-seahorse creature called the Fish-Knight — the Lady of the Blonde Hair prepares a special bedroom in which she can show her appreciation to her rescuer. On the first night, they just fool around on her bed, and then to test his devotion she asks him to deliberately perform poorly at the next day's celebratory tournament. He reluctantly does so, and that night she prepares to reward him even further when this shocking scene occurs:

> When the Knight of the Parrot saw that he could do whatever he wished of the lady, without any restraints, he grabbed her with both hands by her tresses and threw her down to the floor, saying to her: "Most evil whore, full of every filthy wile, take this and that! Learn now about the service I promised you, for I promised you today to serve you as the worst knight in all the world. I want you to see how well I follow your orders; for today you stripped me of my reputation and honor, for which I shall be shamed all the days of my life. So now abandon yourself to me so that I may take my pleasure of you, and let you thus esteem me

---

136 Pages 64–65 in Vesce's rather stiff translation; a comic work like this needs a livelier one.

as the worst knight in the whole world; it would have been better for you had you taken me for the best knight of all. Now then do I wish to render you service as the most vile knight in all the world, as it is well fitting to do to you." Then he dragged her by the hair all through the chamber, hitting her and kicking her, . . . (36–37)

There was nothing like that in earlier Arthuriana, nor like the scene that follows, an interior monologue (*avant la lettre*) in which the Blonde goes through a remarkable series of psychological changes all too familiar to those who deal with battered women: at first she's outraged, then ashamed of herself for encouraging this "strange, unfortunate knight whose name I do not even know," then admires him for sticking to his promise to act the vile knight on and off the tournament field, and how proud and brave he must be to "have dared touch me the way he did," then condemns him for blowing his chance to acquire her kingdom, then thanks him for beating her — "He paid me the greatest courtesy that ever a baron did, for he paid me well indeed for my baseness" — and blames herself for forcing him to beat her, and winds up looking forward to "making peace" with him (37–38). The battered woman gets her wish, and the next day they kiss and make up. Things go differently the next time the knight enters her bedroom:

He approached the bed of the lady who could not sleep and who was waiting instead for him with great desire, and she received him in her arms to great satisfaction and delight. Now did the Knight of the Parrot know great joy and great delight with the Lady of the Blonde Hair. They delighted in each other and gave each other great comfort and sport, without hindrance and to their own individual desires like young people are accustomed to when they have the leisure and the place for it. Why should I go on describing this to you?[137] They spent the best night that ever young people could know, and they wished hard that the night could last a year, which was not possible, of course. (45)

This is likewise rather shocking for its candor, though aesthetically its tender remarks about young love balance out the earlier brutal remarks about reputation and honor.

The second half of the novel is more supernatural: Arthur journeys through an enchanted meadowland and then rescues a fellow knight from a giant serpent, then rescues another lady imprisoned in a Perilous Castle (rented from *Lancelot*), and finally journeys to an island inhabited by a dwarf, his giant son, and a unicorn. Despite their fanciful nature, each episode has to do with bonds of trust and proper behavior, lessons that will be valuable to the once and future king. The knight eventually heads back to Britain and stops off in Amorous City for another joust with Blondie before returning home and resuming his kingship. It's a quirky, colorful tale with much comic relief

137 This is an oft-repeated phrase; the author's always in a hurry to get on with his story.

supplied by the ingenious parrot, which may in fact be a portrait of the artist of this late contribution to Arthurian fiction.

Although first-rate works on Arthurian themes would continue to appear until the end of the Middle Ages, like the brilliant narrative poem *Sir Gawain and the Green Knight* (c. 1400), their appearances became more sporadic. The world of Arthur might have disappeared like Tristan's kingdom of Lyonesse had not a disreputable Englishman of the 15th century made a final encyclopedic effort to organize all the Arthurian legends into one masterwork. Stuck in prison for the last 20 years of his life for a variety of crimes and allegations — attempted murder, rape, extortion, theft — Sir Thomas Malory (c. 1400–71) devoted his final days to constructing a large work that was posthumously published as *Le Morte d'Arthur* (completed in 1469, printed in 1485).[138] In this published version, the version read by English audiences for the next four centuries, it resembles a long adventure novel, the result of the editorial work of printer William Caxton, who divided it into numerous books and chapters and gave the work its title. In 1934, however, a 15th-century manuscript was discovered that appeared to be Malory's own version; since it looked more like a collection of seven novellas with a book-length version of the Tristan legend in the middle, Eugène Vinaver entitled his edition simply *The Works of Sir Thomas Malory* (1947), pointing out that only the final novella bore the title "The Death of Arthur." And by then everyone knew that Malory's work was not an original composition but a series of translations and adaptations of earlier (mostly French) works, to wit:

1. "The Coming of Arthur and the Round Table" — from *The Story of Merlin* (in the *Lancelot-Grail*) and the *Suite de Merlin*, a variant written shortly after.
2. "Arthur's War against the Emperor Lucius" — from the alliterative *Morte Arthur* (c. 1350) and John Hardyng's verse *Chronicle* (1465).
3. "Sir Lancelot du Lake" — from the *Lancelot-Grail*.
4. "Sir Gareth of Orkney" — source unknown, apparently Malory's own composition.
5. "Sir Tristram of Lyoness" — abridged from the Prose *Tristan*.
6. "The Quest of the Grail" — from *The Quest of the Holy Grail* (*Lancelot-Grail*).
7. "Lancelot and Guinevere" — from the stanzaic *Morte Arthur* (1390s?), *The Death of King Arthur* (*Lancelot-Grail*), and some untraced sources.
8. "The Death of Arthur" — ditto.

In his splendid Norton Critical Edition of *Le Morte Darthur*, Stephen Shepherd provides a succinct overview of Malory's methods:

---

138 The date of Malory's birth is disputed; some put it around 1415, but I'm following Christina Hardyment's recent biography.

If there is any agreement about general patterns in Malory's handling of sources, it is that he abbreviated extensively, removed the interdispersing of multiple story lines — the *entrelacement* — characteristic of some of his French sources, suppressed expressions of (amorous) sentiment and psychological introspection, reduced passages of religious allegory and other expressions of doctrine, and reduced accounts of magical phenomena; at the same time he emphasized accounts of martial endeavor and knightly values of loyalty and honor, and drew greater attention to the (tragic) heroism of certain characters — in particular Launcelot. Sometimes, however, he produced virtual word-for-word translations or incorporated words and phrases verbatim from his English sources. (703)

In other words, Malory made the material more straightforward and realistic — qualities of the conventional novel — but his text's mongrel status as a patchwork of translations, adaptations, and plagiarisms, with only a little new material, makes its kinship with the novel problematic. And its lack of originality is vexing: if it's the first Arthurian book you read, it's a magnificent pageant of adventures and colorful characters, but if read on the heels of all the other Arthurian novels I've discussed, it's déjà vu all over again.

Malory's personal contribution to the Arthurian mythos, "Sir Gareth of Orkney," is an odd and rather racy tale, more like *The Knight of the Parrot* than the older works he adapts. It has the same kind of opening: a damsel named Lynette comes to Arthur's court to request a knight to rescue her older sister, Dame Lyones. She's given a tall lad nicknamed Beaumains (Nice Hands), who has been living in Arthur's kitchen for the last year but is actually Gareth, son of King Lot of Orkney (the same regent from *The Knight of the Parrot*). On the long trip to her sister's, Lynette taunts him with class-conscious British scorn until he eventually proves himself to her. (She reminds me of Estella in *Great Expectations*.) We are then treated to a startling example of British hospitality when Gareth spends the night at the castle of a knight he has honorably defeated:

> Sir Persaunt had a daughter, a fair lady eighteen years of age. When Beaumains was abed Sir Persaunt called her to him and charged her and commanded her to go with his blessing unto the knight's bed: "And lie down by his side and make him no distant cheer but good cheer, and take him in thy arms and kiss him. And see that this is done, I charge you, if ye wish to have my love and my good will."
>
> So Sir Persuant's daughter did as her father bade her; she went unto Sir Beaumains' bed, and privily she undressed herself and lay down by him.[139]

---

139 Page 185 in Lumiansky's modernized edition. It's a relief to arrive finally at a work written in English, but the original is a little too archaic for quoting at length: "So whan Sir Bewmaynes was abedde, Sir Persaunte had a doughter, a fayre lady of eyghtene yere of ayge, and there he called hir unto him and charged hir and commaunded hir uppon his blyssyng . . ." (p. 193 in Shepherd's edition).

Gareth wakes and naturally is surprised to find a naked girl in bed with him, and when he learns she's a virgin, he vows not to "defile" her. But when she explains she came at her father's command, not by her own choice — that is, she's a dutiful daughter, not a slut — he admits: "I would be a shameful knight if I would do your father any dis-worship." Such a dilemma. He decides to kiss the nude teenager and send her on her way, thereby winning praise for his noble actions. Gareth defeats Dame Lyones's oppressor, then finds himself caught in the middle of a sororal rivalry. Gareth is gobsmacked by Lyones's physical beauty and "could not eat because his love was so hot that he knew not where he was" (197); luckily for him, the lady feels likewise: "They both so burned with hot love that they agreed to abate their hot lusts secretly" (198; remember, this was written by a man in prison). They arrange a midnight rendezvous, but Lynette gets word of it and, disapproving of sex before marriage (and perhaps wanting Gareth for herself?), plans to disrupt it. Big sister sneaks into Gareth's bed wearing only an ermine fur, and as he begins to kiss her, "an armed knight with many lights about him" appears and wounds Gareth in the thigh before he overpowers it and cuts off its head. Then we witness this spooky scene, something the eldritch author of *Perlesvaus* might have come up with:

> Forthwith the Damosel Lynet came and took up the head in the sight of them all and anointed it with an ointment where it was smitten off; and she did in the same wise to the other part where the head should rest. Then she set them together; they stuck as fast as ever they did, and the knight easily arose. The Damosel Lynet then put him in her chamber. (199–200)

No one says a word about the zombie knight with the flashing lights. Gareth recovers, and the couple is still "so hot with burning love" that they schedule another tryst, only to be interrupted again by the strange creature; Gareth beheads it again, this time chopping the head into a hundred pieces and throwing them out the window, but little sister recovers them, anoints them, and puts her Frankenstein monster together again. Only later are we told that we are on the magical Isle of Avalon, and that Lynette is also known as the Savage Damsel — the girl is a witch! His chastity preserved, Gareth then undergoes a rapid series of adventures, arrives at a huge tournament attended by everyone who is anyone (Arthur, Lancelot, Gawain, Tristan, Guinevere, *et al.*), and dazzles everyone with his prowess. (He's able to change colors due to a magic ring Lyones gave him, which earns him extra points.) The novella ends with his fairytale wedding to Lyones, a rarity in the Arthurian canon, with sister Lynette married off to Gareth's brother Gaheris.

Had Malory published only "Sir Gareth of Orkney," both he and it would be as little known today as *The Knight of the Parrot.* But as an interlude between the early glory days of Arthur and his knights, the tragic story of Tristan, and the decline and fall of Camelot, it expands the tonal variety of the work as a whole. And looking at the work as a whole, it does begin to resemble a novel more than an anthology of Arthurian romances. (In fact, Malory's own title for the work is *The Whole Book of King Arthur and of His Noble Knights of the Round Table*.) By the 1460s, Malory had a variety of sources to choose from, and his choices and revisions of those sources reveal a consistent vision more in keeping with a long novel. Like the *Perceforest* author, Malory wanted his readers to relate his ancient story to his own time, the turbulent period of the War of the Roses. Malory compares Mordred's betrayal and the revolt of the English barons to the civil war between the York and Lancaster branches of the royal Plantagenet family, and does so with no subtlety at all, addressing his readers point-blank near the end:

> Lo, all ye Englishmen, see ye not what mischief was here? For he was the greatest king and the noblest knight of the world and most loved the fellowship of noble knights, and by him they were all upheld; yet these Englishmen could not hold themselves content with him. Lo, such was the old custom and usage of this land, and men say that we of this land have not yet lost that custom. Alas, this is a great default of us Englishmen, for nothing may please us for any length of time! (731)

Alas, this is a great default of an author, hectoring the reader so; better authors trust their readers to draw the parallel themselves. But loyalty to the king is another overarching theme that binds the book's many episodes together. The betrayal and death of King Arthur was implicit in the birth of his bastard son Mordred near the beginning of the work, and since everything in it moves toward that Oedipal wreck, perhaps Caxton was right to give the entire work the unifying title of *Le Morte d'Arthur*.[140] So perhaps we should call it a novel after all: Malory shifted the emphasis from the sacred in the Old French originals to the secular, uses more realistic dialogue (especially from shirty Lynette), and dramatizes the messy entanglements of familial and political obligations — all characteristics of the modern novel. But a novel or not, there's no doubting Malory's contribution to English prose style — the prose romance came late to England, and Malory played a large part in legitimizing prose as a valid medium for artistic expression — or the enormous influence of his work. It was the rediscovery of *Le Morte d'Arthur*, not *Perlesvaus* or *The Knight of the Parrot*, that launched the Arthurian revival in Victorian England and that continues to inspire countless imitators to this day.

---

140 For a closely argued defense of Caxton's choice, see the last few pages of William Matthews's posthumously published essay "The Besieged Printer," *Arthuriana* 7.1 (Spring 1997): 63–92.

Not all medieval French writers were smitten with Arthurmania, however. Some drew less upon chivalric romances than on the more realistic stories featured in older French *fabliaux* — brief, amusing (usually bawdy) verse narratives — and folktales similar to those Boccaccio and his followers adapted. Jean Renart (fl. 1200–22), for example, rejected the high, mystical tone of his predecessor Chrétien de Troyes and wrote picaresque novels in verse (*L'Escoufle, Guillaume de Dôle, Galeran de Bretagne*) that took a more down-to-earth view of aristocrats and their romantic flings, with none of the religious concerns of the Arthurian novelists. Clerics and copyists amused themselves with things like *Solomon and Marcolf* (*Salomon et Marcolphus*, c. 1200), a short, anonymous work in Latin that may have originated in France and that has been called a "proto-picaresque novel."[141] It consists of two parts: in the first, King Solomon engages in a battle of wits with a clever, ugly peasant, trading one-liners as Marcolf undercuts the king's sententious proverbs. In part 2, Marcolf plays a number of tricks on his king, most based on taking the king's words literally to a comic extreme. It's a coarse, scatological work — far inferior to the superficially similar *Alphabet of Ben Sira* — and is notable only for its subversive quality: the language of the Bible is mocked by the language of the barnyard, and Solomon's legendary wisdom is no match for peasant cunning. Rabelais quotes it in *Gargantua and Pantagruel* (1.33), and Bakhtin cites it a few times as an example of carnivalization.[142]

Other writers retained the romance and adventure of Arthurian novels but put them to other uses. The most brilliant and innovative example of this alternative approach is *Aucassin and Nicolette*, written sometime in the 13th century by an anonymous minstrel from northeastern France. This charming and subversive novella is mostly in prose but with occasional poems expanding upon the narrative, reminiscent of medieval Irish fiction but to a modern reader sounding like songs in a musical. The plot is a variation of the popular Old French narrative poem *Floire et Blancheflor*: a girl named Nicolette is kidnapped from her Saracen kingdom and sold to a nobleman of Beaucaire in southern France. Aucassin, the son of the Count of Beaucaire, falls in love with her but is prevented from marrying her by his father, who assumes Nicolette is just a slave-girl. When Aucassin persists, the two are imprisoned separately; Nicolette escapes and hides in the forest, where Aucassin (released because everyone assumes the girl is dead) eventually finds her, and they spend three idyllic years there. They decide to leave and sail to a land called

---

141 By its English translator Jan M. Ziolkowski (p. 2), whose recent edition is a monumental work of scholarship; imagine a 450-page book devoted to one episode of *South Park*.
142 *Rabelais and His World*, 20, 350.

Torelore, where they are captured by Saracen pirates. Aucassin is set adrift in a boat (there are several parallels to the Tristan and Iseut story) and eventually arrives back at Beaucaire, but Nicolette is taken back to her hometown of Carthage, where she is recognized as the king's daughter. When he decides to marry her to another king, she escapes, disguises herself as a minstrel, and returns to Beaucaire, which Aucassin now rules. Incognito, she serenades Aucassin with a song promising his love will soon return to him; after washing off her dark disguise and changing back into a dress, she presents herself to him, and after a night of bliss, they marry.

What would be merely a pleasant tale in a lesser writer's hands became an innovative tour de force by our anonymous author, whom some critics suspect to have been a woman (dressed as a male minstrel?). S/He calls the novella's mixture of prose and poetry a *chantefable*, a unique word meaning "song-tale," and even abandoned the standard octosyllabic meter of the *fabliaux* for an unusual seven-beat line in the poetic interludes. More daring is the subversion of most of the moral and literary standards of the day: Aucassin, a strapping youth, neglects his duties as a nobleman's son and delivers a notorious rejection of Christian aspirations; warned by his father that if he takes up with Nicolette against his wishes he will go to Hell and never see Paradise, Aucassin hotly retorts:

> "What would I do in heaven? I have no wish to enter there, unless I have Nicolette, my own sweet love, whom I love so dearly. For to heaven go only such people as I'll tell you of: all those doddering priests and the halt and one-armed dotards who grovel all day and all night in front of the altars and in fusty crypts, and the folk garbed in rags and tatters and old, worn cloaks, who go barefoot and bare-buttocked and who die of hunger and thirst and cold and wretchedness. These are the ones who go to heaven, and I want nothing to do with them. Nay, I would go to hell; for to hell go the pretty clerks and the fine knights killed in tournaments and splendid wars, good soldiers and all free and noble men. I want to go along with these. And there too go the lovely ladies, gently bred and mannered, those who have had two lovers or three besides their lords, and there go gold and silver, and silk and sable, and harpers and minstrels and all the kings of this world. I want to go along with these, provided I have Nicolette, my own sweet love, with me."[143]

That must have shocked the audiences for whom the story was first performed, but this reversal of expectations persists throughout the novella. It is the pretty blue-eyed blonde Nicolette who is the resourceful one in this work, not passive Aucassin. She's the one who makes a daring escape from prison, then builds a lodge in the forest and figures out a way to contact her boyfriend;

---

143 Section 6 in Pauline Matarasso's translation, which occupies pp. 24–57 of her anthology *Aucassin and Nicolette and Other Tales*. Her translation, out of print for years, is much better than Eugene Mason's more widely available version.

when the lug finally finds her, he trips and dislocates his shoulder, which she pops back into place; after her return to Carthage, she quickly learns to play the viol, disguises herself as a man, and makes her way back to France. In Boccaccio's later adaptation of this tale (*Filocolo*), as in most romances of the period, it's the guy who tracks down the girl, not the other way around. The author further subverts things when the protagonists arrive in Torelore (i.e., Topsy-Turvy), which resembles Alice's Wonderland. There, the king is lying in childbed while the queen is out fighting a war, and the war is conducted with such "weapons" as crabapples, eggs, mushrooms, and fresh cheese. This combination of formal innovation and subversion of traditional values (religion/gender roles/warfare) is more characteristic of Renaissance works than medieval ones, indicating the arbitrariness of these chronological divisions. Like Nicolette in minstrel drag and stained face, the novella is charming and pretty as well as slyly subversive: a remarkable feat. Ford Madox Ford, who read the sole surviving French manuscript, rightly praises the author for achieving "a high narrative form approaching that of the best of subsequent novelists" (*The March of Literature*, 325).

Though not as innovative or subversive as *Aucassin and Nicolette*, another anonymous 13th-century novella called *The Story of King Florus and of the Fair Jehane* likewise features a resourceful girl who challenges traditional gender roles and class distinctions.[144] The narrative employs the enlacement pattern of Arthurian romances, juggling three related story-lines, while the plot was appealing enough to be adapted indirectly by both Boccaccio in the *Decameron* (2.9) and Shakespeare in *Cymbeline*. It begins by introducing King Florus of Ausay (perhaps Ausonia, a poetic name for Italy), deeply in love with his wife but sad that she is barren; after a single paragraph they are put on hold until the second half of the novella as the narrator whisks us off to northwestern France to introduce a 12-year-old girl named Jehane. Wondering how the narrator will link these two disparate individuals up by the end of the novella is part of the fascination of this convoluted work, too complex to summarize in the detail it deserves. Briefly, Jehane's mother is anxious to marry her daughter off, so to shut her up her husband marries her to his squire Robert, who he promotes to knighthood. Robert is tricked into thinking his child-bride has been unfaithful and so abandons her, only to adopt a disguised Jehane as his squire, who helps him become a successful businessman and return home, where she surprises him in a closely fitted dress after living with him for eight years dressed as a guy. At this point, we return to King Florus, who reluctantly abandoned his beloved wife to take on another who he had hoped would be fertile, but who likewise proved barren; both women die, leaving him a widower without an heir to his kingdom. Robert and Jehane experience some years of wedded bliss, but he too dies without producing

144 It occupies pp. 98–138 of Mason's anthology.

any children. The widower Florus learns of the widow Jehane, and after she teaches him a few lessons in courtship, they marry and produce a girl and a boy named Florence and Flora, and these floral siblings eventually become queen of Hungary and emperor of Constantinople, respectively.

In addition to providing an enjoyably intricate plot, the author challenges class snobbery by showing that a lowly squire can not only become a noble knight — more noble than one to the manor born like sleazy Raoul, the knight who tricks Robert into thinking he's slept with his bride and then breaks his vow to a priest — but also that a lowly squire might even be a girl in disguise destined to be the mother of royalty. Like Nicolette, resourceful Jehane drives the plot and is responsible for making her first husband a success and giving her second husband the heir he longed for. And while young love is the stuff of romance, it's heartening to read a story of middle-aged people who have loved and lost but have a second chance to love again. It's a clever, charming novella that deserves to be better known.

During the transition from the Middle Ages to the Renaissance, French writers continued to produce novel-length works of romance and wonder. In 1392, a nobleman named Jean de Berry wanted to legitimize his connection with the Lusignan family, whose fortified castle he had captured nearly 20 years earlier, and so commissioned a man named Jean d'Arras to write a family history. The result is known both as *Le Roman de Mélusine* and *L'Histoire de Lusignan* (1393), an experimental hybrid of novel (*roman*), fairy tale, and history (*histoire*, which also means "tale" in French). Its attempt to historicize myth and mythify history isn't entirely successful, but *Mélusine* is intriguing nonetheless.

Melusine, one of three daughters of a Scottish king, is cursed because she punished her father for violating her fairy mother's taboo: the king was never supposed to watch her during childbirth. Consequently, every Saturday Melusine turns into a serpent from the navel down. One day by a fountain, she convinces a French noble named Raymondin to marry her, promising him riches and success as long as he allows her to spend Saturdays in privacy. After their marriage, Melsuine builds the fortress of Lusignan (just outside Poitiers in west-central France) and other structures, and begins providing him with a number of sons, each with a bizarre facial defect (different colored eyes, or three eyes, a lion's-claw birthmark, huge ears, a protruding tooth, a patch of fur on the nose, etc.). When the eldest sons are in their teens, they go off to fight the Muslims in Cyprus and the Near East, or to fight giants, most of them winning kingdoms and 15-year-old brides. (The exploits of the sons occupy the bulk of the 350-page novel.) Raymondin is content to let Melusine run things (she finances her sons' adventures) until one day, misled by his brother into suspecting his wife is cheating on him on Saturdays, Raymondin carves a peephole in her bedroom door and spies her taking a bath, vigorously splashing the water with her enormous tail. Raymondin keeps the revelation to himself at first. Then Geoffroy, the most brutish of his sons (the one with the protruding tooth), flies into a rage when he learns one of his brothers has decided to become a monk; he burns the monastery to the ground, killing everyone therein. Raymondin is convinced Geoffroy did this because he's the tainted seed of a demonic snake-woman and blurts out his secret. Melusine, her chance at a normal Christian life ruined by her mistrustful husband, turns into a winged dragon and flies away, promising to return every time a family member's death is imminent to shriek a lament, like an Irish banshee.

As a commissioned writer, Jean faced several challenges: reconciling family legends about supernatural women with well-chronicled historical personages (the male characters mentioned above fought in the Crusades two centuries earlier); reconciling Celtic lore with Catholic doctrine (this is a very religious novel), and casting Jean de Berry's ancestors in a favorable light despite some very brutal acts. To accomplish this, he downplayed Melusine's role and exaggerated that of her sons, betraying (like Raymondin) the feminine and exalting the masculine, even if he had to fudge the historical record to do so. Signs of Jean's uneasiness with his task are everywhere: oft-repeated claims he is following verified chronicles closely, various mistakes and anachronisms, jerky transitions, problems with pacing, and other signs he was not fully in control of his material. (He wrote it, he tells us, in little over seven months — November 1392 to August 1393 — a rushed first draft that needed revision.)

It's a clumsy work, then, but an intriguing one because of the remarkably suggestive figure of Melusine. Though forced to respect this matriarch of the Lusignon family, the French-Catholic Jean clearly mistrusted this Celtic pagan witch: whereas *she* proposes marriage to Raymondin, Jean makes sure his sons' teen brides are *given* to them by their fathers or other patriarchal figures. Their relatively young ages assure virginity, whereas Melusine has a shady past: on the night of her marriage, she is taken aside for a motherly sex talk: "Then the countess of Poitiers and the other high ranking ladies came, led her aside, and instructed her on certain matters — as was fitting — even though she was quite knowledgeable of these things already."[145] Hence Melusine might "serve as metaphor for that shadowy, secret, unsettling side of sexuality that a woman must carefully conceal if she is to preserve her happiness."[146] She is punished for supporting her mother over her father, and Jean implies her serpentine nature and her sons' animalistic birth defects mean women are barely human and need to be tamed and civilized by Christian men. Jean dutifully notes her architectural erections (while her

---

145 Page 131 in Morris's translation. Another English translation is forthcoming by Donald Maddox and Sara Sturm-Maddox, editors of a useful collection of essays on *Mélusine*.
146 Emmanuèle Baumgartner, "Fiction and History: The Cypriot Episode in Jean d'Arras's *Mélusine*," in Maddox and Sturm-Maddox, 185.

husband does nothing) but devotes much more space to her sons' violent adventures and religious probity. Despite the mixed signals and muzzled misogyny, Melusine remained a fascinating figure over the centuries, launching various undines and little mermaids, until she eventually found an author worthy of her: A. S. Byatt makes brilliant use of the Melusine myth in *Possession* (1990).

There are other novels from this period, but they're down at the entertainment end of the fiction spectrum and don't require much comment. David Aubert's *Trois fils de roi* (1463) is a routine adventure novel, and several authors wrote chivalric romances set in the time of Charlemagne, most notably Philippe Camus's *Le Livre du Olivier de Castille*, the anonymous *Valentin et Orson* (1489), and *Les quatre filz Aymon*, translated by Malory's publisher William Caxton as *The Four Sons of Aymon* (c. 1489).

The most interesting of these late medieval romances is *Guy of Warwick* (*Le rommant de Guy de Warwick et de Herolt d'Ardenne*), which began as a 12th-century verse narrative but was reworked sometime in the early 15th century by an anonymous Anglo-Norman author as a novel (but not printed until 1525). An English translation appeared in 1560 and, in chapbook form, the story remained a favorite with English readers for centuries, for reasons that will soon become apparent. Set in England during the reign of King Athelstan (ruled 924–40), it begins with the birth, accompanied by portents, of a British hero named Guy. The son of a Northumberland gentleman who, down on his luck, now serves as steward to the Earl of Warwick, Guy grows into a fine lad and falls for the earl's daughter, Phælice (i.e., Phyllis), so beautiful that the only difference between her and Venus is "Venus had a mole."[147] The haughty beauty spurns the steward's son until she has an erotic dream in which Cupid "sends from his bow a golden-headed shaft, and wounded Phælice in her maiden bed" and advises her to give herself to Guy instead of marrying for money (2). Like a damsel in an Arthurian romance, Phælice commands Guy to justify her love by performing acts of valor, so Guy dutifully sails for France and engages in a variety of knightly adventures. When he returns to England and Warwick castle, Phælice is impressed but demands "far greater and more worthy deeds" (6), so first Guy "destroys a monstrous dun cow upon Dunsmore Heath" — not exactly a fire-breathing dragon, but still dangerous — and then returns to France for further adventures with his doughty companion Heraud, and eventually goes to Byzantium to fight against infidels. He returns to Europe, fights an actual dragon in Germany, and then makes his way to England and kills another one in Northumberland before reuniting with his beloved but exacting Phælice. She teases him charmingly — "What! seek a dragon ere thou lookest for me!" (11) — but

---

147 From chapter 1 of the anonymous Elizabethan translation in Thoms's *Early English Prose Romances*, 329–408; hereafter cited by chapter.

finally gives him her hand in marriage. Her father conveniently dies soon thereafter, and Guy the steward's boy is now Earl of Warwick, an early blow against the British empire of class distinctions.

In the final chapters of the novella, which became the most popular part, Guy defends England against foreign invaders. Getting religion and deciding his earlier exploits were done for the wrong reason — "a woman's face; for beauty I have shed a world of blood, hating all others for one mortal creature" (12) — Guy goes on a pilgrimage to silent Palestine, dominion of the blood and sepulcher, for the welfare of his soul. On his way, he kills an evil giant — old habits die hard — then spends years wandering around the Holy Land and entertaining gloomy thoughts. When he eventually returns to England to die, he discovers that it has been invaded by Danes. They have fought the English to a standstill and have proposed deciding their conflict by single combat, and for that purpose send out a Danish giant named Colbron, who talks trash about English cowardice. This is more than Guy can take, so he shrugs off his pilgrim's garb, suits up for combat, and with patriotic furor slaughters the giant. (This is a romanticized version of Athelstan's defeat of the Danes at Brunanburh in 937.) Only then does Guy reveal himself to his king, but rather than return to his wife and earldom, he lives as a hermit nearby, occasionally begging alms from his own wife, who doesn't recognize him and grieves for her absent husband — an irony only a smug religious nut could enjoy. Guy eventually reveals himself to her too, but dies within minutes of doing so; she survives for another 15 days, and then dies of grief.

It's an unexpectedly somber end to what had been an entertaining story of romance and adventure, winningly narrated with rhetorical flourishes and each chapter ending in a verse couplet (vestiges of the old poetic version, apparently), and may betray the same guilt many of the clerical Arthurian romancers felt when they let their tales get too profane, obligating them to rein in their characters by sending them to a monastery or convent to be reminded of the sacred origin of chivalry. But it's not the religious message that appealed to readers of *Guy of Warwick*, especially English readers; as John Simons notes,

> Above all Guy is an English hero. His battles are not only to gain knightly reputation and to further the cause of Christendom: they are also designed to spread the name of England as a country of heroes and, eventually, to save the land from foreign invaders and other dangers. . . . Guy offers a simple model of how English virtue can be depended on to triumph over the chicanery of a variety of foreigners.[148]

In the earlier Arthurian romances, the hero was usually of aristocratic, if not

---

148 Simons, *Guy of Warwick and Other Chapbook Romances*, 20–21. (Simons is speaking of the later English chapbook versions, but his remarks also apply to the French original.)

mythic, origins, "but Guy is not a hero of this kind," Simons continues; "his ascent to an Earldom is fuelled by his ability to act out all the roles expected of a knight by means of natural ability, strength and talent, and not by accident of birth" (21–22). Set in the 10th century but reflecting the growing nationalism and individualism of the 15th, *Guy of Warwick* dramatizes the transition from the feudal Middle Ages to the glorious cultural awakening known as the Renaissance.

CHAPTER 3

The Renaissance Novel

The Renaissance — which for my purpose began in Italy in the middle of the 14th century and ended in England with the death of Queen Elizabeth in 1603 — was a fertile time for the novel. There was growing confidence in and acceptance of vernacular languages for serious literature (instead of Latin); the invention of the printing press in the mid-15th century greatly expanded the audience for books; and the rehabilitation of ancient Greek and Roman texts from maligned "pagan" works to cherished classical literature led to the first printed editions of the early novels: *The Golden Ass* was published in Rome in 1469, the remains of the *Satyricon* in Milan around 1482, Lucian in Florence in 1496, and the Greek romances in the following century (except for Chariton's *Chaereas and Callirhoe*, which didn't appear until 1750).[1] Especially influential were the new editions and translations of Heliodorus's *Ethiopian Story* (Greek 1534, French 1547, Latin 1552, Spanish 1554, Italian 1556, German 1559, English 1569), the model for almost every important novelist from Rabelais until Fielding. The renewed study of classical texts led some to begin chafing under the yoke of Catholic doctrine and to begin favoring secular values over sacred ones, rational humanism over supernatural theism. And no one better exemplifies this new attitude than the co-father (with Petrarch) of the Italian literary renaissance, Giovanni Boccaccio (1313–75).

RENAISSANCE ITALIAN FICTION

The Italian novel begins with Boccaccio, a born writer. "I well remember," he tells us in his *Genealogy of the Pagan Gods*, "that before seven years of age, when as yet I had seen no fictions, and had applied to no masters, I had a natural turn for fiction, and produced some trifling tales."[2] Everyone knows of his *Decameron* but not everyone knows he wrote three novels prior to that

---

1 Doody speculates that this was due to its blasphemous nature: "the near-crucifixion of Chaireas could pose problems for the writer seeking a Christian public and not wishing to be accused of heresy" (254).
2 Quoted in Dunlop, 2:51 n1; hereafter cited parenthetically.

masterpiece — the romantic *Filocolo*, the pastoral *Ameto*, and the psychological *Elegy of Lady Fiammetta* — and one after it, the satiric *Corbaccio*. Had
they not been obscured in the shade by the towering *Decameron*, they would
undoubtedly be better known today for the outstanding novels they are.

In his early 20s, ridiculously well-read and anxious to show off his learning,
Boccaccio wrote his first novel, *Filocolo* (*Il Filocolo*, c. 1338), an adaptation
of the same Old French narrative poem, *Floire et Blancheflor*, that inspired
Aucassin and Nicolette. In Boccaccio's version, set in the 6th century, an
Italian nobleman named Lelio Africano and his wife Giulia make a pilgrim-
age to the shrine of Santiago de Compostela in Spain to thank the gods for
granting them a child, but are attacked en route by the army of the king of
Spain, misled by a devil into thinking the pilgrims were an invading force.
Lelio is killed and pregnant Giulia becomes a servant to the Spanish king's
wife, also pregnant, and both give birth on the same day: the Spanish queen to
a boy named Florio and the Italian noblewoman to a girl named Biancifiore
(White Flower), and then dies. The two children are raised together and,
at the age of 14, fall in love with each other. The Spanish king and queen
disapprove of their son's interest in a mere servant girl — they oddly keep for-
getting that she's descended from the famous Roman consul Scipio Africanus
(237–183 BCE) — so they send Florio to a nearby town to be educated,
hoping he'll forget about her amid the distractions of "the lovely girls going
barefoot in the crystal fountains, crowned with Ceres' garlands and singing
amorous verses."[3] (You can tell we're no longer in the Middle Ages because
he plans to study "the experimental sciences" [2.10].) Instead, Florio pines
away for his flower-white girlfriend, so the king and queen frame the girl for
attempted murder (via poisoned food, exactly like Guinevere in *Lancelot of
the Lake*) and try to burn her at the stake, but she is rescued by a disguised
Florio (Lancelot redux) and is temporarily reconciled to her foster parents.
Next they sell her to some merchants who take Biancifiore to Alexandria and
imprison her in a tower full of virgins reserved for the sultan of Babylonia.
When Florio learns of this, he sets off to find her with a band of followers
and assumes the nom de guerre "Filocolo" (roughly, Frustrated Lover); after
many adventures, he rescues her, beds her, and marries her. They return to
Italy, get baptized (the Spain of that time still worships the Roman pantheon),
and then are reconciled with Florio's parents, who repent of everything once
they learn of Biancifiore's nobility and of her baby boy, named Lelio after
his grandfather. After the Spanish king dies, Florio succeeds to the throne,
converts his subjects to Christianity, and lives happily ever after with his wife
and child.

---

3 Book 2, section 1 of Cheney's translation. It has been criticized for being only serviceable
and occasionally misleading by Victoria Kirkham ("Two New Translations"), author of a
superb book on *Filocolo* entitled *Fabulous Vernacular*, but it's the only one in English.

But as always, it's not the story but what a writer does with the story that interests us. Boccaccio took the 40-page original and expanded it to a 470-page tour de force of rhetoric, a showpiece for his burgeoning talent. First, he supplied a frame for the tale: Boccaccio tells us he found himself one day in a church in Naples where he spotted a young woman and fell instantly in love with her; a few days later he runs into her again at a convent and joins in the conversation she's having with some nuns about the old tale of Florio and Biancifiore. She turns her sparkling eyes on him and says it's a shame "their fame is not exalted in a suitable memorial," and asks him "to take the trouble to compose a little book in the vulgar tongue, in which the birth, the falling in love, and the adventures of those two lovers should all be contained, to the very end" (1.1). Like any man in love, he considers her request a command and, praying to "not err through excessive and unbridled enthusiasm," he begins writing not the "little" book she requested but — through excessive and unbridled enthusiasm — a big one ten times longer than the original.[4] In the closing pages, he addresses his completed book with the hope "she takes you in her soft hands and says with a gentle voice, 'Welcome.' [¶] And perhaps she will offer you a kiss or two, with her sweet lips. . . . And where would you do better than to be in her lap?" (5.97), outlining the amorous welcome he himself hopes to receive with this offering.[5] What's most surprising in the frame is Boccaccio's overlay of Roman mythology on 14th-century Catholic Italy, which has the same jarring effect as a Renaissance pietà enclosed in an elaborate gilt frame depicting drunken satyrs lusting after the auric buttocks of naked nymphs. The first page of the novel unveils an Italy ruled over by the goddess Juno, preceded by "the daughter of Thaumas" (Iris), served by Neptune, Aeolus, and Mars; Boccaccio finds himself not in a Catholic church but in a "gracious and handsome temple in Parthenope" (the ancient name of Naples), and a few days later in "a holy temple named after the chief of the heavenly birds" — his cheeky way of referring to the convent of Sant'Arcangelo at Baiano, dedicated to wingèd Gabriel — surrounded not by nuns but "priestesses of Diana." When he prays for assistance in writing his book, he addresses not the Catholic god but "O mightiest Jove" (1.1).

As I said, one of the defining characteristics of the Renaissance is the revival of our classical heritage, and in this frame Boccaccio goes so far as to de-convert Catholic Italy and return it to its glorious pagan original, the land lauded by Virgil and Ovid, and in his novel still watched over by their colorful if touchy gods. Pushing this reclassification further, he next retells the Old

---

4 "Every word a writing man writes is put down with the ultimate intention of impressing some woman" — William Faulkner, *Mosquitoes* (1927).

5 The woman has been identified as Maria d'Aquino, the daughter of King Robert of Naples and Sicily, and as "Fiammetta" (Little Flame) she appears in most of Boccaccio's fiction. (I like the story she got that nickname because she was a flaming redhead.) On the other hand, Fiammetta may just be an imaginary muse.

Testament story in classical terms (YHWH=Jove, Satan=Pluto, Hell=Dis, Noah=Deucalion, etc.), reversing the procedure Christians would later take when converting foreign gods into demons and hijacking pagan holidays for their own use (Christmas from the winter solstice celebrating the birth of the Sun, Easter from the vernal equinox celebrating Eastre, the Germanic goddess of dawn, etc.). But this isn't as blasphemous at it sounds; one senses Boccaccio did this simply because he could, showing off his immense classical learning and his schoolboy cleverness at rewriting mythology in Christian terms. He boasts that his work will be a "new song" from a "new teller of this tale" (1.2), and one of the first novelties of his novel is the stereographic effect of merging two separate mythologies to create a third: his own private Italy where both co-exist in humanist accord.

Even after he begins the tale proper — set mostly in Italy during the pontificate of Vigilius (538–55), who has a cameo near the end — Boccaccio populates it with participating Roman gods. Pluto initiates the plot by deceiving the Spanish king; Venus tells her son Cupid to envenerate the teenagers with his arrows; Mars has Florio's back in several battles; Venus and Diana come down from heaven occasionally to move the plot along; and even at the end of the novel, after everyone has been converted to Christianity, the references continue to Apollo, Cytherea, Aurora, and others. Admirably free of theological narrow-mindedness, Boccaccio apparently found the classical heritage too rich to be abandoned merely on the grounds of dogma. As a writer, he was more indebted to Roman literature than to Scripture — Florio and Biancifiore study not the Holy Bible but "the holy book of Ovid" (1.45; i.e., *The Art of Love*) — and was cheerfully indifferent to any incongruity that resulted.

Boccaccio seems primarily interested in showing off his wide reading and superior prose style; the simple story of two lovesick teenagers is merely an excuse for this young man to show he could write anything: a love story containing battle scenes (cribbed from Lucan and Virgil), an abduction from the seraglio, mythography, travelogue, letters, apostrophes to the gods, Ovidian metamorphoses (and even de-metamorphoses, returning a man who had been turned into a fountain back into a man), theology, symbolic dreams (as in *Perlesvaus*, items bestowed in dreams are brought back to the waking world), allegories, theophanies, essays on love and political theory, along with countless literary allusions and elaborate rhetorical speeches on any topic: love (pro, con, unrequited), jealousy, exile, loss, death, fate, the Seven Deadly Sins — prolix arias that are largely responsible for the novel's length. At one point, Filocolo has a rather schizophrenic dialogue with himself (4.89) that recalls the dialogues with the soul in Egyptian and Akkadian literature, and there are erotic scenes as hot as any of those written by Byzantine novelists a few decades earlier. (Like them, Boccaccio deprives his heroine of her clothing whenever possible; the attempted seduction of Florio by two beautiful women bent on "carnal conjunction" [3.9–11] reads like a letter to *Penthouse*; and Florio's deflowering of Biancifiore is so graphic that it was expurgated in some early editions.) His pièce-de-résistance is a 55-page symposium on love held while Florio is stuck in Naples (4.17–71), in which 13 participants ask Fiammetta to pass judgment on questions of love given in story form, a kind of mini-*Decameron*. (Indeed, Boccaccio would recycle two of these short tales there: day 10, stories 4 and 5.) As Dunlop observed nearly two centuries ago, *Filocolo* "presents an example of almost every species of fiction" (2:404); nearly everything that had been accomplished in fiction up to Boccaccio's time is represented somewhere in this multifarious work. Ultimately, *Filocolo* may be more style than substance, too blatantly the work of a young man flexing his literary muscles, but it announces at the very beginning of the Renaissance that the novel could be anything it wanted to be in the hands of a gifted writer.

Boccaccio's second novel, *Ameto* (*L'Ameto*, aka *Comedia delle ninfe fiorentine* [The Comedy of the Florentine Nymphs], c. 1342), is even more stylized and mannered, but also more tightly structured and considerably shorter. It's the first pastoral novel since *Daphnis and Chloe* a millennium earlier, though Boccaccio was inspired not by Longus but, once again, by Virgil.[6] Just as *Filocolo* alludes constantly to the *Aeneid*, *Ameto* echoes the *Eclogues*, Virgil's complex allegories in pastoral settings. Boccaccio sets his pastoral in Tuscany (specifically Florence, hence its Italian title); the shepherd Ameto falls in love with a nymph named Lia, whom he finds in the company of six other nymphs, Fiammetta among them. Thinking them goddesses, he keeps his distance but follows them until winter sets in. The following spring, on a holy day devoted to Venus, he comes upon the seven nymphs, each dressed in a different (and symbolic) color, and joins them for an afternoon of conversation. They decide to honor Venus by telling him of their love lives, which takes up the bulk of the novel. (This framed cycle of stories looks back to the symposium in *Filocolo* and of course forward to the grander cycle in the *Decameron*.) As the seven nymphs relate their True Confessions, Ameto comes to realize they represent the seven virtues — the four cardinal ones (wisdom, justice, temperance, fortitude) and the three Christian-specific virtues (faith, hope, and charity) — and that the afternoon has been designed as a spiritual lesson teaching him to sublimate *eros* into *agapē*. Fourteen of the novel's 50 chapters are in verse, bringing the work even closer to its Virgilian inspiration.

The odd thing is, many of these exemplary tales range from seamy to steamy, usually dealing with bad marriages and adultery. (The seven nymphs

---

6 Critics are uncertain whether Boccaccio knew any of the Greek romances, but he definitely knew Apuleius's *Golden Ass* — alluded to twice in *Ameto* — and some Arthurian novels.

are based on women Boccaccio knew in Florence, making *Ameto* a kind of Florentine *Sex in the City*.) For example, the first nymph up is Mopsa, who studies (and represents) wisdom. She is married off to a man of "base appearance, given to me as an eternal penitence and not as a husband."[7] Walking by the seashore one day, Mopsa spots a handsome youth on a little boat near the shore "both eager for the delights of the water and fearful at the same time." (She later learns his name is Affron, Greek for "crazy" or "stupid.") Venus fires Mopsa up with lust, so she invites him to come ashore for some sex on the beach, but he ignores her. She pleads, makes promises, threatens to sic the gods on him, but to no avail. Realizing men are visual creatures, she changes tack:

> "I must tell then that with my long garments belted above the hip and touching the ground as they do now, I acted almost fearful of the water, and I pulled them much higher than is seemly, so that my white legs were visible. I noticed that he looked at them with avid eye, yet he remained firm in obstinate opposition to my desires. Then, set on conquering him, I raised my rather light mantle from off my shoulders as if overcome by the heat; and having opened my pretty bosom, bending down rather low, without a word I uncovered its beauties to him. And no sooner did he see this, than with all his cruelty dissolved, he turned the bow of his boat toward me with these words: 'Wait, young maiden. I am vanquished by your beauty. Look, I am hurrying to your delights.'" (18)

Performing a striptease to attract a dumb sailor is a strange way to exemplify wisdom; after sex, she cleans him up and makes a successful artist of him, which is apparently the point of the story, and it is indeed wiser to leave a bad marriage than to stay and be miserable, but the racy exemplum is typical of *Ameto*. The nymph Agapes, who represents charity, is married off to an old man and tells us of his hopeless amatory skills in comically appropriate pastoral imagery: "he tried in vain to cultivate the gardens of Venus; and seeking to cleave the earth of those gardens, which longed for gracious seeds, with an old ploughshare, he worked uselessly; for that plough, eroded by age, moving its pointed part in a circle like the loose willow, refused to carry out its due office in the firm fallow" (32). Agapes finds relief first in nude lesbian fantasies, and then in a shy young man who she initiates into the joys of adulterous sex. I don't think this is what Paul had in mind when commending charity (1 Cor. 13:13); he'd be agape at Agapes' *agapē*.

The seriousness of the moral lectures is further undercut by Ameto's reactions to the nymphs. As each one is introduced, he devours her with his eyes, favoring us with detailed, head-to-toe inventories of her physical attributes, with special attention to her breasts, or "heavenly fruits" as he calls them. In the interludes between speakers, he confesses he wasn't paying much

---

7 Chap. 18 in Serafini-Sauli's translation, hereafter cited by chapter.

attention to their lessons because he was lost in sexual fantasies about his pretty teachers. These gradually dissipate, and by the time Lia delivers the final story on faith — a cold shower of history and theology — he's all ears (rather than all eyes) and learns his lesson: "And in brief, from brute animal he watched himself become a man" (46). But following this Christian conclusion, the author again changes tack: confessing he had been hiding in the bushes to eavesdrop on Ameto's rainbow party, Boccaccio is first filled with happiness at the sight of the lovely girls, but then is overcome with gloom, partly because the nymphs are beyond his grasp (as their counterparts were in real-life Florence), and partly because of the contrast between his imaginary pastoral world and the real one he lives in:

> In that place [his *Ameto*] are beauty, gentility, and worth, charming words, examples of virtue, and supreme pleasure along with love; there is desire that moves man to salvation; there is as much good and gaiety as man can know; there the worldly delights are fulfilled, and there sweetness is to be contemplated and enjoyed; and where I go is melancholy and eternal sadness. Here one never laughs, or rarely; and the house, dark, mute, and exceedingly sad, receives me and keeps me against my will, where the crude and horrible sight of a cold man [his father], rough and miserly, saddens me ever more; so that having seen a happy day, the return to such a hostel indeed changes that sweetness into sad bitterness. (49)

The confessional note is surprising. A brief final chapter compares his completed book to a "rose, which was born among the thorns of my adversities," and on that conflicted note the novel ends.

It's a dazzling work, and once again displays Boccaccio's encyclopedic knowledge of Greek and Roman mythology, though reversing the procedure of *Filocolo*: instead of superimposing classical mythology on Catholic Italy, he overlays Catholic theology on classical pastoral, and complicates orthodox theology by testing it against some highly unorthodox situations. The mythological detail can be overwhelming — the translator appends 24 pages of very necessary notes to the 145-page novel — and this roman à clef depends a little too heavily on obscure biographical details, but *Ameto* is another tour de force from a young author with talent to burn.

Boccaccio's most daring literary experiment is *The Elegy of Lady Fiammetta* (*L'Elegia di Madonna Fiammetta*, c. 1344). This is the first-person confession of a young Italian noblewoman who has an adulterous affair with a man who then leaves promising to return, but never does. The narrator pours out her misery in a 160-page monologue, hoping her story will win her the sympathy she feels she deserves. Boccaccio's sources were various: Dante's concept of elegy (from his *De vulgari eloquentia*), both Ovid's *Metamorphoses* and his *Heroides* (narrative letters from classical women like Penelope and Dido),

Seneca's tragedies, and perhaps Andreas Capellanus's *Art of Courtly Love*, which defines love as suffering. But it reads like a modern confessional novel along the lines of Elizabeth Smart's *By Grand Central Station I Sat Down and Wept* or Carole Maso's *American Woman in the Chinese Hat*, for what predominates are not the classical sources but the naked emotions of a dumped woman.

The Elegy of Lady Fiammetta is a torch song of a book that has been called the first psychological novel in a modern language.[8] That may be overstating the case, but the first-person monologue allows Boccaccio to explore motivation more attentively, and with more immediacy, than any Western novelist before him. Our narrator describes herself as an upper-class beauty, married at the usual age (around 15) to a suitable husband about whom she tells us nothing — he's so far beside the point he doesn't deserve it — and who one day at church spots a man "alone and leaning against a marble column" (1). She falls instantly in love, makes him aware she's available, and then enjoys a few months of adulterous bliss with him. "He named me Fiammetta and himself Panfilo," she tells us, which should have tipped her off, for "Panfilo" means "Loves everyone." We later learn he's a smooth-talking rake who is having a simultaneous affair with another woman, and his farewell speech promising to return sounds a little too slick to be sincere. When she realizes he's not coming back, and then learns he has a new lover, she's devastated. But we need to remember that Fiammetta is probably only 16 or 17 by this time and relatively inexperienced. She displays the boundless egotism of a teenage girl who interprets romantic disappointment as the end of the world, a tragedy of epic proportions from which she'll never recover. She wastes away, spends most of her time weeping and fretting with jealousy, fantasizing about his return, and of course eventually attempts suicide before experiencing a total emotional meltdown.

But she survives to tell the tale, and her novel can be considered a kind of Portrait of the Artist as a Dumped Girl. She begins her story by saying she merely wants to share her story with other women — she explicitly states she doesn't want any men to read it — so that "you may know me to be more unhappy than any other woman" (prologue). Her first chapter opens modestly with a brief, conventional description of spring, then plunges into self-pity by way of a classical reference:

> At that season when the newly clad earth displays her beauty more than at any other time of the year, I came into the world born of noble parents and welcomed by a benign and

---

8 By older Italian critics as well as by the co-translator of the English version I'll be citing, Mariangela Causa-Steindler, in her introduction (xi), hereafter cited parenthetically by chapter. In their enthusiasm, some "boccaccisti" likewise claim *Filocolo* as "perhaps the first novel of modern Europe" (Bergin 73, quoting Thomas C. Chubb).

generous Fortune. Cursed be the day I was born, more detestable to me than any other! How much luckier it would have been if I had not been born or if I had been led from that wretched birth to my tomb, or if I had not lived longer than the teeth sown by Cadmus and if Lachesis had cut her threads as soon as she had spun them! (1)

She gets the reference wrong — it's Clotho and Atropos who spin and cut the threads of fate, not Lachesis — not the kind of mistake erudite Boccaccio would make but understandable from a conventionally educated upper-class girl. But compare this passage to the opening of chapter 7, 16 months after Panfilo skipped town:

In spite of the hope I had placed in the future journey [she planned to track him down], my anguish continued, and as the sun traversed the sky with ceaseless motion, drawing day after day with it without interruption, I was kept in vain hope for much longer than I wished, anxious and as much in love as ever. And Phoebus with his light was already in Taurus, which had captured Europa; the days took time away from the nights, and from being very short they became very long; Zephyrus arrived bedecked with flowers, quited Boreas' violent blows with his mellow and tranquil breath, and chased the mist from the cold air and the white snow from the high peaks; having dried the rain-soaked fields, he adorned anew every place with grass and flowers, replacing the cold winter's lingering whiteness with a green garb that covered the trees all over. In all places it was already that time in which joyful Spring graciously spreads around its riches everywhere and when the earth, a virtual constellation of violets, roses, and flowers of all sorts, competes in beauty with the eighth heaven. Narcissus was in every pasture, and Bacchus' mother, already show-ing signs of her pregnancy, leaned more heavily on her companion elm, which had itself now become more heavily laden with its acquired garb. Dryope and Phaeton's unhappy sisters rejoiced too, after having shed the mean garments of hoary winter; everywhere the joyous birds filled the air with their delightful songs, and Ceres was gaily covering anew the open fields with her fruit. But beyond all this, my cruel master [Cupid] made his arrows burn more fiercely in longing minds, so that young men and charming maidens, all adorned according to their natures, sought to attract the object of their love. (7)

What a world of difference! Note how fulsome the description is, how she links the stars above with the "constellations" of flowers below, how confident (and accurate) she is in her use of classical allusions, how sparse the first-person pronouns have become. Throughout the second half of the novel her rhetorical skills improve as her physical condition deteriorates, resulting in operatic tirades and erudite expressions of despair. She mentions reading French romances, specifically that of Tristan and Iseult (8), and it's clear she's educated herself in the Greek and Roman classics as well, building her case as the unhappiest girl of all time with the rhetorical cunning of a Cicero. She even displays a modern-sounding awareness of the materiality of her medium, insisting that the plain appearance of her manuscript is an example of form as content. Addressing her finished book (like Boccaccio at the end of *Filocolo*) and incidentally revealing she's been spending a lot of time in the library, she tells it:

> Therefore, do not concern yourself with any ornamentation such as other books are accustomed to have, namely, with elegant covers, painted and adorned with various colors, with clean-cut pages, pretty miniatures, or grand titles; such things do not suit the grave lamentation you bear; leave these things to happy books, and with them the broad margins, the colorful inks, and the paper smoothed with pumice; it is fitting that you go where I am sending you discomposed, with your hair uncombed, stained and full of gloom, to awaken by my misfortunes blessed pity in the minds of those women who will read you. (9)

Fiammetta has learned no moral lessons from her experience — she admits at the beginning that she remains tragically in love with Panfilo — and is as egotistical as ever, but she has become one hell of a writer for a teenage girl, anticipating some genuine female prodigies of the future.[9] But not as good as Boccaccio himself, who challenged himself to write from the point of view of a young woman and succeeded brilliantly, with only a few slips: at one point Fiammetta claims "the avarice innate in women fled from me" (1), which sounds more like the increasingly misogynistic Boccaccio than something a girl would say, and the author of the panting *Ameto* lets his wig slip in this description: "In some places an extremely desirable sight appeared before the young men's eyes: beautiful women covered by sheer, silky tunics, barefooted, and with bare arms, walking in the water, picking sea shells from the hard rock, and as they bent in their task they revealed the hidden delights of their ripe bosoms" (5).[10] But not only does Boccaccio convincingly impersonate a woman, he strikes a few feminist blows. Often Fiammetta chafes against the conventional "female dignity" that requires her to walk slowly or keep her temper. (One of her tirades begins: "with a voice enraged beyond ladylike dignity and wailing beyond any other wailing, I said:" [6].) Her suicidal attempt to jump off her roof is impeded when her long, trailing dress gets caught on "a sharp piece of wood and halted my impetuous flight," and she hits upon "the alternative of disrobing" before her nurse and a mob of maids take her down

---

9 Mary Shelley was 19 when she began writing *Frankenstein* (1818), Françoise Sagan a year younger when she wrote *Bonjour Tristesse* (1954), the same age Polish motormouth Dorota Masłowska wrote *Snow White and Russian Red* (2002); Jane Austen was only 16 when she wrote her epistolary novella *Lesley Castle* (1792), as was Melissa Panarello when she shocked Europe with *100 Strokes of the Brush before Bed* (2003). Daisy Ashford was only nine when she wrote *The Young Visiters* (1919), but that novel is on a different plane of artistic achievement.

10 The previous owner of my copy of the novel, apparently a female college student, wrote a big "HA!" in the margin at this point, rightly incredulous that a heterosexual woman would write such a thing.

(6). Her egotism and continuing devotion to the man who dumped her make her a questionable feminist icon, but it's refreshing to read of such a woman in trecento Italy. I'm probably readings things into it that Boccaccio never intended — he was no feminist, and Fiammetta's style is not substantially different from his — but *The Elegy of Lady Fiammetta* is one of the most striking novels to appear during the Renaissance, and it's a tribute to its timeless concerns that it's probably the only Renaissance novel that a contemporary teenage girl could read with pleasure and, like, totally relate to.

At one point in her misery, Fiammetta tells us, "I gathered my maids together in my chamber and recounted, or had them recount, all sorts of stories . . ." (3). *Filocolo, Ameto,* and *Lady Fiammetta* all feature a sequence in which a group of people tell stories to each other, and it's this formal device that Boccaccio used to create his longest, most ambitious fiction, and one of the greatest works in world literature: the *Decameron.*

When the Black Death struck Europe in 1347 — which the Catholic Church quickly spun as a punitive attack from their god, the same spin some heartless religious leaders put on disasters in our own day — it had the same effect on people that the 9/11 attacks did on many Americans. Florence was hit especially hard, causing some to get out of town and others to abandon themselves to hedonism, taking as their motto "Eat, drink, and be merry, for tomorrow we die." But it gave Boccaccio an idea for a new kind of work, written in a different style than his previous novels, which would give a sharper edge to the *carpe diem* theme and doubts about institutional religion that he already dealt with. So during the plague years he began writing an enormous work, completed around 1352, to which he gave the Greek title *Decameron,* or "Ten Days."[11] The structure is simple and elegant: in the summer of 1348, 10 young Florentine aristocrats leave diseased Florence for the abandoned palaces in the countryside, where they amuse themselves over a two-week period by telling 100 stories over 10 days. (They take Fridays and Saturdays off for religious reasons.) The storytellers — seven women and three men — impose further order on their disrupted lives by assigning a queen or king (moderator) to each day to chose the themes for the stories, and narrator Boccaccio frames the whole event with an introduction, conclusion, and occasional commentary. The result is an 800-page work structured like this:

Author's Preface and Introduction

Day 1   (Wednesday): free choice, though mostly stories hinging on witty remarks (moderated by Pampinea)

---

11 The title is most likely a takeoff on the 4th-century *Hexameron* of Ambrose, six commentaries on Genesis. Boccaccio creates an alternative paradise to the one depicted there.

Day 2 (Thursday): stories of unexpected happiness after a period of misery (Filomena) (Friday and Saturday off)

Day 3 (Sunday): stories about attaining difficult goals (Neifile)

Day 4 (Monday): Author's Prologue, followed by love stories with unhappy endings (Filostrato)

Day 5 (Tuesday): love stories with happy endings (Fiammetta)

Day 6 (Wednesday): stories extolling intelligence as a way to avoid misfortune (Elisa)

Day 7 (Thursday): stories about tricks women play on their husbands (Dioneo) (Friday and Saturday off)

Day 8 (Sunday): stories about tricks men and women play on each other (Lauretta)

Day 9 (Monday): free choice (Emilia)

Day 10 (Tuesday): stories about generosity (Panfilo); storytellers disperse

Author's Conclusion

Is it a novel, or just a tightly structured anthology of stories? Definitely a novel, partly by analogy — one of Boccaccio's sources was Apuleius's *Golden Ass*, a collection of linked stories but considered a novel, and the *Decameron* was the direct inspiration for John Barth's structurally identical *Tidewater Tales* (1987), subtitled "a novel" — and partly by contrast to the superficially similar anthologies of Boccaccio's time. One predecessor and source for the *Decameron* was *Il Novellino*, aka *Cento novelle antiche*, a collection of brief, artless anecdotes pulled together by an anonymous anthologist near the end of the 14th century.[12] There's no frame, no recurring characters, no iterative imagery, no overarching themes — all characteristics of the novel and of the *Decameron*. Same with other medieval anthologies like Petrus Alfonsi's *Disciplina clericalis* (The Scholar's Guide, c. 1100), Walter Map's *De Nugis curialium* (Courtiers' Trifles, c. 1200), Gervase of Tilbury's *Otia imperialia* (Recreation for an Emperor, 1215), the *Gesta romanorum* (Roman Deeds, c. 1300), and other collections of Latin *exempla* and French *fabliaux* that Boccaccio acknowledges in his prologue as his sources. But it is the combination of expressive form, unifying themes, ironic authorial stance, and subtle character development that tags the *Decameron* as a novel rather than a story-cycle — not a conventional novel, to be sure, but happily we are still centuries away from that commercial product: at this time, there was still no such thing as a conventional novel.

12 For an English translation, see Edward Storer's *Il Novellino: The Hundred Old Tales* (London: Routledge, 1925).

It's that carefully constructed structure, in fact, that tells us how to interpret the multifarious work. A reader can easily get distracted by the wide variety of tales the storytellers tell: love stories, tragedies, farces, supernatural tales, adventure stories, clerical satires, and more sex scenes than in any European work of fiction written before it. First, it's worth noting the polite, formal-sounding frame, which stands in stark contrast to the riotous tales within. Recalling how his friends once comforted him during a period of erotic anguish, Boccaccio now offers to comfort those who may be in a similar situation, especially women. Polite, reverent, modest, the narrator sounds like a smooth operator making a good impression on his date's parents before roaring off with her for a night of debauchery. Boccaccio then gives a grim account of the Black Death, with plenty of gruesome details of the physical effects of the bubonic plague, before he takes us to the church of Santa Maria *Novella* (my italics, but the actual name of a church in Florence) and introduces us to his 10 storytellers.[13] Significantly, the seven women are between the ages of 18 and 27, beyond the marriageable sell-by date of that time but still single, suggesting Boccaccio planned to make the same allegorical use of them as he did the seven virtuous nymphs of *Ameto*. (Similarly, the three young men, also single, may represent the three divisions of the soul according to medieval theology: reason, anger, lust.) Though one of them, Dioneo, is a live wire and tells many of the racier stories, all of them are cultivated and well-behaved, and there's no hanky-panky during their unchaperoned fortnight in the country. Similarly in the conclusion, the author expresses his hope that he has provided some solace for his female readers, and then self-defensively defends his work against possible criticism before concluding, unctuously, "[I] offer my humble thanks to Him who assisted me in my protracted labour and conveyed me to the goal I desired. May His grace and peace, sweet ladies, remain with you always, and if perchance these stories should bring you any profit, remember me."[14] After the stories he has told, we can't take this seriously; it's the chaste kiss the smooth operator places on the cheek of his date in full view of her parents later that evening, after getting their daughter drunk and having his way with her. You can almost see Boccaccio winking when he boasts on the last page of his literary talents: "I was told by a lady, a neighbor of mine, that I had the finest and sweetest tongue in the world"; "what is implied here," translator McWilliam assures us, "is an act of cunnilingus" (870).

So how exactly does Boccaccio hope his female readers will profit from

---

13 Many have names from his earlier works, but they apparently are different characters: Fiammetta and Panfilo are here but there's no reference to their relationship in the *Elegy*; Filomena and Filostrato are from a narrative poem Boccaccio wrote when younger; Emilia is also a character in *Ameto*.

14 From G. H. McWilliam's fine translation, hereafter cited by day/story; references to his book-length introduction and invaluable notes will be by page number.

these impious stories exposed from inside his pious raincoat? Let's step inside the frame and look at the first and last stories, which by virtue of their placement should offer us a clue. The first story is about an old criminal who, shortly before he dies, makes a flamboyantly false confession to a naïve priest, who not only absolves him but turns him into a saint, whose relics the populace come to worship. Like the *Decameron* itself, this story begins and ends with sickly-sweet acknowledgments of "God's loving-kindness towards us" while exposing his clergy and followers as credulous fools. It's a comic story, a parody of hagiography, and completely opposite in tone from the hundredth story, a version of the patient Griselda story best known to English readers from "The Clerk's Tale" in Chaucer's *Canterbury Tales*. An arrogant aristocrat named Gualtieri, under pressure from his followers to marry, selects a beautiful peasant and subjects her to a series of tests of her fidelity: first he strips her naked in public (Chaucer left that part out), then hides their two children and tells her he's killed them, and finally tells her he's divorcing her to marry a younger girl. Griselda objects to none of this and remains steadfast in her love for him, so he rewards her at the end by telling her it was all just a test, presents her with the two children she thought were long dead, and restores her to splendor. The story is so horrendous that it can't be taken at face value — the replacement bride Gualtieri shows off to everybody is his own 11-year-old daughter — so how *do* we take it? Most commentators agree with translator McWilliam that the story "should be read rather as an elaborate parable on obedience to the Lord's will" (868), which is borne out by Griselda's numerous quotations from the Bible, identifying herself with both Job and Mary (upon being ordered by Gabriel to serve as a surrogate mother). In back of the story is Abraham's sheep-like response to YHWH's demand that he kill his son. But the narrator, sardonic Dioneo, says Gualtieri's actions "were remarkable not so much for their munificence [the tenth day's theme] as for their senseless brutality. Nor do I advise anyone to follow his example, for it was a great pity that the fellow should have drawn any profit from his conduct" (10.10).

So, the first story exposes Christians as fools and hypocrites, and the last story implies the Christian god's requirement of unquestioning obedience is indistinguishable from the senseless brutality of an arrogant aristocrat, and that only an emotionless doormat like Griselda would submit to such treatment.[15] At least a third of the stories in the *Decameron* feature hypocritical, dishonest priests and nuns, and though there is almost every kind of story within its pages, there's not a single conversion story, not one — unless you count that of Abraham, a Jew who goes to Rome and sees so much depravity among the

---

15 Boccaccio's nonfiction *Famous Women* ignores Christian women in favor of "pagans" because, as Virginia Brown explains in her introduction, "the former sought eternal glory by means of an endurance that was often contrary to human nature" (xvi).

clergy that he becomes a Christian; he figures any religion that continues to grow despite its clergy "doing their level best to reduce the Christian religion to nought and drive it from the face of the earth" must have something going for it, so he joins the winning side (1.2).

If a third of the stories in the *Decameron* mock religion, two-thirds celebrate sex.[16] Here too the structure focuses our attention on Boccaccio's intentions: at the exact center of Dante's *Divine Comedy* is a discourse on love (*Purgatory* 17), by which Dante means the desire to do good; at the center of the *Decameron* — which has quite rightly been called the Human Comedy in contrast to Dante's otherworldly one — is a day devoted to sexy love stories, significantly concluding with the ribald tale of a buxom, passionate redhead who is married off to a guy name Pietro who turns out to be gay. Frustrated by his neglect and considering herself "a fair and lusty wench, blooming with health and vitality," she enlists the help of an old bawd — outwardly very pious, of course — who sends her one stud after another after another to satisfy her needs. One night, she has just welcomed "one of the prettiest and agreeable youths in Perugia" into her house when her husband unexpectedly returns. She tries to hide him, the husband discovers him and is struck by his beauty, and they all climb into bed together. It must have been quite a night, "for the young man was found next morning wandering about the piazza, not exactly certain with which of the pair he had spent the greater part of the night, the wife or the husband" (5.10). Which kind of love, dear reader, would you prefer: Dante's Boy Scout variety or Boccaccio's wild ride?

That seems to be what Boccaccio is asking his female readers throughout the *Decameron*; with conventional religious sentiments banished to the margins of the book (its introduction and conclusion) and lust erected joyously in the middle, Boccaccio seems to be recommending lawless sex over lawful religion, and nowhere is this more apparent than in the tales that combine the two. There are plenty of stories here of nuns or priests caught in the act with laypeople or each other — it's their hypocrisy about it Boccaccio derides, not their natural itch for sex — but the most notorious is the final story of day 3, a third of the way through the novel — another structurally significant location.[17] Waggish Dioneo tells the story of a 14-year-old Arab girl named

---

16 Literally: Bergin calculates "of the one hundred tales told 67% present situations where a sexual relationship (one cannot always call it love) is central to the action" (289–90).

17 Like *The Divine Comedy*, the *Decameron* (100 stories vs. 100 cantos) is divided roughly into thirds: after the third day there's an authorial intervention (prologue to day 4), and at the end of the sixth, there is an extended description of a worldly paradise just at the point where Dante unveils his unworldly one. But I don't want to imply that Boccaccio was parodying Dante: he revered him, wrote the first biography of him, and spent the final years of his life writing and lecturing on his work. Nevertheless, Boccaccio is the anti-Dante. The latter's "divine" realm is imaginary, the bizarre fantasy of brainsick theologians, whereas Boccaccio's realm is comparatively real. There's nothing wrong, of course, with creating and describing an imaginary realm, à la Swift or Tolkein. But they didn't mistake

Alibech who, impressed by the behavior of the local Christians, asks one for the best way to "serve God." He sends her into the desert to consult a hermit. "On observing how young and exceedingly pretty she was," each monk she encounters, terrified of temptation, sends her off to another, until she comes to the cell of a young monk named Rustico. He is quickly overcome by her toxic nubility and tells her the best way to "serve God" is to "put the Devil back in Hell."

The girl asked him how this was done, and Rustico replied:

"You will soon find out, but just do whatever you see me doing for the present." And so saying, he began to divest himself of the few clothes he was wearing, leaving himself completely naked. The girl followed his example, and he sank to his knees as though he were about to pray, getting her to kneel directly opposite.

In this posture, the girl's beauty was displayed to Rustico in all its glory, and his longings blazed more fiercely than ever, bringing about the resurrection of the flesh. Alibech stared at this in amazement, and said:

"Rustico, what is that thing I see sticking out in front of you, which I do not possess?"

"Oh, my daughter," said Rustico, "this is the devil I was telling you about. Do you see what he's doing? He's hurting me so much that I can hardly endure it."

"Oh, praise be to God," said the girl, "I can see that I am better off than you are, for I have no such devil to contend with."

"You're right there," said Rustico. "But you have something else instead, that I haven't."

"Oh?" said Alibech. "And what's that?"

"You have Hell," said Rustico. "And I honestly believe that God has sent you here for the salvation of my soul, because if this devil continues to plague the life out of me, and if you are prepared to take sufficient pity upon me to let me put him back into Hell, you will be giving me marvellous relief, as well as rendering incalculable service and pleasure to God, which is what you say you came here for in the first place."

"Oh, Father," replied the girl in all innocence, "if I really do have a Hell, let's do as you suggest just as soon as you are ready."

"God bless you, my daughter," said Rustico. "Let us go and put him back, and then perhaps he'll leave me alone."

At which point he conveyed the girl to one of their beds, where he instructed her in the art of incarcerating that accursed fiend. (3.10)

---

it for real. What would be your opinion of Swift if he went to his grave insisting *Gulliver's Travels* was a factual account? Exactly. Dante may not have been mad, as Voltaire suggests, but he apparently believed hell, purgatory, and heaven were real places, not metaphors for spiritual states. A comparable modern pair is Joyce and Eliot; both are consummate artists, but the Irishman is greater than the expatriate American because his art is rooted in the real world, whereas Eliot got lost in a fantasy world of Anglican mysticism. That doesn't invalidate his considerable artistry any more than it does Dante's, but it compromises it and makes it, finally, inferior to the art of those who see clearly, not through a glass darkly.

Boccaccio's daring use of "the resurrection of the flesh" to describe an erection is only one reason why earlier translators either skipped this story, resorted to libertine French, or left it in the original Italian. The blasphemous subversion of the defining feature of Christianity is not just a dirty joke: Boccaccio is replacing something unreal and unnatural (a resurrection that never happened) with something real and natural, just as in *Filocolo* he superimposed the more earthy classical gods on the ghostly ones of Christianity. Throughout the *Decameron*, a capitalized Nature is acknowledged as the true force that drives the world, not a god, and sexuality is so obviously a part of nature — as central to it as the resurrection is to Christianity — that Boccaccio condemns no one who goes with that flow. Like Pynchon, he is "always happy to see young people get together" (*GR* 498), and the *Decameron* features story after story in which teenagers follow the promptings of nature and seek out a mate, usually in defiance of churchly convention or parental expectations.

All of which makes us wonder about the seven unmarried women that make up Boccaccio's "happy band" (*lieta brigata*). The three men don't change throughout the novel, but it's worth tracking the ladies' responses to the racier stories told by the men: their development is what makes the *Decameron* a novel rather than a collection of stories. After the first one, in which a monk is caught screwing a girl by his abbot, who is then caught screwing her by the monk (1.4), we're told:

> As they listened to Dioneo's story, the ladies at first felt some embarrassment, which showed itself in the modest blushes that appeared on all their faces. Then, glancing at one another and barely managing to restrain their laughter, they giggled as they listened. When it came to an end, however, they gently rebuked him with a few well-chosen words, in order to show that stories of that kind should not be told when ladies are present. (1.5)

On the second day, Panfilo tells a long story about an Egyptian girl named Alatiel who, "*Owing to a series of mishaps, . . . passes through the hands of nine men in various places within the space of four years*" (headnote to 2.7 — notice how Boccaccio gives the plot away? Again, it's not the tale but the telling that's important). At the end of this sexual Odyssey about a teenage girl who had sex "on thousands of different occasions" with eight different men before marrying the ninth, we're told: "The ladies heaved many a sigh over the fair lady's several adventures: but who knows what their motives may have been? Perhaps some of them were sighing, not so much because they felt sorry for Alatiel, but because they longed to be married no less often than she was" (2.8).[18] No blushing or rebukes this time at this Iliad of illicit sex. By the time they reach the end of Dineo's story of the Arab girl with the salubrious

---

18 McWilliam notes "Alatiel" "happens to be an anagram of La Lieta ('The Happy Woman'), offering a possible clue to the way in which the story is intended to be read" (816).

hellmouth, false modesty and embarrassment are gone with the wind: "So aptly and cleverly worded did Dioneo's tale appear to the virtuous ladies, that they shook with mirth a thousand times more" (3.10).[19]

The cumulative effect of these stories and the relaxing attitudes of the women can best be seen at another structurally significant point: two-thirds of the way through the *Decameron*, the happy band decamps for a new location, near which is a paradisaical Valley of the Ladies, "the work of Nature rather than of man" (6.conclusion). The women go off alone into this valley, and after admiring the beauty of the landscape, they come to a limpid pool, whereupon "all seven of them undressed and took to the water, which concealed their chaste white bodies no better than a thin sheet of glass would conceal a pink rose." Given the progress of their sexual education so far, one might reasonably expect the *Decameron* to turn into an orgy between the seven women and three men (the Hugh Hefner ratio for a successful party), but, alas, nothing of the sort happens. At the end of the two-week getaway, the women head back to grim Florence without getting so much as a peck on the cheek. A missed opportunity? Boccaccio told us in the prologue that the breakdown of law after the plague meant "everyone was free to behave as he pleased." But the reason his female characters don't embrace this dangerous freedom is because the sexual education has been intended all along not for them but for the female readers Boccaccio addressed in his prologue, urging them to shrug off their false modesty and repressed instincts. Could be that some of his liberated female readers will go so far as to turn pro, in which case, as Boccaccio says in the last line of the novel, "if perchance these stories should bring you any *profit*, remember me" (my italics; Richard Kuhns's recent book on the *Decameron* is subtitled *Author as Midwife and Pimp*). The concluding line takes us back to the opening of the book, which doesn't have an actual title page: "*Here begins the book called* Decameron, *otherwise known as Prince Galahalt.*" Galahalt is of course the noble friend from *Lancelot of the Lake*, the one who facilitated the adulterous meeting of Guinevere and Lancelot and as a result got branded as a pimp by later authors, most significantly by killjoy Dante (*Inferno* 5). So the lesson of the *Decameron*, derived as much from its cunning structure as from its cunning linguistics, is to forsake religion and embrace sexuality, especially while you're still young. Like so much of English Cavalier poetry, it's a wake-up call to virgins to make much of time, to gather ye rosebuds while ye may. There is more to the *Decameron* than that — it is large, it contains multitudes — but this oversimplification underscores the subversive nature of the novel; no wonder it was one of the

---

19 "Cleverly worded" indeed — in his *Mimesis*, Auerbach takes what looks like an average passage from the *Decameron* and performs a brilliant close reading to show how artfully every word is chosen, how carefully the syntax is structured (chap. 9).

first books the Catholic Church put on its *Index of Prohibited Books*, and no wonder it is still banned in some school libraries today.

Boccaccio's final novel is as short as the *Decameron* is long, as bitter as it is sweet. *Corbaccio* ("Ugly Crow," c. 1355)[20] is a kind of companion piece to the *Elegy of Lady Fiammetta*; instead of a young girl bewailing a bad romance, we have an older scholar complaining about being spurned by a widow. Like Fiammetta he is tempted to commit suicide, but then falls asleep and has a therapeutic dream: he finds himself in a "desolate wilderness" where he is approached by a spirit, who turns out to be the widow's ex-husband, who sets him straight not only about the widow but women in general with a sarcastic misogynistic lecture. He urges the scholar not only to get over the widow (the ugly bird of the title) but to avenge himself by writing a bitter satire against her, which turns out to be the novella we've just read, and which is so harsh that it too deserves the title "ugly crow." It's the literary equivalent of giving her the bird.

Aside from a brief preface and briefer envoi, the narrative is not divided into chapters, but like *Lady Fiammetta* it consists of nine sections, cleverly organized in chiasmic form (the ninth part inverts the first, the eighth the second, etc.) as Robert Hollander shows in his short but smart book on *Corbaccio*:

(1) narrator's preface
   (2) narrator's initial situation (waking world)
      (3) dream vision (Hell)
         (4) narrator's biography
            (5) spirit's lecture
         (6) spirit's biography of ex-wife
      (7) dream vision (Paradise)
   (8) narrator's final situation (waking world)
(9) narrator's envoi (3)

Corbaccio is notorious for being a classic of misogyny because of the ferocity with which the spirit attacks women, which he defends as rhetorically necessary:

> . . . to sweeten your disordered appetite, I have to dwell even more extensively on things such as you have heard because these words spoken thus are the pincers with which one must break and cut the hard chains which have dragged you here; and these words thus spoken are the reaping hooks and the hatchets with which one chops down the poisonous shrubs, the spiny thornbushes, and the twisted brushwood which have massed in a hedge

---

20 Both the exact meaning of the title and the date of composition are uncertain; the title means something like evil bird, or bird of ill omen, and it is generally believed Boccaccio wrote this right after the *Decameron*.

before you to prevent your seeing the way out. These words thus spoken are the hammers, the picks, the battering rams which must break the lofty mountains, the hard rocks, and the precipitous cliffs to make a road for you . . .[21]

This rhetorical tough-love attitude allows such extravagant passages as this, a Swiftian description of the widow's makeup: "After she had smeared and painted herself with these concoctions as if she had to go and sell herself, often it would happen that, not being on my guard while I kissed her, my lips got all caught in the glue; and better sensing that greasy mess with the nose than with the eyes, not only did I have trouble keeping down the food in my stomach, but could scarcely retain the soul in my breast" (42). And speaking as only an ex-husband can, the spirit pulls out all the stops for this geographical description of the widow's vagina:

> I do not quite know where I should begin to speak of the Gulf of Setalia, hidden in the Valley of the Acheron beneath its dark woods, often russet in color and foaming with foul grime and full of creatures of unusual species, but yet I will tell of it. The mouth through which the port is entered is of such size that although my little bark sailed with quite a tall mast, never was there a time, even though the waters were narrower then, that I might not have made room for a companion sailing with a mast no less than mine without disturbing myself in the least. Ah, what am I saying? King Robert's armada all chained together at the time that he enlarged it could have entered there with the greatest of ease. . . . That gulf, then, is certainly an infernal abyss which could be filled or sated as the sea with water or the fire with wood. I will be silent about the sanguine and yellow rivers that descend from it in turn, streaked with white mould, sometimes no less displeasing to the nose than to the eyes, because the style I have picked draws me to something else. What shall I say further to you therefore about the village of Evilhole? . . . Nor can I otherwise tell of the goaty stench which her whole corporeal bulk exudes when she groans excited sometimes by heat, and sometimes by exertion; this is so appalling that, combined with the other things I have already spoken of, it makes her bed smell like a lion's den, so that any squeamish person would stay with far less loathing in the Val di Chiana [a malarial swamp] in midsummer than near that. (55–56)

This is so over-the-top that we can't take it seriously — or the spirit's diatribes against women in general — as an expression of Boccaccio's personal views on women. It's easy to find misogynistic sentiments elsewhere in his works — an owl-eyed feminist critic can find misogyny in *any* man's work — but it's worth noting that in later years Boccaccio wrote the first biographical collection in Western literature devoted exclusively to exemplary women. (True, some are *bad* examples, but most are admirable.) It's more important to realize that Boccaccio was merely indulging in a *rhetorical* performance of

---

21 Pages 52–53 in Cassell's rather stiff translation, hereafter cited by page number.

a time-honored theme; nearly all his jibes against women can be traced back (as translator Cassell shows in his introduction and notes) to Ovid's *Remedies for Love*, Juvenal's sixth *Satire*, the writings of Church fathers, the *Roman de la Rose*, and other works. Today, hardly any novelist, with the brilliant exception of Alexander Theroux,[22] works in this mode; *Corbaccio's* modern-day equivalent would be the blue routine of a foul-mouthed stand-up comic, and like those performances, it is simply to be laughed at, not taken seriously as social commentary. Give it up, folks, for Gianni Boccaccio, the Florentine Fluffer, two shows nightly.

Just as an art critic can dispassionately admire a superb painting of a bloody massacre as much as one depicting a vase of flowers, the subject matter of a novel shouldn't distract us from the artistry that went into it. So if we judge *Corbaccio* the least impressive of Bocaccio's five novels, it's not for its misogyny but for its inferior artistry. Despite the tight structure and rhetorical flamboyance, it's not that engaging. It does show that the dream-vision common to religious writings can be incorporated into the novel form, but it would require further refinement before it could work effectively: it's a long road from the spirit's harangue to "The Legend of the Grand Inquisitor" in *The Brothers Karamazov*. Not surprising, Boccaccio turned away from fiction at that point and devoted the rest of his writing career to scholarly works, but not before demonstrating in his five fictions that the novel was a viable form for ambitious writers and an excellent vehicle for what would become known as Renaissance humanism, a bracing and necessary alternative to the moribund theology of his time.

Boccaccio was a tough act to follow, so the Italian novelists that succeeded him mostly just imitated his greatest work for a while. In 1378, three years after Boccaccio's death, Ser Giovanni of Florence composed a work called *The Pecorone* (The Simpleton — literally "sheep's head") that is not only patterned after the *Decameron* but plagiarizes a few stories from it.[23] His frame-story is promising: an honorable young man named Auretto hears wonderful things about a beautiful young nun named Saturnina and falls in

---

22 Not surprisingly, *Corbaccio* is listed in the bibliographic chapter "The Misogynist's Library" in *Darconville's Cat* (1981), which, like Theroux's more recent *Laura Warholic* (2007), is more a learned exercise in an old genre than an expression of personal bias. Nevertheless, no writer takes up this topic with complete disinterest; something angry and spiteful draws him to it.

23 Nothing is known about Ser Giovanni, except that his title suggests he was a notary. Some scholars feel the 1378 date given in the book's opening sonnet is a ruse and that it was actually written a century or two later. It was first published in book form in 1558. I'll be quoting W. G. Waters's old 1890s translation.

love with her sight unseen. He takes holy orders and contrives to become the chaplain of her convent, and wins her love when they finally meet. Unlike the horny monks and nuns in the *Decameron*, they decide to sublimate their love by telling stories to each other, 50 stories over 25 days. How sweet.

Now, fiction as foreplay, equating "lovemaking, language making" as in Carole Maso's story-cycle *Aureole*, is a fine conceit; we speak of going to bed with a good book. And the first story in *The Pecorone* nicely dramatizes the loving but chaste relationship between Brother Auretto and Sister Saturnina. He tells her there once was a noble youth named Galgano who fell for a married woman and tried to attract her, but with no luck. Galgano later meets and impresses her husband so much that he in turn praises him to his wife, who *now* suddenly decides she wants him. (I know what the spirit in *Corbaccio* would say about that type.) The adulteress-to-be invites Galgano to her home when her husband is away and throws herself at him, then undresses and invites him to join her in bed. Galgano first wants to know what made her change her mind about him — *she* first wants him to get in bed and embrace her, which he does — and then she explains she was moved by her husband's high praise of him. Galgano is so honored that he refuses to dishonor him by screwing his wife, so he leaves.

The erotic but ultimately virtuous story is exactly the sort of thing a religious couple who love each other but want to stay true to their religious vows might tell each other, a kind of literary flirting. Saturnina tells Auretto, "This tale indeed pleased me greatly when I learned the constancy of this gentleman at the moment when he held in his arms her whom he had admired for so long a time. If I had been in his place, I know not what I should have done" — which must have raised Auretto's eyebrows, if not another part of his anatomy. But Ser Giovanni doesn't keep it up; by the fifth day he's run out of love stories and resorts to miscellaneous tales of intrigue, and then just pads out the remainder of his book with transcriptions from Giovanni Villani's historical chronicles of Italy written earlier in the 14th century. Nothing develops between the monk and nun; at the end of the 25th day they simply hug and go their separate ways. For the most part, Ser Giovanni avoids the licentiousness and irreligion of the *Decameron*, but doesn't offer much to take their place. The one exception might be the scandalous tale Auretto tells on the third day (apparently one of Ser Giovanni's originals) about a priest on his way to the papal court in Avignon who has sex with another traveling friar who not only turns out to be a woman in disguise (and who just misses a lesbian encounter with a maid) but is also the mistress of an influential cardinal. Auretto had warned Saturnina that she might be offended by the story, but she isn't fazed at all. Perhaps she's sending signals that Auretto is too much of a *pecorone* to pick up; that may be one explanation for the book's title, though I suspect the real simpleton is the reader who comes to it expecting another *Decameron*.

The *Pleasant Nights* (*Le Piacevoli notti*, 1550–53) of Milanese writer Giovanfrancesco Straparola (c. 1480–c. 1557) was one of the most popular and influential of these anthology-novels. Using actual historical figures, Straparola begins by describing how an aristocrat and his widowed daughter left troublesome Milan for carefree Venice, where the daughter assembled a brilliant salon of sophisticated ladies and gentlemen (including the writer Pietro Bembo [1470–1547]). During the 13 days of Carnival preceding Lent, her entourage takes turn telling five tales a night, with 13 tales on the final night, punctuated with songs, dances, and riddles — a literary carnival to match the more boisterous one going on in Venice. Only about a half-dozen tales are tragic; the rest are pleasant (*piacevoli*) and fanciful. Straparola favors the supernatural more often than other Italian novelists and was especially fond of fairy tales: he gave us the original versions of "Puss in Boots" and "Beauty and the Beast," which along with similar tales eventually found their way into the fairytale collections of Charles Perrault, the Countess d'Aulnoy, Hans Christian Andersen, and the Brothers Grimm.

Straparola drew inspiration from everywhere, not only from his Italian predecessors (the earlier *Novellino*, Boccaccio, Ser Giovanni) but from *The Arabian Nights* and other Oriental sources. A number of his stories expose the licentiousness of monks and nuns (and were duly expurgated by church authorities in later editions) and there are the usual bedroom farces, but they are milder than those in the *Decameron*, R-rated rather than X-rated. Translator W. G. Waters notes that Straparola was a sloppy writer — more interested in entertainment than art — but his tales are fun to read. One even anticipates the Freudian equation of money with excrement: in the second fable told on the fifth night, we learn of a poor girl named Adamantina who trades some yarn for a doll; she anoints it with oil and goes to bed with it, and soon the doll cries out for the chamber pot, into which she voids "a great quantity of coins of all sorts." (The story was later cleaned up as "The Goose That Laid the Golden Egg.") Then it really gets weird: the doll is stolen, then abandoned in a field; the king of Bohemia happens by, relieves himself, and — lacking anything to wipe himself with — picks up the doll and tries to put it to that purpose, whereupon she bites him on the ass and won't let go. The king promises to marry any girl who can remove the doll from his ass, so when Adamantina hears of the proclamation, she retrieves her doll, marries the king, and lives happily ever after. (The magic doll disappears "after the common fashion of phantoms.") But *Pleasant Nights* barely qualifies as a novel, for Straparola doesn't do anything with his frame-narrative; the narrators remain well-behaved during Carnival, and at the end of the 13th night everyone leaves to endure Lent. *Pleasant Nights* is a major work in the history of fairy tales — see Bottigheimer's *Fairy Godfather* — but a minor work in the history of the novel. Other similar collections of tales from this period — Masuccio di Salerno's *Novellino* (1476), Matteo Bandello's *Novelle* (1554–73), Cinthio's *Ecatommiti* (The Hundred Tales, 1565) — lack a framing narrative and thus belong to the history of the short story, though they all attest to the huge appetite for popular fiction at the time.[24]

Going back, Italian audiences were not immune to the charms of the chivalric novels sweeping through Europe in Boccaccio's time. A Florentine author who called himself Andrea da Barberino (né Andrea Mangiabotti, c. 1370–c. 1431) produced a huge cycle of novels based on the Matter of France, that is, legends that accrued around Charlemagne and his Twelve Peers. One of these heroes, Guérin, duc de Lorraine (featured in *The Song of Roland*), became the protagonist of Andrea's most popular novel, *Il Guerrin meschino* (Guerino the Wretched, 1391). Although Andrea has been praised for his verisimilitude and attention to historical detail in his other novels, he took his inspiration for this one from the fanciful travelers' tales found in the *Letter of Prester John* (c. 1165) and Sir John Mandeville's *Travels* (1357), freeing his hero from history to send him on a fantastic voyage of self-discovery. Get a load of this:

Guerino is born to the king and queen of Albania, but at birth is whisked away from them by his nurse to avoid the invading Turks; she dies en route to Greece, where he is raised by a merchant, grows up to attract the attention of the son of the Greek emperor, and is attracted in turn to his snooty princess sister. Despite proving himself in tournaments and battles, he is dismissed as a "Turk" by the princess, encouraging him to leave and discover his true parentage. Astrologers advise him to consult the trees of the sun and moon at the eastern edge of the world, so armed with a fragment of the True Cross, he heads east, fights and kills a Christian-hating giant, has a three-month dalliance with an Indian princess, sees monsters and hears of dog-headed tribes and people whose feet are so large they use them as umbrellas, learns his real name from the oracular trees, returns to Greece and saves a different princess from real Turks, goes off to the Holy Land, heads south to visit Prester John in Ethiopia, treks across Africa converting the natives, visits the 1,200-year-old sibyl of Cumae (who supplies the epigraph to Eliot's *Waste Land*) for further information about his parents, is warned by a talking snake about the sibyl, who tells Guerin what he wants to know and then tries to seduce him, after which he travels to Rome for cleansing by the pope, who sends him off to do penance at the shrine of Saint James in Spain and Saint Patrick's Purgatory in Ireland, where he descends into a subterranean world for a Dantesque vision of purgatory and hell, after which he returns to Rome, where the pope

---

24 All of these *novellieri* were an important influence on English drama: in 1566 and 1567 William Painter published an enormous anthology of translated Italian novellas under the title *The Palace of Pleasure*, which was ransacked for plots by Shakespeare and other dramatists for decades. It's why so many of their plays are set in Italy.

now sends him to Albania to expel the endlessly marauding Turks, where lo! Guerino discovers his parents in a dungeon (where they have been confined since his birth), frees them, learns of his royal heritage, spurns the snooty princess, and marries the princess of Persepolis.[25]

It's a literally extravagant example of the quest for identity, 566 pages long in the modern Italian edition, and remained enormously popular for centuries. The Italian cultural theorist Antonio Gramsci wonders about "*Guerino* as a 'popular encyclopaedia'; observe how low the culture must be of those strata who read *Guerino* and how little interest they take, for example, in 'geography' for them to be content with *Guerino* and to take it seriously" (351). The unlettered audiences of Andrea's day who attended recitations of his novels derived their conception of the world from imaginative but inaccurate works like this, just as their counterparts today derive their shaky sense of history from the movies.

While some Italian authors were writing such entertainments for the masses, a few others were writing erudite, sometimes experimental novels for the elite. Aeneas Sylvius, the pen name of Enea Silvio de Piccolomini (1405–64), wrote in Latin a sophisticated novel about adultery entitled *The Tale of the Two Lovers* (*De duobus amantibus*, 1444), which became something of a best-seller (35 editions by 1500). It's easy to see why: it's smart, urbane, and sexy. Eurylus, a 32-year-old member of Emperor Sigismund's entourage, visits Siena and is struck by the beauty of a young married woman named Lucrecia, a tall blonde considered the belle of Tuscany. She is likewise struck by his good looks and noble bearing, and the short novel charts their epistolary flirtation and eventual consummation. The prose is graceful and poetic — unless I'm being misled by Flora Grierson's 1929 translation, which has a charming, Yellow Nineties tint — and shot through with literary allusions and psychological insights. The lovers are never found out, despite some close shaves, but Eurylus, much to his and Lucrecia's despair, eventually has to return to Germany. Lucrecia dresses in black and wastes away, her death announced to Eurylus in his dreams. The novel concludes, partly tongue in cheek: "Shattered by this great sorrow, he put on mourning and would not be consoled, until the Emperor wedded him to a maiden of ducal rank, most beautiful, and chaste, and virtuous" (135). The conventional happy ending is undercut by the thrilling unconventional affair preceding it; Lucrecia's willingness to defy convention, her bravery in doing so, and her erudite letters will no doubt be preferred in Eurylus's memory over the conventional attributes of his socially acceptable, nameless bride.

In addition to this novel, Sylvius wrote poetry — he was Emperor

---

25 Adapted from Dunlop's summary, 2:271–80. Though translated into many European languages — a Spanish version is condemned in *Don Quixote* (1.49) — it has never been translated into English.

Frederick III's poet laureate — history, even a work on geography said to have influenced Columbus, but in 1458 he threw it all away and went over to the dark side: with a learned pun on his given name and Virgil's "pious Aeneas," he became Pope Pius II. During his pontificate he tried to suppress his racy novel, but without success. There were apparently many readers who relished the irony that Christ's representative on earth once promised "I'll make the grey hairs of your sickly lust to itch" (xix) and delivered with passages like this about an adulterous couple in bed:

> And now he praised her mouth, now her cheeks, and now her eyes. And sometimes, raising the blanket, he gazed at those secret parts he had not seen before, and cried:
> "I find more than I had expected. Thus must Diana have appeared to Actaeon, when she bathed in the spring. Could anything be lovelier or whiter than your body? Now I am rewarded for all perils. What would I not suffer for your sake? Oh lovely bosom, most glorious breasts! Can it be that I touch you, possess you, hold you in my hands? Smooth limbs, sweet-scented body, are you really mine?" (120–21)

Leon Battista Alberti (1402–72), a Florentine who was even more versatile than Sylvius, the very model of a Renaissance man in fact — he wrote plays, poems, essays, studied scientific topics, designed buildings, both painted and wrote art criticism, all while participating in papal politics — also composed an outlandish comic novel entitled *Momus* (1450). Set in mythic Greece but satirizing figures of Alberti's own day, it lies halfway between Lucian's comic dialogues about the gods and John Barth's postmodern makeovers of Greek mythology. Momus, the god of criticism, shuttles between Olympus and the newly created human realm, criticizing everything and everyone he sees, causing turmoil for the hell of it, earning everyone's ire, and yet is the only one smart enough to know how a state should be run. He not only writes down and publicizes all the transgressions of the gods, but his adventures among the philosophers inspire him to compile a manual for princes that is ignored initially by Jupiter (i.e., Pope Nicholas V, whom Alberti advised) but is later recovered and used by Jupiter to regain and maintain his royal power.

Written in unorthodox Latin, *Momus* is an academic, philosophical comedy that anticipates Erasmus's *Praise of Folly* and More's *Utopia*, but its broad humor also anticipates the picaresque novel that would soon emerge in nearby Spain. The 175-page novel isn't as funny as Alberti keeps claiming it is, though it may have been to his original audience, who had never seen anything like this before. Its audacity must have been shocking, but I'll skip over the complicated, farcical plot to focus on Alberti's most important contribution to the novel: a new conception of the artist. Momus is an obnoxious gadfly who mocks the status quo, a role more and more authors will assume over the centuries. The writer as social critic, as agitator, even as outcast is familiar enough in 20th-century literature but was something of an innovation in 15th-century Europe. It wasn't entirely new — as I said, the satirist Lucian was an important model, and Alberti often quotes that trickster Apuleius — but the bold idea of the artist as someone who questions the very foundations of civilization is expressed with anarchic zeal in Alberti's novel. A large part of the plot concerns Jupiter's plan to destroy the world and create a new one — just as Pope Nicholas V was keen on renovating Rome at that time — and in a sense Alberti does the same thing: razing the conventional pieties and verities of society and replacing them with a new, skeptical attitude based on irony, uncertainty, confusion, and especially paradox: Momus is a god yet encourages atheism; condemns all occupations and praises beggary; mocks philosophers but steals their ideas. It's the anarchic, satiric voice we'll hear later in Rabelais, Swift, Voltaire, Melville, Wilde, up to Gaddis, one of whose surrogates insists that the artist's cause (like that of Momus) "is turmoil. . . . the artist comes among us not as the bearer of idées reçues embracing art as decoration or the comfort of churchly beliefs in greeting card sentiments but rather in the aesthetic equivalent of one who comes on earth 'not to send peace, but a sword.'"[26] *Momus* is a spirited, slash-and-burn achievement, avoiding any moral norm, "taking up no fixed or consistent position" (2.77) until the final pages, in which the author suddenly grows serious and gives some sober advice on statecraft. Momus winds up emasculated by the crowd and imprisoned by the state even though his writings ultimately prove to be accurate and useful, the fate — metaphorical or otherwise — that often awaits the artist who attacks his society.

Needless to say, *Momus* wasn't nearly as popular as books like Straparola's *Pleasant Nights*, but Alberti was proud to be different and struck one of the first blows for difficult, experimental, unpopular novelists everywhere:

> To put other cases aside, how many works by ancient writers, do you suppose, would win approval if they left an impression of banality and the commonplace? On the other hand, what will not be read with the greatest pleasure and admiration if it is understood to belong to the class of things that are unpredictable and difficult, not to say neglected and jeered at by the rest? So I think it is the duty of the writer to undertake nothing that his prospective readers will find predictable and obvious. (preface)

Alberti overestimates the tastes of the reading public, which generally prefers the "familiar and obvious," but *Momus* announces the arrival of a new kind of novelist: a captious misfit whose profane writings show more insight into the human condition than the sacred writings society allegedly follows.

Alberti is also considered by some to be the author of the strangest, most

---

26 *A Frolic of His Own*, 39. The concluding phrase is of course from Matt. 10:34, a verse Christians always conveniently forget when praising Jesus as the god of love.

exotic novel of the Renaissance, the extraordinary *Hypnerotomachia Poliphili* (Poliphilo's Erotic Dream-Quest, 1499).[27] But while it draws upon Alberti's treatise on architecture, the scholarly consensus is that *HP* (as I'll abbreviate it henceforth) was written by a Dominican friar named Francesco Colonna (1433–1527). For the last five centuries *HP* has attracted the attention of bibliophiles — the original edition printed by Aldus Manutius in Venice is considered one of the most beautiful books ever — and students of architecture, art, botany, Neoplatonism, alchemy, and other esoteric traditions, even Jungian psychology, but apparently few students of the novel. This is probably because it doesn't resemble the standard novel, though it has several antecedents in the fictions I've discussed so far: to go no farther back than Boccaccio, *HP* combines genre features of the dream-vision (*Corbaccio*), the pastoral (*Ameto*), and the romantic adventure (*Filocolo*), and as in all of Boccaccio's novels it favors classical mythology and pagan values over Christian. Colonna's style is much more ornate than Boccaccio's, however; it recalls the maximalist prose of Alharizi, of *The Battle of Magh Rath*, and the rarefied style of Apuleius. (There are several references to *The Golden Ass* in the text.) But Colonna goes further than any of them: his language is an artificial one, even more extreme than Moses de León's, mixing Greek and obscure Latin words with his own Venetian dialect of Italian. This macaronic language anticipates that of another huge dream-novel, *Finnegans Wake*; in fact, though other antecedents for *HP* can be found — *The Book of Enoch* and the *Sefer Hekalot*, Zabara's *Book of Delight*, Dante's *Divine Comedy*, the dream-laden *Quest for the Holy Grail* — it better resembles various exotic novels closer to our own time that privilege elaborate description and flamboyant language over plot, such as Flaubert's *Temptation of Saint Anthony*, Huysmans's *Against Nature*, Rolfe's *Don Tarquino* and *The Weird of the Wanderer*, Lovecraft's *Dream-Quest of Unknown Kadath*, Theroux's *Darconville's Cat*, Coover's *Lucky Pierre*, and Danielewski's *Only Revolutions*, as well as Joyce's *Wake* and Schmidt's analogous *Zettel's Traum*. It is illustrated with 172 black-and-white drawings integral to the novel (artist unknown), recalling Lewis Carroll's Alice novellas, Beardsley's *Under the Hill*, even Gorey's quaint novelettes. Heady company.

The plot of *HP*, what little there is of it, is fairly straightforward. The narrator, an erudite, hypersensitive aesthete named Poliphilo, suffers from two unrequited loves: one for a woman named Polia, the other for the vanished glories of the classical era, especially its architecture. After a white night

27 The standard English translation of the title is *The Strife of Love in a Dream*, but since *-machia* can mean *quest* as well as *strife, struggle, battle*, etc., I prefer my rendering. (Something Joycean would be ideal, like *Poliphilo's Wetdreamwork*.) All page references are to Joscelyn Godwin's translation, which appeared on the 500th anniversary of the original Italian publication. (Reportedly there is an excellent translation by Ian White awaiting publication.)

of insomnia, he finally falls asleep on the first morning of May, 1467, and dreams of both unrequited loves melding into one. Critic Liane Lefaivre, admitting the plot sounds "absurd," describes the rest of Poliphilo's adventures in wonderland:

> Poliphilo is transported inside a wild forest. He gets lost, escapes, and falls asleep again. He awakens in a second dream, dreamed inside the first. Within it, he is taken by some nymphs to meet their queen. There he is asked to declare his love for Polia, which he does. He is then directed by two nymphs to three gates. He chooses the third, behind which he finds his beloved. They are taken by more nymphs to a temple to be engaged. Along the way they witness five triumphal processions celebrating their union. Then the lovers are taken to the island of Cythera by barge, with Cupid as their boatswain; they see another triumphal procession. The narrative is interrupted, and a second voice takes over, as Polia describes the erotomachia from her own point of view. This takes up one-fifth of the book, after which the hero resumes his narrative. They are blissfully wed, but Polia vanishes into thin air as Poliphilo is about to take her in his arms.[28]

Though accurate, that's like describing *Ulysses* as a day in the life of a Jewish-Irish adman. The reason *HP* is 466 pages long is because of its elaborate use of *ekphrasis* — the descriptive set-piece favored by ancient Greek novelists — pushing it to unheard-of extremes. Let me quote Lefaivre again, who provides this useful inventory of the novel and index of its concerns:

> These architectural surroundings and design artifacts in which the plot of the *Hypnerotomachia* unravels are described at such length that they take up more than half of the book. Two hundred pages out of 370 are exclusively devoted to architectural descriptions. No fewer than 78 of the first 86 pages are occupied by the painstakingly minute detailing of the *boschetto* [a garden landscaped to look like a wilderness], the palm grove, the giant pyramidal building, the bridge, the octagonal baths, and the palazzo. Indeed, the great pyramidal building alone monopolizes almost 50 pages: and of these, 5 pages, in turn, record nothing but the measurements of the triumphal arch that serves as its entrance. The temple of Venus fills an additional 18 pages, the *nymphaea* [nymphs' shrine] and the aquatic labyrinth 12, the ruins 35. Descriptions of various landscapes and gardens run to close to 60 pages, the gardens on the island of Cythera alone absorbing 36 of them. Of the remaining 150 or so pages of Poliphilo's tale, 63 are occupied with the description of chariots in the triumphal arches, 14 with the food and place settings at what surely must be the most copious banquet ever described, 4 with a ballet, 20 with music, and 20 with

---

28 Lefaivre, 8. Favoring a different author for *HP*, she defiantly entitled her superb book *Leon Battista Alberti's* Hypnerotomachia Poliphili: *Re-Cognizing the Architectural Body in the Early Italian Renaissance*; hereafter cited parenthetically. Godwin reviews all the candidates for the authorship of *HP* — and reinforces Colonna's claim — in chapter 4 of his *The Real Book of Four*, a quickie guide produced to cash in on the best-selling novel *The Rule of Four* (2004) but nonetheless a good overview of *HP*.

the ceremonial rituals at a temple. The descriptions of precious stones, gems, and metals consume 8 pages. Finally, 60 pages are taken up with the description of botanical lore; they constitute a veritable encyclopedia of every plant known during the Renaissance. A mere 30 pages at most are left to the actual action of the love story, to its dialogue and inner monologue, and to the devices usually associated with the genre. (9)

The most common strategy of the experimental novel is the inversion of "the devices usually associated with the genre": Colonna's extended descriptions are not due to the lack of an editor, or being paid by the word like authors of pulp fiction, but a daring experiment to reverse foreground and background: those aspects of the novel usually mentioned in passing (setting, descriptions of clothes, etc.) are given all the attention usually lavished on character and plot development. Any building or statue in *HP* is described in more detail than its nominal hero and heroine, and not only in technical but highly sensuous detail — so sensuous that the novel must be like porn for architecture students.

The style Colonna uses is no less elaborate and unconventional than the extensive descriptions. It's a sterling example of gigantism — the name Joyce gave to the style of the "Cyclops" chapter of *Ulysses* — and accounts for the numerous descriptions of enormous buildings and colossi. He never uses one adjective where two will do, is overly fond of the superlative case and classical allusions, and loves to spin out long, grammatically complex sentences. A typical one reads: "On this horrid and sharp-stoned shore, in this miserable region of the icy and foetid lake, stood fell Tisiphone, wild and cruel with her vipered locks and implacably angry at the wretched and miserable souls who were falling by the hordes from the iron bridge on to the eternally frozen lake" (249). Note that nearly every noun has two adjectives, with three given to the Greek Fury, and how nouns are converted to adjectives ("vipered"); note the careful use of parallelism. But this swatch of purple prose is actually a pale imitation of the original; as Godwin points out in the introduction to his translation, an accurate re-creation of Colonna's trilingual vocabulary would read: "In this horrid and cuspidinous littoral and most miserable site of the algent and fetorific lake stood saevious Tisiphone, efferal and cruel with her viperine capillament, her meschine and miserable soul, implacably furibund . . ." (x–xi). Godwin stops there, as if afraid his computer's Spell-Check program will throw a rod. Now I may be one of the few readers who wishes the entire novel had been translated this way — that is, faithfully — but it does underscore the radical nature of Colonna's fictional experiment and, when adding the dream factor, justifies calling it a Renaissance *Finnegans Wake*.

The most radical inversion of genre and reader expectations in *HP* is the erotic element. Four hundred years before Freud, Colonna realized that erotic urges are sublimated into symbolic forms in dreams. Throughout his dream-novel, Poliphilo's ardor for Polia is displaced onto architectural wonders; since she is absent and "untouched" (64) during the first quarter of the novel, he finds her everywhere in his feminized dreamscape, a land ruled by a queen, containing "no steep mountains, only shapely hills" (78), and populated by countless virginal but erotic nymphs sporting the same blonde hair as she does. (For the first 142 pages, it's the only physical attribute of Polia we're given.) It's significant that the first two structures he encounters and describes are a pyramid and an obelisk: a triangular female symbol and a blatantly phallic one. As he works himself up into a state of arousal at these and other huge erections, Poliphilo often drops Polia's name in passing; one chapter concludes: "I could not satisfy my hungry eyes and my insatiable appetite for looking again and again at the splendid works of antiquity. I was deprived and as though sequestered from every other thought, except that my beloved Polia often came graciously and helpfully into my tenacious memory. But for all that, it was with a loud sigh that I painfully recalled her, then continued admiring these most welcome antiquities" (57). Polia comes and goes in these descriptions of antiquities, which he sexualizes with phrases such as "the solid body of a building" (47), likening "a building to a human body with well-proportioned parts and decorously dressed" (52). When Poliphilo notes that Praxiteles' statue of Venus "was of such beauty that men burned with sacrilegious lust for it and ravished the statue by masturbating" (71), it's clear that Poliphilo's *hypnerotomachia* is one long wet dream for his beloved.

Even when the sexual content becomes manifest in his dream, Poliphilo struggles to sublimate it back into the landscape. The first people he meets are five nymphs, whose names indicate they represent not the seven cardinal virtues (as in Boccaccio) but the five senses. Talk about five easy pieces! These party girls take Poliphilo to their bathhouse, leading him "on with voluptuous movements, virginal gestures, engaging manners, girlish graces, lascivious looks and sweet words of comfort and flattery" (80), but as soon as they get there, he forgets all about them and goes off on a four-page description of the building. The nymphs jerk his attention back by stripping and wading into the bath, but even then "I stood apart blushing with my eyes wandering over these splendid and alluring objects" (83); it's unclear whether he's admiring them or the colonnettes. The naked nymphs then subject poor Poliphilo to merciless cock-teasing, first by flaunting their "divine little bodies" and asking what he'd do if Polia were there naked in the bath with them, and then, after they dry off, by naughtily slipping him some kind of Renaissance Viagra:

I suddenly began to be sexually aroused and lasciviously stimulated to the point of total confusion and torment, while these wily girls, knowing what had happened to me, laughed unrestrainedly. It increased so that I felt the irritation within me growing stronger at every moment. I do not know what curb or bit restrained me from flinging myself upon them like a raving, hungry eagle swooping down on to a flock of partridges: the urge to rape was no less strong in me. I felt this desire continuously increasing, torturing me with prurience and lust, and was all the more venereally inflamed because I was offered such opportune and suitable victims. It was like the spreading of a pernicious plague, inciting me to desires I had never felt before. (86–87)

One of the "inflammatory nymphs" adds more wood to the fire by asking again what he'd do if his dream-girl were there in his aroused state, which almost causes Poliphilo to explode. This causes the girls to laugh so hard "they tumbled down on the fragrant flowers and rolled on the grassy ground, breathless from laughter so violent that they had to untie and loosen their tight transverse girdles" (87), which unleashes another surge of lust in Poliphilo. After chasing them around a bit as they lose more articles of clothing, Poliphilo is given an antidote and soon is back to his sublimated, masturbatory descriptions of the landscape: "I saw an extraordinary fountain spurting clear water through narrow pipes as high as the enclosing bridge" (89) and so on. The novel is all titillation, foreplay, and postponement; it is one of the most erotic novels ever written but lacks a single orgasm — and perhaps that's exactly why it's one of the most erotic novels ever written.

It's an amusing and sexy scene, but Poliphilo's plague simile indicates his conflicted feelings about Polia, which redouble when he finally meets her. For an inexplicably long period, he's not sure if the blonde nymph he meets is actually her, and he seesaws between experiencing overpowering lust for her and feeling guilty that his love for her isn't more spiritual and noble. (Colonna, we should remember, was a monk.) In the passage above, he compares sexual arousal to "a pernicious plague" and later calls female beauty an "infectious artifice" that leads to death and destruction (336–37). When Polia tells her side of the story in the last quarter of the novel, she is literally infected by the plague, which has caused "a tumour in the groin" and which causes her to dedicate her life to chastity. That this occurs right after her menarche suggests she suffers from a similar erotic panic to that which grips Poliphilo from time to time, when he's not ogling flirty nymphs.

But these occasional warning buoys are submerged beneath the novel's tidal waves of eroticism, which apparently escaped the censors because the diction is so difficult; the graphic woodcuts, on the other hand, are defaced in many surviving copies. The novel is set in a prelapsarian sexual paradise where "shameless" and "immodest" are used as terms of praise, not censure, when describing girls who let their beauty shine rather than hide it beneath a bushel. It is packed wall-to-wall with "delicate and divine nymphs . . . of tender years, redolent with the bloom of youth and beautiful beyond belief, together with their beardless lovers who were the perpetual inhabitants of this worthy place" (182). These are the wonder years of teenagers, which

Polia is later warned by her nurse not to waste in unnatural chastity (410–17). Poliphilo (and Colonna, and the reader) looks on enviously, wistfully, at the uninhibited teens' May Day party:

> Others were standing outside the flowing streams on the soft grasses, busily weaving garlands from the fragrant, varicoloured flowers which they then presented familiarly to their lovers, not refusing them afterwards the addition of succulent and savorous kisses. On the contrary, they kissed each other more tightly and mordantly than the suckers of an octopus's tentacles; more than the shells that adhere to the Illyrian rocks or to the Plotae Isles. They kissed with juicy and tremulous tongues nourished with fragrant musk, playfully penetrating each other's wet and laughing lips and making painless marks on the white throats with their little teeth. . . . And beneath the shady arbours they were clinging to one another like the vipers in Medusa's hair, in delectable embraces more intricate than bindweed and tighter than the ivy that snakes around antique elms and ancient buildings.[29] The nymphs were not cruel or resistant to their revered lovers, but purely benign and affable in their reciprocal affections, consenting to their desires by exposing their naked and generous breasts, for which the youths appeared extremely grateful, to judge by their gestures, which were more delectable and welcome than flowing tears are to cruel and impious Cupid; much more so than the fresh brooks and the daybreak dewfall are to the grassy meadows; and still more than the desire of matter for form. (182–83)

That last phrase elevates eroticism to an elemental force. Nor is this merely Colonna's private fantasy; others during his time were calling for more openness in sexual relations. Lefaivre informs us that Lorenzo Valla scandalized Italian society in the 1480s with a free-love manifesto entitled *De voluptate* (76). That Colonna probably agreed with Valla is suggested by the pivotal scene where Polipholo must choose a door to decide his fate. Behind each is a woman symbolizing a destiny, and the author is not subtle in his symbolism. The woman behind the door leading to the religious life is "an aged dame with a spinsterish air. . . . She was in rags, squalid, skinny, poor, with downcast eyes. . . . She dwelt at the entrance to a stony road . . . beneath a troubled, rainy sky and looming dark clouds" (136). Like any healthy, sane person, Poliphilo is appalled by the idea of religious renunciation and tries the next door; this one represents worldly success and he is greeted by an ambitious, no-nonsense career woman: "Her eyes were fierce, her face set. . . . She showed by her face that no arduous or difficult task could daunt her" (137). Polipholo is tempted by fame and riches, but first wants to see who is behind door number three. Turns out her stage-name is Philtronia (Seductive), described as wanton, capricious, joyful, and although one of Polipholo's nymph-guides warns him that Philtronia and her ilk are "deceitful, insipid and vain" and begs him not

---

29 Note the consistent metaphoric (and erotic) equation of bodies with buildings, and vice versa.

to "be lured by so slight and poisonous a pleasure and by deceptive goodness into a morass of evils" (138–39), Polipholo chooses a life of pleasure over religion or riches. He first enters Philtronia's chamber where her girls quickly arouse him "with their lascivious looks, their pert breasts, their flattering eyes" and so on (140), and in this tumescent state he finally meets his Polia, whose charms are spread over five pages of overheated description. They don't consummate their love; for the next 300 pages they remain in this aroused condition, Polia occasionally granting him a grinding hug and/or lascivious open-mouthed kiss, as they travel to the isle of Venus — in a ship piloted by a crew of cute sailor-nymphs — and eventually get married via pagan rites. Even then they don't go to it; dazzled by his beloved as well as by dozens more hot nymphs in haute couture, blue-balled Polipholo remains on edge as Polia tells the nymphs how she fell in love with him, and only after her long story (pp. 381–462) is the couple left alone. Polipholo takes his bride in his arms, begins kissing her, and then — she vanishes, and he awakes to the glaring light of day, alone and utterly forlorn.

It then becomes clear that Polia's story of falling in love with him was merely a fantasy, and that the entire dream was a taunting reminder of his unrequited love. The novel expresses other things, especially the superiority of classical architects and artisans over those of Colonna's day, and maybe even some of the esoteric doctrines scholars have read into it. But ultimately, *HP* is less a symbolic representation of, say, the alchemical *mysterium coniunctionis* or Neoplatonic idealism than the despairing fantasy of an unrequited lover dying of erotic despair, putting into the coral mouth of his dream-girl the words he longs to hear but never will:

> "I am without a doubt your Polia, whom you love so much. A love so worthy should not be left unrequited and denied equal reciprocation and recompense; and consequently I am all prepared for your inflamed desires. Look: I feel the fire of fervent love spreading and tingling throughout my whole being. Here I am, the end of your bitter and frequent sighs. Here I am, dearest Polipholo, the healing and instant remedy of your grave and vexing pains. Here I am, a ready consort for your amorous and bitter suffering and a sharer in everything. Here I am with my profuse tears to quench your burning heart, and to die for you promptly and most devotedly. And as proof of it, take this!" She hugged me close and gave me, mouth to mouth, a luscious biting kiss full of divine sweetness, and also a few pearls in the form of tearlets, wrung by singular sweetness from her starry eyes. Inflamed from head to foot by her charming speech and by the mouth-watering and delicious savour, I dissolved in sweet and amorous tears and lost myself completely. (218)

There were probably "a few pearls in the form of tearlets" in the author's eyes as he wrote this (as there were in mine the first time I read it). At the very beginning of the novel, while still awake, Poliphilo had wondered "how best to love someone who does not love in return" (12), and his answer is a work of art that would immortalize his love for her. And not just any work of art: a splendiferous 466-page Olympus of a novel, a polymorphously (and polylinguistically) perverse Elysian Fields of fantastic erudition, rhetorical fireworks, and elegant eroticism, preserving for the ages his love for the girl who captivated him. The initial letters of the novel's 38 chapters form an acrostic reading: POLIAM FRATER FRANCISCVS COLVMNA PERAMAVIT — that is, "Brother Francesco Colonna loved Polia madly." And who was Polia? The novel takes place, as I noted earlier, in 1467; Colonna spent that year as a teacher of novices, nuns-to-be. Was "Polia" one of his pretty, untouchable pupils? I'd bet anything she was. If he couldn't make her part of his world, he would "re-make the world in a form nearer to the heart's desire,"[30] the motivation for much great art.

The *Hypnerotomachia Poliphili* is a grand synthesis of almost everything that came before it — there are echoes of Homer's epics, Ovid, Apuleius, Pliny's *Natural History*, Dante (*HP* can be read as a pagan alternative to his Catholic fantasy), Arthurian romances — and continues Boccaccio's overturning of Christian values for classical ones. (In this novel, the Christian god and his son are supplanted by Venus and her son, Cupid.) He not only admired the great works of antiquity but shows that similar works can still be constructed; when describing architectural marvels, Poliphilo always praises the creators of such works: "From all of this I could well judge how fertile the learned architect's mind must have been; how careful, studious and industrious he was, and how vigilant his inventive mind; how hard he had worked to achieve so voluptuous an effect; what eurhythmy had informed the subtleties of the stone-carver's work, and what artistry the sculptor showed in his stone" (56). There are dozens such encomia in the novel, and in each one Colonna is proudly describing his own voluptuous achievement.

"Take this!" says impassioned Polia, Bette Davis–style. Take this, Colonna told readers of his no less seductive novel. But there were few takers; like many daring, experimental novels, it was a flop. Ten years after its publication, it had sold so poorly that the publisher had to ask for an extension of the license to keep selling it in the vain hope of at least earning back its enormous printing costs. It eventually found favor with architects and landscape artists, and bibliophiles savored its production values, but it found no literary followers, with the possible exceptions of Rabelais's equally extravagant work a few generations later and maybe Robert Burton a century later in *The Anatomy of Melancholy*. But with a complete English translation finally available, and some free publicity from a 2004 best-seller based on it, there's no longer any excuse for not recognizing the *Hypnerotomachia Poliphili* as a collosal landmark in innovation fiction.

30 Godwin's *Pagan Dream of the Renaissance*, 39.

Erotic despair, sensuous nymphs, and dream-visions also characterize Jacopo Sannazaro's exquisite *Arcadia* (1504), a Renaissance revival of the pastoral novel, "the first in this age to reawaken the slumbering woods, and to show the shepherds how to sing the songs that they had forgotten," as its narrator boasts in the epilogue.[31] Sannazaro, a well-off Neapolitan poet, probably knew Boccaccio's *Ameto* because he names one of his own shepherds after him, but he probably regarded his own novel not as a traditional work in the spirit of Theocritus and Virgil but, as his own translator puts it, an "experiment in allegorical pastoral" (202). Indeed, while the first half of *Arcadia* reads like a traditional pastoral, the second half is even more experimental than Boccaccio's.

A would-be poet named Sincero has left his hometown of Naples for Arcadia in Greece to recover from a broken heart. He joins the local shepherds, listens to their songs, attends their festivals, and watches their games. The tone darkens during the second half, however, when Sincero tells the story of his failed relationship, which is followed by a similar tale of loss by the shepherd Carino. Another lovelorn shepherd, Clonico, is in even worse shape, spotted on his way to a witch to seek an occult remedy for *his* erotic despair, but he is shepherded instead to a rustic magician named Enareto, who explains his elaborate cure in great detail, stirring a cauldron of occult lore for several pages with hair-raising stuff like: "And that the strange and various shapes of the assembled deities may not frighten you, I shall place on your back a tongue, an eye, and a shedded skin of a Libyan serpent, along with the right section of the heart of a lion, aged and dried in the shadow of the full moon only" (10). The funeral rites for the mother of another shepherd darken the mood even further, and that night Sincero dreams of "a solitary place I had never seen before, among abandoned tombs," which somehow reminds him of Naples and his need to return there. He wakes (apparently, though what follows suggests he has descended to a deeper dream level), and wanders through the night until he finds himself at dawn at a river, where he is greeted by an outré woman not unlike those in Colonna's *Hypnerotomachia*:

> But from the river nearby, without my perceiving how, all at once there presented herself before me a young damsel most beautiful of feature, and in her walk and her gestures truly divine, whose garment was of a cloth most subtly thin and so lustrous that, except that I saw it was soft, I would have said for certain that it was of crystal; with a strange coil of hair, on which she bore a green garland, and in her hand a vase of whitest marble. This creature coming toward me and saying to me — "Follow my steps, for I am the Nymph

---

31 In Ralph Nash's very literal translation, hereafter cited parenthetically by chapter (except for his editorial apparatus, cited by page). Sannazaro wrote the novel in the 1480s solely for himself and his circle of friends; a bootlegged publication in 1502 of the first 10 of the novel's 12 chapters prompted him to issue an authorized edition in 1504.

of this region" — implanted in me so much veneration, and at the same time of fear, that struck with astonishment (without making answer to her, and I myself not knowing how to tell if I were indeed awake or in actual truth yet sleeping) I set myself to follow her: and being arrived with her at the river's brim, suddenly I saw the waters shrinking back on the one side and the other, and making a way for her through their midst: a thing truly strange to see, horrifying to consider, fantastic and perhaps incredible to hear. (12)

After this parody of Moses parting the Red Sea it gets even more fantastic and incredible. The nymph leads him underground, past other nymphs and wonders, until Sincero comes to the origins of the world's rivers in the hollow earth.[32] In literally no time this underground passage takes him back to Naples, where he hears Italian shepherds singing. In a sequence filled with Freudian and Jungian symbols, Sincero progresses from a funeral in Arcadia to a rebirth in his native land, his poetic vocation renewed, ready now to write both this novel pastoral and the poetry he hopes will make him immortal.[33]

The pastoral usually presents the simple, rustic life as an attractive alternative to hectic, corrupt city life, but for Sannazaro Arcadia is not a place to *live* — at one point he sneers, "I can hardly believe that the beasts of the woodlands can dwell with any pleasure [here], to say nothing of young men nurtured in noble cities" (7) — but a place to *create*. Not only do the shepherds themselves create art with their songs — each chapter contains a long eclogue in a variety of verse forms — but examples of art are everywhere: paintings, decorations on cups and bowls, even a shepherd's staff has a carved knob "out of which came forth a wolf who was carrying off a lamb; made with such artifice that you would nearly have set the dogs on it" (9). The word *artifice* is used often, always in a positive sense. Early on, Sincero comes upon a flock of shepherdesses, "very beautiful, who were strolling hither and thither making fresh garlands; and setting these in a thousand strange fashions on their blonde tresses, each one exerted herself with masterly art to surpass the gifts of Nature" (3). To *surpass* Nature, not to live in it or hold up a mirror to it, is the goal and purpose of Arcadia, a place to create art and magic. It's why Enareto describes his magic rather than performs it: the language itself is the magic. In a realistic sense, Sincero never left Naples in the first place, but merely traveled to that mental place where art is created, the Yaddo of the mind, and through the process of imagining his own private Arcadia overcame his sorrow by weaving in words "a web of wondrous artifice" (12). Sannazaro's translator Ralph Nash puts it nicely: "And thus Arcadia becomes

---

32 A hollow earth would become the setting for various fantasy novels by Jules Verne and Edgar Rice Burroughs centuries later, but this may be its first appearance in literature — unless one counts Dante's journey to the center of the earth.

33 Sannazaro wrote a good deal of Latin poetry in later life, but the reading public preferred his novel, much to his chagrin. It went through numerous editions, and influenced later pastoral novels like Montemayor's *Diana* and, of course, Sidney's *Arcadia*.

a country of the mind, a symbol of dedication to poetry, to pleasure, to love, to contemplation" (23).

Sannazaro and Colonna got away with describing luscious nymphs in erotic settings by cloaking them in a poetic or artificial language, like Gibbon claiming for his *Decline and Fall of the Roman Empire* that "all licentious passages are left in the decent obscurity of a learned language." The Italian poet and dramatist Pietro Aretino (1492–1556) felt no need for any such dissembling, boldly blasting away at his corrupt society with the earthy language of common people. The only nymphs in his work are what the French call *nymphes du pavé*: streetwalkers. Recalling both Alberti's freewheeling satire and Boccaccio at his bawdiest, Aretino's *Dialogues* (*Ragionamenti*, 1534–36) is a 400-page novel in dramatic form spread over six days in the summer of 1533. A successful Roman whore named Nanna is undecided what to do with her 16-year-old daughter Pippa; the choices for well-to-do girls of that time were limited to nun, wife, or whore. Nanna has been all three, and asking her friend Antonia (a less successful whore) to help her choose the best course for her daughter, Nanna relates her experiences in a convent (day 1), her marriage to a rich old codger and the tales of unfaithful wives she heard while living out in the country (day 2), and her experiences as a whore (day 3). Nanna and Antonia agree that prostitution is the most sensible career choice for Pippa, who enthusiastically agrees and is eager to hop to it. In part 2, Nanna insists she must be trained first, as for any profession, so she begins by explaining all the tricks of the trade and the different kinds of customers Pippa can expect (day 4), then warns her of all the tricks men play on women (day 5), and finally mother and daughter sit in on a discussion of the bawd's role by a local midwife/madam (day 6). Pippa passes this course of instruction in the whorish arts and we leave her ready to launch her raunchy career.

Each day is filled with a dozen or more tales and anecdotes, resulting in a Hexameron that gives the *Decameron* a run for its money, which was apparently Aretino's intention. After one scandalous tale Antonia says, "May Boccaccio forgive me, but now he can go into retirement," to which Nanna responds: "That's not my opinion. But I do think that he should at least admit that my things are alive and breathing, whereas his are painted."[34] Referring to a convent painting depicting one of his episodes, Nanna apparently feels Boccaccio is a little too refined. Like Chaucer's wife of Bath and Defoe's Moll Flanders, Nanna is an entertaining raconteur, her language a pungent mixture of racy narrative, colorful metaphors, and flippant blasphemy. Out-Boccaccioing Boccaccio, she tells us that on the night of her initiation into nunhood, she discovered that nuns and priests indulge not merely in furtive

---

34 From part 1, day 1 of Raymond Rosenthal's spirited translation, cited hereafter by part/day. For a good biography of this larger-than-life writer, see James Cleugh's *Divine Aretino* (1965).

sex (as in his tales) but in sumptuous banquets and orgies; as she peers through a chink in the wall, the convent's General, three young monks, and four nuns give young Nanna this glimpse of the holy life:

[T]he reverend father summoned the three friars and leaning on the shoulder of one of them, a tall, soft-skinned rascal who had shot up prematurely, he ordered the others to take his little sparrow, which was resting quietly, out of its nest. Then the most adept and attractive young fellow of the bunch cradled the General's songster in the palm of his hand and began stroking its back, as one strokes the tail of a cat which first purrs, then pants, and soon cannot keep still. The sparrow lifted its crest, and then the doughty General grabbed hold of the youngest, prettiest nun, threw her tunic over her head, and made her rest her forehead against the back of the bed. Then, deliberately prying open with his fingers the leaves of her asshole Missal and wholly rapt in his thoughts, he contemplated her crotch, whose form was neither close to the bone with leanness nor puffed out with fat, but something in between — rounded, quivering, glistening like a piece of ivory that seems instinct with life. Those tiny dimples one sees on pretty women's chins and cheeks could also be seen on her dainty buttocks, whose softness was softer than that of a mill mouse born and raised in flour, and that nun's limbs were all so smooth that a hand placed gently on her loins would have slid down her leg as quickly as a foot slides on ice, and hair no more dared grow on her than it would on an egg.

ANTONIA So the father General consumed his day in contemplation, eh?

NANNA No, I wouldn't say he consumed it, because placing his paintbrush, which he first moistened with spit, in her tiny color cup, he made her twist and turn as women do in the birth throes or the mother's malady. And to be doubly sure his nail would be driven more tightly into her slit, he motioned to his back and his favorite punk pulled his breeches down to his heels and applied his clyster to the reverend's *visiblium*, while all the time the General himself kept his eyes fixed on the two other young louts, who, having settled the sisters neatly and comfortably on the bed, were now pounding the sauce in the mortar to the great despair of the last little sister. Poor thing, she was so squint-eyed and swarthy that she had been spurned by all. So she filled the glass tool [dildo] with water heated to wash the messer's hands, sat on a pillow on the floor, pushed the soles of her feet against the cell wall, and then came straight down on that great crozier, burying it in her body as a sword is thrust into a scabbard. Overcome by the scent of their pleasure, I was more worn out than pawns are frayed by usury, and began rubbing my dear little monkey with my hand like cats in January rub their backsides on a roof. (1.1)

This represents a remarkable advance in descriptive writing. Note the careful eye for detail (that gangly look of teenage boys who experience growth spurts), the extensive use of gentle, furred animal imagery (sparrow, cat, mouse, monkey), the cumulative metaphors for whiteness for the nun's flanks (ivory, flour, ice, egg), the references to everyday life (slipping on ice, driving a nail, using a paintbrush, the apothecary's mortar), and the inversion of religious terms and items, making a mockery of the "contemplative" life. Aside from Colonna's technical observations on architecture, this sort of rich, detailed description is new to the novel, more vivid. The nun's buttocks are not merely soft, nor merely soft as a mouse, but softer than "a mill mouse born and raised in flour"; the cat doesn't just rub its backsides, but does so "in January," when it's coldest. Aretino may have been the first writer to note that sexual activity produces a scent; all five senses are alive in this passage, "alive and breathing" as Nanna boasted earlier. And the *Dialogues'* dramatic form — which had its immediate source in some Spanish novels I'll discuss in the next section but also looks back to Lucian's *Dialogues of the Courtesans* and forward to Sade's *Philosophy in the Bedroom* — takes full advantage of the immediacy of dialogue.

But the *Dialogues* is not merely a collection of shocking anecdotes. Aretino was a satirist on the noble if futile quest to reform his corrupt society by shoving its face in its worst excesses. (Futile because has any society ever reformed itself after being shown the error of its ways by a satirist? anywhere? ever?) In his preface, Aretino expresses the hope "that my book will be like the scalpel, at once cruel and merciful, with which the good doctor cuts off the sick limb so that the others will remain healthy." However, not many limbs are left after he finishes: religion, marriage, politics, language, literature — all go under the knife. What he finds is not merely a diseased appendage that can be amputated, but a cancer that runs through the body politic. Religious orders break their vows, married couples break theirs, politicians misuse their office, people misuse language, and writers betray literature by composing poems merely to seduce women and flatter their patrons. "Take my word for it," Nanna says on the first page of the novel, "this world is a filthy place," too far gone to benefit from the satirist's scalpel, too mired in hypocrisy and brutality and, above all, avarice.

Nanna's reference to usury near the end of the lengthy passage quoted above is an instance of Aretino's use of iterative imagery throughout the arc of the novel to complement the local imagery of this or another passage. His society, like ours, was corrupted by people who placed making money above all else, and he underscores the cost to values and principles with extensive monetary imagery. When Pippa asks her mother, "how should I behave when I am under some slobbering farter who stinks above and below," Nanna answers: "My dear daughter, the sweet smell of money prevents the stench of rotten breath or filthy feet from reaching your nose" (2.1). The three occupations for women are based on financial reckoning, Nanna explains; parents back then often pushed their daughters into nunneries not for religious reasons but to avoid paying a marriage dowry; when they did marry, they were encouraged to marry not for love but for money, to seek out a rich man, despite the age or personality differences (and which led to wives finding sexual satisfaction outside of marriage); and of course prostitution is strictly about money, sex as commerce. In such a society, making money justifies anything: the midwife admits that, as a whore, she always resented anal sex, "But if money is the do-all and be-all, where's the miracle if we even turn our assholes to be screwed?" (3.3), a question that could be put to any pro-capitalist free-market advocate obsessed with profit margins and shareholder value. Aretino had nothing against honest mercantile exchange or simply making a living, but found whoredom the perfect analogy for the compromises some people make in pursuit of power and/or excessive profits, and thus resorts to fiscal imagery often, even for casual observations: Nanna says that people are like coins — sometimes you have to take them on faith and hope they're not counterfeit (1.2).

Aretino himself is certainly no fake. He insists on using the language of the people, even their obscenities, rather than the counterfeit language of polite society, nor do the niceties of literary decorum prevent him from attacking the aristocracy (he dedicates his book to his pet monkey instead of a nobleman because he doesn't see any difference between the two) or exposing hypocritical Catholics, which pretty much encompasses everyone in the book (except for Franciscans, whom he excuses for some reason). Aretino's descriptions of the debaucheries within convents have been dismissed as exaggerated by some, and while such exaggeration is expected in comic writing, historical evidence suggests he wasn't far off the mark.[35] But to actually describe such debaucheries, and in the kind of detail seen in the lengthy quotation above, took daring. Aside from Petronius and the Spaniard Delicado (see next section), no novelist before him would have included a sentence like: "They celebrated a little wedding there and then, and he fucked her so many times that he almost passed out on top of her" (2.2), and few novelists (to be distinguished from pornographers) after him would dare do so, or be allowed to do so, until the second half of the 20th century.

Nanna justifies her observation about the filthy world with tales of spouse abuse, gang rapes, the ravages of sexually transmitted diseases, and the desperation of poverty. Men come off worse than women; Aretino's whores may be crafty, but Nanna maintains they're just fulfilling an unpleasant but necessary

35 See Mary Laven's *Virgins of Venice: Broken Vows and Cloistered Lives in the Renaissance Convent* (NY: Viking, 2002). She states that "Nanna's recollections do not provide an accurate picture of life in an Italian nunnery" (146), but then provides 50 pages of evidence of similar sexual transgressions by priests and nuns, and cites contemporaries of Aretino's who described nuns as "public prostitutes" and convents as "whore-houses." (When Hamlet tells Ophelia to get herself to a nunnery, he's telling her to join a brothel; "nun" was Elizabethan slang for a whore.) The convent Colonna worked at was described by one shocked visitor as overrun by "nymphs of Venus sent by Satan," the nuns "decked out in all kinds of finery and pomp," with noisy banquets lasting all night and the vow of chastity more honored in the breach than the observance (Lefaivre, 98).

duty, like soldiers, and selling what customers demand, like shopkeepers. It's men, "suffering under the hammer of pounding passion" (2.1), who are really to blame for creating the sex industry and for making it such a dangerous occupation. But the *Dialogues* isn't a gloomy tract of social criticism: it displays all the exuberance we associate with Renaissance writers — Aretino was an exact contemporary of Rabelais and in fact published the *Dialogues* at the same time the Frenchman brought out the first installments of *Gargantua and Pantagruel* — and is frequently laugh-out-loud funny. Aretino clearly had a blast writing it, inserting parodies of the Dido and Aeneas story and of hagiography, making facetious references to other literary works (including his own poems), and inserting metafictional asides on his own narrative. Antonia occasionally interrupts Nanna to point out an inconsistency or to complain about her goofy metaphors — referring to the convent General's penis as a sparrow or a paintbrush, for example — and near the end Aretino acknowledges how artificial and self-referential art is:

MIDWIFE Painters and poets can get away with any sort of lie, and it is just a way of expressing themselves when they praise and magnify the women they love and the passion they suffer in loving them.

WETNURSE Get a rope and tie together all the painters, sculptors, and poets, for they're all crazy.

MIDWIFE Painters and sculptors, except for Baccio Band[i]nelli's grace, are all voluntary madmen, and you can see that this is true by the fact that they take their own privates and bestow them on their paintings and marble statues. (2.3)

"Much madness is divinest sense," Emily Dickinson assures us, and though the "divine" Aretino's madcap novel may seem like the equivalent of an exhibitionist opening a stained raincoat to expose himself to shocked observers — it's been treated that way by critics for centuries — the *Dialogues* is a breakthrough work of fiction and a searing indictment of the mores of his time. Like Samson, Aretino pulls down the pillars of respectability on which Roman society was based — the institution of marriage, its religious practices, the patronage system — deploying a slashing, take-no-prisoners approach that is refreshing after the pious works of the Middle Ages, which rarely challenged the status quo. As a result, he was prized by European intellectuals, Titian painted his portrait, and of course his works were among the first to be placed on the Catholic Index by the policemen of the status quo.

Among Aretino's many correspondents was a brilliant Paduan named Giulia Bigolina (ca. 1518–ca. 1569), whose poems he praised. Bigolina was the first Italian woman to write a novel, an extremely interesting romance entitled *Urania* (ca. 1555) that existed only in manuscript until its Italian publication in 2002, followed by an English translation three years later.[36] It's a feminist recasting of the usual romantic plot: a smart, virtuous, but plain-looking woman named Urania — a common name in pastorals; there's a Uranio in Sannazaro's *Arcadia* — loses her admirer Fabio to a vacuous but pretty young thing named Clorina. Bitterly disappointed at Fabio's preference for beauty over brains, Urania decides to drown her sorrows not by pining away, like Boccaccio's Fiammetta and her type, but by leaving town and wandering throughout Italy, for safety's sake dressing as a man and calling herself Fabio after her superficial ex-admirer. Before she leaves, she sends Fabio an eight-page letter on a variant of what philosophers call the mind–body problem, arguing that a man should be attracted to a woman's mind, not her body. (One wants to take her aside and say, "Sister, if you have to *argue* that point with a man, he's not for you.")

On the road, Urania/Fabio first encounters a group of five women who, assuming she's a he, ask him a number of questions about love, an episode very reminiscent of the symposium on love in Boccaccio's *Filocolo*. (Bigolina was extremely well read and draws upon Boccaccio, Dante, Petrarch, and especially Ariosto's epic poem *Orlando furioso*, among others.) She next encounters the five men in love with those five women, who ask Urania what women want, which she is happy to explain at length. The novel has been a series of rhetorical set-pieces up to this point; a more complicated plot begins to unfold as a suicidal Urania/Fabio is rescued by a young Florentine widow named Emilia, who rather quickly falls in love with him/her. Urania puts her off, explaining she needs to return to her hometown (she's still in love with Fabio and wonders about him), so Emilia accompanies her likewise dressed as a man. Back home, Urania learns that Fabio is in prison because of a dumb scheme Clorina put him up to, and — continuing to reverse traditional roles — the heroine rescues the man by kissing a "wild woman," a savage the prince of this kingdom keeps for sport. (In a subplot, the prince — in love with a virtuous woman like Urania — is tempted by a beautiful duchess who sends him a nude portrait of herself. The prince handles the mind–body problem better than Fabio, and though naturally aroused by the erotic painting, he eventually marries the virtuous woman. Bigolina kills off the daring duchess, not surprisingly.) With all the principals present in the prince's court, Urania then doffs her man's drag and reveals herself, much to everyone's shock and confusion (especially Emilia), tells her story, and then takes part in a quadruple marriage on the novel's last page: Urania to Fabio (who has come to his senses), Emilia to Fabio's brother (with whom she likewise falls in love

---

36 Both were edited by Valeria Finucci. In addition to poetry, Bigolina also wrote a *Decameron*-like story-cycle, only one tale from which survives, unfortunately: it appears in a bilingual format on pp. 44–69 of the English edition of *Urania*. The novel itself occupies pp. 73–174 and will be cited parenthetically by page number.

quickly), the prince to his beloved, and the troublesome beauty Clorina to an ill-mannered braggart who had been pursuing her.

It's an appealing novel in many ways, and Bigolina persuasively makes the case that women are more sensible about matters of the heart than men and less superficial about physical appearances. Nor does she make the heavy-handed feminist mistake of arguing that *all* women are superior to men in these matters: Clorina and the duchess trade on their looks rather than their virtues, and as a result both come to a bad end. (The "wild woman," erotically attracted to men and murderous toward women, represents a mythological extreme.) Bigolina doesn't make much of the homoerotic possibilities of women dressed as men, and Urania's adoption of a man's name and garb seems more a matter of expedience than, say, envy of a man's greater freedom, two points medieval Japanese novelists explored. But what makes *Urania* especially intriguing is the lengthy "Dedicatory Epistle" with which the novel begins, and which is an integral part of the novel, not just the unctuous front matter of similar dedications. It is addressed to a young lawyer named Bartolomeo Salvatico, some 14 years younger than Bigolina, and there is every indication she wrote the novel for his eyes only — one reason it wasn't published in her lifetime. A married woman of about 37 when she wrote this for the 23-year-old bachelor of law, Bigolina explains that she wanted to give him something expressing "the great and pure love" she had for him (74), and hopes that he'll love her in return for her mind rather than her (presumably fading) looks. Her muse is as unconventional as the novel that follows; while brooding on what kind of book to write, she feels someone tugging on her skirt:

> I saw that it was a very deformed little fellow, smaller than a pygmy is said to be. He was completely naked, with a head so large that it would have been almost big enough for a giant. He had only one eye in the middle of his forehead, which was quite large and bright like a mirror, and in turning I saw myself in it entirely from head to toe. It seemed a marvelous and strange thing to perceive myself mirrored in that large eye not, as I was, fully dressed, but as naked as when I was born. I noticed my flesh was so white everywhere (except to the left, where I seemed to spot a stain), that it looked like snow. (75)

After flashing the young lawyer this mental picture of her snow-white body — she may be 37 but she's still got it going on; the spotted "stain" is a sign of being in love — Bigolina listens as the one-eyed dwarf argues that the mind is more important than the body and that consequently she should present Salvatico with a product of her mind (as opposed to a nude portrait like the duchess sent the prince). After he vanishes, she decides to write a novel demonstrating "that wise and shrewd young men sometimes do not know how to dispense their love well, although you men insist that it is always the women who choose poorly in love, as if this were their lot" (84). Whether the recent graduate took the hint and favored sophisticated Mrs. Bigolina over younger women his own age is unrecorded, but it adds extra poignancy to this clever, untraditional challenge to the literary and social status quo.

A too timid deferral to the status quo compromises the only other Italian Renaissance novel of note:[37] another dream-quest, less known than the *Hypnerotomachia* but even more innovative in some ways. In 1578, an Italian Jew named Abraham Yagel was thrown into prison for some irregularities in his banking business, essentially a frame-up by rival bankers. He apparently experienced a nervous breakdown there, brought on by the recent death of his father and having to take over his father's business, for which the young scholar was ill-equipped. Like others before and after him (Boethius, John Bunyan), he claims to have had a dream in prison and wrote a book about it, calling it *A Valley of Vision* (*Gei Hizzayon*) after a phrase in Isaiah 22:1. It's an innovative fusion of several genres, including autobiography, dream-vision, Italian *novelle*, rabbinical midrash, heavenly journey, and philosophical consolation. As its English translator rightly claims, *A Valley of Vision* exhibits "imaginative playfulness and bold experimentalism,"[38] though, like some experimental novels, it may be more interesting for what it attempts than what it accomplishes.

In part 1, Abraham (the protagonist has the same name as the author) relates how, one night in prison, his father appeared to him in a dream, demanding to know how his son got there. Before the young man can answer, his father lectures him on the meaning of life and offers to take him on a tour of heaven. Abraham begins to detail his financial mishaps, but his long account is continuously interrupted by various wandering souls in heaven: a former schoolteacher, a gambler, a rhetorician, an adulterer, a pair of Siamese twins, the biblical character Job (who tells an Italian *novelle*), two contrasting women (one obedient, the other dis-), and finally a caravan of angels, all imparting words of wisdom. Because of these frequent interruptions, Abraham is unable to finish his own account before awaking from his dream. In part 2, he dreams again of his father, this time accompanied by three women who represent philosophy, astrology, and theology, who lecture Abraham on these topics at length. He then concludes the story of his business problems as his father leads him to a hill of frankincense on the summit

---

37 I should say, the only other Italian Renaissance novel available in English: Finucci gives the titles of a dozen more written during the 16th century (19 n51), but they all sound like routine romances.

38 Page 16 in David R. Ruderman's 70-page introduction to his translation, hereafter cited parenthetically by page number. All bracketed words in quotations are Ruderman's, who overdoes it at times.

of a mount of myrrh,[39] where they meet a woman representing language, who lectures him on grammar and the superiority of Hebrew. They enter a palace that reveals the ultimate secrets of the universe, but just as Abraham asks to learn more, his father disappears and he awakes in his prison cell, in "time for the recitation of the *Shema* [prayer] of the morning service" (340).

Both Abraham's long account of his business problems and the numerous lectures are rather tedious, but *A Valley of Vision* remains interesting because of its technical daring. Yagel's language is highly allusive, echoing not only the Tanakh and a wide range of rabbinical writings but also gentile writers like Aristotle, Ovid, Boethius, Henry Cornelius Agrippa, and Isidore of Seville (from whom Yagel nicked most of his linguistic material). Though written in Hebrew, the novel is peppered with Italian words and in a few places even imitates the Aramaic of the *Zohar*. The tone ranges from realistic to abstruse, and his ambition to reconcile recent discoveries in science and medicine with Jewish doctrine is valiant, if doomed. Though Yagel was something of a Renaissance man — he was a highly regarded physician as well as an expert in astrology/astronomy (he didn't distinguish between the two), religion/occult (ditto), and later compiled several encyclopedias — he was still committed to the medieval, not to say archaic, worldview of the rabbinical tradition, which gives his novel a schizophrenic feel. This led him not only to reject the recent findings of Copernicus for the older Ptolemaic view of the universe, but to take seriously any number of Jewish superstitions. For example, he attributes deformities in children to their parents' indulgence in different sexual positions; citing rabbinical authorities as well as Maimonides, one of the Siamese twins (obviously the result of some kinky coupling) explains how parents who stray from vanilla sex maim their children:

> "The rabbis also stated in the second chapter of *Nedarim* that R. Yohanan b. Dehavai said: 'People are born lame because they overturned their tables [i.e., practiced abnormal intercourse]; dumb, because they kiss in "that place"; deaf, because they speak at the time of intercourse; blind, because they look at "that place," etc.'" (150)

This is a trained physician in 1578 speaking! Did he actually believe that talking during sex would result in a deaf child? Elsewhere Yagel defends astrology, kabbalah, metempsychosis, and all sorts of occult nonsense in a futile attempt at synthesis with natural science, while at the same time being warned by his father and other heavenly souls against delving too deeply into these things. (In a sense, Yagel is arguing with himself in another indication of schizophrenia.) There are some inklings of the Faust theme here as

---

39 From Song of Songs 4:16; the editors of *The Jewish Study Bible* say the two mounds "most likely refer to [a] woman's breasts," but here, as elsewhere in theology, the original meaning is subverted for religious purposes.

Abraham pushes against the boundaries of knowledge while his father pushes back and warns him near the beginning of the novel: "'Do not let your heart entice you to investigate what is above you. For the Ancient of Days [God] covered ancient matters from [His] creatures, and it is impossible to fathom their mystery and comprehend their truth'" (76). One of the Siamese twins even mocks him for his curiosity with one of the novel's many allusions to the book of Job: "'Who gave you the credentials to investigate such concealed and esoteric matters. . . . You rather should go and ask the Creator who made you'" (140). Despite Abraham's Renaissance spirit of inquiry, his medieval spirit-guides prevail, and he wakes and prepares obediently to chant the Shema, the traditional proclamation of Jewish faith. Several times in the novel the Torah is described approvingly as a yoke (118, 121, 122) and at the end of the novel Abraham remains penned up like a domestic animal. And Yagel seems to regard that as a happy ending!

Abraham claims his anguish is due to being swindled by his business partners, but the mental breakdown that precipitates his dream-vision is more likely due to this doomed attempt to reconcile the irreconcilable, and to his unwillingness to abandon his father and the patriarchal system he represents. At one point Abraham quotes Ecclesiastes 5:2 — "dreams come with much brooding" (273) — and it could be this long brooding on the differences between new science and old religion that drives him around the bend. This inner turmoil has its formal counterpart in Yagel's unusual juxtaposition of heterodox genres (Italian *novelle* vs. rabbinical sermon, personal autobiography vs. impersonal philosophical discourse, etc.), resulting in a Frankensteinic novel made of incongruous parts. While superficially affirming the rabbinical tradition, it is compromised by too many contradictions to be judged a success in terms of what Yagel apparently thought he was writing — something along the lines of Boethius's *Consolation of Philosophy*.[40] He even allows a character to lecture Abraham against writing about his miseries (227), thereby undermining his own project right in the middle of the novel. One would like to think Yagel was operating at some ironical distance from all this, mocking those who would try to reconcile Judaism with science and the impulse to create art, pretending to be an orthodox Jew while following in Faust's heterodox footsteps, but his later writings indicate he wasn't. At any rate, the *idea* of what may be going on in this unusual novel is more absorbing than actually reading *A Valley of Vision*, which even its sympathetic translator calls tedious in parts. For example, after the story of the obedient vs. disobedient women, the moral of which is obvious, the father enumerates 17 moral lessons to be learned from it, which takes up almost as much space as the

---

40 Written c. 524 while the Roman philosopher was in prison awaiting execution, it alternates between prose and poetry as the author has a vision of conversing with a woman who symbolizes philosophy.

story itself. The numerous learned discourses seem largely an excuse for Yagel to show off his extensive erudition — admittedly remarkable in a 25-year-old author — and while some of them have antiquarian interest, they get old in a hurry, especially since most merely reaffirm the self-medicating bromides of religious belief. A *Valley of Vision* is a Rube Goldberg-like novel, a complicated contraption for delivering a simple message; it was a bold experiment, but not a very successful one, as Yagel himself seemed to realize: he didn't publish the work (it wouldn't be printed until 1880) and wrote no fiction after that. But even if not entirely successful, it underscores the tumultuous intellectual birth pangs taking place in the Renaissance for scholars like him and the growing pains of the novel as it continued to evolve.

For some reason, after this strong start Italian fiction dried up after Yagel. The first pastoral novel written by a woman, Lucrezia Marinella's *Arcadia felice* (*Happy Arcadia*), appeared in 1605, and the Neapolitan Giambattista Basile published one more story-cycle in 1634, *The Tale of Tales* (*Lo cunto de li cunti*, aka the *Pentamerone*), noteworthy for its famous fairy tales (Puss in Boots, Rapunzel, Cinderella, Beauty and the Beast), but after that, there is not much of note until the 19th century — unlike their neighbors on the Iberian Peninsula, who would hit their stride just as the Italian novel was petering out.

RENAISSANCE SPANISH FICTION

Before King Ferdinand and Queen Isabella homogenized Spain in the 1490s by driving out the Jews and Muslims, the Iberian Peninsula was a melting pot of cultures, which is reflected in the diversity of its earliest novels, ranging from Lull's Catalan Christian fantasy *Blanquerna* to Ibn Tufayl's *Hayy Ibn Yaqzan* (an Arabic *Robinson Crusoe* written in Granada in the 11th century) to those dazzling contributions from the Jewish community: Zabara's *Book of Delights*, Alharizi's *Book of Tahkemoni*, and de León's *Zohar*. Another ingredient was added to the pot in the 14th century when Spanish readers fell under the spell of Arthurian romance. Countless translations and knockoffs of the French originals were quickly churned out by Spanish litterateurs, and the aristocracy so enjoyed these works that they even began naming their children and pets after Arthurian characters. Most of these Iberian imitations are negligible, but in the middle of the 14th century an anonymous writer, possibly from Galicia (in northwest Spain), wrote the basis for what would become the most influential chivalric novel of the Renaissance, *Amadis of Gaul* (*Amadís de Gaula*). A second author added more material to the original later that century, and then at the end of the 15th century, a writer named Garci Rodríguez de Montalvo reworked this material into a huge, 1,400-page novel that was eventually published in 1508, four or five years after his death.

The valiant knight Amadis is closely patterned after Lancelot. He is born under mythy circumstances, set adrift in an ark, rescued by a Scottish knight and named "Child of the Sea" (cf. Lancelot "of the Lake"), becomes a knight at an early age, and devotes himself to his lady Oriana, the Danish-born daughter of the king of Great Britain. This is Montalvo's first significant departure from his model: where Lancelot fell in love with another man's wife, the 13-year-old Amadis falls for a 10-year-old girl, their presexual state sidestepping the adulterous theme of the *Lancelot-Grail*. Montalvo's novel is also set earlier than Arthurian times, in fact "not many years after the passion of our Redeemer and Savior" the author says in the prologue.[41] *Amadis* is a G-rated version of the R-rated tales of Lancelot and Tristan, one chronologically closer to Christ and ethically closer to Christian doctrine. And while the early relationship between Amadis and Oriana is sweet — imagine a handsome eighth-grader and the prettiest girl in fifth grade in a school production of *Camelot* — it signals that *Amadis* won't grapple with adult themes as the superior *Lancelot of the Lake* did. Montalvo clearly disapproves of such material he inherited from the original version of *Amadis*; when Amadis's brother Galaor gets lucky with a gorgeous princess, the narrator sniffs: "And they having gone out, Galaor dallied with the damsel that night at his pleasure, and without any more about it being recounted to you here, because from such acts, which do not conform to good conscience or virtue, one should rightly pass on quickly, holding them in that small esteem they deserve" (12). That sort of authorial comment was rare in the Arthurian romances, and though it doesn't amount to much here, it will become increasingly common as the novel progresses.

Amadis follows the standard career path of a knight — fighting malefactors, rescuing damsels, leading armies — is reunited with his parents, goes mad like Tristan, and eventually marries Oriana (though they keep it secret for much of the novel) and produces a son, Esplandián. Like Lancelot's son Galahad, Esplandián represents a purer version of the knightly ideal; near the end of the original version of the novel, father and son unknowingly engage in mortal combat, their faces concealed by their helmets, and the son kills the father, a distant echo of the Mordred–Arthur conflict in the *Lancelot-Grail*, but in Montalvo's family version, Amadis is still standing at the end, ready for the sequel. Amadis is sometimes assisted by an enchantress named Urganda the Unknown (obviously modeled on Morgan le Fay), and there is the occasional giant and dragon, but overall *Amadis* lacks the power of the French originals. It's too prissy, too far removed from the mysterious Celtic mythology that

---

41 All references are to the Place-Behm translation, cited by chapter. Their translation is a little stiff, containing such lines as: "'Sir knight, exert yourself and tell me, if you please, what plight this is in which you are'" (4).

haunts the earlier romances. (Amadis wouldn't last a week in the wild world of *Perlesvaus*.) The author handles the interlacement technique well enough as he juggles various subplots, but the predictability of his material and his moralizing tone become tiresome. Nevertheless, *Amadis of Gaul* became a huge success, the *Star Wars* of Spanish literature; it was translated into several European languages (even Hebrew) and spawned numerous sequels. Before he died, Montalvo himself wrote a sequel featuring the son, published posthumously as *Las Sergas de Esplandián* (The Exploits of Esplandián, 1510), which is remembered today only because one episode takes place on an imaginary island called California, a nation of war-like women ruled by a statuesque pagan queen. When Spanish explorers reached the southwest coast of North America in the 1540s, some wag who had read *Esplandián* suggested calling it California, and it stuck.[42]

In the famous chapter of *Don Quixote* in which the priest and the barber consign most of the mad knight's books of chivalry to the flames, they agree to spare *Amadis of Gaul* only because it was the first of its kind in Spain, though Cervantes dismissively notes that neither of his characters had ever bothered to read it. But the priest goes wild when he spots another fat novel:

> "God help me!" said the priest with a great shout. "Here is Tirant lo Blanc. Let me have it, friend, for I state here and now that in it I have found a wealth of pleasure and a gold mine of amusement. . . . I tell you the truth, my friend, when I say that because of its style, this is the best book in the world: in it knights eat, and sleep, and die in their beds, and make a will before they die, and do everything else that all the other books of this sort leave out. For these reasons, since the author who composed this book did not deliberately write foolish things but intended to entertain and satirize, it deserves to be reprinted in an edition that would stay in print for a long time. Take it home and read it, and you'll say that everything I've said about it is true."[43]

I second the priest's recommendation. *Tirant lo Blanc* (Tirant the White — *not* The White Tyrant, as sometimes rendered) is a major, encyclopedic novel, not quite in the same class as the *Decameron*, *Gargantua and Pantagruel*, and *Don Quixote* as its champions insist, but close. Its haphazard manner of composition and erratic publication history are somewhat to blame for the relative obscurity of this novel. It was begun around 1460 (if not earlier) by a Catalan aristocrat of Valencia named Joanot Martorell, born in 1413 or 1414,

---

42 For a two-page excerpt from this episode, see *The Literature of California, Volume 1: Native American Beginnings to 1945*, ed. Jack Hicks et al. (Berkeley: U California P, 2000), 76–77.

43 Part 1, chap. 6 in Grossman's translation. The penultimate sentence is obscure and is translated different in other editions; Raffel renders it: "Despite all that, let me tell you, we'll send the man who wrote it, who didn't deliberately perpetuate all those other absurdities, to the galleys for the rest of his life."

but who died in 1468 before he could finish it. The manuscript sat around for a decade or two until another Valencian aristocrat, Martí Joan de Galba, was asked by the manuscript's owner to complete the work. Apparently Martorell had written about three-fourths of the 800-page novel and left notes and drafts behind for the remainder, so Galba, a lesser writer, finished it and may have gone back to revise Martorell's earlier work, though he failed to clear up some inconsistencies and errors.[44] At any rate, the complete novel was published in November 1490, several months after Galba died. Unfortunately, the work was written in Catalan, a language and culture that would soon go into hibernation, not to be revived until the 20th century (only to be repressed for decades more under Franco's dictatorship). There had been translations into Castilian (which is what Cervantes read), Italian, and French, but none in English until 1974, when Ray La Fontaine submitted one as his dissertation. A decade later, David H. Rosenthal published his slightly abridged translation — La Fontaine's is unabridged and was eventually published in book form in 1993 — and though it was favorably reviewed and reissued in paperback, *Tirant* remains unknown even to most educated readers.

Martorell, fed up with his culture and devastated by the fall of Constantinople in 1453 to the Muslims, turned to fiction to create an alternative world more to his liking, one that, like Nabokov's Antiterra (in *Ada*), both resembles and dissembles the real world. A knight himself, he was convinced the old code of chivalry, with some modifications, could provide solutions to the various sociopolitical problems of his time, and so set out to write a modern, more realistic novel of chivalry. For a protagonist, he didn't reach back to the Dark Ages for a model but looked instead at some recent examples of heroes who had fought successfully against the Muslims, such as the Catalan Roger de Flor (1267–1305), the Hungarian János Hunyadi (1407?–56), and the Albanian Scanderbeg (1405–68). Martorell wanted a knight engaged with history and realpolitik, not courtesy and emblems, and though his protagonist's career resembles those of earlier chivalrous heroes, it is more attuned to the political realities of his time.

Set more or less in the 1440s,[45] *Tirant lo Blanc* begins with an updated version of the medieval Anglo-Norman romance *Guy of Warwick*, with which

---

44 Scholars are uncertain how much Galba actually contributed; the final quarter contains so many passages from the works of the Valencian poet and priest Joan Roís de Corella (1433–97) that one critic has suggested it was Corella who finished and revised the novel: see Josep Guia i Marín's *De Martorell a Corella: Descobrint l'autor del Tirant* (Catarroja-Barcelona: Editorial Afers, 1996). But this is no place for a nonspecialist, so I'll follow the convention of considering Martorell the key author.

45 At one point, a character states that it's been 492 years since Caesar left Britain (chap. 96), meaning the novel takes place around 440 rather than 1440, but this seems like a glitch Martorell would have corrected had not death surprised him with a deadline.

my previous chapter ended.[46] Martorell starts at the point late in the novella when Guy, here called William, decides to go to the Holy Land, then returns in disguise to live as a hermit. Instead of a Danish invasion, Muslims invade England and are defeated only with the help of William's superior knowledge of weaponry and military tactics. The king of England follows the victory with marriage to a French princess — apparently based on Henry VI's marriage to Margaret of Anjou in 1444 — and throws a year-long celebration, which attracts knights from all over. One of these, a young man from Brittany named Tirant lo Blanc, comes across the hermit William reading from a manual of chivalry — Martorell calls it *The Tree of Battles* but the quotations are from his fellow Catalan Ramón Lull's *Book of the Knightly Order* — and is so impressed by the old man and the concept of chivalry that he vows to become an ideal knight. A year later, he returns with some friends from the king's celebrations; like a good knight, Tirant is too modest to tell how he performed at the various jousts and tournaments, so his cousin Diaphebus gives a lengthy account of Tirant's triumphs, which pleases William and convinces him that Tirant will carry on the chivalric code.

Shortly after he returns to Brittany, Tirant learns that Rhodes is under siege by the Muslims, so he and Diaphebus sail there to help; more triumphs follow. Then they travel to Constantinople, which is also under siege by the Muslims; while there fighting the enemy, they also fall in love with two nubile girls: Tirant with the Byzantine emperor's daughter Carmesina, and his cousin with a duke's daughter named Stephanie, both age 14.

A Brief Digression on Sexual Attitudes

Some readers may be shocked at the young ages at which girls in premodern novels become sexually active, but remember, we're on the *other* side of the Puritan Ice Age; before that, and elsewhere in the world until recently, puberty was considered Mother Nature's signal that a person was ready for sex. In an English novel set in the 1540s, a singer improvises this timetable for a girl's sexual development:

> You were a maid at three years old.
> From three to four, five, six, and seven,
> But when you grew to be eleven,
> Then you began to breed desire;
> By twelve your fancy was on fire:
> At thirteen years desire grew quick,
> And then your maidenhead fell sick:

---

46 This is only the first of many texts Martorell appropriates for his own uses. Scholars have uncovered an elaborate web of intertextual references beneath the novel's surface, from Boccaccio to *The Travels of Sir John Mandeville*.

But when you came unto fourteen,
All secret kisses was not seen:
By that time fifteen years was past,
I guess your maidenhead was lost.[47]

And we haven't even reached Oriental fiction yet, where 16 is the age a courtesan might *retire* from business. Older cultures would be shocked at how we infantilize our young adults. The artificially prolonged childhood imposed on them by the Puritans' sex-negative descendants has done catastrophic physiological and psychological damage, as can be seen in today's happy, well-adjusted teens. (It's not nice to fool Mother Nature, as a TV ad from the 1970s pointed out.) For a sensible book on the hysteria and idiocy surrounding this issue, see Judith Levine's *Harmful to Minors: The Perils of Protecting Children from Sex* (Minneapolis: U Minnesota P, 2002).

A temporary truce with the enemy is called, which allows the Breton boys to lay siege to the Byzantine beauties instead (Martorell skillfully illustrates the adage "All's fair in love and war" by mixing martial and marital imagery) and which allows other romantic complications to unfold: a widow falls for Tirant and so tries to turn Carmesina against him; the Byzantine emperor falls for Carmesina's clever sidekick Plaerdemavida (Pleasure-of-my-life), while the empress falls for Tirant's young companion named Hippolytus (with the same incestuous overtones as in Euripides' tragedy of that name). Just as the truce ends and Tirant sets sail to resume the conflict, he is blown off course to North Africa for a few years' adventures fighting and converting Muslims before he makes it back to Constantinople, where he defeats the invaders and becomes engaged to Carmesina. And just at that point, when on top of the world, he suffers what seems to be an attack of appendicitis and dies in Adrianople (where Roger de Flor was assassinated). Carmesina is grief-stricken, the emperor dies, his daughter perishes the same day, and the Byzantine Empire is inherited by Hippolytus, who shares it for a while with the woman old enough to be his mother until she dies and he marries an English princess. This relatively minor character, not the great hero Tirant, is the one who lives a full, happy life.

As this unexpected, ironic ending suggests, *Tirant lo Blanc* is not a typical chivalric romance. Modernizing the code of chivalry means facing some ugly realities, and as Tirant matures during the long novel from an untested aspirant to knighthood to an experienced military leader, the traditional chivalry story matures from romance to realism. The early chapters of *Tirant* retain vestiges of medieval romance: when Tirant tells the hermit William that

---

47 Modernized from Thomas Deloney's *Gentle Craft, part 2* [1598?] chap. 2, discussed at the end of this chapter.

"when the princess drank red wine, her whiteness was so extreme that one could watch it go down her throat,"[48] one can consider it a fanciful metaphor rather than a supernatural phenomenon, but it's harder to account for the tamed lions that deliver letters of challenge in their jaws, bowing politely as they present them. On the other hand, when Tirant fights a dangerous beast in London, it's not a dragon but a large dog, which he kills by biting it on its jowl. This Man Bites Dog story is not parody but urban realism. When Tirant is challenged to a duel, the terms are as strange as anything in *Perceforest* — the combatants are to wear "French linen shirts, paper bucklers, garlands of flowers, and nothing else" (65) — but the actual duel is a bloody knife-fight in which Tirant plunges a dagger into his opponent's heart just as he stabs Tirant in the head. Medieval fancy and gritty realism alternate in Martorell's world as the flower of nobility rub shoulders with "prostitutes, kept women, and pimps, dancing to tambourins" (42; *sic*). Even the dialogue reflects this, as lofty sentiments are adulterated with slang and clichés; when Stephanie tries to patch up a tiff between Tirant and Carmesina, the princess snaps at her:

> "Shut up, Stephanie, and do not inflame my wrath, for the lofty saints in Heaven are little troubled by our sorrows, and we must strive through good deeds to win those rewards reserved for the virtuous. Not all those who glitter with love are gold. That metal pleases everyone, great and small, rich and poor, but some men prefer words and are full of hot air." (218)

"Shut up, Stephanie" — that's the voice of a modern girl, not a medieval damsel.

As the novel progresses, the medievalisms fall away and we get a more realistic account of life in the 15th century. Old-fashioned tournaments and duels are shouldered aside by more modern war stories, filled with enough complex strategies, acts of guerrilla warfare, espionage, disinformation, psychological warfare, and ordnance-porn to excite any Tom Clancy fan. Tirant's development as a military leader and diplomat, however, is offset by his failure as a lover. He falls in love at first sight of Carmesina — largely because "It had been so hot with all the windows closed that she had half-unbuttoned her blouse and he could see her breasts, which were like two heavenly crystalline apples" (118) — and she reciprocates his feelings, but he insists on wooing her with stilted declarations and moping rather than with decisive action. Though Martorell admired the militant and spiritual aspects of chivalry, he despised its elaborate rituals of courtly love and especially its toleration for secret marriages, in which a couple (like Amadis and Oriana) could make

---

48 Chap. 29 in Rosenthal's translation (because more accessible than La Fontaine's), hereafter cited parenthetically by chapter. (Both translations use the same chapter numbering as the original.)

vows to each other without the benefit of clergy.[49] On the battlefield, Tirant is a man of action, but around women (as Carmesina complains above) he prefers words and is full of hot air. Pleasure-of-my-life chastises him during one of her many attempts to hook him up with the princess: "'No man alive is brave in arms but afraid of women. In battle you are not daunted by all the knights in creation, and here you tremble at the sight of a mere damsel'" (231), and even urges him with military imagery to play rough if he has to:

> "Tirant, Tirant, never will you be feared in battle if you refuse to use a little force with reluctant damsels! Since your wishes are honorable and your beloved is worthy, go to her bed when she is naked or in her nightshirt and attack bravely, for you can invite a friend to dinner even if you lack clean tablecloths. Should you refuse, I shall quit your bailiwick, as I have known many knights whose hands were quick and courageous enough to win honor, glory, and fame from their ladies. Oh God, what a wonderful thing it is to hold a soft, naked, fourteen-year-old damsel in one's arms, and still better if she is of royal blood!" (229)

But throughout this long section of the novel Tirant never avails himself of that pleasure, despite many comic attempts to do so. When Cervantes's priest declared *Tirant* "a gold mine of amusement" he probably had this section in mind, because Martorell's deployment of this extended battle of the sexes is masterful, and more sexually graphic than any chivalry novel before it. As the Peruvian novelist Mario Vargas Llosa observes in a brilliant essay on *Tirant*, "The love scenes succeed one another till they constitute a veritable erotic explosion: sensual parties, fetishism, lesbianism, adultery, threats of rape, symbolic incest, voyeurism, techniques of pimping, erogenous play."[50] Carmesina won't allow Tirant to take her virginity, but she allows everything else; at one point she is entertaining him in her bedroom: "Then she pulled the covers over her head and told Tirant to put his head under them, saying, 'Kiss my breasts for your consolation and my repose'" (175), not something Clarissa would invite Lovelace to do in Richardson's interminable novel, but acceptable in Martorell's world. Carmesina is overly concerned with her reputation and avoiding scandal, which plays into Tirant's shyness and old-fashioned courtly notions, and as a result they never experience the wedded bliss that the other more down-to-earth characters do. They do exchange vows in a secret marriage, but since the author kills them off before they celebrate

---

49 Martorell's sister got entangled in one of those clandestine arrangements, and he spent years trying to arrange a duel with her seducer, traveling to England to find a judge and getting embroiled in all sorts of legal hassles. He was more concerned for his honor than hers, and because of all the bad publicity, she wound up a spinster.

50 "A Challenge on Behalf of *Tirant lo Blanc*," 7. This is the first of three essays Vargas Llosa has written on the novel, which are gathered in his *Carta de Batalla por* Tirant lo Blanc (Barcelona: Seix Barral, 1991).

a public wedding, he apparently regards that as a tactical error of the sort that would have gotten Tirant killed on the battlefield.

As frank as the sex scenes are, as realistic as Martorell's detailed picture of the world is — critic Edward T. Aylward notes that "Martorell was virtually a walking encyclopedia" of history, food, occupations, customs, ceremonies, military tactics, fashion, forms of writing, all of which are poured into this capacious novel (197) — he periodically reminds the reader that this is all an illusion, his alternative to a disappointing reality. "Great novels are great fairy tales," Nabokov lectures us.[51] At the king's wedding party in England, Tirant tells William, "we found a big rock made of wood so cunningly crafted that it made one continuous surface, and on the rock stood a high castle with mighty walls, guarded by five hundred men in shining armor." A mock battle ensures, "but at first we thought it real. Many of us dismounted, drew our swords, and hastened to aid the duke, but then we realized that it was only a masque" (53). *Tirant lo Blanc* is an elaborate masque, made of one continuous surface — its 487 chapters run together with relentless narrative momentum — and while deceptively realistic, it is ultimately an artificial construction. Martorell may have begun the novel as "a program for military and social reform in fifteenth-century Christendom" (the subtitle of Aylward's book), but one senses that as he progressed he became more interested in constructing a "big rock" of a novel to delight and amaze. About halfway through the novel, the Byzantine court receives a visit from "a black ship without masts or sails" transporting Morgan the Fay and some allegorical figures, who have come to visit King Arthur, who is sitting imprisoned in a cage with silver bars with the sword Excalibur on his knees. Even some critics have been taken in by this elaborate masque, wondering what King Arthur is doing in 15th-century Constantinople, overlooking a sentence at the end of the bizarre episode: "Afterward the emperor's retinue left feeling dazzled by what they had seen, as everything seemed to have been done by magic" (202). An artificial world that seems so real that it fools spectators, dazzling us into suspending disbelief, is the goal of every artist, and it is for that reason Vargas Llosa claims "Martorell is the first of that line of God-supplanters — Fielding, Balzac, Dickens, Flaubert, Tolstoi, Joyce, Faulkner — who set out to create in their novels a 'total reality,' the most distant case of an all-powerful, disinterested, omniscient, and ubiquitous novelist" (2). Had Martorell lived long enough to complete the novel himself, it would rank among the greatest novels of world literature, but even in its current form it is a stupendous achievement and compulsively readable. Martorell's radical renovation of the chivalric novel didn't suit all tastes, of course; old-fashioned ones like *Amadis of Gaul* proliferated for another century, growing sillier and more outlandish until Cervantes finally made a bonfire of them in *Don Quixote*. But heed

51 *Lectures on Literature*, 2.

his priest's advice about *Tirant*: "Take it home and read it, and you'll say that everything I've said about it is true."

The Castilian Diego de San Pedro took a different approach to saving the novel of chivalry from hacks: instead of making it more realistic, as Martorell did, he made it even more artificial. His *Prison of Love* (*Cárcel de Amor*, 1492) is a ballet of rhetoric, flaunting its artifice in a style that anticipates John Lyly's ephuism. About San Pedro, little is known except that he wrote an earlier novella entitled *Arnalte and Lucenda* and some poetry. He wrote for aristocrats, not the general public, though both of his novellas became extremely popular in the 16th century and were widely translated before falling into obscurity. The more ambitious of the two, *Prison of Love* may be the most rarified expression of courtly love ever written, or more precisely, of the literary conventions of courtly love. It features a perfect knight and lover (Leriano) and a perfect lady (Laureola), betrayed by a perfect villain (Persio), and ending with the martyrdom of the perfect lover to the religion of courtly love.

It begins in real-life Spain but quickly transforms into a dream of Macedonia, where the narrator spies the allegorical figure of Desire dragging Leriano to Love's Prison, where he is surrounded by other figures such as Understanding, Reason, and Sorrow, all personifications of rhetorical abstractions and psychological states. Leriano explains to the narrator that he has been imprisoned for falling in love with the king's daughter Laureola, and convinces the narrator to go to her and apprise her of the suffering she has caused him. He does so but gets a cold reception from Laureola, who insists she's done nothing to encourage Leriano and can't risk her reputation by showing interest in his situation. The narrator then carries letters back and forth between them as Leriano petitions her to show compassion; he claims he will die without it, so she relents only to the extent that she tells him not to die on her account. This sends Leriano's spirits soaring and frees him from his psychological prison, but no sooner does he return to the king's court than a jealous suitor named Persio spreads lies that L & L are meeting secretly, which causes the tyrannical king to throw his daughter in prison (a real one) to await execution. To make a short story shorter, Leriano raises an army, breaks her out of prison, and eventually exposes Persio's perfidy. But Laureola maintains her icy distance — "Do not think that people live so innocently that, if they learned that I had talked with you, they would believe our intentions to be pure, for we live in so wicked an age that goodness is slandered sooner than virtue is praised"[52] — which sends Leriano to his deathbed. A companion tries to cheer him up by maligning women, but Leriano responds with an elaborate defense of the fair sex. Unsure what to do with the three precious letters he received from Laureola, he tears them into pieces, drops them into a cup of

---

52 Page 64 in Whinnom's translation, hereafter cited by page number.

water, and drinks down his lady's words. And then he dies, literalizing the traditional lover's threat to die if his lady does not succor him.

The characters are stereotypes, the narrative moves from set-piece to set-piece like an old-fashioned ballet, and for all its talk of love there's no eroticism whatsoever: no crystalline breasts are exposed here, much less kissed. But what makes all this palatable, in fact aesthetically blissful, is San Pedro's exquisite style — brilliantly rendered by Keith Whinnom — and the novel's expressive formal structure. The novella is filled with balanced sentences like these (Laureola is addressing the narrator, who is asking for Leriano's release): "If you seek further to secure his release, you will find that in seeking remedy for him you have found only peril for yourself. And I give you notice that, though you may be a foreigner by birth, you will be a naturalized Macedonian in your grave" (15). "Remedy for him/peril for yourself"; "foreigner . . . birth/ Macedonian . . . grave," and note the pun on naturalized/return to nature. The narrator realizes "that while her speech was short, her anger was great." Thesis, antithesis, San Pedro's sentences seesaw with grace. While the characters follow the rigorous rules of courtly love, San Diego replicates this on the stylistic level by following equally rigorous rules of rhetoric, adorning his balanced constructions with alliteration, chiasmus, zeugma, and other fancy turns. Again, it's like watching a story ballet, where you ignore the simplistic plot and focus on the dancers' dazzling technique. And the novella itself is as tightly structured as its sentences; in his introduction, Whinnom notes that critics have shown that these paired phrases are doubled at the narrative level by "two allegorical sections, two assaults to release a prisoner, two false friends, two mother's laments, two reasoned discourses, etc.," and that overall the novella is structured like a formal oration (xxix–xxx). By 1492, few readers could still take seriously the courtly ideal of dying to show one's constancy — as Rosalind cracks in *As You Like It*, "Men have died from time to time, and worms have eaten them, but not for love" (4.1.91–92) — but San Pedro demonstrates that a gifted writer could still mine gold from the literary conventions that glorified those ideals. *Prison of Love* is a delicate music-box of a novel.

Less artificial, more sentimental romances in Catalan and Spanish appeared throughout the 1490s, but were upstaged by the 1499 publication of the sensational *Comedia de Castilo y Melibea*, better known as *Celestina*.[53] The first edition appeared anonymously, but the second, expanded edition of 1502 revealed the author to be Fernando de Rojas (c. 1465–1541), a lawyer and, more important, the son of Jewish parents who had been forced to convert to

---

53 Actually it's best known as "the" *Celestina*. Many critics follow the continental practice of using a definite article before some novels — the *Celestina*, the *Ameto*, the *Quixote* — in emulation of the *Iliad*, the *Aeneid*, and so forth. But since in English we don't refer to "the" *Emma* or "the" *Ulysses*, I'm ignoring this custom. It sounds natural in English only when referring to a truncated title, as when calling Joyce's last novel "the *Wake*."

Christianity. In form *Celestina* resembles a play — divided into acts and with speakers' names given, though no stage directions — but in fact it's a novel in dialogue, or "dramatic novel," a form that would soon be adopted (as we've seen) by Pietro Aretino in Italy, Jorge Ferreira de Vasconcelos in Portugal (he wrote three dramatic novels in the 1540s and '50s, most famously *Eufrosina*), several Spanish novelists of the 16th and 17th centuries, the Marquis de Sade in France (*Philosophy in the Bedroom*), and eventually by novelists such as Peacock, Firbank, Compton-Burnett, and Gaddis. But *Celestina*'s greatest innovation is the focus on lower-class characters and the vicissitudes of every-day life. The novel features a typical aristocratic couple, but the real stars are the supporting players: the servants, whores, and, manipulating them all, the crafty old bawd Celestina.

Celestina begins like a typical romance but ends like a pulp fiction. In search of his escaped falcon, a rich young dandy named Calisto strays into a garden and beholds Melibea, falls head over heels, and declares his love for her. As a virtuous young lady, she professes outrage at his effrontery and tells him to leave (though we find out later she's likewise smitten with him). Calisto goes mad with love in typical fashion, so his scheming servant Sempronio volunteers to help him win the lady, and to that end enlists the services of an old procuress named Celestina, who also happens to be a witch. With the help of other servants and some of her whores, Celestina arranges for a rendezvous in Melibea's garden, where overeager Calisto deflowers her. But while leaving over the garden wall, he falls and kills himself; in a dispute over a valuable gold chain Calisto had given the bawd, Sempronio and another servant named Parmeno stab Celestina to death; immediately captured and tried, they are beheaded by the authorities; and then capping these atrocities, Melibea commits suicide by throwing herself off a tower, leaving her bereaved father Pleberio to close the novel with a diatribe against romantic love.

If *Prison of Love* is a delicate music-box, *Celestina* is a blaring boombox. It's a noisy, talkative novel ringing with the rude vitality of common speech: char-acters argue, rave, lie, sing, speechify, interrupt each other, make wisecracks, toss off proverbs and clichés, quote the classics, indulge in reminiscences, even call up the devil with a formal incantation. Rojas gives voice to charac-ters who had been mostly silent in previous novels, and they let us know in no certain terms what they think of their "betters." Here's Areusa on why she quit as a lady's maid and became a prostitute:

> You waste the best part of your life working for them, and they pay you with a ragged cast-off skirt for ten years of service! They do nothing but insult you and scold you and keep you down, and you don't dare open your mouth in front of them. . . . Don't ever expect them to call you by your right name, only: "Come here, you whore! Go there, you slut! Where are you going, you rascal? Why did you do this, you dirty tramp? . . . Where's that cold

chicken? Go and find it at once! If you don't, I'll take it out of your wages!" And along with this, it's nothing but blows with their slippers, and pinching and beating and whipping from morning till night! You can never please them. They love to scream at you and scolding is their delight. They're least pleased with what you do best. And that's why, mother, I chose to live in my little house by myself, owing nothing to anyone, my own mistress, rather than live a prisoner in a palace.[54]

Thirty-five years later Aretino (who surely read *Celestina*) would allow his characters to talk this way, but no novelist before Rojas did, with the exception of Petronius. He mocks the conventions of courtly love by letting us hear what the servants think of it all, as here, when Calisto launches into the traditional enumeration of his beloved's beauty:

> CALISTO. Well then, just to please you, I'll describe her to you in detail.
>
> SEMPRONIO. *God help us! I'm in for it! But his fit won't last forever!*
>
> CALISTO. I'll begin with the hairs on her head. Have you ever by chance seen the skeins of golden threads they spin in Araby? Hers are more beautiful and shine no less. They reach to the very soles of her feet. And then, when they're curled and tied with a fine ribbon, as she wears them, they turn men into stones.
>
> SEMPRONIO. *Into asses, rather!*
>
> CALISTO. What's that?
>
> SEMPRONIO. I said her hairs could hardly resemble asses' bristles.
>
> CALISTO. What a vile figure! What an idiot!
>
> SEMPRONIO. *If I'm an idiot, what is he?* (1.2)

That's probably what the servants of Tirant and Leriano were muttering under their breath, but they were invisible, inaudible before now. The very language of traditional literature gets heckled:

> CALISTO. . . . I'll not eat until then, even though Apollo's horses have been put out to pasture after their daily run.

54 Act 9, scene 2 in Simpson's translation, hereafter cited by act/scene. He translates the original 16-act version; the second edition added five more acts after Calisto's death in act 14 — a subplot concerning a braggart named Centurio — as well as an author's note and prologue, but I agree with Simpson that these "interpolations and additions are impertinent and obtrusive" (ix). Even the translator of the 21-act version, Mack Hendricks Singleton, confesses he does "not care very much for these extra acts" (xi). Singleton's edition is useful, but since he treats *Celestina* as a play, I'm going with Simpson, who considers it a novel, and "assuredly one of the finest" (ix). I learned too late of two recent translations, by Peter Bush (2008) and Margaret Sayers Peden (2009).

SEMPRONIO. Leave off these high-flown phrases, sir, this poeticizing. Speech that's not common to all, or shared by all, or understood by all, is not good speech. Just say "until sunset" and we'll know what you mean. (8.3)

And sentimentalism is mocked throughout, as when a teary-eyed Celestina tells Parmeno about the mother he never knew:

> Let me tell you something to show you what a mother you lost, although it shouldn't be told, but then I can be free with you. Well, she extracted seven teeth from a hanged man with a pair of tweezers while I was removing his shoes! She was better at calling up the devil than I was, although I was better known for it then than I am now, because her art perished with her, for my sins. In short, the very devils themselves were afraid of her, she scared them so with her blood-curdling screams. (7.1)

Not the kind of praise you'd find on a Mother's Day card. This represents a reversal of values, a repudiation of tradition that was daring for its time.

Technically, *Celestina* is an impressive feat, for Rojas relies solely on dialogue to convey what his characters look like, how they act, their background, and the nature of their personalities. Without a traditional narrator to guide us, the novel is also more open to interpretation. Are we to take Pleberio's concluding sermon on the dangers of love as the theme of the novel? Or should we follow the prostitute Elicia's advice:

> For God's sake let's drop the arguments and sermons and enjoy ourselves while we may! Eat today and let tomorrow take care of itself! The man who makes a lot of money dies as quickly as the poor man, the doctor as quickly as the shepherd, the pope as the sexton, the lord as the serf, the man of high station as the villain, you with your trade as I without it. We can't live forever. Let's be merry, for few of us will reach old age and none of those who do will have died of hunger. And now to bed; it's time! (7.3)

When Celestina thinks back on her long, unconventional life, her biggest regret is not that she strayed from Christian principles but that she didn't take more advantage of her youth. "Enjoy yourselves while you're young," she tells a gathering of the servants and whores before the final calamity, "for whoever gets a chance to do so but waits for a better one will regret it, just as I regret the few hours I wasted when I was a girl and had admirers and lovers" (9.2). For the father who kept his daughter walled within a garden, passion is simply wrong, but Celestina eloquently notes its paradoxical nature: "Love is a hidden fire, a pleasant canker, a savory poison, a sweet bitterness, a delightful distress, a joyous torture, a grateful and cruel wound, a gentle death" (10). She has a rapturous appreciation of the female form and function that flies in the face of Christian austerity; as she tells a naked Areusa:

And how plump and fresh you are! What breasts! Beautiful! I thought you were good-looking before, seeing only the surface, but now I can tell you that in this whole city, so far as I know, there aren't three such figures as yours! You don't look a day over fifteen! I wish I were a man and could look at you! By God, you're committing a sin not to share your beauty with those who love you! God didn't give you such youthful tenderness to hide under six layers of wool and linen. (7.2)

Ultimately her worldly wisdom seems superior to Pleberio's sour conviction (derived from Plato and seconded by medieval theologians) that "Love is the enemy of all reason and gives its gifts to those who serve it least, until they too are caught in love's mournful dance" (16). He gets the final word, but it's the magnificent Celestina we remember. Just as Areusa wanted to be independent of her cruel mistress, Celestina urges the others to make their own way, to live according to their own lights and not by the dreary morality of their social superiors. Rojas may be speaking to the reader when Celestina tells Parmeno *carpe diem*: "One of these days you'll be a man with a riper understanding and you'll say: 'Old Celestina was right!'" (7.1).

But like the scorpion, *Celestina* has a sting in its tail end. Pleberio lashes out with Lear-like rage not only at romantic love but at the entire world, which the earlier part of *Celestina*, for all its humor and exuberance, has been systematically exposing:

When I was young I thought the world was ruled by order. I know better now! It is a labyrinth of errors, a frightful desert, a den of wild beasts, a game in which men run in circles, a lake of mud, a thorny thicket, a dense forest, a stony field, a meadow full of serpents, a river of tears, a sea of miseries, effort without profit, a flowering but barren orchard, a running spring of cares, a sweet poison, a vain hope, a false joy, and a true pain. (16)

The world according to *Celestina* is driven by self-interest and money, ruled over not by Our Father Who art in heaven but by "Sad Pluto, lord of the underworld" (3.2). Money especially contaminates everything; as Parmeno notes before killing Celestina, "There's no friendship where money's concerned" (12.3). The clergy provide no guidance; they're Celestina's best customers, and she does much of her business at church. Class distinctions are meaningless: the aristocratic Calisto is as amoral as his servants, and according to Celestina, the only difference between prostitutes and upper-class ladies like Melibea is that the latter play harder to get. In a fine essay written to commemorate the 500th anniversary of the publication of *Celestina*, Spanish novelist Juan Goytisolo notes that the persecution of Rojas's Jewish parents no doubt left him contemptuous of Christian society and its consecrated values, so he set out in this novel "to attack them and to destroy existing social and literary hierarchies and subvert their meaning. It is the most audacious, virulent work in Spanish literature."[55]

Celestina offered a brash alternative to the sentimental and courtly romance, especially for persecuted Jews and Moors, and cleared the ground for the picaresque novel that would sprout in Spain later in the 16th century. It was a huge success, and — then as now with any successful work — it was followed by a number of cheap knockoffs and imitations. The best novel inspired by it is Francisco Delicado's outrageous *Portrait of Lozana, the Lusty Andalusian* (*Retrato de la Lozana andaluza*, 1528). Like Rojas, Delicado (c. 1480–c. 1535) was the son of Jewish converts to Catholicism, but left Spain and moved to Rome for its greater freedom and tolerance. He tells us he wrote the novel between June and December of 1524 to cheer himself up during an illness (probably syphilis), but he didn't published it until 1528, by which time he was living in Venice. (Rome had been sacked the year before by the Holy Roman emperor Charles V, which inspired Delicado to go back to his manuscript and insert some lines "foretelling" this event, a punishment for Rome's many sins.)

Adapting the dramatic form of *Celestina*, buttressed with all sorts of paraliterary bells and whistles,[56] Delicado divides his 300-page novel into 66 "sketches" (*mamotretos*, or memoranda) chronicling the career of an unflappable adventuress who calls herself Lozana ("Lusty"). Celestina was a successful whore in her younger days, and in a sense Delicado's heroine is what Celestina might have been like as a young woman. Born in Andalusia with the given name Aldonza, she admits she was sexually precocious — in contrast to the walled Melibea, our girl "climbed the garden wall without her mother's knowledge and lost the flower of her innocence" (1) — but was left an orphan after her mother died. She falls for an Italian merchant and pimp named Diomedes and has children by him while traveling the Mediterranean region turning tricks, but before he can marry her Diomedes' disapproving father steps in and arranges for her to be killed. She escapes and arrives in Rome in 1513, heads for the Spanish quarter, changes her name to Lozana, and quickly becomes a successful whore/cosmetician/bawd/quack doctor. A well-endowed young lad named Rampin, who she meets and seduces her first day in Rome in an X-rated scene (sketch 14), becomes her servant and protector. After a decade of whoring and grifting, Lozana, like Moll Flanders,

---

55 "In the Realm of the Senses," trans. Peter Bush, *Los Angeles Times*, 20 June 1999. (I want to thank Spanish novelist Julián Ríos for alerting me to this essay, and for general advice on this section.)

56 The novel is preceded by a dedication and a "Discussion of the Topics Treated in the Present Work," which are followed by (1) an apology, (2) an explication, (3) an epilogue, (4) a mock "Letter of Excommunication against a Cruel, but Healthy Damsel," (5) "Lozana's Letter to All Women Who Have Decided to Come to See Campo di Fiore in Rome," and (6) a "Digression That the Author Narrated in Venice." All quotations are from Damiani's translation, cited parenthetically by "sketch" (chapter).

repents of her ways, changes her name, again, to Vellida (graceful, beautiful), and retires with Rampin to the island of Lipari, her nose eaten away by
syphilis but otherwise a successful survivor of the Roman underworld.

In contrast to *Celestina*, a compact work taking place over a week's time
with only a dozen characters, *Lozana* is a sprawling carnival of a novel with
125 speaking parts representing everyone from aristocrats to a talking donkey,
a melting pot of nationalities, and written in a racy Spanish laced with proverbs, puns, slang, and spiced with Italian, Portuguese, Hebrew, and Catalan
words. The language is vigorously vulgar: "Lozana, I'd like for you to shave
my cunt because I want to leave and see some gentlemen friends" is a typical
line of dialogue (54), Lozana makes a casual reference to her "monthly flow"
(42), and she is amused by Rampin's phallic follies:

> The other day we had a row, because he put his cock into a pot that I had half filled with
> May water. It got hard inside and he brought the pot over dangling in front of himself. Of
> course I was much happier to lose the crockery and the May water than to hurt him. The
> other day when two girls with skin like gold were here, he got so hard that both leather
> straps on his codpiece broke, for they were made of cat skin. (46).

(I hate when that happens.) Delicado re-introduced dirty realism into the
novel, which had been dormant since Petronius's *Satyricon*, and uses it to rub
our noses in the cesspool that was Rome in the early 16th century. Lozana's
various cons are amusing — never vicious, and usually at the expense of the
mark's vanity — but the world she lives in is as morally bankrupt as Rojas's
Spain, so much so that Delicado clearly feels Rome deserved the punishment
it received at the hands of Charles V's army in 1527. It's the same Rome
Aretino would skewer a few years later in his *Dialogues*, which in form and
language was obviously influenced by Delicado's indelicate novel.

But while holding our nose at the world he portrays, we have to admire
the techniques he uses to portray it. The novel is jerkily episodic, edited
with jump cuts like a music video, each "sketch" a snapshot of a moment in
Lozana's colorful life, with characters coming and going at a dizzying rate.
Like a postmodernist author, Delicado occasionally steps into the novel,
chatting with his heroine or addressing the reader before retiring to continue
taking memos about her life. And like Charles Bukowski, whose gutter realism he anticipates, Delicado is smarter than he lets on. There are numerous
literary allusions, ranging from Apuleius's *Golden Ass* to San Pedro's *Prison
of Love*, and he takes intertextuality to a playful extreme by having Lozana
own a copy of *Celestina*, the novel that created her. *Lozana* is divided into
three parts, and some scholars have seen in that and other trinities a mockery
by this forced convert of the tripartite god of the Catholics, with broad hints
that the "virgin" Mary was not much different from those clients of Lozana

who want their maidenheads "repatched" so that they can claim to be virgins.[57] And finally, by showing how a resourceful orphan negotiates her way through a corrupt world, Delicado encouraged (if not invented) the concept of the *pícaro/-a*, the Spanish delinquent whose low-life adventures would be Spain's longest-lasting contribution to the novel. *Lozana* is a delightfully iconoclastic work, and enjoyed some success: it went through two dozen editions, was translated twice into French — the second time Frenched by Guillaume Apollinaire — and into Italian as well. It wasn't until 1987, however, that it was finally translated into English (albeit published by an obscure academic press); apparently British and American readers before that needed to be shielded from a spunky heroine who, in addition to being intelligent, beautiful, and independent, is also capable of asking her beau, "Isn't the pleasure of kissing me enough? Must you have fondling and fucking too?" (14).

The Life of Lazarillo of Tormes (*La vida de Lazarillo de Tormes*, 1554) is considered the first true picaresque novel, and given *Lazarillo*'s subversive appeal, it's easy to see why it became such a popular genre. It was published anonymously — Diego Hurtado de Mendoza and Alfonso de Valdés are the leading candidates for authorship — partly because of its harsh criticism of Catholicism but largely because the author wanted to fob it off as a nonfiction book by one "Lázaro de Tormes."[58] A series of letters to an unidentified authority, it forms a first-person account of an urchin from around the age of 10 until he marries a decade later. His father a thief who was killed in battle, his mother too poor to support both him and his illegitimate little brother, young Lázaro goes in quest of a master who can provide for him. The novella gives a chapter each to the succession of Spanish scoundrels from various professions he hooks up with: (1) a stingy blind man who make a living providing prayers for credulous Catholics, but who also teaches Lázaro how to live by his wits; (2) an even stingier priest who almost starves Lázaro to death;[59] (3) a proud but penniless *hidalgo* who goes to ridiculous lengths to keep up appearances; (4) a worldly friar whom Lázaro quickly leaves "because of one or two other things I'd rather not mention";[60] (5) a pardoner who sells papal indulgences to

---

57 In *The Art of Subversion in Inquisitorial Spain*, Manuel da Costa Fontes decodes and details both Delicado's and Rojas's various attacks on Christian dogma, reminding us that both wrote at the height of the Inquisition and had to hide their blasphemies beneath the skirts of bawdiness.

58 Francisco Rico explains the game the author played on his first readers in his informative essay on *Lazarillo* in Moretti's *Novel*, 2:146–51.

59 At one point, Lázaro is reduced to pretending he's a mouse nibbling on the priest's bread, which recalls the etymological origin of *pícaro* (literally, kitchen boy), from the verb *picar*, to nibble at food.

60 From Alpert's smooth translation in *Two Spanish Picaresque Novels*, where *Lazarillo* occupies pp. 21–79; hereafter cited parenthetically by chapter (except for Alpert's introduction, cited by page number).

credulous Catholics (you can see a theme developing here); (6) "an artist who painted tambourines for a living," then a priest who makes money by selling water to his parishioners; and (7) a constable briefly, and then his final master, the Civil Service, for whom he works as Toledo's town crier. The archpriest of San Salvador then cons Lázaro into marrying his mistress so that he can silence gossip, reducing our antihero to a complacent civil servant and "what the Spanish call a *cabrón*, a man who permits his wife's infidelity not only shamelessly but for his own profit" (Alpert 9).

Until that conclusion, the reader's sympathies are with Lázaro because of the incredible hardships he endures and the contemptible masters he is saddled with. He steals from the worst of them, but is sympathetic to the *hidalgo*, and never becomes the heartless rogue of later picaresque fiction. His search for a master can easily be read as a quest for authority, for something genuine he can believe in and rely on, but no such authority is to be found in chaotic 16th-century Spain. The aristocratic class is ridiculed in the person of the proud *hidalgo*; of the two representatives of the legal system in the novella, one's a conman and the other an ineffective constable who gets beaten up by the fugitives he's pursuing; and of course the state religion is the most contemptible of all. It is difficult to say who the author despises more, the various priests and pardoners who fleece their flock, or the dumb flock of Catholics themselves. Lázaro's quest for authority fails, but rather than continuing the quest, he joins the corrupt system by settling for a cushy government job, turning a blind eye to his wife's infidelity and illegally profiting from his position: "So if anybody anywhere in Toledo has wine to sell or anything else," he boasts in the final chapter, "he won't get very far in this business unless Lázaro de Tormes has a finger in the pie" (7).

The representatives of the aristocracy, the law, and religion all fail him. The only representative of the arts seems to be the tambourine painter, until one realizes he represents the author of *Lazarillo of Tormes* himself, the most reliable authority in this corrupt, credulous world. He's the one who sees through the other representatives of the social order and who provides the most accurate and honest view of the way things are. Painting tambourines sounds like a trifling way to make a living, but Mr. Tambourine Man's art provides the authenticity Lázaro needs, as well as a magic swirlin' alternative to the world that is crushing his young soul; but like many people, he ignores the artist, leaving him for yet another religious huckster.

The author's greatest achievement is not the invention of a genre that could document the lives of rogues, however, but his brilliant decision to convey his social criticism from the point of view of a child. Even though Lázaro is narrating his story years later (writing it on company time, no doubt, while neglecting his official duties), he tells it with the innocent candor of a child, which allows the author to give a stronger bite to his ironies. Huckleberry Finn may be the most famous example of the advantage in using a narrator too young to fully understand what he's reporting, but Lázaro is the first in the history of the novel. After his father dies, young Lázaro notes that a Negro named Zaide "used to come to our house occasionally and leave in the morning," but makes no connection between those nocturnal visits and the baby boy his mother produces nine months later. And since Zaide steals to provide for his family out of love, the boy states with a straight face, "we ought not to be surprised that a priest robs his flock and a friar his convent for the benefit of his female devotees and others" (1). It's fitting that Lázaro becomes a town crier at the end; one of his duties is to "accompany criminals being punished for their misdeeds and shout out their crimes" (7) without knowing the particulars of their cases. The author uses Lázaro the same way as a conduit for his scathing social criticisms, and even though the lad doesn't always understand what he's reporting, the attentive reader does.

Lazarillo is an innovative and subversive novel, as the author well knew. In the prologue, Lázaro admits his story may not appeal to all readers, "especially as tastes vary and one man's meat is another man's poison," but hopes that readers will give it a chance. It was popular with a large number of readers — the inevitable spurious sequel followed quickly — but it cut too close to the bone for two other groups: Catholic authorities, naturally (who placed it on the Index in 1559), and those who read novels to escape from life rather than to confront injustices. That group, mostly women, preferred writers who imitated not a town crier, shouting out society's criminal deeds, but a shepherd with a flute.

The pastoral novel was introduced to Spanish readers in 1559 by a Portuguese-born courtier and musician named Jorge de Montemayor (c. 1520–61). His *Diana* (*Los siete libros de la Diana*) was an instant success, spawned numerous sequels and imitations, and offered Spanish readers an alternative to the novel of chivalry, which was growing tired and predictable by that time. *Diana* isn't the first modern pastoral novel, of course: Boccaccio revived the genre in the 1340s with *Ameto*, and Sannazaro's *Arcadia* was available to Montemayor in a 1547 translation. His Portuguese countryman Bernardim Ribeiro brought out a pastoral novel in 1557 known as *Meina e moça* (actual title *Livro das saudades*, Book of Yearnings), probably Montemayor's most immediate inspiration, along with the pastoral tradition established by Theocritus and Virgil.[61] But *Diana* is truly modern in that it introduces some degree of realism, psychology, self-consciousness, and cultural commentary into the artificial, timeless world of the traditional pastoral.

---

61 I don't believe Ribeiro's novel has ever been translated into English, despite its reputation as a masterpiece of Portuguese literature.

To be sure, *Diana* is spun from the same cotton candy as any pastoral, a fantasy world of noble shepherds and beautiful shepherdesses singing songs while tending well-behaved flocks in perfect weather. But rather than set his novel in a mythological Arcadia, Montemayor places his rustics in recognizable places — by the banks of the Esla river in León and later in Portugal — and even the one enchanted palace in the novel is furnished not unlike an aristocratic Spanish reader's own palace. And rather than pretending he's describing a fantasy world, the author tells us in his preface that the incidents he will describe "have really taken place, although they go disguised under pastoral names and style."[62] The Diana of the title is a beautiful shepherdess who had been in love with (and loved by) a shepherd named Sireno until he was forced to go abroad for a while; during his absence, she forgot about him and married instead a prosperous shepherd named Delio. When Sireno returns, he is devastated by the news, which is where the novel opens. He learns that Diana is miserable in her marriage — she doesn't appear herself until book 5 of the seven-book novel, a clever ploy on the author's part to maintain mystery about her and whet expectations — but that's cold comfort to Sireno or his companion Sylvano, who had also been in love with (but unloved by) Diana. Unrequited love and the inconstancy of women, rather than the innocent joys of the rustic life — "playing, singing, wrestling, twirling our crooks, dancing with the maidens on Sunday" (1) — emerge as the themes of the tearful novel as, one by one, various other characters confess their romantic losses.

Each book of the novel features a story within the story. After Sireno and Sylvano take turns pouring out their hearts over Diana in song — poems occupy about 40 percent of the text — they meet a shepherdess named Selvagia, who tells a gender-confusing tale of how she had fallen in love with a woman pretending to be a man, who thus set her up as a joke to fall for her look-alike male cousin, who falls for her in turn before spurning Selvagia for his cross-dressing cousin with the queer sense of humor. In book 2, we get another cross-dressing tale — adapted by Shakespeare for his first comedy, *Two Gentlemen of Verona* — in which a woman named Felismena disguises herself as a male page to be close to the man she loves. He courts a noblewoman named Celia, who falls instead for the pretty pageboy, but when Celia realizes Felismena is unobtainable, she dies of grief, which causes the grieving man to disappear in exile. Felismena has saved three nymphs from being raped by some wild, hairy men, so to reward her, the nymphs offer to take her, Selvagia, and the two shepherds to a wise woman named Felicia, who can cure all their sorrows. During the ensuing *Wizard of Oz*-like journey in book 3, they come upon a shepherdess crying in her sleep named Belisa,

---

62 "The Summary of This Book," in Mueller's translation, hereafter cited parenthetically by book (i.e., chapter).

who wakes and tells her sad tale of falling for both a father and his son simultaneously, only to apparently witness the father kill his son in jealousy and then commit suicide. She too joins the traveling party.

In book 4, the middle of the novel, the grieving group reaches the enchanted palace of the wise Felicia. (The author is careful to emphasize she's a sage, not a sorceress.) Felicia entertains them lavishly in her palace, where they listen to Orpheus — whether an ingenious artifice or the actual Greek god, we're not told — who sings of the virtues of the ladies at the Spanish court; that is, at the most artificial, unrealistic point in the novel, Montemayor introduces flesh-and-blood women of his own society, a jarring reminder he's actually writing about the affairs of real people. Felicia gives a seminar on the difference between love and desire — love lasts and is thus more admirable, while desire fades after it attains its carnal goal — and in book 5 she cures the unrequited lovers by having them drink a potion, which in effect radically speeds up the time that heals all wounds. In the same book we get the sequel to Belisa's story — the father and son were phantoms, the creations of an evil necromancer — and she is reunited with the son, the father having conveniently retired from the world. And at this point we finally meet Diana, who insists she married another not because she fell out of love with Sireno but because her father insisted. In book 6 we get another story within a story, but more important, Sireno finally confronts Diana for her betrayal; she weakly defends herself by appealing to customary obedience:

> "And what role could love play," said Diana, "if I had to obey my parents?"
>
> "But how can parents, obedience, time, and good or bad twists of Fortune overcome a love as true as the one you showed me before I left? Ah, Diana, Diana, I never thought anything in the world could shake so firm a faith! So much so, Diana, that you could have married and still not forgotten the one who loved you." (6)

That is, if she truly loved him she would have either defied her parents or at least married the other for show and kept Sireno on the side for love — as in chivalric novels — though Sireno quickly admits his jealousy would have ruined that alternative. He is more disappointed at her submission to authority ("parents, obedience") and her unwillingness to exert her independence, another instance of the growing anti-authoritarianism that characterizes the bolder Renaissance novels. But Sireno insists he's over her now, and to her acute embarrassment he and Sylvano sing a four-page duet *pretending* they are still in love with her. "While the shepherds were singing this, the shepherdess Diana stood with her fair face cupped in her hand" (6), and after that humiliation they all part ways to tend to their neglected flocks. The concluding book 7 sees Felismena reunite with her exiled lover in Portugal, and we're given a final story within the story and the promise it will be continued in the sequel. Montemayor died in a duel before he could write one, but a scribble of hacks quickly filled that void.[63]

Although critics have suggested Montemayor wrote *Diana* in revenge against a woman who dumped him after he had to leave Spain for England as part of the future Philip II's wedding party, writing the novel seems to have had the same cathartic effect on him that the magic potion has on Sireno, after which the shepherd merely feigns sadness to justify performing a sad song. There's such an emphasis on artifice that *Diana* reads more like an example of art for art's sake than a vehicle for personal revenge. "All art is quite useless," Oscar Wilde tells us in the preface to *The Picture of Dorian Gray*; art is to be admired for its own sake, not *used* for something else, a sentiment that runs throughout the second half of *Diana*. In book 5, Arsileo (the son whom Belisa loves) is urged to sing a sad song purely for aesthetic reasons: "The shepherd sang this with many tears and the shepherdess heard it with much contentment witnessing the grace with which he played and sang." The aesthetics of the performance, not the song's content or moral, is what matters, just as Sireno and Sylvano later pretend to be still in love with Lady Di only to get into character to sing their sad number. In the final book, another character warns against taking art seriously: "If you become enamored with words and think that carefully written sonnets are good arguments, you deceive yourself" (7), and on the novel's final page, when Felismena tells her lover the story of what happened after he left her, the author suggests how we should take his creation: "He *marvelled* at all of it . . . and everything else that occurred in this book" (7, my italics). Even though Montemayor makes a case for considering nobility a matter of deeds rather than lineage, and another against blindly obeying authority, he ultimately hopes the reader will simply *marvel* at his creation, his alternate universe. Just as Cervantes's priest saved *Amadis* from the flames for being the first of its kind, he exempts *Diana* for the same reason, though he objects to the supernatural elements and most of the longer poems.[64] Montemayor's self-conscious artistry and his use of the pastoral as a stage for literary performance rather than as a viable lifestyle choice (which is what Don Quixote's niece fears her uncle will use *Diana* for) justify the high regard with which the novel was held for centuries after its publication and make it one of the few examples of this outworn genre that can still be read with pleasure today — though I'm with the priest on those long poems.

Cervantes himself wrote a pastoral novel, rarely read today except by specialists, which may be the most complicated and subversive example of

---

63 The one exception is Gaspar Gil Polo's well-regarded *Diana enamorada* (Diana in Love, 1564), in which Diana's husband dies and she makes up with Sireno.

64 In his novella *The Dialogue of the Dogs*, Cervantes has the dog Berganza likewise note with apparent disapproval how easily Felicia's magic potion solves everyone's problems.

the genre. Begun while Cervantes was in prison in Algiers, it was published in 1585 as *Primera parte de la Galatea*. Like *Diana*, it has a recognizable setting — on the banks of Spain's Tagus River — and opens with two swains professing their love for an elegant shepherdess named Galatea, who (as one of them hyperbolically gushes) possesses "the sun's rays in her locks, heaven in her forehead, stars in her eyes, snow in her complexion, pomegranate in her cheeks, ruby in her lips, ivory in her teeth, crystal in her neck, and marble in her breast."[65] Galatea appreciates the attention of one of them, the sensitive Elicio — the other, Erastro, is too rustic, more like a sidekick than a rival — but she doesn't want to encourage him because it would endanger her reputation for "discretion," a vital concern of upper-class señoritas at that time. Cervantes unexpectedly tracks mud into this decorous world as early as page 10, when a fleeing man bursts onto the scene, followed by another who stabs him to death. Such violence was unheard of in the pastoral novel, occurring only in recollected stories set offstage, never in the primary narrative. Elicio and Erastro follow the murderer and ask him to explain himself, at which point we're given the first of many interpolated tales, which dominate the novel.

The dozen or so such tales that follow, all from characters in the "real" world who have fled to the bucolic world for one reason or another, are too complex to summarize. They all deal with the messier aspects of love: jealousy, misunderstanding, betrayal, familial interference, abductions, attempted suicide, mistaken twins, and other soap-opera dramatics. There is little progress in the relationship between Elicio and Galatea; instead, they listen separately to these object lessons in love — Elicio hears stories told by men at night, Galatea those by women during the day — living vicariously through them. Near the end of the novel, just when the couple might apply the lessons they've learned to their own relationship, we're told Galatea's father has decided to marry her to a wealthy Portuguese shepherd. Unlike Montemayor's Diana, Galatea doesn't obediently follow orders, but instead slips Elicio a note asking if he can get her out of that commitment. He promises to do his best, planning first to reason with her father, but ready to use violence if reason fails. And there the novel ends. Again like Montemayor, the author promises a sequel but never wrote one, even though Cervantes planned on doing so up until the day he died.

Like *Diana*, *Galatea* contains reams of poetry in a variety of forms and meters, some several pages long. In fact, Cervantes seems to have regarded his novel largely as a vehicle for his verse and as a defense of poesy: in the

---

65 Book 3 in Gyll's antique Victorian rendition (1867), apparently the last time the novel was translated into English. It's too fusty to be read with pleasure today, though it does occasionally yield unexpected felicities, as when a character tells an agitated woman, "Calm your breasts, Rosaura."

prologue he insists studying and writing poetry is the best way for a writer to appreciate "his mother tongue, and so to rule over the artifices of eloquence therein comprised" (xi). Many of the shepherds in the novel are thinly disguised representations of Cervantes' fellow poets, and structurally the climax of the novel isn't Galatea's unwanted marriage announcement (as one would expect) but the supernatural appearance of the muse Calliope in book 6 (like Orpheus in *Diana*), who praises a hundred or so Spanish poets over the course of a 23-page hymn. Those who have read the original claim "the abundant poetry in *Galatea* is relatively pedestrian, with a few bright spots" (Mancing 137), though Ruth El Saffar brilliantly defends Elicio's first-page song as an ingenious encapsulation of all the thematic concerns and formal devices that will shape the novel.[66]

But the true achievement of *Galatea* is not the poetry but Cervantes' subversive attempt to open up the confined, sentimental, pastoral genre to admit more realism into it, and to allow the genre to teach as well as to entertain. Although the interpolated tales are larger than life, they do bring the outside world into the rarified pastoral domain, and give a more mature view of the vicissitudes of love than earlier idylls in Arcadia did. And unlike the tales in earlier pastorals, given in full at one sitting, Cervantes often interrupts the tales, to be concluded later, which makes greater demands on the reader's memory but strengthens the work's organic unity. There is no wise woman like Felicia to magically solve the characters' problems; they have to work them out for themselves by listening critically to the tales outsiders tell and applying them to their own situations.[67] The same applies to readers of *Galatea*, as few as they may be today.

Antonio de Villegas also wrote a pastoral novel, *Ausencia y soledad de amor*, but he is best known for his version of *The Abencerraje* (*El Abencerraje*), published in his collected works in 1565. This early example of the Moorish novel (*novela morisca*) was apparently written some 15 years earlier by an anonymous author and appeared in print in various redactions in 1561 and 1562 — it was even inserted in later, unauthorized editions of *Diana* — but Villegas's is the most refined version of this idealistic tale of Christian–Moorish relations. (Remember that the Moors had been subjugated by Spanish Christians in 1492 after much bitter warfare; writing about them in 1550s would be like a modern American novelist writing about the Apache.) Set in the early 15th century along the border of Moorish Granada and Catholic Andalusia in southern Spain, *The Abencerraje* is (as its opening line announces) "a living portrait of virtue, liberality, prowess, gallantry and loyalty" on both sides of the

---

66 "*La Galatea*," 342–45. See also Mary Randel's "The Language of Limits and the Limits of Language," where she argues *Galatea* is "primarily a defense of poetry" (256).

67 I'm paraphrasing Elizabeth Rhodes's similar observation in her fine essay on *Galatea*.

religious divide.[68] Rodrigo de Narváez is governor of a frontier fortress and is patrolling one night when he comes across a well-dressed Moor on horseback, who valiantly fights off the Spanish patrol until he is captured. He identifies himself as Abindarráez of the illustrious Abencerraje family, who had been all but wiped out by a Muslim tyrant. Asked where he was going, the Abencerraje unfolds a tale of how he had been separated from his family at an early age and raised by another Moorish family, whose daughter Jarifa he assumed was his sister. The boy and girl are inseparable, and when they reach their teens they began feeling sexually attracted to each other; their relief upon learning they're not actually related is short-lived, however, when Jarifa's father is transferred to another city. Jarifa promises to send for Abindarráez if her father ever goes out of town, and the night he is captured by Rodrigo he had received just such a summons and was speeding toward her. Touched by this tale, Rodrigo offers to free the ardent Abencerraje if he promises to return in three days and surrender himself. The Moor reunites with his sweetheart, exchanges marriage vows in the presence of her duenna, and the couple consummate their love (presumably *not* in the duenna's presence).

Afterward, Abindarráez explains his situation to Jarifa, who offers to ransom him with daddy's treasure, but the last of the Abencerrajes insists on fulfilling his vow: he may be a figurative prisoner of love, but he is a literal prisoner of war and wouldn't dream of sullying his reputation, so he returns with Jarifa to surrender himself to Rodrigo. Asking what kind of man this Rodrigo is, Jarifa is told an anecdote about his valiancy that is similar to (if not plagiarized from) the first tale in Ser Giovanni's *Pecorone*: the husband of a lady Rodrigo once fancied ignored him until her husband praised him, and when she then made herself available, Rodrigo refused to dishonor a man who spoke so highly of him. Rodrigo patches things up between Abindarráez and Jarifa's father, and the novella ends happily as an example of mutual Christian–Moorish respect.

It's a slight but well-told tale, expertly handling flashbacks within an ongoing narrative, and its romanticized vision of Islamic and Catholic cooperation stands in marked contrast to the bitter and more realistic animosity displayed by the Jewish writers Rojas and Delicado. Though *The Abencerraje* is little read today, like *Diana* it was very popular and influential, leading to numerous adaptations and translations, all the way up to Washington Irving's late *Spanish Romance* (1839). It is of course mentioned in *Don Quixote* — the mad knight ludicrously identifies with Abindarráez (1.5) — and a variant of *The Abencerraje* also appears in the last Spanish novel I want to consider, the most ambitious example of the picaresque novel in Spanish literature.

Guzman of Alfarache (*Guzmán de Alfarache*, 1599) was written by a hard-luck case named Mateo Alemán (1547–1614?). Ashamed of his Jewish

---

68 In Keller's translation, a bilingual edition with an extensive introduction.

heritage, he avoided his *converso* father's medical profession — which exposed young Alemán to all sorts of misery and suffering — in favor of various ventures that merely landed him in debt and eventually in prison (ironically, the same one his father worked at). He published his novel in 1599 and a sequel in 1604 but made little money from them, and in 1608 emigrated to Mexico, where he died six or seven years later. He drew upon his difficult life for his lengthy novel about a protagonist who is likewise ashamed of his heritage and who scams his way through life, often trading on the discrepancy between appearance and reality.

Like *Lazarillo de Tormes*, which Alemán knew and alludes to, *Guzman* is a first-person confession by a repentant looking back on his disreputable career from a later vantage point of semi-respectability.[69] He quickly, guiltily, passes over his family's origin: they were from "the Levant" (i.e., were Jews) and became successful moneylenders in Genoa, where they somehow became "incorporated" into Italian nobility.[70] Forsaking (or hiding) his Judaism, Guzman's father made a great show of piety at Mass, leading the narrator to wink: "Is it not doing him a horrible injustice to believe that, with such a beautiful exterior, he was capable of the evil traffic of which he was accused?" (5). Throughout the novel, characters with "beautiful exteriors" are more often than not whited sepulchers disguising moral corruption, and Guzman's father is no different. Sailing for Spain to confront a dishonest partner, he is shipwrecked in Algiers, where he quickly changes religion again and marries a rich woman, whom he robs and dumps at the first opportunity to continue on to Spain, where he becomes a successful financier again and seduces the concubine of an old dandy to produce our hero. (The woman later tells Guzman she wishes he were a girl so that she could rent her out as a prostitute, as her mother did with her at age 12.) When he reaches 14 — his father dead and his mother desperate — Guzman decides to leave home and seek his fortune in Genoa, hoping to be incorporated into their wealthy ranks. But he experiences one setback after another on the road, is mistreated by almost everyone, and quickly learns that he will survive only if he becomes as duplicitous as everyone around him. "Being amongst wolves, I began to howl as well as they" (141), and he quickly becomes an accomplished beggar and thief. When he reaches Genoa he is rejected by his relatives because of

69 As Joan Ramon Resina points out in "The Short, Happy Life of the Novel in Spain," the confessional mode of both *Lazarillo* and *Guzman* reflects the growing use of confession by the Jesuits to regulate Spanish society (in Moretti's *Novel* 1:298–99).

70 All quotations are from Edward Lowdell's 1883 translation, the last to be made into English, hereafter cited parenthetically by page number. At 478 pages it contains the bulk of the original; the translator admits he has omitted the many "disquisitions on morality and religion with which the author, in accordance with the spirit and custom of his time, has interlarded and overloaded his subject" (iv). The only other English translation, James Mabbe's *The Spanish Rogue* (1622–23), contains many inaccuracies and interpolations as well as deletions; a new English translation is obviously needed.

his trampy appearance, which leads him to scam his way through the rest of Italy, eventually making enough money to return to Genoa and fleece his sniffy relations in revenge before heading back to Spain.

Following in his father's crooked footsteps, Guzman becomes a successful businessman, marries, but soon goes bankrupt, which causes his wife to die of shame. He studies for the priesthood — "More rogues than one have made their fortunes by taking such a course" (433) — but forsakes orders at the last minute to marry a "dangerous beauty," then moves to Madrid and lives (like Lázaro) as a *cabrón* while various gallants flirt with his wife and shower her with gifts. Eventually she runs off with an Italian sea captain, much to Guzman's relief, but his final job as a steward to a rich widow tempts him with embezzlement, which gets him thrown into prison and later sentenced as a galley-slave on a ship. After snitching to the captain about a planned revolt, he is rewarded with his freedom and vows "to lead a more reasonable life in the future" (478).

It's always a guilty pleasure to read of grifters and their clever schemes, and on that superficial level *Guzman of Alfarache* is hugely enjoyable. But look closer and the novel begins to resemble one of Guzman's elaborate scams. Are we to take his final conversion and moralizing tone seriously?[71] True converts ashamed of their past usually don't recall it with so much gusto. Or was Alemán going out of his way to broadcast his Christianity and condemn his Jewish characters because that was his only ticket to Mexico? Guzman's repudiation of social concepts of honor in favor of private notions of integrity smacks of individualism, not of submission to authority. The novel is not as anticlerical as *Lazarillo*, but Christianity is hardly shown the respect a convert would give it. A Franciscan monk gives the lad food and comfort after he is spurned by some Spanish merchants, but this looks less like an example of Christian charity than another lesson in the contradiction between appearance and reality: the men who spurn him "had the *appearance* of being rich merchants" while the poor monk "himself *appeared* to want assistance" (130–31, my italics). A cardinal takes pity on Guzman and hires him as a page, but treats him more like a jester than a soul to be saved, and Guzman's greatest scam is carried out while impersonating a young abbé, with all the egotism and vanity he had seen in them while in Rome. The church, the law, and the nobility are invariably exposed as corrupt; only particular individuals

---

71 Yes, says Alexander A. Parker in his well-informed study of the picaresque novel, *Literature and the Delinquent*. He argues Guzman represents Original Sin-stained humanity and that his tribulations "may well be symbolical of mankind's spiritual odyssey" (40), which would limit the novel's interest to reactionary Catholics. (He also regards *Guzman* as the first true picaresque, and *Lazarillo* merely a "precursor.") Others, like Richard Bjornson in *The Picaresque Hero in European Fiction*, consider *Guzman* more a defense of *conversos*. (Bjornson provides helpful maps of the protagonists' travels in both *Lazarillo* and *Guzman*.)

emerge as decent. Like *Lazarillo*, *Guzman* is as much about a broken social system as it is about the scoundrels suffering at the bottom of that system. "Are we then among barbarians here?" Guzman asks his lawyer of Catholic Italy. "'Among barbarians,' he replied, 'the laws of nature at least are followed, whereas none are observed at Bologna'" (327–28).

While Guzman often suffers at the hands of corrupt magistrates and lawyers, this particular lawyer is decent, as is the generous Franciscan monk and the cardinal. Individuals — not institutions or professions — alone are worthy of respect, Guzman learns, and long before he vows to reform himself he demonstrates he is among these decent individuals: he is robbed by a gang of thieves in Rome, but when he catches up with them, he decides to make one of them his friend, a fellow rogue named Sayavedra, forgiving his trespasses, undeceived by appearances for once, and refusing to betray him when his case finally comes to trial. They remain fast friends until Sayavedra dies in a storm while they are returning to Spain, but they are criminals in the eyes of the law and church, complicating any urge to put a Christian spin on Guzman's charitable friendship.

Alemán warns the reader in his introduction that he won't be telling the whole truth: he intends to pass over some things, overemphasize others, and fabricate still others. As to how to read his novel, he tells the story of a noble-man who commissioned two artists to paint portraits of his two favorite horses; the first paints an excellent rendition of the horse, but leaves the background vague; the other doesn't do as well with the horse itself,

> but, as a recompense, he ornamented the top of his picture with trees, clouds, admirable prospects, and ruined edifices; and at the bottom he depicted a landscape full of shrubs, meadows, and ravines. In another place might be seen the trunk of a tree from which depended a horse's harness, and at the foot a Turkish saddle, so well represented that art could go no farther. (2)

The nobleman rewards the first, but the other painter, "for having done more than was required of him, was not paid for his trouble" (3). Alemán is the second painter, leaving Guzman ambiguously indistinct but filling his broad canvas with so many colorful details about life in Spain and Italy during the second half of the 16th century and digressions on all manner of topics that it is easy to lose sight of the ostensible Christian moral of the story. More likely, the author, like his tricky protagonist, is distracting our attention the better to pull off his scam, complicating our response to his novel, confounding any easy interpretation. As Rabelais did in his preface, Alemán offers the reader two ways of looking at his novel: you can look at the horse — a Christian con-version story — or at the background: a scathing indictment of the Spanish "Golden Age," inherently as phony as the gilt copper chain that Guzman passes off as pure gold to his relatives (367). Once he fooled the authorities, the rogue Alemán was off for Mexico, putting an entire ocean between him and the apartheid Catholic nation that persecuted his ancestors and made him ashamed of his own heritage. He never came back.

Guzman of Alfarache was an enormous success, running through two dozen editions by the time its author left for Mexico, to be followed by translations into all major European languages, even Latin. One reader who took careful note of the novel's popularity was 52-year-old Miguel de Cervantes. He had written nothing of substance after *Galatea* in 1585, but Alemán's success encouraged him to try his hand at another novel: not a copycat picaresque — a writer named José Martí published a sequel to *Guzman* in 1604 before Alemán could finish his own continuation — and not another pastoral romance, but something different for the new century, something novel.

RENAISSANCE FRENCH FICTION

While other French writers in the 15th century were still producing medieval tales of Charlemagne, one Frenchman decided — like Martorell down in Catalonia — to modernize the chivalric novel. Straddling the Middle Ages and Renaissance like *Tirant lo Blanc* is a 300-page novel by Antoine de La Sale (c. 1386–1462) entitled *Little John of Saintré* (*Le petite Jehan de Saintré*, 1455). It belongs to the genre of education novel, which began with Xenophon's *Cyropaedia*, is parodied in the education of the giants in the first two books of Rabelais's *Gargantua and Pantagruel*, and expanded in France during the 18th century with novels like Fénelon's *Telemachus* and Rousseau's *Julie* and *Emile*. La Sale was a tutor to French aristocracy and in *Little John* describes the education of an ideal knight. At age 13, young John catches the eye of a young widow known only as My Lady; after her husband's death, she decided to remain single, "perchance in the intent to be like to the faithful widows of aforetime, whereof the Roman histories, which are the worthiest of all, make such glorious mention,"[72] a statement that later turns out to be mordantly ironic. Both John and My Lady are attached to the court of King John II of France (reigned 1350–64), and My Lady decides to sponsor John and help him rise through the ranks from page to squire, chamberlain, and valiant knight-errant. She helps him financially, tutors him in theology as well as court manners, and encourages him when older to go on adventures to prove his worth, acting like a cross between mentor and stage mother. For reasons of her own, My Lady keeps all this secret from the rest of the court,

---

72 Chap. 2 in Irvine Gray's 1931 translation, hereafter cited by chapter. Unfortunately, he thought he was doing the novel a favor by giving it "an archaic flavor" with pseudo-15th-century English.

seeking clandestine meetings with her young friend at night to celebrate his progress. (Her signal to him that she wants to rendezvous is to clean her teeth with a toothpick.) We're told they exchange kisses at these meetings, but it's unclear whether they go further than that, partly due to La Sale's Icelandic reserve and party thanks to the translator's archaic language. ("Then to kissing and kissing again, and playing and sporting at such plays and disports as the god of love bade them" [66].) This goes on for 16 years until John is nearly 30 and My Lady *d'un certain âge*, as the French gallantly say. She is enormously proud of him and seems to be deeply in love with him as well, and John — Lancelot to her Guinevere — does her proud and loves her even more.

The first three-fourths of the novel is a pleasant, rather predictable tale of John's progress, and the reader learns much about court life in the 15th century. (Though the novel is set in the mid-1300s and is based on historical figures, La Sale describes his own time a century later.) My Lady has some interiority, but John is all surface, like Galahad in the *Lancelot-Grail*, following the program without a murmur. There's almost no dramatic tension: though John is overmatched in his first few tournaments, he predictably wins every one, and even the tournaments are rather mild, more like officiated fencing matches than the brutal encounters in Arthurian fiction. But then at chapter 65, the novel makes an abrupt turn, leaving the dirt path of the Middle Ages for the stone-paved road of the Renaissance.

John realizes he has never undertaken a deed of arms on his own, but always at the prompting of My Lady, and so sends challenges to the courts of Rome and England. Both My Lady and the king are sorely wroth at his initiative, My Lady so much so that she sickens of grief and worry after he departs and decides to go to her country estate to recuperate. At her local church there, she runs into the new abbot, "who was of the age of five-and-twenty years, stout of body, strong and lusty; at wrestling, leaping, tossing the bar or the weight, or playing at tennis, in his leisure time, there was neither monk, knight, squire, nor townsman that could match him" (69). My Lady — a noble, intelligent, sympathetic character until this point — falls immediately for this lusty clergyman and they begin an affair; La Sale isn't as forthright as Boccaccio or Aretino, but the couple is clearly living out one of their bawdy tales. After John returns (triumphantly, of course) from his adventures and learns to his disappointment that My Lady is out in the country, he goes to visit her to share his good fortune, for Little John the page is now the Seigneur de Saintré. In a scene that is shocking because of the genteel respectability of the novel until then, My Lady coldly spurns him, flirts openly with the abbot in front of John, and lets the abbot humiliate him both verbally and in an impromptu wrestling match. La Sale gives no explanation for My Lady's change of heart, but his crack at the beginning about faithful Roman widows now makes sense, and this older woman's original interest in an underage boy now seems more predatory than pedagogical. The reader also remembers that she harshly condemned six of the Seven Deadly Sins during her theological lecture, but downplayed the sin of lust. And that signal: a phallic toothpick — after all, he is *Little* John — playing about her mouth? *Mais oui.* The novel suddenly has tension, psychological depth, barbed dialogue, unpredictability.

Though shocked and hurt at My Lady's actions, and deeply insulted by the abbot's disparaging remarks about knights, John remains cool — her lessons in conduct were not lost on him — and invites the couple and their entourage to his lodgings for dinner the next day, where he plots a satisfying revenge. After feeding them, he loans the abbot a suit of armor and suggests a rematch, to which the vain clergyman foolishly agrees. As a trained knight John easily defeats him and is on the verge of killing him when he remembers My Lady's teachings from the Bible, and instead merely stabs his tongue through his cheeks. He then lets My Lady have it with a volley of insults, grabs her and nearly smacks her, but desists and only strips her of a blue sash (here called a girdle), for "the color blue doth signify loyalty," he tells her, "and you are the most unloyal: verily you shall wear it no more" (82). He returns to court and leaves the couple behind, who feel no remorse, and in fact "who for the space of two months more took their pleasure together, as well as ever they had done, or better" (83).

Then La Sale delivers the coup de grâce. John says nothing about My Lady at court, and when she finally returns at the queen's insistence, John tells a story to the assembled court in her presence. Pretending that he is relating the contents of a letter from Germany, he gives a capsule version of their entire relationship, concluding with the violent revenge taken against her. He asks the ladies of the court their opinion of the unfaithful widow, and each one condemns her roundly. When he reaches My Lady and asks her opinion of the story, she says stiffly, "Sith that I must speak, I say that this lover, be he knight or squire, was passing discourteous to have ungirded the Lady and borne away her girdle, as you did say" (86). That's brilliant, perfectly capturing in one sentence the impregnable egotism of people who never feel at fault, never admit they're wrong, and even consider themselves the victim in tragedies they create. You know the type. Having given her this chance to admit her guilt, he produces the blue girdle and exposes her in front of the court, who now realize My Lady was the faithless widow of John's story; "and no need to ask if she was shamed: certes she would fain have been far away overseas; and there lost she all joy and honour" (86). John, thanks to My Lady's early training, ends his days as one of the noblest knights of his age, but not before learning one final paradoxical lesson: a person can be simultaneously a good teacher and a bad person. What starts like a late Arthurian romance ends like an early modern novel of psychological insight and understated irony. It's a valuable record of courtly life during the waning of the Middle Ages but also points the way of future French fiction, and for that reason *Little John of Saintré* is considered an important milestone in the development of the French novel.

One curious formal device in La Sale's novel is the inclusion of many lists — of books My Lady wants John to read, of gifts, of nobles going to war — which is about the only thing it has in common with the greatest novel of the French Renaissance, and one of the greatest of world literature, François Rabelais's *Gargantua and Pantagruel*.[73] Taking note of the brisk sales of an anonymous chapbook about a giant entitled *The Great Chronicles of Gargantua*, this priest-turned-physician (1483?–1553) decided to cash in on its popularity by writing a sequel called *Pantagruel* (1532?), a short novel about the giant's son. It sold well enough to inspire him to write his own version of that original chapbook, published as *Gargantua* in 1534. (Though written second, it is usually placed first in the completed work.) A dozen years passed before he resumed the story with the unimaginatively titled *Third Book* in 1546. This was followed by *The Fourth Book* in 1552, published the year before his death. In 1564 there appeared *The Fifth Book*, allegedly worked up from Rabelais's drafts and notes (which don't survive) by an anonymous but empathetic author, perhaps Jean Turquet. Together, the five sections make up an outrageous, encyclopedic, 800-page novel unlike anything that had preceded it.

The plot is episodic, improvised, full of inconsistencies, but it doesn't matter; it's merely a rickety stage for Rabelais's burlesque revue of linguistic

---

73 Unlike most of the novels I've been discussing, there are several English translations of this novel to choose from, though none is ideal. The early translation begun by Sir Thomas Urquhart and completed after his death by Peter Motteux is an exuberant masterpiece of 17th-century prose, but they took too many liberties with the text and made too many mistakes. W. F. Smith's 1893 translation, on the other hand, stuck *too* closely to the original, rendering it obscure and convoluted. Samuel Putnam produced a readable, extensively annotated edition in 1929 that unfortunately was never reprinted; selections from it were published in *The Portable Rabelais* (1946), but that too is out of print. Jacques Leclercq's Modern Library translation (1936) — the one I read in my twenties — is excellent but inserts too much explanatory matter into the text, misrepresenting Rabelais's style and making him sound like a pedantic village explainer. J. M. Cohen's 1955 translation for Penguin is also excellent, though specialists have noted some errors, and his edition contains only a pattering of little footnotes. (Great introduction, though.) Same with Burton Raffel's 1990 version: lively, reads well, but even fewer footnotes (and a negligible introduction). Donald Frame's 1991 edition is admirable (though not entirely free from errors, typos, and poor word choices), with the extensive notes Rabelais demands for any but the most superficial reading; but the style is often pedestrian rather than fleet, flat instead of bubbly, like a society dance band trying to play rock 'n' roll. (In Frame's defense, he died before he could see the book through the press, depriving him of time for a final polish.) M. A. Screech's recent Penguin translation (2006) is the most accurate and complete, but it switches the traditional order of the first two books, and the scholarly apparatus is obtrusive. But since it is the most faithful, I'll be citing it by page number, followed by the traditional book/ chapter divisions for ease of reference to other editions.

performances, a makeshift platform for his humanistic philosophy. The story seems simple enough: Gargantua is the boisterous offspring of the giant Grandgousier and his wife Gargamelle; after a wild youth he becomes a great scholar in Paris, then is called home to help his father defend his country from an invasion. He is aided in the battle by a colorful, motormouthed monk named Jean, whom he rewards afterward by building him an abbey called Thélème ("Will") — Rabelais's vision of a humanist paradise — whose motto is "Do What You Will." Gargantua later marries and begets Pantagruel ("All thirst"), a giant who likewise becomes a wise scholar, makes a great friend in the raffish, irrepressible Panurge ("All will"), and is called upon by his father to voyage to his mother's land of Utopia to defend it from an invading army.[74] Like the father, the son is successful in war as well as learning. The rest of the novel is largely concerned with Panurge's indecision whether to marry or not; after consulting all sorts of authorities without receiving a satisfactory answer, Panurge talks Pantagruel and others into voyaging to India to consult the Oracle of the Holy Bottle, where, after many bizarre adventures, he finally receives an answer: "Drink!" And with that ambiguous response, the novel ends.

On the surface, *Gargantua and Pantagruel* seems like merely a long cock-and-bull story, the only theme Pantagruel's laid-back approach to life: "He took everything in good part: every deed he interpreted favorably. He never tormented himself: he never took offence" (418/3.2). And even at the surface level the reader is dazzled by a carnival of literary forms, parodies of genres, and novelties. There is a poem with words missing because rats and moths have nibbled them away; a chapter consisting entirely of drunken dialogue; genealogies; farcical essays on various topics; formal letters and orations; typographical high jinks; songs and riddles; debates in pantomime; a legal case given in gobbledygook; prose translations of narrative paintings; and numerous surrealistic flights of fancy. One character speaks in an almost unintelligible Latinized French,[75] while Panurge introduces himself in 13 different languages. There is a chapter of dialogue in which each new line echoes the concluding syllables of the last, a philosophical exchange in imitation of a Platonic dialogue, a four-chapter parody of legal proceedings, choked with Latin citations, a dialogic chapter in which a monk answers his interlocutor only with monosyllables, and a poem in the shape of a wine bottle. There are ludicrous variants of the bildungsroman, the war narrative, utopian fiction, the daring escape story, the infernal descent, the animal fable, and the

---

74 Rabelais borrowed the country from Sir Thomas More's *Utopia* (1516), but while the Englishman's imaginary land is set off the coast of South America, the Frenchman's is apparently off the eastern coast of Africa.

75 It closely resembles Colonna's Latinized/Hellenized Italian. Rabelais read the French translation of the *Hypnerotomachia* that appeared in 1546, too late to have suggested the episode here (34–36/2.6) but in time for the architectural wonders in books 4 and 5.

fantastic voyage. And *lists!* There are long lists and catalogs of giants, games, books, the contents of Panurge's pockets, methods for reading invisible writing, famous heroes doing menial labor in Hell, hot mineral baths in France and Italy, methods of divination, slangy epithets, noble attributes (of a fool), the botanical properties of the fictitious herb Pantagruelion, ludicrous deaths, anatomical similes, cooks' nicknames, food offerings to a god, venomous creatures, and of dishes served at a banquet and of the dances that followed — many of which go on for pages and/or are printed in two or three columns. And the *language!* Rabelais employs every style from the most formal to the most obscene, incongruously mixing registers high and low, delighting in puns and neologisms, a racy rhetoric at once earthy and erudite that gleefully violates virtually every stricture in Strunk and White's *Elements of Style*. Here, for example, is how the monk Jean responds to Panurge's question whether he should get married or not:

> "Get yourself married, for the devil's sake; get yourself married, and ring me a double carillon with your balls. As soon as you can, I say, and I mean it. The evening of this very day order the banns and the bedstead! Mighty God! What are you keeping yourself for? Don't you know that the end of the world's drawing nigh? We're nearer to it by two poles and one yard than we were yesterday. Antichrist has already been born, so they tell me. True, he is still only pawing at his nurse and his governesses, for he's but a toddler and has yet to display his riches. As long as a sack of corn costs less than three silver patacoons, and a cask of wine but six copper blanks, *Go forth — we that live — and multiply*. Scripture that is: Breviary stuff. In the Day of Judgement, *when He shall come to judge*, do you really want them to find you with your balls full?" (511–12/3.26)

The monk speaks like both a priest and a peasant, punching out alliteration (balls, banns, bedstead), mixing up measurements for time and space, mangling Scripture, and tossing in for good measure an obscure literary allusion that would have been puzzling even in Rabelais's day. (Frame: "The poet Eustache Deschamps [1346–1406], in his 'Ballade d'Antichrist,' wrote that the Antichrist, on coming, will enjoy Solomon's treasures" [853].) This playful, self-consciously literary language is what the adjective "Rabelaisian" *should* mean (as opposed to merely "bawdy"); as J. M. Cohen writes in the introduction to his translation: "it should be made to denote the writer who is in love with his medium, the man for whom words call up associations, in contrast to the man who employs them to express previously conceived notions" (17). With the motto "Do What You Will," Rabelais gave himself permission to do anything he damn well pleased with the language and the form of the novel; as a result, every author of an innovative novel mixing literary forms and genres in an extravagant style is indebted to Rabelais, directly or indirectly. Out of his codpiece came Aneau's *Alector*, Nashe's

Unfortunate Traveller, López de Úbeda's *Justina*, Cervantes' *Don Quixote*, Béroalde de Verville's *Fantastic Tales*, Sorel's *Francion*, Burton's *Anatomy*, Swift's *Tale of a Tub* and *Gulliver's Travels*, Fielding's *Tom Jones*, Amory's *John Buncle*, Sterne's *Tristram Shandy*, the novels of Diderot and maybe Voltaire (a late convert), Smollet's *Adventures of an Atom*, Hoffmann's *Tomcat Murr*, Hugo's *Hunchback of Notre-Dame*, Southey's *Doctor*, Melville's *Moby-Dick*, Flaubert's *Temptation of Saint Anthony* and *Bouvard and Pecuchet*, Twain's *Adventures of Huckleberry Finn*, Frederick Rolfe's ornate novels, Bely's *Petersburg*, Joyce's *Ulysses*,[76] Witkiewicz's *Insatiability*, Barnes's *Ryder* and *Ladies Almanack*, Gombrowicz's Polish jokes, Flann O'Brien's Irish farces, Philip Wylie's *Finnley Wren*, Patchen's tender novels, Burroughs's and Kerouac's mad ones,[77] Nabokov's later works, Schmidt's fiction, the novels of Durrell, Burgess (especially *A Clockwork Orange* and *Earthly Powers*), Gaddis and Pynchon, Barth, Coover, Sorrentino, Reed's *Mumbo Jumbo*, Brossard's later works, the masterpieces of Latin American magic realism (*Paradiso*, *The Autumn of the Patriarch*, *Three Trapped Tigers*, *I the Supreme*, *Avalovara*, *Terra Nostra*, *Palinuro of Mexico*),[78] the fabulous creations of those gay Cubans Severo Sarduy and Reinaldo Arenas, Markson's *Springer's Progress*, Mano's *Take Five*, Ríos's *Larva* and *otros libros*, the novels of Paul West, Tom Robbins, Stanley Elkin, Alexander Theroux, W. M. Spackman, Alasdair Gray, Gaétan Soucy, and Rikki Ducornet ("Lady Rabelais," as one critic called her), Mark Leyner's hyperbolic novels,[79] the writings of Magister Gass, Greer Gilman's folkloric fictions and Roger Boylan's Celtic comedies, Vollmann's voluminous volumes, Wallace's brainy fictions, Siegel's *Love in a Dead Language*, Danielewski's novels, Jackson's *Half Life*, Field's *Ululu*, De La Pava's *Naked Singularity*, and James McCourt's ongoing Mawrdew Czgowchwz saga.

If *Gargantua and Pantagruel* were no more than a linguistic Godzilla that bestrode the Renaissance and spawned a boisterous line of descendants including some of the greatest novels ever written (as well as some criminally neglected ones), that would be enough to assure its historical importance. But there's much more to it. *Gargantua and Pantagruel* is above all a gonzo study in hermeneutics — that is, the art of interpretation, chiefly of texts, but by extension, of all phenomena. During the Renaissance, everything was being

76 Joyce said he never actually read Rabelais, only a book about his language, but he must have at least started it once because an incident in 1.6 (around page 20 in most translations) is quoted by Molly in her concluding monologue (18.488–90). Merely flipping through *Gargantua and Pantagruel* would have sufficed to inspire Joyce's use of different genres, styles, and catalogs in *Ulysses*.

77 When Dean comes for Sal near the end of *On the Road*, "It was like the imminent arrival of Gargantua; preparations had to be made to widen the gutters of Denver and foreshorten certain laws to fit his suffering bulk and bursting ecstasies" (4.2, pp. 360–61 in *The Original Scroll*).

78 García Márquez once said, "The Latin American reality is totally Rabelaisian."

79 Come back to the raft ag'in, Mark honey, and quite writing those jokey doctor books.

reexamined and reinterpreted: the Bible, which led to the Reformation; celestial movements, which led to junking the Catholic-favored Ptolemaic system for the Copernican; geography, due to the voyages of exploration; the human body, which revolutionized medicine; and everyday life, the reinterpretation of which began the slow process of clearing away the cobwebs of folk beliefs, astrology, divination, religion, and other delusions and superstitions in favor of empirical scientific observation — a work still in progress, unfortunately.

The challenge of accurate interpretation, and the pitfalls of misinterpretation, is Rabelais's grand theme, announced at the very beginning in his prologue to *Gargantua* (pp. 205–8 in Screech's translation, book 1 in most others). Like Apuleius's announcement on the first page of *The Golden Ass* that his novel can be read on two levels, Rabelais addresses two audiences: the common reader can peruse his novel for enjoyment, but the sophisticated reader can study it for enlightenment.[80] He illustrates this with an anecdote about deceptive appearances: Socrates, like a Silenus (a little box decorated on the outside with playful figures of satyrs and flying goats, etc., but inside containing rare medicines), had a repulsive "external appearance . . . ever hiding his God-sent wisdom." He tells this anecdote so that readers of his own books don't "too readily conclude that nothing is treated inside save jests, idiocies and amusing fictions" — which is how most readers over the centuries have regarded Rabelais's work. "And even granted that you do find, in its literal meaning, plenty of merry topics entirely congruous with its name," he goes on to warn, "you must not be stayed there as by the Sirens' song but expound the higher meaning of what you had perhaps believed to have been written out of merriness of mind," a warning that has fallen on too many deaf ears. He boasts that his superficially funny book actually contains "hidden instruction which will reveal to you the highest hidden truths and the most awesome mysteries touching upon our religion as well as upon matters of state and family life." But then he turns on a centime and mocks those who find elaborate allegories in Homer's epics or try to prove that Ovid's *Metamorphoses* concerns "the mysteries of the Gospel," and claims that his "merry new Chronicles" have no allegorical meanings. The canny doctor uses these reversals to prepare the reader, hinting that his work does indeed have depths, but that it can't be interpreted any which way; he is also protecting himself in case his satires rub the authorities the wrong way, for people were still being burned at the stake in his day for expressing countercultural opinions. (The book was added to the Index in 1564 and Rabelais headed the list of "heretics of the first class." Luckily he was dead by then.)

---

80 Apuleius is named in *Gargantua and Pantagruel* and is an obvious influence. Among other ancient novels, Lucian's *True History* was a major inspiration for the fantastic voyage in books 4 and 5, and Pantagruel is depicted holding a copy of Heliodorus's *Ethiopian Story* in 4.63. (A French translation was published in 1547, if Rabelais didn't already know the Greek original.)

Thus alerted, the careful reader will proceed with caution, assuming Rabelais's wild tales allude to philosophical issues and current events in France, but careful not to misinterpret them.[81] Rabelais tests his readers as early as the second chapter, entitled "The Antidoted Bubbles" in Screech's translation, which consists of a four-page prophetic poem à la Nostradamus that is impossible to interpret (though that hasn't prevented some from trying). Many chapters in books 1 and 2 are dramatizations of acts of interpretation — of legal cases, of color symbolism, of pantomimes — and book 3 is entirely about hermeneutics. Wanting to know if his marriage will turn out bad, Panurge employs every means of divination available and consults with all manner of advisors and fortune-tellers; everyone and everything predicts he will be cuckolded, but he consistently (and comically) insists on reinterpreting the prophecies in his favor, like those 16th-century astronomers who came up with increasingly elaborate Rube Goldberg models for the Ptolemaic system because they couldn't accept the more accurate Copernican explanation (and its implied repudiation of the biblical worldview). Books 4 and 5 concern Panurge's trip to the Oracle of the Holy Bottle, and the novel ends as he and the others dispute the interpretation of the oracle's puzzling answer. While reading *Gargantua and Pantagruel*, we are being entertained on one level, but tested on another on our ability to interpret texts like this one, and by extension, all phenomena. Test results vary: many have failed to see anything in Rabelais's novel beyond tall tales and scatological jokes, while others have misinterpreted Rabelais as a heretic or an atheist, a radical occultist or a babbling drunk.

"Drink!" the oracle says. Bacbuc, the priestess who presides over the oracle, tells Panurge that drinking wine is a metaphor for seeking truth — over the shrine is a Greek inscription that translates "In wine there is truth" — and that each person is responsible for deciding what is truth. This represents a daring rejection of authority, both divine and secular, and acceptance of full responsibility for one's actions and morality — too great a responsibility for most people, who would rather let others (the church, the state, the community) tell them how to live. The denizens of the abbey of Thélème exemplify the happy few capable of taking on that responsibility and relying on their own moral compass. One might say, with Bakhtin, that Rabelais's elite "builds its own world versus the official world, its own church versus the official church,

---

81 This didn't work, of course, and in fact Rabelais was so disgusted with misinterpretations of his work that he planned to abandon the novel after book 3. His critics accused him of various heresies, but he insisted this was not the case "unless by perversely inferring, against all rational and routine linguistic usage, things I would never have allowed to enter my mind . . ." (642/prefatory letter to book 4). But of course Rabelais doesn't adhere to "rational and routine linguistic usage." Less convincingly, he claims some of the alleged heresies are the result of typos, "an N for an M through the compositor's misprint and carelessness" (643), as in one instance *asne* (ass) for *âme* (soul).

its own state versus the official state."[82] "Do what you will" is not a license to run wild or to indulge oneself at the expense of others.[83] As Pantagruel tells Panurge on several occasions, first he must identify the nature of his will — the self he is intended to be, not the person others expect him to be — and then develop that self. "Are you not sure of your will?" Pantagruel asks him at the beginning of Panurge's quest (416/3.10), and at the end advises him to follow "what your mind tells you to do" (1014/5.46). Not what the Church tells him to do, or the State, or classical authors; Rabelais razes those authorities with his relentless satire. Although he doesn't reject the basic tenets of Christianity, Rabelais mocks both Catholics and nascent Protestants, takes the usual pot shots at gluttonous monks and wayward nuns, and derides most theological re-/misinterpretations of the Bible. The library at Saint Victor's abbey in Paris (39–44/2.7) is filled with ludicrous theological treatises like *The Preachers' Fox-tail Duster*, *The Testes of Theology*, *The Crucible of Cuntemplation* [*sic*], *The Bagpipes of Prelates*, Bishop Boudarinus's *Nine Enneads on Profits to Be Milked from Indulgences, with a Papal Privilege for Precisely Three Years*, *The Theologians' Cat-door*, *The Manacles of Devotion*, and Magister Noster Fripesauce's *On Finely Sifting the Canonical Hours* (in 40 volumes), among others — many based on real books by theologians. Politics and warfare are belittled by way of the ludicrous conflicts throughout *Gargantua and Pantagruel*, and the laws by which the State exercises its authority are exposed as scams run by judges and lawyers drunk with greed and power. Even the authority of classical writers like Plato, Aristotle, Ovid, Pliny, and others is undermined when their various misinterpretations of natural phenomena are cited to verify the bizarre sights seen during the fantastic voyage in books 4 and 5. Who's left to provide guidance? On several occasions Rabelais sneaks in a line from Romans 14:5, "Let each one be convinced in his own mind," to suggest all authorities are suspect and that each individual is ultimately responsible for his or her interpretation of the world. "Rabelais's basic goal was to destroy the official picture of events," Bakhtin writes (439), which leaves it up to the individual to construct a new, more accurate one. This calls for drinking in vast quantities of knowledge (the wine metaphor the priestess used)[84] and then interpreting it all as carefully as possible without recourse to received opinion. Such radical individualism is a momentous departure from the tradition-bound Old World and the first step toward the New World of

---

82 *Rabelais and His World*, 88. Or one might say, with Bob Dylan, "To live outside the law you must be honest" ("Absolutely Sweet Marie").

83 Magician Aleister Crowley adopted his motto "Do What Thou Wilt" from Rabelais and founded his own Thelemic abbey in Sicily, where he could indulge in lots of sex and drugs with his disciples.

84 For the numerous symbolic meanings of wine in *Gargantua and Pantagruel*, see Weinberg's *The Wine and the Will*, and to see how deeply Rabelais himself drank of the wine of knowledge, see Screech's *Rabelais*.

modernism and, eventually, postmodern relativism. We never learn whether Panurge finds a wife; he now has bigger problems, greater responsibilities: to encounter for the first time the reality of experience and to forge in the smithy of his soul an authentic self, and to remain true to that self despite the nets flung at him by the church, the state, and tradition.

Rabelais's symbolism and erudite allusions are complex enough to admit other interpretations; the more time one spends unpacking that symbolism and tracing those allusions, the more profound the novel becomes. All the dick jokes and farting donkeys fade into insignificance for the attentive reader, but the surface risibility and its *toujours gai* attitude prevented *Gargantua and Pantagruel* from being taken seriously by most readers for centuries, for much the same reason that literary but comedic literature today is undervalued by those who feel that only serious fiction on serious themes qualifies as great literature. P. G. Wodehouse often mocked the kind of novel in which a Russian peasant spends 300 pages bemoaning his miserable life before hanging himself, and yet such novels, not those like his own highly wrought works, usually get the respectful reviews and win the prizes.[85] As the Rabelaisian Tom Robbins writes (another gifted novelist spurned by the literary establishment because of his ludic style), "the notion that inspired play (even when audacious, offensive, or obscene) enhances rather than diminishes intellectual rigor and spiritual fulfillment; the notion that in the eyes of the gods the tight-lipped hero and the wet-cheeked victim are frequently inferior to the red-nosed clown, such notions are destined to be a hard sell to those who have E. M. Forster on their bedside table and a clump of dried narcissus up their ass" (*Wild Ducks*, 187). For this reason, what Bakhtin wrote 70 years ago is even more true today: "Of all great writers of world literature, Rabelais is the least popular, the least understood and appreciated" (1).

Rabelais's world is a man's world; aside from Gargantua's mother and the priestess Bacbuc, the women in his novel are mostly anonymous butts of sexual jokes. Whenever an accounting is given of people involved in some event, Rabelais always adds a pointedly dismissive parenthetical aside like "(not counting the women and little children)." There are some ladies at the ideal abbey of Thélème, but for the most part, women literally don't count. But several female French writers of this period objected to that official picture of their status and started giving their side of the story, which came to be called the *querelle des femmes* (the women question: equal to men or inferior?). Christine de Pisan wrote a prose work (not really a novel) entitled *The Book of the City of Ladies* (1405) in defense of women to counter the widespread misogyny of the time. The first female French novelist appears to be Marguerite Briet (c. 1515–50), who under the pseudonym Hélisenne de

---

85 Wodehouse's novels are filled with fictitious examples of such dour fare: *Offal* by Stultitia Bodwin, *Deadly Earnest* by Adela Bristow, *Songs of Squalor* by Ralston McTodd.

Crenne published the earliest "sentimental" novel in French literature, *The Torments of Love* (*Les Angoysses douloureuses qui precedent d'amours*, 1538). The novel of sentiment, which peaked in the 18th century, features tender souls discussing their feelings, at great length, rather than acting on them; in *The Torments of Love*, the two protagonists discuss their overpowering love for each other for 200 pages without so much as sharing a kiss.

Part 1 of the novel sounds very much like Boccaccio's *Elegy of Lady Fiammetta*, which our well-read author undoubtedly knew. As in that novel, the protagonist is both a participant in, and the future author of, a narrative larded with classical allusions. At age 11, an upper-class girl named Hélisenne is married "to a young gentleman whom I did not know" but whom she comes to love.[86] By 13 she has blossomed into a buxom beauty — in public, crowds actually form around her and praise her body — and she attracts the attention of a 21-year-old man-about-town named Guenelic. The feeling is more than mutual: Hélisenne is overcome with lust at the mere sight of Guenelic, for this novel is all about looking, gazing, visual appearances, "in accord with the nature of the feminine sex, which never gets enough of seeing and being seen" (1.2). As her body goes wild with increased levels of dopamine, testosterone, and especially norepinephrine — which not only strengthens the sex drive but also the memory, important for a budding writer like Hélisenne — and her defenses go down due to decreased activity in the amygdala (the part of your brain associated with fear) and lower levels of serotonin (which keeps us calm and content), she gets reckless and angers her husband with the obsessive attention she starts paying to Guenelic, seizing every opportunity to gaze at him. Knowing nothing of these mood-altering chemicals the body produces when sexually aroused, Briet paints a convincing picture of a young girl gone "boy-crazy." (We have to remember she's still only 13 at this point; Briet was in her twenties when she wrote the novel.) Hélisenne knows nothing about this handsome stranger — the few conversations they eventually have are just exchanges of platitudinous declarations of love and formulaic accusations of neglect — but that doesn't prevent her from throwing operatic tantrums (like Boccaccio's Fiammetta) until her long-suffering husband decides to send her to a castle in the country to cool off, where his harpy sister can keep an eye on her.

In part 2, Guenelic goes in search of her, accompanied by a dashing friend named Quezinstra, and they travel throughout the Mediterranean area performing chivalrous feats until they get word of Hélisenne's whereabouts at the beginning of part 3. Locating the castle, Guenelic climbs a ladder to

---

86 Cited by part and chapter (here, 1.1) in the Neal-Rendall translation. The translators are to be congratulated for faithfully reproducing Briet's erudite, Latinate style, more of which anon. Though the novel was published under the name Hélisenne de Crenne, I follow their example of using Briet for the author and Hélisenne for the character.

hold another stilted conversation with the imprisoned girl, telling her of their adventures, and together they concoct a plan for escape. No sooner do they make their escape than Hélisenne, pleading poor health, dies, but not before expressing her relief that they never actually had sex and advising her beloved to cleanse himself of "the poison of concupiscence" (3.8). Then Guenelic dies — whether from a broken heart or a lethal case of blue balls, we're not told — and Quezinstra concludes the novel by telling how Mercury came down from the heavens to spirit them away to the Greek Elysian Fields, and explaining how *The Torments of Love* came to be published: the manuscript of the book was at Héliesenne's side, so (like an agent) Mercury took it up to Olympus; after Minerva vetted it, Jupiter declared it worthy of being published. In Paris.

As ludicrous as that last bit sounds — reminiscent of the Akkadian Kabti-ilani-Marduk boasting that the gods *loved* his "Erra and Ishum" — it's only the last of many daring narrative choices Briet makes. Part 1 is narrated by Hélisenne, and was written just before her exile (she tells us) in the hope Guenelic would read it and understand how she feels. Instead, the narrative is intercepted by her evil sister-in-law and used against her. (A harsh critic would say it's Hélisenne's obstreperous prose style that justifies her imprisonment.) Part 2 is ostensibly narrated by Guenelic, but the half-title informs us it was "Composed by Lady Hélisenne, Speaking in the person of her beloved Guenelic"; it seems that in the 24 hours between the time Guenelic told her of his adventures and when they make their escape, the sickly girl wrote the 40,000-word narrative of his Mediterranean tour. Part 3 is likewise narrated by Guenelic, but since it includes an account of his and Hélisenne's death, its authorship is unclear. And then Quezinstra steps in with his mythological cadenza. Either this is a novice writer experiencing technical difficulties, or (as cotranslator Lisa Neal argues in her advocative introduction) a clever author deliberately forcing the reader to reevaluate the reliability of the various narratives. It could be that Guenelic told Hélisenne only the gist of his adventures, which she then elaborated by way of her readings of ancient Greek novels and Arthurian romances. (References in the text indicate Briet was well acquainted with such works, along with Boccaccio, Sylvius's *Tale of the Two Lovers*, La Sale's *Little John of Saintré*, and quite a bit more.) When Hélisenne's husband confiscates a copy of her letter to Guenelic in part 1 — that is, a first draft of the letter that appears in the novel — she insists that it "was composed only as an exercise and to avoid idleness" (1.11). The girl is lying in this instance, but in a larger sense *The Torments of Love* is not an autobiographical account (as its first readers, like her husband, assumed) but an elaborate literary "exercise" in which Briet appropriates older male models of fiction and makes them her own, "speaking in the person" of these forbearers. This would align her closer to 20th-century experimentalists like Kathy

Acker than to 18th-century sentimental novelists, and while I'm not entirely convinced that's what Briet was about, it's an intriguing notion to entertain.

To show she can write as well as the boys can — or as badly, in some cases — Briet concocted an elaborate, allusive style, deploying countless classical allusions along with (as Neal explains) "the use of semisynonymous qualifiers or 'doublets,' Latinate syntax, diction, and spelling, as well as frequent neologisms" (xxix). A typical sentence: "Then I was very frightened, and trembling and fear seized my heart not otherwise than does Zephyr when it blows upon the waves, or when it shakes the dry and sylvan herbage" (1.22). Addressed to female readers, she didn't try to write down to them, a compliment many of these "gracieuses Damoyselles" didn't appreciate, for a dozen years after the first edition appeared, a poet named Claude Colet was asked to edit a simpler version for female readers. In fact, one contemporary of hers named Etienne Pasquier claimed the unintelligible scholar spouting Latinate French in *Gargantua and Pantagruel* (2.6) is a parody of Briet.[87] Too often, her classical allusions are trite — "They fought so hard one might have imagined it was Hercules and Antaeus struggling against each other" (2.10) — and her style occasionally approaches self-parody, as when Quezinstra, speaking "with an eloquence equal to Cicero's," refers to "the exiguity, debility, and humbleness of my style" (2.10), the very diction mocking his claim. (Here, as when earlier in the same chapter Quezinstra's speech is said to have "exceeded Virgilian eloquence," it's possible Briet is mocking her classical models, not aspiring to them, but if so, she was kidding herself.) But writing like a man also allows Briet to make some unladylike observations. She's wise to the sexual symbolism of chivalric tournaments — "Some of the princes armed themselves to go joust; the new bridegroom refused to go along, for he was far more interested in the nocturnal joust" (2.11) — and engages in scholarly discussions of Neoplatonism and theology that were almost exclusively the province of men at the time. Though ostensibly written to warn female readers of the dangers of illicit love, *The Torments of Love* surreptitiously encourages them to crash the men's club of literary production.

Briet followed it a year later with a companion volume, *Personal and Invective Letters* (*Les Épistres familieres et invectives*, 1539), which is considered the first epistolary novel in French literature. It consists of 18 letters to a variety of correspondents — 13 personal, 5 invective — written by a Hélisenne who is and isn't the same character as the protagonist of *The Torments of Love*. Like a woman on the verge of a nervous breakdown, Hélisenne calmly dispenses good advice to troubled friends, playing Dear Abby with sententious reminders from Scripture and the classics, while repressing her own problems. In the first letter, she thanks an abbess for her recent stay at a convent and admits she's attracted to that life, a troubling admission from a young wife.

---

87 Cited in the Boni & Liveright edition of Rabelais, 252 n1.

Something is wrong with her marriage, but Hélisenne devotes her energy to advising others until, in the ninth letter, she has a change of heart and tells a female friend to go ahead and enjoy that illicit affair she had earlier advised against, and then admits in the tenth letter that she too has fallen in love with another man. When she writes to Quezinstra in letter 12, and then notes in the final personal letter that her husband has locked her up in a castle, we seem to be back in part 1 of *The Torments of Love*.

But in the five invective letters that follow, Hélisenne the author (rather than the character) defends the publication of the *Torments* against both her husband and the citizens of the town in which the novel was set, who feel she slandered their fair city. These final letters constitute a spirited defense of women in general and of a woman's right to practice literature, but their relationship to the quasifictitious material that precedes them is puzzling, and Hélisenne's repeated assertion that her erotic novel was written "only to pass the time" (letter 14) is hypocritical in light of her very real erotic torments. Nonetheless, the character development from conventional wife to fire-breathing feminist without any connective expository material is an impressive technical feat, and though some still had problems with her mannerist prose, the novella was another popular success.

Rabelais may have mocked Marguerite Briet but he admired Marguerite of Navarre, opening book 3 of *Gargantua and Pantagruel* with a poem dedicated to her. Born Marguerite d'Angoulême (1492–1549), the older sister of King François I of France, Marguerite was not only a patron of innovative writers like Rabelais but in her final years assembled a lengthy frame-novel that she called *Histoires des amans fortunez* (Tales of Fortunate Lovers) that came to be known as the *Heptameron*, published posthumously in 1559. Unfortunately, it was left unfinished — she intended it to contain 100 tales like the *Decameron* but didn't live to complete more than about 70 — and it's unclear whether Marguerite wrote the complete work herself or assembled it with the help of a few friends. To confuse matters further, the tales appear in different order in some surviving manuscripts, making it pointless to attempt the kind of structural analysis I performed on the *Decameron*. Nevertheless, the *Heptameron* is not only an assured, entertaining work but provides an instructive illustration of the transition from medieval tale to modern fiction.

The framing narrative is similar to that of the *Decameron*: five men and five women, all French aristocrats modeled on the author's acquaintances, take refuge in an abbey after a storm. Stuck there until the bridges can be repaired, one of the ladies, Parlamente (probably a stand-in for Marguerite herself), proposes passing the time as Boccaccio's characters did — art imitating not life but art — with the difference that the tales be based on true stories. (Scholars have verified that many of them are indeed based on historical circumstances.) Nearly all of the stories are about the sexual relations between men and women, with a large percentage dealing with the unromantic side: with rape, infidelity, the seduction of nuns and wives by monks (everyone in the Renaissance seems to have despised monks), loveless marriages, incest, and borderline necrophilia. The very first story, for example, concerns an adulterous wife who takes up with the bishop of Sées as well as a young stud named du Mesnil, whom she gets her clueless husband to kill after he poses a threat to her relationship with the bishop. In the second, a servant's lust for his employer's wife is thwarted, so he mortally wounds her and has sex with her dying body. (Because of stories like these, most editions of the *Heptameron* were expurgated until recently.) There's little of the joyful bawdiness of the *Decameron*, but plenty of instances of illicit relations, forced sex, frustrated passions, and the tension generated by the friction between the ideals of marriage and the realities of lust.

Where Marguerite also differs from her Italian model is in giving her narrators more space to discuss the tales; in fact, these discussions — some of them nearly as long as the tales they follow — may be the most appealing aspect of the novel for contemporary readers. Like some reading groups today, they discuss not the artistry or technical aspects of the tales but the validity of the characters' actions, and how they themselves would have acted in similar circumstances. Each of these interludes is a battle between the sexes as the men and women argue about the way lovers treat each other, about the social codes they're expected to follow, and even the lies they tell each other. They are remarkably frank, the men in some cases defending the use of rape and the women justifying the dissembling and stalling tactics they use against their suitors. Here's a typical exchange, worth quoting at length; the first speaker, Hircan, is thought be to be modeled on Marguerite's husband, Henri de Navarre; he is addressing the female narrator of a tale about an adulterous wife:

> "It seems to me, Longarine," said Hircan, "that this lady you've told us about was moved more by resentment than by love, because if she'd loved the young gentleman as much as she pretended, she wouldn't have left him for another man. It follows that she could reasonably be said to be resentful, bitter, vindictive, stubborn and fickle!"
>
> "It's easy for you to talk," said Ennasuite [a woman], "but you don't know how heartrending it is to love without having your love returned."
>
> "True," he replied, "because the moment a lady starts to be in the slightest way cold to me, I forget all about love and all about her as well!"
>
> "That may well be so," said Parlamente [Hircan's wife, recall], "for you. All you care about is your own pleasure. But an honest woman shouldn't leave her husband in that fashion."
>
> "However," said Simontaut [♂], "the woman in the story completely forgot she was a woman for a while, for even a man could not have taken his revenge so well!"

"Because one woman is not virtuous," said Oiselle [♀], "one should not think that all others are like her."

"All the same," said Saffredent [♂], "you *are* all women. You can cover yourselves up becomingly with all the finery you like, but the fact remains that anyone who looks carefully underneath all those skirts will find that you *are* all women!"[88]

How modern does that sound? The tonal contrast between the tales themselves — narrated in straightforward chronicle fashion — and these snappy exchanges displays an evolutionary leap from old tales to new fiction; it's like watching a caterpillar turn into a butterfly. In another of the tales, the narrator demurs, "I shall not try to describe Amador's feelings as he listened to these words. It would be impossible to set such anguish down in writing" (1.10). Impossible for the old storytellers, perhaps, but not for the new novelists like Marguerite Briet, eager to "set such anguish down in writing."

Hardly worth mentioning, except for its popularity and influence on English literature, is *The Wandering Knight* (*Le Voyage du Chevalier errant*, 1557) by a Carmelite prior and scholar named Jean de Cartigny (1520?–78). Based on the Parable of the Prodigal Son (Luke 15:11–32), the short novel is a by-the-numbers allegory about a young man who is tempted by his governess Folly to indulge in worldly pleasures until he sees the error of his ways and devotes himself to stringent Catholic dogma. In the preface, the author gives the plot away, so there's no dramatic tension, just clichéd encounters with personifications of the Seven Deadly Sins and other concepts. It was translated into English in 1581 and reprinted frequently thereafter. Edmund Spenser drew upon it for the first book of *The Faerie Queen*, and it used to be considered an influence on John Bunyan's *Pilgrim's Progress*, but not so much anymore. There's nothing original about Cartigny's preachy novel; it is clearly indebted to similar, earlier works by Guillaume Deguileville and Bernard of Clairvaux. The most interesting chapter (1.5) is also the longest, during which Folly retells the history of the world. Like Lucifer in the Rolling Stones' "Sympathy for the Devil," she was present at all catastrophes since the beginning of the world, governess to every sinner and tyrant from Adam on. The chapter shows off Cartigny's wide if indiscriminate reading, a farrago of bad history, mythology, and Catholic doctrine.

A more intriguing farrago is Barthélemy Aneau's *Alector, or The Cock* (1560). As with *Perceforest* in the last chapter, I'm hobbled by the lack of a modern English translation and will have to rely on secondary sources.[89]

---

88 Conclusion of day 2, tale 15, in Paul Chilton's unexpurgated translation.
89 There is an anonymous English translation from 1590, but trying to read a scratchy microfilm of this book printed in a cramped, black-letter font with Elizabethan orthography was too much for me. My sources are three reviews of Marie-Madeleine Fontaine's recent critical edition of *Alector ou Le Coq* (1996) — Tom Conley's in *Renaissance Quarterly* 50.1 (Spring 1997): 253–54; Barbara C. Bowen's in *Sixteenth Century Journal* 28.3 (Fall

Annoyed by the popular success of the 1540 French translation of *Amadis of Gaul* and especially with the feeble sequels and imitations that followed, Aneau (c. 1510–61) — a serious humanist and author of a legal book published in 1554 — sought to rehabilitate a genre that had previously been "the privileged expression of a cultural elite in twelfth-century courtly society" (Krause 45). That is, he wanted to turn entertainment back into art. The result is an outlandishly erudite and bizarre work, a "proto-Freudian rebus-text that analyzes its own enigmatic form" (Conley), "combining the model of Lucianic dialogue with a multi-layered narrative structure" (Bamforth). Barbara Bowen describes the plot as

> an incredible saga in twenty-six chapters of the adventures of the hero Alector, his father Franc-Gal, and a secondary cast of dozens, including: Alector's mother, Priscaraxe, who is half woman and half snake [like Melusine]; a 415-year-old virgin priest called l'Archier Croniel; a venerable lady Anange (meaning "Fate"), with three daughters who distribute life and death to heroes; a flying hippopotamus who carries Franc-Gal round the world; the ghost of a black knight named Gallehault; a professor of lying, cheating, magic, alchemy, counterfeiting, and other evil arts named Pseudomanathon; the sea god Proteus; a centaur and assorted savage wild beasts; and a giant serpent/dragon, from whose body, after Alector has killed it, a miraculous voice utters an omen. (I am not making this up.)

Zut alors! And the structure?

> The adventures of these disparate dramatis personae are curiously structured. The story begins in medias res, with Alector's capture and imprisonment on suspicion of illicit sex with Noémie (chap. 1) and Noémie's death (chap. 2), of which Alector is accused. He is condemned to combat with the serpent two days later, but this combat doesn't take place until chapter 25. All the intervening chapters are flashbacks, stories (and sometimes stories-within-stories) told of the histories of all the main characters and a few minor ones, interrupted by descriptions, laments, poems, omens, and a total of thirty-five prophecies; Franc-Gal's death, in chapter 25, comes as something of an anticlimax after the number of times it has been foretold.

Sacré bleu! Go on.

> But the narrative, which might be an amalgam of *Perceforest* and Folengo's *Baldus*,[90] is only part of the story, as it were. Subtexts provide constant distraction: Franc-Gal is (on one level) obviously Noah, and his son (born with spurs on) is a cock, a symbol of France,

---

1997): 928; and Stephen Bamforth's in *French Studies* 52.3 (July 1998): 334 — along with Virginia Krause's "The End of Chivalric Romance: Barthélemy Aneau's *Alector* (1560)," *Renaissance and Reformation* 23.2 (Winter 1999): 45–60.

90 A lengthy mock-heroic epic in a mixture of Latin and Italian published earlier in the 16th century by the Italian writer Teofilo Folengo (1491–1544). Nearly 500 years later, it

so that Aneau is continuing Lemaire de Belges's embroidering on the mythic origins of the Gauls; the magic swords, talking corpses, beasts and birds, Alector's double birth (his mother produces a transparent egg, out of which he breaks after nine days), and many other details create a mysterious folklore atmosphere; the careful description of the city of Orbe, its administration and its solar cult (well before Campanella and Bacon), make of this book, as Fontaine justly claims, the first urban utopia in French literature.

Although Aneau's *"histoire fabuleuse"* draws upon Heliodorus, the *Lancelot-Grail*, *Perceforest*, the French translation of Colonna's *Hypnerotomachia*, and Rabelais, it also anticipates *Tristram Shandy* and some of the learned Menippean satires of our own time, like Barth's *Giles Goat-boy*. Now that a superb critical edition of the French text is available, it is to be hoped that a new English translation won't be too long in following.

The absence of English translations likewise forces me to pass over some late, derivative French Renaissance novels: Jacques Yver (1520–72) wrote one entitled *Le printemps* (Spring, 1572) that drew upon the same source used by Shakespeare in *Two Gentlemen of Verona*. Nicolas de Montreux (c. 1561–1608), a nobleman who wrote under the anagramed pseudonym Ollénix du Mont-Sacré, was inspired by Montemayor's slim *Diana* to produce the fat *Bergeries de Juliette* (1585–98), remembered today only for inspiring Honoré d'Urfé's even fatter *Astrea* and Charles Sorel's savage parody of them both, *The Extravagant Shepherd* (1627). In the last decade of the 17th century, Montreux published a few other novels modeled on ancient Greek romances, as did François Béroalde de Verville (1556–1626), who published several philosophical romances between 1592 and 1612 that sound similar to (but much lengthier than) Aneau's 200-page *Alector*. (He edited a French translation of the *Hypnerotomachia* and imitated its antiquarian encyclopedism.[91]) It is with some relief, then, that I turn to a group of novels that need no translation.

RENAISSANCE ENGLISH FICTION

For a nation that would dominate the genre within a few centuries, the English were slow to produce their own novels. Most of the book-length fictions published in England before 1500 were translations of continental

---

has been translated into English for the first time: Ann E. Mullaney's two-volume *Baldo* appeared in 2007–08 (Cambridge: Harvard UP).

91 The only book of his to be translated into English is *Le Moyen de parvenir* (c. 1610), which Arthur Machen rendered as *Fantastic Tales, or The Way to Attain: A Book Full of Pantagruelism* (privately printed, 1923). In it a number of historical figures from different eras trade anecdotes, jibes, dirty jokes, and philosophical speculations in the facetious manner of Rabelais.

works, or prose adaptations of metrical romances. The great Chaucer tried his hand at two prose novellas, "The Tale of Melibee" and "The Parson's Tale," both included in *The Canterbury Tales* (1387–1400), but they're tedious religious treatises about patience and penitence, respectively. They're the first to go in any abridged edition of the *Tales* and demonstrate Chaucer was much more comfortable and creative with poetry than prose. (However, as the medievalist William Ker noted a century ago, in the narrative poem *Troilus and Cressida* Chaucer was moving away from the medieval romance in the direction of the modern novel.[92]) As we saw in the previous chapter, Thomas Malory may have made an original contribution to Arthurian fiction with his novella "Sir Gareth of Orkney," but otherwise his *Morte d'Arthur* likewise falls into the translation/adaptation category. Can we call Sir Thomas More's *Utopia* (1516) a novel? If so, this might qualify as the earliest English novel except that, though More was born in England, he wrote it in Latin. (It wasn't translated into his native tongue until 1551, 16 years after this man for all seasons was beheaded.) But the novelistic element is negligible in this mordant work of political theory and social criticism.[93]

The honor of the first English novel belongs to a clever little work entitled *Beware the Cat* (1553, posthumously published 1570), written by William Baldwin (c. 1518–63), better known as the principal author of *The Mirror for Magistrates*, an important source for Shakespeare and other Elizabethan dramatists. Writing during the tumultuous transition from Catholicism to Protestantism in 16th-century England, Baldwin's main motive may have been to satirize the superstitious nature of many Catholic beliefs and practices, but he also showed his countrymen that this newfangled toy called the novel was capable of more than merely recounting medieval tales of heroes and villains.

The plot will sound as silly as *Alector*'s: narrator Baldwin (he uses himself and acquaintances as characters) once found himself lodging with some members of the king's entertainment committee, and one night they fell to talking about "whether birds and beasts had reason."[94] Gregory Streamer, a pedantic theologian, insists not only that animals possess reason but also that they can talk, and in fact he once listened in on a colloquy of cats. Extracting a promise from his fellows not to interrupt him, he launches into a three-part

---

92 *Epic and Romance*, 349. Similarly, Schlauch calls *Troilus* a "great sustained approximation to a modern novel" (29).

93 *The Praise of Folly* (1508), written by the Dutch humanist Desiderius Erasmus a few years earlier while staying with More, is a similar genre-defying work, a comic monologue that doesn't quite fit into the novel tradition. His comic dialogue "Julius Excluded from Heaven" (1513), written just after Pope Julius II's death, is entertaining fiction but not long enough to be considered even a novella.

94 Page 5 in the Ringler-Flachmann edition, hereafter cited parenthetically. Not only is this a model scholarly edition with extensive apparatus, but it contains a long appendix on the early history of the novel that was immensely useful to me.

tale. In the first, he explains that he learned of cats' conversational abilities from some acquaintances, who told him of two felines in Staffordshire discussing the death of the legendary Grimalkin — "*A wonderful wit of a cat*," the author informs us in a marginal note (11) — and tales of a possessed Irish cat that not only could speak but was capable of killing and eating a man, which leads to further tales of possession involving lycanthropy and shape-shifting, whereby witches take the form of cats.[95] All of this leads Streamer in part 2 to concoct a magic potion that will allow him to understand the cats that assemble outside his window every night and keep him up with their chatter. The potion succeeds wonderfully, and in part 3 he listens as the cats conduct a trial. A female named Mouse-slayer defends herself against breaking the cats' code of sexual conduct — "which forbiddeth us females to refuse any males not exceeding the number of ten in a night" (47) — with a long, frequently hilarious account of her life. Streamer goes to sleep afterward and awakens the next day to discover the potion has worn off, but he admonishes his auditors with the ostensible moral of the story: cats communicate with other cats, so "Beware the cat": don't do anything in front of it that you'd be ashamed to have become public knowledge.

But that's only the tip of this cat tale. Every person in the novella who believes that cats can talk is Catholic, or a fledgling Protestant who reverts to his Catholic upbringing in times of fright. In the funniest episode, Mouse-slayer is shoed in walnut shells as a practical joke, but when she clatters on the floor at night her master is convinced it's the devil, and runs for an old priest and his box of tricks (surplice, candle, wafer, chalice, and holy water — "*Holy water was good for conjurers*" says the marginal note), who likewise takes the walnut-shoed cat for the devil, slips and falls among the crowd, and winds up with his face in the "bare arse" of a boy "which for fear had beshit himself" (49). The hocus pocus (*hoc est corpus*) of the Mass, saints' relics, the rosary, the use of an abstruse language instead of the vernacular for religious services, animated statues of the goddess Mary, the infallibility of the pope, apostolic traditions, the celibacy of the clergy, indulgences, Purgatory — all the beliefs that make Catholics essentially indistinguishable from bug-eyed natives in grass skirts shaking their spears at the sun during an eclipse are aligned in *Beware the Cat* with the credulous belief in witchcraft, lycanthropy, demonology, and talking cats. Beware the Cat(holic).

The target of Baldwin's satire is obvious, but to make sure he points the moral and adorns his tale with the ingenious use of marginalia. Baldwin fills his margins with italicized glosses, adages, source notes, catcalls, Latin quotations, and asides, imitating the practice of some religious tracts, and anticipating the use of marginal notes in López de Úbeda's *Justina*, Bunyan's

---

95 The belief that a cat has nine lives originates with Baldwin's observation "a witch may take on her a cat's body nine times" (16). The novella is a litter box of cat lore.

Pilgrim's Progress, Swift's *Tale of a Tub*, Joyce's *Finnegans Wake* (2.2), and in some recent experimental novels.[96] Next to a Catholic Irishman's account of how a witch passes down her shape-shifting ability to her daughter, Baldwin notes: "*Witchcraft is kin to unwritten verities, for both go by traditions*" (19), criticizing the Catholic reliance on religious beliefs not found in the Bible but dreamed up by later theologians. In another anecdote about the ignorance of some of the Catholic clergy, who couldn't name all Ten Commandments or locate the Lord's Prayer in the Bible, Baldwin sneers, "*Railing and slandering are the Papists' Scriptures*" (38). My favorites are his general observations:

Irish curs bark sore. (12)

The best learned are not the greatest boasters. (20)

Strange things are delectable. (30)

Cats are skilled in astronomy. (36)

Women are glorious.[97] (41)

It is as much pity to see a woman weep as to see a goose go barefoot. (43)

With Baldwin heckling Streamer from the sidelines as the credulous theologian tells his story, the reader is being taught how to read critically, how to decode symbolism, and how to maintain aesthetic distance when engaged with a work of art. (Of course, the reader needs to be as critical of Baldwin as he is of Streamer.[98]) And like a ventriloquist with his dummy, Baldwin uses Streamer to show off his stylistic range and outlandish learning. He has great fun imitating his pompous, pious pedant and easily slips into different voices as Streamer relates stories he's heard. His range of reference is impressive; Baldwin worked in a printing shop and had access to many kinds of books, for in addition to the classical and theological references common to educated writers, he draws upon such arcane works as Richard Sherry's *Treatise of Schemes and Tropes*, Giraldus Cambrensis's *Topography of Ireland*, and especially Albertus Magnus's *Book of Secrets of the Virtues of Herbs, Stones, and Certain Beasts*. The most dazzling display of Baldwin's rhetorical skill comes when Steamer uses *The Book of Secrets* to concoct the potion that allows him to understand the speech of cats. It enhances Streamer's sense of hearing to

96 Kenneth Patchen's *Journal of Albion Moonlight*, Malcolm Lowry's *Through the Panama*, Julián Ríos's *Larva* and *Poundemonium*, Douglas Coupland's *Generation X*, Julieta Campos's *Fear of Losing Eurydice*, Janice Galloway's *Trick Is to Keep Breathing*, Stephen Marche's *Raymond and Hannah*, Myla Goldberg's *Wickett's Remedy*, Alasdair Gray's *Old Men in Love*, Reif Larsen's *Selected Works of T. S. Spivet*.

97 They are indeed, but in this case "glorious" means vain, boastful.

98 As Maslen notes, Baldwin as narrator "seems credulous and naïve, and gathers material for his text from the most dubious sources. He takes everything Streamer says at face value, and shows equal confidence in the tall tales of servants and travellers when recording the story of Grimalkin" (81).

almost hallucinatory levels, so that he imagines he can hear the movement of the heavenly spheres in addition to everything happening in London:

> While I harkened to this broil, laboring to discern both voices and noises asunder, I heard such a mixture as I think was never in Chaucer's House of Fame; for there was nothing within an hundred mile of me done on any side (for from so far, but no farther, the air may come because of obliquation) but I heard it as well as if I had been by it, and could discern all voices, but by means of noises understand none. Lord what ado women made in their beds — some scolding; some laughing; some weeping; some singing to their suckling children, which made a woeful noise with their continual crying. And one shrewd wife a great way off (I think at St. Albans) called her husband "cuckold" so loud and shrilly that I heard that plain; and would fain have heard the rest, but could not by no means for barking of dogs, grunting of hogs, wawling of cats, rumbling of rats, gaggling of geese, humming of bees, rousing of bucks, gaggling of ducks, singing of swans, ringing of pans, crowing of cocks, sewing of socks, cackling of hens, scrabbling of pens, peeping of mice, trulling of dice, curling of frogs, and toads in the bogs, chirking of crickets, shutting of wickets, shriking of owls, flittering of fowls, routing of knaves, snorting of slaves, farting of churls, fizzling of girls, with many things else — as ringing of bells, counting of coins, mounting of groins, whispering of lovers, springling of plovers, groaning and spewing, baking and brewing, scratching and rubbing, watching and shrugging — with such a sort of commixed noises as would a-deaf anybody to have heard. . . . (31–32)

"Here the poetical fury came upon him" is Baldwin's dry aside on this vivid passage, but it's a rousing declaration of aesthetic independence from this English writer. Having taken a back seat for centuries to French and Latin, the English language bursts forth here in full glory, capable of mixing rare words (*obliquation*) with nursery rhymes, goofing on alliteration, alluding to English authors (Chaucer) rather than European ones, privileging diction derived from Anglo-Saxon over French and Latin, all enclosed in a multilayered work as aesthetically daring as any produced before it. The English novel has arrived, baby! Hail Britannia!

I could play with this *Cat* all day, but I'll close with one final observation. "The cat" is short for the whip known as the cat-o'-nine-tails, used to scourge malefactors. Baldwin uses the novel as a cat, applying the lash of satire to superstitious Catholics in this instance, but demonstrating how the novel can be used as a weapon against other targets. Like the cats in his tale, novelists observe and report on the silly actions of humans, nor do they need any magic potion to heighten their senses: the gifted writer sees all, hears all, and respects neither person nor office. Beware the cat of the outraged novelist![99]

---

99 Theroux plays on these two meanings in the title of his great satirical novel *Darconville's Cat*, which refers to both the feline the protagonist owns and his use of the novel to scourge those who wronged him.

Baldwin's *Cat* was followed a few years later by the first epistolary novel in English, *The Image of Idleness* (1556) by the pseudonymous Oliver Oldwanton.[100] It purports to be a work translated from the Cornish, but this is merely the first of many learned jokes in this comic novella, a pun on the Italian *cornuto* — the horn of cuckoldry that Elizabethan writers punned on ad nauseam. Oldwanton dedicates his translation to "Lady Lust," suggesting she familiarize herself with the work's misogyny the better to counter its arguments. (A later reference to "her band" implies she's a bawd in charge of a whorehouse, which certainly sets the tone for this bawdy little work.) It seems one Walter Wedlock has upbraided his old friend Bawdin Bachelor for never marrying, and in the novella's first letter Bachelor explains that it has not been for want of trying. He sends Wedlock copies of 10 older letters he wrote while trying to find a wife, most of them dignified but pained responses to the women who turned him down. It quickly emerges that Bachelor is a condescending pedant whom no woman in her right mind would want, and as the letters progress we learn of his increasingly desperate and ludicrous courtships, in which he engaged in a kind of speed-wooing (courting a second woman before the first has refused him, a third during the second, up to eleven candidates), and even wrote to an old army buddy to ask if there were any available women where he is garrisoned, before eventually giving up on his quest.[101] He had hoped to marry partly as field research for a marriage manual he wanted to write as a public service, which he decides to go ahead and write anyway (much as celibate priests consider themselves qualified to give marriage counseling). In the novella's final three letters, Bachelor gives his married friend Wedlock all sorts of advice on how to manage his wife, concluding with the worldly recommendation that he look the other way when she inevitably cheats on him.

Given his many rejections, some harsh, Bachelor not surprisingly becomes vexed at womankind and indulges in a great deal of misogynistic criticism, adding his tuppence to the *querelle des femmes* that was raging in Europe at the time, though coming from such a character it dilutes the misogyny to mere sour grapes. Like *Beware the Cat*, *The Image of Idleness* is an erudite, anti-Catholic work written for an educated, mostly male audience: the novella's first sentence cites the ancient Greek hedonist philosopher Aristippus, which is followed by references to Plato, Ovid, Malory, and figures from Greek history and mythology and the Bible (as well as some made-up authorities and

---

100 In the introduction to his modern edition, Michael Flachmann notes that both William Baldwin and the novella's publisher, William Serres, have been suspected of authorship, but that there is as much evidence against them as for them. The style is certainly different from the *Cat*'s.

101 Flachmann finds a parallel between Bachelor's and Panurge's quest to find a wife; this strikes me as something of a stretch, but Oldwanton was certainly well-read and his bawdiness is consistent with Rabelais's, so it's possible.

mythological figures). The style is rather ponderous, with long, complicated sentences, which suits the character but strains the humor somewhat: the reader has to work to mine the irony and wit from Oldwanton's prose. For example, here Bachelor recommends feigning madness as an excuse for beating one's wife to keep her in line:

> Let the husband fain himself to be sick, complaining altogether in his head and thereupon send for the physician, with whom he must be at point [in agreement] before hand, who at his coming shall in open presence make the matter light and put him in comfort to do well; and then, taking her apart, show her in secret that he is wonderfully inclined to frenzy, ascribing him a special diet for the defense thereof, which as well for dainty feeding under pretense to engender good blood as also for gentle entertainment for doubt to stir up the choleric humours shall be even as the goodman himself had beforehand devised. And if afterwards he shall perceive her to break any part of the same, then must he straight ways seem to be stark staring mad and, among other light and unwonted parts, be sure to beat her well and, to enforce the matter, make as though he would leap out of the chamber window — *but let not her be near at hand, lest she happen to help him outward.* And when he hath a while stormed in his rage, then let the physician come again and, blaming the wife for breaking his order, seem to pacify him by medicines. Yet first, hardly let him be well bound, even after the right Bedlam fashion, but let it not be too straight, *lest finding him at such advantage she happened to be* [get] *even with him.* And afterwards, when he is well come to himself and informed under what manner he misentreated his wife, let him utterly deny it, as though he knew not what he had done in his woodness [madness], swearing and staring that and if he would be so lewd it were pity of his life, affirming that in all the world there is not so benign and loving a woman to her husband nor that so little doth deserve to be under such sort used. But at length, when by his wife's tears, her broken eye, her black sides, and sore bones he must needs be persuaded that it was true, then must he counterfeit such woeful repentance as though he should straight ways out of his wit again for pure sorrow, wishing rather to die a thousand-fold than to be vexed again with the like passion. (letter 13)

I've italicized the funny bits, which might go unnoticed as one flinches from the brutality while trying to parse those long sentences. The italicized lines also suggest the author knows full well that any husband who treats his wife thus deserves to be pushed out a window, and though *The Image of Idleness* sometimes finds itself on lists of misogynistic works, it (and *Beware the Cat*) more properly belong to the nascent genre of British comic fiction.

It wasn't until the 1570s that more English writers took up the novel, largely inspired by the Italian novellas translated by William Painter and Geoffrey Fenton in their anthologies *The Palace of Pleasure* (1566–67) and *Certain Tragical Discourses* (1567), respectively. Roger Ascham warned teachers about the corrupting influence of these racy, sophisticated fictions in his famous pedagogical manual *The Schoolmaster* (1570), but, as usual, students ignored their teachers and embraced these Italian models *con amore*. Sophisticated, racy writing is on display in *The Adventures of Master F. J.* by George Gascoigne (1525–77), which first appeared in a collection of his writings entitled *A Hundreth Sundry Flowers* (1573). It concerns a young man known by the initials F. J. who visits a castle in northern England and promptly falls in love with a married woman named Elinor, daughter of the lord of the castle. He besieges her with letters and poems and eventually enjoys several sexual encounters with her until he learns he has a rival: not her returning husband, whom F. J. rather enjoys cuckolding, but Elinor's male secretary, whom the narrator describes in comically unflattering terms: "He was in height the proportion of two pigmies, in breadth the thickness of two bacon hogs, of presumption a giant, of power a gnat, apishly witted, knavishly mannered, and crabbedly favoured."[102] After realizing Elinor has been screwing her secretary for some time, F. J. takes ill when the secretary returns from a trip to London and resumes his unofficial duties with his mistress, which the narrator describes with the kind of imaginative sexual imagery found throughout the novella: "And in very deed it fell out that the secretary, having been of long time absent and thereby his quills and pens not worn so near as they were wont to be, did now prick such fair large notes that his mistress liked better to sing faburden under him than to descant any longer upon F.J.'s plainsong" (62). The two- (or three-)timing Elinor comforts the ailing F. J. nonetheless until one night he forces sex upon her, after which she understandably becomes standoffish (considering it more an example of bad manners than rape). Soon F. J. realizes nearly everyone at the castle is aware that the older woman has been using the young gallant merely as a plaything, so he writes her a final kiss-off poem and leaves in humiliation.[103]

"A comedy of manners with a sting in its tail" is how editor Salzman describes it, an early example of those British country-house comedies later perfected by Jane Austen and (more aptly) Aldous Huxley. But the most innovative thing about *The Adventures of F. J.* is its narrative structure: the novella begins with a letter from the publisher to the reader explaining that a friend of F. J.'s named G. T. received from the humiliated lover all the letters and poems he wrote during that embarrassing affair, along with a sketchy account of their context. The resulting novella is thus not a straightforward account of what actually happened up there in the north of England but G. T.'s reconstruction of the

---

102 Page 15 in Salzman's *Anthology of Elizabethan Prose Fiction* (where it occupies pp. 1–81), hereafter cited parenthetically. This is the original 1573 version of the novella; in 1575 Gascoigne published a slightly revised and neutered version, set in Italy rather than England, and deleting some of the sexual references, to avoid libelous charges that the novella was based on actual people (which apparently it was).

103 Helen Gardner deemed that final poem worthy of inclusion in *The New Oxford Book of English Verse* (1972).

affair, mostly to provide background for the poems to be published. He comments on the genesis of each poem, offers criticism of them — liking some of them, discounting others — and speculates about the characters. "What was there in him then to draw a fair lady's liking?" he asks after giving his description of Elinor's unattractive secretary, and paints a flattering portrait of the lord of the castle's sensible daughter, Frances, who assists F. J. with his affair even though she comes to love him and would make a much better mate. Sometimes G. T. gets impatient with the story, using an "etc." to speed things along; although he has a flair for sexual imagery and double entendres — lots of swords and pikes in this novella, lots of pricking and thrusting — he becomes coy when F. J. forces himself on Elinor: "he thrust her through both hands and etc.; whereby the dame, swooning for fear, was constrained for a time to abandon her body to the enemy's courtesy" (61; lots of martial imagery too in this battle of the sexes). At times, he seems to misunderstand F. J.'s poems — mistaking an evocation of Helen of Troy for some wench named Helen the poet knows — and often is baffled by the clever characters' use of conceits (elaborate extended metaphors), calling them "dark" or "misty." It's not quite *Pale Fire*, but G. T.'s attempts to grapple with F. J.'s poetry resembles Kinbote's mishandling of Shade's poem in Nabokov's masterpiece. G. T. is Gascoigne's plaything as surely as F. J. is Elinor's, resulting in a dazzling work as aesthetically sophisticated as the socially sophisticated society it treats. "It will please none but learned ears," as G. T. says of one of F. J.'s creations (52), the fate of most innovative fiction, but *The Adventures of F. J.* charts the growing sophistication (in every sense) of the English novelists.

"Sophisticated" needs to be prefixed by a couple of "ultra-"s to describe John Lyly's extraordinary novels, *Euphues: The Anatomy of Wit* (1578) and its sequel, *Euphues and His England* (1580). In a brilliant fusion of style and substance, Lyly (1554?–1606) cast doubt on the eternal verities of his age and revealed a destabilized world where everything resembles its opposite, where change is the only constant, and where people are lost in a maze of words, puzzled by paradox — our postmodern condition *avant la lettre*. Its substance is less noted than its style, its style more often reviled as whimsy than revered as wise. Lyly's cadenced sentences consist of balanced clauses built on antithesis, analogy, assonance, allusion — and alliteration. My penultimate sentence aped the master; here are some actual examples of the style that came to be called euphuism, beginning with its opening sentence:

> There dwelt in Athens a young man of great patrimony and of so comely a personage that it was doubted whether he were more bound to Nature for the lineaments of his person or to Fortune for the increase of his possessions.[104]

---

104 Page 32 in Leah Scragg's superb edition, hereafter cited parenthetically. *Euphues: The Anatomy of Wit* occupies pp. 26–152, the longer *Euphues and His England* pp. 154–354.

"Alas, Euphues, by how much the more I love the high climbing of thy capacity, by so much the more I fear thy fall. The fine crystal is sooner crazed than the hard marble, the greenest beech burneth faster than the driest oak, the fairest silk is soonest soiled, and the sweetest wine turneth to the sharpest vinegar." (37)

"Suppose that which I will never believe [argues Euphues], that Naples is a cankered store-house of all strife, a common stews for all strumpets, the sink of shame, and the very nurse of all sin: shall it therefore follow of necessity that all that are wooed of love should be wedded to lust; will you conclude, as it were *ex consequenti*, that whosoever arriveth here shall be enticed to folly and, being enticed, of force shall be entangled? No, no! It is the disposition of the thought that altereth the nature of the thing. The sun shineth upon the dunghill and is not corrupted, the diamond lieth in the fire and is not consumed, the crystal toucheth the toad and is not poisoned, the bird trochilus liveth by the mouth of the crocodile and is not spoiled, a perfect wit is never bewitched with lewdness neither enticed with lasciviousness." (40–41)

"Although my face cause him to mistrust my loyalty, yet my faith enforceth him to give me this liberty; though he be suspicious of my fair hue, yet is he secure of my firm honesty." (66)

Dig how in the final example Lyly links a pair of single words (assonantal monosyllable + rhyming trisyllable) in the first half of the sentence (faith . . . loyalty/face . . . liberty), then raises the bar to alliterate on pairs of words in the second (fair hue . . . firm honesty) while still alliterating on the adverbs (suspicious . . . secure). This is prose written as carefully as poetry — compare any of the structured sentences above to the rambling prose of Oldwanton quoted a few pages back — and makes far greater demands on the reader than any English prose written before it. Lyly didn't invent this style; San Pedro used a nearly identical one in *Prison of Love*, which Lyly apparently knew from Lord Berners's translation, and it has affinities with the musical style used by Alharizi and some Arab prose stylists. Closer to home, John Grange published an allegorical romance entitled *The Golden Aphroditis* in 1577, a year before *Euphues* appeared, which employs a similar style.[105] Even Queen Elizabeth wrote in this manner long before *Euphues* was published.[106] But Lyly popularized it, and it quickly became so faddish that trendy types at the

---

105 There is no modernized edition of this novel; I tried reading the original black-letter edition, but as its heroine says about halfway through, "words are but winde, although in this case they lie as logs before my feete to stüble at in yᵉ darke." In an excellent essay, Knapp says the young author of this linguistically exuberant work "achieves a nearly modernist concentration on sheer surface and play. His lone opus finally amounts to an oddly frustrating formal contradiction, neither novel nor allegory, just words; the worst of what would later be Euphuism, without Lyly's intellectual and moral subtlety" (270).

106 Tuckerman gives an example from a letter of hers to her half-brother Edward VI in his *History of English Prose Fiction*, 76.

Elizabethan court actually spoke this way for a while; as Lyly's first editor wrote in 1632, "All our ladies were then his scholars, and that beauty in court which could not parley Euphuism was as little regarded as she which now there speaks not French."[107] A few years earlier, though, poet Michael Drayton took a dimmer view, which prevailed until the 20th century; he praises Sir Philip Sidney for rescuing

> Our tongue from Lyly's writing, then in use:
> Talking of stones, stars, plants, of fishes, flies,
> Playing with words, and idle similes,
> As th'English apes and very zanies be
> Of everything that they do hear and see,
> So, imitating his ridiculous tricks,
> They spake and writ all like mere lunatics.[108]

Obsessed with Lyly's style, both his faddish followers and captious critics overlooked the substance of his work: the ambiguity of language and the danger of rhetoric. As the subtitle indicates, the novel is an examination of the nature of wit, both a brilliant demonstration and a subtle condemnation of its uses. Lyly's protagonist is a smooth talker who gets by on his wit, can argue either side of any question, and who over the course of about 10 years changes from a young fop to a middle-aged moralist, ultimately using his facility with rhetoric to convert an agnostic with the same dexterity he once used to seduce a woman. Young Euphues leaves his hometown of Athens for sophisticated Naples — "a place of more pleasure than profit, and yet of more profit than piety" (33) — and one of the first people he meets is an old gentleman named Eubulus, who gives him four pages of Polonius-like advice not to waste his youth; Euphues cheekily responds with a four-page rebuttal, doubting the old man followed his own advice when younger. (In the second half of the novel, the older Euphues will write to Eubulus and admit he was right, and will dispense the same "aged and overworn eloquence" [41] to others without the slightest blush of hypocrisy.) Euphues then becomes best friends with a young man named Philautus, but their friendship turns to rivalry once Euphues gets an eyeful of his girlfriend Lucilla. Euphues betrays Philautus by wooing Lucilla behind his back, then is betrayed in turn by Lucilla when she finds

---

107 Edward Blount, quoted by Scragg, 2. British novelist Anthony Powell recalled the similar impact made by Hemingway's style on his set: "We thought it was absolutely extraordinary. I mean people used to literally talk to each other in Hemingwayese. It became a craze, like the latest dance" (quoted in Barber's *Anthony Powell*, 70).

108 "To Henry Reynolds, of Poets and Poesy" (1627), ll. 90–96, in Alexander's *Sidney's The Defense of Poesy and Selected Renaissance Literary Criticism*, 294. He sounds just like those contemporary critics who mock fancy prose styles, but four centuries later people still read Lyly — who reads Michael Drayton?

a new fool to take Euphues' place in her affections. After some rhetorical flame-throwing, the two young men patch things up but agree to part ways, Euphues back to Athens to pursue a scholarly life and Philautus to become a courtier there in Naples.

That's where the first half of *Euphues: The Anatomy of Wit* ends; the second half consists of Euphues' later writings: essays, pamphlets, and letters on various topics — love, friendship, women, education — mostly modeled on the writings of "heathens" like Ovid and Plutarch. After 10 years, now a professor of philosophy in Athens, he decides to publish his collected lectures, but then asks himself: "Why, Euphues, art thou so addicted to the study of the heathen that thou hast forgotten thy God in heaven? Shall thy wit be rather employed to the attaining of human wisdom than divine knowledge?" (120–21). He turns to theology and becomes a sententious prig, writing letters to old acquaintances and advising them — with less polite sensitivity than pious superiority — not to mourn the death of a child or being forced into exile; telling Philautus to give up his corrupt courtier's life and dismissing his news of Lucilla's death with "a sinful life is rewarded with a sudden death" (141); and, as a final irony, lecturing a young fop lately arrived in Naples in the same vein as Eubulus lectured him years before. The novel ends with Euphues making plans to visit England with his old friend Philautus.

While an obtuse reader might applaud Euphues' "progress" from light-headed hedonist to hardhearted moralist, the more alert reader will realize he has not yet progressed from wit to wisdom. A wit can argue any point while believing in none, and find witty examples to defend any position, no matter how outrageous, and in the course of *Euphues* Lyly piles up so many arguments for so many contradictory positions that one doesn't know where he stands. Early on the narrator confesses, "I have ever thought so superstitiously of wit that I fear I have committed idolatry against wisdom" (43); what passes for wisdom in the novel (as dispensed by Eubulus and the older Euphues) is exposed as rhetorical bromides that can be easily contradicted. The state of doubt expressed in the novel's opening line, quoted above, remains throughout. "For neither is there anything but that hath his contraries" (43): Lucilla is a goddess when Euphues meets her, a harlot when she betrays him; Philautus is his best friend and worst enemy; nothing is as it seems, and no objective judgment is possible. Euphues' wit declines noticeably after he becomes a theologian, betraying his sensible classical authors (as he betrayed Philautus, and as Lucilla betrayed them both) for the hectoring Bible, which he cites not with precision but with the improvisatory prooftexting of a revival-tent preacher. Euphues becomes a rather despicable creature by the end, but readers *loved* the way he talked, and so Lyly obliged with a sequel.

As in its predecessor, the plot of *Euphues and His England* is negligible. Euphues and Philautus take a ship to England and attend the Elizabethan court; the two friends split after another disagreement, Philautus falls for an 18-year-old noblewoman named Camilla, and after she spurns him he makes up with Euphues; Euphues is called back to Athens, but Philautus stays and marries another Englishwoman named Frances.[109] Euphues writes a long, glowing description of England, addressed to the ladies of Italy, then retires to "some uncouth place" as a hermit. With Philautus happily married and Euphues unhappily martyred, the author leaves it to the reader to decide which is better off, ending the second novel on the same note of doubt on which the first novel began. As in the first, there's still no pretense to realism. The English characters have some very unEnglish names — Fidus, Iffida, Surius, Martius — and everyone speaks in the same elaborate style, drawing upon an encyclopedic range of references for their metaphors and analogies (many of them taken from Pliny's popular *Natural History*). The style is as exquisite as ever:

> "Thou art in view of the whole court, where the jealous will suspecteth upon every light occasion, where of the wise thou shalt be accounted fond, and of the foolish amorous. The ladies themselves, howsoever they look, will thus imagine: that if thou take thought for love thou art a fool, if take it lightly, no true servant.
>
> "Besides this, thou art to be bound as it were an apprentice, serving seven years for that which if thou win is lost in seven hours. If thou love thine equal, it is no contest; if thy superior, thou shalt be envied; if thine inferior, laughed at. If one that is beautiful, her colour will change before thou get thy desire; if one that is wise, she will over-reach thee so far that thou shalt never touch her; if virtuous, she will eschew such fond affection; if one deformed, she is not worthy of any affection; if she be rich, she needeth thee not; if poor, thou needest not her; if old, why shouldst thou love her; if young, why should she love thee?" (200–1).

It's like watching a pretty girl on a swing as these poised clauses go back and forth, back and forth, never coming to rest at a conclusive statement. I could watch her all day, read him all night.

The theme remains the same as in the *Anatomy*: "wit shippeth itself to every conceit, being constant in nothing but inconstancy" (236). All is in flux: the swing never comes to rest; each argument is countered by another, every position supplanted by its opposite, which can paralyze a person. In the quoted extract above, whom does one court if every kind of woman is inappropriate? "He that feareth every bush must never go a-birding," Philautus realizes, "he that casteth all doubts shall never be resolved in anything" (265). The distrust of wit in the *Anatomy* grows stronger in the sequel. As witty as ever, Euphues himself admits "talk the more it is seasoned with fine phrases

109 She plays the same role as the Frances in *The Adventures of F. J.*, but that may be only coincidental.

the less it savoreth of true meaning" (242). So why would Lyly work so hard to create fine phrases if they obscure true meaning? A clue can be found in the *Anatomy*'s dedicatory preface, where Lyly complains, "It is a world to see how Englishmen desire to hear finer speech than the language will allow," and insists it is "a greater show of pregnant wit than perfect wisdom in a thing of sufficient excellency to use superfluous elegance" (29). Lyly is mocking those who enjoy "superfluous elegance" by pushing it to such an extreme — "finer speech than the language will allow" — that he hopes such readers will overdose on it, and swear off such rhetoric, like a father who discourages smoking by forcing his son to smoke an entire pack of cigarettes. Englishwomen are worse than Englishmen in their desire for fine speech, pushovers for smooth talkers. "This causeth you, gentlewomen, to pick out those that can court you, not those that love you; and he is accounted best in your conceits that useth most colours [colorful wit], not that showeth greatest courtesy. A plain tale of faith you laugh at, a picked [refined] discourse of fancy you marvel at, condemning the simplicity of truth and preferring the singularity of deceit; . . ." (264). Lyly goes so far as to suggest a fancy prose style is one of the black arts, and poisonous; despairing at winning Camilla, Philautus goes to a magician named Psellus for help; the magician tells him to forget about spells and potions and *write* to her instead, for "there is nothing that more pierceth the heart of a beautiful lady than writing. . . . This is the poison, Philautus, the enchantment, the potions that creepeth by sleight into the mind of a woman and catcheth her by assurance; better than the fond devices of old dreams, as an apple with an Ave Mary, or a hazel wand of a year old crossed with six characters, or the picture of Venus in virgin wax, or the image of Camilla upon a mouldwarp's skin" (262). Lyly didn't need Drayton to condemn his witty style; he did so himself.

Using fancy writing to condemn fancy writing is only one of the many paradoxes of these tricky novels. But there is something else at work here. Lyly had a Truman Capotic relationship with his aristocratic readers, willing to entertain them and desiring their acceptance, but at the same time he was not-so-secretly critical of their vapidity, their showy ostentation, their addiction to fads. The beautiful and the glammed no doubt noticed this critical attitude in *Euphues and His England* and realized Lyly's wit was at their expense more often than not, which is perhaps why the sequel wasn't as popular as the *Anatomy*. And yet Lyly's wit was his only meal ticket, so he continued to perform for this vapid audience: he followed his two novels with eight charming plays written in the same style, all performed in the 1580s, before he eventually fell out of favor, spurned by the very people whose tastes he had courted.[110] The magician Psellus denounces magic as nonsense, but

---

110 The only unpalatable passages in his novels are those in which he flatters British aristocrats and especially Queen Elizabeth, which he does with the flamboyant unctuousness heard

then for the benefit of the "many, without doubt, that have given credit to the vain illusions of witches" (257), he puts on a five-page rhetorical magic show, itemizing various spells, ingredients, and occult beliefs; Lyly likewise played both sides, denigrating "superfluous eloquence" but giving one of the most impressive examples of it in English literature. Though he had his imitators in fiction, Lyly had greater influence on Elizabethan drama than on the novel — *Love's Labours Lost* is perhaps the best example of Shakespeare gilding the Lyly style, but Marlowe, Jonson, and the rest all learned much from him — but his ambiguous attitude toward the unsettling be*witch*ment of language will be shared down through the centuries by writers as different as Swift (especially in *A Tale of a Tub*), Carroll, Wilde, Wittgenstein, and Beckett.

One of those who resisted the bewitchment of Lyly's style was his exact contemporary Sir Philip Sidney (1554–86), the celebrated poet and courtier who during the same years Lyly wrote his novels composed the longest, most ambitious novel in Elizabethan literature at that time, *Arcadia*. The original version, now called the "old" *Arcadia*, was written between 1578 and 1580, and was intended only for the amusement of his younger sister Mary, countess of Pembroke, and her circle (the "fair ladies" Sidney addresses throughout the novel). At around 360 pages, it is longer than any other English novel of the period, but in 1584 Sidney began to rewrite it in an attempt to convert what he had dismissed as a "trifle" into an epic novel. He wrote nearly 600 pages before he was killed in 1586 during a military expedition in the Netherlands, reaching only the middle of his revision.[111] This "new" *Arcadia* was published posthumously in 1590, but because it was incomplete, an editor published in 1593 a version that combined the first 600 pages of the elaborate new *Arcadia* with the last 200 pages of the simpler old *Arcadia*; "it is as if the head and shoulders of a man were grafted on to the hind quarters of a horse," sneers one of Sidney's modern editors of this textual hybrid.[112] Yet for centuries this was the only version that was available until the earlier *Arcadia* was finally published in its original form in 1926.

The old *Arcadia* is a masterful fusion of the ancient Greek romance, the medieval adventure, and the Renaissance pastoral. Sidney knew them all: Achilles Tatius, Heliodorus, Boccaccio, Montalvo, San Pedro, Sannazaro,

---

today only in the praise of Third World dictators by their state-controlled media. Much of Lyly's flattery was no doubt sarcastic, and *everyone* overpraised the Faerie Queen at that time, but still one is embarrassed for him.

111 A century ago, every British schoolchild knew the splendid story of Sidney, mortally wounded at Zutphen, giving his water bottle to another wounded soldier, saying, "Thy necessity is greater than mine." Even as an American schoolboy, I came across the story somewhere, but I suspect no schoolchild, British or American, hears the story today.

112 Katherine Duncan-Jones in her edition of *The Old Arcadia*, ix, hereafter cited parenthetically by page number.

Montemayor.[113] The novel is divided into five books or acts — Sidney uses both terms — and indeed the first book resembles the first act of one of Shakespeare's cross-dressing comedies. Basilius, duke of Arcadia, travels to the oracle at Delphi and hears a disturbing prophecy that causes him to abandon his palace and hide out among the shepherds in Arcadia, taking with him his wife and two teenage daughters. Two adventuring teenage princes learn of the duke's retreat; the younger, named Pyrocles, sees a portrait of the duke's younger daughter, Philoclea, falls instantly in love, and vows to find her; the elder, Musidorus, mocks his plan to disguise himself as an Amazon named Cleophila (flip-flopping *Philoclea*) to get close to her, but when he spots Pamela, the duke's older daughter, he too falls in love and disguises himself as a shepherd to do likewise. When they meet the duke's family, things get more complicated: old Basilius, thinking Pyrocles/Cleophila is a girl, falls in love with him/her, and his wife Gynecia, somehow seeing through his disguise, also falls for the lad. Meanwhile, Cleophila saves Philoclea's life and praises her beauty so ardently that she experiences some "unquiet imaginations" (49) about this handsome Amazon, unaware that her father and mother are her rivals in affection. Musidorus likewise saves Pamela's life, but this aristocratic lass is a bit sniffy toward the rude shepherd, adding class conflict to the transvestite/homoerotic/adulterous/transgeneration mix. Throw in a rustic named Dametas for some broad comic relief and you have a delightful opening act.

Between each book is a lengthy interlude of "eclogues," a series of poems in a variety of complex meters connected by prose passages. In the first of these, we learn from a messenger that a princess of Lydia whose father Pyrocles and Musidorus had once aided has been imprisoned by the queen of Persia, who demands that the two princes return for a duel within two years or else the princess will be burned at the stake. Pyrocles and Musidorus are startled at the news, but "considering they had almost a year of time to succour her" (63), they leave the princess to stew in prison so that they can pursue their Arcadian affairs — one of many indications these noble princes are not as gallant as they might be. (Other clues: Pyrocles feasts his eyes on Philoclea when, "her light nymph-like apparel being carried up with the wind, that much of those beauties she would at another time have willingly hidden were presented to the eye" [43] — a gentleman would have looked away — and after Pamela faints from fear, Musidorus "took the advantage to kiss and re-kiss her a hundred times" [47].) These poetic interludes, much longer and more varied than the eclogues in Sannazaro or Montemayor, allow Sidney to comment on his themes in the person of the melancholy shepherd Philisides, and

---

113 In his *Amadis de Gaule and Its Influence on Elizabethan Literature*, O'Connor makes the case that Montalvo's endless novel was Sidney's principle influence, which if true is a good example of making a silk purse out of a sow's ear.

"under hidden forms utter such matters as otherwise were not fit" for everyday discourse (50) — the perennial appeal of art.

In book 2, Sidney tightens these knotty entanglements as the characters declare their love, which he disturbingly compares to a "cup of poison, which was deeply tasted of all this noble company" (80). Gynecia confesses her love to Cleophila, who then receives a similar declaration from Basilius; Musidorus (who has truncated his name to Dorus) reveals his secret identity to Pamela, which removes the class barrier; and finally Philoclea, after an attack of what queer theorists call "lesbian panic," accepts her Sapphic attraction to Cleophila, only to be told by that much-loved Amazon of his true identity, somewhat to her confused relief.[114] Jealousy between mother and daughter and wife and husband rears its green-eyed head, but is upstaged by an unexpected revolt of drunken peasants, who attempt to kill their duke until Cleophila, in a rousing pro-monarchy speech, manages to defuse the mob, after which the narrator pours out his aristocratic contempt for "the many-headed multitude" (115). In "The Second Eclogues" interlude, amid some high-wire poetry acts in death-defying meters — Anacreontics! Phalucian hendacasyllabics! ascledpiadics! — we hear more early adventures of the wandering princes, in which Sidney's debt to Heliodorus is especially apparent.

The two princes steal away at the beginning of book 3 to compare notes, sometimes in song, and we learn that Dorus had made arrangements to elope with Pamela, who is fed up with living in the sticks and with her father's increasingly strange behavior. In a chapter playfully filled with sexual cliff-hangers, Dorus escapes with Pam, and after she falls asleep in his lap during a rest period, he is so worked up by her sexual allure that he is on the verge of raping the sleeping beauty when he is interrupted by "a dozen clownish villains, armed with divers sorts of weapons" (177). Sidney leaves us hanging there to return to Cleophila/Pyrocles, who plays a dangerous game of enticing first Gynecia then Basilius to meet her that night to satisfy their lusts — Basilius "was old enough to know that women are not wont to appoint secret night meetings for the purchasing of land" (194) — only to play a bedtrick by which the husband mistakenly commits adultery with his own wife. With them out of the way, Pyrocles steals into Philoclea's room, where she is conveniently perched "upon the top of her bed, her beauties eclipsed with nothing but a fair smock" (202). After some narrative foreplay, including a four-page poem cataloging the glories of the teenager's body, Sidney consummates this teasing chapter with their sexual union, appropriately followed in "The Third Eclogues" with poems celebrating the marriage of two shepherds.[115] Later

114 This lesbian episode earned *Arcadia* a place in Terry Castle's massive anthology *The Literature of Lesbianism* (88–93). And here's how clever Sidney is: when Cleophila addresses her first love poem to Philoclea, he uses the meter known as sapphic.

115 These are among the first epithalamia in English poetry; *Arcadia* also contains the first English madrigal, the first sestina, one of the first pastoral elegies in English, a verse *fabliau*

Philoclea will consider this her wedding night, "whereto our innocencies were the solemnities, and the gods themselves the witnesses" (263), the same kind of DIY secret marriages popular in medieval romances.

Book 4 opens with some Three Stoogic shenanigans as Pamela's shepherd-guardian Dametas realizes Dorus tricked him (and his shrewish wife and dumb daughter) into letting the princess escape. But farce turns to tragedy after Dametas comes across Pyrcoles and Philoclea still asleep in bed, and spreads the word that "Cleophila" is actually a man and has "abused" the duke's daughter, only to learn the duke is dead, having drunk a potion that his wife assumed was an aphrodisiac but that was actually poison — literalizing the lust-as-poison metaphor introduced at the beginning of book 2. As it happens, a deputation from Arcadia's capital arrives just then (alerted by the peasants' revolt earlier), which causes Gynecia in an orgy of self-hate to explain what has happened, and Pyrocles to attempt suicide to protect Philoclea's reputation. Philanax, the clearheaded counselor who had tried to talk Basilius out of his flight to Arcadia at the beginning of the novel, now takes charge and puts everyone into custody. Meanwhile, Musidorus and Pamela are attacked by "the scummy remnant" of those rustic rebels from book 2; he dispatches a few of them with Homeric grisliness but surrenders once they capture Pam, and the rebels decide to return both to Basilius for a reward, not knowing of his death. When they return, they find the place in an uproar and Philanax losing control, with factions arguing over Basilius's successor as our two princess and princesses are imprisoned.[116] In the fourth interlude of eclogues, the shepherds retreat to the hills of Arcadia and "used this occasion to record their own private sorrows which they thought would not have agreed with a joyful time" (284), resulting in the longest, most impressive poems in the novel.

In the concluding book/act 5, Pyrcocles's father Euarchus, king of Macedonia, unexpectedly arrives to visit his old friend Basilius and reproach him for his dereliction of princely duty, and is instead convinced by Philanax to restore order to Arcadia. An outdoor court of judgment is convened (reminiscent of the courtroom scenes at the end of many ancient Greek novels), but judge Euarchus fails to recognize the defendants as his son or his nephew Musidorus — or they him — because of their long separation, which strains credibility but is likewise characteristic of Sidney's ancient sources. Acting as prosecutor,

---

in the French manner, and so many other verse forms that it is as important to the history of English poetry as it is to that of the novel.

116 The anarchy that results when Basilius dies without leaving a clear heir is not unrelated to the concern Sidney and other Elizabethans felt at this time at Queen Elizabeth's unmarried state. In 1579, however, in the middle of writing *Arcadia*, Sidney advised the queen against marrying the duke of Anjou, the Catholic heir to the French throne, thereby earning her displeasure. Sidney's close familiarity with political intrigue is evident throughout the novel.

Philanax builds a case against Gynecia and the princes as co-conspirators in Basilius's murder, twisting circumstantial evidence to fit his charge, bent on revenging the death of his beloved king. The princes confess that all their disguises and subterfuges were done for love of the girls, not enmity toward the king, but since they are indeed guilty according to Arcadian law — Musidorus of kidnapping, Pyrocles of seduction — Euarchus sentences both to death in a lengthy opinion worthy of the awful majesty of the law. Even when a surprise witness reveals the princes' true identity, Euarchus doesn't budge from his judicial duty: "No, no, Pyrocles and Musidorus, I prefer you much before my life, but I prefer justice as far before you," he says euphuistically (356). Only a totally unexpected development (which I won't spoil) sorts things out and allows the princes to escape death and to marry their loves. Cleverly fulfilling the oracle given at the beginning, it's an aesthetically satisfying end to a novel that displays considerably more intellectual heft than others of the time: through his characters Sidney discourses brilliantly on political and legal theory, the nature of love, the ethics of suicide, public duty vs. personal desire, and of course on poetics. Consequently this *Arcadia* is considerably more than "a trifle, and that triflingly handled," as he told his sister (3). Sidney's fiercely pro-monarchy, antipopulist stance won't sit well with many readers today, and the novel's elaborate prose style and leisurely pace can be testing, but *Arcadia* is a splendid achievement and required reading for anyone interested in the history of the novel.

Sidney's disclaimer to his sister sounds like false modesty, but apparently he was serious, for a few years later he set out to make the novel more than a trifle, upgrading it from the category of mere entertainment (as he deemed it) to that of high art. Between the two versions of *Arcadia* he wrote *The Defense of Poesy* (posthumously published in 1595), another first for him: the first sustained work of literary criticism in English. In this dazzling manifesto for imaginative fiction, he underscores great literature's didactic properties, its potential to teach readers to be better people. In order to do so, it should be aggressively idealistic, presenting characters at their best, the better to inspire readers to emulate them. Citing Xenophon's *Education of Cyrus*, Sidney says it doesn't matter that the Persian king's actions in that novel don't match the historical record; Xenophon created an ideal and was right "to bestow a Cyrus upon the world to make many Cyruses, if they [readers] will learn aright why and how that maker made him."[117] The artist creates "notable images of virtues" that will inspire the reader to "virtuous action" (12, 13), and thus these images have to be larger than life, unrealistically ideal, to make their pedagogic point.

---

117 *Sidney's* The Defense of Poesy *and Selected Renaissance Literary Criticism*, 9 (hereafter cited parenthetically). By "poesy" Sydney means imaginative fiction, whether in prose or verse; hence he calls Plato, Xenophon, and Heliodorus poets. Unimaginative writers of verse are not poets but mere "versifiers."

As artificial and unrealistic as the old *Arcadia* is, Sidney apparently felt it was insufficiently idealistic to inspire readers to "virtuous action," especially the sexual antics of his two princes. The purpose of great art, he felt, is "to teach and delight" (10), and while the old *Arcadia* certainly delights, it doesn't teach as effectively as it might. Since one advantage fiction has over philosophy and history is that "the feigned may be tuned to the highest key of passion" (20), Sidney decided to maximize the artificiality in his novel and to present idealized images of virtue in idealized English "poesy." In the revised *Arcadia*, his characters will exemplify the ideal lover, the ideal king, the ideal friend, the ideal host; even the animals are idealized examples of their kind. The language is even more artificial and elaborate, "tuned to the highest key of passion," resulting in what one of his editors calls "a gladiatorial display of oratory which outshines anything achieved in English before and perhaps since."[118]

To serve this higher purpose, Sidney turned away from the profane Greek novel as a model and embraced the sacred Arthurian romance, going so far as to array his heroes in armor and have them addressed occasionally as "Sir knight." He also complicated his relatively straightforward narrative structure with the *entrelacement* pattern from Arthurian fiction, introducing and maintaining many more characters and story-lines than in the old *Arcadia*. For example, while the old *Arcadia* begins in chronicle form by describing Arcadia and detailing Basilius's trip to Delphi and what he heard there, the revised *Arcadia* opens in medias res (less like novelist Heliodorus than epic poets Homer and Virgil) with the shepherds Strephon and Claius — mere walk-ons in book 4 of the previous version — at the seashore, bewailing the departure of an über-shepherdess named Urania, whom they both loved in friendly rivalry, and describing her effect on them:

> "Hath not the only love of her made us, being silly ignorant shepherds, raise up our thoughts above the ordinary level of the world, so as great clerks do not disdain our conference? Hath not the desire to seem worthy in her eyes made us, when others were sleeping, to sit viewing the course of the heavens; when others were running at [Prisoners'] Base, to run over learned writings; when others mark their sheep, we to mark ourselves? Hath not she thrown reason upon our desires and, as it were, given eyes unto Cupid? Hath in any but in her, love-fellowship maintained friendship between rivals, and beauty taught the beholders chastity?" (63–64)

Sidney opens with this episode to show the effect he hopes his *Arcadia* will have on readers, as well as to introduce the lesson to be learned (the same as Grange's *Golden Aphroditis*): love needs to be governed by reason, and desire should be ennobling, not debasing. He then relates many of the pre-Arcadian

---

118 Page 15 in Maurice Evans's brilliant introduction to the revised *Arcadia*, hereafter cited by page number.

adventures of the two princes, merely summarized in the older version, to establish their nobility of character *before* they go undercover. The author frequently overdoes it — Pyrocles is described by his benefactors as a "demigod" and "the uttermost that in mankind might be seen" (103) — but Sidney's purpose is not to mirror nature with realistic characters but to outdo it:

> Only the poet, disdaining to be tied to any such subjection, lifted up with the vigour of his own invention, doth grow in effect into another nature, in making things either better than nature bringeth forth or, quite anew, forms such as never were in nature, as the heroes, demigods, cyclopes, chimeras, furies and such like. So as he goeth hand in hand with nature, not enclosed within the narrow warrant of her gifts but freely ranging only within the zodiac of his own wit. Nature never set forth the earth in so rich tapestry as divers poets have done, neither with so pleasant rivers, fruitful trees, sweet-smelling flowers, nor whatsoever else may make the too-much-loved earth more lovely: her world is brazen, the poets only deliver a golden. (*The Defense of Poesy*, 8–9)

In addition to refining his heroes' virtues from brass to gold (to continue his metaphor), Sidney made numerous improvements in plotting that provide more realistic motivation for his characters' actions while, paradoxically, making those actions more unrealistically heroic. In the earlier version, for example, Pyrocles beholds the painting of Philoclea, falls in love and seeks her out, and then explains his cross-dressing plan to Musidorus: simple and straightforward. In the revised version, Musidorus is the one who sees the portrait first; after being reunited with Pyrocles after an absence, his friend begins acting strangely and then disappears, so Musidorus goes in search of him, sometime later resting in an arbor when a beautiful Amazon walks by. Only later does he realize the Amazon is Pyrocles — his surprise is the reader's as well — and only after that do we learn that Pyrocles had seen the portrait and had fallen in love, but not simply because of Philoclea's beauty but because of her resemblance to a former love of his called Zelmane, whose name Pyrocles takes (instead of Cleophila) when he disguises himself. The linear plotting and simplistic motivation of the original is thus replaced by a convoluted series of delays, surprises, and recognitions, complicating and ennobling Pyrocles's attraction to Philoclea: she is a representation of Zelmane just as the portrait is a representation of her, making her an almost literal picture of virtue, an ideal rather than a flesh-and-blood girl. (Fortunately Sidney doesn't overdo this: little sister still dresses suggestively in "nymph-like apparel, so near nakedness as one might well discern part of her perfections" [146].) Dozens of similar revisions enrich the narrative, making it more demanding but also more satisfying to the reader who takes the time (as Sidney recommended in the *Defense*) to "learn aright why and how" the author wove his "rich tapestry."

Had Sidney lived to complete the novel, this *Arcadia* would be a towering achievement to stand beside those of Boccaccio and Rabelais. Superficially completing it by tacking the old version's conclusion onto where the new version breaks off, the Countess of Pembroke changed character names for consistency and deleted the sex scenes — Musidorus's attempted rape of Pamela and Pyrocles's successful seduction of Philoclea — to maintain Sidney's more exalted view of his heroes, but for the poetic interludes my lady often mixed together various of her brother's poems without regard for their thematic relevance. Much later, to link the incomplete version with the conclusion, a Scottish poet and critic named Sir William Alexander wrote a 30-page bridge sequence, published in the fifth edition of 1621 and in most editions thereafter; he does a creditable job, but he's no Sidney, and the stylistic/thematic discrepancies between the two versions fatally compromises the revised *Arcadia*'s artistic integrity.[119] Nevertheless, *Arcadia* is the first clear masterpiece in English fiction, and arguably would remain the greatest one until 1749, when Henry Fielding published a different kind of prose epic. "In the *Arcadia*," Virginia Woolf saw, "as in some luminous globe, all the seeds of English fiction lie latent."[120]

The same year Sidney began revising *Arcadia*, a poet and lawyer named William Warner (1558–1609) published the most formally elegant, most ingeniously structured novel of the Elizabethan era, *Pan His Syrinx* (1584; revised as *Syrinx; or, A Sevenfold History*, 1597). The title is from Ovid, the style from Lyly, and the content from Heliodorus, but the structure is Warner's own. In the myth of Pan as given in Ovid's *Metamorphoses*, the woodland god is smitten by a nymph named Syrinx, a devotee of chaste Diana, and pursues her relentlessly after she spurns him; she reaches the river Ladon and asks the water nymphs to transform her; just as Pan grabs her, she metamorphs into some marsh reeds:

> And while he sighed,
> the reeds in his hands, stirred by his own breath,
> gave forth a similar, low-pitched complaint!
> The god, much taken by the sweet new voice
> of an unprecedented instrument,
> said this to her: "At least we may converse
> with one another — I can have that much."[121]

---

119 Thirty years later, a young woman named Anna Weamys did Alexander one better by publishing *A Continuation of Sir Philip Sidney's Arcadia* (1651), accepting Sidney's invitation in the final sentence of his novel for "some other spirit" to tell the tales he has left untold (848). I'll discuss Miss Weamys's novella in the next volume, along with other sequels to *Arcadia*.

120 "The Countess of Pembroke's Arcadia," in *The Second Common Reader*, 49 — a lovely if ultimately disparaging essay.

121 From Charles Martin's translation (NY: Norton, 2004), 1:976–82.

An allegory of art as a consolation for loss, the episode provided Warner with his structure: the seven reeds of the syrinx (or panpipe) become seven chapters, each called a "calamus" (reed) and focusing on a particular character (just as each reed gives a particular pitch). Panpipes are also known as "quills," the writing instrument Warner would have used. Syrinx is thus a performance by Warner on his quills, and like Pan's in Ovid's *Metamorphoses*, it is a "low-pitched complaint" rather than a sprightly woodland tune.

The story has a vaguely biblical setting (maybe 7th century BCE) around the Ninevah/Black Sea region, and deals with a royal Median family that is dispersed after an Assyrian invasion and is reunited three years later on a desert island. The details are too complicated to summarize; suffice it to say that as the characters search for each other they encounter other characters with interesting stories to tell, and it is these recitations that dominate the novel. For example, while a ship's crew is waiting for its principal passengers to explore an island, one mariner delivers a speech condemning the sailor's life as too dangerous, followed by one arguing that life on land is just as dangerous, followed by a third who insists that both are equally dangerous — all of these supported by various anecdotes. These speeches don't contribute much to the story-line, but that's not the point; each calamus is a performance piece on a standard rhetorical topic: the fickleness of fortune, friendship, and women; the nature of justice and honor, the duties of kingship, the dangers of lust, and so forth. As I said, Warner was a lawyer, and many of these speeches sound like the opening or closing statements of an attorney, one slick enough to argue either side of a case. (A speech condemning women is followed by one praising them.) While characters in Heliodorus (Warner's principal model) likewise filled each other in with long recitations, Warner's novel unfolds more like an Oriental fiction, with the frame-tale of Duke Arbaces and his wife Dircilla enclosing the tale of their son Sorares' search for his father, enclosing the tale of *his* sons' search for him, all of which encloses the stories they hear from other characters during their searches. Though the novel is only 188 pages long, it's challenging to keep track of who is talking to who, where, and when.

Warner's "sevenfold history" portrays a dark, dangerous world. Most of the substories are filled with violence, betrayal, greed, suicide, adultery; there are cases of cannibalism and torture, beheadings and other ghastly deaths, and a few occasions when a character will almost execute someone who turns out to be a relation. "Overcome with the surcharge of this kind sorrow," as he says of one character (chap. 44), Warner himself perhaps saw too much of the seamy side of life in his capacity as a lawyer, because he goes beyond the demands of a genre that thrives on such things. Interestingly enough, when the family is reunited on a semisavage island where Dircilla has been made queen, they decide to stay in that matriarchal Eden rather than return to the civilized world. Despite the "happy" ending, it is a pessimistic, even despairing novel, and perhaps for that reason *Syrinx* remains one of the least known Elizabethan novels.

But Warner's novel was certainly known by other budding novelists of the 1580s, especially those Londoners known as the University Wits, a well-educated, hard-living, prolific brat pack down from Oxford and Cambridge. One of the most colorful, Robert Greene (1558–92) — whom Warner later charged with plagiarizing his *Syrinx* — knocked out three dozen works in the final dozen years of his short, reckless life — plays, journalism, memoirs, poetry — including about 15 short novels. Remembered today mostly for calling Shakespeare "an upstart crow beautified with our feathers" in his *Groatsworth of Wit*, Greene did much to popularize the novel, finding a happy medium between eccentric Lyly and exorbitant Sidney. But he had some nerve accusing Shakespeare of stealing from his work, because Greene shamelessly stole from Warner and especially from Lyly, aping his alliterative style and exotic allusions to animals and nature (which they both stole from Pliny's *Natural History*), and borrowed his plots from the Italian *novellieri* tradition.

In his third novel, *Gwydonius, or the Card of Fancy* (1584), Greene tells the anti-Sidnean tale of a prince who is a scoundrel (much like Greene himself) wasting "his time in roisting and riot, in spending and spoiling, in swearing and swashing, and in following willfully the fury of his own frantic fancy."[122] Following one's personal fancy rather than one's social obligation is the subject of the novel, and it seems to lead to nothing but trouble at first for Prince Gwydonius. Encouraged to travel by his exasperated father Clerophontes, the prince leaves his kingdom of Mytilene (Lesbos) for Barutta (Beirut), where he raises so much hell he gets thrown in prison. He eventually winds up in Alexandria, "pinched with poverty" (96), and slowly works himself into favor with King Orlanio (though he keeps his royal descent a secret). Gwydonius falls for the king's daughter Castania, and realizes he needs to straighten up to win her. Win her he does, to the point where she's ready to elope with him; she knows she is betraying her class obligations by falling for this penniless stranger, following her own fancy rather than marrying a "carpet knight" of her own class who has been wooing her. Just then, her father decides to stop paying the annual tribute to Gwydonius's father, which causes Clerophontes to bring his army down to Egypt and wreak carnage. (He turns out to have as violent a temper as his son, and is just as headstrong, rejecting Orlanio's proposed peace settlement in favor of war.) The two kings decide to settle their disagreement by personal combat; Clerophontes, a hulking warrior still in his prime, will fight his own battle, but Orlanio chooses as his representative a disguised Gwydonius, which means the son must kill his own father to

---

122 Page 84 in Di Biase's modernized edition, hereafter cited parenthetically.

win Castania's hand. In the last of the novel's many soliloquies (reminding us Greene also wrote plays), the dichotomy between fancy and duty reaches a fatal head:

> "Alas, poor Gwydonius," quoth he, "how art thou cumbered with diverse cogitations! What a cruel conflict dost thou find in thy mind between love and loyalty, nature and necessity! Who ever was so willfull as willingly to wage battle against his own father? Who so cruel as to enter combat with his own sire? Alas, duty persuades me not to practice so monstrous a mischief, but the devotion I owe to Castania drives me to perform the deed, were it thrice more dangerous or desperate. The honor I owe to my father makes me faint for fear but once to imagine so brutish a fact. The love I owe to Castania constraineth me to defend the combat if Jupiter himself made the challenge. And is not, fond fool, necessity above nature? Is not the law of love above king or kaiser, father or friends, God or the devil? Yes, and so I mean to take it, for either I will valiantly win the conquest and my Castania, or lose the victory and so by death end my miseries." (195–96)

That "Yes" is revolutionary. Choosing love over every social and religious obligation is anarchistic, a repudiation of every value held sacred by the sensible Elizabethan, and a validation of Sidney's equation of love with poison, and Plato's with madness. Greene's female readers may have considered Gwydonius's declaration wonderfully romantic, but others would have considered it treasonous and blasphemous.

Knowing he couldn't top this bold statement — it occurs on the next-to-last page of the novel — Greene quickly wraps up his story: Gwydonius defeats his father in battle but spares his life, and the king is so pleased to see his worthless son perform like a valiant prince that he forgives him and blesses his proposed wedding to Castania. For good measure, he even allows his daughter to marry Orlanio's son, forcing a happy ending on this Oedipal tale of hedonistic individualism. The narrator is right to call this a "tragical comedy" (138), for though it ends like a comedy with a double wedding, it's a moral tragedy that a selfish party animal willing to kill his own father just to have sex with a beautiful princess he barely knows is rewarded with two kingdoms and the girl of his dreams. No wonder the nascent Puritans of this time condemned novels as well as plays. But apparently Greene wanted to shock his customers, to satirize the romance genre that places love above everything, to mock the "sugared harmony" (156) of euphuism and fancy writing, and to produce a novel that is formally as tight as a drum and just as disruptive. Achilles Tatius's *Clitophon and Leucippe* was a major source for Greene's novel and he follows the Greek author's tendency to indulge in peacock displays of rhetoric. It's still a pleasure to read.

It was followed a year later by Greene's strangest, most fanciful novel, *Planetomachia*, or "the brawles of the Planets" as he translates it in his dedication.[123] A cross between a primer on astrology and an anthology of Italianate novellas, it begins with a six-page defense of "astronomy" (by which he means astrology), followed by a six-page dialogue in Latin further defending that astral superstition, most of it plagiarized from the ancient writings of Ptolemy, Lucian's mock eulogy *De Astrologia*, and French polymath Antoine Mizaud's more recent *Planetologia* (1551). Then we attend a convocation of the seven planets (Sol, Mercury, Venus, Luna, Mars, Saturn, and Jupiter), who are arguing over who has the most pernicious effect on Earthlings. Loving Venus lambastes melancholic Saturn, and then tells a Romeo-and-Juliet-like tale of two young lovers thwarted by the girl's sour, spiteful father. Saturn takes no responsibility for the father's actions, and retaliates with a story set in Egypt about "an infamous strumpet" (50) and her venereal influence on the king, a tale of lust, irresponsibility, and near-incest after the king's son is found in bed with her. Since Mars defends Venus in this instance, Jupiter tells a war story about the kings of Scythia and Libya whose martial anger brought ruin to both countries. Before Mars can retaliate with a tale of Jupiter's malefic influence (pride, ambition), Sol calls it a day and suggests they continue the next morning: a promised sequel that the busy Greene never got around to writing.

The tales are narrated in the Lylian manner and the rest in spirited dialogue that reminds us that Greene was a successful dramatist. Though the front matter defends the legitimacy of astrology, the tales tell a different story about human nature and motivation that has nothing to do with one's astrological sign. As that "upstart crow" would write 14 years later, "The fault, dear Brutus, in not in our stars, / But in ourselves" (*Julius Caesar* 1.2.141–42). Still, *Planetomachia* is an interesting experiment in mixed media and the musical prose remains a delight:

> *Venus*, you play like them which seeking to shoote against the starres, are wounded with their owne Arrowes in the fall: or like the envious Porcuntine, who coveting to strike others with her pennes leaveth her selfe void of any defence: you have here tolde a tale of *Valdracko*, which sheweth not my crabbed influence, but your owne crooked constellation, for it was the wilfull forwardnesse of *Pasylla* in her doting fancies, and her lascivious love in liking her fathers enimy, that procured those haplesse events: yea, it was the unbridled affection of staylesse youth, not the careful wisedome of setled age that wrought this Tragicall discourse. (46)

Pandosto: The Triumph of Time (1588) is Greene's best-known novel, chiefly because Shakespeare based his late play *A Winter's Tale* on it, again justifying Greene's enmity.[124] Like *Gwydonius*, it is named after a despicable

---

123 Page 3 in Das's old-spelling critical edition, hereafter cited by page number.
124 Shakespeare's famous error of giving Bohemia a seacoast comes straight from *Pandosto*. (Shakespeare should have checked a map, for Greene wrote quickly and sometimes

character, and similarly mixes elements of comedy and tragedy. A cautionary tale about jealousy, its plot will be recognizable to anyone familiar with Shakespeare's lovely play. Pandosto, king of Bohemia, receives a visit from his friend Egistus, king of Sicily. Pandosto's wife Bellaria entertains the visitor warmly (but chastely), which poisons Pandosto's mind with jealousy. He decides to kill the "adulterous" couple; Egistus gets wind of the plot and escapes back to Sicily; Pandosto, too cowardly to pursue him, takes it out on his wife and throws her in prison, where she soon realizes she's pregnant. She tells us in a monologue that the child is Pandosto's (and there's no reason to doubt her), but the king assumes it is Egistus's, so after his wife gives birth to a daughter, he sets the baby adrift in a boat in revenge. Calling Bellaria to court to humiliate her further, Pandosto agrees to her suggestion to question the oracle at Delphi to see what the gods say. They verify Bellaria's innocence, but no sooner does her neurotic husband apologize than they get word their son Garinter has died, which causes the queen to fall dead, and Pandosto to rue his lost wife and daughter.

The second half of the novella follows the abandoned baby girl, who arrives in Sicily and is adopted by a shepherd couple, Porrus and Mopsa, who name her Fawnia and raise her as a shepherdess even though she came with tokens identifying her as royalty.[125] Fast-forward 16 years, when this queen of curds and cream catches the eye of Egistus's son Dorastes, age 20 and under pressure from his father to marry the king of Denmark's daughter. He falls in love with the shepherdess with the royal manners — Greene belongs to the nature vs. nurture school of sociology — and plans to elope with her to mainland Italy, but their ship is blown off course to Bohemia, where the couple (and Fawnia's father, abducted because he was on the verge of spilling the beans about her origin) are captured. Dorastes and Porrus are put in prison, but 50-year-old Pandosto is enflamed by Fawnia's beauty and begins pressuring her for sex. At the last minute, Porrus is allowed to explain all, and Pandosto realizes the hot babe he has been romancing is actually his daughter. He is overjoyed to be reunited with her, but after she marries Egistus, he realizes how terrible he has behaved over the years and commits suicide. *The Winter's Tale* concludes in glorious spring with the queen brought miraculously back to life, but Greene's dark tale ends in near-incest, despair, and death.

Though to compare *Pandosto* to *The Winter's Tale* is to compare a robin to an eagle, it does represent an improvement over *Gwydonius*. The narrative is more structured and efficient, less reliant on Lyly-like rhetoric and set-pieces and closer to Sidney's pastoral mode. Greene reiterates his warning

---

carelessly; after his premature death, his friend Thomas Nashe wrote, "In a night and day would he have yarked up a pamphlet as well as in seven year.")

125 The oracle at Delphi, the name Mopsa, and the pastoral setting all suggest Greene saw one of the circulating manuscripts of Sidney's *Arcadia*.

"that love was above all laws, and therefore to be stayed with no law,"[126] the danger of which is titillated by Pandosto's "unlawful lust" for his daughter. He handles the two-part structure nicely, replaying the fatal jealousy at the beginning of the first part as comedy at the beginning of the second part as Mopsa assumes the baby Porrus brings home is the result of treading some "country slut" (180). And as in *Gwydonius*, Greene again insists that nature, not human laws or religion — classical gods are evoked, but there isn't a trace of Christianity — provides the standard by which one should live, "for that nature never framed anything amiss" (*Gwydonius* 162; cf. *Euphues* 39–40). While Shakespeare let his jealous king off the hook, tougher-minded Greene destroys Pandosto as an abomination of nature.

One more of Greene's numerous novels deserves notice. In *Menaphon* (1589) he almost perfected a Lyly/Sidney hybrid; its subtitle, *Camilla's Alarm to Slumbering Euphues in His Melancholy Cell at Silexedra*, means only that Greene is still cashing in on the popularity of euphuism — this isn't a sequel — but otherwise he follows Sidney both in setting his novel in Arcadia and by including several charming songs. (And his are actual songs one could sing, unlike Sidney's elaborate poems.) As in Heliodorus's *Ethiopian Story* (and the revised *Arcadia*), Greene's novel begins with a shipwreck; a shepherd named Menaphon spies three survivors struggling ashore: an older man named Lamedon and a beautiful young woman named Sephestia, nursing an infant. Menaphon, a wise man who had been boasting of his imperviousness to love, is stunned by Sephestia's beauty, so this former "atheist to love" who had of late "thought Venus a strumpet and her son a bastard, now must . . . offer incense at her shrine and swear Cupid no less than a god."[127] Greene doesn't identify the shipwrecked trio further than to hint they're royalty, letting their story unfold gradually. Menaphon offers them shelter and soon declares his love to Sephestia, now calling herself Samela of Cyprus, and while she demurs, she enjoys his hospitality and gamely adapts to the life of a shepherdess. He takes her to a party where learned rustics engage in a Wildean whirl of wit, with some especially waspish remarks coming from peevish Pesana, whose unrequited love for Menaphon is stung by the sight of his new love. Samela is astonished to see a shepherd named Melicertus who closely resembles her dead husband Maximus, and after the party "Melicertus" reflects how closely "Samela" resembles his dead wife Sephestia. Both assume their spouses are dead and thus decide to show favor to these bucolic facsimiles of their lost loves.[128]

---

126 Page 157 in Salzman's *Anthology of Elizabethan Prose Fiction*, where the novella occupies pp. 151–204.
127 Pages 106, 110 in Cantar's critical edition.
128 Near the beginning of the revised *Arcadia* Sidney tells the edifying tale of a woman whose beauty was destroyed by a rival who rubs poison in her face, and who consequently releases her fiancé from his vow and disappears. Sometime later a woman who looks exactly like her shows up and offers herself to the jilted man, but faithful to his first love, he declines. Thus

After this broad wink hinting at how the novella will end, Greene loses control of his narrative, lurching ahead five years to have Sephestia's son Pleusidippus kidnapped by pirates, and then leaping ahead another 11 years and contriving for shock value to have both Sephestia's son *and* her father proposition her (à la *Pandosto*) and abduct her for immoral purposes. Then Pleusidippus winds up in a swordfight with his unknown father (à la *Gwydonius*) among other absurdities until the inevitable recognition/reconciliation scene on the penultimate page, followed by marriages all around. According to Nashe, Greene was a heavy drinker and must have been drunk while yarking up the second half of the novella, which is a shame because the soberly composed first half is quite poised and lyrical. "He had his faults," Nashe admits,[129] one of which seems to have been his inability to break free from the Lyly/Sidney rut he was stuck in, and it's as though he just gave up and impatiently trashed his *Arcadia* in frustration.

Another of Greene's novels, *Philomela, the Lady Fitzwater's Nightingale* (1590), was called "the best of Greene's tales, and approaches more closely the modern novel than any work of the time" by Tuckerman in 1882 (86), but a more recent critic has dismissed it as an "Italianate tale in the euphuistic mode, one of Greene's least inspiring efforts" (Salzman, *English Prose Fiction* 62), so I'm going to pass over it and the other novels by this prolific author. A popular but minor novelist then, but an interesting character; Virginia Woolf had her doubts about Sidney, but she admired Greene enough to make him a character in her *Orlando*.

Thomas Lodge (1558–1625) was Greene's friend and collaborator, and is likewise remembered today chiefly for a novel that influenced Shakespeare. His *Rosalynd* (1590), the source for *As You Like It*, is the best of his half-dozen novels, and is a refinement of, rather than a departure from, the Lyly/Sidney mode Greene developed. Like *Menaphon*, it acknowledges Lyly's influence in its lengthy subtitle: *Euphues' Golden Legacy: found after his death in his cell at Silexedra*, purporting to be a cautionary tale written by Euphues for the benefit of Philautus's sons in England. And like *Arcadia*, it is set in a pastoral sanctuary (the forest of Arden) where affairs of the heart are intermixed with affairs of state, and is liberally sprinkled with a variety of poems, though (it must be said) they are as inferior to Sidney's as the novel itself is to Shakespeare's scintillating play.

---

convinced he was not marrying her solely for her looks, the woman reveals herself as the original, her face restored by a physician (87–92, 103–6). This strange inability of spouses or lovers to recognize each other is a contrived convention carried over from Greek romance and reminds us, yet again, that realism meant little to most novelists until recently, but in Greene's case, the unrealistic crosses over to the unbelievable.

129 All of Nashe's remarks are from his *Strange News* (1592). Nashe wrote a blustery 15-page preface for *Menaphon*, but he barely mentions the novel and instead rails against their alma mater Cambridge for neglecting the classics in favor of theology.

Written while on a long voyage to the Canary Islands, *Rosalynd* shows more care than Greene's rushed productions and moves from scene to scene much more smoothly. The plot is so similar to Shakespeare's that it requires no summary; Lodge foregrounds the political upheaval that Shakespeare leaves in the background after act 1, and his cast lacks a Touchstone or Jacques, but the strange capers in Arden are just as amusing, and cross-dressing Rosalynd's homoerotic flirtations are just as charming, though she lacks the slashing wit of Shakespeare's heroine. It's the polished work of a professional, and not surprisingly went through numerous printings in Lodge's lifetime. Unfortunately, the brilliance of *As You Like It* puts *Rosalynd* in the shade, and by 1590 the novelty of euphuistic pastoral was wearing off.

If Lodge wrote *Rosalynd* in a holiday humor, he was in a fouler mood when composing his last novel, for which he abandoned English pastoral for Italianate tragedy and Oriental wonder. In 1591, he accompanied the doomed explorer Thomas Cavendish on a voyage to South America, and while exploring the Strait of Magellan wrote *A Margarite of America* (1596).[130] Cavendish's crew mutinied and he died at sea; it must have been a harrowing time for Lodge, for his novel is rife with treachery and violence. It's a sermon on tyranny, on the dangers of unlimited power; in *Rosalynd* he had shown his contempt for the tyrant whose overthrow of the rightful king sets much of the action in motion, and here he drives home his point with a Grand Guignol excess of blood and horror.

The novel gets off to a brisk if confusing start as two emperors prepare to lead their armies into battle at dawn: Protomachus of Moscow is set to fight Artosogon of Cusco (capital of Peru) for Mantinea, a battleground in eastern Arcadia. How the Russian and Peruvian armies met up in Greece is never explained, and one suspects Lodge simply wanted some exotic locales to flavor his tale.[131] An old man suddenly strides onto the field and convinces them to negotiate instead, suggesting Protomachus's daughter Margarita marry Artosogon's son Arsadachus to join their kingdoms together. Both parties agree, and the Cuscan prince is sent to the Muscovite court to introduce

130 A margarite is a pearl, so the title means Lodge is offering British readers a pearl from America in the form of a novel. It also refers to the novel's heroine Margarita, "*A precious pearle in name, a pearle in nature*" (p. 225 in Harrison's old-spelling edition of Greene's *Menaphon* and *A Margarite of America*, where the latter occupies pp. 109–226). In his preface, Lodge claims to be translating a Spanish novel he found in a Jesuit library in the New World, but this is probably the same dodge many novelists used at this time to give their works a pedigree, or to avoid blame for any objectionable material.

131 As an explorer of South America, Lodge would have heard of Cuzco, taken by the Spanish in 1533, but since one of the Cuscan emperor's courtiers is the duke of Moravia, Lodge's imaginary kingdom is apparently down in the Balkans somewhere, perhaps near the seacoast of Bohemia. In an otherwise informed essay, Josephine A. Roberts argues unconvincingly that the novel is actually set in South America, ignoring all the European locales and Greek/Latin names.

himself. The narrator tells us in no uncertain terms that Arsadachus is a real snake in the grass, and shortly after he arrives he begins scheming and murdering and framing rivals, all while pretending to woo naïve Margarita. Arsinous, the father of one of the murder victims, tries to expose him to Protomachus but is banished instead to the steppes of Russia, since by then Arsadachus has wormed his way into the emperor's favor. When the emperor decides it is time for marriage, however, Arsadachus gets cold feet — he wants the throne but not the girl — and so uses his father's illness as an excuse to return home, but not before Margarita gives him a jewel-box to be opened only when he begins to miss her.

Back in Cusco, Arsadachus falls for a courtier's daughter named Diana, who impersonates her divine namesake in a masque, dressed to kill:

> her haire scattered about her shoulders, compassed with a siluer crownet, her necke decked with carkanets of pearle, her daintie body was couered with a vaile of white net-work wrought with wiers of siluer, and set with pearle, where through the milke white beauties of the sweete Saint gaue so heauenly a reflexion, that it was sufficient to make *Saturne* merry and mad with loue, to fixe his eie on them: . . . (189)

"The Egyptians (as *Ororius* reporteth) when as they would represent loue do make a net" (177), a character informed us earlier, and Diana's net-work traps Arsadachus instantly. Lodge repeats the word *pearle* twice to contrast this temptress with the pearl of Moscow Arsadachus left behind. He is "stricken so dombe with her diuine beautie" (190) that her scheming father hastily arranges a marriage between the two, but as soon as Artosogon gets wind of this he has the father "torne in peeces at the tailes of foure wilde horses" (197) and threatens to do likewise with Diana for spoiling his scheme to unite the two kingdoms. His viperish son responds by mutilating him and dressing him in fool's motley, much to Diana's amusement. After his death, Arsadachus plays shepherd-and-goddess games with Diana and writes reams of poetry — Lodge gives us 10 of his poems spread out over seven pages — which betrays "the right shape of his dissembling nature" (208).

Impatient Margarita decides to visit Cusco to see what is delaying her fiancé, disguising herself as a peasant and accompanying herself with a friend name Fawnia (after the heroine of *Pandosto*). Along the way, a lion surprises them, and though it devours Fawnia "(in that she had tasted too much of fleshly loue)," as Lodge tells us in a puritan parenthesis (210), the lion places its head gently in Margarita's lap, the king of the beasts sensing a fellow royal. From this point on, the novel grows more fanciful and magical, especially when banished Arsinous returns with his spellbook and performs several tricks after he meets up with Margarita en route to Cusco. It also grows more violent as Protomachus, learning of his daughter's disappearance, "put al her attendants to most bitter and strange death" (211), another example of tyrannical overkill that Lodge adds to his case against absolute power. Back in Cusco, Arsadachus marries Diana in Oriental splendor, then opens Margarita's remembrance box for laughs; "a sodain flame issued thereout, which with a hideous odour so bestraught *Arsadachus* of his senses" (217) that in a frenzy he slaughters everyone around him, including his bride and her child, in ghastly detail. Just then, Margarita arrives in court, and he runs her through with a rapier. "The poor princesse euen when death beganne to arrest her, pursued him," Lodge adds poignantly (219), capturing in a gesture the tyranny of blind love. Coming to his senses later, Arsadachus realizes how terribly he has acted and commits suicide, leaving Arsinous to read the riot act to the Cuscans for allowing such a tyrant to prevail: "beleeue me, beleeue me, your sufferance of such a viper in your realme, is a hainous sinne in you; and as *Dion* saith, it is but meete they be partakers to the paine, who haue wincked at the fault" (221).

A *Margarite of America* is a showpiece for Lodge's wild imagination and especially his rhetorical skills: the novel is filled with orations, poems, a symposium on love, Latin quotations, learned allusions, and detailed descriptions of clothes, furnishings, and pageants. I hear a self-reflexive boast from Lodge when Margarita and the magician talk "merrilie as they rode of such strange things as Arsinous had wrought by his art" (214). But overriding the strange things of this romance is a revolutionary call to citizens to take responsibility for their government and to be critical of their leaders, and a warning to those who misuse their power. *Sic semper tyrannis!*

Greene called him a young Juvenal, Lodge a true English Aretino. Thomas Nashe (1567–1601?) was, like them, a University Wit and a busy polemicist, and after a short, fast life left behind the two most modernistic novels of the Elizabethan era. *Pierce Penniless His Supplication to the Devil* (1592) is a first-person screed by an author angry at his lack of success and failure to find a patron to lift him out of poverty. Desperate, he decides to ask the devil to become his patron, and pens a 66-page letter of application that doubles as an audition piece, a sweeping attack on "the lamentable condition of our times."[132] Searching London for one of Satan's representatives, Pierce first approaches the lawyers at Westminster Hall, then the financiers at the Exchange, and finally finds one in the person of a Knight of the Post (a professional witness paid to give false testimony). The Knight reads Pierce's supplication, answers some questions about demonology, then leaves promising to submit the application to his dark lord.

Like Dostoevsky's *Notes from Underground*, *Pierce Penniless* is a study in frazzled personality, of someone who projects onto the outer world his own

---

132 Page 54 in *The Unfortunate Traveller and Other Works*, where the novella occupies pp. 49–145.

frustrations and neuroses. Pierce's frost-bitten bitterness, his outrage that lesser men than he are more successful, pushes his social criticism over the edge into the realm of grotesque exaggeration — fun to read, but revealing more about Pierce than the targets of his satire. For instance, after criticizing Spaniards, Italians, and the French, he lays into the Danish, of all people:

> The most gross and senseless proud dolts (in a different kind from all these) are the Danes, who stand so much upon their unwieldy burly-boned soldiery that they account of no man that hath not a battle-axe at his girdle to hough dogs with, or wears not a cock's feather in a red thrummed hat like a cavalier. Briefly, he is the best fool braggart under heaven. For besides nature hath lent him a flabberkin face, like one of the four winds, and cheeks that sag like a woman's dugs over his chin-bone, his apparel is so puffed up with bladders of taffety, and his back like beef stuffed with parsley, so drawn out with ribbons and devices, and blistered with light sarsenet bastings, that you would think him nothing but a swarm of butterflies if you saw him afar off.[133] Thus walks he up and down in his majesty, taking a yard of ground at every step, and stamps the earth so terrible, as if he meant to knock up a spirit, when, foul drunken bezzle, if an Englishman set his little finger to him, he falls like a hog's-trough that is set on one end. (74–75)

As this typical passage shows, the main appeal of *Pierce Penniless* is Nashe's flamboyant style, a rich shepherd's pie of beefy English. It's not all invective — Pierce praises poetry and plays (which were under attack at the time) — and it's filled with realistic details that give a better sense of life in Elizabethan England than other novels written at the time.

Because *Pierce Penniless* doesn't resemble those other novels, it is rarely considered a novel by specialists of the era — Paul Salzman feels it's "much too diverse in its aims to be considered a true work of prose fiction" (86) — but a 20th-century specialist has no problem recognizing it as a novel. Novels by/about frustrated writers are legion, ranging from Frederick Rolfe's *Nicholas Crabbe* (1904) to Steve Hely's *How I Became a Famous Novelist* (2009). In many respects it resembles William Gaddis's final novel, *Agapē Agape*, another first-person novella weak on narrative but apoplectic with cultural criticism. I can easily imagine Alexander Theroux or Percival Everett writing something like *Pierce Penniless*, or the late great Gilbert Sorrentino.

But there's less disagreement over the genre of Nashe's most famous novel, *The Unfortunate Traveller* (1594). Subtitled *The Life of Jack Wilton*, it is the first-person confession of a prankish page at the court of Henry VIII. A rogue and gambler, Jack first regales us with several scams he played on people while in France with the armies of his king, then returns to England only to

---

133 "If you know him not by any of these marks, look on his fingers and you shall be sure to find half a dozen silver rings, worth threepence apiece" — Nashe's note, making *Pierce Penniless* perhaps the first novel to use footnotes.

find an epidemic of the sweating sickness has broken out, which causes him to hightail it back to Europe; the French are now fighting the Swiss and he figures he'll join whichever side wins. His first view of the battlefield sets the graphic, impudent tone for the rest of the novel:

> It was my good luck or my ill, I know not which, to come just to the fighting of the battle, where I saw a wonderful spectacle of bloodshed on both sides. Here unwieldly Switzers wallowing in their gore like an oxe in his dung; there the sprightly French sprawling and turning on the stained grass like a roach new taken out of the stream. All the ground was strewed as thick with battle-axes as the carpenter's yard with chips: the plain appeared like a quagmire, overspread as it was with trampled dead bodies. In one place might you behold a heap of dead murthered men overwhelmed with a falling steed instead of a tombstone; in another place a bundle of bodies fettered together in their own bowels. And as the tyrant Roman Emperor used to tie condemned living caitiffs face to face to dead corpses, so were the half-living here mixed with squeezed carcases long putrefied.[134]

There had been countless battle scenes in novels before, some brutal, but this is the first to rub the reader's face in the gory details while disrespecting the dead with flippantly alliterative rhythms ("unwieldy Switzers wallowing . . . sprightly French sprawling"). "Like a crow that still follows aloof where there is carrion" (277), Jack next goes to Münster in Germany, where John Leyden is leading the Anabaptist uprising against the emperor of Saxony (1534; Nashe merrily mixes fact with fiction throughout the novel). Jack mocks this ragtag army and their theology, and after witnessing another slaughter heads back to England and offers his service to the poet Henry Howard, earl of Surrey (1517?–47), who, though in love with a lass named Geraldine, soon leaves with Jack for Italy.[135]

En route, the pair stop over at Rotterdam to visit Erasmus and Sir Thomas More, then pass through Wittenberg, where they are treated to some "scholastical entertainment," including a magic show by Cornelius Agrippa (1486–1535) in which he conjures up the ghost of Cicero. Approaching Italy, Surrey and Jack decide to switch places, and in Venice they indulge in all sorts of antic capers with pimps and whores. Pietro Aretino makes a cameo appearance, and the cheerful vulgarity of his *Dialogues* enlivens this portion of the novel. (Nashe pauses to pay a three-page tribute to him [309–11]: "ne'er a line of his but was able to make a man drunken with admiration.") In Florence Surrey visits the house where his beloved was born, which allows Nashe to

---

134 Page 276 in *The Unfortunate Traveller and Other Works*, where the novel occupies pp. 251–370. It is also included in Salzman (205–309) and in most anthologies of Elizabethan prose.
135 Surrey's sonnet "Description and Praise of His Love Geraldine," which claims Florence as his lady's birthplace, was Nashe's inspiration for this section; Surrey never visited Italy (nor did Nashe).

parody the extravagant prose his fellow University Wits were churning out in their romance novels:[136]

> Oh, but when he came to the chamber where his Geraldine's clear sunbeams first thrust themselves into this cloud of flesh and acquainted mortality with the purity of angels, then did his mouth overthrow with magnificats; his tongue thrust the stars out of heaven, and eclipsed the sun and moon with comparisons. Geraldine was the soul of heaven, sole daughter and heir to *primus motor*. The alchemy of his eloquence, out of the incomprehensible drossy matter of clouds and air distilled no more quintessence than would make his Geraldine complete fair. (315)

Surrey issues a challenge to defend his lady's beauty against all comers, which gives Nashe an excuse to mock chivalric conventions (10 years before *Don Quixote*) with comical descriptions of the knights' symbolic trappings:

> After him followed the Knight of the Owl, whose armour was a stubbed tree overgrown with ivy, his helmet fashioned like an owl sitting on the top of this ivy. On his bases were wrought all kinds of birds, as on the ground, wandering about him; the word, *Ideo mirum quia monstrum* [Thus marvelous because monstrous]. His horse's furniture was framed like a cart, scattering whole sheaves of corn amongst hogs; the word, *Liberalitas liberalitate perit* ["Giving ruins the giver" — Jerome]. (319)

A Monty Pythonesque battle follows, and after Surrey emerges victorious, he is called back to England, leaving Jack to continue on to Rome with a courtesan he has picked up.

Jack does Rome like Hunter S. Thompson doing Vegas: the grandeur that was Rome is just a gaudy amusement park as far as he's concerned (though he's lost in admiration for its artificial gardens). Like a black cloud following our unfortunate traveler, another epidemic descends while Jack is staying at the home of a Roman matron named Heraclide. A Spanish bandit named Esdras is taking advantage of the plague to break into rich men's houses for robbery and rape; he sexually threatens Heraclide, and as the tense narrative unfolds over four pages one expects Jack or someone to come to her rescue, but not in the world according to Nashe: "Whatsoever is born, is born to have an end," Jack preaches from his hiding place. "Thus ends my tale: his whorish lust was glutted, his beastly desire satisfied. What in the house was carriageable, he put up, and went his way" (336). Jack is suspected of her murder and nearly hanged, but is saved at the last minute by a banished English earl who has overheard Esdras's partner confess what really happened, and who lectures Jack on the evils of traveling. Jack is soon captured again by a Jew named

---

136 In his book on Nashe's rhetoric, Crewe labels *The Unfortunate Traveller* an "antiromance" (69).

Zadoch and is nearly sold to a Jewish doctor for anatomical experimentation when he is rescued by Countess Juliana, one of the pope's courtesans, who has her own anatomical designs on the handsome 18-year-old. (Zadoch is eventually condemned and tortured to death in horrific detail.) After toiling for months as the countess's boy toy, Jack finally escapes and in Bologna witnesses yet another grisly execution as a cobbler named Cutwolfe is broken on the wheel, but not before delivering a six-page paean to revenge. (Cutwolfe killed Esdras for killing his brother, which Jack interprets as evidence that his god punishes malefactors.) The savage sight scares Jack straight: "To such straight life did it thenceforward incite me that ere I went out of Bologna I married my courtesan, performed many alm-deeds, and hasted so fast out of the Sodom of Italy, that within forty days I arrived at the King of England's camp twixt Ardes and Guines in France" (370), not far from where his tale began.

Superficially resembling a picaresque novel, *The Unfortunate Traveller* is a collage of many genres: chronicles, gonzo journalism, sermons, stage tragedies, popular novels, exposés of criminal life (like the cony-catching pamphlets his friend Greene excelled at), poetry, and of course travel narratives — all punched up with parody. One critic has said it "begins as a jest book, continues as a mock chronicle, and concludes as an experiment in Italianate melodrama."[137] Nashe himself calls it a "fantastical treatise" (251) and Jack Wilton's "Acts and Monuments" (253), a facetious reference to John Foxe's popular *Acts and Monuments* of Protestant martyrs (1563), whose deaths are described in the same ghastly detail as the executions Jack witnesses. Coincidentally, a comedian's "act" might best describe Jack's presentation: he will introduce a topic like the sweating sickness and then riff and pun on it for a few paragraphs; the banished English earl in Italy does an extended bit on foreigners that surely got some big laughs from Nashe's English audience; and Surrey's challenge is an occasion for Nashe to keep topping himself as he describes one ludicrous knight after another. Many episodes resemble comedy skits, with Jack alternating in the roles of conman and dupe. In this regard the novel resembles popular Elizabethan jestbooks like *A Hundred Merry Tales* (1526) and *The Sackful of News* (c. 1588), though Nashe's juxtaposition of farce and graphic violence is new, more like Burroughs's *Naked Lunch* than *Scoggin's Jests* (c. 1570). The very novelty of these juxtapositions — of humor and horror, of high culture and low comedy — is what Nashe considered his claim to fame with this novel: "A new brain, a new wit, a new style, a new soul I will get me . . ." (252).

That "new style" is Nashe's greatest innovation. He has the largest vocabulary of any Elizabethan writer save Shakespeare, drawn from all quarters of the linguistic globe. Here's Jack on one of the scholars at Wittenberg:

---

137 L. G. Salinger (1956), quoted by John Berryman in the brisk introduction to his edition of the novel (9).

A bursten-belly inkhorn orator called Vanderhulke they picked out to present him with an oration; one that had a sulphurous big swollen large face like a Saracen, eyes like two Kentish oysters, a mouth that opened as wide every time he spake as one of those old knit trap doors, a beard as though it had been made of a bird's nest plucked in pieces, which consisteth of straw, hair and dirt mixed together. He was apparelled in black leather new-liquored and a short gown without any gathering in the back, faced before and behind with a boisterous bear-skin, and a red night-cap on his head. To this purport and effect was this brocking double-beer oration. (292–93)

The oration that follows reaches Joycean heights at times — "Why should I go gadding and fizgigging after firking flantado amphibologies?" (293) — and is only one of dozens of dazzling rhetorical set-pieces. The language is both more realistic and more contrived than that of any other Elizabethan novelist; the critic Walter Raleigh once wrote, "it is the likest of all others to Shakespeare's prose writing. The same irrepressible, inexhaustible wit, the same overpowering and often careless wealth of vocabulary, the same delight in humourous aberrations of logic distinguish both writers."[138] Nashe would push his linguistic innovations even further in his final work, *Lenten Stuff* (1599), an unclassifiable tour de force about the quality of red herring found in the town of Yarmouth, but *The Unfortunate Traveller* pulled the Elizabethan novel out of the Lyly/Sidney rut and gave it a new voice and new content, both unmistakably British, and proudly so. Much of the novel is set in Europe only to expose its inferiority to England, and the protagonist is not named Pyrocles or Arsadachus but plain Jack Wilton. The novel has its faults — the internal chronology is a mess, and too often Nashe imposes his voice on Jack's — but *The Unfortunate Traveller* is a spray-painted milestone in the development of the English novel and richly deserves the Knight of the Owl's motto *Ideo mirum quia monstrum*: it is marvelous because monstrous, wonderful because outlandish.

Nashe's friend Henry Chettle (c. 1564–c. 1607), primarily a dramatist, published in 1595 a clever little novel entitled *Piers Plainness' Seven Years' Prenticeship*. A playful experiment in narratology, Chettle tossed Nashe's realism, Greene's violent romances, and Lyly's style into a blender for a self-consciously literary cocktail. It opens like a pastoral as a Thessalian shepherd named Menalcas tells his neighbor Corydon of a vagabond worker he has just hired, an "exceedingly Satyrical" wag called Piers Plainness.[139] Piers offers to tell the two of his work history, then launches into a story set in Thrace

138 *The English Novel* (1894), quoted in Steane's introduction, 38. Shakespeare, as Berryman notes, "made some use" of *The Unfortunate Traveller* in *1 Henry IV*, and gently satirized Nashe as Moth in *Love's Labours Lost*.
139 Page 123 in Winny's *Descent of Euphues*, where the novella occupies pp. 122–74. Piers' name obviously owes something to Nashe's *Pierce Penniless*, on which Chettle wrote a pamphlet called *Kind-Heart's Dream* (1592).

(NE Greece), where he was a servant to a court hanger-on. There follows a Greenish tale of a king and his two children exiled by his lascivious son (via an evil advisor) to Crete, ruled by a beautiful young queen who is being stalked by her lustful uncle, with all the principals eventually reunited, reconciled, and restored. Piers regularly interrupts this tale with Nashean accounts of his misadventures with various employers, adjusting his language as he switches back and forth between the two narratives, genteel Lylian for the nobility and impudent Nashese for his own activities. Intent on finishing before sundown, Piers often speeds things along with clipped narration like this:

> Dolon at Rhegius Castle finds Aemilius, intertains him, stayes him, betrayes him, and in a deepe dungeon imprisons him, where day equalled the night in darkness, only a small glimmering through a cranny in the wall descended. (172)

Any earlier Elizabethan novelist would have spent a dozen pages on this sequence, but (and this is Chettle's point) by 1595 anyone who has read those novels can fill in the details.

There is a hint of the picaresque as Piers moves from master to master like Lazarillo, witnessing corruption, financial swindling, prostitution, and other criminal activities, though he lacks the innocence of the true *picaro*. As Margaret Schlauch notes (201–3), Chettle is describing the Elizabethan underworld of his own time, which doesn't mesh with the timeless Grecian pastoral/romantic setting of the rest of the novella, and Piers narrates material about the royals he couldn't possibly have known, but this all seems to be part of Chettle's game. Satyrical Piers often interrupts his narrative to point out he is going to switch tales, or his auditors will interrupt him with a question, drawing attention to himself as narrator and raising suspicions about his reliability. It's fun to watch Chettle toy with the conventions of the novel, mashing genres together, switching registers of language, and playing with reader expectations. It's a shame that after this lark Chettle returned to his largely forgotten dramatic work.

Another novelty: We have an Englishman to thank for the sentimental tear-jerker. Nicholas Breton (c. 1550–c. 1625), an Oxford-educated friend of the Sidneys and a mentor to Shakespeare and Jonson, worked like Nashe in a variety of prose forms and like him produced one novella, *The Miseries of Mavillia* (1597). Breton knew Italian literature well and may have come across *The Elegy of Lady Fiammetta*, for like Boccaccio's novel *Mavillia* is a monologue from a young woman convinced she is, in the words of the subtitle, *The Most Unfortunate Lady That Ever Lived*. The short work is divided not into chapters but into five "Miseries": in the first, she tells how her parents were killed by enemy soldiers when she was almost five and how she wound up with a laundress to the defending army; this woman treated her nice at first but then mistreats her until a captain who knew Mavillia's father intervenes and arranges to send her to her uncle. But in "The Second Miserie" her escorts are killed except for a devoted pageboy; they live off the land for a while until they find shelter with a kindly rustic couple, but then the page dies. In "The Third Miserie" the old lady, like the laundress, turns ugly and sends our little heroine into "a Miserie of Miseries."[140] After the old woman dies, the old man treats Mavillia much nicer, and in fact leaves her his goods when he dies, which she is promptly cheated out of in "The Fourth Miserie" by relatives and thrown in jail. Taken to court, Mavillia's Christian resignation to her god's will shames her accusers and they all confess, and Mavillia recovers the old man's inheritance. But there's one more "Miserie" to go: now of marriageable age, Mavillia is courted by a younger and an older man (no one in this novella is named, emphasizing Mavillia's self-pitying egotism — this is *her* show and she's not sharing the spotlight with anyone). Though the younger man is a little slick and speaks like one of Lodge's lovers, the older is repulsive, so she marries the former. The old codger disfigures her in revenge, and some time later her husband kills him; Mavillia is about to give birth, and all these shocks to her system, she implies on the last page of the novella, will kill her as soon as she drops her pen. Ever the Christian martyr, she writes: "since I am borne to miserie, Gods will be done" (165).

A series of unfortunate events, *The Miseries of Mavillia* now reads like a parody, but in the late 1590s it was something new. The use of a child as narrator was still novel (especially a female) and excuses somewhat the excessive tugs on the heartstrings. And the prose is even more realistic than Nashe's; here's Mavillia on the frustration of trying to teach the old lady's spoiled daughter:

> Nowe forsooth, I must attend uppon my young Mistresse, the olde Womans daughter, the most ilfavoured and untowarde urchin that ever was borne: This baggage must I go teach her Booke, and forsooth touch her I must not, but Good Mistresse looke on your Booke: Yea, that is a fayre Gentlewoman, when shee saide never a word, but I was faine to speake for her: If I complained of her, then, Oh you thinke much of your paynes, would you have her reade as well as you the first daye: Go, come not to mee with such twittle twattle, then go to the Gyrle, Ha! Mouse, doth she say thou wilt not learne? Marrie she lyes. Holde heere, wilt thou have a Plum or an Apple? yea, marrie, it is a good Gyrle: then was I glad to get Apples and Peares, and such geere to bring her to the Booke. And then the apish elfe, for my heart would not say a word, so that I could not for my life, but give her a little slap on the shoulders: and if I did but even touch her, the Monkie would set out the throate, and crie so vengeouslie, that to it must the mother come: and then, How now gyrle? tell me, doth she beate thee? Minion, you were not best touch her, see you? the Wench would

140 Page 135 in Kentish-Wright's edition of Breton's prose works, jauntily entitled *A Mad World My Masters*, where the novella occupies pp. 107–66 of volume 2.

learne well inough, and you were willing to teach her, well, you were best use her gently, least yee fare the worse for it, and so away she goes. (136–37)

Now known as "free indirect discourse," such a mode was still a novelty then in fiction, and at other times Breton approaches a stream-of-consciousness style when Mavillia is "prating to my selfe" (153). Breton cleverly and realistically allows the language to grow up with Mavillia — she speaks almost like a cheeky Shakespearean heroine by the time she's being courted — and his gruesome descriptions of illness and prison life set a new standard for squalor. *Mavillia* is no forgotten masterpiece, but it is a fascinating experiment in pathos. The great Saintsbury once said of the English novelists of this era that they "seemed to be conducting a series of blind or half-blind experiments";[141] but critics usually underestimate artists, and I'm sure Breton and the others had their eyes wide open.

But most kept their blinkered eyes down, following the old, familiar roads. By the 1590s, the once purebred strains of the ancient Greek novel, chivalric romance, Italian novella, and European pastoral had mixed to produce such mixed breeds as Chettle's *Piers Plainness* and Emanuel Ford's *Ornatus and Artesia* (1598?), the best of his novels. Though influenced by Sidney and Greene, Ford (d. c. 1607) attempted to reach a broader audience than their erudite, stylish works could, and in this popular novel — "far more popular in his time than any play of Shakespeare's," as his first modern editor says,[142] with some embarrassment, I imagine — Ford found a simplified formula that would be followed by lesser talents thereafter. Two households, both alike in dignity, hold an ancient grudge. A young man named Ornatus belongs to one of them, and while resting from hawking one day he espies a young woman who departs from her father's hunting party to likewise take a breather. With none of his immediate predecessors' sense of decorum, Ford allows us to look over Ornatus's shoulder

whilst she, tying her steed to a bush, laid her delicate body down upon the cooling earth to breathe herself and dry up her sweat, which the sooner to accomplish, she unbraced her garments and with a decent and comely behavior discovered [exposed] her milk-white neck and breast, beautified with two round precious teats, to receive the breath of the cool wind, which was affected with a delight to exhale the moistened vapors from her pure body. Ornatus seeing all, and unseen himself, noted with delight each perfect lineament of her proper body, beauty, sweet favor, and other comeliness, which filled his heart with exceeding pleasure, therewith growing into an unrestrained affection towards her . . .[143]

141 Introduction to *Shorter Novels*, ix.
142 Pages x–xi in Philip Henderson's introduction to *Shorter Novels: Jacobean and Restoration*, where *Ornatus and Artesia* occupies pp. 1–143.
143 Page 114 in Stanivukovic's recent edition, which corrects Henderson's many transcription errors.

This sort of description (especially the detail of the lad's growing, unrestrained erection) is what led John Bunyan to condemn novels as "bad and abominable books . . . beastly romances full of ribaldry, even such as immediately tended to set all fleshly lust on fire."[144] This topless beauty is of course Artesia, and Ornatus's desire to dip into Artesia's well launches a predictable narrative of familial resistance, obstacles, foreign adventures, pirates, disguises, etc., concluding with the inevitable marriage and happy ending. At this point, anyone could write such stuff, so innovative writers looked elsewhere for inspiration.

Thomas Deloney (d. 1600), an educated silk-weaver and ballad-maker who started writing fiction only in the final years of his life, produced four delightful novels that, in their own way, are as radical as Nashe's, for he decided to write about working-class characters in everyday language. The novels of his contemporaries were about the upper classes and royalty; even Nashe's page spends most of his time around titled aristocracy.[145] Deloney's heroes are the members of England's growing middle class: cloth-workers and shoemakers, apprentices and factory workers. And perhaps most revolutionary of all, he treats them with respect and admiration.

Deloney's first novel, *Jack of Newbury* (1597), is set early in the reign of Henry VIII (1509–47), the "good old days" for Elizabethans living in the 1590s. John Winchcombe, Jack to his friends, is a working-class hero who rises from apprentice to rich merchant, and eventually to Member of Parliament, by way of hard work and virtuous living. After his master dies, he catches the eye of his widow, who is so impressed by his work that she fends off the marriage proposals of the local tanner, tailor, and parson in favor of Jack in one of the most charming opening chapters I have ever read. The basic plot is taken from one of the *Hundred Merry Tales*, but Deloney turns it into a witty romance as the widow courts her modest employee, who is uncomfortable with marrying his former boss's wife, especially one "so auncient." Deloney is careful to portray the widow not as the sex-crazed older woman of some novels but as an intelligent if lonely woman seeking companionship. One cold winter's night she makes it clear that she wants Jack to take her husband's place — literally:

> In the ende bed time comming on, shee caused her maide in a merriment to plucke off his hose and shooes, and caused him to bee laide in his masters best bed, standing in the best Chamber, hung round about with very faire curtaines. *Iohn* being thus preferred,

---

144 *The Life and Death of Mr. Badman* (1680), quoted on p. xii of Henderson's introduction.
145 Thomas Lodge provides a questionable exception in his novel *William Longbeard* (1593), about a lower-class rabble-rouser in the time of Richard I. It shows some concern for the abuses heaped on the poor by the rich, but William is portrayed more as a trouble-maker than a social activist and is deservedly hanged at the end. See Schlauch, 235–36.

thought himself a Gentleman, and lying soft, after his hard labour and a good supper, quickly fell asleepe.

About midnight, the Widow being cold on her feet, crept into her mans bed to warme them. *Iohn* feeling one lift vp the cloathes, asked who was there?

O good *Iohn* it is I, quoth the widow, the night is so extreame colde, and my Chamber walles so thin, that I am like to be starued in my bed: wherefore rather then I would any way hazard my health, I thought it much better to come hither and trie your curtesie, to haue a little roome beside you.

Iohn being a kind young man would not say her nay, and so they spent the rest of the night together in one bed.[146]

No rhetorical protests about chastity or reputation, no appeals to "the impediments of honour and the torments of conscience" (as Musidorus says in the new *Arcadia* [222]), just two human beings seeking refuge from the cold outside world. How easily this reads, even in its original spelling, and how poignant the widow's plea. The next morning, she sort of tricks him into marrying her — he doesn't protest much — and after a comic skirmish in which the husband and wife establish their equality, "they liued long together, in most godly, louing and kind sort, till, in the end she died, leauing her husband wondrous wealthie" (1).

The 10 shorter chapters that follow are like scenes in a play, each providing further dramatizations of Jack's good citizenship and/or the virtues of the middle class. Jack raises a small army to serve the queen, then wins the king's approval during a royal visit to Newbury. He later petitions the king for redress for unfair economic competition from foreigners with English clothiers like himself (as Deloney did in 1595) and criticizes Henry's advisor Thomas Wolsey for betraying his humble roots and imposing heavy taxation and restrictions upon the working classes. Jack forgives a huge debt owed to him by a draper and even sets him up in a new business, in which the draper prospers and eventually becomes sheriff of London, one of many rags-to-riches tales in the short novel. In one chapter Jack lectures on the 15 portraits hanging in his parlor, each depicting a king who rose from humble origins. But it's not all inspirational civics lessons: during Henry's visit, the girls who work in Jack's shop play a cruel trick on the king's jester involving "a couple of dogs droppings," and when an Italian merchant tries to seduce one of the local girls, her kinsman arranges a bedtrick involving a drugged sow. In fact, the novel ends with a seedy inversion of the first chapter, in which a shopgirl named Joan allows a visiting aristocrat to knock her up and then tricks him into marrying her, which rounds the square corners of Deloney's otherwise idealistic attitude toward the upward mobility of the middle class.

146 Chap. 1 in Lawlis's critical edition of *The Novels of Thomas Deloney*, all of which I will cite by chapter number.

His worldview "is frankly economic but not selfishly materialistic," the leading authority on his work insists,[147] which is the point of the draper's tale; Jack is even criticized for treating his help too well. But Deloney seems to condone whatever it takes to get to that room at the top.

Jack of Newbury departs from other Elizabethan novels not only in content but in style. As the extract above shows, the language is much simpler and more realistic, and Deloney goes so far as to introduce dialect, broken English (from the Italian merchant), a drunk's slurred speech, and comic malapropisms. He relies heavily on the spoken word — two chapters are entirely in dialogue (8 and 10) — a feature both of jestbooks and of course the popular plays of his day. Deloney will occasionally parody euphuistic diction or pen a formal letter (in chap. 6), and sprinkled throughout the novel are the kinds of ballads he was famous for before he turned to writing fiction. Stylistically variegated, socially engaged, didactic but playful, idealistic but rooted in real life, extolling bourgeois values while relaxing with knavish tricks, *Jack of Newbury* introduced a new paradigm for fiction, one that would reach its apotheosis in Dickens. It is both a nostalgic evocation of merrie olde England with its fairs and folk ballads, and a forward-looking example of proletarian fiction. In a word, revolutionary.

It was followed later in 1597 by *The Gentle Craft*, which proved so popular that Deloney published a sequel a year or two later.[148] The focus here is on shoemakers, for whom Deloney cobbled together a foundation myth from the Christian legends of the Welsh saints Hugh and Winifred (it is royal-born Hugh who names shoemaking "the gentle craft," that is, suitable for a distressed gentleman), the Roman brothers Crispin and Crispinian (considered the patron saints of shoemakers), and the British saint Ursula (she of the 11,000 virgins).[149] After Hugh is martyred, his bones are converted into shoemaking tools, and the Crispin–Ursula romance is an etiological explanation for the saying "a shoemaker's son is a prince born." Deloney handles all this smoothly, and is confident enough to depart from his source to allow Crispin to secretly marry Ursula, who loses any connection to the famous virgin after "he pluckt the rose of amorous delight" (6). The novel enters more familiar territory after Deloney jumps from the mythic 5th century to the historic 15th and introduces Simon Eyre, based on a mayor of London who died in 1458.[150]

---

147 Lawlis in his splendid anthology *Elizabethan Prose Fiction*, 549. He also wrote *Apology for the Middle Class: The Dramatic Novels of Thomas Deloney* (1961).

148 The publication dates of Deloney's later novels are uncertain because no first editions survive; they were so popular they were literally read to pieces. The first two are dated 1597 only because they were entered into the Stationer's Register for that year.

149 Someone who knew how difficult it would be to corral 11,000 virgins eventually realized that the Latin *undecim millia* (11K) was actually the name of one virgin, Undecimilla. Deloney adapted all this mythic material from Jacobus de Varagine's *Golden Legend*.

150 Students of Elizabethan drama will recognize him from Thomas Dekker's delightful play

It's another rags-to-riches story as Simon progresses from humble shoemaker to rich merchant to sheriff and eventually lord mayor of London. His big break involves a fraudulent deception; again, the ethics of upward mobility don't seem to bother Deloney, and in fact Simon later credits his god for his success with no cognitive dissonance. The story of Simon's rise alternates with a comic subplot involving his maid Florence and two foreigners who are dating her — not *courting* her as in days of old, for they go to taverns for drinks just like modern dating couples — though Florence eventually settles for an Englishman, another expression of British patriotism. The novel is notable for its strong female characters: Winifred, though "ouermuch superstitious" (2), inspires Hugh with her bravery in dying for the newfangled Christian cult; Ursula courts Crispin with admirable boldness, and a woman comes up with the plan to hide Ursula's pregnancy; Simon's ambitious wife devises the scam that enables him to become rich; and Florence, nobody's foole, handles her three suitors with aplomb. There are even some gamesome lasses who drink wine straight from the bottle and swear by their maidenheads. It's a pleasant entertainment, no more.

The Gentle Craft, the Second Part (1598?) is a linked trilogy of stories about London shoemakers in the mid-1500s, and opens with the finest thing Deloney ever wrote: the wooing of Richard Casteler, "the cock of Westminster." This prosperous bachelor shoemaker is the envy "of all the pretty Wenches in the Citty," all of whom go to him for shoes so that they can show off their legs. Two girls in particular set their caps at him: known by the inns at which they work, they are called Gillian of the George and Margaret of the Spread Eagle.[151] The first three chapters recount their comically doomed attempts to win Dick (who has his eye on a Dutch girl), a droll sex farce kept in motion by one of Richard's employees, Round Robin, who speaks mostly in verse. Like the fool in Shakespeare's plays, he's full of wit and sexual innuendo, mostly at the expense of the two husband-hungry girls, but also of his rather vacuous master. But the star of the show is Margaret, known as Long Meg (as in Little Richard's tautological Long Tall Sally), a fun-loving, wise-cracking dame with all the best lines. Teasing him for not having a last (a mold for shoemaking) long enough to fit her foot, she winks: "Fie *Richard* fie, thou shouldest neuer be vnprouided especially for women" (2). Her idealistic paean to marriage is touching, but likewise ends with a wink:

The Shoemaker's Holiday (1599), written to capitalize on the popularity of *The Gentle Craft*.

151 Richard Casteler was an actual London shoemaker who died in 1559. Margaret is based on a Renaissance "roaring girl" named Long Meg of Westminster, the subject of ballads and pamphlets; for an example of the latter, see *The Life and Pranks of Long Meg of Westminster* (1590), reprinted (from a later edition) in Mish's *Anchor Anthology of Short Fiction of the Seventeenth Century*, 83–113.

it is the most pleasingst life that may be, when a woman shall have her husband come home and speake in this sort vnto her, How now Wife? how dost thou my sweet-heart? what wilt thou have? or what dost thou lacke? and therewithall kindly embracing her, gives her a gentle kisse, saying: speake my prettie mouse, wilt thou have a cup of Claret-wine, White-wine, or Sacke to supper? . . . At last having well refresht themselues, she sets her siluer whistle to her mouth, and calles her maid to cleare the boord: then going to the fire, he sets her on his knee, and wantonly stroking her cheeke, amourously hee chockes her under the chin, fetching many stealing toutches at her rubie lips, and so soone as he heares the Bell ring eight a clocke, he calls her to goe to bed with him. O how sweet doe these words sound in a womans eares? But when they are once close betweene a paire of sheetes, O *Gillian* then, then.

Why what of that (quoth she)?

Nay nothing (saith *Margaret*) but they sleep soundly all night. (1)

The rivalry between the girls is surprisingly naturalistic, and charmingly rendered. After a number of mix-ups and comic misunderstandings, Meg and Jill lose Dick to the Dutch girl; Meg bounces back splendidly at first and even helps disappointed Gillian recover, but then Deloney suddenly erases the smile that has been on the reader's face throughout this section. After attending the wedding, the vibrant Margaret withers into despondency and decides to ruin herself:

Thus *Margaret* in a melancholy humour went her waies, and in short time after she forsooke *Westminster*, and attended on the Kings army to *Bullen* [in France], and while the siege lasted, became a landresse to the Camp, and never after did she set store by her selfe, but became common to the call of every man, till such time as all youthfull delights was banished by old age, and in the end she left her life in *Islington*, being very penitent for all her former offences.

Gillian in the end was well married, and became a very good house-keeper, living in honest name and fame till her dying day. (3)

Deloney's abrupt transition from farce to tragedy is unexpected and devastating. The emotional impact is difficult to convey to anyone who hasn't read this brilliant 32-page sequence, but the subtle artistry with which Deloney pulls off this pocket tragedy is stunning. Here he's closer to Maupassant than to any of his contemporaries. Chapter 4, a kind of coda, reveals that after many years of marriage Richard was unable to impregnate his wife, providing a wide opening for Round Robin to tease "the cock of Westminster."

Chapters 5 through 9 give us the story of a prosperous shoemaker named Peachie and two of his employees, boastful Tom Drum and Harry Nevell, a distressed gentleman. If the first story was intended for female readers, this one is aimed at their menfolk, with rough-and-tumble adventures and jestbook pranks, all redounding to the credit of the cordwainer fraternity, and ending with another example of a hard-working apprentice marrying his mistress (as in the opening chapter of *Jack of Newbury*). The concluding chapters 9 and 10 concern a jolly but irresponsible shoemaker nicknamed the Green King and his equally oddly named friend, "Anthony now now, the firkin Fidler of *Finchlane*." A sermon on fickle friendship, it has little to do with the gentle craft, but fittingly fulfills what the title page promised would be "a most merrie and pleasant History." Having written a fanciful history of shoemaking (part 1) and its practice in London (part 2), Deloney intended to write a third part on country shoemakers, but death prevented the completion of his trilogy.

In *Thomas of Reading* (1599?), Deloney's most ambitious novel, he not only returns to the clothing industry, but returns in time as well. It opens with a highly symbolic scene: on a trip west to Wales, King Henry I (ruled 1100–35) is forced off the road by a long convoy of wagons loaded with the dry goods of Thomas Cole of Reading. The king watches in annoyance at first, but soon realizes this display of middle-class economic power is significant and needs to be harnessed to state power. It represents a shift from a class-based society to a capital-based one, and — in literature — a shift away from the upper class as the subject of novels toward the middle class. Both classes are represented in *Thomas of Reading*, but in a revolutionary reversal the non-U characters occupy the main plot while the aristocrats are relegated to the subplot.

Both narratives are woven together for the first time in a Deloney novel, replacing the sequential, episodic structure of his other three. The novel is only partly about Thomas Cole; its full title is *Thomas of Reading, or The Six Worthy Yeoman of the West*, and his fellow clothiers in fact get more stage time than he does. All successful merchants, they make periodic trips to London together, where they mix business (suggesting economic reforms to King Henry, which he is happy to authorize) with pleasure: Thomas Dove is a music-loving party animal, and married man Cuthbert of Kendall chases after an innkeeper's wife and gets publicly humiliated. Their wives go on shopping sprees to the big city like their counterparts in New Jersey today. It's all very pleasant for the first half of the novel, except for those trapped in the subplot.

This concerns Margaret, the daughter of the earl of Shrewsbury, left homeless after the king banishes her father. (Introduced as a piece of gossip the clothiers share on the way to London, this information is cleverly integrated into the main plot.) Literally out on the street, Margaret decides to go to a fair where job-seeking servants congregate. Middle-class Deloney has some fun with the uselessness of his "betters" when two other prospective servants ask Margaret about her job skills:

Why what can you do (quoth the maidens) can you brew and bake, make butter and cheese, and reape corne as well?

No verily said *Margaret*, but I would be right glad to learne to do anything whatsoeuer it be.

If you could spin or card said another, you might do excellent well with a clothier, for they are the best seruices that I know, there you shall be sure to fare well, and to liue merily.

Then *Margaret* wept saying, alas, what shall I do? I was neuer brought vp to these things.

What can you doe nothing quoth they?

No truly (quoth she) that is good for any thing, but I can reade, and write and sowe, some skill I haue in my needle, and a little on my Lute: but this, I see will profit me nothing.

Good Lord, quoth they, are you bookish? (3)

Despite this handicap, Margaret becomes a servant in a middle-class household — another symbolic reversal — and eventually attracts the attention of an aristocrat in the area who is under a kind of house arrest. She eventually agrees to elope with him, but the aristocrat is captured and punished harshly: he is blinded in her presence and thrown in jail. Margaret is devastated, and decides to withdraw from the world and join a monastery. Deloney skillfully weaves her story into the fabric of the main narrative, giving *Thomas* a greater unity than any of his other novels. He also shifts language as needed: the dialogue between regular folk is realistic (as in the example above) but when Margaret and her aristocratic paramour are together, the register shifts to the Lyly-lite style of Greene and Lodge. Deloney's versatility is impressive.

Margaret's tragic end is only one of several events that darken the second half of the novel. Cuthbert of Kendall receives permission from the king to institute capital punishment against anyone caught stealing his goods, but when no hangman can be found to execute the culprits, a friar invents a kind of guillotine for him. Fun-loving Tom Dove loses all his money, and is abandoned not only by his friends but by the workers whom he has enriched; they turn on him quicker than union members, revoking Deloney's earlier idealistic view of workers. (In *Jack of Newbury*, they actually sing while they work, as in a Disney movie.) And most surprising of all, Deloney kills off his title character: Thomas is the victim of two evil innkeepers (again it's the wife who comes up with the plan) who dump him in a scalding cauldron; in the events leading up to the murder, and the detection of the crime afterwards, Deloney more or less invents the crime novel. (In a brilliant move that has reminded some critics of the porter scene in *Macbeth*, Deloney follows Thomas's ghastly death with the silly gossip of the clothiers' wives, who exchange wild rumors about it before concluding a talking horse helped solve the crime.)

Where economic prosperity had been the ideal in his earlier novels, Deloney here dramatizes the fact that wealth and position are no guarantees against adversity. "He that is possessed with riches, without content, is most wretched and miserable," Margaret says at one point (10), and even argues it is better to be poor and sure of your position than prosperous and subject to reversals: "pouertie with surety, is better than honour mixed with feare" (3). This is surprising from such a champion of the bourgeoisie as Deloney, and while it results in a more ambiguous novel, *Thomas of Reading* was apparently less popular than his other novels for that reason.

To a contemporary reader, Deloney's are the most conventional of the Elizabethan novels, the closest to the commercial fiction of our day. But in the 1590s, his various innovations — realistic dialogue, middle-class characters, economic issues, equality between men and women — put him in the avant-garde, and not surprisingly few novelists followed his lead. While no single novel of his is a masterpiece, together they represent another paradigm shift in the development of the novel, with farther-reaching consequences than the more polished works of his contemporaries. I'll confess I'd never heard of him before writing this book, but now I'm convinced he's the first Elizabethan novelist a reader needs to know.

In most discussions of Elizabethan literature, novels come in a distant third behind drama and poetry — sometimes even fourth behind nonfiction — and in discussions of the Renaissance in general novels often rate no mention at all. But as I've shown in this chapter, the Renaissance was a robust period for fiction, producing examples of nearly every genre from middle-class escapist fiction to hermetic symbolist works. But for too long I've ignored the adventures of the novel on the other side of the world, which parallel those in Europe and in some cases even surpass them. Like Columbus in 1492, let's set sail for India.

The Mesoamerican Novel

In August 1492, Christopher Columbus left Europe for the Orient, but ran into America instead. (Despite three subsequent voyages, he died believing he had actually visited the east coast of Asia.) En route from Europe to explore the Oriental novel, I want to stop over in America briefly to excavate pre-Columbian literature to see if there is anything resembling a novel. I think there is, maybe even a few, though the Spanish did their damnedest to destroy them.

While European civilization was rejoicing in its rebirth, the civilizations of the Western hemisphere were in their death throes. Within 50 years of Columbus's arrival, the great kingdoms of early America were on the verge of extinction, partly due to the deliberate cultural genocide perpetrated by the Spanish invaders, and partly due to the fatal diseases they inadvertently unleashed on the native population. While many of the Spaniards wanted simply to rob the Indians, some wanted to "save" them — that is, convert them to Catholicism. Like all religious imperialists, they decided the first step was to destroy any traces of "pagan idolatry" in their art and writings. Bartolomé de Las Casas, a sympathetic Dominican missionary writing around 1550, describes what happened to the gorgeous hieroglyphic codices of the Maya that recorded their myths and history: "These books were seen by our clergy, and even I saw part of those which were burned by the monks, apparently because they thought [they] might harm the Indians in matters concerning religion, since at that time they were at the beginning of their conversion."[1] A religious fanatic named Diego de Landa was the worst offender, torturing and burning Mayans as well as hundreds of their books while in the Yucatán in the 1560s: "We found a large number of books of these characters, and as they contained nothing in which there were not to be seen superstition and lies of the devil, we burned them all, which they [the Maya] regretted to an amazing degree and which caused them much affliction." Really — the destruction of their literature caused "much affliction"? Fancy that. I hope

---

1 Quoted in Christenson's preface to his translation of *Popol Vuh*, 21. The next quotation is from the same page.

the fundamentalist bastard is burning in his Catholic hell.[2]

Luckily, a few of these codices survived, and a few others were transcribed before they too were burned by the invading Christians.[3] Among these writings are some extended narratives that can be called novels in the broad sense I've been using the term. Of course, their authors would not have considered them fictions; like their counterparts in the ancient Near East, Mesoamericans didn't distinguish between myth and fiction, theology and history, or even (as I argued at the beginning of chap. 1) between prose and poetry. Archaeologists and epigraphists are still deciphering pre-Columbian writing systems, but the results so far are not that different from the narrative fictions produced by the ancient Egyptians, Babylonians, and Israelites.

The codices are like modern graphic novels without words, or better yet, like the wordless woodcut novels created by some artists earlier in the 20th century — like the Belgian Frans Mesereel, who called them *romans en images*, or the American Lynd Ward — or even the surrealist collage novels Max Ernst created in the 1920s and 1930s. In pre-Columbian days, a performer would use a codex as a promptbook and narrate the tale to an aristocratic audience, often to musical accompaniment or even with performers literally bringing the story to life. All but eight of the codices belonging to the Mixtecs — a group of principalities in the present Mexican state of Oaxaca — were destroyed by the Spanish, but several of the surviving ones tell the story of an 11th-century priest/general/politician named Eight Deer Jaguar Claw. (Mixtecs used their birthdays as personal names, so he was born on the 8th day of the year of the Deer: 1063.) Working from the *Codex Nuttall*, John M. D. Pohl has provided one version of this story in *The Legend of Lord Eight Deer*. Like any historical novel, it is based on actual events but contains obvious fictitious elements, and thus can be called a Mesoamerican novella without too much of a stretch. It's impossible to say when it was composed, other than no earlier than the mid-12th century, around the time Byzantine novelists were narrating their exotic tales to the royal court.

The story begins near the end of a hundred-year dynastic conflict between three Mixtec kingdoms: Tilantongo, Jaltepec, and what Pohl calls Red and White Bundle, "a reference to a sacred object that identifies the place sign

---

2 For a brilliant re-creation of Bishop Landa's mania, see Rikki Ducornet's novel *The Fanmaker's Inquisition* (1999). And for an innovative novel in which the Aztecs defeated the European invaders and went on to colonize Europe, see Sesshu Foster's *Atomik Aztex* (2005).

3 To be fair, Mesoamericans sometimes burned their own writings. Charles C. Mann notes, "In addition to taking slaves and booty, wartime victors in central Mexico often burned their enemies' codices, the hand-painted picture-texts in which priests recorded their people's histories. Tlacaélel [1398–1480, emperor of Mexica] insisted that in addition to destroying the codices of their oppressors the Mexica should set fire to their *own* codices" because they were unflattering; like Soviet-era historians, the priests were encouraged to fabricate more flattering histories (*1491*, 118).

in the codices."[4] The mysterious murder of three Jaltepec princes leads the priestess of the dead to call for a peace conference of the warring parties; representing Red and White Bundle is their aged king Eleven Wind; from Jaltepec comes their child-queen, 10-year-old Six Monkey; while Eight Deer, the 20-year-old son of a priest, represents the underage heir to the Tilantongo throne. The priestess is a fright: "the flesh covering her jaw had been stripped away, leaving her with a permanent and menacing grin" (12), and she is surrounded by the mummies of their royal ancestors. Eight Deer wants to bring the hundred-year conflict to an end by uniting his kingdom with Jaltepec, but the priestess says the ancestors prefer to see Six Monkey marry Eleven Wind, 45 years older than she is. This is a disappointment both for the young queen, who has a crush on Eight Deer and had hoped to marry him someday, and for ambitious Eight Deer, who instead of gaining power is banished to an outpost on the Pacific coast. There he builds up an army, conquers the surrounding region, and returns to Tilantongo seven years later after learning that Eleven Wind has married Six Monkey. (He spots her on his way back, and even though they are now technically enemies, they become lovers.) After a series of further assassinations and betrayals, Eight Deer decides to take control by force. First he enlists the help of the nearby Toltecs by defeating one of them in a kind of one-on-one soccer match, and then makes a supernatural visit to the oracle of the sun, which is guarded by a shadow army of dead warriors. (By this point, Eight Deer has obviously morphed from a historical figure into a mythic hero per Joseph Campbell's taxonomy.) Eight Deer asks to be recast as "a man-god that I may found a new dynasty for my kingdom" (42). His wish granted, he returns to the "world of the living" (43) and eventually conquers his enemies, though he makes the sentimental mistake of sparing one of Six Monkey's sons. Eight Deer unites the three kingdoms and starts a new dynasty, but he is eventually assassinated by Six Monkey's son, who has never forgiven him for indirectly killing his mother. Eight Deer's corpse is taken to the princess of the dead, who mummifies him and places him alongside the other mummies that had frightened Eight Deer at that council 30 years earlier.

It's a compelling story of ambition, thwarted love, triumph, and betrayal, impeccably structured, enlivened by a sports match and a mythic journey, and insightfully underscores how the personal is the political in royal families. Because Pohl's *Legend of Lord Eight Deer* is a 21st-century interpretation of an ancient work in a different medium, one has to be careful about the particulars of its artistry, but the story provides evidence enough that the Mesoamericans had a gift for narrative fiction.

---

4 Page 7 of *The Legend of Lord Eight Deer*, hereafter cited parenthetically. A reproduction of the original pictographic version of Eight Deer's tale can be viewed in *The Codex Nuttall* (pp. 42–84), which incidentally reveals Mixtec fashion was seriously overaccessorized.

We're on surer ground with the greatest literary work of this era, because it comes down to us in a 16th-century transcription made by the Maya themselves. The *Popol Vuh* (Council Book, 1555) might best be described as a communal novel: the protagonist is a Mayan community known as the Quiché (who came to occupy present-day Guatemala), and the 120-page text was compiled by a group of Quiché in the 1550s to preserve their "mythistory," as Dennis Tedlock, one of its English translators, calls this dizzying fusion of theology, mythology, legendry, etiology, poetry, astronomy, calendar lore, and actual history.[5] Thirty years earlier, Pedro de Alvarado — one of Cortés's murderous henchmen — invaded the Quiché's land, torturing and killing many of them and burning their codices, so a group of priests, historians, and performers compiled their stories, some stretching back 800 years, which were then edited into a unified whole by three Masters of Ceremonies representing the principal Quiché lineages.[6] Though based on oral legends and a pictorial codex, the *Popol Vuh* is very much a literary work, and in fact celebrates the power of language.

Beginning with the creation of the world and ending with the Spanish invasion, the *Popol Vuh* is a continuous text that falls into three parts: (1) the creation itself and the unsuccessful attempts by the gods to create intelligent humans; (2) the adventures of the mythic twins Hunahpu and Xbalanque;[7] and (3) the gods' successful creation of mankind and the founding of the Quiché nation. It's written in a style that's been called "poetic" and sometimes translated into couplets — see Edmonson's incantatory version — but its reliance on parallel constructions resembles euphuistic prose as much as verse couplets. (The earliest surviving transcription is written in prose, not verse.) The description of the unformed state of the universe before the act of creation is especially beautiful:

> Now it still ripples, now it still murmurs, ripples, it still sighs, still hums, and it is empty under the sky.
>
> Here follow the first words, the first eloquence:
>
> There is not yet one person, one animal, bird, fish, crab, tree, rock, hollow, canyon, meadow, forest. Only the sky alone is there; the face of the earth is not clear. Only the sea alone is pooled under all the sky; there is nothing whatever gathered together. It is at rest; not a single thing stirs. It is held back, kept at rest under the sky.

5 Tedlock uses "mythistory" on page 59 of the introduction to his translation, hereafter cited by page number. Allen J. Christenson's more recent translation is just as good and is superbly annotated, but Tedlock's version is more accessible.

6 For a detailed account, see Akkeren's "Authors of the *Popol Wuj*" (an alternate spelling); he narrows the completion date to 1555.

7 The *x* in Mesoamerican words is pronounced *sh* (as it was in 16th-century Spanish), and Mayan words tend to be accented on the last syllable; hence Mixtec = meesh-TECK, Xbalanque = shbah-lahn-KAY, Xibalba = sheeb-alb-AH, etc.

Whatever there is that might be is simply not there: only the pooled water, only the calm sea, only it alone is pooled.

Whatever might be is simply not there: only murmurs, ripples, in the dark, in the night. Only the Maker, Modeler alone, Sovereign Plumed Serpent, the Bearers, Begetters are in the water, a glittering light. They are there, they are enclosed in quetzal feathers, in blue-green. (64)

When reading creation stories like this — like the Egyptian "Memphite Theology," the Akkadian "Atrahasis," the Hebrew Genesis — it's easy to forget they are not timeless, autonomous myths but the work of creative individuals at some point in history; someone with a name and literary ambition imagined what the universe might have been like before people, and not uncoincidentally these accounts replicate the conditions of the artist before he or she begins creating: the empty sky and calm ocean here (cf. Gen. 1:2) symbolize the blank page before the writer, the clean staff paper before the composer, the white canvas before the painter, or the empty rehearsal room of the choreographer, where the floor and mirror resemble the sea and sky. In every account the creator — whether Ptah, Anu, YHWH, or the Mayan Maker — then speaks and thereby begins the composition process: "And then the earth arose because of them, it was simply their word that brought it forth. For the forming of the earth they said 'Earth.' It arose suddenly, just like a cloud, like a mist, now forming, unfolding" (65).

The use of "Maker" reminds me of Sidney's definition of the artist as a maker, and of the poet's recourse to metaphor: "So, as Amphion was said to move stones with his poetry to build Thebes, and Orpheus to be listened to by beasts, indeed stony and beastly people . . ." (*The Defense of Poesy*, 5). The first people created by the Quiché gods are rough drafts: the first batch can't speak but only howl, so they become the animals that populate the region. The second are made of mud, and go nowhere. Consulting with other gods, the Makers then create people of wood, but these wooden characters have no spiritual or aesthetic sensibility: "there was nothing in their hearts and nothing in their minds, no memory of their mason and builder" (70). The insensitive masses are wiped out by a flood and by their own materialistic acquisitions: "Their faces were crushed by things of wood and stone. Everything spoke: their water jars, their tortilla griddles, their plates, their cooking pots, their dogs, their grinding stones, each and every thing crushed their faces" (72). One commentator interprets this as a warning against the thoughtless reliance on technology,[8] but I also recognize the tone of an artist railing against

8 León-Portilla and Shorris, *In the Language of Kings*, 398. In their headnote to a section from the *Popol Vuh*, they tell how some modern Mayan students were studying this part: "when a backhoe was brought to the village to dig a trench for a waterpipe, the students pointed to the operators of the roaring, clanging machine, and said, 'Look, the men of wood!'" (398).

an unappreciative audience. The authors of the *Popol Vuh*, like their divine counterparts, want the right kind of readers: "How else can we be invoked and remembered on the face of the earth?" (68).

Before the cigar-smoking gods make their fourth and successful attempt at creating intelligent people with an appreciation of the arts, we are given the stories of various demigods, too complicated to relate here, but closer to standard narrative than the mythy parables that precede them. To those of us unfamiliar with Mayan culture, these adventures are bizarre, like an account of a weird dream or an acid trip. In fact, the Maya had their intoxicants and hallucinogens — some even argue drug abuse played a large part in the fall of the Mayan empire — so we shouldn't rule out the possibility that some of the weirder episodes of the *Popol Vuh* were pharmacologically inspired.[9] But the final result, let me hasten to say, is obviously the polished work of sober artists: in his notes Tedlock explains that most of the episodes in the middle third of the *Popol Vuh* are based on Mayan star lore. Mayans were brilliant astronomers, so an otherwise trippy episode might actually parallel the retrograde motion of Mars in relation to Venus. And while some sections follow a narrative logic alien to anyone unfamiliar with their culture, others are universal, as when the twins Hunahpu and Xbalanque descend into the Mayan underworld of Xibalba and are tested (including another ball game, as in *Lord Eight Deer*) before returning to the surface in triumph.

Having failed to make acceptable people from mud or wood, the gods hit paydirt when they turn to corn, or maize. To this day Mesoamericans refer to themselves as *hombres de maíz* — the title of a celebrated novel by Miguel Angel Asturias (1949) — and the first four men of corn made by the gods become the ancestors of the Quiché. But these humans are *too* perfect, for their power of imagination rivals that of the gods: "They didn't have to walk around before they could see what was under the sky; they just stayed where they were. [¶] As they looked, their knowledge became intense. Their sight passed through trees, through rocks, through lakes, through seas, through mountains, through plains" (147). Like YHWH in Genesis (3:22), the gods fear these new beings will become like them: "Yet they'll become as great as gods, unless they procreate, proliferate at the sowing, the dawning, unless they increase" (148). In essence, these potential gods are then saddled with wives and jobs to distract them, and after they've procreated as directed, their tribes make their slow way toward Quiché, where they are taught how to perform human sacrifices by cutting out the heart as an offering to their makers. We also learn of the origin of prostitution as two "radiant" maidens named Lust

---

9 We're talking about people who ingested intoxicants via ritual enemas: "The substances known to be administered range from alchohol . . . to tobacco, peyote, LSD derivatives, and mushroom-derived hallucinogens" — Jared Diamond, *The Third Chimpanzee* (NY: HarperCollins, 1992), 201.

Woman and Wailing Woman try to seduce the lords of rival tribes. All goes well — except for the sacrificial victims and the prostitutes, that is — until the 12th generation, when the Spanish arrive and begin torturing people. The novel ends in the 1550s with the 13th generation, suffering under the rule of the invading Christians, and expresses the hope that the book will provide "light" for future readers, a word used throughout the heuristic text as a synonym for intelligence and imagination.

Among the authors' many purposes for the *Popol Vuh* was an unsavory political agenda — to validate the divine right of the Quiché leaders and to justify human sacrifice — but it shines as a tribute to creative intelligence. The creation of the world is an act of the imagination, and the successful exploits of the twins Hunahpu and Xbalanque depend on the application of creative solutions to challenging situations. After their initial experience of unimpeded sight, the new humans are plunged into a long-lasting night, starless and bible black, until the sun finally appears to illuminate the long march toward civilization. The three Quiché MCs who completed the mystical novel may have been primarily concerned with preserving their nation's legacy, but their real accomplishment is this stunning demonstration of the power of the imagination, and of the urge to progress from darkness to illumination by those not made of mud or wood. The *Popol Vuh* is often called the Mayan bible; Ovid's *Metamorphoses* is another analogue, but its multilayered symbolism, dark/light imagery, and intellectual concerns make it more like a Mayan *Divine Comedy*.

Unfortunately, no other novel-length narratives survived the Spanish holocaust. In 1558, a Spanish-educated Aztec wrote *Legends of the Suns*, which opens like the *Popol Vuh* with failed attempts to create humans and continues with a surrealistic series of creations and destructions (but with little of the Quiché novel's sublimity). It is crowded with incredibly inventive incidents and features the Mesoamerican hero-god Quetzalcoatl, but only the beginning of the manuscript survives.[10] Speaking of Quetzalcoatl: Among the Toltecs, who occupied central Mexico from around 900 to 1150, there was an epic narrative that one specialist calls *The Topiltzin Quetzalcoatl of Tollan Tale*. Several versions existed in the forms of hieroglyphic codices and narrative chants of the story of this possibly historical Toltec king who instituted religious reforms but was later dethroned and exiled by rivals. Over the centuries his story was expanded and mythologized, though retaining sections that are "too novelistic" for it to be pure myth, according to the same specialist.[11] But the invading Spaniards destroyed the primary documents, so all we know of this tale of a man-god are scattered recollections recorded later

10 Willard Gingerich's translation appears on pp. 132–47 of the Markmans' landmark anthology *The Flayed God.*
11 H. B. Nicholson, in his classic *Topiltzin Quetzalcoatl*, 251.

in the 16th century. Some other narratives that combine "mythistory" and fiction are preserved in the various chronicles written later by the Spanish or by converts, but any extended works of the same caliber as the *Popol Vuh* — and surely there were *some* among the hundreds and hundreds of manuscripts — were burnt to ashes.

And what of the Inca? Were any novels written in Tawantinsuyu (The Land of the Four Quarters), the largest nation on earth in the 15th century? We'll probably never know, because the majority of their records were likewise burnt by Pizarro and his thugs, and the few survivors have resisted translation so far because of their unusual form. The fiber-based Inca recorded their thoughts not in codices but in arrangements of knotted strings called *khipu*; as Charles Mann explains,

> they consist of a primary cord, usually a third to a half an inch in diameter, from which dangle thinner "pendant" strings — typically more than a hundred, but on occasion as many as 1,500. The pendant strings, which sometimes have subsidiary strings attached, bear clusters of knots, each tied in one of three ways. The result, in the dry summary of George Gheverghese Joseph, a University of Manchester mathematics historian, "resembles a mop that has seen better days." (*1491*, 345)

Older readers may be reminded of diagrammed sentences on a chalkboard, with adjectives and clauses hanging from the main <u>noun | verb</u> line. By inspecting the knots and strings, some dyed various colors, and the literally dependent clauses, the Incan *khipukamayuq* (knot-makers/keepers) could read it like a codex. Gary Urton has written a fascinating book entitled *Signs of the Inka Khipu* in which he argues the *khipu* are based on a binary system (like computer language), and that the kinds of knots and variety of fibers and colors encode a huge amount of information — enough for a *Popol Vuh*-sized novel, perhaps. He further suggests this binary code is the textile equivalent of the parallelism that characterizes Mesoamerican poetics. Researchers like Urton are still trying to break the code, but it's exciting to speculate the Great Incan Novel may be concealed in something that looks like a colorful mophead in a museum somewhere. It is sad to speculate, while leafing through the various anthologies of Mesoamerican literature now available, how many pre-Columbian novels might have been lost, victims of religious fanaticism in the never-ending war between dogma and the imagination.

CHAPTER 4

The Eastern Novel

The novel evolved in the East much as it did in the West, and pretty much along the same timeline: it was preceded in the first millennium BCE by religious hymns, etiologies, sacred epics, mythology, and "official" (i.e., fanciful) chronicles. Around the same period the ancient Greek novel came into existence, this literary high road started intersecting with the low road of folklore, fables, historical legends, and tall tales; prose fictions began to appear in India, followed a few centuries later by adventure stories in Arabic, and soon after that by novels in Japan and China. By the time the Greek novel was revived in Byzantium in the 12th century, novels were a flourishing genre in the East, differing from their Western counterparts only in superficial cultural details, and surpassing them in a few cases. It's a literary world that was largely unknown to Western readers until only a century ago, and with a few exceptions (such as *The Tale of Genji*) remains so. But the growing number of translations now available makes it inexcusable for those who profess an interest in the novel as an art form to remain ignorant of the glories of the premodern Eastern novel.

Two procedural matters before we begin: First, the vague chapter title above is meant to encompass the wide sweep of land between Egypt and Tibet, almost corresponding to the southern route of the Silk Road of yore. It's imprecise but better than a pedantic, multihyphenated designation. Second, Oriental languages have been transliterated in a variety of ways over the centuries, creating havoc for nonspecialists. For the most part I've followed the forms used by my sources in this chapter and the next, with these exceptions: as I've done earlier, I've eliminated diacritical marks — useless without elaborate pronunciation charts — except in quoted matter, and favor self-pronouncing forms where they exist. In Sanskrit, that means Shiva rather than Çiva, *Panchatantra* rather than *Pañcatantra*, and forms that vocalize the consonants: Krishna rather than Krsna. For consistency I'll be using compound forms of book titles (*Kathasaritsagara* rather than *Katha Sarit Sagara*), and unless they are already well known, like the *Panchantanra*, I prefer published English titles over the originals to make them look less forbidding (*The Ocean of Story* vs. *Kathāsaritsāgara*). With Arabic, I'm not going to fuss with the *hamza* (') and the *'ayn* (') in most cases, nor with underdots. Japanese is fairly straightforward, but with Chinese there's the discrepancy between two completely different romanization systems. Before the 1960s, the Wade–Giles system was standard, but since then the pinyin system has dominated, which is less intuitive for the untrained reader; for example, the author of *A Dream of Red Mansions* was spelled Ts'ao Hsüeh-ch'in in Wade–Giles days, which gives the reader at least a sporting chance at its pronunciation, but it's spelled Cao Xueqin in pinyin, which requires recourse to a chart to realize it's pronounced something like Tsaow Shew-chin. (The problem is that some Chinese sounds don't have an exact counterpart in English, but why they used *c* to represent *ts* and *q* for *ch* is a mystery — unless it was a Commie plot to frustrate English readers.) In a few instances I will indicate alternative spellings, but I'm not qualified to convert names from one system to another, so the reader will have to settle for some discrepancies. And remember that in these languages the family name comes first; I'm not being overly familiar by referring to this author as Cao, just following standard practice. In Japanese, the family (clan) name likewise comes first, though often individuals go by their given name: Narihira is how scholars refer to the Japanese poet Ariwara no Narihira, with no disrespect intended. (The *no* is an attributive particle like *de*, *von*, or *O'*.) Nowadays they go by their surname; mine not to reason why.

INDIAN FICTION

The earliest Indian novel is no longer extant, but by all accounts it was a whopper, thousands of pages long and written in the language of goblins! Gunadhya's *Brihatkatha* (Long Story) is thought to have been written in the early centuries of our era — scholars' estimates range from the 2nd century BCE to the 5th century CE — and later Indic works based on it give a good indication of its size and scope. Just as Allah is believed by Muslims to be the author of the Quran, the *Brihatkatha* purports to be the work of Shiva, the Hindu god of destruction and creation, the original Lord of the Dance. It came about in this way, a grim parable about authorship:

One day blue-throated Shiva was so pleased by the flattering songs of his wife Parvati, she of the "noose-like glances," that he sat her on his lap and asked what he could do to make her happy.[1] She asks for a story that is "new

---

1 The quoted phrase is from page 1 of Arshia Sattar's translation *Tales from the* Kathasaritsagara (one of the later works based on the *Brihatkatha*), hereafter cited parenthetically. In his summary of this book, John Barth says Shiva "is so delighted at the way Parvati makes love to him that he offers her anything she wishes in reward" (*The Friday Book*, 87); I don't know where he got that — perhaps just a fellow novelist's instinct — but it rings truer than Sattar's "hymns of praise." C. H. Tawney's older translation, which Barth read, refers only to Parvati's "praises"; since Shiva's symbol is the erect phallus, maybe that's what she's singing about.

and amusing," but Shiva tells an old-fashioned tale about loving her in a previous lifetime. Parvati insists she wants something novel, avant-garde, so Shiva promises to tell a new kind of story, not about the gods or about humans, but about the celestial beings in between called *vidyadharas*. With his lovely wife in his lap, he tells seven long tales of these worldly angels amounting to 700,000 couplets — the equivalent of a 30,000-page novel.[2] Although Shiva has banned everyone from the room, a divine retainer named Puspadanta sneaks in and overhears the long tale, and then relates it to his wife, who in turns tells it to Parvati. She's outraged that this "new" story seems to be one people know already, so she curses Puspadanta and another retainer named Malyavan (who tried to intercede for him) to become lowly humans; the curse won't be lifted until Puspadanta locates a similarly cursed outcast named Supratika and relates the entire tale to him, who in turn has to relate it to Malyavan. Puspadanta eventually finds his man, tells the tale, and returns to his heavenly home.

Malyavan, now known by his human name Gunadhya, has a more difficult time of it. He becomes a minister to King Satavahana of Pratishthana (about 200 miles east of Mumbai), who one day joins his wives in a lake, "their wet clothes clinging to their bodies and revealing their curves," and after stripping off their clothes he splashes around with them. "One of the queens, tired from the weight of her breasts, her body as tender as a flower, wearied of the game" (37) and tells the king to stop splashing her. Because the words for "don't splash" and "sweets" sound similar in Sanskrit, the king begins throwing rock candy at the busty beauty, who also happens to be a grammar maven, and she makes fun of his lexical faux pas. Mortified, the king seeks a teacher to polish up his Sanskrit; Gunadhya applies for the job but loses out to another scholar who boasts he can teach the king everything he needs to know much quicker. Despondent, he renounces his three languages (Sanskrit, Prakrit, and his own vernacular) and retires to the forests of the Vindhyas and comes across Supratika, who narrates Shiva's long story to him. It takes Gunadhya seven years to record the whole thing in the Paishachi tongue (called the language of goblins because it was unrefined), and lacking ink, he writes it in his own blood on palm leaves. During Supratika's seven-year narration, various supernatural beings come around to listen to the fabulous tale, and when he's finished Gunadhya naturally wants to publish the work. He figures King Satavahana could spread it around, but when two of his disciples take it to the king, he turns up his royal nose at the bloody manuscript written in gutter

---

2 Shiva, in his capacity as god of generation, is frequently depicted with his wife straddling him in sexual union; most novels follow the rhythm of the sexual act — introductory foreplay, then increasing activity with plot twists and turns leading up to a climax, followed by a brief dénouement — so when Shiva begins his narration with his wife planted in his lap, they are in one sense embarking on an epic fornication — a sense this sensuous book suggests.

language. Like any rejected author, Gunadhya is distraught and decides to burn the manuscript, reading each page aloud before tossing it to the flames. The king meanwhile falls ill from undernourishment because all the animals he feeds on are listening with tears in their eyes to Gunadhya burn through his story. The king hears of this and visits the author, "looking like a forest-dweller with long matted locks, grey like the smoke from a fire" (48), and not only recognizes his former minister but learns he was a divine retainer in his previous life. The king asks for the rejected manuscript, but by then only one of the seven sections remains, and that becomes the *Brihatkatha*.

The historical Gunadhya wasn't the first author to regard his work as so great that it was inspired by the gods, nor to feel it was written with his heart's blood under difficult circumstances, nor the first author to indulge in self-destructive behavior after receiving harsh criticism. Inspired to try something new, and in everyday prose rather than the Sanskrit verse used by professionals — though the story given in later versions speaks of couplets, the scholarly consensus is that the *Brihatkatha* was written in prose — Gunadhya must have been an innovator of huge ambition, and some measure of his success (and validation of the novel's existence) is found in the numerous positive references to the *Brihatkatha* in later Indic literature and the many adaptations that were made from it. Among these are Sanghadasa's *Vasudevahindi* (Vasudeva's Travels), a Jain work from the 6th century or earlier; Budhasvamin's *Emperor of the Sorcerers* (*Brihatkathaslokasamgraha*, literally *Long Story* Abridged in Verse), a Nepalese version from the 8th or 9th century; Konkuvelir's huge but incomplete *Perunkatai* in Pali from perhaps the 10th century; Ksemendra's *Brihatkathamanjari* (Abridged *Long Story*), a Kashmirian digest from the early 11th century, and Somadeva's famous *Ocean of the Rivers of Story*, compiled later in the 11th century, and the source for the tale of Gunadhya I've just related.[3] Except for the *Vasudevahindi*, all of these adaptations are in verse, as though, like King Satavahana, their authors were put off by vulgar prose and wanted to give their work a more elegant form. But by studying these later versions we can partially reconstruct the original, a task worth pursuing because not only is the *Brihatkatha* the foundation of Indic fiction, but it is also the unacknowledged prose leg of India's tripod of gigantic epics with Valmiki's 1,500-page *Ramayana* (Romance of Rama, c. 300 BCE) and Vyasa's 4,000-page *Mahabharata* (Great Epic of the Bharata Dynasty, c. 400 CE), which dominate the field of Sanskrit literature like three royal elephants.

Scholars agree that the version closest to Gunadhya's original is Budhasvamin's *Emperor of the Sorcerers*, which corresponds to the section the despondent author saved from the flames, and which happened to be his

---

3 See Nelson's "*Brhatkatha* Studies: The Problem of an Ur-text" for a succinct assessment of all these texts.

disciples' favorite part. (In all likelihood, this was all Gunadhya wrote, with the story of the lost portions added just to enhance it — authors do that sort of thing.) Unfortunately it breaks off after only 400 pages; internal evidence suggests it went on for another thousand pages at least. It's the tale of a prince named Naravahanadatta who accumulates 26 wives on his way to becoming emperor of the sorcerers, and after 400 pages he's only just met bride #6, which gives some sense of the size of the complete work — and remember, this is only an *abridgment* of Gunadhya's work.

Budhasvamin's verse narrative — and presumably Gunadhya's novel — takes the form of a fantasy quest. It opens with three cantos of background material narrated in the third person, at the end of which Prince Naravahanadatta, emperor of the "sorcerers" (translator Mallinson's too-dark rendition of *vidyadharas*), makes his spectacular entrance at a hermitage:

> In the morning the sages heard in the cloudless sky a rumbling that filled the firmament. They asked Divákaradeva, the sky-ranger, what it was.
>
> He replied, "That is the noise of the drums of the sky-charioteers. It comes from within the sky-chariots so it sounds like thunder. Here comes our master, the emperor of all the sorcerer kings, flying through the air amid clouds of thundering drums. Look!"
>
> Like a bank of clouds filling the sky in every direction, gleaming gold with the dazzle of *róhita* rainbows, lightning and cranes, the ascetics saw arriving from far off in the heavens a fleet of sky-chariots; the lattice of light from its myriad gems was awe-inspiring.
>
> The emperor's sky-chariot landed at the gate of the hermitage; the others came down in the valleys, and on the ridges and peaks of the mountain. The sky-chariot of the emperor of the sorcerers was in the form of a lotus surrounded by twenty-six petals of ruby. He himself sat in the middle of the emerald pericarp; his wives, wearing fabulous jewels, were in the petals. Like a great tusker and his herd of lady elephants, the sorcerer and his wives arrived at the assembly hall, which, with its beaming lotus-faces, was like a lotus pond.[4]

Asked by the sages how he "came by this extraordinary majesty and won these wives" (4:3), Prince N. narrates the rest of the book. As he tells how he met each of his wives, mostly while traveling incognito throughout India with his clever friend Gomukha, he often digresses to relate tales he overheard (and tales within those tales), the embedding structure so characteristic of later Sanskrit and Arabic works. Some of them deal with the fantasy world of the vidyadharas, the "sky-rovers" who zip around in the sky when not traveling in their UFOish "aerial chariots" (which they credit to the Greeks, for

---

4 Canto 3, ll. 97–105, hereafter cited parenthetically. *The Emperor of the Sorcerers* was one of the first volumes in the Clay Sanskrit Library, launched in 2005 and modeled on the bilingual Loeb series of Greek and Latin classics, providing new, much-needed translations of Sanskrit literature. Sponsored by the John and Jennifer Clay Foundation by arrangement with New York University Press, this is literary philanthropy at its best.

some reason).[5] But like the fairies of Celtic mythology, these magical beings interact with humans, and most of the work is set not in a fantasy world but in a Bollywood version of Gupta-era India (320–540). Many of the novel's characters are regular folk — cooks, cowherders, courtesans (*lots* of those), sea captains, ascetics, servants, artisans — with special attention to the mercantile class. Gunadhya's work downplayed the gods and kings of other epics to focus on the merchants of early India, for whom life had three goals: pleasure (*kama*), prosperity (*artha*), and virtue (*dharma*). (A fourth, "liberation" from existence [*moksa*], was only for religious nuts.[6]) Gunadhya focused on the first two; we hear of dangerous ocean voyages undertaken by traders (similar to Sindbad's voyages in *The Arabian Nights*), stories of the lengths to which some people go to amass wealth — some admirable, some criminal — and of the pleasures money can buy. The chief god of this world is not Indra or Shiva but Kubera, the god of wealth and patron of the merchant class, evoked throughout the work. "Our lives will be a wealth of expectation and consummation," says one character eagerly (19.158), and conspicuous consumption and concupiscent consummation intertwine in a heady celebration of the material world. For this reason, courtesans are cherished members of this society; in fact, N.'s first and most beloved wife Madanamanjuka is the daughter of one.[7] Even semi-divine Naravahanadatta, after taking bride #3's hand in marriage "like Indra's son taking that of Kubera's daughter," admits "that worldly existence was vastly superior to liberation" (17.180, 184).

It's a sensuous world: the work is filled with gorgeous sights, with the smell of incense and perfume, with descriptions of food, with the sound of the *veena* — a sitar-like instrument played like a dulcimer; N. wins bride #3 because of his abilities on it — and with touching: characters wash the feet of

---

5 The Sanskrit word for these flying machines is almost literally "spacecraft," and some of them are as big as the starship *Enterprise*. Understandably, those who believe we've been visited by aliens in the past have made much of these descriptions (here and elsewhere in early Sanskrit literature). Gunadhya has been credited with inventing science fiction by at least one critic (Warder, *Indian Kavya Literature* 2:128).

6 Gotta love a society that not only recognized the importance of *kama* — specifically sexual pleasure — but even provided its citizenry with sex manuals like Vatsyayana's *Kamasutra* (3rd century?). Dharma is a more complex matter, ranging from simply doing the right thing, acting responsibly and ethically, fulfilling social duties and religious obligations, to the fundamentalist/totalitarian injunction to obey without question the sacred texts (the Vedas).

7 See Pran Neville's "The Indian Courtesan: Symbol of Love and Romance" in Dehejia's *A Celebration of Love*, a gorgeously illustrated collection of essays on the positive representations of women in Indian art and literature. Unlike the modern sex worker (but similar to the Japanese geisha), the Indian courtesan "occupied an important position in society" and "was expected to be accomplished in the sixty-four arts which included dancing, singing, acting, calligraphy, gambling, distillation of liquours and above all the art of love making. For a courtesan, sex was not only a ritualistic activity but a prime source of bliss and the ultimate form of human recreation" (221). Courtesans retained their high reputation in India until the late 19th century, when they fell victim to Western-inspired reformers.

visitors, bathe often, give massages to each other, and make love at the drop of a turban. (Those who can afford them have multiple wives *and* a harem; those who can't just declare a *gandharva* marriage and go to it.[8]) The superlative case is the only one the author seems to know. But it's also an ethical world: the author forces many of his characters to make difficult decisions between integrity and prosperity, and will introduce digressions that allow characters to debate such matters. At one point N. listens as a wandering ascetic tells his student a story illustrating the power of destiny over free will, concluding: "The king of the elephants, human effort, was conquered in battle by its master, the valiant lion of destiny" (21.172–73), only to hear his student tell a longer story illustrating just the opposite: "the mountain of destiny, dear to beings whose goodness has been worn down by complacency, and cherished by cowards, was uprooted by the hurricane of human effort" (22.315–17). (One of the pleasures of reading foreign literature is being introduced to fresh metaphors.) There are discussions of religious matters, of the validity of holy books, literary theory, philosophy, and other intellectual matters mixed in with romantic escapades and adventure stories.

The essence of the *Brihatkatha* is contained in an entertaining novella-length digression narrated by one of N.'s fathers-in-law, a merchant named Sanudasa. As a young married man, he was reserved and antisocial because of his "constant study of the books of Brahmin, Buddhist and Jaina renouncers" (18.639), so one day a friend of his got him drunk and tricked him into sleeping with a courtesan masquerading as a *yakshi*, a nymph attendant on the god of wealth (i.e., a high-maintenance mistress). He devotes himself to this enchantress and soon depletes his fortune, forcing his family into poverty. Ashamed of himself, he vows to leave and not return until he has earned back his fortune fourfold. He joins a caravan of traders, only to be attacked by bandits. He makes his way to his rich uncle's, who offers to give him the money he needs, but proud Sanudasa insists on earning it the hard way and joins a sailing expedition, only to have his ship destroyed by a whale. He makes his way ashore, where he spots a nearly naked woman, also a castaway. They have sex, are rescued, then are separated after another shipwreck. He makes his way to one country and becomes a jewelry appraiser, then joins an expedition to a land of gold, where his party is attacked, and then is transported by giant vultures (a mode of transportation sometimes used in *The Arabian Nights*). Several times Sanudasa curses himself for his pursuit of gold, but he is finally rewarded for his persistence. He comes across a sage in the forest, who hails him as a great merchant. And then another close encounter of the third kind:

---

8 "Form of marriage in which only the spirits of the air are witness; usually due to an intense sexual attraction between the partners" (Sattar, 256).

One day I saw in front of the great saint a sky-chariot as brilliant as Mount Meru: it was as though his merit had taken physical form and arrived from the sky. Maidens emerged from within, and their radiance lit up the forest like a streak of lightning coming from a rainbow-tinted cloud. They walked reverently around the majestic ascetic and bowed to him before flying into the sky like moonbeams. (18.536–38)

One of these celestial maidens stays behind and is adopted by Sanudasa as a daughter, eventually to become Prince N.'s third wife. The "majestic ascetic" (which sounds like a Hindu wrestler's stage name) bestows a fortune on Sanudasa, so father and daughter return to his hometown only to learn the entire experience has been a set-up: his family only pretended to be destitute, and the whole thing was staged by the king just to shake Sanudasa out of his religious stupor to encourage him to enjoy life. At several points during his ordeal Sanudasa had to make difficult dharmic decisions — whether to lie to save a life, whether he should kill someone begging for mercy who threatens his friends, or kill a faithful goat to further his own desires — which made him wonder if wealth (*artha*) was really a legitimate goal. In this novel, it definitely is, and the story became one of the most popular sections of the long novel, adapted by numerous later writers. Its self-contained form and lively subject matter also suggest that Gunadhya constructed his novel from older stories and travelers' tales, legends and vidyadhara/fairy tales, using Prince N.'s bridal quest as a frame into which he could weave a variety of fictions.

Unfortunately, Budhasvamin's version ends just after N. has married someone who appears to be a man but who in his eyes is a woman. The thought of the wide hips of a new girl in town with the mouth-filling name Bhagirathayashas is tormenting our prince when the manuscript breaks off. In occidental fiction, a protagonist will spend an entire novel pursuing and marrying one woman; Naravahanadatta makes them look like underachievers on his way to racking up 26 brides, and presumably the *Brihatkatha* gave us all their stories, along with delightful digressions on everything else under the Indian sun.

This presumption is confirmed to some extent by the other works based on the *Brihatkatha*. The earliest is a lengthy Jain novel called the *Vasudevahindi* (Vasudeva's Travels), which was left unfinished by a writer named Sanghadesa, and then completed a few centuries later by Dharmasena. (Scholars differ on the date: its English translator assigns part 1 to the 1st or 2nd century, which would push the *Brihatkatha* back to BCE, but another scholar suggests the early 6th century for part 1, with part 2 following perhaps in the 9th.[9]) In this

---

9 Jain, *Vasudevahindi*, 27 (hereafter cited by page number) vs. Jamkhedkar, 8. In Jain's *Prakrit Narrative Literature*, published a few years after his translation, he revised the date to the 3rd century (20). And I should point out that Jain's translation of the *Vasudevahindi* isn't complete, but a confusingly assembled selection-cum-commentary.

version, the narrator is not the earth-dwelling Naravahanadatta but the divine Vasudeva, father of the god Krishna, and though his pan-Indian acquisition of wives still drives the plot, the work has a more religious, didactic tone in keeping with the daffy doctrines of the Jains. (Think naked Amish vegetarians.) For example, the Jain opposition to eating meat is gruesomely illustrated in one digression in which a cook secretly feeds his prince the flesh of a dead child after the cat stole the peacock meat he had prepared. The prince relishes the taste of this new dish, and after the cook confesses to the menu substitution, the prince sends his servants out to scour the city for dead children; "and when unable to find such ones, they killed them secretly" (343). The prince is caught, banished, and ends his days as a cannibal. This probably wasn't part of Gunadhya's original, and the Jain sermons and pious interpretations of events are certainly alien. However, the tales of Vasudeva's romantic conquests seem to pick up where *The Emperor of the Sorcerers* broke off, though many of them are more supernatural in nature. Despite the religious orientation of the *Vasudevahindi*, there's a good deal of sex, and the authors match (if not copy from) Gunadhya's sensuous descriptions of women:

> She was wearing a garland of flowers mingled with the sprouts of *dūrvā* grass earrings of excellent flowers, her ornamented hair shining with the rays of crest-jewel, her lotus-like face brilliant with splendid eyes anointed with the dazzling of the earrings made of gold and silver, her creeper-like arms beautiful with the reddish palm of the hand, shining with the lovely golden armlets, her waist exhausted by the burden of fleshy breasts decorated by a moving necklace, her lotus-like feet afflicted by carrying the weight of large buttocks fastened with a circular girdle. She carried the splendour of the goddess of wealth dispossessed of a lotus, was surrounded by the maid-servants occupied in giving her bath, decorating her and so on, and she put on an upper garment made of fine and white silken cloth. (475)

When Dharmasena completed Sanghada's work he expanded the number of brides from 26 to 100, and inserted many essay-like digressions on topics ranging from archery, dance, and painting to the ideal conduct of courtesans. While both authors knew the *Brihatkatha* and at times followed it closely, it is now difficult to separate their work from Gunadhya's.

Ksemendra's *Brihatkathamanjari* sounds like a Reader's Digest version of the *Brihatkatha*,[10] but since it hasn't been translated, let's return to the gong-tormented *Ocean of Story* that gave us the origin of Gunadhya's long novel. At the beginning of his adaptation, Somadeva — a Kashmiri Brahmin who undertook the work around 1070 to please his queen — invokes the elephant-god Ganesh and then announces:

---

10 For a shirty summary, see Keith's *History of Sanskrit Literature*, 276–80.

I worship the Goddess of Speech who is the light that illuminates everything, and here compose this collection of verses which are the essence of the *Brhatkathā*.

This book is exactly like the one from which it has been taken although the language has been modified so that this book is shorter. As far as possible, the connections between the stories have been maintained and the essence of the stories has been preserved. I have not undertaken this project out of a desire for fame as an original teller of tales. Rather, I have done this so that this vast web of stories, so different and so varied, be remembered. (Sattar trans., 1)

His 1,800-page abridgment is indeed shorter than the lost original, and we do hear some further adventures of Prince Naravahanadatta and how he eventually became emperor of the vidyadharas, which is how the *Brihatkatha* presumably ended. But Somadeva doesn't indicate (or perhaps realize) his work is filled with stories and entire books that were written *after* Gunadhya's time, and which blur the original author's focus on the merchant class. Somadeva apparently worked not from a copy of the actual *Brihatkatha* but from a much later version, by which time the original chapter order had been reshuffled, lots of new material added from a wide variety of sources, and longer episodes in the original reduced to a single summary sentence. In his "Terminal Essay" to the 1928 edition of Charles H. Tawney's English translation (which originally appeared in the 1880s), Norman Penzer details this textual mess with growing exasperation and concludes, "Gunadhya's original must have been very different to what we find in the *Kathā-sarit-sāgara*" (9.107) — "different" as in much, much better. Instead of Gunadhya's presumably coherent work of art, we are left with a poorly assembled Kashmiri anthology of miscellaneous tales, valuable (Penzer concedes) for shedding "light on the manners and customs, the folklore and beliefs of a country so poor in historical documentary evidence" (9.117), but incoherent as a work of art and unhelpful in reconstructing Gunadhya's greater work.[11] Ironically, Penzer's long editorial labor on *The Ocean of Story* only exposed its shortcomings and sharpened his appreciation of the innovative *Brihatkatha*: Gunadhya handled "his subject-matter in a way unheard of and absolutely original. . . . All this must have struck contemporary audiences as most original and novel" (9.120). As so often in literary history, the innovator's work is ignored while that of the imitators prospers. *The Ocean of Story* has its appeal, but apparently it's only a muddy pond compared to Gunadhya's vast meganovel. The loss to Indian literature, and to the history of the novel, is summed up by Anthony

---

11 In his engaging essay on *The Ocean of Story* cited earlier, Barth likewise expresses the disappointment he felt in the vast work once he finally got around to reading it. Tawney's translation, the only complete one until recently, is now being superseded by Sir James Mallinson's *Ocean of the Rivers of Story*; the first of seven projected volumes appeared in the spring of 2007 from the Clay Foundation/New York University Press.

Warder, who gives the best account I've read of this "supreme fiction" in his monumental *Indian Kavya Literature*:

> It was apparently the first great novel produced by a *kavi* [sage/poet], and probably the greatest Indian novel. . . . It was, however, very likely the *Brhatkathā* which for the first time boldly appropriated in a prose fiction the entire scale and scope of the epic: the grand and leisurely manner, the rich detail, the whole range of aspirations and emotions and *rasas* [aesthetic bliss], but with more realism, whilst mingled among its episodes were more marvels as well. Here then was a modern Great Epic, to suit an age when commerce and art and science had replaced heroism; a Great Story of success such as all men dreamed of, to supersede the *Rāmāyana* with its too high-minded hero and too unworldly wisdom. (2.116)

May Ganesh, "who brushes away stars when he dances at twilight and who creates new ones from the spray of his trunk" (1), recover the original *Brihatkatha* from beneath a Hindu temple someday.

One of the books that was swallowed up by Somadeva's *Ocean of Story* is the most influential work in Sanskrit fiction, so popular that it has generated over 200 adaptations and translations into over 50 languages in the last 1,500 years. The *Panchatantra*, or *Five Discourses*, was written sometime in the early centuries of our era (c. 300 is a good guess) and is traditionally credited to a Brahmin named Vishnusharman (or Visnu Śarma), who is also the narrator. The original is no longer extant, but in 1924 Franklin Edgerton reconstructed a hypothetical version that, as translator Patrick Olivelle puts it, "comes as close to the original as we are going to get without the discovery of new evidence."[12] Over the centuries, as with Gunadhya's novel, further stories were added to *Five Discourses*, expanding the 160 or so pages of the hypothetical original to more than 400 pages by the time the Jain monk Purnabhadra published his recension in 1199. This longer version is available in a fine English translation by Chandra Rajan, but I want to work with the shorter one that replicates the original.

Superficially, *Five Discourses* resembles Aesop's fables, but it's more like a cross between Machiavelli's *Prince* and Orwell's *Animal Farm*. A king in ancient India finds himself saddled with three "utterly stupid" sons and wonders how they'll ever learn to rule the country. His ministers tell the king that it usually takes at least a dozen years to learn statecraft, but that an 80-year-old teacher named Vishnusharman can do it within six months. His trick is to teach political science not from the usual textbooks but through

---

12 Page xliv of the introduction to his translation of the *Panchatantra*, herafter cited by page number. First published by Oxford in 1997, it was reissued by the Clay Sanskrit Library in 2006 under the title *Five Discourses on Worldly Wisdom*. For a modern visual interpretation, see Bill Buford's edition of *Walton Ford: Pancha Tantra* (Taschen, 2009).

animal fables. Each book (discourse) opens with a topic and a poetic teaser, which intrigues the dumb princes; for example:

> "We begin here the First Book, named 'On Causing Dissention among Allies.' This is its opening verse:
>
> > In the jungle lived a lion and a bull,
> > with great and ever growing love,
> > But by a jackal their love was undone,
> > by a traitor consumed with greed."
>
> The princes asked: "How did that happen?" Visnuśarman narrated this story. (5)

The stories are populated by animals behaving like people, but these aren't simple fables followed by obvious morals; they are thorny lessons in realpolitik with animals representing every variety of ruler, politician, official, diplomat, minister, and advisor. In book 1, two jackals named Karataka and Damanaka (Prudence and Daring, or Wary and Wily in Rajan's translation) become advisors to a lion king who has befriended a bull. Scheming Damanaka uses deceit to turn them against each other, and though his fellow jackal criticizes him harshly for his dirty politics, Damanaka convinces the lion to kill the kindly bull and then feeds on the carcass. For "saving" the king's life, he becomes his top advisor and enjoys the comforts of the royal life. At every step in this story, the lion king is confronted with problems for which his ministers offer advice ranging from the sensible to the shortsighted, and they often tell other animal stories to support their recommendations. (These embedded stories sometimes go three levels deep, tales within tales within tales.) Expediency clashes with ethics, self-interest with public interest, all of it as sleazy as a presidential election. The eventual triumph of Machiavellian Damanaka would have struck me as cynical when younger, but after the second Bush administration it now strikes me as depressingly realistic.[13]

Book 2 is "On Securing Allies," book 3 "On War and Peace," book 4 "On Losing What You Have Gained," and the brief book 5 "On Hasty Actions." The work ends with the tale of a human who kills three religious mendicants under the stupid assumption the act would make him rich — it doesn't; he is "arrested by the officers of the king and impaled" (159) — without returning to the classroom of Vishnusharman and his slow students, so we don't learn the effect of the stories on them.[14] But if they were paying any attention at

13 If Disney ever makes an animated movie of *Five Discourses*, the voice of deceitful Damanaka the jackal should be supplied by Karl Rove.
14 The later version by Purnabhadra ends simplistically with a public service announcement: "This work on polity, composed by the celebrated Visnu Śarma, consisting of stories linked by wise and good sayings of a good and true poet aims to be of service to others here in this

all they would be masters of political science, for Vishnusharman covers everything from diplomacy to consensus-building to disinformation to military strategy to political wheeler-dealing, all by way of entertaining animal fables. As in the first chapter, victory often goes to the deceitful, and trust is often rewarded with betrayal, but the paradoxical result is that a fantasy about talking animals behaving like Hindus turns out to be a work of dirty realism of contemporary relevance. The characters are faced with the myriad ambiguities of real life, full of contradictions, ambiguities, and confusing options. Can you ever trust a former enemy? If forced to choose, would you kill your spouse or your best friend? Traditional guidebooks are available — there are quotations from Kautilya's *Arthasastra* (on political science) and the *Laws of Manu* (on everything else) — but their theory is often difficult to put into practice. Religion isn't of much use: most of the Brahmins and ascetics are exposed as superstitious and gullible. The author pays lip service to *karma* — the doctrine that past actions influence present ones — but he favors those who take fate into their own hands. The book is filled with useful proverbs, folk wisdom, and homiletic verse, but as in Lyly's *Euphues*, you can find a proverb to illustrate anything. Perhaps that's why the novel lacks a conclusive ending, because ethical behavior is always an open question, and will always be challenged by complex new situations. Dharma is a bhitch.

Is *Five Discourses* a novel? Unlike Aesop's or La Fontaine's *Fables* (the Frenchman acknowledges the influence of a European descendant of the Indian book), it has a single narrator, a unifying structure, and dramatizes the classic theme of moving from ignorance to awareness. True, it's called the *Pancha-tantra* rather than the *Pancha-katha* — "discourses" rather than "stories" — and it's obviously a didactic work. But the sophistication of its frame-narrative technique, its reliance on drama and suspense, its skillful alternation between prose and verse, and its clever association of types of animals with types of people are all qualities that belong more to a talented novelist than a creative educator.

The *Brihatkatha* and *Panchatantra* are both secular Hindu fictions. Buddhists in India, like the early Christians, preferred sacred fictions. It wasn't long after the death of Gautama Siddhartha in 483 BCE that (as always happens in religion) some of his followers began inventing miraculous stories about the Buddha.[15] Siddhartha's original teachings (sutras) were secular and philo-

---

world, and to lead the way to the World of Eternal Light, as the wise and learned declare" (435).

15 To clarify: the Buddha is not a personal name but a title (awakened/enlightened one), like Christ (anointed one). Gautama was the clan name of Prince Siddhartha, heir to the throne

sophical, and like the teachings of Jesus four centuries later offered a different way of looking at the world, one "which is against the current, which is lofty, deep, subtle and hard to comprehend."[16] Nothing supernatural about it, just a realistic assessment of life and how best to negotiate it. The goal is "to see things as they are (*yathābhutam*) without illusion or ignorance (*avijja*)"; as Siddhartha told a follower (according to the *Lankavatara Sutra*), "Nirvāna means to see the state of things as they are." The story goes that three months after his death, his disciples gathered to recall all of his talks (he didn't write anything down) and memorize them in group recitals, so as to pass the oral teachings along — it was 300 years before they were committed to writing. By that time a jungle of commentaries, interpretations, and new sutras had grown around them, some even plagiarized from Hindu writings where an author lazily substituted Buddha's name for Shiva's.[17] Sects arose, the Great Vehicle (the Mahayana faction) drove off in one direction, the Lesser Vehicle (Hinayana) in another, both getting further and further away from Siddhartha's original teachings. As would happen with Jesus, a countercultural philosophy degenerated into a religion with all the trimmings: idolatry, virgin birth, rituals, prayers, miracles, competing doctrines, myths, schisms — the usual nonsense.

Just as early Christians invented tales about the young Jesus making sparrows out of mud, raising the dead, and turning his playmates into goats (*Gospel of Thomas*), some Buddhists concocted stories of Buddha's former lives when he was still a bodhisattva, a potential buddha. (Reincarnation — has there ever been a more pathetic religious notion than that? It's yet another desperate denial of the finality of death.) Some of these stories were allegedly based on Siddhartha's own teachings, others were based on Hindu folktales, and others sheer fiction. Sometime at the beginning of the Common Era they were gathered into a collection called *Jataka* (Former Lives [of Buddha]), 547 stories ranging from a page to 30 pages long, each teaching a Buddhist precept. In some the bodhisattva is a king or a tree-spirit, in others a merchant or stonecutter, and in still others a monkey or a parrot. As fiction, they belong more to folklore than to literature, the Buddhist equivalent of Sunday school lessons. Quite popular, needless to say.

The final story in the collection stands apart from the rest, because of both its popularity in the East and its length: at about a hundred pages, *The Perfect Generosity of Prince Vessantara* (*Vessantara Jataka*) has often been published separately and qualifies as the first Buddhist novel, for whoever wrote it brought a novelist's sensibility to what, in lesser hands, would be merely a

---

of the Sakyas (in southern Nepal), hence his nickname Sakyamuni (Sage of the Sakyas). I'll use Siddhartha to refer to the historical philosopher and Buddha for the fantasy figure.

16 Quoted (without a source) by Walpola Rahula in his deservedly popular *What the Buddha Taught*, 52. The following two quotations are from p. 40.

17 Donald S. Lopez, *The Story of Buddhism* (NY: HarperSanFrancisco, 2001), 13.

sermon on charity. Like the other *Jataka* tales, it was written in Pali — the scholarly language of the conservative Theravada branch of Buddhism — and is quite old: illustrations from the story have been found dating back to the 2nd century BCE (though the text as we have it probably dates from a few centuries later). As for a plot summary, I can't improve on the one Richard F. Gombrich provides in his edition:

> Prince Vessantara, the son and heir of Sañjaya, King of the Sivis, and of Queen Phusatī, lives in the capital with his wife Maddī and their small son and daughter. His munificence is unique. He has a magic white elephant which ensures adequate rainfall, but he gives it away to brahmin emissaries from another kingdom. The citizens are enraged, and force Sañjaya to banish him. Maddī chooses to share his exile with the children. Before leaving he gives away all his possessions, making "the gift of the seven hundreds." After a long journey the family reach a mountain glen, where they settle down. A vile old brahmin called Jūjaka, harried at home by a young wife who demands servants, arrives to ask him for his children, and Vessantara gives them while Maddī is away gathering food. Next morning Sakka, the king of the gods, fears that Vessantara may yet give away his wife and be left all alone; he therefore disguises himself as a brahmin and asks her of Vessantara. On receiving her, he gives her back immediately. . . . Jūjaka and the children come to Sañjaya's court, where Sañjaya ransoms his grandchildren and Jūjaka dies of overeating. Full of remorse, Sañjaya takes his retinue to the mountain and invites Vessantara and Maddī to return. The family is reunited, Vessantara becomes king, and all live happily ever after.[18]

The story is intended to illustrate the importance of giving (*dana*), the first of the 10 perfections in Theravada Buddhism, and at the end the prince is rewarded not only with a kingdom because of his selfless acts of charity, but in his next lifetime will be reincarnated as the Buddha. But at the same time the author seems to be telling a different story, one in which these selfless acts are exposed as selfish and irresponsible. Generous people are admirable, but in real life they are often taken advantage of by opportunists, the role played in this novel by leeching Brahmins, who consider Vessantara a patsy and deprive him of everything. Not only is the bodhisattva naïve and unworldly, but his love of generosity is irresponsible: giving away the elephant deprives his country of rain, and when banished, he is willing to abandon his family, in effect turning his wife into a widow and his children into orphans. (His wife Maddi, who emerges as the most human character in the novel, delivers a lament on the widow's life that paints such a horrific picture it almost makes the murderous practice of suttee understandable. *Almost*, for the practice was probably instituted by some selfish Hindu who simply didn't like the

---

18 Pages xv–xvi in his excellent introduction to this splendid volume, which contains numerous photographs of Indian artwork inspired by the story; hereafter cited by page number. Gombrich is the general editor of the Clay Sanskrit Library.

idea of his wife remarrying after his death, and had the power to enforce his meanness.) At one point the author compares Vessantara's eagerness to give things away to "a drunkard eager for a drink" (54), a blasphemous insult in light of the Buddha's injunction against alcohol. When Jujaka cons him out of his kids (who likewise deliver a heartbreaking lament on being abandoned by their father), Vessantara first lies to his wife about it, then falsely accuses *her* of neglecting her children by running around in the forest with magicians and ascetics. It's her responsibility to gather food for the family while he stays at home seeking "enlightenment," and his despicable subterfuge suggests our author was hip to this whole scam about seeking perfection. Like priests and televangelists, some Buddhists harp on about the importance of giving because that's how they sustain themselves, and a man who abandons familial and social responsibility and depends on others for handouts sounds more like a bum than a buddha. The author keeps referring to Vessantara as the "Great Being," which after a while begins to sound as sarcastic as Mark Antony's repeated references to Brutus as an honorable man.

The author lets Vessantara's dubious actions twist in the ironic tension between theory and practice as he delivers some beautiful descriptions and set-pieces. He writes winningly of rural life and delivers a five-page description of a forest that is a tour de force of nature writing. He milks every ounce of pathos from the children's abandonment, and elevates Maddi's maternal instincts to a formidable force of nature. (Male idealism and female realism is another tension at work.) Though tarted up with miracles and supernatural events, the novel contains some admirably realistic touches, as when the Brahmins who get the elephant flip off the angry townspeople ("mocking the crowd with insulting gestures" [14]), or when a messenger is in such a hurry that he races off "with his hair still wet" from a bath (16). While the happy ending too easily relaxes ironic tensions the author subversively set up earlier, *The Perfect Generosity of Vessantara* is an impressive work of fiction, an interesting study in the competing claims of religious and social obligations.

Less popular than the *Jataka* because more literary is another collection of stories that were written around the same time called *The Heavenly Exploits* (*Divyavadana*), an anthology of 38 Buddhist fictions comparable to Christian legends of the saints. (This collection was assembled later, perhaps as late as the 8th century, but many of the stories were composed much earlier.) These tales are longer, a few approaching the length of a novella, and much more adventurous, albeit weighed down by religious doctrine. They're all set during Buddha's lifetime and include an appearance by him at some point. The first tale in the collection, "The Story of Shrona Kotikarna," features a merchant who gets lost and enters a fantastic world where he encounters cities of iron and floating palaces, invariably featuring "a heavenly nymph, shapely, beautiful and gracious . . . making love and otherwise dallying with" some lucky Indian, though in one instance the nymph morphs into an enormous centipede that "wrapped its body seven times around the man's body and devoured his head from above."[19] Other "characters" in this religious parable about dharma include souls waiting to be reborn and many hungry ghosts, one of the stages on the road to reincarnation.[20]

The inescapability of karma is the theme of one of the most complex novellas, "The Story of Makandika the Wanderer" (no. 36). Makandika wants to marry his daughter Anupama to Lord Buddha, in town bumming alms, but the Enlightened One has forsaken women, and tells several tales to illustrate his contempt for those seductive hindrances to Truth.[21] The first, based on one of the *Jataka* tales, begins very much like Shrona's adventure, except that the merchant in this story, Simhala by name, is stranded on Sri Lanka after a sea monster destroys his ship. On that Circean island, he and his crew marry a group of man-eating sirens; Simhala escapes via a flying horse before his mate can devour him, but she follows him back to India and tries to convince others that she's his wife. Simhala tries to tell everyone she's actually a demoness, but everyone assures him "All women are demons" (345). Buddha reveals that *he* was Simhala in a previous lifetime and coldly rejects Anupama by saying, "this girl, filled with urine and excrement, I could not bear to touch even with my feet" (323) — a real gentleman — so Anupama winds up instead the wife of King Udayana (the father of Naravahanadatta, our future emperor of the sorcerers!). Jealous of the king's principal wife, a Buddhist convert, Anupama talks her father into burning her and the king's 500 other wives to death, which Buddha later dismisses as more or less what they deserve, karmic payback for deeds committed in a previous lifetime. It's a strange brew of adventure story, Buddhist sermon, misogyny, and special effects: "A display of psychic powers quickly secures the favor of ordinary people," Lord Buddha winks (389), and the colorful, supernatural stories comprising *The Heavenly Exploits* are the literary equivalent of displays of psychic powers — a bit tacky, but OK if used for entertainment purposes only.

The first extended-length Buddhist fiction seems to be the anonymous

---

19 Pages 57, 59 in the first volume of Tatelman's translation.
20 Tatelman: "Buddhists believe [*sic* — not "used to believe," but still believe] in six realms of rebirth: in heaven as a god, on earth as a human, on earth as an animal, just under the earth as an anti-god, as a hungry ghost who haunts the earth, or in a hell" (1:418). All of this constitutes *samsara* (literally "the running around"), essentially the messy world we live in. These realms could work as metaphors for a tumultuous life — someone might be wild as a monkey as a child, be treated like a god when famous, become homeless and look like a hungry ghost, and "go through hell," as we say — but I fear many Buddhists take all this literally. "Maybe rebirth is simply HAVING KIDS," Jack Kerouac wrote at the end of his Buddhist period (*Selected Letters 1957–1969*, 206).
21 Siddhartha taught that there are five hindrances (*nīvarana*) to spiritual progress: "(1) Sensuous Lust, (2) Ill-will, (3) Physical and mental torpor and languor, (4) Restlessness and Worry, (5) Doubt" (Rahula, 3 n3).

Entry into the Realm of Reality (*Gandavyuha*), the last and longest section of the immense *Flower Ornament Scripture* (*Avatamsaka sutra*, 1st or 2nd cent. CE), and which sometimes circulated separately.[22] A pilgrim's progress, it concerns a religious boy named Sudhana eager to graduate from a disciple to an "enlightening" being: not merely an enlightened person but someone who enlightens others and facilitates their entry into the realm of reality, meaning not the illusory "reality" perceived by the senses but the ultimate reality perceivable only by those who have overcome the limitations of the senses and cultural conditioning. (Its author would agree with Nabokov that "reality" is "one of the few words which mean nothing without quotes" [*The Annotated Lolita*, 314].) Inspired by a lecture given by a bodhisattva named Manjushri, Sudhana asks him for further enlightenment, and is told to seek out spiritual benefactors across India who can teach him what Manjushri knows. The bulk of the novel records Sudhana's interviews with these benefactors; in addition to the predictable monks, seers, and brahmins, Sudhana confers with a number of laypeople: a grammarian, a mariner, several perfumers and householders, a goldsmith, several children still living with their parents, a few kings, a beggar, even a prostitute. In fact several women become his spiritual benefactors, mostly lay devotees, but also a group of night goddesses with long names (e.g., Sarvajagadrakshapranidhanaviryaprabha) and even longer discourses to relate. Sudhana humbly learns from them all, and finally meets Maitreya (the future Buddha) before returning to Manjushri who, impressed by Sudhana's accomplishments, arranges for an interview with an enlightening being named Universally Good, a hypostatization of Buddhist theology in its entirety.

The novel is carefully structured in decades: the first 10 benefactors Sudhana visits speak of what is called "The Ten Abodes" (the subject of the 15th sutra of *FOS*), the next 10 cover "The Ten Practices" (*FOS* #21), followed by "The Ten Dedications" (#25); next, the night goddesses drone on and on about "The Ten Stages" (#26) and include stories in their discourses similar to those in *The Heavenly Exploits*, and the final 10 subdivide the 11th stage, Universal Good (#36). The theology is stupefying, but the style is intoxicating. The author of *ERR* is a maximalist prose stylist given to spinning out long, additive sentences that use sensory overload to entrance the reader. His style has one reaching for such fancy adjectives as magniloquent, hyperbolic, recherché, altisonant, coruscating, diamondiferous, refulgent. A typical sentence:

> Sudhana saw as many water spirit girls as all worldly events, in inconceivably many forms, emerging from [the monk] Saradhvaja's sides, pervading all universes moment to moment,

---

22 *ERR*, as I'll abbreviate it, occupies pp. 1135–518 of Thomas Cleary's heroic translation of the entire *FOS* (ditto), which will be cited by page number.

showing the miracle of the water spirits, adorning the sky with inconceivable fragrant clouds, adorning the whole sky with inconceivable clouds of flowers, arraying the whole realm of space with inconceivable adornments of clouds of garlands, covering all universes with inconceivable adornments of clouds of garlands, covering all universes with inconceivable adornment of bejeweled parasols, adorning the sky with inconceivable clouds of jeweled banners, inconceivable clouds of jeweled pennants, rain from inconceivable endless clouds of great jewels, rain from inconceivable clouds of jewel necklaces and various flowers, inconceivable clouds of jewel seats with enlightening beings sitting on them teaching the ways of enlightenment, inconceivable clouds of troves of celestial jewels, rain of clouds of sounds of goddesses singing praises of the Teaching, inconceivable raining clouds of jewel lotuses adorned with nets of pearls crowned with diamonds, inconceivable clouds of jewel crowns and rain of clouds of endless lights adorned by all jewels, inconceivable clouds of celestial beings graced with flowers, garlands, parasols, and banners, inconceivable clouds of goddesses, adornments of rain produced by clouds of songs of praise of buddhas' qualities sung by the goddesses on high standing with joined palms or scattering golden flowers, also covering all buddhas' assemblies with clouds of heaps of fragrances the colors of all jewels and clouds of smoke of the finest incense, adorning all worlds, delighting all beings, honoring all buddhas. (1198–99)

This overloaded, incantatory style can become wearying over the course of the 400-page novel, but as an advertisement for the cosmological visions awaiting disciples like Sudhana who want to leave behind the dreary "reality" of ancient India for the ultimate reality, it couldn't be more seductive.

Beyond these psychedelic visions, however, is an admirable emphasis on helping others find enlightenment, and on practicing Buddhist virtues in everyday life — hence Sudhana's interviews with working-class folks like the mariner and the goldsmith. When Sudhana goes to visit the prostitute Vasumitra — whose name aptly means "Friend of the World" — the towns-people are shocked, exhibiting the petty cultural conditioning an enlightened being needs to transcend. But as Vasumitra explains, she helps her customers attain the virtue of dispassion even as she plies her trade, catering to their various preferences:

"Some attain dispassion as soon as they see me, and achieve an enlightening concentration called 'delight in joy.' Some attain dispassion merely by talking with me, and achieve an enlightening concentration called 'treasury of unimpeded sound.' Some attain dispassion just by holding my hand, and achieve an enlightening concentration called 'basis of going to all buddha-lands.' Some attain dispassion just by staying with me, and achieve an enlightening concentration called 'light of freedom from bondage.' Some attain dispassion just by gazing at me, and achieve an enlightening concentration called 'tranquil expression.' Some attain dispassion just by embracing me, and achieve an enlightening concentration called 'womb receiving all sentient beings without rejection.' Some attain dispassion just by kissing me, and achieve an enlightening concentration called 'contact with the treasury of virtue of all beings.' All those who come to me I establish in this enlightening liberation of ultimate dispassion, on the brink of the stage of unimpeded omniscience." (1272)

Sudhana just talks with her, opting for "treasury of unimpeded sound" — me, I would have jumped at "womb receiving all sentient beings without rejection" — but the point is that any activity or occupation can be imbued with spiritual value, not merely the ostensibly religious ones. (It's significant that an enlightening *nun* sends Sudhana along to the prostitute.) True, *ERR* lacks conflict — Sudhana faces no obstacles in his quest, and it's a foregone conclusion that he will become an enlightening being — a major drawback of all early Buddhist novels. Nonetheless, the novel shows that it's not enough simply to hear or read edifying discourse; one must go out into the world like Sudhana and talk to people, specifically those who have incorporated religious values into mundane activities like sailing, goldsmithing, or even prostitution, not hole up in a cave and seek "some kind of loincloth nirvana."[23] Since the novel genre dramatizes activity in the world, it was an inspired choice by the author of *ERR*, and an influential one. As a Buddhist scripture, *ERR* has been called "the most imposing monument erected by the Indian mind to the spiritual life of all mankind";[24] but as fiction, it encouraged other Buddhists to use narrative form to convey their theology. Its elaborate, cosmological style would be adopted by secular Indian novelists in later centuries, as we'll see. Translated into Chinese at an early date, *ERR* eventually influenced some of the great Chinese novelists as well, specifically Wu Chengen, who refers to Sudhana and *ERR* in his parody of the religious quest, *The Journey to the West* (c. 1570), and Cao Xueqin, author of the monumental *Dream of Red Mansions* (c. 1760).

Moving on from the sublime to the ridiculous takes us to the anonymous *Lalitavistara*, a florid, 400-page fantasy of Buddha's life assembled in the 3rd century from earlier traditions, and like *The Heavenly Exploits* written in Buddhist Hybrid Sanskrit. It begins, as does *Entry into the Realm of Reality*, with the formulaic opening of the canonized sutras — "Thus have I heard" — which is rather cheeky given what follows, but that seems to be the point: the title means the "Elaborated Sports" of Buddha, "sports" (*lila*) being a playful equivalent to the "acts" used by the dour New Testament authors. These are the "acts" of Buddha as Busby Berkeley production numbers.

The author follows the traditional story of Buddha's life: royal birth, sheltered upbringing, early marriage; his epiphanic confrontation with old age,

---

23 Plaks, *The Four Masterworks of the Ming Novel*, 276.
24 D. T. Suzuki, *Essays in Zen Buddhism* (1953), quoted in Li's *Fictions of Enlightenment*, 30.

disease, and death; his adoption of the ascetic life, temptation by Mara (the Buddhist devil), and eventual enlightenment; and his decision to share his insights with others, beginning with five old companions, and then with all classes of people. But like the authors of the *Jataka*, like Asvaghosa in his verse narrative *Buddhacarita* (1st or 2nd cent. CE), like the authors of *The Heavenly Exploits*, the author is less interested in giving an accurate account of Siddhartha's life than in inspiring monks to adore Buddha, and thus indulges in vulgar hero-worship and outlandish exaggeration. It begins not with Buddha's birth but a dozen years earlier, as the bodhisattva is cooling his heels in Tusita (a Buddhist heaven), where he decides to be reborn for a final time as a prince. Meanwhile, he lectures the gods and divine nymphs, which gives our myriad-minded author an opportunity to unfurl his peacock tail of rhetoric:

> There, Bodhisattva sat on the throne, decked with the emanations of the fruits of his own virtues, its legs studded with many gems, adorned by strewing many flowers, fragrant with many divine scents, aromatic with the best incense, beautified with the strewing of divine flowers and perfumes of many colours, irradiated by the hundred thousand rays of many jewels, covered with a net of many jewels, ringing with the waving net of many bells, resounding with the clanging of many hundred thousand jewelled gongs, clear with many hundred thousand jewels, hung with many hundred thousand cloths, decked with many hundred thousand cloths and garlands, sung to by the dancing, singing and music of many hundred thousand nymphs, described with many hundred thousand qualities, served by many hundred thousand Lokapālas, saluted by many hundred thousand śakras, bowed to by many hundred thousand Brahmās, surrounded by many *koti niyuta* [billion] hundred thousand Bodhisattvas, inviting many *koti niyuta* hundred thousand Buddhas from the ten quarters, and attended by the essence of the fruits of the load of *Pāramitās* [perfections] and virtues for the innumerable *koti niyuta* hundred thousand *kalpas* [aeons].[25]

A full house, then. These compound descriptions, mounting in scale, are typical of the author; he glories in two-page sentences, long catalogs, and in creating a hall of mirrors where Buddha's qualities can be multiplied into infinity. Having chosen his ideal mother — Maya, wife of King Suddhodana — the bodhisattva decides for reasons of his own to assume the form of "a baby white elephant with six tusks, its head the colour of *indragopa* [a reddish insect], the set of tusks made of gold, complete in every limb, and entered on the right side, the womb of his mother who had undertaken the *posadha* rite in the star *Pusya*" (6). Ten months later he'll be born out of her right side, "not smeared by the uterine dirt" (7), a virgin birth betraying a puritanical disgust with the body that runs throughout this novel. The author goes out of his way to praise Maya's sexlessness, her complete lack of interest in sensual

---

25 Chap. 4 in Goswami's stiff translation, hereafter cited by chapter.

pleasure, even her inability to incite lustful thoughts in men.[26] But while still in the womb, the bodhisattva has already begun to attract attention, which the author dramatizes in atrociously bad taste: the fetus receives visitors, sticking his golden arm out of his mother's vagina to greet them, point to chairs, and later to dismiss them — like Thing from his box in *The Addams Family*.

Because the author has already announced many *koti niyuta* times that Prince Siddhartha will become Buddha, aka the Tathagata (the one who has found the Truth), there's no drama, no epiphany at his life-changing encounter with suffering and impermanency, just intoxicating flights and fantasy at every stage of his career. T. S. Eliot once complained that reading Swinburne was like downing repeated shots of gin; Siddhartha discouraged drinking, so the author gets us drunk with words instead. Much of the novel is ludicrous, and some passages read like thesaurus entries ("His speech was instructive, authoritative, clear, pleasant to each of many people, pretty, pleasant on the ear, inspiring, satisfying . . ." [19]), a bad stylistic tic the author may have picked up from *ERR*. But at its best, *Lalitavistara* exhibits some truly imaginative writing. The longest and most spectacular chapter is "The Defeat of Mara" (21), which deserves a psychedelic title like "Purple Modal Strobe Ecstasy with the Daughters of Destruction."[27] The evil Mara arrives to prevent Buddha from achieving enlightenment under the *bodhi* tree, so Buddha "emits a ray named Sarvamāramandhalavidhvamsanakari, from the circle of hair between his eyebrows" that lights up the tri-state area and broadcasts Buddha's intention to stand his ground.[28] Mara has 32 bad dreams, then amasses an army

> of gods and men, their hands, feet, and bodies encircled by the coils of hundreds and thousands of serpents, . . . their terrible fangs bared, their thick and long tongues hanging out, their tongues the colour of a turtle's neck, their eyes red as fire, as though filled with cobra-venom. Some vomited forth venom, some caught serpents in their hands and ate them. Some like Garuda, raised human flesh, blood, hands, feet, heads, liver, entrails and fecal matter, and ate them . . .

26 Earlier I identified Mara as the Buddhist devil; specifically, he is the god of sex/vice/ disease/death. For the Hindus, sensual pleasure (*kama*) was one of the three aims of life, but Buddhists were told to avoid it like the plague.

27 The subtitle of a version of Terry Riley's *Poppy Nogood and the Phantom Band* (1968), a mesmerizing soundscape of tape-looped soprano saxophone and organ drone.

28 By the time this was written, Buddha's ray was legendary. In the introductory chapter of *The Lotus Sutra*, probably written a few centuries earlier, we're told (in the same big-top style): "At that time the Buddha emitted a ray of light from the tuft of white hair between his eyebrows, one of his characteristic features, lighting up eighteen thousand worlds in the eastern direction. There was no place that the light did not penetrate, reaching downward as far as the Avichi hell and upward to the Akanishtha heaven" (6). *The Lotus Sutra* is a long, fictitious discourse by the Buddha near the end of his life that has just enough narrative continuity and interaction with characters that it could be considered a novel, but one has to draw the line somewhere.

which occupies three pages. Then Mara's thousand sons join the fray, but Buddha scares them off with a glance. Mara then tries to tempt Buddha with his daughters:

> Approaching, they stood before Bodhisattva and exhibited the thirty-two types of feminine guile. Which thirty-two? Some covered half their faces. Some showed high and firm bosoms. Some showed rows of their teeth in a half-smile. Some raised their arms and revealed their bare armpits. Some showed their *bimba*-like lips.[29] Some looked on Bodhisattva with half-open eyes, and on seeing him, closed them quickly. Some showed half-revealed breasts. Some with dishevelled robes revealed their hips with the waistband . . .

and so on, through all 32 recognized forms of flirtation. But Buddha shuts them down:

> "Your beauty is like foam or bubbles. Like a magic show, it becomes false by itself. Like play, or like a dream, it is non-eternal, transient. It deludes the minds of the foolish and the ignorant.
> "Eyes are like bubbles held by the skin, like hard pustules of clotted blood. The belly is a repository of urine and fecal matter, impure, a machine of sorrow, arising out of the pain of action."

Again with the urine! It's easy to make fun of such writing, but the author's over-the-top style is actually appropriate: if Buddha is a superhero, then this hyperactive video-game gusto does justice to his struggle in this chapter with his inner demons and with the armies of competing religions and philosophical systems he hopes to vanquish.

Following his enlightenment, we are given some passages from Buddha's earliest teachings — a few sparks from the famous Fire Sermon, and all of his introductory lecture, "Turning the Wheel of Dharma" — before the author concludes audaciously with a blurb from Buddha himself recommending the book we've just read: "This, Sirs, is the exposition of *Dharma*, the *sūtrānta* named Lalitavistara, the great *Vaipulya* of Bodhisattva-sport, the beautiful entrance into the subject of Buddha, relating to himself, narrated by Tathāgata.[30] Accept it, bear it, read it" (27). Surprisingly, this religious jeu d'esprit was actually adopted as one of the Vaipulya sutras (like the *Lankavatara Sutra* cited earlier), which is as ludicrous as adding Buck Mulligan's "Ballad of Joking Jesus" to Christian hymnals (see *Ulysses* 1.584–99). But when we

29 No, not a Buddhist bimbo but "the red fruit of Momordica monadelpha, a species of amaranth" (*Mahavastu* 1.97, n1).
30 The author switches between third and first person, but in one sense the entire novel is being narrated by Buddha to his bhikkus (monks).

remember that the equally ludicrous Acts of the Apostles were considered holy writ by some early Christians, we shouldn't be surprised.

On the last page of his lengthy *Some of the Dharma*, Jack Kerouac wonders if his book on Buddhism hasn't in fact "been mighty preparations for the Epic Novel THE TATHAGATA?" (420). Actually, that epic novel had already been written. In the 3rd or 4th century, an author or authors compiled a 1,200-page book entitled the *Mahavastu* (Great Story, as in "The Greatest Story Ever Told"). This was an attempt to gather every story, legend, and myth about the Buddha into a definitive work. Like the author of the *Lalitavistara*, the authors were interested in inspirational stories, not doctrine, which is why it belongs more to literature than to religion. As its translator J. J. Jones dryly notes, "There may not be much in the work that reminds us that originally Buddhism was a code of morals."[31] They scooped up everything they could find: fables from the *Jataka*, holy lives (*avadana*) like those in *The Heavenly Exploits*, and exaggerated accounts of Siddhartha's life as in the *Lalitavistara*, beginning with a lengthy section on the stages in a bodhisattva's life and the story of *a* buddha who proclaimed the coming of *the* Buddha: Dipamkara.[32] It's an incongruous work, lurching from one genre to another and often giving multiple accounts of events (as in the Hebrew Genesis, the authors wanted to preserve all the different traditions, despite the contradictions.) It has some of the linguistic exuberance of the *Lalitavistara*, but the authors were too respectful of their various sources to make the material their own. So: an epic novel of the Tathagata? Yes, but not a very good one. Kerouac would have done better.

An example of an author taking traditional material and making it his own is supplied by Arya Sura in his *Jatakamala* (Garland of Former Lives [of Buddha], 4th cent.?). Sura adapted 30 *Jataka* tales, wrote four of his own, then organized them carefully to make his case for self-sacrifice, asceticism, and "complete faith in Lord Buddha."[33] According to his translator, Sura pays close attention to style and expertly mixes poetry with prose in 30 different meters. Unfortunately, his examples of self-sacrifice are so extreme as to render them void of any real interest or application. In the first, the bodhisattva was a Brahmin who came across a starving tigress on the verge of eating her offspring; rather than see that happen, he killed himself so that the tiger could devour him and live. In another, he was a king who so loved giving alms that he even gave his own eyes to a beggar who requested them. Even

---

31 Foreword to vol. 2, pp. xii–xiii.
32 When Buddhists upgraded Siddhartha from man to god, they outfitted him with all the traits of a savior, including a John the Baptist figure to announce his coming; in the myth of Buddha, Dipamkara plays that role; in the traditional (if not historical) version of Siddhartha's life, it's a colleague named Ananda. See Campbell's *Oriental Mythology*, 252–55.
33 Page 9 in Khoroche's fine edition entitled *Once the Buddha Was a Monkey*.

the animals display this neurotic love of mortification; an ascetic hare comes across a Brahmin who is starving, and selflessly throws himself into a fire to roast himself for the holy man. (In these last two cases, the supreme god Sakra impersonated the beggar and the Brahmin in order to test them.) The stories are well written and show some wit — in the story about the king who sacrifices his eyesight, there are several puns on being blinded by passion and not believing one's own eyes — but this is a violation of Siddhartha's warning against extreme asceticism. In his very first lecture, "Turning the Wheel of Dharma," he advocates the Middle Path of responsible, compassionate living and condemns the two extremes of living *la vida loca* or indulging in extreme asceticism and "self-mortification, which is painful, unworthy and unprofitable."[34]

Indeed the *Jatakamala* indicates why the Buddhist novel fizzled out (just as the early Christian novel did around this time): of the four goals of life — pleasure, prosperity, virtue, and liberation — it places all its emphasis on the last two, and rigs the game by letting the reader know in advance that all these tests of one's virtue are superfluous; you *know* the bodhisattva will someday become the Buddha, which deprives the book of what the novel as a genre thrives on: drama and real conflict. There is a moment of doubt in *Prince Vessantara* when the ascetic suspects he may have gone too far after giving away his children, but there's no hesitancy, no doubt, no conflict in these later Buddhist works. Novelists find these tensions wherever people pursue pleasure and love (*kama*) and social and material advancement (*artha*), rarely in the fantasy world of religious observance (*dharma*) and the downright unhealthy realm of suicidal "liberation" (*moksa*). In his story of the hare, Sura writes of his friends (an otter, a jackal, and a monkey), "Contrary to animal nature, they showed pity to living things" (32); all of these Buddhist fictions, from the *Jataka* to the *Jatakamala*, are contrary to nature, both human and animal, and contrary to the nature of the novel, which deals with samsara, not nirvana. I'm sure Siddhartha intended his philosophy as a guide to living deliberately in this world, not as an escape plan from it. The fundamental error of his followers — that our phenomenal world is transitory and thus unreal, and that their hallucinatory spiritual cosmos is the real, permanent one (technically known as getting it ass-backwards) — reduces the appeal and relevance of their fiction. To be fair, the novel's dramatic structure is inimical to Buddhist theology; as translator Brother Anthony of Taizé explains, "One of the challenges to the novel that [Buddhist writers] cannot avoid is the fact that the Buddhist vision of the nature of things virtually denies the reality of progress and the possibility of ending."[35] One can admire the imagination and

---

34 The text of this lecture, the *Dhammacakkappavattana-sutta*, is given in Rahula, 92–94.
35 Page 375 of his afterword to South Korean poet Ko Un's novel *Little Pilgrim* (*Hwaomgyeong*, 1991), a modern adaptation of *Entry into the Realm of Reality*. Two recent scholarly

stylistic verve with which Indian Buddhists dressed up their delusions, but it wouldn't be until writers in Tibet and the Far East brought conflict and realism back that the Buddhist novel would continue its cycle of rebirths.

After Gunadhya's tidal wave of stories subsided, the Hindu novel entered its classic phase, beginning with one of the most extraordinary works in Sanskrit literature. *Vasavadatta* was composed by a brilliant, erudite writer named Subandhu, about whom we know nothing except that he was familiar with the *Brihatkatha* and apparently everything else written in Sanskrit before his time. Scholars are unsure of when he existed; one confidently gives 385–465 as his dates, others place him a century later.[36] A rather slight love story, the novella is almost a Sanskrit *Finnegans Wake* in the density of its language: nearly every word is a pun — even a double or triple pun — extended metaphors reach Himalayan heights, and many sentences carry double meanings, so as we follow the main narrative we are also taking an encyclopedic course in Indian history, theology, science, geography, and social customs.[37] Actually, "we" doesn't include most of us, for the two English translations available only hint at the multiple meanings in Subandhu's text. When we read a punny phrase in *Finnegans Wake* like "they were yung and easily freudened" (115), we recognize the words "young" and "frightened" beneath the distorted names of the two most famous psychoanalysts of the 20th century; but any attempt to translate that phrase into another language — and into a culture unfamiliar with modern psychology — would be doomed. Louis Gray's old translation of *Vasavadatta* relies on brackets to indicate multiple meanings (single brackets for one pun, double for double puns), resulting in unwieldy sentences like this: "Thus, even though a <Bhīma>, he is <<no foe of Baka>>, for he is <horrible> and a <<foe of them that praise him>>; though a <fire>, he is a <<wind>>, for he is a <devourer of his own place of refuge> and a <<dog in his mother>>" (63–64). To a Sanskrit reader, this is presumably as clear and clever as "yung and easily freudened," but it would take half a page to unpack that portmanteau sentence for the English reader. The other English

---

books that address the same question are *Reading Emptiness: Buddhism and Literature* by Jeff Humphries (Albany: State U New York P, 1999), who insists there's no place "in a genuine Buddhist practice for literature" (xxi), and *Buddhist Scriptures as Literature: Sacred Rhetoric and the Uses of Theory* by Ralph Flores (Albany: State U New York P, 2008), who argues Buddhist sacred writings do qualify as literature, if not as novels.

36 Maan Singh is the confident one; see chap. 1 of his slim monograph. Warder, whom I mostly follow in this section, places him at the end of the 6th century.

37 This was not an innovation in Sanskrit literature — translator Gray mentions a similar double-entendre work, Ramacandra's *Rasikaranjana*, "which may be read as a laudation either of asceticism or of eroticism" (32) — but Subandhu pushes the technique to an unheard-of extreme.

translation, completed by Harinath De in 1908 but not published until 1994, explains things as it goes along; the same sentence in Dr. De's translation reads: "The wicked man combines the incompatible appellations of being *Bhīma* and yet no foe to the demon *Baka* in the sense that he is terrible and hostile to those worthy of praise; of being *āśrayāśa*, fire, yet *Matariśvā* in the sense of being a destroyer of shelters and adopting a canine behaviour towards his own mother" (18) — hardly an improvement. And some of his sentences go on like that for pages as Subandhu describes cities, scenery, cemeteries, battles, and the seasons.

Fortunately, it's not all that dense, and enough of Subandhu's story emerges from his complex raga of language to allow an appreciation of his achievement. It concerns a young prince named Kandarpaketu who one night near dawn (like Poliphilo in Colonna's equally complex novel) dreams of his ideal mate, who is described in terms that recall those erotic sculptures adorning some Hindu temples:

> then (Kandarpakētu) saw in a dream a damsel about eighteen years of age[38] with her hips girt round with the bond of a girdle which was the gate of the city of delight of her thighs; which was the golden rampart of the great treasure-house of the city of joy; which was a trench for the line of the tendril of down; which was a halo for the disc of the moon of her hips; which had a golden inscription consisting of a line of down that proclaimed victory over the triple world; which was the line of the moat of the prison of the hearts of all men; and was as the bar of the chamber of a flock of birds which were the glances of the world.
>
> (She was) adorned with a waist which seemed full of sorrow through failure to see her moon-like face that was hidden by the burden of her swelling breasts; which appeared to be filled with weariness from the oppression of the urns of her bosom and the circlets of her heavy hips; which had apparently conceived a deep resentment for her massy buttocks; which seemed filled with exhaustion from the restraining hand of the Creator who had compressed it exceedingly; and which had become extremely slender, as if on account of its anxious thought: "Suppose mine own breasts should fall on me like projections from a height?" (58–59)

This is ludicrous, but wonderfully so — and lest the description seem unflattering, this was a culture in which it was a *compliment* to tell a woman she had thighs like an elephant's trunk. K. goes in search of his dream-girl with his friend Makaranda, and at night they overhear a lovers' spat between a mynah bird and a parrot; the latter explains that his long absence was due to his stay

---

38 This is the American Gray's translation; the Hindu De doesn't give her age in his, and I suspect Gray wanted to make Vasavadatta of legal age before launching into this lascivious description of her nubile body. Elsewhere in Sanskrit literature (as in world literature generally, as we've seen), the heroine is much younger.

in Pataliputra, where he heard of a princess named Vasavadatta who dreamed of a perfect lover named Kandarpaketu. The prince, delighted by the news, goes to Pataliputra and, turning on his subcontinental charm, has no trouble convincing V. to elope with him on a flying horse, especially since the next day her father was going to force her to marry someone, ashamed that she has reached the age of puberty without a husband. They spend the night in the forest, but when K. wakes the next morning she has disappeared; unable to find her, he wanders in desolation to the sea and is about to commit suicide when a cosmic voice tells him to hang in there. Shortly afterwards he comes across a statue that resembles Vasavadatta, and as soon as he touches it, she comes back to life. Seems she went off looking for food, got mixed up in a battle (which Subandhu describes splendidly), and angered a monk whose grounds were destroyed by the armies, and who cursed her to remain in stone until rescued by her prince — an Eastern prototype of the Sleeping Beauty story, and which has probably inspired more than one Hindu to caress those stone beauties engaged in acrobatic sex acts on the sides of the temples in Khajuraho in the hope of reviving one. They return to the prince's city and "lived enjoying blisses as his heart desired" (141).

Kama is not merely an aim in life in this novel, but is capitalized as a god, and the *Kamasutra* cited like Scripture. "Red-eyed with lust, . . . wearied with the exhaustion of excessive love" (108), all of the females in the novel are sexually active, and every man is measured by his success with them. It's a very sensuous novel, with much of the wordplay providing sexual double entendres. Subandhu's many descriptions of nature are highly sexualized, with phallic and vulval imagery abounding, as in "showers of sap passing out through holes in the stems of buds of trumpet-flowers cloven by the tips of the claws of koels; that medlar-trees horripilate [grow erect] from sprinkling with rum in mouthfuls by amorous girls merry with wine" (83–84). Nights are filled with women racing to assignations, with the moans of lovers, with the dirty songs of harlots. It approaches sensory overload at times as Subandhu piles on his detailed descriptions and overextended metaphors, enabled by Sanskrit's capacity for lengthy compound words; when K. arrives at the seashore, he notes the "multitude of lions illumined with beautiful heavy manes smeared with quantities of blood from must elephants' frontal-lobes split open by terrible blows from masses of claws sharp as the tips of the thunderbolt" (126), which is complicated enough, but a literal translation of the Sanskrit is one gigantic word-image: "thunderboltpointsharpclawcollectionfurious-blowtornopenwantonelephantfrontallobeplacestartingbloodspurtanointed-beautifulmanemassterriblelionmultitude" (Warder 3:239). Translator Gray compares Subandhu's style to Lyly's, which is certainly apt, but he was writing in 1913; had he lived longer, *Finnegans Wake* with its hundred-letter thunderwords would have provided a better parallel. Just as the *Wake* has attracted a small band of devotees, *Vasavadatta* would fascinate a small audience of Sanskrit writers and scholars for centuries; but like a tourist in Khajuraho, the Western reader can only gawk in awe.

One of the first to praise and imitate Subandhu was the great writer Bana (sometimes Banabhatta: *-bhatta* is a respectful title), author of the two finest novels of this period. In the introductory verses to his first novel, *The Deeds of King Harsha* (*Harshacarita*), he claims "the pride of poets verily melted away" when they read *Vasavadatta*.[39] Bana took up the challenge by mastering Subandhu's *gaudiya* style — which looks aptly enough like "gaudy" but means sentences that enclose two or more meanings — and applying it not to a fairytale world of talking birds and flying horses but to the historical India of the early 7th century. Harshavardhana was a king in northern India, born around 590, who ascended the throne in 606 and greatly expanded his kingdom before his death in 647. Bana was born around 600 to a good family, and after losing his parents at age 14 he took up *la vie bohème*, wandering throughout India with an artsy band of poets, painters, musicians, comedians, and dancing girls, until he finally decided to seek the patronage of King Harsha. The king was initially suspicious of this rakish Brahmin, so Bana charmed the socks off him by writing this highly stylized account of the king's early life, from his birth to his ascension of the throne, a fanciful and dazzling display of his literary skills (and gift for flattery). Though mislabeled a biography by some historians of India — even as they identify its many departures from recorded history — it is clearly a historical *novel*, expanding the king's actual deeds to legendary proportions. Bana's purpose was not to supply an accurate chronicle or explore the king's character but to celebrate him in a series of rhetorical showpieces.[40]

Structurally, *The Deeds of King Harsha* resembles the *Brihatkatha*: the first two and a half chapters are narrated in the third person and deal with Bana's mythological ancestry and early life (while supersizing his king's deeds the author also fictionalizes his own background) and his frosty reception at the court of King Harsha. Then in the middle of chapter 3, Bana takes over as narrator and tells his kinsmen the story of their magnanimous king, beginning with his ancestors. In chapter 4 he relates the births of Harsha and his siblings — an older brother named Rajyavardhana and a younger sister named Rajyacri — their childhoods, and Rajyacri's marriage to a neighboring prince. Their father dies in chapter 5 while Rajyavardhana is up north repelling an invasion, but not before naming Harsha as his successor, contrary to primogeniture. (Historians suspect Bana of playing loose with facts here to justify the younger son's claim to the throne.) Both sons are devastated by

---

39 From the old Cowell/Thomas translation, hereafter cited by chapter.
40 Nevertheless, it is treasured by historians of the era for its countless cultural details, itemized in Vasudeva Agrawala's fascinating *Deeds of Harsha*.

their father's death — Bana's description of their profound grief is devastating — and then they learn their sister's husband has been killed by an enemy king and that she has been imprisoned. Raj goes off to fight, subdues the enemy, but then is killed during a treacherous act. In chapter 6 Harsha vows to avenge his brother's death, but then learns his sister has escaped and is lost somewhere in the Vindhya mountains and decides in chapter 7 to rescue her first. (He needs to maintain the alliance with her dead husband's kingdom.) In the concluding eighth chapter, he rescues his sister just before she is about to commit suttee (burn herself to death, as Harsha's mother did), and assumes the reins of power over his father's kingdom as the moon rises in the night sky, a symbol of future glories.[41]

As in *Vasavadatta*, the various events in *King Harsha* are merely excuses for Bana's rhetorical displays, which even in translation are stupendous. In fact, the novel resembles a series of tableaux from the king's life, pictures at an exhibition that Bana describes in sumptuous detail. Professor Agrawala puts it another way: "Bāna acts like the curator of a big palace rich in every way who takes delight and interest in acquainting the visitor with minute details of all that comes before him without showing the least hurry" (3). Nightfall, dawn, the splendor of King Harsha's court, a horripilating demonic ceremony, a wedding, a forest fire, and other events are described in a mixture of vivid, realistic detail and erudite, mythological allusion; as each new character is introduced, a three-page portrait in superlative terms follows, often pushed (as in Subandhu) to almost absurd lengths. (In fact, Bana inserts a few passages from *Vasavadatta* verbatim into his novel.) Allowances must be made for a different culture that placed a great emphasis on ceremony and formality, but even by Oriental standards Bana's elaborations seem extreme.[42] Harsha's mother, for example, "was endowed with the gait of a *hamsa* [swan], the voice of a cuckoo, the answering love of a ruddy-goose, the full bosoms of the rainy season, the laugh of wine," and so on, concluding that she was the very "quietude of quiescence, the decorousness of decorum, the nobility of high birth, the temperateness of temperance, the stand of steadfastness, the witchery of grace" (4). Some of the descriptions are rather cloying, like the Champa incense I burned while reading this novel. But Bana is also capable

---

41 Some critics feel Bana left the novel unfinished because he didn't continue with Harsha's reign, but it seems obvious Bana meant to bring his hero only to the threshold of adulthood, like Stephen Dedalus in Joyce's *Portrait* or George Willard in Anderson's *Winesburg, Ohio*.

42 The author shows his awareness of this when the character Bana receives a letter and summarizes it: "'When they have once learned the news from Mekhalaka, the wise will avoid all delay as hindering success'; this is the real essence of the writing, — all else is mere rhetorical compliment" (2). But there's a difference between conventional rhetorical compliment and Bana's word-pictures, which is why he doesn't bother to reproduce the entire letter.

of detailed observations of mundane life that are extraordinarily vivid, as here when Harsha's army departs:

> The low people of the neighborhood, running up as the elephants and horses started, looted heaps of abandoned grain. Donkeys ridden by throngs of boys accompanied the march. Crowds of carts with creaking wheels occupied the trampled roads. Oxen were laden with utensils momentarily put upon them. Stout steers, driven on in advance, lagged out of greed for fodder lying near them. In front were carried the kitchen appliances of the great feudatories. First ran banner-bearers. Hundreds of friends were spectators of the men's exits from the interior of their somewhat contracted huts. Elephant keepers, assaulted with clods by people starting from hovels which had been crushed by the animals' feet, called the bystanders to witness the assaults. Wretched families fled from grass cabins ruined by collisions. Despairing merchants saw the oxen bearing their wealth flee before the onset of the tumult. A troop of seraglio elephants advanced where the press of people gave way before the glare of their runners' torches. Horsemen shouted to dogs tied behind them. Old people sang the praises of tall Tangana horses which by the steady motion of their quick footfalls provided a comfortable seat. Deckhan riders disconsolately contended with fallen mules. The whole world was swallowed up in dust. (7)

"No Kipling, no Rushdie better evokes India's heaving vitality or the lifelong industry of its people," one recent historian has said of this novel.[43]

While *The Deeds of King Harsha* is obsequiously flattering to its subject, there are hints that Bana never abandoned a bohemian's distrust of pomp and authority. The excessively fawning nature of his praise for Harsha is suspicious if not tongue-in-cheek, and in the extract above, he made sure to note that the king's glorious army negligently crushes the hovels of hapless peasants. He lashes out at court life and the abominable practice of suttee with a vehemence seen nowhere else in Sanskrit literature. And what seems like praise for Harsha's ecumenism (an orthodox Hindu, he welcomed Buddhists) sounds more like mockery when the young monarch, searching for his sister in the forest, comes across a holy man who has attracted

> various Buddhists from various provinces seated in different situations — perched on pillars, or seated on the rocks or dwelling in bowers of creepers or lying in thickets or in the shadow of the branches or squatting on the roots of trees — devotees dead to all passion, Jainas in white robes, white mendicants, followers of Krisna, religious students, ascetics who pulled out their hair, followers of Kapila, Jainas, Lokāyatikas [atheists], followers of Kanāda, followers of the Upanishads, believers in God as a Creator, assayers of metals, students of the legal institutes, students of the Puranas, adepts in sacrifices requiring seven ministering priests, adepts in grammar, followers of the Pancarātra and others besides, all diligently following their own tenets, pondering, urging objections, raising doubts,

43 John Keay, *India: A History* (NY: HarperCollins, 2000), 161.

resolving them, giving etymologies, disputing, studying, and explaining, and all gathered here as his disciples. Even some monkeys who had fled to the "three Refuges" were gravely busy performing the ritual of the caitya, while some devout parrots, skilled in the Çākya çāstras, were explaining the Koça, and some mainas, who had obtained calm by expositions of the duties of monastery life, were giving lectures on the law, and some owls, who had gained insight by listening to the ceaseless round of instruction, were muttering the various births of the Bodhisattva, and even some tigers waited in attendance who had given up eating flesh under the calming influence of Buddhist teaching . . . (8)

Bana may or may not be mocking Sura's Buddhist animals and the *Jataka*, but his talk of grave monkeys and devout parrots seems to reveal a typical bohemian disdain for religious orthodoxy. Passages like this, and all the mythological/supernatural material, limit the novel's use to historians of the period, I would think, but with a writer as subtle as Bana I'll defer to someone who has actually studied the novel in the original and is better qualified to have the final word: "What is most gratifying in the *Harshacharita* is the amalgamation of the historical and poetical styles, namely a combination of factual details recorded by a sparkling imagination . . . of the highest order which at every step produces fine intellectual ecstasy" (Agrawala 10).

Having mastered Subandhu's extravagant style, Bana decided next to adapt his fairytale setting for an ambitious novel about everlasting love entitled *Kadambari*, named (like *Vasavadatta*) after its heroine. Joining Buddhist concepts of karma and reincarnation with older Hindu myths of metamorphosis and transmigration, Bana tells of two young men who undergo two rebirths, one in animal form, before they can be united with their lovers. Bana could have narrated his story chronologically, as Subandhu did, but intent on "surpassing the other two" as he says in an introductory verse — that is, Subandhu and Gunadhya — he chose to challenge himself and his readers with an achronological narrative in an embedded structure five levels deep.[44] Unfortunately, he was able to complete only about two-thirds of it before he died; the final third was finished by his son Bhushana, but it's unclear whether the father left instructions for the son, or whether Bhushana came up with his own complicated solution to his father's convoluted tale.

The novel begins (level one) at the court of King Sudraka, an ideal king in all respects but one: he has yet to produce an heir, and doesn't seem to have any desire to do so. Indeed, there's something queer about the king and his court: we're told he considers "womankind as worthless as straw," preferring to spend his time with his witty male friends, "who were expert in various games

44 The quoted phrase and its explication are from C. M. Ridding's 1895 translation, still in print in India, which abridges the 350-page novel by about 30 percent; Gwendolyn Layne's more complete translation leaves these verses out, but will be cited hereafter. (David Smith's new translation appeared too late to use.)

and pastimes" (9–10). His porter is not a man but a woman of "frightening mien" who wears a phallic "scimitar at her left side, a practice forbidden to most women" (10), before whom the king's chiefs bend in submission. But before we learn more of this curious situation, the dominating porter ushers in a beautiful "untouchable" — a woman from the caste that cremates corpses for burial — who presents the king with a parrot in a golden cage. Named Vaisampayana, this is no ordinary parrot: not only can he talk, he can compose stories and poems, paint, dance, settle quarrels, and lecture on a variety of subjects, like any of Sudraka's courtiers. The king is intrigued by the colorful stranger and asks him to tell his story.

Vaisampayana begins the second narrative level, explaining how his father was killed while he was still a fledgling, how he was rescued and taken by an ascetic to the ashram of an all-knowing monk named Jabali, who peered closely at him and revealed that in a previous life he had been a human. Jabali then begins the third narrative level, explaining that Vaisampayana was once the companion of an ideal prince named Candrapida, who was well educated in all the arts, including lovemaking — the Hindus believed in hands-on sexual education for its boys, unlike our squeamish, clinical approach (or avoidance) — and who set forth at age 16 to conquer the world. At one point he chases after some centaur-like creatures (horse heads on human bodies) and stumbles upon a supernaturally beautiful lake, where a nun named Mahasveta, a nymph descended from the Moon, is grieving for a lost love.

Asked by Candrapida for her story, Mahasveta begins the fourth narrative level (all this is still being narrated by the parrot to King Sudraka), which is the chronological beginning of the whole story. In happier days, she once spotted by this same lake an ascetic named Pundarika, and flirted with him by coquettishly putting his rosary around her neck and bathing in the lake in his presence. Pundarika falls hard for her, and she for him, but he's torn between his sexual attraction and his vow of celibacy. His wingman Kapinjala, in a fifth narrative level, tells Mahasveta about Pundarika: he was conceived when his mother Lakshmi (the goddess Fortune) admired a similar ascetic by the same lake so intensely that she experienced an orgasm while squirming on a white lotus, and later gave birth to him. (Pundarika means "white lotus" in Sanskrit; earlier we were told that Vaisampayana was conceived after his father placed in his mother's lap a white lotus dripping with nectar; your sharp Sanskrit reader would realize the two are connected.) Kapinjala now tells Mahasveta that Pundarika will die if he can't have sex with her; she's more than willing to save the handsome ascetic from this fate, but just then her mother arrives for a long visit, and the dutiful daughter stays with her. As a result, Pundarika actually dies from frustrated desire, and guilt-ridden Mahasveta almost kills herself before a cosmic voice tells her to be patient and her love will be returned to her. She takes a vow of chastity, which so impresses her friend, the

Princess Kadambari, that she too vows to remain chaste until her girlfriend is reunited with her love.

We then return to the third-level narrative (Jabali's, that is, as narrated by Vaisampayana), in which Mahasveta takes Candrapida to meet Kadambari to persuade her to give up her sympathetic but unnecessary vow. The sheltered princess falls in love at first sight with the prince; he is appreciative of her beauty, especially her huge breasts and big butt, but is not quite as smitten, and seems to welcome a message from his father to return home. This crushes Kadambari, who was willing to defy her parents and break her vow of chastity for Candrapida's sake. Duty to one's parents is a recurring theme, and in each instance it causes misery.

This is where Bana left off. In his son's conclusion, Vaisampayana visits the same supernatural lake and is dumbstruck by Mahasveta for reasons he can't explain — he was her love Pundarika in his previous life — and pesters her to the point where she curses him to become a parrot before she realizes who he is. Jabali finishes his tale, and with his backstory revealed to him the parrot is anxious to visit Mahasveta and explain matters. When Candrapida learns of Vaisampayana's metamorphosis, he drops dead, and the rest of the novel is a convoluted account of how these various transmigrated souls are eventually reborn and reunited, Candrapida with Kadambari, and Vaisampayana (Pundarika) with Mahasveta. The cemetery girl turns out to be Lakshmi, and King Sudraka turns out to be the reincarnation of Candrapida, not gay after all but simply holding out until the cycle of rebirths had run its course and he could be reunited with Kadambari. It's all rather confusing, but no more confusing, the author chides, than similar tales told in the Vedas that are believed "on the authority of tradition" (325); if you believe *those* tales, he implies, you shouldn't have any trouble with *Kadambari*.

The plot may sound preposterous — I've left out many details, like Kapinjala's transformation into Candrapida's magnificent horse — but the artistry is amazing. As his translator Gwendolyn Layne notes, Bana's aesthetic "might be likened to a literary high-wire act in which the performer/poet inches along a cable made of traditional story lines and poetic conventions, all the while juggling an array of rhetorical devices" (xiii). Bana handles his multilevel narrative structure with aplomb, and as in his first novel he unfurls extended metaphors and similes to dizzying lengths. Sometimes he offers the reader a variety of fanciful (but mythologically significant) images to choose from, as when Candrapida first beholds Mahasveta and is struck by her whiteness (indicating her glory and association with the moon rather than her skin tone):

"'She looked like a troop of celestial elephants fallen in their speedy descent to the Sky River. She looked like the beauty of Mount Kailāsa tumbled there after experiencing tremors when uprooted by the Ten-faced One. She looked like the beauty of the White Continent, come there curious to see the other continents. She looked like the blooming loveliness of *kāśa* blossoms waiting for the advent of autumn. She looked like the sheen on Śeṣa's body, leaving the Nether Region and coming there. She looked like the luster of the Club-armed One's body, dislodged by the exertions of his staggerings when drunk on wine. She looked like a collection of all the bright phases of the month. She looked as if all geese had bestowed on her their whiteness. She looked as if she had sprung forth from the God of Duty. She seemed to be carved out of conch, extracted from pearl, or as if she had limbs made out of lotus fibers. She appeared to have been fashioned with pieces of ivory, washed with brushes of moonbeams, covered with layers of whitewash, whitened with wisps of foam of the Elixir, laved in streams of liquid mercury, cleansed with molten silver, carved out of the lunar orb, or ornamented with the lusters of *kutaja*, *kunda*, and *sinduvāra* blossoms. She was, as it were, the acme of whiteness.'" (133)

Elsewhere he forgoes his usual elaborate description of a palace and instead reveals it through the excited exclamations of its residents, piling on the details until his picture of this artificial paradise is complete:

He [Candrapida] walked a ways into the residence and wandered around, overhearing various very charming conversations between the servants who closely attended on Kādambarī: "Lavalikā, make basins at the roots of the *lavalī* creeper with *ketakī* pollen." "Sāgarikā, scatter jewel-dust on the ponds of scented water." "Mrinālikā, sprinkle handfuls of saffron powder on the pairs of toy *cakravāka* birds in the beds of artificial lotuses." "Makarikā, perfume the scent pots with the juice of camphor sprouts." "Rajanikā, place jewel lamps in the avenues of *tamāla* trees." "Kumudikā, cover the pomegranates with netted pearls to protect them from the flocks of birds." "Nipunikā, draw decorations with saffron juice on the breasts of the jewelled *śāla* wood dolls." "Utpalikā, sweep the emerald dais in the banana house with golden brushes." "Kesarikā, sprinkle wine on the houses made with garlands of *bakula* blossoms." [Ten more of these follow, concluding:] "Harinikā, give the caged parrots and mynahs their lesson." (184–85)

Sometimes Bana will describe a character indirectly via her reflection in a mirror, or by spinning a web of mythological allusions. Though the novel is set in a timeless fantasy world, he addresses timely, mundane concerns like the idiocy of committing suicide after losing a parent or husband — unfortunately suttee, though outlawed by the British in 1829, has continued to this day in some parts of India — or of taking up an ascetic life while still young and beautiful: in Hindu society, the ascetic life was for one's golden years, not for golden youths. The protagonists are types rather than well-rounded characters, yet there are nice distinctions between impetuous Vaisampayana and prudent Candrapida, between flirty Mahasveta and innocent Kadambari. And who doesn't love a parrot for a narrator? There are veils between a modern Western reader and this ancient Hindu work that obscure its full brilliance, but even in translation *Kadambari* is obviously a first-rate novel of exceptional daring and creativity. It's no surprise to learn that in India Bana became known as *the* novelist by the time he died, that *kadambari* became the generic term for a novel, or that for centuries afterward Sanskrit literary artists insisted "*Banochhishtam jagat sarvam*" — "The whole world subsists on Bana's leavings."[45]

The third member of the power trio of novelists from this era is Dandin, who apparently lived during the second half of the 7th century.[46] Author of one of the earliest Sanskrit works on poetics (*Kavyadarsa*), Dandin wrote the most readerly of these learned, writerly novels, *What Ten Young Men Did* (*Dasakumaracarita*). Unfortunately, the complete work hasn't survived; the first fifth has been supplied from a Telugu translation, and the concluding dozen pages are attributed to one Chakrapani Dikshita. Compounding the problem is the possibility that *Ten Young Men* may be only a subsection of a much longer novel by Dandin entitled *Avantisundari* (the name of the wife of the protagonist), which exists only in fragmentary form. It's even been suggested that Dandin first wrote the fairly straightforward *Ten Young Men*, then revised it into the more elaborate *Avantisundari*, a course similar to Sidney's revision/expansion of *Arcadia*. But even in the hybrid form it's come down to us, the novel is a delightful, action-filled example of the kind of frame-tale narrative that would become so popular in succeeding centuries.

Set in the same era as Gunadhya's *Brihatkatha* — Dandin name-checks Prince Naravahanadatta and clearly knew the great tale — it begins with the traditional problem of a king who has everything but a son. But after paying "constant worship to Vishnu Naráyana, the one and only creator of all creatures," the king is pleased to learn his queen has become pregnant.[47] Moreover, he is told that when his son reaches age 16, he will defeat his long-time enemy, a rival king. As it happens, when Prince Rajavahana is born, four wives of the king's ministers likewise give birth to boys; even more coincidental, five foundlings are presented to the king by various travelers at this time. The prince is reared with these nine companions, and at age 16 they all set out to conquer the world. But no sooner do they depart than Rajavahana gets sidelined by a Brahmin who requests his help, which involves a midnight trip to the netherworld. (The magic-realist mode is established early, and thereafter supernatural events alternate with such mundane matters as a detailed description of how to prepare a rice meal from scratch.) The next morning,

45 Naravane, *Three Novels from Ancient India*, 12.
46 We can date Bana to King Harsha's reign, but critics disagree on when Subandhu and Dandin actually lived, some arguing that Dandin preceded the other two. I'm following Warder and Gupta by placing him last.
47 Chap. 1 in Onians's translation — another fine volume in the Clay Sanskrit Library — hereafter cited by chapter.

the nine teens wake to find their prince missing and go off in all directions to find him, agreeing on a time and place to regroup. When the prince resurfaces and finds his chums gone, he too goes in search of them. After a while, he arrives at a pleasure garden outside the city of Ujjayini (modern Ujjain, and Candrapida's residence in *Kadambari*, which Dandin likewise knew), where he runs into one of his lost boys. Asked by his prince where he's been, Somadatta proceeds to tell him, establishing the structure for the rest of the novel: thereafter each of the other teens reappears and gives a chapter-long account of what he's been up to, usually an outlandish tale in which he has overcome difficult odds to win a kingdom and a wife. After the ninth has completed his story, the 10 young men defeat the enemy of the prince's father and disperse to rule the kingdoms they've won during their adventures.

The individual episodes are a riot of wild adventures, in which our sheltered teens hit the road running in a world filled with thieves, gamblers, cruel kings, prostitutes, weeping mothers, maidens in distress, monsters, magical nymphs, people falling out of the sky, naïve monks, murderers, greedy merchants — characters from every class of Indian society. There are shipwrecks, duels, elephant-jackings for dramatic getaways, fake magic tricks and impersonations, and many instances of penetrating a king's harem. They're like the boys' adventure novels of yore, except with lots of sex. Not only are the tales rather outlandish, but each of the five foundlings runs into his parents at some point, straining credulity even further.

There's more to the novel than just an anthology of wild boys' stories, however. *What Ten Young Men Did* is a group-bildungsroman about some teenagers encountering the reality of experience for the first time and triumphing because of their wit and creativity. It's significant that half of the boys are orphans: cut off from their families, they cannot rely on traditional parental support or a hereditary place in their society. Somadatta runs into a group of "motherless sons" at the beginning of his adventure (2), and from *Avantisundari* we learn that Dandin himself was orphaned around the age of seven. Thus our 10 boys form a kind of alternative family, "brothers in spirit" (2), display an orphan's hard-knocks sense of self-reliance, and rely on nontraditional, even criminal methods to survive and prosper. "Extraordinary! Your ruthlessness surpasses even that of wily Karnisuta, patron of thieves," the prince praises Apaharavarman at the end of his lengthy recitation (7), and after hearing what Upaharavarman did, the prince smiles and says,

> "Take note how seducing another man's wife twinned with fraud has reinforced in abundance both material profit and religious merit. For thanks to these crimes you could procure your parents' release from the oppression of captivity, slay the wicked enemy and win back a kingdom. Whatever an intelligent man does becomes a noble act." (8)

Beyond good and evil, freed from traditional strictures, and possessing a strong sense of entitlement, the über-teens don't shy away from Machiavellian methods to achieve what they want, convinced the end justifies the means, no matter how criminal. "After all," one character notes, "here in the real world fortune does not favor those who do not strive to achieve her. And every felicity is always within reach of energetic hands" (12). And these boys will stop at nothing to get their hands on the lotus-faced girls who tickle their fancy; Prince Raj uses the old "I think we were married in a previous life" line to seduce his target, and the other guys are as crafty as characters in a teen-sex movie. Outwardly a devout Hindu (though essentially a fatalist), Dandin shows contempt for fanatical Jains and for goody-goody Buddhists and their notions of right conduct, though he also shows how easily Hindu ascetics can be duped. (Apaharavarman's story concerns a prostitute who seduces one just to win a bet.) More than the Vedas, Dandin seems to value the *Arthasastra*, the same political manual that inspired the *Panchatantra*, even though he parodies it in one chapter (13). Perhaps he held nothing sacred, except art.

Dandin's rhetorical feats are what elevate this amoral adventure novel to high art. He is as fluent as Subandhu and Bana at double-entendred prose, where a sentence like "the monsoon spread its circles on heavy rain-bearing clouds in the sky" can also be read via paronomasia as "she spread the heavy spheres of her milk-bearing breasts on her beloved's chest" (6). His descriptions of nature and especially of women are just as metaphoric as theirs, and he makes some interesting narrative choices: instead of simply relating a scam pulled by one of the boys, he usually has his protagonist explain what he *plans* to do, like an author devising a plot; afterward he will simply say everything went according to plan, thereby placing the emphasis on the imaginative act itself.

In several of the chapters the protagonists put on a performance — impersonating a magician or an acrobat — and Dandin is very self-conscious about himself as a performer. During the second half of the novel, each chapter seems to be an effort to top the previous one, leading the reader to wonder if the boys are simply making up these increasingly outlandish stories to impress their prince. In chapter 11, Mitragupta is captured by "a hideous-looking brahmin demon," whom Mitragupta beguiles by telling a series of stories, like Shahrazad postponing her death with tales. In chapter 12, however, Mantragupta tops that, even though (or rather, because) he can't speak properly. "For his ruby lips were in an agony of agitation, perforated with bite marks that his beloved had bestowed in her forceful love-play. Hence he was compelled to speak without using the labial lip sounds: *p*, *b* and *m*" (11). Labials are even more plentiful in Sanskrit than English, yet Mantragupta tells an entire story without them (cleverly matched by Onians in her translation). As soon as he finishes, the missing labials begin popping: "His li*p*s *b*athed in a *b*rilliant s*m*ile, the *p*rince Rajavāhana and all their friends a*pp*lauded Mantragu*p*ta's skill" (12, my italics) — which of course doubles as self-congratulation for Dandin's own skill. And how does he top that? The following chapter is a satire of the *Arthasastra*, mocking the venerable book that informs the earlier part of his novel, and dismissing "the supreme felicity to be had in the hereafter" as a "mirage" (13), leaving us wondering, again, what if anything he believed in.

"Sharp and of untrammelled tongue, he was clever at paronomasia and double entendre, and loved to spy out other people's weak points," Dandin says of a courtier (13), perhaps another self-reference. Like Apuleius in *The Golden Ass*, he keeps us guessing about his motives, but not about his rhetorical abilities, and even in its patchwork form *What Ten Young Men Did* is serious fun, the last great masterpiece from the fruitful 7th century.

Indian authors continued to produce novels in the succeeding centuries, though none of them are considered to be in the same aesthetic league as those by Subandhu, Bana, and Dandin, and perhaps for that reason few of them have been translated into English. (I'll be relying on my guru A. K. Warder and other critics for those that haven't.) For example, in the 8th century Kutuhala wrote a novel in Prakrit entitled *Lilavai* that, like Bana's *Kadambari*, mixes supernaturalism and reincarnation with more realistic elements; from Warder's description (4:477–98) it sounds convoluted and delightful. It is a novel in verse, a form that became increasingly popular during this time, and which Sanskrit critics distinguish from verse narratives like the *Ramayana*.[48]

The Jains, mocked in some previous Brahmin novels, began writing their own novels during this period, usually of a didactic nature in keeping with their austere religion.[49] The earliest, like Mahasena's *Sulocana* and Prabhanjana's *Jasaharacariu*, are lost, but the latter's popularity is attested by the numerous adaptations that have survived, most notably Somadeva Suri's *Yasastilaka*

---

48 Two verse narratives written in Tamil in southern India in the early centuries of the Common Era — Ilango Adigal's *Shilappadikaram* (The Ankle Bracelet) and its sequel, Shattan's *Manimekhalaï* (The Dancer with the Magic Bowl) — are called novels by translator Alain Daniélou in his introductions to each (New Directions, 1965 and 1989) and presented in prose, but in Rajagopal Parthasarathy's definitive English translation of the former, he demonstrates its adherence to Tamil verse forms so thoroughly that I decided against my original plan to include these two in my discussion of the Indian novel. See *The Cilappatikaram of Ilanko Atikal* (NY: Columbia UP, 1993).

49 Occasionally they could loosen up, as can be seen in Granoff's Jain anthology *The Clever Adulteress and Other Stories*, but even in these medieval tales the aim was to teach a lesson rather than provide aesthetic delight.

(959). Prabhanjana's original was apparently a religious romance in which a king converts from Brahminism to Jainism. Another Jain novelist of the 8th century named Haribhadra wrote two novels: *Samaraicca*, a religious novel that follows a hero of that name through nine reincarnations, during which he develops from "a thoughtless, though apparently sincere, person into a philosopher" (Warder 4:519); and *Dhuttakkhana* (The Rogues' History), a novel in verse that satirizes Brahminism. Haribhadra's student Uddyotana, impressed by *Samaraicca* and anxious to outdo his teacher, wrote a novel entitled *Kuvalayamala* (779) featuring not one but five characters undergoing reincarnation. In his critical study of the novel, A. N. Upadhye gives a 40-page plot summary that leaves the head spinning, and in his preface to this book, Ludwig Alsdorf adds: "As their histories are not connected to begin with but interlace only at a later stage; and as, moreover, they are not told in a tedious systematic or chronological order but — by a device common also in modern literature — are often put into the mouths of different characters of the story who tell them in retrospect, the plot of the novel becomes involved to a degree and is . . . difficult to follow."[50] It is a very erudite work, linguistically diverse (Uddyotana alternates between Sanskrit, Prakrit, and various dialects), and filled with strange characters: one is an alchemist, perhaps the first in fiction, and once again a talking parrot helps with the narration. It was an influential novel and sounds richly deserving of translation. Can't say the same for the Jain monk Siddha's lengthy *Upamitibhavapancakatha* (Novel of Differentiation in Existence by Analogy, 906), another reincarnation novel that slavishly imitates those by Haribhadra and Uddyotana. The characters are allegorical figures with names like King Result of Action and Queen Ripening in Time, and the work sounds more didactic than most Jain novels.

A more worldly approach was taken by Dhanapala, a Jain writer of the later 10th century, who went back to the celebrated *Kadambari* and even the *Brihatkatha* for inspiration for his novel *Tilakamanjari*, a romance about two pairs of lovers. He attempted to outdo Bana with his own elaborate prose style — which he compares to a multicolored tiger lurking in an impenetrable forest and striking terror in its beholders — but even a sympathetic critic admits the result is "ornate verbal jugglary" that tries too hard to be original, unusual, and provocative.[51] Warder, who devotes 40 pages to it (5:759–800), expresses a much higher opinion of *Tilakamanjari* than earlier critics. And finally, there is a kind of historical novel entitled *Prabandhacintamani*, translated by C. H. Tawney under the winsome title of *The Wishing-Stone of Narratives*, which was completed by a Jain monk named Merutunga in 1306. It traces the

---

50 Page xxvi in Upadhye's *Uddoyotana-Suri's* Kuvalayamala.
51 Sharma, 45–46. In the preface (dated 2002), Sharma says his English translation of *Tilakamanjari* has been accepted for publication, but as of this writing it has yet to appear, which is just as well: Sharma's grasp of English is weak, and his earlier translation of Soddhala's *Udayasundari* (see below) is almost unreadable.

history of India — or more specifically, the western kingdoms of Gujarat and Malwa — from the time of King Vikramaditya (a legendary ruler we'll hear more about) down to King Kumarapala, who died in 1286. Though it contains much fictitious material drawn from legends and oral traditions, some poetry, and rewrites historical material to favor the Jain religion, Merutunga made little effort to give aesthetic form to his material, unlike Bana in the even more historical *Harshacarita*. It reads more like a plodding chronicle than a novel, though that may be partly the fault of Tawney's fusty translation ("The king was inly wroth" [19]); or perhaps that's what Merutunga intended, despite his reliance on fictitious, even supernatural material.

Returning to Brahmin writers, several of them adapted the frame-tale structures of *Ten Young Men* and especially the popular *Panchatantra* to pleasing effect. In the final decades of the 8th century, a court minister named Damodaragupta composed a comic narrative entitled *The Bawd's Counsel* (*Kuttanimata*), which, though written in verse, has been considered a novel ever since the influential Sanskrit critic-king Bhoja pronounced it one in the 11th century. A courtesan named Malati is failing at her profession, so she goes to an old bawd named Vikarala "for instruction in the science of harlotry," as Warder puts it (4:568). Like Aretino's *Dialogues*, *The Bawd's Counsel* is mostly a dialogue about the tricks of the trade, but it includes two longish stories that Vikarala tells to illustrate her lessons. One concerns a harlot who makes the mistake of falling in love with a customer, while the other is about one who plays her cards right and succeeds in her profession. At the conclusion, Malati has learned how to be a better whore, and the reader has wised up to those in her profession. *The Bawd's Counsel* is both pornographic and satiric, a new mode for the Sanskrit novel. Unlike Aretino, who was shunned by prudish critics because of his subject matter, Damodaragupta was celebrated for his wit and artistry *despite* his subject matter, and quoted with approval by critics for centuries thereafter.

Narayana's *Friendly Advice* (*Hitopadesa*, 9th or 10th cent.) was even more popular, and still is in India, though it's essentially an adaptation of the *Panchatantra*, in four books instead of five, but structured the same way: a king named Sudarsana is concerned that his wayward sons are unprepared for statecraft, so he hires Visnu Sarma to instruct them, which he does mostly by way of animal fables. The worldview is just as realistic, the moral similar: "friendly advice" is often given by people bent on your destruction, as the fable of the scripture-quoting tiger in book 1 demonstrates. We're told at the end that the princes are grateful for the instruction, but we don't see them put it to use. Instead of drawing upon the *Arthasastra*, Narayana drew upon a similar political primer entitled *Nitisara*, which was based on the *Arthasastra*, making *Friendly Advice* a doubly derivative work. It was translated into many languages and was in fact the second Sanskrit work to be translated into English (in 1787, three years after the *Bhagavad Gita*), but it contains much more poetry than the *Panchatantra*, resulting in something closer to an anthology of folk wisdom than a novel.

Considerably more novelistic is the weird and fascinating *Five-and-Twenty Tales of the Genie* (*Vetalapancavinsati*), a hermeneutical text of remarkable sophistication. This is one of several cycles of tales that accrued around King Vikramaditya; like King Arthur, he was a semilegendary figure that has been associated with both a Hindu king of the 1st century BCE and another of that name from the Gupta era five centuries later. This particular cycle developed orally over time until the 11th century, when four versions were committed to paper. One was included in Ksemendra's *Brihatkathamanjari*, another was added near the end of Somadeva's *Ocean of Story*, and there are two stand-alone versions: a readerly one by a defense minister named Jambhaladatta — which "makes little claim to ornateness and is at times monotonously bald and undistinguished," as its translator admits[52] — and a writerly one by an author who called himself Shivadasa, possibly a pseudonym. For the latter, imagine Kafka adapting the tales of King Arthur.

In Shivadasa's hands, these weird old folktales celebrating King Vikramaditya's wisdom became unsettling and complicated, "burdened by an awareness of the presence of wrongdoing, even evil in the stark sense of the term, and of subsequent moral retribution."[53] He maintained the basic frame-tale from the older oral version(s): once a skyclad yogi named Ksantisila came to the court of King Vikramaditya and presented him with a piece of fruit as a gift, and continued doing so for 12 years, until one day the king noticed each piece of fruit contained a gemstone. Asked how the king can repay him for all these gems, the yogi requests the king to assist him in a magic ritual that will allow him to attain "the eight great Siddhis," or supernatural powers:

> "To be minute as an atom,
> or enormous as a mountain,
> light as air or heavy as a rock,
> to be invisible at will,
> to have all one's desires fulfilled,
> to subject others to one's will
> and to have lordship of the world;
> know these to be the eight Siddhis." (15–16)

(Though written primarily in prose, *Tales of the Genie* contains much poetry, and of much higher quality than the doggerel in *Friendly Advice*.) Instead of

---

52 Page xix in Emeneau's introduction to Jambhaladatta's version.
53 Page xxxiv in Rajan's long introduction to Shivadasa's version, hereafter cited by page
    number. (I would cite them by tale but their order differs from version to version.)

sensing danger in this request, the king is seduced by the promise that he too will gain powers, and so agrees to help. He meets the yogi at a graveyard and is told to retrieve the corpse of a hanged man, necessary for the ceremony. The king finds and takes down the corpse, which turns out to be possessed by a genie.[54] As soon as the king throws the corpse over his shoulder to head back to the ceremony, the genie speaks up with a riddling tale and a question at the end. The king answers correctly, and the genie escapes back to the *sinsipa* tree; the king takes him down again, and again the genie tells a story, and again he returns to the tree after the king answers his riddle. For the next two hours or so, the king and genie repeat this routine, until the king is stymied by the 24th tale, a real brainteaser involving patrimony. Nevertheless, the genie is impressed by the king's ability to answer all the preceding questions and warns him that Ksantisila plans to kill him after the magic ceremony. So Vikramaditya kills the yogi, and the heavens burst forth with praise. The whole thing has been a test of his suitability to continue reigning as king; he appoints the genie as his chief minister and goes on to rule in great glory.

The tales themselves pose ethical dilemmas, questions of dharma, which the ideal king should be able to handle. But the tales are bizarre and nightmarish, and seem to follow some sort of irrational dream-logic, not the types of realistic situations a king is likely to encounter during the course of his reign. They are set in the same fairytale world as the *Brihatkatha*, upping the challenge because normal rules don't always apply to that supernaturally enriched realm. In tale 6, for example, a prince falls in love with a princess and vows to worship the goddess Candika "with my head as oblation" (66) if she helps him win her. He's successful, and one day as the prince is traveling with his bride and his best friend he stops at a shrine dedicated to Candika, and fulfils his vow by cutting off his own head with a dagger. After a while his friend enters the shrine to look for him, sees the headless corpse and fears he'll be accused of murder, so he too decapitates himself. Then the bride enters the shrine, sees the corpses, and in despair decides to hang herself, at which point the goddess intercedes; impressed by the princess's courage, Candika grants her wish to revive the two men. But in her confusion, the bride puts the wrong head on the wrong body, and when they come back to life, they argue over which of them is now the woman's husband. That's the question

54 "Genie" is Rajan's translation of *vetala*, which (like *vidyadhara* earlier) is a supernatural creature without an exact counterpart in Western mythology. Elsewhere in Sanskrit literature it's usually translated as "vampire" — Sir Richard Burton entitled his translation of this book *King Vikram and the Vampire* (1870) — but that's too evil. Spirit, specter, sprite, and goblin have also been used, but originally the *vetala* was a kind of woodland deity, akin to the Classical term "genius," the attendant spirit of a place, neither good nor evil, making "genie" the best choice, despite its *Arabian Nights/I Dream of Jeanie* associations. Burton's translation, incidentally, is to be shunned like a vampire: he translates only 11 of the 25 tales, yet pads them out so much that his abridged edition is longer than the complete version.

the genie puts to the king; if you guessed the body with the prince's head, you have royal potential. That is, intelligence (the head) is more important to a king than passion or emotions (the body), but self-decapitation and supernatural reanimation involving mismatched heads sounds like the plot of a bad sci-fi movie rather than a case study in ethical philosophy. The other tales feature a queen so sensitive that moonbeams cause her skin to blister, four foolish Brahmins who use their expertise to reanimate a dead lion (which promptly devours them), another genie who enters the corpse of a woman's dead lover in order to have sex with her, a man who builds his own "sky chariot," fairy brides who float on the sea, a Wishing Tree, and a few trips to the underworld. There are all sorts of things that would be symbolically sublimated in traditional fairy tales — lots of sex and violence, realistic details like a menstruating woman and a pooping baby — which is why these stories feel more like surrealistic parables than folktales, or like a disturbing dream that keeps repeating itself.

Nevertheless, a rigorous and conservative doctrine of ethics emerges from this carnival of weird tales. There is an emphasis on strict adherence to principles (often Buddhist) even in the strangest of circumstances, on intelligence over book-learning, and especially on the need for a careful examination of all available facts over jumping to conclusions based on appearances. The lessons are intended as much for the reader as for the king, and the complicated scenarios are necessary to exercise the reader's intellect: just as the king needs to display intelligence to qualify as a great ruler, the reader must do likewise to appreciate a novel like this.

In addition to adapting the old tales, Shivadasa added his own preamble to the book that, in retrospect, poses a riddle for the reader like those the genie poses for the king. Before Vikramaditya was born, his father King Gandharvasena came across a thousand-year-old ascetic named Valkalashana who was so deep in meditation that he failed to acknowledge the king, which he interpreted as a deliberate insult. Back at court, he asks for a volunteer to interrupt the monk — dangerous because, as we've seen, monks are apt to utter curses when annoyed — and the only one who steps up is a courtesan. She manages to seduce the monk not with her beauty but with sweets (balls of melted cream, butter, and crystallized sugar), which she slips him a few at a time. His hunger breaks his meditation, and when he opens his eyes and beholds the sweet temptress — who claims to be an *asparas*, a celestial dancing girl — he falls in love and soon impregnates her. After their child is born, the courtesan convinces the hermit to visit the court of King Gandharvasena, who mocks him for breaking his penance. In a predictable rage, Valkalashana unpredictably grabs his son by his feet and smashes him on the floor. "The child's head fell inside the palace; the trunk in a potter's house; the feet in the house of an oil merchant" (7–8). That day, the queen and the wives of a potter and an oil merchant conceive, and all three give birth at the same time. A prediction is made: "Of these three, one will slay the other two; one alone shall remain" (8). The queen's son is of course Vikramaditya, who succeeds to the throne at an early age upon his father's death; the potter's son, hearing the prediction given at his birth, lures the oil merchant's son into the woods, strangles him, and hangs the corpse from a *sinsipa* tree. Vikramaditya gets wind of the murder, but the murderer escapes, so instead the king orders "that the escaped murderer's house be ransacked, his possessions confiscated and his house and other properties be torn down and razed to the ground. [¶] After this, King Vikramāditya sighed with relief, confident now that his realm was rid of thorns; and he rejoiced in his heart" (11).

By adding this preamble, Shivadasa creates an air of dread that hangs over the rest of the narrative. How can the king be content knowing there's a murderer loose who wants to kill him? Will the potter's son be caught? Will the oil merchant's son be avenged? Is all this the fault of Gandharvasena's irrational anger at a hermit minding his business? And what of the courtesan's dirty trick, and the hermit's ghastly slaughter of his own son? Set on edge, the reader begins to wonder as the frame-tale is introduced: are the gem-filled fruits the yogi offers the king the same kind of temptation that the courtesan offered the hermit? Is the corpse hanging from the *sinsipa* tree the oil merchant's son? If so, what is the symbolic importance of his association with the dismembered child's feet? (Is that why he needs to be carried?) If not, was the genie sent down by the gods to see if the son is as rash as the father (which seems to be the case after the son rashly agrees to help the yogi with his necromantic rites)? As the genie unfolds one bizarre tale after another, a Kafkaesque uneasiness persists up to the supposedly triumphant end, when the king kills the sorcerer-yogi and obtains the eight Siddhis the yogi yearned for. Then Sivadasa quotes the old proverb:

> Pay a man back in his own coin;
> do harm unto him who has done harm to you;
>   I see no harm in that;
> adopt foul means toward an evil man. (180)

— which seems to contradict the high principles espoused earlier throughout the novel. Now in possession of magical powers and unafraid to "adopt foul means" when necessary, is King Vikramaditya really on his way to becoming a just ruler? This ambiguity is exactly what Shivadasa promised in his introductory verses:

> A simple and straightforward narrative
> pleases some learned readers;

some, wiser, delight in the figurative —
irony, ambiguity, metaphors. (12)

The other versions of these tales are simple and straightforward narratives; Shivadasa's brilliant use of "irony, ambiguity, metaphors" guarantees that readers would continue contemplating this bizarre bildungsroman, which is what he wanted: for when the gods invite the king to name a favor at the end, he replies, "Grant that this work, the *Five-and-Twenty Tales of the Genie* may become celebrated and gain renown" (181). He got his wish.

Less celebrated and renowned is *Thirty-two Tales of the Throne of Vikramaditya (Simhasana Dvatrimsika)*, a kind of sequel to the *Tales of the Genie* that was composed sometime in the late 13th or early 14th century. The anonymous author of this playfully didactic work found a novel way to praise the virtues of King Vikramaditya and to offer him as a model for future rulers. He begins the novel with an account of Vikramaditya's succession to the throne after his half-brother abdicated, his encounter with the vetala that established his worthiness to reign, and then of the time Vikramaditya was taken up to heaven to judge a dance competition between two nymphs. (He awards the prize to the one who literally dances by the book — the dance manual *Nrityasastra* — instead of the one who has her own style; this novel is about following the edicts of the wise, not glorifying the self.) The god Indra is so pleased that he gives Vikramaditya a jewel-encrusted throne supported by 32 female stuatuettes made of moonstone; the king takes it back to earth and uses it until his death, when a voice from heaven instructs his ministers to bury the throne until someone as worthy as Vikramaditya comes along.

The author then jumps ahead a thousand years to the reign of King Bhoja of Dhar (ruled c. 1010–55), who discovers and unearths the throne, returns it to his capital, and at an auspicious moment attempts to mount it. But one of the statuettes suddenly speaks up: "O King! Do you possess valour, magnanimity, daring, nobility and other such qualities like *him*? If so, then mount the throne. Not otherwise!"[55] She gives an example of Vikramaditya's generosity, which is so far beyond anything Bhoja has done that he retreats in shame. On the next auspicious day, he attempts to ascend the throne again, and the second statuette speaks up, tells another anecdote about the former king's generosity, and the present king again retreats. So it goes 30 more times — 32 is the number of "auspicious marks of virtue" a king should possess, mentioned

---

55 Page 44 in Haksar's translation. As with *Tales of the Genie*, there are numerous variant manuscripts but no surviving ur-text. Haksar assembled his translation from the four main recensions edited and translated by Franklin Edgerton in 1926 as *Vikrama's Adventures*. Haksar adds an interesting historical note: "Edgerton's own work utilized thirty-three manuscripts originating in different parts of India over a period of nearly four hundred years, if not longer. Another fourteen manuscripts sent from Bombay were lost in the shipwreck of the *Titanic*" (xvi).

in many Sanskrit works — until the 32nd statuette has told her tale, at which point all the statuettes magically become life-size and announce that Bhoja is now ready to ascend Vikramaditya's throne. They reveal that the goddess Parvati once caught them all making eyes at her husband and reduced them to statuettes until such time as they could recount their tales and thus break the curse. We are then told (or reminded) that this entire novel has been a tale told to Parvati by Shiva (here called Paramesvara), the same narrative frame used in *The Ocean of Story*.

The various vignettes of Vikramaditya range from the comic — in #3 a "rogue of a weaver" seduces the king's daughter by impersonating the god Vishnu, who then covers for him to preserve his divine reputation — to the supernatural: in #19 the king descends to the netherworld, where "perfumed and passionate youths delighted in breezes wafting fragrance from the mouths of serpent maidens" (123). In almost every instance, whatever gift or boon Vikramaditya wins through his valor he simply gives away to the first needy person he meets on his way home. *That* act of generosity, more than the heroic deed preceding it, is what counts in the author's eyes. Vikramaditya's magnanimity is superhuman and unrealistic at times, but the principles of charity and generosity he exhibits have a real-world relevance lacking in the Buddhist novels I discussed earlier, such as *The Perfect Generosity of Prince Vessantara* and Arya Sura's *Jatakamala*. Nor is Vikramaditya a self-righteous prig; he keeps a well-stocked harem, with whom he "gathered flowers, dallied in the water, made music, sported on the swings, and played woman's house and other games. He enjoyed there the most exquisite delights of this earthly existence" (65). That final sentence is not one seen in most didactic novels promoting selfless virtue, which is one reason why *Tales of the Throne* makes for delightful reading (and instruction). In the penultimate tale #31, we get another version of his encounter with the evil yogi and riddling vetala from *Tales of the Genie*, but the novel is free of the eeriness and moral ambiguity of the earlier, admittedly superior work. It too ends with the hope that Vikramaditya's "deeds remain forever famous on earth" (179).

There's no air of dread or ambiguity hanging over the bawdy *Seventy Tales of the Parrot* (*Shukasaptati*), another contribution to the select list of great psittacine fiction.[56] Like *Tales of the Genie*, it's a cycle of older tales that was organized and written down much later, probably in the 11th or 12th century, and exists in three versions. The frame-story is delightful: a merchant, disappointed in his wayward married son Madan Vinod, gives him a worldly-wise parrot, which soon talks him out of his bad ways. When Madan needs to leave

---

56 Bana's *Kadambari*, Nakhshabi's *Tales of a Parrot*, the Arthurian *Knight of the Parrot*, Flaubert's "A Simple Heart," Queneau's *Zazie in the Metro*, Barnes's *Flaubert's Parrot*, Robbins's *Fierce Invalids Home from the Hot Countries*, Paul's *Elsewhere in the Land of Parrots*.

on a lengthy business trip, he assigns the parrot to chaperone his lusty young wife, named Prabhavati. After a few days she gets restless, and "some women friends of questionable character" advise her to seek a lover, arguing "your body will stay young only for a short while, enjoy the fruit of your youth in love with another man."[57] Deciding not to waste the pretty, she gets dolled up and is ready to go out when the parrot warns her that if she's going to start fooling around, she'd better be smart enough to get out of a jam if necessary. The parrot gives an example of a lady named Lakshmi who managed to fool her husband through some quick thinking, which persuades slow-thinking Prabhavati to stay home that night. Next day she's hot to trot again, so the parrot tells another tale, and so on for 70 days, at which time her husband returns to find his wife's "virtue" intact, thanks to the parrot's prophylactic tales.

Most of them involve smart women fooling dumb men; as Lee Siegel points out in his fine book on humor in Sanskrit literature, here "cunning can be a greater virtue than chastity, and stupidity a greater sin than adultery."[58] Most of the tales are short, short enough that a typical one can be quoted in full as an example:

> "Slim waisted one," replied the parrot when asked by Prabhávati the next day, "go out this evening if you know what to say like Devika did in the past while she was with her lover."
>
> In the big village of Kuhad there lived a householder named Jaras who was a mighty fool. His wife Devika was an adulteress. A brahmin called Prabhakar would merrily make love to her in a quiet place by a plum tree in the middle of a field.
>
> Jaras heard about this occurrence from other people, and went to the field to see it for himself. He climbed up the tree and saw exactly what he had been told. "You minx!" he cried out while sitting on his perch, "today I have at last caught you after a long time!"
>
> "Now then," asked the parrot, "how should she convince her husband?"
>
> "I do not know!" said Prabhávati. "Tell me yourself!"
>
> "I will tell you if you do not go out," said the parrot, and when she promised this, the bird continued.
>
> "O my lord!" exclaimed Devika, "this tree is bewitched! Whoever climbs it sees some lovemaking in progress."
>
> "All right," said her husband. "You climb and see." And, going up the tree, she said wickedly: "After a long time I see you lying with another woman."
>
> "This must be true," the fool concluded, and he pacified his wife and took her home. Prabhávati went to sleep after listening to this story. (106–7)

Upon her husband's return, Prabhavati confesses she was tempted to take a

---

57 Page 5 (prologue) in Haksar's translation, hereafter cited by page number. He translates the "simple" version; an English translation of a later, more ornate version ascribed to Cintamani Bhatta is forthcoming from the Clay Sanskrit Library.

58 *Laughing Matters*, 129. In addition to being an Indian scholar, Siegel has written some dazzling novels that I'll discuss when I reach the 20th century.

lover, but following the parrot's advice Madan forgives her, realizing it is only natural for a young woman to crave sex. In fact, the author's attitude toward lust is refreshingly positive, even more so than that of most Sanskrit authors. As in the frame-tale, there are other stories in which young women bursting with vitality are advised: "do not let your looks and years go to waste. For

> Listen, you lovely-legged girl,
> spring has sounded on the earth
> Káma's royal proclamation
> with the koel's song:
> let gallants all shed haughtiness
> and enjoy their mistresses;
> for youth is transient in this world
> and life is fleeting." (61)

Ostensibly, Prabhavati wins a moral victory by remaining faithful to her husband, but the subversive author broadly hints that such traditional morality is only for dull women like her not smart enough or bold enough to take the initiative to satisfy their sexual needs. The author turns the narrative focus from Prabhavati to the audacious women of the parrot's tales; the clever adulteresses and sensuous party girls in the novel are held up for admiration, not reprobation, except for a few greedy prostitutes who try to take advantage of their customers. Pro-sex, the author is not surprisingly anti-religious; he signals his attitude toward religion in the prologue: "Once, while the young ascetic was sitting by the riverside, telling his beads, a stork flying overhead happened to shit upon him" (3). In fact, as A. Berriedale Keith noted long ago, in this novel "religion plays its part in helping immorality; religious processions, temples, pilgrimages, marriages, sacrifices, all are convenient occasions for assignations, the fleeing lover is declared by the ingenious wife to be the ghost of the paternal ancestor, and so forth."[59]

In the longest chapter of the novel, Prabhavati's friends praise the joys of sex in verse, to which the parrot responds by quoting "from the book of proper conduct" (87); that is, he literally parrots the official view of morality, which rings hollow after the lovely paeans to sensuality and "nature's course" uttered by the women (86–87). The author seems to suggest monogamy is against nature, and that there's no harm seeking sexual fulfillment when a spouse is away. (Although we hear nothing of Madan while off on his business trip, it's highly unlikely *he* was faithful.) *Seventy Tales of the Parrot* both challenges the sexual mores of its time and offers storytelling as a sexual surrogate — after each of the parrot's erotic tales, Prabhavati goes to sleep, temporarily satisfied — and along with the earlier *Bawd's Counsel* of Damodaragupta shows that

---

59 *A History of Sanskrit Literature*, 291; published in 1920, this is still a useful survey.

Sanskrit novelists were way ahead of their European counterparts in sporting an enlightened view of sex, considering it a gift from the gods, not a curse from the devil. They order this matter better in India.

Another frame-tale narrative that assumed its final form at this time (1150–1250) is the gigantic *Vasistha's Yoga* (*Yogavasistharamayana*, literally "The Great Story of Rama in Which Vasistha Teaches His Yoga"). Even longer than the *Ramayana* it purports to supplement, this verse-novel takes the form of an extended lecture delivered by a primordial sage named Vasistha, called in to counsel young Prince Rama after he returns from a religious pilgrimage convinced the world is pointless. Vasistha *praises* the 15-year-old for this insight, and lectures him (and a group of listeners) on how to attain liberation by recognizing the illusory nature of the external world. He illustrates this with over 50 stories, ranging from hagiographies of men and women who have attained "supreme infinite consciousness" and can thereby zip around the universe and behold its wonders, to animal fables, to stories about vidyadharas and vampires (the latter indebted to *The Five-and-Twenty Tales of the Genie*), to numerous tales of people who dream of living totally different lives, which dramatize the sage's thesis: "What is experienced as the waking life is not entirely different from the dream-experience."[60] Nothing is real, all is illusion — including gender, caste, and the world itself — life is but a dream, aummmmmmm. . . . It's possible to compare the seeker's liberated state with the power of the imagination, and because of its use of stories Wendy Doniger claims *Vasistha's Yoga* influenced *The Arabian Nights*.[61] Nonetheless, the stories are so overwhelmed by the yogic commentary surrounding them that it's probably better to classify this vast work as theosophy rather than literature.

Though these frame-narratives or anthology-novels became India's most popular exports, more traditional novels continued to be written in the 11th century, the last great era of Indian fiction. This century saw not only the publication of the verse abridgments we've already encountered (Ksemendra's *Brihatkathamanjari* and Somadeva's *Ocean of Story*) and the commitment to paper of the oral vetala and parrot story-cycles, but also novels in the tradition of earlier classics. King Bhoja of Dhar (the protagonist of *Tales of the Throne*), a patron of the arts and a prolific writer on many topics, composed

---

60 Pages 548–49 (6.2.63 in the original) in Swami Venkatesananda's abridged translation, which even at 725 pages represents less than half of the original. There is a complete translation in English dating from the 1890s, but it is reportedly of poor quality.

61 *The Hindus: An Alternative History* (NY: Penguin, 2009), 518. She deals with *Vasistha's Yoga* more extensively in *Dreams, Illusions, and Other Realities* (Chicago: U Chicago P, 1984).

a novel similar to *The Bawd's Counsel*; but while Damodaragupta's harlot is down on her luck and in need of career counseling, Bhoja's *Shringaramanjari* features a successful prostitute of that name. Most of the novel consists of 13 stories her mother tells concerning the hazards of "the life," and it has been suspected that Bhoja was writing about his favorite courtesan. Soddhala's *Udayasundari* (c. 1040), likewise named after its heroine, is a romance modeled on *Kadambari*, including a narrating parrot, but is even more self-consciously literary and reliant on fantasy.[62] Around the same time, a Jain author named Jinesara wrote a novel called *Nivvanalilavai*, similar to Uddyotana's *Kuvalayamala*, which is lost but was highly regarded by later authors. Dhanesara followed in the footsteps of both Uddoyotana and Jinesara with his *Surasumdari* (1038), a Prakrit novel in verse that also harks back to the *Brihatkatha*, another testament to the enduring influence of that foundational supernovel. Even more dependent upon Gunadhya's great tale is the not-so-great *Gadyacintamani* of Odayadeva (alias Vadibhasaimha). Written in the mid-11th century, this retells the Jain legend of Jivaka, a model of ethical behavior "despite his weakness for women, repeated absorption in love-making and utter infidelity" (Warder 6:321). It features a flying "peacock machine" and other wonders as Jivaka weds and beds a number of women before finally abandoning them all to become a Jain monk. But after Vardhamana's *Manorama* (1083), another Prakrit novel (but mostly in prose) featuring a series of sages teaching Jain doctrine by way of edifying stories (yawn), the novel seems to have fallen out of favor. Of course by that time India had its hands full with the invading Muslims, who stupidly destroyed many of its libraries and books, including many of the novels I've described as lost. Warder adds with justifiable bitterness: "the plundering barbarians were in this case also religious fanatics, for whom looting the infidel was an act of piety and massacre an act of faith" (6:151). We've seen this before, and will see it again.

The closest contributions the invading Arabs made to the Indian novel were several Sufi verse romances, influenced in equal parts by Sanskrit novels and Persian romances, and written in Hindavi. Maulana Dauda's *Candayan* (1379) is the first example of the genre, in which the romantic yearning of a young man for a beautiful girl is spiritualized and sublimated via Sufi theology into an allegory of the soul's yearning for ecstatic union with the divine. Qutban's *Mirigavati* (1503) and Malik Muhammad Jayasi's *Padmavat* (1540) are later examples, and the best example of this genre is Mir Sayyid Manjhan Rajgiri's *Madhumalati* (1545).[63] While it could be titillating to hear Allah

---

62 As noted above, an English translation of this novel by Dr. Sharma is available, but it's so bad as to be unintelligible.

63 Manjhan's *Madhumalati* is available in a fine verse translation by Aditya Behl and Simon Weightman, whose introduction supplied all the details in this paragraph. Annotated selec-

described as a hot babe and religious yearning in terms of sweating with lust, the careful attention these writers paid to versification means these works should be categorized as poetry rather than fiction, of more interest to the student of Sufi mysticism and religious psychopathology than to the historian of the novel.

Most of the novels I've discussed so far were written in northern India; in southwestern India in the 16th century a literary renaissance was under way that produced the most technically sophisticated novel in Indian literature, *The Sound of the Kiss* (*Kalapurnodayamu*) by Pingali Suranna. Attached to the court of King Krishna of Nandyala (in modern Andhra Pradesh), Suranna wrote in the Telugu language either in the late 16th or early 17th century, and made his debut with a tour-de-force narrative poem that managed to tell the stories of the *Mahabharata* and the *Ramayana* simultaneously. *The Sound of the Kiss* is a novel in verse (as its most recent translators insist, not a verse narrative) distantly related to *Kadambari* in that it too features a pair of lovers who undergo several lives before finding each other (and likewise includes a talking parrot). But in Suranna's hands, the myth of reincarnation becomes a metaphor for the erotic quest, while eroticism itself becomes the source of language and literature.

"The story is a new one, utterly unlike anything told before, and compelling in its beauty," a character quite rightly boasts.[64] The frame-story itself is reminiscent of the *Brihatkatha*, but the ensuing narrative is mind-boggling. One day Brahma the creator was sporting with his wife Sarasvati, goddess of language, and bit her on the lower lip. "As pleasure awoke inside her, a soft moan of enchantment slipped from her throat. . . . She was pressing her thighs together and closing her eyes. It was a textbook case" (5). Embarrassed by her orgasm, Sarasvati resists Brahma's further advances, so he diverts his erotic drive into fiction and procreates the story of a king named Kalapurna and how he eventually married a girl named Madhuralalasa, all the while continuing to fondle his wife. But after two pages Sarasvati stops him, realizing the story has been a coded account of Brahma's love for her. He fesses up to his sharp critic, and then explains that his story, told in the past tense, will come true in the future. This is the narrative seed from which the entire novel grows, though it is not related at the beginning of *The Sound of the Kiss* but at its very center. Sarasvati's moan creates a two-level story (like Suranna's earlier tour de force) that radiates backward and forward from the center of the novel, meaning that when we begin reading it, we are hearing a story that has already happened but, simultaneously, has yet to happen. And when we

---

tions from Behl's translation of Qutban's *Mirigavati* can be found in Dehejia's *Celebration of Love*, 60–73.

64 Chap. 5 in the Narayana/Shulman translation, cited hereafter by chapter. This excellent rendition is slightly abridged, for some of Suranna's punning sentences resist translation. (Pingali is the author's family name, but I follow the translators in using his given name.)

reach the big bang at the center of the novel, we realize (like Sarasvati) that everything that has come before it is a code for something else, every character an earlier incarnation of a later character. The courtesan Kalabhashini we meet at the beginning of the novel, for example, was once a parrot that overheard the Brahma–Sarasvati sex-story incident, and will be reborn as Madhuralalasa, Kalapurna's bride.

If it sounds confusing, it is. (And a detailed plot summary would only make it worse, so I won't bother.) But Suranna wanted to tell a new story in a new way, to reinvigorate what by then was a thousand-year tradition of writing fiction in India. He wanted to play with the relation between lovemaking and language-making (as Carole Maso says in *Aureole*), with the generative power of speech, and to examine the nature of a reader's response to literature, what stories can tell us about ourselves. "This story you told is about us," the goddess realizes after she decodes Brahma's figurative language, and throughout the novel there are other occasions when a narrator is describing the previous lives of characters when one of them, in a moment of recognition, realizes the story is about him. It's easy enough for us to identify with a character in a novel who has a personality similar to ours or dilemma we've faced, but harder to see ourselves in superficially dissimilar characters who, in actuality, may be closer to our true selves, exhibiting traits we weren't aware we shared until that moment of recognition. Characters in Suranna's novel recognize themselves from previous lives, and alert readers may recognize themselves in a 16th-century Telugu novel if they pay close enough attention, and not necessarily in the hero but perhaps in a mad magician or porcupine-demon.

Related to the difficulty of self-recognition in Suranna's novel is the difficulty of recognizing one's true soulmate, the tendency to fall for someone for superficial reasons. At the beginning of the novel we are introduced to the beautiful courtesan Kalabhashini, who falls for a semidivine man named Nalakubara; she is studying music with another *gandharva* named Manikandhara, but she is so obsessed with Nalakubara that she transforms herself into a double of his lover Rambha to have sex with him; but she later learns that Manikandhara has transformed himself into Nalakubara, meaning the couple fated to be together — they eventually reincarnate as Kalapurna and Madhuralalasa — had to work through superficial relationships based only on appearances before finding their true loves. Reincarnation is a metaphor for maturation, which is perhaps all that Siddhartha meant in the first place. Suranna handles all this with much more subtlety and aplomb than my blunt rendition indicates; these transformations and mistaken identities have reminded some critics of Shakespeare's *Comedy of Errors* or *A Midsummer Night's Dream* — written at the same time Suranna was at work — though metempsychosis and Suranna's nonlinear structure make them harder to keep track of.

Like Brahma, Suranna is capable of some amazing linguistic feats: at one point, some boys want to slip a secret message to the king, so they utter a sentence that means one thing in Telugu but something entirely different in Sanskrit. Impressed, Kalapurna asks them for another example, so one of them tosses off a Telugu poem that, if read backwards and in Sanskrit, reveals a second poem! When Kalapurna's other wife feels neglected, he recites a poem (as the translators explain) "using only two consonants — *m* and *n* — as if conjuring up the resonance of *mana*, 'we,' reassuring her that they are together" (142 n13). Some of Suranna's wordplay is so complex and dependent upon what the translators call "phonoaesthetic effects" that it can't be translated. Throughout the novel there are stories within stories, a lecture on yoga, and the kind of elaborate, metaphoric descriptions Sanskrit novelists favored — but with fresh metaphors, not the same ones recycled from Bana & Co. — and towards the end Suranna seems to parody their typical plot devices as he describes Kalapurna's expedition to conquer the world — not undertaken for the lofty, empire-building reasons of earlier kings, but merely to collect jewels for an anklet for his newest queen. (Structurally, this section functions like the rude mechanicals' play in act 5 of *A Midsummer Night's Dream*, a parody that's enjoyably overdone.) And then there's the explicit eroticism that has shocked some readers and delighted others. The saris of female characters are always slipping down to expose their pendulous breasts, and the author refuses to draw the curtain after Kalapurna marries Madhuralalasa (young enough to be his daughter), gleefully giving a blow-by-blow account as he initiates her into the joys of *kama*. Sarasvati's erotic moan (*manita*) is like a tambura drone throughout the novel as Suranna puns on it with character names like Manigriva, Manikhandhara, Manistambha, and the magical necklace (*manihara*) that bestows omniscience on anyone who wears it over the heart. No one is deaf to the sound of *eros*, as indicated in my favorite line in the novel: "God was watching the dancing women" (2).

The Sound of the Kiss is an amazing novel, "ahead of its time" if that phrase had any real meaning. If published today, it would be praised (or more likely dismissed) as a postmodern, experimental, paronomastic, achronological prose poem on the synergetic relationship between *logos* and *eros*, with enough sex and blasphemy to get it banned in many schools. That such a novel could appear in the 16th century, in India, *in Telugu*, is surprising, once again revealing how uninformed conventional wisdom is regarding the historical development of the novel.

Pingali Suranna followed this brilliant novel with a shorter, less ambitious one entitled *The Demon's Daughter* (*Prabhavati-pradyumnamu*), based on an old story in the *Harivamsa*, a supplement to the *Mahabharata*. In contrast to the mazy *Sound of the Kiss*, it's a single-level story narrated in linear fashion, superficially a throwback to the Sanskrit novels of the 7th century. Blurring

the distinction between the divine and human realms, the god Indra's kingdom has been taken over by Vajrapuri, an obnoxious *asura* (an "anti-god,"
the demon of the novel's title), so Indra appeals to his fellow god Krishna for
help in expelling the invader. (Though the kings are based on Hindu gods,
the situation reflects the political reality of 16th-century Deccan India, made
up of small rival kingdoms.) Thanks to a boon granted by Brahma, no one
can enter Vajrapuri's fortress without an invitation, so Krishna comes up with
the idea of sneaking someone into the city under cover of an invited acting
troupe, and nominates his son Pradyumna for the role. To sweeten the pot,
Pradyumna is told of the demon's beautiful daughter Prabhavati (no relation
of the restless housewife with the guardian parrot), who has already fallen
in love with him by way of a portrait of Pradyumna given to her in a dream.
Pradyumna successfully sneaks into the city, performing on stage for the
demon king by day and performing in bed with his daughter by night (after
a DIY *gandharva* marriage), until the subterfuge is exposed and Pradyumna
kills his lover's father, with her steely blessing.

Faced with a genre that by then was over a thousand years old, Suranna
was challenged to make it new (as Ezra Pound recommends). He displays
an ironic, postmodern attitude to the conventions of the genre, as when one
character begins to describe Prabhavati to the prince by rattling off all the
traditional clichés:

> What images can I conjure up
> to describe the beauty of her body, from toe to tip?
> Lotus blossoms, crescent moon, banyan fruits,
> tortoise shell, a quiver of arrows, banana plants,
> sandbanks, whirlpools, a lion's waist, golden pots,
> fresh lotus stalks, leaf buds, the conch of the Love God,
> jeweled mirrors, red coral, a sesame flower,
> darting fish, a bow of horn, a piece of the moon,
> the curves of the letter Sri, black bees —
> it's a shame we can't do better.[65]

These shorthand similes ("whirlpool"=navel; "golden pots"=breasts; "darting
fish"=eyes) had been used by everybody, so Suranna attempts to "do better"
by playing with them over the next two pages, breathing new life into these
dying similes. In the chapter that follows, the same narrating character begins
to tell a story to Prabhavati and her friend Ragavallari that displays a similar
disregard for convention:

---

65 Chap. 2 in the Narayana/Shulman translation. Another novel in verse, their translation
alternates between prose and poetry.

She looked at Prabhavati. "Here's the story of the man who stole your heart. In the Bharata land, there's a city called Dvaraka. Not even the Creator can describe it to the end, for its splendor has no end. If I were to attempt to describe it to you to the best of my abilities, even a little, you'd find it would distract you from the main story. So let it go."

They giggled. "You're right about that. You're obviously a good storyteller." (3)

In Subandhu and Bana, the approach to a city would be an occasion for a splendid five-page description, but our po-mo narrator and audience have no patience for such stuff. And the narrator? She's a goose named Sucimukhi, a learned bird who doesn't simply recite the narrative but plays an active part in it, spying on the enemy for the king, acting as the go-between for the two lovers, advising them, and in one comic episode getting the best of a parrot in a fight, as though Suranna were telling Bana: "My goose can beat your parrot at narration!" This mother goose is the author's persona: creative, mellifluous, and clearly in charge.

Most of the novella tracks the affair between P & P; the conflict between the two kings at the beginning is essentially an excuse for Suranna to indulge in more spicy eroticism, which is both R-ratedly explicit and imaginatively poetic. Before Pradyumna enters the city, he prepares himself "for both love and war," and after his first night with Prabhavati, she surveys herself like a soldier looking at a battlefield the day after a vigorous engagement:

> Prabhavati, meanwhile, was looking at herself in the standing mirrors. At her breasts that still showed the marks of her husband's armlets. At the scratches left by his nails on her body, still glowing with the dried-out flakes of sandalpaste. At her cheeks bearing the impress of his earrings, and her lips that showed his bites. (5)[66]

In contrast to the playful eroticism and ironic narrative tone, however, is a more serious concern with fatherhood. Suranna begins his novel by announcing that he is writing it in honor of his father, hoping thereby to make his father as proud of him as Krishna is of Pradyumna. To a devoted son, a father is a god, as he states at both the beginning and end of the novel. But to please his father, Pradyumna must kill his lover's father; when he tells Prabhavati of his dilemma, we have this chilling scene:

> She looked intently at her husband, who was torn at the prospect of having to kill the demon king. From where she stood she could see her father already scaling the walls with his heavily armed soldiers. She tried to find some other way to save her husband, her children, and herself. Finding none, she cut her love for her father from her heart.
>
> She went herself and brought the sword from the corner. Placing it in her husband's hands, she said, "Kill the king of the demons. Doubt no more. No more." (5)

---

66 These Indians love to bite; the *Kamasutra* devotes two chapters to scratching and biting.

It would probably be going too freuding far to read an Oedipal conflict into Pradyumna's patricidal act, or to argue that Suranna had to kill the fathers of the Sanskrit novel to make way for his more innovative ones, or to make anything of the phallic sword. Still, placed two pages before the end of the novel, Prabhavati's cold decision to "cut her love for her father from her heart" clashes with the novel's warm conclusion: "There Pradyumna played endlessly while remaining ever devoted to his father, who is God" — an intriguingly ambiguous ending to an otherwise delightful romance.

Pingali Suranna's two novels pointed the way for the future of Indian fiction, but there were no immediate followers; though some writers continued to produce novels in verse and prose, they were not advances but retreats to old forms and older beliefs. It would be centuries before any Indian writer produced a novel as interesting as his.[67]

TIBETAN FICTION

Besotted by Buddhism from the 8th century onwards, Tibetans never really developed any art forms (or much of anything) that didn't concern their religion, a more esoteric, idolatrous doctrine than Siddhartha ever intended. Consequently, except for the *Epic of Gesar* — a *Mahabharata*-sized collection of oral legends about a heroic king — and some indigenous folk tales, there's no secular Tibetan literature to speak of.[68] Those stuck in the Land of Snow who wanted something more cosmopolitan had to rely on translations from the Sanskrit — there's a Tibetan version of *Tales of the Genie*, for example — and it wasn't until the 18th century that a resident produced a bona fide novel, *The Tale of the Incomparable Prince* by Tshe ring dbang rgyal. I'll discuss him in the next volume, but there is one earlier Tibetan writer I want to shanghai for my crew of innovators who thought like a Buddhist but wrote like a novelist, a colorful character known as Tsang Nyön Heruka: the Mad Yogi of Tsang.[69]

Born in 1452 in Tsang (in southwestern Tibet), he was ordained at the immature age of seven and given the first of many names, Sang gye Gyaltsen. At age 18 he had "a vision of fifteen strange girls" urging him to go on a pilgrimage; meeting his guru (or lama, as they're called in Tibet) he was given yet another name and immersed himself in solitary meditation before joining

---

67 Although I didn't have occasion to cite it, I want to acknowledge Sures Chandra Banerji's encyclopedic *Companion to Sanskrit Literature*, which was an invaluable guide during my Hindoo holiday.

68 This is the gist of Cabezón and Jackson's *Tibetan Literature: Studies in Genre*, though its contributors offer some scattered examples of belles lettres, mostly ornate poetry.

69 Tibetan names are complicated — a traditional transcription of this author's name would be gTsan sMyon Heruka — so I'll be using the most familiar forms I can find.

a religious college to study the tantra. He mastered that over-intellectualized hooey, and then snapped. "He began behaving strangely," his biographer tells us, "chattering aimlessly, laughing madly. His break with the monastery and its stifling discipline was spectacular. On the day that the prince and his court paid a visit to the monastery, Tsang Nyön behaved in the wildest and most insulting manner. His monastic career was at and end."[70] Now calling himself Durto Rolpai Naljorpa, "The Yogi Who Wanders in Cemeteries" (a name he claimed the gods gave him), he began a peripatetic life as a religious mad-man, a respected occupation in 15th-century Tibet. He lived in cemeteries and created fashion accessories from what he found there: "He wore neck-laces of fingers, intestines and toes, and had a robe made from human skin. He was also known on occasion to eat the remains of the dead."[71] He mingled with Tibetan nobility, but is also reported to have exorcised a zombie. Waving his freak flag high, he soon found his vocation as a writer.

During his wanderings he visited many of the holy places made famous by an earlier monk and poet named Milarepa (1040–1123, or 1052–1135 accord-ing to a different tradition). As with any charismatic religious figure, stories and legends about Milarepa had begun circulating after his death, growing more fanciful over the centuries. Strongly identifying with Milarepa, and claiming to possess "the secret oral tradition," Tsang Nyön wrote two narratives about him that are considered hagiographies by some, expositions of Tibetan Tantrism by others, but which contain so many imaginative, fictitious elements that the most accurate classification for them would be religious novels.

The shorter of the two, *The Life of Milarepa* (*Mila Khabum*, 1488) is a chronological account of his spiritual quest, dramatizing how a troubled youth who messed around with black magic and killed some people became one of Tibet's most beloved religious figures. But the structure shows a novelist's touch: rather than recount his life from birth to death, as most hagiographers would, Tsang Nyön begins at the end, when Milarepa is an old man, surrounded by disciples. One of these, a historical figure named Retchung Dorje Drakpa (1084–1161), has a dream in which the Buddha promises to tell him the inspiring story of Milarepa the following night. When Retchung wakes at dawn, still half-asleep, he confuses a rainbow with five beautiful girls, who encourage him to ask Milarepa to tell his story. When he does, the sage is reluctant to comply, but upon further prompting launches into a first-person account that occupies most of the book. Tsang Nyön's use of Retchung to introduce the autobiographical tale is bookended in the long final chapter, after Milarepa's death. Retchung was elsewhere when his master died, and it becomes a question of some dramatic import whether he

---

70 Smith, *Among Tibetan Texts*, 64, paraphrasing a 16th-century biography.
71 Peter Alan Roberts, "The Kagyu School," in Dinwiddle's *Portraits of the Masters*, 154. This art book reproduces a few copper bronzes of the mad yogi.

will arrive in time to view the body before it is cremated. Again we see him at dawn, halfway between dream and contemplation, when "he perceived a host of dakinis who were about to carry away to another realm a crystal stupa radiating light throughout the heavens."[72] Retchung dreams that Milarepa leans out from the stupa and gives him a special blessing. So thrilled is he that "Retchung, in an act of devotion, drew air into his body and, retaining it, with the force of a well-shot arrow covered in one morning a distance that for ordinary travelers would take two months" (2.9).[73] Consequently, Retchung is there to witness the psychedelic light show that accompanies Milarepa's passage to nirvana. Retchung is a surrogate for the enthusiastic reader, for whom Milarepa "performs" his life — a much more effective narrative strategy than an unmediated account, and one that justifies considering the book a novel rather than a hagiography.

The story Milarepa tells is a variation on the sinner-who-finds-religion theme. Born into a religious family, he had a happy childhood until age seven, when his father died. His evil uncle and aunt force the boy and his mother and sister to become their servants and cheat him out of his inheritance. Vowing revenge, his mother White Jewel sends her son at age 15 to a lama to learn sorcery, and when the uncle throws a wedding party for his eldest son, Milarepa works his black magic on their house:

> The uncle and aunt had gone out to discuss the meal to be served and the speech to be given. At this moment a former servant of ours who was now with my uncle had gone to draw water. She did not see the many horses tied up in the stable, but instead she saw scorpions, spiders, snakes, and tadpoles. She saw a scorpion as big as a yak which grasped the pillars between its claws and tore them out. At this sight, the servant fled, terrified. Hardly was she outside when the stallions in the stable began mounting the mares and the mares began kicking the stallions. All the rearing, kicking horses struck against the pillars of the house, which then collapsed. Under the debris of the fallen house, my uncle's sons, his daughters-in-law, and the other guests, thirty-five in all, lay dead. The inside of the house was filled with corpses buried in a cloud of dust. (1.3)

Several interesting things going on here: note how sexual frenzy is partly responsible for the destruction; Milarepa doesn't undergo any hard-core

---

72 Part 2, chap. 9 in Lhalungpa's translation (hereafter cited by part/chapter). A dakini — literally, "she who travels in the sky" — is a prim version of a vidyadhara, pretty but not as sexual as her Sanskrit cousin. A stupa is a reliquary containing sacred relics; some are buildings, but this one is only a foot high, and later will house a doll-sized Milarepa.

73 This is one of many supernatural incidents in the novel, yet many readers — including the book's 20th-century translator — consider *The Life of Milarepa* to be a "true account," a "genuine autobiography" (Introduction, vii, viii). Lhalungpa admits many of the novel's gods are to be understood as "psycho-cosmological symbols" (xxiv), but he seems to think that overall it is closer to history than fiction. Unbelievable.

sexual temptations as in many hagiographies — he's been engaged since childhood to a girl named Zessay, a routine social arrangement — but lust is one of the Three Poisons he'll need to resist during the course of his spiritual adventures (the others being hatred and ignorance). And note how Tsang Nyön conveys the incident from the servant's point of view, which heightens the drama and personalizes it in a manner similar to Retchung's in the framing narrative. The thing is, Milarepa was in another town when he cast this long-distance spell; three paragraphs earlier, he said, "Meanwhile I wondered how the spell had manifested itself in my village of Kya-Ngatsa." So the giant scorpion and mating horses are simply what he *imagined* might have happened, even though the episode is recounted as though it were a factual account. Tsang Nyön is waving a big banner announcing the book's fictionality, a point lost on his credulous readers but reiterated near the end when Milarepa sings to Retchung from the crematorium:

> In the invisible realm of the heavens,
> There is a Buddha who skillfully uses falsehoods,
> Guiding sentient beings toward relative truth.
> Little time have they to realize ultimate truth. (2.9)

Like Buddha, and like any pedagogic novelist, Tsang Nyön (as Milarepa) "skillfully uses falsehoods" to guide his readers toward *relative* truth — which is all we can know; "ultimate truth" is claimed only by deluded solipsists and fanatics — and gives yet another indication we're reading fiction rather than nonfiction.

When the townspeople threaten harm to Milarepa's family, he responds with another incantation that causes a hailstorm to ruin their crops. Though he has avenged his family's honor, he's ashamed of his actions and fears he'll spend several low lifetimes repaying the karmic consequences. He is also disgusted by the world he's seen so far, filled with greed, duplicity, vengeance, arrogance, and mob violence. Part 2 of the novel recounts his search for the right lama to teach him religious principles, and finding one in Marpa the Translator (1012–97) — so named because he brought back many Sanskrit sutras from India to translate — who tests his sincerity by putting him through a series of exasperating, symbolic ordeals before giving him the keys to enlightenment. (At the end of Milarepa's apprenticeship, Marpa explains the symbolism behind his ordeals, which again alerts the reader that everything in the novel is to be interpreted, not taken literally.) Milarepa then spends many years wandering through southern Tibet, meditating in caves and imposing such severe austerities on himself that he is reduced to a bag of bones. Hallucinating with hunger, he imagines he can fly and converse with supernatural beings. (Milarepa composes poems throughout this period, giving us another variation on the poet-as-madman theme; Marpa brought poetic forms back from India in addition to religious texts, and thus acts as Milarepa's writing instructor as well as religious advisor.) Over the years, people from his early life seek him out: his sister Peta, now a homeless wanderer; his fiancée Zessay, still single; and even the evil aunt who mistreated him as a child, and whose remorse for her actions and decision to pursue dharma completes that particular narrative arc. Milarepa begins to attract disciples and eventually becomes a spiritual celebrity (against his wishes), which brings us to the point where the novel began: Milarepa, in a cave surrounded by a mob of followers — yogis, bodhisattvas, lay disciples (male and female), even some dakinis and gods — one of whom asks him for his story.

Milarepa's spiritual quest is set against the social consequences of the religious life; Tsang Nyön allows the men to babble on about the Three Levels of Enlightenment, the Five Skandas, the Eight Perfect Attributes, the Three Modes of Time, and so on, while his female characters raise more practical questions about the wisdom of withdrawing from society. Milarepa's not-to-be-messed-with mother, skeptical sister, and jilted fiancée all remind him what it means to be human, and Marpa's wife lavishes lower-case compassion on the young disciple while her seemingly hard-hearted husband torments him in the name of Cosmic Compassion. Though the women respect Milarepa's decision to lead a religious life, they wonder about the extremes he goes to and resist his invitation to do the same: after he sings a song to Peta inviting her to renounce the Eight Worldly Reactions (pleasure, praise, gain, delightful words; displeasure, criticism, loss, dreadful words) and join him in austerity, she tells her naked brother to put some clothes on and brings him down to earth:

> "What my brother calls the Eight Worldly Reactions, people call worldly happiness. We have no happiness to give up. Your high-sounding words are an excuse to cloak your realization that you will never be like Lama Bari Lotsawa. I will not go to Lachi to buy misery and deprive myself of food and clothing. I do not even know where Lachi is. Rather than running away and hiding in the rocks like a deer pursued by hounds, stay in one place and your practice will intensify and also it will be easier for me to find you." (2.7)

Both she and Zessay repeatedly check his spiritual arrogance, his undisguised pride at being a filthy, naked, emaciated, hallucinating religious nut, and his egotistic assumption that by meditating in isolation he is helping all sentient beings. Though Tsang Nyön identified with Milarepa and obviously intended him to be an admirable figure, his use of compassionate and skeptical female characters complicates the idealized, uncomplicated genre of hagiography and brings *The Life of Milarepa* within the domain of the novel. One critic has claimed it "is arguably Tibet's greatest literary work."[74]

Near the end of the 200-page book, after Milarepa has finished with his autobiography, the author announces: "I am now going to enlarge a little on the Master's life," and gives a sketchy summary of Milarepa's wandering years; the real enlargement comes in the 700-page companion volume Tsang Nyön wrote at the same time, *The Hundred Thousand Songs of Milarepa* (*Mila Grubum*). Just as Jack Kerouac rewrote the fairly conventional *On the Road* as the longer, more experimental *Visions of Cody*, this unconventional, episodic work tracks Milarepa's career as a dharma bum, going from cave to cave to meditate, and blowing the minds of everyone he encounters. Like the *Life*, it is structured in triads: part one concerns the malevolent nonhuman beings he overcomes, part two the dedicated disciples he instructs, and part three the lay followers he encounters during his travels.[75] It's significant to me, though it probably wasn't to our author — for whom all is illusion: Maya — that on the very first page, Milarepa faints "due to weakness from lack of food," and then awakes to a psychedelic vision of his lama Marpa "on a cluster of rainbow clouds resembling a robe of five colors . . . and riding a lion with rich trappings," who encourages him to continue with his solitary meditations.[76] It's as though everything that follows is a dream, or more likely a series of hallucinations induced by extreme hunger. As soon as Marpa vanishes, Milarepa returns to his cave and is "startled to find five Indian demons with eyes large as saucers." In the second chapter, en route to Lashi (where sister Peta refused to go), the Jetsun (Reverend) Milarepa imagines goddesses paying tribute to him and then has this religious experience:

> As Milarepa proceeded on his way, a host of demons assembled and conjured visions of huge female organs on the road to shock him. Then the Jetsun concentrated his mind and exposed his erected male organ with a gesture. He went farther, and passing an apparition of nine female organs, reached a place with a rock shaped like a vagina standing in its center — the quintessence of the region. He inserted a phallic-shaped stone into the hollow of the rock, [a symbolic act] which dispersed the lascivious images created by the demons.

74 Roberts 125, yet it is mentioned only in passing in Cabezón and Jackson's 550-page *Tibetan Literature*. These Tibetan scholars need to get their story straight.

75 The *Life* consists of 12 chapters: three on Milarepa's early life (part 1), three on his apprenticeship to Marpa (part 2, chaps. 1–3), three on his wandering years (4–6), and three on his path to nirvana (7–9).

76 Chap. 1 in Chang's translation, hereafter cited by chapter. (Chaps. 28–31 were written by others, perhaps two of Tsang Nyön's many disciples; the long chapter 41 also feels like an interpolation.) Like Lhalungpa, Chang has his own name on the book's cover, not Tsang Nyön's; both translators refer to him only briefly, as though he were merely the compiler of a sacred work rather than the creative artist who carefully crafted these two novels. Both are eager to expound the books' religious significance but are indifferent to their status as literary compositions. Chang's translation was brutally criticized upon its original appearance by D. L. Snellgrove in *Asia Major* 10 (1963): 302–10.

The embarrassed translator attaches this note to the bracketed phrase: "The meaning of this passage in the text is esoteric and therefore obscure; it may thus be subject to different interpretations." I'll say. One interpretation is that food is not the only thing the body of this virgin needs. Another is that Milarepa is clinically insane, pushed over the edge by his austerities, and now unable to distinguish between reality and fantasy. "One day a monkey came to Milarepa's hut riding on a rabbit, wearing mushroom armor and carrying a bow and arrow made from stalks" (6) — who needs LSD when religious devotion provides hallucinations like that? The most likely interpretation is that the author is playing up his "mad yogi" rep — "I sing as you requested; / These are my mad words" (4) — putting on the same outrageous show that got him thrown out of his monastery. (What do you want to bet Tsang Nyön exposed himself to his prince as Milarepa does here?) The madcap laughs at his readers, expounding complex religious doctrines by way of surreal adventures and Tantric psalms:

> Myriad visions and various feelings all
>   appear before me —
> Strange indeed are Samsāric phenomena!
> Truly amusing are the dharmas in the
>   Three Worlds,
> Oh, what a wonder, what a marvel!
> Void is their nature, yet everything is manifested. (5)

Consequently, perhaps it's best for the reader just to sit back and enjoy the trip rather than get hung up on Chang's copious notes explicating the intricacies of Tibetan Tantrism, most of which sound crazy anyway. ("To avoid involvement in the world, a technique for eating stones in place of food is provided for determined Tantric yogis" [5 n12] — who, to avoid involvement with Tibetan women, can also have sex with stones, as Milarepa does.)

And what a long strange trip it is. Milarepa is attacked by a demon army, attracts pigeons who metamorphose into goddesses, meets his future disciple Retchung as a boy (who abandons his family to follow the older man), spots teenage girls and seduces them with song into joining his cult, walks on water, dreams often of beautiful dakinis, wins a "miracle contest" against a priest of Tibet's aboriginal religion, debates all comers, communicates with animals, enjoys "the company of some low-born fairies in the forest of Sen Ding" (27), refuses an invitation from the king of Nepal, flies through the air, runs like the Flash, reads others' minds, transforms his body into water, continues to expose himself on sundry occasions, and throughout sings about 400 didactic songs (not the 100K promised by the title). Despite the variety of incidents, the long novel lacks the dramatic tension between self and community that humanizes *The Life of Milarepa*, and in fact lacks drama of any sort: Milarepa has already achieved enlightenment when the novel opens, and easily overcomes all challengers to his doctrine in the boringly predictable way of Christian hagiography. There is a subplot involving his mild troubles with Retchung, who grows up, goes to India, returns a little too proud of himself, and occasionally questions his lama, but it falls short of the more interesting relationship between Milarepa and his sister in the *Life*. Milarepa's songs display an encyclopedic knowledge of Buddhist Tantrism, but like an annoying televangelist the guru too often pitches his defeatist solution to life's challenges: "abjure the world, renounce all thoughts and wishes of this life, and devote oneself to meditation" (25).[77] Still, *The Hundred Thousand Songs of Milarepa* is an impressive achievement. Near the end of the novel, Milarepa delivers a Ginsburg-like poem on holy madness, and his auditor responds, "Your kind of craziness is very good" (53); our author may have deserved the nickname "The Mad Yogi of Tsang," but his kind of craziness is likewise very good.

Near the end of his life, long after he had recovered from the "yogic-madness" he warned potential disciples against (*Songs* 17), Tsang Nyön wrote one more biographical novel, *The Life of Marpa the Translator: Seeing Accomplishes All* (*Marpa Mamthar*, c. 1505). Unfortunately this represents a decline in Tsang Nyön's literary powers. It's a straightforward chronicle of Milarepa's lama, from birth to death, written in a plain style (the translation appears to be very faithful), with little of the drama or wildness of his earlier novels. Born to wealthy landowners, Marpa is a headstrong youth, and at age 12 is sent to cool off at religious school, where he learns Sanskrit and other Indian languages. Eager for further teachings, he makes three trips to India over the next 30 years, finding his true teacher in the guru Naropa (1016–1100), and ends his life in Tibet, dazzling his disciples with vulgar miracles to reinforce his teachings before dying at the age of 88.

Only two sections show Tsang Nyön's old flair: on his third trip to India, Marpa seeks out Naropa for the ultimate teachings, but the guru has "entered the action," a hip-sounding phrase meaning he has abandoned conventional life and is experiencing the world directly from a different dimension, as it were. Marpa's desperate quest for Naropa involves several symbolic episodes that allow the Mad Yogi to return to the hallucinatory imagery of the *Songs*.[78]

---

77 I suspect these songs came first; Tsang Nyön probably gathered all the songs of Milarepa passed down via bardic tradition and invented prose anecdotes to dramatize them, as Indian and Irish writers did with their ancient materials.

78 Stunning examples of this sort of hallucinatory writing can also be found in *The Tibetan Book of the Dead*, especially chapters 11 ("The Great Liberation by Hearing") and 13 ("A Masked Drama of Rebirth"). This work, originating in India in the 6th century and achieving its present form in the hands of Rigdzin Nyima Drakpa (1647–1710), has recently appeared in a definitive English translation by Gyurme Dorje (NY: Viking, 2006).

The other is the account of the death of Marpa's son, Tarma Dode, which is so much more novelistic than the rest of the book that I wonder if Tsang Nyön contributed only these two episodes and let his disciples write the rest, just as some 17th-century European artists would paint the face in a portrait after their students had filled in the background. Perhaps he wrote the songs as well; in one of them, Marpa exhorts: "Be carefree; eat flesh; be a madman" (46), no doubt Tsang Nyön harking back to his cemetery days amidst the rotting viscera. Good times.

Though it lacks much artistry, *The Life of Marpa* doesn't lack historical interest concerning the religious life. The author doesn't hide the fact that the pursuit of dharma was a business: lamas required pre-payment before they would pass on their teachings, and each of Marpa's trips to India is preceded by raising the necessary financing. (For this reason, young Milarepa had complained, "Religion is forbidden to the poor" [*Life* 2.2].) When a fellow student heads back to Tibet before him, Marpa even wonders if the market for his teachings will thereby be diminished. He translates manuscripts for his Tibetan audience with the avidity of a publisher signing up potential best-sellers. These mystics weren't above exchanging ethnic slurs and insults either: one Nepalese nirvana-junky sneers, "Tibetans are like oxen," and later one of Marpa's relatives observes, "His breath has a rotten stench. His crotch stinks. He lives by devouring gifts from his devotees."[79] We also learn that the quest for enlightenment needn't be as ascetic and lonely as it was for Milarepa: Marpa not only has a wife but enjoys other "authentic consorts possessing good qualities," including a "dark-skinned daughter of the merchant" who accompanies him during his wanderings in India (56, 104). Marpa sensibly argues "if one does not enjoy meat, liquor, and women, it is a disservice to oneself," and justifies his enjoyment of these "sense pleasures" by insisting that "I am not fettered by them" (153). Tantric sex with his consorts or with fantasy figures is also part of his religious discipline, as he notes in song: "On the occasion of upāyamarga, I meditate on another's body. / Arousing bliss again and again, I meditate" (154).[80]

A few years after dictating this work to his students, Tsang Nyön died (1507), perhaps as the result of poisoning, which, ironically, is how he imagined Milarepa died. He left behind a school of students who wrote similar biographies — Lhatsün Rinchen Namgyal produced a *Life and Teaching of Naropa* that is available in an English translation by Herbert V. Guenther

---

79 Pages 10, 148 in the Nalanda translation, an outstanding edition with useful scholarly apparatus.

80 *Upāyamarga* means "path of skillful means." This is a meditation exercise with form (as opposed to formless abstraction), apparently the warm form of another body, also called *karmamudra*, the "tantric practice involving the union of male and female" (from the glossary to *The Life of Marpa*, 235). Unfortunately these "meditations" are not depicted in the novel.

(1963) — and perhaps some of these exhibit novelistic qualities, but as with Christian hagiographies, I'll leave them to other sentient beings.

ARABIC FICTION

As we've seen, the earliest novelists in many cultures often appropriated the narrative models provided by their sacred writings, but Islamic writers had to look elsewhere. Their Quran (Recitation, 610–32, final recension c. 651) is not a narrative but a series of hectoring sermons allegedly delivered by their god Allah via an angel to an illiterate merchant named Abu al-Qasim Muhammad (c. 570–632), nearly identical in form and threatening content to prophetic books of the Jews, Muhammad's models. It consists of 114 semi-independent sections (suras) ranging from a few lines to 30 pages in length, which are organized not by chronology or theme but simply by length, with the longest first and tapering to the shortest at the end. (The oldest suras are mostly at the end, making a sequential reading of the book disorienting, for it begins with later suras referring to themes and events that occurred much earlier.) The fatalistic theology is a combination of boot-camp Judaism and apocalyptic Christianity, denigrating this world for the world to come, which Muhammad shamelessly baits with sexual lures. (True believers will be hooked up in heaven with beautiful, high-breasted virgins with big, dark eyes, reportedly a major motivation for today's suicide bombers.) Although there are a few narrative anecdotes, the majority dumbed down from the Tanakh, the suras consist mostly of commands, threats, boasts, and reminders, reiterating the same points with little variation. The bulk of the book rails against disbelievers and polytheists, and the tone is unfortunately a familiar one: Allah is the kind of person who thinks highly of himself and then becomes angry when he doesn't get the respect he feels he deserves, and so goes home to plot revenge. The Quran is filled with gloating reminders of societies Allah has destroyed in the past and revenge fantasies planned for the future for those who don't take him seriously, giving the book a petulant, "I'll show you!" tone that no doubt derives from the poor reception Muhammad received when he first delivered these suras. Hell hath no fury like an author scorned.[81]

Like all religious scriptures, the Quran promotes some admirable virtues

---

81 See the first chapter of Efraim Karsh's *Islamic Imperialism* (New Haven: Yale UP, 2006) for an account of how Muhammad, acting more like a Mafia don than a religious leader, used his invented religion "to cloak his political ambitions with a religious aura" (5), which he achieved with the usual tactics of tyrants — robbery, assassination, extortion — and how his followers used it as an excuse to go looting and pillaging. In *Muhammad: Islam's First Great General* (Norman: U Oklahoma P, 2007), Richard A. Gabriel further details the "calculated butchery" (xix) Muhammad sometimes employed, inflicting levels of bloodshed and brutality previously unknown to Arabs and justifying genocide against unbelievers.

— generosity, hospitality, gracious manners, compassion for the needy — but as Asma Afsaruddin points out, these virtues were merely carried over from those of the earlier "pagan" Arabs.[82] (Besides, one shouldn't need the promise of heaven or the threat of damnation to act decently.) The oldest suras in rhymed prose have some striking imagery, which led some contemporaries to the natural conclusion Muhammad was simply a poet recycling ancient fables. Muhammad insisted he was reporting fact, not creating fiction, and thereafter dropped the poetic tone in the more prosaic later suras, where he goes out of his way to distance himself from poets (sura 26; cf. 36:69). Nevertheless, Muhammad betrays an artistic temperament from time to time, as when he says (in the persona of Allah), "When Our verses are recited to him [a disbeliever], he turns away disdainfully as if he had not heard them, as if there were heaviness in his ears. Tell him that there will be grievous punishment!" (31:7).[83] In fact, the poor reception of the early suras is a recurring theme in the book and accounts for the disproportionate amount of material devoted to trashing disbelievers, both those of Muhammad's time and those in the past who likewise scorned the warnings of Noah, Abraham, Moses, Jonah, and Jesus, giving the Quran its unsympathetic tone of bullying and intimidation. Still, Muhammad couldn't resist the occasional flash of authorial imagery; in fact, in the very first sura traditionally dictated to Muhammad, Allah proclaims: "Your Lord is the Most Bountiful One who taught by [means of] the pen. . . ." (96:3–4). In sura 18, which contains more narrative than most, Allah prompts Muhammad to say, "If the whole ocean were ink for writing the words of My Lord, it would run dry before those words were exhausted" (18:109), and elsewhere Allah promises that on the day of reckoning, "We shall roll up the skies as a writer rolls up [his] scrolls" (21:104), which conjures up the image of the world as a text. In other hands, this would be a celebration of the writer's godlike ability to create and populate a world, aligning the artist (and Allah) with other creators like Ptah, Anu, YHWH, Shiva, Akongo, et al. But not here. Muhammad claimed to be a medium, not a poet, which led his critics to the only other assumption: that he was mad. The truth, obscured by the unreliability of the original texts and commentaries, is probably somewhere in between.[84]

82 *The First Muslims: History and Memory* (Oxford, UK: Oneworld, 2008), 3.
83 All quotations from the Quran are from M. A. S. Abdel Haleem's translation (NY: Oxford UP, 2004). The term "Allah," by the way, is derived from the Canaanite god El, and as Coogan points out, "the epithets 'the Merciful' and 'the Kind' used of Allah are strikingly close to the Ugaritic designations of El as 'the Kind, the Compassionate'" (*Stories from Ancient Canaan*, 12).
84 For the problems associated with these writings, see any of the handy collections of essays edited by Ibn Warraq: *The Origins of the Koran* (1998), *The Quest for the Historical Muhammad* (2002), and *Which Koran? Variants, Manuscripts, and the Influence of Pre-Islamic Poetry* (2010), all published by Prometheus Books. See also Mondher Sfar's compact *In Search of the Original Koran: The True History of the Revealed Text* (2007) from

So, as I say, Islamic writers had to look elsewhere for inspiration. Just as Muslims adapted their religion from the West, from Judaism and Christianity, they adapted their fiction from the East, from India and Iran. After the Quran, the most popular book with Arab readers in the Middle Ages was *Kalilah and Dimnah*, an adaptation of the *Panchatantra* made around 750 by a scholar named Abdullah ibn al-Muqaffa (c. 722–c. 758), who adapted it from a Pahlavi (Middle Persian) translation of the Sanskrit original. Ibn al-Muqaffa was born in Iran and after moving to Iraq converted to Islam from Zoroastrianism, though his commitment to reason and free inquiry led some of his detractors to question the sincerity of his conversion. (The Quran doesn't exactly encourage freedom of thought: "When God and His Messenger [Muhammad] have decided on a matter that concerns them, it is not fitting for any believing man or woman to claim freedom of choice in that matter" [33:36].) The Pahlavi version of the *Panchatantra* Ibn al-Muqaffa used hasn't survived, but it's fairly clear he made the text his own; he adapted the original animal fables to suit his own political philosophy, and invented some others. He dispensed with the frame-tale about a teacher instructing a king's dull sons and instead has the king himself question the teacher on various ethical points, who replies with fables. The names have changed — the Sanskrit jackals Karataka and Damanaka are called Kalilah and Dimnah, and the Brahmin teacher Vishnusharman goes by the name Bidpai — but the stories remain much the same.

What's most interesting about *Kalilah and Dimnah* is the paraliterary additions. The tales are preceded by 50 pages of introductory material, nearly a quarter of the book, namely: (1) an introduction by Ibn al-Muqaffa, insisting his work is to be read on two levels: the animal fables are meant to entertain, but they conceal philosophical issues a reader needs to uncover; (2) a second introduction by Bahnud ibn Sahwan (aka Ali ibn al-Shah al-Farisi, who may also be our author), which gives the background to the fables, beginning with Alexander the Great's conquest of India centuries earlier, and explaining why the Indian philosopher Bidpai wrote the Sanskrit original; (3) the long

---

the same brave publisher. The most eye-opening study to have appeared in recent years is Christoph Luxenberg's *Syro-Aramaic Reading of the Koran* (Berlin: Hans Schiler, 2007), which shows the Quran has been misread since its inception because its earliest transcribers and editors didn't realize its indebtedness to Syriac, the lingua franca of Muhammad's time, and consequently they mistranslated the prophet's original revelations. (Those dark-eyed virgins in paradise? A mistranslation of "white grapes" [251]. Sorry, fellas.) Even today, at least a quarter of the Quran remains puzzling to scholars because of their ignorance of its Syriac roots, and in addition "a considerable number of passages that were thought to be certain have in reality been misunderstood" (108). To put it bluntly, an entire culture was based on a botched editing job, and Muhammad's revelations mangled in translation from the oral to the written word. But for one-stop shopping, read F. E. Peters's *The Voice, the Word, the Books: The Sacred Scripture of the Jews, Christians, and Muslims* (Princeton: Princeton UP, 2007), a lucid account of how the Tanakh, the New Covenant, and the Quran were created and edited.

story of how a Persian king learned of the book and sent a physician/scholar named Barzawayh to India to make a translation and return with it; and (4) a short biography of Barzawayh's early years by the Persian king's vizier, Buzurjmihr.[85] All this seems to have interested Ibn al-Muqaffa more than the fables; a scholar himself, he stresses the importance of scholarly advisors throughout, and with the example of Barzawayh places the scholarly quest for knowledge and enlightenment above all other duties, including those owed to one's king or god. He makes some rather slighting remarks about religion and asceticism, and may even be mocking the origin of the Quran by claiming the fourth part of the introduction was "dictated" by Barzawayh even though it's clearly Buzurjmihr's own invention.[86] Rather than blindly following authority, the author advocates scholarly inquiry, self-examination, and personal responsibility for one's choices, paying only lip service to the Islamic doctrine of destiny. Since the stories of Barzawayh and Bidpai are fictitious, and since Ibn al-Muqaffa inserts several fables into this introductory matter, he complicates the distinction between nonfiction and fiction, and by insisting on the various levels of meaning in his work he raised the quality and expectations of imaginative prose at a time when poetry was considered the only serious form of literature — an opinion most Arabs continued to hold for centuries, unfortunately.

But his insistence on the importance of scholars to the state, and the respect due to them, was in vain. At age 36, Ibn al-Muqaffa got mixed up in some political intrigue and was tortured and killed by the new governor of Basra at the prompting of Caliph al-Mansur, "Commander of the Faithful." Nevertheless, *Kalilah and Dimnah* survived and spread throughout the Middle East and Europe in various translations and adaptations, eventually influencing La Fontaine's *Fables* and perhaps even the Br'er Rabbit fables African slaves brought to America.

Around the time Ibn al-Muqaffa was murdered, a sharp rise in literary production began because of the availability of paper — courtesy of some Chinese paper manufacturers the Arabs captured during one of their endless wars of expansion — which replaced parchment and papyrus. Book-collecting, library-building, and book-selling likewise encouraged literary creativity; by the time the Baghdad bookseller al-Nadim compiled his *Fihrist* (Index) in 987, thousands of books were available to Arab readers, though fiction still ranked low on the list. After cataloguing all the books in print on language, religion, grammar, history, humor, poetry, law, philosophy, mathematics, astronomy, and medicine, al-Nadim finally deigns to offer a short

---

85 This introductory material can be found in Jallad's recent translation (2002), but not in Irving's superior translation of the fables (1980) or in most earlier ones.

86 Robert Irwin notes that Ibn al-Muqaffa "was accused of having written a heretical imitation of the Qur'an which began, 'In the name of the Light, the merciful, the compassionate . . .'" (*Night and Horses and the Desert*, 75–76).

section on books written by storytellers, whom he lumps in with exorcists, jugglers, and magicians. He names *Kalilah and Dimnah* and other adaptations from Persian literature, and then catalogs a wide assortment of pop fiction: fables, story-cycles, historical novels, romances, novels named after "Loving and Fickle Girls," others about humans who fall in love with the jinn (genies) or vice-versa, sea sagas, humorous tales, and erotica (*The Daughter of Bilyan*; *Martus the Greek*; *The Capable Woman*; *Jaded Harlots and Adulterers*; *La'ub the Head Woman and Husayn the Homosexual*; *Concubine Mistress*) (2:712–36). Among the earliest of Persian imports, al-Nadim notes,

> was the book *Hazār Afsān*, which means "a thousand stories." The basis for this [name] was that one of their kings used to marry a woman, spend a night with her, and kill her the next day. Then he married a concubine of royal blood who had intelligence and wit. She was called Shahrāzād, and when she came to him she would begin a story, but leave off at the end of the night, which induced the king to spare her, asking her to finish it the night following. This happened to her for a thousand nights, during which time he [the king] had intercourse with her, until because of him she was granted a son, whom she showed to him, informing him of the trick played upon him. Then, appreciating her intelligence, he was well disposed towards her and kept her alive. The king had a [female] head of the household named Dīnār Zād who was in league with her in this matter. (2:713–14)

That the fabled *Arabian Nights* (*Alf Layla wa Layla*) was actually Persian in origin is the first of many surprises about the most famous Islamic contribution to world literature. That it is not a gigantic supernovel written by one person but a vast collection of Eastern tales assembled over many centuries is the second. A minor third is that some of its most popular stories — like those of Aladdin, Sindbad, and Ali Baba and the 40 thieves — were never part of the original. The fourth, and most disappointing, is that there *is* no original: every extant Arabic version is a farrago of texts based on the editorial taste of whoever assembled it, meaning every version differs from the others in numerous ways. But the extraordinary influence *The Arabian Nights* has had on Western novels (rarely Eastern, paradoxically) is too important to let a textual mess like this deter us.

In his wonderful book on the *Nights*, Robert Irwin gives this compact account of how the Persian *Hazar Afsan* became the glorious if ramshackle *Book of a Thousand and One Nights* we now have:

> Most scholars agreed that the *Nights* was a composite work and that the earliest tales in it came from India and Persia. At some time, probably in the early eighth century, these tales were translated into Arabic under the title *Alf Layla*, or "The Thousand Nights." This collection then formed the basis of *The Thousand and One Nights*. The original core of stories was quite small. Then, in Iraq in the ninth or tenth century, this original core

had Arab stories added to it — among them some of the tales about the Caliph Harun al-Rashid. Also, from perhaps the tenth century onwards, previously independent sagas and story cycles were added to the compilation, such as the epic of *Omar bin al-Nu'uman* and the *Sindibadnama* (or, as the latter cycle features in the Burton translation, "The Craft and Malice of Women").[87] Then, from the thirteenth century onwards, a further layer of stories was added in Syria or Egypt, many of these showing a preoccupation with sex, magic, or low life. In the early modern period yet more stories were added to the Egyptian collections so as to swell the bulk of the text sufficiently to bring up its length to the full 1,001 nights of storytelling promised by the book's title. At the same time older stories were modernized in small ways, so that one finds references to guns, coffee-houses and tobacco in some stories, which certainly pre-date the invention or discovery of those things. (*Companion*, 48)

After that, various Arab editors compiled different versions of all this material, changing the language and the order of the stories as they saw fit, a process later mirrored by the *Nights'* Western translators. The French Orientalist Antoine Galland introduced the book to Europe, publishing a French version in many volumes beginning in 1704 based on a Syrian text of the 14th or 15th century (as luck would have it, the earliest extant version), which was quickly translated into English by an anonymous Grub Street hack as the *Arabian Nights' Entertainment* (c. 1706–21). Galland's manuscript reached only the 282nd night (the core of older stories Irwin refers to above), so he continued to publish volumes based on other Oriental tales, including a few dictated to him by a Syrian Christian informant, and even a few of his own invention. This version, which runs to about 900 pages, wasn't supplanted in England until Edward Lane published his longer version in 1838–42. A prudish man, he left out the erotic and scatological bits, as well as stories he deemed inferior. John Payne published an even longer, more complete version between 1882 and 1884, but imposed a polished literary tone on the racy vernacular of the original. (Because it was published in a limited edition of 500 sets that quickly disappeared into the hands of collectors and libraries, Payne's translation never caught on, despite its many merits.) A year later came Sir Richard F. Burton's notorious translation (1885–88), partly plagiarized from Payne; it is the most expansive edition available in English — in addition to the main text that runs to about 3,000 pages, he published six volumes of supplementary tales — but also the hardest to read because of Burton's bizarre stylistic decision to mate Malory's 15th-century idiom with Urquhart's Rabelaisian English, with some 19th-century slang thrown in. The French finally replaced Galland's courtly translation with a fin-de-siècle one by Joseph Charles Mardrus published in 1899–1904, which enchanted Proust and impressed T. E. Lawrence ("of Arabia") but outraged most specialists because, like Galland, Mardrus felt free to move stories around and write a few of his own. (Though born in Cairo,

87 I discussed the Hebrew version of this book, *Tales of Sendebar*, in chap. 2.

his command of Arabic was rather shaky as well.) His version was translated into English in 1923 by Powys Mathers, who made a few "improvements" of his own (though not to the Arabic errors). Nevertheless, the Mardrus/Mathers version "is the most readable of them all" in the weighty opinion of Jorge Luis Borges,[88] and has been almost continuously in print. In the 1990s, Husain Haddawy published a fluent, reliable, two-volume selection from the *Nights*; the first volume translates the original core text as reconstructed by Muhsin Mahdi in 1984, which ends with the 271st night (basically the same core Galland worked from before he decided to expand); in 1995, Haddawy published a second volume that contains one further core story (that of Qamar al-Zaman) plus the extracurricular stories that most people associate with the *Nights* (Sindbad, Ali Baba, Aladdin), albeit mostly from the movies.[89] Finally, in November 2008, Malcolm Lyons published an accurate, complete translation of *The Arabian Nights* in three fat volumes, which also includes the two most popular "orphan" stories (those of Ali Baba and Aladdin, translated by his wife Ursula). Although it lacks "the decorative elaboration of the original," it is now *the* English translation of choice for those who want to attend all thousand and one nights.[90]

Given this chaotic bazaar of competing texts and translations, it's foolish to expect the aesthetic consistency of a single-authored novel in *The Arabian Nights*. But by taking a roc's-eye view, it's possible to see the entire thing as a long novel — encouraged by the absence of section titles from Lyons's translation, which are present in virtually all others — or at least to extract a few novel-length works from it. It's not surprising that Proust felt an affinity with *The Arabian Nights* as he worked through more than a thousand and one Parisian nights on his long novel.

All of the complete editions contain the essentials of a novel: they introduce a set of characters — King Shahriyar, his vizier's daughter Shahrazad, her kid sister Dunyazad — and give them a dramatic conflict to face: Shahriyar has been sexually betrayed by his wife and becomes convinced all women are unfaithful, and so begins bedding a different virgin every night and beheading her the next morning (before she has a chance to betray him), keeping it up until his country is nearly void of virgins. How to stop this practice? The

---

88 "The Translators of *The Thousand and One Nights*" (1936), in *Selected Non-Fictions*, 106.

89 Like many Americans of a certain age, I learned of the *Nights* through old movies and Rimsky-Korsakov's *Scheherazade*. (My father had an LP picturing Shahrazad as a belly-dancer on the cover, as though she conveyed her tales through interpretive dance.) Jane Seymour in *Sinbad and the Eye of the Tiger* (1977) is a cherished memory, but it was Proust who led me to read the work in my mid-twenties, all 10 volumes of Burton's obstreperous translation.

90 "A Note on the Translation," 1:xx. All citations will be to this edition (by volume/page) unless otherwise noted. Like Lane and Burton, Lyons follows the Arabic text edited by W. H. Macnaghten published in Calcutta in 1839–42.

well-read Shahrazad valiantly volunteers to marry the sultan, confident that she, aided by her sister, can escape beheading by beguiling him with stories. She does so for a thousand and one nights, reciting an encyclopedic range of tales of every kind — romantic, magical, religious, erotic, historical, comic, tragic, animal, detective, along with thousands of lines of poetry — and with dramatic tension effectively maintained because she needs to keep topping herself to prevent the sultan from getting bored and resuming his gynocidal rampage. (As John Barth mordantly notes, it's a literal case of publish or perish.)[91] But she overcomes these obstacles, finally convincing the king to abandon his murderous policy. Shahriyar, in turn, has matured; as the 18th-century version puts it, Shahrazad's tales "contributed so much towards removing the sultan's fatal prejudice against all women, and sweetening the violence of his temper" (*Arabian Nights' Entertainment*, 892). In most versions of the conclusion, Shahriyar simply exempts Shahrazad from other women, for her many tales of cunning adulteresses and wily women probably did little to change his misogyny. These versions trot out the three children the sultan has unknowingly fathered on Shahrazad — how her three pregnancies went unobserved is not explained — but he downplays this sappy ploy: "Even before the arrival of these children, I had intended to pardon you, as I have seen that you are a chaste and pure woman, freeborn and God-fearing" (3:734). As in most romantic novels, they marry — Dunyazad, now of age, marries the sultan's brother in some versions — and all live happily ever after, "until they were visisted by the destroyer of delights and the parter of companions" (3:734). In essence, "*The Arabian Nights* is the story of a conjugal union ruptured by one female and restored by another,"[92] not unlike, say, *Jane Eyre*.

So, we have all the essential ingredients of a novel: recurring characters, dramatic complications, and resolution. The only difference is that instead of *participating* in dramatic incidents, as in a conventional novel, our female protagonist *relates* dramatic incidents; instead of a knight facing one challenge after another, every night Shahrazad faces a new narrative challenge. Storytelling itself, not the actual stories, becomes the focus of this novel, which Shahrazad cleverly reinforces with various stories in which a character's fate depends on his ability to tell a good story. The very first tale Shahrazad tells, no doubt deliberately, exemplifies this: a demon threatens to kill a merchant who accidentally killed the demon's son, but three travelers who become interested in the merchant's fate manage to dissuade the demon by telling fantastic tales of metempsychosis. In "The Story of the Three Apples"

91 "Muse, Spare Me" (1965), in *The Friday Book*, 58. Barth's love for Shahrazad and for the narrative conceit of *The Arabian Nights* is evident from several of his essays and brilliant fictions, especially the "Dunyazadiad" (in *Chimera*) and *The Last Voyage of Somebody the Sailor*.
92 Ghazoul, *Nocturnal Poetics*, 32.

(1:123–72), another of the original core tales, Caliph Harun al-Rashid threatens to kill his vizier's slave unless he can tell a good story; as determined as Shahrazad, the vizier complies with a 50-pager, after which the grateful caliph frees and befriends the slave and orders that the tale be recorded. Even some of the late, foreign additions to the *Nights*, like the *Sindibadnama* Irwin mentions above, feature characters telling stories to save their lives, mirroring the situation of the frame-tale and keeping Shahrazad's death sentence in the reader's mind despite the absorbing distractions of the exotic stories. Nor is storytelling to be confused with creativity: Shahrazad retells stories she has learned from books, and other characters tell "true" stories of events they've witnessed, not fanciful lies they hope will get them off the hook. *The Arabian Nights* is about narrativity, not creativity or originality, which is one reason it has attracted metafictionists like Borges and Barth.

Early European readers of the *Nights* who considered it a collection of droll *contes* objected to the nightly interruptions when "Morning now dawned and Shahrazad broke off from what she had been allowed to say" (1:13). Galland dropped this device about halfway through his edition, his English translator even sooner (see his "Advertisement" after the 27th night on pp. 65–66), and Payne after only the fourth night, thereby converting the work from a novel to an anthology. (Selections from the *Nights*, like N. J. Dawood's popular Penguin edition, obviously do likewise.) But those nightly interruptions, usually at a cliffhanging point in the story, keep the narrative spotlight on Shahrazad: *her* predicament, *her* relationship to her murderous lover, *her* need to keep the stories novel.[93] There's a reason why this is called *The Arabian Nights*, even though most of the tales take place during the day: the real story is taking place at night. Those nocturnal intermissions also remind us of the sexually charged circumstances of Shahrazad's storytelling, which takes place in the sultan's bed, often after sex, with the nymphet Dunyazad lolling at the foot of the bed, and which again brings to mind Professor Maso's axiom lovemaking ≈ language-making. At first, Shahrazad tells each night's story after she's had sex with the sultan — and given the brevity of some of the installments, they must have been going at it for hours on some nights — but as the book progresses, that detail is dropped, as though the oral tales themselves have become a form of sex, a "thousand one nightinesses" (nighties + naughtiness), as Joyce puns it in *Finnegans Wake* (51). Even if dropped by editors because sex is implied, there's an obvious analogy between keeping sex fresh and interesting in a relationship and Shahrazad's narrative challenge. Her dazzling tales, full of variety and surprises and postponed climaxes (narrative coitus interruptus), may be analogous to her dazzling sex skills. (Given

93 This is why the most faithful film version is *Arabian Nights* (1999), a spectacular television miniseries written by Peter Barnes that begins with Shahrazad's situation and features her throughout struggling to keep one story ahead of her psychopathic husband.

the tales' Indic–Persian origins, the *Kamasutra* was undoubtedly one of the thousand books she boned up on in preparation.) Irwin notes that despite all the erotic incidents in the book, "detailed information about normal copulation is hard to glean from the *Nights*, because of the linguistically ingenious and metaphorical modes of describing the sex act favoured by the storytellers, as they move smoothly from the description of foreplay to word-play. What we are offered are displays of rhetorical skill, not documentary accounts of fucking" (*Companion* 175–76). The erotic content of many of the tales, coupled with the bedroom setting, blur the distinction between lovemaking and language-making and provide the enormous work with the unifying, iterative symbolism more characteristic of a novel than an anthology.

Were any of the *Nights'* editors conscious of this, and did they organize their versions accordingly? Perhaps. I'd like to think of the book as a communal novel, like the *Lancelot-Grail* that was being assembled in France at the same time as the core collection of *Nights*, or a big project constructed over a period of time by various hands like the Great Pyramid of Cheops or the Chartres cathedral. Borges demurs: "the artisans and craftsmen of the cathedrals knew what they were making. In contrast, *The Thousand and One Nights* appears in a mysterious way. It is the work of thousands of authors, and none of them knew that he was helping to construct this illustrious book. . . ."[94] The Argentine exaggerates — hundreds at most (not thousands) may have been involved — but there is considerable evidence that intelligent shaping by a small number of editors took place, especially with the core selection that Mahdi reconstructed.[95] There's a certain amount of literary self-consciousness in the text indicating the editors did indeed know what they were making, as when Harun al-Rashid orders that the vizier's story be written down. Whoever contributed the novella-length tale of Hasan of Basra (3:145–261) was especially proud of his achievement; in some versions, Shahrazad prefaces it with the story of a king who so loved tales of adventure that he threatens his favorite storyteller (experiencing writer's block) with impalement on a stake unless he brings him a fantastic new story — another tale mirroring Shahrazad's situation. The storyteller sends his agents to the four corners of the earth, and finally one returns with the manuscript of *The Adventures of Hasan of Basra*, which the storyteller transcribes in his best calligraphy and reads to the king, who is so ravished by it that he makes the storyteller his grand vizier on the spot (Mathers 3:151–57). Only after this celebration of imaginative literature does Shahrazad begin telling the actual tale. (It's a corker all right, though derivative of Gunadhya's *Brihatkatha*.)

94 *"The Thousand and One Nights"* (1977), in *Seven Nights*, 48.
95 Mahdi goes so far as to suggest a single storyteller may have edited the core collection: see his essay "Exemplary Tales in the *1001 Nights*" in the special issue of *Mundus Arabicus* entitled *The 1001 Nights: Critical Essays and Annotated Bibliography* (dated 1983 but published in 1985).

Irwin points out another instance of narrative self-reflexivity worthy of Borges or Barth:

> In "The Tale of Attaf" (also known as "The Power of Destiny"), Harun visits a library, consults a volume at random, falls to laughing and weeping and dismisses the faithful vizier Ja'afar from his sight. Ja'afar, disturbed and upset, flees Baghdad and plunges into a series of adventures in Damascus, involving Attaf and the woman whom Attaf eventually marries. Returning to Baghdad, he reports back to Harun, who takes him into the library. Now Ja'afar is allowed to consult the book which caused his master such grief and mirth, and in it Ja'afar finds the story of his own adventures with Attaf, those same adventures which were provoked by Harun's reading of the story in the book. (*Companion* 198–99)

This self-awareness of the massive mosque of texts the editors were building persists to the end, when Shahriyar "summoned chroniclers and copyists and bade them write all that had betided him and his wife, first and last; so they wrote this and named it *The Stories of the Thousand Nights and A Night*" (Burton, 3641). True, this detail is only in Burton's and Mardrus's translations; the lickerish Englishman expands on the laconic conclusions of his predecessors to include a sexually ambiguous fashion show put on by Shahrazad; after modeling seven feminine outfits, she is clad

> in youth's clothing, whereupon she came forward swaying from side to side and coquettishly moving and, indeed, she ravished wits and hearts and ensorcelled all eyes with her glances. She shook her sides and swayed her haunches, then put her hair on sword-hilt and went up to King Shahryar, who embraced her as hospitable host embraceth guest, and threatened her in her ear with the taking of the sword; . . . (3640)

This tacky scene suggests the sultan prefers Shahrazad's sexual skills over her textual ones, reducing her from a feminist heroine to a hootchy-kootchy dancer. Still, even this conclusion supports the thesis that *The Arabian Nights* is essentially a multiplex novel about the complicated domestic relationship between a hot-tempered misogynist and a clever young woman who brings him to his senses with a combination of great tales and great tail.

No? Then let's reverse figure and ground to look at three extended narratives within *The Arabian Nights* that are more easily recognizable as novels. Right after the tale that so impressed Harun al-Rashid, Shahrazad begins a novella entitled *The Story of the Hunchback*, which takes her a week and a half to narrate (1:173–243). It starts off with a brisk if brutal whirl of screwball comedy: a tailor and his wife are returning from a day in the city when they spot a drunken hunchback singing and playing a tambourine, and naturally invite him home for further laughs. While feeding him, a fish bone gets stuck in the hunchback's throat and he collapses; afraid they've killed him, the wife suggests they drag the body to the door of a Jewish doctor, tell the maid it's a sick child, and run off; as the doctor comes out, he knocks the body over and likewise thinks he's killed him. Now at *his* wife's suggestion (women are the clever, scheming ones) the doctor then goes onto the roof of the house of a Muslim neighbor (the steward of the king's kitchen) and lowers the body into his house; returning at night, the steward mistakes the shadowy figure for a thief and clubs him a few times. When the body doesn't move, he too panics and drags the body outside and props it up against an alley wall. A drunken Christian comes along, and while urinating spots the hunchback and assumes he's going to steal his turban (as another thief attempted to do earlier that day) and begins beating him while yelling for the police. Suspicious of a Christian beating a Muslim, the police notice the hunchback isn't moving and arrest the Christian for murder. (All this is taking place in China, for no discernible reason.)

The next day the king is informed that a Christian has killed the hunchback, who happens to be his jester, and orders him to be executed. A crowd gathers as the hangman puts the noose around the Christian's neck. From out of the crowd comes the Muslim steward, who admits he, not the Christian, killed the hunchback, and explains what happened. Also feeling guilty, the Jewish doctor then steps forward and does likewise; then the Chinese tailor appears and takes responsibility. Informed of this strange situation, the king orders all four men to appear before him, along with the body of the hunchback. The police chief recounts the whole story to the king, who laughs and declares it the most amazing thing he's ever heard. (The whole frantic sequence flies by in five pages.) The Christian, sober and sensing a challenge, boasts he can tell an even more amazing story, and with the king's permission tells of a merchant he once knew in Cairo whose right hand was chopped off for theft as a result of a sexual intrigue he got mixed up in. (Or rather, that Allah planned for him: everything that happens in this novella, good or bad, is ascribed to their god, the author of the book of life.) Asked by the Christian if his story isn't even more amazing than the hunchback's, the king answers no and decides to hang all four suspects. The steward then asks whether the king will pardon them all if *he* tells an even more amazing story, and given permission, he launches into another pulp fiction of sexual intrigue that results in the loss not of a hand but of both thumbs and toes for the hapless protagonist. *I* was impressed, but not the king of China, so the Jewish doctor takes the stage and tells of another young man with a missing hand involved in a web of sex and murder. A tough critic, the king says it's still not as amazing as what happened to the hunchback.

The tailor is the group's last hope, so he pulls out all the stops with a hilarious tale of a lame man who broke his leg as a result of (you guessed it) a sexual intrigue, largely the fault of a meddlesome blabbermouth of a barber nicknamed the Silent — one of the great comic inventions of world literature. After the tailor finishes the primary tale, he recounts the barber's own tale of how he was almost executed once by Caliph al-Mustansir Billah (ruled 1226–42) but talked his way out of it by regaling the caliph with madcap stories of his six brothers, each of them "with some physical deformity. One of them has lost an eye, while another is completely blind, a third is semi-paralysed, a fourth has had his ears and a fifth his lips cut off, while the sixth is a hunchback" (219). In keeping with the preceding tales, most of them suffer because of a woman's wiles and/or their own foolishness, and the Commander of the Faithful falls over laughing and pardons the barber. The king of China is likewise delighted, and not only pardons the four suspects but summons the barber for further entertainment. When the barber learns what all the commotion is about, he examines the hunchback, removes the fish bone from his throat, and restores him to consciousness, to the further amazement of all. The king orders that the entire tale of the hunchback be written down and makes the barber his constant companion "until they met death, the destroyer of delights and parter of companions" (243).

The embedded structure of this masterpiece of black humor is cleverly constructed and paced.[96] Whereas Sanskrit aesthetics recommended that a work be shaped like a cow's tale, "ending in a bushy flare of surprises,"[97] the author of this novella begins with a bushy flare of incidents at breakneck speed, then slows down for the leisurely tales unfolded by the four suspects, drawing out the final one by the tailor and the loquacious barber the longest (nearly half of the novella). Despite the variety of narrators and incidents, the work is unified by recurring motifs of lust at first sight, sexual betrayal, violence, and physical deformation and mutilation — but played for laughs rather than for tears. And despite the wackiness of most of the episodes, the novella is highly realistic: we get details of what the characters are wearing, the cost of goods and merchandising practices, the various kinds of food they eat, and so forth. (The tale of the barber's sixth brother contains the famous feast of the Barmecide, in which a rich man pretends to feed a beggar an imaginary meal, describing the items on the menu with mouthwatering specificity; only after the beggar decides to play along does the man drop the farce and feed him a real meal.) The Christian describes Cairo in such detail that his story can be followed on old maps of the city, according to Irwin (126), and in one story we are given

---

96 In an otherwise unconvincing Lacanian reading of this novella, Daniel Beaumont notes that it "is often cited by theorists of narrative like Todorov and Genette for its formal brilliance; no other story group in the *Nights* joins so many different narratives in a complex artistic whole" (*Slave of Desire*, 105). Todorov in particular has an interesting chapter on the *Nights* in his *Poetics of Prose* (66–79), reprinted in Marzolph's *Arabian Nights Reader* (226–38), which conveniently collects many of the best essays written on the *Nights* over the last century.

97 Layne's introduction to *Kalambari* (xv), citing the 4th-century critic Bharata.

the exact date of an incident: the barber shaves the soon-to-be lame man on "Friday, that is the tenth of the month of Safar in the year 653 of the Prophet" (208), or April 1255. While the choice of China as a setting and the various religious persuasions assigned to characters seem arbitrary — they all act like Muslims and swear Islamic oaths, except for once when the Jew swears by "Joshua, son of Nun" (174) — these realistic details anchor the farcical events in the observable world of the novella's original audience, and give us a better view of medieval Arab life than tales of the jinn and mermaids. The mutilations and physical humor at the expense of the handicapped will bother some modern readers — the soft-hearted will want to skip over the outrageous tale of the barber's semi-paralyzed brother, which few shock-comics even today would dare tell — but *The Tale of the Hunchback* is a masterfully structured, richly entertaining example of knockabout farce.

From cruel comedy we turn to dark romance in *The Story of Qamar al-Zaman and His Two Sons* (1:693–832), a novel that concludes the original core of *The Arabian Nights* according to Mahdi. It's an intriguing, if occasionally clumsy novel about fathers and sons and the perfidy of women, a kind of brutal fairy tale in which a fanciful romantic story is often interrupted by scenes of graphic sex and violence. Though the plot is similar to that of "The Story of the Two Viziers," the one Ja'far wows Harun al-Rashid with, and shares elements with the Joseph story in Genesis, it most closely resembles Sanskrit novels like *Kadambari* and *What Ten Young Men Did*; not only are the plots similar, but the poetic descriptions of the zaftig protagonists use exactly the same idiosyncratic tropes, suggesting our author either knew them or had them in translation. Like Dandin's *Ten Young Men*, *Qamar al-Zaman* opens with a king, Shariman of Persia, who lacks a son but is granted one after he performs some rituals, though this blessing soon becomes a curse. Reaching marriageable age, his son Qamar al-Zaman tells his father that he doesn't want to have anything to do with women (cf. Sudraka in *Kadambari*), for he has "found much that has been written and said about their guile and treachery" (694). This so enrages his father that he imprisons his son in a tower. In the first of many plot doublings, we soon learn a king in China has a daughter named Budur who likewise doesn't want to marry: "As a princess, I am a mistress of power and authority, ruling over the people, and I have no wish for a man to rule over me" (705), so she too is confined. To a modern reader, such independence and confidence may sound admirable, but in the Arabic context of the novel, two teenagers who defy their fathers and refuse to play their allotted roles in society spell trouble, which calls forth the demonic jinn. One night a jinniya (female genie) named Maimuna notices Qamar in his cell and is so struck by his beauty that she spends an hour contemplating him in mute admiration. Flying up into the heavens, she runs into a jinni (male) named Dahnash, who has just returned from China where he was similarly admiring Budur. They argue over which is more beautiful, and to settle it Dahnash transports the sleeping Budur to place her at the side of sleeping Qamar. They look so much alike the jinn can't decide, so they enlist the help of a hideous demon named Qashqash, who suggests a test: wake each one in turn, and the one who shows more lust for the other will be judged inferior. Dahnash turns himself into a flea and bites Qamar on the neck, who wakes to find a beautiful girl next to him "wearing a Venetian chemise but no drawers" (713). He opens her blouse and wakes her for sex, but when she doesn't respond, he suspects something, so turns over and goes to sleep. Maimuna then turns herself into a flea, "went into the clothes of Dahnash's beloved, Budur, and walked from her leg up to her thigh and then, going on, she bit her on a spot four inches below her navel" (714). Budur wakes and is equally impressed by the handsome guy sleeping next to her; she likewise fails to wake him, but instead of suspecting anything, the bold girl helps herself:

> She opened the collar of his shirt, and leaning over him, she kissed him and then stretched out an exploring hand to see whether he had anything with him that she could take. When she found nothing, her hand went down to his chest and then, thanks to the smoothness of his skin, it slipped to his belly. From his navel it passed to his penis, at which her heart shook with palpitations and her lust was stirred, as lust is stronger in women than in men. This was followed by a feeling of shame and, removing the seal ring from his finger, she put it on her own as a replacement for hers. She kissed his mouth and his hands and then every part of his body, after which she took him in her arms and hugged him. With one of her arms beneath his neck and the other beneath his armpit, she embraced him and then fell asleep by his side. (716)

Because she couldn't control her lust, she's judged inferior in beauty by the jinn and returned to China.

The next day, both wake and try to find out who their nocturnal visitor was. Their guards know nothing about what happened and assume they're mad, so Qamar, after a few scuffles, is moved to house arrest in a palace overlooking the sea. The hellcat Budur, on the other hand, goes wild and actually kills one of her nurses and has to be chained against a palace wall with an iron collar around her neck. By way of the ring she took from Qamar's finger the two are eventually brought together after Budur's brother Marzawan helps bring Qamar to China, where they are wed. On their way back to Persia, however, they are separated after a curious incident; resting en route, Qamar notices a jewel in his sleeping bride's waistband and takes it outside to decipher the inscription on it. A bird snatches it, so Qamar follows it and gets lost, eventually making his way to a city inhabited by fire-worshiping Magians (i.e., Zoroastrians), where he takes refuge with a friendly gardener. Meanwhile, Budur discovers her husband is missing, so to protect herself (and perhaps to fulfill that deep-seated urge to rule over men) she disguises herself as a man and continues the journey, eventually winding up in the Ebony Islands, where she is mistaken for a prince and (in order to maintain her cover) allows herself to be married to the king's daughter, Hayat al-Nufas. Budur kisses her bride at night but avoids consummating the marriage with the puzzled girl, though this gender confusion is nothing compared to what follows. After various plot twists and turns, Qamar winds up in Budur's new kingdom, and though she recognizes him, he doesn't recognize his bride in sultan drag, so she decides to have some fun with him. The "prince" invites him up to the bedroom and confesses to a homosexual desire for him, and won't let him leave the kingdom until he submits to sodomy. She tries to seduce him by quoting some obscene poems, even resorting to blasphemy in one of them:

> She said when I refused to sleep with her,
> "How you persist in your folly, you fool!
> If you reject my cunt as Mecca to your cock,
> I will then show you a more pleasing tool."[98]

Gives a whole new meaning to the hajj. Qamar reluctantly bends over to take it like a man and is invited by butch Budur to take hold of her "tool" when lo! "he came to a dome full of blessings and of movement" instead (771). Budur falls on her back laughing, reveals her true identity, and the reunited couple make love, rendered obliquely in a 23-line poem. The next morning they reveal all to the royal court, Qamar takes Hayat al-Nufus as a second wife — Budur doesn't object, and Hayat is relieved to get a real man this time — and is crowned king of the Ebony Islands, sleeping with his wives on alternate nights (never together, apparently, though Budur doesn't seem the type to object to that either). But what seems like a happy ending is negated by the line, "his cares and sorrows cleared away, and he forgot his father, King Shahriman, and the royal dignity that he had enjoyed" (773). In a fiercely patriarchal society like Qamar's, that neglect demotes him from romantic hero to ungrateful wretch.

The second half of the novel concerns Qamar's two sons, one from each wife. But when the boys reach 17, Budur falls in love with Hayat's son As'ad, and Hayat falls for Budur's son Amjad. When the boys refuse their stepmothers' advances, the cougars accuse *them* of unnatural lust, so their father orders one of his slaves to take them out to the forest and execute them. They escape, become separated, and have adventures that replicate their father's, though a little more realistic, less supernatural than Qamar's. His early mistrust of women is confirmed as each of his sons gets involved with a dangerous

---

98 This is from Haddawy's translation of the novel in *The Arabian Nights II*, 218. Lyons's rendition is milder.

woman who nearly kills him. Amjad manages to become a vizier and is able to rescue his brother from a Magian named Bahram, who converts to Islam and then puts the primary narrative on hold to tell "The Tale of Ni'ma and Nu'm," a 15-page story of two underage lovers separated and reunited that is so different in tone and setting that it must be an interpolation by a later editor, who thought this would be a good home for this orphan story.[99] When the story resumes, the armies of three kings arrive in clouds of dust one after the other, that of Budur's father looking for his daughter, Qamar looking for his two sons (he has come to realize his wives duped him), and Shahriman looking for Qamar. Fathers and sons are reunited, the two evil queens sent away, the sons enthroned in kingdoms of their own, and Qamar succeeds to his father's kingdom, presumably without the burden of a woman, for verily as the poet saith:

> Women have been created for us as devils;
> I take refuge in the Lord from devilish wiles.
> From them spring the misfortunes of mankind,
> In matters of the world and in religion. (785)

Patriarchy and arranged marriages are re-established, and sexual adventurism condemned as the work of the jinn. As Andreas Hamori puts it, "It is as though the erotic desire must be dismissed for the patrimonial desire to come to fulfillment."[100]

Misogynistic? Yes, but in a curious way, because what is most reprehensible about the women in the novel is that they act like men at their worst. Budur is a sexual predator, kills an attendant for angering her, knows more dirty ditties than a sailor, and is so wild she snaps the chains that bind her in prison. When As'ad is captured by the Magians, he is beaten and tortured not by a man but by a slave-girl. When his brother Amjad picks up a woman, it is *her* idea to break into someone's house, and then *she* tries to kill the owner when he unexpectedly returns. In a novel filled with gender reversals and cross-dressing, the traditional roles of men and women are redistributed, and women are exposed as "devils" (as in the poem above) not so much for being women as for acting like men. It's more about power than gender, and if anything the novel is more misanthropic than misogynistic. The putative hero Qamar's disrespect for his elders at the beginning of the novel would be rude in any society, and though he learns some humility while working as the gardener's assistant — he misses a rare chance to return home by remaining to

---

99 It doesn't appear in Galland's translation; either it wasn't part of his source text, or he had the good editorial sense to leave it out.
100 "The Magian and the Whore: Readings of *Qamar al-Zamān*," *Mundus Arabicus* 3 (1985): 28.

see the gardener decently buried — his continued neglect of his father and his overhasty decision to execute his sons disqualify him from being any kind of hero. Joseph Campbell includes him in his *Hero with a Thousand Faces*, but I think he misreads Qamar's actions: his quest for Budur turns out to be a bad idea based on superficial attraction, not a heroic pursuit of personal destiny.

Aside from the beauty contest staged by the jinn, the most fanciful and mythically suggestive episode is when the bird steals the jewel Qamar has taken from the waistband of Budur's trousers — "a stone as red as the dragon's blood gum that was fastened to it . . . [with] two lines engraved in a script that he could not read" (748) — and leads him off on his post-honeymoon adventure. When Budur wakes, she says, "It looks as though he took the ring stone and went off, but he doesn't know its secret" (752). We're never told what the lines mean, or what the secret power is. Given its location, the jewel is likely a metonymy for Budur's sex — she passes as a man while the jewel is missing — and Qamar's inability to read its inscription suggests he doesn't comprehend the nature of sex. The alternating sexual dynamics in the novel and numerous instances of transvestism and homosexuality (feigned or otherwise) further suggest sexuality is always hard to read, even in societies where gender roles are clearly defined.[101] Though the author's plotting is sometimes awkward and overly reliant on coincidence, here he subtly honors the mysterious, sometimes fatal allure of sex by leaving it mysterious, which is as it should be.[102]

Comedy! Romance! and now *Adventure!* Top billing for our triple feature at the Aladdin Theatre goes to *The Tale of King Umar ibn al-Nu'man and His Sons*, the longest self-contained narrative in *The Arabian Nights* (1:304–613), which takes Shahrazad a full hundred nights to recite, and which at more than 300 pages can be considered a full-length novel. In addition to being an entertaining, action-packed read, it may be the richest Arabic novel for study from this period; as critic Wen-Chin Ouyang states, it "is practically a bottomless well of topics not only for researchers interested in storytelling in medieval Arabic Islamic culture, but for those interested in such topics as 'gendered thinking' in general, or gender roles in medieval Islam in particular, or the interaction and intersection between 'popular' and 'elitist' literatures, or the dichotomy between materialism and spirituality, or the tension between

---

101 See Beaumont (82 and 177 n20) for his and other critics' explanations of the jewel, none entirely convincing — not that mine is any better.

102 Heath argues the use of coincidence here isn't a lazy narrative shortcut but an affirmation of Allah's divine plan: "In short, *Nights* romances use chance, coincidence, surprise, and reversal to affirm that order and organization, not chaos, prevail in the world." He goes on to suggest that this is what appealed to European readers of the 18th century, when the old Judeo-Christian divine plan was being displaced by Newton's mechanical universe ("Romance as Genre," in Marzolph, 196, 211).

metropolis and nomadism, to name but a few."[103] Apparently composed in the middle of the 13th century and inserted into the *Nights* much later (for reasons more significant than to help expand the collection to 1,001 nights), *Umar al-Numan* is a military family saga set against the Muslim–Christian wars, a patriotic story that became revered by many Arabs despite what Ouyang calls "the deadly sins committed by 'Umar al-Nu'mān and his sons: jealousy, greed, rape, impatience, incest and treachery" (12).

The patriarch of the family, Caliph Umar of Baghdad, rules over a huge kingdom that stretches from China to Abyssinia, matched by a huge, unruly appetite for sex; in addition to the four wives allowed by the Quran, he "had three hundred and sixty concubines, equaling the number of the days of the Coptic year" (305). He spends one night a year with each of his calendar girls, each of a different nationality, until one of them — a Greek slave named Sophia — becomes pregnant. Umar's grown son Sharkan, worried about a potential rival heir to the throne, threatens to kill the child if it's a boy; the moment he hears Sophia has given birth to a girl named Nuzhat al-Zaman, he dashes off to the wars in Turkey; but then Sophia delivers a twin, a boy named Dau' al-Makan.

On the eve of an attack on the Byzantine army, Sharkan falls asleep on his horse and wakes to see a strange sight: 10 beautiful Christian girls are watching an even more beautiful one wrestle an old woman, whom she defeats. She then spots Sharkan and invites him for a tumble, but he's too aroused by her to fight and is beaten three times. The beautiful wrestler takes him to a nearby monastery and chastely entertains him, but the next day the Byzantine troops arrive to capture the Arab prince, tipped off by the old woman, Dhat al-Dawahi (Mother of Calamity), the villainess of the novel. It is then revealed that Sharkan's beautiful hostess is Abriza, daughter of the king of Caesarea (Palestine) and Calamity Dhat's granddaughter, and Umar's concubine Sophia the abducted daughter of the king of Constantinople, the two Christian kingdoms Umar's family will fight throughout the novel. By the time Abriza realizes who Sharkan is, she has fallen in love with him and is ready to convert to Islam, so they escape back to Baghdad — but not before Abriza and her troop of virgins engage in a mock battle with Sharkan and his Arabian knights, proving their equality. In Baghdad, lecherous old Umar is struck by Abriza's beauty, and her resistance to his advances drives him to drug and rape her when his son is away. (Later, Mother Calamity will get her revenge by distracting him with five "swelling-breasted virgins" posing as Islamic schoolgirls, and will poison him with a drug. So much for the progenitor of this proud Muslim family.) Nine months later, pregnant Abriza escapes from Baghdad, but just as she's ready to give birth, she is rudely propositioned

---

103 Ouyang, "Romancing the Epic," 17 n2. My reading of the novel is greatly indebted to this provocative essay.

by her black slave; angered at her refusal, he slays her moments after she's given birth to a boy that her servant will spirit away and raise until his return at the end of the novel.

At age 14, the twins Nuzhat and Dau' run away from home to join a pilgrimage heading west, but become separated in Jerusalem; the girl is abducted and taken to Damascus, where her older half-brother Sharkan is now governor. They have never met, and he winds up marrying and impregnating her before they realize they're related. Sharkan quickly marries her off to his chamberlain, and then the married couple heads back to Baghdad. Dau' al-Makan has been taken under the wing of a kindly bathhouse stoker and they unknowingly join the caravan for Baghdad that his sister happens to be leading. On the outskirts of Baghdad they learn that Umar has died, the brother and sister are reunited, and Dau' succeeds to the throne, promoting his older brother to king of Damascus. A chip off the old block, first thing Dau' does is do a doxy, who becomes pregnant, and then joins up with his brother to resume the wars against the infidel Christians. The Muslims are victorious at first, but Mother Calamity infiltrates their camp in the guise of an Islamic ascetic and causes setbacks, including the death of Sharkan, whose throat she slits with a poisoned knife.

Despondent outside the walls of Constantinople, the war bogged down, Dau' takes comfort in a long, convoluted love story told by his vizier Dandan, "The Tale of Aziz and Aziza, and of Prince Taj al-Muluk." After four years, the Muslim army decides to retreat to Baghdad, where Dau' learns he has a son named Kana-ma-Kana, who grows up with Nuzhat's daughter Qudiya-fa-Kama.[104] Still despondent, Dau' dies young, and though he appointed Kana as his successor, the throne is seized by Nuzhat's husband. Angered, Kana begins a nomadic life as a brigand with a Bedouin companion, amassing great booty after numerous adventures. Eventually his father's loyal vizier Dandan raises an army, dethrones the usurper, and puts out a call for Kana, who returns to Baghdad in triumph. During the final pages, virtually every character in the novel still alive appears and gets what he or she deserves in a satisfying display of poetic justice. Final closure comes as Abriza's son Rumzan, who was raised a Christian but retained his allegiance to Islam, kills Mother Calamity, his great-grandmother. "She was crucified on the gate of Baghdad, and when her [Christian] companions saw what happened to her, they all embraced Islam" (613).

The author's symbolism is clear. Abriza's defeat of Mother Calamity in the wrestling match at the beginning of the novel presages Islam's eventual

104 All these names have allegorical significance: Nuzhat al-Zaman = Glory of Time, Dau' al-Makan = Light of Place, Kana-ma-kana = There Happened What Happened, Qudiya-fa-Kama = It Was Decreed and It Was. Mother of Calamity has already been noted, and shifty Sharkan is derived from the English word *shirk* (Ouyang, 14–15).

overthrow of Christianity, and Umar's impregnation of two Christian virgins to produce Islamic offspring projects the hope for the Islamic infiltration of Christian Europe and eventually the world. (We remember that Umar had 360 concubines of all nationalities.) The author seems untroubled by the reprehensible qualities of this founding family: Umar is a sex maniac and rapist, Sharkan was willing to kill his baby half-brother and commits incest with his half-sister, Nuzhat and Dau' defy their father and run away from home, and Dau' especially is a weakling: he owes his life to the stoker, is unable to win his war, and after retreating from Constantinople, he seems to wither away in depression. His son Kana, the hope for the future, is a thief who preys on innocent travelers. Hard to say if the author was being subversively ironic or was blinded by patriotism, but this dysfunctional family (like Faulkner's Sutpens) seems to be a rotten foundation on which to build a nation's hopes for the future.

Like any patriot, the author apparently felt the official moral values of his nation excused the actual practices of its citizens, and celebrates those values in the tale of Aziz and Prince Taj al-Muluk. Unlike the digression at the end of *Qamar al-Zaman*, the long tale Dandan tells near the end of *Umar* functions as an ethical balance to the unethical actions of the Umar family. Prince Taj of Persia one day happens upon a merchant named Aziz who tells a sad tale of how he abandoned his family-approved engagement to his selfless cousin Aziza in favor of two strange women who make a fool of him. He winds up castrated, loses Aziza, and is kicked out of his house. Aziz tells Taj of a lovely princess of the Camphor Islands who has refused to marry, but Taj patiently wins her over and is married with the approval of both families. The 70-page novella isn't as pat as that, for it contains numerous bizarre plot twists and turns, but it illustrates many points made back in the main part of the novel. For example, to prove her worth, Nuzhat gives a lecture on Islamic values, paraphrasing the Caliph Umar: "There are three types of women. First comes the true Muslim — pious, loving and prolific [like Aziza], who helps her husband against fate rather than helping fate against her husband. The second looks after her children and does no more [the second strange woman Aziz meets], while the third is a fetter placed by God on the neck of whomever He wills" (371), like the first strange woman Aziz encounters, the one who castrates him. Nuzhat and Dau' defy their parents as Aziz did his, but Dau"s son Kana-ma-Kana is more like Prince Taj, patiently biding his time. Dau' hears this story during a stalemate in the war against the Christians, but the moral is that the Believers will triumph over the Unbelievers if they are patient enough — and can resist strange women.

The author has quite a bit of fun at the expense of Christians, whom he calls *al-'isaba al-salibiyya*: "the crucifix gang." With a straight face he tells us that the bowel movements of the High Patriarch of Constantinople are collected, dried into a powder, and used as incense; sometimes it is spat upon and made into a paste to daub on the faces of Christian soldiers marching off to war.[105] On the other hand, the gullible Muslims are easily duped by Christian women on several occasions, and the most pious expounders of Islamic doctrine turn out to be female frauds. Outwardly patriotic and pious, the author may be thumbing his nose in both directions. As Eva Sallis notes, the *Nights* evolved "as a response or reaction to a rigid social and spiritual structure, and satisfies a need similar to that which generates carnival and carnivalesque inversions in popular cultures" (1). The author seems to have been more devoted to constructing an ingenious, inverted, ironic novel than to toeing the party line, and his brilliance isn't lost on the listening king after Shahrazad concludes the long tale, signalling a turning point in their relationship; as Dunyazad tells her big sister, "In all this time, it is only tonight that I have seen the king looking happy, and I hope your affair will turn out well" (613).

During this discussion of these three novels I've refrained from noting their relationship to the larger frame-tale that encloses them, but their points in common should be obvious. King Shahriyar's pre-Shahrazad practice of sleeping with a different girl every night differs from Umar's only in literalizing *la petite mort*, Nuzhat's display of learning mirrors Shahrazad's own while her death sentence resembles that hanging over the culprits in *The Story of the Hunchback*, and all three novels reinforce the prejudice against women that darkens the *Nights*. But as impressive as these individual novels may be, it is the complete *Arabian Nights* that seduced European audiences and inspired legions of writers. Because of its communal composition over a period of centuries it lacks the artistic coherence of similar, roughly contemporary works like the *Decameron* and *The Canterbury Tales* — both of which contain imported versions of some its tales — but the influence of the *Nights* is far greater than those European works. The last chapter of Irwin's *Companion*, wittily entitled "Children of the *Nights*," discusses dozens of the writers it has inspired, ranging from forgotten scriveners like Thomas Simon Guellette to early modernist masters like Proust and Joyce, to postmodernists of our own day. (Eastern novelists have finally come round to confronting it as well, most brilliantly in the novels of Naguib Mahfouz, Salman Rushdie, and Vikram Chandra.) There are more artistically refined Arabic works from the Middle Ages, even some novels longer than the *Nights*, but none of them approaches the seductive appeal of this vast work, this Arabian nightmare, this dark carnival, this . . .

But morning overtook the scholar, and he lapsed into silence.[106]

---

105 In Arabic and Indian novels, characters often take baths, but Christians rarely did during this period and thus stank to high heaven, which was likewise noted by the hygienic American Indians upon the arrival of the filthy Europeans and Pilgrims.

106 OK, I stole that from William H. Gass, *il miglior fabbro*, who thus ended his review of Irwin's *Companion*, reprinted in his *Temple of Texts* (87–95).

Among those more artistically refined works are two picaresque novels composed in rhymed prose, a style disliked by Muhammad (even though some of the Quran uses it) but popular with both pre-Islamic poets and later orators because of its euphony and ease of memorization. Around 994, a young Iranian rhetorician named al-Hamadhani (969–1008), nicknamed Badi al-Zaman (Wonder of the Age) for his verbal skills, composed a work named after the genre he created, the *Maqamat*.[107] It consists of a series of encounters, recalled by a narrator named Isa ibn Hisham fond of fine phrases and rare words, with a mysterious, silver-tongued vagabond in different parts of the Middle East who always turns out to be Abu al-Fath al-Iskandari, a wandering scholar who ekes out a living by dazzling folks with his rhetorical skills. "I roam about the interiors of the countries, in order that I might light upon the dish of a generous man," he replies when asked his occupation. "I have a mind served by a tongue, and rhetoric which my own fingers record."[108] Most of the episodes are only a few pages long; for example, here's a short one in which Abu al-Fath charms a gold coin from his mark with a fanciful extended metaphor:

Isa ibn Hisham related to us and said: When I desired to return from the Pilgrimage there came into my presence a youth and he said: "I have a young man of yellow origin who invites to unbelief and dances upon the finger. Exile has disciplined him. The desire for recompense has brought me to thee that I might represent his case before thee. He has demanded of thee in marriage a yellow damsel that pleaseth the company and rejoiceth the beholders. Now, if thou dost assent, there will be begotten of them both an offspring [praise] that will fill the regions and men's ears. And when thou hast folded this robe and rolled up this thread it will have preceded thee into thy country. Therefore now decide regarding the unfolding of what is in thine hand."

Said Isa ibn Hisham: I was astonished at his narration and his witticism in his solicitation, so I complied with his request. Then he recited saying: —

"By the lower hand, glory is duped,
But the hand of the generous man and his judgement are supreme." (41)

---

107 *Maqamat* is the plural of *maqama*, an occasion when one stands to address an assembly. It's been suggested "that it represents an informal, or disreputable, parallel to the *majlis* ('sitting, session') of the proper Muslim or Arabic scholar" (Meisami and Starkey, *Encyclopedia of Arabic Literature* 1:123).
108 Chap. 14 in Prendergast's stiff old translation, hereafter cited by chapter (i.e., maqama). However, Prendergast does offer copious annotations, which are absolutely necessary to appreciate al-Hamadhani's allusions and rhetorical devices.

In the longer ones, Abu al-Fath — usually dressed like a bum, a Beat Arab — improvises and/or parodies religious sermons, critiques of poets, a father's advice to his son, philosophical disputes, praise of horses, riddles, anecdotes about generous benefactors, and so on, each a "lavish display of erudition, intellectual obscurities, and the use of words of doubtful meaning," as his translator notes (20). The work even flirts with blasphemy, for the formulaic opening "Isa ibn Hisham related to us and said" imitates (if not parodies) the hadith, the records of Muhammad's sayings and activities. In one episode, Abu al-Fath serves as imam in a mosque and denounces wine-drinkers, per the Quran (5:90), then afterward skips off to a tavern.

At times Abu al-Fath comes across as little more than a conman, hustling people for money with his rhetorical tricks, and in one chapter is caught performing with a trained monkey, as though that's all he amounts to. Some critics are reminded of the anti-hero of a Spanish picaresque;[109] to Lenn Goodman he sounds like a Wildean dandy, delighting in acting out "the conflict between reality and appearance."[110] But at his best, Abu al-Fath is "a kind of knight-errant of literature" to quote his translator again (15), traveling the Arab world to display doughty deeds of rhetoric, jousting with opponents (maqamat 43 is a hilarious cursing contest) and glorifying the Arabic language with amazing verbal pyrotechnics.

Apparently his *Maqamat* consisted of 400 episodes; only 52 survive, so it is impossible to tell whether the work possessed an overall structure. We saw in Alharizi's similar *Book of Tahkemoni* a progression on the narrator's part from admiration to suspicion of his too-clever friend, but the surviving episodes give no indication of such growth on the part of Isa ibn Hisham. And as entertaining as the *Maqamat* is, it's not as dazzling as it could have been; as Prendergast notes in his introduction, al-Hamadhani boasted in his letters "of his ability to employ no less than four hundred artifices in writing and composition, such as the writing of a letter which, if read backwards, furnishes the required reply, or an epistle containing no dotted letters, or without using [certain letters], or a letter which if read one way constitutes an elegy, and, if taken in another, is a satire; . . ." (21). He refrained from such artifices in this novel, but later writers of maqamat wouldn't, so while al-Hamadhani can be credited with inventing the genre, others developed its full potential.

A century later, an Arab poet and philologist named al-Hariri (1054–1122) wrote a similar work, also called the *Maqamat*, that not only flaunted the artifices his predecessor used only in correspondence, but made the genre more novelistic by expanding the characterization and relationship of his two

---

109 Abdelfallah Kilito in Moretti's *Novel* 2:141, who cites James T. Monroe's *The Art of Badī' az-Zamān al-Hamadhānī as Picaresque Narrative* (Beirut: American University of Beirut, 1983).

110 "Hamadhani, *Schadenfreude*, and Salvation through Sin," 29.

protagonists, narrator al-Harith and the rogue rhetorician Abu Zayd. Instead of merely reporting on his chance encounters with the wandering wordsmith, as Isa ibn Hisham had, al-Harith also interacts with Abu Zayd, enjoying his company at times, condemning him at other times for his scams, alternately admiring Abu Zayd's wisdom and deploring the disreputable use to which he puts it. Although the novel doesn't progress chronologically, the penultimate maqama has Abu Zayd on his deathbed passing along his tricks of the trade to his son, and the final one features a touching reunion of the two protagonists, both weeping as they make their final farewells.

Abu Zayd is more than a literary conman; he is a born outsider, in self-imposed exile from society, almost a Byronic hero doomed to wander the earth. He is also that rarest of creatures in Arabic culture, an individualist. Asked his ancestry at one point, he sneers at the importance of family and fate:

> "A curse on him who boasts of mouldering bones!" said he. "There is no glory but in piety and choice scholarship. By your life, man is but the son of his own day, according as that day displays itself, he is not the son of his yesterday. There is no boast in rotten bones; there is only the glory of him who seeks glory through himself."[111]

More often than Abu al-Fath, a performer rewarded for his displays of wit, Abu Zayd uses his gift of gab to play confidence games. Many of his hustles involve impersonating a preacher or mullah, using Islamic doctrine to con his devout listeners out of their money, which he'll then blow in a tavern that night, breaking every rule in the Quran. Usually dressed as an old beggar, he'll also fake blindness or lameness, disguise himself as an old woman, and occasionally enlist his son in his scams. When not fleecing regular folks or conning a magistrate, Abu Zayd will seek out an assembly of the learned, listen to their literary talk until they "empty their quivers" of wit, and then outdo them in critical ingenuity or challenge them with linguistic riddles. Although the entire novel is written in imagistic, musical prose, these are the chapters in which al-Hariri shines: in one maqama, Abu Zayd delivers a 200-word palindrome, in another recites a poem in which every other line avoids the dots that define Arabic letters, in yet another he astounds a group of grammarians with a dozen riddles based on abstruse points of Arabic

---

111 Chap. 25 in Amina Shah's translation, hereafter cited by chapter (maqama). Except for some notes on a few of the more difficult maqamat, her translation lacks annotations, essential for an allusive work like this. The older translation by Chenery and Steingass has annotations galore, but tends toward the Burtonesque ("I wept by reason of the weeping of his eyne, as I had wept heretofore anent him"); plus it's impossible to find outside of the largest academic libraries. (This is an appropriate place to acknowledge the fabulous Harlan Hatcher Graduate Library at the University of Michigan in Ann Arbor, where I did all the research for this book. Its Asian collection in particular is a veritable Ali Baba's cave of treasures.)

philology (al-Hariri gives the answers in an appendix), and in maqama 32 he impersonates a mullah and gives what appear to be shocking answers to 100 thorny religious questions, each redeemed by a rare or obsolete meaning of a word. (It's as though a priest today, asked if it's OK to have intercourse with a neighbor's wife, were to answer Yes — meaning *intercourse* in its original sense of *conversation*.) Others consist of riddles based on wordplay that is baffling even to Arabic readers because of their reliance on uncommon words and obscure idioms. Most of this is lost in translation, of course, but Abu Zayd's linguistic circus acts must be quite a show in the original.

Though his topics are usually edifying and steeped in the Quran, there's something subversive about using noble thoughts to dupe the unwary and confound the learned, making a mockery of the grammarians and religious scholars who argue over recondite points of language and law. As in Lyly's novels, style is privileged over substance, and the substance often compromised by the rhetorical hoops the author puts it through. In the 50th and final maqama, set in Basra (where al-Hariri lived), Abu Zayd ostensibly repents; for once he appears undisguised, and after delivering an encomium on Basra and its citizens, he apologizes for his wayward ways. The populace "doled out to him whatever each had at hand" — the same reward he used to get after his scams — and Abu Zayd returns to his hometown of Seruj. Al-Harith tracks him down there, and listens as his old friend utters a lovely, Whitmanesque farewell to his soul, repenting for the nights he spent "in sins that none before had dared," and asking Allah for forgiveness. He seems to be sincere, but given everything that has gone before this, one cannot help but suspect the wily word-slinger is staging his greatest imposture of all, conning Allah himself out of a place in paradise.

The scholarly community loved al-Hariri's *Maqamat* from the start, despite its mockery of their pedantry, and it became the subject of more commentaries than any other book after the Quran. (The example of Joyce comes to mind, both the difficulty of his work and the avidity with which some scholars have tackled that difficulty.) As noted in chapter 2, the novel so impressed the Spanish Jew Judah Alharizi that he not only translated it into Hebrew, but went on to compose his own maqamat, attempting to outdo al-Hariri by as much as he did al-Hamadhani.

While Abu Zayd goes into self-imposed exile, the protagonist of *Hayy ibn Yaqzan* has exile forced upon him. Written sometime in the 12th century by an Arab physician of Andalusia named Abu Bakr ibn Tufayl (c. 1116–85), this short novel introduced a popular topos of later novels: the desert island story, in which an individual or group, cut off from civilization, reenacts the origins of civilization. *Hayy ibn Yaqzan* takes the form of a long letter from the author to a disciple eager to learn about the mystical teachings of the Persian philosopher Ibn Sina (aka Avicenna, 980–1037). Avicenna had written some short "visionary recitals" featuring characters on a mystical quest, so his admirer Ibn Tufayl borrowed the names of a few of them to tell his correspondent an allegorical tale of the growth of a soul.[112]

Set on "a certain equatorial island, lying off the coast of India," the tale concerns an individual named Hayy ibn Yaqzan (literally Alive, son of Awake), the sole inhabitant of the island. There are two versions, Ibn Tufayl writes, of his birth: spontaneous generation (which the author favors) and a romantic tale of a baby abandoned, like Moses and Amadis of Gaul, in a small boat that made its way to this island, where the baby was rescued and nourished by a doe.[113] Thereafter, Hayy develops in seven-year installments: until the age of seven he is reared by his "foster-mother" and imitates other animals; at age seven he realizes he is different from the other animals, specifically in lacking cover for his private parts, which makes him "very unhappy" and spurs him to create clothes for himself, whereby he discovers the superiority of his hands and toolmaking abilities, which restores his self-esteem.[114] From seven to 21 he learns to become more independent, especially after the doe dies, and becomes more inquisitive: he performs a rough autopsy on his foster-mother, which gives him the first inkling of some animating spirit apart from the body; then becomes fascinated with fire as a symbol of that spirit; and then makes the metaphoric leap to assume stars are similar fire spirits, or mystical beings. From 21 to 35 he develops a system of metaphysics — paralleling the historical development of metaphysics from Plato and Aristotle to Avicenna and al-Ghazali — and from 35 to 49 seeks and attains enlightenment, specifically that of a Sufi mystic/whirling dervish. (The reaction of the island's animals to Hayy's trance-dances is not recorded.) Starving himself and retiring to a cave, he spends his time in self-induced hallucinatory ecstasies until one day, at age 50, during one of his rare excursions from the cave, he spots another human.

Absal had been living on the nearby island where Hayy was born, but unlike his brother Salaman preferred private contemplation to public forms of worship and sailed to Hayy's island to live in isolation and tearful prayer. When the two religious nuts first behold each other, Absal assumes he has encountered another anchorite and runs away, but curious Hayy tracks him down, watches him pray, and assumes he is "one of those beings who know the Truth," just as he does (158). Hayy makes friends with Absal, who in turn teaches him to speak and fills him in on Islam, which just happens to correspond with Hayy's own revelations of the Truth. After Absal tells him of the

112 A translation of Ibn Sina's "Recital of Hayy ibn Yaqzan" can be found in Corbin's *Avicenna and the Visionary Recital*, 137–50.
113 Thus in Goodman's translation (106), though Corbin says the Arabic word *zabya* means "gazelle" (225 n26), a common synonym in Arabic and Persian for a young woman.
114 In *Gilgamesh* it was sex that made Enkidu realize he was different from the animals, but this is a religious novel, so there's no sex, only shame.

Muslims back on his home island, and "how stupid, inadequate, thoughtless, and weak willed they are, 'like sheep gone astray, only worse'" (162, quoting Quran 7:179), Hayy is bitten by the preaching bug and wants to go to the island to "save" them. But the sheep don't respond, so Hayy and Absal return to the uninhabited island, reveling in religious ecstasies "until man's certain fate overtook them" (165).

Since Ibn Tufayl wanted to impart a religious philosophy rather than tell an adventure story, we shouldn't fault him for not taking more advantage of his promising topos. After Hayy learns to fend for himself as a child we hear nothing about his daily life on the island, only his endless metaphysical musings. Nor was the author concerned about realism: Hayy's shame at his exposed genitals wouldn't occur to a feral child, none of whom (in the accounts I know) ever developed a religious sensibility either. Religion is a social construct, not a natural instinct; even Muhammad is alleged to have said, "Every infant is born in a natural state. It is his parents who make him a Jew or a Christian or a Magian."[115] Rather, Ibn Tufayl wanted to show that Sufi mysticism is the logical result of the metaphysical tradition and the highest form of worship, implying that any intelligent individual, completely isolated, would reach the same conclusion even without all the books of philosophy and religion Ibn Tufayl himself used to reach that conclusion. As a result, *Hayy ibn Yaqzan* belongs more to the history of Islamic theology than to literature, but it has its place in the history of the novel, both for its own sake and for its influence: it was translated into Hebrew in 1349, into Latin in 1671, into Dutch in 1672, and three times into English between 1674 and 1708 — the third and best known version, Simon Ockley's, appearing 11 years before the publication of *Robinson Crusoe*.[116]

The erudite fictions of al-Hamadhani, al-Hariri, and Ibn Tufayl were aimed at the elite; the masses preferred to hear stories from *The Arabian Nights* and especially the long adventure novels known as *siyar*, of which a dozen survive. Similar in content (if not religiosity) to the lengthy Arthurian novels of the later Middle Ages, the typical *sira* features a heroic Arab who fights in countless battles, romances at least one wife, engages occasionally in supernatural adventures, and finally dies a heroic death. (*The Adventures of Dhat al-Himma* is about a warrior queen, but all of the others are male-dominated.) The earliest were based on oral tales that originated in pre-Islamic Arabia, the later ones based on more recent historical events, and all were expanded upon (and sometimes anachronistically updated) by generations of anonymous

115 Ibn Khaldun, *Muqaddimah* (14th century), as quoted by Goodman, 69.
116 Pastor, *The Idea of Robinson Crusoe*, a leisurely account of Ibn Tufayl's novel.

storytellers and editors until they were committed to written form between the 13th and 16th centuries. They weren't studied as literature — even though they used the same rhyming-prose style of the maqamat and included reams of poetry — but used largely as promptbooks by coffeehouse performers, right up to the last century in some places (like Egypt), when serial radio programs and then television soap operas took their place as the preferred entertainment of the masses.

Only two of these siyar have been translated into English, and only in greatly abridged form. The most famous is *The Adventures of Antar* (*Sirat 'Antar*), which is gigantic: about 6,000 pages long, more than twice the length of *The Arabian Nights*.[117] In 1819 and 1820 Terrick Hamilton published a four-volume English translation, but it covers only the first third of an *abridged* version. (Despite being hyped as even better than *The Arabian Nights*, his *Antar* had a lukewarm reception, so Hamilton abandoned his plan to translate the rest.) In 1980, Harry Norris published a hundred-page selection of passages, including the protagonist's famous death scene. There are some lengthy summaries of the entire novel in English,[118] but it seems unlikely we'll ever have a complete translation.

The Adventures of Antar is based loosely on a historical figure named Antara ibn Shaddah, a warrior and poet who lived a generation before Muhammad. The son of an Arab chieftain and a black slave-girl, baby Antar is a fright: "black and swarthy like an elephant, flat nosed, blear eyed, harsh featured, shaggy haired; the corner of his eyes bloated" (Hamilton, 1:25). As a boy he's a bully and a brute, but eventually his strength and fearlessness endear him to his tribe. He falls in love with his (white) cousin Abla, which inspires him to become a poet, but because of the racial and class differences, his romance is put on hold and he goes off to become a marauder in the desert. Still technically a slave, Antar eventually wins both his freedom and Abla after a series of escapades. Thereafter, it's the usual stuff of military adventure novels: raids and retaliations, escapes and pursuits, betrayals and reconciliations, insults and reprisals, alarums and excursions, and endless warfare, both intertribal and foreign, which takes Antar all over the Muslim world, from Ethiopia to India. Much of the narration is merely expository, though the many battle scenes feature some imagistic writing, as in this encounter between the Ethiopian army and Antar's Arabs (Banū = tribe):

That battle raged from the first third of the night until sunrise. When it was light the negroes attacked again. They were met by Antar and the Banū 'Abs. Spears were pointed at

---

117 And *The Adventures of Baybars* is even longer than *Antar*! A French translation is being published by Editions Sindbad in Paris that is expected to reach 60 volumes.
118 Lyons, *The Arabian Epic*, 3:17–76, and Heath, *The Thirsty Sword*, 168–231. In fact, Lyons's massive book provides detailed summaries of the dozen surviving siyar.

their chests and blood flowed like a river. The earth trembled, and the crow hovered above the corpse. There was a flash of blade and spear-point. Spears were aligned like serpents at the heart. The Banū 'Abs shrieked aloud. The coward sought to flee. The bodies of the negroes were heaped in the sandy valleys. The wind from the spears blew above them, and death's clouds shed their rain. The goblet of mortality was drunk to its last drops. Both sides were finely balanced, and men's souls were sold cheap after they had offered them for a high price. (Norris, 113)

This led some early European admirers to declare *Antar* the *Iliad* of the Arabs, though that's overly generous. What I read of it was entertaining in a B-movie sort of way, and the development of Antar from a racist stereotype to a noble hero is admirable, but I can't say I'm disappointed there's no complete translation available.[119]

On the other hand, I wish there were more of the hugely entertaining *Adventures of Sayf ben Dhi Yazan* (*Sirat Faris al-Yaman al-Malik Saif ibn Dhi Yazan*); Lena Jayyusi's translation covers only the first 500 of this 2,000-page novel, relating the early years of this heroic king of Yemen. If *Antar* is Arabic literature's *Iliad*, then *Sayf* is its *Odyssey*: its protagonist wanders all over the known and imaginary world, confronts all sorts of supernatural creatures and malignant spells, and survives not because of his wit (like the wily Greek) but because of his Penelope, a jinniya named Aqisa who loves and watches over him.

First a word about the novel's chronology, which then needs to be ignored: it's a mess, no doubt because of multiple authorship. *Sayf* apparently began, like *Antar*, as a fictionalized account of an actual Yemeni king of the 6th century famous for driving the invading Ethiopians out of his country. Then, a later author decided to mythologize this conflict by aligning it with the Jewish explanation for the origin of the black race, namely, Noah's curse on his disrespectful son Ham (progenitor of the black Ethiopians) and his prophecy that the black race would be subservient to the offspring of his respectful son Shem (progenitor of the white Arabs).[120] Another more pious author, uncomfortable with Sayf's pre-Islamic status as a pagan, probably wrote the opening pages of the novel, in which it is firmly stated that Sayf's father had a wise minister who "had found — in the Torah, and the Bible, and the writings of Abraham the Friend of God, and the scrolls of David — the name of our master Muhammad" (1). Hence the novel is anachronistically filled with Muslims praising Allah and infidels converting to Islam long before Muhammad was

---

119 Peter Heath's *Thirsty Sword* not only makes a measured case for *Antar*'s importance but is also an ideal introduction to popular Arabic fiction of the Middle Ages.

120 At one point the protagonist is told his lineage: "your name is King Sayf Ben Dhi Yazan, son of the Tubba'i Yemeni king, son of King Asad al-Baida', son of King Shem, who was brother to King Ham, and your grandfather was Noah" (95). If taken literally, this would place the novel in biblical times, which would create an even greater chronological mess.

even born. The original 6th-century setting receded even further when the novel's final author/editor gave the same name to Sayf's archenemy as that of the Ethiopian king who was harassing Muslim kingdoms in the 14th century. Apparently the authors/editors wanted merely to establish the transhistorical opposition between black/pagan and white/Arab for narrative tension while they focused on their real goal: to tell the most outlandishly imaginative tale in Arabic literature, outdoing even *The Arabian Nights* in magic and wonder.

Malcolm Lyons's succinct summary of the entire novel occupies 55 pages of small type in *The Arabian Epic* (586–641), but it can be boiled down to two major narrative arcs, one political, the other romantic: Sayf's rocky path toward kingship, which is opposed by his evil mother Qamariyya and the Ethiopian king's two evil wizards, Saqardis and Saqardyoun; and Sayf's no less rocky acquisition of about a dozen wives over the course of his adventures. This bride quest, and the extensive reliance on the supernatural, recalls Gunadhya's *Brihatkatha*, which may have been a distant source; but while Prince Naravahanadatta actively wooed his wives, Sayf passively receives proposals by virgins he meets and marries them usually out of a sense of obligation.

In fact, women play a surprisingly active role in this novel: Sayf's mother's selfish and "unnatural" desire to rule the kingdom alone after her husband dies kick-starts the plot. After failing to cut off her baby's head, Qamariyya abandons Sayf in the desert, where he is first suckled by a gazelle (like Hayy), then by a passing jinniya — whose daughter Aqisa thus becomes his foster-sister — before he is found and delivered to a black king named Afrah, who rears the boy alongside his daughter Shama. Sayf grows up and goes off to train as a warrior, and returns just in time to save grown-up Shama from a forced marriage. *She* then suggests he ask her father for her hand, but to forestall the marriage the sorcerer Saqardyoun — Afrah's advisor — sets two difficult tasks for Sayf by way of a dowry. Shama helps him achieve the first, but he refuses her suggestion of an elopement and leaves to accomplish the second task alone: locating the magical *Book of the Nile,* which will allow the river — currently blocked in Ethiopia — to flow up to Egypt and enable the founding of Cairo. He meets a holy man named Jiyad who converts him to Islam and tells Sayf he is destined to marry a girl named Tama, the daughter of a sorceress. (Every other character in this novel seems to be a magician.) Shortly afterward, he literally runs into her disguised as a mounted knight, a trick Shama had also played on Sayf and typical of the many role-reversals in this novel, where women act like men and Sayf relies on them for advice and protection. (Predictably, he later dresses as a woman during one of his adventures.) Tama's mother Aqila devises several clever schemes to help passive Sayf obtain *The Book of the Nile,* and he becomes engaged to Tama, though insisting he is obligated to marry Shama first. He soon meets fiancée #3, the daughter of a king of China, then reunites with his foster-sister jinniya Aqisa, who rescues him again and again — and so it goes, as Sayf undergoes every conceivable fantastic adventure while being manipulated by women, both the mother who continues to try to kill him and the resourceful girls who save him.

The authors apparently intended this to be the ultimate Arabian fantasy novel, for virtually every magical device, trope, and mythic motif is included: the jinn, sea monsters, talking birds, flying horses, magical rings and swords, a cap that confers invisibility, flying machines, bizarre cities, ghouls, giants, dwarfs, mermaids, and magical journeys through the air (measured in time rather than distance). As in the James Bond movies, Sayf's captors often devise needlessly complicated ways of killing him, which he always foils, often with the help of magic. It's an enchanted, bewitched world that would seem to be at odds with the dour monotheism of Islam, but the authors cleverly insist that all things are possible with Allah, and portray him as the ultimate wizard. At one point Sayf wants to steal the magical robe that allows a beautiful woman to fly, and without a jinniya or magician nearby, he prays to Allah to help him on what amounts to a panty-raid; waiting until she has disrobed and is playing in a lake,

> Then King Sayf Ben Dhi Yazan reached out and took the feather robe, placing it within his garments, while the All-Compassionate and All-Concealing One kept him hidden; and he made his way back from the shelter of the trees till he reached the place beneath the wheel, his tongue never ceasing or forgetting all the while to invoke the Lord of Lords who had aided him in seizing that robe. (176)

In this novel, there is a deadly opposition between Islam and paganism — those who don't convert are mercilessly killed — but not between Islam and magic. (The Quran acknowledges the existence of the jinn.) Religion has always been the official, institutionalized version of magic and superstition, so as with many folks today there's no conflict in Sayf's mind between magic spells and prayers, between supernatural wonders and the ways of Allah. At times, the authors seem to be taking this position merely as a cover for their outlandish fantasies, even teasing the faithful about their credulity; it's hard to believe the All-Compassionate One would claim as one of his creations the islands of Waq al-Waq, where women grow on trees and can be eaten like fruit, though Sayf's giant guide insists otherwise when Sayf hesitates:

> "One would think," said the giant, "that you doubt their nature as fruit. Do you not know that God has power to make all things? Was it not He who created the Universe?"
> And so King Sayf Ben Dhi Yazan asked the giant to bring him one. "I hear and obey," said the giant; then, approaching a tall tree, he seized a maiden by the hair, plucked

her from the branch where she was, and brought her to King Sayf, saying: "Take it, my lord."

King Sayf contemplated her hands and her feet and the green-black color of her eyes, and said: "Praise be to the One who shaped her and gave her being."

Then the giant advanced and, taking her in his hands, broke her in two pieces, then removed the peel from the sides, so that a fragrance rose from her sweeter than heavy musk; and he saw that the inner part was laid out in segments like an orange, each the full length of the body, like the ribs of a human being, and that her right arm was like jasmine and her left likewise. And when King Sayf Ben Dhi Yazan ate from it, he found the taste to be like the taste of tender walnut, and sweeter than honey, finer than all other foods. (249)

The giant also notes that one can have sex with these sweeties before turning them into a snack — the ultimate frat-boy fantasy. But at this point our authors turn coy; Sayf plucks one tasty-looking maiden from the tree, and then? "He had been some time absent from his womenfolk, and it is said by some that he joined with her forthwith, as the Sovereign Lord decreed; but others say he declined to do so out of decency before God the Ruler of All Realms" (258). Note how Allah would approve either way since Sayf is a good Muslim.

Setting such nonsense aside, it's obvious that the true wizards here are the authors, who have conjured up an extraordinary world with ink and paper that overshadows the real one:

And so the eighty magicians entered their place of divination, remaining there all that day and night; then, on the second day they came out with their enchantment set down on a piece of white paper inscribed with charms and Syriac names and Hebrew writings, and murmured their spells over this till it soared up in the air, rising still till it reached at last to the top of the palace in which Qamariyya lay. Then it spread itself, growing ever larger till it covered the very turrets of the palace, and folding down its edges all around, it descended to the earth; and every spot of the darkness rose to the upper side of the paper, leaving none remaining within the palace. Then the paper itself rose up, so that the darkness wrought by Barnoukh [another sorcerer] was lifted, and light returned to the palace just as before, and Queen Qamariyya was afflicted no more. (191)

"It spread itself, growing ever larger" — just as this novel did over the centuries. And the authors leave no doubt who the real heroes are in this heroic tale:

> A hero's sword that lopped ten peaks;
>> that's a thing we have not known.
> But we have known a drop of ink
>> that could a thousand flags haul down. (227)

496

The pen is mightier than even the sword of Shem that Sayf wins. Writing as magic, as enchantment, as a rival creation emerges as the main activity of the novel, a magic show performed with words rather than props. After Sayf marries the half-dozen fiancées he has racked up so far — he takes the maidenheads of two of them on the same night — and after Aqisa kills his mother, Sayf's subsequent adventures have more to do with converting the heathen, and as he ages we begin to hear of his sons' adventures. But the ostensible history lesson of how a pious Yemeni king drove out the blacks, founded Cairo, and spread Islam throughout the world takes a back seat to the jaw-dropping descriptions of more mysterious cities, a fire-breathing elephant, a green horse, a parallel universe where Sayf and his court visit their "duplicates," more brides (including a few giantesses), snakes that turn into beautiful girls, man-eating ghouls, Saif's season as a crow, his further rescues by and fights with Aqisa (his gal Friday starts pressuring him for marriage), magic cows and mules, a fruit that causes a sex change, the City of Brass from *The Arabian Nights*, invisible beings, a magic mirror, Satan (Iblis) himself, and "a chest that distracts anyone who enters it from the cares of the world" (Lyons, 637), another analogue for the novel itself. The unflagging creativity and unbounded imagination at work here is astounding; there are literary and folkloric antecedents for some of these things, but about halfway through the novel one of the authors drops a hint about another likely source for their creativity: as Lyons notes, "There follows an interjected episode of two opium eaters who try out the baths in the new quarters. One agrees that his hair is too long, and promptly has it removed and his scalp cauterised, while the other is dismayed by a jinni who elongates his arm to fetch him a bowl" (613). Whoa, dude! At a realistic level, the whole novel could be considered a long opium dream experienced by the historical King Sayf of Yemen after a tough day. But wherever the inspiration came from, *The Adventures of Sayf ben Dhi Yazan* is one of the great fantasy novels of world literature; as with its contemporary counterparts in France (e.g., the *Lancelot-Grail* and *Perceforest*) the religiosity can become tiresome — Sayf robotically repeats "God is great" at every crisis — but passages like the following remind us who the real authors of creation are:

> With that she [Tama] raised the veil from her face to reveal a countenance like the full moon, round as a shield of bright crystal, with cheeks on which roses were strewn, fashioned by the All-Forgiving Sovereign, and eyes like the eyes of the gazelle, with glances darting arrows and lances that had power to strike the boldest of men, and a neck like a pillar of precious stone set on a bosom smooth as marble, on which were set breasts before which a lion might bow its head. (39)

Allah akbar!

None of the other surviving siyar contains as much magic as *Sayf*, but they all sound like entertaining adventure novels, and it's a shame none of them has been translated. But instead of progressing from these to more sophisticated novels as their European and Chinese counterparts did at the end of the Middle Ages, Arabic novelists gave up, part of the general stagnation of Arabic culture that had set in by that point.[121] Besides, fiction had always been frowned upon by most Arab rhetoricians, who insisted any writing not based on truth or history was merely a lie, and so of no redeeming social (i.e., theological) value. Irwin quotes a 14th-century Syrian religious scholar who told his copyists to ignore "deceptive books 'by which Allah does not offer any useful thing, such as *Sirat 'Antar* and other fabricated things.'"[122] Fiction was taken about as seriously then as comic books are today by most of our cultural mullahs. It didn't help that lofty religious sentiments were sometimes used merely as props in literary magic acts, as in the maqamat, or that Allah's creation was recklessly expanded to include hallucinatory fantasies, as in *Sayf* and the *Nights*. There were cultural reasons as well: Most novels are about individuals at odds with their community standards; Muslim culture is very community-minded, to put it mildly — the most successful and frightening brainwashing operation in human history is more like it — and doesn't encourage individualism. Most characters in Arabic fiction are stock figures — the ambitious king, the beautiful princess, the evil mother, the gallant prince, the crafty advisor — whose actions are either black or white, "without our hesitating retinue of finer shades," as T. E. Lawrence once put it.[123] The Quran always speaks of *groups* of people, usually reduced to believers and unbelievers, rarely individuals, aside from some historical models like Abraham and Noah. Even then, these figures have none of the personal quirks of their counterparts in the Tanakh, and there's nothing in the Quran remotely like the psychologically subtle travails of David or Job. In a totalitarian culture where imagination is distrusted and individualism discouraged, it's no surprise that the novel didn't flourish. The jinni went back into his magic lamp and wouldn't come out again for centuries.

121 For succinct explanations, see Bernard Lewis's *What Went Wrong? The Clash between Islam and Modernity in the Middle East* (NY: Oxford UP, 2002) and Dan Diner's *Lost in the Sacred: Why the Muslim World Stood Still* (Princeton: Princeton UP, 2009).

122 *Night and Horses and the Desert*, 417.

123 In *Seven Pillars of Wisdom*, Lawrence observed that the Arabs "had no half-tones in their register of vision. They were a people of primary colours, or rather of black and white, who saw the world always in contour. They were a dogmatic people, despising doubt, our modern crown of thorns. They did not understand our metaphysical difficulties, our introspective questionings. They knew only truth and untruth, belief and unbelief, without our hesitating retinue of finer shades" (chap. 3).

PERSIAN FICTION

"The divers in the ocean of historiography, and those who have plunged into the sea of stories of the past, obtain the pearls of narrative in this manner:"[124] The Arab/Islamic conquest of Iran in the middle of the 7th century dealt a severe blow to Persian culture: that a 1,300-year-old civilization could be over-run by a horde of religious fanatics with no previous culture to speak of was deeply humiliating and was followed by what the late Iranian scholar Abdol-Hussein Zarrinkoub called the "two centuries of silence."[125] Much early Persian literature disappeared during this period, partly due to the switch from Pahlavi to Arabic script, leaving earlier works to fade into oblivion, and partly due to Muslim depredations (as would happen in India a bit later). A 9th-century Muslim governor of Khurasan (in northeast Iran) — I'm not going to preserve the barbarian's name — said of one early Persian romance:

"'We are men who read the Qur'ān, and we need nothing beside the Qur'ān and the Traditions of the Prophet. Of such books as this we have no need, for they are compila-tions of the Magians, and are objectionable in our eyes.' Then he ordered the book to be thrown into the water, and issued orders that wherever in his dominions there should be any books composed by the Persians and Magians, they should all be burned. Hence till the time of the House of Sāmān [10th century], no Persian poems were seen, and if now and then poetry was composed [in Persian], it was not collected."[126]

When Persian writers recovered their voices in the 10th century, it was to compile story-cycles like the *Hazar Afsan* and *Sindibadnama* — the originals of *The Arabian Nights* and *Tales of Sendebar*, respectively — many translated from or inspired by Sanskrit fiction. Another durable literary model for the Persian novelists who would emerge in the 10th and 11th centuries was the ancient Greek novel. Persia and Greece had of course been in contact with each other almost from the beginning of Persian civilization; the Greek his-torians Herodotus and Ctesias wrote about Persia in the 5th century BCE, and you'll recall that the first Greek novel, Xenophon's *Education of Cyrus*, was about a Persian emperor. Greek culture was especially influential in Persia during the Parthian period (c. 250 BCE–225 CE), the same period in which most of the classic Greek novels were written. Just as the Byzantines would

---

124 From the *Dastan of Amir Hamzah* (see below), 109.
125 Quoted (but not named) in Dick Davis's introduction to his translation of *Shahnameh*, xvii. This *Book of Kings* is a vast epic poem covering Persian history from the creation of the world to the Muslim conquest. Written by Abolqasem Ferdowsi between 975 and 1010, it has influenced virtually every Persian writer since. (Though Iran has always been the correct name for the nation, I'll be using it and Persia interchangeably, as do most writers on the premodern period.)
126 Browne, *A Literary History of Persia*, 2:275–76, quoting a 15th-century scholar named Dowlatshah.

soon do, Persian writers rediscovered these romances and began writing their own, the better (writerly) ones in verse — again like the Byzantines — the others in readerly prose.

A direct line of influence, for example, has been traced from the early Greek romance *Metiokhos and Parthenope* (1st century BCE) to the 11th-century verse-novel *Vamiq and Adhra* by the Ghaznavid court poet Abu al-Qasim Unsuri (c. 970–c. 1040), a later version of the novel thrown into the water by that Muslim governor. Unfortunately, both novels survive only in fragments, but what remains indicates that they told a love story set in Greece during the time of Alexander the Great.[127] Another Persian novel that used the Grecian formula, Ayyuqi's *Varqah and Gulshah*, was written around the same time as *Vamiq and Adhra*, but has not yet been translated into English. In this case, however, the resemblance is coincidental: *Varqah* reads like a standard Greek novel but was likely based on an Arabic source.[128]

The first major Persian novel is Fakhr ud-Din Gurgani's *Vis and Ramin*, another 11th-century novel in verse that fortunately is both complete and available in a lovely English translation in prose by George Morrison.[129] Though it too has elements in common with the Greek novel, the first thing that strikes the reader is its remarkably close resemblance to the legend of Tristan and Iseut. Vis is a young woman promised in marriage to Shah Moubad, old enough to be her father. But she catches the eye of Prince Ramin, the king's younger brother (not nephew, as in the Tristan story), and thereafter Vis and Ramin have a series of clandestine affairs while Moubad tries to catch them at it, just like the Cornish king Mark. And just as Tristan later leaves the Irish Iseut to marry the Breton Iseut of the White Hands, Ramin temporarily leaves Vis and marries a beautiful princess named Gul ("Rose") before realizing he needs to return to his first love. Translator Morrison provides dozens of other parallels in his introduction and footnotes, giving credence to the belief of some literary historians that this old Persian romance made its way to Europe (possibly via the Seljuk court of Syria) and helped shape the better-known Celtic version of the tale of the tragic lovers. The principal difference, however, is the ending; instead of dying young, like Tristan and Iseut, Ramin marries Vis after Moubad is killed by a boar, and they live happily for 80 years thereafter.

127 In *The Virgin and Her Lover* Hägg and Utas give a fascinating account of how the two remote fragments were eventually matched up. They also provide translations of the surviving portions of both.

128 Davis, *Panthea's Children*, 6 and n2. Graham Anderson finds numerous parallels, not all convincing, between the ancient Greek novel and Oriental fiction in general in his *Ancient Fiction* (1984).

129 Published in 1972, it will be cited by chapter hereafter. (After I wrote this section, a verse translation by Dick Davis appeared in early 2008, but since Davis omits some useful material at the beginning and end, I decided to retain the citations to Morrison's fuller version.)

The story may have originated as early as the Parthian period, and remained popular even after the Islamic takeover of Iran, despite its pagan (Zoroastrian) elements. Gurgani, a court poet, composed his highly polished version of the tale sometime between 1050 and 1055; as he explains in chapter 7, the Muslim governor of Khurasan — whose name, unlike the earlier one, I'm happy to preserve: Amid Abu'l-Fath Muzaffar — once asked him what he thought of the old tale of Vis and Ramin. Gurgani admitted it was a fine story, but that it was written in Pahlavi (a dying language by that time) and was rather artless: a readerly work rather than a writerly one. "If a scholar were to apply himself to it," he observed, "it would become as pretty as a treasure full of gems; for this is a famous story, whose incidents contain numberless marvels." So his patron told him: "Beautify this story as April the garden," planting the seeds for the horticultural imagery that flourishes throughout the novel.

It is indeed filled with numberless marvels, but marvels of language rather than supernatural marvels (as in much Arabic fiction). Before Vis was born, Shah Moubad wanted to marry her mother Shahru, princess of Media, who puts him off by claiming she is too old for him (i.e., pushing 30), but nevertheless taunts him with her former glory, a typical specimen of Gurgani's superlative style:

> "You did not see me in my young days, all charm and willfulness and gaiety, grown as straight as the lofty cypress; the breeze wafted scent from my twin forelocks, I was in the springtime of my life, like the willow bough by the stream. In broad daylight the sun lost its way at the sight of me, the moon missed its way by night. Many a face lost its radiance because of me, many an eye became sleepless! If one day I so much as passed along a lane, it would smell of jasmine for a whole year! My beauty made slaves of kings, my scent brought the dead back to life." (10)

(All of the women in this novel are supremely confident of their beauty.) Instead of marrying the shah, she promises him he can have the next daughter she gives birth to. (She seems to have a very open marriage with a man named Qarin; much later during a fight, the shah tells Vis that "Shahru has had more than thirty children; she has not borne two children to one single husband!" [48].) This rash promise, the author tells us, is the source of all the woe that follows: "See into what tribulation they fell from giving away an unborn child as a bride!" (10).

By the time Vis reaches marriageable age, Shahru has forgotten her promise and instead weds the girl to Viru, Vis's brother.[130] They fail to consummate the marriage because the incompetent astrologers recommended a wedding

---

130 "Now brother and sister marriage was not only possible in pre-Islamic Iran," Davis says, "it was held to be meritorious" (67).

day on which Vis would be menstruating, which is described with the same decorative beauty Gurgani brings to everything in this novel: "Indisposition broke from the body of the beauty of silvery frame; the wild lily became dabbled with blood. That Moon of two weeks became for one week as if a mine of rubies was aflow" (25). Coincidentally, Moubad has sent a messenger to remind Shahru of her old promise, and when the shah learns of her alternative arrangement, he attacks her land, drives Viru off, and abducts the virgin bride and marries her. He too is frustrated in his desire, for Vis gets her resourceful nurse to cast an impotence spell on him. Thus, she is twice married but still virginal when she meets the king's younger brother Ramin, who is so stunned by the sight of her that he literally falls off his horse.[131] Ramin is temporarily torn between his desire for Vis and his loyalty to his brother (and king), but desire trumps duty once he gets her into bed, where Gurgani gives us another surprisingly frank but beautiful description:

> As he pranced in the lists of happiness he put the key of desire in the lock of happiness: his delight in the lover grew the more when he saw the seal of God was as yet intact upon her. He pierced that soft pearl of great price; seduced a saint from her virginity. When he drew the arrow from the wound, target and arrow alike were covered in blood. Vis of the rosy limbs was wounded by the arrow, her heart's desire was realized in that wounding. (46)

To hide her unsealed state from her husband the king, Vis gets her nurse to play a bedtrick on him, just as Brangain does in *Tristan*.

Thereafter the plot follows the usual trials and tribulations of secret lovers, but the real appeal is Gurgani's voluptuous style. His characters, like figures in Persian paintings, lack depth but are gorgeously colored, clothed in a choice set of metaphors drawn from horticulture, astronomy, and jewelry that are repeated to intoxicating effect. (There is also a Rabelaisian amount of wine-drinking to enhance the mood.) He sometimes pushes his similes to bizarre extremes, reminiscent of the English metaphysical poets, as in this dreamlike battle scene:

> Now the sword slipped into armor like water; now the arrow slid into the eyes like sleep; now the spearpoint glided into the heart like love; now the axe cracked into the head like wit. You would have sworn the bloodthirsty sword knew where the Creator had disposed the soul in the body! The soul escaped from men by the same road as the sword had entered. The Indian blade was like a lily; a flood the hue of Judas blossom raining from it; like a myrtle branch with pomegranate petals hanging from it; like pomegranate petals

---

131 Actually this is a reunion, for the two were raised together as children for a while, in fact like brother and sister, making Ramin a symbolic substitute for Viru but morally acceptable to the Muslim audience Gurgani was writing for. Islam of course forbids brother–sister marriages (Quran 4:23).

with seeds upon them. The javelin was like a tailor in the battle; it kept sewing warriors to the saddle! (20)

When Ramin sees his temporary lover Rose for the first time — he doesn't fall off his horse, but his knees go weak and he drops the arrows he's holding — Gurgani favors us with an elaborate description of this Persian kitten that transforms her into a verbal icon made up of letters of the Persian alphabet and poetic code words:

> Her twin locks had conned the recipe of every spell, copied the curve of every *jīm* [j] and *nun* [n]. Her lips had become the cure of every hurt, had robbed all honey and sugar of glory; her mouth narrow like a *mīm* [m] of cornelian; her twin teeth peeping from it like the glittering Pleiades. In her eye she affected an archer from Abkhāz; in her locks a scorpion of Ahvāz; her cheeks were a bale of Shushtar brocade; her lips a bale of 'Askarī sugar cane; the one like roses on which musk has been scattered, the other like pearls over which wine has been poured. Her hyacinth [her curls] had become an armorer working upon roses [her cheeks]; her narcissus [eye] a bowman working upon the moon [her face]; the Pleiades were cast among chain-mail, musky bark was fitted to her bow. Her cheek earned the name of "pomegranate blossom of Barbary"; her locks merited the byname of "sweetheart's chain." One had been watered by the spring of the elixir of life, the other twisted by the hand of captivation. Her cheeks all snow and blood, milk and wine; her mouth all sugar, nectar, honey, and pearls. . . . (74)

You get the picture; or rather, you don't. It's nearly impossible to visualize Rose from this description, but that's not the point; this is beauty by association, an impressionistic attempt at the heady *effect* her beauty has on Ramin, not a realistic portrait. Gurgani's thousand words are worth more than a picture.

Gurgani apparently used the old story of Vis and Ramin to show off his virtuosic writing skills and to produce aesthetic bliss, not to illustrate any particular thesis about love, as the later European writers would. He does toss out a perfunctory warning at the end not to become "the slave of desire" like Ramin, yet the prince's success is entirely due to following his desires and natural sex urges (the point of all the nature imagery?) rather than remaining loyal to the state and observing civilized morality. So either Gurgani is sending a mixed message, or didn't think too much about it, preferring to concentrate on imagery rather than ideology. During the last quarter of the novel Gurgani overdoes it somewhat, staging tiffs between his lovers merely as an excuse for them to exchange (and for him to compose) lengthy accusations and protestations — Vis writes a long letter to Ramin in which "the words of the letter were so pathetic that blood dripped from their very letters" (96) — but ultimately he earns the praise he bestows on himself at the end: "They [future generations] shall tell of us in the world as we have told the tale of Vīs and Rāmīn. I have told a tale as fresh as spring blossom: each verse in it as gorgeous as a bloom. My fine fair friend, perfect in beauty and of pure-based nature; read out this pretty story, for your friends' happiness will be increased thereby, a story far pleasanter to scholars than a gorgeous garden!" (104)

The silly but popular *Alexander Romance* was the next to be given a Persian makeover. The anonymous *Iskandarnama* (Book of Alexander) is an 11th- or 12th-century abridgment of an earlier, much longer work — it breaks off after 770 pages with the end nowhere in sight, so the original must have been enormous — and shows a disregard for history that is breathtaking. In this version of the ancient Greek novel, Alexander is the son of the Persian king Darab (Darius III), though he winds up being raised by his historical father Philip of Macedon, and then he somehow becomes an observant Muslim a thousand years before the time of Muhammad. (This is probably due to a figure in the Quran named Dhu 'l-Qarnayn — literally, "the two-horned one" — who is traditionally associated with Alexander the Great, and who acts as Allah's emissary: see 18:83–98.) The episodic novel deals mostly with Alexander's adventures in the East, searching for the Water of Life that will supposedly make him immortal while collecting brides like Sayf ben Dhi Yazan. (Alexander was no slouch back in Greece either, where once "he had taken the seal off forty maidens in one night."[132]) The author took advantage of the novel's expansive form to include many digressions on Persian-Islamic culture that are of interest to historians today, and during a stopover in Cairo the "Chief of Egypt" beguiles Alexander with a number of entertaining stories à la Shahrazad. But ultimately *Iskandarnama* is an artless, careless work of pop fiction, filled with inconsistencies and anachronisms. At one point the scribe himself concludes an episode with the skeptical observation: "this tale belongs to a later date than the time of Alexander the Great, but God knows best" (52). Despite its origin, *Iskandarnama* is more like an Arabic sira than a Greek novel, and a bad one at that.

Even closer to the siyar are the long Persian adventure novels known as *dastans* (stories) that began to be compiled in the 11th and 12th centuries. One commentator describes them as "combining the extravagant fantasy of Tolkein with the fast action of James Bond."[133] The *Dastan of Amir Hamza* (11th cent.?), the most popular example of the genre, was inspired by the life of Muhammad's paternal uncle, Hamza ibn Abdul Muttalib (569?–625). But the hero of this anonymous, communal novel is a typical adventurer, dividing his time between *razm o bazm* — peace and war, the boudoir and

---

132 Page 25 in Southgate's translation; at 164 pages it represents only a fraction of the original, but that's more than enough.
133 Pritchett, *The Romance Tradition in Urdu: Adventures from the* Dastan of Amir Hamzah, 28.

the battlefield. The novel begins with his birth in Mecca, and alternates between there and the capital of Iran, Ctesiphon (now a ruined city 20 miles southwest of Baghdad), until he comes of age, then follows him on various adventures from India to Greece to the magical land of Qaf, where he fights giant demons called *devs* and gets engaged to several peris (beautiful Persian fairies). (The Qaf sections are apparently later additions, designed to draw out the story.) Like all romantic protagonists, Hamza accumulates wives as well as kingdoms during the course of his adventures, and finally suffers a gruesome death at the hands of a woman, who then rips him open and devours his liver, but who escapes punishment by converting to Islam.[134]

Until that grisly death, the *Dastan of Amir Hamza* is a lively, enjoyable novel, albeit rather cartoonish at times. There's a good deal of humor — sometimes scatological — thanks to Hamza's sidekick Amar, a prankster, and Aadi Madi-Karab, a glutton who provides comic relief. The novel shows the usual medieval indifference to accurate geography and chronology, and anachronisms regarding Islam abound, which crept in during later revisions.[135] The tale became a staple of Persian storytellers, who added more adventures before passing it along to the next generation, who did likewise. (Some of the expansions were drug-inspired, for many storytellers would do opium before their recitals.) It was translated into many Eastern languages and was especially popular in Muslim India, where it was known as the *Hamzanama*. The emperor Akbar (ruled 1556–1605) was so enamored of it that shortly after he assumed the throne he commissioned a gigantic illustrated edition; for the next two decades a team of painters produced a "book" of 1,400 folios, each more than two feet high, with text on one side and a detailed painting on the other. As the emperor and his court studied each painting, the dastan-narrator would glance at the corresponding text and improvise upon it.[136] But since the novel continued to grow and didn't assume its final form until the 19th century, I'll postpone further discussion of it until the next volume.[137]

I described Hamza's clever sidekick Amar as a prankster, but he is more specifically an *ayyar; ayyari* is the "special art of trickery, deceit, dirty tricks,

---

134 This incident is based on the historical Hamza's death at the battle of Uhud; the woman thus avenged her relatives whom Hamza had killed a year earlier at the battle of Badr.

135 When the Safavids, a Turkish dynasty, ruled Iran (1501–1736), "they vigorously promoted Shi'i Islam as the state religion, using every means at their disposal, including the storytellers. The didactic function of the romances, i.e., to preserve and transmit certain cultural values, was turned to use and some of the pre-Safavid romances such as *Iskandar Namah* and *Qissah-i Hamzah* were recast with a strong Shi'i coloring" (Hanaway, "Formal Elements in the Persian Popular Romances," 159 n7). *Qissah* means "story" and is an alternative title for the *Dastan of Amir Hamza*.

136 See John Seyller's glorious, oversized edition of *The Adventures of Hamza* (2002), which reproduces all the surviving paintings, with translations provided by Wheeler M. Thackston (288–312).

137 In the meantime, treat yourself to Musharraf Ali Farooqi's recent translation of the 19th-century version, *The Adventures of Amir Hamza*.

disguises, espionage, reconnaissance, and guerilla warfare . . . a profession," Pritchett explains, "with its own dress and private language" (259). *Samak-i Ayyar* (Samak the Brigand) is a 2,000-page novel from the 12th century starring a member of that profession; it differs from most siyar and dastans in featuring a commoner rather than a prince or a king, and one engaged in more realistic adventures such as "helping people in trouble, kidnapping enemy leaders, spying, carrying messages through enemy lines, and various commando-like deeds" (Hanaway, 160 n15). The only English translation I know of is a 35-page episode in an old anthology of Persian fiction, in which Samak assists a Syrian prince to win the hand of a Chinese princess.[138] The novel includes a large number of letters as narrative devices, and is the only dastan to use flashbacks rather than plain linear form. A French translation by Frédérique Razavi was published in 1972, but *Samak* remains a closed book to English readers.

More ayyari action enlivens what may be the best example of the *razm o bazm* genre, the *Firuzshahnama* (Book of Firuz Shah), which apparently originated at the same time as *Samak* but achieved its final form in 1483 in the hands of Sheik Bighami, probably a professional storyteller. William Hanaway's 175-page abridgment represents less than a tenth of Bighami's huge work, but it's an attractive mix of adventure, romance, magic, humor, and a pinch of pedagogy. Set vaguely in pre-Islamic times but displaying the attitudes and manners of 12th-century Iran, it doesn't have a particularly original plot, though it complicates the linear dastan form with an enlacement pattern similar to that of Arthurian narratives. King Darab of Iran (more or less the character of the same name in the *Iskandarnama*) longs for a son, and is granted one after his Greek vizier finds a Barbary princess for him. Firuz Shah grows up to be the typical accomplished prince, and one night dreams of a princess named Eyn al-Hayat (Well in Darkness), with whom he falls in love and goes in search of. Meanwhile Eyn, daughter of the king of Yemen, has fallen in love with a portrait of Firuz. (Seduction by art: the writer's goal, the reader's wish.) His quest for her — and their usual separations and reunions — activates the story, which soon brings kingdoms into conflict after Eyn's father promises her to another king's son. Sorcerers, devs, and peris join the show, and the centuries-old secrets of Solomon are revealed as the story complicates itself further, sending its characters all over the known world and to its edge, the magical land of Qaf. Firuz and Eyn eventually marry and produce a son named Malek Bahman, and once he comes of age, he too falls in love, goes off on adventures (including a fight with an enormous dragon), and otherwise follows in his father's footsteps. The novel resists resolution, which is one of its themes (and a justification for its endless length): "The

138 "Khurshidshah and the Princess of China," in Levy's *Three Dervishes and Other Persian Tales and Legends*, 175–210.

affairs of the world are never the same, not for an hour, not for a moment. Every instant they change."[139]

The novel is especially notable for its bold, adventurous female characters; these virgins are the dynamos that generate the plot by inspiring men to risk all for their love, and they are not afraid to take an active, even lethal part in the romance. When Firuz arrives at her palace in Yemen, Eyn sneaks out at night to spy on him (to see if he matches his portrait); like any teenage girl sneaking out of her house, she took "what she would need for going about at night, such as a dagger, a rope, and a sword" (44). On her way back, she encounters a guard and slices him in half "like a cucumber." The next night she kills four guards, and even more the night after that. She *had* to, she explains to her nurse, to avoid the scandal that would have ensued had she been captured, and this makes sense to the nurse — and presumably to Persian readers. Later a mysterious warrior kidnaps both Eyn and Firuz and takes them to a castle, then reveals herself to be a beautiful woman, who strips and bathes Eyn but really wants to be a second wife to Firuz, whom she has been stalking. A sorceress near the end of the novel almost destroys the Persian army in China, and a peri named Ruhana helps many of the mortals at crucial points in the novel. The novel may be named after Firuz Shah, but the novel is largely about his relationships with these entrancing women.

Bighami's opiate wand casts a spell over the entire novel, which contains more supernatural elements than the average dastan, yet is magically realistic as well. For example, when Malek Bahman approaches the dragon, his horse smells the beast before it sees it, and refuses to go further, just as a real horse would react. As Hanaway notes in his introduction, the narrator occasionally stops the narrative for a descriptive passage "to display his skill with words and dazzle his audience" (19), as when peacock-proud Eyn al-Hayat claims like a rap diva

> that the moon in the heavens was lighted by her beauty, that the sun was jealous of her loveliness, that the partridge had learned its bearing from her, that the straight-standing cypress at the edge of the brook bowed before her fir-like stature, that a hundred thousand hearts were bound by her tresses, that the shining sun was a cavalier on the battlefield of her comeliness, that the radiant moon was envious of the sun of her fairness . . . (41)

Eyn (and Bighami) could go on, I'm sure: sometimes Persian storytellers would stop a narrative for days with such descriptions, holding their audiences in thrall with their endless verbal invention. Perhaps its charms wear thin in the complete 2,500-page version, but the *Firuzshahnama* is a splendid example of Persian pop fiction.

Much shorter but just as entertaining is *The Adventures of Hatim Tayy*

---

139 Page 182 in Hanaway's translation, hereafter cited parenthetically.

(*Qissai-i Hatim Ta'i*, 12th cent.?). Like *Amir Hamza* it too features an Arabic folk hero of the 6th century, celebrated in particular for his generosity. While hunting one day, Hatim comes across a prince who is frustrated in his desire to marry a rich merchant's daughter because she requires her future husband to go in quest of the answers to seven riddles. Hatim generously volunteers to do so for him, which results in seven longish tales in which he encounters talking animals, is swallowed and regurgitated by a dragon, is kidnapped by a mermaid and taken to her underwater boudoir, marries a bear's daughter, and experiences a thousand and one equally outlandish adventures. After answering the seventh riddle, Hatim sees the couple happily wed and returns to Yemen, where he soon succeeds to the throne. It's fun in a cartoonish way, and unlike the spiritual work of later Persian writers, it shows a refreshing contempt for dervishes, exposed literally as thieves in the very first chapter. Hatim is a moral hero, a Muslim *avant la lettre*, though he allows himself to get into a few compromising situations; for example, Hatim agrees to spend three days with the mermaid, which his English translator (writing in 1830) passes over with winking italics: "For particular reasons, the *whole truth* of the original is *not* given here."[140] Like the mermaid's sea palace, most of the novel's settings are labeled "enchantments" or "delusions," which Hatim can enjoy as long as he doesn't mistake them for reality — presumably the attitude Persian audiences took toward entertainments like this.

The artsy blood-and-roses verse-novel of Gurgani was revived and surpassed a century later by Ilyas ibn Yusuf Nizami Ganjavi (1141?–1209?), an Azerbaijani poet widely considered the greatest and most innovative Persian writer of the Middle Ages. In addition to his shorter poetry, Nizami wrote five book-length narratives in verse, collectively known as the *Khamsa* (Quintet): the first and last are a philosophical treatise and a study of Alexander the Great, respectively; the other three are novels in verse after the manner of *Vis and Ramin*: the earliest, *Khasrow and Shirin* (c. 1180), about a cruel king and his long-suffering wife, was adapted from an episode in Ferdowsi's *Shahnameh* (pp. 810–31 in Davis's translation). It has not been translated into English, so I want to concentrate on the remaining two that have, *Layla and Majnun* and especially his masterpiece, *Seven Beauties*.[141]

"Layla, got me on my knees!" Many Westerners unwittingly know of Nizami's second novel by way of Eric Clapton's sweaty guitar epic (1971), which he wrote after reading a 1966 translation of the novel. (The flipside of

---

140 Page 29, note, in Forbes's careful translation — and it does appear to be a close translation, not a free adaptation like so many early European efforts. This and many other older translations are available online at the Packard Institute's "Persian Literature in Translation" Website at http://persian.packhum.org/persian.

141 There are 20-page précis of all three, along with numerous full-page reproductions of Persian miniatures illustrating the tales, in a gorgeous book entitled *Mirror of the Invisible World: Tales from the* Kamseh *of Nizami*, which is highly recommended.

the "Layla" single, "I Am Yours," takes its lyrics directly from chapter 23 — Nizami even gets a songwriting credit.) Written around 1192 at the suggestion of a local chieftain, *Layla and Majnun* was based on a popular Arabic legend of a pair of star-crossed lovers. A prince named Qays falls hard for a classmate named Layla, makes a spectacle of himself with the intensity of his love, and is thus nicknamed Majnun ("madman"; Layla means "night"). He does indeed begin to act crazy after Layla's parents remove her from school: he begins stalking her tent at night, wandering in the nearby desert, letting his hair grow wild, and (most importantly) composing poems about her. Failing to restore him to reason, his parents reluctantly suggest that the two marry, for Layla shares Majnun's passion, but her parents naturally don't want their daughter to marry a madman. This pushes Majnun over the edge and out into the wilderness, where he wastes away while continuing to compose songs; an early animal rights advocate, he attracts sympathetic animals that watch over him. A Bedouin prince discovers Majnun and takes an interest in his case by leading an army against Layla's tribe, but after the shedding of much blood, Layla remains with her people. She is then forced to marry another man, but refuses to relinquish her virginity or her devotion to "my wild love in his wilderness."[142] This stalemate causes misery all around and leads to a series of deaths: first Majnun's father, then his mother, then Layla's husband, then Layla herself, and finally Majnun, who decomposes atop Layla's grave, protected by his bodyguard of animal companions.[143]

Layla and Majnun is a superbly poised work, written in demonstration-class metaphoric style, and capable of being read on several levels. Its powerful if bathetic evocation of frustrated love and the pain of separation has a primal appeal, similar to that of *Romeo and Juliet* or *Wuthering Heights*. Religious readers have interpreted it as an allegory of the dark night of the soul and a Sufic renunciation of the world, but that's the least developed or engaging aspect, and even seems to be contradicted by some elements: early on, Majnun's father takes him to the holy Kaaba in Mecca hoping for Allah's aid, but once there, Majnun impiously laughs and pounds on the temple door, demanding of his god to make his love for Layla even stronger (8); later, in a letter to his beloved, Majnun blasphemously declares Layla is "my Kaaba . . . my altar" (41). No; like many great works of art, the novel is primarily about the workings of art; it doesn't represent "the experience of the soul in search of God," as one commentator enthused, so much as the experience of the poet in search of metaphors. Consider this passage from near the center of

---

142 Chap. 45 in Gelpke's translation (the same Clapton read), hereafter cited by chapter. This translation omits the introductory chapters — unctuous invocations of Allah and his prophet, Nizami's patron, etc. — no great loss.

143 Other manuscripts add a concluding scene in which a character named Zayd has a vision of Layla and Majnun happily united in heaven, but this sounds specious, like the happy ending Nahum Tate tacked onto *King Lear*.

the novel; Majnun has entered the wilderness and feels something watching him:

> By chance, his eye fell on the crown of the date-palm in whose shade and protection he had rested. There, in the green trelliswork of the fan-shaped branches, he saw a black shadow: a big raven squatted motionless, staring at Majnun, eyes glowing like lamps.
>
> Dressed in mourning, he is a wanderer like myself, thought Majnun, and in our hearts we probably feel the same. Aloud he said to the bird:
>
> "Blackfrock, for whom are you mourning? Why this sombre color of the night in the light of day? Are you burning in the fire of my grief, or have I disguised my soul with your blackness?"
>
> When the raven heard the voice, he hopped on to another branch without taking his eyes off Majnun who continued:
>
> "If you, like myself, belong to those whose hearts have been burned, why do you shun me? Or are you a Khatib, who on Fridays preaches from the pulpit of a mosque? Is that why you are wearing this sombre garb? Or are you a negro watchman? If so, whom do you fear? Perhaps I am a shah and you are my princely protector? Heed not! If, in your flight, you happen to see my beloved, tell her this from me:
>
> [poem omitted]
>
> As Majnun recited these lines, the raven fluttered farther and farther away until he finally took wing from the crown of the palm tree, vanishing into the fading light, which seemed to swallow him up.
>
> It was no longer day, but not yet night: the hour of the bats' awakening. The darkness grew until it was as black as a raven's plumage. What a giant raven this night was. When its wings were spread they reached right across the sky and yellow ravens' eyes stared down on Majnun as before, only now there were thousands of them, great and small, a countless multitude.
>
> To hide from their gaze, Majnun covered his face with his hands, and wept bitterly. (24)[144]

As the raven is transformed from an actual bird to a foreboding metaphor, we witness Majnun the poet playing with imagery, trying this simile out, then that one, creating a poem, and progressing from looking up and being inspired, to looking down in despair after his giant raven of night masses into a menacing multitude. "Layla," we recall, means "night," and the raven's lamp-like eyes remind us of young Qays's first glimpse of Layla: "Under the dark shadow of her hair, her face was a lamp, or rather a torch, with ravens weaving their wings around it" (2). After showing us how Majnun creates metaphors, Nizami shows us who the greater poet is.

---

144 A more literal translation of this final line is: "Like a night whose light is dead / Majnūn had fallen down, a raven had stolen his eyes" (Seyed-Gohrab, *Layli and Majnun*, 33; this fine study explores the mystical implications of the novel I've impatiently dismissed).

Majnun treats Layla much the same way, transforming her from a person to a poem. Her separation from him inspires him to become a poet — "for sorrow is the cause of immortal conceptions," Edward Dahlberg tells us — and as he continues to write poems about her in his self-imposed exile, she becomes more and more abstract to him. Towards the end of the novel, the married Layla arranges to meet her childhood admirer in a garden at night, but they both sense that he lives in a different world now, the world of art. "Only ten paces separated her from her beloved, but he was enveloped by a magic circle she must not break" (45). As Coleridge says of the visionary artist:

> And all should cry, Beware! Beware!
> His flashing eyes, his floating hair!
> Weave a circle around him thrice,
>   And close your eyes with holy dread,
>   For he on honey-dew hath fed
> And drunk the milk of Paradise.

Layla asks him to recite some of the poems he has written about her, which he does. He too keeps his distance in order to maintain his idealized vision of her; he has transformed her into art just as he transformed the raven into a metaphor. "Suddenly he fell silent, jumped up and fled from the garden into the desert like a shadow" (46), and the two never see each other again. They are no longer lover and beloved, but creator and creation, Qays a martyr to the madness of art and Layla his symbol for the mysteries of the universe. And while Layla resents the cultural fact that, as a woman, *she* didn't have the option of fleeing society and becoming a poet, she accepts her role as muse. On her deathbed, she reveals her own gift for abstract metaphor as she tells her mother:

"When I am dead, dress me like a bride. Make me beautiful. As a salve for my eyes, take dust from Majnun's path. Prepare indigo from his sorrow, sprinkle the rose-water of his tears on my head and veil me in the scent of his grief. I want to be clad in a blood-red garment, for I am a blood-witness like the martyrs. Red is the color of the feast! Is not death my feast?" (50)

These two martyrs to art have their counterparts elsewhere in world literature — Majnun's poetic madness recalls that of Sweeney and Tristan, Layla is Pygmalion's Galatea in reverse, and they are joined in death like Cathy and Heathcliff — but Nizami's compact novel is one of the finest treatments of this theme I've read. It was a sensation in Persia, spawning countless adaptations, illustrations, and translations throughout the East, and as Slowhand

Clapton demonstrated, it can still inspire the lonely to artistic heights.

The second word in the title of Nizami's third novel in verse, *Haft Paykar* (1196), has several meanings: the title has been translated as *Seven Beauties* — as its first English translator, C. E. Wilson, called his 1924 version — but it also means *Seven Portraits* or *Planets*; the title refers to the novel's central episode, which as been translated separately as *The Seven Princesses*. All of these possibilities reveal the polysemy of this complex text: nearly every line contains allusive puns and metaphors that allow it to be read several ways, and the entire work lends itself to multiple interpretations, even more so than *Layla and Majnun*. For this reason Wilson attached over 2,000 explanatory notes to his translation, which take up almost as many pages as the novel itself. Its most recent translator, Julie Scott Meisami, makes do with only 35 tightly printed pages of notes, but gives the best description of the novel I've seen: "The *Haft Paykar* is an allegorical romance of profound dimensions, constructed according to a plan which echoes the design of the cosmos itself, filled with a universal and syncretic symbolism, and evoking a wide network of intertextual allusion. Rich in fantasy, evoking the world of faerie, of magic, and of dream, it is charged with a powerful eroticism expressed in vivid sensuous imagery. All these elements are bound together in a whole of unparalleled richness and diversity."[145]

Like the *Cyropaedia*, like the tales of Vikramaditya, *Seven Beauties* is about the education of a king. Bahram — based on a 5th-century Persian king of that name, featured in the *Shahnameh* (622–78) — is born, as usual, to an aging, childless king, then sent off to an Arab king named Numan to be reared and prepared for kingship. (Numan hires an architect named Simnar to build a marvelous palace called Khavarnaq for the Persian prince, the first of many self-reflexive creations by Nizami.) After Bahram proves his worthiness by killing a dragon and recovering treasure from a cave, he returns to his palace and notices for the first time a locked room. Opening it, he sees that it contains portraits of seven princesses, one from each of the world's seven "climes": India, China, Khwarazm (modern Uzbekistan), Russia, the Maghreb (north Africa), Byzantium, and Iran. In the center is a portrait of the prince himself, foretelling his acquisition of all seven beauties (and by extension his domination of the world). After his father dies, Bahram returns to Iran, deposes a usurper, and assumes the throne. He is a just ruler, but apparently rather irresponsible: as fond as Omar Khayyam of the juice of the grape, he spends his days drinking wine and pressing lips.[146] The emperor of

---

145 Pages xxiv–xxv of her edition, hereafter cited by chapter and verse (except for editorial matter). She decided to retain the Persian title for her translation, probably one reason why it disappeared after one printing and is now extremely hard to find.

146 Omar Khayyam (1048–1131), author of the *Rubaiyat*, was a contemporary of Nizami's and just as formidably erudite, though that erudition led him in a different direction, toward agnostic hedonism.

China hears of this dereliction of duty and tries to invade Iran, but is repulsed by the bibulous shah, who then "unsheathed his tongue's sharp blade" (28:4) and rebukes his generals, insisting his hedonism was just a ploy: "Only fools drink and lose their wits; / quite otherwise are those with sense" (28:23). With the kingdom back to normal, he recalls the portraits of the seven princesses, and arranges for all seven women to be brought to his palace to be wedded, and for their benefit seven stately pleasure-domes decrees.

The grand centerpiece follows, occupying nearly half the novel's 270 pages. Each beauty is settled in her own palace, and over a week's time the king spends a day with each to make her acquaintance, listen to her narrate an erotic tale of a man tempted by a woman, and then have sex with her. This sequence is elaborately structured with a variety of concepts based on the number seven: each princess represents one of the seven days of the Islamic week (which begins on Saturday), one of the seven climes, one of the seven planets, and one of the colors (her dress and surroundings are color-coordinated), thus:

	1	2	3	4	5	6	7
princess	Furuk	Yaghma-Naz	Naz-Pari	Nasrim-Nush	Azaryun	Humay	Durr-Siti
country	India	China	Khwarazm	Russia	Maghreb	Byzantium	Iran
day	Saturday	Sunday	Monday	Tuesday	Wednesday	Thursday	Friday
planet	Saturn	Sun	Moon	Mars	Mercury	Jupiter	Venus
color	black	yellow	green	red	turquoise	sandal	white
protagonist	Turktazi	Iraqi king	Bishr	"King of Red"	Mahan	Good	nameless
temptress	Turktaz	Chinese slave	married woman	"Lady of the Fort"	Chinese demoness	Kurdish girl	Bakht

All of these elements are loaded with Islamic symbolism — the planets have astrological significance, the colors represent a number of things — and have additional implications based on numerology: the perfect number 7 is made up of 3 + 4 (which are represented by a triangle and square), so there are further allusions to the three aspects of the Islamic soul (vegetative, animal, rational), the "three kingdoms" of creation (animal, plant, mineral), and to a number of quartets: the four directions, four seasons, four elements, four humors, and so on, as well as combinations of 3 and 4, like the scholastic trivium (grammar, rhetoric, poetry) and quadrivium (arithmetic, geometry, astronomy, music), and the human body (head, chest, belly, and the two arms and legs).[147] The narration of the seven tales also evokes the seven stages of alchemy, of special significance because this entire sequence has a

147 For further explication, and an even more complex chart, see Krotkoff's "Colour and Number in the *Haft Paykar*."

hermeneutic purpose: to refine Bahram from a pleasure-loving prince into a mature king, hence the progression from black (the first story) to white (the final one). The novel is as carefully structured as *The Divine Comedy* or *Ulysses* (whose Linati schema inspired the chart above), and functions almost as an encyclopedia of Persian–Islamic thought: read Wilson's 2,000 notes explaining all this and you'll almost be qualified to teach a course on medieval Persian civilization.

This complex mathematical/astronomical/alchemical structure is upstaged by the tales themselves, each one a real beaut. (These tales, not their pretty narrators, are the real beauties.) Each one concerns a man tested on his sexual manners; only those who display patient, responsible behavior are rewarded, which is the lesson Bahram is expected to take away from his week-long sex holiday. In the first story, for example, a king learns of a city where everyone dresses in black for some mysterious reason; consumed by curiosity, he travels there and convinces a saturnine citizen to tell him why. The man takes him to a ruin and an isolated column (a phallic foreshadowing of his lonely fate), from the top of which a giant bird carries him off to a magical garden, where a beautiful woman surrounded by pretty companions excites his lust. She allows him all sorts of liberties — "Caress my curls while you are calm; / steal kisses, bite my lips" (32:285) — but she won't go all the way; if he can't control himself, she'll allow him to use one of her companions to "put out your burning flame" (32:292), which he does — every day for a month. On his final visit, she tells him she will personally douse his flame if he can wait one more day; he can't, and is on the verge of raping her "when she perceived my harshness, my / impatience, my anxiety" (32:488) and asks him to close his eyes so she can undress. When he opens them a moment later, he's alone back in those ruins. He's so depressed he vows to wear black thereafter to symbolize his crushing disappointment. In all but one of the succeeding tales, on the other hand, sexual success comes to those men who display patience, honesty, wit, intelligence, and devotion. (The exception is the one told by Wednesday's child, a woeful tale of an Egyptian youth who forsakes women for the religious life.) And just as history repeats itself, first as tragedy, then as farce, the final tale is a comic version of the first: a man finds a garland of girls in a garden, falls in love with the most beautiful of them, Bakht ("fortune"), but each time he tries to mate with her there's a ludicrous interruption of some sort. "Impatient with desire . . . all grace abandoned him" (38:152, 157), resulting in the funniest tale of the septet, something Boccaccio might have written. But unlike the king in black, he doesn't force the issue; instead, after realizing he's been acting irresponsibly, he marries Bakht, after which "with coral pierced the pearl unbored" (39:316).[148]

---

148 Nizami uses a variety of ingenious metaphors to describe sex acts, but they were a little too racy for translator Wilson, who rendered those bits in Latin.

All seven tales are enjoyable and cleverly made — the fourth became the basis, via adaptations and translations, for *Turandot*, Puccini's last and most experimental opera — and since each one is followed by Bahram sleeping with its narrator, there's the same language-making as lovemaking motif as in *The Arabian Nights*. Fiction as foreplay. But while Bahram was enjoying these sex fantasies, his wicked vizier had been ruining the kingdom, and once again an invasion by China is imminent. (Although the tales occur over seven days, the real world has aged seven years.) To clear his mind the shah goes hunting and comes across a shepherd who tells a story implying Bahram has not been a very good shepherd to *his* flock, so Bahram returns and executes his vizier, staves off the Chinese invasion, abandons his seven brides, and devotes himself to becoming an ideal king. At the end of a prosperous reign, though, he abandons his kingdom as he did his international brides and disappears into a cave; as a young prince he had found treasure in a cave, and now the old king has found some sort of heavenly treasure, it seems. His mother arranges for one of Bahram's heirs to become shah, and Nizami concludes the novel with some well-earned self-praise of his literary performance and hints at how to read it, comparing his book to both a fruit and a virgin:

> From my mind's garden I have brought
> to you a fruit as rich and sweet
> as honeyed milk. Its seeds of figs
> Do taste; its centre almond-pith.
> For lesser men its outside's fine,
> for those who see, the pith's within.
> . . . .
> All that you see, in this broad space,
> that I've thrown wide to ears and eyes,
> are meaning's beauties, narrow-eyed,
> their faces veiled from narrow sight;
> Each bride a treasury shut fast,
> the golden key beneath her locks.
> He will find gold who opes this mine;
> who finds the door fair pearls will gain. (53:23–25, 40–43)

A mirror for princes, a kamasutra, a pilgrim's progress, an astrological allegory — *Seven Beauties* is all of these and more. But I like to think of it as a meditation on art and even a challenge to the Quranic assertion that creation is solely a divine prerogative. Nizami sought to create a universe on paper to rival the real one, just as intricately structured, and announces this ambition ("for those who see") early on with the architect Simnar's creation of

Khavarnaq.[149] He builds "a palace with a heavenly dome / round which the heavens' nine spheres turned; / A pole formed like those south and north" (10:26–27), a microcosm of the cosmos itself. But Nizami is of course describing his own work as well; he's the real architect of Khavarnaq, and just as that palace contains within it the room of the seven beauties (a room Nizami calls Paradise), the novel contains a section that brings those beauties to life. In one of the Quran's many bullying threats, Muhammad warns, "if He wills, He can do away with you and bring in a new creation" (35:16). So can Nizami.

Bahram commissions a painter to fill Khavarnaq with additional paintings representing his various feats: pictorial versions of the verbal paintings Nizami narrates. Even nature participates in artistic creation: "The morning wind, a painter, limned / upon the water, chain-like rings" (30:8). Bahram then hires an architect named Shida to build the seven domes for his seven fiancées, who admits he will be emulating Allah and explains that a work of art can not only rival the real world but also function as protection against that messy, dangerous place:

> [Shida] said, "If the king gives me leave,
> I'll keep the Evil Eye away.
> For I can weigh the sky, and know
> the stars; my wit their work does show.
> In painting, building, you would say
> God's art inspires me. I will make
> a likeness of the heavenly sphere,
> that it not bring him harm; and nor,
> while he dwells in earth's picture-house,
> need he have fear of Heaven's stars.
> He'll dwell protected all his life; (30:77–82)

Perhaps the translation is misleading, but it sounds as though the Evil Eye belongs to Allah, and at any rate this is a pretty defiant, if not blasphemous, claim for human art. (Nizami covers himself by having Bahram ask "where is the house of the Creator?" Shida says he can be worshipped anywhere [30:95–98].) As Shida goes on to describe his plans for the seven domes, Nizami is explaining how he constructed his novel, and the result is "an Eden wrought / that men from Eden knew it not" (30:110).

At the same time, Nizami acknowledges the dangers of art. Upon completion of the seven-domed palace, he expresses doubts about his creation: "Nizâmî, flee the rose garden: / its roses are but sharpest thorns. / In such a

---

149 Interestingly enough, Simnar is a Greek, not an Arab, and in fact later the Arab king kills the Greek, perhaps an allegory of how the Arabs ultimately treated the Greek culture they preserved during the Middle Ages.

realm, a two-days' rest, see what befell Bahrâm at last" (31:25–26). The shah's kingdom descends into chaos during his long sojourn in the "rose garden," and ultimately he dismisses the seven beauties and converts their domes to Zoroastrian fire temples. At age 60 he regrets being "charmed by idle tales" and "turned, sincere, to worship God" (52:5, 12) — for Zoroastrians, that would be Ahura Mazda, the star of a collection of idle tales called the *Avesta*. While it's true that a king has responsibilities that preclude spending too much time in the rose garden of art, and while it was considered admirable in the East to devote oneself to religion after a lifetime pursuing love and fame, Nizami concludes his novel by politely telling his patron that *his* achievement will outlast anything his Seljuk king can offer:

> Although your banquets are unmatched,
> yet *this* is an eternal feast.
> Men reckon gems and treasures wealth:
> *this* is true ease, the rest all trial.
> That, should it last five hundred years —
> May you live long! — will not endure;
> *This* treasure, destined for your court,
> will ever be your firm support. (53:69–72)

Of course there are those who would clothe *Seven Beauties* in the burqa of religious allegory, yet another example of the soul's progression from the darkness of ignorance (the black first story) to the clear light of revelation (the white final story). Nizami allows that option, but the more complicated ways of love and art fill most of the novel's pages and exert the greater appeal. The novel is too delirious with the joys of sex and artistic creation to be reduced to something as routine as a theological allegory, and it's that brilliant engagement with the challenges of love and art that makes *Seven Beauties* the equal of anything comparable written in Europe during the Middle Ages, and deserving of the attention paid to Khavarnaq:

> Hearing of it, from near and far
> Flocked thousands just to gaze and stare.
> All those who saw sang praises loud,
> and humbly at its threshold bowed. (11: 3–4)

A few decades after Nizami finished *Seven Beauties*, another Azerbaijani writer named Sa'd al-Din al-Varavini (or Warawini) compiled *The Tales of Marzuban* (*Marzuban-nama*). Superficially, it too is a novel teaching kings how to rule responsibly, though its most obvious predecessors are books like the *Panchatantra*, Narayana's *Friendly Advice*, and *Kalilah and Dimnah*

— that is, didactic novels made up of animal fables. Varavini lived during the reign of the Atabeg sultan Uzbek ibn Muhammad ibn Ildigiz (1210–25) and observed enough of court life to know of its dangers. "There is a saying," a character notes at the end of the book, "that association with a king, and close familiarity with him, resembles the hot chambers in the baths — those who are outside have great impatience to enter, while those who have been settled inside for some time, being scalded by the heat of the water and distressed by the unhealthy atmosphere, desire to emerge as quickly as possible."[150] He based his work on a lost *Marzuban-nama* written in verse a few centuries earlier, attributed to a king of Tabaristan (northwest Iran) named Marzuban. Like Gurgani before him, Varavini found this early version to be uncouth and decided to beautify it with all the flowers of Persian rhetoric. In his introduction, he states that he also drew inspiration from *Kalilah and Dimnah*, the *Sindibadnama*, the Arabic maqamat, and other story collections.[151] Though most of the tales feature animals, there are some human actors, including several clever adulteresses who could have snuck out of the *Seventy Tales of the Parrot*.

In the novel's frame-narrative, a vizier tells the king of Tabaristan that one of his younger brothers, the noble-minded Marzuban, has designs on his throne, though the case is just the opposite: Marzuban wants to leave the court to avoid just these sorts of machinations. Marzuban and the vizier have a rhetorical joust in front of the king in which the vizier is exposed as a liar and thrown in prison. The king grants Marzuban his own country, but before he leaves, Marzuban is asked to compile his wisdom in a book, and *The Tales of Marzuban* is the result.

As in the *Panchatantra*, the various lions, jackals, dogs, and camels in Varavini's exemplary tales portray every kind of political animal, with the focus on scheming opportunists. In one of the longest episodes, a goat turns an ineffective dog (which lost the flock he was supposed to be guarding) into a dictator by way of political chicanery that anticipates *Animal Farm* (not to mention the Rove–Bush relationship). But what arrests the reader's attention is not so much the insights into the seamy underside of politics as Varavini's outlandish metaphors and doughty diction. A sampling:

> A tongue of flame from the tormenting fire in his heart shot out upon the whip-lash of his speech. (25)

---

150 Page 249 in Levy's translation; he omitted Varavini's introduction and "some of the more easily identifiable additions and insertions made by editors" (10). He also glossed over some bawdy humor, declaring "There are parts of this story in which the author indulges in a realism that need not be reproduced in translation" (149 n1), referring to an incident where a bird bites an adulterer's penis.
151 Arberry summarizes Varavini's introduction (181).

. . . he abandoned his hopes of Naw-Khurrah, to whom he bade farewell, setting fire to the load of gratitude he owed him and lengthening against him the tongue of impudent objurgation. (48)

. . . let the honeyed droplets of lust so trickle from the branches of anticipation that he will fail to see the serpent of destiny waiting open-jawed at his feet. (83)

Yet the one who is veritably courageous is he who, when confronted by necessity, ties the baggage of determination upon the camel humps of departure, sets out like the moon to traverse the plain of the easts and the wests and like the sun seats himself in the saddle laid upon the backs of the stars. (88)

Dates and grapes hung, like round-bosomed maidens, with the seal of their virgin bloom upon them. Except the sun and moon which peered through the lattices of the boughs, no one glimpsed their breasts shapely as pomegranates or their chins of apple roundness; only the cool north breeze and the zephyr ever raised a corner of the leafy veil covering them there, with their lips shaped like pistachios and their eyes of almond form. Greedy teeth never reached the lip of the citron or the dewy throat of the orange there, no one came to bite into the skin of the blue grape or the cheek of the apple, none ravished its peaches, its clusters perceived no harm or ever heard a word of disparagement. (99–100)[152]

There he concealed himself under the bed, and, as he did so, destiny felled the tree which would provide the timber for his gallows. (104)

In the bear's heart the fires of wrath spurted out flame when he heard this speech, and he set about hurling naphtha-bottles of scorn upon Dāstān's speech. (117)

"To-morrow, when the manservant of destiny applies the comb to your hair and you behold in the mirror of fortune the images of your greatness and my significance, you will be driven to extract from me the teeth of ambition, which still exist, in you and me alike, as equal in size and length as the teeth of a comb." (137)

At dawn, when the negro of night raised his head from the pillow of the east and displayed his white teeth in the mouth of the horizons, he sent in search of the weaver. (225)

He spent some time setting the outposts of cleverness and the spies of observation upon the highways of perception and the roads of understanding . . . (233–34)

"Scattering lavishly before them pearls of phrases from the jewel-box of his mind and the casket of his heart" (156), Varavini had an appreciative audience in Azerbaijan; although my bumper sticker reads I ♥ INGENIOUS IMAGERY, I suspect most modern readers would regard such "pearls" as egregious examples of overwriting. And while it may be unintentionally amusing to hear a bear and a camel converse like a pair of Victorian MPs, Varavini had a pedagogical purpose behind his purple prose: "And it is especially

---

152 Cf. the women-as-fruit trope in *The Adventures of Sayf ben Dhi Yazan*.

probable," says one character, speaking for the author, "that if the words uttered are pleasantly modulated, the phrases well turned and the language steeped in sugar, the style will find a home in the very heart of one's liking" (82). Varavini's sweet style masks some sour observations about the nature of tyranny and the willingness of some people to exchange their freedom for security: a group of beasts about to submit to their dog-king say (in unison): "and even though he should from time to time contemplate some injury to us, such injury would not greatly affect us, since we live secure against the harm of others in the area which is under his protection. That degree of injury from him would indeed appear to us the very acme of comfort" (157). A hare upbraids the animals for their spinelessness, but is discredited by a pigeon, appropriately enough.

It's easy enough to apply Varavini's animal fables to human situations, but he hints that his tales are deeper than that. After giving a strange account of a temporary kingship like a case study from Frazer's *Golden Bough*, Marzuban explains the symbolism behind the story, which involves the growth of a soul from an embryo to the afterlife. The embryonic journey would never have occurred to me, and I would have scoffed at any scholar extracting that from the tale, but coming from the author, it stands as a warning that his subsequent tales hide secret meanings. (Marzuban doesn't explicate any further stories; he gives us one freebie, and after that we're on our own.) This particular tale occurs early in the book (pp. 37–42); it is bookended near the conclusion with a tale of false interpretation: a serpent gives one set of readings for a series of dreams, which satisfies everyone, but later gives the true interpretation of the dreams, which he had kept to himself to test others. Varavini is the complete teacher: instructing us, testing us, tricking us if necessary to make us better citizens, and better readers. The didactic novel observes Islamic orthodoxy — even a duck quacks the Quran — but *The Tales of Marzuban* is a subtle, subversive work nonetheless.

Tales of a Parrot (*Tutinama*) is a similar aesthetic makeover of an earlier work, in this case the Sanskrit *Seventy Tales of the Parrot*, along with a few stories borrowed from the *Panchatantra*, *Sindibadnama*, and *Kalilah and Dimnah*. It was compiled around 1330 by Ziya al-Din Nakhshabi (d. 1350), who lived in present-day Uzbekistan. Although the frame-tale is essentially the same — a merchant leaves a parrot behind to watch over his frisky wife while's he's gone — Nakhshabi borrows the narrative tactic of *The Arabian Nights*: the parrot tells the wife a tale not to dissuade her from seeking a lover, as in the original, but to delay her; by the time his long tale is finished, "the dawn unveiled its brilliant face, and her departure was delayed," a recurring formula. The snappy Sanskrit is replaced by plummy Persian, as in the opening of the 10th night, when once again Khojasta (the wife) asks permission of the parrot (Tuti) to skip out:

When the sun, like a cup of sparkling wine, was poured into the wine barrel of the west, and the crescent moon, like a half-filled cup visible to the world, emerged from the assembly of the east, Khojasta, who was intoxicated with the desire for love and drunk with emotion, went to Tuti to ask permission to leave.

"Oh reliable consultant and illustrious counselor!" she said, "the disastrous wind of love has broken the branch of my patience and calmness, the gusty storm of yearning has uprooted my reason and judgment. Grant me permission so that I may go to my lover's house for our rendezvous in order that I may brighten my bedimmed eyes with the radiance of my beloved."[153]

Nakhshabi was the author of a Persian sex manual (modeled on the Indian *Kokashastra*), but he was also a devout Sufi, and perhaps for that reason gave his novel a harsher ending. The worldly Hindu husband in *Seventy Tales of the Parrot* forgave his wife, who was only responding to nature's promptings; but as Khojasta's metaphors indicate, lust was considered a natural disaster by her society, and after her Muslim husband returns and learns from the parrot of his wife's yearnings, he "decapitated Khojasta, shaved his hair, put on woolen clothes [the garb of Sufis], entered a hermitage and devoted his life to the worship and service of God" (331). I'll let the reader decide which husband acted more intelligently.

Most of the remaining Persian prose fictions of the later Middle Ages are likewise variants and adaptations of earlier works. The *Bakhtyarnama* (13th or 14th century) is another version of the *Sindibadnama*, and the anonymous *Palace of Nine Pavilions* (pp. 102–74 in Levy's *Three Dervishes*) is a low-rent expansion of the seven-domes sequence in Nizami's great novel. Amir Khusraw Dihlavi (c. 1253–1325) also ripped off Nizami with a *Hasht bihisht* (Eight Paradises), but he also wrote some verse-novels set in his own time, none of which has been translated into English. (The original of the Urdu classic *A Tale of Four Dervishes* [*Qissa Chahar Darvesh*] was traditionally ascribed to him, but it is now thought to be a later work of Turkish origin.) A few more adaptations of the much-imitated *Kalilah and Dimnah* appeared in the 15th and 16th centuries, like the *Lights of Canopus* (*Anvar-i Suhayli*) by Husain Va'iz Kashifi, and the *Touchstone of Knowledge* (*Ayar-Danish*) by Abu'l Fazl (who also adapted Nakhshabi's *Tutinama*). But one final adaptation of an old, old story commands our sustained attention.

The biblical story of Joseph as given in the Quran (sura 12) has always been a favorite with Muslims; at only eight pages, it is less detailed than the one given in the Tanakh (Gen. 37–50), and places so much emphasis on the lad's appearance that "as beautiful as Joseph" became a standard simile. In 1484, Nur al-Din al-Rahman Jami (1414–92) produced an allegorical romance that

---

153 Page 75 in Muhammad Simsar's faithful translation, which is accompanied by 50 gorgeous color reproductions from a 16th-century manuscript of the *Tutinama*.

opens up the rather clunky quranic version in a number of fascinating ways. An Afghan Sufi, Jami took Joseph's beauty to symbolize the beauty of his god, but shifts the focus from Joseph to the woman so dazzled by that beauty that she became in his hands the greatest tragic heroine in Persian literature. She's unnamed in the Quran, called merely Potiphar's wife in Genesis, but Jami follows Arabic tradition in calling her Zulaikah.

Yusuf and Zulaikah begins with all the usual Persian prelims (invocations, prayers, dedications, etc.), gives a brief account of Yusuf's childhood, and then provides a long account of Zulaikah's girlhood, the first departure from scriptural tradition and the first indication this novel will be more about her than Yusuf. The daughter of a king of Barbary, Zulaikah is as beautiful as the boy she will later try to seduce; Jami gives an elaborate head-to-toe description of her, like Gurgani comparing certain of her features to letters of the alphabet as he composes his verbal icon, seducing the reader with her beauty and establishing her as a good character, not the desperate housewife of tradition. Like many other characters in Eastern fiction, she then falls in love with a man she sees in a dream, the erotic nature of which is signaled by Jami's typically elaborate chapter heading: "The Seeing by Zuleikha for the First Time of the Sword of the Sun of the Beauty of Joseph in the Sheath of a Dream, and Her Being Killed with Love of Him by That Sword."[154] This vision of beauty astounds her, but in the wrong way, the author tells us: "She was beside herself with shock; but she stopped short of grasping the true significance of her experience. If only she had been aware of that deeper meaning, she would have numbered among those who have joined the path of Truth; but being captivated by the outward form, she was oblivious at first to the underlying reality" (15). Real-world appearances are unreal, dream visions are real; beauties like Yusuf and Zulaikah are merely mirror reflections of the source of beauty, Allah; the path of Truth is mapped by a fiction about people who never existed; the erotic resembles the spiritual: Jami piles on the paradoxes to warn us early on not to mistake the "outward form" of this narrative — apparently a romance about obsessive love — with the underlying reality proposed by Sufi mystics. Jami's canny strategy will be to tease the reader by making the world of appearances as seductive to us as it is to Zulaikah by way of lush descriptions and erotic episodes so that her struggle to apprehend "the underlying reality" is ours as well — or would be if

---

154 From Alexander Rogers's verse translation of 1892. Though complete, this admirable attempt to imitate Jami's intricate verse — like R. T. H. Griffith's 1881 version before it — results in many forced rhymes and makes for plodding reading. Consequently I will be citing David Pendlebury's prose translation of 1980 (by page number), which abridges the novel by about a third but retains all the key scenes. In his afterword, Pendlebury makes a convincing case for prose as the appropriate contemporary medium for Jami's work.

we accepted Jami's Sufism, which is nonsense, of course.[155] The phenomenal world is the real one; his Sufi fantasy world, like the Muslim god at its center, never existed. But let's play along.

A tortured year later, Zulaikah has a second dream, in which her dreamboat tells her to save herself for him: "Let no tooth bite that sugared lip, nor any diamond pierce that pearl!" (21). This sends the poor girl into a tizzy of erotic derangement — "Like a bursting bud, she tore her robe open; and each time she thought of her beloved's face and locks, she ploughed her nails into her own face and tore her own hair" (21) — and so, like Budur in *The Story of Qamar al-Zaman*, she is chained up by her concerned father and treated like a madwoman. A year later she has a third dream, in which the man identifies himself as the grand vizier of Egypt. With that info, she springs into action: she announces to her father that she is cured and willing to start considering the marriage proposals that have been pouring in ever since word of her beauty got out. She's disappointed that there isn't one from the vizier, so her father informs the Egyptian that his daughter would like to marry him. Turns out the current vizier is someone else — the dream-Yusuf had been speaking from the future — which devastates the girl until "the bird of divine pity" announces that the vizier is the means by which she'll finally meet Yusuf, and that the vizier (a eunuch in some traditions) poses no threat to her virginity: "he will leave your silver lock untouched, for his key is of the softest wax. Have no fear: from an empty sleeve no hand can emerge, brandishing a dagger" (34). Mollified, she marries the vizier, who one day acquires Yusuf on the slave block at her prompting. Overjoyed that she has finally met Yusuf in the flesh, she impiously proclaims, "Now that I have become the companion of this gorgeous being, I can flaunt my fortune to the very heavens" (53).

Just at that point, Jami inserts a brief tale of a woman named Bazigha, who hears of the handsome Hebrew slave and wants to buy him. She literally loses consciousness at the sight of Yusuf, and after she comes to, she asks him, "Who was it that endowed you with such perfect beauty? . . . What artist is the author of your image?" (56). Yusuf replies with a short homily encapsulating Sufi theology; it's worth quoting in full because it both compactly expresses the thesis behind the novel and continues the idea of Allah as author:

> "I am the handiwork of that Creator, in whose ocean I am content to be the merest droplet. The whole sky is nothing but a dot from the pen of his perfection; the whole world is merely a bud in the garden of his beauty; the sun is but a single ray of the light of his wisdom; the vault of heaven a mere bubble in the sea of his omnipotence.

---

155 Fear of/obsession with sex? Check. Disgust with the body and life itself? Check. Uncritical acceptance of a "sacred" text? Check. Confusion of subjectivity with objectivity? Check. Self-absorption mistaken for selflessness? Check. Displacement of eros onto a paternal (and in this case homoerotic) fantasy figure? Check. Yep, it's the usual religious bullshit.

"Hidden behind the veil of mystery, his beauty was ever free of the slightest trace of imperfection. From the atoms of the world he created a multitude of mirrors, and into each of them he cast the image of his face; for to the perceptive eye, anything which appears to be beautiful is only a reflection of that countenance.

"Now that you have seen the reflection [i.e., Yusuf], make all haste to its source; for in that primordial light, the reflection is entirely eclipsed. Beware of lingering far from that primal source; or else when the reflection fades you will be left in darkness. The reflection is as ephemeral as a rose's blush: if you want permanence, turn towards the source; and if you want faithfulness, seek it there also. Why tear your soul apart over something that is here one moment and gone the next?" (56)[156]

Bazigha responds as Zulaikah *should* have: "the wise girl rolled up the carpet of her passion for Yusuf," thanks him for having "pierced the pearl of mystery" (a recurring sexual metaphor), gives away all her possessions, and becomes a hermit on the banks of the Nile "steadfastly devoting herself to piety" (57).

But even Jami realizes how unrealistic that is, so he resumes his narrative. Several chapters follow in which Zulaikah tries to seduce the boy — no ages are given, but Zulaikah is around 18, Yusuf maybe 12 (not 17, as in Genesis) — and when that doesn't work she tries to prime the pump by sending him "a hundred pretty, fragrant-breasted maidens," encouraging him to "choose whichever one of these beauties pleases you, and satisfy your desire with her. Enjoy your youth, for it is a time of voluptuous delights" (72). Hear hear! Zulaikah's plan is to wait until Yusuf takes one of these "ravishing creatures" to bed and then play the old bedtrick and slip in beneath him. But even though the century of cock-teasers do their best — and Jami details their "flirtatious words and gestures" with near-pornographic avidity — our priggish hero preaches to them instead and by dawn has converted them all to his religion. Jami intends thus to establish Yusuf's superiority to mere mortals, and while every Muslim reader would grant this in theory, few would have reacted the same way. "All of us are like Zulaikha," Jami scolded earlier: "slaves of opinion and victims of appearances" (15). Jami seems to enjoy taunting his readers, daring them to disagree with his ethics as he excites them with paper dolls like the one "who made a loop with her black and perfumed tresses, and said, in a pleading voice: 'Can you not open a door for me to union with you? Please do not leave me hanging helplessly outside, like the ring on the door'" (73). Jami cleverly sets this scene in a garden, anticipating the virgin-stocked garden of paradise that allegedly awaits the Muslim who can resist such temptations in this world.

---

156 I once asked a dancer if he thought it was a drawback that choreography couldn't be transcribed and preserved, but he replied that ballet's ephemeral nature — "here one moment and gone the next" — was one of its many attractions. Put another way, "Death is the mother of beauty" (Stevens, "Sunday Morning").

Zulaikah next builds a palace for Yusuf filled with paintings depicting them engaged in sex — she ain't subtle — and when she contrives to get herself in his arms, he is tempted: "But Yusuf did not let the arrow fly, or break open the oyster for the pearl. He would have dearly loved to pierce that pearl with his diamond; but the command to preserve his purity held him back" (85). There follows the famous scene where Yusuf flees and Zulaikah grabs the back of his cloak, and then is accused by the spurned woman of attempted rape. The affair is hushed up, but after Zulaikah becomes the laughingstock of the town for making a fool of herself over a Hebrew slave, she invites the women who have been laughing over for a banquet. When Yusuf is brought before these ladies just as they are about to peel their dessert oranges with a knife, they are so stunned by his beauty that they accidentally cut their hands.[157] A couple of the women die on the spot, some go mad and run into the street, others faint, and those who survive the sight forgive Zulaikah for her passion.[158] They even chastise Yusuf for withholding himself from his mistress, though adding that any one of them would be happy to fill her place should he desire someone else. Predictably, Yusuf shuts them down too.

Annoyed at the loss of her reputation, Zulaikah gets her husband to send Yusuf to prison, where we're told the pretty boy was rapturously received — I'll bet he was — but she remains tragically in love with him, and Jami maintains the reader's sympathy for her despite her transgressions. Later Yusuf is released from prison because of his knack for interpreting dreams and eventually becomes grand vizier. Zulaikah's limp husband has died in the meantime and over the succeeding years she wastes away in erotic despair until she becomes a bent-over, white-haired woman sunk in poverty, living only for those rare moments when she can catch a glimpse of Yusuf in a procession. One day as he passes her on the road he hears this old woman praising their god, and after inviting her for a personal audience, he is surprised to learn that this is the woman who tried to seduce him 20 years earlier. Offering to grant her any wish, she asks for her youth back, and in a fairytale transformation Yusuf miraculously changes her back to an 18-year-old and then is instructed by the angel Gabriel to marry her. Once again approaching pornography in this spiritual allegory, Jami describes their wedding night in graphic but crucially symbolic detail:

157 Though not in Genesis, this scene became part of the Midrash and was adapted by Muhammad for his account. But compare his clumsy handling of the scene — there's no motive given for Zulaikah handing the ladies knives (12:31) — with Jami's superior rendition. I don't care how devout he was, Jami must have known he was a better writer than his god, who tells the story via Muhammad. In fact some translators of the Quran (like Yusuf Ali) cite Jami to explain what Muhammad intended in sura 12.

158 Max Beerbohm reverses this in his delightful novel *Zuleika Dobson* (1911), in which the visiting Zuleika lays waste to the boys at Oxford, who drown themselves out of love for her.

Then with his arms entwined about her, he felt below her waist, where he found signs of an intact and undiscovered treasure.

Quickly he sought the jewel casket in that treasure trove: it was shut tight with a silver lock; neither trusty guard nor traitorous intruder had ever laid a hand on it. With a glistening ruby for a key, he unlocked that casket and slipped the jewel in. To and fro his charger sped along that narrow course, until in the end it galloped itself lame. Thus the unruly carnal soul starts out on its impetuous career — only to come at last to rest, shorn of all selfishness. (127)[159]

The Persian word *nafs*, translated here as "carnal soul," means both "penis" and "the unregenerate self" in Sufi theology. (Cf. the American slang term "dickhead.") That is, sexual passion is selfish, and only when all passion is spent does one attain the selfless state necessary to find *true* love with the divine. This is why Bazhiga thanked Yusuf for the spiritual orgasm he gave her. Even though this sex scene is told from Yusuf's point of view, it is implied Zulaikah experiences something similar. Asked by Yusuf (after he goes back for seconds) wasn't it better that they waited until her soul had been purged of selfish lust before uniting in this divinely sanctioned marriage, Zulaikah deliriously agrees, the implications being that lust has refined itself to love during her long ordeal, that she has come to value Yusuf's inner beauty over his outward appearance, and that all beauty is a manifestation of Allah. Jami ignores the rest of the traditional story of Joseph and his brothers and kills him off instead, allowing Zulaikah to take center stage for a final aria of bereavement. Visiting his grave, she gouges out her eyes — the root cause of her attraction to physical beauty — and dies upon his grave, which leads Jami to make a startling statement in the context of his patriarchal culture: "No man, let it be said, ever stepped more heroically to his own death than did this lioness. First she made herself blind to all that was not the beloved [both Yusuf and Allah]; then she laid down life itself for him" (136). This is yet one more reversal of the reader's expectations; the hero of the novel turns out to be not the prophet Yusuf, whose life was scripted for him from the beginning, but Zulaikah, the nameless temptress of scripture reviled by conservative Muslims, who displays more passion, individuality, and heroism than any other character.

159 Victorian translator Rogers omits all this as being "unsuited to European ideas." This is an example of the stupid prudery that Burton quite rightly criticized in his "Terminal Essay" on *The Arabian Nights*: "Moslems and Easterns in general study and intelligently study the art and mystery of satisfying the physical woman . . . a branch of the knowledge-tree which our modern education grossly neglects, thereby entailing untold miseries upon individuals, families and generations. The mock virtue, the most immodest modesty of England and of the United States in the nineteenth century, pronounces the subject foul and fulsome: 'Society' sickens at all details; and hence it is said abroad that the English have the finest women in Europe and least know how to use them" (3744).

But Jami saves his biggest surprise for last. In a lengthy epilogue, he points the moral of his tale — "Everything which appears desirable to you and captivates your heart will in the end only be grievously wrenched from you with a hundred regrets" (138) — and recommends detachment from the world and its many attractions. Except for books: "Remember that knowledge is vast and life is short. Life does not come again for anyone; so go in search of indispensable knowledge" (140). He then offers one of the loveliest paeans to the allure of books I've heard:

> A book is the companion of solitude, the brilliant light of the dawn of wisdom, forever opening new vistas of knowledge. It is a favoured adviser, clad in buckskin, full of good sense, silently counselling his master. It is a palanquin of colourful moroccan leather, sheltering two hundred beauties dressed in pink with musk-flecked faces, all of them lying tenderly cheek to cheek. If someone places a finger on their lips, they open them and display thousands of subtle gems of inner meaning. (141)

But then he renounces writing as yet another worldly distraction, then flipflops and praises *Yusuf and Zulaikah* for the "precious" work it assuredly is, then reverses tack again and advises himself (punning to the end) to "close your book on the melancholy business of writing. Bid your tongue be silent, for silence is worth more than anything you could ever say" (146). The conflicted novel is filled with rapturous celebrations of beauty, but we are told to shun it; knowledge and books are indispensable companions, but he ends his brilliant book with a repudiation of writing. Jami was a genius — *Yusuf and Zulaikah* is only one of his *Haft Awrang* (Seven Thrones, verse-narratives modeled on Nizami's) — but that didn't prevent him from getting it all wrong: beauty may be impermanent (even culturally constructed) but it is real nonetheless, unlike his silly Sufic system, and had he remained silent and not penned this and other books, Jami would never have attained the only real form of immortality: the creation of a work of art that will survive as long as there is a reader to place a finger on the lips of his beautiful pages.

CHAPTER 5

The Far Eastern Novel

Around the same time as European Christians brought literacy to the island of Ireland, thereby enabling written Irish literature, China brought the same gift to the island of Japan, which was slower than most countries to develop a high culture. Although Chinese literature was well under way by the 5th century, it wasn't until the Japanese adopted Chinese ideographs that their written literature began. (Even so, Chinese remained the lingua franca of the educated classes in Japan for centuries, like Latin in Europe.) The Japanese even adopted the Chinese name for their country, Nihon (i.e., Nippon, "origin of sunrise"), relegating the old name Yamato to a single province, and welcomed Buddhism to augment their native religion of Shinto. Despite China's thousand-year head start, however, the novel bloomed first in Japan and peaked before the first substantial Chinese novels started appearing in the 14th century. But between the two, Japan and China produced the greatest novels before the modern era.

JAPANESE FICTION

As in many cultures, the earliest Japanese fictions can be found embedded in sacred writings and mythology. The two oldest surviving books in Japanese literature, the *Kojiki* (Records of Ancient Matters, 712) and the *Nihongi* (or *Nihon shoki*: Chronicles of Japan, 720) are, like the Hebrew Tanakh and the Mayan *Popul Vuh*, farragoes of mythology, genealogy, etiology, theology, and idealized history — or, as the Victorian translator of the *Nihongi* (who would have preferred reliable history) says with some exasperation, "a very complete assortment of all the forms of the Untrue of which the human mind is capable, whether myth, legend, fable, romance, gossip, mere blundering, or downright fiction."[1] But as the modern translator of the former allows, more comfortable with "downright fiction," the *Kojiki* contains "the first Japanese

---

1 Aston's introduction, xvii. Here's a delicious example of his dry British wit: in one episode, a man tries to wake a sleeping monkey, who startles him by singing a 7-line lyric, of which Aston says: "The metre belongs to no recognized standard. The text of this song is probably corrupt. As it stands it is very obscure, though, perhaps, not more so than we should expect from a drowsy monkey" (2:187 n1).

short stories . . . [and] the beginning of recorded Japanese poetry."[2] Both are substantial works (400 and 800 pages, respectively) with interesting fictional episodes, but since they were compiled from miscellaneous sources with the political purposes of establishing an "official" history (not abandoned until the dedeification of the emperor in 1945) and clarifying the nobility's ranks and titles based on accurate genealogy (rather than family legends), we should look elsewhere for the first Japanese novel. But it is worth noting the heterogeneous nature of these two foundational works; perhaps because of them, Japanese novelists felt free to mix poetry, history, criticism, diaries, sermons, and other genres into their works, often with surprisingly modern-looking results.

A perfect example is the *Indications of the Goals of the Three Teachings* (*Sango shiki*, 797) by the Buddhist scholar Kukai (774–835), which defies neat genre classification. Some critics consider it the first Japanese novel — though at 40 pages it barely qualifies as a novella — but *Indications* has also been called the first Japanese drama because of its reliance on dialogue, as well as a theological treatise because of its content. Written in highly ornate Chinese, the novella begins with a visit paid by a Confucian named Kimo to his friend Tokaku, who is upset with his nephew Shitsuga for spending all his time drinking, gambling, and whoring. Tokaku asks his erudite friend to talk some sense into Shithead (actually, his name means "Leech's Tusk"), so Kimo obliges with a recruitment speech for Confucianism, arguing that its precepts are a recipe for success in life. Shitsuga is sold, but then a Daoist named Kyobu — who had been silently listening to all this — speaks up and says detachment from the world, not worldly success, should be one's goal, and that Shitsuga should devote himself to learning how to prolong his life and attain immortality. All three are won over and vow to become Daoists, but outside Tokaku's house a Buddhist mendicant named Kamei-kotsuji has overheard both pitches and invites himself in to argue that both are wrong. He delivers a lecture on the impermanence of life, the horrors of hell, and the need to transcend the phenomenal world and escape the cycle of trans-migration. His four auditors are converted and make a vivid promise: "From now on we will observe faithfully your teaching with our whole beings — by writing it on the paper of our skins, with pens of bone, ink of blood, and the inkstone of the skull."[3]

As that sentence indicates, the didactic novella is enlivened by some strik-ing imagery, and the erudition on display is astounding. Kukai was 24 when he wrote *Indications* and wanted to show off his extensive reading in Chinese literature and Sanskrit theology, despite his disingenuous claim at the end

2 Philippi's introduction, 15.
3 Page 139 of Hakeda's translation of Kukai's *Major Works*, where *Indications* occupies pp. 101–39.

of the preface "I am writing just to express my own unsuppressible feelings and not in order to be read by others" (103).[4] As a dramatized primer on the differences between Confucianism, Daoism, and Buddhism it serves its purpose (though too prejudiced in favor of the latter), but as fiction it's not as successful. Only the mendicant is given enough backstory to make him a character rather than a type — Kamei-kotsuji is likewise 24 and is obviously the author's alter ego — and the ease with which the others convert to various faiths is utterly unrealistic. But *Indications* is interesting on a formal level for gathering sermons, poetry, and two show-stopping *fu* (prose poems) under one fictional tent. Kukai's motives were more practical than aesthetic — as he tells us in the preface, he wanted to justify to his irate relatives and teachers his conversion from their Confucianism to esoteric Buddhism, plus he really did have an out-of-control nephew to admonish — but in its extensive use of dialogue it resembles the conversational novels of Plato, Athenaeus, Delicado, Aretino, Peacock, and Firbank (whose *Inclinations* rhymes with Kukai's *Indications*), and in its use of fiction to examine three branches of religion with ostentatious erudition it even anticipates Swift's *Tale of a Tub*, another youthful tour de force.

Those who demur from calling *Indications* the first Japanese novel point instead to *The Tale of the Bamboo Cutter* (*Taketori monogatari*, c. 900), a novella of about the same length — but written in simple Japanese instead of ornate Chinese — that brilliantly fuses fantasy, romance, comedy, etiology, poetry, and political satire. Like most early Japanese novels, it is anonymous. The tale falls into thirds: an old bamboo cutter named Miyakko one day finds among the stalks a three-inch girl; being childless, he takes her home where, after barely three months, she grows to full size. She's obviously not from around there, so he names her Nayotake no Kaguya-hime (Shining Princess of the Supple Bamboo). Word of her unearthly beauty spreads and she attracts numerous suitors, but the icy princess doesn't allow them so much as a glimpse. Five members of the nobility are especially persistent, so her stepfather encourages her to pick one to marry. In order she says to test their sincerity — an important quality in Japanese culture but just a delaying tactic here, for the girl doesn't want to marry anyone — she sets the suitors five impossible tasks:

> Kaguya-hime declared: "I should like Prince Ishizukuri to obtain for me from India the stone begging-bowl of the Buddha. Prince Kuramochi is to go to the mountain in the Eastern Sea called Hōrai and fetch me a branch of the tree that grows there, with roots of silver and trunk of gold, whose fruits are pearls. The next gentleman is to bring me a robe

4 Cf. Cecily on her diary in Wilde's *Importance of Being Earnest*: "You see, it is simply a very young girl's record of her own thoughts and impressions, and consequently meant for publication."

made of the fur of Chinese fire-rats. I ask Ōtomo, the Grand Counsellor, please to fetch me the jewel that shines five colors, found in a dragon's neck. And Isonokami, the Middle Counsellor, should present me with a swallow's easy-delivery charm."[5]

The lively middle third of the novella recounts the attempts by the five suitors to meet these demands; while the fairytale beginning and ending were probably derived from an early source, the author was free to improvise in the middle, as translator Donald Keene notes.[6] (Formally the novella resembles a jazz composition; as storytellers retold the story in later centuries, they too improvised in the middle while sticking closely to the written theme at the head and conclusion.) The two princes, unwilling to make the long journeys, try to fool the girl by substituting imitations, but she sees through them and dismisses them in disgrace. (The second prince makes up an especially elaborate lie about his quest, a fiction within this fiction.) The gentleman assigned the fire-retardant rat-fur coat is swindled in turn by a fake, so he's out. The Grand Counsellor at least tries to find a dragon's jewel — how hard can that be in the land of Godzilla? "Dragons are constantly rising from the sea and descending from the mountains in this country," he casually remarks (71) — but he almost dies in the attempt, and the Middle Counsellor actually does die from injuries sustained from trying to steal the mythical charm in the stomachs of swallows that allows them to lay eggs with ease. Each anecdote ends with a play on words, and all five are imaginative, frequently funny demonstrations of the unreliability and fiscal irresponsibility of aristocrats and of the lengths to which men will go to please a lady.

In the final third, the emperor of Japan learns of Kaguya-hime and commands her to join his harem, but she refuses, spending her nights watching the moon and weeping. The emperor comes to the bamboo cutter's house to seize her, and then it is revealed she is not of this earth: born on the Moon, she was sentenced to a period down below as punishment for some sin. Having served her time on the big rock, she reluctantly prepares to return to the Moon, having grown accustomed to the place. The stepfather and emperor vow to protect her from the lunar legation that comes down from the sky one night — an impressive scene like something out of a sci-fi movie — but the Moon people paralyze the Earthlings and give her a feathered robe to wear as she's transported in a flying chariot.[7] Kaguya-hime leaves the emperor with

---

5 Pages 25/29 of Keene's translation, a beautifully illustrated bilingual edition. The text alone can be found as an appendix to Rimer's *Modern Japanese Fiction and Its Traditions*, 275–305.
6 *Seeds in the Heart*, 437. I am deeply indebted to this superb history of early Japanese literature.
7 This feathered robe also appears in *The Adventures of Sayf ben Dhi Yazan* (173); Kaguya belongs to the mythical sorority that visit the human world for a short time before returning to their origin (in the moon, the sea, the otherworld, the grave).

the elixir of immortality, but having lost the selenic beauty he loses his will to live and takes the elixir to the top of the mountain closest to the Moon: "Ever since they burnt the elixir of immortality on the summit, people have called the mountain by the name Fuji, meaning immortal. Even now the smoke is still said to rise into the clouds" (145).

"The ancestor of all tales," as Murasaki Shikibu calls it in *The Tale of Genji*,[8] *The Tale of the Bamboo Cutter* is the earliest surviving example of the *tsukuri monogatari* (invented tale), but later in the 10th century a more curious genre appeared, the *uta monogatari* (poem-tale). Most novels are about people; these are novels about poetry, at which every member of the fantastic court society of the Heian period (794–1185) was expected to be proficient.[9] This was a hyperaesthetic elite devoted to decorous elegance, witty sophistication, and the arts; Oscar Wilde advised young people, "One should either be a work of art, or wear a work of art" — these Japanese dandies did both. In addition to mastering fashion, flower arranging, and etiquette, they were expected to be able to compose and to analyze poetry, which by this time meant the formal *waka*: a 5-line poem of 31 syllables on a limited range of topics, most having to do with a self-conscious, often sentimental sensitivity to impermanence and the evanescent nature of beauty, the seasons, and love — in a phrase, *mono no aware*, the pathos of life, Lucretius's "tears of things" (*lacrimae rerum*). The idea of impermanence causes religious people to despise this world and pin their hopes on a permanent afterlife, but the more sensible Japanese made it an occasion for art, cherishing the beauty of this world all the more *because* of its impermanence. "Were they, when one called 'Stay!' to linger on and never fall, why would one ever prefer cherry blossoms?"[10]

The earliest and most famous *uta monogatari* is *Tales of Ise*, an 80-page novella edited during the first half of the 10th century by an unknown author. If published today, it would be called a nonlinear, pointillist, experimental metafiction, for it recounts the life of an unnamed character from youth to death by way of 125 discrete, nonsequential anecdotes about occasions on which he wrote a poem, usually during one of his many affairs with women. The opening section is typical:

> Once a man who had lately come of age went hunting on his estate at Kasuga village, near the Nara capital. In the village there lived two beautiful young sisters. The man caught a glimpse of the sisters through a gap in their hedge. It was startling and incongruous indeed that such ladies should dwell at the ruined capital, and he wished to meet them. He tore

---

8 Chap. 17 in Tyler's translation.
9 *Heian* is both an adjective and the name of the Japanese capital established in 794 (modern Kyoto), which remained the capital until 1869.
10 An anonymous poem (#70) collected in the famous anthology *Kokinshu* (c. 905), as translated by Tyler in *The Tale of Genji* (35, n100).

a strip from the skirt of his hunting costume, dashed off a poem, and sent it in. The fabric of the robe was imprinted with a moss-fern design.

> Like the random pattern of this robe,
> Dyed with the young purple
> From Kasuga Plain —
> Even thus is the wild disorder
> Of my yearning heart.

No doubt it had occurred to him that this was an interesting opportunity for an adaptation of the poem that runs,

> My thoughts have grown disordered,
> As random patterns dyed on cloth
> Reminiscent of Shinobu in Michinoku —
> And who is to blame?
> Surely not I.

People were remarkably elegant in those days.[11]

The young man is traditionally understood to be Ariwara no Narihira (825–80), a courtier and poet who soon after his death became idealized as the perfect gentleman, especially in matters of the heart. About 30 of his own poems are scattered throughout *Tales of Ise*; the rest are anonymous love poems of the time taken from anthologies. The poems are so dependent upon wordplay, allusion, and cultural subtleties that they obviously lose much in translation and require extensive annotation to be appreciated, and what passes for narrative is lost on anyone not already familiar with Narihira's life (as its intended audience was), so for the Western reader *Tales of Ise* offers little more than fleeting glimpses of a Japanese Don Juan with a gift for improvising allusive poems. But it had an enormous influence on later Japanese fiction, especially *The Tale of Genji*. (The Japanese word for "purple" used in the first poem above is *murasaki*, and Genji himself was modeled on Narihira.)

Two other poem-tales appeared in the middle of the 10th century, when Heian culture was at its most sophisticated under Emperor Murakami (ruled 946–67). *Tales of Yamato* (*Yamato monogatari*, c. 952) differs from *Tales of Ise* in featuring the poetic activities of a group of aristocrats rather than of one particular individual. It's twice as long as the earlier work and often gives more prose background to the poems, but without the individual focus (however blurry) of *Tales of Ise*, it reads more like a poetry anthology with

---

11 From McCullough's translation, 69–70.(I've eliminated the Japanese originals of the poems.) Helen Craig McCullough (1918–98) was the grand dame of medieval Japanese translation, and several of her works will be quoted in this section.

chatty headnotes, which perhaps is all it was intended to be. The novella is somewhat unified by the recurring imagery and the relationships between the characters — they all belonged to the courts of emperors Uda and Daigo (ruled 887–97, 897–930) — but this is weakened at the end by the addition of some longer episodes based on romantic legends rather than on court life.

Taira no Sadafun (870?–923?), a famous courtier/poet/lover who appears here and there in *Tales of Yamato* under his nickname Heichu, takes center stage in *Tales of Heichu* (*Heichū monogatari*, c. 960–65). Two-thirds of the poems in this 70-page novella are attributed to him, and like *Tales of Ise* it benefits from keeping its focus on a single protagonist. Though the least famous of the *uta monogatari* — the manuscript wasn't discovered until 1931 — it is the most novelistic in having a higher proportion of prose to poetry and in offering a well-rounded view of a ladies' man. Although he occasionally scores, Heichu more often strikes out with the objects of his affections, or loses them to a rival (even to a priest in one episode), or is frustrated by protective parents, or is the victim of lies and unflattering rumors. The novella is episodic and simply stops rather than concludes — there's no death scene as in *Tales of Ise* — but *Tales of Heichu* is a pleasant, sometimes comic look at the vicissitudes of romance and the important part poetry played in aristocratic flirtation in the 10th century, yet another demonstration of Maso's Axiom lovemaking ≈ language-making. (One lady who doesn't know how to write poetry is summarily disqualified from the game of love.) Although *Tales of Heichu* itself wasn't too popular, the figure of Heichu appealed to later Japanese writers who exploited his reputation in such a way that he degenerated over the centuries into a profligate clown and even appeared in a few pornographic works, more like Coover's Lucky Pierre than the legendary Don Juan he originally resembled. The great 20th-century Japanese writer Tanizaki Junichiro made a novella out of Heichu's post-*Tales* appearances entitled *The Mother of Captain Shigemoto* (1950), a far cry from the endearing romantic of a millennium earlier.[12]

Yet another genre added to the mix of Japanese fiction in the 10th century was the war story (*gunki monogatari*). *The Story of Masakado's Rebellion* (*Shomonki*, 940?) fictionalizes the last five years of the life of Taira no Masakado (903?–40), a historical figure related to the imperial family. A landowner in the eastern provinces — which, because of a weak central government more interested in aesthetic ritual than national administration, were run by corrupt officials and powerful families with their own armies — Masakado gets involved in some family feuds and property disputes and

---

12 Both *Tales of Yamato* and *Tales of Heichu* are available in excellent scholarly editions by Mildred Tahara and Susan Downing Videen, respectively. One further *uta monogatari* is sometimes mentioned in conjunction with them, *The Tale of Takamura* (*Takamura monogatari*), but it's only a dozen pages long, and though it may have originated in the 10th century, it apparently didn't achieve its final form until the 13th.

begins waging war on his enemies, winning enough victories that he soon gets the vainglorious idea (seeded by a shamaness) of taking over all of Japan — the only man in Japanese history who dared to dethrone the "divine" emperor. He becomes "New Emperor" of the Bando region, but is soon killed in battle by the allied armies of two rivals. The anonymous author says Masakado was "struck by a stray arrow from one of the gods" as punishment for rebelling against the divine order, and the brief novella ends with the rebel's damned spirit speaking from hell, describing his torments and advising the living to "show compassion toward your fellow man and accumulate good deeds to compensate for past evil!"[13]

It's a clumsy work in most respects, alternating between a documentary style and patches of purple prose, frequently getting names and dates wrong, introducing new characters out of nowhere, leaving motives unexplained, and written in a hybrid Sino-Japanese style that its English translator describes as "difficult and uneven — sometimes broken, awkward, or barely intelligible," yet possessing "a rustic charm that is one of the work's most appealing features" (2). Since it was apparently written later the same year Masakado was killed, perhaps it is a rushed first draft that the author never revised. Whoever he was, the author was very well read, lacing the novella with numerous allusions to Chinese history and Buddhist lore, the latter influencing his pacifist view toward Masakado's disruptive rebellion. The author takes special care to remember the victims of war — peasants burned out of their huts, wives stripped naked and raped, families scattered, exhausted soldiers forced to fight yet another battle, even a weary horse "licking the thin snow at its hooves" (97) — and portrays Masakado as a good man turned villain, undeserving of the deification he later enjoyed from the Japanese people. (Even today there are shrines devoted to him in Tokyo.) *The Story of Masakado's Rebellion* is the earliest example of a genre that wouldn't come into fruition in Japan until the 13th century, but it offers a bracing change from the exclusive world of the *uta monogatari* and adds one more room to the growing house of fiction under construction in 10th-century Nippon.

All of the works I've discussed so far are short — bonsai novels. The earliest surviving extended-length novel is *The Tale of the Hollow Tree* (*Utsubo* [or *Utsuho*] *monogatari*), traditionally attributed to Minamoto no Shitago (911–83), a poet and scholar. Apparently written in the 960s and '70s, this 600-page novel is a transitional book, linking folkloric works like *The Tale of the Bamboo Cutter* to the more realistic novels that followed, of which this may be the first.[14]

---

13 From Rabinovitch's translation (pp. 131, 139), another model scholarly edition.
14 Many other novels written in the 10th century have not survived — or, like *The Tale of Sumiyoshi*, exist only in later versions — so it's impossible to make definitive claims for any of them.

The long opening chapter — an old-fashioned *monogatari* on its own — is set in the early 9th century and tells of a musical prodigy named Toshikage, who is asked by the emperor to join at age 16 an embassy to China. His ship is blown off course and wrecks on the coast of "Persia" (i.e., the Malay Peninsula), a wonderland filled with flying horses and peacocks, where he meets some celestial koto players who pass along their divine technical skills. Toshikage eventually meets the Buddha himself, a huge fan of koto music, then returns to Japan 23 years later with 12 kotos (two of them magical), which will be passed along to other characters later in the novel. Toshikage's parents have died by then, but the emperor is impressed by his adventures and favors him. "After that, Toshikage was married to the daughter of a prince of fine character who had become a commoner with the name Genji" — a name worth remembering.[15] He and his wife produce a daughter whom he teaches the koto from age four; he dies when she is 15, and shortly afterward she has a one-night stand with a young noble that results in a son named Nakatada, the principle protagonist of the novel. Mother and son leave their dilapidated house in Kyoto to live in the mountains nearby, where she teaches the boy the koto, which has a magical effect on listeners and the elements themselves.

In chapter 2, the author leaves the fairytale mode for a more realistic one, but with one foot still in folkloric tradition. Chapters 2 through 12 concern the courtship of a 12-year-old *fille fatale* named Atemiya, who is wooed by 16 men of all ages: our hero Nakatada along with married men, bachelors, a Buddhist monk, even one of Atemiya's own brothers. The heartless tween ignores them all, indifferent to (or unaware of) the devastating effect her budding beauty has on men, and the author effectively alternates between eliciting pity, outrage, and scorn for the various suitors. This sequence is distantly related to the wooing of Kaguya-hime, but realistically dramatizes the actual courtship habits of Heian Japan. Eventually the teenaged Crown Prince — who already has a harem ranging in age from 17 to "old" — pulls rank and claims Atemiya, now 15. News of this causes havoc among the suitors: one dies of disappointment, another (her brother) nearly dies, another burns his house down and retreats to the hills to become a hermit, and others are ruined for years by unrequited love.

The last part of the novel (chaps. 13–20) is the most realistic and deals with the machinations of dynastic succession (apparently based on a similar situation in Japan in 967). One faction wants Atemiya's son to become the

---

15 From Ziro Uraki's translation, published in Tokyo apparently without the benefit of an English-speaking editor: it's frequently unidiomatic, and a comparison with two sections translated earlier in *Monumenta Nipponica* by Cranston (1969) and Lammers (1982) reveals Uraki streamlined the text by eliminating sentences, poems, and entire paragraphs along the way. Even his title is off: he called it *The Tale of the Cavern*, but the incident that gives the novel its name takes place in the hollow of four cedar trees, not in a cavern. To complicate matters, the Japanese text is a mess, with countless variants and difficulties.

next emperor, while another favors the son of a different concubine of the Crown Prince. Throughout, the power of music unites the various strands of the novel's plot; rejected by Atemiya, Nakatada marries someone else, has a daughter, and begins teaching her the koto, just as his mother did when he was a child, preserving the teachings Toshikage learned back in "Persia." During this section, Nakatada discovers a cache of manuscripts his grandfather left behind, including an account of his time in Persia; it is tempting to regard the first chapter, so different in style and technique from the rest of the novel, as a re-creation of Toshikage's diary, old-fashioned to the point of parody, but that may be giving the author too much credit. The novel ends pleasantly as the question of succession is settled amicably in favor of Atemiya and as Nakatada's daughter Imumiya gives her first koto concert, an affirmation that artistic expertise is as important as political connections in achieving success and respect at the Heian court.

The Tale of the Hollow Tree is filled with realistic touches from everyday aristocratic life: there are countless domestic details, lots of scenes with babies and children, political procedures, and interesting facts such as Heian women sought to increase their appeal by blackening their teeth (with a fluid made by steeping iron in sake), which seems pointless given that they spent much of their lives indoors concealed behind fans, curtains, and screens, swimming in voluminous robes, and living in darkness like weird deep-sea creatures. There are about a thousand poems in the novel, but none memorable (says Keene, 445); perhaps Shitago merely wanted a permanent place to park his own poems. The respect and attention paid to music, especially to the koto, is remarkable; if not intended as a metaphor for art in general, koto music must at least have been dear to the author. But ultimately it's a rather bland, rambling novel, the work of someone who was feeling his way toward a modern alternative to the old *monogatari* without a firm idea of what the end product should be. Not a great novel, then, but it unquestionably smoothed the way for the Japanese to produce a great novel eventually.

Half the length of *The Tale of the Hollow Tree* but twice as accomplished, *The Tale of the Lady Ochikubo* (*Ochikubo monogatari*) is a delightful, Nancy Mitfordesque satire on the upper classes written by an unknown author during the final decade of the 10th century. The plot elements introduced in its opening pages will be familiar to the Western reader: Beautiful stepdaughter treated as a drudge? Evil stepmother? Haughty sisters? Yes, it's a Japanese version of the Cinderella story, one of the earliest in world literature.[16] "Lady Ochikubo" is a derisive title rather than a personal name, meaning "Miss

16 The earliest is said to be a Chinese tale recorded by Tuan Ch'eng-shih around 850; it's possible the anonymous author of *The Tale of Ochikubo* knew it, but the brief Chinese fable has little in common with the 260-page novel, and evil stepmothers are a staple of Oriental fiction anyway. In a Japanese novel set in the 12th century, we're told young Huang-li's "stepmother so detested him that she fed him poisoned food. Huang-li, however, merely

Basement," which is where our heroine is forced to live by the principal wife of a middle-level imperial counselor named Tadayori, her father. He once had an affair with a princess, and Ochikubo was the result; after the princess died, Ochikubo was relegated to the lower level of his house and forced to sew clothes for Tadayori's legitimate daughters, who now, having reached the ages of 12 and 13, are ready to find husbands. Ochikubo is about 15 when the novel opens, her only friend a quick-witted servant named Akogi, a girl around the same age who is largely responsible for the happy ending our Cinderella will eventually enjoy.

Though it consists of four long chapters, *The Tale of Ochikubo* falls neatly into thirds. In the first third we watch as Akogi gets her newly acquired boyfriend Tachihaki to encourage an up-and-coming nobleman named Michiyori to become Ochikubo's lover and rescue her from her awful situation. This waggish bachelor, still in his teens, plays along and visits the girl one night, who is more mortified at her shabby clothing than at a stranger joining her in bed. Michiyori enjoys his one-night stand more than he expected and comes back the second night, when he hides under the covers and gets a load of the evil stepmother and learns how poorly Ochikubo is being treated. Then he returns — in pouring rain, a measure of his devotion — for the all-important third night: at this time in Japan, a man taking a wife or lover would have sex with her the first night — often without ever having laid eyes on her before — come again the second night, and then, if he wanted to establish a relationship, would return the third night and be treated to traditional foods signifying the union. (Even after the marriage, the man would often continue to live on his own and only visit his wife at her parents' house.) The stepmother, suspecting something, not only locks Ochikubo in a storeroom but "gives" her to her uncle, a repulsive man in his sixties, whose disgustingly comic attempts to seduce the teenager lead to a daring rescue by Michiyori, who installs Ochikubo in a spare house, bringing along Akogi because she stage-managed the whole affair with considerable aplomb for a teenager.

In the middle third of the novel, Michiyori systematically avenges Ochikubo's mistreatment by publicly humiliating the counselor's family in as many ways as he can. (Tadayori is fond of his little princess but was easily duped by his scheming, henpecking wife into thinking Ochikubo was a brat and thus went along with her punishments.) Meek Ochikubo is willing to forgive and forget, but Michiyori delights in making the family miserable, going so far as to trick one of the counselor's daughters into marrying a dunce nicknamed the White-faced Colt, taking over a house (through a legal loophole) just after the counselor had refurbished it, and stealing away his prettiest

---

regarded her deed as that typical of any stepmother, and he bore her no grudge" (*The Tale of the Soga Brothers*, book 2).

servants. He's careful not to let the family know he's behind all these reversals, and it's wicked fun to read of his machinations.

Michiyori then summons Tadayori for a long talk, confessing to his schemes and explaining why he wanted to avenge his wife's honor — all news to the befuddled counselor. But to show their filial piety, Michiyori and Ochikubo spend the last third of the novel showering the family with gifts and honors, killing them with kindness. Now one of the most powerful men in Japan, Michiyori even gives up his post for a while so that Tadayori can take it and thereby fulfill his lifelong ambition. Slowly, even the stepmother realizes that her stepdaughter is the most devoted of her children. By this time Ochikubo has produced several beautiful children of her own, one of whom eventually becomes empress of Japan. But the novel's final line is given to resourceful Akogi, who is now the Naishi no Suke (supervisor of the female palace staff): "And it is said that the Naishi no Suke lived to the age of two hundred years."[17]

The fairytale ending is surprising because until then the novel has been fairly realistic. True, Michiyori's steadfast devotion to the girl from the basement is unusual — he takes no further wives or concubines — and his meteoric rise to power is a little too spectacular.[18] But the novel is filled with realistic touches new to the Japanese novel: Akogi claims to be menstruating in order to get out of going on an excursion, and note the marital intimacy of this passage, in which Akogi's new boyfriend watches her get ready:

> "There must be a basin in the main building. I will go and fetch the Third Lady's for the Lord [Michiyori] to use," she said, letting down her hair again. Having made a grand toilet, with her *obi* loosely tied around her, and her hair, about three feet longer than her height, hanging down her back, she looked very pretty to Tachihaki as he followed her with his eyes as she went into the next room where the Lady [Ochikubo], still in great distress, lay in bed. (31)

There's a naturalness, even sassiness to the dialogue, as in this snappy exchange between Akogi and Michiyori, when the traditional rice-cakes

---

17 Page 258 in the Whitehouse/Yanagisawa translation. As in this sentence, most of the characters are referred to by their titles, and since these often change as people marry or get promoted — Michiyori ascends through a half-dozen ranks — it is challenging to keep track of who's who. The personal names I've been using above occur only once in most cases.

18 Promotions were based on rank and cronyism, not on ability; see chapter 3 of Ivan Morris's *World of the Shining Prince*, an engrossing companion to *The Tale of Genji* that, perhaps inadvertently, exposes the aristocracy of that time to be arguably the most ridiculous society in human history, despite its artistic achievements: superstitious, insular, incurious, unintellectual, snobbish, conformist, superficial, mawkish, impractical, and gossipy. "People were remarkably elegant in those days," as *Tales of Ise* says, but aside from an aversion to violence and an admirably relaxed attitude toward sex, there's not much to commend.

served on the third night of intimacy become metaphors for sex:

> "Oh, it's the rice-cakes, is it?" he said, finding it all rather amusing. "Is there any special way of eating them? What must I do?"
>
> "Haven't you learned yet what you have to do?" asked Akogi.
>
> "How could I have learned? I have remained single up till now. So I have never eaten them."
>
> "You must take three," said Akogi, on hearing this.
>
> "This is like a child's game," he said. "How many does the Lady [Ochikubo] take?"
>
> "As many as she pleases," answered Akogi laughing.
>
> "Take these," said the Lord to the Lady but she was too shy to take them. (41)

Characterization is more realistic and richer than in previous Japanese fiction. Shy, meek Lady O remains so throughout the novel, even though her later success and position would have emboldened most women. The evil stepmother finally comes around to appreciating Ochikubo, but her suspicious, ornery nature persists: she accepts her advice to become a Buddhist nun after her husband dies, "But when she was angry, she said, 'She made me become a nun. And she knows how fond I am of fish. Step-children are very crafty'" (257).[19] That's her last line in the book, consistent to the end. There's even some realistic scatological humor in the novel, as when the creepy uncle beshits himself while trying to get at Ochikubo in the storeroom. All of these touches are new to the Japanese novel, resulting in an urbane novel of manners that is smart and sophisticated. Since the English translation of *The Tale of the Lady Ochikubo* has been around since 1934, I don't know why this appealing novel isn't better known.

There is one more genre that blossomed during the cultural flowering of the 10th century worth mentioning before moving on: the diary (*nikki*), or journal. Diaries had been kept in the past — factual accounts written mostly by men and in Chinese — but after the appearance of *The Tosa Diary* around 935, women took over the genre, writing in Japanese instead of Chinese and borrowing elements from current *monogatari* to create books that read more like first-person novels than diaries. Although narrated by a woman, *The Tosa Diary* was actually written by a man named Ki no Tsurayuki (872?–945); grieving over the death of his daughter, he apparently felt a female persona would better allow him to express his "womanly" grief, though he lets the mask slip so many times nobody was fooled.[20] *The Tosa Diary* is only a 30-page account of the narrator's trip from Tosa (on the island of Shikoku) to

---

19 Monks and nuns kept a strict vegetarian diet. Several times in this novel a woman expresses a desire to become a nun, but only to hide away from the world — never for religious reasons — or, as here, as part of a retirement plan.

20 This subtle little work can be found in Miner's *Japanese Poetic Diaries* (59–91) and in McCullough's *Classical Japanese Prose* (73–102).

the capital in Kyoto, and is apparently historically accurate, but the female persona and the large number of poems inserted in the work blur its genre, resulting in a hybrid of travel journal, *uta monogatari*, and primer on Japanese verse. (During the trip, the narrator and her fellow passengers write poems, which are freely criticized by the narrator; Tsurayuki wrote the introduction to an important imperial anthology of poetry called the *Kokinshu*.)

This typically Japanese indifference to genre distinctions is even more apparent in the first major "art diary" written by a woman, *The Gossamer Years* (*Kagero nikki*, 974).[21] The author's personal name is unknown, so she's called Michitsuna no haha: the Mother of Michitsuna (her most famous son). Beginning in the third person, she explains why she wrote her book:

> These times have passed, and there was one who drifted uncertainly through them, scarcely knowing where she was. . . . Yet, as the days went by in monotonous succession, she had occasion to look at the old romances [*monogatari*], and found them masses of the rankest fabrication. Perhaps, she said to herself, even the story of her own dreary life, set down in a journal, might be of interest;[22]

The dreariness of her life stems from being only the second wife of a nobleman named Fujiwara Kaneie and being often neglected by him not only in favor of his principal wife but a cornucopia of concubines and courtesans. This diary of a mad housewife is thus rooted in fact but reads like fiction, especially when one learns that Mrs. Michitsuna wildly overdramatized her situation, casting herself as the star of her own soap opera. (As the translator notes in his introduction, "For someone in her class to be taken as the second wife of such a well-placed young gentleman as Kaneie would have been considered a fine stroke of luck by most Heian ladies" [9].) Although the work has dates like a diary, it is made up of long dramatized narratives that are obviously fictionalized to some extent. But since the author deliberately distanced herself from "the old romances," perhaps we shouldn't try to turn her into a novelist — she had enough grief in her life.

But translator Edwin A. Cranston had no qualms about subtitling *The Izumi Shikibu Diary* "A Romance of the Heian Court," and contemporary critics agree it has more in common with a novel than a diary. The Anaïs Nin

---

21 Japanese critics have proposed a number of terms for these novel-like diaries such as *tsukuri nikki, nikki bungaku*, and my favorite (because it sounds like the name of a Japanese pop idol), *nikki monogatari*. Miner provides an informative overview of the genre in his lengthy introduction to *Japanese Poetic Diaries*. But *nikki* is not to be confused with the "pillow book," like the famous one by Sei Shonagon (c. 1005), which is a miscellany of observations, poetry, dramatized scenes, and lists of likes and dislikes — superficially resembling a modern teenage girl's diary or MyFace profile.

22 From Seidensticker's translation, 33. The work breaks off mid-sentence after about 130 pages.

of Nippon, Izumi Shikibu (c. 975–after 1033) was a celebrated poet with a reputation as a femme fatale. After an affair with one prince of the realm ended in 1002 with his premature death — and which got Izumi divorced from her husband and disinherited from her father — she began an affair with his half-brother Atsumichi in May 1003 that she dramatized a few years later in a 60-page work that has been called both a *nikki* and a *monogatari*. (Its title, like that of nearly every Japanese work I've discussed so far, is a descriptive term used by later commentators, not the author's choice.) As translator Cranston points out, its story conforms to the known facts of this Heian hellion's scandalous life, but: "The narration is in the third person, and the point of view is not limited to that proper to a diarist. There are simultaneous or almost simultaneous scenes in different places, imagined conversations, and descriptions of the thoughts and feelings of different people. The work is at least partially one of imaginative fiction."[23] To a reader unacquainted with its history, it sounds like a work of imaginative fiction, beginning with its lyrical opening paragraph:

> Frailer than a dream had been those mortal ties for which she mourned, passing her days and nights with sighs of melancholy. And now the tenth of the fourth month had come and gone, and the shade beneath the trees grew ever deeper. The fresh green of the grass on the embankment — though most people would hardly have given it a glance — somehow aroused an emotional awareness within her, and, as she sat gazing out at it, she noticed a movement at the nearby openwork fence. Who could it be, she wondered, only to discover a moment later that it was the young page who used to wait on the late Prince. (131)

The page brings a note from the late prince's half-brother, testing the waters, and when she responds favorably — though wondering if it is too soon to stop mourning her old love and to seek a new — the delicate affair is off and running. Or halting, for it proceeds at a very slow pace, with much hesitation and many exchanges of allusive poems, both parties paralyzed by the fear of gossip. (She's trying to repair her bad reputation and he has a jealous wife to consider.)

Both follow the rules of Heian courtship as laid down in the love poems in anthologies like the *Kokinshu* already mentioned — every aristocrat memorized its thousand or so poems — which challenged Izumi to align those rules with the actual events she lived through — another reason for calling the result a novel rather than a diary.[24] They occasionally spend the night watching the moon together and speaking "of all the touching sadness of this

---

23 Introduction, 26. (The novella occupies pp. 131–91 and will be cited by page number.) For these same reasons, some commentators insist the work was written by someone other than Izumi.
24 See Janet A. Walker's fine essay "Poetic Ideal and Fictional Reality in the *Izumi Shikibu nikki*"; she too treats it "as a work of Heian fiction" (154).

life" (162) and the prince soon falls in love with her for a poignant reason: "The more he studied her, the more he realized that she had never been hardened by the world" (163). He invites her to move in with him — that is, into a secluded wing of his mansion — which leads to further doubts, poems, and hesitations, for the world's mistreatment has Izumi considering a retreat to the religious life. She finally agrees to the move, but her arrival is met with chattering disapproval from the servants and the principal wife. The novella ends abruptly with the wife threatening to leave the prince; it's implied the "romance" stage of Izumi's relationship with the prince has ended and that the only thing to be salvaged from the affair is the telling of it:

> "Will I alone be left
> To tell the story of our past —
> Destined to be numbered
> With old tales of painful loves,
> Many as the nodes of black bamboo?" (186)

Izumi asks in her final poem, and it's obvious this melancholy baby is to be numbered with the old *monogatari* rather than with diary literature.[25] All it lacks is a novelistic title; just as *The Sarashina Diary* (which I'll discuss later) sounds much more like a novel (which it is) under its current English title *As I Crossed a Bridge of Dreams*, *The Izumi Shikibu Diary* should be replaced by something more evocative — given the pervasive moon imagery and stylized melancholia, perhaps *The Serious Moonlight* (with apologies to David Bowie).

It remains an open question whether this and the other *nikki* can be classified as novels, but there is no disputing their enormous influence on the developing Japanese novel. They legitimized introspection, shifted the focus from public events to private matters, and allowed women to join the ranks of authors, still a rarity at this point in history. The first-person psychological novel especially in later Japanese fiction is deeply indebted to the pioneering efforts of these Heian diarists.

In the spring of 1009 Izumi Shikibu joined the brilliant court of Empress Shoshi (aka Akiko), which included another lady who wrote a *nikki* still read today. But she was also putting the finishing touches on a monumental *monogatari* — longer and more ambitious than any previous one and destined to become the greatest novel in Japanese literature.

---

25 In real life Izumi stayed with Prince Atsumichi until his death in 1007 at age 27. The novella's ambiguous ending is one more reason to classify it as fiction rather than as a diary.

The Tale of Genji (Genji monogatari, c. 1010) would be an extraordinary novel in any time or place, but all the more so for appearing in the 11th century, and in Japan. As we've seen, Japanese fiction was only a century old when *Genji* was written, and consisted mostly of compact, stylized works of considerable surface charm but of little depth. How then to account for the quantum leap to this elegantly erudite, psychologically profound, thousand-page tragicomedy of manners? Genius, suggests Harold Bloom; he includes the author in his book of that name, calling her "the genius of longing" (297), and in the absence of any other explanation, it's hard to disagree.

Who was she? We don't know her personal name, only the nickname she later acquired: Murasaki Shikibu literally means "Violet of Ceremonial," and is apparently derived from the name of the novel's young heroine, Murasaki (purple/violet, after the plant that produces purple dye) and the post the author's father once held at the Bureau of Ceremonial (Shikibu-sho). She was born around 973, married a man twice her age around 998 (and produced a daughter a year later), and was widowed by 1001. In the lonely years that followed, she began writing her novel. Around 1006 she joined the entourage of the young, straitlaced Empress Shoshi, just as Izumi Shikibu did shortly after, and was already known for her work in progress, which she apparently finished around 1010. The last anyone heard from her was in 1013, and she is presumed to have died a year or two later in her early forties — the same age as her fictional namesake, as it happens.

The Tale of Genji is a novel written by an aristocratic woman for other women of her rank — men at this time read history and poetry, sometimes theology, but not fiction — which presents the first challenge to reading it. It wasn't written for you, dear reader, but for select contemporaries who instinctively understood everything that now needs to be spelled out in annotations and commentary. Like the woman in chapter 38 who "could not bring herself to speak plainly and instead touched only obliquely on the matter," Murasaki relies on understatement, indirection, suggestion, a coded language made up of poetic allusions and a complex pattern of floral and seasonal imagery to relate her tale, which seems to be addressed to a superior (like Empress Shoshi). The modern reader doesn't so much listen to the story as eavesdrop on it, spy on it, like the courtiers in *Genji* always peeking through gaps and peepholes to catch glimpses of the young beauties indoors.[26] The reader of *Genji* is not an invited guest but a voyeur.

Adding to the challenge is the unprecedented complexity of the novel, the result of highly detailed accounts of the interactions of some 500 characters over a 60-year period. Like the elaborate outfits Heian women wore, it has

---

26 The Japanese had a word for this lustful male spying, *kaimami*, first base in the game of seduction. To take a frank look at a woman up close was an act of violation tantamount to rape.

many layers.[27] The outermost layer is a study of the manners and sexual politics of the imperial court during the first half of the 10th century — that is, a few generations before Murasaki's time. Beneath that is a dazzling and erudite display of Heian aesthetics, and beneath that (but carefully harmonized with these aesthetics, especially by way of poetry) is a dramatization of "the conflict between prudent restraint and passionate feeling" in a society that encouraged extremes of both behaviors.[28] Filling out the novel are several case studies of desire, more specifically of the metamorphoses of desire, of how unrequited love for one person is transferred to another, and another, in an endless quest for an ideal forever out of reach. Although the stuff of poetry, desire is portrayed here as a disruptive force, its fleeting joys usually outweighed by the misery caused to the unwilling victims of others' desires, by the jealousy that often results — so virulent in some women that it takes the form of spirit possession — and by the frustration of unfulfilled longings. (Suffusing the novel like the incense with which the nobility perfumed their clothes is the Buddhist view of desire as the cause of all suffering.) And beneath it all, like the transparent shift of silk gauze Japanese women wore in summer, are occasional glimpses of Lady Murasaki herself, commenting on her novel as it progresses, comparing it to older novels, and confidently intimating that her novel (like Genji's paintings), "done at undisturbed leisure by a genius at the art, was beyond anything" (17).

The outermost layer of the novel, like all public displays, is deceptive. Although it may seem (especially in Waley's winsome translation) like "a beautiful sad story populated by languorous princes and princesses who console themselves for unrequited and perhaps even tragic love by refining their already exquisite sensibilities vis-à-vis the affectingly mutable manifestations

27 "The full-dress costume worn by women at court or by gentlewomen in an aristocratic household" consisted of the following: "The Chinese jacket (*karaginu*) was worn over a train (*mo*) tied at the waist over an outer gown (*uwagi*) that was the most elaborate of a layer of gowns of identical shape (*uchiki, kinu, onzo*) worn over a shift (*hitoe*) and long, ample trousers (*hakama*) tied at the waist with a sash. The layers of gowns were cut smaller as they reached the outside so that the edges of the underlayers could be seen" — Tyler (see next note), 1155.

28 From chapter 34 in Royall Tyler's translation (2001), hereafter cited by chapter (and by page for editorial matter). This translation is more faithful to the original than Edward Seidensticker's excellent translation (1976) by referring to characters by their rank or position; Murasaki did not give personal names to most of them, though later commentators assigned them ones (based on key images) for ease of reference, which Seidensticker follows. (I too will follow this practice, going so far as to refer to the female character Murasaki as "Violet" to distinguish her from the author.) Tyler's translation is thus more challenging to read, especially since the novel's characters frequently change rank, but he offsets that with copious notes, glossaries, maps, etc. Arthur Waley's old translation (1925–33) is no longer viable; not only did he eliminate one entire chapter (38), but he cut and expanded passages freely, turning this alien Japanese work into a romantic Edwardian novel. Nevertheless (as Mike Dirda reminded me) Waley performed a great service to literature by introducing this masterpiece to Western readers in the first place.

of nature," in Norma Field's deliberate caricature (297), *The Tale of Genji* is primarily a mordant exposé of the nature of desire. Unlike the Buddha, Murasaki doesn't deliver a fiery sermon against desire, but rather a complex, nuanced look at how it affects a society that has aestheticized desire to a dangerously sentimental degree. She begins her novel by reminding readers that while desire may seem to be a personal matter, at an imperial court the personal is the political:

> In a certain reign (whose can it have been?) someone of no very great rank, among all His Majesty's Consorts and Intimates, enjoyed exceptional favor. Those others who had always assumed that pride of place was properly theirs despised her as a dreadful woman, while the lesser Intimates were unhappier still. The way she waited on him day after day only stirred up feelings against her, and perhaps this growing burden of resentment was what affected her health and obliged her often to withdraw in misery to her home; but His Majesty, who could less and less do without her, ignored his critics until his behavior seemed bound to be the talk of all.
>
> From this sad spectacle the senior nobles and privy gentlewomen could only avert their eyes. Such things had led to disorder and ruin even in China, they said, and as discontent spread through the realm, the example of Yōkihi came more and more to mind, with many a painful consequence for the lady herself; yet she trusted in his gracious and unexampled affection and remained at court. (1)

Yokihi was a beauty who so bewitched Emperor Xuanzong (685–762) that he abandoned his duties and provoked a rebellion, as Murasaki's readers would have known from the Chinese poet Bo Juyi's 9th-century ballad "Song of Lasting Pain," which is alluded to throughout *The Tale of Genji*.[29] Things don't get that bad in the Japanese emperor's case, but it doesn't bode well for the beautiful son his lady soon provides him, who is called Genji — not a personal name but a proper noun indicating membership in the Minamoto clan. His almost supernatural beauty earns him the nickname "the Shining Prince," after the Shining Princess of *The Tale of the Bamboo Cutter*.

The novel can be divided into three unequal parts: chapters 1 through 33 (the first half of the book) tracks Genji's career from birth to age 39, when he is at the apex of personal and political success. Things begin to go wrong in chapter 34 and get worse until chapter 41, when Genji is 52. Chapter 42 resumes eight years later, several years after Genji's death, with no explanation of how he died.[30] The remainder of the novel (through chapter 54) concerns

29 An English translation can be found in Stephen Owen's *Anthology of Chinese Literature*, 442–47.

30 Between chapters 41 and 42 in some editions (and in Tyler's translation) there is a blank chapter with only a title: "Vanished into the Clouds" (*Kumogakure*), in which the reader can speculate on the manner of Genji's death, reminiscent of the blank page in Sterne's *Tristram Shandy* where the narrator invites the reader to write his own description of the

the romantic rivalry between two young men — Kaoru, thought by everyone to be Genji's son but actually the grandson of Genji's closest friend, and Genji's grandson Niou — for the love of the daughters of Genji's younger half-brother Hachi no Miya: Oigimi, Naka no Kimi, and their half-sister Ukifune. (I promise there won't be many more sentences like that; as the narrator herself admits at the end of chapter 39, "The relationships between these people are all too complicated to explain.") The long novel ends appropriately on a note of romantic disappointment.

"Importunate in his desires" (7), Genji is the author's principal instrument for her variations on the theme of desire. In the first nine chapters, she portrays this charming man as a young playboy; blessed with devastating looks, wit, and aristocratic immunity, he develops an appetite for romantic intrigues shortly after coming of age. (In chapter 2 he sits in on a kind of locker-room discussion of which kind of women make the best game.) Convinced he's Buddha's gift to women, Genji is attracted to a wide variety of all ages but ultimately wants to marry a girl just like the girl that married dear old dad. Genji's mother died when he was three, but after his father married a young girl called Fujitsubo (about five years older than Genji) who closely resembled his dead wife, the deprived boy developed a passionate desire for her — that is, for his stepmother because she resembles his dead mother, introducing the near-incestuous nature of many relationships in this novel.[31] "Ah, he thought, she is the kind of woman I want to marry" (1), but instead Genji was forced at age 12 to marry a 16-year-old cousin called Aoi, who is naturally miffed at being saddled with a mere boy and remains cold and distant throughout their brief marriage.

Stuck with an unwanted wife, denied the girl he really wants, Genji indulges in romantic escapades, often in rivalry with his best friend, Aoi's brother To no Chujo. While the author makes plain her disapproval of Genji's promiscuity, she also displays a worldly woman's tolerance for a rakish bad boy, especially since he doesn't love 'em and leave 'em but remains faithful, in his fashion, to all of them, eventually even building a house where all of his ex-girlfriends can stay — something few men would contemplate doing.

Nevertheless, Murasaki dramatizes the consequences of irresponsible desire early on when, at age 17, Genji becomes attracted to a slightly older

---

Widow Wadman, "as like your mistress as you can — as unlike your wife as your conscience will let you" (6.38), or the four blank pages following the half-title promising "Some Revelations" in Cabrera Infante's *Three Trapped Tigers*.

31 The Heian Japanese concept of incest was different from ours — see Bargen's "The Problem of Incest in *The Tale of Genji*" — but Murasaki toys with the taboo nonetheless. In this instance, the emperor complicates matters by promising "that she [Fujitsubo] would be to him as a daughter of his own" (1), meaning she wouldn't have to rely on her mother for support, but also underscoring the fact Fujitsubo is indeed young enough to be his daughter.

woman called Yugao, largely because he suspects To no Chujo has already enjoyed her favors. He seduces her easily, and after several clandestine visits to her home, abducts her one night to take her to an abandoned house where they can enjoy greater privacy. On their second night there, however, Genji dreams of a former lover called Rokujo berating him for abandoning her for this younger woman, and wakes to find Yugao dead, the apparent victim of "spirit possession" by the jealous Rokujo, the first of four such supernatural attacks in the novel.[32] Genji is shaken by the incident and falls ill, but by the end of the same chapter he returns to his wicked ways. "No," the narrator comments, "he had not yet learned his lesson, and he seemed as susceptible as ever to the perils of temptation" (4).

Reckless desire gets him exiled from court seven years later, after he is caught in the act with a palace woman called Oborozukiyo by her father, who complains to the Empress Mother — the same woman who humiliated Genji's mother to death — who "could not have Genji pointedly mocking and belittling her by brazenly invading her house while she herself was at home, so nearby, and this gave her a fine reason to set in train the measures to accomplish his downfall" (10). Yet even in exile (on the coast southeast of the capital) Genji pursues further affairs; he impregnates a local girl who subsequently gives birth to a daughter who will eventually become empress of Japan, a stupendous honor for Genji and typical of the mixed messages the author sends about him. After his pardon and return to the capital, Genji exerts greater control over his desire, pursuing an affair only with a former girlfriend named Asagao, which goes nowhere. (Here as elsewhere I'm grossly oversimplifying Murasaki's intricately plotted narrative.) But Genji doesn't need to chase after more women at this point because he has the perfect woman at home, one of his own creation: *Wakamurasaki*, the young Violet.

Several years earlier, when he was 17, Genji had gone on a religious retreat and noticed a girl of about 10 who reminded him of both Fujitsubo and his mother. (He later learns she's Fujitsubo's niece, hence the family resemblance, and that like Genji she too lost her mother at an early age.) "He now longed for the pleasure of having her with him day and night, to make up for the absence of the lady he loved" (5), which again refers primarily to Fujitsubo but secondarily to his mother. Genji's initial attempt to adopt the young girl scandalizes her custodians, who assume he wants her for a mistress — which he does, but not yet. During a rare opportunity back in the capital he sneaks into Fujitsubo's room and makes love to her, which stiffens his determination to adopt her younger look-alike as a substitute. He then abducts the girl and

---

32 Morris rightly dismissed spirit possession as one of Japan's many "superstitions," a judgment that has been condemned by some recent, politically correct critics as outdated, imperialistic, and/or condescending. Come on, people: *spirit possession*? It's a powerful metaphor for female rage against repression (as I'll argue later), or for a psychotic meltdown, but just a metaphor.

installs her in his house, determined to groom her into the perfect daughter/ mistress/wife/mother. (If Freud had had access to this novel, Genji would be as iconic as Oedipus in psychology.) Although they undergo a symbolic marriage, Genji acts at first like a father to Violet (as she eventually comes to be called), though in a way most readers today would find creepy: they play dolls together — she even has a Genji doll — cuddle together through the night, and as early as age 11 Violet starts wearing makeup at Genji's prompting. "They made a delightful couple" the narrator states (6), apparently without irony or censure. *Autres temps, autres mœurs.*

When Violet is 15, and shortly after Genji's wife Aoi gives birth and dies (another instance of spirit possession by jealous Rokujo), the 23-year-old Genji decides to consummate his play-marriage in a superb example of Murasaki's oblique artistry:

> It was a pleasure to see that his young lady had turned out to be all he could wish, and since he judged that the time had now more or less come, he began to drop suggestive hints, but she showed no sign of understanding.
>
> He spent whole days with her, whiling away the time at Go or at character-guessing games, and such were her wit and grace, so enthralling in quality her every gesture, that after those years of forbearance while her charm had offered nothing more, he could endure it no longer; and so despite his compunction it came to pass one morning, when there was nothing otherwise about their ways with each other to betray the change, that he rose early while she rose not at all. (9)

Violet is shocked and angered by this change in their relationship, but as she grows older she accepts it and indeed becomes the perfect wife, just as Genji had hoped. For the rest of the novel — she doesn't die until chapter 40, about two-thirds of the way through, in her early forties — she is no Stepford wife but a paragon of manners, intelligence, and understanding by the standards of her day. (The validity of those standards, and Murasaki's attitude toward them, are separate questions.) Say what you will about their unorthodox relationship — some will be reminded of *Lolita* or "Tandy" in *Winesburg, Ohio* (but with happy endings), others of *Pygmalion* or tabloid-grade pedophilia — Genji and Violet are one of the most fascinating, psychologically complex couples in world literature.

Genji is devastated by Violet's death — my sleeves too were wet with tears — and although he finds some comfort in the arms of a waiting woman named Chujo, it is "only because she reminded him of her" (41). The love of his life gone, Genji disappears from the novel at this point. The fact that there was nothing more to his life than love is driven home in the career-summarizing chapter 41, and just as the first chapter reminded readers of the irresponsibly sex-crazed Chinese emperor in the "Song of Lasting Pain,"

Murasaki cunningly makes another reference to Bo Juyi's ballad in the last chapter in which Genji appears, thereby encouraging us to consider whether Genji's charmed life could have been spent more wisely.

Erotic transference is the theme of the remaining third of the novel as well, though played as tragedy rather than romance. Kaoru and Niou are friends and romantic rivals much like their grandparents Genji and To no Chujo, but completely different from each other: Kaoru is serious and unworldly, whereas Niou is a sensuous aesthete: "To him life meant shivering with delicious pleasure before the dew on a flower" (49). They learn of two sisters in their early twenties living down in the village of Uji (about 10 miles southeast of the capital), and get involved with them with disastrous results. Kaoru, as cultured as Genji but lacking his confidence, falls for the older of the two, Oigimi, who is shy and tries to interest him instead in her sister Naka no Kimi, going so far as to arrange for him to spend the night with her. Naka no Kimi puts up the kind of ladylike resistance that Genji would have ploughed straight through but that stops Kaoru cold. Increasingly obsessed with Oigimi, Kaoru gets Niou to seduce Naka no Kimi in the desperate hope that Oigimi will reconsider him, but this morbidly shy woman disobliges him by starving herself to death to avoid dealing with the problem. Later, Niou marries Naka no Kimi and takes her back to the capital, where she begins to appreciate Kaoru more; he in turn transfers his desire for her dead sister to her, especially since he now sees the family resemblance. (Their earlier encounters were conducted in the dark, as are almost all the love affairs in this novel — which sometimes results in awkward cases of mistaken identity.) Sensing this, Naka no Kimi uses the same strategy on him as her sister did and tells Kaoru she has a mysterious half-sister named Ukifune who resembles Oigimi even more than she does. Kaoru predictably becomes obsessed with this woman, who is attracted to (and has sex with) both Kaoru and Niou and, unable to choose between the two, decides to drown herself — an option for young women in difficulties mentioned several times in the novel. Kaoru especially is upset by the news, but is then relieved to learn later that she didn't die after all. But by this point Ukifune, suffering from partial amnesia after her weird adventure (attempted suicide, spirit possession), has become a nun and wants nothing further to do with desire. Desire-wracked Kaoru is left hanging, as is the reader; the novel's inconclusive ending has frustrated many readers over the centuries, but it is fitting for us to remain as frustrated by desire (for narrative closure) as Kaoru.

These final nine chapters of *The Tale of Genji* are superb, and benefit from the smaller cast of characters and the dramatic contrast between the worldly capital and the otherworldly village of Uji, a site of magic and religion. (At 300 pages, this section forms a novel within the novel.) The tone is darker, sadder, even neurotic, a Japanese *Wuthering Heights*. Desire is just as important here as in the earlier part of the novel, but while Genji was able to transfer his desire from his mother and Fujitsubo to an unorthodox but satisfying substitute (not to mention having a number of enjoyable flings along the way), religious-minded Kaoru doesn't know what to do with his desire, displacing it on unsuitable substitutes and tempted to extinguish it altogether by taking Buddhist vows. As Richard Bowring notes, "In the beginning an excess of passion was seen as a dangerous but grand thing; now it is seen as little more than a troublesome appetite, a problem to be solved."[33] Unlike most of the women in the first half, the three daughters featured in the final chapters are scared to death of desire — literally in Oigimi's case, and almost in Ukifune's. Though in their twenties, they are consistently berated by their (older) waiting women for being so timid, desperately shy, childishly unworldly, and incapable of responding to men in a mature way. They prefer to hide, to waste their youth and looks, to pine away alone. "As far as [Ukifune] was concerned, she preferred to be left as solitary as a stump" (53). These aren't women looking for a room of their own to assert their independence, or for an alternative lifestyle, but are dysfunctional, cowering creatures who are frightened to death of life. (What kind of culture would do that to its people?) Murasaki's impatience with them is palpable.[34]

Murasaki's insight into erotic transference is profound; the above examples are only a few of the many metamorphoses of desire in the novel. At the end of chapter 2, denied the woman he wants to sleep with, Genji makes do with a 12-year-old boy. Genji's brother "missed the wife he had lost, and he only wanted another like her. There was nothing wrong with his new one, but he did not find in her the resemblance he sought" (35). Kaoru's father Kashiwagi provides the funniest example. (Like father like son.) He yearns for an unobtainable woman, so turns instead to her cat: "To relieve his powerful feelings the Intendant [Kashiwagi] called the cat and cuddled it, and with its delicious smell and its dear little mew it felt to him naughtily enough like its mistress herself" (34). He then takes her pussy home, which results in this amusing scene:

33 *Murasaki Shikibo: The Tale of Genji*, 55. This compact book may be the best introduction to *Genji*.
34 From her diary: "For example, whenever the Master of Her Majesty's Household arrives with a message for Her Majesty, the senior women are so helpless and childish that they hardly ever come out to greet him; and when they do, what happens? They seem unable to say anything in the least bit appropriate. It is not that they are at a loss for words, and it is not that they are lacking in intelligence; it is just that they feel so self-conscious and embarrassed that they are afraid of saying something silly, so they refuse to say anything at all and try to make themselves as invisible as possible" (52). There are some refreshing exceptions, from the sassy, whip-smart Sei Shonagon, to "the careless, fun-loving" Taifu, a gal pal of Genji's whom he chides for being as promiscuous as he is. (She appears only in chap. 6; how I wish there were a *Taifu monogatari* of her amorous adventures.)

So he had the cat at last, and he got to sleep with him at night. By day he caressed it and fussed over it. Soon it was no longer shy, and it curled up in his skirts or cuddled with him so nicely that he really did become very fond of it. He was lying against a pillar near the veranda, lost in thought, when it came to him going Meow! Meow! ever so sweetly.

My, we *are* eager, aren't we![35] He smiled and stroked it, then gazed into its eyes:

> "You I make my pet, that in you I may have her, my unhappy love:
> what can you be telling me, when you come crying this way?

This is destiny, too, I suppose." It meowed more endearingly still, and he clasped it to him.

"How odd of him all at once to take such a liking to a cat!" the old women muttered. "He never cared about such creatures before!"

The Heir Apparent sent for the cat, but the Intendant never returned it; instead he kept it to whisper sweet nothings to all by himself. (35)

Amusing, yes, but also tragic: conflicted Kashiwagi later kills himself because, as Bowring puts it, "he knows he cannot deal with the consequences of his own desire" (47).

If Murasaki's understanding of sexual pathology sounds remarkably modern, her attitude toward fiction sounds positively postmodern. Several times in *Genji* she draws attention to the fictionality of her novel by self-consciously evoking older *monogatari*:

". . . as she sat in her poor house [says To no Chujo of his neglected wife], I felt as though I must be living in some old tale." (2)

Why [thinks Genji], in the old tales this is just the kind of place that provides the setting for all sorts of moving scenes! (6)

It may be cruel to go through her costume, but the old romances always start out by describing a character's clothes. (6)

The happy fate of Genji's darling was just like a fiction in a tale. (10)

"In this sort of thing, my lord [says a nursemaid], the old tales suggest that even a Sovereign's cherished daughter may go astray, but then someone privy to the affair is generally the one to arrange it for her." (21)

[On To no Chujo's daughter Tamakazura:] the more her reading of old tales taught her what people are like and what the ways of the world are, the more timid she became . . . (24)

---

35 "The cat's meow (in Heian pronunciation something like *nyon nyon*) apparently sounds to Kashiwagi like *nen nen*, 'Let's go to bed, let's!'" (Tyler's note).

As usual on the nights when [Genji] was away, [Violet] sat up late and had her women read her tales. These old stories are all about what happens in life, she thought, and they are full of women involved with fickle, wanton, or treacherous men, and so on, but each one seems to find her own in the end. (35)

When [Kaoru] heard young gentlewomen read old tales with scenes like this, he always assumed disappointedly that nothing of the kind could actually happen, but there were after all such corners in real life! (45)

[On a young woman named Roku no Kimi:] Why, she had always wondered, reading an old tale or listening to talk about somebody else, why does this aspect of life [jealousy] upset people so? (49)

The idea that her daughter might have drowned herself had not occurred to her [Ukifune's mother], since she knew nothing about her anguish over what had been going on, and she could only suppose that a demon had devoured her or that some fox-like creature had made off with her — she remembered strange things just like that turning up in old tales; (52)

"How extraordinary! [says Kaoru] Who can she be? I suppose that she must have decided to hide there because she wants no more of the world. It sounds like an old romance, doesn't it!" (53)

"The young woman appeared to be dead" [says an old priest of Ukifune], but she was still breathing, and I was reminded in my astonishment of that old tale about someone's coming back to life after being put in the soul sanctuary." (54)

Why so many references (and there are many more) to older tales? Aside from the obvious answer — novels are based as much on other novels as they are on "real life" or the imagination, and Murasaki's characters in particular are associated by way of allusion with figures in Japanese and Chinese literature and history — several others suggest themselves. Murasaki wanted to legitimize the *monogatari* genre, to elevate it from light entertainment to high art, to modernize it by revealing its relevance to contemporary life, and lastly to take control of the genre (previously written by men but intended for ladies) to show that not only could a woman do a man's job, but in this case do it better — spectacularly better.

When Murasaki was growing up, novels were held in low esteem; like today's trashy romances, they were considered (by most men) to be not only silly but dangerous. In 984 a killjoy named Minamoto Tamenori wrote a primer on Buddhism entitled *Illustration of the Three Jewels* (*Sanboe-kotoba*) that had this to say about novels:

Then there are the so-called *monogatari*, which have such an effect on ladies' hearts. They flourish in numbers greater than the grasses of Ōaraki Forest, more countless than the sands on the Arisomi beaches. They attribute speech to trees and plants, mountains and rivers, birds and beasts, fish and insects that cannot speak; they invest unfeeling objects with human feelings and ramble on and on with meaningless phrases like so much flotsam in the sea, with no two words together that have any more solid basis than does swamp grass growing by a river bank. *The Sorceress of Iga, The Tosa Lord, The Fashionable Captain, The Nagai Chamberlain,*[36] and all the rest depict relations between men and women just as if they were so many flowers or butterflies, but do not let your heart get caught up even briefly in these tangled roots of evil, these forests of words.[37]

Murasaki was aware of this attitude and dramatized it in chapter 25 of her novel, deep within its forest of words. Genji is raising his friend To no Chujo's unknown daughter by Yugao (the woman who died at Genji's side in chap. 4), a beautiful 22-year-old named Tamakazura, pert as a schoolgirl, who has already fended off one attempted rape by her surrogate father. ("He had a very strange way of being a father," the author says of Genji [24], again toying with the incest theme.) Noting Tamakazura's fondness for novels, Genji begins by berating them à la Tamenori but then comes around to what is obviously Murasaki's own view, a famous passage worth quoting at length because it is one of the earliest defenses anywhere of fiction as a legitimate form of art:

Finding her enthralled by works like these, which lay scattered about everywhere, Genji exclaimed, "Oh, no, this will never do! Women are obviously born to be duped without a murmur of protest. There is hardly a word of truth in all this, as you know perfectly well, but there you are caught up in fables, taking them quite seriously and writing away without a thought for your tangled hair in this stifling warm rain!"[38] He laughed but then went on, "Without stories like these about the old days, though, how would we ever pass the time when there is nothing else to do? Besides, among these lies there certainly are some plausibly touching scenes, convincingly told; and yes, we know they are fictions, but even so we are moved and half drawn for no real reason to the pretty, suffering heroine. We may disbelieve the blatantly impossible but still be amazed by magnificently contrived wonders, and although these pall on quiet, second hearing, some are still fascinating. Lately, when my little girl has someone read to her and I stand there listening, I think to myself what good talkers there are in this world, and how this story, too, must come straight from someone's persuasively glib imagination — but perhaps not."

"Yes, of course, for various reasons someone accustomed to telling lies will no doubt take tales that way [*zing!*], but it seems impossible to me that they should be anything other than simply true." She pushed her inkstone away.

36 None of these novels has survived; from other contemporary works we know the names of many more vanished 10th-century novels — *The Tale of Josanmi, The Tale of Kumano, The Princess Who Sought a Corpse,* et al. — attesting to the genre's popularity.

37 From the "General Preface," p. 93 in Kamens' translation. This attitude is one more reason why the Buddhist novel went nowhere.

38 Tamakazura is copying a manuscript, not actually "writing" one, but she represents the struggling female novelist vs. the condescending male critical establishment of the day.

"I have been very rude to speak so ill to you of tales! They record what has gone on ever since the Age of the Gods. *The Chronicles of Japan* and so on give only part of the story.[39] It is tales that contain the truly rewarding particulars!" He laughed. "Not that tales accurately describe any particular person; rather, the telling begins when all those things the teller longs to have pass on to future generations — whatever there is about the way people live their lives, for better or worse, that is a sight to see or a wonder to hear — overflow the teller's heart. To put someone in a good light one brings out the good only, and to please other people one favors the oddly wicked, but none of this, good or bad, is removed from life as we know it. Tales are not told the same way in the other realm [China], and even in our own the old and new ways are of course not the same; but although one may distinguish between the deep and the shallow, it is wrong always to dismiss what one finds in tales as false. . . . To put it nicely, there is nothing that does not have its own value." He mounted a very fine defense of tales.

"But do any of these old tales tell of an earnest fool like me?" He moved closer. "No, no cruelly aloof heroine in any of them could possibly pretend to notice nothing as heartlessly as you do. Come, let us make our story one like no other and give it to all the world!" (25)

Genji may be saying all this only to get into his ward's gathered trousers, but fewer critics in Japan were likely to dismiss *monogatari* after this.[40] Murasaki knew she was writing a new kind of novel, more artistically rigorous and realistic, and distances herself somewhat from older tales, which (if Tamenori is to be trusted) relied too much on the romantic and supernatural. (Chapter 17 describes a picture contest in which old-fashioned paintings are pitted against those that are "more brilliantly modern"; like the present chapter 25, it is a metafictional vehicle for Murasaki's views on art and a defense of her own "brilliantly modern" approach to fiction.) Murasaki created a fictional world that was contemporary and realistic, but that still retained enough of the magic of older *monogatari* for To no Chujo to feel as though he's "living in some old tale."

Adding to *The Tale of Genji*'s curiously postmodern aura are the narrator's

39 I.e., the *Nihongi*. In her diary Murasaki records the time "His Majesty was listening to someone reading the *Tale of Genji* aloud. 'She must have read the *Chronicles of Japan*!' he said. 'She seems very learned'" (57). She was. As Shirane notes, "The *Genji* alludes to, cites, and draws upon a staggering body of literary and religious texts: Chinese literature, including the *Shih chi* (*Records of the Grand Historian*), the *Wen hsüan* (*Anthology of Literature*), and Po Chü-i's [Bo Juyi] collected works; a wide range of Buddhist scriptures; *waka* from a multitude of collections; and a variety of tales (*monogatari*), poetic diaries (*nikki*), songs (*kayō*), poetry contests (*uta awase*), and histories" (*The Bridge of Dreams*, xvii).

40 After Tamakazura rejects his advances at the end of this scene, Genji tells Violet not to read her any more romantic novels. "'Not that a heroine secretly in love is likely to catch her interest, but she must not come to take it for granted that things like that really happen.' The lady in the west wing [Tamakazura] would have been outraged to hear him talk that way" (25), repudiating his "fine defense of tales."

frequently expressed doubts about the authenticity of her tale. There are dozens of instances where she says things like: "Having got wrong everything I have written, I must have made him seem even odder and more foolish than he was" (13); "there are many things here that I have patched together and that may easily be wrong" (20); or "I remember only bits and pieces of what I heard then, and all this may be wrong" (29). One entire chapter (44) is based on "gossip volunteered by certain sharp-tongued old women" who wanted to correct earlier lies spread by "women older and more muddled than they. . . . One wonders which side to believe." Indeed. In fact, the author admits at the beginning of the second chapter that the entire tale is the work of "a terrible gossip." Along with irony, self-deprecation, and admissions of omissions, the author undercuts her authority so often that the resulting text is unstable, open to endless interpretation, resistant to closure — one reason why the concluding chapter *must* be open-ended. And this is why *The Tale of Genji* over the last thousand years has generated commentaries in numbers greater than the grasses of Ōaraki Forest, mostly by men entranced by this gifted woman who made a story like no other and gave it to all the world.

Reviewing the first volume of Waley's translation in *Vogue* in the summer of 1925, Virginia Woolf was gobsmacked (well, impressed) by the novel, but predicted "the lady Murasaki is not going to prove herself the peer of Tolstoy and Cervantes or those other great story-tellers of the Western world. . . ."[41] She was wrong. *The Tale of Genji* can hold its own with *War and Peace*, *Don Quixote*, or any other novel produced by Western novelists.

<hr/>

Following Murasaki's example, Japanese women took possession of the *monogatari* genre — they would write most of the hundreds that followed over the next few centuries, not men — and in their hands the novel became a species of spirit possession, a ventriloquist act by which they could attack Heian attitudes toward women via the characters in their fiction. In *Genji* and these later novels, when a woman becomes possessed, an exorcist transfers the attacking spirit into a nearby woman medium who then begins ranting, thrashing about, disordering her clothes, and in general acting very unlady-like. Murasaki and the women novelists who followed are like those mediums, expressing under the cover of court romances the rage and resentment Heian women were unable to express under normal circumstances. (This rage targeted not only men but women who mindlessly complied with their

41 *The Essays of Virginia Woolf* 4:267. To be fair, Woolf may not have read the five succeeding volumes — there's no indication in her published journals or letters — otherwise she would have found the vigor, richness, and "maturity of the human spirit" that she admires in those Western storytellers.

subjugation.) In her book on this subject, Doris Bargen calls spirit possession "a woman's weapon" and argues "spirit possession is not merely a conflict between the possessed and the possessor; it also tests the values of the whole society. In other words, the intensely private experience of spirit possession makes a public statement. The spirits' complaints and wishes, voiced directly through the possessed or indirectly through a medium, are a challenge to the social order."[42] Those "complaints and wishes" are ultimately voiced by the novelist herself, of course, and the growth of the Japanese novel hereafter would be nourished by the urge to find different and more subversive ways to use this feminine medium to rage against the machine.

One of the earliest readers (as opposed to courtly auditors) to be seduced by the great *Genji* was a woman known only as Takasue's daughter (Takasue no musume), after her father Sugawara no Takasue, a provincial official. The miserable author of *The Gossamer Years* was one of her aunts. Born in 1008, she began reading scattered early chapters of *Genji* at age 12. (The chapters first circulated as chapbooks.) Tantalized, she prayed "to see the entire *Tale of Genji* from beginning to end," and her prayers were answered by an affectionate aunt:

> And so it was that she presented me with fifty-odd volumes of *The Tale of Genji* in a special case, together with copies of *Zai, Tōgimi, Serikawa, Shirara, Asauzu*, and many other Tales.[43] Oh, how happy I was when I came home with all these books in a bag! In the past I had been able to have only an occasional hurried look at fragments of *The Tale of Genji*, and much of it had remained infuriatingly obscure. Now I had it all in front of me and I could sit undisturbed behind my curtain, bent comfortably forward as I took out the books one by one and enjoyed them to my heart's content. I wouldn't have changed places with the Empress herself.[44]

This passage comes from a lovely 80-page work of indeterminate genre that later came to be called *The Sarashina Diary* (*Sarashina nikki*, c. 1060). As its English translator Ivan Morris (who preferred to call the author "Lady Sarashina") explains in his introduction, it was categorized as a diary but its artistic nature

> makes the book a work of literature rather than a mere record of facts or a collection of random jottings. In her youth, works of romantic fiction had often been more important for Lady Sarashina tha[n] the "real" world about her; now in *Sarashina Nikki* she deliberately shaped the events of her actual life into a sort of Tale. The modern Japanese genre it most

---

42 A *Woman's Weapon: Spirit Possession in* The Tale of Genji, 12. (I want to thank my friend Rikki Ducornet for recommending this book to me.)
43 *Zai* is probably *Tales of Ise*; the rest are lost novels.
44 As *I Crossed a Bridge of Dreams*, 46–47 (hereafter quoted by page number).

resembles is the ever-popular *shi-shōsetsu* or "I-novel," in which the author uses the facts of his own life to create a work of quasi-fiction. (14)

And since the title some cataloguer gave it is irrelevant — the Sarashina district is merely alluded to in a poem near the end of the book — Morris gave it a novelistic title, *As I Crossed a Bridge of Dreams*, alluding to the final chapter of *Genji*, "The Floating Bridge of Dreams." Like the diary of Izumi Shikibu, it works best as an autobiographical novella, specifically as a kind of Portrait of the Artist as a Young Woman.[45]

Written when the author was in her fifties, the novella concerns a dreamy, hypersensitive woman lured in opposite directions by literature and religion as she seeks an escape from a harsh world filled with disappointment and death. After reading *Genji* late into the night, the young narrator dreams "that a handsome priest appeared before me in a yellow surplice and ordered me to learn the fifth volume of the Lotus Sutra as soon as possible" (47), but she is too enthralled by the handsome heroes of Murasaki's novel to heed the call to religion and instead daydreams that, "when I grew up, I would surely become a great beauty with long flowing hair like Yūgao, who was loved by the Shining Prince, or like Ukifune, who was wooed by the Captain of Uji. Oh, what futile conceits!" (47) the older author says of her 12-year-old self, and she will continue to ignore other religious dreams in favor of the waking dreams of fiction. As Keene points out (386), it's significant that the narrator identifies herself not with Genji's beloved Violet but with the spirit-possessed Yugao and especially with the suicidal Ukifune.

The novels she reads develop her capacity for imaginative thinking — in one charming section she becomes convinced a stray cat is a metamorphosed princess — and she begins writing poetry to preserve her thoughts and impressions. (Much of the novella resembles an *uta monogatari*.) But the years pass and no shining prince comes to rescue her from her drab life, and in her thirties she finally asks herself:

> How could I have let all those years slip by, instead of practising my devotions and going on pilgrimages? I began to doubt whether any of my romantic fancies, even those that had seemed most plausible, had the slightest basis in fact. How could anyone as wonderful as

---

45 To belabor the point, it was not based on an actual diary the author kept, but rather written from memory much later in life. On the last page of the work, she writes, "Many years have passed, but whenever I think about that sad, dreamlike time my heart is thrown into turmoil and my eyes darken, so that even now I cannot clearly remember all that happened" (110) — meaning she *invented* what she could not remember. In her searching analysis of the work, Edith Sarra doesn't actually call it a novel but admits it uses "a *monogatari*-like narrative medium" (*Fictions of Femininity*, 111), which is close enough for me.

Shining Genji or as beautiful as the girl whom Captain Kaoru kept hidden in Uji really
exist in this world of ours? Oh, what a fool I was to believe in such nonsense! (79–80)[46]

But soon after she renounces fiction, she ironically encounters a dashing
nobleman "as wonderful as Shining Genji." However, nothing comes of this
brief encounter, so she abandons the "nonsense" of fiction for the nonsense
of religion, spending the succeeding decades going on religious pilgrimages.
Even so, one of her pilgrimages takes her through Uji, where she can't help
gawking like a literary tourist at the house Ukifune may have lived in. She
marries, has children, but never finds anything approaching the happiness
she experienced as a teenager absorbed in novels. In fact, she blames novels
for her misspent life: "If only I had not given myself over to Tales and poems
since my young days but had spent my time in religious devotions, I should
have been spared this misery" (106) she says a few pages before the end of
the book.

Of course, if she had abandoned *Genji* for the *Lotus Sutra* as that dream-
priest had urged, she would never have become such a good poet — many
of her poems became enshrined in anthologies — or developed the lyrical
sensibility that allowed her to write *As I Crossed a Bridge of Dreams*. There's
a highly symbolic scene near the end when the narrator decides to leave on
a pilgrimage on the same day people from all over the country are swarm-
ing into the capital to witness an elaborate ceremony called the Sacred
Purification for the Great Festival of Thanksgiving. People can't believe she's
leaving the city at the one time of year everyone wants to *enter* it, but she
firmly goes against the human tide and dares to be different. It's that difference that marked her to become a writer, a vocation apparent in the opening
pages of the novella in which the 12-year-old narrator describes her trip from
the provinces to the capital in a dozen-page sequence that is considered a
classic example of Japanese travel writing, and in which her gift for metaphor
is already apparent. (She describes Mount Fuji as "wearing a white jacket
over a dress of deep violet" [39].) During this trip, three professional female
entertainers emerge mysteriously from the mountains one night to sing for
the travel party, almost as if these weird women were calling the girl to join
their ranks as an artist. But mundane disappointments cause the narrator to
doubt her artistic vocation — in Campbell's hero paradigm, there's an early
stage where the hero refuses the call to adventure — and the entire novella
can be read as a fascinating dramatization of someone becoming an artist in
spite of herself.

46 These lines occur near the beginning of a long, three-page sentence in the original, "many
parts of which are extremely obscure," says the translator (133), who breaks it into conventional sentences and paragraphs. How daring of the author to convey her narrator's moment
of crisis in a rambling stream-of-consciousness monologue à la Molly Bloom! (And how
traitorous of the translator to normalize it.)

There's a biographical note at the end of the earliest surviving manuscript of *As I Crossed a Bridge of Dreams* (c. 1230) stating Takasue's daughter also wrote four novels. While some scholars have doubted these attributions, others find them plausible given her obvious talent for writing and her close acquaintance with earlier *monogatari*. Of the four, two are lost — *Misukara kuyuru* (Filled with Regret) and *Asakura* (the protagonist's name) — less than half remains of another, and the fourth lacks its opening chapter. They are usually dated after *The Sarashina Diary* — that is, after 1060 — but since the narrator renounces novels near the end of that work, I think it's more likely she wrote them earlier while still single and under their spell. At any rate, they can't be dated any more precisely than the mid-11th century.

The Tale of Nezame (*Yowa* [or *Yoru*] *no nezame*) originally consisted of four long parts that apparently ran to 600–700 pages, of which only parts 1 and 3 survive. Thanks to medieval commentaries and adaptations, scholars have been able to reconstruct the contents of parts 2 and 4, though this obviously precludes a confident evaluation of the entire novel. Nevertheless, Keene confidently praises *The Tale of Nezame* as "an extraordinary work, as close as the Heian storytellers ever came to creating what even purists might call a novel" (536).

Nezame, the aristocratic heroine of the novel, takes her name from the phrase *yowa no nezame*, meaning "wakefulness at night," referring to the sleepless nights she endures because of her complicated relationship with a courtier whose rank is Naidaijin (Minister of the Center). "Of all stories about relations between men and women," the narrator sighs in the novel's opening line, "rarely has one brought with it such sleepless nights for its lovers as that which I am about to tell."[47] Raised by a widowed ex-prime minister along with her older sister Oigimi (the older of the Uji sisters, you'll recall), Nezame becomes a prodigy on the koto and at age 13 dreams of a heavenly figure who teaches her some koto secrets to improve her playing even further; a year later the divine being returns in another dream and, after a final koto lesson, prophesies that Nezame is fated "to suffer remorse" all her life (R 56). While the supernatural koto lessons recall the opening of *The Tale of the Hollow Tree*, the dire prediction recalls those delivered to the oneiromantic narrator of *As I Crossed a Bridge of Dreams*. Because of her musical abilities and stunning beauty, Nezame might have had a brilliant career at court, but at age 16 she gets knocked up by Naidaijin, which fills her with intense shame and initiates her life of constant sorrow.

In soap-operatic fashion, Naidaijin happened to be engaged to Nezame's older sister when this happened. (He had heard a woman playing a koto, and

---

47 Page 52 in Richard's translation; for reasons of my own, I'm going to alternate between his translation (R) and Hochstedler's (H) from a slightly different manuscript tradition, and will be using the latter's names for characters.

thinking her a mere commoner, snuck into her house and had his way with her — by modern standards, most Heian rakes were rapists.) Nezame has their child in shameful secrecy while Naidaijin goes ahead with his marriage to Oigimi, though as soon as he discovers Nezame's identity he declares her the love of his life and devotes himself wholeheartedly to her. After that, it's one damned thing after another for poor Nezame: Oigimi learns of N & N's fling and becomes sick with rage; her father (who doesn't find out until much later) marries Nezame to an older man, who generously raises her *second* child by Naidaijin; stung by this marriage, Naidaijin retaliates by marrying the daughter of the retired emperor, which causes his first wife Oigimi to die of jealous grief after giving birth to his daughter. Later, when Nezame is in her late twenties, the reigning emperor tries to rape her; frustrated, he makes do with her 10-year-old son Masako in a transgenerational homosexual relationship that doesn't seem to bother anyone, least of all the boy.[48] Nezame and Naidaijin continue their on-again/off-again relationship, complicated by endless misunderstandings, false accusations, and a mother-in-law making life hell for both of them, all of which drives Nezame to the brink of nunhood, pulled back only when she learns she is pregnant yet again by the fertile Naidaijin.[49] Part 3, the last section extant, ends with the dour prediction, "The lady Nezame is said to have spent endless nights of wakeful anguish" (R 410). In the concluding part 4, apparently Nezame's children all prosper, but she finds life so trying that she pulls a Ukifune and fakes her own death so that she can crawl off and become a nun at last, to the disappointment of everyone.

In much of the extant novel, Nezame bewails her fate and constantly worries what others might think of her. There is more brooding on events than on the depiction of the events themselves, a greater emphasis on interiority than on the external world, though the interior monologues here are much stiffer than the more realistic ones in *The Tale of Genji*, more like stage soliloquies. It has fewer poems than *Genji*, and the style isn't as elaborate and allusive as Murasaki's, which was apparently intentional; as the emperor says of one of Nezame's letters, "She uses simple and ordinary phrases, yet they perfectly express the strong emotions she must feel. That is the touch of a genuine artist" (H 26). But one extraordinary phrase sticks out: when the author states Naidaijin introduced Nezame to "the ways of love" (H 87), she literally says he took her to "the floating world." Though this evocative term (*ukiyo*) is usually associated with the hedonistic world of Genroku Japan (roughly 1680–1740), it originated as a Buddhist term signifying "the sad impermanence of earthly

---

48 "Masako had learned artful ways of pleasing him and had become increasingly gentle, till now he did seem very much like a girl" (H 139). When he grows up, Masako goes straight and falls for the retired emperor's favorite daughter. Unfortunately this occurs in the lost part 4; I would have liked to see how the author handled *that* about-face.

49 Here as elsewhere in Japanese fiction, taking religious vows is portrayed not as an admirable spiritual step but as a cowardly retreat from the challenges of life.

things," as Howard Hibbett notes. "The Chinese had also used it to imply the transiency of life, as in a line by the T'ang poet Li Shang-yin [9th cent.], 'In this floating world, there are many meetings and partings.'"[50] By the 11th century, the Japanese were using *ukiyo* as both a sexual metaphor *and* a religious concept, paradoxically enough.[51] Conventional folks continued to use *ukiyo* in the Buddhist sense, but the demimonde converted the idea of the floating world from sad to glad, recognizing that the impermanence of this world is all the more reason to seize the day, to go out with a bang, not a whimper.

Though Nezame is the heroine of the novel, she is hardly an admirable character: she allows that early dream to become a self-fulfilling prophecy, and her instinctive reaction to difficulties is to whimper, hide, fake illness, remain silent, refuse food, and/or regress to a childish state. She prefers security to excitement, resignation to courage, conformity to individuality. She has a paralyzing fear of gossip and of the opinions of others — Naidaijin, in refreshing contrast, grows increasingly indifferent to what others think — and nowadays her pathological lack of confidence and self-esteem would scream out for prescription drugs and long-term counseling. In the introduction to her translation of part 3, Carol Hochstedler feels "the heroine is doomed by the tricks of fate and the weakness of men to a life of suffering and disappointment," but I join nearly all the characters in the novel in holding this sob sister responsible for her own misery. (As her dream originally predicted, Nezame would torment *herself* with remorse, not be tormented by others.) The author continually insists on how beautiful she is, on how devoted Naidaijin is to her, even on the retention of her divine koto skills, but Nezame considers herself a total failure by the standards of her culture. Whether the author intended her novel to be an attack on those standards and practices — the narrative equivalent of spirit possession — or, like *The Gossamer Years* and *As I Crossed a Bridge of Dreams*, a *cri du cœur* from someone trapped by those values, is hard to say, especially since half of the novel is missing. But the half that remains is intriguing, and builds nicely on both the confessional *nikki monogatari* and Murasaki's psychologically realistic fiction.

A Brief Digression on Translation

So why didn't the translator say Naidaijin introduced Nezame "to the floating world" instead of paraphrasing it as "the ways of love"? Why replace a striking image with a bland phrase? When caught in a comically compromising situation with a woman in her late 50s, why does the 18-year-old Genji tell her "You

50 *The Floating World in Japanese Fiction*, 11. In *The Tale of Genji*, Murasaki's use of *ukiyo* in one of Genji's poems is translated "this sorry world" (41).
51 Cf. the French slang term for orgasm *voir les anges* (to see the angels), or the American habit of calling on one's maker in the throes of passion.

undoubtedly knew quite well that this gentleman was coming" in Tyler's translation, when what he literally says (as Tyler explains in a footnote) is "I am sure the
spider's behavior was perfectly clear" (7) — an allusion to the proverbial poem
stating that a spider's sudden activity foretells a lover's visit. That is, why didn't
Hochstedler and Tyler translate their texts literally and put the paraphrases in their
footnotes, rather than the other way around? Undoubtedly for the same reason
Morris gives after he translates a line in *As I Crossed a Bridge of Dreams* as "What
good does it really do us to see the Purification [ceremony]?": "The original text,"
he tells us in a note, "has the rather charming idiom, 'What good does it do to
fatten one's eyes temporarily?' i.e., to feast one's eyes on something that will give
no lasting nourishment. It is tempting to retain such exoticisms in a translation
— tempting but unwise" (140). I wish translators succumbed to that temptation
more often. These Japanese texts in particular are filled with poetic allusions,
figurative language, and "charming" idioms that would make them immeasur-
ably richer and more appealing if translators didn't strip them down to plain
sense. There is one school of thought that holds a translation should be so free of
any linguistic peculiarities that one forgets one is reading a translation; another
school (which I attend) feels one should *never forget* one is reading a translation,
especially if the original uses a peculiar style and/or figurative language. People
are shaped by their language as much as by anything else, and to ignore this is
like asking a visiting shadow dancer from Bali to disguise her accent and dress like
an American when she performs. Of course there are many idioms that would
be nonsensical if translated literally, but are "fatten one's eyes" or "the floating
world" really that incomprehensible, especially in context? An American writer
known for playful language (Tom Robbins, say) could use either phrase without
his readers batting an eyelash. One of the pleasures of reading a foreign novel is
the immersion in different customs and attitudes, which should also include different idioms and metaphors. Yet too many translators deprive us of that pleasure,
making all of their characters speak as if they're from Denver and the texts blander
than the originals, often without telling us. In his older translation of *Genji*, Arthur
Waley renders the line above, "What possessed you to let me in on a night when
you knew that someone else was coming?" without a word about early-warning
spiders. Edward Seidensticker uses the method I prefer: he has Genji say, "This is
a fine thing. I'm going. The spider surely told you to expect him, and you didn't
tell me" and then appends a note explaining what the spider reference means —
though in many other instances he resorts to paraphrase without notes. When
I visit a foreign country, I want to see the real land and its people, not take an
official, sanitized tour, to sample the local cuisine rather than eat at McDonald's,
and when I read a translation I want to fatten my eyes on the country's linguistic
sights and treasures. And if I get lucky, I want to be shown "the floating world,"
not "the ways of love."

Only the first chapter is missing from the other novel Takasue's daughter may have written, the *Hamamatsu chunagon monogatari*, which is shorthand for "The Tale of the Middle Counselor [known for his poem with the phrase *Mitsu no*] *hamamatsu*," meaning "the pine pining [for me on the beach] at Mitsu," i.e., present-day Osaka. Let's just call it *Hamamatsu*. It's about half the length of *The Tale of Nezame*, and is a curious amalgam of several types of fiction then in circulation: Murasaki's psychological novel (erotic transference with incestuous overtones), older supernatural novels like *The Tale of the Bamboo Cutter* and *The Tale of the Hollow Tree* (including a fantastic voyage), sanctimonious religious novels (all of them, like *The Tale of Oi* mentioned in the text, thankfully lost), and Buddhist tales of karma and reincarnation, mostly derived from the *Lotus Sutra*.[52] It's an interesting if sometimes ludicrous mix. In the missing opening chapter (as reconstructed by scholars), the reader was introduced to a pious young man in his late teens referred to only by his title, Chunagon (Middle Counselor). He lost his father at an early age, and became upset when his mother remarried a widower named Lord Taisho. Keene, who doesn't much like the novel, sneers, "This sounds like *Hamlet*, but there are no further resemblances" (537), but there are: Like Hamlet, Chunagon is "the glass of fashion, and the mould of form," admired by everyone who sees him. (Regarding fashion, he is once seen sporting "light purple trousers of Chinese damask with a yellow shirt lined in red," a color combination few men before Jimi Hendrix could have pulled off.[53]) And like the melancholy Dane, he also suffers from indecision, believes in supernatural revelations, and has a problematic relationship with his (step)sister. Although he doesn't get along with his new father, he is attracted to his new sister, Taisho no Kimi. Along about the time she becomes engaged to heir-apparent Shikibukyo (Niou to Chunagon's Kaoru in romantic rivalry), Chunagon receives word that his dead father has been reborn as a prince in China! He gets permission from the emperor for a three-year visit, and just before Chunagon leaves he and Taiso no Kimi have a farewell tryst that gets out of hand; after he leaves for China, she discovers she's pregnant, is dumped by Shikibukyo in favor of her *un*pregnant sister, and in shame cuts her hair and becomes a nun.

The extant portion of the novel (presumably chapter 2) begins with Chunagon en route to China to express his "deep sense of filial piety" (55). He is pleased to be reunited with his father, even though the latter is only seven

---

52 See, for example, Yoshiko K. Dykstra's translation of *Hokke genki* (c. 1040), *Miraculous Tales of the Lotus Sutra from Ancient Japan* (1983), as well as the *Lotus Sutra* itself, which is filled with such tales. It is mentioned in Heian fiction more often than any other sutra, and apparently was the Japanese equivalent of the family Bible.

53 Page 184 in Rohlich's faithful translation, hereafter cited by page number because he uses chapter 1 to refer to the surviving second chapter, etc., which can be misleading. (I happen to own the copy Rohlich inscribed to his indexer, Debby.)

or eight years old and looks nothing like him, but he is even more pleased by Chinese women. In most works of art — ancient novels as well as sci-fi films — the exotic is erotic, a site of sexual fantasy free of the restrictions back home, and the bold and beautiful women he meets there create stumbling blocks for this priggish nobleman whose heart belongs to Taisho no Kimi (the beach pine pining for him in the novel's title). He is like a Henry James character visiting Paris for the first time. Matters aren't helped by Chinese fathers, who are so impressed by Chunagon they push their daughters at him in the hope he will impregnate them and leave behind a little souvenir of his visit. Chunagon is especially taken with his reincarnated father's mother, known as the Hoyang Consort. She is his age, but as his father's mother she is in one sense his grandmother, which makes his eventual tryst with her complicated, to say the least. She too bears him a child just before Chunagon leaves to return to Japan, so he takes the boy back to spare the mother's shame, along with a letter she wants him to deliver to her Japanese mother.

Back home, Chunagon is shocked to discover Taisho no Kimi has become a nun, but they live together nonetheless in a nonsexual arrangement that threatens to turn sexual at any moment, given her beauty and his passion. Chunagon seeks out the Hoyang Consort's mother, living in religious seclusion in the mountains. (There are more unwed mothers in this novel than married ones.) To make a long story short, the Consort's mother has another daughter, a 17-year-old *naïf* named Yoshinohime whom Chunagon adopts as a surrogate for her older sister in China. A monk predicts Yoshinohime will die if anyone impregnates her before she reaches 20, to the considerable chagrin of Chunagon, already feeling deprived by his live-in nun. For relief, Chunagon cuckolds his uncle by impregnating his new bride (another girl pushed at him by her father earlier on, when he wasn't interested), and then his old rival Shikabukyo abducts Yoshinohime and impregnates her. The novel ends with a heartbroken Chunagon biding his time until Yoshinohime gives birth to a girl and raises her to marriageable age, because Chunagon is convinced she will be the reincarnation of the Hoyang Consort, whose death was announced by a supernatural voice in the sky, you see.

Hamamatsu's interest for the modern reader depends on how much tolerance one has for its supernatural elements — closer to what we now call magic realism — and on how much irony we can credit the author with. Chunagon claims, "All I really want in this world is to be left alone to spend my time in devotion to the Buddha, a wandering monk in the mountains" (164), but he spends most of his time wandering into women's bedrooms, especially if they are engaged or married to someone else. Whenever they become pregnant, he blames "the predestined bonds of former lives" (118) instead of what the narrator calls "his irrepressible passion" (239). A romantic hero, or a pious hypocrite? Or perhaps, as the narrator says, Chunagon is "trapped between two worlds" (95), the floating world of pleasure (China) and the fixed world of duty and Buddhist sorrow (Japan). Perversely combining the two, Chunagon (like some of Poe's characters) is most attracted to a woman when she is sickly or near death, as is Yoshonohime most of the time: his praise of her beauty escalates as her health deteriorates. Granted, these shrinking violets were a popular romantic type in Heian fiction, but nearly all the Japanese women in *Hamamatsu* are female eunuchs who hide behind fans, obsess over what others might think of them, or renounce the world and become nuns. Perhaps it would be better, the author might be suggesting, to emulate the confident women of China: "The Prime Minister's daughter lifted the curtain surrounding her dais and, toying with her fan as she lay in bed, stared at Chūnagon" (72)? And perhaps it is better, Chunagon wonders, "to speak one's mind directly" as Chinese men do, as opposed to "his countrymen's tendency to dress and embellish each phrase" (71)? It is difficult to say whether the novel is an ironic attack on silly Japanese customs and irrational beliefs (karma, reincarnation, the Dragon King of the Sea, voices from the sky), or an unironic sermon on irresponsible passion dressed up with inaccurate accounts of decadent Cathay and comforting testimonials to the validity of dreams and reincarnation. Unfortunately, the author probably intended the latter — the view taken by the twisted Japanese novelist Yukio Mishima, who said the *Hamamatsu chunagon monogatari* inspired his *Sea of Fertility* tetralogy (1965–70), which he completed just before disemboweling himself.

The most accomplished of the post-*Genji* novels is reportedly *The Tale of Sagoromo* (*Sagoromo monogatari*), written in the 1060s by Rokujo Saiin no Senji, or "Senji [scribe] of the Sixth Street Kamo Priestess's household" (c. 1020–92), the title of a court lady who served Princess Baishi. Even though the complete novel survives and has been praised as "the second *Tale of Genji*," it hasn't been translated into English yet, so I'll have to take the words of other critics.[54] Keene gives this succinct plot summary:

> Although most manuscripts divide *The Tale of Sagoromo* into four books, each with an elegantly written introductory section, it is from beginning to end an uninterrupted account of ten years in the life of Sagoromo, a prince of the highest rank (the son of the kampaku [chancellor] and the nephew of the emperor). He is blessed with extraordinary beauty and intelligence, as the author frequently reminds us, but to the end is unsuccessful in his love for his cousin, Princess Genji.[55] Other loves or worldly honors, even

54 Keene (518–30) and the fabulously named Charo D'Etcheverry, who devotes a chapter to *Sagoromo* in her book *Life after* The Tale of Genji (58–87). D'Etcheverry also translated a few excerpts from the novel for Shirane's anthology *Traditional Japanese Literature* (504–18) but (she told me in an e-mail) doesn't plan to translate the entire novel. A few doctoral candidates have tackled the project, but without publishable results so far.

55 "Although the name is the same as that of the hero of *The Tale of Genji*, and for this reason somewhat confusing, there is no connection between the two characters" (Keene's note,

becoming emperor, give him no pleasure because of this frustration, and as his despair accumulates, his thoughts turn incessantly to "leaving the world" as a Buddhist priest. The work concludes as Sagoromo gazes out over an autumn garden in the deepening twilight, and wonders about the nature of the karma that has caused his life in the present world to be so unsatisfying. (519)

Aside from a few blatantly supernatural intrusions — near the beginning the 18-year-old Sagoromo plays the flute so beautifully for the emperor that it attracts the god of music Amewakamiko in the form of a child, who tries to pull the flutist up to heaven, losing in a tug-of-war as the emperor pulls him back to earth — the novel is much more realistic than other Heian novels, especially the dialogue; according to Keene, "the conversations sometimes seem remarkably close to colloquial speech, and there are even a few coarse words" (529). The descriptions of characters are more sensuous — Keene lingers over the sight of Princess Genji sitting in the sunlight, her figure illumined under the diaphanous white shift she's wearing — and there are some comic lowlife characters who are new to the Japanese novel's dramatis personae. "The plot is carefully constructed and better organized than that of *The Tale of Genji*," Keene feels (527), and notes how well the 200 or so poems are integrated into the text. D'Etcheverry praises Senji for exposing "the essentially exploitative nature of the midranks relationship" (79), that is, the habit of nobles preying on socially inferior women found in almost every Heian novel from *The Tale of Lady Ochikubo* onward. The sample excerpts D'Etcheverry has translated are lively and appealing — the dialogue is snappy and the interior monologues much better than the stiff ones in *Nezame* and *Hamamatsu* — so I hope readers won't be kept waiting too much longer for a complete translation.

The most subversive *monogatari* of this period has to be *The Changelings* (*Torikaebaya*, literally "If only I could exchange them"), the world's first transgender novel. An early version appeared near the end of the 11th century, but the surviving version is a revision made apparently sometime between 1160 and 1180. The author is anonymous but was probably a woman, or — given the autobiographical nature of Heian fiction — someone who had gender issues like those dramatized in the novel.

Beginning with a take-off on *Genji*'s opening sentence ("Once, we know not when . . ."), the author introduces us to a court official called Sadaijin — his eventual rank (Minister of the Left) — who has two unnamed wives, neither of whom interests him much. Nevertheless, each provides him with a child at the same time who resemble each other so closely as to pass for twins. They instinctively abandon their society's gender assumptions at an early age:

---

544). D'Etcheverry adds that Princess Genji was based on Senji's employer, Princess Baishi (85).

"the boy became surprisingly shy," hides behind curtains, and plays with dolls, while the girl becomes "quite mischievous," plays male sports, and masters the phallic flute (girls are associated with the recumbent koto); in the presence of her father "she was more restrained and did not display her unladylike behavior," but when that patriarchal symbol isn't around "she would promptly join the rest of the men and lark about with them quite as she pleased."[56] Sadaijin, to his credit, tolerates their unconventional behavior, but is saddened by it. "'If only I could exchange them,' he mused [hence the title], 'my son for the daughter and my daughter for the son'" (16). He hopes they'll soon revert "to the behavior of their own sexes," that is, become conventional: the word used in the original to describe their condition is *yozukazu*, literally "not adhering to the ways of the world."[57] But they don't straighten out, and when they become teenagers the narrator performs some sexual reassignment surgery: "Hereafter I shall refer to the children as the others had come mistakenly to do; the son I shall call the daughter, and the daughter the son" (16).

What follows is not a comedy of sexual errors like *As You Like It* or *Twelfth Night* but a more somber look at the extraordinary inequality of the sexes in medieval Japan. The biological girl-turned-boy, called Chunagon after the rank he eventually holds, is free to move around as he pleases, to study the Chinese classics (off-limits to girls[58]), and even to flirt with the ladies, though Chunagon's heart isn't really in that male prerogative. The biological boy-turned-girl, called Naishi no Kami, becomes a companion to the "weak and childish" crown princess and virtually disappears from the first half of the novel. As they mature, Chunagon in particular faces challenges: "four or five days each month he was unable to conceal the strange ailments about which he could do nothing. 'I am afflicted by evil spirits,' he would say, as he secretly went off to his wet nurse's to hide" (29), and at age 16 he is married off to a 19-year-old named Yon no Kimi, but doesn't consummate the union. "Some thought something lacking in him," the narrator winks (38), but Chunagon's transvestism fools almost everyone.

Then Chunagon's oversexed friend Saisho throws his spanner in the works. He finds Chunagon so handsome and alluring that "he yearned for a woman comparable to this man" and transfers his yearning to Chunagon's half-sister, who he assumes is "all the more lovely" (25). This too travesties *The Tale of*

---

56 Pages 14–15 in Willig's translation; I follow her fixed designations of characters' names, though as usual in Heian fiction these change during the course of the novel as characters assume new ranks and stations.

57 Pflugfelder, "Strange Fates," 351. In this excellent essay on the novel, Pflugfelder warns that the Heian perception of gender was more fluid than ours, and that Westerners should therefore resist the sort of sweeping judgments I'm prone to make.

58 In her diary Murasaki recalls eavesdropping as her slow brother was taught Chinese literature and mastering the subject more quickly than he did. "Just my luck," she remembers her father saying, anticipating Sadaijin. "What a pity she was not born a man!" (58).

Genji, where there are many instances of a man admiring another man and wishing he were a woman. First, however, Saisho assaults Chunagon's wife — "wearing so many layers of kimono that there did not seem to be a body within them" (42) — and impregnates her. (He is surprised she's still a virgin, and she is surprised real men want to do more than just talk.) Then one hot afternoon with his friend, both partly undressed because of the heat, Saisho becomes so fired up by his yearning for the sister that he gropes Chunagon and learns he is a she. Saisho then takes full advantage of his embarrassed friend.

Chunagon becomes pregnant, and when he grows too big to conceal the fact, he and Saisho escape down to fabled Uji, where Chunagon begins reverting to his original sex and the behavior expected of women. Conforming to current standards of feminine beauty, he lets his hair grow long, plucks his eyebrows, and blackens his teeth.[59] His disappearance worries his half-sister, so she summons the strength (from her innate masculinity, it is implied) to go look for him, disguising herself as a man to do so. In a conceptually brilliant scene halfway through the novel, Naishi no Kimi (the biological boy/turned girl/now dressed as a man, remember) catches a glimpse of Chunagon (girl/man/woman) in Uji (an incestuous instance of *kaimani*) and comes into his view. "It then occurred to Chunagon that this man was the mirror image of himself when he had been a man" (132). Like Alice going through the looking-glass and finding everything "as different as possible," the twins pass each other through the mirror and revert to their biological sexes and socially prescribed roles. Chunagon gives birth and returns to the capital as Naishi no Kami, while her half-brother returns to take Chunagon's place. During the second half of the novel, they exchange names and the reader has to keep reminding him/herself who belongs to which sex.

The Changelings is a fascinating (if somewhat predictable) exploration of the social construction of gender, and would be even more pertinent to current debates on gender theory if the twins' inversion were not blamed on Buddhist superstition about "sins in their previous lives" (21). Their father Sadaijin later has a dream in which a priest informs him, "In previous lives their paths were crossed, and in retribution a goblin changed the boy into a girl, the girl into a boy, and caused you no end of sorrow" (149). Perhaps this was a sop thrown to conventional readers who wouldn't acknowledge the reality of gender dysphoria — or perhaps it's merely a vestige of the

---

59 In "The Lady Who Preferred Insects," a story written around this time, a smart noncon-formist doesn't bother with her hair and refuses to blacken her teeth, calling it unsanitary. This refreshingly *yozukazu* gal is depicted as more sensible than the conformist drones around her, and her example gently mocks Japanese cultural assumptions. This delightful tale is part of a collection entitled *The Riverside Counselor's Stories* (*Tsutsumi chunagon monogatari*), and this particular one can be found in most anthologies of early Japanese literature.

folkloric original, which reportedly was cruder — but the author makes it clear that life for Heian women was a drag. During his confinement in Uji, after 17 years of male freedom, Chunagon begins feeling his "life is coming to an end" (115) as he reverts to womanhood. Symbolically losing "the flute he had been attached to since childhood" (116), the pregnant Chunagon becomes depressed, frail, codependent on fickle Saisho (whom he now feels "it was not his place to criticize" [126]), anxious, and mindless: "Chūnagon arose less and less often, and quiet and lonely, would gaze blankly at nothing" (134). Her misery is reinforced by her religion: "How wretched it is to have become the woman I now am," he thinks. "Even the Buddha claimed woman is sinful" (143).[60]

Naishi no Kimi, on the other hand, having acted like a girl all her life, finds his new male persona liberating. S/he realizes "to be cared for by others, and to remain hidden from the world are wretched and lamentable things to do" (127). He enjoys moving about freely, speaking his mind, and begins to find other women "unexpectedly interesting" for the first time (though s/he did have confused feelings for her royal companion). He takes up the flute, takes on a second wife, fathers several children, and eventually, it must be admitted, becomes something of a dick.

It may be considered another sop to the status quo to have Chunagon and Naishi no Kimi revert to their biological sexes and become conventionally successful — she becomes empress, and he becomes a high-ranking official — rather than to seek out an alternative gay/lesbian/bisexual/transgender community (which surely existed in a city as artsy as Kyoto). But their walk on the wild side has taught them what it's like to live as the opposite sex, and they are more sensitive to gender differences as a result. There's no call for women's liberation in the novel, but *The Changelings* is a clever critique of the status quo, using the only means available to a woman then: writing. When one character is mistakenly praised, the wet nurses in the know write corrective "detailed accounts" and "dropped these notes where they would be found" (120–21). Those who found *The Changelings* in the 12th century enjoyed it, but it later fell from favor and went underground, eventually acquiring a reputation as pornography. Keene-san, who has a low opinion of the novel, notes: "The distinguished historian of Japanese literature Fujioka Sakutarō (1870–1910) was so appalled by the work that he wrote a denunciation which

---

60 In chapter 12 of the popular *Lotus Sutra*, one of the Buddha's chief disciples lectures the Dragon King's daughter that she can never attain Buddhahood "because a woman's body is soiled and defiled" and is "subject to the five obstacles" (188). The dragon girl shows him by attaining Buddhahood, but only *after* transforming herself into a man. In chapter 25, the Buddha promises, "If there is a woman who hears this chapter . . . and is able to accept and uphold it, that will be her last appearance in a woman's body and she will never be born in that form again" (287). This is the kind of crap that was fed to Japanese women in Heian society.

concluded, 'It makes me want to vomit'" (541). That homophobic remark makes *me* want to vomit, for *The Changelings* is a touching, insightful work that deserves a place on the narrow shelf of tranny classics along with Honoré d'Urfé's *Astrée*, Théophile Gautier's *Mademoiselle de Maupin*, Virginia Woolf's *Orlando*, Gore Vidal's *Myra Breckenridge*, Brigid Brophy's *In Transit*, Will Self's *Cock & Bull*, and L. Frank Baum's *Marvelous Land of Oz*.

⸺⸙⸺

"The world is coming to its end," intones the emperor at the conclusion of *The Changelings* (237), and in 1185 the superb/absurd Heian era came to an end, to be followed by the Kamakura era (1185–1333) of military dictatorships under various shoguns. The Japanese novel survived the regime change, but the earliest extant example of a Kamakura novel, *The Tale of Matsura* (*Matsura no miya monogatari*, c. 1190), is quite different from the Heian *monogatari*. The first difference is that it was written not by a woman but by a man, and no ordinary man. Fujiwara Teika (or Sadaie, 1162–1241) is one of the greatest and most influential poet/scholars in Japanese literature. As a young man he wrote poetry so difficult and innovative it was called "crazy Zen poetry" (*daruma-uta*), and his prowess at improvising poems was legendary. He was one of the editors of a major imperial anthology, the *Shin Kokinshu* (1205), and he expanded both the subject matter and vocabulary of the traditional *waka* — his motto was "Give new meanings to old words."[61] He devoted his later years to collecting and editing classic Heian literature, including both *The Tale of Genji* and Murasaki's diary, *Tales of Ise*, the works of Izumi Shikibu and Takasue's daughter — he wrote the biographical note identifying the latter's novels — and much else. As Keene says, "It is not much of an exaggeration to say that what we know of the literature of Teika's day and earlier is mainly what he thought was worthy of preservation" (674).

The second difference is the setting: Most *monogatari* were set in and around the Heian capital in the recent past, but *The Tale of Matsura* takes place mostly in China in the early 8th century; in addition, Teika pretends he is merely transcribing a partly damaged manuscript from the 9th century and uses archaic diction to further the subterfuge. And instead of dramatizing and critiquing Heian values in a realistic manner, Teika wrote a patently unrealistic novel that appropriates material from a wide variety of Japanese and Chinese sources to test the applicability of his poetic principles to the *monogatari* form. Wayne Lammers subtitles his translation of the novel

---

61 A few days after typing this sentence I opened the latest issue of the *New York Times Book Review* to find Teika's 21st-century countryman Haruki Murakami expressing the same aesthetic: "Our job is to give new meanings and special overtones to absolutely ordinary words" ("Jazz Messenger," 8 July 2007, p. 27).

"Fujiwara Teika's Experiment in Fiction," and it's an enjoyable if not entirely successful one.[62]

The plot is fairly simple: Ujitada at an early age displays all the qualities of a storybook hero — he is "unparalleled in beauty and temperament" (57) and excels at poetry and music — but suffers from romantic disappointment when the princess he loves is pressed into service as the emperor's concubine. The heartbroken 17-year-old is then ordered to accompany an embassy to China, much to the disappointment of his mother, who vows to wait for him on the coast of Matsura (hence the novel's title). In China, Ujitada wanders away from the court one night and meets an old musician who prophesizes that Ujitada will introduce koto music to Japan. He is told to go to Mount Shang to receive instruction from Princess Hua-yang; they make sweet music together, then she ends the course and explains she'll die soon, but that they'll meet again when he returns to Japan. She launches her koto into space, which will be retrieved later. Teika's sources so far are blatantly clear: he's borrowing from the first chapters of both *The Tale of the Hollow Tree* and *The Tale of Nezame* for the supernatural koto lessons, and from *The Tale of the Hamamatsu Counselor* for the trip to China.

At this point the Chinese emperor dies and a dynastic struggle ensues, which thrusts Ujitada into battle defending the emperor's young heir and his beautiful mother, the dowager empress. Even though he had "never even learned to tell which way an arrow should fly" (103), he is put in charge of her army and at a crucial point is assisted by nine supernatural warriors to defeat the rebel leader. (This is another radical difference from the Heian *monogatari*, which contain virtually no scenes of violence or warfare.) This earns the Japanese teen the gratitude of the Chinese empress, with whom he falls in love. They have an affair similar to (read: ripped off from) that of Chunagon and the Hoyang Consort in *Hamamatsu*, during which Ujitada isn't sure whether he is romancing the empress herself or a supernatural being resembling her. The time comes for his return to Japan, which he delays as long as possible to continue the affair. Back home, he is reunited with the reincarnated Princess Hua-yang, hears from his first love, and conjures up the Chinese empress by way of a magic mirror, which doesn't please his wife Hua-yang. And at this sticky point, the novel breaks off with a note from the author/transcriber: "Here, too, the binding is damaged and the remaining pages have been lost" (162).

Scholars have speculated why Teika ended his short novel this way. Had he grown bored with the project? Had he painted himself into a narrative corner? Or, given the nature of this "experiment in fiction," was this a snarky disruption of readers' expectations, just as the preceding narrative was a pastiche of earlier *monogatari* clichés? I like to think it was the latter. It would

62 His well-annotated edition will be cited by page number.

anticipate such ploys as the moth-damaged poem in Rabelais's *Gargantua and Pantagruel*, the gaps in the texts of Swift's *Tale of a Tub* and Danielewski's *House of Leaves*, the blank chapters in Sterne's *Tristam Shandy*, the missing conclusion of Poe's *Narrative of Arthur Gordon Pym*, and weird stories like Lovecraft's "Haunter of the Dark" that break off just as some eldritch horror overcomes the narrator ("I see it — coming here — hell-wind — titan blur — black wings — Yog-Sothoth save me — the three-lobed burning eye . . .").

Here, as in *Hamamatsu*, exotic China is an erotic fantasy. Still pining for the Japanese princess he left behind, Ujitada is not aroused by the "countless lovely dancing girls, all decked out as colorfully as flowers," and the "beguiling beauties" whom the emperor provides for his entertainment (77), but after one glimpse of Hua-yang he forgets about not only the dancing girls but his first love as well. "Back home he had thought no one could match the beauty of Princess Kannabi, who had so stirred his heart; now he could see that next to this lady she would be like the unkempt daughter of a provincial rustic" (82). As Hua-yang begins to play her koto, Ujitada joins her on his, and their playing produces erotic overtones of the sort Teika used in his poetry. One of his most famous poems reads as follows:

> When the floating bridge
> Of dreams of a night in spring
> Was interrupted,
> In the sky a bank of clouds
> Was taking leave of the peak.

After providing this translation, Keene writes, "commentators agree that, despite the imagery drawn from nature, the poem is not about the seasons but about love" (659–60), specifically about an interrupted erotic dream. (As noted earlier, "The Floating Bridge of Dreams" is the title of the final chapter of *The Tale of Genji*, and like "the floating world" signified both an erotic experience and the transcience of the world.) Similarly, Ujitada's first music lesson doubles as a lesson in love as he accommodates himself to his partner's rhythm:

> He followed [her playing] with ease from the first, not missing a single note, and as the music gradually cleared his heart of all other thoughts and concerns he found that he was able, quite naturally, to match the subtlest tones of the princess's playing; before long their performances had become indistinguishable. Playing together in this way they moved from one piece to another, and by the time the night was over Ujitada had mastered a great many pieces perfectly. (82)

The erotic nature of their performance is confirmed when "from the sash of her underrobe she took a crystal jewel nearly large enough to fill the palm of her hand, and gave it to Ujitada" (92) to remember her by, the same vaginal symbol as the jewel from Budur's waistband in the Arabic *Story of Qamar al-Zaman and His Two Sons* discussed in the previous chapter. But once Ujitada tastes the charms of the disguised dowager empress (who likewise seduced him with music via the *sho*, a mouth organ) he ungallantly forgets all about Hua-yang. The fantasy nature of his relationship with the empress is underscored by his recurring suspicion that she is "a manifestation of some demonic spirit" (137) — which doesn't deter him and may in fact add a terrible thrill to it all. (The vaginal symbol she leaves him is the peony blossom.) When she finally reveals herself as his mystery lover, she also explains that she had been sent down from heaven to quell the revolt, that Ujitada was likewise sent by the Japanese god Sumiyoshi to assist her, and that they had been lovers in a previous life. Having elevated his tale to this supernatural plane, Teika might understandably not have known how to continue with the more mundane situation of Ujitada juggling a jealous wife, an exotic mistress, and an old flame who comes back into his life. So he ended it. Fujiwara Teika reportedly wrote several other novels in his younger days, but they haven't survived, which is a shame, for *The Tale of Matsura* is a seductive experience, rich in literary allusions, and a charming effort at infusing the novel with the "ethereal beauty" (*yoen*) for which his poetry is celebrated.

The supernatural likewise dominates another unconventional novel written in the 1190s, *Partings at Dawn (Ariake no wakare)*, author unknown but assumed to be a woman in Teika's circle. It features a protagonist no doubt unique in the annals of literature: a transvestite with the power of invisibility. And it is unique among *monogatari* for not beginning with the protagonist's birth and upbringing but with the unusual crisis faced by a courtier named Ariake on the edge of 17 — following a brief prologue that one of its translators calls "a tour de force of intertextuality . . . a tone-setting introduction to the theme of fickleness of male lovers."[63] Ariake had been born a girl but raised a boy by an ambitious father who claimed the gods instructed him to do so. (It later turns out the father probably dreamed this, but so strong is his desire for the prestige only a male heir can bring that he believes the dream

---

63 Khan, 200 n2. For his dissertation Khan translated all of book 1, two chapters from book 2, and most of the concluding book 3, working from the old Japanese version. There is a complete translation by a three-person team that was serialized in the Tokyo magazine *The East* in 1992–94, but it was based on a modern Japanese translation of the original; it is bland and lacks notes, whereas Khan's translation is very authentic and is well (even over-) annotated. Since neither is completely satisfactory I'll be switching between Khan (K) and *The East* (E) as needed, and dispensing with page references. I'll be using Khan's names for characters, which as usual are either ranks or poetic tags associated with them. Ariake, for example, comes from a famous poem in the *Kokinshu* that supplies the novel's title and opening imagery: "Since parting at dawn / when the pale moon appeared / so indifferent, / compared with the day's first light / there is nothing so wretched" (K).

was indeed divinely inspired.) Ariake is an accomplished young man on the road to success, and plays the flute so beautifully as to cause atmospheric disturbances. "His taste in the robes and decorated carriages he provided was simply fabulous" (K), but he is tired of his impersonation act and especially of the way men treat women in his society, which he learns by wandering around at night under the cloak of invisibility. (This was apparently inspired by a lost novel entitled *Kakuremino* about a man with a garment that made him invisible.) First he spies on his uncle, who is sexually abusing his stepdaughter Tai no Ue; then he watches a fellow courtier named Sanmi no Chujo butter up a mistress, fabricate a phony excuse for leaving, then sneak over to the house of a "quite voluptuous and ostentatiously attractive" (K) young woman who was once offered as a wife to Ariake, who is now disgusted by her sensuality. With brilliant, bitter irony, the author has an old man in another room reciting that misogynistic part in the *Lotus Sutra* where the Buddha says a woman needs to change into a man before she can attain salvation, which adds to our transvestite's gender confusion. He later overhears some women gossiping about him, wondering why he hasn't married yet. Topping things off, Ariake serves a young emperor who is smitten with him and wishes Ariake were a woman.

So Ariake takes action: disgusted at Tai no Ue's abuse, he abducts her and installs her in his family home, then puts the word out they're married. Sealing the subterfuge, she gives birth to a son, who Ariake allows others to think is his (actually the son of her wicked stepfather; Tai no Ue goes along with all this just to get away from him). But this stopgap measure doesn't resolve Ariake's gender crisis, which comes to a head when the aroused emperor — like Saisho in *The Changelings* (which is often quoted and was an obvious inspiration) — assaults the androgynous courtier and discovers he is a woman. The emperor is delighted by this discovery, so Ariake's family pretends that their son dies and presents his hitherto-unseen "sister" to the court. The openminded emperor is even more delighted by the female Ariake and makes her his Junior Consort. (Now a widow, Tai no Ue decides to "throw herself away as a nun," as the frequently irreverent author puts it, but not before giving birth to a daughter, the result of a one-night stand with her marauding stepbrother Sanmi no Chujo.) Ariake now finds herself married and pregnant, which leads the narrator to make this interesting observation:

Furthermore — perhaps because the Junior Consort was now involved in a more conventional relationship — all that wandering around completely invisible by some supernatural means or other no longer happened any more. Without that ability, she thought, even if the Emperor should no longer love her as much as he did now, he would probably not allow her the freedom of behaviour that Ariake had had before, whether invisible or visible, and she felt listless and forlorn as she remained sunk in thought. (K)

Invisibility in *Kakuremino* sounds like a gimmick, but in *Partings at Dawn* it is a multivalent metaphor: it signifies the invisibility of virginal girls in Japanese society (which is why Ariake's parents can produce a teenage daughter out of nowhere), the invisibility of transgendered and differently oriented individuals in a conformist society (there's certainly no mention of them in any work prior to *The Changelings*), and even the invisibility of a writer — what else does a novelist do but spy on others and tap into their thoughts? (One of the few benefits of becoming a woman is that Ariake can now read novels.) In male drag Ariake is invisible to horndogs like Sanmi and can thus protect her virginity. Consequently, the loss of invisibility means the loss of the freedom enjoyed by any male in a patriarchal society, which Ariake now misses as much as Chunagon did in *The Changelings* after he switched places with his sister. They both miss their flutes.

Ariake still has "intense feelings of love" (K) for bewildered Tai no Ue, and it could be that her/his true orientation is bisexual: "she earnestly wished to play both male and female roles. She thought that she would attain distinction in various ways if she were able to do this" (E). But this isn't an option, so she resigns herself to her female role and quickly reaches the pinnacle of distinction for a woman in her society: she bears her husband a son and becomes empress of Japan.

At this point, about halfway through the novel, the story jumps ahead a decade or so to deal with the next generation, just like *The Tale of Genji*. But unlike *Genji*, the second half isn't as captivating as the first. Gone are the powers of invisibility and other supernatural manifestations. (True, there are two cases of spirit possession, but these are regarded as annoying but mundane matters, like a power outage — which they kind of are: a temporary female disruption of patriarchal power.) Instead we have a morality tale about the consequences of reckless male desire like Sanmi's: he seems to have planted bastards in half of the aristocratic families of Kyoto, and as a result his younger half-brother the Sadaijin — who believes he's Ariake's son by Tai no Ue but is the son of her wicked stepfather — winds up romancing girls who are actually his half-sisters; that is, when he's not mooning over Empress Ariake, who he thinks is his aunt but is actually no relation. (The complicated genealogical relationships in this novel are maddening — even with the color-coded chart provided in one of the issues of *The East* — especially since everyone keeps changing titles/names.) Twenty-year-old Sadaijin dominates the second half of the novel, yearning for the "impossible woman" (E) and feeling a bit guilty about being as fickle as his half-brother Sanmi, who in turn begins feeling remorseful about his reckless youth as he discovers his grown-up by-blows around town. The theme here is not so much gender inequality (as in *The Changelings*) as the damage done by promiscuous men who (like so many in *Genji*) can't control their lawless desires.

Linking both halves of *Partings at Dawn* is the deceptiveness of appearances: no one is who he thinks he is, or who society thinks she is. Even Ariake, the one character the reader knows best, holds a surprise for us at the end: now called the Former Empress, she passes along her old flute to the Crown Prince (her *legitimate* son by the emperor), who plays it divinely at a gathering. She joins him on the biwa (a four-stringed lute), and the effect catches the ear of heaven, as music often does in these novels. Just when the reader thought the supernatural was a thing of the past, the author stages this *coup de théâtre*:

I cannot tell you how beautifully her biwa-playing blended with the flute-playing of the Crown Prince. And then how could words describe the extraordinary sight of seven radiantly beautiful maidens descending. They walked on a bank of cloud trailing on the uppermost branches of that stand of cherry trees in the garden whose blossoms were scattering down and swirling indescribably, and as they danced in formation together, waving their sleeves, with their celestial nape-ribbons fluttering dazzlingly in the breeze, I cannot tell you how utterly charming it was. . . . As if unable to pass up the opportunity, one of the seven heavenly maidens plucked a spray of blossom for a hair garland, and stepping down from the trailing clouds, approached the Former Empress's blinds [behind which she is playing]. Then, as the breeze swirled around her, she went right up to them, and placing the spray of blossom on the sleeve of her robe as an offering, said,

> How are you able
> to remain in such a world?
> It was you and I
> who, those many years ago
> plucked a single blossom spray

With the blossom still in her hand, the Former Empress played her biwa all the more spontaneously and unhesitatingly — perhaps she was not feeling her usual self — and as if quite disoriented, she said,

> The scent of blossoms
> on sleeves that never forget
> — let it remain here
> until the time I return
> to the cloud realm I once knew

Hearing this the maiden wiped the tears from her face and then straight away the palace was suffused with perfumed breezes as the maidens ascended back to the heavens leaving only a mist lingering in the sky. (K; Japanese verse omitted)

Apparently Ariake too is a heavenly maiden, not a human girl, these intimations of immortality recalling the revelation of the Shining Princess in *The Tale of the Bamboo Cutter*. The author had been dropping hints about this as early as book 1, stating, "Major Captain Ariake gave an outward impression of being distinctly forceful, but he was actually quite delicate, and the moonlight quite unsettled him, so anyone watching might have wondered whether he was indeed a heavenly maiden who had descended" (K). The novel ends with one more revelation, which is handled so brilliantly it too deserves to be quoted. Ariake's old lady-in-waiting, Jiju no Naichi — who translator Khan thinks is the implied narrator of the novel — knows the secret of Sadaijin's patrimony and, near death, decides to break it to him. The novel ends:

> The Sadaijin was overcome with pity at the sight of Jiju, who was worn out from her illness. She said tearfully, "I am terrified at the mere thought of revealing the circumstances surrounding your birth. . . ."
>
> Afterward, the Sadaijin muttered to himself:
>
> > The temple bells ring with pathos
> > Never have I tasted
> > Grief as bitter
> > As I tasted this evening. (E)

Khan and other critics suspect there might be a lacuna in the manuscript after Jiju's line, but the ellipsis is a wonderfully understated effect and was probably intentional — why would the author spell out what the reader already knows? — and the novel's final line about evening elegantly bookends the novel's opening line about parting at dawn. But Khan is right in noting that the novel provides several instances of "female solidarity and women performing as surrogate fathers" (402 n78), from Ariake's early rescue of Tai no Ue, to several cases in the second half of women providing for children abandoned by their fathers, to the heavenly maiden who restores the Retired Empress to something of her old self ("not her usual self"). Working invisibly behind the scenes, the women hold society together while the men indulge in socially sanctioned rape. Despite Ariake's youthful cross-dressing adventure, *Partings at Dawn* belongs not on the shelf of tranny novels but in the canon of feminist classics.

It is mentioned in passing in a transgenre work written a few years later, *The Story without a Name* (*Mumyozoshi*, c. 1200), probably written by Fujiwara Teika's sister, an extremely well-read woman known only as Shunzei's daughter (Shunzeiko no musume, 1171?–1252?). This delightful, 70-page work takes the form of a first-person account by an 83-year-old nun, who once served at the imperial court but now wanders around Kyoto chanting the

Lotus Sutra. She comes across a rundown house inhabited by some bluestockings, one of whom spots the old nun and invites her in to tell her story and to recite chapter 2 on "expedient means" from the *Lotus Sutra*, in which the Buddha says it's kosher to use "words of simile and parable," even fictions, to expound the more esoteric aspects of Buddhist doctrine. (In his discussion of novels with Tamakazura, Genji allowed that *monogatari* could qualify as "expedient means.") The ladies invite the nun to "stay up all night talking" with them, and begin by asking each other "what is the most difficult thing to give up in the world?"[64] The ladies suggest things like the moon, letters, dreams, tears, even the *Lotus Sutra*, but they all finally agree the hardest thing to give up would be novels.

In the second chapter of *The Tale of Genji*, the Shining Prince listens as three men discuss women; here, in a playful homage, the nun listens as three or four women discuss not men but literature. The first third of the novella is given over to praising *The Tale of Genji*, which they revere. In 2004 Karen Joy Fowler published a clever novel entitled *The Jane Austen Book Club*; this one could be called *The Murasaki Shikibu Book Club* for all the space it devotes to *Genji*, which one woman feels is such a masterpiece it "cannot be the work of an ordinary being" (137). During the middle third they discuss other novels: *The Tale of Sagoromo* is ranked second to *Genji* (though faulted for its supernatural scenes), and *The Tale of Nezame* ranked third. Most of the novels I've discussed are dissected, and there are tantalizing references to a dozen or so lost novels. I especially mourn the loss of *The Tale of Tamano* — starring a woman who displays "bold behavior" and "a strange disposition" (409) — and *A Swamp of Straps* (*Odae no Numa*), "written in an exaggerated, up-to-date style" (417), indicating even medieval Japan had its avant-garde writers. The author makes this coy reference to her brother Teika's efforts:

> "The Minor Captain Teika appears to have written many novels, but they have only the outward appearance of novels and are quite devoid of realism. The poems of *Matsura no Miya* were composed after the fashion of *Man'yōshū*, while its plot tends to make me feel as if I am reading *Utsubo Monogatari* [the fanciful *Tale of the Hollow Tree*]. Its style is too lofty to appeal to a talentless person like myself." (418)

That must have caused some family arguments. In the last third the women discuss poem-tales and poetry anthologies, and then literary women: though no woman had edited any of Japan's many anthologies, one lady pointedly remarks, "Well, surely compiling an anthology is not all that wonderful.

---

64 Page 133 in Marra's translation, serialized in *Monumenta Nipponica* in 1994, hereafter cited by page number. Marra doesn't translate the title *Mumyozoshi*; other critics have called it *Untitled Book*, *A Nameless Text*, or *Untitled Leaves*, but I prefer Keene's *Story without a Name*.

Starting with Murasaki Shikibu, who wrote *Genji*, and Sei Shōnagon, the author of *Makura no Sōshi* [her famous *Pillow Book*], weren't most of the novels we've just been talking about written by women? And so it is difficult for anyone to underestimate women" (422). The other ladies chime in with praise for women poets as the nun continues to listen, pretending to sleep. Only on the final page does someone casually notice, "We've spent the entire night here talking of women and haven't even touched at all on the subject of men. How very unfair!" (434). How very catty!

The Story without a Name has long been revered as "the earliest extant example of prose criticism in the history of Japanese literature" (as translator Marra writes in his introduction), and it's certainly the earliest theoretical essay on the novel. But its fictional format also makes it the first example of what we might call "critifiction" (to borrow experimental novelist Raymond Federman's coinage), a work of fiction in the form of criticism, or vice versa. Oscar Wilde's *Portrait of Mr. W. H.* may be the most famous example of this rarefied genre, to which we can add Ki no Tsurayuki's *Tosa Diary*, Joseph ben Zabara's *Book of Delight*, George Gascoigne's *Adventures of Master F. J.*, Clara Reeve's *Progress of Romance* — similar in form to *The Story without a Name*: three readers discuss the history of fiction over a dozen evenings — William Carlos Williams' *Spring and All*, Arno Schmidt's radio dialogs, Julian Barnes' *Flaubert's Parrot*, A. S. Byatt's *Possession*, Lee Siegel's *City of Dreadful Night*, Lance Olsen's *Girl Imagined by Chance*, the book-mad novels of Roberto Bolaño and Enrique Vila-Matas, Nicholson Baker's *Anthologist*, Fowler's novel mentioned above, and perhaps David Markson's later, unclassifiable novels.[65]

65 Critifiction could also include works of fiction that display formal elements of criticism and pedagogy, such as the analyses of chivalric novels in Cervantes' *Don Quixote*, of pastoral and mythology in Sorel's *Extravagant Shepherd*, and of baroque sermons in Isla's *Friar Gerund*; the essays in literary criticism that preface each book of Fielding's *Tom Jones*; the Qing-era scholarly novels of Xia Jingqu, Li Ruzhen, Tu Shen, and Chen Qiu; the footnoted essays on architecture in Hugo's *Notre-Dame de Paris* and cetalogy in Melville's *Moby-Dick*; the 40-page essay on history at the end of Tolstoy's *War and Peace*; the "night studies" chapter of Joyce's *Finnegans Wake*; the critical-edition format of Vladimir Nabokov's *Pale Fire*, Herbert Lindenburger's *Saul's Fall*, Milorad Pavić's *Dictionary of the Khazars*, David Mamet's *Wilson*, and Samuel Delany's *Phallos*; the scholarly apparatus attached to some of the novels of Julián Ríos and William T. Vollmann; the endnotes in the novels of Lawrence Durrell and Alasdair Gray, in Carol Maso's *AVA*, David Foster Wallace's *Infinite Jest*, Ciaran Carson's *Shamrock Tea*, Albert Goldbarth's *Pieces of Payne*, and Paul Anderson's *Hunger's Brides*; the comically erudite index to Lewis Carroll's *Sylvie and Bruno*, and the more functional ones at the ends of Harry Mathews' *Sinking of Odradek Stadium* and Jeremy M. Davies's *Rose Alley*; the footnotes in Thomas Nashe's *Pierce Penniless*, Jonathan Swift's *Tale of a Tub*, Eliza Haywood's *Adventures of Eovaai*, Thomas Amory's *John Buncle*, Sir Walter Scott's *Waverley*, Joseph Perl's *Revealer of Secrets*, in Thomas Love Peacock's novels, Jack London's *Iron Heel*, Flann O'Brien's *Third Policeman*, Samuel Beckett's *Watt*, John Fowles's *French Lieutenant's Woman*, Ignácio de Loyola Brandão's *Zero*, Manuel Puig's *Kiss of the Spider Woman*, Robert Grudin's *Book*, John Barth's *Sabbatical*, Augusto Roa Bastos's

Although the ladies are unnamed and don't emerge as identifiable characters, they *are* characters, not talking heads: like the members of a reading group, they disagree with one another, sometimes make uncritical judgments based on personal prejudices, and occasionally get plot details wrong. But they share the same aesthetic expectations of novels: they should feature admirable characters and deep emotions, demonstrate masterful diction, and ultimately should comfort and console. None of them cares for supernatural effects in fiction; one lady categorically states, "A novel is surely absurd if it isn't realistic" (295). Shunzei's daughter probably exaggerated this point to redeem the novel from critics like Minamoto Tamenori, quoted earlier scoffing at *monogatari* for their fairytale elements. The author clearly wanted to assert the legitimacy of fiction, and perhaps even propose its equality (if not superiority) to religious writings, a bold response to the religious fever that sickened Japan at the end of the Heian era. The ladies' initial praise for the

---

I the Supreme, Nicholson Baker's *Mezzanine*, Rikki Ducornet's *Phosphor in Dreamland*, Geoff Ryman's *253*, in Roger Boylan's novels, Mark Z. Danielewski's *House of Leaves*, Susanna Clarke's *Jonathan Strange & Mr Norell*, Shirow Masamune's *Ghost in the Shell: Man-Machine Interface*, Michael Cox's *Meaning of Night*, Stephen Graham Jones's *Demon Theory*, E. Lockhart's *Boyfriend List*, Michele Jaffe's *Bad Kitty*, Junot Díaz's *Brief Wondrous Life of Oscar Wao*, Andrew Foster Altschul's *Lady Lazarus*, Lawrence Shainberg's *Crust*, Josh Bazell's *Beat the Reaper*, Matthew Flaming's *Kingdom of Ohio*, and many other novels by authors seduced by the "aesthetic evil of a footnote," as J. D. Salinger demonized it in *Franny and Zooey* (in a footnote); the appendices to John Sladek's *Müller-Fokker Effect*, Borislav Pekić's *How to Quiet a Vampire*, Greg Boyd's *Nambuli Papers*, Scarlett Thomas's *PopCo*, and Zach Plague's *boring boring boring boring boring boring boring*; the formal lectures and essays in the Marquis de Sade's fictions, Hermann Broch's *Sleepwalkers*, J. M. Coetzee's *Elizabeth Costello*, and Alexander Theroux's schoolmasterly novels; the mock *Paris Review* interview and Nabokovian afterword in Donald Harington's *Ekaterina*; the imitations of academic writing in the fictions of Harry Mathews, Gilbert Sorrentino, Umberto Eco, and Steven Milhauser; Lee Siegel's scholarly translation-cum-commentary-cum-confession *Love in a Dead Language*; Benjamin Zucker's Talmudic novels; the intra-chapter supplementary materials in Alan Moore and Dave Gibbons's *Watchmen*; the Japanese flash cards and job guidelines provided in the front of Hilary Raphael's *I ♥ Lord Buddha*; the test questions at the end of Jacques Roubaud's *Princess Hoppy* and Marisha Pessl's *Special Topics in Calamity Physics*; the advice columns and heuristic quizzes in *How to Meet Cute Boys* by Deanna Kizis; novels in the form of historical studies (Washington Irving's *History of New York*), academic biographies (Thomas Carlyle's *Sartor Resartus*, Milhauser's *Edwin Mullhouse*, Wolfgang Hildesheimer's *Marbot*), scholarly editions of letters (Ingo Schulze's *New Lives*), literary interviews (Bohumil Hrabal's *Pirouettes on a Postage Stamp*), Ph.D. theses (R. M. Koster's *Dissertation*), college quarterlies (Jerome Charyn's *Tar Baby*), literary anthologies (Stephen Marche's *Shining at the Bottom of the Sea*), mathematical treatises (Suri and Bal's *A Certain Ambiguity*), travel guides (Jean Ricardou's *Place Names*, Chandler Brossard's *Postcards*, Karen Gordon's *Paris Out of Hand*, Michael Martone's *Blue Guide to Indiana*, Aravind Adiga's *Between the Assassinations*), foreign-language phrasebooks (Norah Labiner's *German for Travelers*), appendices (A. M. Homes's *Appendix A*), pedagogical handbooks (Jean-Jacques Rousseau's *Emile*, Stanley Crawford's *Some Instructions to My Wife Concerning the Upkeep of the House and Marriage and to My Son and Daughter Concerning the Conduct of Their Childhood*), and dictionaries and encyclopedias (see chap. 2, n69), not to mention the maps, glossaries, marginal notes (see chap. 3, n96), and genealogies some novelists provide.

Lotus Sutra pales in comparison with their praise for *Genji* and other novels. There is a legend that Murasaki began writing *Genji* on the back of a temple scroll, symbolically overturning sacred scripture in favor of a secular scripture that could convey truths more accurate than those in books like the *Lotus Sutra*. Towards the end of the novella the ladies begin speaking of a capitalized Way of Poetry to rival the Way of Buddha or the Dao. "I hear that in these Latter Days when everything is bad," someone says, "only the Way of Poetry continues without interruption and without ever becoming exhausted" (421). As writers elsewhere have suggested, the only true immortality is literary; of poets, one of the ladies boasts, "Their work has perpetuated their name for a hundred, even a thousand years, and this is a very impressive feeling. How wonderful to compose something, even only a single word, that will last into the future" (429). The silent nun wisely doesn't try to counter this with any quotations from the *Lotus Sutra*.

With the indifference to genre distinctions that characterizes early Japanese literature, *The Story without a Name* changes hats from fiction to criticism to feminist manifesto and back again, all while building a narrative arc whereby religion is supplanted by literature. The dialogue is lively, the criticism sharp, the counter-theology inspiring, and the defense of women's contributions to Japanese literature unassailable. The author's name has been lost, but the work has lasted 800 years into the future, just as she hoped.

One reason *The Tale of Genji* is praised so highly by the ladies is that, unlike her successors, Murasaki knew only a handful of novels like *The Tale of the Hollow Tree*, *The Tale of the Bamboo Cutter*, and *The Tale of Sumiyoshi* (137). The 10th-century version of the latter that Murasaki knew is lost, but sometime in the early 13th century someone wrote a new version that has survived. Like the 10th-century *Tale of Lady Ochikubo* it is a variation of the Cinderella story, but it's a simplistic, sentimental novella lacking *Ochikubo*'s adult situations and humor. (It doesn't help that the only English translation of *Sumiyoshi* was made over a century ago, and in an antique style that was old-fashioned even then.) The ladies of *The Story without a Name* skip over it, and I'll follow their example.

Sometime in the middle of the 13th century, an anonymous writer revived the *uta monogatari* genre for *The Tale of Saigyo* (*Saigyo monogatari*), a novella based loosely on the life of the famous poet Saigyo (1118–90). It's a typical religious conversion story — a young aristocrat becomes convinced of the evanescence of the world after his friend dies, then abandons his family to become a wandering dharma bum — and is as sanctimonious as most conversion stories. And it's a typical *uta monogatari* in that the prose narrative mostly provides a context for the historical Saigyo's woeful *waka*. But what makes the novella interesting is the fictional Saigyo's conflicted feelings about poetry: as a Buddhist, he struggles to detach himself from the illusory beauties of the phenomenal world, but as a poet he is inspired to write about them. One famous poem encapsulates his struggle:

> A curlew lifts from the marsh
> in autumn twilight —
> and even my heart,
> which should no longer feel,
> feels the moment touch it.[66]

Not only does he still "feel" for the world, but he's driven to write poems about his feelings. As he wanders over Japan, he more often visits places that inspired earlier poets than religious shrines, and virtually everything he experiences becomes the occasion for poetry rather than religious meditation. Shortly before he dies, Saigyo convinces himself that writing poetry has aided his religious quest:

> Thus more than fifty years had flown by. He now thought, "One day and night of life contain myriad wayward thoughts. But I have devoted myself to the thirty-one syllables of the *waka* as a way of purifying myself of transgressions committed, and it has been the means whereby my heart has followed the Buddhist way." (8)

The pursuit of poetry has in fact *prevented* his complete detachment from the world: two pages earlier he lamented, "I thought I was past caring / for the spring, / but the frozen water in my water pipe / has made me yearn for it again" (8). Instead, the novella implies religious discipline is a metaphor for an artist's discipline, which is much more convincing than Saigyo's self-defensive rationalization. (The historical Saigyo was much more worldly than his fictional counterpart.) *The Tale of Saigyo* is set during the final years of the Heian era, and its autumnal mood and sense of loss also make it an elegy for an era that had already assumed legendary status by the time the novella was written.

Court romances continued to be written during the 13th century as a narrowing circle of nostalgic aristocrats tried to hold on to Heian ideals — an anthology compiled in 1271 entitled *Fuyo waka shu* (Wind and Leaves Collection) drew its poems from nearly two *hundred* novels, and those are just the ones the editor liked — but most of them perished in the civil wars that left the Heian capital in ruins. Of the later Kamakura novels, only the first two of eight books remain of *Iwade shinobu monogatari* (A Tale of

---

66 Chap. 3 in McKinney's translation (hereafter cited by chapter). Coincidentally, McKinney's version appeared within months of Gustav Heldt's "Saigyō's Traveling Tale: A Translation of *Saigyō Monogatari*" in *Monumenta Nipponica* 52.4 (Winter 1997): 467–521. Both have fine introductions and are well annotated.

Unspoken Yearning, c. 1235–50), possibly by Shunzei's daughter, which must have been a major work (see Keene, 808–14). In 1933 a huge novel entitled *Wagami ni tadoru himegimi* (The Princess in Search of Herself, c. 1245–70) was discovered, but it was not printed until 1956 and has yet to be translated into English. Keene finds it "decadent" but notes that "some enthusiasts now claim that it is the finest of all the pseudoclassical tales" (804). But such novels became rare by the end of the 13th century, shouldered aside by a more masculine genre, the war novel (*gunki monogatari*).

The civil wars of the 12th century that led to the end of the Heian era and the continuing wars of the Kamakura era were first recorded by historians and diarists, then embellished by wandering minstrels over the next few centuries, and eventually compiled into novels. Like the prototypical *Story of Masakado's Rebellion*, they hew closely to recorded history and use fiction mostly for flavoring, and for that reason I'll limit myself to only a few remarks on most of them.[67]

The anonymous *Tale of the Disorder in Hogen* (*Hogen monogatari*, 1221?) is the earliest example, and centers on a one-day battle in July 1156 that changed the course of Japanese history, leading to the downfall of the Heian aristocracy and the ascendancy of the military classes, and inspiring the militaristic spirit that bedeviled Japan until recently. The hundred-page novel is divided into thirds (three scrolls originally): part 1 recounts the events leading up to the battle, part 2 portrays the battle itself in Kyoto, and part 3 concerns the aftermath. You can see the *gunki monogatari* genre develop before your eyes as the chronicle-like first third becomes more fiction-like as the novel progresses, concluding with a dramatic scene that is completely fictitious, though this oversimplifies the actual genealogy of the text. Hogen is not a person or place but the name of a brief period (1156–59), and the "disorder" was caused by an imperial family squabble over who should occupy the throne. The clash was between two clans, the Heike (aka the Taira) and the Genji (the Minamoto), but members of those clans supported different candidates for the throne, which pitted father against son, and brother against brother. The civil war also raised questions of Confucian and Buddhist ideals regarding government and personal conduct, elevating the conflict to a disorder in the cosmos itself, a deviation from "Universal Law," all of which provided the tale's shapers with rich dramatic possibilities.

---

67 For a similar reason I'm passing over the genre known as "historical tales" (*rekishi monogatari*), which includes such works as Akazome Emon's *Tale of Flowering Fortunes* (*Eiga monogatari*) and *The Great Mirror* (*Okagami*, both late 11th century), because they are considerably more history than tale.

Hogen's hero is a fierce warrior named Tametomo (1139–77), a member of the Genji clan. His real-life counterpart is barely mentioned in the earliest accounts of the Hogen disturbance, but here he looms as large as Achilles in the *Iliad*. His father had "chased him off to the West Country in his youth" for being "too wild";[68] but the 17-year-old comes to his rescue when he learns his father has been stripped of his office, and in Kyoto he finds himself facing his brother in battle (whom he spares). Tametomo's side is defeated, so he lights out for the wilds, eventually discovering and taming "the Isle of Devils," a fan-service episode added later. Attesting to his importance, the finished novel ends not with the death of the defeated emperor (as earlier versions probably did) but with Tametomo's act of hara-kiri. After *Tale of the Disorder in Hogen*, the noble samurai, not the aesthetic aristocrat, would dominate the Japanese novel.

The Heike and Genji butted topknots a few years later in the winter of 1159–60, which became the basis of the *Heiji monogatari* (Tale of the Disorder in Heiji, mid-13th century). This slightly longer novel resembles the *Hogen monogatari* in so many ways that it's been suspected the earliest written version was either prepared by the same person or by someone who used it as a template. It too is structured in thirds (origins/battle/aftermath), is pro-Genji, is written in a style MSG'd with Chinese vocabulary, and is dependent upon Chinese literature for its allusions and references (as opposed to Japanese poetry, as in the court romances). *Heiji* is a little more digressive than *Hogen*, and introduced some much-needed humor into the Japanese novel. The following scene is unimaginable in any Japanese novel after *Lady Ochikubo*:

Frightened by the battle cry, Lord Nobuyori, who had seemed so awesome until then, grew pale and became [as green] as grass. He descended the south steps [of the Shishinden {the main building of the imperial palace}], but his knees trembled so that he could scarcely get down. He intended to mount his horse like the rest and had it brought up, but, fat and bloated as he was and clad in heavy armor, and his horse being big, he had difficulty mounting. Furthermore, [the horse], unlike his master, was a fine and high-spirited creature, continually straining to be away. Seven or eight footmen approached and restrained him. If they had let him go, he might have flown up to heaven. He made one think that the colts of the eight heavenly horses of King Mu might have been like this. Since [Nobuyori] was unable to mount him, two of his retainers came up at once and saying, "Quickly mount," pushed him up. Perhaps because they shoved too much, he went over on the left

---

68 Page 20 in Wilson's translation. This is another superb scholarly edition and the translation seems quite faithful, though Wilson's dialogue is a bit stilted, sounding at times like a poorly dubbed martial arts movie ("So since it would be regrettable should I lose my present good repute, well then, good!" [38].)

side and fell flat on his face with a thud. They quickly raised him up and looked. He was a frightful sight, his face covered with sand and blood streaming from his nose.[69]

This fat courtier is the instigator of the disorder in the Heiji period, and is aligned with the Genji; he opposes a wise scholar named Shinzei, who sides with the Heike. Because of resentments left over from the Hogen disturbance, the two clans clash again, with the heroic role of Tametomo taken by a young man named Yoshihira. The Heike capture and execute Nobuyori, but not before he kills his enemy Shinzei, and then they execute Yoshihira, who (like Tametomo) is splendidly defiant to the end. The novel ends with the story of Yoshihira's father's mistress and her sons, two of whom, Yoritomo and Yoshitsune, will eventually avenge this second defeat of the Genji in the greatest of the medieval Japanese war novels.

The magnificent *Tale of the Heike* (*Heike monogatari*) is not only the greatest of the *gunki monogatari*, but synthesizes elements of the realistic (*tsukuri*) and historical (*rekishi*) genres as well to give it a scope and grandeur second only to *The Tale of Genji*. Historically, it covers the period after the disturbances in Hogen and Heiji, especially the Genpei War of 1180–85 that brought a formal end to the Heian era. But it expands on history when necessary to dramatize the transition from a courtly society to a military one in 12th-century Japan and to illustrate the Buddhist doctrines of karma and the impermanence of all things.

Accounts of this civil war began circulating shortly after the events themselves and soon entered the repertoire of wandering minstrels (*biwa hoshi*). Written versions began appearing in the 13th century — one by a courtier named Yukinaga, another a 2,000-page account entitled *Genpei josuiki* (The Rise and Fall of the Genji and the Heike) — but the version of *The Tale of Heike* read today (in English as well as Japanese) is the work of a blind priest named Kakuichi, who after 30 years' work completed the 500-page novel a few months before he died in 1371 — that is, nearly two centuries after the events it describes. Kakuichi was a member of a guild that specialized in Heike recitations and had developed a reputation for being "different" according to one diarist, "a comment" (one of his translators explains) "probably inspired not only by his textual revisions but also by his performance style, which seems to have been more complex, colorful, and melodic than anything previously attempted by the guild members."[70] Kakuichi's approach has been called revo-

69 As translated by Reischauer in *Translations from Early Japanese Literature*, 439–40 (his brackets, except for my explanation of the Shishinden). This is only a partial translation, most of book 1 and scenes from books 2 and 3. Marisa Chalitpatanangune translated books 1 and 2 for her dissertation, but not the third. The novel is only about 125 pages long, so perhaps someday a hardier translator will take on the entire work.

70 From page 8 of the introduction to McCullough's excellent translation, hereafter cited by book/chapter. There are two earlier complete English translations of the *Heiki*, one made

lutionary and innovative, his history inverted and heterodox;[71] though more or less historically accurate, the *Heike* more closely resembles golden-era Heian novels like *The Tale of Genji*, which Kakuichi obviously knew, except with a level of violence unthinkable in those earlier romances.

Following the defeat of the Genji in 1160, the Heike began lording it over them, especially in the person of Taira no Kiyomori (1118–81), head of the clan and virtual dictator of Japan for the next 20 years. The first half of the novel deals with his heavy-handed regime, held in check only by his high-minded son Shigemori (who, like many of *Heike*'s characters, first appeared in the *Hogen* and *Heiji monogatari*). In the second half, the Genji half-brothers Yoritomo and Yoshitsune revolt against the Heike, first driving them out of the imperial city of Kyoto, and then further west until the Genji defeat the Heike at the naval battle of Dan-no-ura in 1185. The victors begin exterminating the remaining Heike until they did "vanish forever from the face of the earth," as the concluding chapter mournfully states (12.9).[72]

By the time Kakuichi composed his definitive version, everyone knew the basic story, so he let the military plot take care of itself to concentrate on the human element by way of innumerable biographical vignettes, after the manner of Chinese history books. Although there were complicated political reasons for the regime change, Kakuichi blames the fall of the house of Heike on a failure of character. In an early episode (1.2), we're shown how Kiyomori's father Tadamori wheedles a political favor out of the emperor that so outrages his courtiers they try to assassinate the schemer, which Tadamori avoids by committing a crime that is later dismissed on a technicality. That this sort of brash behavior would be tolerated, much less rewarded by the emperor spells the beginning of the end as far as the old-fashioned courtiers (and the author) are concerned. His son Kiyomori establishes the equivalent of a police state — his Gestapo consists of 300 teenagers with pageboy haircuts — and makes nepotistic appointments that further alienate the old guard. Needless to say, the Genji, who used to share power with them, are left out completely.

Political wrongdoing is aligned with personal wrongdoing throughout the novel. Early on, the author tells us of one "freakish caprice" Kiyomori indulges in (1.6). He falls for a dancer named Gio, which sort of means Art Girl. (She is now considered the first geisha; like them, her name more broadly signifies

---

during World War I by A. L. Sadler (published in a scholarly journal but never in book form) and one by Hiroshi Kitagawa published in Japan in 1975, with a brief but instructive foreword by Edward Seidensticker.

71 The first pair of adjectives is McCullough's, the second pair from Bialock's *Eccentric Spaces, Hidden Histories*, 190, 299.

72 This is followed by an epilogue entitled "The Initiates' Chapter," which was apparently Kakuichi's own contribution to the source material and was conveyed only to special members of the *Heike* guild.

"performance artist.") Kiyomori takes care of her and her younger sister Ginyo for three years, but ditches them when a 16-year-old dancer who cheekily calls herself Buddha (Hotoke) sashays into town. Humiliated, the sisters become nuns and seclude themselves in the Saga mountains, where they are eventually joined by Hotoke, who was miserable in Kiyomori's palace and has likewise become a Buddhist nun. The ex-dancers "achieved their goal of rebirth in the Pure Land" (1.6), whereas heartless Kiyomori adds one more debt of bad karma to his doom.

Kakuichi proceeds in this manner, contrasting bad behavior with good, alternating between corrupt actions (usually by Kiyomori and other men in power) and the consequences of those actions on others (usually women and children), each episode a sermon on the transience of mundane life and the promise of eternal life dangled by Buddhist doctrine. Each episode is a microcosmic example of the novel's macrocosmic themes, and while one sadly shakes the head at these delusions of an afterlife via renunciation of the only life there is, one admires the thoroughness with which the author pursues his theme. He begins the novel with "the sound of the Gion Shōja bells" in India, allegedly the first Buddhist monastery, and concludes with the tolling of the Jakkoin bell north of Kyoto, where Kiyomori's daughter Kenreimon'in (and mother of the last Heike emperor) has sought religious refuge, reenacting the historical movement of Buddhism from India to Japan, where it mixed with animistic Shinto beliefs to create an especially superstitious if colorful brand of Buddhism. There are references throughout to various Buddhist tenets and sutras, mingling promiscuously with native myths, miracles, ghosts, spirit possessions, and old legends, as though in an encyclopedic attempt to encompass all of Japan's religious beliefs. Near the end (11.14) Kakuichi even tells a cleaned-up version of the story of the sun goddess Amaterasu, from whom the imperial Japanese family claim descent to this day.[73]

How seriously Kakuichi took this is hard to say, especially given his Confucian outlook. One section features two island exiles slowly going crazy and spouting all sorts of Buddhist nonsense about fish-gods and "Thousand-Armed Kannon" and seeing poetic answers to their prayers spelled out in insect-gnawed leaves (2.15–16). Kakuichi relates with a straight face how one samurai was a fifth-generation descendant of a giant snake, "the divinity worshipped at Takachio in Hyūga Province" (8.3), and after a quotation asks

---

73 It's quite a story: bugged by her brother's Bart Simpson-like behavior (involving excrement, among other things), the sun goddess shuts herself inside the cave of heaven, plunging the world into darkness. To lure her out, the other gods set up a mirror and hire Uzume, the goddess of pleasure, to perform a raunchy striptease outside the cave, which the gods greet with all the enthusiasm of frat boys at a strip club. Wondering at the commotion, Amaterasu peeks outside her cave and catches her reflection in the mirror. It's love at first sight. She had never seen herself before and is so dazzled by her own beauty that she remains in the world and thus restores the light. The myth is told in both the *Kojiki* and the *Nihongi*.

with what I hope is unctuous irony, "Since that is the miraculous language of the *Lotus Sutra*, the scripture containing the Buddha's golden words, how could it be even a tiny bit wrong?" (7.13). That was for the church ladies in the audience; for more sophisticated members Kakuichi often uses ironic juxtaposition to undercut "conventional wisdom." In one of his many historical asides, he politely notes that "although the power of Buddhism may have decided the succession in Emperor Seiwa's case [ruled 858–76], it is the Sun Goddess who has selected every other sovereign," which he *immediately* follows with this backroom politicking:

> "This is infuriating!" the Heike said when they heard the news in the west. "We ought to have brought the Third and Fourth Princes with us."
>
> "If we had, the Retired Emperor would probably have elevated Kiso no Yoshinaka's patron, Prince Takakura's son, who was made a monk and taken north by his guardian, Shigehide," Major Counselor Tokitada said.
>
> "He could not have given the throne to a Prince who had pronounced religious vows," someone said.
>
> "You are mistaken," Tokitada said. "I believe there is a Chinese precedent. . . ." (8.2)

In other words, the emperor of Japan was usually selected by those in power for political reasons, and as in *Genji* the "divine" emperor could even be someone's unacknowledged bastard. The sun goddess and "the power of Buddhism" obviously had nothing to do with it, and are just the snake-oil rhetoric of patriotism that medicates the gullible portion — i.e., the majority — of any nation's population. (See Yukio Mishima's beautifully perverse story "Patriotism" for a more recent Japanese expression of this con.) Kakuichi knew all this, but he also knew what his audience and patrons expected, so we don't need to take the Buddhist blab any more seriously than we do the gods and goddesses in the *Iliad* or the *Popol Vuh*. That many Japanese today still take Buddhist mythology seriously is, dare I say, inscrutable.[74]

Befitting *The Tale of the Heike*'s original status as a performance piece, Kakuichi filled it with numerous rhetorical showpieces. The battle scenes, it goes without saying, are vivid, but he also captures the chaos of war in general, as when the Heike are surprised by a Genji attack:

---

74 Some of these beliefs are not without their charm. There are shrines in Japan today where unwanted dolls can be sent for the benefit of their "souls." According to a 2004 issue of *Asian Sex Gazette*, this service has even been extended to sex dolls; one such dollmaker says that in addition to taking exhausted sex dolls off the hands of his customers, "Twice a year we also arrange for a *kuyo* (Buddhist memorial service) for discarded dolls at the special bodhisattva for dolls at the Shimizu Kannon-do in Ueno Park" (quoted in David Levy's *Love and Sex with Robots* [NY: HarperCollins, 2007], 249), which I find strangely touching.

They fled in desperate haste, abandoning their belongings. Some seized bows and left arrows in the confusion; some seized arrows and left bows; some mounted others' horses; some saw their horses mounted by others. Some leaped onto tethered beasts and rode in circles around picket stakes. There were screams from great numbers of courtesans and harlots, brought in as entertainers from nearby post stations, who sustained grievous injuries from kicks in the head or suffered broken hips from being trampled underfoot. (5.11)

There are bathetic scenes in which husbands say farewell to their wives and/ or children, many scenes of operatic suicide — in Japan a noble failure was more admirable than an easy victory — and passages where Kakuichi pulls out all the stops with one of his many transhistoric overviews, as in this description of Kyoto after the Heike torch it and flee from the approaching Genji, which ends with evocations of similar scenes from ancient Chinese history:

Some of those places had been honored by imperial visits. Of their phoenix gates, only the foundations remained; of the simurgh palanquin, only the resting place was visible.[75] Some had been the sites of Empresses' banquets. Storm winds wailed where pepper rooms had stood; dew lay heavy in lateral courtyards. Chambers hung with embroidered curtains and patterned draperies, estates with hunting groves and fishing ponds, locust and jujube seats, phoenix dwellings — all those structures so long in the building were reduced to ashes in an instant. And how much swifter was the devastation of the Taira retainers' mugwort and brushwood cottages! How much swifter the disappearance of the commoners' humble abodes! The spreading flames laid waste an area of twenty-five or thirty acres outside the city. It was sad to think that it must have been even thus when the sudden destruction of mighty Wu left dewdrops moistening brambles where once they had formed on the Gusutai Palace, or when the decline of tyrannous Qin caused smoke from the Xianyang Palace to shroud the parapets. (7.15)

This is impressive even in translation, but those who have read the original are unstinting in their praise of Kakuichi's command of the language and its "exceptional aural beauty" (Keene 636). In an appendix to her translation entitled "The 'Heike' as Literature," McCullough extols the author's

concern for the nuances of diction, his masterly exploitation of the full range of the Japanese language and his careful matching of style to content. Merely to describe the *Heike* as "*wakan-konkōbun* narrative prose" is to do less than justice to its linguistic and

---

75 "The language in this passage draws heavily on Chinese literary convention," McCullough explains in a note. "As used here, 'simurgh palanquin' means the Emperor's equipage, 'pepper rooms' the Empress's apartments, 'lateral courtyards' women's quarters, 'locust and jujube seats' houses of Ministers of State and other senior nobles, and 'phoenix dwellings' courtiers' houses" (245).

tonal complexity.[76] The language of official documents, letters, prayers, and Buddhist homilies is sonorous and dignified, with much use of parallelism, difficult words, and Chinese allusions; the occasional dated notations concerning official appointments, ceremonies, and other court events are succinct and colorless, like entries in a court noble's diary; the pathetic stories about women adopt the elegant prose, leisurely pace, and lyricism of the Heian monogatari style; the military setsuwa [tales] incorporate many conventional oral storyteller's phrases and make free use of colloquialisms, especially for dialogue, and of onomatopoeia. (464)

As in the Heian romances, there are dozens of intricate poems throughout the novel, emotional responses to the changing of the seasons, paeans to the power of music, and even a few comic scenes. Like them, but unlike other *gunki monogatari*, the *Heike* features several memorable female characters: the geisha dumped by Kiyomori, a temple virgin who gets to make a spectacle of herself via spirit possession — she dances for an hour, then makes an oracular speech (1.14), probably the high point in her sequestered life — several noble wives and their loyal ladies-in-waiting, a beautiful warrior named Tomoe who makes an all-too-brief appearance on the battlefield before galloping off toward the eastern provinces with my heart (9.4), a brothel-keeper's daughter named Jiju considered "the best poet on the Eastern Sea Road" (10.6), and concluding with the touching death of the superb imperial lady Kenreimon'in, the epitome of everything that was lost with the defeat of the Heike. It's as though Kakuichi wanted not only to compose the best account of the Genpei War, but to compose the Great Japanese Novel, one that would outdo its predecessors in style and technique and enshrine everything that defined Japan in his time, good and bad. If so, he succeeded brilliantly.

Around the time Kakuichi died (1371), another priest named Kojima was putting the finishing touches on a huge, 1,500-page war novel called the *Taiheiki* (Chronicle of the Grand Pacification), which covers the civil wars that ravaged Japan from 1322 to 1367. Even more so than in Kakuichi's case, Kojima (d. 1374) should be regarded more as an adapter than an author: by the 1340s the bulk of the novel already existed in some form, and was revised during that decade by two Buddhist priests named Echin and Gen'e, both erudite Confucians.[77] Kojima obviously extended the novel to include

---

76 "*Wakan-konkōbun*, a precursor of modern Japanese," McCullough footnotes, "combines classical Japanese syntax and vocabulary with colloquialisms, many Chinese loan words, and elements of Chinese syntax. *Heike monogatari* is probably the finest example of the style, which at its best exhibits the elegance and grace of classical language, the strength and lexical richness of Chinese, and the freshness and vigor of everyday speech" (464).

77 There's a scholar named Gen'e in the first chapter of the *Taiheiki* who delivers a lecture at a boisterous literary party; perhaps Gen'e wrote himself into the novel to show off his knowledge and to attend his idea of a great party: "The wine was served by more than twenty maidens of sixteen or seventeen years, clear-skinned and superior in face and figure,

later events, but his other contributions to the work are hard to ascertain (though I'll hold him responsible for its final form). Of the novel's 40 long chapters, only the first 12 have been translated into English, amounting to a still-substantial 400-page work; translator Helen McCullough suggests this self-contained section may have been the original version of the *Taiheiki* anyway, and that the rest is "devoted to episodic, disorganized accounts of fighting in local areas; . . . These episodes are not subordinated to a central unifying theme, and they are so similar to one another as to be dull reading for any but the specialist."[78]

Like Kakuichi, Kojima wanted to give cosmic significance to the political squabbles of his country. Under the shogunate, emperors had been playing only a ceremonial role since 1185, but in 1322 one of them, Emperor Go-Daigo, decided to regain complete power. For the next 10 years, his followers fought against the Hojo family that ran Japan; in 1333, his side triumphed and he was able to restore the power of the imperial throne, ending the Kamakura era and beginning the Muromachi (1333–1600). This is where McCullough's abridged edition leaves off; but in 1336 Go-Daigo was deservedly driven out of Kyoto for his extravagance and for stiffing his samurai supporters, and for the rest of the century — and for the rest of the *Taiheiki* — Japan had two rival governments. For the author, however, these power struggles were the result of a loss of virtue and a deviation from the cosmic Way, as he announces in the opening paragraph; McCullough omits this without explanation, so it's presented here as a public service:

> When one carefully considers the changes from ancient times to now and the sources of safety and peril, what covers all things, good and evil, is the Virtue of Heaven. The Enlightened Sovereign, embodying this, maintains the nation. What bears up all things, rejecting nothing, is the Way of Earth. Loyal subjects, conforming to this, protect the Gods of the Land and of Grains [i.e., the country]. When that Virtue is lacking, though the Sovereign has high place, he cannot maintain the rule. It is related, Chieh of the Hsia fled to Nan Ch'ao, Chou of Yin was smashed at Mu Yeh. When that Way is transgressed, though the subject has power, he will not last long. It was heard of old, Chao Kao was executed at Hsien Yang, Lu Shan perished at Feng Hsiang. The Former Sages, giving these examples due weight, were able to hand down these principles to future generations. How can later generations fail to look back and heed these admonitions of the past?[79]

---

      through whose unlined robes of raw silk the snowy skin gleamed fresh as lotus blossoms newly risen from the waters of the T'ai-i."

78 Page xvi of her lengthy introduction; the novel will be cited by chapter. One of her earliest translations, McCullough adopted a faux-antique style that fortunately she dropped in her later translations. Comparing her version to the selected translations by Paul H. Varley in *Traditional Japanese Literature* (858–74) suggests Kojima wrote with some flair, but too often McCullough makes him sound like Malory.

79 As translated by Wilson in the afterword to *Hogen monogatari*, 117.

The Chinese allusions and Confucian principles are typical of the erudite author, who often interrupts his chronicle of battles and skirmishes with episodes from Chinese history, edifying examples that his countrymen often ignore at their peril. He also inserts a few *michiyuki* — travel accounts thick with puns and literary allusions — and seems to have invented some incidents merely as an excuse for a poem on the topic. Finally, he gussies up his tale with Buddhist fables, "strange portents," and outlandish supernatural events, much to the irritation of historians. In 1891 one Japanese scholar published a series of articles with the harsh title "The *Taiheiki* Is Worthless as a Historical Source," and while that overstates the case — the novel is reasonably true to history, though the author likes to throw impossibly big troop numbers around — it's clear Kojima had a novelist's sensibility and took full advantage of the poetic license granted to writers of historical fiction.[80] He was deeply read in the "strange happenings of antiquity, recorded in old chronicles" (11), and Kojima's evocations of these happenings and his other literary flourishes enhance what otherwise would be a tedious tale of endless military excursions, aside from the exploits of a few memorable characters like the loyal samurai Kusunoki Masashige, a hero to this day in Japan.

Even though Go-Daigo eventually triumphs, albeit briefly, the *Taiheiki* has a defeated, even apocalyptic tone. Several characters express their conviction that "This is the end for this world" (10), and there is a decadent obsession with suicide; ghastly scenes like the following are typical, in which a young man named Tadayori speaks of the necessity of avoiding dishonor and thus begins a daisy chain of death:

> Nor did he finish [speaking], but drew forth his dagger from beneath his sleeve, secretly plunged it into his belly, and died where he knelt.
>
> Beholding this, Tadayori's younger brother Shiaku Shirō thought to cut his belly after him. But his father admonished him sternly, saying:
>
> "Let me go before you, as is fitting in a filial son. You may take your life when I have done."
>
> Thereupon, Shiaku Shirō put away his dagger to kneel before his father the lay monk. The lay monk caused a monk's chair to be brought to the middle gate, whereon he sat with legs crossed and soles upturned, as on his widemouthed trousers he wrote a death song in praise of the Buddhist Law.

> Holding the trenchant hair-splitter,
> He severs emptiness.
> Within the mighty flames —
> A pure cool breeze.

80 Whoever at the Library of Congress classified the *Taiheiki* as history (DS861) obviously didn't read it; it belongs in medieval Japanese literature (PL790).

> He folded his hands, stretched out his neck, and commanded his son Shirō, "Strike!" And when Shirō had laid bare the upper half of his own body, he struck off his father's head. After he had made the sword right again, he thrust it into his body up to the hilt and fell on his face. Moreover, three retainers ran forward to be pierced by the same sword, falling down with their heads in a row like fish on a skewer. (10)

In other instances, hundreds of retainers follow their fallen lord in suicide, usually by disembowelment; women take the more ladylike route of drowning themselves. (I'm with the sensible author of Ecclesiastes: "even a live dog is better than a dead lion" [9.4].) "A death song in praise of the Buddhist Law" is one way to describe the *Taiheiki*; a vivid illustration of samurai ethics and methods of Japanese warfare — from strategic battles to ninja-style assassinations — is another. It's an ambitious, encyclopedic work, very clever in its use of figurative language; perhaps the lengthy remainder of the novel isn't as interesting, but it would be good to have a complete English translation of the *Taiheiki* someday.

The shambolic *Tale of the Soga Brothers* (*Soga monogatari*, c. 1400?) is ranked with the *gunkimono* because it dramatizes samurai values and takes place during the same warring period as *The Tale of Heike* (that is, the second half of the 12th century). But like many Japanese novels it borrows from several genres, though in this case not by design but by accident. It apparently began as a short, factual account of how two brothers named Juro and Goro avenged the death of their father over a land-inheritance dispute; it was taken up by storytelling priests, who added numerous religious digressions and sermons, then by nuns and other adherents of "Pure Land" Buddhism — a fundamentalist sect that promised absolution of all sins and eternal life merely through the robotic repetition of the name Amida Buddha. The tale then became a specialty of blind female performers called *goze*, who added (or gave greater prominence to) the female characters — the brothers' grieving mother and two heart-of-gold harlots — and apparently under the influence of the last chapter of the *Heike* spun the tale beyond the deaths of the avenging brothers to conclude with the religious careers of two prostitutes who became nuns and were eventually reborn in the Pure Land. As a result of two centuries of oral transmission by storytellers with different agendas, *The Tale of the Soga Brothers* is an episodic jumble lacking any aesthetic finesse. It's like watching a kung-fu movie on broadcast TV with too many Buddhist product placements and irritating commercial interruptions.

Nonetheless, the novel has its moments. It effectively dramatizes the implications of the regime change following the Genpei War; before that, the Soga brothers' quest for revenge would have been acceptable, but under the shogunate it was illegal. Their actions also exemplify the conflict in medieval Japan between aggressive, worldly Confucianism and passive, otherworldly

Buddhism. One of the novel's many authors contributed a brilliant scene in the middle of the novel in which the brothers confront an enemy who is attracted to Juro's lover, a courtesan named Tora who has the tastes and comportment of an old-fashioned Heian heroine. "Violence hung over the room" as this tense, Hemingwayan scene plays out, the political and sexual rivalry between the males beautifully controlled.[81] And the final extended episode in which the brothers exact their revenge is very well done, all Buddhist pieties shoved aside as the brothers show what it meant to be a samurai. Tora and the other courtesans are sympathetically drawn; they are treated with respect by everyone in the novel, and the only condemnation of their trade is an elegantly sad aria from an ex-courtesan named Shosho, Goro's former lover:

> "Our sins are even greater [than those of other women], for we, as courtesans, have spent our lives intent only on enticing men. We gave our love to men coming and going along the road. When the sun set over the western mountains, we dressed as though life were as fleeting as a dream. When the moon rose over the eastern ridge, we waited for an unknown person. Every night the scent of a different man clung to our bodies, and we grieved over this. Every morning our pillows were soaked with tears, and our hearts were singed with sadness when we bid farewell to our guest. How regrettable it is to be a courtesan! This world is not our final home, for it is more fragile than the dew on the grass and more evanescent than the moon on the water." (12)

But these fine moments are outnumbered by too many unnecessary digressions, repetitive sermons, clichés, contradictions, and overreaching attempts to give cosmic significance to a family squabble. (Chapter 1 actually begins with the creation of the Japanese gods.) Translator Cogan argues that the novel "contributed to the development of a national literature, for it is a work that embodies the themes, emotions, beliefs, and ideals of the nation. . . . [namely] self-sacrifice, filial piety, duty, courage, and tenacity" (xl). One critic even suggests the novel "can also be read as narrative shorthand for the ritual slaying of the king whose death brings about the reinvigoration of diminished royal mystique."[82] I suppose it can, though the conclusion of the novel shows no interest in the political aftermath of the death of the "king" (in this case, just a retainer of the shogun), only with personal renunciation of public life. The novel is too sloppy and heterogeneous to support any nuanced readings, but it's been big in Japan from the beginning; as Cogan points out, "The Soga brothers figure more prominently in subsequent plays and stories than anyone else in Japanese history except Yoshitsune" (xl) — who happens to be the protagonist of the last Japanese novel before the modern era.

    Yoshitsune (*Gikeiki*, c. 1411) is set during the same Genpei War period and

---

81 Book 6 in Cogan's translation, yet another model scholarly edition.
82 Bialock, *Eccentric Spaces* 113.

contains some of the same characters as the *Heike* and *Soga monogatari*. With his older half-brother Yoritomo, Minamoto Yoshitsune (1159–89) defeated the Heike in a series of daring military maneuvers, but after the victory of 1185 his suspicious brother turned against him and forced Yoshitsune into exile, hounding him until he committed suicide four years later. *Yoshitsune* is the least historical of the *gunkimono*, but is the most imaginative; the anonymous author evaluated all the legends that had grown around the noble hero over two centuries, omitted the outlandish ones and abridged the actual historical events (readily available in the *Heike*), and concentrated instead on Yoshitsune's youth and especially on his later fugitive years. By narrowing his focus on Yoshitsune and a few of his followers, and by resisting the digressive and religious tendencies of his predecessors, the author produced a tight, engaging narrative that more closely resembles a modern novel than any other Japanese fiction. As with the Greek *Chaereas and Callirhoe*, a mass-market edition with handsome Yoshitsune and his concubine Shizuka on the cover could sell boatloads today, especially in Helen McCullough's fluent translation.

More than any other Japanese character from this period, Yoshitsune exemplifies "the nobility of failure," as Ivan Morris calls it in his book of that name, a man who "was undone at the very height of his glory and plummeted to total disaster, a victim of his own sincerity, outwitted by men more worldly and politic than himself and betrayed by those whom he had trusted."[83] Yoshitsune did more than his half-brother Yoritomo to win the Genpei War, so the unfairness of his treatment and the deprivations he faces while on the run are particularly galling; the author reinforces this by surrounding Yoshitsune with admirable concubines and supporters who give up their lives for him. (One, an enormous, resourceful samurai named Benkei, plays Sancho Panza to Yoshitsune's Don Quixote.) The novel ends not with Yoshitsune's return to power, as many a Western or Near Eastern work of this period would, but in further betrayals and an orgy of suicides.

Though less historical than other war tales, *Yoshitsune* is the most realistic, with many naturalistic touches new to the Japanese novel. When Yoshitsune first visits Hedehira — a warlord who will later briefly give him shelter — the old man is suffering from a cold and asks his sons to help him up and dress him, domestic details earlier novelists wouldn't have bothered with. At one point, Yoshitsune stoops over to retie his shoelace; some passengers on a ship vomit in the hold; we're told exactly how Japanese women gave birth (from a sitting position, reportedly more natural and efficient than the recumbent position modern women use). The dialogue is much more natural too: one

---

83 *The Nobility of Failure*, 67. Morris devotes a chapter to Yoshitsune, and closes his book with a chapter on kamikaze pilots of World War II, showing how such nobility can deteriorate into fanatical self-destruction.

character calls another a "stupid ass," and a husband tells his wife, "You talk too much; shut up!"[84] She doesn't, so he starts beating her, which the neighbors ignore, saying, "Ōtsu Jirō's woman is raving drunk again, yelling because her husband is beating her up," something you'd never hear in *The Tale of Genji*. This synthesis of legendary material and dirty realism is one of the many attractions of the novel.

Yoshitsune isn't great art, but it's great entertainment, with all the strengths of popular fiction: a propulsive plot, colorful characters, clear moral distinctions, exciting adventures and close calls, cinematic violence, tearful farewells, noble sacrifices, even some cross-dressing and sexual ambiguity. (Young Yoshitsune is as beautiful as a girl and serves as a monk's boy toy; both of Yoshitsune's principal courtesans wear men's clothes to escape detection.) There is a lovely homage to *Genji* at one point and some learned allusions, as well as some errors and contradictions, but they were probably lost on the tale's audience, for by this time most Japanese were illiterate — even the nobility — and *Yoshitsune* would have been read aloud to folks, not studied in written form. Unlettered, benighted by Buddhism and superstition, few Japanese by then could appreciate anything more demanding than pop fiction like this. But even *Yoshitsune* proved a little too demanding; there would be no further book-length fictions in Japan until the middle of the 17th century.

Yoshitsune's simplicity and realism resemble the short stories of the day, called *otogi-zoshi*, and though the distance between *Genji*'s genteel "Oh, no, this will never do!" and *Yoshitsune*'s "Shut up!" may seem like a regrettable degradation, the naturalistic mode of the latter could have reinvigorated the Japanese novel had any author chosen to forget the Genpei War and write instead about modern life. Here's a Célinesque screed someone scribbled on a wall in Kyoto in 1334:

> Current fashions in the capital: attacks by night, burglary, forged edicts, prisoners, swift horses, brawls over nothing, freshly severed heads, apostate clergy and self-ordained holy men, overnight lords, lost wanderers, . . . monks mingling among the flatterers and slanderers at court, upstarts outdoing their betters, . . . swaggering warriors wearing hats fashionably askew, crowds of rakes with lecherous intent prowling at nightfall, wives turning tricks under the guise of sightseeing, . . . starving horses, thin robes, old armor pawned and redeemed in installments, hick samurai off to work in palanquins, . . . archery contestants unable to pull their bows, tumbles from their steeds outnumbering arrows launched, . . . poetry parties everywhere, a world of open mayhem where everyone's a judge, . . . tea and incense competitions held even in the stronghold of warrior power, . . . loafing warriors throughout the city exchanging greetings on every street corner, . . . what a wonder that

---

84 Chap. 7 in McCullough's translation.

the country has been unified at all! Born in this imperial reign, you hear and see all sorts of amazing things. This is just a fraction of the chatter on the lips of the city's children.[85]

What a shame the author of that scrawl of Japanese graffiti didn't write a novel! But as it happens, just as the novel was dying out in Japan, it was coming to life in China. So like Chunagon in *Hamamatsu* or Ujitada in *The Tale of Matsura*, let us journey, finally, to far Cathay.

CHINESE FICTION

Unlike the Indian novel, which began big and ended small, the Chinese novel began small but grew to enormous lengths during its heyday in the Ming dynasty (1368–1644) with several novels in the 2,000-page range, a great wall of Chinese fiction that is a wonder to behold. But in the beginning, Chinese fiction faced the same uphill battle for respectability that fiction faced everywhere: early Chinese literature is distinguished by numerous works of history, philosophy, military theory, theology, literary criticism, philology, divination, and of course by a sunflower splendor of poems, but no fiction to speak of, aside from compilations of mythology. And when the first fictions did begin to appear, they were dismissed as *xiashuo*, "small talk," especially by historians. (Similarly, the Japanese term *monogatari* originally meant "desultory conversation.") In fact throughout most of Chinese history, one critic goes so far as to say, "Historiography is to *xiashuo* as a government is to a rebellious force," underscoring the often subversive role of fiction everywhere.[86] But this disregard is somewhat understandable: the earliest Chinese fictions were brief and anecdotal: humorous incidents, episodes from myths and legends, encounters with gods and demons, fantasies about fox-women, and *lots* of ghost stories. Indeed, the Chinese had a fascination with the supernatural, the uncanny, the miraculous, and many early stories bear such titles as "Chi Kang and the Headless Ghost" and "The Fairy of Chiangshi Temple." The tales that survive from the earliest period (3rd through 6th centuries) are all short, entertaining but rather artless.

Chinese fiction grew in quality if not length during the Tang dynasty (618–906); most writers were still penning things like "The Dragon King's Daughter" — the term for fiction was now *chuanqi*, "weird tales" — but some became ambitious to provide something more than mere entertainment. The earliest Chinese fiction long enough to be considered a novel — or at least a novelette, as its translator calls it — is *The Dwelling of Playful Goddesses* (*You*

---

85 "The Nijo Riverbed Lampoon," as translated on page 1 of Skord's introduction to *Tales of Tears and Laughter*, a good anthology of *otogi-zoshi*.
86 Gu, *Chinese Theories of Fiction*, 5.

xianku, c. 678?) by Chang Wen-ch'eng (aka Zhang Zhuo, c. 657–c. 730).[87] And what a sexy little novel it is, though hardly the sort of thing the present regime would want to acknowledge as China's first contribution to the art of the novel. The plot is simple and sounds like a letter to *Penthouse*: a minor official named Chang is traveling on government business in an unfamiliar landscape when he comes across an isolated mansion belonging to two beautiful young widows, Tenth Sister and Elder Brother's Wife (her sister-in-law). Chang is sexually attracted to the ladies, who let him know the feeling is mutual as they entertain him with food, music, and dance, during which all exchange poetry tumescent with sexual double entendres. Chang is hoping for a threesome, but settles for Tenth Sister; after they have sex, described bluntly and briefly, both sadly exchange gifts, and Chang continues on his official business.

Variously described as "hot-tempered and reckless" and "somewhat flippant and unsteady in character,"[88] Chang Wen-ch'eng was an erudite, sarcastic nonconformist, which is reflected in his experimental novel. Rather than write in the stereotyped classical style of most Tang authors, he used a euphuistic style called *pien wen*, in which balanced sentences alternate between pairs of four and six characters; he enlivened this stilted form with racy vernacular, unusual locutions, and with numerous poems ranging from sweet to sassy. Like the elaborate entertainments the merry widows stage for their handsome visitor, Chang seduces the reader with all manner of literary foreplay, postponing the actual sexual act for as long as he can. First, he deliberately blurs the setting so that the reader isn't sure if this is a realistic encounter with two lonely widows, an otherworldly visit to the realm of goddesses, or simply a night at a brothel or nunnery. The term *xian* in the title means not only goddesses or fairies, but also prostitutes and even wayward Daoist nuns,[89] and the author keeps all possibilities on the table by way of his extravagant, figurative language.

Everything Chang sees and hears becomes an occasion for elaborate, sophisticated praise, with similes drawn from Chinese history, literature, and nature. For example, our Chinese Cole Porter flatters Tenth Sister that she

---

87 With Chinese names and terms, I generally use pinyin spellings but on occasion defer to the usage of my translators; in this instance, Chang Wen-ch'eng is the Wade–Giles version of the author's honorific and Zhang Zhuo the pinyin of his given name. (Zh is pronounced as j; other pinyin oddities to remember are c=ts, q=ch, and x=sh.) Henceforth, P and W-G will be used to identify pinyin and Wade–Giles spellings.

88 By Ch'ên Shou-yi (277) and Lu Hsun (88), respectively.

89 As in Boccaccio, nuns in Chinese literature are often depicted as more sensual than spiritual. Howard S. Levy, who translated *The Dwelling of Playful Goddesses*, also co-translated an anonymous 17th-century collection of erotica entitled *Monks and Nuns in a Sea of Sins* (Warm-Soft Village Press, 1971).

is without an equal in Heaven and is the only one among mortals. The supple and delicate willow is restrained into becoming your waist; the brilliant, side sweeping waves are turned into your side-long glances. A slight relaxation of both cheeks, and the onlooker suspects that every flower on earth has vanished; a sudden display of two eyebrows, and he gradually perceives that the moon in Heaven has been eclipsed. You could cause Hsi She, the superlative beauty of antiquity, to hide her face and burn her make-up a hundred times, and make the beauties of the south so distressed at heart that they would smash their mirrors a thousand-fold. The Lo River Goddess, who danced like the whirling snows, would barely be fit to fold away your garments; the Immortal of Shaman Gorge, who manifested herself in clouds, would not [even] dare to remove your embroidered shoes. (14)

Chang flatters beautifully, Tenth Sister flirts charmingly, Elder Brother's Wife gooses them along with risqué remarks, and de-lovely maids with names like Green Bamboo and Petite Fragrance flutter around as the principles feast, drink, and dance; it is all so exquisite and seductive that the reader likewise becomes intoxicated by the author's language, letting him have his way with us. Chang is sad to leave his playful goddesses, and we're sad to close the cover of this winsome work.

But the Chinese literati were not amused, too distracted by the eroticism to see the artistry, and ignored the work. But some visiting Japanese got hold of it and took it back with them to Japan, where it became widely read and studied, exerting a palpable influence on Japanese literature for centuries to come. (Translator Levy includes a 24-page appendix tracking its influence there.) As a result, this brilliant mixture of eroticism and erudition, of high style and low puns, of traditional themes and modern attitudes, didn't influence any subsequent Chinese authors, who continued to restrict themselves to short forms. This is a shame, for there are a few Tang authors who display a novelistic imagination. The superb "Ying-ying's Story" ("*Ying-ying chuan*") by Yuan Zhen (779–831), for example, modernizes the old divine encounter motif for an almost Jamesian study in moral complexity. A priggish scholar named Zhang, still a virgin at 23 due to his Confucian rectitude, is introduced to a distant cousin named Ying-ying, a melancholy 17-year-old beauty who at first wants nothing to do with him, not even bothering to dress properly for their introduction. But he is bewitched by her unstudied glamour and promptly falls in love with her. (Sad, artistic, and complex, Ying-ying is a character type that would reach its apotheosis in Lin Dai-yu, the moody teen heroine of the monumental *Dream of Red Mansions*.) Too impatient to go through the formalities, Zhang tries to get Ying-ying's maid to convey his feelings, but she is scandalized at this breach of etiquette and suggests he send a poem instead. Ying-ying replies with a poem proposing a rendezvous at night on the western porch, to which Zhang eagerly agrees, but she arrives dressed severely and lectures him on impropriety. But then she falls for him, and a few nights later arrives for some "clouds and rain," an old euphemism for sexual intercourse. The next morning Zhang wonders if she was "one of those goddesses or fairy princesses" of yore who would grant their favors to mortals, and begins a long poem entitled "Meeting the Holy One." But Yuan Zhen makes it clear this is a realistic, possibly autobiographical story, set in the datable present. (Ying-ying first visits Zhang on the evening of 15 April 800.) After several wet months of "clouds and rain," Zhang leaves to take an examination and never returns. The jilted Ying-ying writes him a two-page letter that its translator describes as "a remarkable piece of prose, with the most complicated twists and turns of the heart working at cross purposes with the Tang delight in formal eloquence."[90] Unmoved, Zhang shows her letter around and eventually marries someone else, explaining that Ying-ying's beauty and brilliance scared him; alluding to older tales for metaphoric purposes, he says if he had married her she would have become "a serpent or a fierce dragon — I do not know what she would have been transformed into" (548). This Tang Portrait of a Lady questions conventional ethics, mocks literary assumptions, and dramatizes the conversion of experience into art before our eyes — a remarkably sophisticated and touching performance, and only 10 pages long.

Hundreds and hundreds of tales were written during the Tang and Song dynasties (960–1279) — including the world's first detective stories, preceding Poe's "Murders in the Rue Morgue" by six centuries — but apparently nothing long enough to be called a novel. As in the Middle East during this period, however, storytellers who spun out longer tales were active in China during the late Song and especially the Yuan dynasty (1279–1368). Embellishing famous episodes from Chinese history, they would stretch their stories out for weeks or months, and when their promptbooks were eventually fleshed out and reworked by writers for publication beginning in the 14th century, they provided a prototype for the sophisticated novels that would follow later in the century. They are divided into *yishi* (unofficial histories), *pinghua* (historical novellas), and *cihua* (prosimetric tales, i.e., alternating between prose and verse), and conveniently one anonymous example of each has been translated into English.

Proclaiming Harmony (*Xuanhe yishi*, c. 1300 — literally *Neglected Events of the Reign Period "Proclaiming Harmony"*) is a 180-page novel about the final decades of the Northern Song dynasty, and specifically about the emperor responsible for the dynasty's collapse, Huizong (ruled 1101–25). Stylistically it's an odd mix, ranging from dry, chronicle-like accounts to

---

90 Stephen Owen, *An Anthology of Chinese Literature*, 540; "Ying-ying's Story" occupies pp. 540–49 of this excellent anthology. Yuan Zhen's story became the basis of one of the most famous Chinese plays, Wang Shifu's *Western Wing* (c. 1300), available in an English translation by Stephen H. West and Wilt L. Idema as *The Moon and the Zither: The Story of the Western Wing* (Berkeley: U California P, 1991).

fleshed-out novelistic episodes, and drawing freely (to the point of plagiarism) on earlier histories of this period. The novel is divided into two parts, the first detailing Huizong's dereliction of duty, and the second the punishment he endures as the prisoner of the invading Manchurians.

It's another example of an author at an early point in a nation's culture discovering the art of fiction while writing something else. He begins with a recital of examples of earlier Chinese emperors who failed their country by either devoting themselves to a favorite concubine, or by allowing corrupt officials to run things (or both). He then tells of the repressive neo-Confucian "reforms" Grand Counselor Wang Anshi introduced around 1070, and eventually of Huizong's ascent to the Dragon Throne in 1101. The emperor is an intelligent man and a patron of the arts, but is a sucker for occult Daoism, sorcery, alchemy, and the lies of his sycophantic ministers. He then falls for a talented prostitute named Li Shishi, and the author's chronicle style blossoms into romantic fiction. Here's a typical paragraph from early in the novel:

> On the fifteenth day of the first month, the emperor accepted the imperial seals in the Palace of Grand Celebration and issued a general amnesty throughout the empire. Cai Jing made known a list of eighty-seven favorable portents throughout the realm and offered his formal congratulations. He was made grand tutor. Tong Guan was made military commissioner in addition to his position as pacification commissioner.[91]

Yawn. Now compare this paragraph 35 pages later:

> Even as he was finishing this proclamation, a man stepped out from the ranks. Reversing his insignia wand and bowing his head, he began his address. "All hail to His Majesty! I beg to risk punishment and submit a memorial to the imperial throne!" As the emperor read through the memorial, he became so appalled he began to break out in a sweat. For the longest time he was dumbstruck. Then he glanced over at Cai Jing and said, "What do you make of this?" What did the memorial say? (58)

The memorial follows (an inauspicious report by the royal astronomer) and a lively discussion ensues between everyone of what it means. Thereafter, the author switches between the two modes: annalistic accounts with occasional supernatural events recorded with a straight face ("That summer, a kraken made a malevolent appearance in the salt marsh at Jiezhou" [21]), and dramatized episodes enlivened with novelistic details and realistic dialogue. There is a beautifully staged dream-sequence that takes the reader by surprise (83–85) and several eerie, *Twin Peaks*-like scenes. For these reasons *Proclaiming Harmony* was long ignored by historians, but it played an important role in the development of the Chinese novel. Two of the greatest novels in Chinese

---

91 Page 22 in Hennessey's fluent but underannotated translation, hereafter cited by page.

literature are set in the same 12th-century period, one (*The Water Margin*) drawing directly on *Proclaiming Harmony* for part of its plot, and the other (*The Plum in the Golden Vase*) dramatizing at epic length how personal failings can have national consequences.

The author seems to take grim glee in detailing all the humiliations forced on the emperor during the second half as he's hauled all over northern China, and drives home the ironic contrast between the official view of China promulgated by the emperor and his corrupt cronies — reflected in the patriotic era-titles of the period such as "Harmonious Reign" and "Proclaiming Harmony" — and the ugly reality of a country so weakened by political mismanagement and religious hucksterism that the northern region is easily conquered by some "barbarians" from Manchuria. Aesthetically *Proclaiming Harmony* is rather inharmonious — the author can't seem to decide if he's writing history, fiction, or pastiche — but it's an appealing work and establishes one of the personae of future Chinese novelists: the honest counselor who warns the government of its failings, only to be ignored (if not punished) for his candor.

King Wu's Expedition against Zhou (*Wu wang fa Zhou pinghua*, c. 1322) goes further back in history for a fanciful tale of the fall of the Shang dynasty in the 11th century BCE.[92] Lascivious King Zhou comes under the influence of an evil concubine named Daji (actually a nine-tailed fox-spirit in human form), for whom he neglects his official duties and commits atrocities against his subjects.[93] His noblemen decide to rebel, and eventually the forces led by the future King Wu defeat the king's army and execute the ruthless royal couple. This fairytale version of historical events originated at least as early as the Tang dynasty and was a popular subject of ballads and puppet shows. Unfortunately, it's about as subtle as a puppet show, just an artless recitation of events spiced with some gratuitous violence and nudity but with no attempt at characterization or depth. The novella is remembered today only because it inspired a more ambitious novel of the 16th century entitled *Creation of the Gods*, which we'll witness later. It does, however, introduce a theme that will bedevil other Chinese novels, namely the notion of filial respect at the heart of Confucianism. Confucius (Kong Fuzi) felt a society would achieve harmony by honoring filial duty (father-son, subject-ruler, husband-wife,

---

92 It occupies pp. 10–75 of Liu Ts'un-yan's *Buddhist and Taoist Influences on Chinese Novels*. (This is a large book with small type; the novella would be about 100 pages long in a standard setting.)

93 See Rania Huntington's *Alien Kind* for a fascinating study of the fox-spirit in Chinese literature. She notes that tradition credits Daji with China's bizarre practice of footbinding: "Since she had not yet changed her small fox paws to human feet, she wrapped them in bandages to conceal them. Thereafter all the palace women imitated her" (177). For a postmodern example of a fox-spirit, ogle A Hu-Li in Victor Pelevin's *Sacred Book of the Werewolf* (2005).

older sibling-younger, friend-friend) but didn't account for bad rulers, abusive husbands, shiftless older brothers, and so on.[94] Chinese novelists challenged this notion by introducing moral complexity into the argument. Near the end of this novella, a general loyal to King Zhou boasts, "I have heard that one who exerts himself for his home is filial, and one who dies for his country is loyal" (70) — the brainlessly patriotic "My country, right or wrong" view — whereas his opponent justifies supporting the rebellious King Wu with: "I assist a moral King and fight against a ruthless ruler" (71), inserting adjectives to qualify the limits of filial duty: if a king isn't moral and kind, he deserves no respect. Like many novelists, the author of *King Wu's Expedition* challenges the status quo and welcomes change, innovation; as this same rebel said earlier, "You do not know that the times have changed and you do not understand the rotation of the pivot of heaven" (69).

A favorite setting for these proto-novels was the period of the Three Kingdoms, between the fall of the Han dynasty in 220 and the reunification of the empire by the Jin dynasty in 280. This is the backdrop to a 200-page *cihua* entitled *The Story of Hua Guan Suo* (*Hua Guan Suo zhuan*), which was first published in the middle of the 14th century but undoubtedly written sometime earlier.[95] It's not particularly good, just an entertainment that would have competed with jugglers, acrobats, and puppeteers for the attention of a Chinese city-dweller out for a good time. It's the archetypal story of a boy who loses his father, later goes in quest of him, and eventually assumes his patrimony by avenging his father's death, the kind of skeletal plot that drives a typical martial arts movie.

Wobbling between history and folklore, the story begins with the narrow escape of the protagonist's pregnant mother, spared from a family slaughter instigated by her husband, of all people. Guan Yu (a historical figure who lived from 160 to 219) has sworn a pact with two others to put down a revolt against the Han empire, and to show that he will not let family ties distract him, he allows one of his oath-brothers to kill his family. The murderer spares Guan Yu's wife, Hu Jinding, because she is three months pregnant. After she gives birth to our hero, the boy gets lost, adopted by another family, and then apprenticed to a Daoist master, who teaches him the martial arts. At age 18, Hua Guan sets out to find his father, now an important commander in the ongoing wars, and en route has many opportunities to show off those martial arts against outlaws and enemies, and even uses them to acquire a few brides.

---

94 A rash statement, no doubt; perhaps somewhere in Confucian writings this problem is addressed, but all I've read emphasizes filial piety and ancestor worship, no matter what kind of scoundrels they might have been.

95 This work was lost until the 1960s, when some peasants unearthed it from a Ming-era graveyard near Shanghai. It was found with a few other novels in a tomb thought to belong to the wife of a minor official; see Gail King's "Discovery and Restoration of the Texts in the Ming Chenghua Collection," *Ming Studies* 20 (Spring 1985): 21–34.

A confident young woman named Bao Sanniang has proclaimed she will marry only a man capable of defeating her in combat, so the two teens suit up for a violent mating ritual, which ends predictably with her defeat and marriage. A little later, Hua Guan comes across two female generals blocking his way, sisters Wang Tao and Wang Yue (ages 18 and 16), and after another extreme courtship, the latter gamely announces: "Elder sister today will be your wife, / And I will be one who holds aloft the stars and lifts up the moon" — that is, his concubine, but it's a lovely expression, I must say, of what the right woman can mean to a man.[96] Hua Guan and his mother eventually reunite with the surprised father, and the young man spends the next 18 years fighting alongside Guan Yu and the other oath-brothers. Though regularly successful in battle, he is almost killed in one of them, but is resuscitated by his three wives; the Wang sisters continue to command armies, and all the women in this novel play admirably strong roles. Only the death of his father stops Hua Guan short, and he dies of grief.

Like a martial arts movie, *The Story of Hua Guan Suo* is lively and filled with special effects — a metallic horse, a flame-shooting sword, ghosts, a woman who turns to stone — and since it was never meant to be anything more than entertainment, we shouldn't judge it too harshly. After all, as translator King points out, "It was so treasured by one woman that it was buried with her" (14). But one writer decided that the Three Kingdoms period deserved something more majestic, and that an extended narrative could be more than mere entertainment.

Three Kingdoms (*Sanguo yanyi*) is the first major Chinese novel, deservedly praised as one of the "four extraordinary books" (*si da qishu*) of the Ming era, and might just be the greatest war novel ever written. It is a historical novel that covers the hundred-year period from the decay of the Han dynasty that set in around the year 180, through the empire's dissolution into three warring kingdoms in 220, to the eventual reunification of China in 280. Tradition attributes it to Luo Guanzhong (W-G Lo Kuan-chung, c. 1315–c. 1400), a scholar and playwright who presumably wrote it sometime after the Ming dynasty came to power in 1368. Recent scholars have suggested other dates of composition ranging from the 1330s to the 1490s, when the preface for the first printed edition was written (though that edition didn't appear until 1522), but since no definitive evidence against Luo's authorship has been presented, it's convenient to regard him as the author.

Though he was familiar with the vernacular versions of the Three Kingdoms story and may have even written a play on the topic, Luo Guanzhong decided to go back to the original sources, namely Chen Shou's *Sanguozhi* (Records of the Three Kingdoms, c. 280), Pei Songzhi's expansion of that work,

---

96 Page 92 in King's translation. Most of the writing isn't this poetic; King admits "the verse is often doggerel, the prose is clumsy, and the plot repetitive" (14).

Sanguozhi zhu (The Annotated *Sanguozhi*, 429), and Liu Yiqing's *Shishuo xinyu* (New Account of Tales of the World, 430). He also consulted later historical works such as Sima Guang's *Zizhi tongjian* (General History for the Aid of Government, 1066–84) and especially Zhu Xi's revised version of that work (1172), resulting in a novel that has been famously described as "seven parts fact and three parts fiction."[97] The fictitious elements came from poems that had been written on the conflict over the centuries, many by Du Fu (712–70), generally considered China's greatest poet; from popular novels like *The Story of Hua Guan Suo* and especially the *Sanguozhi pinghua* of 1321–23; and from Yuan plays dramatizing colorful legends from the Three Kingdoms period that Luo found useful for his theme.

The conflicted relationship between loyalty and honor, between public duty and personal ambition, is Luo's grand theme, and like many writers before and after him, he realized these values are tested hardest during times of war. Fed up with the imperial government, which was being run at the end of the 2nd century not by the Han emperor Ling but by his corrupt eunuchs, a group of peasants calling themselves the Yellow Scarves revolt; three of the novel's most important characters — Liu Xuande, a distant relation of the imperial family; Guan Yu, a proud warrior (and the absentee father of *The Story of Hua Guan Suo*); and Zhang Fei, a hotheaded pig butcher — take a vow in a peach orchard to put down the revolt and to clean up the government, swearing loyalty to each other as well as to the empire. Ostensibly the heroes of the novel, each displays a different combination of loyalty and honor: Xuande, the compassionate, levelheaded man who eventually becomes emperor of the breakaway kingdom of Shu, is guided by loyalty to the Han dynasty until he hears of the death of Guan Yu late in the novel, at which point he angrily decides that loyalty to his oath-brother takes precedence over loyalty to the imperial cause, consequently making a tactical blunder that dooms any hope of reunification. Guan Yu himself gets himself killed because he allows personal honor — or "willful arrogance," as another character bluntly puts it (78) — to cloud his judgment. And Zhang Fei is assassinated because he's a brute and an angry drunk — lost to all honor. Each of the novel's thousand other characters dramatize some aspect (or absence) of loyalty and/or honor, from a wife's concern for her personal honor to patriotic appeals to honor the sacred shrines of the Han and the Mandate of Heaven.

Two other characters dominate the novel along with the three oath-

---

97 So said the 18th-century critic Zhang Xuecheng, quoted on p. 939 of Moss Roberts's afterword to his definitive translation of *Three Kingdoms* as published by the University of California Press (revised version of 2004); quotations from the novel itself will be by chapter number. By using a large page format and a tiny point size, this edition manages to pack the novel into 936 pages; the four-volume Foreign Languages Press edition of the same translation runs to 2,034 pages.

brothers. One is a brilliant, Napoleonic commander named Cao Cao, who under the pretense of protecting the interests of the Han emperor paves the way for his own dynasty in Wei after the empire breaks apart. (The three kingdoms of the title are Wei in north-central China, Shu in the southwest, and Wu in the southeast.) Cao's loyalty to the Han is hypocritical, a cover for his own personal ambitions, and he exemplifies on a grand scale the petty ambitions of hundreds of other officers and soldiers who juggle their own loyalties according to which side appears to be winning and which side gives them more scope for attaining fame. The other principal character, the real hero of the novel as Luo Guanzhong positions him, is a young Daoist hermit named Zhuge Liang, aka Kongming, whom Liu Xuande recruits to his cause (with much comic difficulty) because of his expertise in military theory. In contrast to scheming Cao, Kongming has no personal ambitions and wants only to serve the Han empire. He possesses supernatural abilities (which Luo borrowed from folklore) and can foresee that his efforts are doomed to fail, but he knows Xuande's cause is just and dutifully applies his considerable talents to battling the enemies of the old Han empire.[98] A cool character who plays the zither, rides in a tricked-out cart, and dresses like a Daoist immortal — strange headwear, a cloak of crane plumes, and always carrying a feather fan — Kongming is dismissed by some aristocratic warriors as a "hill-town hick" and a "mere plowman from Nanyang who knows nothing of the Heavenly-appointed course of events" (99, 100), but he proves to be the wisest, most loyal, and hardest-working character of all, serving the empire with aplomb until dying from overwork at the age of 54.

"The possibilities in warfare are manifold," says Cao in the middle of the novel (59), and every form of warfare, every branch of military theory, is here: from elaborate field maneuvers to one commander chasing another around a tree with a sword, from brilliant strategies to improvised guerrilla tactics, along with naval battles, espionage, betrayals, professional rivalries, propaganda and disinformation, diplomatic ploys, supply logistics, a wide variety of weaponry (including wild animals unleashed on the enemy), brutal executions, and public relations with civilians. It's mostly a man's world, but the women fight in their own way: in chapter 8 a loyal 16-year-old named Diochan uses her seductive charms to arrange for the murder of a Han traitor; the 17th-century editor of the definitive edition of *Three Kingdoms* praises her act in military terms: "The couch was her battleground, cosmetics her armor, glances her spear and dagger, frowns and smiles her bows and arrows. With pleasing words and humble phrases she arranged surprise attacks and ambushes — a female

---

98 In most Chinese novels of this era, Daoists are portrayed not as philosophical seekers of the Way as expounded in the *Daodejing* and *Zhuangzi*, but more like the wonder-working saints of Catholic mythology. It's the same degradation that befell Buddhism, and that befalls all subtle, abstract ideas after the masses drag them down to their level.

general truly to be feared and respected."[99] An epic elaboration of Sunzi's terse *Art of War* (often mentioned in the novel), *Three Kingdoms* is not merely a novelization of a bloody century of Chinese history but an encyclopedic treatment of the causes and effects of war that is as relevant to our own time as it was to Luo Guanzhong's.

Unlike the Western war novel, which usually climaxes with a major battle, *Three Kingdoms* is cyclical rather than linear, with one conflict leading to another, every action causing a reaction, like the tides of the ocean breaking and receding endlessly. (In this regard it resembles the Japanese *gunki monogatari* being written at this time.) Luo begins his novel with the observation, "The empire, long divided, must unite; long united, must divide" (1), and then reverses it at the end: "The empire, long united, must divide, and long divided, must unite" (120); writing from the vantage point of the 14th century (after a long struggle to expel the Mongols from China), Luo knew there is no such thing as a war to end all wars, and recognized that warfare seems to be the natural state of mankind. Indeed, at the end of the novel a new generation of corrupt eunuchs is back in charge and the hard-earned unification of the empire is already on the rocks. This is not a pessimistic judgment, only a Buddhist recognition of the ways things are; the best any individual can do is to align himself with a legitimate cause or leader and to serve honorably, like Kongming.

Like the authors of the Icelandic sagas, Luo Guanzhong is a laconic writer, emulating the factual style of the historians he drew upon; he rarely comments on his characters' actions, letting their deeds and words speak for them. (His dialogue is quite natural and realistic, not the stilted eloquence of many older epics.) Even the many supernatural elements — sorcery, astrology, consultations of the *I Ching*, portentous dreams, ancestral retribution, numerous ghosts, reports of dragons, phoenixes, and unicorns — pass without comment. But the performing artist in him contrives several scenes where he can show off his erudition and linguistic skills. In chapter 23, for example, a character named Mi Heng is summoned to Cao Cao's court; "a sort of Confucian beatnik," as one critic describes him,[100] this young scholar mocks Cao and his courtiers with some clever put-downs, strips naked in front of them after being humiliated by Cao, and then like a Shakespearean fool once again flames everyone with his caustic wit — which allows Luo to express what were probably his own

---

99 In the 1660s Mao Zonggang examined the various editions of *Three Kingdoms* and edited the version that has been read ever since (and upon which Roberts's translation is based). In addition Mao provided a running commentary on the novel that is extraordinarily insightful and cited by critics to this day. Roberts quotes hundreds of his observations in the extensive notes to his translation; this one is from p. 1012. An annotated translation of Mao's enthusiastic preface to *Three Kingdoms* can be found in Rolston's *How to Read the Chinese Novel*, 152–95.

100 Hsia, *The Classic Chinese Novel*, 55.

feelings toward these characters. But the scene is functional as well: Mi Heng could have been Cao's Kongming, for he's a brilliant young scholar despite his "sharp tongue," but Cao craftily arranges to have the "rotten pedant" killed by a rival (not wanting to damage his reputation by executing Mi Heng himself), thereby harming his cause. Scholar-pedant Luo seems to have had fun writing for Mi Heng and inserts similar scenes later in the novel where someone wows others with language games or explications of difficult texts (chaps. 56, 71, 72, 79, 86, 93). In a novel filled with swordplay, Luo wanted to demonstrate that the pen is as mighty as the sword and has Kongming literally kill an opponent with words at the end of a rhetorical duel:

> At Kongming's denunciation Wang Lang's chest heaved with rage. A loud cry broke from him, and he fell dead from his horse. A poet of later times wrote of Kongming thus:
>
>> Forth from a land once known as Qin
>> With mettle to match a thousand times ten[,]
>> He came with his light and limber tongue
>> And lashed to death the false Wang Lang. (93)[101]

Kongming is obviously an author surrogate, for Luo is of course the one with the "light and limber tongue," and the one who devises Kongming's brilliant military plans. "Kongming's maneuvers are as subtle as those of gods and demons," one opponent laments (101), which is Luo's way of praising his own subtle ingenuity.

Luo Guanzhong established the formal template for the classic Chinese novel that would be followed for the next 400 years. He was the first to divide a lengthy narrative into chapters, each of which contained two episodes. The chapter titles have two lines announcing them, often giving away the plot — e.g., "On Seven Star Altar Kongming Supplicates the Wind; At Three Rivers Zhou Yu Unleashes the Fire" (49) — and each chapter ends on a cliffhanger with a poetic two-line teaser for the next chapter and an injunction to read on. Scholars from Mao Zonggang onward have noted how carefully *Three Kingdoms* is structured: the 120 chapters can be divided into thirds (like the tripartite division of the three kingdoms), then into narrative groups of 10, and each chapter divided in half. Luo bookends the novel so that the final chapter mirrors the first, the penultimate the second, and so on. (For example, two minor characters appear in chapter 9 who are not mentioned again until chapter 112, nine chapters from the end.) Although the novel seems to move at a steady pace, time moves quickly during the opening and closing chapters, slowing down during the middle 60; at the exact center we

---

101 In chap. 100, Kongming writes an insulting letter to a Wei commander that has the same lethal effect.

have a detailed description of the battle of Wei River, a major turning point in the novel.[102] "In warfare," a character says at that point, "there can never be too much trickery" (59), and while *trickery* is not the best word for Luo's structuring devices, the statement serves as another self-referential boast from the ingenious author. Another character's remark "There's a scheme hiding in all of Kongming's arrangements" (102) is seconded by translator Roberts, who writes, "The more one studies the patterns of the novel, the more it seems like a grand cathedral designed by an intelligence purposefully placing even the smallest, most innocent details, not only to create satisfying patterns but also to make a point or suggest a judgment" (972).

In his annotations Mao points out hundreds of examples of these details and patterns, especially regarding foreshadowing and cross-referencing, which frequently drive him into heightened states of aesthetic bliss. ("Such twists and turns! Truly a master storyteller!" [1015].) Luo took some liberties with documented history to achieve this tight aesthetic structure (and Mao helped him by taking some editorial liberties with the received text), but that structure, its encyclopedic treatment of all things military, and Luo's deep insights into the personal dynamics of warfare are what make this perhaps the greatest war novel ever written. It can be a demanding read for Westerners — Chinese readers know the story from childhood on from a variety of media[103] — because of its inordinate length, complexity, and gigantic cast of characters (not to mention the difficulty of keeping characters straight with names as similar as Sun Quan and Song Qian, or Dong Cheng and Chen Deng). *Three Kingdoms* has been called China's *Iliad*, but Homer dealt only with the final year of the decade-long Trojan War; imagine if he had covered the entire conflict in as much detail. To modern readers of any nationality, the brutality and carnage are shocking: when a traitor is exposed, not only is he executed, but his entire clan as well. Hardly a page goes by without someone getting beheaded for something or other, and tens of thousands die in battles. *Three Kingdoms* has the highest body count of any novel I've read. There are numerous scenes like this:

> [Ma] Chao rode through the night, arriving at daybreak at the gates of Jicheng; demanding entrance, he was met with a storm of arrows and curses from Liang Kuan and Zhao Qu standing on the wall. They brought out his wife, Lady Yang, cut her down, and flung her

---

102 These observations are drawn from Plaks's *Four Masterworks of the Ming Novel* (386–89), who drew some of his observations from an insightful dissertation that unfortunately was never published in book form, Andrew Lo's "*San-kuo chih yen-i* and *Shui-hu chuan* in the Context of Historiography" (1981).

103 See the second half of Besio and Tung's *Three Kingdoms and Chinese Culture* (2007). Young Americans are likewise learning of *Three Kingdoms* by way of video games based on it; on Amazon.com several gamers have testified to seeking and devouring Luo's novel because of PlayStation's *Dynasty Warriors* and *Romance of the Three Kingdoms* series.

corpse from the wall. Next, three of Ma Chao's infant sons and a dozen close kin were butchered one by one and pieces of their bodies were thrown to the ground. His bosom bursting, Ma Chao nearly toppled from his mount. (64)

Earlier, a hunter wants to offer Xuande "fresh game but, unable to find any, butchered his wife" and cooks her up for his guest. "Then Xuande realized what he had eaten and tears of gratitude streamed from his eyes" (19).[104] Though most of the female characters are admirable, a few can be just as cruel as men: after her husband's death, "Lady Liu had all five of Yuan Shao's favored concubines put to death. Driven by jealousy, she had their heads shaved, their faces slashed, and their corpses mutilated, lest they try to rejoin their master in the netherworld" (32). Luo recounts all this without comment; there's even a *Heart of Darkness*-like excursion among some Chinese aborigines, whom Luo describes with the same objectivity he uses to describe the customs of his more "civilized" characters:

> A native suffering from an affliction rarely took medicine, praying instead to a shaman master known as the "medicine spirit." Criminal laws did not exist; those who committed offenses were executed immediately. When women grew to maturity, they bathed in a stream where male and female mixed freely and coupled without parental prohibition, a practice called "learning the art." (90)

No indication whether Luo considers this a sensible approach to sex education or a barbaric practice. He never condemns any actions outright, though he does use irony throughout the novel "to subtly turn the reader's attention to the discrepancy between the simplistic surface of noble aims and heroic deeds, and the underlying complexities of historical judgment."[105] It's the author's subtle complicating of his materials that elevates *Three Kingdoms* from edifying entertainment (as it has traditionally been treated) to art: the book's mastery of complex military theory has long been acknowledged — Chinese commanders through the centuries have consulted it — but not the complicated relationship between history and the popular legends of the Three Kingdoms period, nor the irony forged by its characters' stated aims and their private motives, even neuroses. These are the complications we associate with the modern novel, not a 14th-century "romance," and *Three Kingdoms* deserves to be ranked among the greatest novels ever written.

Luo Guanzhong is also credited with the composition of the second of

104 Translator Roberts notes: "Frightful though it is, this scene shows the readiness of a true brother to sacrifice his family to the cause" (1019). But Luo left out the scene in *The Story of Huan Guan Suo*, right after Xuande, Guan Yu, and Zhang Fei take their oath, where Xuande wonders if the family obligations of the other two will compromise their pact, whereupon these two dutifully agree to slaughter each other's family.
105 Plaks (404), who develops this argument at great length (399–495).

the "four extraordinary books" of the Ming era, a huge, rambunctious novel generally known as *The Water Margin (Shuihu zhuan)*.[106] Tradition has it that a shadowy figure named Shi Nai-an prepared the raw materials and Luo arranged them into a coherent novel, but the evidence is inconclusive. Both names could be pseudonyms for an author reluctant to take credit for such a subversive work. Even if Luo did write it, the text we now have went through the hands of many editors with their own ideas of how the novel should read; there are versions ranging in length from 70 to 120 chapters, with some obvious interpolations in the later chapters.[107] But as with *Three Kingdoms*, the present editions agree in most respects and are probably close enough to the putative 14th-century original for a general overview.

Three Kingdoms opened with three heroes who took it upon themselves to suppress a peasant rebellion against the empire; *The Water Margin* tells of the formation of a band of rebellious outlaws and its valiant resistance to the empire's attempts to suppress them. It too is based on historical events: in the early 12th century, a man named Song Jiang led a revolt in northeast China; he and his band of 36 men outwitted the imperial army for years and soon became folk heroes similar to England's Robin Hood and his merry men. During the Yuan dynasty they became the subjects of many ballads, plays, and story-cycles — they play a small role in *Proclaiming Harmony* — all of which (as the story goes) Shi Nai-an compiled and Luo Guanzhong then organized into a novel — make that a *gigantic* novel, over 2,200 pages in the most recent English translation. But the popular revolt, their 120-chapter length, and Luo's possible authorship are about all the two novels have in common. *Three Kingdoms* is dependent on recorded history and deals with the upper classes in dignified prose, while *The Water Margin* draws upon imaginative folklore and deals with the middle and lower classes in appropriately informal language. *Three Kingdoms* flows seamlessly while *The Water Margin* is more episodic — cleverly linked, it is true, but betraying its motley origin as many separate tales. The former is majestic, serious, tragic; the latter is subversive, lurid, often comic. *Three Kingdoms* is classical music, *The Water Margin* rock 'n' roll.

---

106 The title literally means "Marsh Chronicles" and has been translated into English under the titles *All Men Are Brothers* (Pearl Buck, 1933), *Water Margin* (J. H. Jackson, 1937), *Outlaws of the Marsh* (Sidney Shapiro, 1981), and *The Marshes of Mount Liang* (John and Alex Dent-Young, 1994–2002). The earlier two are based on the 70-chapter version of the novel, the later two on the 120-chapter version. Specialists have frowned upon Shapiro's composite text — a slightly abridged version of the 70-chapter version followed by selections from the remaining chapters — whereas the Dent-Youngs present an unexpurgated translation of the full 120-chapter version. For that reason, I've chosen it as my text (cited by chapter) over Shapiro's otherwise fluent translation.

107 In *The Evolution of a Chinese Novel* Richard Irwin suggests Luo wrote chapters 1–82 and 111–20, with the rest added in the 16th century (114; I can't resist noting I own the copy Irwin inscribed to his mother).

But as the long novel unwinds, *The Water Margin* reveals the same distrust of hero worship; by the 14th century, the oath-brothers of *Three Kingdoms* had reached godlike status, so Luo took them down a peg; in *The Water Margin* he does the same with the folk "heroes" of the 12th century. The popular and/or official version of things is always to be distrusted, an attitude Luo displays in the opening pages of *The Water Margin*. The novel begins with some rhetorical flourishes suggesting this will be more than just a historical account of a populist uprising. First there is a cryptic song about the novelist's role in interpreting history and instructing readers, and a boast that he will be trying something novel: "So just drink the cup, and lend an ear / To the new melody sounding here." To demonstrate the need for a new approach, the author then follows with a prologue in the old-fashioned style of the annals (bordering on parody), an obsequious, officialese account of the events leading to the uprising. The tone is formal, flat, and unenlightening. But in chapter 1, the author switches from the historical mode to that of fiction, showing rather than telling, and suddenly the story comes alive. To ward off the plague that has infected the land, the emperor of China sends an envoy named Hong Xin to find and bring back a holy man to perform the necessary purification ceremonies. As soon as Hong Xin leaves the court, we begin seeing things through his eyes, hearing through his ears, following him up a treacherous mountain in search of the Daoist monk. As Deborah Porter notes, "The author thus reveals to the reader his belief that narrative should strive to represent an event as it is experienced and not just provide an account of the event," as a historian would.[108] Earlier I quoted Gu on the "rebelling force" of fiction versus the "government" of history, and in these opening pages, Luo is clearly siding with the literary rebels.

Further availing himself of the advantages of fiction, Luo then introduces the first of many supernatural elements. After Hong Xin descends the mountain, he comes across a temple called the Hall of the Vanquished Demons, which contains a stone slab "covered in dragon script and phoenix characters, magic signs and ciphers," and which Hong insists on opening despite the terrified monks' warnings. (How many horror movies have begun thus?) The stone slab is removed to reveal a deep pit, out of which a black cloud suddenly rises and ascends to the heavens: the spirits of 108 demons imprisoned centuries earlier who will descend to earth 60 years later during the reign of Huizong (the failed emperor of *Proclaiming Harmony*). These will be our outlaws of the marsh. Demons, not angels, it's worth remembering.[109]

---

108 "The Style of *Shui-hu chuan*," 61. I am indebted to Porter's insightful analysis of the novel's prologue.
109 Why 108? In Kukai's *Indications*, the Buddhist says, "The flames of greed, hatred, and stupidity burn day and night, and the thicket of the 108 defilements flourishes throughout the four seasons" (131).

The author then switches from the supernatural mode to the realistic and introduces a minor character who, in a sense, generates the rest of the novel. Gao Qiu is a young lout good at martial arts and soccer, "but of generosity, virtue, the rites, wisdom, trustworthiness, reliability, loyalty, or excellence he knew absolutely nothing" (2). He manages to leech on to the imperial court and soon joins the other dissolute advisors to the emperor who are ruining the country (much like the eunuchs in *Three Kingdoms*). We see Gao only intermittently thereafter, but the author introduces him to characterize the officials in charge of China at that time, who drive his characters into becoming outlaws and eventually rebelling against the empire. "Fear not the law but the one who wields the law" (2) is a recurring proverb; Shapiro translates it "Fear not officials — except those who officiate over you!" The future rebellion will not be against the emperor, a good but clueless man, but against "those fucking officials," as one character bluntly calls them (52). Its salty, realistic dialogue is one of the many attractions of *The Water Margin*.

Another minor character is introduced in the second chapter to characterize the nature of the outlaws who eventually join up on Mount Liang. Shi Jin is a tattooed teenager likewise into martial arts; he becomes lord of the manor after his father dies, but neglects his duties, preferring to practice with the staff and sword. Nicknamed the Tattooed Dragon, he one day encounters three robbers who have been working the area. But once he captures them, he is impressed by their brotherhood — which they compare to that of the oath-brothers of *Three Kingdoms*, one of many references to Luo's other novel — and not only releases them but later defends them from the police force that comes to arrest them. This entails killing innocent men and burning down his own house, after which he has one of those What-was-I-thinking? moments: "Just because I once decided to save three lives, I have had to burn my house and estate. Although I rescued a few valuables, the stuff that can be carried, everything more substantial is gone" (3). Shi Jin is typical of those who wind up on Mount Liang: talented in some ways, brave, loyal, but also irresponsible, hotheaded, and (in some cases) a few eggrolls short of a General Tso's Delight. As we are introduced to new characters, we usually see them do something stupid or impulsive that dampens our sympathy for whatever injustice drove them to become outlaws.

Nonetheless, the mini-biographies that make up the first half of the novel are wonderfully done. Chapters 3 through 7 (an 85-page picaresque novella) feature a garrison commander named Lu Da, whom Tattooed Dragon meets on the lam. Lu Da kills a butcher for taking advantage of an old man and his daughter (another example of vigilante justice) and then joins a Buddhist monastery to hide from the law, taking the name Zhishen, or Profound Wisdom. But Lu has trouble adjusting to monastic discipline — "What a fucking awful life!" he observes (4) — and proceeds to engage in some un-

Buddhist behavior that gets him transferred to another monastery, where he gets in further trouble. Much sport is made of the contrast between his thuggish looks and foul mouth and his Buddhist robes and shaved head, one of many instances in the novel of the deceptiveness of appearances.

At the second monastery Lu befriends an imperial arms instructor named Lin Chong, whose chaste wife is fending off the advances of the adopted son of dissolute Gao of chapter 1. Lin is one of the novel's most moral characters, and his story (chaps. 7–12) reminds us of the kind of official corruption that can drive even a decent man into outlawry. Framed by the seducer and sentenced to exile, Lin eventually encounters the true hero of the novel, not a person but a place: the Marshes of Mount Liang in the Jizhou district of Shandong, currently the headquarters of an outlaw gang, but soon an alternative community whose sense of honor and brotherhood stands in marked contrast to the corrupt imperial court. One by one, other renegades, misfits, and victims of official injustice make their way there, and in chapter 18 we are introduced to the novel's most important and complicated character, Song Jiang, a county clerk whose practice of helping people out of jams has earned him the nickname Welcome Rain. What we'd now call a fixer, he is especially drawn to the "heroes of the rivers and lakes" — that is, clever outlaws — and like a Mafia lawyer has a reputation for solving their legal difficulties. He is forced to join his heroes because of problems with a woman: he is pressured into taking a concubine, an airhead named Poxi, who cheats on him and one day threatens to blackmail Song Jiang, who in a rare fit of rage kills her. Because of his reputation, he is not only welcomed by the rebels on Mount Liang but is asked to become their leader after their former one is killed by Lin Chong, now going under the nom de guerre Leopard's Head.

Over the next 50 chapters, more characters arrive at Mount Liang until all 108 demons foretold in chapter 1 have descended to earth, as it were. Many are petty criminals with police-gazette backstories, others commit crimes because of a woman — the novella-length story of Wu Song and his brother's cheating wife Pan Jinlian (Golden Lotus) would inspire the plot of one of China's greatest novels, *The Plum in the Golden Vase* — some are shanghaied into joining the band because they possess special skills, and others join merely for the adventure. It's a colorful crew, some admirable, some despicable, with nicknames like Madcap, Morbid, Iron Ox (aka the Black Whirlwind, a brutal buffoon but a fan favorite to this day in China), the Magic Messenger (who can travel hundreds of miles a day with the aid of amulets), Hasty, Short-Arse, Blue-Faced Beast, the Flea, Winged Ghost, Yellow Dog, Scarface, Cave Dragon, and Red-Haired Devil (who sounds like a Viking that somehow wound up in Cathay). There are only a few women, including the admirable warrior Hu Sanniang, nicknamed Steelbright (much better than Shapiro's translation Ten Feet of Steel, which is too butch),[110] and the disgusting Sun Erniang, called the Ogress for her penchant for cannibalism, a taste shared by other characters in this often shocking novel.

But no matter how bad some of them are, they become convinced they are doing heaven's work, for after all 108 are assembled they have a celebration (chap. 71) and lo! the stone slab from chapter 1 falls from heaven like a meteor; the "dragon script and phoenix characters" that Hong Xin had puzzled over turn out to be the names and titles of the 108 outlaws of the marsh, and Song Jiang interprets this as a sure sign his band of renegades is fulfilling the Mandate of Heaven. The 70-chapter version of the novel ends here in triumph, and as critic Jing Wang points out, the return and deciphering of the mystic stone "creates a kind of textual symmetry that the 120-chapter edition of The Water Margin fails to achieve" (261). But that shorter version is the work of a 17th-century editor who wanted to turn these rebellious demons into obedient angels, good Confucian subjects of the state. The longer version is darker and more realistic, and has its own aesthetic form in the rise and fall of the outlaw band.

They progress from banditry to insurgency, defeating every imperial army sent out to destroy them, but Song Jiang resists the suggestion of some of his men to overthrow the emperor; he sees himself and his band as loyal sons of the empire and wants only to be granted amnesty and the opportunity to serve the emperor. He gets his wish in chapter 82 when the emperor declares amnesty and promises rewards, but a gang of four ministers postpones those rewards by sending Song Jiang and his now-imperialized army to suppress other rebellions in China. They are victorious against some invading Tartars and two other outlaw bands, but during their final campaign against a rebel lord named Fang La, they begin to fall apart: one by one the 108 are killed off until only 36 are left. They manage to defeat Fang La, but instead of enjoying the bitter fruits of their pyrrhic victory, the remaining band drifts apart, either to return home, to join monasteries, to die of illness, or to seek further adventures elsewhere. Song Jiang and a few others are given official posts, but the emperor's evil ministers manage to slip Song Jiang some poisoned wine, and the novel ends with the last of the heroes joining him in death, buried on their beloved Mount Liang, and haunting the emperor in a dream that reveals how "those fucking officials" triumphed over these loyal patriots.

It's a tragic end to a magnificent, swashbuckling novel, as good as, if not better than, anything Dumas ever wrote. (Three Musketeers? Try writing for 108!) But it's also a fascinating study of authorial manipulation, of giving the reading public what they want and subtly mocking them for wanting it. Like the director of a gangster movie who despises the scum he depicts, Luo Guanzhong

---

110 In the Shaw Brothers' movie Water Margin (1972), Steelbright is played by a radiant Lily Ho, who kicks ass most elegantly.

makes us root for characters who are often brutal and given to delusions of grandeur. In the course of the novel, his "heroes" guzzle a Yangtze river of wine and go on drunken rampages; resort to murder to achieve their ends, not sparing children or innocent bystanders; and engage in numerous acts of sadism, arson, and cannibalism.[111] Like many patriots, they are too naïve to realize they're being used by the government to do its dirty work during the last third of the novel, and can't see the irony in suppressing in the name of the empire rebel bands like their own. Their self-aggrandizement grows to ridiculous proportions in the celebratory chapter 71, in which Song Jiang claims they have been granted "the protection of heaven" and his outlaws are now "celestial stars." Here's one of the stars doing heaven's work:

> So there was Wu Song, with this big yellow dog yapping at his heels. He was very drunk and needed no excuse for a quarrel. This dog that went on barking and barking infuriated him, so he drew the sword from his left-hand scabbard and bounded after it. The dog fled along the bank of the stream, still barking. Wu Song struck out at it, but he struck empty air. He used such wild force that he went head over heels into the stream and couldn't get out. (32)

And here's how another star behaves in a teahouse:

> As they enjoyed their wine, each of the four men told of something close to his heart, and everything was going swimmingly, when a young girl of about fifteen in a gauze dress suddenly appeared and, having softly wished them all a thousand happinesses, opened her mouth and proceeded to sing. Iron Ox was just on the point of telling them boastfully about various feats of daring when this singing burst out. Since the other three all started listening to the song, he had lost his audience. A fury seized him and jumping up he thrust his parted fingers into the girl's face. With a scream she collapsed on the floor. Everyone gathered around the girl. Her face was the color of earth and no sound issued from her lips. (38)

Luo had warned us at the beginning that these were demons, not angels, and keeps reminding us by placing such scenes throughout the novel — and there are far worse examples than these two — as though rubbing his readers' faces in their tendency to idolize such lowlives. By Luo's time the 12th-century outlaws of the marsh had become folk heroes, so he simultaneously inflates their exploits to mythic proportions while mocking them with incidents like these and with ironic asides. As a result, the rebel army comes across more like an urban gang than the heaven-sent patriots they come to regard themselves as. Scholars in Luo's time who failed to find official positions often had to

---

111 In his entry for the year 1120, the author of *Proclaiming Harmony* writes: "At that time, Song Jiang was attacking prefectures west of the capital and in Hebei, robbing, raping, and murdering hordes of people" (49).

resort to writing fiction to make a living, sometimes venting their frustration in this way for having to compete with storytellers, biting the hand that fed them by denigrating popular heroes.[112]

As if to exert his superiority over mere storytellers, Luo fills his novel with aesthetic delights: beautiful descriptions of nature, sharply observed details of provincial life, fresh vernacular rather than formulaic storytelling, subtle characterization, symbolic supernatural effects and dream sequences, and the ability to control an often convoluted plot. At times he pretends to have difficulty, but only to remind the reader that the story isn't telling itself and that there's an artist at work:

> You know, friends, telling this story is like flinging a handful of sand. When my predecessors recorded the events, they wanted to tell it all, every detail, but you simply can't tell everything at once. But gradually the plot will unfold and you shall know all. For the moment just try to remember the general direction. Later all that is most hidden will be revealed. (114)

What exactly is revealed has been debated for centuries. French sinologist André Lévy has noted, "Considered an incitement to banditry, in 1642 *Water Margin* was the first of the great novels to be banned."[113] Chinese communists of the 20th century at first praised it as revolutionary — that monster Mao Zedong loved it — then condemned it as a revisionist work, insisting the brutal buffoon Iron Ox is the only true revolutionary in the novel. C. T. Hsia feels it exposes "the darker aspects of the Chinese mentality" and "a peculiar insensibility to pain and cruelty on the part of the Chinese people in general" (76, 96), though he is surely wrong to assert "the novelist unambiguously sides with the heroes in all their actions" (103). Luo's ironic distance from his characters seems clear enough, and if not, Andrew Plaks drives the point home in chapter 4 of his formidable book, a chapter appropriately subtitled "Deflation of Heroism." A reader's response to *The Water Margin* probably depends on whether it is approached as entertainment — rebel heroes sticking it to the Man — or as art: a literary exercise blending several genres for a critique of political corruption and macho gang mentality in the guise of a patriotic, kick-ass adventure novel, written out of contempt for its ostensible audience but with the hope more sophisticated readers will uncover its hidden meaning. It succeeds on both counts and is a monumental achievement by whoever wrote it, for whatever reason.

If Luo Guanzhong did indeed write *The Water Margin* as well as *Three*

---

112 See chap. 5 of Ge's *Out of the Margins* for the touchy relationship between failed scholars and successful storytellers.

113 *Chinese Literature*, 136. The following remarks on its communist reputation are from the same page.

Kingdoms, he deserves to be ranked among the world's greatest novelists. Other novels have been ascribed to him, but they survive only as chapters in expanded works by later novelists.[114] No matter; every Chinese reader already knows these two major novels, and a thousand happinesses await Western readers encountering them for the first time.

❧

Just as Gunadhya in India and Boccaccio in Italy left behind shoes too big for anyone to fill for a while, no Chinese novelists of note followed in Luo's footsteps. "Master Luo compiled *Water Margin* and sired three generations of deaf-mutes," wrote Ueda Akinari in the preface to his *Tales of Moonlight and Rain*.[115] The 15th century "constitutes a curious blank in the history of Chinese fiction," as Wilt Idema once observed,[116] but the 16th century saw the dawning of the golden age of the Chinese novel. In the first half of the century, Hsiung Ta-mu produced four historical novels set in the 10th century (none of which has been translated, however). They were popular for about a century before falling out of favor, the fate of similar novels written in the 1500s, because Chinese critics (who appreciated the novel as an art form long before anyone else did) later in the century began making a distinction between art and entertainment. I'd like to quote Idema at length to show this distinction is not a modern prejudice, as some contemporary critics allege:

> To me, the novels by Hsiung Ta-mu and other novels from the first three quarters of the 16th century seem to stand at the beginning of two quite distinct traditions within the development of Chinese fiction. One tradition is that of the literary novel, the other that of the chapbook, the military romance, the *wu-hsia hsiao-shuo* [martial arts adventure]. The point where these two traditions divide would [be] as early as the last quarter of the 16th century. The contrast between these two traditions is very clear from this date onward. On the one hand we have the literary novel with its original theme and imaginative style, on the other hand the subject matter follows the popular theatre, and the language is a dreary "novelese." For the literary novels we often know the names of the authors, who, possibly without exception, belonged to the official and gentry class; the novels that belong to the other tradition are almost all anonymous. The novels of the first tradition were read by the élite, who left us their desultory notes, but they ignored the *wu-hsia hsiao-shuo*.

114 Only one of these, *The Sorcerers' Revolt* (*Ping yao zhuan*), has been translated into English, but the 17th-century author Feng Menglong added so much to the original that it will be discussed in the next volume as one of his works. There are doubts Luo actually wrote this anyway.

115 Trans. Anthony H. Chambers, 49. *Ugetsu monogatari* is a Japanese collection of occult tales first published in 1776.

116 *Chinese Vernacular Fiction*, 105. He is my source for Hsiung Ta-mu's novels, which he discusses at length (106–16).

These novels apparently had a public of their own, of a different and lower class-nature. (*sic*, 119)

One genre that has always appealed to readers high and low is erotica, and in the 1520s an unusual example appeared entitled *The Lord of Perfect Satisfaction* (*Ruyijun zhuan*), which its English translator has anointed "the fountainhead of Chinese erotica."[117] It is unusual both for describing sexual acts more explicitly than any Chinese work before it, and for its X-rated stars: a 70-year-old empress and a 30-year-old virgin, seven feet tall and endowed with a "meaty implement" of gigantic proportions. It is also unusual for its erudition, alluding to a wide variety of Chinese classics of history, philosophy, and poetry, mostly by way of ironic double entendres. The well-read author is unknown, but his translator makes a good case for attributing it to a brilliant scholar named Huang Xun (1490–c. 1540), an expert in the early Tang era in which the novella is set.

The Lord of Perfect Satisfaction adheres closely to recorded history, specifically that of the notorious Empress Wu Zetian (624–705), China's first and only female emperor. As with much erotica, the narrative begins with a sketchy plot, as if in a hurry to get to the sex scenes. At age 14, pretty Wu Zetian becomes one of the concubines of Emperor Taizong, serving under him until he falls ill a dozen years later. Knowing that concubines are discarded after their emperor's death, she allows herself to be seduced by the emperor's son Gaozong. After he ascends the throne, he ungallantly dumps her in a nunnery, but a year later has a change of heart and makes Wu his official consort. Over the next 20 years she gradually takes over the government and after his death becomes the sole ruler. She's had several lovers but never a man able to completely satisfy her, so her pandering minister suggests a commoner named Xue Aocao, still unmarried at the age of 30 because women are frightened of his uncommon wang.[118] But Wu regards this as an exciting challenge, and halfway through the novella they become lovers. She nicknames him "the lord of perfect satisfaction" and he seems content to serve his empress in this capacity, but while locked in carnal embrace he politely lectures her on mending her tyrannical ways. The second half of the novella describes in lubricious detail their epic fornications — Wu is well into her seventies by now but has retained her youthful looks, Dorian Gray-wise — the last of which almost kills the old lady. Consequently, she puts Xue out to pasture, but after copulating with two lesser-endowed boy toys, the brothers Zhang, she sends for Xue, who realizes if he returns he'll be stuck there for

117 Charles S. Stone's translation appeared under this title in 2003. The novelette occupies only pp. 133–60 of his 271-page book; the rest is valuable scholarly apparatus.
118 Xue is the author's invention, one of the few departures from history. Xue becomes the moralizing author's mouthpiece, so perhaps it's not surprising the author would give him(self) a giant dong. Men!

life (and no doubt killed once she dies), so he disappears. Disconsolate Wu returns to the Zhang brothers (who have taken a South Seas aphrodisiac to keep up with the spry octogenarian), and Xue is last spotted some 50 years later, looking not a day over 20, a follower of the Dao.

As I said, *The Lord of Perfect Satisfaction* is unusual in many ways, all of which elevate it from pornography to art. Although the novella begins with the usual situation of an older man smitten by a beautiful teenager, it doesn't become a typical tale of a king ruined by a crafty concubine. In *Proclaiming Harmony* and *The Water Margin*, for example, Emperor Huizong spends more time with his luscious mistress Li Shishi (heavenly sibilants in a world of gutturals) than on affairs of state, thereby allowing his corrupt ministers free rein. Here, a powerful woman becomes a predator of young males, and far from ruining things, Xue encourages her to become a more sensible ruler. Nor does the author describe any of Wu's sexual activities when she was in her teens or twenties, as a typical pornographer would; he waits until she's a senior citizen before giving us the graphic details — so graphic I'm too embarrassed to transcribe any of them; no pretty euphemisms like "clouds and rain" here. Even more unusual is the high density of intertextuality; as translator Stone documents in his extensive annotations, there are about a hundred allusions, quotations, or parodies of Chinese classics in the short work, many so obscure only the best-educated readers at that time would have recognized them. The author is as erudite and allusive as Joyce or Nabokov, both of whom were likewise accused of writing "dirty books" by those blind to all their literary qualities. Both Wu and Xue are widely read in the classics and often bandy quotations at times when other copulating couples would be moaning or talking dirty. But she always misunderstands or subverts the quotations, and it is that failure, more than her voracious sexuality, that condemns her.

It's a strange way to deliver lectures on Confucian morality, but *The Lord of Perfect Satisfaction* is nonetheless a highly innovative addition to Chinese fiction. Unfortunately, many later writers would misconstrue it (as Empress Wu does the classics) and borrow only its graphic vocabulary for their pornographic novels; a special few, however, learned from it how to combine intertextuality, erotic realism, even surrealism to take literature to a new level. Those few include Tang Xianzu, author of the great play *The Peony Pavilion* (*Mudan ting*, 1598), and Xiaoxiaosheng, the pseudonymous author of *The Plum in the Golden Vase*, both of whom allude to *The Lord of Perfect Satisfaction*. It may be the fountainhead of Chinese erotica, but it is also the fountainhead of avant-garde Chinese fiction.

Creation of the Gods (*Fengshen yanyi*), on the other hand, is a flamboyant throwback to the weird tales of the Tang era. Apparently written in the 1550s and tentatively attributed to Xu Zhonglin (d. c. 1566), it is another huge, 100-chapter novel, ostensibly set in the 11th century BCE but actually adrift in the timeless wonderland of Chinese mythology.[119] A brief summary of the first half-dozen chapters tells us what kind of novel we're dealing with. Wicked lusty King Zhou, the last of the Shang dynasty (c. 1600–c. 1020 BCE), has to be persuaded to pay his respects at the temple of the snail goddess Nu Wa. At the altar before her statue, a sudden draft blows her protective curtain aside to reveal Nu Wa in all her supernatural beauty. Zhou is overcome with lust for her and scribbles a poem to that effect on the wall next to the idol, then returns to his court for a "happy reunion" with his queen and concubines. Goddess Nu Wa then visits her temple, is outraged by the graffiti, and vows vengeance. She summons all the demons of the world, then selects a thousand-year-old fox-spirit as the instrument of her revenge. Meanwhile Zhou, still aroused by Nu Wa, puts out a call for a hundred beauties to come serve him; a minister points out the king already owns a thousand concubines, and that this concupiscent conscription will only cause civil unrest, so Zhou settles for one new girl, the daughter of Duke Su Hu. The duke puts up a fight — we witness a few battle scenes like those in *The Water Margin* — but capitulates and sadly sends his daughter Daji to the king's palace. One night during the journey, the fox-spirit "sucked out Daji's soul and then occupied her body. Her purpose was to seduce King Zhou and overthrow the Shang Dynasty, as Goddess Nu Wa ordered" (4).

When this faux Daji arrives at the capital, Zhou is smitten by the foxy lady, as who wouldn't be?

> She had soft black hair, cheeks as pretty as peach blossoms, a body slender as a tender willow branch, and was dressed as elegantly as floating clouds. She gave one the impression of a begonia drunk with sunshine, or a pear blossom drenched in rain. She was as ethereal as a fairy from either the Ninth Heaven, or the moon palace. When she parted her cherry lips, she gave a breath of perfumed fragrance. Her eyes were like autumn ripples, radiating coquettish charm. (4)[120]

Zhou beds her that night and "began to spend all of his energy and time taking pleasure in her. He lost his patience for state affairs and his civil and military officials, and mountains of reports, petitions and documents piled up awaiting his decision. . . . The kingdom rapidly sank into chaos" (4).

---

119 Others, like Liu Ts'un-yan in his *Buddhist and Taoist Influences on Chinese Novels*, ascribe it to a Daoist priest named Lu Xixing (1520–1601). The fullest English translation is that by Gu Zhizhong (1992), which is "slightly abridged" and runs to a little over 1,000 pages; I'll be citing it by chapter. A comparison with the two chapters translated in Owen's *Anthology of Chinese Literature* (pp. 771–806) reveals it's merely serviceable. Katherine Liang Chew's translation, *Tales of the Teahouse Retold: Investiture of the Gods* (2002), is somewhat better, but she gives only the first half of the novel and sums up the rest in a two-page epilogue.

120 Comrade Gu leaves out a crucial detail that Mrs. Chew supplies: "curvaceous bosom like high mountains in the spring."

Ten months later, in another part of the kingdom, a Daoist immortal named Master of the Clouds notices "the emanation of an evil sprite shooting high into the sky in the southeast" and realizes what's happening. He travels on his cloud to the court and gives the king a pine sword to hang before the Central Palace Tower, which will turn the sprite to ashes within three days. After giving a charming pitch for the wandering Daoist life, the Master leaves and the sword has the predicted effect, but Daji talks the king into removing it before it kills her. The 'whipped king doesn't make the connection between the sword and her sudden illness, and in fact follows her advice to start eliminating all court officials who are spreading "rumors" about her. She even designs a special torture device, a burning brass pillar that could be a symbol of the king's inflamed phallus if the author went in for that sort of thing. (Hard to say; subtlety or even verisimilitude is not his strong suit.) At any rate, the rest of the novel concerns the civil war that ensues, with Zhou and Daji pitted against a wide array of rebels, monks, demons, sorcerers, strange creatures, giants, dwarfs, and numerous Daoist immortals who, like the gods in the *Iliad*, take sides in the cascading conflict. In fact, the civil war also becomes a sectarian struggle between the Chan and Jie schools of Daoism. It's all totally unhistorical, of course; Daoism didn't appear until many centuries after the fall of the Shang dynasty, and even its most outlandish adherents didn't look like this member of the Jie sect:

> The Taoist was just about eight feet tall, had a face like the skin of a water melon, and a mouth full of fangs. Dressed in red, he wore a rosary made of parietal bones and a gold-inlaid container made of a skull around his neck. Flames leapt from the sockets where his eyes, ears, and nose should have been. (60)

It's lots of fun. Drawing upon the *pinghua* described earlier, *King Wu's Expedition against Zhou*, Yü Shao-yü's *Lieh-kuo chih-chuan* (Chronicle of the Feudal States, mid-16th century), and on centuries of folklore, mythology, and superstition, supersizing the hoary cliché of a lusty king and his scheming concubine (which *The Lord of Perfect Satisfaction* had tried to subvert), Xu Zhonglin provides a noisy arcade of fantasy entertainment. Characters shoot paralyzing rays from their nostrils or beams of light from their "third" eye; travel by cloud, crane, swan, or by "Wind-Fire Wheels"; ride unicorns, tigers, and oxen that can cover 300 miles a day; resort to divination and sorcery for all their needs; employ a variety of magic rings and mirrors; and interact with fairies, genii, sea monsters, dragons, a nine-headed pheasant-spirit, drunken ghosts, and a buddha named Candi. It's not surprising that in recent years *Creation of the Gods* has been adapted for Chinese television, video games, and manga.

Though clearly intended as entertainment — it's been said Xu Zhonglin wrote *Creation of the Gods* for his daughter's trousseau — the novel is carefully structured (in thirds) and dramatizes a serious theme: the perennial question of loyalty to a bad ruler. Does loyalty to the office extend to anyone who inhabits it, no matter how corrupt or incompetent, or does it insist on someone worthy of the office? The novel's cast is divided between those who blindly support King Zhou simply because he *is* the king, and those who feel he has disgraced the crown and must be replaced. This divides fathers and sons, masters and acolytes, and drives the civil war that occupies most of the long novel.[121] Those who oppose the king, as the author clearly does (following the Confucian philosopher Mencius [Mengzi, 4th cent. BCE], who often uses Zhou as an archetype for a bad ruler), point to historic models of good behavior and stress the importance of precedents and tradition, but they also insist on personal responsibility. There are several variations throughout the novel on the proverb "A worthy minister selects the master he'll serve" (61), *selects* being the operative word. Those ministers who blindly serve the king aren't exercising any faculty except mindless obedience, and only in religion and totalitarian systems is that expected. It's a simple dramatic conflict that the author doesn't develop much — characters keep repeating the same arguments for and against King Zhou with little variation — but it gives a certain weight to the otherwise fanciful conflict, which too often reads like this:

> Zheng Lun was afraid of Nezha. He fought with caution, ready to bolt if Nezha used his magic weapon again. Yang Jian and Huang Tianhua battled with Lu Yue, and soon Earth Traveler Sun joined in. Lu Yue then shook himself and instantly transformed into a three-headed, six-armed creature, holding the Heaven Shocking Stamp, the Pestilence Bell, the Plague Spreading Pennant, the Plague Sending Sword, and a pair of swords. His face turned green, long fangs protruding over his lips.
>
> Jiang Ziya [the rebel leader] was terrified. Yang Jian saw this and quickly galloped out of the circle. He ordered the Golden Fleece Lads to bring his bow and gold ball, and he shot Lu full on the shoulder. Huang Tianhua hurled his Fire Dragon Javelin and hit Lu Yue on the thigh. Encouraged, Jiang Ziya cast up his Staff for Beating Gods and struck Lu Yue a heavy blow, bringing him down from his camel. Lu Yue was severely wounded and fled back to his camp on the dust. (58)

Incidentally, the Earth Traveler Sun mentioned above is a repulsive dwarf who tricks an aristocrat into giving his only daughter to him in marriage. In a rare break from the battle scenes, we are privy to their wedding night, when the dwarf forces himself on the shy virgin.[122] Along with the scene near the

---

121 For more on the ethical dimensions of the novel, see Karl Kao's essay "Domains of Moral Discourse."

122 In "The Military Romance: A Genre of Chinese Fiction," Hsia calls this "an amatory episode of the comic variety," though I don't think many Western readers would find it funny. He compares it to the "romance" between lusty Short-Arse Wang and noble Steelbright

beginning where Su Hu is forced to give up his lovely daughter for the king's pleasure, the reader wants to credit that story of Xu writing this for his newly married daughter: it certainly expresses the disappointment a father might feel for his new son-in-law, who is never good enough for his princess.

After the rebels defeat all 36 expeditions the king sends to crush them, and after the king and Daji have committed some ultimate atrocities — the tender-minded will want to skip the chapter "Cutting Open the Bellies of Pregnant Women" — the rebels attack the capital. In the Wagnerian closing chapters, the goddess Nu Wa from the first chapter punishes Daji, bewitching to the end, for excessive cruelty by turning her over to Jiang Ziya, who executes her in a surrealist manner, and then King Zhou sets himself and his palace on fire. Virtuous King Wu establishes the Zhou dynasty, which would last for eight centuries, and all the dead combatants of the long civil war — whose souls have been in a kind of celestial holding pen called the Jade Emptiness Palace — are elevated to gods, hence the novel's title.

Like *The Water Margin*, *Creation of the Gods* is a violent novel, but a fantastically imaginative one. There's a character who owns a magic map that can "instantly produce any phenomenon one thought of or desired" (61); *Creation of the Gods* is the author's magic map. If *The Lord of Perfect Satisfaction* is the fountainhead of Chinese erotica, it would be tempting to call *Creation of the Gods* the fountainhead of Chinese fantasy if a far greater novel written around the same time didn't have a lock on that claim.

The Journey to the West (*Xiyou ji*, W-G *Hsi-yu chi*) is the third of the "four extraordinary books" of the Ming era, and like *Three Kingdoms* and *The Water Margin*, its author and date of composition are uncertain. Traditionally it has been attributed to Wu Chengen (1506?–82?), a minor official whom a 17th-century source described as "a man of exceptional intelligence and many talents who read most widely; able to compose poetry and prose at a stroke of the brush, he also excelled in witty and satirical writing."[123] Like the earlier two, it is a mammoth novel, 1,700 pages long in Anthony Yu's splendid, doggedly faithful translation. And like them, it is based on history — the expedition made by a Chinese Buddhist monk named Hsüan-tsang (P Xuanzang, 596–664) to India to collect religious manuscripts — and draws upon numerous chronicles, tales, plays, and earlier novels about Hsüan-tsang's famous pilgrimage. As Glen Dudridge shows in *The Hsi-yu chi: A Study of Antecedents to the Sixteenth-Century Chinese Novel*, nearly all of the plot elements were already in place for the author; but in his treatment of these materials, Wu Chengen is more akin to the creative author of *Creation*

---

in *The Water Margin*, which isn't much funnier (*On Chinese Literature*, 158). There are references to outlaw bands in *Creation of the Gods* that recall those of the earlier novel.

123 *Gazetteer of Huai-an Fu*, quoted in Yu's introduction to his translation of *The Journey to the West*, 17 (hereafter cited by chapter except for editorial matter). Yu uses the older Wade–Giles romanization, as do the translators of the remaining novels in this section.

of the Gods, deploying his extravagant imagination and wide erudition to transcend his sources and transform a book-hunting trip into a symbolic voyage of psychological integration.

While *Creation of the Gods* is structured evenly in thirds, *The Journey to the West* consists of three uneven sections. Chapters 1 through 7 (a hundred-page novella in itself) are a wild parody of every creation myth ever written. It features a restless individual who shares traits with many mythic heroes of world literature: like Gilgamesh, he is unsatisfied with impermanent earthly life and yearns for the secret of immortality; like Faust, he has an unquenchable thirst for knowledge, especially for the occult doctrines of magic; like Lucifer, he revolts against a bland, conformist heaven and engages in war against the divine legions; and like Prometheus, his defiance of the gods results in imprisonment, not enchained to a mountain like the Greek but confined beneath one. The only difference is that Wu Chengen's defiant mythical hero is not a daring man but a mischievous monkey.

After narrating the creation of the universe, Wu tells how a stone nurtured by the rays of the sun and moon engendered a monkey, an energetic simian who soon becomes king of a tribe of monkeys. Called Stone Monkey at first, then just Monkey, his premonition of death sets him apart from his carefree subjects and causes him to leave his kingdom on a spiritual quest, which involves mastering Chinese alchemy, Daoist magic, and the secret of transformation. He's given the religious name Sun Wu-k'ung and sets his sights on heaven, where the Jade Emperor placates him for a while with unimportant functions. Monkey soon creates so much havoc in heaven — including eating the forbidden fruit of the Garden of Immortal Peaches, which should sound familiar — that he is expelled and sent back to his planet of the apes, where he vows revenge. He becomes such a nuisance that the heavenly Powers That Be decide to destroy him. After Monkey defeats the first group sent against him, they send an immortal named Erh-lang, who pursues Monkey through numerous transformations that recall tales from Irish mythology and *The Arabian Nights.* When he fails to subdue the pesky primate, they send in Lao Tzu, the semilegendary founder of Daoism, who also fails, so finally they call on the godfather himself, Buddha, who is able to capture Monkey and imprison him beneath a mountain range.

All of this is narrated with infectious exuberance and stylistic brio, a spirited romp through Chinese and Buddhist mythology with a character who is both a parody of mankind and an admirable example of the few who detach themselves from the tribe and strive for a more meaningful life. In his first encounter with his human cousins, he scares most of them off:

> One of them could not run and was caught by the Monkey King, who stripped him of his
> clothes and put them on himself, aping the way humans wore them. With a swagger he

walked through counties and prefectures, imitating human speech and human manners in the marketplaces. He rested by night and dined in the morning, but he was bent on finding the way of the Buddhas, immortals, and holy sages, on discovering the formula for eternal youth. He saw, however, that the people of the world were all seekers after profit and fame; there was not one who showed concern for his appointed end. (1)

The next section (chapters 8 through 12) takes place five centuries later and introduces the other principal character of the novel. Buddha decides to share his teachings with the heathen Chinee, and asks for a volunteer to go to China to find a worthy pilgrim willing to make the long, dangerous trip to India to collect Mahayana manuscripts and bring them back. The goddess Kuan-yin volunteers, and as she makes her way eastward (mostly by air) she encounters the trapped Monkey as well as a few monsters — former residents of heaven punished, like Monkey, for transgressions — whom she converts to Buddhism, instructing them to wait until she returns with a Chinese pilgrim for them to serve as penance for their former lives. The mythy ninth chapter relates the birth and upbringing of that future pilgrim, Hsüan-tsang. His father murdered and his mother abducted, the baby is set adrift on a river (cf. Moses, Amadis, Hayy ibn Yaqzan, et al.) then rescued and raised by monks until he reaches the age 18, when he avenges his father's death and reunites with his mother. His story and religious devotion reach the ears of the Tang emperor of China in a leisurely, roundabout way during which the reader is treated to a dialogue between a fisherman and a woodsman on who has the more idyllic life, several ghost/nightmare stories, and the emperor's hair-raising descent to the underworld. The emperor decides to build a Buddhist temple for Hsüan-tsang in Changan (modern Xian in north-central China) and make him its abbot; shortly after, the low-flying goddess Kuan-yin arrives and asks the emperor for his holiest subject to travel to India. He recommends Hsüan-tsang and confers upon him the new name Tripitaka, in reference to the three collections of scriptures he is to collect, and treats him to a farewell dinner featuring a hideous-sounding "vegetarian wine," in deference to his religious vows.

Road trip! The rest of the lengthy novel (chaps. 13–100) narrates Tripitaka's 14-year, 1,200-mile journey to India and the 81 ordeals he must overcome (9×9: a mystical number for perfection) before he can meet the Buddha and return to China with the scriptures, which he doesn't accomplish until the novel's final three chapters. In other words, the novel is about the *journey* toward enlightenment, not the enlightenment promised by those scriptures. Raised by monks, brainwashed by Buddhism, Tripitaka's sheltered upbringing has left him ill-equipped to face the challenges of the real world, so his journey is the archetypal one from innocence to experience — though, as we'll see, he doesn't mature much.

His unworldliness causes problems from the start: unacquainted with travel, he and two companions leave a temple too early (while it is still dark) and promptly get lost, which results in capture by ogres, who devour Tripitaka's companions. He is rescued by a divine old man — the first of many deus-ex-machinations in this novel — then taken under the wing of a hunter. As a vegetarian, Tripitaka won't eat the hunter's game, causing further problems. Luckily, by then he has reached the Chinese border and encounters Monkey, and by freeing the born-again simian from his mountain prison, he acquires a guardian who will protect the naïve pilgrim.[124] The naked ape first slays a tiger that threatens them, skinning it to create a kilt for himself, and then foils six robbers, who symbolize (the author plainly tells us) the six senses that impede enlightenment, cluing the reader in on the allegorical nature of the novel. Tripitaka is especially impressed with the weapon Monkey used to kill the tiger and the robbers (a souvenir from his rebellious youth): an object as tiny as a needle when unneeded but that can erect into "an iron rod with the thickness of a rice bowl. . . . 'Master,' said [Monkey] laughing, 'you have no idea what that rod of mine really is'" (14). I have no idea what this might symbolize, but Monkey's magically expanding rod will get the pair out of many a tight spot in the course of the novel.

The earliest English adaptation of *The Journey to the West* was entitled *A Buddhist Pilgrim's Progress*, which it is, but it's closer to a Buddhist *Don Quixote*, with the worldly Monkey and his bookish master in the roles of Sancho Panza and the book-mad knight. This Chinese odd couple is one of the great pairings in world literature, and their differences create much of the humor in the novel: Monkey is impulsive, reckless, self-reliant, versatile, bold but wary, and streetwise, while Tripitaka is timid, impractical, whiny, haughty, booksmart but naïve, and unworldly. The monkey and the monk exasperate each other, and the sparks that fly provide much of the light in this brilliant novel.

In chapters 15 through 22, the pair pick up the rest of their road crew, in each case a monster that is later revealed to be one of those that bodhisattva Kuan-yin had converted, and each an allegorical representation of a human drive that must be mastered by the would-be bodhisattva: a dragon (symbolizing will) transformed into a white horse for Tripitaka to ride; Pigsy, a porcine monster (appetite) who abandons his wife to join the expedition; and finally Sandy (habit?), a river-monster. Many chapters after they're introduced, the last two are described; Tripitaka warns an Indian king:

124 At this point in his translation, Yu begins to use the name Tripitaka bestows on Monkey, Pilgrim Sun (adapted from his religious name Sun Wu-k'ung). But to distinguish between the simian pilgrim and the human one, I'll continue using Monkey, as Arthur Waley did in his popular abridgment (*Monkey*, 1943). I also prefer Waley's names for Tripitaka's two future companions, Pigsy and Sandy, rather than Yu's Pa-chieh (aka Hog, Idiot) and Sha Monk (*sha* = "sand").

"My elder disciple [Pigsy] . . . has a long snout and fang-like teeth, tough bristles on the back of his head, and huge, fan-like ears. He is coarse and husky, and he causes even the wind to rise when he walks. My second disciple [Sandy] . . . is twelve feet tall and three span wide across his shoulders. His face is like indigo, his mouth, a butcher's bowl; his eyes gleam and his teeth seem a row of nails." (29)

Together with Monkey (symbolizing the overactive mind) they face a variety of ordeals involving other monsters, larcenous monks, shiftless Daoists, a marriage proposal by a widow with three teenage daughters, demons, peony-pretty temptresses, maligned ghosts, dragons, spirits, impassible rivers, ill winds, a mountain of flames, brambles, a, um, poetry discussion group, female soccer players in clingy sweat-wet jerseys, and other obstacles to the ideal of Buddhist mindlessness. The pilgrims are helped out by gobs of gods and bodhisattvas, and they need all the help they can get because word has spread to the monster community that eating Tripitaka will confer immortality. Alternatively, insemination by the monk — the extraction of his "primal yang" — will make a woman eternally young, which is why all the female characters hound him for his semen, often with a boldness not usually associated with modest Chinese maidens. When the queen of one country gets a look at Tripitaka, she resorts to a Chinese sexual metaphor and calls out, à la Mae West, "Royal Brother of the Great T'ang, aren't you coming to take and ride the phoenix?"; and after he leaves her yangless at the end of the chapter, another hussy yells, "Royal Brother T'ang, where are you going? Let's you and I make some love!" (54). True to his name (and allegorical function), only Pigsy is tempted by the novels' many temptresses, but he is prevented from any yin-yanging by the others. In almost every case, it is Monkey's ingenuity and prowess that saves Tripitaka from man-eaters of all kinds.

The novel has been read by the Asian multitudes for centuries merely as a colorful adventure novel — which it certainly is — but the Chinese cognoscenti have read it as an allegory, encouraged by Wu's far-flung references to Buddhism, Daoism, Chinese alchemy (what Jung called "the integration of the personality" rather than the transformation of base materials into gold), and Confucian philosophy. There's no doubt about Wu's erudition, but some doubt about what it all means. Tripitaka makes no progress in his Buddhist goal to transcend suffering and extinguish the senses — the advice of the *Heart Sutra* he receives in chapter 19 and recites thereafter — and while "the monkey of the mind and the horse of desire" are condemned throughout the novel, on a literal level it's Monkey's mind that saves T and the white horse that transports him on his long journey. Pigsy's Rabelaisian appetite for food and sex is funny and life-affirming rather than disgusting, but whatever it is Sandy represents, it isn't appealing. He's gloomy, suspicious, a stickler for procedure, and seems to personify deadening habit.[125]

And Monkey? He represents the restless mind that Buddhism seeks to quiet, yet he is obviously the hero of the novel and the most admirable character, which suggests this ostensibly Buddhist novel might just be an anti-Buddhist allegory — a paradox like the *Heart Sutra*'s dictum "form is emptiness, and emptiness is form."[126] On the one hand, Monkey's conversion to Buddhism is sincere, he understands the *Heart Sutra* better than Tripitaka does, and he sees through the veils of maya, the illusory nature of the phenomenal world. (Most of the monsters are animals in disguise.) On the other, it's his active mind and ingenuity that ensure the journey's success, and he's usually the only one who appreciates the scenery along the way (conveyed by Wu in lovely verse), the same sensual world your true Buddhist should shun. He acknowledges the Buddhist gods and their heaven, but also recognizes their occasional malice — he calls his sponsor Kuan-yin a "rogue" for sending demons to test him (35) and wonders why all-powerful Buddha didn't simply send the scriptures to China himself (77) — and sneers at the boring conformity and bureaucratic pettiness of the Buddhist heaven. His faith forbids killing, yet Monkey slaughters thousands of life-forms (humans, animals, demons, fiends) in the course of the novel. Of course it could be argued that these contradictions mean Monkey is still struggling with his inner demons; Chen Yuan-chih, editor of the first printed edition of the *Journey* (1592), assures us in his preface that no actual demons were harmed in the making of the novel:

> For demons are the miasmas caused by the mouth, the ears, the nose, the tongue, the body, the will, the fears and the illusions of the imagination. Therefore, as demons are born of the mind, they will be also subdued by the mind. This is why we must subdue the mind in order to subdue the demons: we must subdue the demons in order to return to truth; we must return to truth in order to reach the primal beginning where there will be nothing more to be subdued by the mind. This is what is meant by the accomplishment of the *Tao*, and this is also the real allegory of the book.[127]

This return-to-the-womb fantasy has been sensibly rejected by others, who argue that the paradoxes in Monkey's behavior invalidate a strict Buddhist

---

125 I'm reminded of the important role habit plays in Proust's great quest, especially as he resorts to adventure-fantasy imagery when Marcel muses, "Would I now, I had said to myself, unsuspecting of the abrupt change that lay in wait for my soul, have to go into yet other hotels, where I would dine for the first time, where habit would not yet have slain, on each floor, before each door, the terrifying dragon that had seemed to stand watch over an enchanted existence . . . ?" (*Sodom and Gomorrah*, 162).

126 Quoted in its entirety in chapter 19, the *Heart Sutra* is a concise distillation of Mahayana Buddhism, which the historical Hsüan-tsang swore by.

127 Quoted in Yu's introduction, 1:34.

interpretation, and point instead to the Daoist and Confucian elements as the keys to the allegory. Wu Chengen makes enough references to the pilgrims as a "single body" to justify regarding all five as facets of a single personality attempting to integrate those disparate psychological elements into a coherent self, and then attempting "the harmonizing of the self within a network of human relations in a society and the world at large."[128] An 18th-century critic named Liu I-ming felt the novel is about "the proper way to conduct oneself in the world" and argues "against complete immersion in one's own mind and thoughts and the mere playing with the concepts of vacuity and nirvana."[129] This seems to be the author's intention, for he tells us bluntly at the beginning of chapter 23: "The principal aim of this chapter is to make clear that the quest for scriptures is essentially the same as the need to attend to the fundamentals in one's life." Today, this is the most relevant aspect of the *Journey*. Most of the ordeals encountered by Wu's Tang clan are recognizable from everyday life: selfishness, inhospitality, corruption (even at the end, Buddha's librarians need to be bribed before they'll turn over the scrolls), false accusations, miscarriages of justice, ingratitude, cruelty, and lust. There's no need to evoke the veils of maya to realize people aren't always what they appear to be, or consult the *I Ching* to tell when someone's talking nonsense.

For a modern reader, Monkey is the unconventional, creative individual living in a conservative, conformist world, forced to work for a soulless corporation or a bad boss, hemmed in by oppressive "community values," and he pays a price for his independence. After Monkey is recruited for the journey, Kuan-yin (working for the Man) attaches a steel headband to his skull; every time the macaque asserts himself, Tripitaka need only recite a spell to cause him excruciating pain — a thought-control device common in modern dystopian fiction. The conservative monk thereby keeps the independent monkey on a leash, sometimes punishing him unfairly for actions that later turn out to be life-saving. I can't help but think that Wu Chengen felt like Monkey during the autocratic Ming regime, which didn't tolerate dissent. Wu's "boss" was Emperor Chia-ching (P Shizong), who sounds like a character out of his own novel; can you imagine trying to lead a meaningful life in a country ruled by a nutcase like this?:

> During his years of seclusion, following the abortive attempt by palace women to kill him, the Emperor, deep into his long-held Taoist beliefs and alchemy, based important decisions on divination. One of the methods consisted of two mediums holding the short

128 Plaks (264), who offers a convincing neo-Confucian interpretation of the novel's allegorical elements.
129 "How to Read 'The Original Intent of the *Hsi-yu chi*,'" in Rolston's *How to Read the Chinese Novel*, 301. Liu thought so highly of the novel that he advised, "The reader should purify his hands and burn incense before reading it, and it should be read with the utmost reverence" (299).

arms of a T-shaped object from whose long arm a suspended awl traced out, on a platter of sand beneath it, the answers to supplications that had been written in gold ink on dark blue paper, addressed to a certain Taoist deity and then burnt, for the smoke to rise up to the deity. The Emperor's chief Taoist adviser, one T'ao Chung-wen, also prescribed aphrodisiac pills made largely of red lead and white arsenic, to which Chia-ching became addicted, gradually poisoning himself. For the attainment of immortality T'ao also recommended sexual intercourse with virgins, and in 1552 he collected eight hundred girls aged between eight and fourteen to serve the Emperor, adding one hundred and eighty more in 1555. None of this availed against the poisoning effect of the elixirs. Insomnia plagued him, and swings of mood from depression to rage. From 1564 his eunuch attendants put peaches — symbols of longevity — in his bed, saying they were gifts from the immortals, which much pleased him. His mental capacity shrank, and as his condition deteriorated he was moved from the Palace of Everlasting Longevity back to the Forbidden City, where he died at midday on 23rd January 1567, ending a forty-four-year reign of more oddity than achievement.[130]

Tripitaka's emperor, T'ai-tsung (P Taizong), is just as barmy about Buddhism, and decrees "any person who denounces a monk or Buddhism will have his arms broken" (12). Living under an autocratic Daoist, writing about a brutal Buddhist, Wu Chengen had to be careful with his freewheeling satire, and thus loaded the novel with so many references, positive and negative, to so many doctrines that commentators have read all sorts of things into it. Chinese communists considered Wu a Marxist critic of a corrupt social system, while a recent Japanese critic named Miki Katsumi praised Wu for championing (like his Renaissance contemporaries) "human liberation from mystery and progress from the medieval world to the spirit of modernity."[131] After Grove Press reissued Arthur Waley's abridged version in paperback in 1958, Monkey became a countercultural trickster-hero to Western dharma bums and creative hippies, especially in England.[132] In recent years, The Journey to the West has been adapted for so many television shows, movies, musicals, cartoons, and video games that it's become all things to all people.

Though there may be questions about Wu's allegorical intention, there can be no question as to his aesthetic achievement. One of the grandest works of world literature, The Journey to the West introduced satire and humor to the Chinese novel on a much larger scale than any work before it, and brought

---

130 Rayne Kruger, *All under Heaven: A Complete History of China* (Chichester, UK: Wiley, 2004), 295–96.

131 Quoted with astonished reservations by Yu in his introduction, 1:35.

132 The British rock group Small Faces got their song/album title "Autumn Stone" (an alchemical term) from chapter 2, and the ape's original name Stone Monkey was appropriated by a dance troupe that accompanied the Incredible String Band on a brief tour in 1970 (and pictured on the sleeve of their brilliant album *U* later that year). A hip generation later, Damon Albarn of the Britpop band Blur debuted his opera *Monkey* in 2007.

Sanskrit luxuriance to Chinese prose. (Wu alludes to *Entry into the Realm of Reality* a few times, and was obviously acquainted with other flowery sutras.[133]) Like earlier Chinese novels, the *Journey* contains hundreds of poetic passages, but while Luo Guanzhong mostly inserted older poems into his novels, Wu wrote many of his own, which are so good, says C. T. Hsia, that he "must be considered one of the most skilled descriptive poets in all Chinese literature."[134] Like his Sanskrit predecessors, Wu resorts to all sorts of wordplay and paronomasia, especially in the poetry, and gives himself set-pieces to show off his extensive knowledge in a variety of disciplines. "To tell is to exaggerate," says Monkey at one point (74), and there is a delirious verbal exuberance to the novel as Wu describes epic battles, feasts, ornaments, a festival of lanterns, the beauties of nature, and the seductive charms of women. Monkey and Pigsy frequently roar with laughter, and many of the demons they encounter turn out to be divine animals who escaped boring heaven to go live it up on the good earth, displaying a rage for life that may be at odds with Buddhist ideals but is completely understandable. The novel has its faults: there are way too many plot recapitulations (perhaps a vestige of its oral origins), a sameness to some of the ordeals after a while, and a wanton indifference to animal life and to the destruction of the environment that doesn't sit well with a 21st-century sensibility. Female readers will be hard-pressed to find a sympathetic character of their gender anywhere in the long novel, though this has less to do with misogyny than with adherence to the novel's symbolism. (Most of the demons live in caves into which they lure our pilgrims to try to kill them; they parallel the human females' numerous attempts to entice Tripitaka into their anatomical caves.) But these are minor qualms, hardly worth mentioning in light of Wu Chengen's stupendous achievement. Monkey and the others journey 14 years to acquire a bundle of Buddhist sutras, but I doubt anything in those scrolls could match this novel *about* the journey. As Liu I-ming put it over 200 years ago, "The acquisition of the true scriptures by means of the journey to the West actually means the acquisition of the true scripture of *The Journey to the West*" (303).

A severely abridged version of *The Journey to the West* is included in an omnibus volume compiled by Yang Chih-ho entitled *Ssu-yu chi* (Four Pilgrimages), novella-length accounts of religious journeys in all four directions, probably assembled in the last quarter of the 16th century. One of these, *Journey to the North* (*Pei-yu chi*) is available in an English translation by Gary Seaman (cited hereafter by chapter) and offers a ludicrous example of pop Chinese religious fiction. Though anonymous, it may be based on (if not

133 Li discusses the influence of the *Entry* and other sutras on the *Journey* in chapter 3 of his *Fictions of Enlightenment*.
134 *The Classic Chinese Novel*, 120. Yu notes there are 33 poems in the *Journey* that also appear in *Creation of the Gods*, but since the two novels were written at roughly the same time, it's impossible to say who originated them.

identical to) *T'ai-ho chuan* (The Tale of Wu-tang Mountain) by Kuo Hsün, a close friend of crazy Emperor Chia-ching who took part in those royal divination ceremonies, and to whom other pop novels are attributed.

Set during the Sui dynasty (589–618), the novel opens at a banquet in the Thirty-third Heaven, where the Jade Emperor becomes so enamored of a Magnificent Flowering Tree that he sacrifices one of his three souls to be reborn as the son of the owner of the tree so that he can enjoy it better. Because he has thus given in to his "avaricious heart" (1), the Jade Emperor, now called Firstborn, is then sent down to earth to expunge desire and cultivate the Way (*Dao*). Twenty-six years later, now living on Paradise Peak in the country of Ko-ko (Tibet), Firstborn impresses a hunting king, who takes him back to his palace, where the Daoist is propositioned by the queen. He turns her down, but since he gallantly adds "ask me again in a life to come" (2), a patrolling deity chastises Firstborn, who dies of shame seven days later, as does the queen shortly after. Firstborn is then reborn as the child of the hunting king's new wife Teng; the ex-queen is also reborn, and at age three the two are betrothed, fulfilling Firstborn's former offer.

Like a Sanskrit novel it continues in this vein, a farrago of reincarnation, Daoist magic, Buddhist mythology, and supernatural adventure. Firstborn, now called the Venerable Teacher, inherits the throne of Ko-ko, then abdicates to continue following the Way, agrees to marry a pretty peach-seller in a future life (a Daoist sting to test him) and consequently needs to be re-reborn, inherits another throne at age 15 (and is given 32 wives and 72 concubines as a graduation present), and so on through another reincarnation until VT winds up on sacred Wu-tang Mountain in northeast China (a destination for pilgrims to this day). A Mother Goddess is sent to watch over him, and after observing 20 years of impeccable behavior, she decides to test him. Like one of the bold hussies in *The Journey to the West*, she says to herself: "I think I must change this very evening into the form of a beautiful maiden and go flirt with him. If I can move his heart to lust, then I will fornicate with him. If I can seduce him in this way, then my Supernatural Powers will be great and I will become famous throughout all the world! Wouldn't that be wonderful!" (9). The Venerable Teacher not only resists her but this time avoids making any promises about calling her in a future life, indicating he is indeed well on the Way.

But I'm going into way too much detail for what is at bottom a simple-minded if diverting novel. It's all an allegory of how "worldly desires" prevent one from "realizing his Original Identity" (6) — that is, immortal soul (or trinity of souls in this case) — the whole thing a Buddhist recruitment document for abandoning the material world and joining the Way. The rest of the novel tells how VT became one of the Jade Emperor's celestial officials, descended to earth to subdue demons and accumulate merit, and how he became the god Chen-wu, aka Emperor of the Dark Heavens, who is still worshiped in China. (A 1960 survey found 260 temples dedicated to him on Taiwan alone.) Most of VT's battles against demons are pale imitations of Monkey's, though there is one interesting twist in chapter 19, in which an immortal's writing brush comes to life and begins trapping people in a notebook, including the Venerable Teacher. The immortal owner of the brush needs to rescue VT from the demon's book, which recalls some 20th-century novels in which characters try to escape from their author. But perhaps in this instance, as Horatio warns Hamlet, 'twere to consider too curiously to consider so; our anonymous author doesn't go in for this sort of literary self-referentiality, or for much literary finesse at all. Like *Journey to the West*, *Journey to the North* is a didactic religious novel, but with none of the complications, gusto, irony, and artistry of Wu Chengen's masterpiece. Go *West*, young reader, not *North*.

In 1597 an otherwise unknown author named Luo Maodeng brought out a novel as long as Wu Chengen's entitled *Adventures in the Western Ocean* (*Xiyangji*), based on the travels of Zheng He (1371–1433), a Chinese Muslim who explored the Indian Ocean and may have reached as far as Africa. Although Luo followed the records of Zheng He's explorations, he felt free to embellish his imperialistic narrative with all sorts of supernatural and folkloric elements. The result sounds fun — Ch'ên Shou-yi describes it as "a peculiar combination of *Gulliver's Travels* and *Robinson Crusoe*" (488), and other critics are reminded of Sindbad's voyages — but since this long yarn has never been translated, we'll have to move on.

A section break is needed to cleanse the palate for the last and greatest Chinese novel of this period, arguably the greatest novel written before *Don Quixote*.

⚜

> The telling of this tale is enough to knock the peak
> of Mount Hua askew;
> Its revelation is sufficient to make
> the Yellow River flow backward.

This boastful quatrain concludes the prologue to *The Plum in the Golden Vase* (W-G *Chin p'ing mei*, P *Jin ping mei*), the fourth and longest of China's "four extraordinary books," in David Tod Roy's new translation.[135] As with its predecessors, the novel's exact date of composition and author are not known

---

135 Since only the first three of his projected five volumes have appeared so far, I'll cite his translation through chapter 60, and the remaining 40 in Clement Egerton's older, inferior one entitled *The Golden Lotus*, both by chapter (except for editorial matter, cited by volume/page). Egerton has only a few explanatory notes, whereas Roy provides hundreds of pages of detailed annotations that suggest he has read every scrap of Chinese literature.

for sure; most of the evidence indicates it was written in the 1590s (though not published until 1617) by someone who called himself the Scoffing Scholar of Lanling (W-G Lan-ling Hsiao-hsiao-sheng, P Lanling Xiaoxiaosheng). A contemporary of his named Yüan Chung-tao (1570–1624) gave this account of the origin of the novel: "Long ago there was a captain Hsi-mên in the capital, who engaged an old scholar from Shaohsing to serve in his household. The scholar had little to occupy his time, and so day by day recorded the erotic and licentious things that went on there. In the figure of [Hsi-]mên Ch'ing, he portrayed his master, and in the other figures, his master's various concubines."[136] Over 30 candidates for authorship have been proposed by scholars — Roy favors T'ang Hsein-tsu (1550–1616), the leading playwright of the time — but since his identity hasn't been conclusively proved, I'll refer to him by the very apt pseudonym Scoffing Scholar. Given his scorching criticism of Chinese culture (not to mention his graphic eroticism), it's not surprising that the author concealed his identity under a nom de guerre; in the culture wars of his time, this novel would have been grounds for death. For though he set his story in the early 12th century, Scoffing Scholar was writing about his own debased era with a hard-core realism that was revolutionary, and used the entire body of Chinese literature to condemn it by way of allusion, quotation, and appropriation. T. S. Eliot did something similar in *The Waste Land*, but imagine writing a 2,300-page novel that weaves in quotations from the entire body of English literature, from *Beowulf* to *Darkmans*, irreverently putting them into new contexts that resulted in a mordantly ironic condemnation of modern England. That boastful quatrain above? Not his own, but taken from an early Ming novel entitled *San Sui p'ing-yao chuan* (The Three Sui Suppress the Demons' Revolt), a minor action novel whose vaunting claim, Scoffing Scholar decided, better suited his own revelatory novel than that ghostbusters yarn. PGV is filled with appropriations like this — today we'd call them "samples," if not plagiaries — "a marquetry of texts cleverly joined and adapted to the needs of the narration," as its French translator observes.[137]

Scoffing Scholar also has a Shakespearean penchant for punning, beginning with the novel's title. *The Plum in the Golden Vase* sounds like a pretty piece of chinoiserie, but as translator Roy explains,

136 From Yüan's diary *Yu-chü shih-lu*, as translated by Patrick Hanan in "The Text of the *Chin p'ing mei*," 44. Others feel that's just a story invented to account for the novel's verisimilitude; see Chang Chu-p'o's remarkably perceptive "How to Read the *Chin p'ing mei*" (c. 1695), in Rolston, 238.

137 Lévy, *Chinese Literature*, 141. (His two-volume *Fleur en Fiole d'Or* appeared in 1985.) Hanan provides a survey of these texts in "Sources of the *Chin p'ing mei*," which Roy drew upon for many of his annotations. Hanan emphasizes "the degree to which the author has relied on literary experience rather than on personal observation" (65) — that is, what the scholar saw in Hsi-men's household was only the starting point for the novel — and marvels at "the breadth of the author's borrowing. The copied sourceworks represent the whole spectrum of Ming dynasty literatures" (66).

It is made up of one character each from the names of three of the major female protagonists of the novel (P'an *Chin*-lien, Li P'*ing*-erh, and P'ang Ch'un-*mei*) that would literally
mean *Gold Vase Plum*; it can be semantically construed as *The Plum in the Golden Vase*,
or *Plum Blossoms in a Golden Vase*; and it puns with three near homophones that might
be rendered as *The Glamour of Entering the Vagina*. (1:xvii)

Scoffing Scholar's largest and most blatant literary appropriation is from
The Water Margin. The first 10 of PGV's 100 chapters rework a novella-length
story from chapters 23–26 of Luo Guanzhong's novel, a sordid account of
small-town adultery. An "empire-toppling" beauty named P'an Chin-lien
(meaning Golden Lotus) escaped a wayward and abusive childhood by marrying a dim dwarf named Wu Chih, who makes a living peddling steamed
wheatcakes on the street. When his brawny, tiger-killing brother Wu Sung
happens to get a job in the same town and moves in with his brother, sex-
starved Chin-lien tries to seduce him but fails; he moves out in disgust (but
without exposing her to his brother) and then goes on a long business trip,
during which Chin-lien catches the roving eye of Hsi-men Ch'ing, the
main character of the novel. A spoiled, 27-year-old party-animal/ex-jock who
inherited a wholesale pharmaceutical business and bribes his way into getting whatever he wants, Hsi-men begins an affair with Chin-lien (now 24), is
caught in the act by her husband, and nearly kills him by kicking the wee man
in the solar plexus. The adulterous couple decides to finish him off, so Chin-
lien poisons Wu and cremates the body to hide the evidence while Hsi-men
bribes the officials to look the other way. At this point in *The Water Margin*,
Wu Sung returns, learns of the scandal, and brutally kills Chin-lien (then
makes his way to join the other outlaws on the marsh). But Scoffing Scholar
has Chin-lien move in with Hsi-men, who already has a principal wife — Wu
Yüeh-niang, a pious lady who likes to listen to nuns recite Buddhist sutras —
and three secondary ones (concubines), but who always has room for one
more. Even these "bedmates," as he calls them, aren't enough to satisfy him;
he seduces maidservants and spends a lot of time with his leeching buddies
in the town's red-lantern district, the victim of an insatiable lust that will
eventually kill him.

Structured in 10-chapter units — usually with narrative bumps in the fifth
and seventh and a climax in the tenth — the novel switches gears in the next
10 chapters from pulp fiction to the novel of manners to relate the growing
tension between Hsi-men's five wives, his unabated whoring in the licensed
quarter, and further examples of his bullying methods to keep his women
compliant and his business growing. Bored Chin-lien seduces a 15-year-old
— "Almost before they know it, a glob / of donkey's spunk, / Has been depos-
ited in Chin-lien's jade-like body" is the author's ironic/poetic description of

their tryst (12)[138] — while her husband seduces her maid P'ang Ch'un-mei (the *Plum* [*Blossom*] of the novel's title) as well as the rich, flirty wife of his next-door neighbor, *plus* her maids. (In other households as well, maids are considered the sexual property of their owners.) After the cuckolded neighbor dies, the H-Man — as his counterpart today would be nicknamed — promises to marry someday the debauched widow, Li P'ing-erh (the *Vase*), who gets tired of waiting and instead marries a meek pharmacist (who owns a wide variety of sex toys), whom Hsi-men ruins Mafia-style in revenge. At that point Hsi-men agrees to marry P'ing-erh: "Let her pick a good day and I'll have the whore carried across my threshold, and be done with it," he says romantically. Meanwhile, jealous Chin-lien nags and sexually humiliates herself in a vain attempt to retain Hsi-men's affections, alienating most of his other wives in the process. Chapter 20 culminates in the scandalous wedding — Hsi-men keeps his bride waiting three nights to teach her who's boss, and P'ing-erh attempts suicide in response — and dramatizes Hsi-men's growing reliance on his son-in-law Ch'en Ching-chi, who will become the novel's second principal male character.

With six wives now in his harem, Hsi-men plays one against the other while continuing to seduce his employees' wives.[139] Chin-lien, now 27, becomes the queen bitch of the brood, lashing out against everyone with her tart tongue, flirting with young Ch'en Ching-chi, and engaging in increasingly acrobatic sex acts with her wayward husband. (The orgiastic chapter 27 is heavily indebted to *The Lord of Perfect Satisfaction*, and wouldn't be out of place in the pages of *Penthouse*.) Failed-suicide Ping-erh becomes pregnant — the absence of any previous pregnancies despite Hsi-men's rampant coupling symbolizes the sterility of his life — and chapter 30 ends with the birth of a son just after Hsi-men receives an important promotion to "battalion vice-commander in the Imperial Insignia Guard" and, closer to home, "assistant judicial commissioner of the local office of the Shantung Provincial Surveillance Commission."

The latter post broadens Hsi-men's opportunities for bribery and corruption, which the author pursues with prosecutorial detail over the next 10 chapters. Hsi-men also acquires a new secretary, a handsome, 15-year-old former "gate boy" named Shu-t'ung, a homosexual transvestite who submits to his master's expanding sexual tastes as he coordinates Hsi-men's expanding official calendar. The author cleverly links Hsi-men's official and sexual corruption by way of a joke one of his drinking buddies tells (punning on the phrase *hsing-fang*, which can mean both "sexual intercourse" and "Office of Justice"):

---

138 Also not his own but appropriated from a 10th-century Buddhist monk named Chih-ts'ung by way of a 12th-century book on prostitutes.

139 For a close (if overly academic) examination of the sexual politics and intradomestic power plays between Hsi-men's women, see part 2 of Naifei Ding's *Obscene Things*.

"A magistrate was interrogating a suspect in a case of illicit sexual intercourse and asked him, 'Initially, how did you go about violating her?' To which the man replied, 'Her head was facing east, and her feet were also facing east, when I did it.' 'Nonsense,' the magistrate responded. 'How could you do justice to the office with anybody in such a crooked position?' At which point a bystander came forward, knelt down, and said, 'Your Honor, as for that crooked position in the Office of Justice, if there are any openings in that body, I would be happy to fill them'" (35).

Hsi-men begins ignoring his former friends and the "painted faces" of the licensed quarter (two of whom cleverly arrange to be "adopted" by his family to continue profiting from his lust), and even tortures a few servants for imaginary derelictions of duty. He participates in further shady doings in the bureaucratic and religious spheres — he sponsors a Daoist ceremony for his son that resembles medieval Catholicism at its simoniac, indulgence-selling worst — and in chapter 40 watches in amusement as the two principal rivals for his affection, P'ing-erh and Chin-lien, play dress-up for him: the mother dresses their baby boy in a cute little Daoist costume, which warms Hsi-men's heart, while the mistress slips into a saucy maid's outfit, which warms a different organ. We also hear of some Buddhists who traffic in fertility drugs, foreshadowing things to come.

With a luxuriance of detail that rivals an overstuffed Victorian novel, the author continues to track the social lives of his characters, though in language no Victorian novelist would have dared to use.[140] Hsi-men Ch'ing takes one bribe too many in chapter 47 and nearly gets impeached, then impenitently runs another scam resembling insider-trading, greasing palms with silver and sing-song girls.[141] He buys some aphrodisiacs from an Indian monk, a grotesque personification of Hsi-men's overworked phallus:

His leopard-shaped head with its sunken eyes was the color of purple liver and was crowned with a cock's comb-like chaplet. He wore a long flesh-colored gown. The whiskers beneath

140 Which demonstrates how artificial and unrealistic some allegedly realistic Victorian novels are. Given the underworld setting of Dickens's *Oliver Twist*, for example, the air should be blue with foul language, but there isn't a single obscenity in it, not even the common intensifier "bloody." And Nancy? Scoffing Scholar would have called her a "splay-legged whore," as Hsi-men calls Chin-lien after she taunts him by saying of his maids: "If they don't laugh at you with their mouths, / They'll certainly laugh through their cunts" (43; bold Chin-lien lifts her dress and exposes her beautiful gams to show she is not, in point of fact, "splay-legged"). To attempt a realistic description of a milieu without reference to the language that characterizes, if not shapes, that milieu is bloody unrealistic.

141 Like their Indian and Japanese sisters, these women were trained entertainers as well as prostitutes and were accepted members of society, not outlaws as in our less sophisticated one. They are everywhere in this novel, sporting names like Jade Darling, Tung the Cat, and Crape Myrtle Fairy.

his chin bristled unevenly, and he had a shiny annular ridge around the base of his head. Truly, he was:

> An authentic arhat, of the most
> extraordinary aspect;
> A one-eyed dragon, undivested of
> his fiery temperament.

He had fallen into a trance on his meditation couch, so that his head was drooping, his neck subsided into his upper trunk, and a trickle of jade-white mucus was dribbling from his nostrils. (49)

In the literally climactic chapter 50 Hsi-men tries the stimulants out on an employee's wife (who likes anal sex) and, later the same night, on a reluctant P'ing-erh during her period. The next night (and chapter), it's Chin-lien's turn, and with this "past mistress of the intimate arts" (51) he engages in epic fornications over the succeeding chapters, in addition to drug-enhanced bouts with his other concubines and even with his principal wife, Lady Wu, who so longs for a child of her own that she has scored some fertility drugs from a Buddhist nun. At this point, the sarcastic author begins repeating a four-character phrase that translates "this culture of ours," which translator Roy explains "stands for the value system of the educated Confucian elite" (3:560 n59); the author implies he's not simply telling a story about a 12th-century parvenu but instead condemning his own culture for drifting so far from Confucian ideals. In chapter 59 Hsi-men's baby son dies — he had been sickly from birth, but the proximate cause is Chin-lien's vicious cat, which she had trained to attack the baby (have I mentioned she's insanely jealous?) — but in a brilliant example of letting form determine meaning, the concluding chapter 60 celebrates the opening of Hsi-men's new silk-goods store. The corrupt wheeler-dealer coldly dismisses the death of his son — "Think of him as an alien rascal," he comforts the devastated mother. "Seeing that: He is not fated to be our child, we have raised him in vain" (59) — but is delighted by the first day's receipts, an unsubtle indication of the priorities of this "famed exemplar of this culture of ours" (56).

But Hsi-men Ch'ing's delight quickly fades. Still desolate at the loss of her child, P'ing-erh sickens and dies at age 27, giving Scoffing Scholar an opportunity to deride the medical establishment (and to show off his own knowledge of the subject). Next, Hsi-men's catamite Shu-t'ung steals some money and runs away, and then his doctor warns him he's run-down and overweight, even though Hsi-men is only 32 at this point. (He relies on aphrodisiacs for nearly all his sexual activities now.) No sooner is P'ing-erh buried than the H-Man shacks up with his dead son's wet-nurse Ju-i, though he genuinely misses the concubine: still she haunts him, phantomwise. Meanwhile Chin-lien, desperately trying to remain in favor, buys some fertility drugs from the same Buddhist nun that hooked up Lady Wu, who is now pregnant. Hsi-men reverts to slipping off to the licensed quarter for kicks and begins an affair with Chin-lien's former foster-mother, the rich and randy widow Lin — "a voluptuous lover of sex in plush apartments, a goddess of fornication in the inner chambers" (69)[142] — while continuing to misuse his position for personal gain. Then, in the middle of these debaucheries and miscarriages of justice, Hsi-men gets official word he has been promoted to magistrate for his "pre-eminent virtue," and the heavily ironic chapter 70 ends with his visit to the Eastern Capital (modern Kaifeng) to meet the emperor, where he indulges in an orgy of obsequiousness and empty ceremony.

Back home in Ch'ing-ho, Chin-lien and Ju-i get into a catfight, and after Hsi-men's return Chin-lien sinks to a new low to maintain her sexual hold on him; after he lies about missing her — he was too busy sodomizing his new catamite while in the capital — they have sex, and during the oral phase (Chin-lien's specialty),

> Ximen Qing [Hsi-men Ch'ing] felt the need to get down from the bed to urinate. But the young woman refused to let go of [the penis still in her mouth].
>
> "My dear," she said to him, "piss in me, if that is troubling you. I will swallow it all! It's good to stay warm, you should avoid the cold. It would be better than getting down and freezing your balls off."
>
> "My dear little cookie, no one loves me like you do!" Ximen Qing exclaimed, immensely happy with such attention.
>
> At this he pissed to his heart's content into her mouth. She actually drank it, slowly, mouthful after mouthful, without losing a drop.
>
> "Is it good?" Ximen asked her.
>
> "A little bitter. If you have some jasmine tea, it would help to make that taste go away."[143]

After she munches on some tea leaves, they resume and "enjoyed ecstasies of pleasure that night" (72). Attending to business by day, upending women by night, drinking heavily both day and night, the H-Man begins to suffer from exhaustion and various aches and pains. After a particularly grueling double-header — first with an employee's wife, and later that night with insatiable Chin-lien, who overdoses him with his Indian Viagra in what Andrew Plaks rightly calls "a scene of sexual horror scarcely matched in all literature" (141) — Hsi-men dies at age 33, his penis covered in boils and leaking blood. (There are deliberate verbal parallels between Chin-lien's poisoning of her

---

142 As translated in Plaks's *Four Masterworks*, 94; Col. Egerton's version lacks va-voom.
143 As translated in Lévy's *Chinese Literature*, 141–42; again, Egerton's version is too bland.

first husband in chapter 5 and her overdosing of Hsi-men in chapter 79. In the earlier chapter, Hsi-men had insincerely told her: "If I ever betray you, may I suffer the same fate as your Wu the Elder.") Ironically, Lady Wu gives birth to his son a few hours after his death.

The novel's remaining 20 chapters recount the dissolution of Hsi-men's family and business, just as the first 20 showed the growth of both. His second wife, a former sing-song girl, returns to the licensed quarter; while the corpse of her former husband is still warm, Chin-lien begins humping his son-in-law Ching-chi; Hsi-men's various debtors blithely default on the loans he had generously given them; an employee and his wife (the one Hsi-men had been treading) embezzle a large sum of money and escape to the Eastern Capital; followed by similar disgraceful betrayals. Ching-chi soon impregnates his mother-in-law Chin-lien, who aborts the fetus to save face, though word gets out anyway. Several chapters are devoted to their doomed love — it does seem to be love rather than mere lust — and in chapter 86 Lady Wu kicks them both out of her house. Ching-chi goes off to the Eastern Capital to raise the money to buy and marry Chin-lien, but at this point Scoffing Scholar returns to his source and brings back Wu Sung, brother of her first husband Wu Chih, whom she and Hsi-men murdered six years earlier.[144] As in *The Water Margin*, Wu Sung brutally kills Chin-lien and escapes to join the outlaws on Mount Liang.

The last 10 chapters of *PGV* mark the fall of the house of Hsi-men Ch'ing. His various concubines scatter — some to make better marriages, some not — leaving Lady Wu alone with her servants. Feckless Ching-chi is distressed to hear of Chin-lien's death, but soon takes up with a sing-song girl and drives his wife (Hsi-men's daughter) to suicide; losing everything thereafter, he becomes a monk at age 24 and promptly gets buggered by a fellow novice. Of the trio of women alluded to in the novel's title, only Ch'un-mei (Plum Blossom) survives and prospers after Hsi-men's death, but even she eventually dies while copulating with a servant 10 years her junior, yet another martyr to the "fires of passion" (100). The magnificent final chapter, set 15 years after Hsi-men's death, is filled with signs and portents. The invading barbarians from the north — the same that Song Jiang and his rebel band fight in *The Water Margin* — disrupt China and leave it without an emperor, and chaos comes to Ch'ing-ho. Everyone seeks sanctuary at the Buddhist Temple of Eternal

144 Or eight years earlier, by another reckoning. There are some chronological inconsistencies that suggest Scoffing Scholar didn't give the work a final polish, though his early defender Chang Chu-p'o insists the author deliberately took liberties with the chronology for artistic purposes (223–24). In addition, "chapters 53–57 are not extant in their original form," Roy notes. "Textual evidence and linguistic analysis indicate that they must have been supplied by two or more editors, on the basis of clues contained in the chapter titles, which are probably genuine. They are demonstrably inferior to the rest of the work in terms of both internal consistency and literary quality" (3:576–77).

Felicity, where a priest summons the ghosts of all the characters killed in the novel and sends them to the Eastern Capital to be reincarnated — the only supernatural scene in the long novel. Lady Wu fulfills an old vow by giving her son to the priest to become a monk, and after civic order is restored, the pious, conventional lady lives the rest of her life with Hsi-men's crafty but loyal page-boy Tai-an, who inherits his master's property.

The beautifully choreographed barbarian invasion in the final chapter reminds us once again that Scoffing Scholar's theme is the decline not merely of a family but of an empire, and not just the Northern Song empire of the early 12th century but his own *fin-de-siècle* Ming era.[145] Moreover, he uses literary allusion to assert this has been a recurring problem throughout Chinese history: Hsi-men Ch'ing is associated with every bad ruler from King Zhou (of *Creation of the Gods*) and Ying Cheng, first emperor of the Qin dynasty (ruled 221–07 BCE), up to the Emperor Wan-li of the author's own time; similarly, Chin-lien is linked with Zhou's foxy Daji, the goddess of Witch's Mountain who seduced King Huai of the 4th century BCE, Empress Wu (of *The Lord of Perfect Satisfaction*), and every other femme fatale in Chinese history or literature who exerted undue influence over a man. Like Leopold and Molly Bloom, Hsi-men and Chin-lien are archetypes as well as well-rounded characters in a recognizable historical setting; and like Joyce, Scoffing Scholar draws upon an encyclopedic range of references to give his Chinese soap opera some sort of epic grandeur.

Most of the allusions and references are deployed ironically not only to mock the characters but also to deflate Chinese culture in general. Poetic euphemisms like "the world of breeze and moonlight" or "mist and flowers" cover up the sleazy bordello scene like a cheap air-freshener, where Kuan-yin is not the name of a goddess (as in *The Journey to the West*) but of a hooker (13). Hsi-men is often compared to exalted emperors of the past, arousing the suspicion that those emperors were no better than he once stripped of the exaggerated praise bestowed upon them by later poets and historians. Romantic heroines from Chinese literature, it is smugly implied over and over again, were merely horny teenagers, their wistful lovers as duplicitous and sex-crazed as Hsi-men. The ease with which the unqualified, poorly educated Hsi-men attains official appointments due to bribery and cronyism casts a pall on China's political institutions past and present, and China's rich religious history is reduced to tatters after Scoffing Scholar exposes the fraudulent nature of Daoist and Buddhist practices. From the novel's 12th-century setting, he casts a cold eye both forward to his own century and backward over China's past and sees little to admire in a land that paid only lip service to the

---

145 The emperor at this time, Wan-li (ruled 1573–1620), was remote, lascivious, avaricious, and indifferent to his duties, leaving his eunuchs in charge. The Manchu attacked China during this time just as the Tartars do at the end of *PGV*.

Confucian ideals of moderation and self-cultivation.

But sometimes Scoffing Scholar deploys allusions and references for fun, simply to show off his amazing linguistic skills. In one parlor game, "Each player in turn must come up with the name of a song tune, the names of two domino combinations, and a line from the *Hsi-hsiang chi* [*The Story of the Western Wing*], strung together as to make some semblance of sense," as in "'The Sixth Lady,' like a 'Drunken Yang Kuei-fei,' drops her 'Eight-pearled Bracelet,' 'Gossamer strands catch on the rose-leaved raspberry trellis'" (21). (Roy's annotations have to work overtime to explain what *that* means.) In another instance, Chinese literature is the subject of a drinking game:

> "When I throw the dice," Scholar Wên said, "we will have a quotation from some poem, or song, or some classical work, which must have the word 'snow' in it. If we can think of one, we drink a small cup; if not, a large one." He threw a one. "I know," he said, "it is long since snow fell on the wild bird's island." (67)

Elsewhere characters recite poems that work on two levels, a literal one and a figurative one based on specialized terminology. On the one hand, these are occasions for Scoffing Scholar to strut his stuff for the scholarly audience for whom his novel was intended (which justifies Roy's comparisons to Joyce and Nabokov), but on the other, that these characters have reduced China's literary heritage to game clues contributes to his ironic view of "this culture of ours."[146]

Scoffing Scholar uses juxtaposition to achieve his ironic effects. In a comic scene that anticipates the famous one in *Madame Bovary* where Flaubert contrasts Rodolphe's romantic rhetoric with Councilor Lieuvain's speech on patriotic agriculture (2.8), Hsi-men and Chin-lien have noisy sex while a Buddhist ceremony for her dead husband is going on next door (8). (When the bonzes realize what's going on, they're tickled rather than outraged, one of Scoffing Scholar's many assaults on Buddhists in the novel.) Most chapters begin with a lovely poem that violently clashes with the contents that follow; for example, chapter 36 opens with this wistful poem about the wish to send a friendly letter:

> From Fu-ch'uan gazing into the distance
> west of Chien-chiang;
> I see only a solitary cloud formation
> blocking the sunset.
> The tears that I am wont to shed, are
> lost amid the misty trees;

---

146 For more on the novel's puns and puzzles, see Katherine Carlitz's fine book on *The Rhetoric of Chin p'ing mei*, especially pp. 77–82.

> There is no way to transmit a letter,
>> geese and fish are scarce.
> My wish to enquire after you is impeded
>> by three thousand li;
> Separated as we are, I only long in vain
>> all twenty-four hours.
> Broad as the sea and high as Heaven
>> are my thoughts of you;
> On whom can I rely to let you know
>> the fate of my return?

We are then told Hsi-men receives a letter from an important official remind-ing him to supply a teenage girl "for the purpose of procreation" in exchange for some underhanded favors, putting Hsi-men in the role of pimp and caus-ing the reader to wonder how many other letters in Chinese poetry likewise masked sordid agendas.

Scoffing Scholar's most damning juxtaposition is that of money and sex, of conspicuous consumption and erotic excess — in a word, *spending*. Though not used much in the sexual sense since the heyday of Victorian erotica, "to spend" has meant "to have an orgasm" since Shakespeare's time; similarly, the Chinese word *yin* can mean both "licentiousness" and "silver," the primary currency of the novel, and throughout Scoffing Scholar linguistically and structurally juxtaposes Hsi-men's lavish spending and his overactive libido. "In this way," translator Roy explains, "the sexual transactions for which the novel is so notorious are symbolically equated with the economic, politi-cal, and spiritual transactions that also play such a conspicuous part in the narrative."[147] Consequently, readers should be as shocked by a passage like the following — a lavish reception thrown by Hsi-men for some corrupt officials — as by any of the sexual scenes:

> As they proceeded inside, Regional Investigating Censor Sung Ch'iao-nien and Salt-Control Censor Ts'ai Yün were both garbed in robes of scarlet brocade, decorated with an embroidered *hsieh-chih*, a mythical one-horned goat that was said to gore wrongdoers, black silk caps, black shoes, and official girdles featuring plaques of "crane's crest red," and were accompanied by attendants bearing two large flabella.
>> They saw before them a thirty-foot-wide reception hall, in which:
>>> Speckled bamboo blinds were rolled high, and
>>> Brocaded standing screens were arrayed,
>> while in the place of honor there stood two fancy table settings, of a kind intended as much for display as for eating, replete with:

147 1:491 n26, which follows an explanation of how the author symbolically equates semen with silver money. Carlitz notes the two meanings of *yin* (45).

> High-stacked pyramids of square-shaped confectionary,
> Ingot-shaped cakes, and cone-shaped piles of fruit,

all of them meticulously arranged.

The two officials, politely deferring to each other, entered the reception hall in order to exchange amenities with Hsi-men Ch'ing. Salt-Control Censor Ts'ai Yün ordered his retainers to proffer:

> The customary presentation gifts,

consisting of two bolts of Hu-chou silk, the collected literary works of a well-known author, four bags of tender leaf tea, and an inkstone from Tuan-ch'i. . . .

After Hsi-men Ch'ing had seen to the serving of the wine, and sat down to preside over the feast, the various courses were presented from below.

Words are inadequate to describe the scene:

> Only the rarest delicacies are arrayed;
> The soup shows off its peach-red waves;
> The wine overflows with golden ripples.

Truly:

> The singers and dancers display voice and color;
> The tables, ten-foot square, are laden with food.

Hsi-men Ch'ing was aware of the large number of attendants that had accompanied his visitors, so, for the retinues of each of the two sedan chairs, he set aside fifty bottles of wine, five hundred snacks, and a hundred catties of precooked pork, which were duly accepted and taken outside. The personal servants, secretaries, "gate-boys," etc. were separately entertained in an antechamber, but there is no need to describe this in detail. Suffice it to say that it cost Hsi-men all of a thousand taels of silver to put on the banquet that day. (49)

— the cost of a nice house in Ch'ing-ho. Readers should recoil from this no differently than from the scene in which Chin-lien consumes Hsi-men's urine, as the author's ironically juxtaposed allusions suggest. (All those double-indented lines above are quotations from various works.) For example, "The tables, ten-foot square, are laden with food" is from the writings of Mencius, who in his eponymous book is reported to have said:

> "When speaking to men of consequence it is necessary to look on them with contempt and not be impressed by their lofty position. Their hall is tens of feet high; the capitals are several feet broad. Were I to meet with success, I would not indulge in such things. Their tables, laden with food, measure ten feet across, and their female attendants are counted in the hundreds."[148]

Scoffing Scholar's ideal reader would have caught the reference, and a little later would have relished the fact that Hsi-men's lavish reception occurs in

---

148 *Mencius*, trans. D. C. Lau (NY: Penguin, 2004), 165 (7B 34).

the same chapter in which he acquires the aphrodisiacs that will kill him. The stringently moral author sees no difference between the two expenditures. If we're not shocked or disgusted by the above description, it's because we too live in a land of conspicuous consumption, where the lifestyles of the rich and famous are more often envied than scorned, and where captious authors like Mencius and Scoffing Scholar are irrelevant. (Note that among the tainted gifts the Salt-Censor brings are "the collected literary works of a well-known author.") Four centuries later, Bret Easton Ellis would shock readers with the same juxtaposition of conspicuous consumption and sexual violence in *American Psycho* (1991) to satirize the amoral commodity culture of the Reagan Eighties.

Scoffing Scholar's moral philosophy, plainly stated in poems and in asides to the reader, is obvious: live simply and modestly, respect filial relations, read and study, shun excess, and so on. They're simple enough to be stitched on a sampler:

> Worldy wealth, painted faces, and wine
> in the sing-song houses.
> Who is there who is not deluded
> by these three things? (18)

His philosophy is based on neo-Confucianism, particularly the pessimistic views of Hsün Tzu (P Xun Zi, 3rd cent. BCE), but it boils down to living sensibly and avoiding extremes. (Moderation, not abstinence or renunciation; the author's no prude.) Siddhartha, Confucius, Mencius, Aristotle, Jesus, Thoreau, and almost every moral philosopher would side with Scoffing Scholar, but no matter; I'm sure the author wasn't naïve enough to think his novel would change anyone's behavior. What matters is the cunning artistry with which Scoffing Scholar builds his case, marshaling every formal and literary device at his disposal to indict his culture. The ubiquitous singing girls in the novel reinforce Scoffing Scholar's conviction that everyone is a whore to some degree; the girls are more upfront about selling their favors, but as Scoffing Scholar extends his symbolic equation of sex and money to encompass nearly all activities, prostitution becomes the dominant metaphor for his debased society, precious few of whose members cannot be bought.

Other Chinese novelists used similar symbolism and ironic allusions, as we've seen, and paid just as close attention to mathematical structures. Scoffing Scholar's most daring innovation is the one modern readers now take for granted: the novel's realism. Some of the short stories being written at this time are fairly realistic, but *PGV* is the earliest full-length novel to detail the domestic lives of the Chinese: what they ate, what they wore, their pets, religious practices, dishware, how they disciplined servants, renovated houses, arranged marriages, tried law cases, conducted business, the games they played, their hygienic habits, holiday outings, medical practices, the pop songs they listened to, the slang they used, and especially their sexual activities. There are a few novels before this that are sexually candid — Petronius's *Satyricon*, Delicado's *Portrait of Lozana*, Aretino's *Dialogues*, and closer to hand, *The Lord of Perfect Satisfaction* — but not like this. The first time Hsi-men and Chen-lien undress for sex, we're told he wears a cock-ring and she shaves her pubic region as casually as if we're being told the color of their eyes. Most of the sex acts are narrated in lubricious detail — but in no more or less detail than any other activity, it should be noted — and include almost every motive people bring to sexual encounters: tenderness, recreation, drunken lust, loneliness, dominance, self-abasement, self-advancement, procreation, duty, and so on, to which Hsi-men adds various perversions, fetishes, sex toys, role-playing, and experimentation as his sex addiction rages out of control. It wouldn't be until the 20th century that Western novelists dared to write this candidly and insightfully about this most common if complicated of human interactions. Of course Scoffing Scholar's sexual realism was dismissed as pornography by most early readers and his novel banned in China until only recently.[149] When Colonel Egerton published his English translation in 1939, he had to render the sexual passages in Latin to avoid legal prosecution by an immature society *still* too scared of this basic activity to read about it in plain language.[150]

Realism is what many critics insist separates the true, modern novel from older book-length fictions, and for that reason usually assign the honor of the first novel to Defoe's *Robinson Crusoe* (1719) or Richardson's *Pamela* (1740). In Ian Watt's opinion, "the novel is surely distinguished from other genres and from previous forms of fiction by the amount of attention it habitually accords both to the individualisation of its characters and to the detailed presentation of their environment" (*The Rise of the Novel*, 17–18). Even granting that premise — other critics (like myself) feel realism is merely one of many modes of the novel, not the only or defining one — any reader who turns from *The Plum in the Golden Vase* to either of those two novels will immediately be struck by how many details are missing from them, especially concerning physical/sexual matters, how quaintly *un*realistic they are, displaying a faux-realism at best. If a detailed presentation of characters' environment defines a novel, we have to go back more than two centuries to Scoffing Scholar's

---

149 Today apparently everyone knows the novel in China (if only by reputation), where there are betel-nut stands and sex-toy stores named after the novel (Ding xv). Even the Chinese-American waitstaff at the Chia Shiang Restaurant here in Ann Arbor know the novel. I was reading it over dinner there one night, and my waitress agreed Hsi-men had way too many wives.

150 When the book was reprinted in 1972, J. M. Franklin translated the Latin into English, but timidly and quaintly, as though nervously looking over his shoulder for a policeman.

exhaustively detailed presentation of life in old China for the first true novel. Professor Gu, equally at home with Western and Eastern fiction, argues *PGV* not only "conforms to the modern notion of the novel [but] even anticipates some postmodern fictional techniques of fiction-writing" (126, redundancy *sic*). It's not necessarily the *first* realistic novel — see those by Petronius, Murasaki, the Icelanders, Martorell, Aretino, Deloney — but it's the *most* realistic. And regarding "the amount of attention" a novel "accords the individualisation of its characters," the two Englishmen can't hold a candle to their Chinese predecessor. Mr. Robinson Crusoe of York, as Coleridge noted, "is merely a representative of humanity in general; neither his intellectual nor his moral qualities set him above the middle degree of mankind; his only prominent characteristic is the spirit of enterprise and wandering, which is, nevertheless, a very common disposition."[151] If he's a type rather than a well-rounded character, Miss Pamela Andrews is a stereotype: a proper, prudish virgin, culturally constructed to within an inch of her life.

Ah, but P'an Chin-lien, the Golden Lotus! There's a well-rounded, completely realized *individual*. Although Scoffing Scholar didn't invent her, he lavished all his considerable artistry on her to create a richly complex character, one who fascinates as much as she repulses, who earns both our sympathy and antipathy, a difficult feat to pull off. The author began by taking special pains over her background, discarding the one given in *The Water Margin* — a pretty maid put off by her master's advances complains to his wife, who forces her husband to sell her to a midget in revenge — and instead drew upon other literary sources. He makes her the daughter of a poor tailor, after whose death she is sold at age eight into the household of an imperial commissioner, where she learns music and drawing, not to mention the art of seduction; "She was adept at:

> Painting her brows and making up her eyes,
> Applying powder and putting on rouge,
> Combing her hair into a chignon,
> Wearing form-fitting gowns,
> Putting on airs,
> And making a spectacle of herself. (1)

The author took these lines from a Ming short story entitled "Lovers Murdered at a Rendezvous" (*Wen-ching yüan-yang hui*), "which has for heroine a *femme fatale* of inordinate sexual appetite who ruins physically or financially all the

---

151 From *Coleridge's Miscellaneous Criticism* (1936), as abridged in the Norton Critical Edition of *Robinson Crusoe*, 268.

men she captivates."[152] After the commissioner dies, her mother recovers Chin-lien and resells her to a prosperous merchant named Chang, whom Scoffing Scholar found in another story, "Zhang Zhicheng the Manager Escapes an Extraordinary Calamity" (*Chih-ch'eng Chang chu-kuan*).[153] In this story, Chang is over 60 years old, "but instead of reconciling himself to his age, he indulged in the pleasures of the flesh until he dissipated all his family fortune and almost ended up a ghost in an alien land," which of course foreshadows Hsi-men's fate. In *PGV*, Chang rapes Chin-lien when she's 17, after which he sickens with syphilitic symptoms and dies, the first of the half-dozen people our fatal femme kills directly or indirectly over the course of the novel. Before he dies, Cheng sells Chin-lien to the dwarfish peddler Wu, a highly inappropriate match for a young lady now possessing a fine education, artistic talents, and stunning beauty. To expect such a woman to accept a mundane marriage would give even Confucius pause, and in this way the author cunningly creates a cognitive dissonance in the mind of the reader, who knows that Chin-lien deserves a better life after such a harsh upbringing, yet is aware of the red flags the author has raised with those two background stories, which his readers would have recognized. (In the second story, the young wife tries to seduce her old husband's young employee; he resists, and later learns she died earlier and is now a tempting ghost.) Stuck in an unsatisfying relationship and bored to death, this desperate housewife spends her days standing behind the bamboo door-curtain to her house, all dolled up and trying to attract attention, "cracking melon seeds with her teeth, and revealing her tiny lotuses [feet] for all to see" (1), and soon catches the eye of Hsi-men; the rest you know. Her actions are disgraceful but thoroughly understandable, and Scoffing Scholar skillfully maintains this balancing act throughout the long, long novel.

She's the smartest woman in the novel, the most sensuous, well-read and accomplished in embroidery and on the *p'i-p'a* (a kind of lute), nobody's fool, and even though she's a kind of bride of Frankenstein assembled from parts of other Chinese vixens, she's the most realistic character in the novel (in Watt's sense), the most lifelike. She resembles the portrait of Ch'un-mei that Hsi-men commissions after her death: "the only thing it lacked was breath" (63). More often than with any other character in the novel, we are privy to her thoughts and see her alone, seething with anger, boredom, jealousy, despair, or erotic longing. This Chinese Madame Bovary, this Lady Macbeth

---

152 Hanan, "Sources of the *Chin p'ing mei*," 34. English translations of the story are available in McLaren's *Chinese Femme Fatale* (41–57) and Feng Menglong's *Stories to Caution the World* (649–61).

153 Also in *Stories to Caution the World*, 250–60. (The quotation that follows is on pp. 250–51.) Although they are outside the scope of this study, I can't say enough about these Chinese short stories: each one I've read is wonderful. Feng's three 17th-century anthologies gather the bulk of them (see bibliography).

of Ch'ing-ho, this Salome of Shantung Province is one of the most fully real-ized characters in world literature. Just as Scoffing Scholar revived her from her premature death in *The Water Margin*, others would revive for sequels, adaptations, and — in our day — movies. A great character needs a great novel to support her, and in *The Plum in the Golden Vase* we have perhaps the greatest novel written before the modern era — only *The Tale of Genji* rivals it — and an aesthetic delight for those willing to plumb its depths. Truly:

> The burden of the tale contains
> a deep meaning;
> The topic of the story conceals
> a hidden intent.

Yüeh-niang, however, was a straightforward person. How could she be expected to understand:

> The story within the story?

We will say no more, at present, about how the ladies ate their crabs. (35)

Had someone in 1600 been able to acquire and read all of the fiction published up to that time — from the proto-novels of the Egyptians and Assyrians to the early novels of the Greeks and Romans, the later novels of the Irish, Icelanders, medieval Jews, and Spaniards, the tales of Arthur, the accomplished novels of Renaissance scriveners, the spicy novels of India, the vast adventure novels of the Arabs, and the sophisticated works of Persia and the Far East — that person might have guessed that the future of fiction lay in China. But that person would have been wrong. Though the Chinese continued to produce fine novels for another century and a half, the novel would show the greatest growth not in the East but in the West, beginning in Spain, as it happens, where a failed writer imagined a man of La Mancha who had been driven loco by reading too many novels.

Bibliography

PRIMARY WORKS: FICTION AND ANTHOLOGIES

Achilles Tatius. *Leucippe and Clitophon.* Trans. Tim Whitmarsh. NY: Oxford UP, 2001.

Adomnán of Iona. *Life of St. Columba.* Ed. Richard Sharpe. NY: Penguin, 1995.

The Adventures of Amir Hamza, Lord of the Auspicious Planetary Conjunction. Ed. Ghalib Lakhnavi and Abdullah Bilgrami. Trans. Musharraf Ali Farooqi. NY: Modern Library, 2007.

The Adventures of Antar. Trans. H. T. Norris. Warminster, UK: Aris & Phillips, 1980.

The Adventures of Hamza. Trans. Wheeler M. Thackston. Ed. John Seyller. London: Azimuth/Washington, DC: Smithsonian Institution, 2002.

The Adventures of Hatim Tai. Trans. Duncan Forbes. London: Oriental Translation Fund, 1830.

The Adventures of Sayf ben Dhi Yazan: An Arab Folk Epic. Trans. Lena Jayyusi. Bloomington: Indiana UP, 1996.

Akinari, Ueda. *Tales of Moonlight and Rain.* Trans. Anthony H. Chambers. NY: Columbia UP, 2007.

Alberti, Leon Battista. *Momus.* Trans. Sarah Knight. Cambridge: Harvard UP, 2003.

Alemán, Mateo. *The Amusing Adventures of Guzman of Alfaraque.* Trans. Edward Lowdell. London: Vizetelly, 1883.

al-Hamadhani. *The Maqamat of Badīʿ al-Zamān al-Hamadhānī.* Trans. W. J. Prendergast. London: Luzac, 1915.

al-Hariri. *The Assemblies.* Trans. Thomas Cheney and F. Steingass. 2 vols. London: Royal Asiatic Society, 1867, 1898.

———. Trans. Amina Shah. London: Octagon, 1980.

Alharizi, Judah. *The Book of Tahkemoni: Jewish Tales from Medieval Spain.* Trans. David Simha Segal. Oxford, UK: Littman Library of Jewish Civilization, 2001.

Alter, Robert. *The David Story: A Translation with Commentary of 1 and 2 Samuel.* NY: Norton, 1999.

———. *The Five Books of Moses: A Translation with Commentary.* NY: Norton, 2004.

al-Varavini, Sa'd al-Din. *The Tales of Marzuban.* Trans. Reuben Levy. Bloomington: Indiana UP, 1959.

Andrea da Barberino. *Il Guerrin meschino.* Ed. Mauro Cursietti. Rome: Antenore, 2005.

Aneau, Barthélemy. Αλεκτορ: *The Cock.* Trans. anon. London: Thomas Orwin, 1590.

Antar: A Bedoueen Romance. Trans. Terrick Hamilton. 4 vols. London: John Murray, 1819–20.

Apuleius. *The Golden Ass*. Trans. Robert Graves. 1950. NY: Pocket, 1954.

———. Trans. Jack Lindsay. Bloomington: Indiana UP, 1960.

———. Trans. P. G. Walsh. NY: Oxford UP, 1994.

———. Trans. E. J. Kenney. NY: Penguin, 1998.

———. *The Golden Ass, or, A Book of Changes*. Trans. Joel C. Relihan. Indianapolis: Hackett, 2007.

The Arabian Nights. Trans. Husain Haddawy. 1990. NY: Everyman's Library, 1992.

The Arabian Nights II. Trans. Husain Haddawy. 1995. NY: Everyman's Library, 1998.

The Arabian Nights: Tales of 1001 Nights. Trans. Malcolm C. and Ursula Lyons. 3 vols. London: Penguin, 2008.

Arabian Nights' Entertainments. Trans. anon. (from the French translation of Antoine Galland). 1704–17. Ed. Robert L. Mack. Oxford: Oxford UP, 1995.

Aretino, Pietro. *Dialogues*. Trans. Raymond Rosenthal. 1971. NY: Marsilio, 1994.

Arrow-Odd: A Medieval Novel. Trans. Hermann Pálsson and Paul Edwards. NY: New York UP, 1970.

Ashley, Robert, and Edwin M. Moseley, eds. *Elizabethan Fiction*. NY: Rinehart, 1953.

Athanasius. *Life of Antony*, 7–70. In *Early Christian Lives*. Ed. Carolinne White. NY: Penguin, 1998.

Athenaeus. *The Deipnosophists, or Banquet of the Learned*. Trans. C. D. Yonge. 3 vols. London: Bohn, 1854.

———. *The Learned Banqueters*. Trans. S. Douglas Olson. 7 vols. Loeb Classical Library. Cambridge: Harvard UP, 2006– .

Austen, Jane. *Northanger Abbey, Lady Susan, The Watsons, Sandition*. Ed. James Kinsley, John Davie, and Claudia L. Johnson. NY: Oxford UP, 2003.

The Bakhtyar Nama: A Persian Romance. Trans. Sir William Ouseley. Larkhall, UK: W. Burns, 1883.

The Balavariani (Barlaam and Josaphat): A Tale from the Christian East. Trans. David Marshall Lang. Berkeley: U California P, 1966.

Baldwin, William. *Beware the Cat: The First English Novel*. Ed. William A. Ringler, Jr., and Michael Flachmann. San Marino, CA: Huntington Library, 1988.

Ballaster, Ros, ed. *Fables of the East: Selected Tales 1662–1785*. NY: Oxford UP, 2005.

Bana. *The Harsa-carita*. Trans. E. B. Cowell and F. W. Thomas. 1897. Delhi: Motilal Banarsidass, 1961.

———. *The Harshacarita of Bāṇabhaṭṭa*. Ed. P. V. Kane. 1918. Delhi: Motilal Banarsidass, 1965.

———. *The Kadambari*. Trans. C. M. Ridding. 1895. New Delhi: Oriental Books Reprint Corp., 1974.

———[Banabhatta]. *Kādambarī: A Classic Sanskrit Story of Magical Transformations*. Trans. Gwendolyn Layne. NY: Garland, 1991.

———. *Princess Kadambari*. Trans. David Smith. 3 vols. NY: New York UP/Clay Sanskrit Library, 2009– .

Bandello, Matteo. *The Novels*. Trans. John Payne. 6 vols. London: Villon Society, 1890.

The Banquet of Dun na n-Gedh and The Battle of Magh Rath: An Ancient Historical Tale. Trans. John O'Donovan. Dublin: Irish Archaeological Society, 1842.

Barnstone, Willis, ed. *The Other Bible*. San Francisco: HarperCollins, 1984.

———. *The New Covenant: The Four Gospels and Apocalypse*. NY: Riverhead, 2002.

———. *The Restored New Testament: A New Translation with Commenatry*. NY: Norton, 2009.

———, and Marvin Meyer, eds. *The Gnostic Bible*. Boston: Shambhala, 2003.

Basile, Giambattista. *The Tale of Tales, or Entertainment for Little Ones*. Trans. Nancy L. Canepa. Detroit: Wayne State UP, 2007.

Beowulf: A Dual-Language Edition. Trans. Howell D. Chickering, Jr. 1977. NY: Anchor, 2006.

Betts, Gavin, trans. *Three Medieval Greek Romances*: Velthandros and Chrysandza, Kallimachos and Chrysorroi, Livistros and Rodamni. NY: Garland, 1995.

Bialik, Hayim Nahman, and Yehoshua Hana Ravnitzky, eds. *The Book of Legends / Sefer Ha-Aggadah: Legends from the Talmud and Midrash*. Trans. William G. Braude. NY: Schocken, 1992.

Bighami, Muhammad ibn Ahmad. *Love and War: Adventures from the* Firuz Shāh Nāma *of Sheik Bighami*. Trans. William L. Hanaway, Jr. Delmar, NY: Scholar's Facsimiles & Reprints, 1974.

Bigolina, Giulia. *Urania: A Romance*. Trans. Valeria Finucci. Chicago: U Chicago P, 2005.

Black, Jeremy, Graham Cunningham, Eleanor Robson, and Gábor Zólyomi, eds. *The Literature of Ancient Sumer*. 2004. Oxford, UK: Oxford UP, 2006.

Bloom, Harold, ed., and David Rosenberg, trans. *The Book of J*. NY: Grove Weidenfeld, 1990.

Boccaccio, Giovanni. *Il Filocolo*. Trans. Donald Cheney with the collaboration of Thomas G. Bergin. NY: Garland, 1985.

———. *L'Ameto*. Trans. Judith Serafini-Sauli. NY: Garland, 1985.

———. *The Elegy of Lady Fiammetta*. Trans. Nariangela Causa-Steindler and Thomas Mauch. Chicago: U Chicago P, 1990.

———. *The Decameron*. Trans. Mark Musa and Peter E. Bondanella. NY: Norton, 1977.

———. Trans. G. H. McWilliam. 2nd ed. NY: Penguin, 1995.

———. *The Corbaccio, or The Labyrinth of Love*. Trans. Anthony K. Cassell. Rev. ed. Binghamton, NY: Pegasus, 1993.

The Book of Counsel: The Popol Vuh of the Quiche Maya of Guatemala. Trans. Munro S. Edmonson. New Orleans: Middle American Research Institute/Tulane University, 1971.

The Book of Enoch or Enoch I. Trans. Matthew Black. Leiden: Brill, 1985.

The Book of Sindibad; or, The Story of the King, His Son, the Damsel, and the Seven Viziers. Trans. W. A. Clouston. Glasgow: J. Cameron, 1884.

The Book of the Thousand Nights and a Night. Trans. Richard F. Burton. 1885–86. 3 vols. NY: Heritage, 1962.

The Book of the Thousand Nights and One Night. Trans. John Payne. 1882–84. 9 vols. London: privately printed ("Herat Edition"), 1901.

———. Trans. Powys Mathers (from the French translation of J. C. Mardrus). 1923. 4 vols. NY: Routledge, 1986.

Breton, Nicholas. *A Mad World My Masters and Other Prose Works*. Ed. Ursula Kentish-Wright. 2 vols. London: Cresset, 1929.

Budhasvamin. *The Emperor of the Sorcerers.* Trans. Sir James Mallinson. 2 vols. NY: New York UP/Clay Sanskrit Library, 2005.

Buile Suibhne (The Frenzy of Suibhne) being the Adventures of Suibhne Geilt: A Middle-Irish Romance. Trans. J. G. O'Keeffe. London: Irish Texts Society, 1913.

Caldwell, Ian, and Dustin Thomason. *The Rule of Four.* NY: Dial, 2004.

Campbell, Anthony F., and Mark A. O'Brien, eds. *Unfolding the Deuteronomistic History: Origins, Upgrades, Present Text.* Minneapolis: Fortress Press, 2000.

Cartigny, Jean [de]. *The Wandering Knight.* Trans. William Goodyear. Ed. Dorothy Atkinson Evans. Seattle: U Washington P, 1951.

Castle, Terry, ed. *The Literature of Lesbianism: A Historical Anthology from Ariosto to Stonewall.* NY: Columbia UP, 2003.

Cervantes Saavedra, Miguel de. *Galatea: A Pastoral Romance.* Trans. Gordon Willoughby James Gyll. London: Bell and Daldy, 1867.

———. *Don Quijote.* Trans. Burton Raffel. Ed. Diana de Armas Wilson. NY: Norton, 1999.

———. *Don Quixote.* Trans. Edith Grossman. NY: Ecco, 2003.

Chandra, Vikram. *Red Earth and Pouring Rain.* Boston: Little, Brown, 1995.

Chang Wen-ch'eng. *The Dwelling of Playful Goddesses: China's First Novelette.* Trans. Howard S. Levy. Tokyo: Dai Nippon Insatsu, 1965.

The Changelings: A Classical Japanese Court Tale. Trans. Rosette F. Willig. Stanford: Stanford UP, 1983.

Chariton. *Callirhoe.* Trans. G. P. Goold. Cambridge: Harvard UP, 1995.

Charlesworth, James H., ed. *The Old Testament Pseudepigrapha.* 2 vols. NY: Doubelday, 1983, 1985.

Chaucer, Geoffrey. *The Canterbury Tales.* Ed. Jill Mann. NY: Penguin, 2005.

Chettle, Henry. *Piers Plainness: Seven Years' Prenticeship,* 122–74. In *The Descent of Euphues: Three Elizabethan Romance Stories.* Ed. James Winny. Cambridge: Cambridge UP, 1957.

Chrétien de Troyes. *The Complete Romances.* Trans. David Staines. Bloomington: Indiana UP, 1990.

The Codex Nuttall: A Picture Manuscript from Ancient Mexico. Ed. Zelia Nuttall. NY: Dover, 1975.

Colonna, Francesco. *Hypnerotomachia Poliphili: The Strife of Love in a Dream.* Trans. Joscelyn Godwin. NY: Thames & Hudson, 1999.

Coogan, Michael David, ed. *Stories from Ancient Canaan.* Louisville: Westminster, 1978.

Crenne, Hélisenne de. *The Torments of Love.* Trans. Lisa Neal and Steven Rendall. Minneapolis: U Minnesota P, 1996.

———. *A Renaissance Woman: Helisenne's Personal and Invective Letters.* Trans. Marianna M. Mustacchi and Paul J. Archambault. Syracuse: Syracuse UP, 1986.

Cross, Tom Peete, and Clark Harris Slover, ed. and trans. *Ancient Irish Tales.* NY: Holt, 1936.

Dalley, Stephanie, ed. and trans. *Myths from Mesopotamia: Creation, the Flood, Gilgamesh, and Others.* Rev. ed. Oxford: Oxford UP, 2000.

Damodaragupta. *The Art of the Temptress.* Trans. B. P. L. Bedi. Bombay: Pearl, 1968.

————. *The Bawd's Counsel*. Trans. Csaba Dezső and Dominic Goodall. NY: New York UP/Clay Sanskrit Library, forthcoming.

Dandin. *Daśakumāracarita*. Trans. M. R. Kale. 1925. Delhi: Motilal Banarsidass, 1966.

————. *What Ten Young Men Did*. Trans. Isabelle Onians. NY: New York UP/Clay Sanskrit Library, 2005.

The Death of King Arthur. Trans. James Cable. NY: Penguin, 1971.

Defoe, Daniel. *Robinson Crusoe*. Ed Michael Shinagel. 2nd ed. NY: Norton, 1994.

de León, Moses. *Zohar: The Book of Enlightenment*. Trans. Daniel Chanan Matt. Mahwah, NJ: Paulist Press, 1983.

————. *Mystic Tales from the Zohar*. Trans. Aryeh Wineman. 1997. Princeton: Princeton UP, 1998.

————. *The Zohar*. Pritzker Edition. Trans. Daniel C. Matt. 10 vols. Stanford: Stanford UP, 2003–.

Delicado, Francisco. *Portrait of Lozana: The Lusty Andalusian Woman*. Trans. Bruno M. Damiani. Potomac, MD: Scripta Humanistica, 1987.

Deloney, Thomas. *The Novels*. Ed. Merritt E. Lawlis. Bloomington: Indiana UP, 1961.

Dickens, Charles. *Our Mutual Friend*. NY: Penguin, 1997.

Eco, Umberto. *The Name of the Rose, Including the Author's Postscript*. Trans. William Weaver. San Diego: Harvest, 1994.

Erasmus, Desiderius. *The Praise of Folly and Other Writings*. Ed. and trans. Robert M. Adams. NY: Norton, 1989.

Erman, Adolf, ed. *The Literature of the Ancient Egyptians*. Trans. Aylward M. Blackman. NY: Dutton, 1927.

Eugenianos, Niketas. *A Byzantine Novel: Drosilla and Charikles*. Trans. Joan B. Burton. Wauconda, IL: Bolchazy-Carducci, 2004.

Euthymius; see John Damascene

Feng Menglong, ed. *Stories Old and New: A Ming Dynasty Collection*. Trans. Shuhui and Yunqin Yang. Seattle: U Washington P, 2000.

————. *Stories to Caution the World: A Ming Dynasty Collection, Volume 2*. Trans. Shuhui and Yunqin Yang. Seattle: U Washington P, 2005.

————. *Stories to Awaken the World: A Ming Dynasty Collection, Volume 3*. Trans. Shuhui and Yunqin Yang. Seattle: U Washington P, 2009.

Ferdowsi, Abolqasem. *Shahnameh: The Persian Book of Kings*. Trans. Dick Davis. NY: Viking, 2006.

The Flower Ornament Scripture: A Translation of the Avatamsaka Sutra. Trans. Thomas Cleary. Boston: Shambhala, 1993.

Ford, Emanuel. *The Most Pleasant History of Ornatus and Artesia*. Ed. Goran Stanivukovic. Ottawa: Dovehouse, 2003.

Foster, Benjamin R., ed. *From Distant Days: Myths, Tales, and Poetry of Ancient Mesopotamia*. Bethesda, MD: CDL Press, 1995.

Foster, John L., ed. and trans. *Ancient Egyptian Literature: An Anthology*. Austin: U Texas P, 2001.

Fox, Everett, trans. *The Five Books of Moses*. NY: Schocken, 1997.

————. *Give Us a King! Samuel, Saul, and David*. NY: Schocken, 1999.

Friedman, Richard Elliott, trans. *In the Day*. In *The Hidden Book in the Bible*. San Francisco: HarperCollins, 1998.

————. *The Bible with Sources Revealed.* San Francisco: HarperCollins, 2003.

Fujiwara Teika. *The Tale of Matsura: Fujiwara Teika's Experiment in Fiction.* Trans. Wayne P. Lammers. Ann Arbor: Center for Japanese Studies/University of Michigan, 1992.

Gaddis, William. *The Recognitions.* 1955. NY: Penguin, 1993.

————. *J R.* 1975. NY: Penguin, 1993.

————. *Carpenter's Gothic.* NY: Viking, 1985.

————. *A Frolic of His Own.* NY: Poseidon, 1994.

Gantz, Jeffrey, ed. and trans. *Early Irish Myths and Sagas.* NY: Penguin, 1981.

Giovanni Fiorentino, Ser. *The Pecorone.* Trans. W. G. Waters. 3 vols. London: Society of Bibliophiles, 1898.

Gorgani, Fakhraddin. *See* Gurgani, Fakhr ud-Din.

Grange, John. *The Golden Aphroditis and Grange's Garden.* NY: Scholars' Facsimiles & Reprints, 1939.

Granoff, Phyllis, ed. *The Clever Adulteress and Other Stories: A Treasury of Jain Literature.* Oakville, Ontario: Mosaic, 1990.

The Greek Alexander Romance. Trans. Richard Stoneman. NY: Penguin, 1991.

Greene, Robert. *Gwydonius, or The Card of Fancy.* Ed. Carmine G. Di Biase. Ottawa: Dovehouse, 2001.

————. *Planetomachia.* Ed. Nandini Das. Aldershot, UK: Ashgate, 2007.

————. *Menaphon: Camilla's Alarm to Slumbering Euphues in His Melancholy Cell at Silexedra.* Ed. Brenda Cantar. Ottawa: Dovehouse, 1996.

————, and Thomas Lodge. *Menaphon* [and] A *Margarite of America.* Ed. G. B. Harrison. Oxford: Basil Blackwell, 1927.

Grettir's Saga. Trans. Denton Fox and Hermann Pálsson. Toronto: U Toronto P, 1974.

Gurgani, Fakhr ud-Din. *Vis and Ramin.* Trans. George Morrison. NY: Columbia UP, 1972.

————. *Vis and Ramin.* Trans. Dick Davis. Washington, DC: Mage, 2008.

The Heavenly Exploits: Buddhist Biographies from the Dívyavadána. Trans. Joel Tatelman. NY: New York UP/Clay Sanskrit Library, 2005.

"*Heiji monogatari*: A Study and Annotated Translation of the Oldest Text." Trans. Marisa Chalitpatanangune. Ph.D. diss., University of California at Berkeley, 1987.

Heliodorus. *An Ethiopian Romance.* Trans. Moses Hadas. Ann Arbor: U Michigan P, 1957.

Henderson, Philip, ed. *Shorter Novels, Volume 2: Jacobean and Restoration.* London: Dent/Everyman's Library, 1930.

The High Book of the Grail: A Translation of the Thirteenth Century Romance Perlesvaus. Trans. Nigel Bryant. Cambridge: Brewer, 1978.

The History of Fulk Fitz Warine: An Outlawed Baron in the Reign of King John. Trans. Thomas Wright. London: The Warton Club, 1855.

Hōgen monogatari: Tale of the Disorder in Hōgen. Trans. William R. Wilson. 1971. Ithaca: East Asia Program, Cornell U, 2001.

Huang Xun (attributed). *The Fountainhead of Chinese Erotica: The Lord of Perfect Satisfaction (*Ruyijun zhuan). Trans. Charles R. Stone. Honolulu: U Hawaii P, 2003.

Ibn al-Muqaffa, Abdullah. *Kalilah and Dimnah.* Trans. Thomas Ballantine Irving. Newark, DE: Juan de la Cuesta, 1980.

————. *The Fables of Kalilah and Dimnah*. Trans. Saleh Sa'adeh Jallad. London: Melisende, 2002.

————. *The Fables of Kalilah and Dimnah*. Trans. Saleh Sa'adeh Jallad. London: Melisende, 2002.

Ibn Tufayl, Abu Bakr. *Hayy ibn Yaqzān*. Trans. Lenn Evan Goodman. 4th ed. Los Angeles: gee tee bee, 1996.

Irwin, Robert, ed. *Night and Horses and the Desert: An Anthology of Classical Arabic Literature*. Woodstock: Overlook, 2000.

Iskandarnamah: A Persian Medieval Alexander-Romance. Trans. Minoo S. Southgate. NY: Columbia UP, 1978.

Izumi Shikibu. *The Izumi Shikibu Diary: A Romance of the Heian Court*. Trans. Edwin A. Cranston. Cambridge: Harvard UP, 1969.

Jacobsen, Thorkild, ed. *The Harps That Once . . . : Sumerian Poetry in Translation*. New Haven: Yale UP, 1987.

Jambhaladatta. *Jambhaladatta's Version of the* Vetālapañcaviṅśati. Trans. M. B. Emeneau. New Haven: American Oriental Society, 1934.

Jami, Mawlana Nur al-Din Abd al-Rahman. *The Book of Joseph and Zuleikha*. Trans. Alexander Rogers. London: David Nutt, 1892.

————. *Yusuf and Zulaikha*. Trans. David Pendlebury. London: Octagon, 1980.

Jātaka Tales. Ed. H. T. Francis and E. J. Thomas. Trans. E. B. Cowell. Cambridge: Cambridge UP, 1916.

Jean d'Arras. *A Bilingual Edition of Jean d'Arras's* Mélusine *or* L'Histoire de Lusignan. Trans. Matthew W. Morris. 2 vols. Lewiston, NY: Edwin Mellen, 2007.

The Jewish Study Bible (New JPS *Tanakh* translation [1985]). Ed. Adele Berlin and Marc Zvi Brettler. NY: Oxford UP, 2004.

John Damascene (attributed). *Barlaam and Ioasaph*. Trans. G. R. Woodward and H. Mattingly. Cambridge: Harvard UP, 1967.

Journey to the North: An Ethnohistorical Analysis and Annotated Translation of the Chinese Folk Novel Pei-yu chi. Trans. Gary Seaman. Berkeley: U California P, 1987.

Joyce, James. *A Portrait of the Artist as a Young Man*. 1916. NY: Penguin, 2003.

————. *Ulysses: The Corrected Text*. Ed. Hans Walter Gabler. 1922. NY: Random House, 1986.

————. *Finnegans Wake*. 1939. NY: Viking, 1960 ("embodying all author's corrections").

Judah ha-Levi. *See* Yehudah HaLevi.

Kakuichi. *The Tale of the Heike*. Trans. Hiroshi Kitagawa with Bruce T. Tsuchida. Tokyo: U Tokyo P, 1975.

————. Trans. Helen Craig McCullough. Stanford: Stanford UP, 1988.

Kerouac, Jack. *On the Road: The Original Scroll*. NY: Viking, 2007.

King Artus: A Hebrew Arthurian Romance of 1279. Trans. Curt Leviant. 1969. Syracuse: Syracuse UP, 2003.

King Vikram and the Vampire. Trans. Sir Richard F. Burton. 1870. Rochester, VT: Park Street, 1992.

King Wu's Expedition against Zhou, 10–75. In Liu Ts'un-yan, *Buddhist and Taoist Influences on Chinese Novels, Volume 1: The Authorship of the* Feng Shen Yen I. Wiesbaden: Otto Harrassowitz, 1962.

The Knight of the Parrot. Trans. Thomas E. Vesce. NY: Garland, 1986.

Kojima. *The Taiheiki: A Chronicle of Medieval Japan.* Trans. Helen Craig McCullough. 1959. Rutland, VT: Tuttle, 1979.

Ko Un. *Little Pilgrim.* Trans. Brother Anthony of Taizé and Young-Moo Kim. Berkeley: Parallax, 2005.

Kritzeck, James, ed. *Anthology of Islamic Literature.* NY: Mentor, 1966.

Kukai. *Major Works.* Trans. Yoshito S. Hakeda. NY: Columbia UP, 1972.

Lalitavistara. Trans. Bijoya Goswami. Kolkata: The Asiatic Society, 2001.

Lancelot-Grail: The Old French Arthurian Vulgate and Post-Vulgate in Translation. Ed. Norris J. Lacy. Various translators. 5 vols. NY: Garland, 1993–96.

The Lancelot-Grail Reader: Selections from the Medieval French Arthurian Cycle. Ed. Norris J. Lacy. Various translators. NY: Garland, 2000.

Lancelot of the Lake. Trans. Corin Corley. Oxford: Oxford UP, 1989.

La Sale, Antoine de. *Little John of Saintré.* Trans. Irvine Gray. London: Routledge, 1931.

Lattimore, Richmond, trans. *The New Testament.* NY: North Point, 1996.

Lawlis, Merritt, ed. *Elizabethan Prose Fiction.* Indianapolis: Odyssey, 1967.

Lazarillo de Tormes, 21–79. In *Two Spanish Picaresque Novels.* Trans. Michael Alpert. NY: Penguin, 1969.

The Legend of Lord Eight Deer: An Epic of Ancient Mexico. Retold and illustrated by John M. D. Pohl. NY: Oxford UP, 2002.

León-Portilla, Miguel, ed. *Pre-Columbian Literatures of Mexico.* Trans. Grace Lobanov and the author. Norman: U Oklahoma P, 1969.

———, and Earl Shorris, eds. *In the Language of Kings: An Anthology of Mesoamerican Literature — Pre-Columbian to the Present.* NY: Norton, 2001.

Levy, Reuben, trans. *The Three Dervishes and Other Persian Tales and Legends.* Oxford: Oxford UP, 1923.

Lewis, Bernard, and Stanley Burstein, eds. *Land of Enchanters: Egyptian Short Stories from the Earliest Times to the Present Day.* 1948. Rev. ed. Princeton: Markus Wiener, 2001.

Lichtheim, Miriam, ed. and trans. *Ancient Egyptian Literature.* 3 vols. Berkeley: U California P, 1973–80.

Lodge, Thomas. *Rosalynd.* Ed. Brian Nellist. Keele, UK: Keele UP, 1995.

———. *A Margarite of America;* see under Greene, Robert.

Longus. *Daphnis and Chloe.* Trans. J. M. Edmonds; Parthenius, *Love Romances and Other Fragments.* Trans. Stephen Gaselee. Cambridge: Harvard UP, 1916.

The Lotus Sutra. Trans. Burton Watson. NY: Columbia UP, 1993.

Lovecraft, H. P. *Tales.* Ed. Peter Straub. NY: Library of America, 2005.

Lucian. *Chattering Courtesans and Other Sketches.* Trans. Keith Sidwell. NY: Penguin, 2004.

Lull, Ramón. *Blanquerna.* Trans. Edgar Allison Peers. 1925. London: Dedalus, 1997.

Luo Guanzhong (attributed). *Three Kingdoms: A Historical Novel.* Trans. Moss Roberts. 2 vols. 1994. Berkeley: U California P, 2004.

———. Introduction by Shi Changyu. 1995. 4 vols. Beijing: Foreign Languages Press, 2004.

———— and Shi Nai-an (attributed). *Outlaws of the Marsh*. Trans. Sidney Shapiro. 1981. 4 vols. Beijing: Foreign Languages Press, 2003.

————. *The Marshes of Mount Liang*. Trans. John and Alex Dent-Young. 5 vols. Hong Kong: Chinese UP, 1994–2002.

Lyly, John. *Euphues: The Anatomy of Wit* and *Euphues and His England*. Ed. Leah Scragg. Manchester: Manchester UP, 2003.

Ma, Yau-Woon, and Joseph S. M. Lau, eds. *Traditional Chinese Stories: Themes and Variations*. NY: Columbia UP, 1987

Machado de Assis, Joaquim Maria. *Quincas Borba*. Trans. Gregory Rabassa. NY: Oxford UP, 1998.

The Mahavastu. Trans. J. J. Jones. 3 vols. London: Luzac, 1949–56.

Mahfouz, Naguib. *Voices from the Other World: Ancient Egyptian Tales*. Cairo: American U in Cairo P, 2002.

Malory, Sir Thomas. *Le Morte Darthur*. Ed. R. M. Lumiansky. NY: Scribners, 1982.

————. Ed. Stephen H. A. Shepherd. NY: Norton, 2004.

Manjhan. *Madhumalati: An Indian Sufi Romance*. Trans. Aditya Behl and Simon Weightman. NY: Oxford UP, 2000.

Marguerite de Navarre. *The Heptameron*. Trans. Paul A. Chilton. London: Penguin, 1984.

Markman, Roberta H., and Peter T. Markman, eds. *The Flayed God: The Mesoamerican Mythological Tradition*. NY: HarperCollins, 1992.

Martorell, Joanot, and Martí Joan de Galba. *Tirant lo Blanc*. Trans. David H. Rosenthal. 1984. Baltimore: Johns Hopkins UP, 1996.

————. Trans. Ray La Fontaine. NY: Peter Lang, 1993.

Maso, Carole. *Aureole*. Hopewell, NJ: Ecco, 1996.

Mason, Eugene, trans. *Aucassin and Nicolette and Other Medieval Romances and Legends*. 1910. NY: Dutton, 1958.

Masuccio. *The Novellino*. Trans. W. G. Waters. 2 vols. London: Lawrence & Bullen, 1895.

Matarasso, Pauline, trans. *Aucassin and Nicolette and Other Tales*. Harmondsworth, UK: Penguin, 1971.

Matthews, Victor H., and Don C. Benjamin, eds. *Old Testament Parallels: Laws and Stories from the Ancient Near East*. Mahwah, NJ: Paulist Press, 1997.

McCullough, Helen Craig, ed. *Classical Japanese Prose: An Anthology*. Stanford: Stanford UP, 1990.

McLaren, Anne E., trans. *The Chinese Femme Fatale: Stories from the Ming Period*. Sydney: Wild Peony, 1994.

Melville, Herman. *Moby-Dick*. Ed. Hershel Parker and Harrison Hayford. 2nd ed. NY: Norton, 2002.

Merutunga Acarya. *The Prabandhacintāmani, or Wishing-Stone of Narratives*. Trans. C. H. Tawney. 1901. Delhi: Indian Book Gallery, 1982.

Minamoto no Shitago (attributed). "'Atemiya': A Translation from the *Utsubo monogatari*." Trans. Edwin A. Cranston. *Monumenta Nipponica* 24.3 (1969): 289–314.

————. "'The Succession' (*Kuniyuzuri*): A Translation from *Utsuho monogatari*." Trans. Wayne P. Lammers. *Monumenta Nipponica* 37.2 (Summer 1982): 139–78.

———. *The Tale of the Cavern.* Trans. Ziro Uraki. Tokyo: Shinozaki Shorin, 1984.

Miner, Earl, ed. *Japanese Poetic Diaries.* Berkeley: U California P, 1969.

Mish, Charles C., ed. *The Anchor Anthology of Short Fiction of the Seventeenth Century.* Garden City, NY: Anchor, 1963.

Montalvo, Garci Rodríguez de. *Amadis of Gaul.* Trans. Edwin Place and Herbert Behm. 2 vols. Lexington: UP of Kentucky, 1974, 1975.

Montemayor, Jorge de. *The Diana.* Trans. RoseAnna M. Mueller. Lewiston, NY: Edwin Mellen, 1989.

Moore, Steven, ed. *Medieval Epics and Sagas.* Ann Arbor: Borders Classics, 2005.

More, Sir Thomas. *Utopia.* Ed. and trans. Robert M. Adams. 2nd ed. NY: Norton, 1992.

Mostow, Joshua S., ed. *At the House of Gathered Leaves: Shorter Biographical and Autobiographical Narratives from Japanese Court Literature.* Honolulu: U Hawaii P, 2004.

Murasaki Shikibu. *The Tale of Genji.* Trans. Arthur Waley. 1925–33. NY: Modern Library, 1960.

———. Trans. Edward Seidensticker. NY: Knopf, 1976.

———. Trans. Royall Tyler. 2 vols. NY: Viking, 2001.

———. *A String of Flowers, Untied . . .: Love Poems from* The Tale of Genji. Trans. Jane Reichhold with Hatsue Kawamura. Berkeley: Stone Bridge, 2003.

Nabokov, Vladimir. *Laughter in the Dark.* 1938. NY: New Directions, 1960.

———. *The Annotated* Lolita. Ed. Alfred Appel, Jr. 1955. NY: McGraw-Hill, 1970.

Nakhshabi, Ziya al-Din. *The Cleveland Museum of Art's Tūtī-nāma: Tales of a Parrot.* Trans. Muhammed A. Simsar. Cleveland: Cleveland Museum of Art, 1978.

Naravane, Vishwanath S. *Three Novels from Ancient India: Abridged and Retold with an Introductory Essay.* New Delhi: Vikas, 1982.

Narayana. *Hitopadeśa.* Trans. A. N. D. Haksar. New Delhi: Penguin, 1998.

———. *Friendly Advice & King Víkrama's Adventures.* Trans. Judit Törzsök. NY: New York UP/Clay Sanskrit Library, 2007.

Nashe, Thomas. *The Unfortunate Traveler: or The Life of Jack Wilton.* Ed. John Berryman. NY: Putnam Capricorn, 1960.

———. *The Unfortunate Traveller and Other Works.* Ed. J. B. Steane. NY: Penguin, 1972.

The New Jerusalem Bible. Ed. Henry Wansbrough. NY: Doubleday, 1985.

Nihongi: Chronicles of Japan from the Earliest Times to A.D. 697. Trans. W. G. Aston. 1896. Rutland, VT: Tuttle, 1972.

Nizami Ganjavi. *The Story of Layla and Majnun.* Trans. Rudolf Gelpke, with E. Mattin and G. Hill. 1966. New Lebanon, NY: Omega, 1997.

———. *The Haft Paikar (The Seven Beauties).* Trans. C. E. Wilson. 2 vols. London: Probsthain, 1924.

———. *The Story of the Seven Princesses.* Trans. Rudolf Gelpke, with Elsie and George Hill. London: Bruno Cassirer, 1976.

———. *The Haft Paykar: A Medieval Persian Romance.* Trans. Julie Scott Meisami. Oxford: Oxford UP, 1995.

———. *Mirror of the Invisible World: Tales from the* Kamseh *of Nizami.* Ed. Peter J. Chelkowski. Trans. Vernon Newton. NY: Metropolitan Museum of Art, 1975.

Njal's Saga. Trans. Robert Cook. NY: Penguin, 2001.

O'Brien, Flann. *The Complete Novels*. NY: Everyman's Library, 2007.

Ólason, Vésteinn, ed. *Gisli Sursson's Saga* and *The Saga of the People of Eyri*. NY: Penguin, 2003.

Oldwanton, Oliver. *The Image of Idleness*. Ed. Michael Flachmann. *Studies in Philology* 87.1 (Winter 1990): 1–74.

Ō no Yasumaro, ed. *Kojiki*. Trans. Donald L. Philippi. Princeton: Princeton UP, 1969.

Owen, Stephen, ed. *An Anthology of Chinese Literature: Beginnings to 1911*. NY: Norton, 1996.

Painter, William, trans. and ed. *The Palace of Pleasure*. Ed. Joseph Jacobs, 1890. 3 vols. NY: Dover, 1966.

Parkinson, R. B., ed. and trans. *The Tale of Sinuhe and Other Ancient Egyptian Poems 1940–1640 B.C.* Oxford: Oxford UP, 1997.

[*Partings at Dawn*] *Ariake no wakare*. Trans. Masayuki Ikeda, Monden Hideo, and Ujiie Yoko. *The East* 28.4–30.2 (1992–94).

———. Trans. Robert Omar Khan. In *"Ariake no wakare*: Genre, Gender, and Genealogy in a Late 12th Century Monogatari." Ph.D. diss., University of British Columbia, 1998.

The Perfect Generosity of Prince Vessantara: A Buddhist Epic. Trans. Margaret Cone. Ed. Richard F. Gombrich. Oxford: Clarendon, 1977.

The Petese Stories II: The Carlsberg Papyri 6. Ed. Kim Ryholt. Copenhagen: Museum Tusculanum, 2006.

Petronius. *The Satyricon*. Trans. William Arrowsmith. 1959. NY: Meridian, 1994.

———. *The Satyricon*/Seneca, *The Apocolocyntosis*. Trans. John P. Sullivan. Rev. ed. NY: Penguin, 1986.

———. Trans. Michael Heseltine and W. H. D. Rouse; rev. ed. by E. H. Warmington. Cambridge: Harvard UP, 1969.

———. *Satyrica*. Trans. R. Bracht Branham and Daniel Kinney. Berkeley: U California P, 1997.

Philostratus, Flavius. *Apollonius of Tyana*. Trans. Christopher P. Jones. 2 vols. Cambridge: Harvard UP, 2005.

Piccolomini, Aeneas Sylvius. *The Tale of the Two Lovers*. Trans. Flora Grierson. London: Constable, 1929.

Pingali Suranna. *The Sound of the Kiss, or The Story That Must Never Be Told*. Trans. Velcheru Narayana Rao and David Shulman. NY: Columbia UP, 2002.

———. *The Demon's Daughter: A Love Story from South India*. Trans. Velcheru Narayana Rao and David Shulman. Albany: State U New York P, 2006.

Pirkê de Rabbi Eliezer (The Chapters of Rabbi Eliezer the Great). Trans. Gerald Friedlander. 1916. NY: Benjamin Blom, 1971.

Plato. *The Collected Dialogues*. Ed. Edith Hamilton and Huntington Cairns. NY: Pantheon, 1961.

Popol Vuh: The Definitive Edition of the Mayan Book of the Dawn of Life and the Glories of Gods and Kings. Trans. Dennis Tedlock. Rev. ed. NY: Touchstone, 1996.

Popol Vuh: The Sacred Book of the Maya. Trans. Allen J. Christenson. NY: O Books, 2003.

Pritchard, James B., ed. *The Ancient Near East: An Anthology of Texts and Pictures.* Princeton: Princeton UP, 1958.

Proclaiming Harmony. Trans. William O. Hennessey. Ann Arbor: Center for Chinese Studies/University of Michigan, 1981.

Proust, Marcel. *Sodom and Gomorrah.* Trans. John Sturrock. NY: Viking, 2004.

Pynchon, Thomas. *Gravity's Rainbow.* NY: Viking, 1973.

The Quest of the Holy Grail. Trans. P. M. Matarasso. NY: Penguin, 1969.

Quirke, Stephen, ed. *Egyptian Literature 1800 BC: Questions and Readings.* London: Golden House, 2004.

Rabelais, François. *Complete Works.* Trans. Sir Thomas Urquhart and Peter Motteux. 2 vols. NY: Boni & Liveright, 1927.

———. Trans. Donald M. Frame. Berkeley: U California P, 1991.

———. *Gargantua and Pantagruel.* Trans. J. M. Cohen. NY: Penguin, 1955.

———. Trans. Burton Raffel. NY: Norton, 1990.

———. Trans. M. A. Screech. NY: Penguin, 2006.

Reardon, B. P., ed. *Collected Ancient Greek Novels.* Berkeley: U California P, 1989.

Recognitions. Trans. Thomas Smith. In *The Ante-Nicene Fathers.* Ed Alexander Roberts and James Donaldson. 1886. Peabody, MA: Hendrickson, 1994. 8:75–211.

Reischauer, Edwin O., and Joseph K. Yamagiwa, eds. *Translations from Early Japanese Literature.* Cambridge: Harvard UP, 1951.

The Report of Wenamun. Trans. Hans Goedicke. Baltimore: Johns Hopkins UP, 1975.

Róbert, Friar. *The Saga of Tristram and Ísönd.* Trans. Paul Schach. Lincoln: U Nebraska P, 1973.

Robert de Boron. *Merlin and the Grail: Joseph of Arimathea / Merlin / Perceval.* Trans. Nigel Bryant. Cambridge: Brewer, 2001.

Rojas, Fernando de. *The Celestina: A Novel in Dialogue.* Trans. Lesley Byrd Simpson. Berkeley: U California P, 1955.

———. *Celestina: A Play in Twenty-one Acts.* Trans. Mack Hendricks Singleton. Madison: U Wisconsin P, 1958.

The Romance of Tristan: The Thirteenth-Century Old French Prose Tristan. Trans. Renée L. Curtis. Oxford: Oxford UP, 1994.

The Romance Tradition in Urdu: Adventures from the Dastan of Amir Hamzah. Trans. Frances W. Pritchett. NY: Columbia UP, 1991.

Rosenmeyer, Patricia A., ed. *Ancient Greek Literary Letters: Selections in Translation.* NY: Routledge, 2006.

Sade, Marquis de. *The 120 Days of Sodom and Other Writings.* Trans. Austryn Wainhouse and Richard Seaver. NY: Grove, 1966.

The Saga of the Volsungs: The Norse Epic of Sigurd the Dragon Slayer. Trans. Jesse L. Byock. Berkeley: U California P, 1990.

Saintsbury, George, ed. *Shorter Novels, Volume 1: Elizabethan and Jacobean.* London: Dent/Everyman's Library, 1929.

Salzman, Paul, ed. *An Anthology of Elizabethan Prose Fiction.* NY: Oxford UP, 1987.

Sanghadasa. *The Vasudevahindi: An Authentic Jain Version of the* Brhatkathā. Trans. Jagdishchandra Jain. Ahmedabad: L. D. Institute of Indology, 1977.

Sannazaro, Jacopo. *Arcadia & Piscatorial Eclogues.* Trans. Ralph Nash. Detroit: Wayne State UP, 1966.

San Pedro, Diego de. *Prison of Love.* Trans. Keith Whinnom. Edinburgh: Edinburgh UP, 1979.

Schmidt, Arno. *Nobodaddy's Children.* Trans. John E. Woods. Normal: Dalkey Archive, 1995.

Schneemelcher, Wilhelm, ed. *New Testament Apocrypha,* vol. 2. Rev. ed. Trans. R. McL. Wilson. Louisville: Westminster John Knox, 2003.

Shirane, Haruo, ed. *Traditional Japanese Literature: An Anthology, Beginnings to 1600.* NY: Columbia UP, 2007.

Shōmonki: The Story of Masakado's Rebellion. Trans. Judith N. Rabinovitch. Tokyo: *Monumenta Nipponica*/Sophia University, 1986.

Shuka Saptati: Seventy Tales of the Parrot. Trans. A. N. D. Haksar. New Delhi: HarperCollins, 2000.

Shunzeiko no musume (attributed). *Mumyōzōshi.* Trans. Michele Marra. *Monumenta Nipponica* 39.2–4 (1984): 115–45, 281–305, 409–34.

Sidney, Sir Philip. *The Countess of Pembroke's Arcadia (The Old Arcadia).* Ed. Katherine Duncan-Jones. NY: Oxford UP, 1985.

———. *The Countess of Pembroke's Arcadia.* Ed. Maurice Evans. NY: Penguin, 1977.

Simhāsana Dvātrimśikā: Thirty-two Tales of the Throne of Vikramaditya. Trans. A. N. D. Haksar. New Delhi: Penguin, 1998.

Simons, John, ed. *Guy of Warwick and Other Chapbook Romances: Six Tales from the Popular Literature of Pre-Industrial England.* Exeter: U Exeter P, 1998.

Simpson, William Kelly, ed. *The Literature of Ancient Egypt: An Anthology of Stories, Instructions, and Poetry.* 3rd ed. New Haven: Yale UP, 2003.

Sîn-leqi-unninnī. *The Epic of Gilgamesh: A New Translation.* Ed. Andrew George. NY: Penguin, 2000.

———. *The Epic of Gilgamesh.* Ed. Benjamin R. Foster. NY: Norton, 2001.

Śivadāsa. *The Five-and-Twenty Tales of the Genie.* Trans. Chandra Rajan. New Delhi: Penguin, 1995.

Skord, Virginia, ed. *Tales of Tears and Laughter: Short Fiction of Medieval Japan.* Honolulu: U Hawaii P, 1991.

Soddhala. *Udayasundari Katha.* Trans. Sudarshan Kumar Sharma. Delhi: Parimal, 2004.

Solomon and Marcolf. Trans. Jan M. Ziolkowski. Cambridge: Harvard UP, 2008.

Somadeva. *The Ocean of Story.* Trans. C. H. Tawney. Ed. N. M. Penzer. 10 vols. 1928. Delhi: Motilal Banarsidass, 1968.

———. *Tales from the Kathāsaritsāgara.* Trans. Arshia Sattar. London: Penguin, 1994.

———. *The Ocean of the Rivers of Story.* Trans. Sir James Mallinson. 7 vols. NY: New York UP, 2007– .

Steinhauer, Harry, ed. and trans. *Twelve German Novellas.* Berkeley: U California P, 1977.

Stephens, Susan A., and John J. Winkler, eds. *Ancient Greek Novels: The Fragments.* Princeton: Princeton UP, 1995.

Stern, David, and Mark Jay Mirsky, eds. *Rabbinic Fantasies: Imaginative Narratives from Classical Hebrew Literature.* Philadelphia: Jewish Publication Society, 1990.

Sterne, Laurence. *The Life and Opinions of Tristram Shandy, Gentleman.* Ed. Melvyn New. NY: Penguin, 1997.

The Story of Hua Guan Suo. Trans. Gail Oman King. Tempe, AZ: Center for Asian Studies, 1989.

Straparola, Giovanni Francesco. *The Facetious Nights.* Trans. W. G. Waters. 4 vols. London: Society of Bibliophiles, 1898.

Subandhu. *Vāsavadattā: A Sanskrit Romance.* Trans. Louis H. Gray. NY: Columbia UP, 1913.

———. Trans. Harinath De. Calcutta: Sanskrit College, 1994.

Sullivan, Thelma D., trans. *A Scattering of Jades: Stories, Poems, and Prayers of the Aztecs.* Ed. Timothy J. Knab. Tucson: U Arizona P, 2003.

The Sumiyoshi Monogatari. Trans. Harold Parlett. *Transactions of the Asiatic Society of Japan* 29.1 (1901): 37–123.

Śūra, Ārya. *Once the Buddha Was a Monkey: Ārya Śūra's Jātakamālā.* Trans. Peter Khoroche. Chicago: U Chicago P, 1989.

Sweeney Astray: A Version from the Irish. Trans. Seamus Heaney. NY: Noonday, 1984.

The Táin. Trans. Thomas Kinsella. 1969. NY: Oxford UP, 1970.

The Táin: A New Translation of the Táin Bó Cúailnge. Trans. Ciaran Carson. NY: Viking, 2008.

Táin Bó Cúalnge from the Book of Leinster. Ed. and trans. Cecile O'Rahilly. Dublin: Dublin Institute for Advanced Studies, 1967.

"Takamura Monogatari." Trans. Ward Geddes. *Monumenta Nipponica* 46.3 (Autumn 1991): 275–91.

Takasue no musume. *As I Crossed a Bridge of Dreams.* Trans. Ivan Morris. 1971. NY: Penguin, 1975.

———(attributed). *The Tale of Nezame.* Trans. Kenneth L. Richard. In "Developments in Late Heian Prose Fiction: *The Tale of Nezame.*" Ph.D. diss., University of Washington, 1973.

———. *The Tale of Nezame: Part Three of* Yowa no Nezame Mongatari. Trans. Carol Hochstedler. Ithaca: China–Japan Program/Cornell U, 1979.

———(attributed). *A Tale of Eleventh-Century Japan:* Hamamatsu Chūnagon Monogatari. Trans. Thomas H. Rohlich. Princeton: Princeton UP, 1983.

The Tale of Saigyō. Trans. Meredith McKinney. Ann Arbor: Center for Japanese Studies/University of Michigan, 1998.

The Tale of the Bamboo Cutter. Trans. Donald Keene. Illus. Miyata Masayuki. Tokyo and New York: Kodansha, 1998.

The Tale of the Lady Ochikubo. Trans. Wilfred Whitehouse and Eizo Yanagisawa. 1934. Garden City, NY: Doubleday, 1971.

The Tale of the Soga Brothers. Trans. Thomas J. Cogan. Tokyo: U Tokyo P, 1987.

A Tale of Woe: From a Hieratic Papyrus in the A. S. Pushkin Museum of Fine Arts in Moscow. Trans. Ricardo A. Caminos. Oxford: Giffith Institute/Ashmolean Museum, 1977.

Tales of Heichū. Trans. Susan Downing Videen. Cambridge: Harvard UP, 1989.

Tales of Ise: Lyrical Episodes from Tenth-Century Japan. Trans. Helen Craig McCullough. Stanford: Stanford UP, 1968.

Tales of Sendebar. Ed. and trans. Morris Epstein. Philadelphia: Jewish Publication Society of America, 1967.

Tales of the Elders of Ireland (Acallam na Senórach). Trans. Ann Dooley and Harry Roe. NY: Oxford UP, 1999.

Tales of Yamato: A Tenth-Century Poem-Tale. Trans. Mildred M. Tahara. Honolulu: UP of Hawaii, 1980.

Thackeray, William Makepeace. *Vanity Fair: A Novel without a Hero.* 1848. NY: Penguin, 2004.

Theroux, Alexander. *Darconville's Cat.* Garden City, NY: Doubleday, 1982.

Thoms, William J., and Henry Morley, eds. *Early English Prose Romances.* New Edition, Revised and Enlarged. London: Routledge, n.d. [1906?]

Thorsson, Örnólfur, ed. *The Sagas of Icelanders.* Various translators. NY: Viking, 2000.

The Thousand and One Nights. Trans. Edward Lane. 1838–42. 3 vols. London: John Murray, 1859.

Tóruigheacht Dhiarmada agus Ghráinne: The Pursuit of Diarmaid and Gráinne. Ed. and trans. Nessa Ní Shéaghdha. Dublin: Irish Texts Society, 1967.

Tsang Nyön Heruka. *The Life of Milarepa.* Trans. Lobsang P. Lhalungpa. 1977. NY: Penguin, 1992.

———. *The Hundred Thousand Songs of Milarepa.* Trans. Garma C. C. Chang. 1962. Boston: Shambala, 1999.

———. *The Life of Marpa the Translator: Seeing Accomplishes All.* Trans. Nālandā Translation Committee. 1982. Boston: Shambala, 1995.

Vanstiphout, Herman, ed. *Epics of Sumerian Kings: The Matter of Aratta.* Atlanta: Society of Biblical Literature, 2003.

Vasistha's Yoga. Trans. Swami Venkatesananda. Albany: State U New York P, 1993.

Villegas, Antonio de. *El Abencerraje.* Trans. John Esten Keller. Chapel Hill: U North Carolina P, 1965.

Visnu Śarma. *The Pañćatantra.* Trans. Chandra Rajan. London: Penguin, 1995.

———. *The Pañcatantra.* Trans. Patrick Olivelle. NY: Oxford, 1997.

———. *Five Discourses on Worldly Wisdom.* Trans. Patrick Olivelle. NY: New York UP/ Clay Sanskrit Library, 2006.

Vonnegut, Kurt. "Harrison Bergeron." In *Welcome to the Monkey House.* NY: Delacorte, 1968.

Warner, William. *Syrinx; or, A Sevenfold History.* Ed. Wallace A. Bacon. Evanston: Northwestern UP, 1950.

Weldon, Fay. *Mantrapped.* London: Fourth Estate/NY: Grove, 2004.

Wills, Lawrence M., ed. and trans. *Ancient Jewish Novels: An Anthology.* NY: Oxford UP, 2002.

Wu Chengen (attributed). *Monkey.* Trans. Arthur Waley. 1943. NY: Grove, 1984.

———. *The Journey to the West.* Trans. Anthony C. Yu. 4 vols. Chicago: U Chicago P, 1977–83.

Xenophon. *The Education of Cyrus.* Trans. Wayne Ambler. Ithaca: Cornel UP, 2001.

Xiaoxiaosheng. *The Golden Lotus.* Trans. Clement Egerton (with Lao She). 4 vols. 1939. London: Routledge & Kegan Paul, 1972.

———. *The Plum in the Golden Vase.* Trans. David Tod Roy. 5 vols. Princeton: Princeton UP, 1993– .

Xu Zhonglin (attributed). *Creation of the Gods.* Trans. Gu Zhizhong. 2 vols. Beijing: New World Press, 1992.

————. *Tales of the Teahouse Retold: Investiture of the Gods*. Trans. Katherine Liang Chew. Lincoln: iUniverse, 2002.

Yagel, Abraham. *A Valley of Vision: The Heavenly Journey of Abraham ben Hananiah Yagel*. Trans. David B. Ruderman. Philadelphia: U Pennsylvania P, 1990.

Yehudah HaLevi. *The Kuzari: In Defense of the Despised Faith*. Trans. N. Daniel Korobkin. Jerusalem: Feldheim, 2009.

Yoshitsune: A Fifteenth-Century Japanese Chronicle. Trans. Helen Craig McCullough. 1966. Stanford: Stanford UP, 1971.

Zabara, Joseph ben Meir. *The Book of Delight*. Trans. Moses Hadas. NY: Columbia UP, 1932.

Zenkovsky, Serge A., ed. *Medieval Russia's Epics, Chronicles, and Tales*. 2nd ed. NY: Dutton, 1974.

SECONDARY WORKS: NONFICTION

Adams, Alison, et al., eds. *The Changing Face of Arthurian Romance: Essays on Arthurian Prose Romances in Memory of Cedric E. Pickford*. Cambridge, UK: D. S. Brewer, 1986.

Agrawala, Vasudeva S. *The Deeds of Harsha: Being a Cultural Study of Bāna's Harshacharita*. Ed. P. K. Agrawala. Varansi, India: Prithivi Prakashan, 1969.

Akenson, Donald Harman. *Saint Saul: A Skeleton Key to the Historical Jesus*. NY: Oxford UP, 2000.

Akkeren, Ruud W. van. "Authors of the *Popol Wuj*." *Ancient Mesoamerica* 14 (July 2003): 237–56.

Alexander, Gavin, ed. *Sidney's* The Defense of Poesy *and Selected Renaissance Literary Criticism*. NY: Penguin, 2004.

Allaire, Gloria. *Andrea da Barberino and the Language of Chivalry*. Gainesville: UP Florida, 1997.

al-Nadim. *The Fihrist of al-Nadīm: A Tenth-Century Survey of Muslim Culture*. Trans. Bayard Dodge. 2 vols. NY: Columbia UP, 1970.

Anderson, Graham. *Ancient Fiction: The Novel in the Graeco–Roman World*. London: Croom Helm, 1984.

Andersson, Theodore M. *The Growth of the Medieval Icelandic Sagas (1180–1280)*. Ithaca: Cornell UP, 2006.

Andreas Capellanus. *The Art of Courtly Love*. Trans. John Jay Parry. NY: Columbia UP, 1960.

Arberry, A. J. *Classical Persian Literature*. London: Allen & Unwin, 1958.

Arbuthnot, F. F. *Persian Portraits: A Sketch of Persian History, Literature, and Politics*. London: Bernard Quaritch, 1887.

Auerbach, Erich. *Mimesis: The Representation of Reality in Western Literature*. 1946. Trans. Willard R. Trask. Princeton: Princeton UP, 2003.

Aylward, Edward T. *Martorell's* Tirant lo Blanch: A *Program for Military and Social Reform in Fifteenth-Century Christendom*. Chapel Hill: North Carolina Studies in the Romance Languages and Literatures, 1985.

Bakhtin, Mikhail Mikhailovich. *Rabelais and His World*. Trans. Hélène Iswolsky. 1968. Bloomington: Indiana UP, 1984.

————. *The Dialogic Imagination: Four Essays*. Trans. Caryl Emerson and Michael Holquist. Austin: U Texas P, 1981.

Ballaster, Ros. *Fabulous Orients: Fictions of the East in England 1662–1785*. NY: Oxford UP, 2005.

Banerji, Sures Chandra. *A Companion to Sanskrit Literature*. 2nd ed. Delhi: Motilal Banarsidass, 1989.

Barber, Michael. *Anthony Powell: A Life*. London: Duckworth, 2004.

Barber, Richard. *The Holy Grail: Imagination and Belief*. Cambridge: Harvard UP, 2004.

Bargen, Doris G. "The Problem of Incest in *The Tale of Genji*," 115–23. In *Approaches to Teaching Murasaki Shikibu's* The Tale of Genji. Ed. Edward Kamens. NY: Modern Language Association of America, 1993.

————. *A Woman's Weapon: Spirit Possession in* The Tale of Genji. Honolulu: U Hawaii P, 1997.

Barrier, Jeremy W. "A Critical Introduction and Commentary on the *Acts of Paul and Thecla*." Ph.D. diss., Brite Divinity School, 2008.

Barth, John. *The Friday Book: Essays and Other Nonfiction*. NY: Putnam, 1984.

————. *Further Fridays: Essays, Lectures, and Other Nonfiction, 1984–1994*. Boston: Little, Brown, 1995.

Barthelme, Donald. *Not-Knowing: The Essays and Interviews*. Ed. Kim Herzinger. NY: Random, 1997.

Barthes, Roland. *S/Z*. Trans. Richard Miller. NY: Farrar, Straus & Giroux, 1974.

————. *The Pleasure of the Text*. Trans. Richard Miller. NY: Farrar, Straus & Giroux, 1975.

Beaton, Roderick. *The Medieval Greek Romance*. 2nd ed. NY: Routledge, 1996.

Beaumont, Daniel. *Slave of Desire: Sex, Love and Death in* The 1001 Nights. Madison, NJ: Fairleigh Dickinson UP, 2002.

Bergin, Thomas G. *Boccaccio*. NY: Viking, 1981.

Besio, Kimberly, and Constantine Tung, eds. Three Kingdoms *and Chinese Culture*. Albany: State U of New York P, 2007.

Bialock, David T. *Eccentric Spaces, Hidden Histories: Narrative, Ritual, and Royal Authority from* The Chronicles of Japan *to* The Tale of the Heike. Stanford: Stanford UP, 2007.

Bjornson, Richard. *The Picaresque Hero in European Fiction*. Madison: U Wisconsin P, 1977.

Bloom, Harold. *Genius: A Mosaic of One Hundred Exemplary Creative Minds*. NY: Warner, 2002.

Boccaccio, Giovanni. *Life of Dante*. Trans. J. G. Nichols. London: Hesperus, 2002.

————. *Famous Women*. Trans. Virginia Brown. Cambridge: Harvard UP, 2001.

Bonz, Marianne Palmer. *The Past as Legacy: Luke-Acts and Ancient Epic*. Minneapolis: Fortress, 2000.

Booker, Christopher. *The Seven Basic Plots: Why We Tell Stories*. London: Continuum, 2004.

Borges, Jorge Luis. *Seven Nights*. Trans. Eliot Weinberger. NY: New Directions, 1984.

————. *Selected Non-Fictions*. Ed. Eliot Weinberger. Trans. Esther Allen, Suzanne Jill Levine, and the editor. NY: Viking, 1999.

Bottigheimer, Ruth B. *Fairy Godfather: Straparola, Venice, and the Fairy Tale Tradition*. Philadelphia: U Pennsylvania P, 2002.

Bowring, Richard. *Murasaki Shikibu: The Tale of Genji*. Cambridge: Cambridge UP, 1988.

Boyd, Brian. "Getting It All Wrong." *American Scholar* 75.4 (Autumn 2006): 18–30.

Braund, David, and John Wilkins, eds. *Athenaeus and His World: Reading Greek Culture in the Roman Empire*. Exeter: U Exeter P, 2000.

Browne, Edward G. A *Literary History of Persia*. 4 vols. Cambridge: Cambridge UP, 1928.

Burns, E. Jane. *Arthurian Fictions: Rereading the Vulgate Cycle*. Columbus: Ohio State UP, 1985.

Cabezón, José Ignacio, and Roger R. Jackson, eds. *Tibetan Literature: Studies in Genre*. Ithaca: Snow Lion, 1996.

Callahan, Tim. *The Secret Origins of the Bible*. Altadena, CA: Millennium, 2002.

Calvino, Italo. *The Uses of Literature*. Trans. Patrick Creagh. NY: Harcourt Brace, 1986.

Campbell. Joseph. *The Hero with a Thousand Faces*. 1949. Commemorative Edition. Princeton: Princeton UP, 2004.

————. *Oriental Mythology*. The Masks of God, vol. 2. 1962. NY: Penguin, 1976.

Carlitz, Katherine. *The Rhetoric of Chin p'ing mei*. Bloomington: Indiana UP, 1986.

Ch'ên Shou-yi. *Chinese Literature: A Historical Introduction*. NY: Ronald Press, 1961.

Chrisafis, Angelique. "Overlong, Overrated and Unmoving: Roddy Doyle's Verdict on James Joyce's *Ulysses*." *Guardian*, 10 February 2004.

Cleugh, James. *The Divine Aretino*. 1965. NY: Stein & Day, 1966.

Clute, John, and John Grant, eds. *The Encyclopedia of Fantasy*. NY: St. Martin's, 1999.

Corbin, Henry. *Avicenna and the Visionary Recital*. Trans. Willard R. Trask. NY: Pantheon, 1960.

Costa Fontes, Manuel da. *The Art of Subversion in Inquisitorial Spain: Rojas and Delicado*. West Lafayette, IN: Purdue UP, 2005.

Courtney, Edward. A *Companion to Petronius*. NY: Oxford UP, 2001.

Crewe, Jonathan V. *Unredeemed Rhetoric: Thomas Nashe and the Scandal of Authorship*. Baltimore: Johns Hopkins UP, 1982.

Damiani, Bruno M. *Francisco López de Úbeda*. Boston: Twayne, 1977.

Damrosch, David. *The Buried Book: The Loss and Rediscovery of the Great* Epic of Gilgamesh. NY: Holt, 2007.

Davis, Dick. *Panthea's Children: Hellenistic Novels and Medieval Persian Romances*. NY: Bibliotheca Persica, 2002.

Dehejia, Harsha V., ed. A *Celebration of Love: The Romantic Heroine in the Indian Arts*. New Delhi: Roli & Janssen, 2004.

Delcourt, Denyse. "The Laboratory of Fiction: Magic and Image in the *Roman de Perceforest*." *Medievalia et Humanistica* n.s. 21 (1994): 17–31.

De Rougemont, Denis. *Love in the Western World*. Trans. Montgomery Belgion. Rev. ed. Princeton: Princeton UP, 1983.

D'Etcheverry, Charo B. *Love after* The Tale of Genji: *Rewriting the World of the Shining Prince*. Cambridge: Harvard U Asia Center, 2007.

Dillon, Myles. *Early Irish Literature*. Chicago: U Chicago P, 1948.

Ding, Naifei. *Obscene Things: Sexual Politics in* Jin Ping Mei. Durham: Duke UP, 2002.

Dinwiddle, Donald, ed. *Portraits of the Masters: Bronze Sculptures of the Tibetan Buddhist Lineages*. London: Oliver Hoare, 2003.

Dirda, Michael. *Classics for Pleasure*. NY: Harcourt, 2007.

Doniger, Wendy. *The Bedtrick: Tales of Sex and Masquerade*. Chicago: U Chicago P, 2000.

Doody, Margaret Anne. *The True Story of the Novel*. New Brunswick: Rutgers UP, 1996.

Dooley, Ann. *Playing the Hero: Reading the Irish Saga* Táin Bó Cúailnge. Toronto: U Toronto P, 2006.

Dover, Carol, ed. *A Companion to the* Lancelot-Grail Cycle. Cambridge, UK: Brewer, 2003.

Dudbridge, Glen. *The* Hsi-yu chi: *A Study of Antecedents to the Sixteenth–Century Chinese Novel*. Cambridge: Cambridge UP, 1970.

Dunlop, John Colin. *The History of Fiction*. 1814. Rev. ed. [retitled *History of Prose Fiction*] ed. Henry Wilson. 2 vols. London: George Bell, 1888.

Eagleton, Terry. *After Theory*. London: Allen Lane, 2003.

Ehrman, Bart D. *Misquoting Jesus: The Story behind Who Changed the Bible and Why*. NY: HarperSanFrancisco, 2005.

El Saffar, Ruth. "*La Galatea*: The Integrity of the Unintegrated Text." *Dispositio* 3.9 (Autumn 1978): 337–51.

Federman, Raymond. *Critifiction: Postmodern Essays*. Albany: State U New York P, 1993.

Field, Norma. *The Splendor of Longing in the* Tale of Genji. Princeton: Princeton UP, 1987.

Finkelstein, Israel, and Neil Asher Silberman. *The Bible Unearthed: Archaeology's New Vision of Ancient Israel and the Origin of Its Sacred Texts*. NY: Simon & Schuster, 2001.

———. *David and Solomon: In Search of the Bible's Sacred Kings and the Roots of the Western Tradition*. NY: Free Press, 2006.

Ford, Ford Madox. *The March of Literature: From Confucius' Day to Our Own*. 1938. Normal: Dalkey Archive, 1994.

Forster, E. M. *Aspects of the Novel*. NY: Harcourt, Brace, 1927.

Franzen, Jonathan. "Mr. Difficult." *New Yorker*, 30 September 2002, 100–111. Rpt. in *How to Be Alone*. NY: Picador, 2003.

———, and Ben Greenman. "Having Difficulty with Difficulty." *New Yorker Online*. Posted 23 September 2002.

Friedman, Richard Elliott. *Who Wrote the Bible?* 1987. Rev. ed. San Francisco: HarperCollins, 1997.

Frye, Northrop. *Anatomy of Criticism*. Princeton: Princeton UP, 1957.

———. *The Secular Scripture: A Study of the Structure of Romance*. Cambridge: Harvard UP, 1976.

Funk, Robert W., and the Jesus Seminar. *The Acts of Jesus: What Did Jesus Really Do?* NY: Polebridge Press/Harper SanFrancisco, 1998.

Gardner, John. *On Moral Fiction*. NY: Basic Books, 1978.

Gass, William H. *A Temple of Texts*. NY: Knopf, 2006.

Ge, Liangyan. *Out of the Margins: The Rise of Chinese Vernacular Fiction*. Honolulu: U Hawaii P, 2001.

Geoffrey of Monmouth. *The History of the Kings of Britain*. Trans. Lewis Thorpe. NY: Penguin, 1966.

Ghazoul, Ferial. *Nocturnal Poetics:* The Arabian Nights *in Comparative Context*. Cairo: American University in Cairo P, 1996.

Godwin, Joscelyn. *The Pagan Dream of the Renaissance*. 2002. Boston: Weiser, 2005.

———. *The Real Rule of Four*. NY: Disinformation, 2004.

Goethe, Johann Wolfgang von. *Conversations with Eckermann (1823–1832)*. Trans. John Oxenford. 1850. San Francisco: North Point, 1984.

Goodman, Lenn Evans. "Hamadhānī, *Schadenfreude*, and Salvation through Sin." *Journal of Arabic Literature* 19 (March 1988): 27–39.

Gramsci, Antonio. *Selections from Cultural Writings*. Trans. William Boelhower. Ed. David Forgacs and Geoffrey Nowell-Smith. London: Lawrence & Wishart, 1985.

Green, Arthur. *A Guide to the Zohar*. Stanford: Stanford UP, 2004.

Green, Jack. *Fire the Bastards!* 1962. Normal: Dalkey Archive, 1992.

Gu, Ming Dong. *Chinese Theories of Fiction: A Non-Western Narrative System*. Albany: State U New York P, 2006.

Gupta, Dharmendra Kumar. *A Critical Study of Dandin and His Works*. Delhi: Meharchand Lachhmandas, 1970.

Hägg, Tomas. *The Novel in Antiquity*. Rev. ed. Oxford: Blackwell, 1983.

———and Bo Utas. *The Virgin and Her Lover: Fragments of an Ancient Greek Novel and a Persian Epic Poem*. Leiden: Brill, 2003.

Halpern, Baruch. *David's Secret Demons: Messiah, Murderer, Traitor, King*. Grand Rapids, MI: Eerdmans, 2001.

Hanan, Patrick. "The Text of the *Chin p'ing mei*." *Asia Major* 9 (1962): 1–57.

———. "Sources of the *Chin p'ing mei*." *Asia Major* 10 (1963): 23–67.

———. "The Composition of the *P'ing yao chuan*." *Harvard Journal of Asiatic Studies* 31 (1971): 201–19.

Hanaway, William L., Jr. "Formal Elements in the Persian Popular Romances." *Review of National Literatures* 2.1 (Spring 1971): 139–60.

Hardyment, Christina. *Malory: The Knight Who Became King Arthur's Chronicler*. London: HarperCollins, 2005.

Heath, Peter. "Romance as Genre in *The Thousand and One Nights*." *Journal of Arabic Literature* 18 (1987): 1–21; 19 (1988): 1–26; rpt. in Marzolph's *Arabian Nights Reader*, 170–225.

———. *The Thirsty Sword: Sīrat 'Antar and the Arabic Popular Epic*. Salt Lake City: U Utah P, 1996.

Heiserman, Arthur. *The Novel before the Novel: Essays and Discussions about the Beginnings of Prose Fiction in the West*. Chicago: U Chicago P, 1977.

Hellner-Eshed, Melila. *A River Flows from Eden: The Language of Mystical Experience in the Zohar*. Trans. Nathan Wolski. Stanford: Stanford UP, 2009.

Helms, Randel McGraw. *Who Wrote the Gospels?* Altadena, CA: Millennium, 1997.

Herodotus. *The Histories*. Trans. Aubrey de Sélincourt. Rev. ed. John Marincola. NY: Penguin, 2003.

Hibbett, Howard. *The Floating World in Japanese Fiction.* 1959. Rutland, VT: Tuttle, 1975.

Hirsh, John C. *Barlaam and Iosaphat: A Middle English Life of Buddha.* Oxford: Oxford UP, 1986.

Hofmann, Heinz, ed. *Latin Fiction: The Latin Novel in Context.* London: Routledge, 1999.

Hollander, Robert. *Boccaccio's Last Fiction:* Il Corbaccio. Philadelphia: U Pennsylvania P, 1988.

Holtz, Barry W., ed. *Back to the Sources: Reading the Classic Jewish Texts.* NY: Summit, 1984.

Hsia, C. T. *The Classic Chinese Novel: A Critical Introduction.* NY: Columbia UP, 1968.

————. *On Chinese Literature.* NY: Columbia UP, 2004.

Huizinga, Johan. *The Autumn of the Middle Ages.* Trans. Rodney J. Payton and Ulrich Mammitzsch. 1919. Chicago: U Chicago P, 1996.

Huntington, Rania. *Alien Kind: Foxes and Late Imperial Chinese Narrative.* Cambridge: Harvard University Asia Center, 2003.

Huot, Sylvia. *Postcolonial Fictions in the* Roman de Perceforest. Cambridge, UK: D. S. Brewer, 2007.

Idema, W. L. *Chinese Vernacular Fiction: The Formative Period.* Leiden: E. J. Brill, 1974.

Ikegami, Keiko. *Barlaam and Josaphat: A Transcription of MS Egerton 876 with Notes, Glossary, and Comparative Study of the Middle English and Japanese Versions.* NY: AMS Press, 1999.

Irwin, Richard Gregg. *The Evolution of a Chinese Novel:* Shui-hu-chuan. Cambridge: Harvard UP, 1953.

Irwin, Robert. The Arabian Nights: *A Companion.* 2nd ed. London: Taurus, 2004

Jain, Jagdishchandra. *Prakrit Narrative Literature: Origin and Growth.* New Delhi: Munshiram Manoharlal, 1981.

Jamkhedkar, A. P. Vasudevahimdi: *A Cultural Study.* Delhi: Agam Kala Prakashan, 1984.

Jung, Emma, and Marie-Louise von Franz. *The Grail Legend.* Trans. Andrea Dykes. 2nd ed. Princeton: Princeton UP, 1998.

Kahane, Ahuvia, and Andrew Laird, eds. *A Companion to the Prologue to Apuleius'* Metamorphoses. NY: Oxford UP, 2001.

Kao, Karl. "Domains of Moral Discourse: Self, History, and Fantasy in *Fengshen yanyi.*" *Chinese Literature: Essays, Articles, Reviews* 24 (December 2002): 75–97.

Kawashima, Robert S. *Biblical Narrative and the Death of the Rhapsode.* Bloomington: Indiana UP, 2004.

Keene, Donald. *Seeds in the Heart: Japanese Literature from Earliest Times to the Late Sixteenth Century.* 1993. NY: Columbia UP, 1999.

Keith, A. Berriedale. *A History of Sanskrit Literature.* London: Oxford UP, 1920.

Kennedy, Elspeth. *Lancelot and the Grail: A Study of the Prose* Lancelot. Oxford: Clarendon, 1986.

Ker, William. *Epic and Romance: Essays on Medieval Literature.* 1911. NY: Dover, 1957.

Kerouac, Jack. *Some of the Dharma.* NY: Viking, 1997.

———. *Selected Letters 1957–1969.* Ed. Ann Charters. NY: Viking, 1999.

Khosla, Sarla. Lalitavistara *and the Evolution of Buddha Legend.* New Delhi: Galaxy, 1991.

———. Brhatkatha *and Its Contributions.* Delhi: Agam Kala Prakashan, 2003.

Kibler, William W. *The* Lancelot-Grail Cycle: *Text and Transformations.* Austin: U Texas P, 1994.

Kirkham, Victoria. "Two New Translations: The Early Boccaccio in English Dress." *Italica* 70.1 (1993): 79–89.

———. *Fabulous Vernacular: Boccaccio's* Filocolo *and the Art of Medieval Fiction.* Ann Arbor: U Michigan P, 2001.

Kirsch, Jonathan. *God against the Gods: The History of the War between Monotheism and Polytheism.* NY: Viking, 2004.

Knapp, Robert S. "Love Allegory in John Grange's *The Golden Aphroditis.*" *English Literary Renaissance* 8.3 (Autumn 1978): 256–70.

Koester, Helmut. *Ancient Christian Gospels: Their History and Development.* London: SCM, 1990.

Kraemer, Ross S. *When Aseneth Met Joseph: A Late Antique Tale of the Biblical Patriarch and His Egyptian Wife, Reconsidered.* NY: Oxford UP, 1998.

Krotkoff, Georg. "Colour and Number in the *Haft Paykar,*" 97–118. In *Logos Islamikos: Studia Islamica in Honorem Georgii Michaelis Wickens.* Ed. Roger M. Savory and Dionisius A. Agius. Toronto: Pontifical Institute of Medieval Studies, 1984.

Kuhns, Richard. Decameron *and the Philosophy of Storytelling: Author as Midwife and Pimp.* NY: Columbia UP, 2005.

Kundera, Milan. *The Curtain: An Essay in Seven Parts.* Trans. Linda Asher. NY: HarperCollins, 2006.

Lacy, Norris J., ed. *The New Arthurian Encyclopedia.* NY: Garland, 1996.

Lane Fox, Robin. *The Unauthorized Version: Truth and Fiction in the Bible.* 1991. NY: Vintage, 1993.

Lawrence, D. H. *Studies in Classic American Literature.* 1923. NY: Viking, 1964.

Lefaivre, Liane. *Leon Battista Alberti's* Hypnerotomachia Poliphili: *Re-Cognizing the Architectural Body in the Early Italian Renaissance.* Cambridge: MIT Press, 1997.

Levine, Amy-Jill, Dale C. Allison, Jr., and John Dominic Crossan, eds. *The Historical Jesus in Context.* Princeton: Princeton UP, 2006.

Lévy, André. *Chinese Literature, Ancient and Classical.* Trans. William H. Nienhauser, Jr. Bloomington: Indiana UP, 2000.

Li, Qiancheng. *Fictions of Enlightenment:* Journey to the West, Tower of Myriad Mirrors, *and* Dream of the Red Chamber. Honolulu: U Hawaii P, 2004.

Lo, Andrew Hing-bun. "*San-kuo chih yen-i* and *Shui-hu chuan* in the Context of Historiography: An Interpretive Study." Ph.D. diss., Princeton University, 1981.

Loomis, Roger Sherman. *The Grail: From Celtic Symbol to Christian Symbol.* 1963. Princeton: Princeton UP, 1991.

Loprieno, Antonio, ed. *Ancient Egyptian Literature: History and Forms.* Leiden: Brill, 1996.

Lüdemann, Gerd. *The Acts of the Apostles: What Really Happened in the Earliest Days of the Church.* Amherst, NY: Prometheus, 2005.

Lu Hsun. *A Brief History of Chinese Fiction*. Trans. Yang Hsien-yi and Gladys Yang. 1930. Beijing: Foreign Languages Press, 1959.

Lyons, M. C. *The Arabian Epic: Heroic and Oral Story-telling*. 3 vols. Cambridge: Cambridge UP, 1995.

Maan Singh. *Subandhu*. New Delhi: Sahitya Akademi, 1993.

MacAlister, Suzanne. *Dreams and Suicides: The Greek Novel from Antiquity to the Roman Empire*. London: Routledge, 1996.

MacDonald, Dennis R. *Does the New Testament Imitate Homer? Four Cases from the Acts of the Apostles*. New Haven: Yale UP, 2003.

Mack, Burton L. *Who Wrote the New Testament? The Making of the Christian Myth*. NY: Harper SanFrancisco, 1995.

MacKillop, James. *A Dictionary of Celtic Mythology*. NY: Oxford UP, 1998.

Maddox, Donald, and Sara Sturm-Maddox, eds. *Melusine of Lusignan: Founding Fiction in Late Medieval France*. Athens: U Georgia P, 1996.

Magnusson, Magnus. *Iceland Saga*. London: Bodley Head, 1987.

Mancing, Howard. *The Cervantes Encyclopedia*. 2 vols. Westport, CT: Greenwood, 2004.

Mann, Charles C. *1491: New Revelations of the Americas before Columbus*. NY: Knopf, 2005.

Marzolph, Ulrich, ed. *The* Arabian Nights *Reader*. Detroit: Wayne State UP, 2006.

———, and Richard van Leeuwen. *The* Arabian Nights *Encyclopedia*. 2 vols. Santa Barbara: ABC-CLIO, 2004.

Maslen, Robert W. *Elizabethan Fictions: Espionage, Counter-Espionage, and the Duplicity of Fiction in Early Elizabethan Prose Narratives*. Oxford: Clarendon, 1997.

McBride, Richard D., II. "A Koreanist's Musings on the Chinese *Yishi* Genre." *Sungkyun Journal of East Asian Studies* 6.1 (2006): 31–59.

McClure, Laura K. *Courtesans at Table: Gender and Greek Literary Culture in Athenaeus*. NY: Routledge, 2003.

McKeon, Michael, ed. *Theory of the Novel: A Historical Approach*. Baltimore: Johns Hopkins UP, 2000.

McNerney, Kathleen. Tirant lo Blanc *Revisited: A Critical Study*. Detroit: Michigan Consortium for Medieval and Early Modern Studies, 1983.

Meisami, Julie Scott, and Paul Starkey, eds. *Encyclopedia of Arabic Literature*. 2 vols. London: Routledge, 1998.

Melnikoff, Kirk, and Edward Gieskes, eds. *Writing Robert Greene: Essays on England's First Notorious Professional Writer*. Aldershot, UK: Ashgate, 2008.

Mentz, Steve. *Romance for Sale in Early Modern England: The Rise of Prose Fiction*. Aldershot, UK: Ashgate, 2006.

Michitsuna no haha. *The Gossamer Years: The Diary of a Noblewoman of Heian Japan*. Trans. Edward Seidensticker. Rutland, VT: Tuttle, 1964.

Minamoto Tamenori. *The Three Jewels: A Study and Translation of Minamoto Tamenori's Sanbōe*. Trans. Edward Kamens. Ann Arbor: Center for Japanese Studies/U Michigan, 1988.

Moore, Steven. *William Gaddis*. Boston: Twayne, 1989.

———. "Dalkey Archive: The Tradition of the New." *Dalkey News* 2.1 (Fall 1993): 1.

————. "A New Language for Desire: *Aureole*." *Review of Contemporary Fiction* 17:3 (Fall 1997): 206–14.

Moretti, Franco, ed. *The Novel.* 2 vols. Princeton: Princeton UP, 2006.

Morgan, J. R., and Richard Stoneman, eds. *Greek Fiction: The Greek Novel in Context.* London: Routledge, 1994.

Morris, Ivan. *The World of the Shining Prince: Court Life in Ancient Japan.* 1964. NY: Kodansha, 1994.

————. *The Nobility of Failure: Tragic Heroes in the History of Japan.* NY: Holt, Rinehart and Winston, 1975.

Murasaki Shikibu. *The Diary of Murasaki Shikibu.* Trans. Richard Bowring. NY: Penguin, 1996.

Murphy, Gerald. *The Ossianic Lore and Romantic Tales of Medieval Ireland.* Dublin: At the Sign of the Three Candles, 1955.

Myers, B. R. *A Reader's Manifesto.* Hoboken, NJ: Melville House, 2002.

Nabokov, Vladimir. *Lectures on Literature.* Ed. Fredson Bowers. NY: Harcourt Brace Jovanovich, 1980.

Nelson, Donald. "*Brhatkathā* Studies: The Problem of an Ur-text." *Journal of Asian Studies* 27.4 (August 1978): 663–76.

Nicholson, H. B. *Topiltzin Quetzalcoatl: The Once and Future Lord of the Toltecs.* Boulder: UP of Colorado, 2001.

Nietzsche, Friedrich. *Basic Writings of Nietzsche.* Ed. and trans. Walter Kaufmann. NY: Modern Library, 2000.

Nilsson, Ingela. *Erotic Pathos, Rhetorical Pleasure: Narrative Technique and Mimesis in Eumathios Makrembolites'* Hysmine & Hysminias. Uppsala: Acta Universitatis Upsaliensis, 2001.

————. Review of Joan B. Burton, trans., *Drosilla and Charikles. Ancient Narrative* 4 (2005): 159–69.

O'Connor, Frank. *The Backward Look: A Survey of Irish Literature.* London: Macmillan, 1967.

O'Connor, John. Amadis de Gaule *and Its Influence on Elizabethan Literature.* New Brunswick: Rutgers UP, 1970.

O'Donoghue, Heather. *Old Norse–Icelandic Literature: A Short Introduction.* Oxford: Blackwell, 2004.

O'Gorman, Richard. "The Prose Version of Robert de Boron's *Joseph d'Arimathie*." *Romance Philology* 23.4 (1970): 449–61.

Orwell, George. *Essays.* Ed. John Carey. NY: Knopf/Everyman's Library, 2002.

Ouyang, Wen-Chin. "Romancing the Epic: '*Umar al-Nu'mān* as Narrative of Empowerment." *Arabic and Middle Eastern Literatures* 3.1 (January 2000): 5–18.

Ozick, Cynthia. *Metaphor & Memory.* NY: Knopf, 1989.

Parker, Alexander A. *Literature and the Delinquent: The Picaresque Novel is Spain and Europe 1599–1753.* Edinburgh: Edinburgh UP, 1967.

Parrinder, Patrick. *Nation & Novel: The English Novel from Its Origins to the Present Day.* NY: Oxford UP, 2006.

Pastor, Antonio. *The Idea of Robinson Crusoe.* Watford, UK: Gongora, 1930.

Patai, Daphne, and Will H. Corral, eds. *Theory's Empire: An Anthology of Dissent.* NY: Columbia UP, 2005.

Peavler, Terry J. *Julio Cortázar*. Boston: Twayne, 1990.

Peck, Dale. "The Moody Blues." *New Republic*, 1 July 2002. Rpt. in *Hatchet Jobs: Writings on Contemporary Fiction*. NY: New Press, 2004.

Pervo, Richard I. *Profit with Delight: The Literary Genre of the Acts of the Apostle*. Philadelphia: Fortress, 1987.

———. "Romancing an Oft-Neglected Stone: The Pastoral Epistles and the Epistolary Novel." *Journal of Higher Criticism* 1 (Fall 1994): 25–47.

Pflugfelder, Gregory M. "Strange Fates: Sex, Gender, and Sexuality in *Torikaebaya Monogatari*." *Monumenta Nipponica* 47.3 (Autumn 1992): 347–68.

Pierce, Frank. *Amadís de Gaula*. Boston: Twayne, 1976.

Plaks, Andrew H. *The Four Masterworks of the Ming Novel: Ssu ta ch'i-shu*. Princeton: Princeton UP, 1987.

Porter, Deborah Lynn. "The Style of *Shui-hu chuan*." Ph.D. diss., Princeton University, 1989.

Power, Arthur. *Conversations with James Joyce*. London: Millington, 1974.

Prasad, S. N. *Studies in Gunādhya*. Varanasi: Chaukhambha Orientalia, 1977.

Prophet, Elizabeth Clare. *The Forbidden Mysteries of Enoch: Fallen Angels and the Origins of Evil*. Livingston, MT: Summit UP, 1994.

Rahula, Walpola. *What the Buddha Taught*. Rev. ed. NY: Grove, 1974.

Ram-Prasad, Chakravarthi. *Eastern Philosophy*. London: Weidenfeld & Nicolson, 2005.

Randel, Mary Gaylord. "The Language of Limits and the Limits of Language: The Crisis of Poetry in *La Galatea*." *Modern Language Notes* 97.2 (March 1982): 254–71.

Rhodes, Elizabeth. "Sixteenth-century Pastoral Books, Narrative Structure, and *La Galatea* of Cervantes." *Bulletin of Hispanic Studies* 66.4 (October 1989): 351–60.

Rimer, J. Thomas. *Modern Japanese Fiction and Its Traditions: An Introduction*. Princeton: Princeton UP, 1978.

Robbe-Grillet, Alain. *For a New Novel: Essays on Fiction*. Trans. Richard Howard. NY: Grove, 1965.

Robbins, Tom. *Wild Ducks Flying Backward*. NY: Bantam, 2005.

Roberts, Josephine A. "Lodge's *A Margarite of America*: A Dystopian Vision of the New World." *Studies in Short Fiction* 17.4 (Fall 1980): 407–14.

Roilos, Panagiotis. *Amphoteroglossia: A Poetics of the Twelfth-Century Medieval Greek Novel*. Washington, DC: Center for Hellenic Studies, 2005.

Rolston, David L., ed. *How to Read the Chinese Novel*. Princeton: Princeton UP, 1990.

Romano, Carlin. "William Gaddis: His Legacy on the Line." *Philadelphia Inquirer*, 21 December 1998.

Rosenmeyer, Patricia A. *Ancient Epistolary Fictions: The Letter in Greek Literature*. Cambridge: Cambridge UP, 2001.

Saintsbury, George. *A History of the French Novel, vol. 1: From the Beginning to 1800*. London: Macmillan, 1917.

Sallis, Eva. *Sheherazade through the Looking Glass: The Metamorphosis of the Thousand and One Nights*. Richmond, Surrey: Curzon, 1999.

Salzman, Paul. *English Prose Fiction 1558–1700: A Critical History*. Oxford: Oxford UP, 1985.

Sante, Luc. "Inside the Time Machine." *New York Review of Books*, 11 January 2007, 8–10, 12.

Sarra, Edith. *Fictions of Femininity: Literary Inventions of Gender in Japanese Court Women's Memoirs.* Stanford: Stanford UP, 1999.

Schlauch, Margaret. *Antecedents of the English Novel 1400–1600.* Warsaw: PWN/ Oxford: Oxford UP, 1963.

Schniedewind, William M. *How the Bible Became a Book.* Cambridge: Cambridge UP, 2004.

Screech, Michael. *Rabelais.* London: Duckworth, 1979.

See, Carolyn. "No, I Liked It. Really." *Washington Post Book World,* 7 May 2004, C8.

Seyed-Gohrab, Ali Asghar. Laylī and Majnūn: *Love, Madness and Mystic Longing in Nizāmi's Epic Romance.* Leiden: Brill, 2003.

Shadduck, Gayle. *England's Amorous Angels, 1813–1823.* Lanham, NY: University Presses of America, 1990.

Sharma, Sudarshan Kumar. Tilakamañjarī *of Dhanapāla: A Critical and Cultural Study.* Delhi: Parimal, 2003.

Shirane, Haruo. *The Bridge of Dreams: A Poetics of* The Tale of Genji. Stanford: Stanford UP, 1987.

Shklovsky, Viktor. *Theory of Prose.* Trans. Benjamin Sher. Elmwood Park, IL: Dalkey Archive, 1990.

Showalter, Elaine. "The Literary Tradition of Women." Interviewed by Karen J. Winkler. *Chronicle of Higher Education,* 10 April 2009, B12.

Siegel, Lee. *Laughing Matters: Comic Tradition in India.* Chicago: U Chicago P, 1987.

Silesky, Barry. *John Gardner: Literary Outlaw.* Chapel Hill, NC: Algonquin Books, 2004.

Smiley, Jane. *Thirteen Ways of Looking at the Novel.* NY: Knopf, 2005.

Smith, E. Gene. *Among Tibetan Texts: History and Literature of the Himalayan Plateau.* Boston: Wisdom, 2001.

Stevick, Philip, ed. *The Theory of the Novel.* NY: Free Press, 1967.

Tanner, Tony. *Adultery in the Novel: Contract and Transgression.* Baltimore: Johns Hopkins UP, 1979.

Tarnawsky, Yuri. "The Mininovel and Negative Space." *American Book Review* 28.4 (May/June 2007): 3, 15.

Tatum, James, ed. *The Search for the Ancient Novel.* Baltimore: Johns Hopkins UP, 1994.

Thompson, Thomas L. *The Messiah Myth: The Near Eastern Roots of Jesus and David.* NY: Basic Books, 2005.

The 1001 Nights: *Critical Essays and Annotated Bibliography. Mundus Arabicus* 3 (1983 [i.e., 1985).

Todorov, Tzvetan. *The Poetics of Prose.* Trans. Richard Howard. Ithaca: Cornell UP, 1977.

Toorn, Karel van der. *Scribal Culture and the Making of the Hebrew Bible.* Cambridge: Harvard UP, 2007.

Trilling, Lionel. *The Liberal Imagination.* NY: Viking, 1950.

Tripathi, Jayashankar. *Dandin.* Trans. Deepali Bhanot. New Delhi: Sahitya Akademi, 1996.

Tuckerman, Bayard. *A History of English Prose Fiction.* NY: Putnam's, 1882.

Ugrešič, Dubravka. *Thank You for Not Reading*. Trans. Celia Hawkesworth. Normal: Dalkey Archive, 2003.

Upadhye, A. N. *Uddyotana-Sūri's* Kuvalayamālā. Vol. 2. Bombay: Bharatiya Vidya Bhavan, 1970.

Urton, Gary. *Signs of the Inka Khipu: Binary Coding in the Andean Knotted-String Records*. Austin: U Texas P, 2003.

Vanstiphout, Herman. "The Craftsmanship of Sîn-leqi-unninnī." *Orientalia Lovaniensia Periodica* 21 (1990): 45–79.

Vargas Llosa, Mario. "A Challenge on Behalf of *Tirant lo Blanc*." Trans. Robert B. Knox. *Research Studies* 37.1 (March 1969): 1–16.

Varley, Paul. "Warriors as Courtiers: The Taira in *Heike monogatari*," 53–70. In *Currents in Japanese Culture: Translations and Transformations*. Ed. Amy Vladeck Heinrich. NY: Columbia UP, 1997.

Walker, Janet A. "Poetic Ideal and Fictional Reality in the *Izumi Shikibu nikki*." *Harvard Journal of Asiatic Studies* 37.1 (June 1977): 135–82.

———. "On the Applicability of the Term 'Novel' to Modern Non-Western Long Fiction." *Yearbook of Comparative and General Literature* 37 (1988): 47–68.

Wallace, David Foster. *Consider the Lobster and Other Essays*. NY: Little, Brown, 2005.

Wang, Jing. *The Story of Stone: Intertextuality, Ancient Chinese Stone Lore, and the Stone Symbolism in* Dream of the Red Chamber, Water Margin, *and* The Journey to the West. Durham: Duke UP, 1992.

Warder, A. K. *Indian Kāvya Literature*. 8 vols. Delhi: Motilal Banarsidass, 1972– .

Warren, F. M. *A History of the Novel Previous to the Seventeenth Century*. NY: Holt, 1895.

Watt, Ian. *The Rise of the Novel: Studies in Defoe, Richardson and Fielding*. 1957. Berkeley: U California P, 2001.

Weinberg, Florence M. *The Wine and the Will: Rabelais's Bacchic Christianity*. Detroit: Wayne State U P, 1972.

Wheeler, Bonnie, ed. *Arthurian Studies in Honour of P. J. C. Field*. Cambridge: Brewer, 2004.

White, L. Michael. *From Jesus to Christianity*. NY: HarperSanFrancisco, 2004.

Wilson, A. N. *Paul: The Mind of the Apostle*. NY: Norton, 1997.

Winkler, John J. *Auctor & Actor: A Narratological Reading of Apuleius's* The Golden Ass. Berkeley: U California P, 1985.

Wood, James. *The Irresponsible Self: On Laughter and the Novel*. NY: Farrar, Straus and Giroux, 2004.

———. *How Fiction Works*. NY: Farrar, Straus and Giroux, 2008.

Woolf, Virginia. "The Tale of Genji," 264–69. In *The Essays of Virginia Woolf, Volume 4: 1925–1928*. Ed. Andrew McNeillie. London: Hogarth, 1994.

———. *The Second Common Reader*. 1932. Ed. Andrew McNeillie. San Diego: Harcourt, 1986.

Wright, J. Edward. *Baruch ben Neriah: From Biblical Scribe to Apocalyptic Seer*. Columbia: U South Carolina P, 2003.

Yarshater, Ehsan, ed. *Persian Literature*. Albany: Bibliotheca Persica, 1988.

Chronological Index
of Novels Discussed

Date	Title	Author	Language	Pages
BCE				
20th C	"Tale of Sinuhe"		Egyptian	39–41
20th C	The Matter of Aratta		Sumerian	50–52
19th C	"The Tale of the Eloquent Peasant"		Egyptian	41
19th C	"The Tale of the Shipwrecked Sailor"		Egyptian	41
19th C	The Tale of King Cheops' Court		Egyptian	41–44
c. 1700	"Atrahasis"	Ipiq-Aya	Akkadian	52–53
16th C	Gilgamesh	Sîn-leqi-unninnī	Akkadian	53–55
14th C	Enuma Elish		Akkadian	55
13th C	"The Tale of Two Brothers"		Egyptian	44
13th C	"The Contendings of Horus and Seth"		Egyptian	44–45
12th C	"The Report of Wenamun"		Egyptian	45
11th C	"A Tale of Woe"		Egyptian	45–46
early 8th C	"Erra and Ishum"	Kabti-ilani-Marduk	Akkadian	55–56
8th/7th C	In the Day	"J"	Hebrew	59–63
late 7th C	Deuteronomistic History	Baruch ben Neriah?	Hebrew	63–69
4th C	The Story of Petese		Egyptian	46–48
c. 360	The Education of Cyrus	Xenophon	Greek	73–75
3rd C	Setna Khaemuas cycle		Egyptian	48–49
3rd-2nd C	The Alexander Romance		Greek	78–79
2nd C	The Book of Enoch		Aramaic	70–73
1st C	Metiokhos and Parthenope		Greek	500
CE				
early 1st C	Chaereas and Callirhoe	Chariton	Greek	79–82
c. 60	Satyricon	Titus Petronius	Latin	100–5
c. 90	Luke-Acts		Greek	111–17
1st/2nd C	Entry into the Realm of Reality		Pali	415–18

General Index